Street by Street

WEST YORKSHIRE

PLUS BARNSLEY, LITTLEBOROUGH, MILNROW, PENISTONE, SHAW, SKIPTON, TADCASTER

Enlarged Areas Bradford, Halifax, Huddersfield, Keighley, Leeds, Wakefield

Ist edition May 2001

© Automobile Association Developments Limited 2001

This product includes map data licensed from Ordnance Survey® with the permission of the Controller of Her Majesty's Stationery Office. © Crown copyright 2000. All rights reserved. Licence No: 399221.

Published by AA Publishing (a trading name of Automobile Association Developments Limited, whose registered office is Norfolk House, Priestley Road, Basingstoke, Hampshire, RG24 9NY. Registered number 1878835).

Mapping produced by the Cartographic Department of The Automobile Association.

A CIP Catalogue record for this book is available from the British Library.

Printed by G. Canale & C. S.P.A., Torino, Italy

The contents of this atlas are believed to be correct at the time of the latest revision. However, the publishers cannot be held responsible for loss occasioned to any person acting or refraining from action as a result of any material in this atlas, nor for any errors, omissions or changes in such material. The publishers would welcome information to correct any errors or omissions and to keep this atlas up to date. Please write to Publishing, The Automobile Association, Fanum House, Basing View, Basingstoke, Hampshire, RG21 4EA.

Ref: MX016

Key to map pages	ii-iii
Key to map symbols	iv-1
Enlarged scale pages	2-15
Street by Street	16-271
Index – towns & villages	272-273
Index – streets	274-336
Index – featured places	336-344

ii

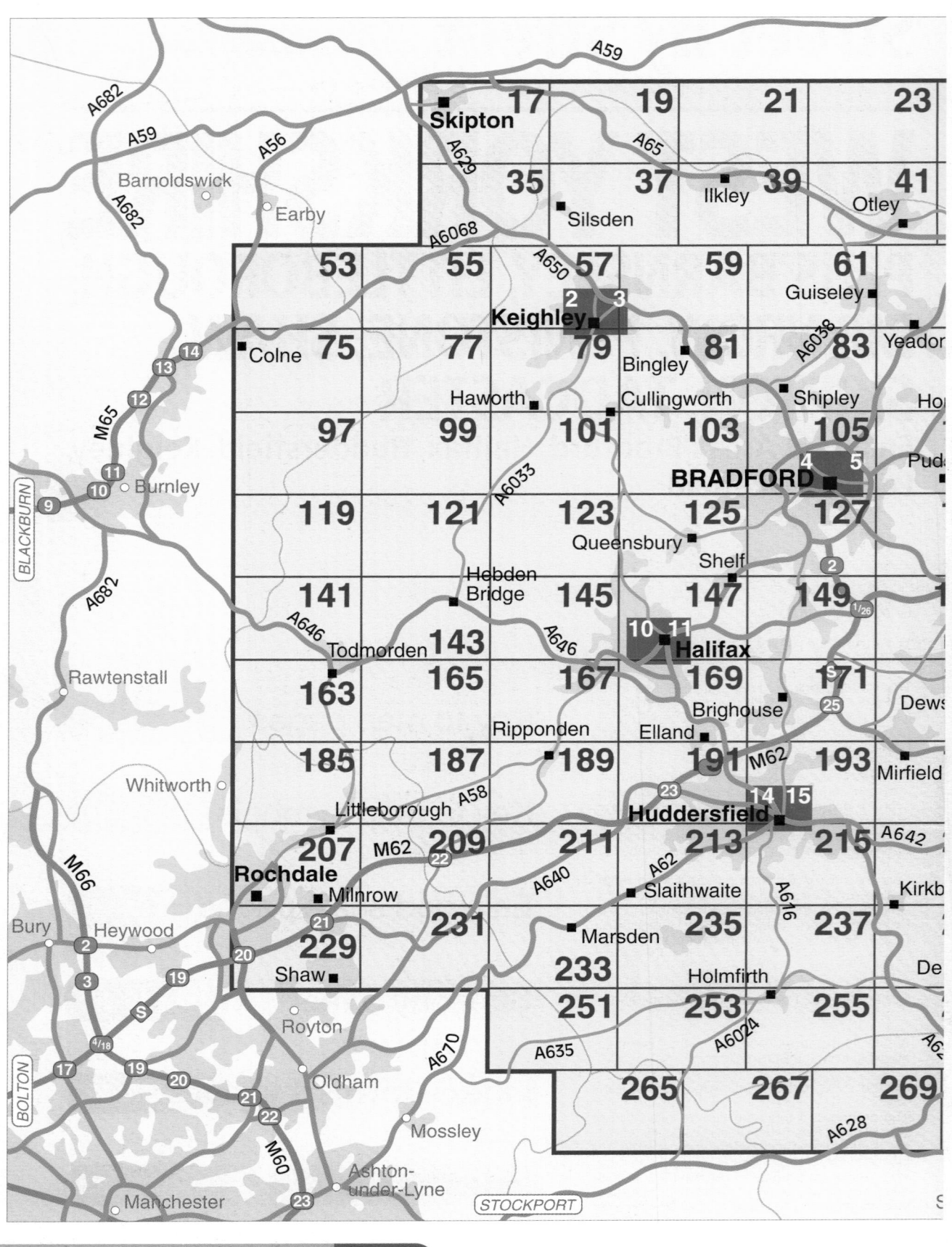

Enlarged scale pages   **1:10,000**   6.3 inches to 1 mile

miles
1/4   1/2   3/4

kilometres
0   1/4   1/2   3/4   1   1 1/4

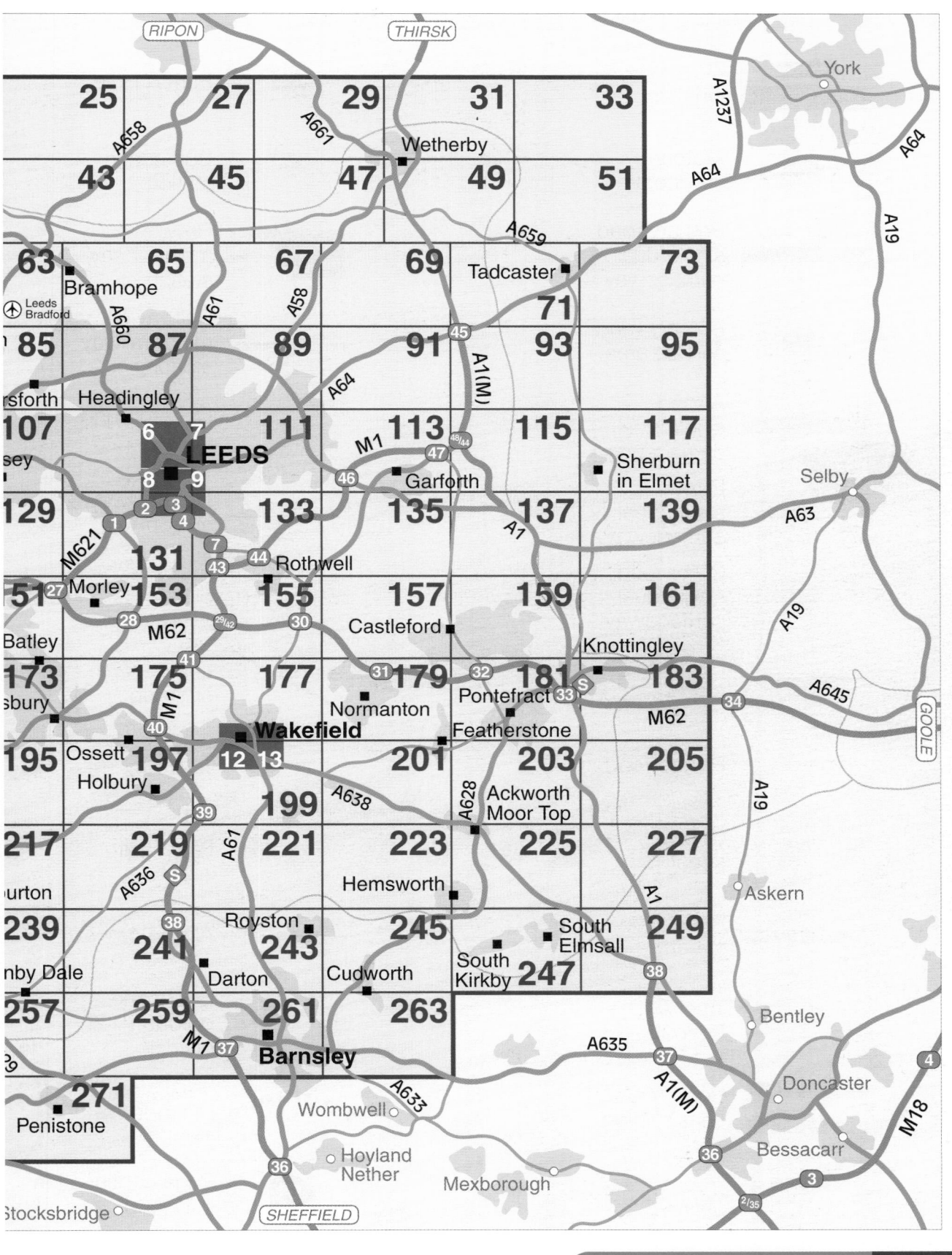

Scale of main map pages 1:17,500

Junction 9	Motorway & junction	P+	Park & Ride
Services	Motorway service area		Bus/coach station
	Primary road single/dual carriageway		Railway & main railway station
Services	Primary road service area		Railway & minor railway station
	A road single/dual carriageway		Underground station
	B road single/dual carriageway		Light railway & station
	Other road single/dual carriageway	+++++++	Preserved private railway
	Restricted road	LC	Level crossing
	Private road	•–•–•–•–•	Tramway
← ←	One way street	-------	Ferry route
	Pedestrian street	....	Airport runway
-------	Track/ footpath	–·–·–·–	Boundaries- borough/ district
■■■■■■	Road under construction	▼▼▼▼▼	Mounds
[=====]	Road tunnel	93	Page continuation 1:17,500
P	Parking	7	Page continuation to enlarged scale 1:10,000

Symbol	Description
	River/canal lake, pier
	Aqueduct lock, weir
465 ▲ Winter Hill	Peak (with height in metres)
	Beach
	Coniferous woodland
	Broadleaved woodland
	Mixed woodland
	Park
	Cemetery
	Built-up area
	Featured building
	City wall
A&E	Accident & Emergency hospital
	Toilet
	Toilet with disabled facilities
	Petrol station
PH	Public house
PO	Post Office
	Public library
i	Tourist Information Centre
	Castle
	Historic house/ building
Wakehurst Place NT	National Trust property
M	Museum/ art gallery
†	Church/chapel
	Country park
	Theatre/ performing arts
	Cinema

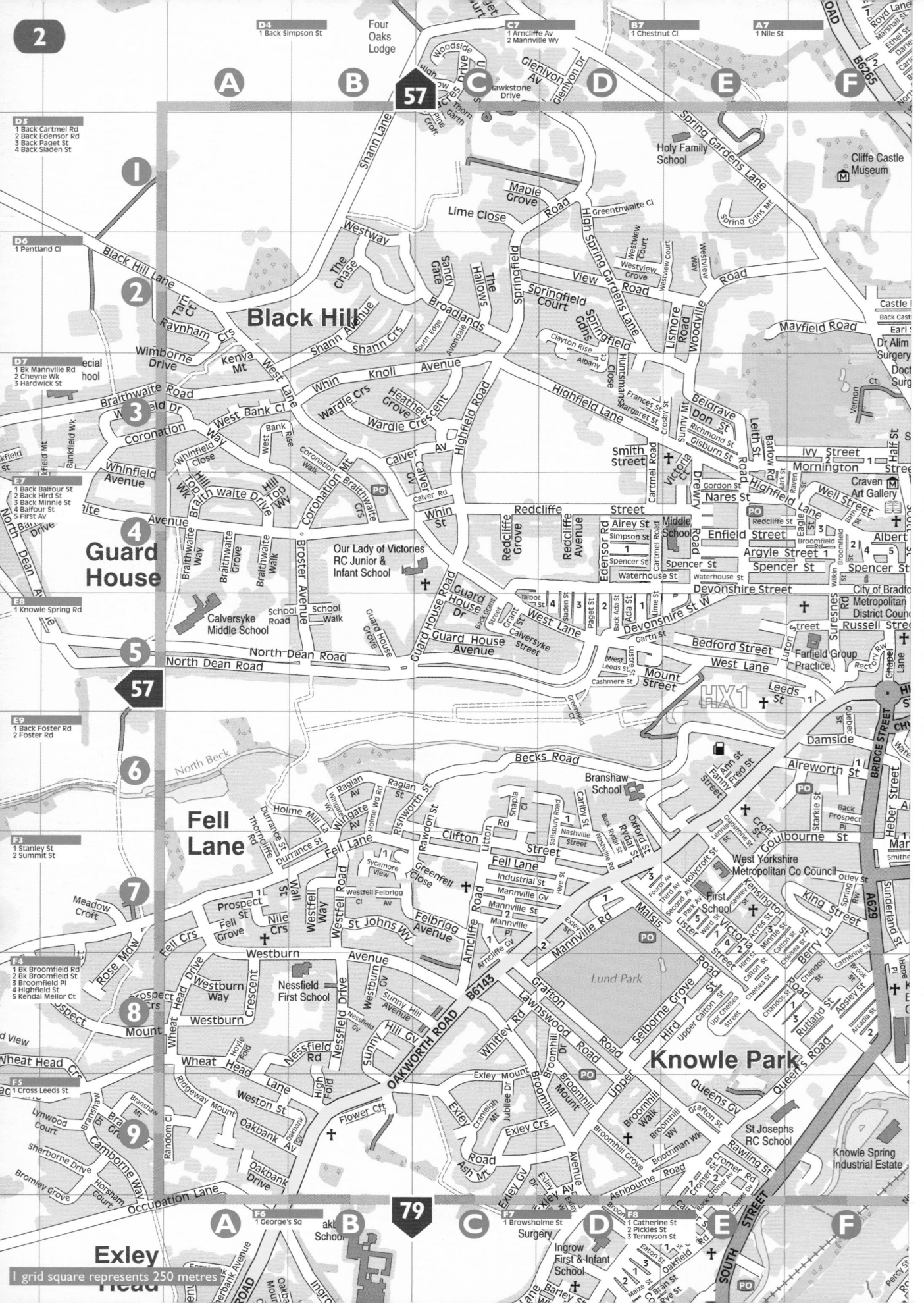

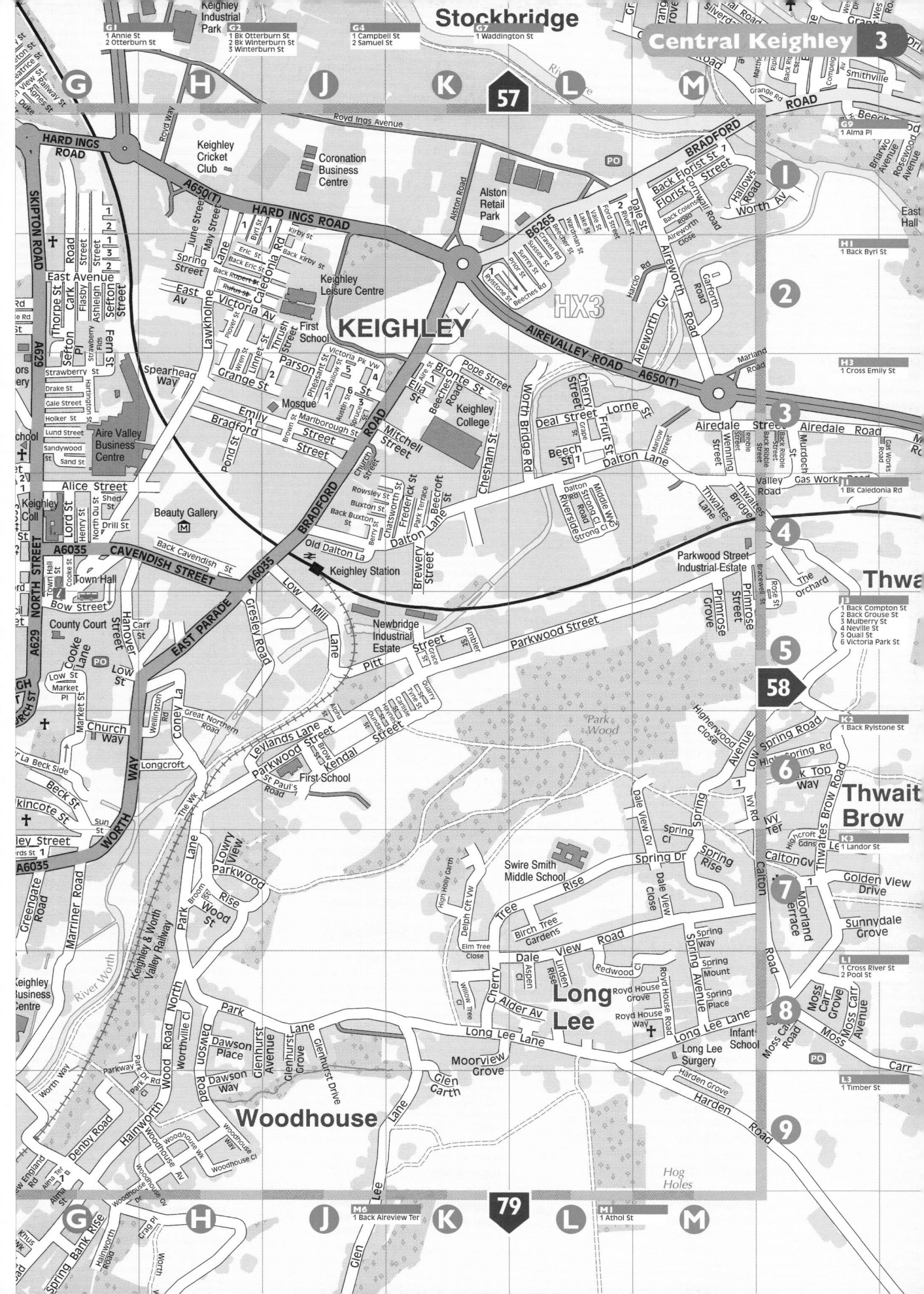

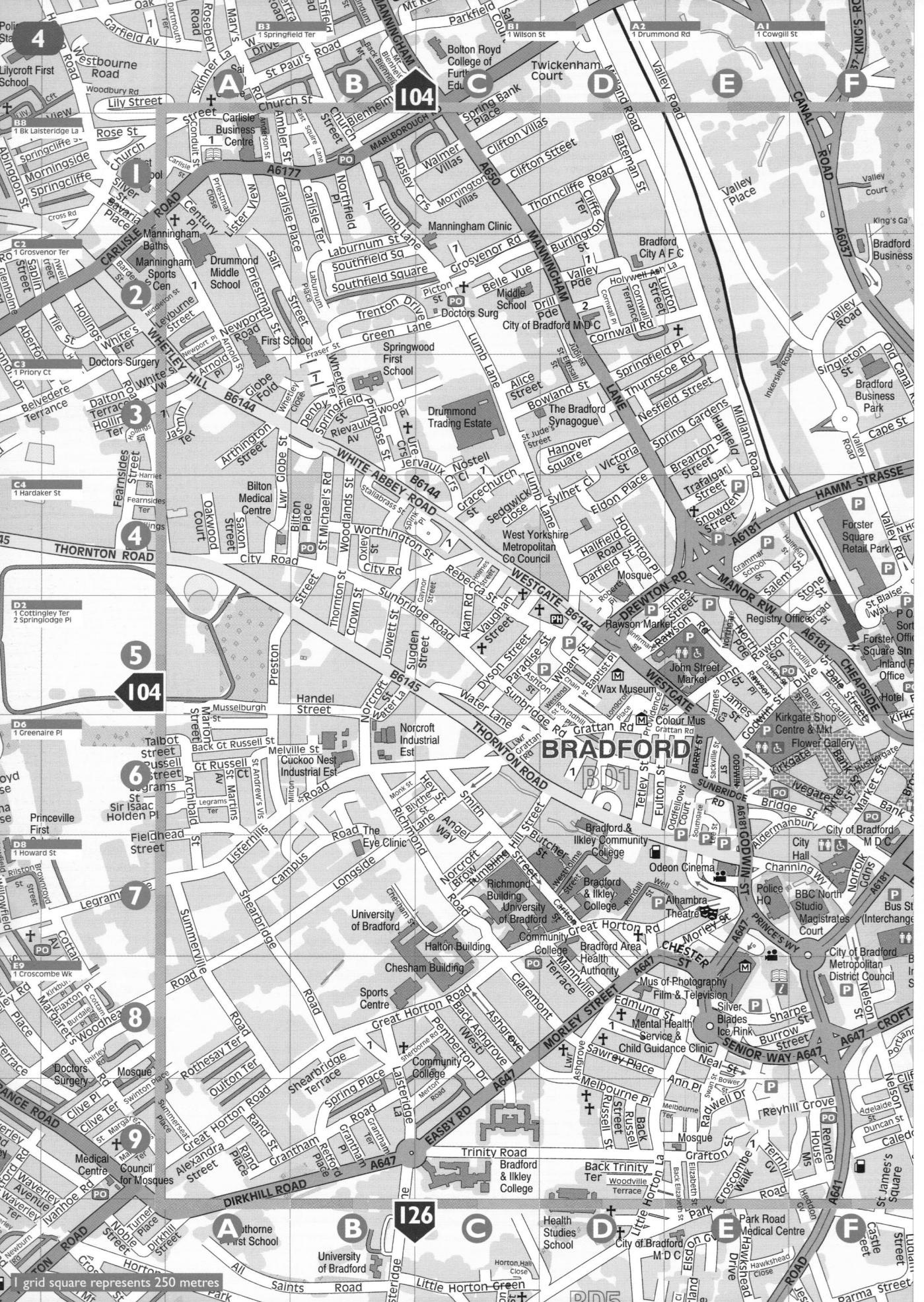

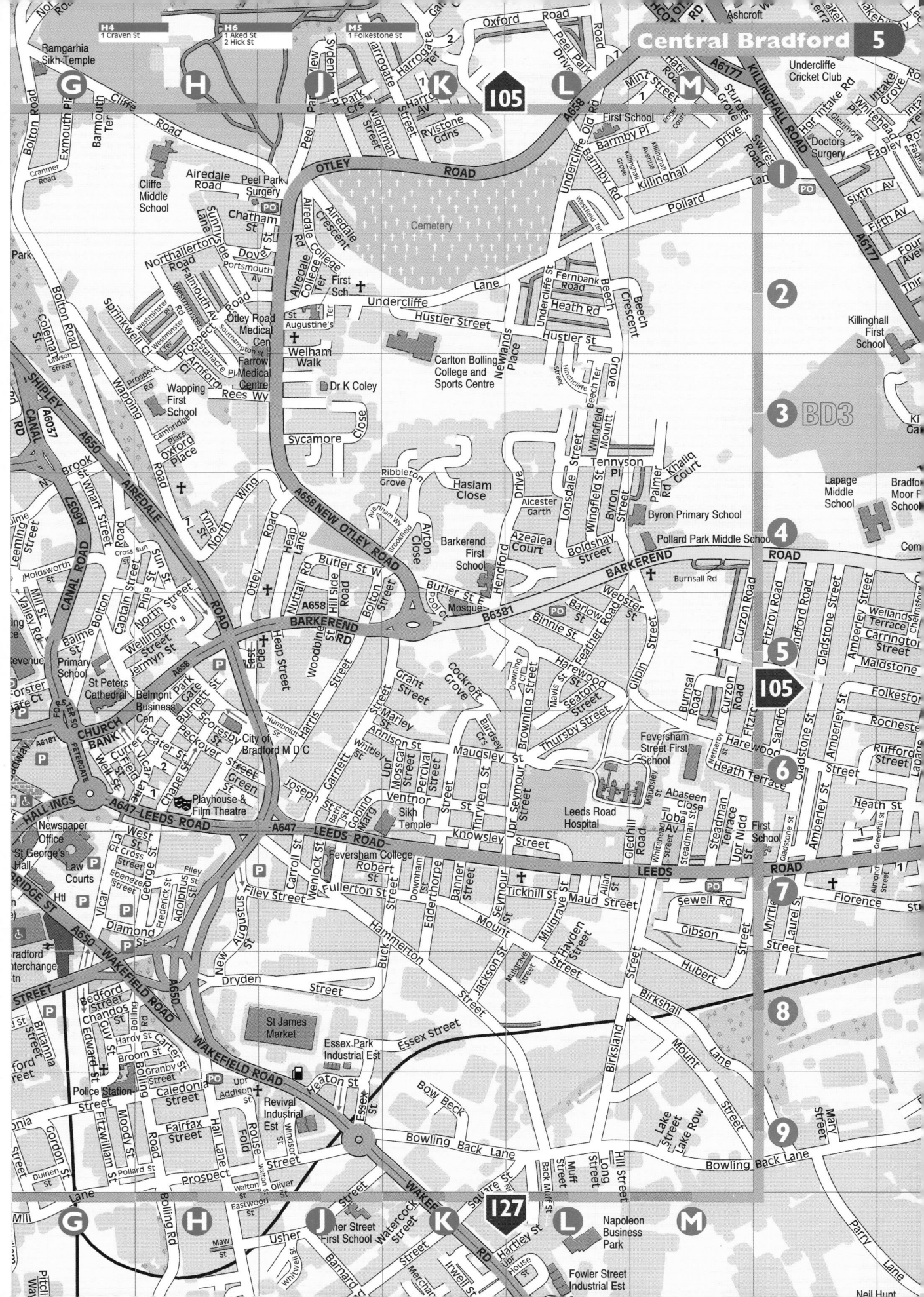

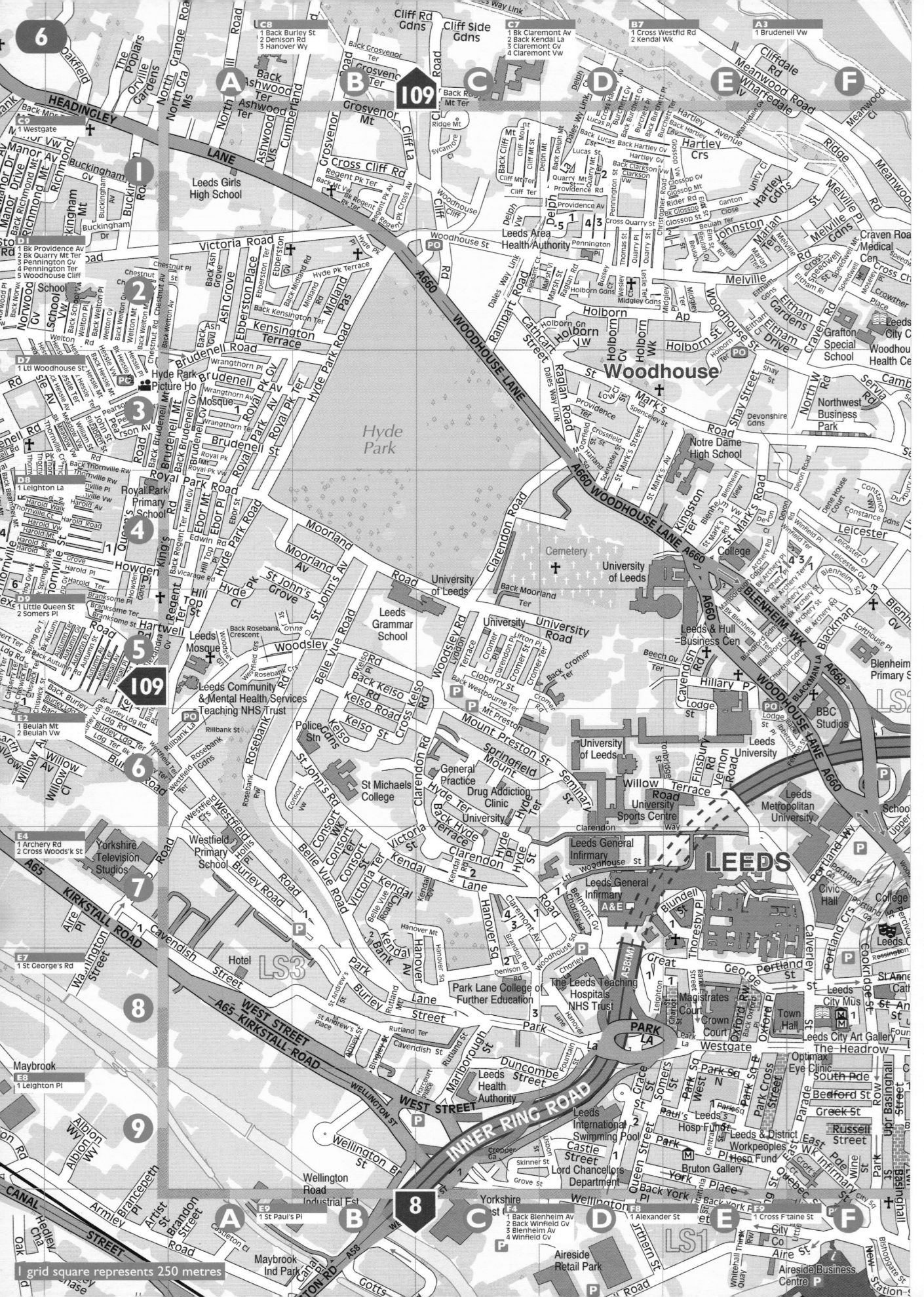

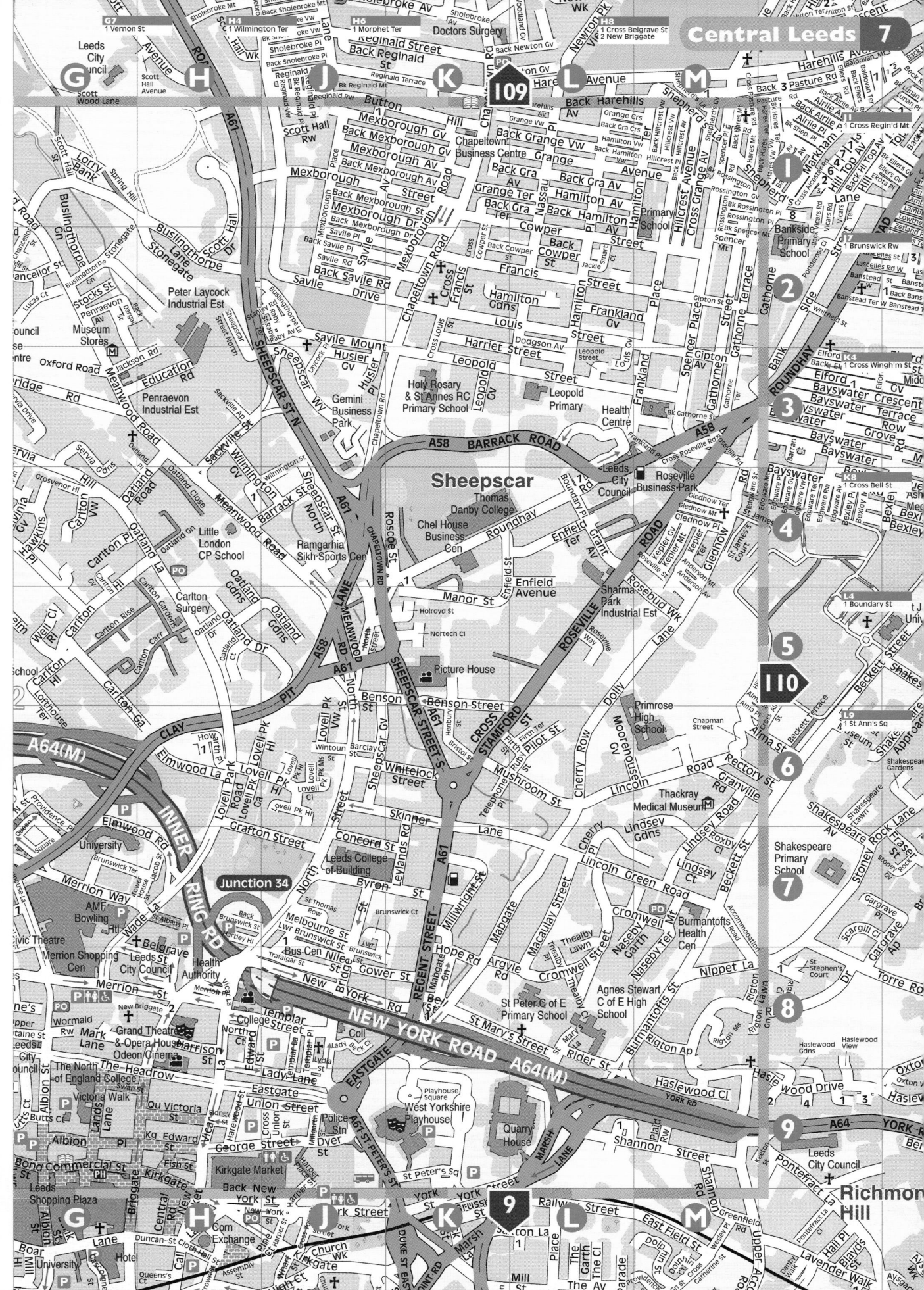

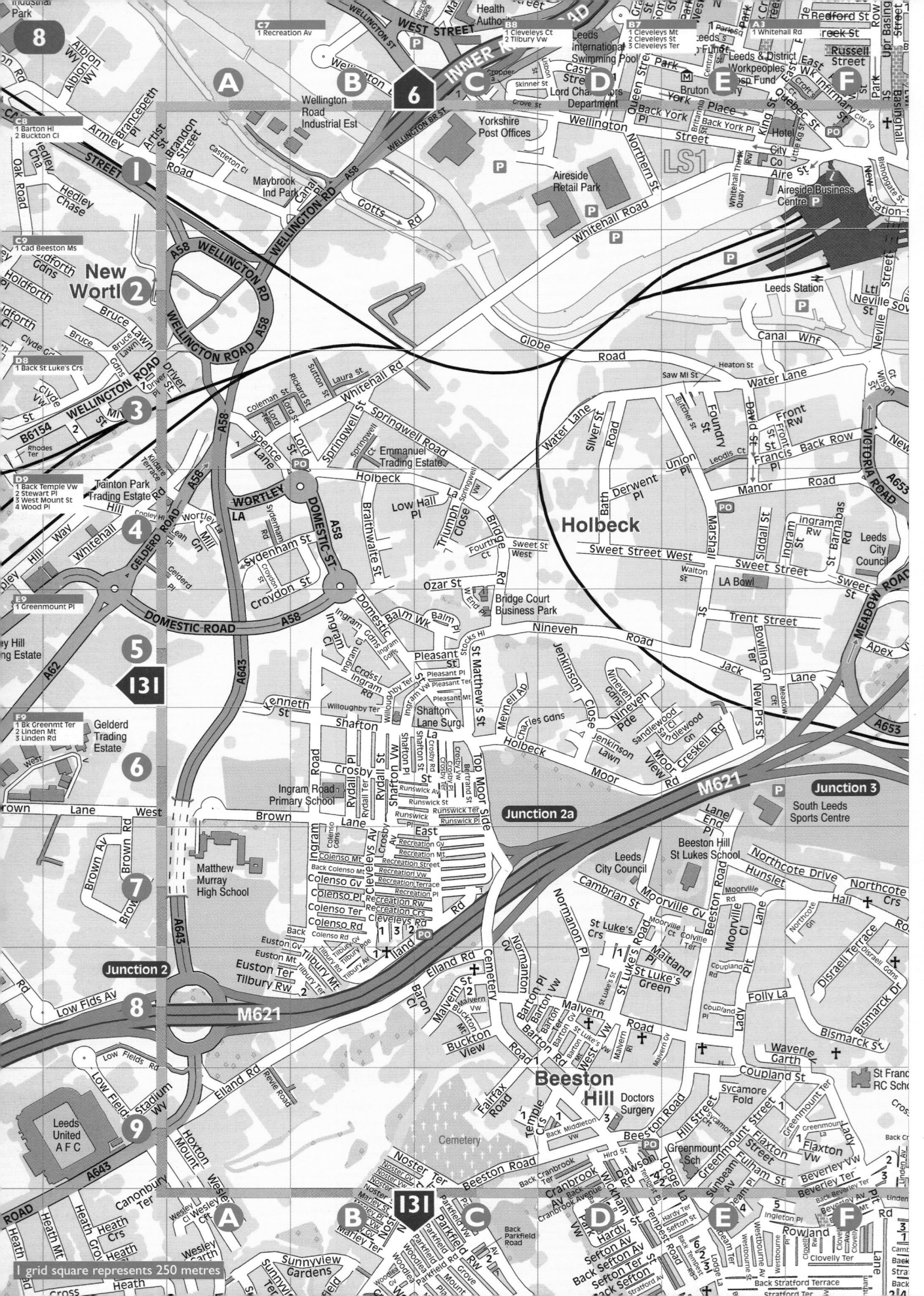

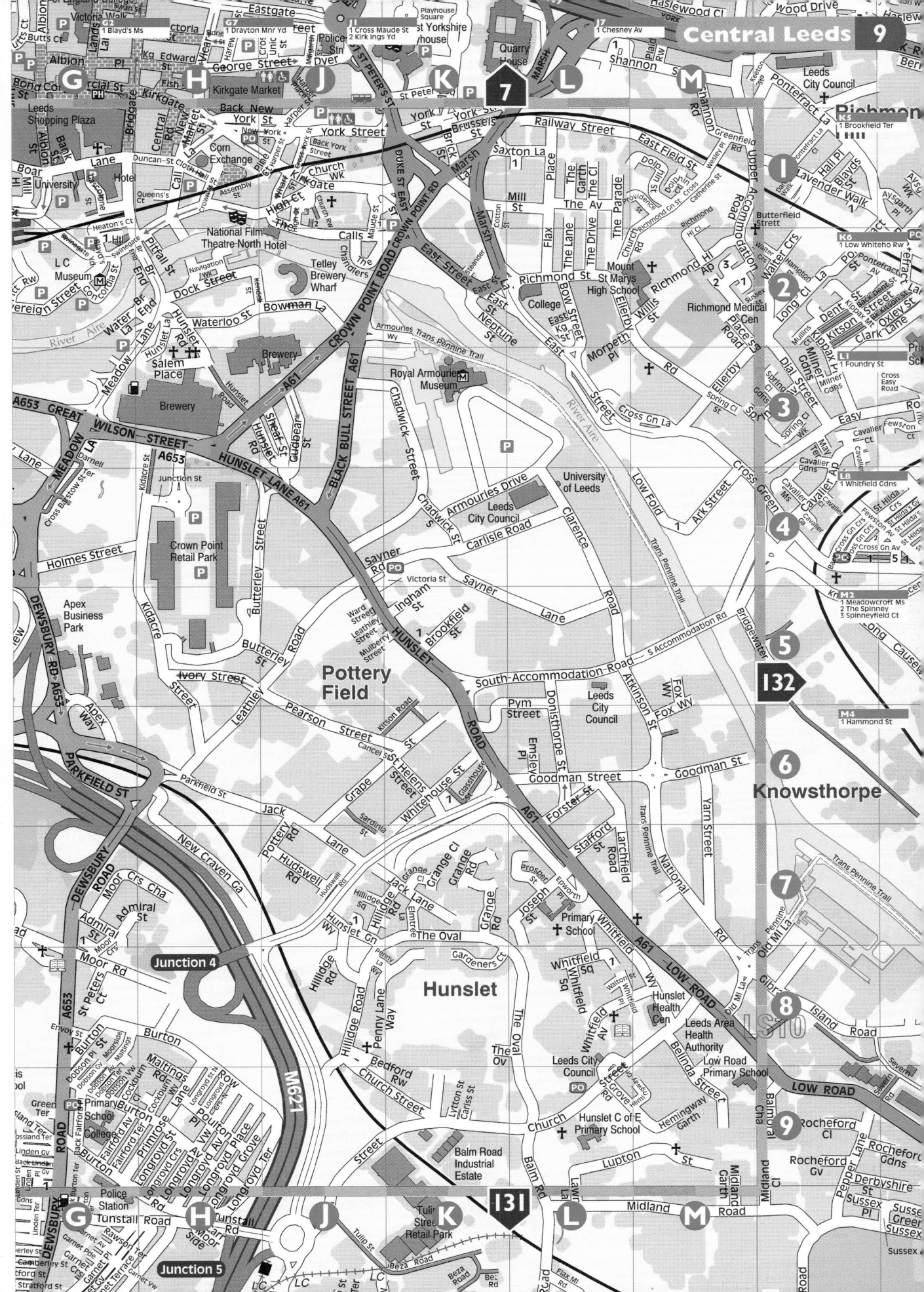

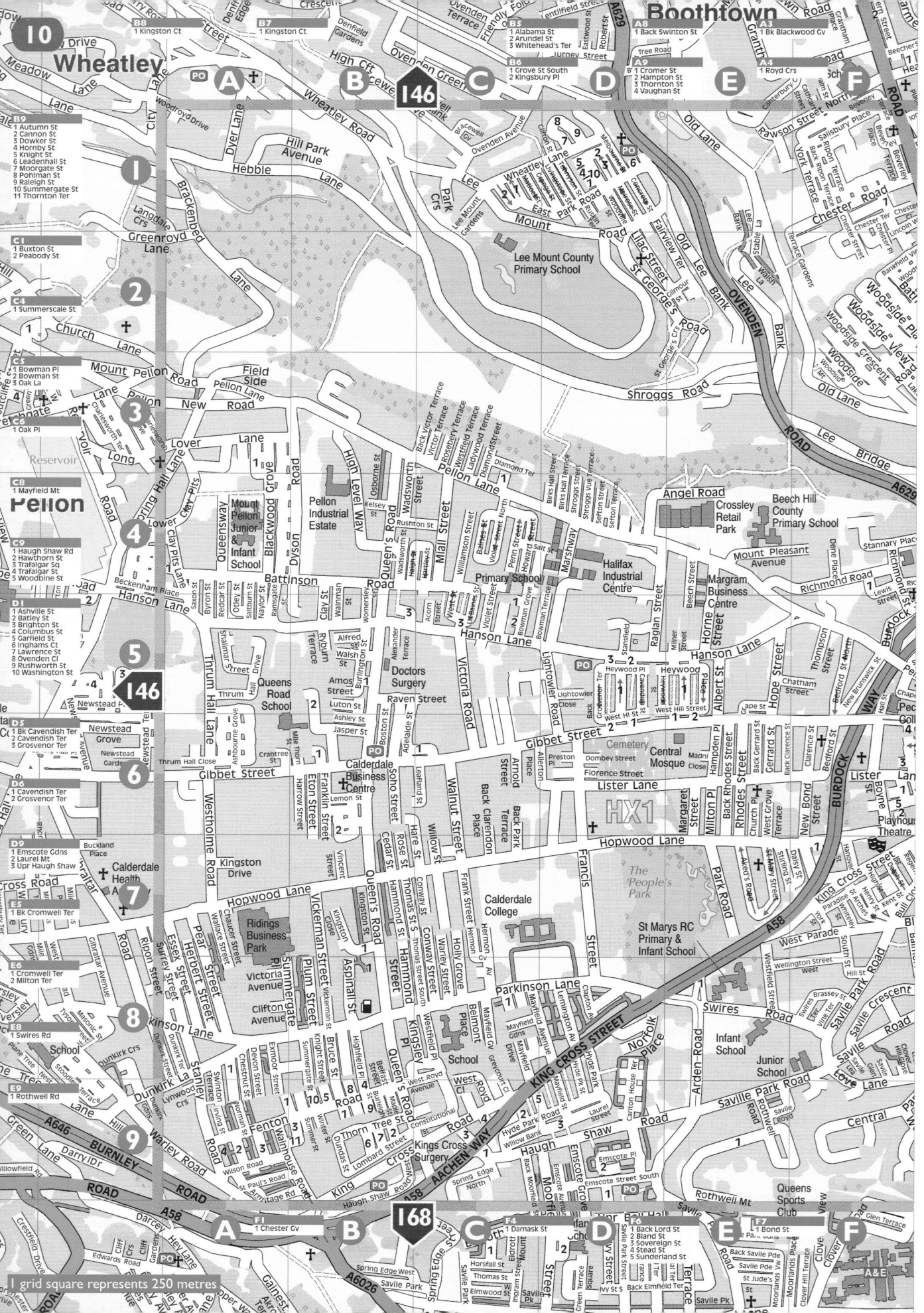

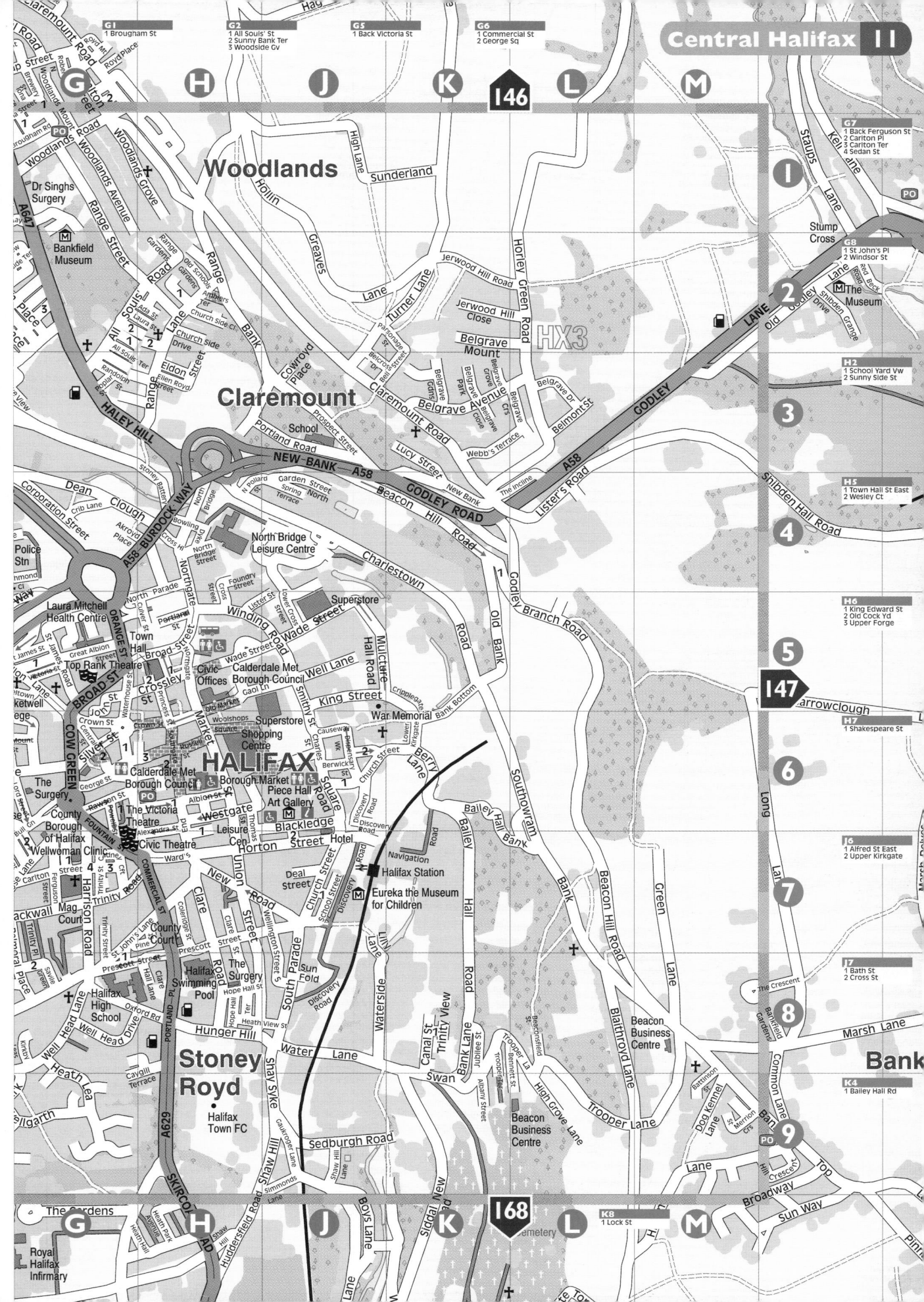

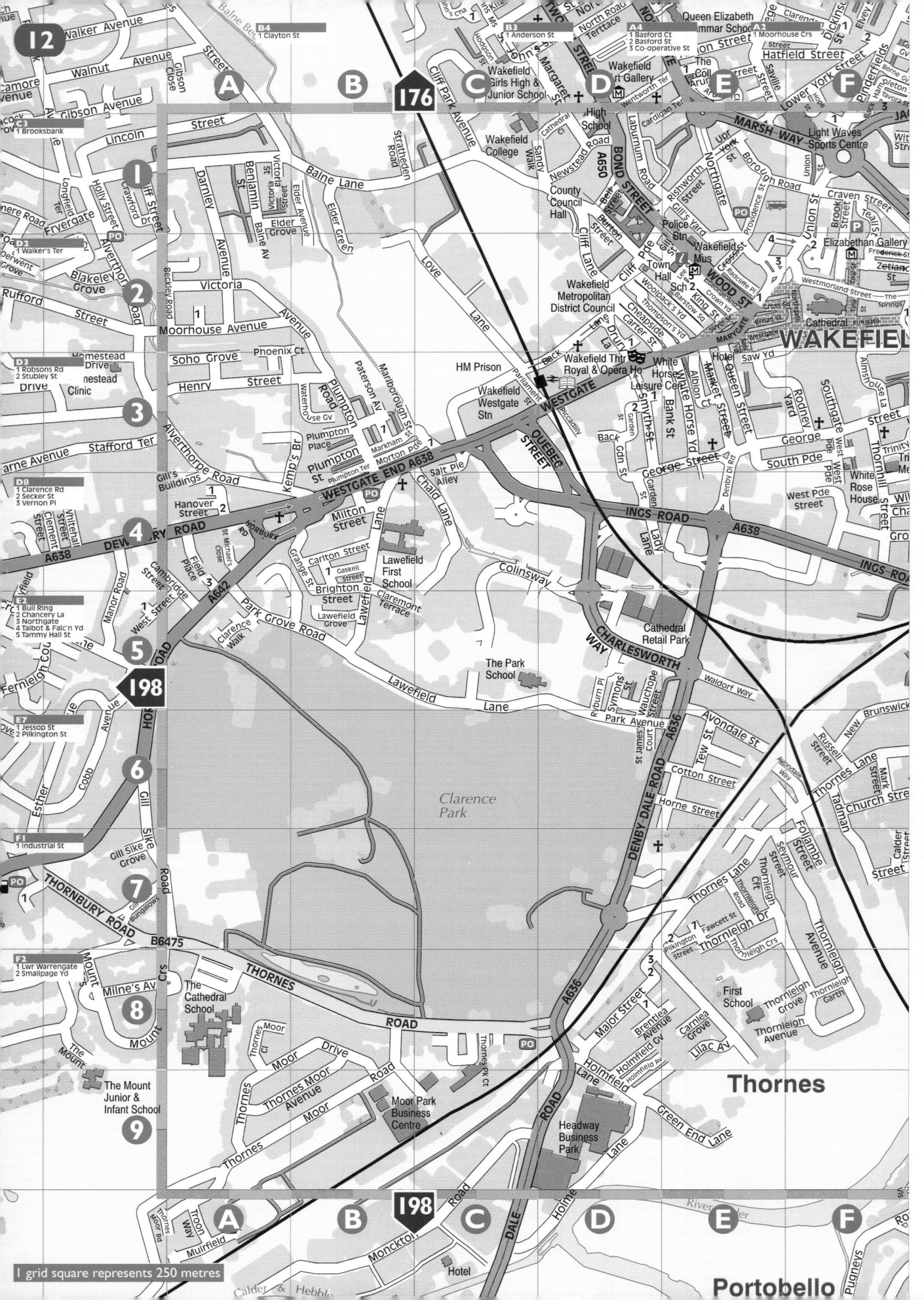

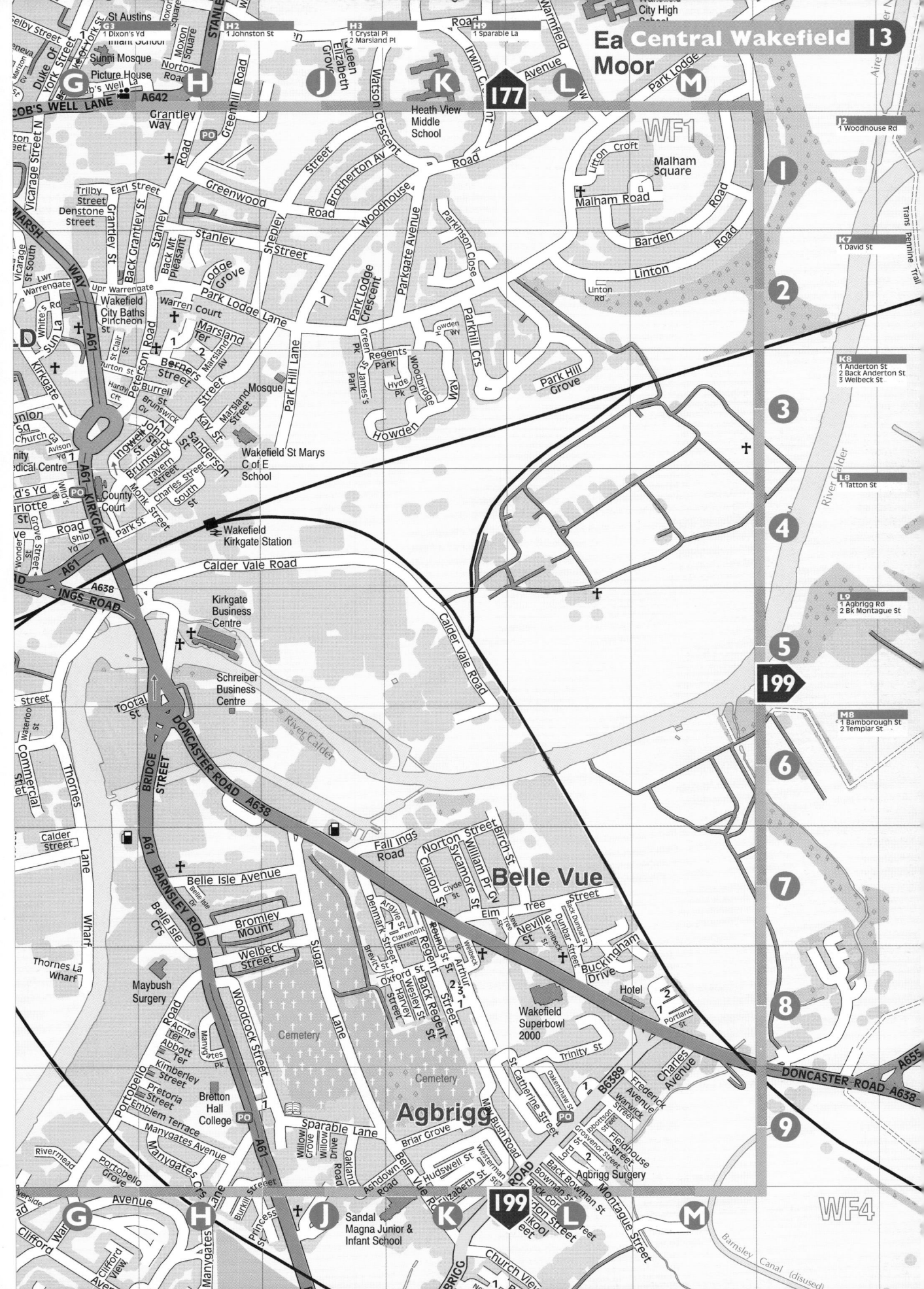

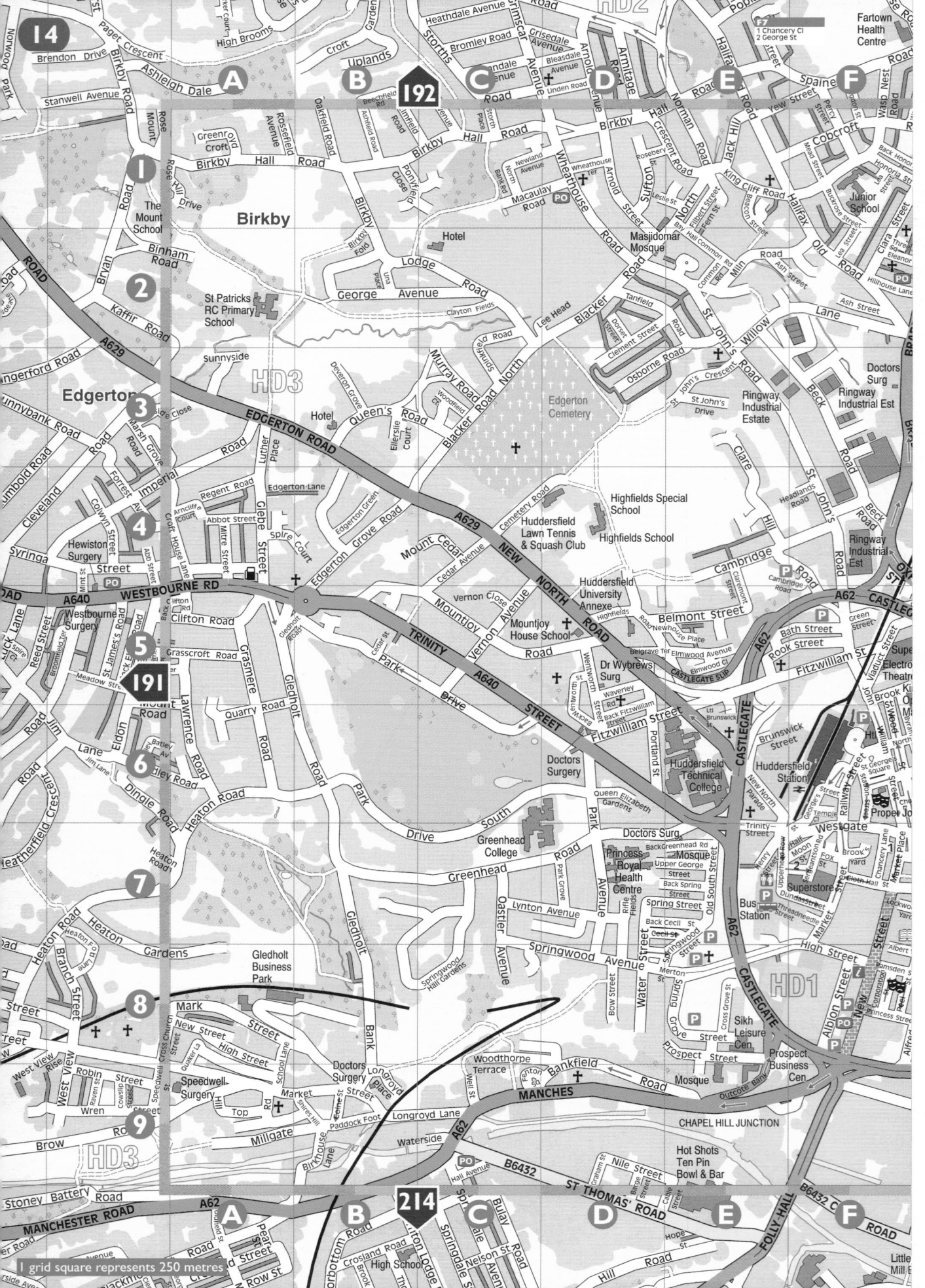

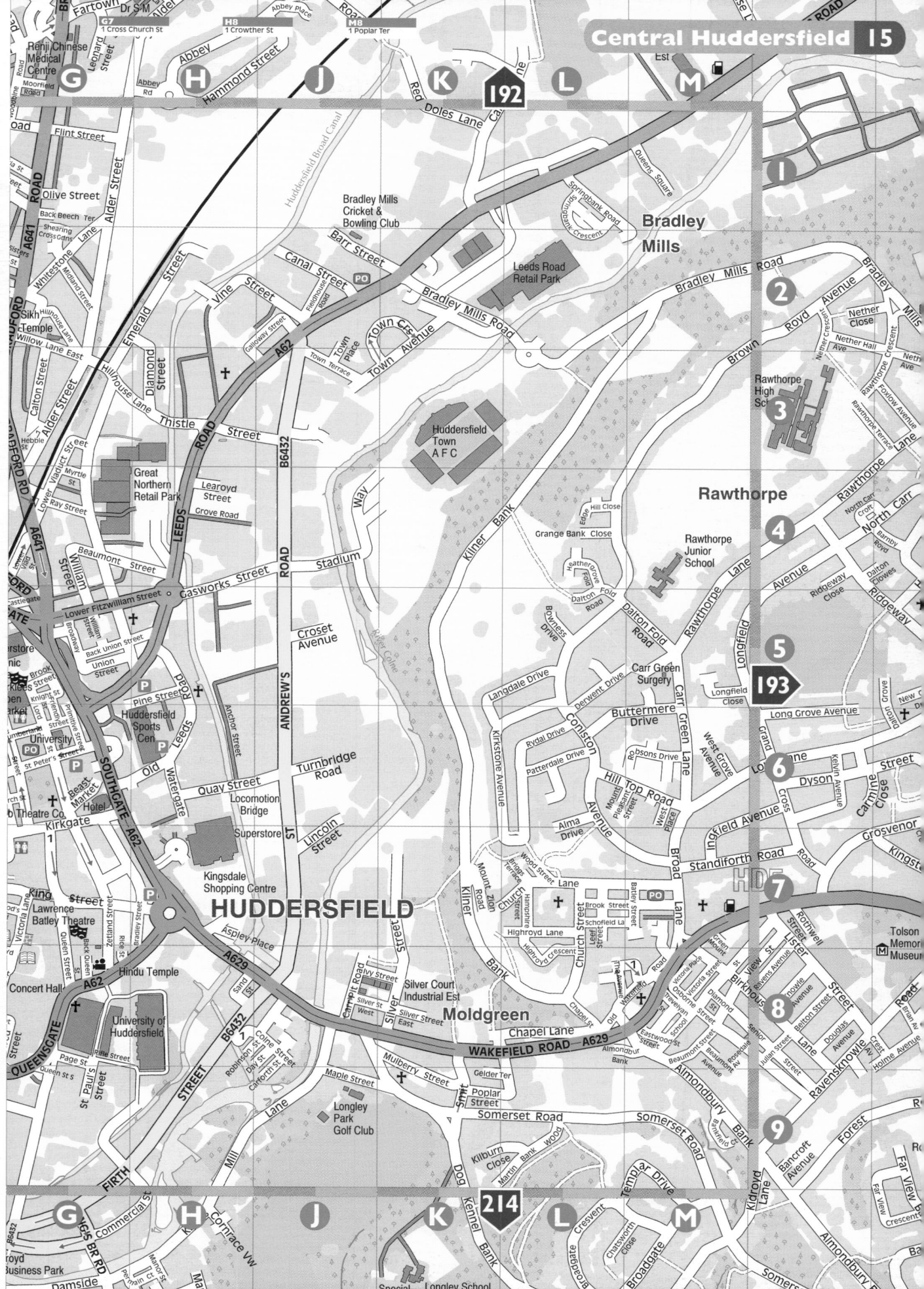

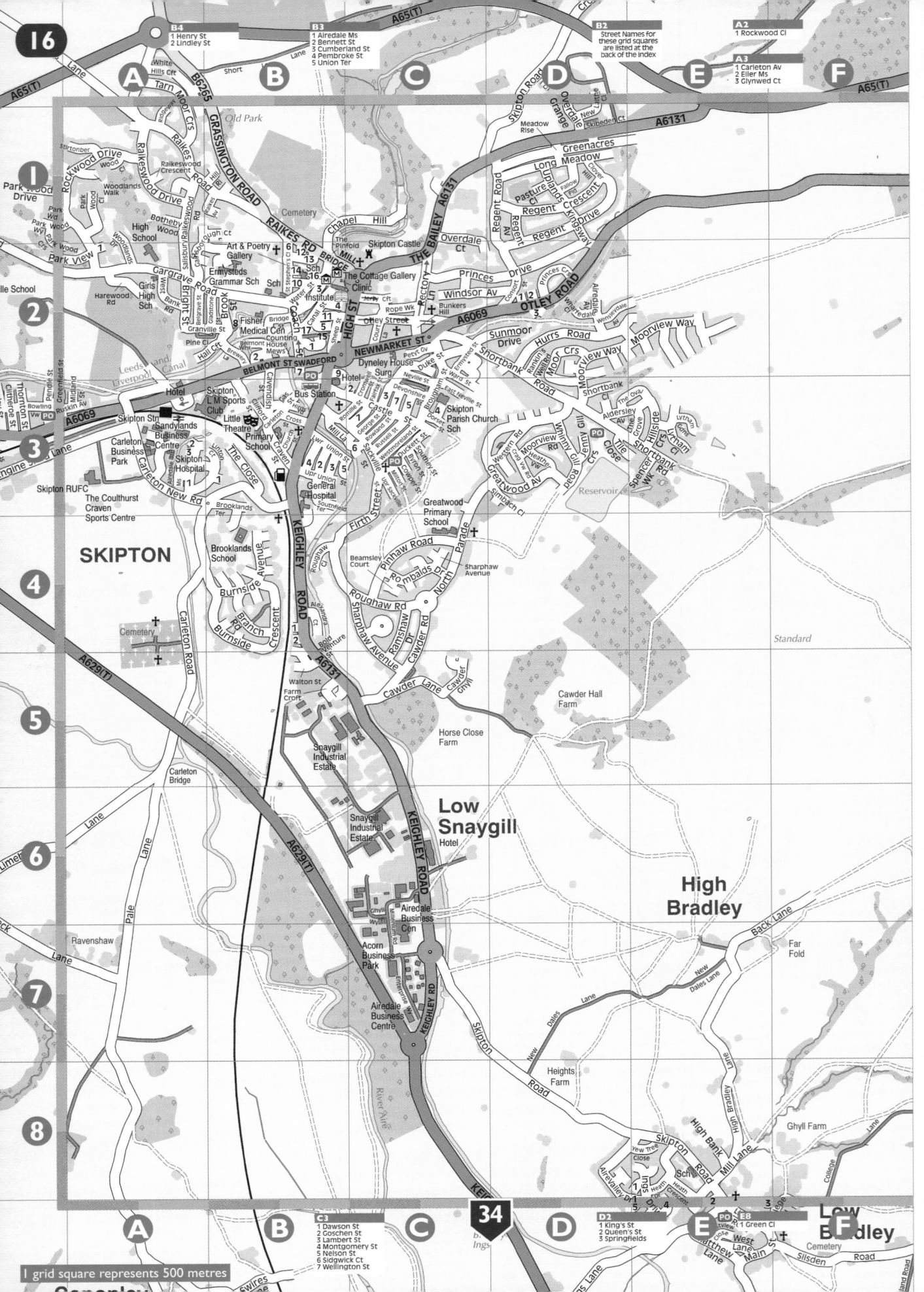

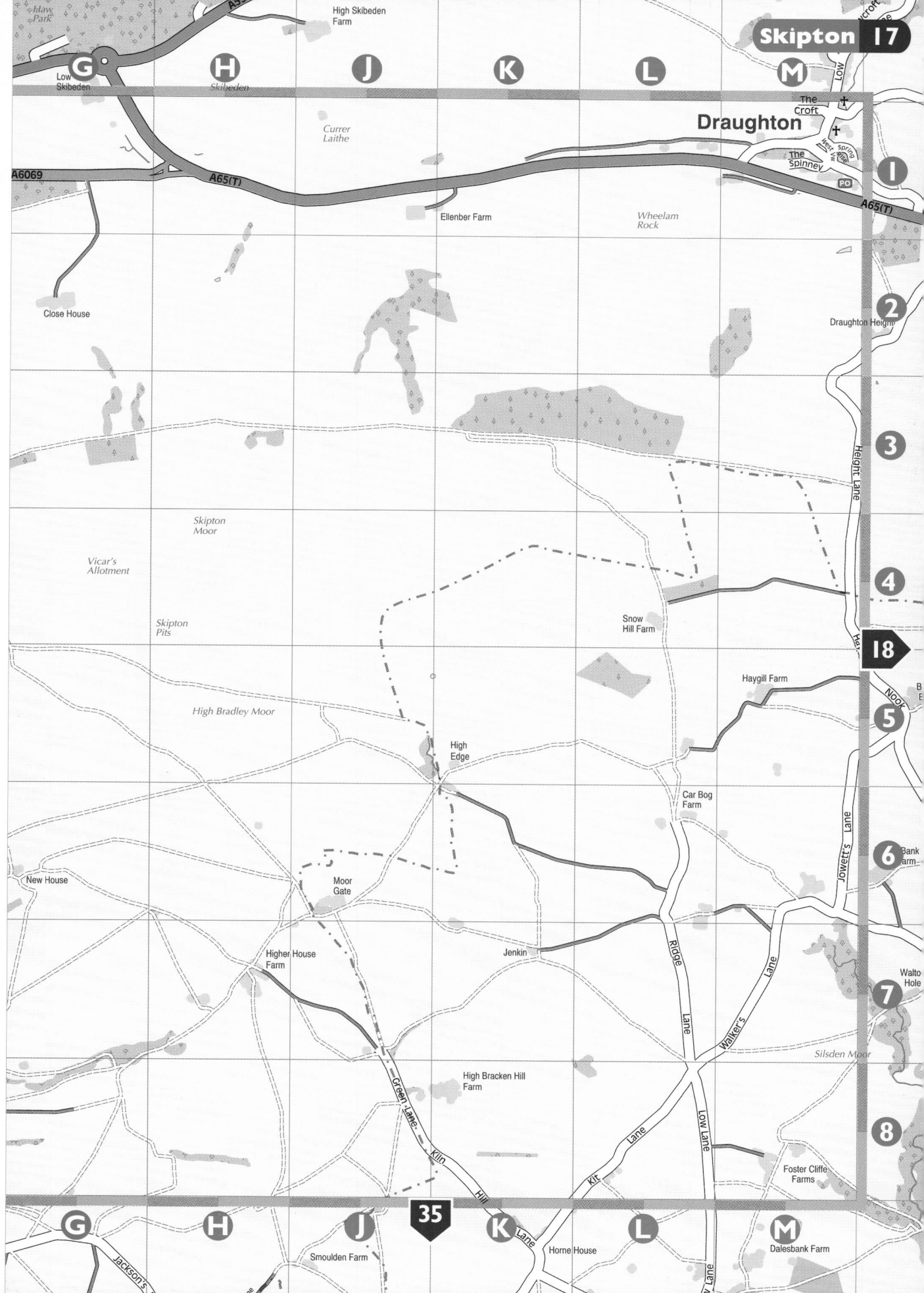

Haw Park

Low Skibeden

G

High Skibeden Farm

H

Skibeden

Currer Laithe

J

K

L

Draughton

M

The Croft

West WW spring

The Spinney

PO

I

A6069

A65(T)

A65(T)

Ellenber Farm

Wheelam Rock

Close House

Draughton Heigh

2

Height Lane

3

4

Skipton Moor

Vicar's Allotment

Snow Hill Farm

18

Skipton Pits

Haygill Farm

Nook

5

High Bradley Moor

High Edge

Car Bog Farm

Jowett's Lane

Bank Farm

6

New House

Moor Gate

Jenkin

Ridge Lane

Walker's Lane

Walto Hole

7

Higher House Farm

Silsden Moor

8

Green Lane

High Bracken Hill Farm

Kiln Hill

Kit Lane

Low Lane

Foster Cliffe Farms

G

H

J

35

K

Lane

L

M

Jackson's

Smoulden Farm

Horne House

Dalesbank Farm

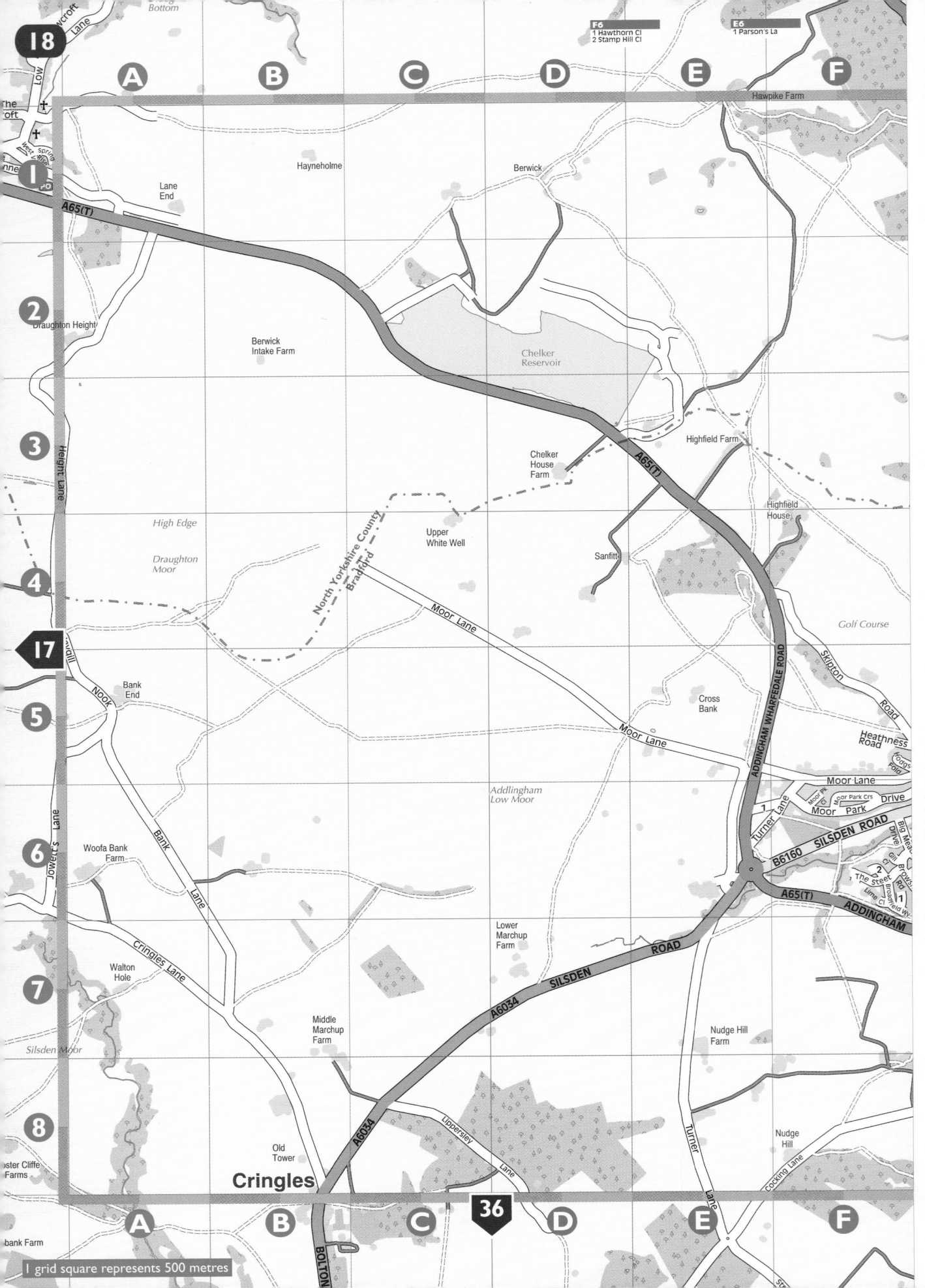

A   B   C   D   E   F

Hawpike Farm

The
oft

Hayneholme

Berwick

Lane
End

A65(T)

Draughton Height

Berwick
Intake Farm

Chelker Reservoir

Chelker
House
Farm

Highfield Farm

A65(T)

High Edge

Upper
White Well

Highfield
House

Height Lane

Draughton
Moor

North Yorkshire County
Bradford

Moor Lane

Sanfitt

Golf Course

17

Bank
End

Moor Lane

Cross
Bank

Skipton Road

Heathness Road

Hoggs Fold

Moor Lane

Nook

Addlingham
Low Moor

Moor PK

Moor Park Crs

Drive

Addingham Wharfedale Road

Turner Lane

1

Moor Park

Big Mea

Brows

Drive

Woofa Bank
Farm

B6160

SILSDEN ROAD

The Steet

Broadfield Rd

Lune Cl

Broadfield Wy

Jowett's Lane

Bank Lane

A65(T)

ADDINGHAM

Lower
Marchup
Farm

Cringles Lane

Walton
Hole

SILSDEN   ROAD

A6034

Nudge Hill
Farm

Middle
Marchup
Farm

Silsden Moor

Turner Lane

A6034

Old
Tower

Uppersley Lane

Nudge
Hill

oster Cliffe
Farms

Cocking Lane

Cringles

A   B   C   36   D   E   F

BOLTON

bank Farm

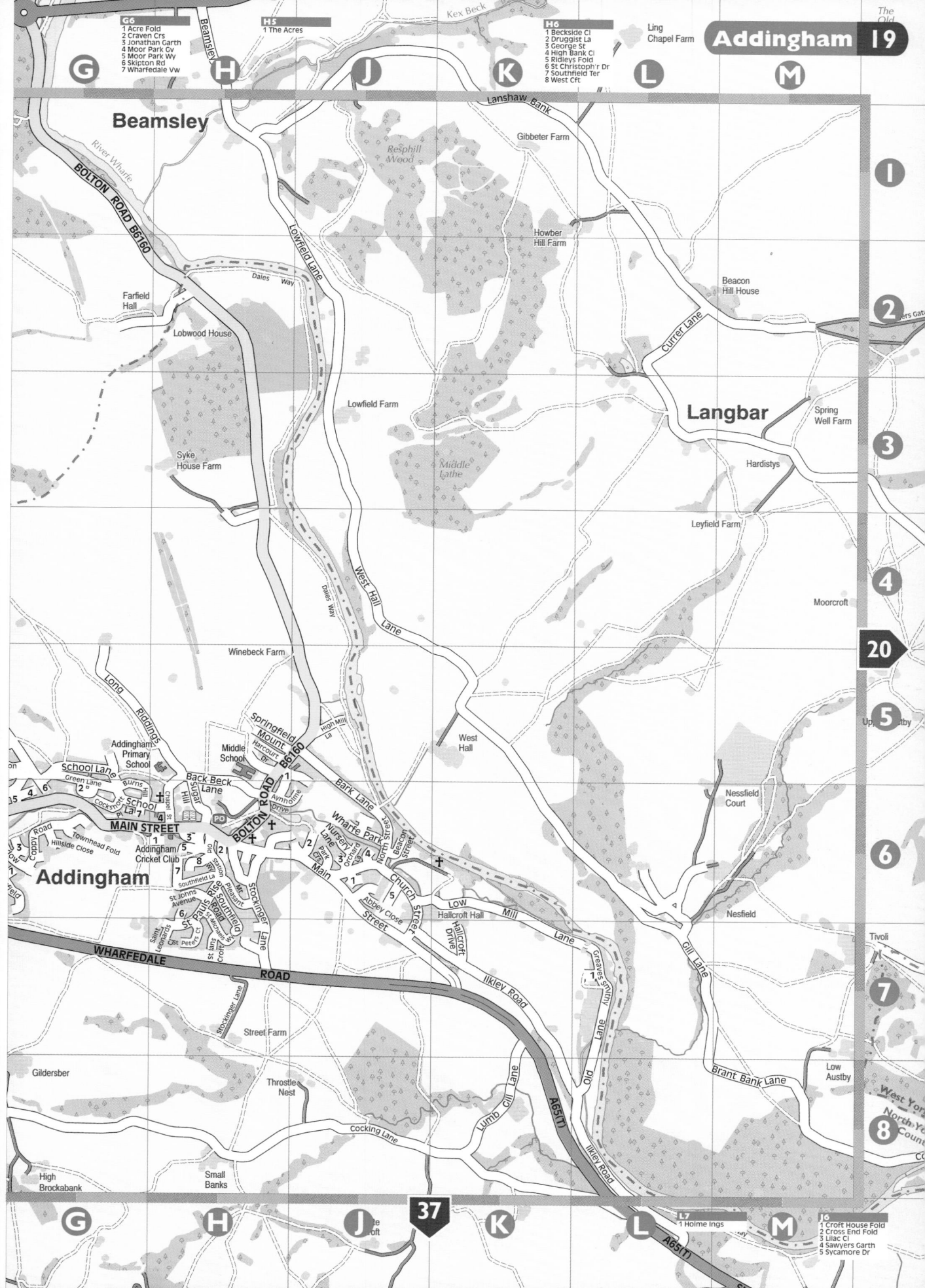

G6
1 Acre Fold
2 Craven Crs
3 Jonathan Garth
4 Moor Park Gv
5 Moor Park Wy
6 Skipton Rd
7 Wharfedale Vw

H5
1 The Acres

H6
1 Beckside Cl
2 Druggist La
3 George St
4 High Bank Cl
5 Ridleys Fold
6 St Christoph'r Dr
7 Southfield Ter
8 West Cft

L7
1 Holme Ings

J6
1 Croft House Fold
2 Cross End Fold
3 Lilac Cl
4 Sawyers Garth
5 Sycamore Dr

Beamsley

Langbar

Addingham

River Wharfe

BOLTON ROAD B6160

Farfield Hall

Lobwood House

Syke House Farm

Lowfield Lane

Dales Way

Lowfield Farm

Middle Lathe

West Hall Lane

Dales Way

Winebeck Farm

West Hall

Lanshaw Bank

Gibbeter Farm

Resphill Wood

Howber Hill Farm

Ling Chapel Farm

Beacon Hill House

Currer Lane

Spring Well Farm

Hardistys

Leyfield Farm

Moorcroft

The Old

Long Riddings

Addingham Primary School

Middle School

Springfield Mount

Harcourt

High Mill La

School Lane

Green Lane

Burns

Cockshott Pl

School La

Chapel St

Back Beck Lane

Sugar Hill

Avenholme Drive

BOLTON ROAD B6160

Bark Lane

Wharfe Park

North Street

Nessfield Court

Up Austby

Nesfield

Main Street

Townhead Fold

Hillside Close

Copy Road

Saint Leonards

St Pauls Rise

St Michaels

St Crofts

St Ians

St Peters

Addingham Cricket Club

Southfield La

Mt Pleasant

Station Rise

Stockinger Lane

Southfield Lane

St Johns Avenue

Nursery Lane

Park Orchard

Main

Church Street

Low Hallcroft Hall

Abbey Close

Hallcroft Drive

Greaves smithy Lane

Low Mill Lane

Gill Lane

Tivoli

WHARFEDALE ROAD

Stockinger Lane

Street Farm

Throstle Nest

Gildersber

Cocking Lane

Lumb Gill Lane

Gill Lane

Ilkley Road

A65(T)

Brant Bank Lane

Low Austby

West Yor North Yo Coun

High Brockabank

Small Banks

PO

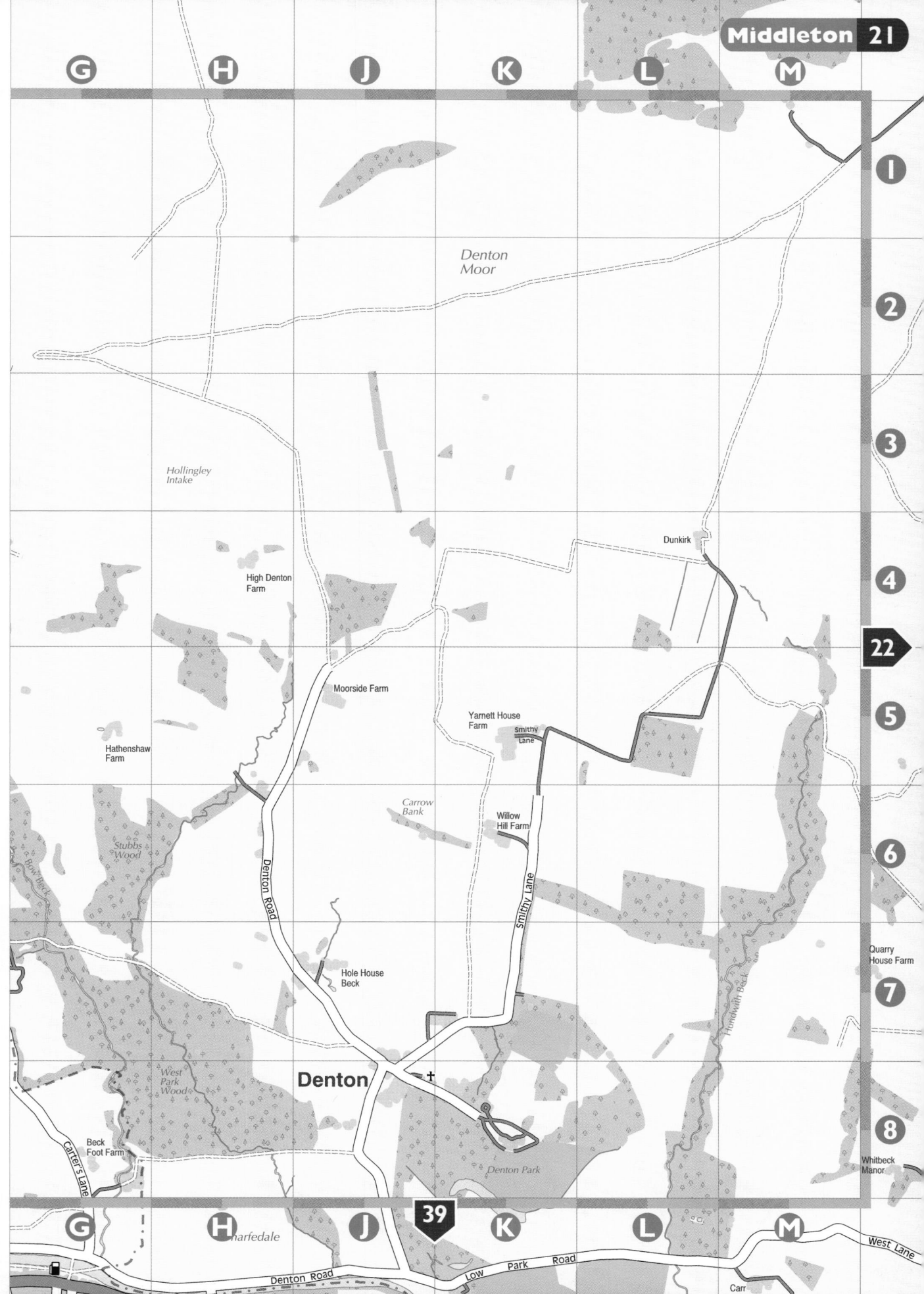

G   H   J   K   L   M

Denton
Moor

Hollingley
Intake

High Denton
Farm

Moorside Farm

Dunkirk

Yarnett House
Farm

Smithy
Lane

Hathenshaw
Farm

Carrow
Bank

Willow
Hill Farm

Stubbs
Wood

Denton Road

Smithy Lane

Bow Beck

Hole House
Beck

Hindwith Beck

Quarry
House Farm

West
Park Wood

Denton

Beck
Foot Farm

Carter's Lane

Denton Park

Whitbeck
Manor

Wharfedale

Denton Road

Low Park Road

West Lane

Carr

I

2

3

4

22

5

6

7

8

G   H   J   39   K   L   M

G   H   J   K   L   M

I
2
3
4
24
5
6
7
8

Reservoir

Cooper House

Scow Hall

Brat Lane

Jack Hill Lane

Maud Lane

Jack Hill

Hambleton House Farm

Top Lane

Brass Castle

Folly Hall

Norwood Bottom Road

River Washburn

Hunter's Stones

Prospecthouse Farm

B6451

Norwood Hall

Low Park

Norwood Bottom

Dobpark Wood

Middle Farm

River Washburn

Park Road

Bride Cross House

Rose Tree Farm

Lindley Wood Reservoir

Lindley Wood

Dob

Farnley Moor

FARNLEY LANE   B6451

Lin

Higher Carr Farm

Newall Carr Road

Crag Farm

G   H   J   K   L   M

Clifton

Lane

41

Haddockstones Farm

Farnley C of E Primary School

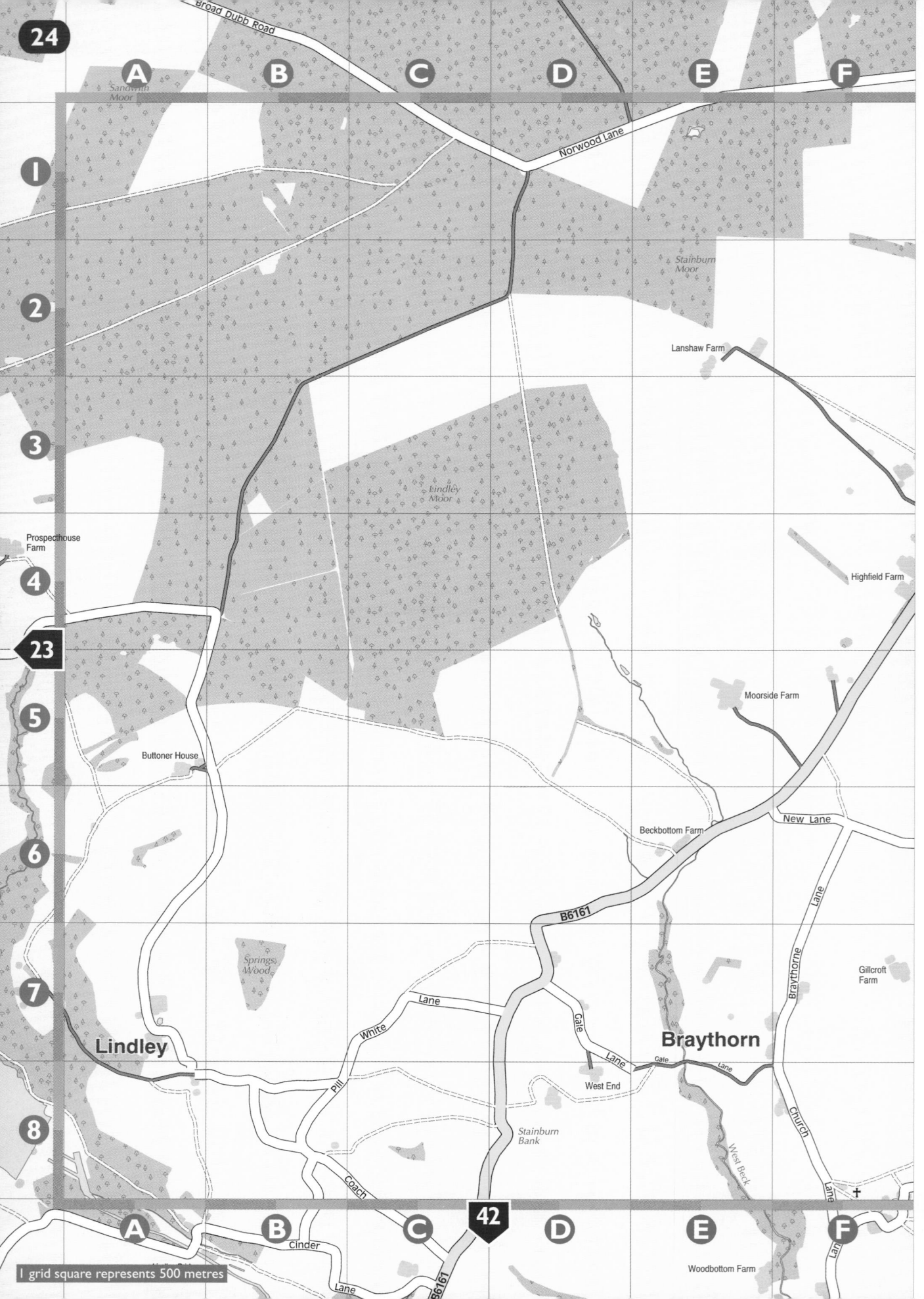

A   B   C   D   E   F

Broad Dubb Road

Sandwith Moor

Norwood Lane

1

2

Stainburn Moor

Lanshaw Farm

3

Lindley Moor

Prospecthouse Farm

Highfield Farm

4

Moorside Farm

5

Buttoner House

6

Beckbottom Farm

New Lane

B6161

Braythorne Lane

Springs Wood

Gillcroft Farm

7

Lindley

White Lane

Gale Lane

Braythorn

West End

Gale Lane

Church Lane

8

Stainburn Bank

West Beck

Pill

Coach Lane

Cinder Lane

Woodbottom Farm

A   B   C   D   E   F

1 grid square represents 500 metres

B6161

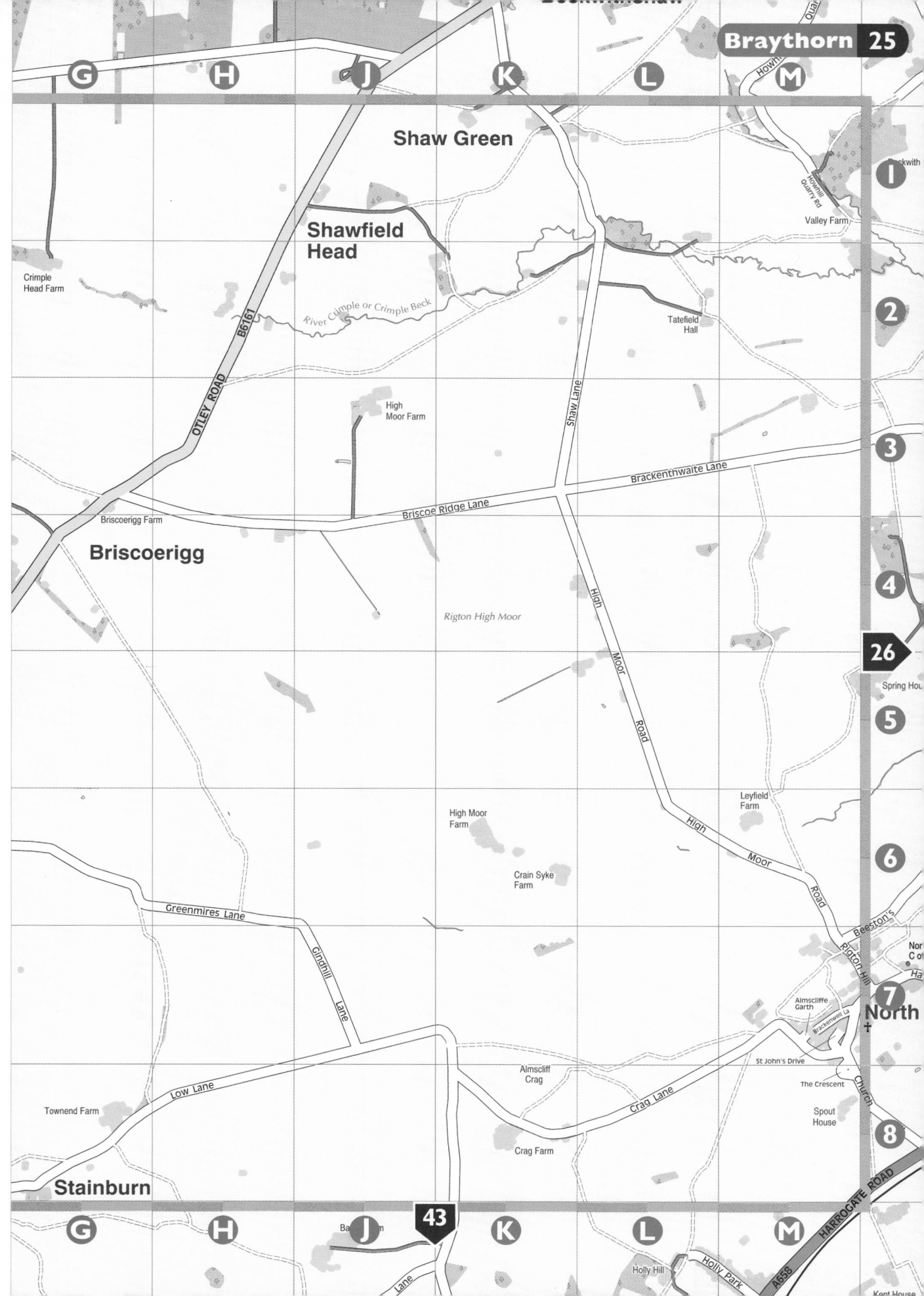

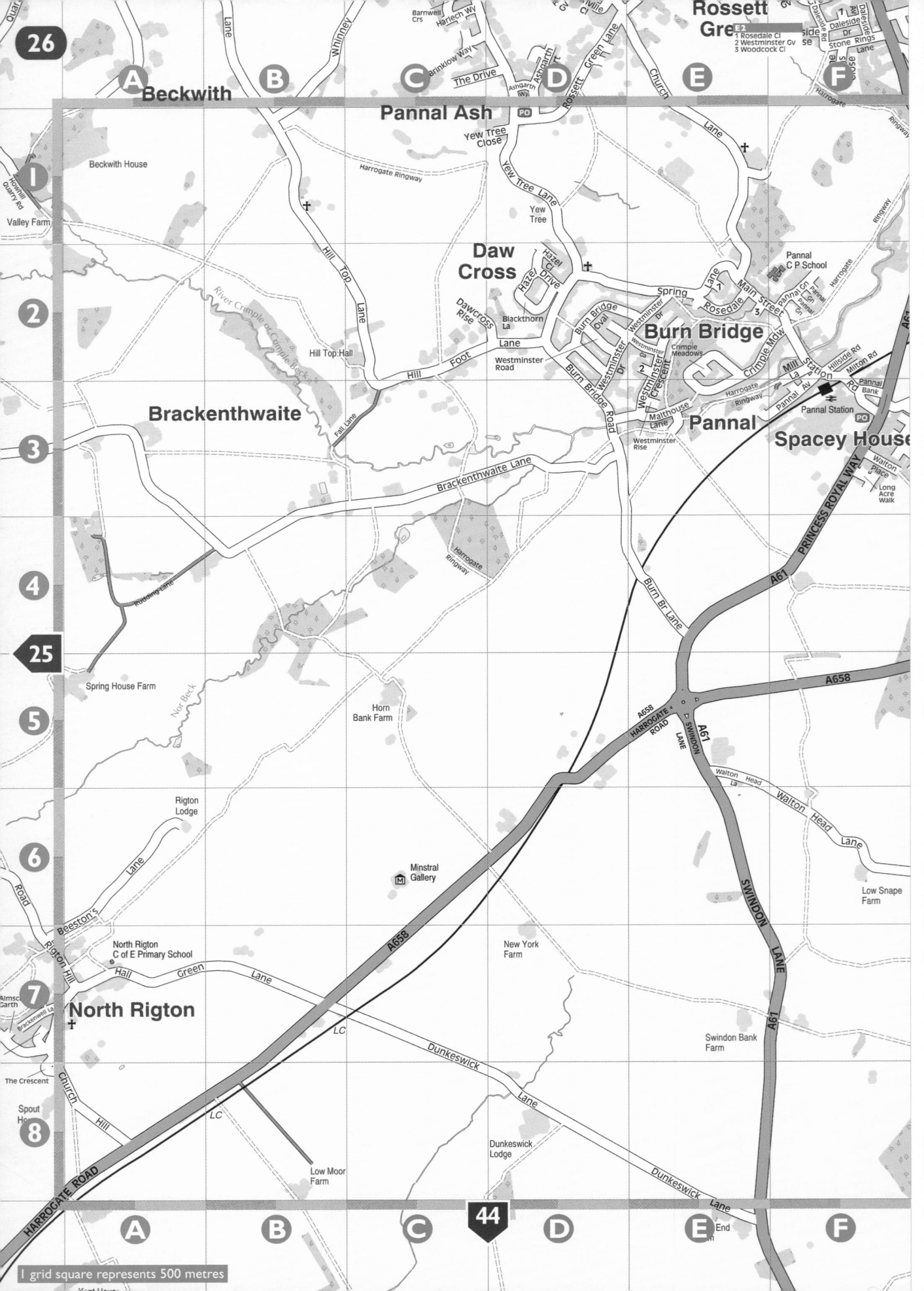

G H J K L M

Fulwith Lane
Fulwith Gate
Fulwith Close
Fulwith Drive
Fulwith Grove

Rudding Lane

Primary School
Freehold Garth
Main St.
The Paddocks
Valentine Rd

River Crimple or Crimple Beck

LC

Pannal Road

Haggs Road

A658

Pannal Road

Follifoot Road

Follifoot Lane

Spofforth Moor

Haggs Road

Drury Lane

Pannal Golf Club

Walton Avenue

Walton Park

Oakwood Farm

Spa Bottom Farm

Haggs Business Park

Haggs Farm

Spofforth Haggs

Follifoot Lane

28

Sunrise Farm

High Snape

Parks Farm

High

Follifoot Lane

Cemetery

Low Hall

Walton Head Lane

Kirkby Overblow C of E Primary School

Cemetery

Kirkby Overblow

Birdwell Farm

Wharfe View

Jasper Lane

Barrowby Lane

Swindon Lane

Swindon Wood

Swindon Hall

Lund Head

Barrowby

Rd Lane

1 2 3 4 5 6 7 8

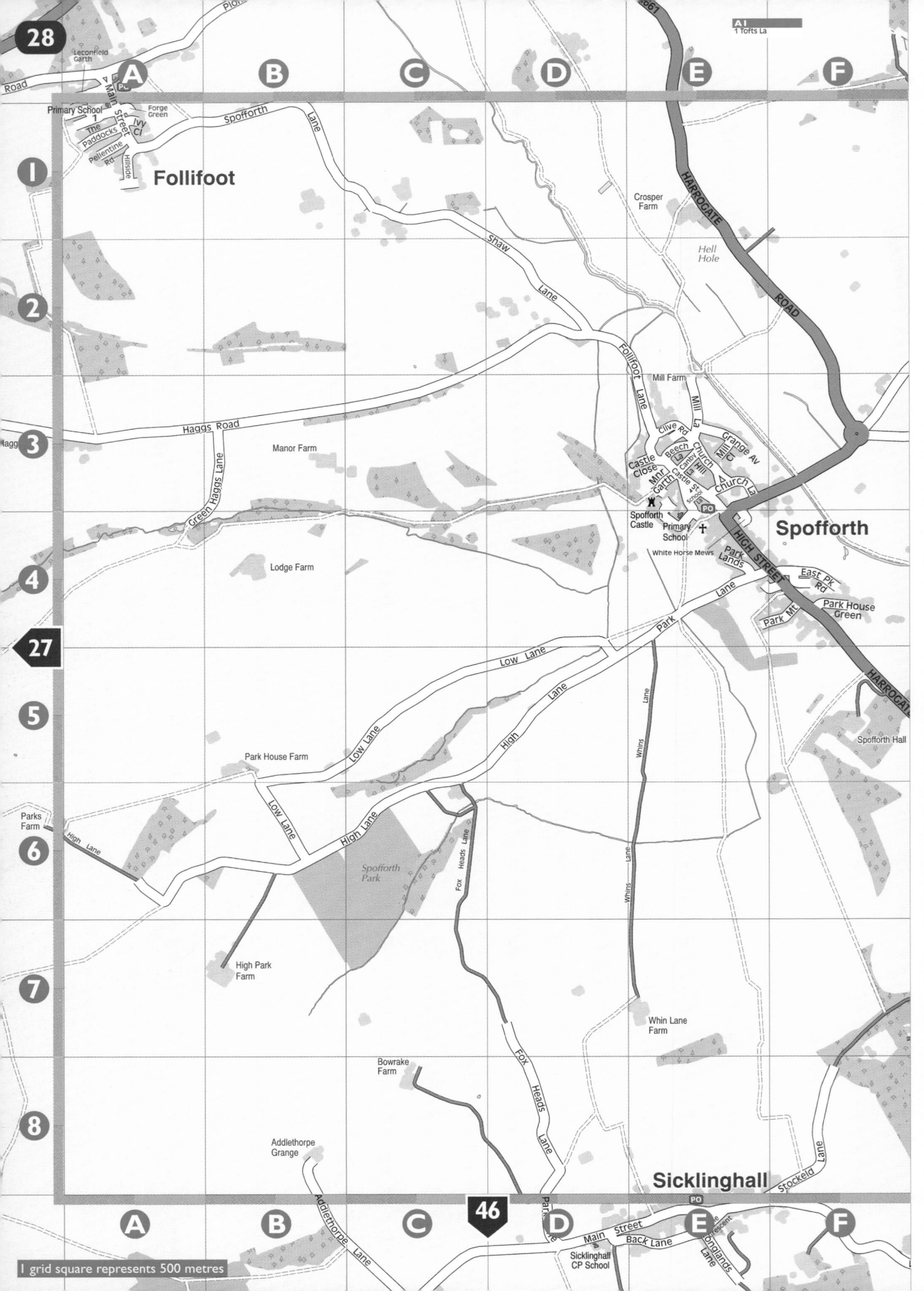

Leconfield Garth
Road
Primary School
The Paddocks
Pellentine Rd
Ivy Cl
Forge Green
Spofforth Lane
Main Street
Hillside

Follifoot

A B C D E F

I

2

Shaw Lane
Crosper Farm
Hell Hole
HARROGATE ROAD
A1 1 Tofts La

Haggs Road
Manor Farm
Green Haggs Lane
3
Mill Farm
Follifoot Lane
Clive Rd
Beech Castle Close
Mnr Garth
Castle
Church Hill
Grange Av
Mill La
Mill Cl
Church La
Church
PO
Spofforth Castle
Primary School
White Horse Mews
Park Lands
Spofforth

4
Lodge Farm
Park Lane
HIGH STREET
East Pk Rd
Park House Green
Park Mt

5
Low Lane
Lane
Whins Lane
HARROGATE
Spofforth Hall

Park House Farm
High Lane
Low Lane
High Lane
Parks Farm
High Lane
6
Spofforth Park
Fox Heads Lane

High Park Farm
7
Whin Lane Farm

8
Bowrake Farm
Fox Heads Lane

Addlethorpe Grange
Addlethorpe Lane
Sicklinghall
Stockeld Lane

A B C D E F
Main Street
Back Lane
PO
Sicklinghall CP School

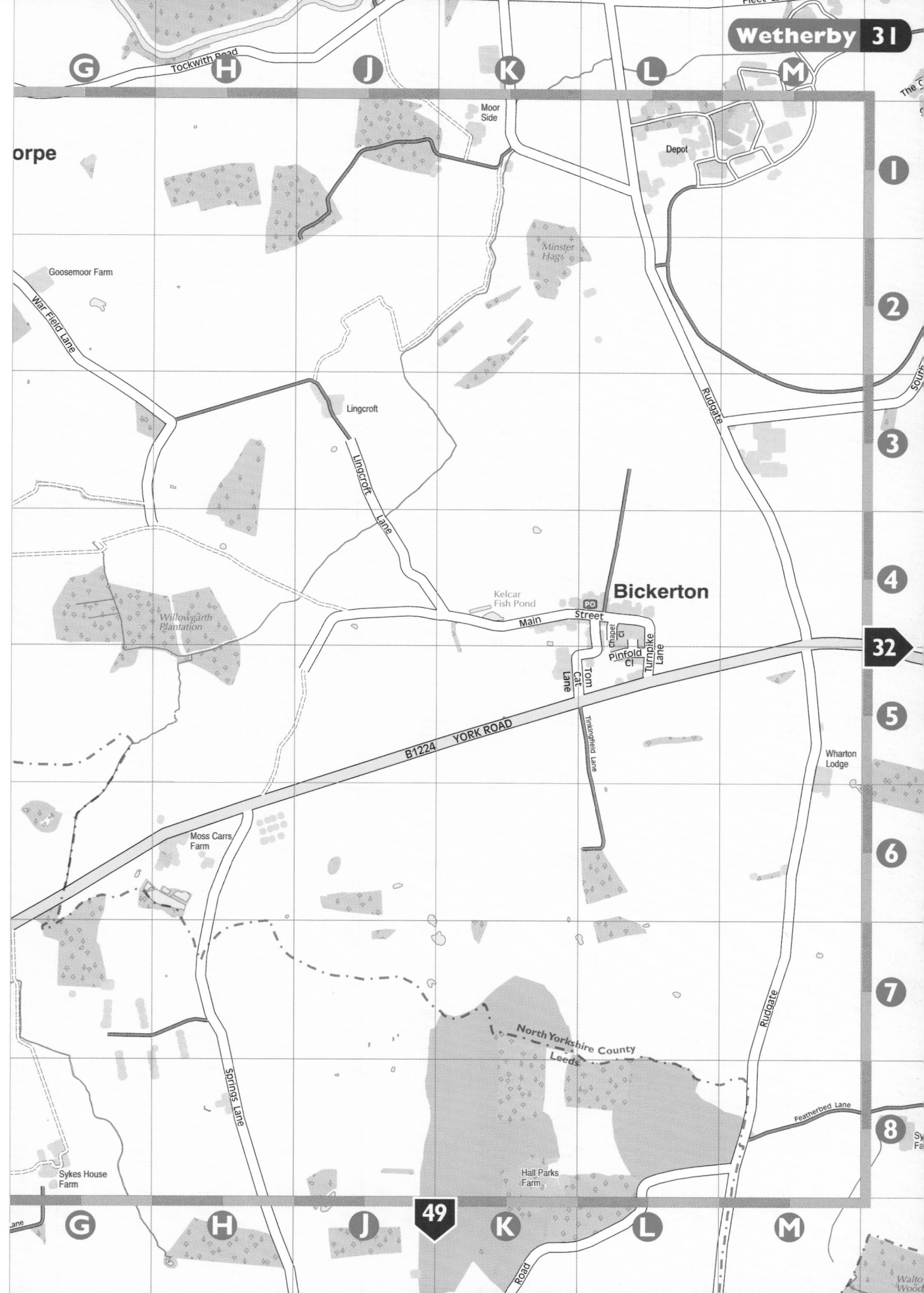

To B with

A B C D E F

Marston
Grange

The Green

Crawford
Close

Prince Rupert

Fairfax Drive

Westfield

Norfolk
Cardens

PO

Kendal Lane

Westfield Road

Kirk Lane

Kendal
Gardens

Ralph Garth

Tockwith Road

Marston Road

1

Lucas Rd

Lucas Grove North

Lucas Grove

Tockwith C of E
Primary School

2

South Field Lane

Tockwith Lane

Bilton
Grange

3

West
Grange

Moor Lane

4

B1224   WETHERBY   ROAD

Church Street

Marston
Wyes

Bilton in Ainsty

5

Wharton
Lodge

Manor Farm

Westlands

6

Bilton
Haggs

7

Nova
Scotia
Wood

The
Loft

Featherbed Lane

8

Syningthwaite
Farm

Waller House
Farm

A B C **50** D E F

1 grid square represents 500 metres

Wood

Battle
1644

G   H   J   K   L   M

York North Yorks) Council

Atterwith Lane

Mill Lane

Rufforth Hall

Atterwith Lane

B1

Moor Drain or New Cut

Hutton Thorn

Moor Drain or Old Cut

Manor Cha

YORK   ROAD

Tockwith Road

Old Lane

B1224

† **Long Marston**

WETHERBY ROAD   PO   Saddlers Way   Long Marston C of E Primary School

Butt Hedge

Angram Road

Hillside Farm

Hutton Wandesley

†

Hutton Street

Spring Lane

Healaugh Lane

Healaugh Lane

The Dam

Speng Lane

Healaugh Lane

Marston Lodge

Dam Bridge

Dam Hill

Collier Hagg Lane

Hutton Grange

Angram

Healaugh Grange

The Rash

G   H   J   K   L   M   New Lane

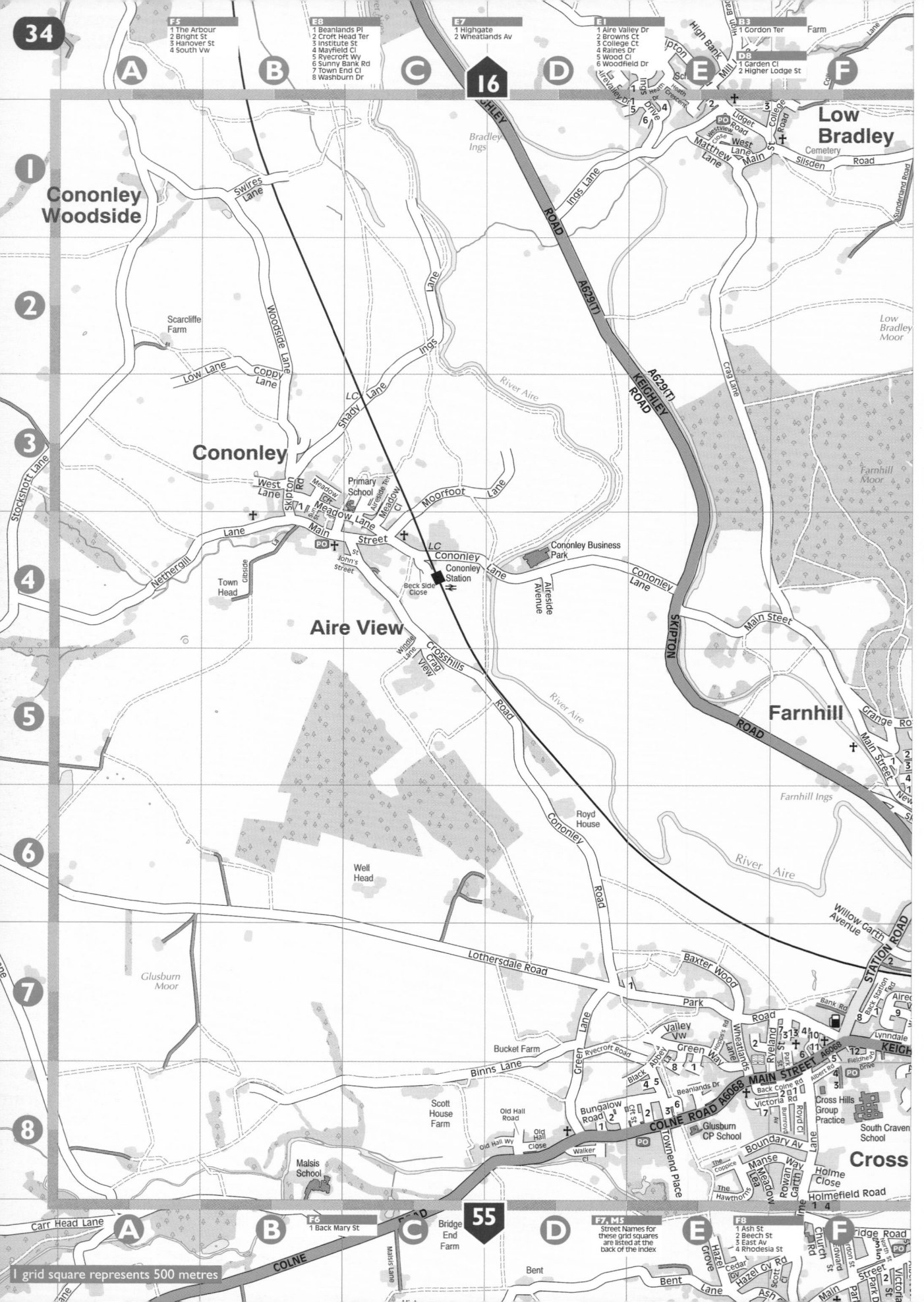

G5
1 The Crofts
2 High Croft Wy
3 Lang Kirk Cl

G6
1 Kirkgate

G7
1 Spencer Cl

G8
1 Keighley Rd
2 Ravensville
3 Westland Cl

H8
1 Greenfield Gdns
2 North Vw
3 Shoebridge Av

G H 17 J K L M

Smoulden Farm

Horne House

Dalesbank Farm

er Cliffe Farms

1

Jackson's Lane

Wilcock Lane

Low Lane

Horn Lane

2
Hay Hills Farms

Delph Farm

Hayhills Lane

Coate's Lane

Heights Lane

Bloomer Hill

Hole Lane

Lane

3

Hole Farm

Bridge House

Kildwick Moor

Dennis Lane

Raikes Head

Burnsall Mews

Bradford North Yorkshire County

Low Bracken Hill Farm

Bradley Road Bradley Brop Bradley Rise Bradley Av

3

N Dene Av sackvill

4
13

New Lane

High Cross Moor Farm

Crag Top

Skipton Road

Kildwick Grange

Bracken Gv Drive High Green Drive Green Cv Bracken Ml Foster Avenue

Park Green Cll Croft
Hawkcliffe Vw Lower Grn

Cornwall Av Gloucester Avenue Kent Av

Elliott St

Woodside Road

36

New Rd

KIRKGATE

5
Infant Schl

Hall Gdns.

Starkey Lane Mary Street rby Rd

Lane House

Kildwick C of E Primary School Bank

Priest Bank Rd

Leeds and Liverpool Canal

PO

Woodside

Airedale House Farm

Silsden Health Centre

Taylor St Millfields

10

South Vw Ter Vale Junior Sch

Aire Pl St

12

Low H Drive

6

Kildwick

BD20

Grange Bridge

Airedale

Cowling Bridge

Silsden Cricket Club

Sykes

A603A

Silsden Bridge

KEIGHLEY ROAD

7

A629(T)

Hardings Lane

LC

Churchill Wy

dale W
kipton Av
Elmfield Rd
Av

Junction

SKIPTON RD

KEIGHLEY ROAD

Steeton & Silsden Station

8

Rivock Avenue

LEY ROAD
ire Aire St
Crs
Clayton
Hall Road

SKIPTON ROAD B6265

Eastburn Bridge

Lyon Road

Green Lane

Eastburn Junior & Infant School

Ings Rd

Wilson Av

Thornhill

Camel Road

Currer Wk

Teal Ct

Heron Close

Robin Dr

Steeton Grove

St Stephen's Court

Summerhill Lane

Hills

B6265

Green Rw Close

Mill

Eastburn

Styveton Way

Elm View

Station Road

Halsteads Way

Fortia Aire Vlly

Cemetery

Clough Av

Ennsley

St Stephen's

PO

Low Fold
Fast Pde

Steeton Junior & Infants School

Steeton

Cricketers Walk

56

SKIP

Chapel Road

Steeton Health Centre

Bank House

M8
1 Summerhill Av
2 Summerhill Dr

M4
1 Fardene St
2 Green Av
3 Kilnsey Fold
4 Newton Cl
5 Throstle Nest Rd
6 Tillotson St

L8
1 Gare Forth Av
2 Steeton Hall Gdns

K8
1 Curlew Ct
2 Tewitt Cl
3 Thornhill Gv

G H 56 J K L M

Sutton Mill

The Knott F

Sutton Mill

Eastburn

Steeton

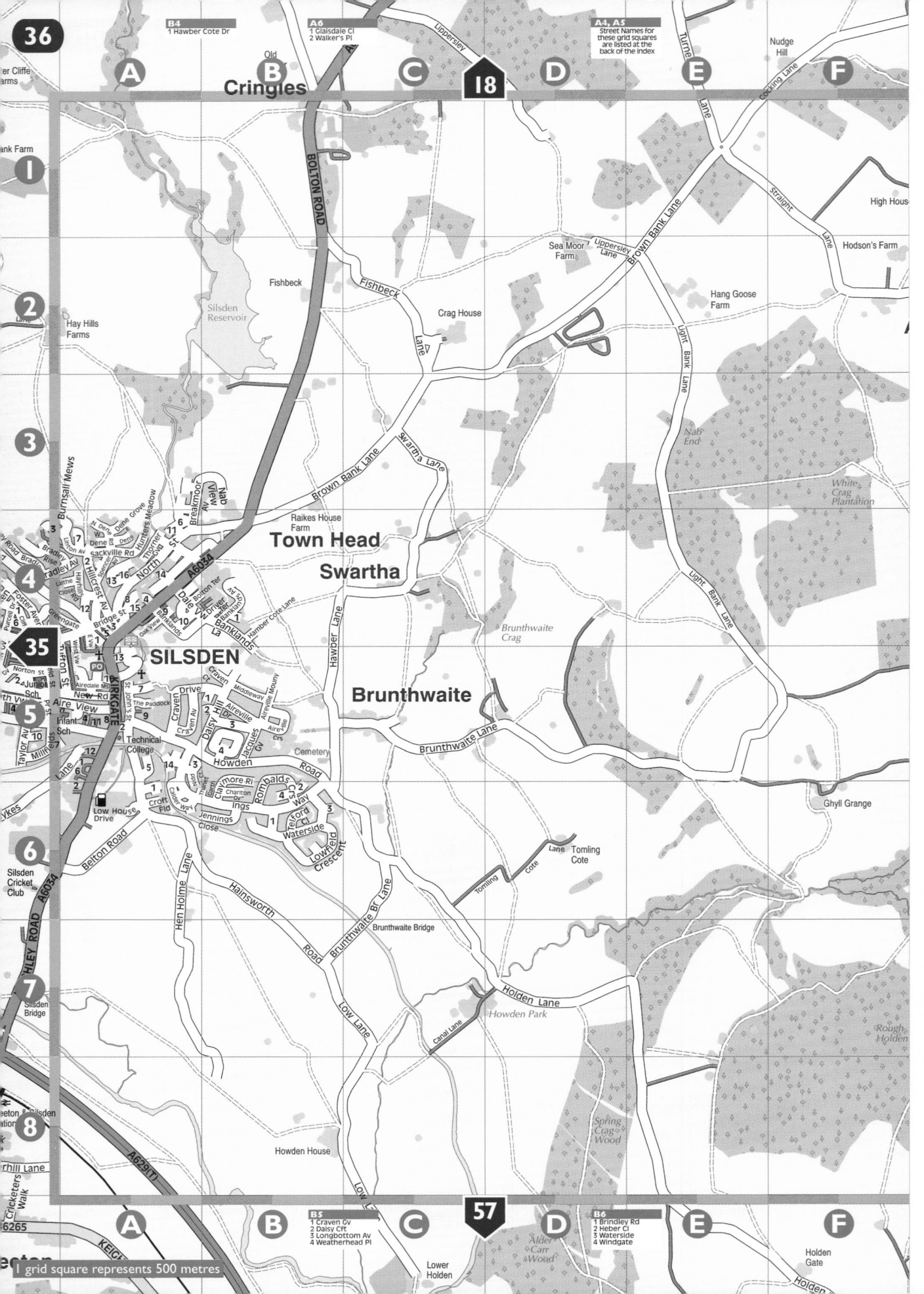

B4
1 Hawber Cote Dr

A6
1 Glaisdale Cl
2 Walker's Pl

A4, A5
Street Names for
these grid squares
are listed at the
back of the index

Nudge Hill

A B C **18** D E F

Cringles

I

High House

Bolton Road

Lippersley Lane

Sea Moor Farm

Lippersley Lane

Brown Bank Lane

Turner Lane

Cooking Lane

Straight Lane

Hodson's Farm

Fishbeck

Fishbeck

Crag House

Hang Goose Farm

Silsden Reservoir

Hay Hills Farms

Lane

2

Light Bank Lane

Nab End

3

Brown Bank Lane

Swartha Lane

Raikes House Farm

White Crag Plantation

Town Head

Swartha

Burnsall Mews

Breakmoor Av

Nab

North St

A6054

Dene Grove

Hunters Meadow

Thorper

Bradley Rise Av

Hillcrest Av

Larkfield

sackville Rd

Dene Rd

Bolton Ter

Driver

Hamber Cote Lane

Hawber Lane

Brunthwaite Crag

Light Bank Lane

4

Foster

Greengate

Banklands

Banklands

Oak View

Aireville

SILSDEN

St John's

Kirkgate

PO

Craven Drive

Middleway

Aireville Av

Aireville Mount

Brunthwaite

35

Junior Sch

New Rd

Aire View

Infant Sch

The Paddock

Daisy Hill Dr

Jacques Gv

Aire Cre

Aireville Crs

Brunthwaite Lane

5

Taylor Av

Millfields

Technical College

Howden

Sycamore Ri

Charlton Gv

Cemetery

Romdalds

Rombalds Way

Ghyll Grange

Croft Fld

Canal Way

Jennings

Close

Waterside

Telford Cl

Lowfield Crescent

Tomling Cote

Cote Lane

Low House Drive

Belton Road

Hen Holme Lane

Hainsworth

Road

Brunthwaite Br Lane

Brunthwaite Bridge

Tomling

6

Silsden Cricket Club

A6034

7

Silsden Bridge

Low Lane

Holden Lane

Canal Lane

Howden Park

Rough Holden

HLEY ROAD

8

eeton & Silsden ation

A629(T)

Howden House

Low Lane

Spring Crag Wood

hill Lane

Cricketers Walk

6265

KEIGH

A B **B5** C **57** D **B6** E F

B5
1 Craven Gv
2 Daisy Cft
3 Longbottom Av
4 Weatherhead Pl

B6
1 Brindley Rd
2 Heber Cl
3 Waterside
4 Windgate

Alder Carr Wood

Lower Holden

Holden Gate

Holden

1 grid square represents 500 metres

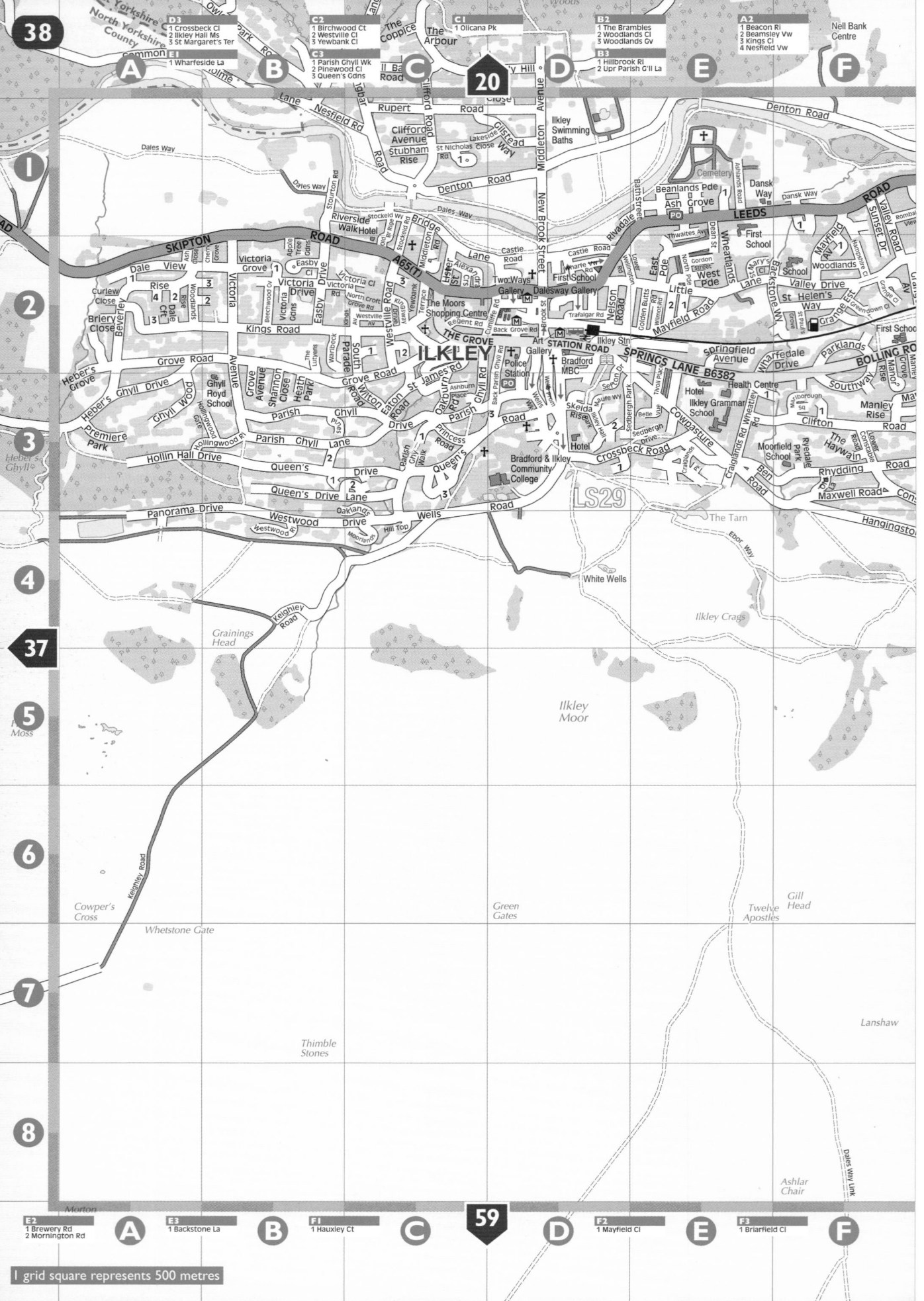

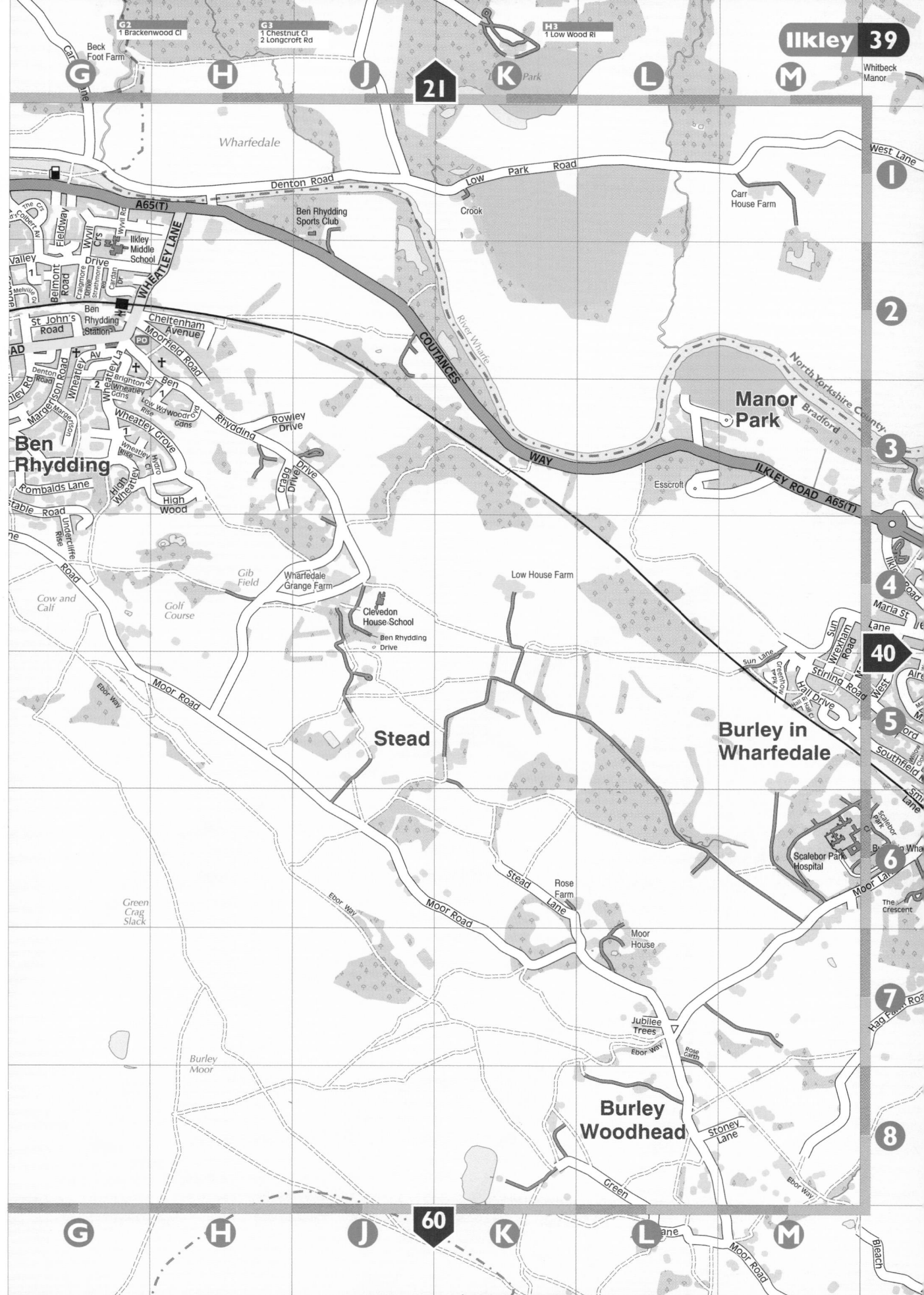

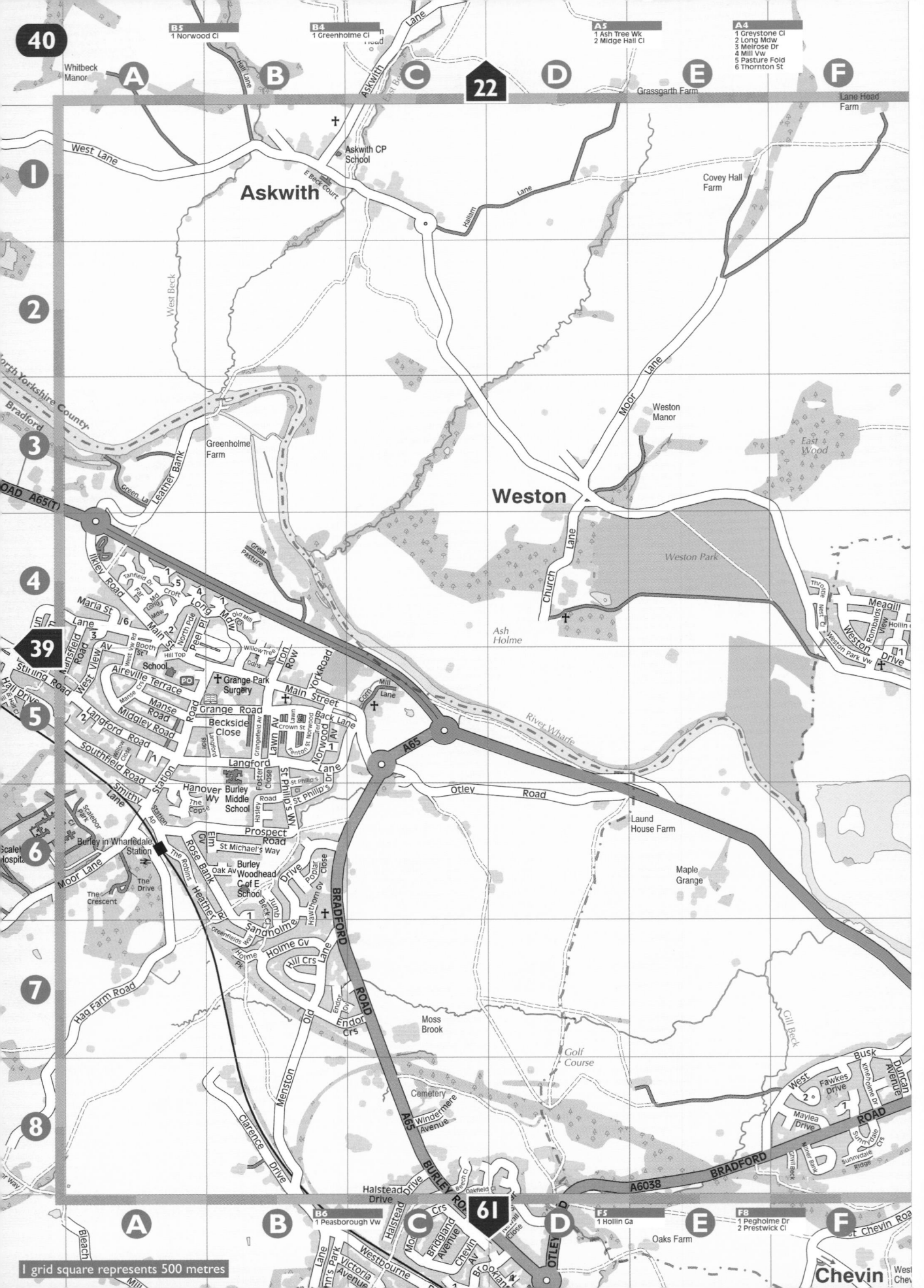

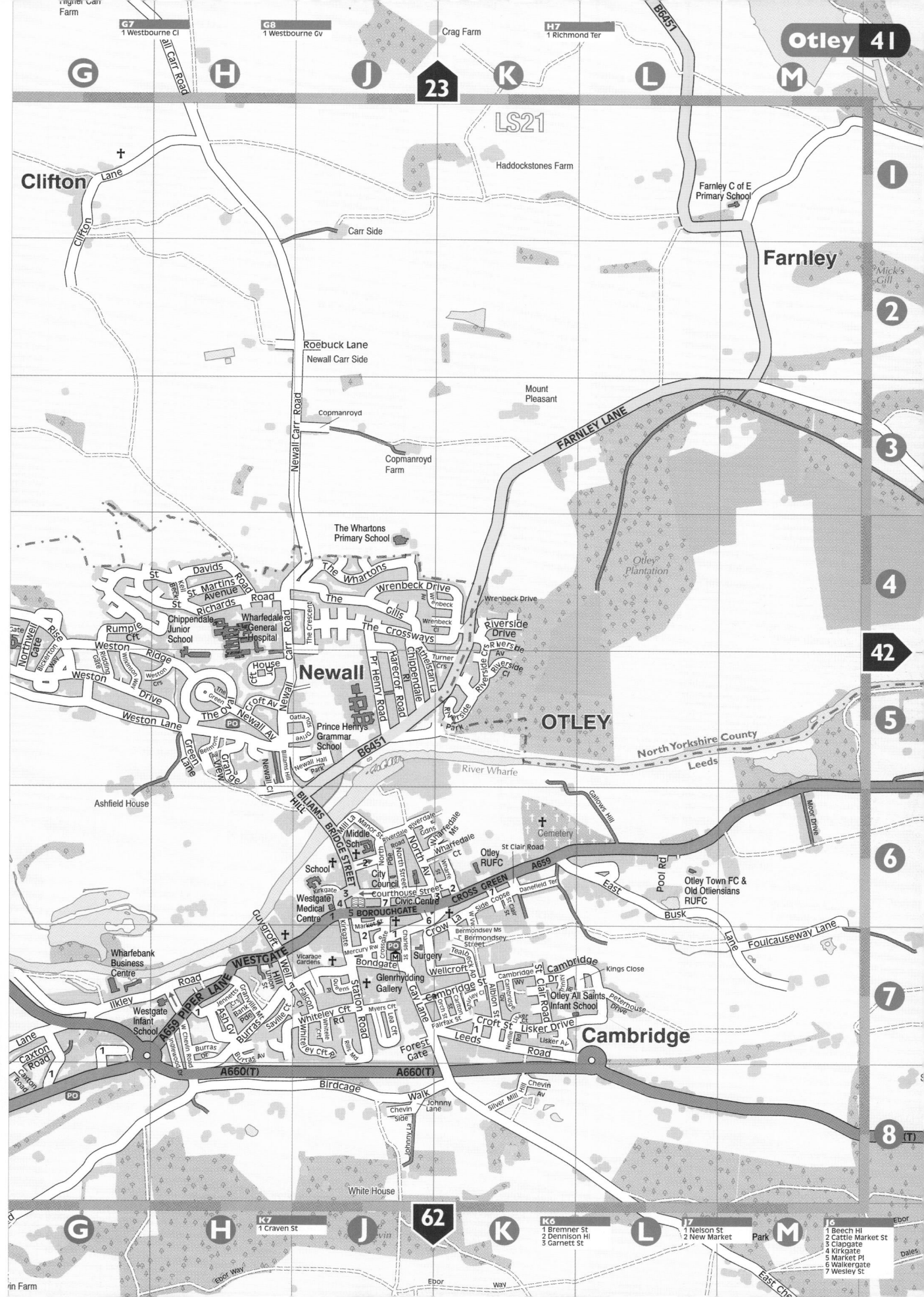

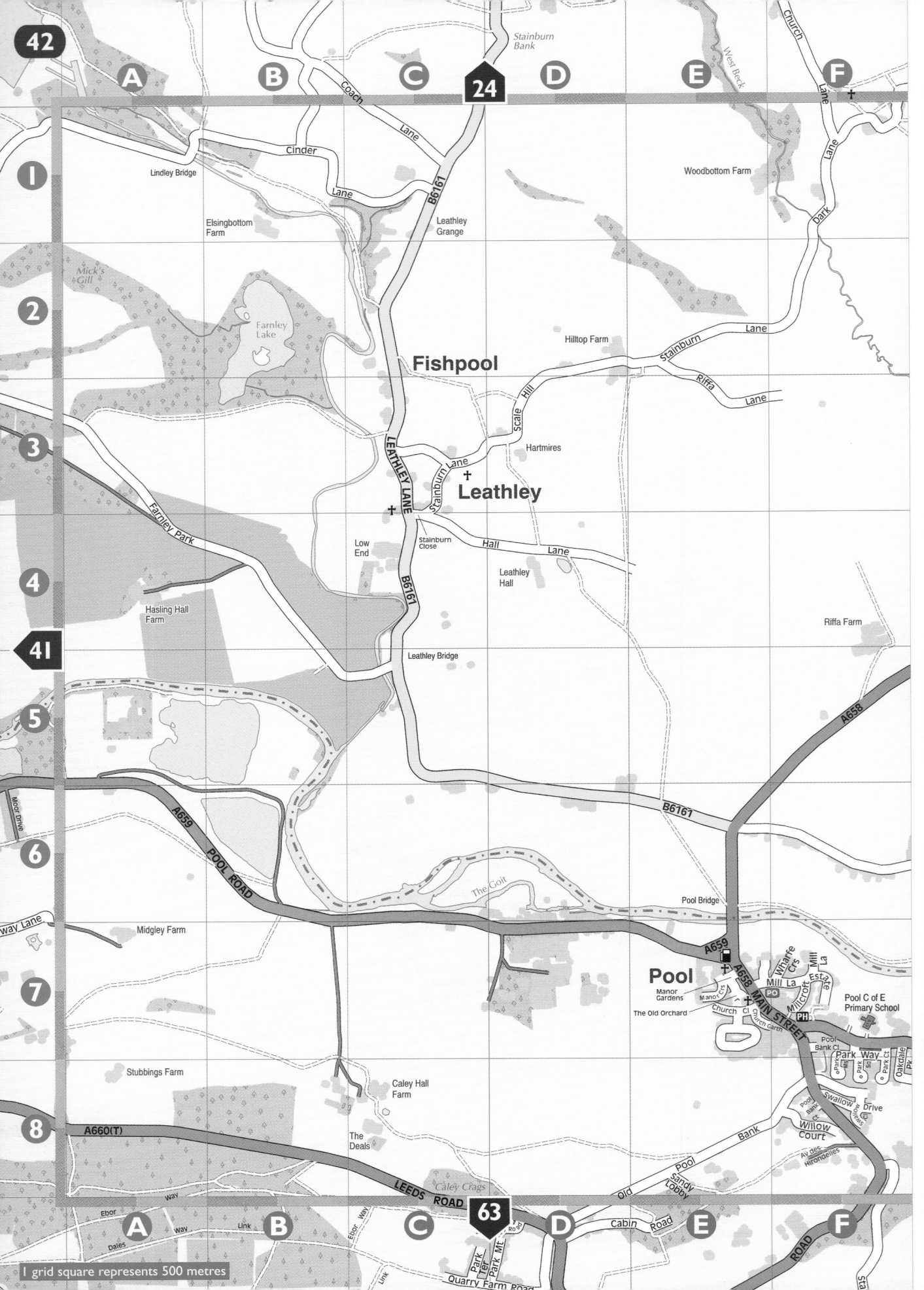

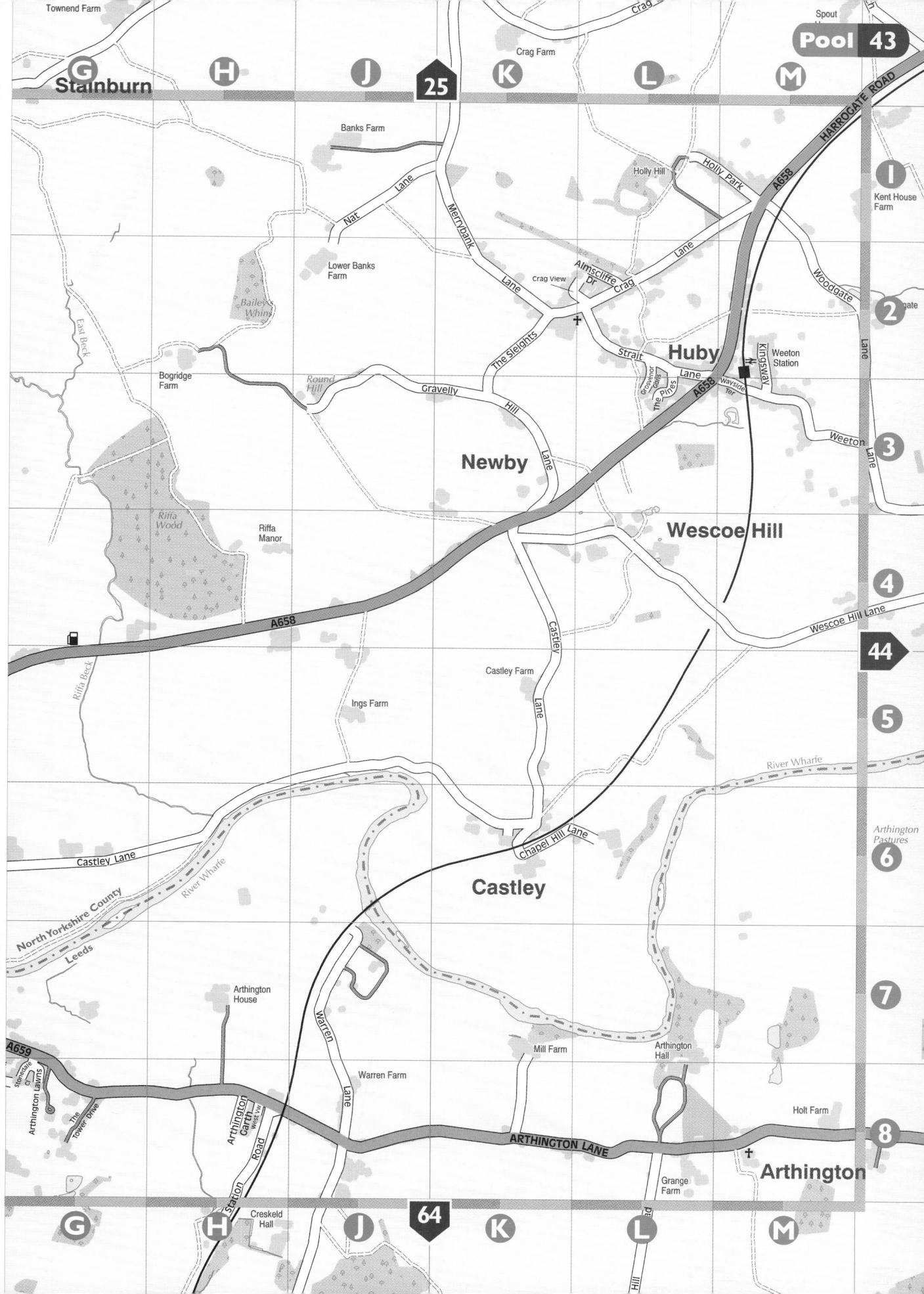

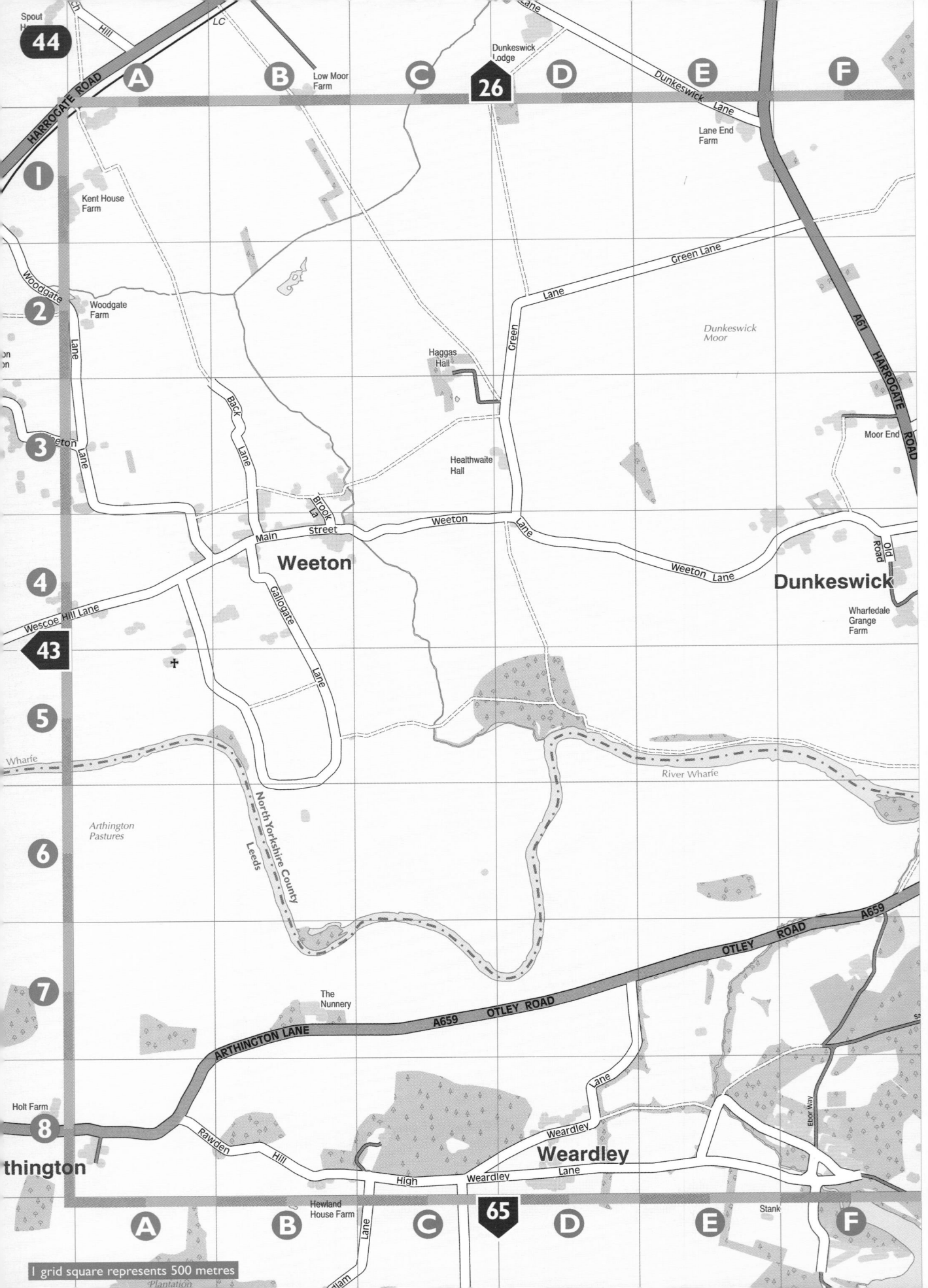

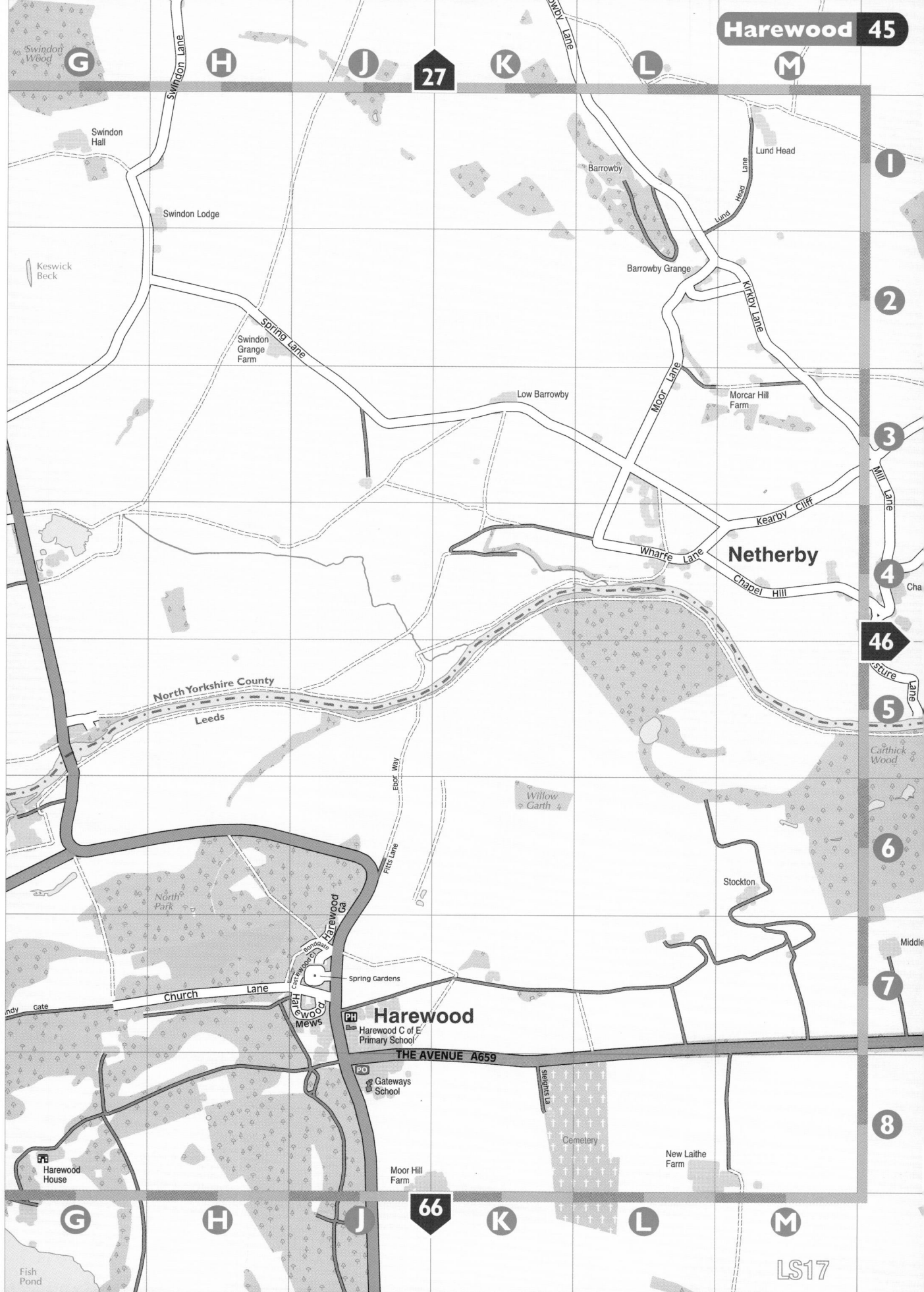

G H J K L M

27

I
2
3
4
46
5
6
7
8

Swindon Wood

Swindon Hall

Swindon Lodge

Keswick Beck

Swindon Lane

Spring Lane

Swindon Grange Farm

Barrowby

Lund Head

Barrowby Grange

Morcar Hill Farm

Low Barrowby

Moor Lane

Kirkby Lane

Lund Head Lane

Mill Lane

Kearby Cliff

Wharfe Lane

Netherby

Chapel Hill

Cha

North Yorkshire County

Leeds

Carthick Wood

Willow Garth

Ebor Way

Fitts Lane

Stockton

Middle

North Park

Harewood Ga

Bondgate

Castlewood

Church Lane

Spring Gardens

Harewood Mews

PH **Harewood**

Harewood C of E Primary School

PO Gateways School

THE AVENUE A659

Sleights La

Cemetery

New Laithe Farm

Harewood House

Moor Hill Farm

Fish Pond

Andy Gate

G H J K L M

66

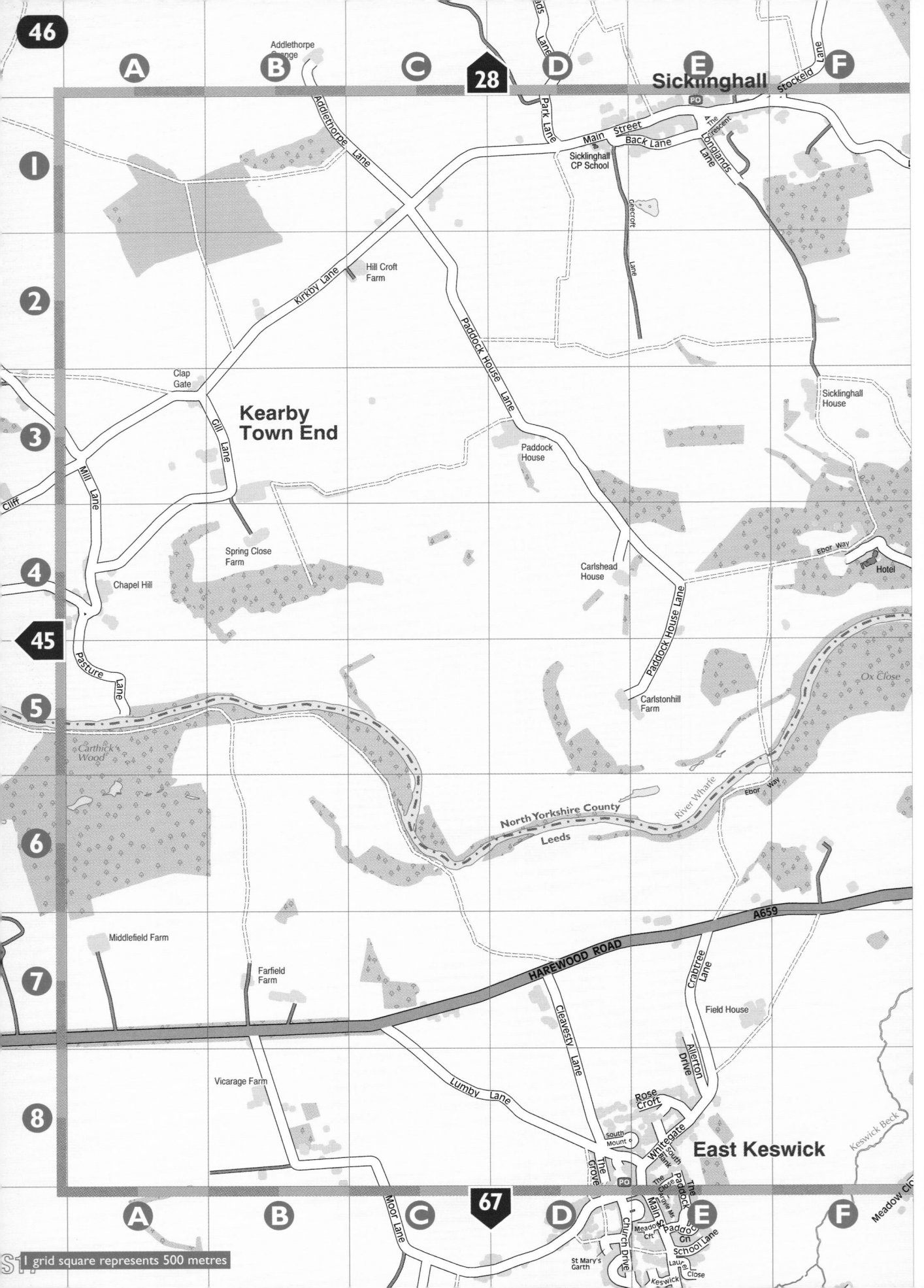

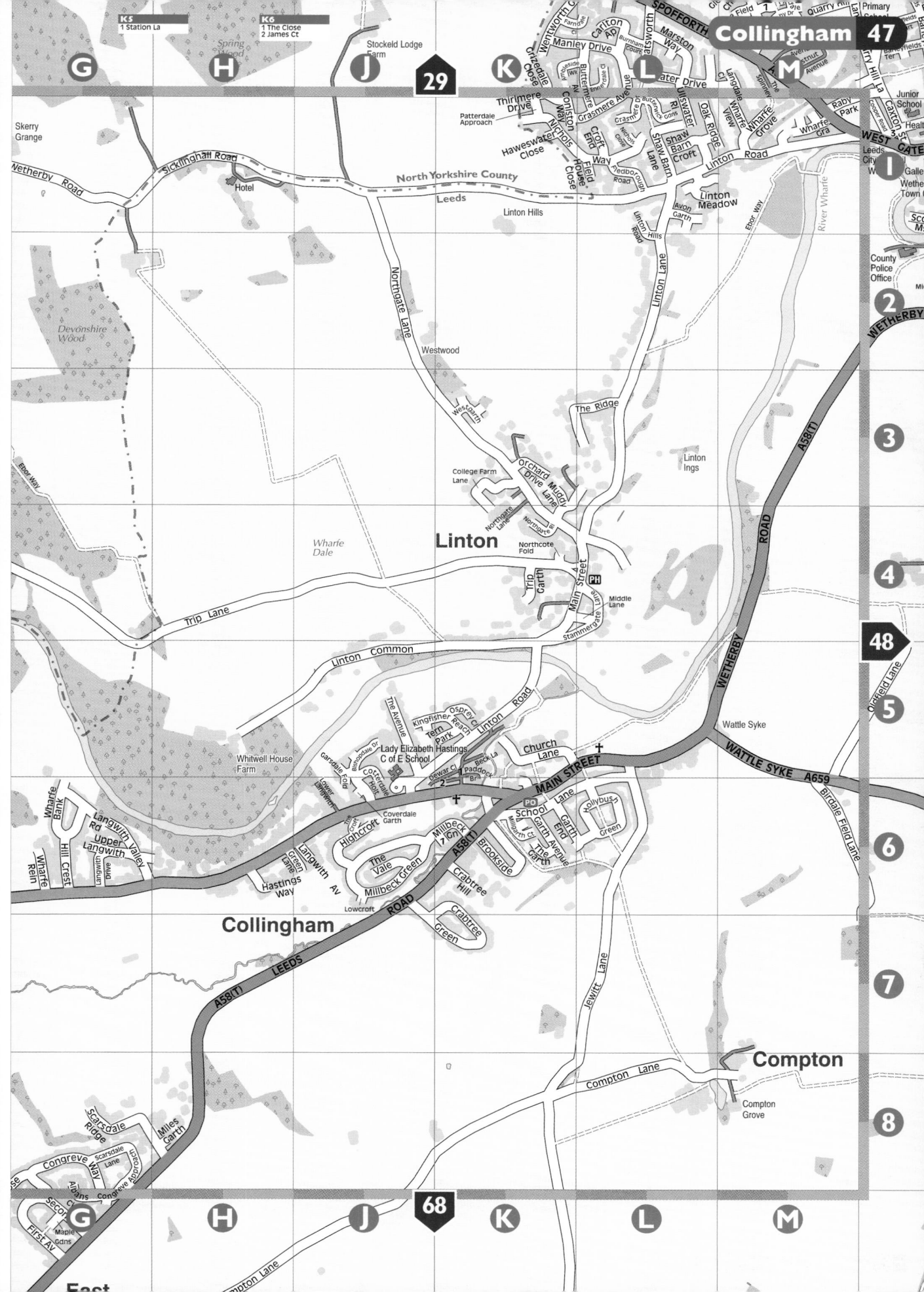

G6
1 Royal Ter

G7
1 Greystone Cl
2 Grove Pl
3 Holly Bush Ct
4 Spa Ms

G H J 31 K L M

I

2

3

4

50

5

6

7

8

Walton Wood

Walto Wood

Sy House Farm

Wetherby Road

School Lane

Main

Croft Lane Street

Smiddy Hill

Walton

Hall Parks Farm

Hall Park Road

Inholmes Lane

Rudgate

Rudgate

North Yorkshire Coun

Grange Avenue

Northfields

Rudgate Park

Walton Chase

Road

Walton Lodge

Wood Lane

Avenue A

Street 7

Wighill Lane

Walton Road

Trading Estate

Av C East

Street

Avenue G

Trading Estate

Street 5

Avenue C West

Street 7

Avenue F

Wood Lane

Dowkell Lane

Causeway

Church

Lady Elizabeth Hastings C of E School

Mulberry Garth

Whins Lane

Avenue B

Street 3

Avenue D

Street 5

Avenue E

East

Avenue E West

Ings Lane

Thorp Arch Park

Pear Tree Acre

The Village

Thorp Arch Park

Thorp Arch

Street 7

Avenue

Street 2

Avenue E

Avenue West

Spa Baths

Mill Lane

Bridge Foot

Orchards

Bridge Rd

Pine Tree Av

PO

Hotel

HIGH STREET

Clifford Road

Hall Ms

Hall Close

Spa Lane

Stables Lane

Lime Tree Gdns

Beeches End

Hudson

1

3

The Square

River Wharfe

Green Lea Close

Grove Crescent

Grove Crs

Grove Green

Grove

Road

River View

Gas Works Lane

Grove Gardens

Cinder Lane

HighTrees School

Spa Lane

A659

Works

Firgreen Bridge

Bar Lane

A659

Croft La

Main

G H J 70 K L M

Oglethorpe Hall Farm

Watson's Lane

Rudgate

Lucerne Farm

New Mil La

Oxfield Mill

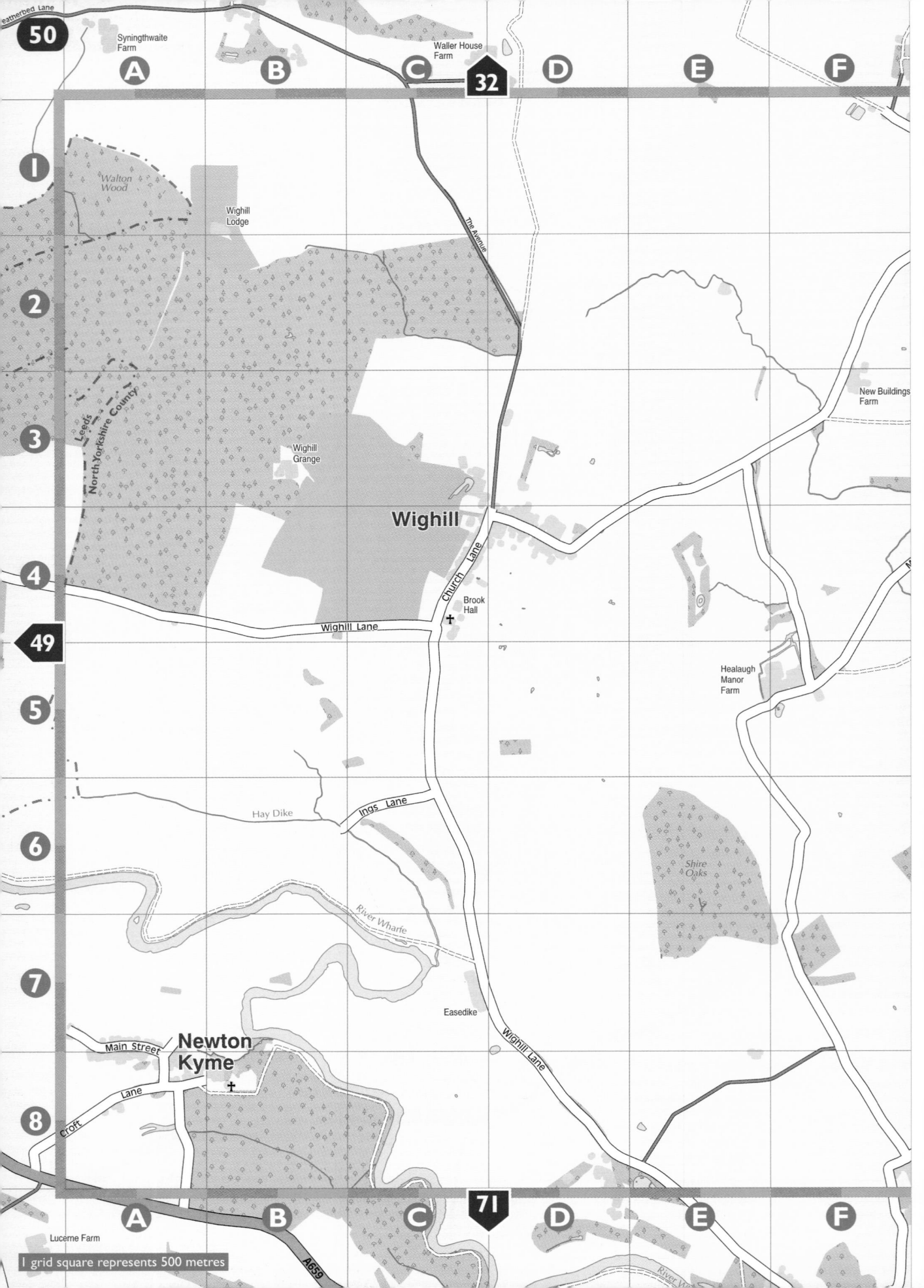

Ⓐ　　　　Ⓑ　　　　Ⓒ　　Ⓓ　　　　Ⓔ　　　　Ⓕ

32

Syningthwaite
Farm

Waller House
Farm

The Avenue

① Walton
Wood

Wighill
Lodge

②

Leeds
North Yorkshire County

③ Wighill
Grange

Wighill

Church Lane

④ Wighill Lane
Brook
Hall ✝

49

⑤ Healaugh
Manor
Farm

New Buildings
Farm

⑥ Hay Dike
Ings Lane
Shire
Oaks

River Wharfe

⑦
Easedike

Wighill Lane

Main Street
**Newton
Kyme**
✝

Croft Lane

⑧

Lucerne Farm

Ⓐ　　　　Ⓑ　　　　Ⓒ　　Ⓓ　　　　Ⓔ　　　　Ⓕ

71

A659

1 grid square represents 500 metres

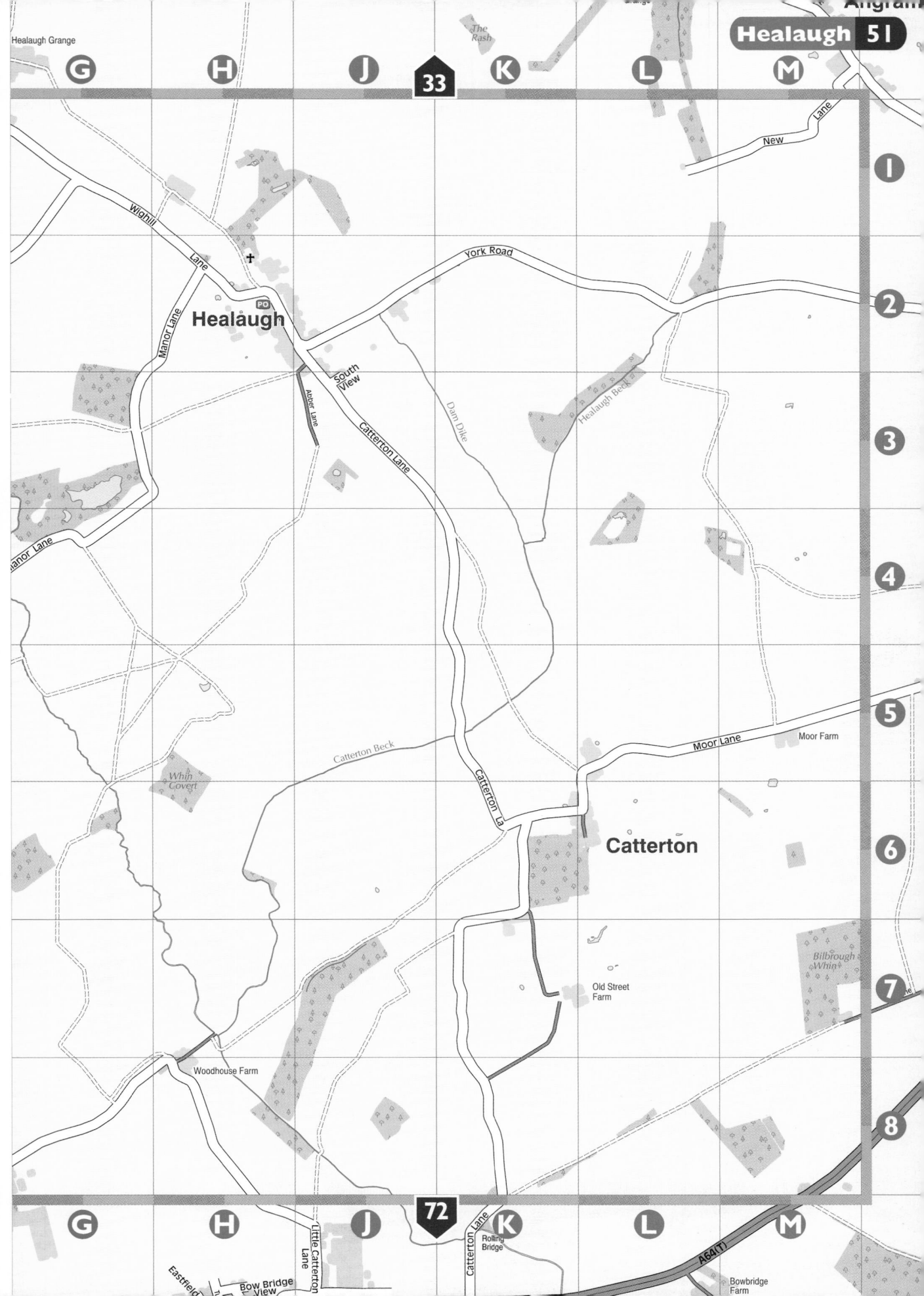

G H J 33 K L M

1
2
3
4
5
6
7
8

Healaugh Grange

Wighill Lane

Manor Lane

Healaugh

PO

South View

Abber Lane

Catterton Lane

Dam Dike

York Road

The Rash

Healaugh Beck

New Lane

Manor Lane

Whin Covert

Catterton Beck

Catterton La

Catterton

Moor Lane

Moor Farm

Bilbrough Whin

Old Street Farm

Woodhouse Farm

Little Catterton Lane

Catterton Lane

Rolling Bridge

A64(T)

Bowbridge Farm

Eastfield

Bow Bridge View

Bashfield Farm

C8
1 Derwent Cl

B8
1 Buttermere Av
2 Coniston Gv
3 Hawes Dr
4 Langdale Ri
5 Thirlmere Av

A8
1 Bristol St
2 Chatham Crs
3 Cranbourne St
4 Douglas St
5 Lark St
6 New Bath St
7 New Oxford St
8 Percy St
9 Regent Av

A5
1 Breeze Cl
2 Chapel St
3 Ivegate
4 Stoney La

A   **B**   **C**   **D**   **E**   **F**

Heads

Dotcliffe

Yorkshire Dales
Land Mining Museum

Primary Sch

Kelbrook

I

Old Lane

Cob Lane

Thick Bank

Roger Moor

2

Great Hague

COLNE ROAD

A56

Old Stone Trough Lane

Old Stone Brow

Old Stone Trough

Hague House

3

Accornlee Hall

Skipton Old Road

Oxenards

Earl Hall

4

New Road

Trent Farm

Great Edge

SKIPTON

PO

Noyna Bottom

Flass Bent

Foulridge

5

Archery Av

BUSWAY

Noyna Av

Lower Broach

Noyna Hall

Bent Laithe

Salter Syke

6

St Michael & All Angels C of E Primary School

Cock Hill

Cockhill Lane

Colne Golf Club

Long Lane

Flass

The Manor

Brown Hill Lane

7

Foulridge Upper Reservoir

Noyna Vw

Manor Rd

Castle Road

Blue Bell

Lane Head

Emmott

A56

Castle Road

Venables Rd

Park High School

Heyroyd

Hill Lane

Laneshawbridge CP Sch

8

SKIPTON ROAD

Snell Gv

Casserley Rd

Thorn Gv

Fern Street

Bent Lane

Sheridan Road

Alma Rd

Vernon Rd

KEIGHLEY

Chatham St

Temple St

Elm St

Lilac Oak

Vincent St

Cleveland St

Windermere Rd

Ryda Pl

Favordale

A6068

KEIGHLEY ROAD

Colne

ROAD A6068   **WINDSOR**   **LANGROYD RD**   SKIPTON RD

F8
1 Kingsley Rd

St Church E School

St Stephen's Wy

Colne Cricket Cl

74

St Church E School

BairGrove Dr

A   **B**   **C**   **D**   **E**   **F**

Norfolk St

KEIGHLEY

B6250

COTTON TREE

Craven

Standroyd Drive

Clarence

Keighley

Ing Heys

I grid square represents 500 metres

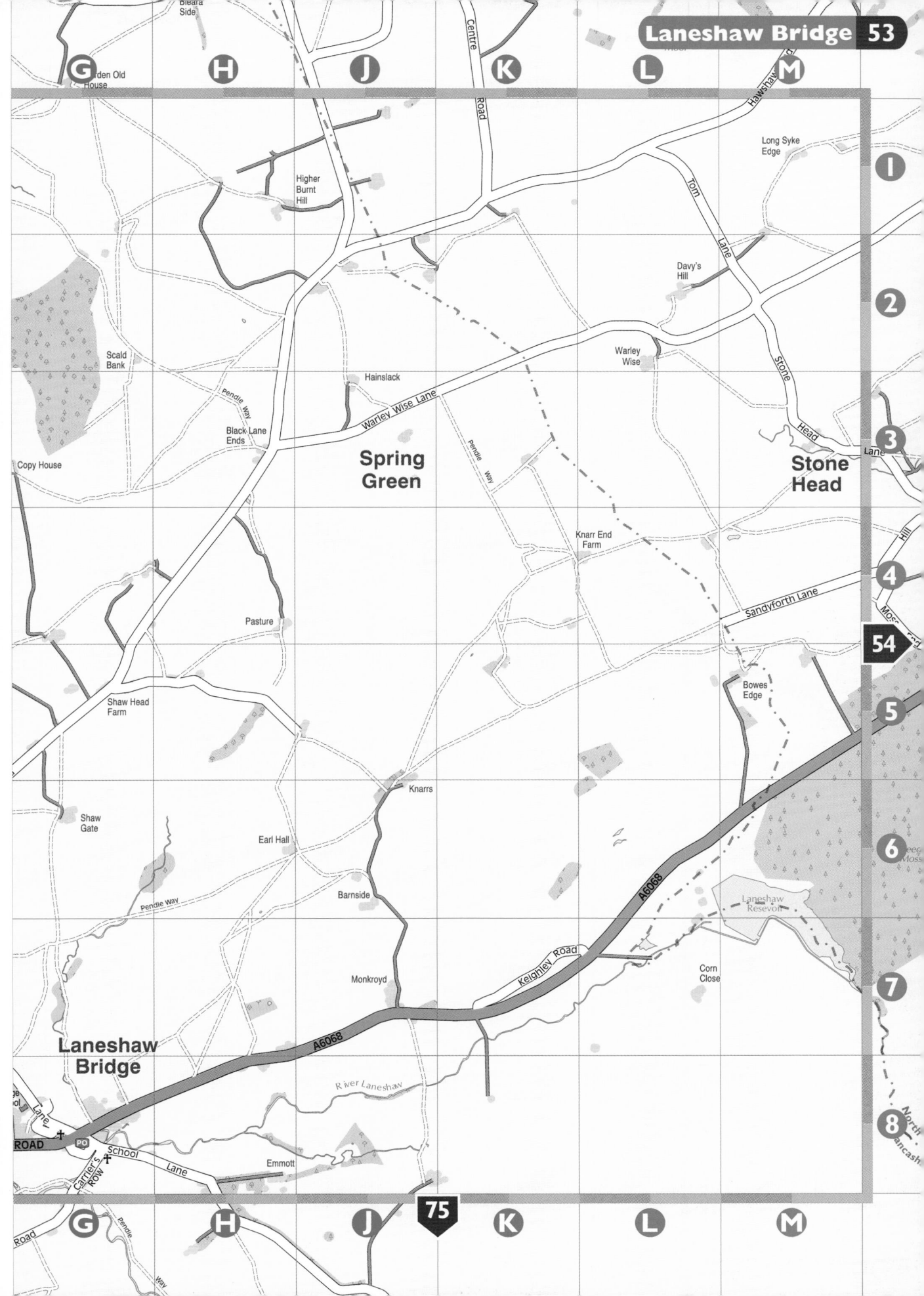

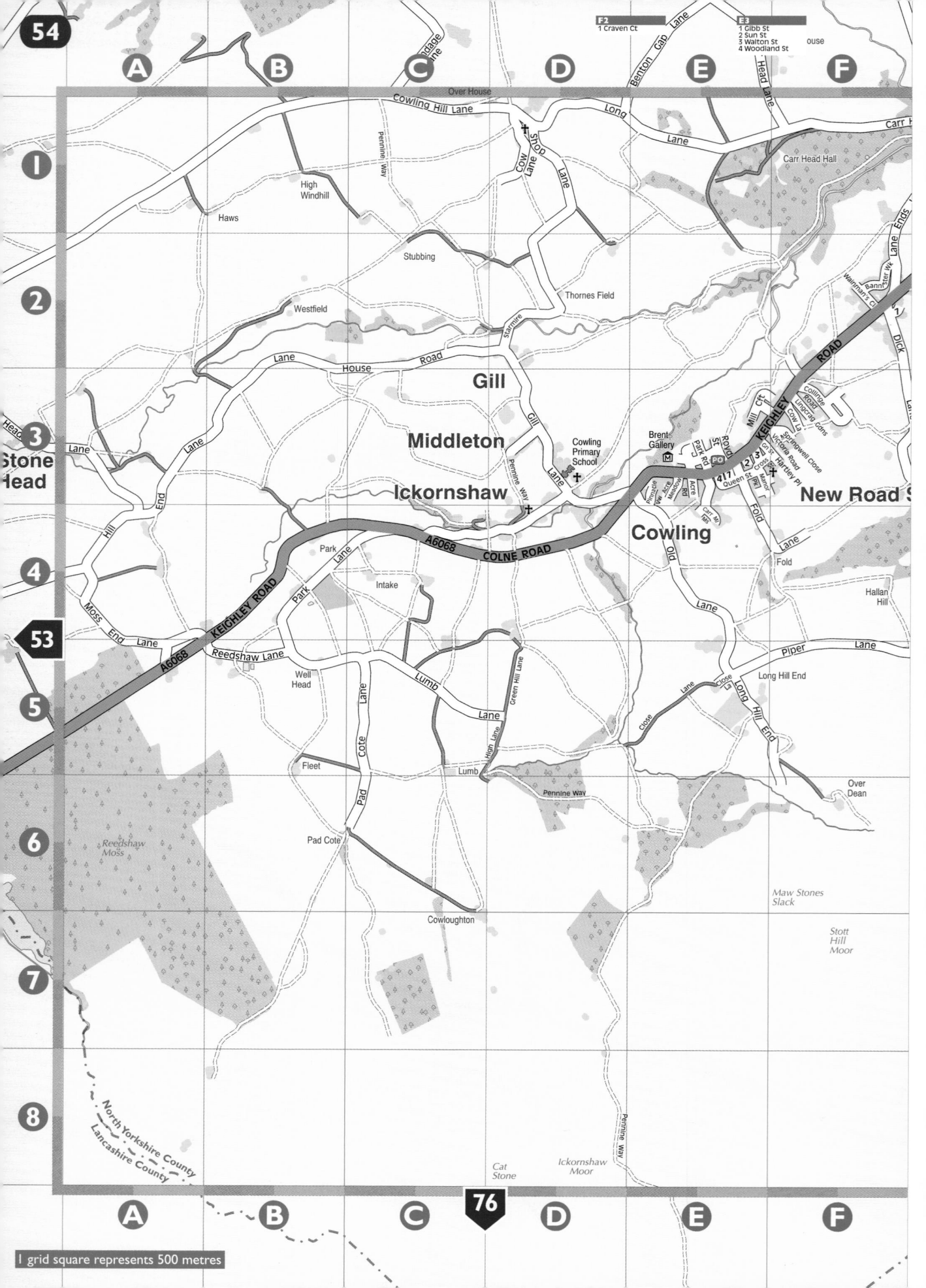

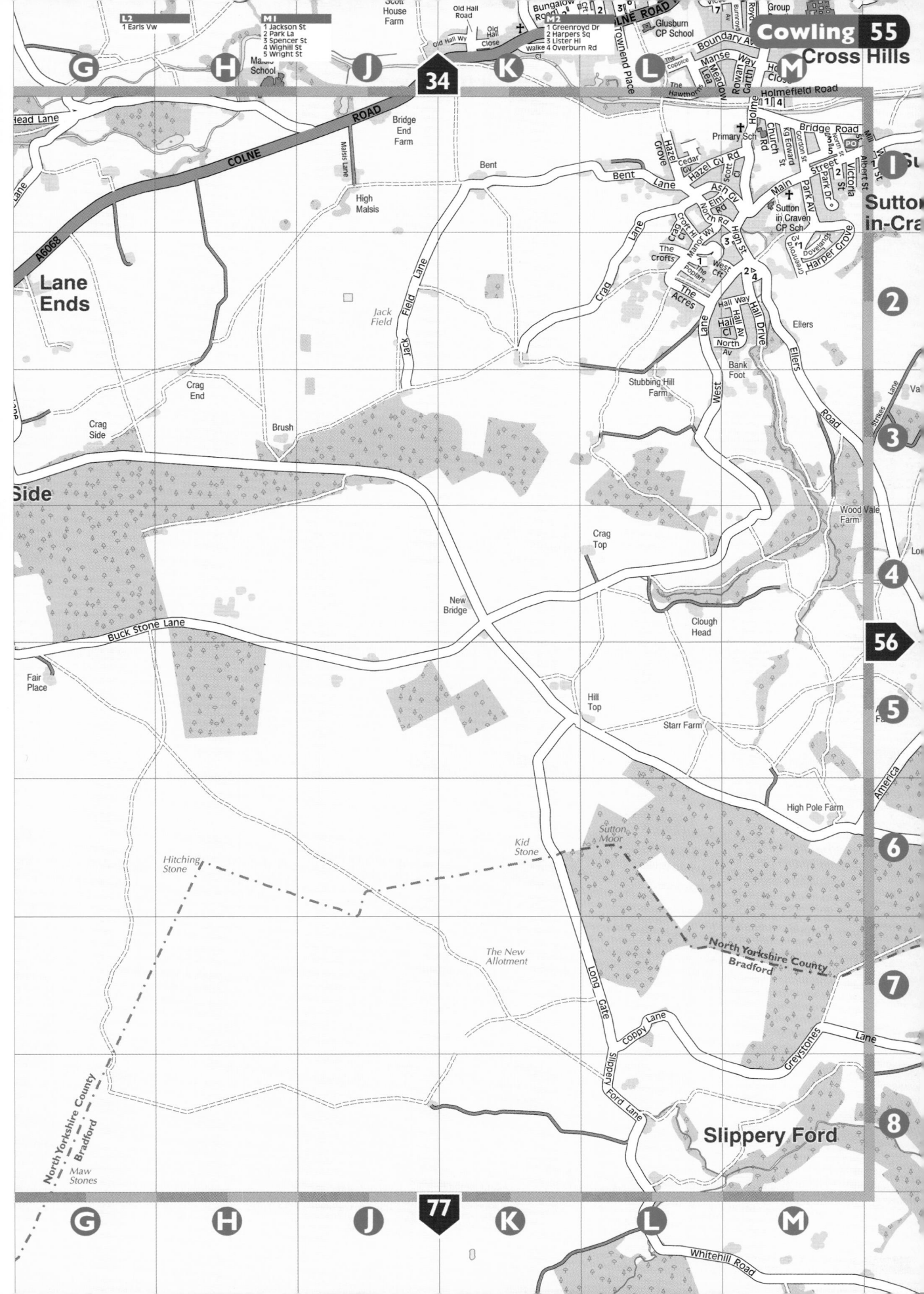

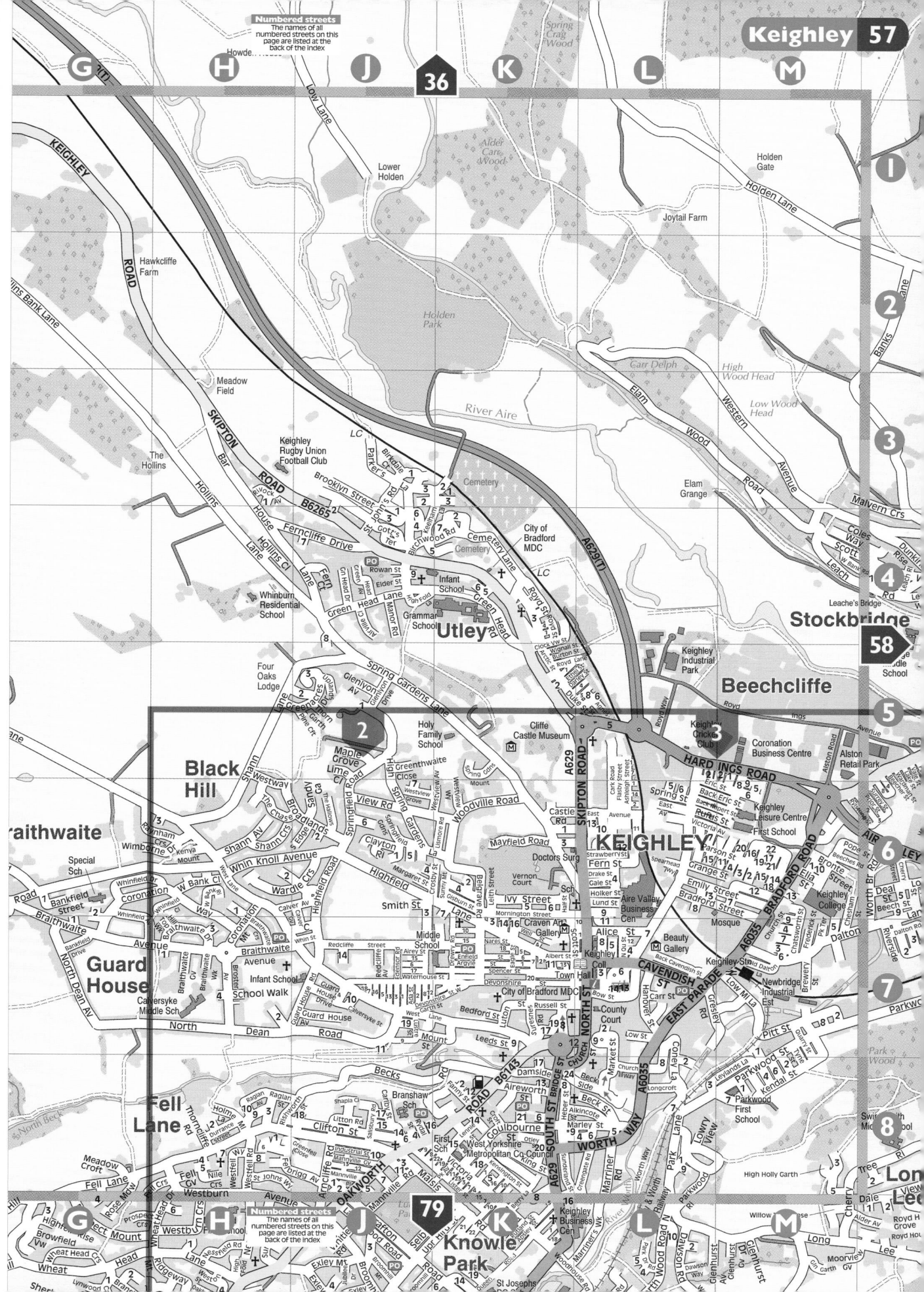

A7
1 Bracewell St
2 Strong Close Gv
3 Strong Close Rd

A8
1 Back Aireview Ter
2 Birch Tree Gdns
3 Spring Wy

A6
1 Aireworth Cl
2 Back Rylstone St
3 Beeches Rd
4 Craven Rd
5 Grape St
6 Marlow St
7 Ribble St
8 Sussex St
9 Timber St

A5
1 Arnside Av
2 Athol St
3 Back Colenso Rd
4 Back Florist St
5 Cornwall Rd
6 Cross River St
7 Matthew Cl
8 Pool St

A4
1 Leach Crs
2 West Bank Gv

37

Rivock Over

Rivock

Bradup

Low
Bradup

Brass Castle

Bradup

The
Glen
Beck

Silsden Road

Banks
Lane

Moorcock Farm

Upwood

Ilkley Road

Ilkley Road

Street Lane

West Morton

Malvern Crs

Coles
Way

Scott

Stockbridge

57

Leache's Bridge

Dunkirk
Rise

Ridgemount
Rd

Slade La

Banks Lane

Scott
Lane

Canal
Road

Grange
Middle
School

Grange
Road

Grange Crs

Silverdale

Granby Drive

Granby
Lane

Riddlesden
Infants
School

School

St Mary's
Rd

Ilkley

Bank Top
Dr

Barleycote

Barley
Cote Av

Southfield
Drive

Southfield Av

Fieldedge Lane

Southlands Road

Southlands Mt

Southlands Gv

Carr
Lane

Dean
Hole

Carr
Lane

Studley C

Altar
Drive

Hospital   Road

Newlyn
Rd

Daleside

Riddlesden

Carr Bank

Highfield Mews

Highfield Close

East Morton
First School

Elm
Gv

Morton

Dimples
Lane

Bradford Road

3

PO

Alston
Retail Park

Aireworth
Rd

Beechwood Av

Briarwood Av

Rosewood Av

Westlea Avenue

B6265

Kingsway

Ashwood
Drive

Hawkcliffe
Avenue

Cliffe
Crs

Cem

south Vw

Carr
Lane

Sunnycliffe

The Spinner

Cliffestone
Dr

Airevalley Road

Pope St

Keighley
College

Worth Br

Deal
St

Cherry
Tree

Lorne
St

Fruit
St

Dalton

Airedale St

Airedale
Rd

Marley Rd

Gas Works

Swine
Lane

B6265

Swine
Lane Bridge

Maxville
Av

Golf Course

Mayfield Drive

Airedale Mount

Aireville
Mt

Mt Pleasant

Bradford Road

Poplar
Drive

Waverley Av

Heston

Aire Vw Dr

Poplar Ter

Sunnycliffe

The Spinner

Brewery

Parkwood Street

Parkwood-Street
Industrial
Est

Primrose St

Primrose
Gv

Rose
Street

Thwaites
Brow
Rd

Thwaites

Airevalley

Road

Hollinwood Vw

Marley
Court

Marley
Vw

River Aire

A650(T)

Crossflatts
Cricket
Club

Croft Road

Croft Av

Castlefields

Swire Smith
Middle School

Higherwood
Close

Spring

High Spring Rd

Bank Top
Way

Ivy Ter

Lee Court

Golden View Drive

Sunnydale
Grove

Currer
Laithe

Thwaites
Brow

Marley

Long
Lee

View La

Tree

Dale

Calton
Road

Moorland

Spring

Spring Mt

Spring Av

Raven

B4
1 High Banks Cl
2 Westfield Crs

B5
1 Back Ripley St
2 Compeigne Av
3 Hazelwood Av
4 Riddlesden St
5 Ripley St
6 Westfield Dr
7 Westfield Rd

B7
1 The Orchard

Upper Transfield

B6
1 Back Ribble St

B8
1 Calton Gv
2 Fairmount Ter
3 Highcroft Gdns

C4
1 Barley Cote Gv
2 Southfield Mt
3 Southfield Wy
4 Southlands Gv W

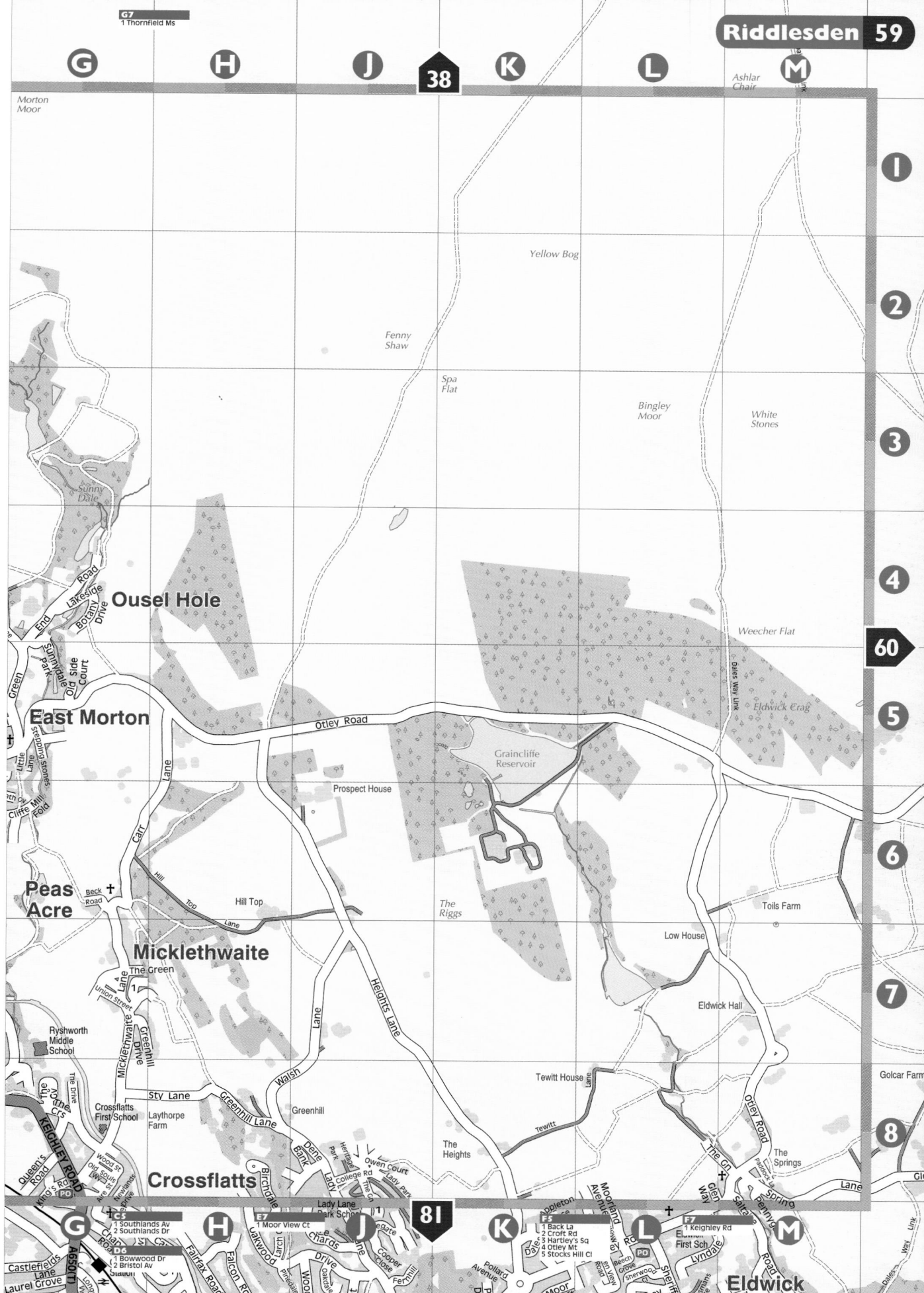

G7
1 Thornfield Ms

G **H** **J** **38** **K** **L** **M**

Ashlar Chair

1

Morton Moor

2

Yellow Bog

3

Fenny Shaw

Spa Flat

Bingley Moor

White Stones

4

60

Weecher Flat

Sunny Dale

Ousel Hole

Eldwick Crag

5

Lakeside
Botany Drive
Road
End
Green
Sunnydale Park
Old Side Court

East Morton

Otley Road

Graincliffe Reservoir

Little Lane
Stones
Cliffe Mill Fold

Prospect House

6

Toils Farm

Low House

Peas Acre

Beck Road
Carr Lane
Hill Top Lane

Hill Top

The Riggs

Eldwick Hall

7

Micklethwaite

The Green
Union Street
Lane
Heights Lane

Tewitt House

Tewitt Lane

Golcar Farm

Otley Road

Ryshworth Middle School
The Drive
Thorpe Crs

Greenhill Drive
Micklethwaite Lane

Sty Lane
Greenhill Lane
Walsh Lane

Greenhill

Eldwick Hall

The Gn
Eldwick Hall

The Springs
Spring

8

Keighley Road
Queen's Road
King St
Wood St
old Souls Lwy
Newlands Drive
Crossflatts First School
Laythorpe Farm
Dene Bank

Crossflatts

Birchdale
Larch
Chards
Lady Lane Park School

Owen Court
Hertford Park
Lady Park
College Rd
The Gn

The Heights

Appleton
Pollard Avenue
Moorland Avenue

Sheriff
Glen Way

Elwick First Sch

G7
1 Southlands Av
2 Southlands Dr
D6

E7
1 Moor View Ct

F5
1 Back La
2 Croft Rd
3 Hartley's Sq
4 Otley Mt
5 Stocks Hill Cl

F7
1 Keighley Rd

Castlefields Lane
Laurel Grove

Eldwick

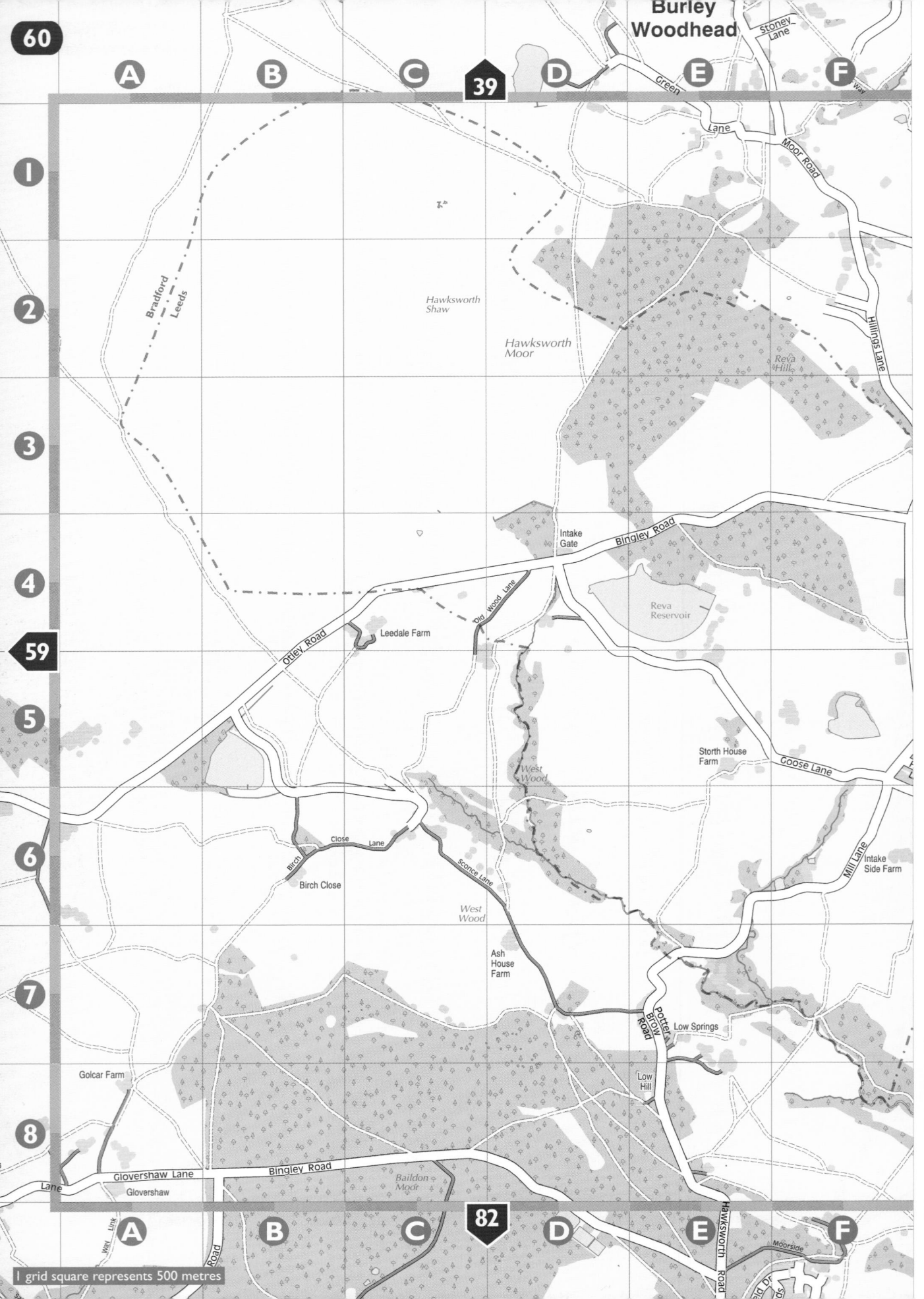

A B C **39** D E F

Burley
Woodhead

Stoney
Lane

green

Moor Road

Lane

Way

1

Hillings Lane

2

Bradford
Leeds

Hawksworth
Shaw

Hawksworth
Moor

Reva
Hill

3

Intake
Gate

Bingley Road

4

Old Wood Lane

Otley Road

Leedale Farm

Reva
Reservoir

5

West
Wood

Storth House
Farm

Goose Lane

Close   Lane

6

Birch

Birch Close

Scance Lane

Mill Lane

Intake
Side Farm

West
Wood

Ash
House
Farm

7

Golcar Farm

Potter
Brow
Road

Low Springs

Low
Hill

8

Glovershaw Lane

Bingley Road

Baildon
Moor

Hawksworth Road

Lane

Glovershaw

Way Link

Road

A B **82** C D E F

Moorside

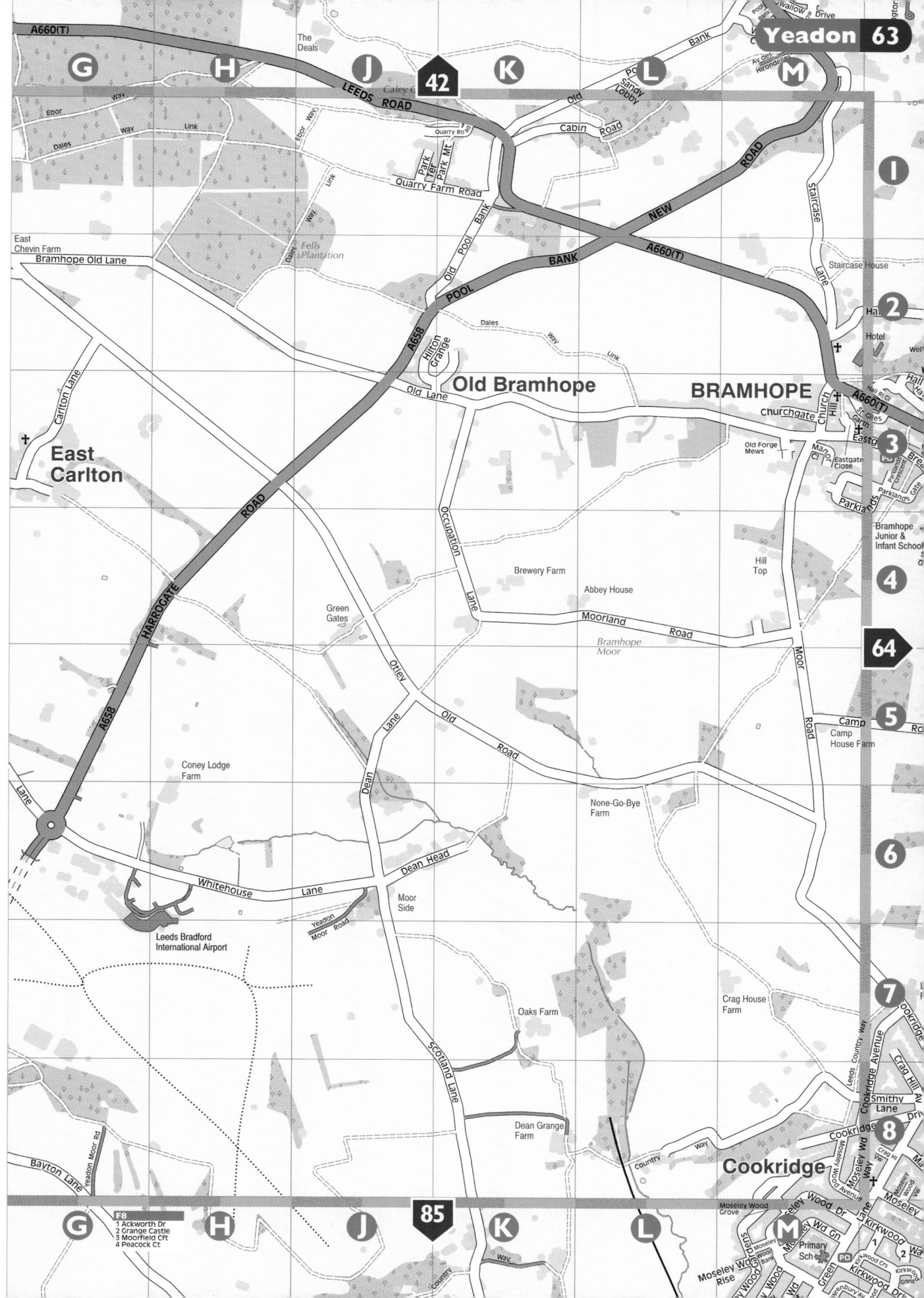

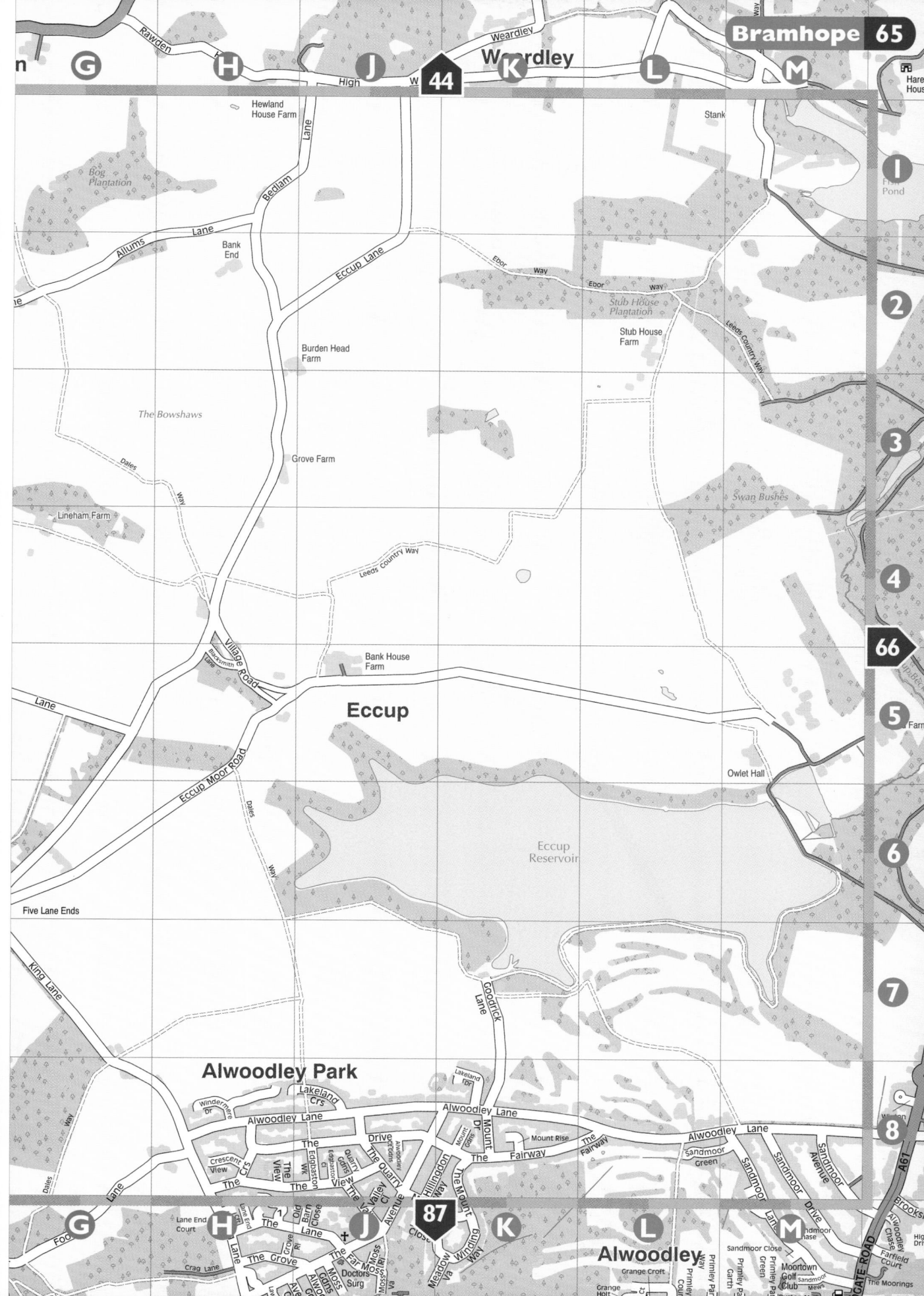

G H J 44 K L M

Weardley

Weardley

High

W

Stank

Hewland
House Farm

Bedlam Lane

Eccup Lane

Bog
Plantation

Allums Lane

Bank
End

Ebor Way

Ebor Way

Leeds Country Way

Stub House
Plantation

Stub House
Farm

I
Fish Pond

Harew
House

2

Burden Head
Farm

The Bowshaws

Grove Farm

Dales Way

Swan Bushes

3

Lineham Farm

Leeds Country Way

4

66

Lane

Village Road

Blacksmith Lane

Bank House
Farm

Eccup

Owlet Hall

5

Farm

Eccup Moor Road

Dales Way

Eccup
Reservoir

6

Five Lane Ends

King Lane

Goodrick Lane

7

Alwoodley Park

Windermere Dr

Lakeland Crs

Alwoodley Lane

Lakeland Lor

Alwoodley Lane

Mount Gdns

Mount Dr

Mount Rise

The Fairway

The Fairway

Alwoodley Lane

Sandmoor
Green

Sandmoor Avenue

Sandmoor Drive

A61

8

Dales Way

Foo...

Crescent View

The Crs

The View

The View

Quarry Gdns

Edgbaston Wk

Edgbaston Cl

The Quarry

Accordion

Alwoodley...

Hillington Way

The Mount

Winding Way

Sandmoor Chase

GATE ROAD

Brookside

High Dr

Farfield Court

The Moorings

G H 87 J K L M

Crag Lane

The Grove

The Far Moss

Doctors Surg

Meadow Va

Closes

Alwoodley

Grange Croft

Grange Holt

Primley Park

Moortown
Golf Club

Sandmoor Close

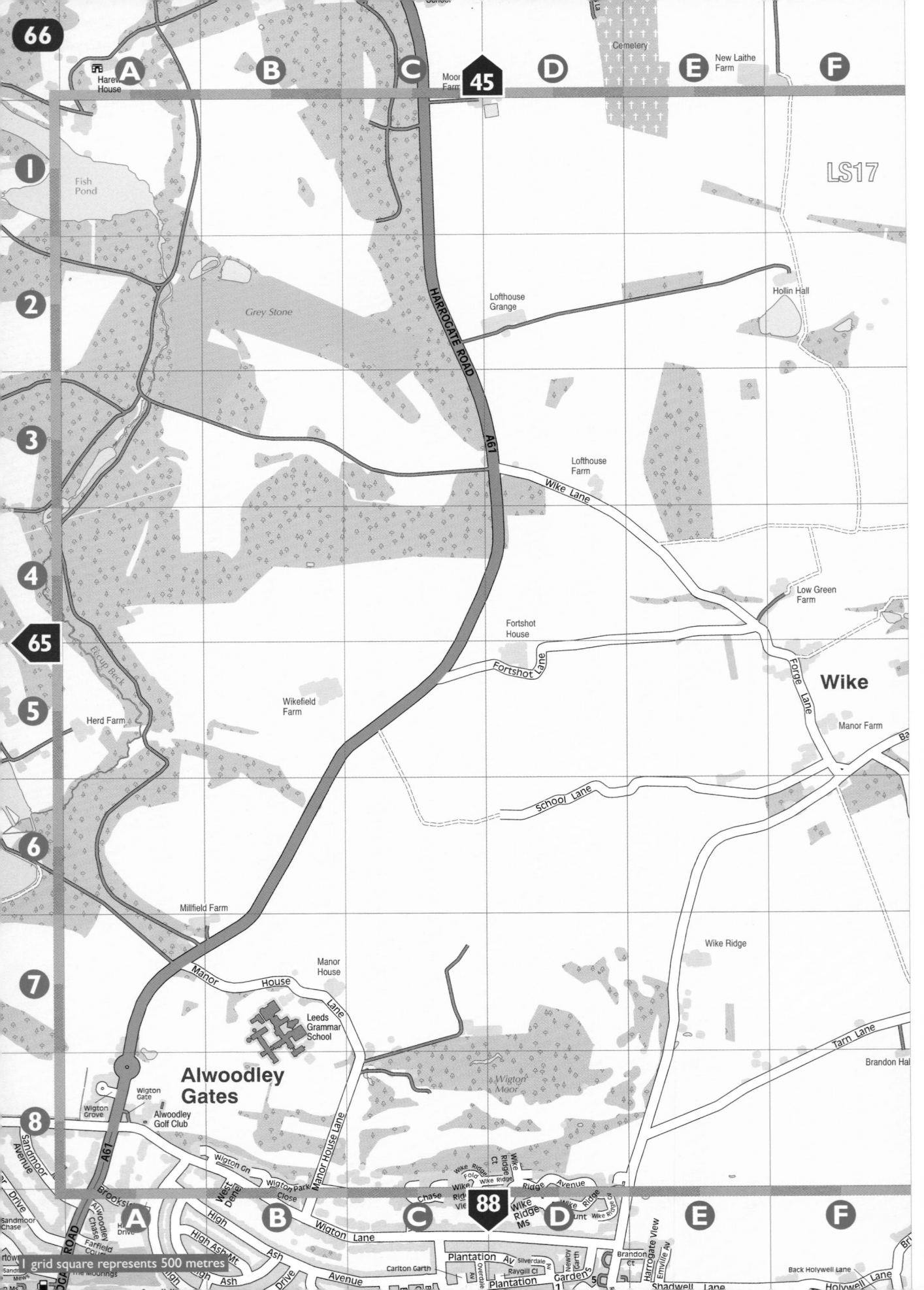

L3
1 Bradfords Cl
2 Lyndon Crs
3 Lyndon Sq
4 Milnthorpe Cl
5 Milnthorpe Gdns
6 Milnthorpe Garth
7 Milnthorpe Wy

M1
1 Albion Cl
2 Ashmead
3 Church View Ms
4 St Luke's Cl

M3
1 Church Mdw
Rho 2 Croft Rd

M4
1 Cropstones

LS23

West Woods

West Woods Farm

Clifford

Bramham CP School

Bramham

Hope Hall

Thorner Lane

Dalton Lane

Thorner Road

Thorner Road

Tenter Hill

Milnthorpe Lane

Lyndon Way
Lyndon Road
Lyndon Avenue
Wetherby Road
Croft Drive
Clifford
Firbeck Road
Fine Garth
Garth Close
Prospect Bank
New Rd
Front St
Back St
Low Way
Church Hill
Vicarage
High St
Low Town
Back La
Lane
Windmill
AlmsHouse
Gdns
Folly Lane
Folly View
Orchard Ct
Freely Lane
Aberford Road
Bowcliffe Road
Bramham Lodge

Terry Lug

Bramham Biggin

Bowcliffe Hall

Wellhill Farm

South Approach

Bramham Park

Rakes Wood

Whittle Car

Black Fen

New Black Fen

Paradise Farm

Mangrill Lane

South Approach

Windsor Farm

Junction 45

Crescent
Willow
Willow AV
Bellwood
Willow
Lairum Rd
Lane
Low Way
Burns Wy
Albion Ter
Nursery
Albion St
Chapel Lane
High
New Rd
Lea Croft
Springfiel
Mill Dam
Bramham Road
Windmill
Headley

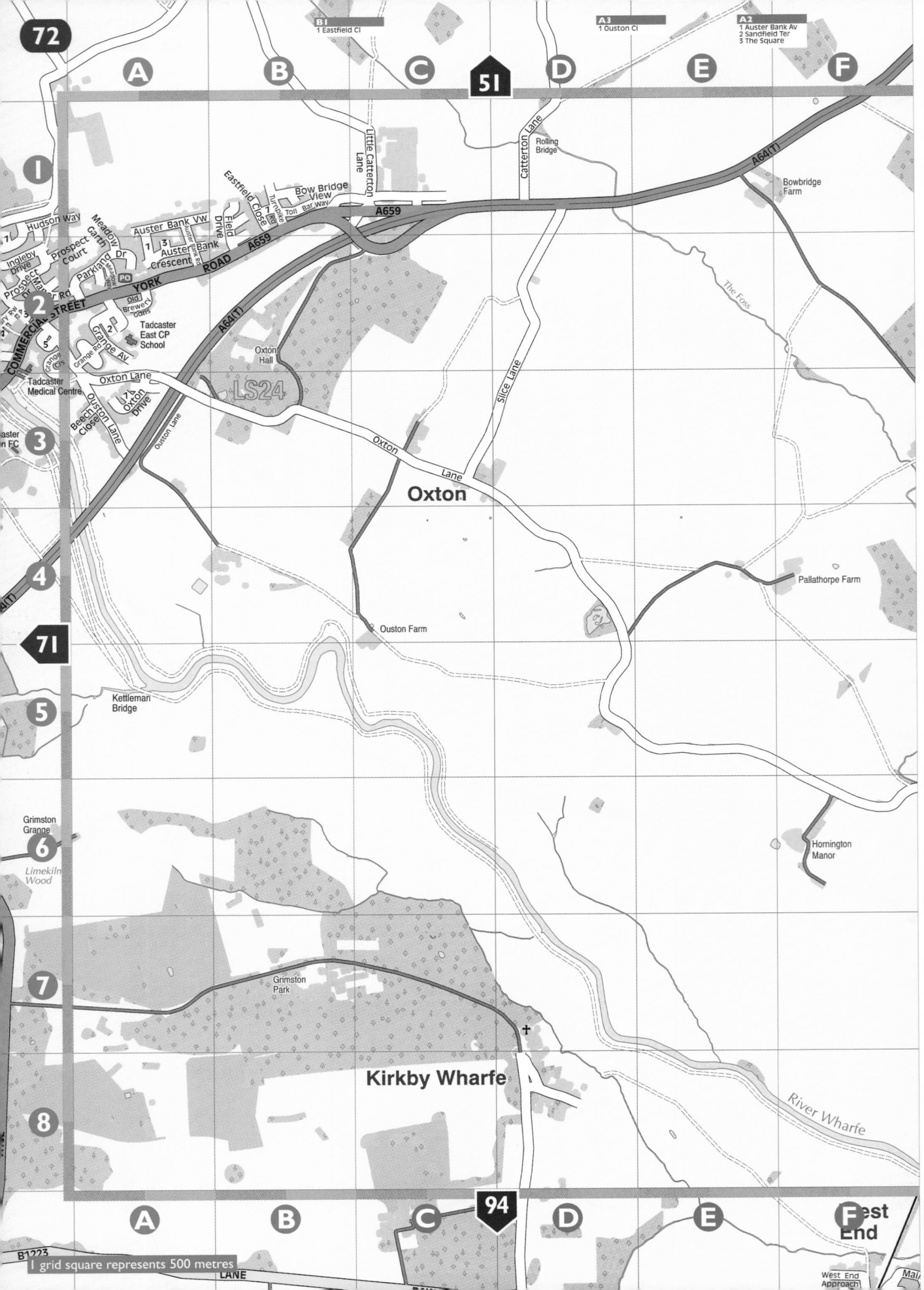

G H J K L M

Colton

I

2

3 No
Ha

4

**Appleto
Roebuck**

5

6

7

8

1 Fairfax Cl
Steeton
Grange

New
Plantation

Pickering
Wood

Steeton
Hall Farm

Lowmoor
Farm

Brumber
Hill

Colton Bridge

Street Lane

Steeton Lane

Braegate Lane

PO

New Road

Colton Lane

Main Street

Orchard Close

Briars Drive

Briars Court

Hornington Bridge

Old Road

Church Lane

Mill Cottage

The Foss

Glebe
Close

Low Farm
Close

Regent
Cl

† Bolton
Percy

PO

The Rampart

Marsh
Lane

Bolton
Lodge

Scotland
Wood

Oak Avenue

Bolton
Grange

Jew Leys Lane

PO †
Hall Garth

Ozendyke

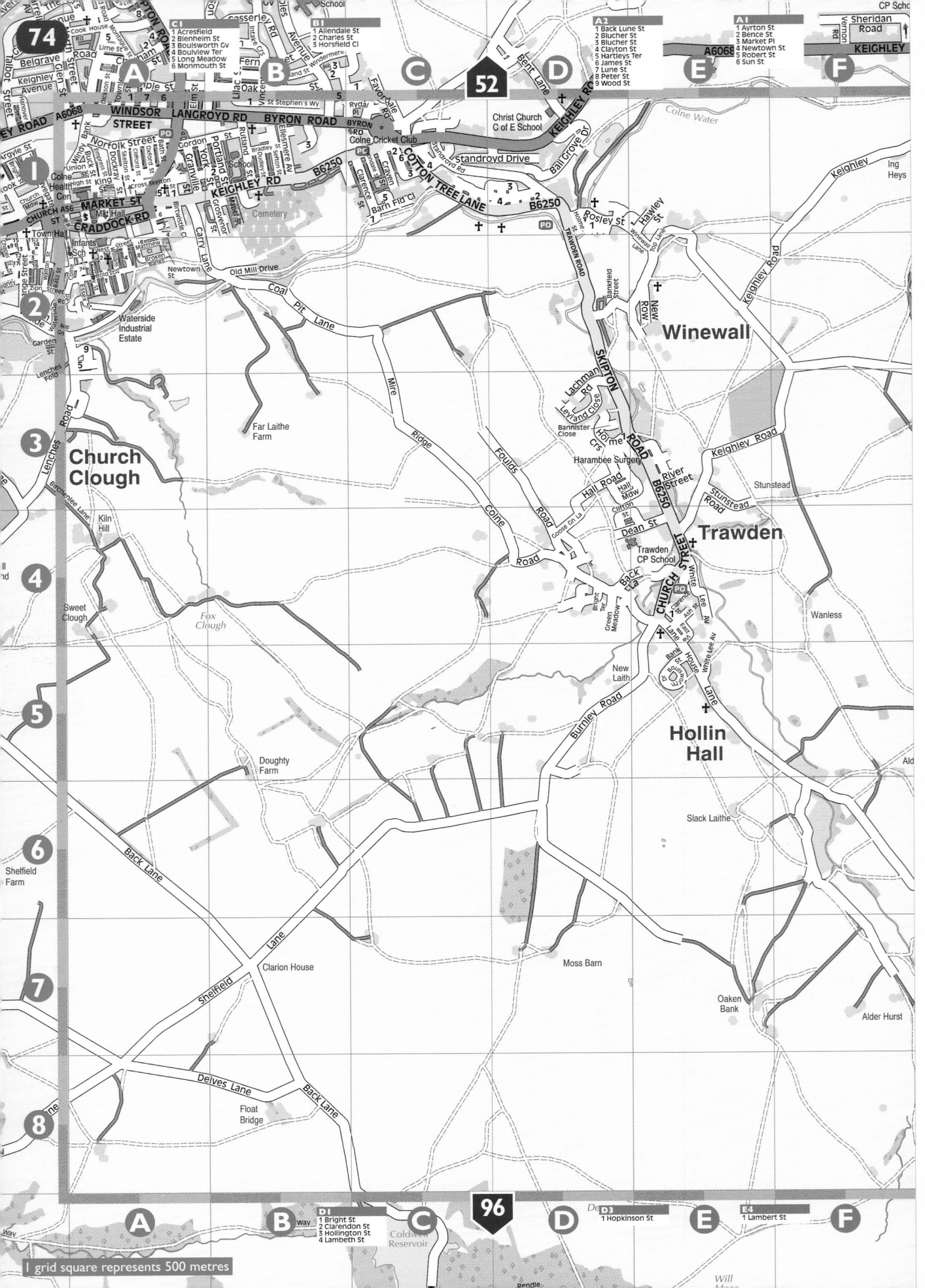

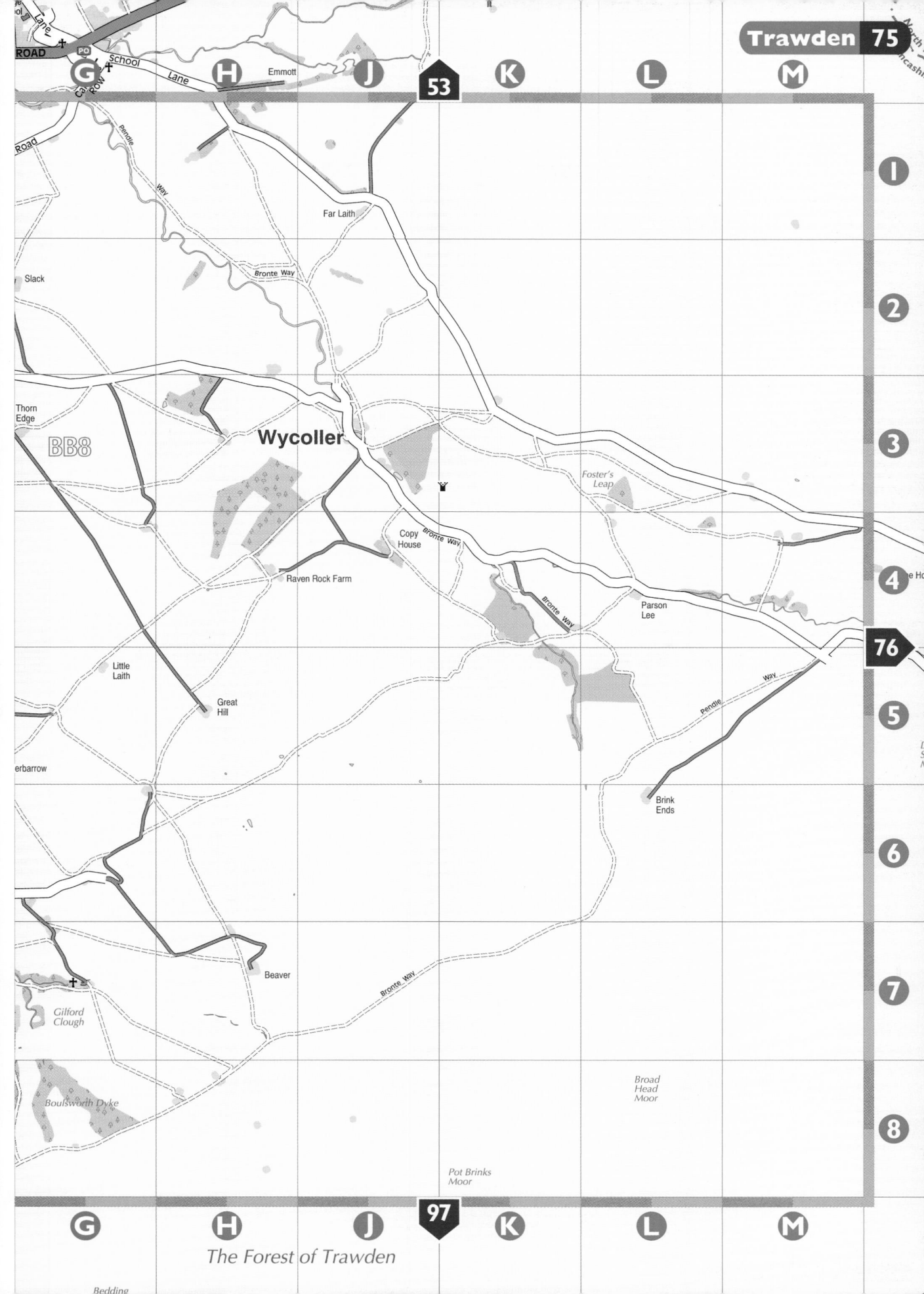

G H J K L M

53

I
2
3
4
76
5
6
7
8

ROAD

School Lane

Emmott

Pendle Way

Far Laith

Bronte Way

Slack

Thorn Edge

BB8

Wycoller

Foster's Leap

Copy House

Bronte Way

Raven Rock Farm

Bronte Way

Parson Lee

Pendle Way

Little Laith

Great Hill

Brink Ends

erbarrow

Gilford Clough

Beaver

Bronte Way

Boulsworth Dyke

Broad Head Moor

Pot Brinks Moor

G H J K L M

97

The Forest of Trawden

Bedding

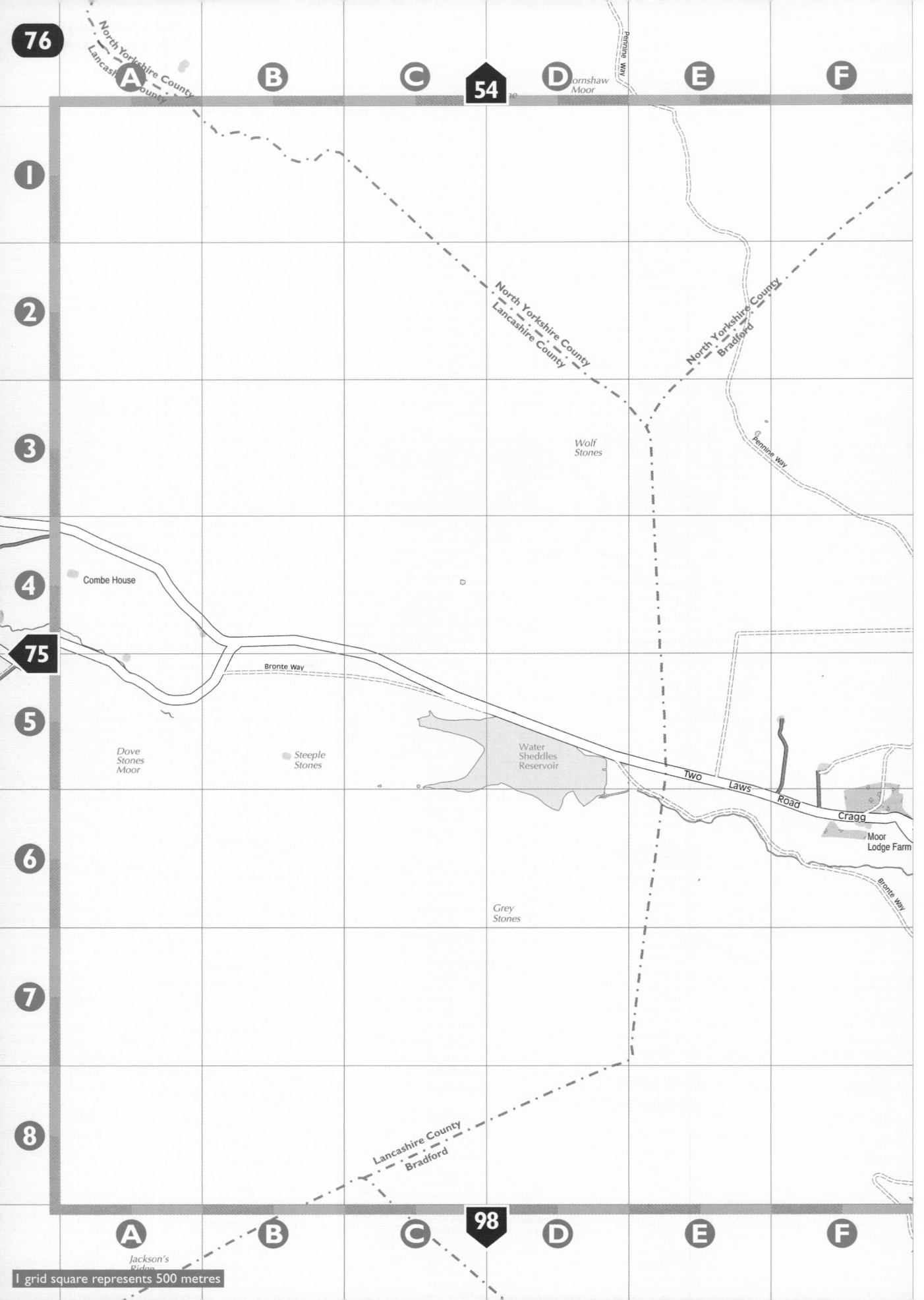

 54

North Yorkshire County
Lancashire County

Pennine Way

Dornshaw
Moor

1

North Yorkshire County
Lancashire County

North Yorkshire County
Bradford

2

Wolf
Stones

Pennine Way

3

Combe House

4

75

Bronte Way

Two Laws Road

Cragg

Dove
Stones
Moor

Steeple
Stones

Water
Sheddles
Reservoir

Moor
Lodge Farm

5

6

Grey
Stones

Bronte Way

7

8

Lancashire County
Bradford

 98

Jackson's
Ridge

1 grid square represents 500 metres

G H J **55** K L M

Slipp... **Oldfield 77**

Whitehill Road

White Hill

Keighley Moor

Clough Hey

Keighley Moor Reservoir

Broad He... Farm

Clough Hey Allotment

Old Bess

Oakworth Moor

Flask

78

Dean Clough Head

Harehills Lane

Hill Top

Oldfield First School

West House Farm

Bottom Road

Crag Bottom

Dean Edge Road

Mean Lane

Oldfield Lane

Oldfield

Griffe Road

New

Laithe Road

Pennine Way

Scar Top

Scar Top Road

Old La

Old Snap

Whitestone Farm

Ponden Reservoir

Ponden Lane

Rush Isles

Hob Lane

Stanbury

Main Street

Pennine Way

Buckley

Ponden Clough

Pennine Way

Cold Knoll

Back Lane

Enfield Side

Bully Trees

G H Master Stones J **99** K L M Enfield Side

Stanbury Moor

Bottoms

The Height

North Yorkshire Co... Bradford

Stones

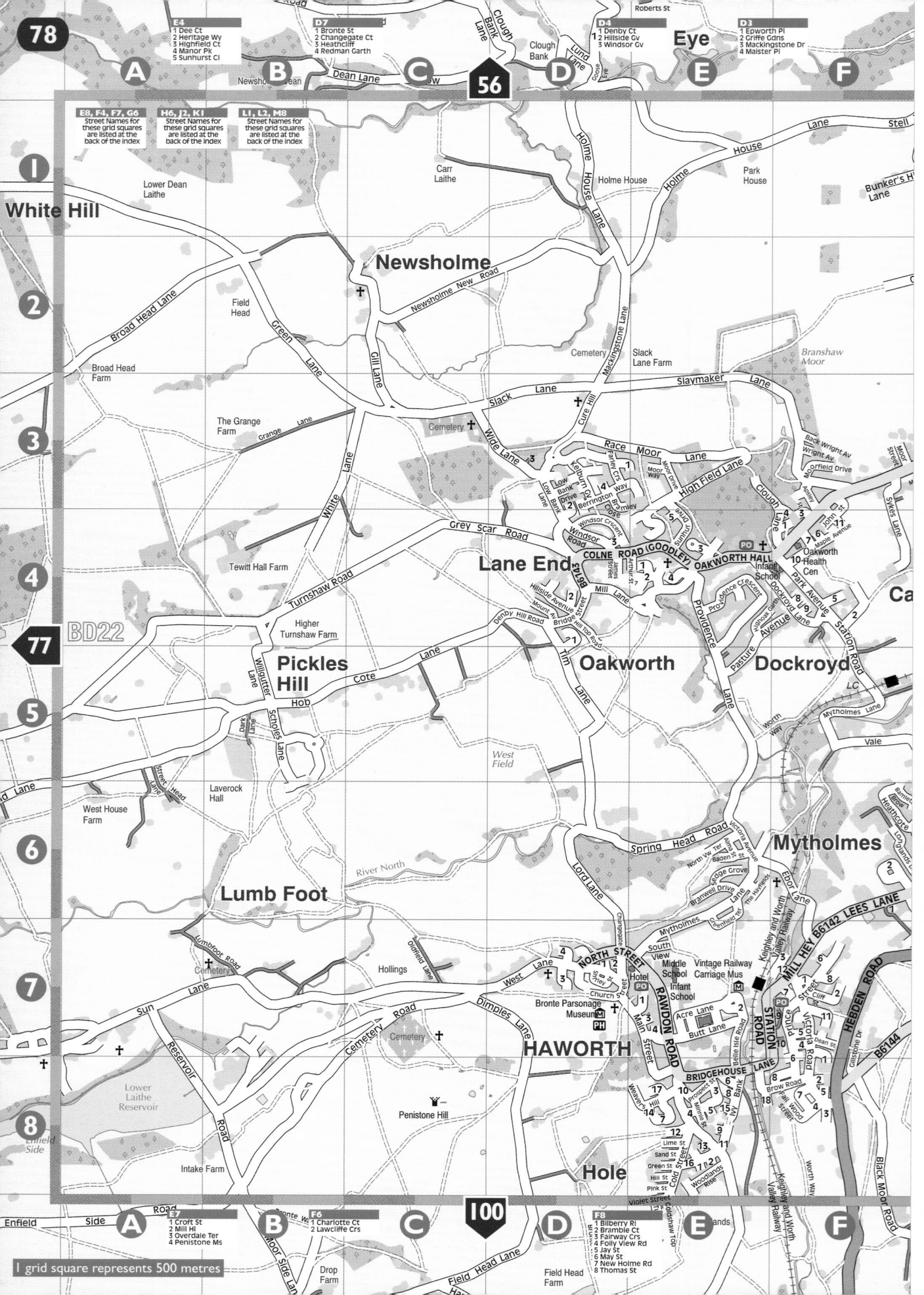

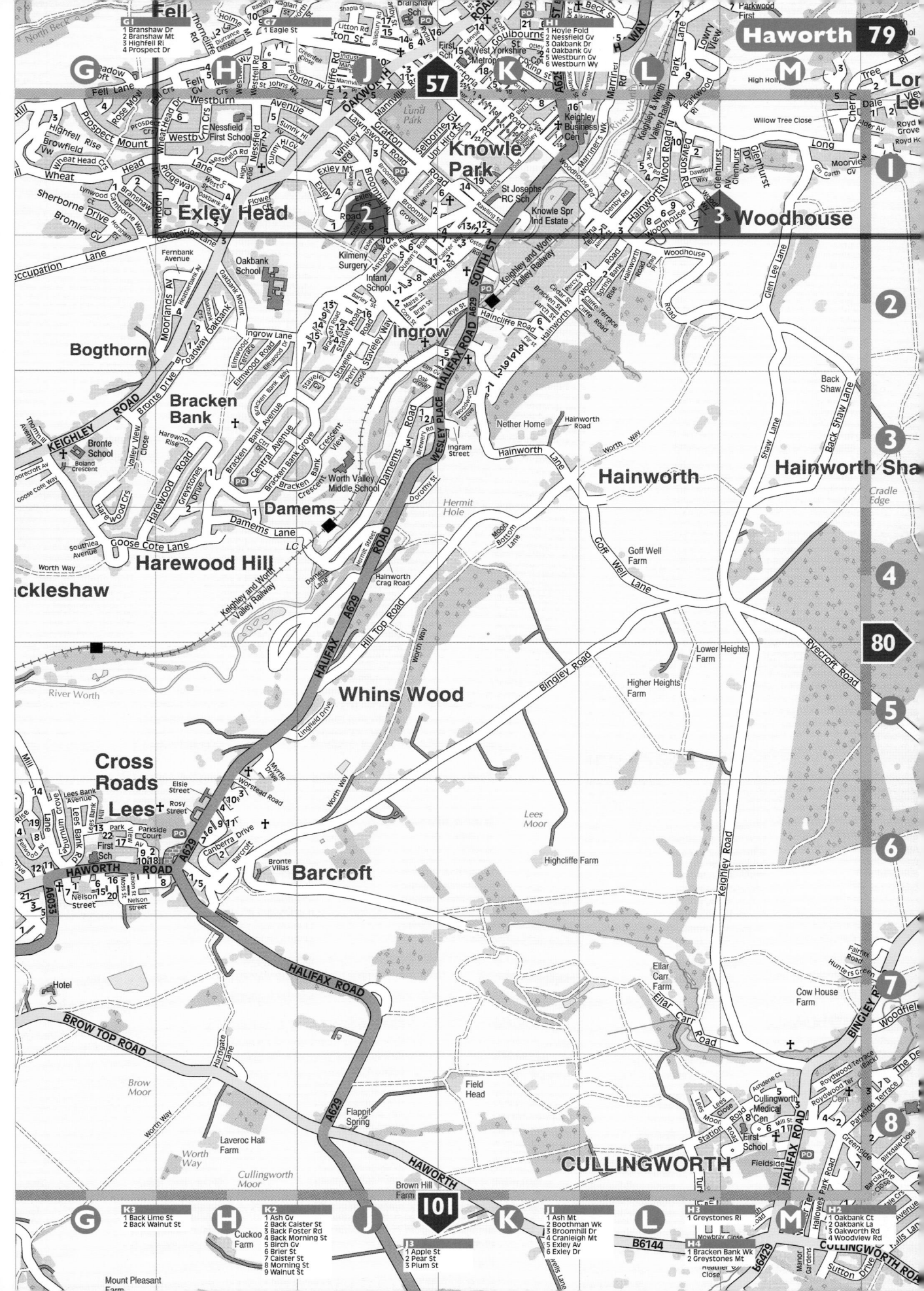

Map labels

Fell

G   H   57   J   K   L   M

1

Knowle Park

Woodhouse

Exley Head

2

Bogthorn

Ingrow

3 Woodhouse

Bracken Bank

Damems

Hainworth

Hainworth Sha

2

3

Harewood Hill

ackleshaw

4

80

Whins Wood

5

Cross Roads Lees

6

Barcroft

80

7

River Worth

CULLINGWORTH

8

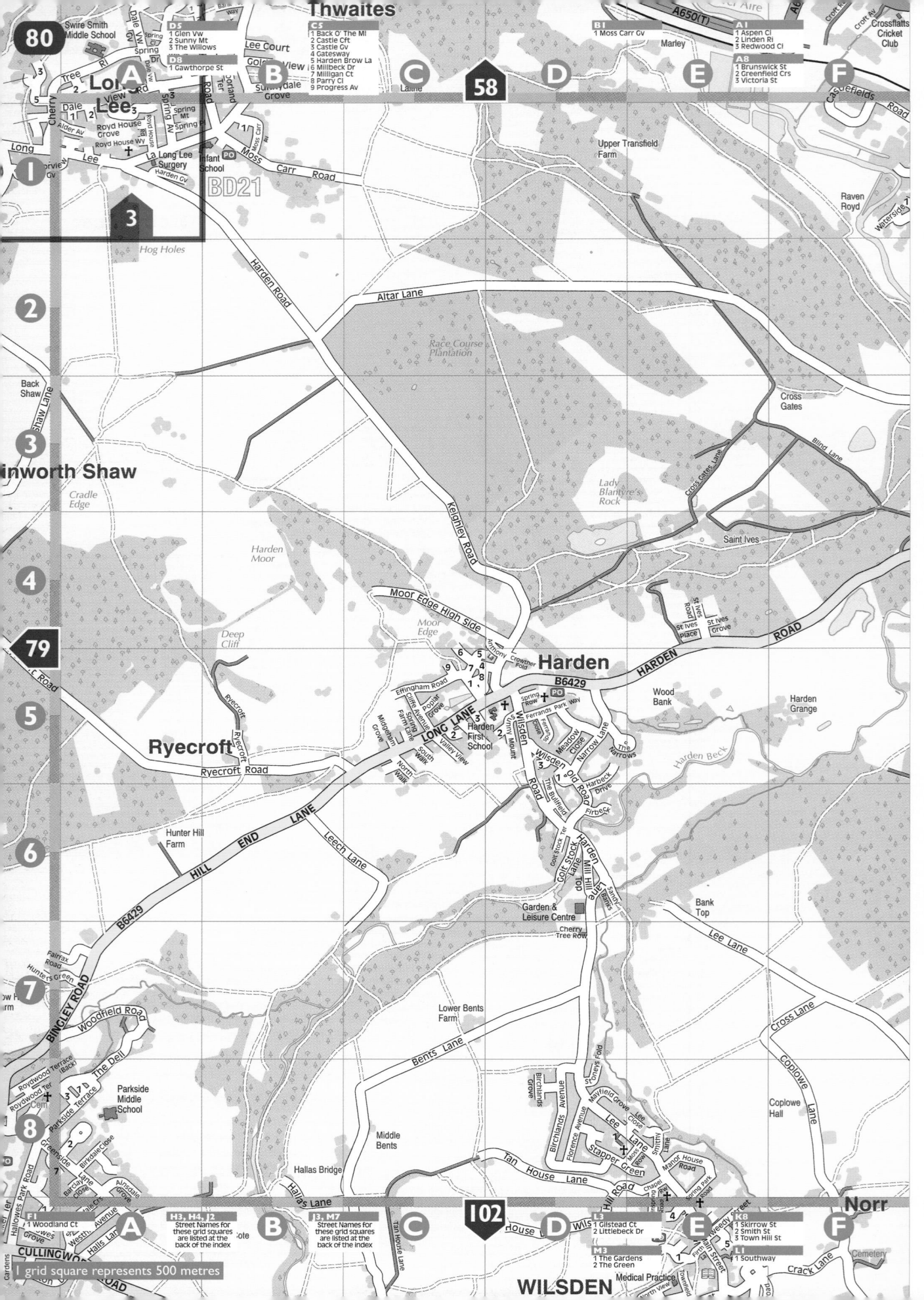

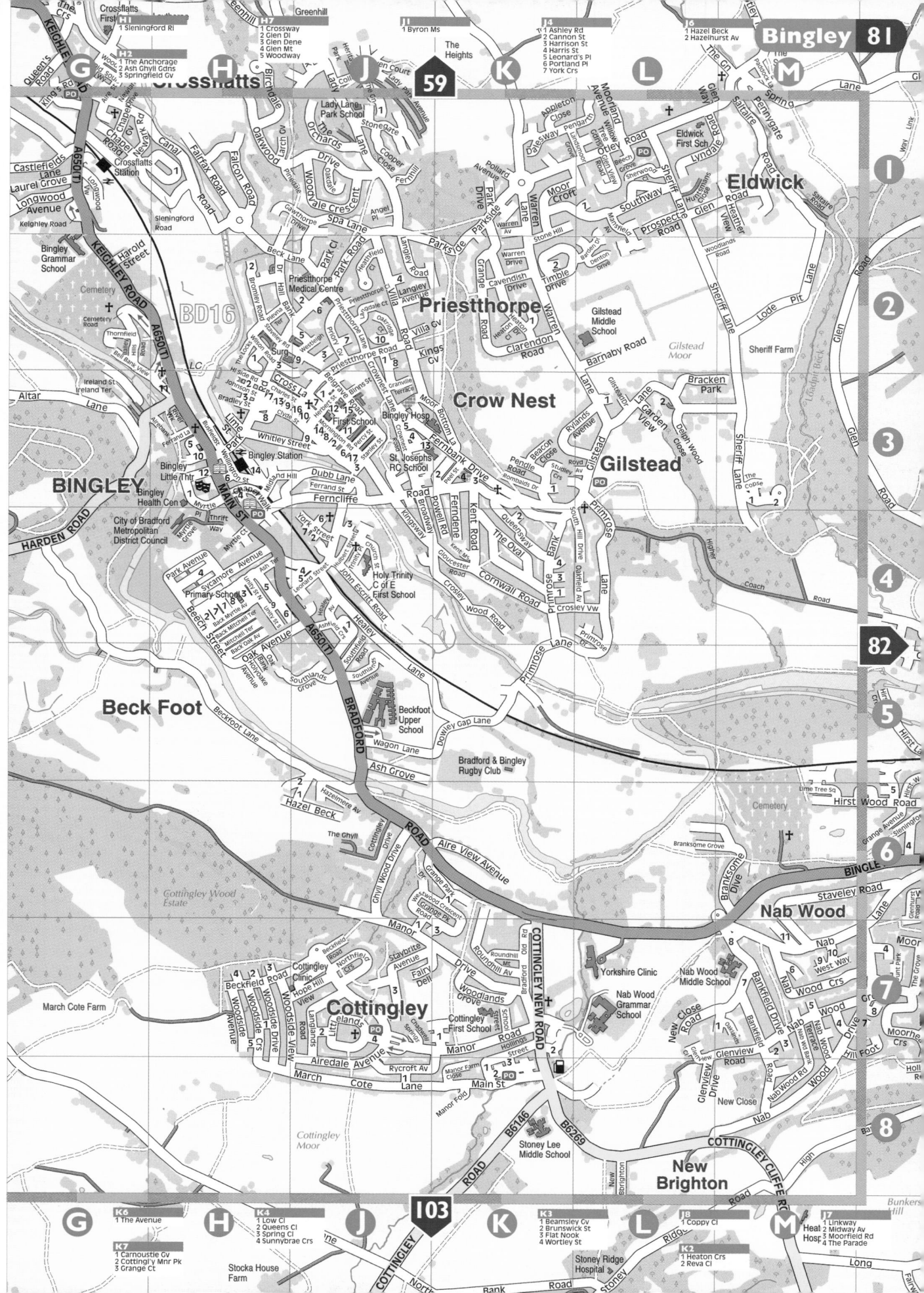

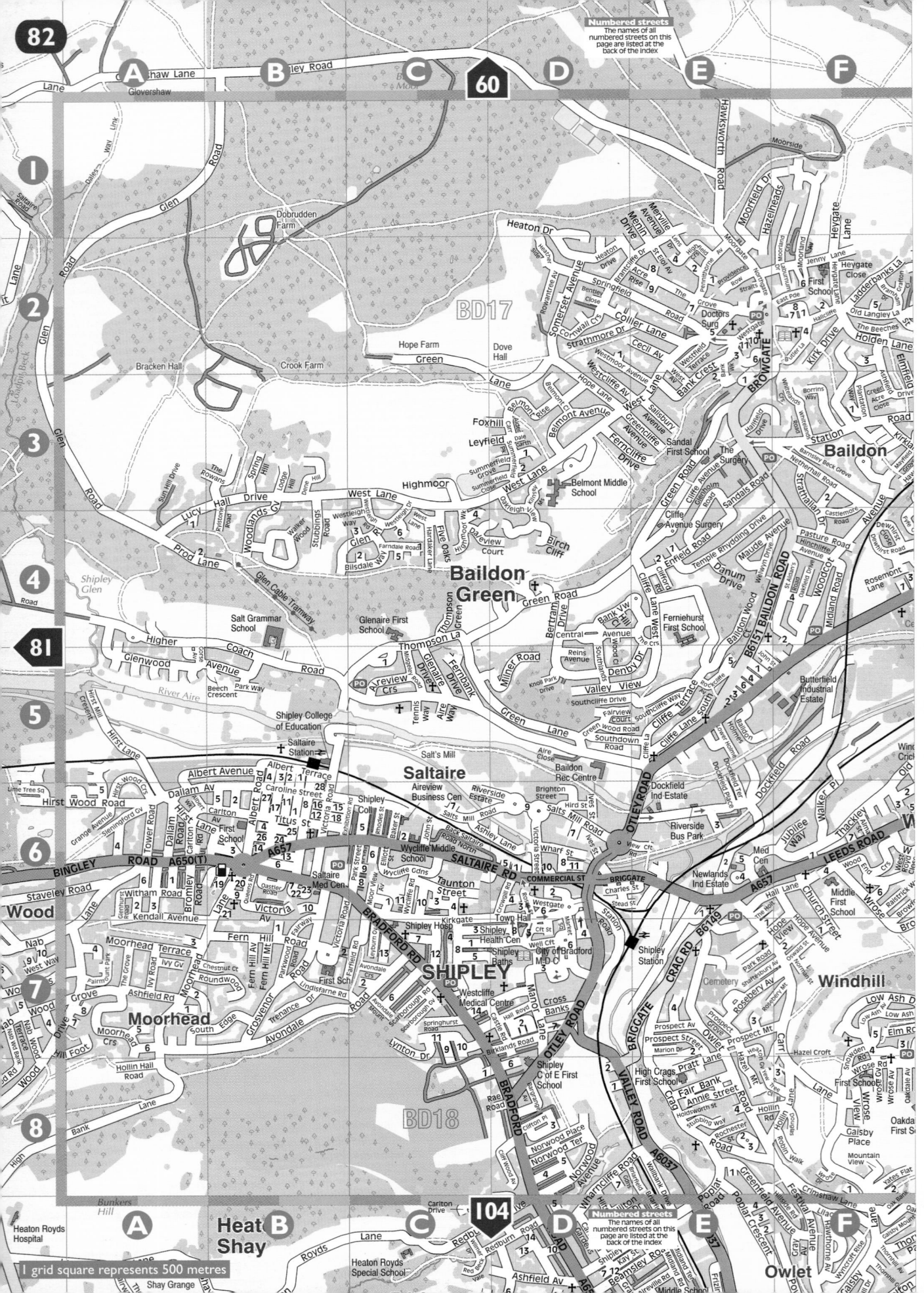

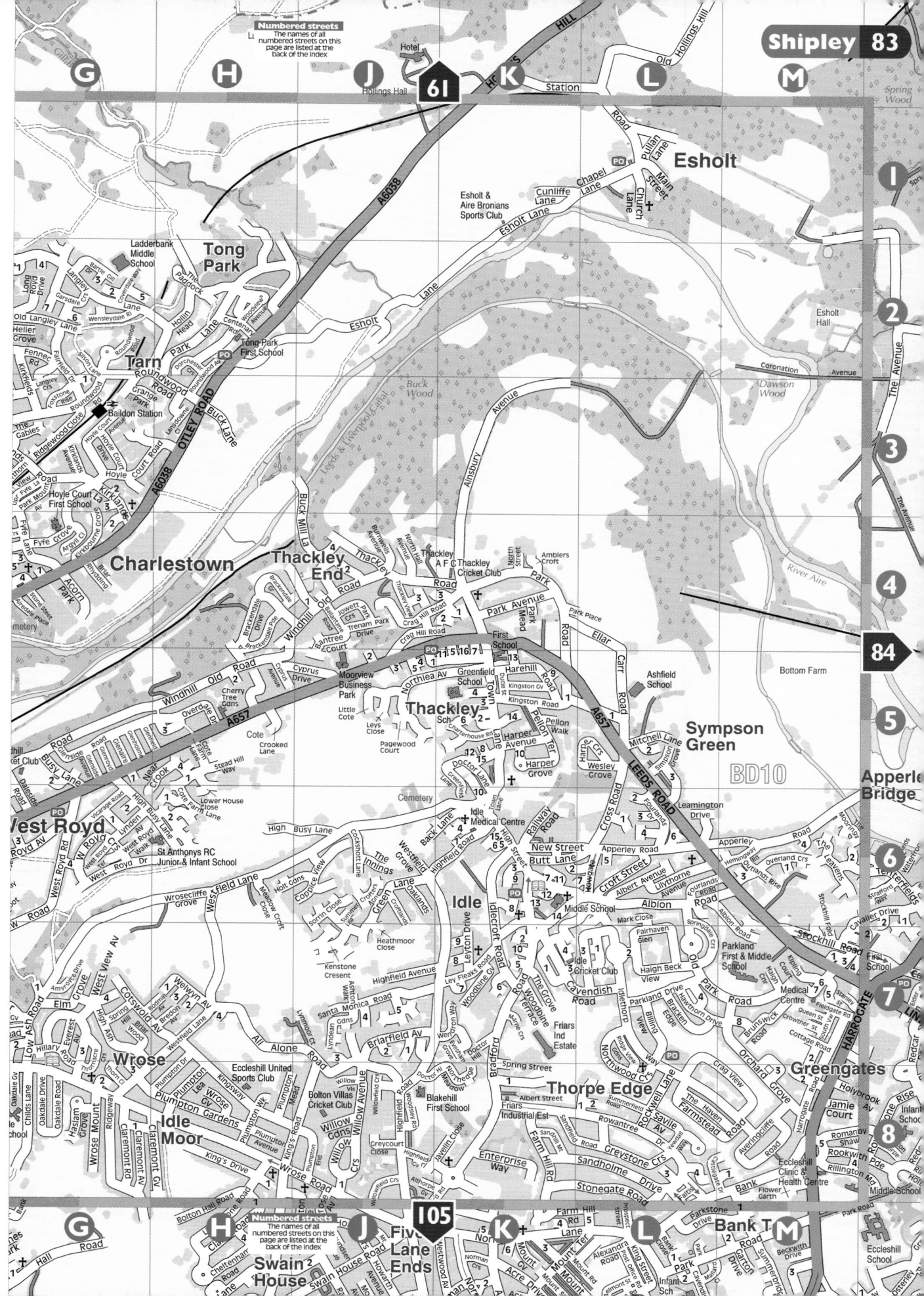

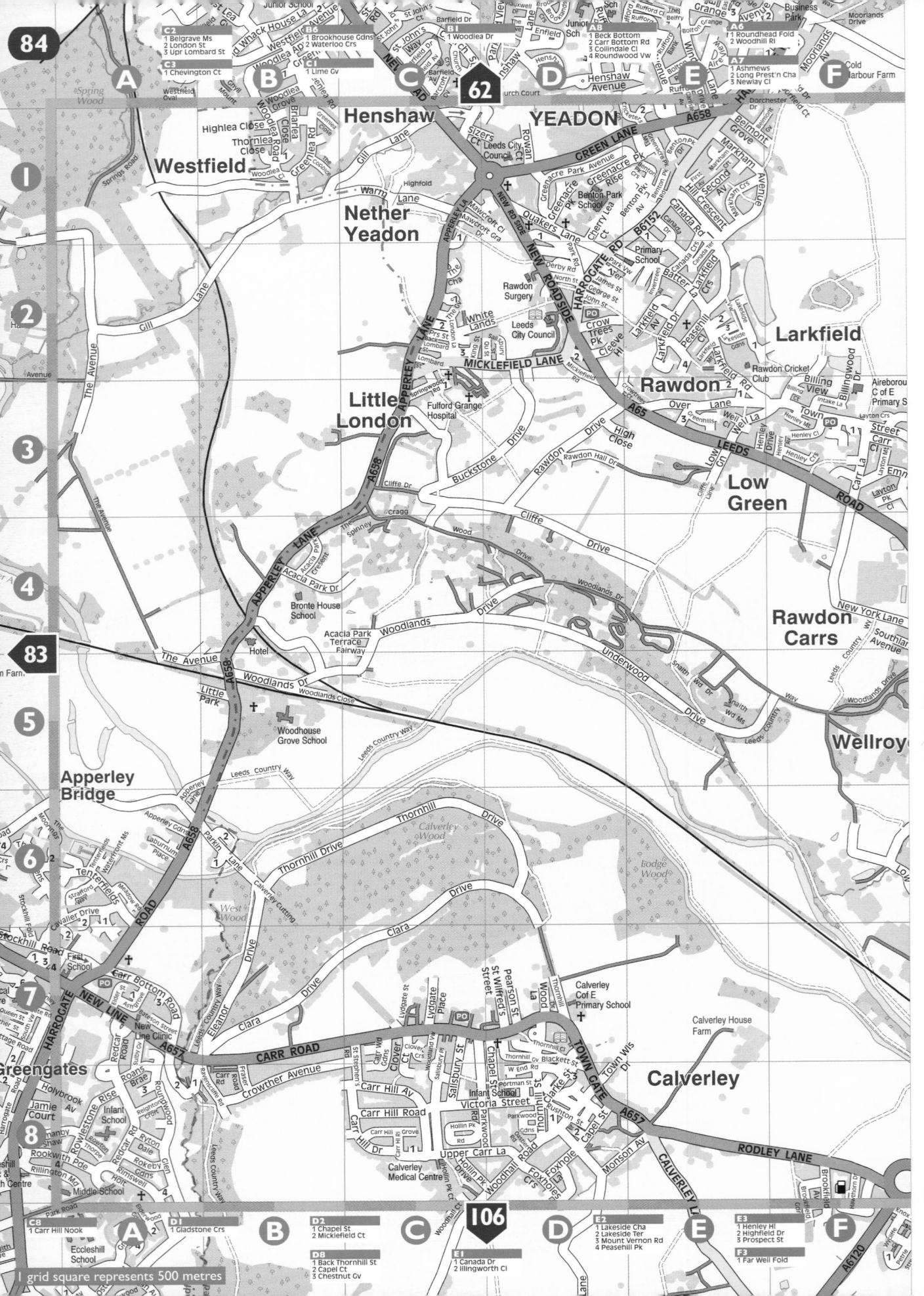

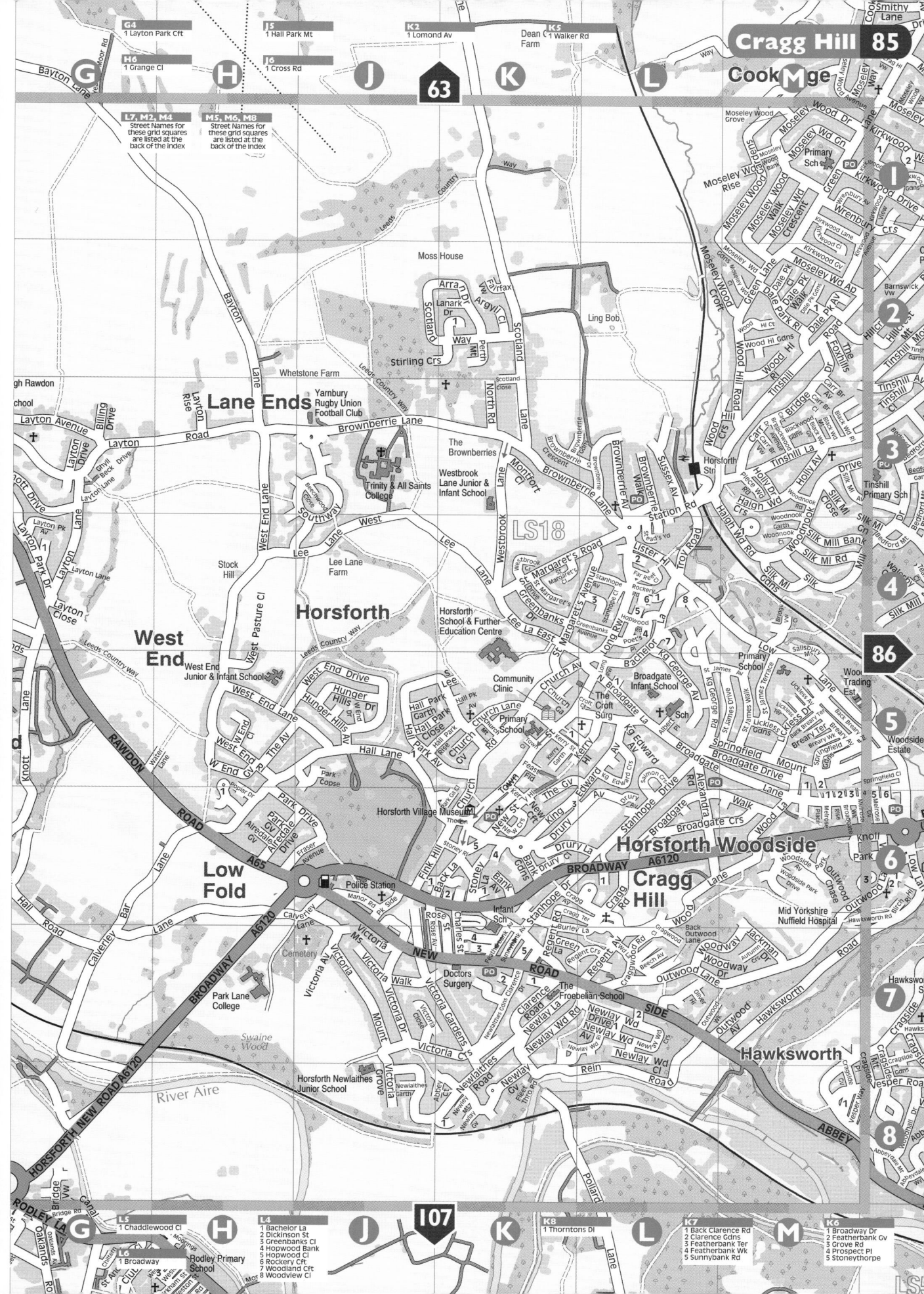

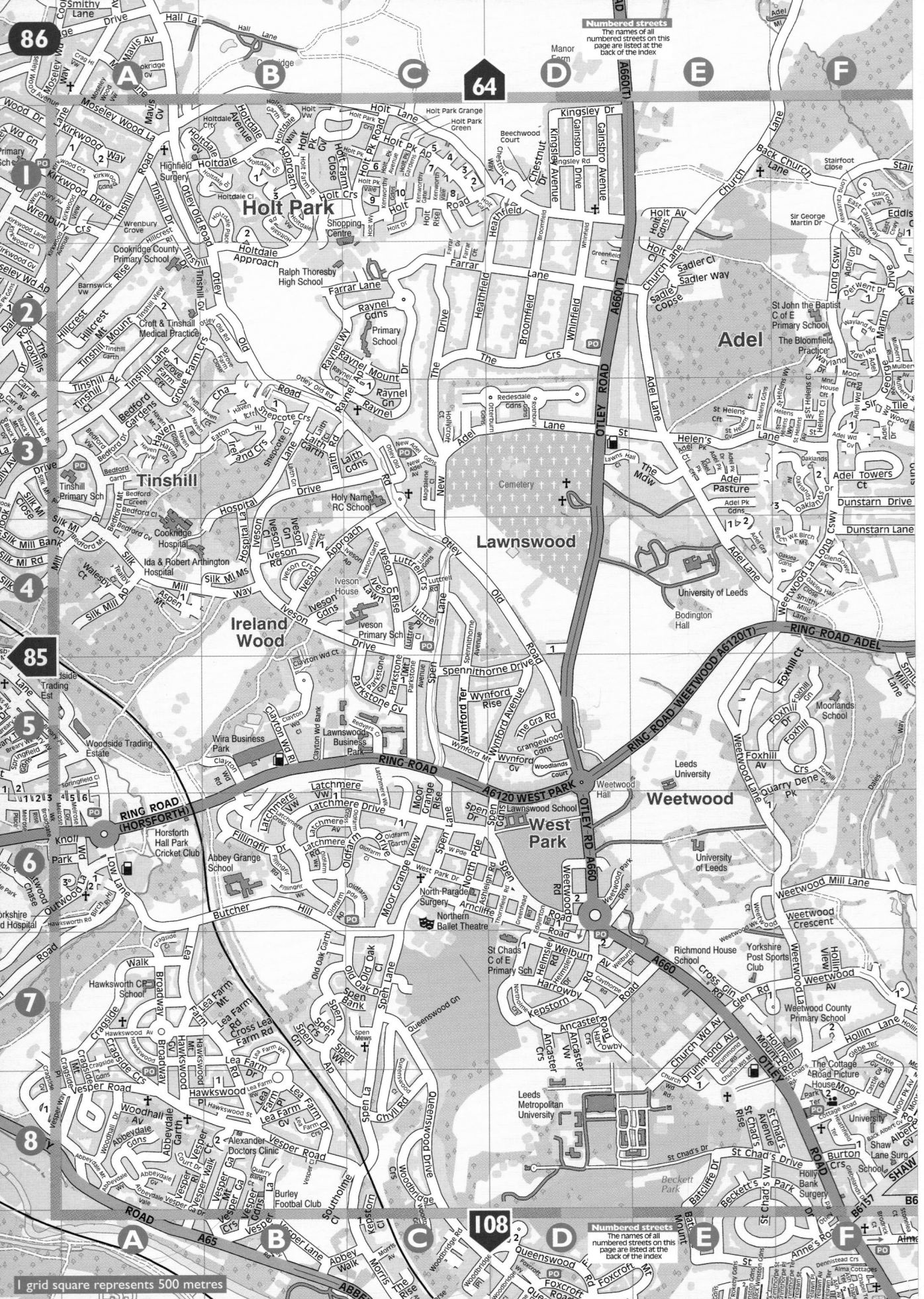

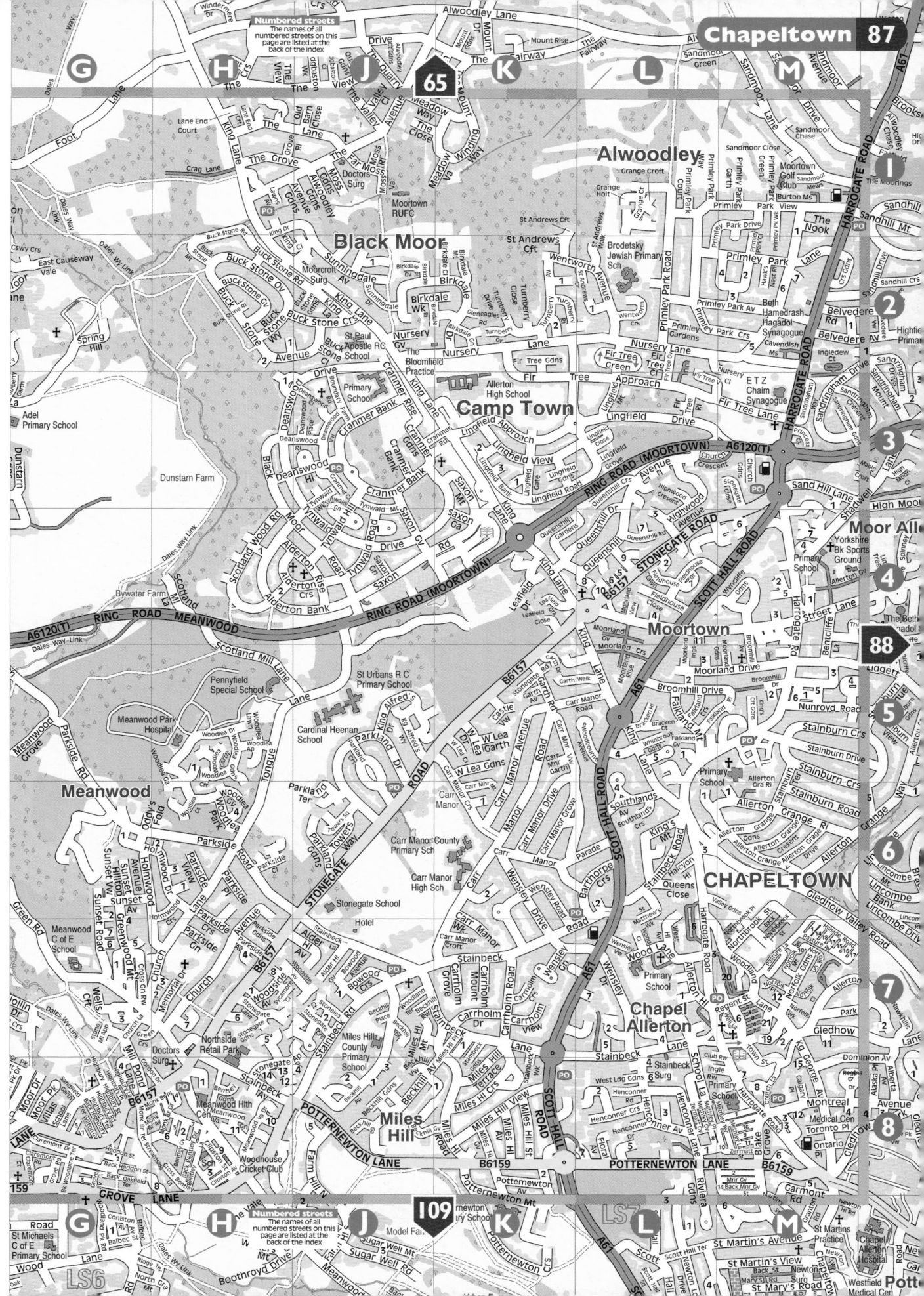

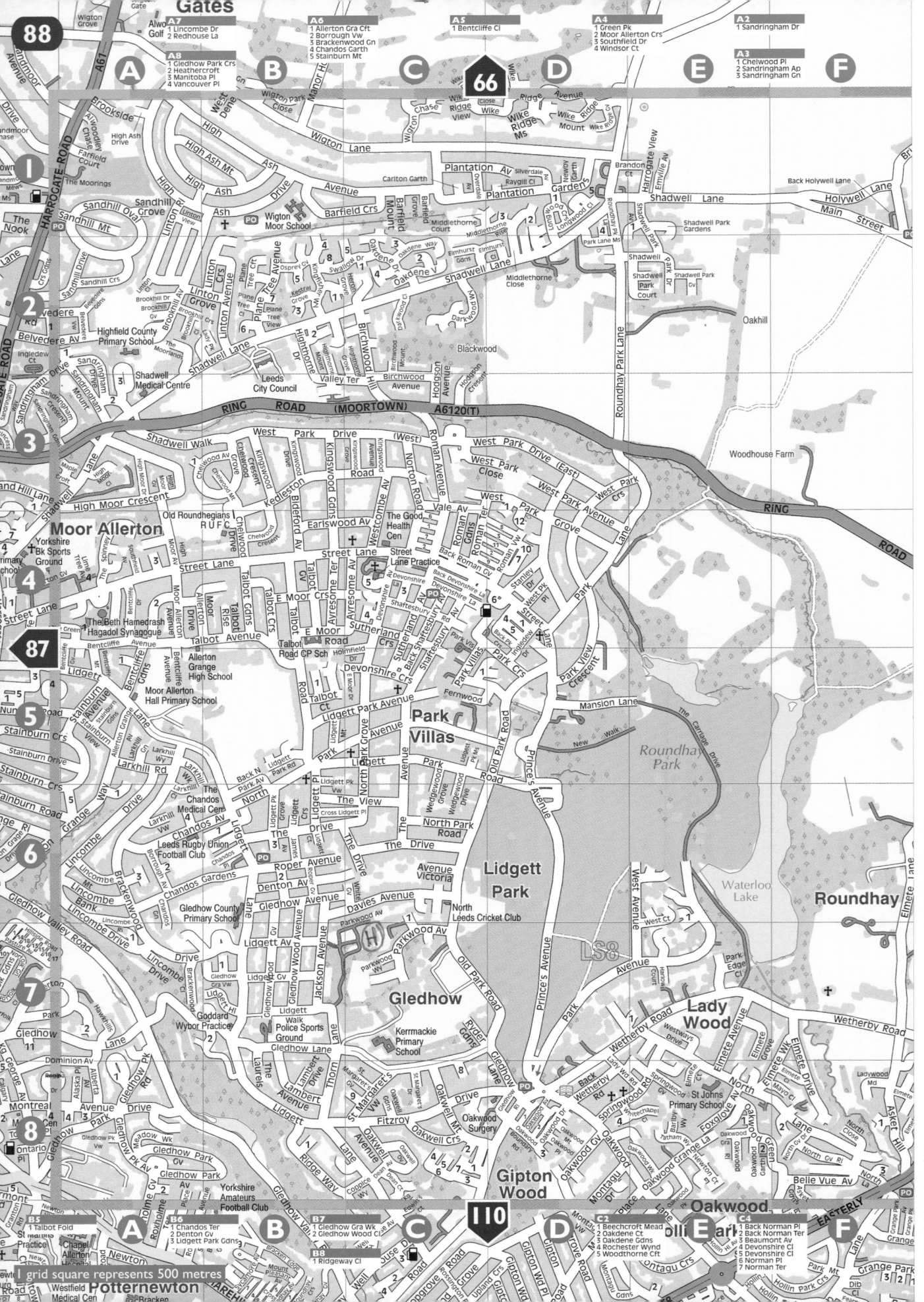

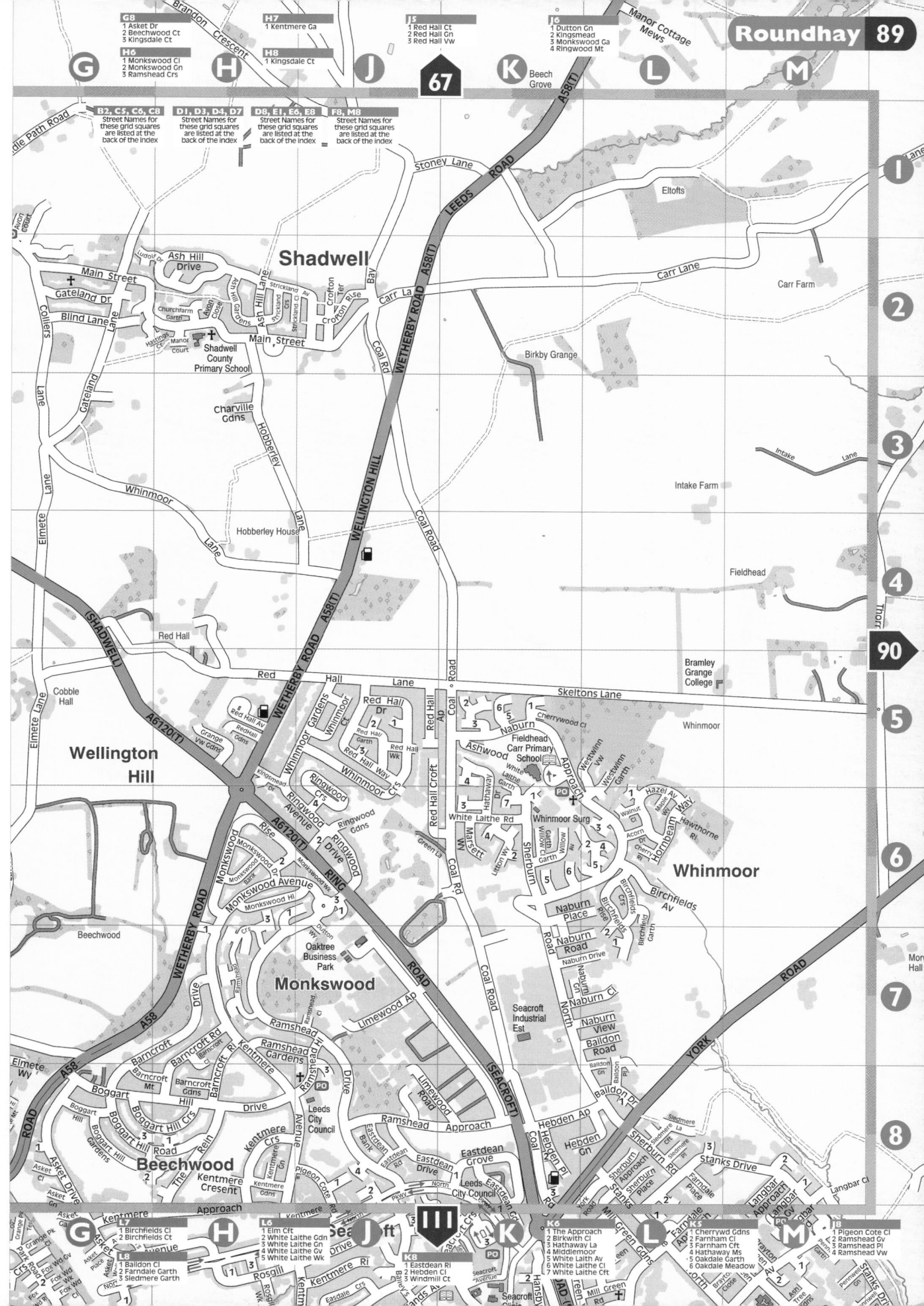

67

90

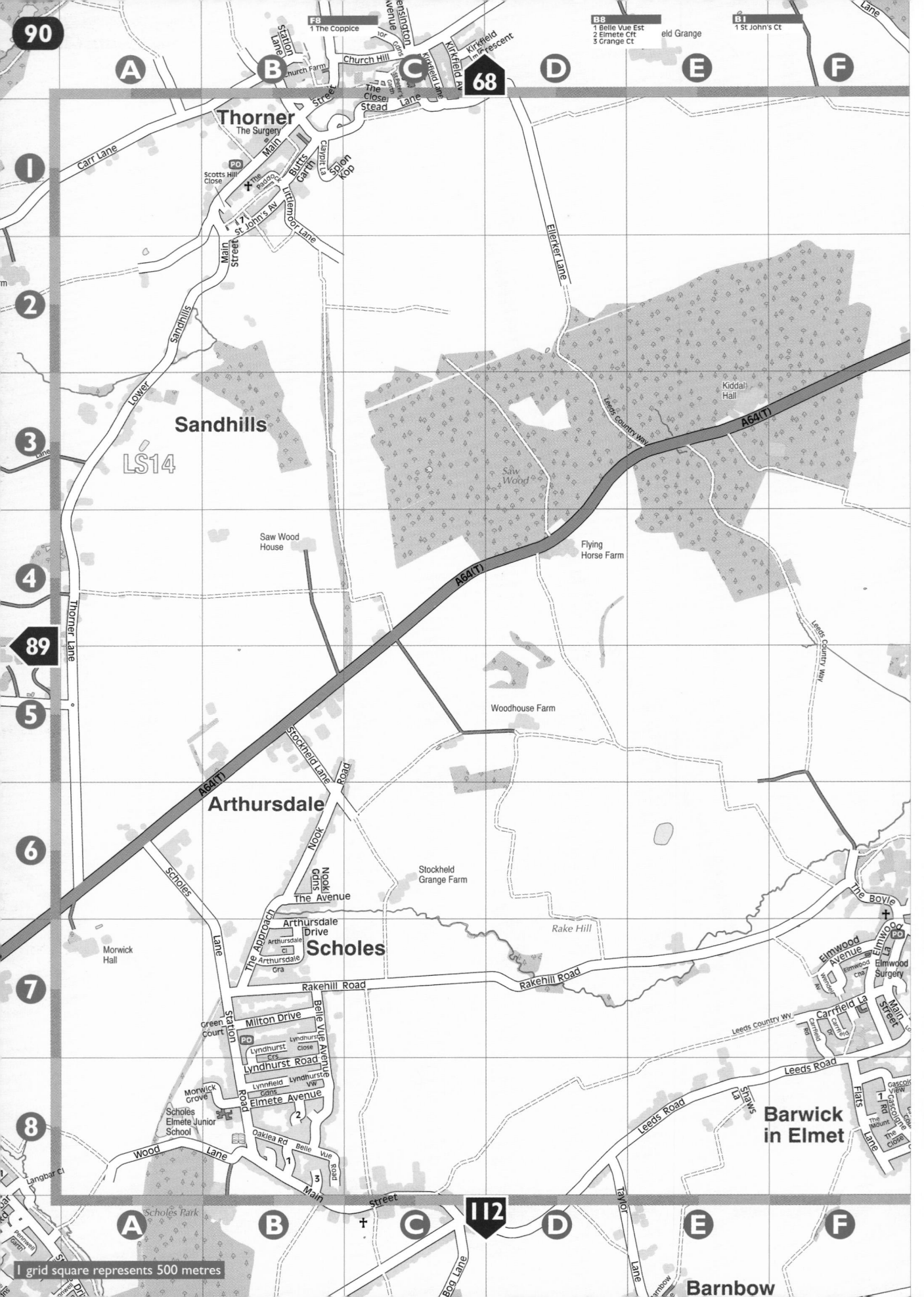

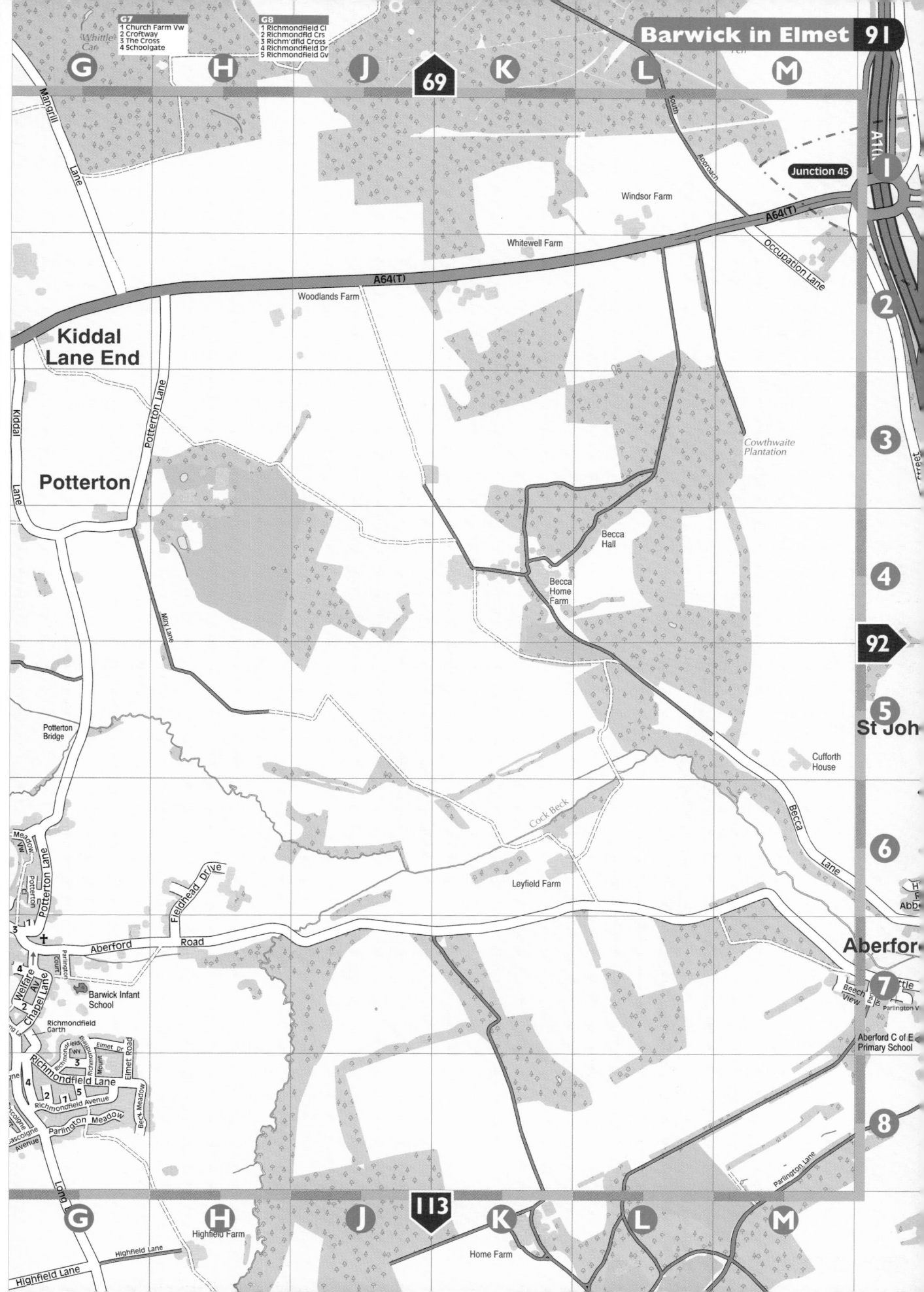

G7
1 Church Farm Vw
2 Croftway
3 The Cross
4 Schoolgate

G8
1 Richmondfield Cl
2 Richmdfld Crs
3 Richm'dfld Cross
4 Richmondfield Dr
5 Richmondfield Gv

G H J K L M

69

I

Junction 45

A64(T)

South Approach

Windsor Farm

Whitewell Farm

Occupation Lane

2

A64(T)

Woodlands Farm

Kiddal
Lane End

3

Cowthwaite
Plantation

Kiddal Lane

Potterton Lane

Potterton

Becca
Hall

Becca
Home
Farm

4

92

Miry Lane

5

St Joh

Potterton
Bridge

Cufforth
House

Becca Lane

6

Cock Beck

Meadow Vw

Potterton Lane

Fieldhead Drive

Leyfield Farm

Abb

Aberfor

Aberford Road

Parlington Court

Welfare

Chapel Lane

Parlington Av

Barwick Infant
School

Beech
View

7

Parlington V

Richmondfield
Garth

Richmondfield
Lane

Aberford C of E
Primary School

Richmondfield Avenue

Elmet Dr

Elmet Road

Elmet Mount

Beck Meadow

Gascoigne

Gascoigne Avenue

Parlington Meadow

8

Long Lane

Parlington Lane

G H J K L M

113

Highfield Farm

Home Farm

Highfield Lane

Highfield Lane

G   H   J   **71**   K   L   M

White Quarry
Farm

Cock Beck

B1223   **1**

Old London

Cocksford   Cocksford
Golf Club
Limited

Road   Grange View   **2**
Rockingham   The Close
Towton

B1217   **3**

Cock Beck

Harper
Rash

A162   **4**

Mawfield
Spring   **94**

Saxton
Grange   **5**

Newstead
Farm   Castle Hill
Wood   Towton
1461   **6**

Carr
Wood

Lead Mill
Farm   A162   **Scar**

Cotchers Lane   **7**

Scarthingwell

Lead Hall
Farm   †   B1217   Milner Lane   Walnut Close
Saxton Court
Scarthingwell Crescent
Saxton Lane

Cock Beck

Hungate Close   Saxton
Dacre Court   Walnut
Close

Dam   Lane   Saxton C of E
Primary School
PO   Main Street   **8**

Saxton

G   H   J   **115**   K   Headwell Lane   L   M   A162

Coldhill Lane   Orchard Cl
Ash Tree
Barkston Ash

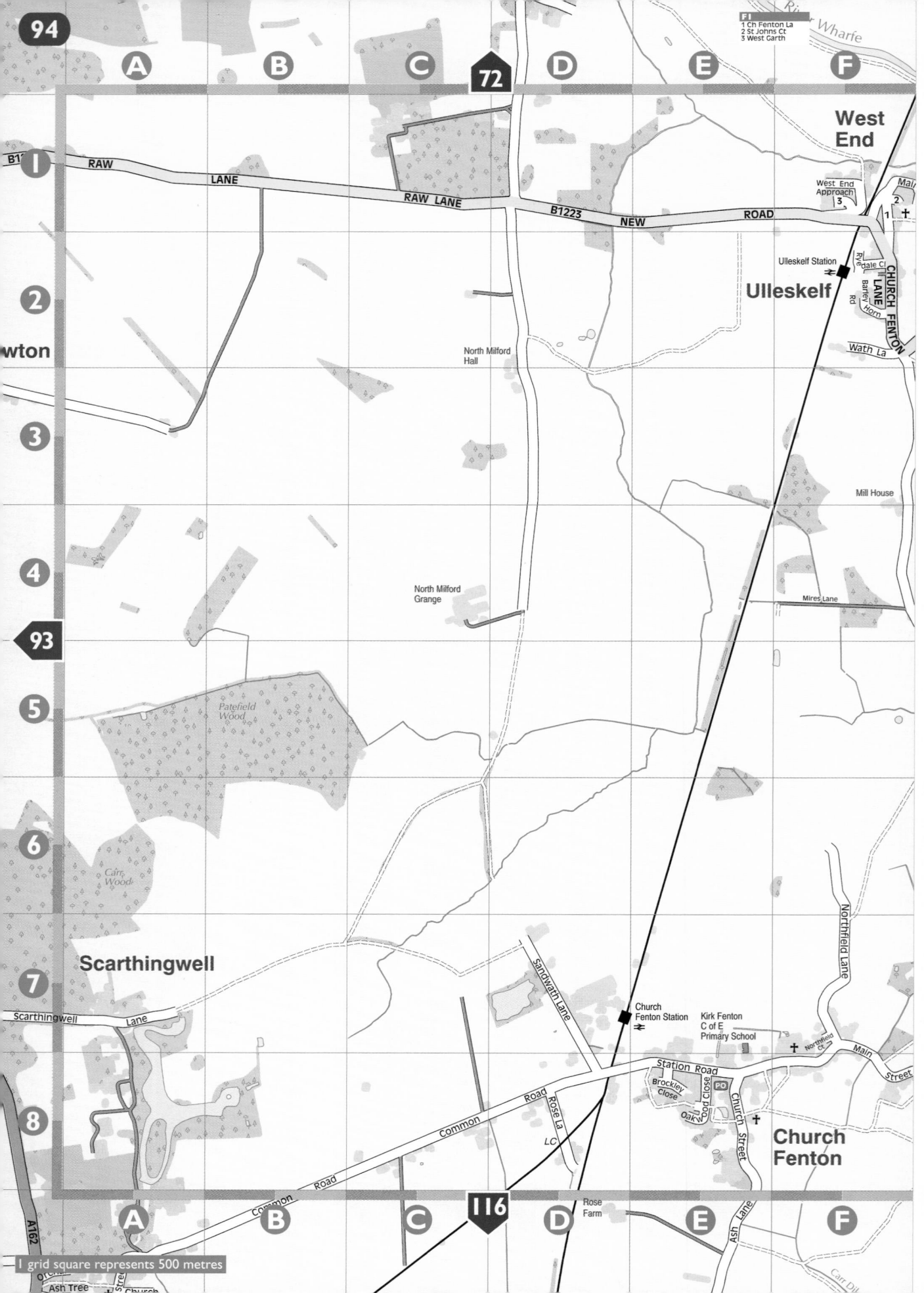

G   H   J   **73**   K   L   M

I

Scotland Wood

Ozendyke Ings

River Wharfe

River Wharfe

PO

Hall Garth Close

1/2 Street

Ings Road

Bell Lane

BOGGART   LANE

2

B1223

Common Lane

Ozendyke House Farm

B1223

3

Woodbine Grange

Ryther

Outwood   Lane

Mill Lane

Ozendyke Grange

4

Moor Lane

Cawood Crs

Skelf St

Dorts Crs

Ulla

Trans Wk

Ltt Ings Cl

Poplars Farm

5

Airfield

6

Busk Lane

Paradise Wood

7

Brackenhill Lane

Paradise Lodge

Nanny Lane

Partridge Hill Farm

Oxmoor Lane

8

Gay Lane

Great Lawn Wood

Hall La

Hall Farm   G   H   J   **117**   K   L   M

Broad Lane

Meeke Wood

Lodge

G1

1 Church St

2 Smithy La

Jew Leys Lane

Bolton Grange

Jew Leys Lane

A B C D E F

I Catlow Brook

Foulds House Farm

Pendle Way

Coldwell Reservoir

Deerstone Moor

Will Moor

Pendle Way

Back Lane

2 Shuttleworth Pasture

Bronte Way

Red Spa Moor

3 Halifax Road

High Ridehalgh

Ridehalgh Lane   Ridehalgh Lane

Thursden

Maulf Road

4 Burnley Way

Monk Hall

Thursden Brook

Burnley Way

Bronte Way

Halifax Road

5

6 Extwistle Moor

Swinden Reservoirs

7 Swinden Water

8 Hameldon

A   Gorple Rd   B   C   D   E   F

Burnley Way

I grid square represents 500 metres

G   H   J   75   Brinks   K   L   M

The Forest of Trawden

Bedding
Hill
Moor

518
▲
Boulsworth
Hill

Dove
Stones

Hole Sike

The Plain

Rushy
Clough

Foul Sike

Field of
the Mosses

Lancashire County
Calderdale

Widdop
Moor

Greave
Clough

Pisser
Clough

Widdop

Burnley Way

Widdop
Lodge

Widdop
Reservoir

Flask

I
2
3
4
98
5
6
7
8

G   H   J   119   K   L   M

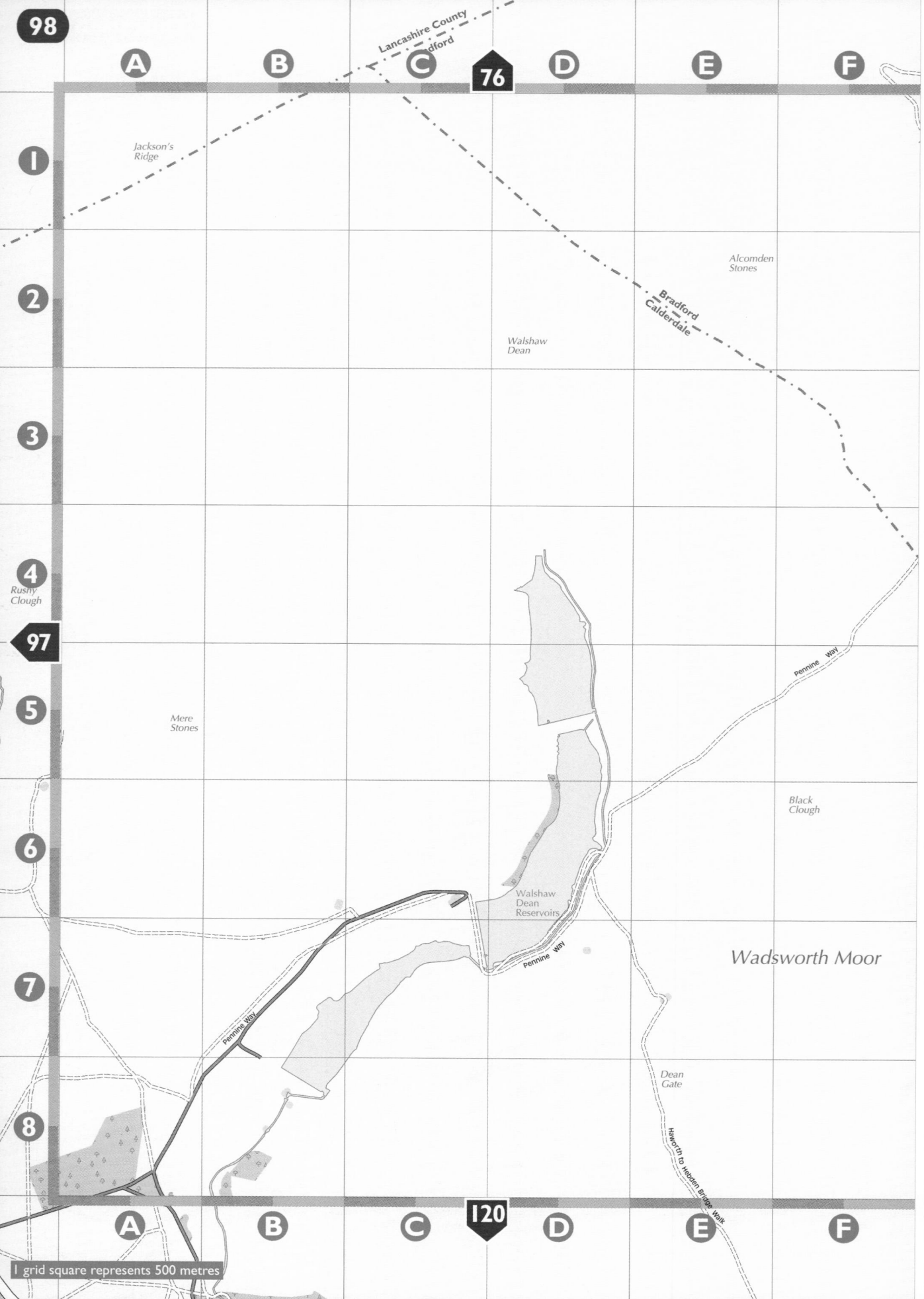

A B C D E F

76

Lancashire County
...dford

1

Jackson's
Ridge

2

Walshaw
Dean

Alcomden
Stones

Bradford
Calderdale

3

4

Rushy
Clough

97

Pennine Way

5

Mere
Stones

6

Black
Clough

Walshaw
Dean
Reservoirs

Pennine Way

Wadsworth Moor

7

Pennine Way

Dean
Gate

8

Haworth to Hebden Bridge Walk

A B C D E F

120

1 grid square represents 500 metres

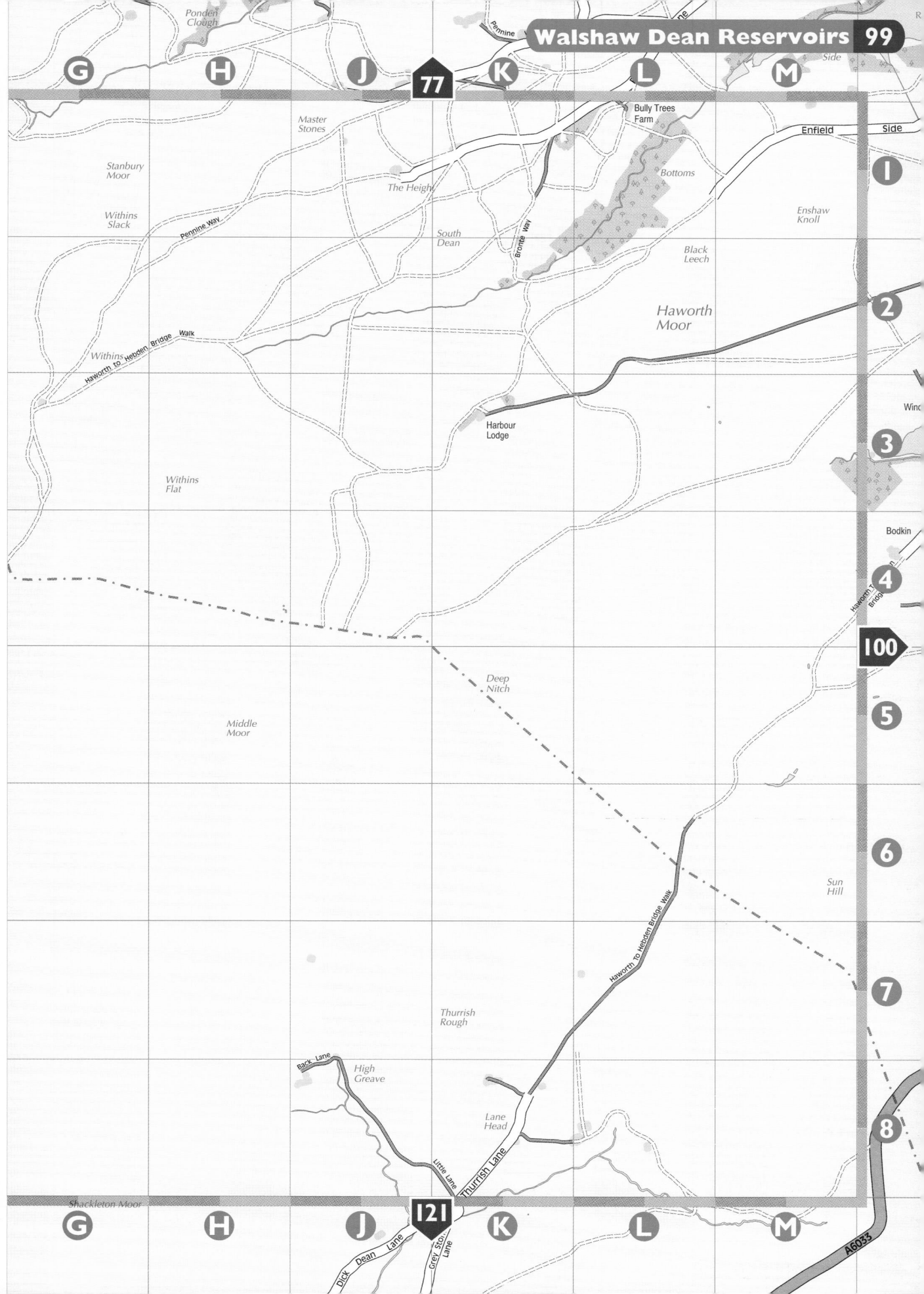

G   H   J   **77**   K   L   M

Ponden Clough

Master Stones

Bully Trees Farm

Enfield   Side

I

Stanbury Moor

The Height

Bottoms

Enshaw Knoll

Withins Slack

Pennine Way

South Dean

Brontë Way

Black Leech

2

Withins to Hebden Bridge Walk

Haworth to Hebden Bridge Walk

Haworth Moor

Wind

Harbour Lodge

3

Bodkin

Withins Flat

Haworth To Bridge

4

100

Deep Nitch

5

Middle Moor

6

Sun Hill

Haworth To Hebden Bridge Walk

7

Thurrish Rough

Back Lane

High Greave

Lane Head

8

Shackleton Moor

Thurrish Lane

Little Lane

Grey Stone Lane

Dick Dean Lane

A6033

G   H   J   **121**   K   L   M

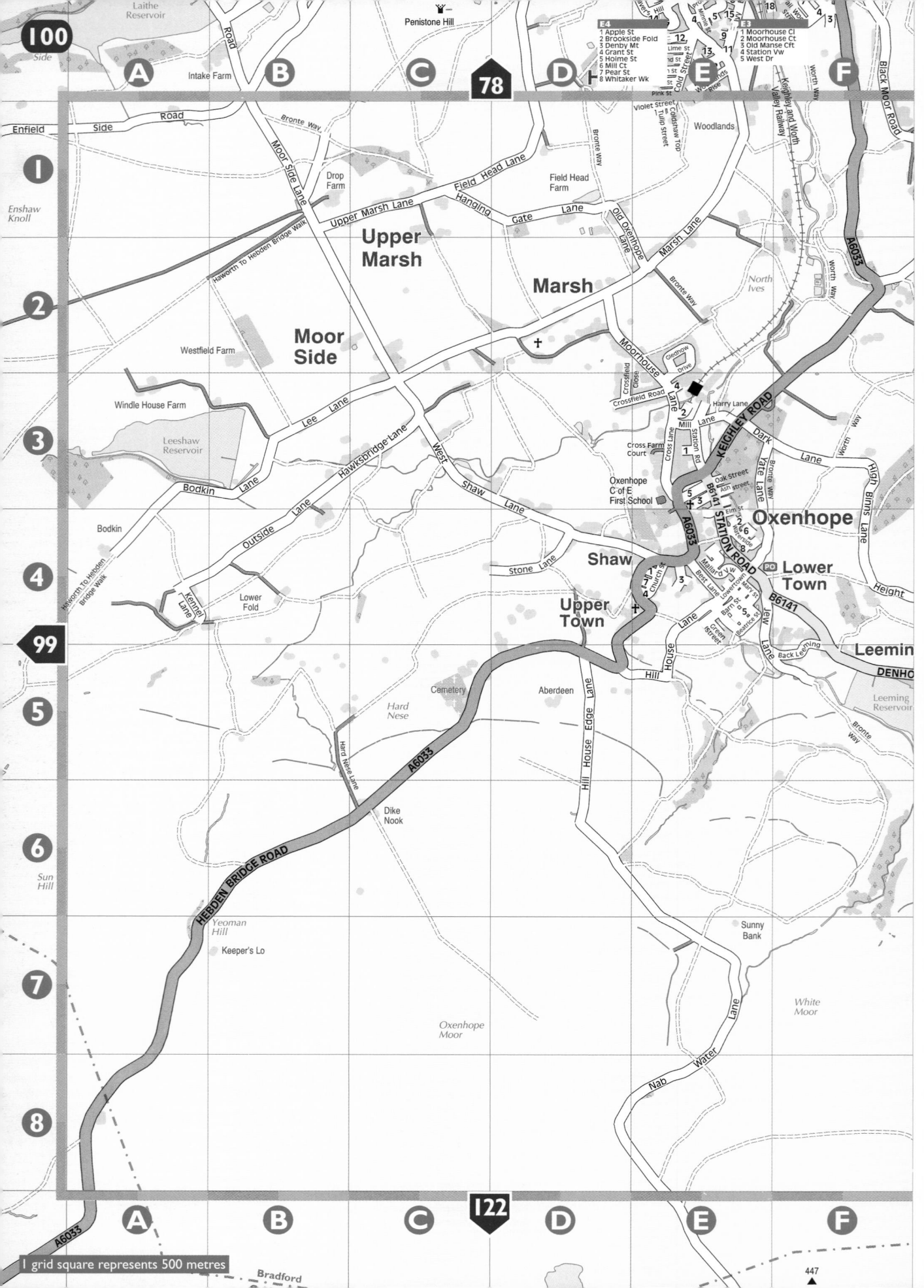

Side

Enfield

Enshaw
Knoll

**Upper
Marsh**

**Moor
Side**

Marsh

Intake Farm

Side   Road

Bronte Way

Moor Side Lane

Field Head Lane

Field Head
Farm

Hanging   Gate   Lane

Drop
Farm

Upper Marsh Lane

Haworth To Hebden Bridge Walk

Old Oxenhope Lane

Marsh Lane

Bronte Way

North
Ives

Woodlands

Violet Street
Tulip Street
Coldshaw Top
Pink St

Keighley and Worth
Valley Railway

Black Moor Road

A6033

Worth Way

E4
1 Apple St
2 Brookside Fold
3 Denby Mt
4 Grant St
5 Holme St
6 Mill Ct
7 Pear St
8 Whitaker Wk

12
Lime St

13
11

E3
1 Moorhouse Cl
2 Moorhouse Ct
3 Old Manse Cft
4 Station Vw
5 West Dr

Westfield Farm

Windle House Farm

Leeshaw
Reservoir

Lee   Lane

Hawksbridge Lane

West shaw Lane

Gledhow
Drive

Moorhouse Lane

Crossfield Close
Crossfield Road

Harry Lane

Keighley Road

Dark   Lane

Worth   Way

High Binns Lane

Bodkin   Lane

Bodkin

Outside   Lane

Oxenhope
C of E
First School

Cross Farm
Court

Mill
Station Rd
Cross Lane

B6141
Oak Street
Ash street

Bronte Way
Yate Lane

Oxenhope

Shaw

Stone Lane

A6033

STATION ROAD

Riverside

Lower
Town

Height

**Upper
Town**

Lower
Fold

Kennel Lane

Haworth To Hebden Bridge Walk

Church St
Church St

Hill

Hill House Edge Lane

House Lane

Mill St
Best Lane
Elm St
Mary St
Barn St
Green Street
Beatrice St

PO
Lowertown

B6141

Back Leeming

New Lane

Leemin

DENHO

Leeming
Reservoir

Cemetery

Hard
Nese

Aberdeen

Hard Nese Lane

A6033

Sunny
Bank

Sun
Hill

HEBDEN BRIDGE ROAD

Dike
Nook

Oxenhope
Moor

Water
Lane

White
Moor

Yeoman
Hill

Keeper's Lo

Nab   Water

I grid square represents 500 metres

Bradford

Penistone Hill

A6033

E2
1 Badgergate Av
2 Burniston Cl
3 Kingston Cl
4 Moorside Rd
5 St Matthews Gv

E1
1 Briggland Ct
2 Cranford Pl
3 School St
4 Spring Farm Ms
5 Village Ms
6 Well St

A6
1 Carperley Crs
2 Clapham St
3 School St

A5
1 George St
2 Mary St

80

Norr

WILSDEN

Wilsden Primary School

Wilsden Medical Practice

Hare Croft

New Holland

Lingbob

Meadow Green

B6144

HAWORTH ROAD   LANE SIDE

Station Road

B6144

BD15

Harrop Lane

Allan House Farm

Harrop Edge

Mutton Lane

Allerton Road

Long Lane

Buck Park

Whalley Lane

Whalley Lane

Tewitt Lane

Old Allen Road

Dean Lane Head Farms

Hollin Park

101

Ten Yards Lane

Allen Park Farm

Black Dyke Lane

High Stream Head Farm

Dean Lane

Upper Pikeley

Foster Park Road

Foster Park View

Doe Park

Reservoir

Law Farm

Egypt

Egypt Road

Lower Heights Road

Upper Heights Road

Bell Dean

Station Road

Old Road

HALIFAX ROAD A629

Denholme House

Spring Hall Farm

Back Hts Road

Half Acre

Well Heads

BD13

Hill Top

Spring Holes Lane

Hill Crest Road

Leaside Drive

Denholme Clough

Bronte Way

Well Heads

Close Head

Close Head Lane

Cemetery

Hill   Top   Road

Bronte Way

Windy Ridge

Ash Tree Avenue

Wensley Bank Ter

Wensley Bank West

First School

B6145

Royd Mount Middle School

John St

Alderscholes Lane

SMITHY HILL

BRIGHOUSE

Cragg Lane

Keelham First School

THORNTON ROAD

124

Green Clough

L3, L5, L6, L7
Street Names for these grid squares are listed at the back of the index

E7
1 Cliffe St
2 Moss St
3 Reservoir Vw

F7
1 Lyon St
2 Oakhall Pk
3 South St

Keelham

1 grid square represents 500 metres

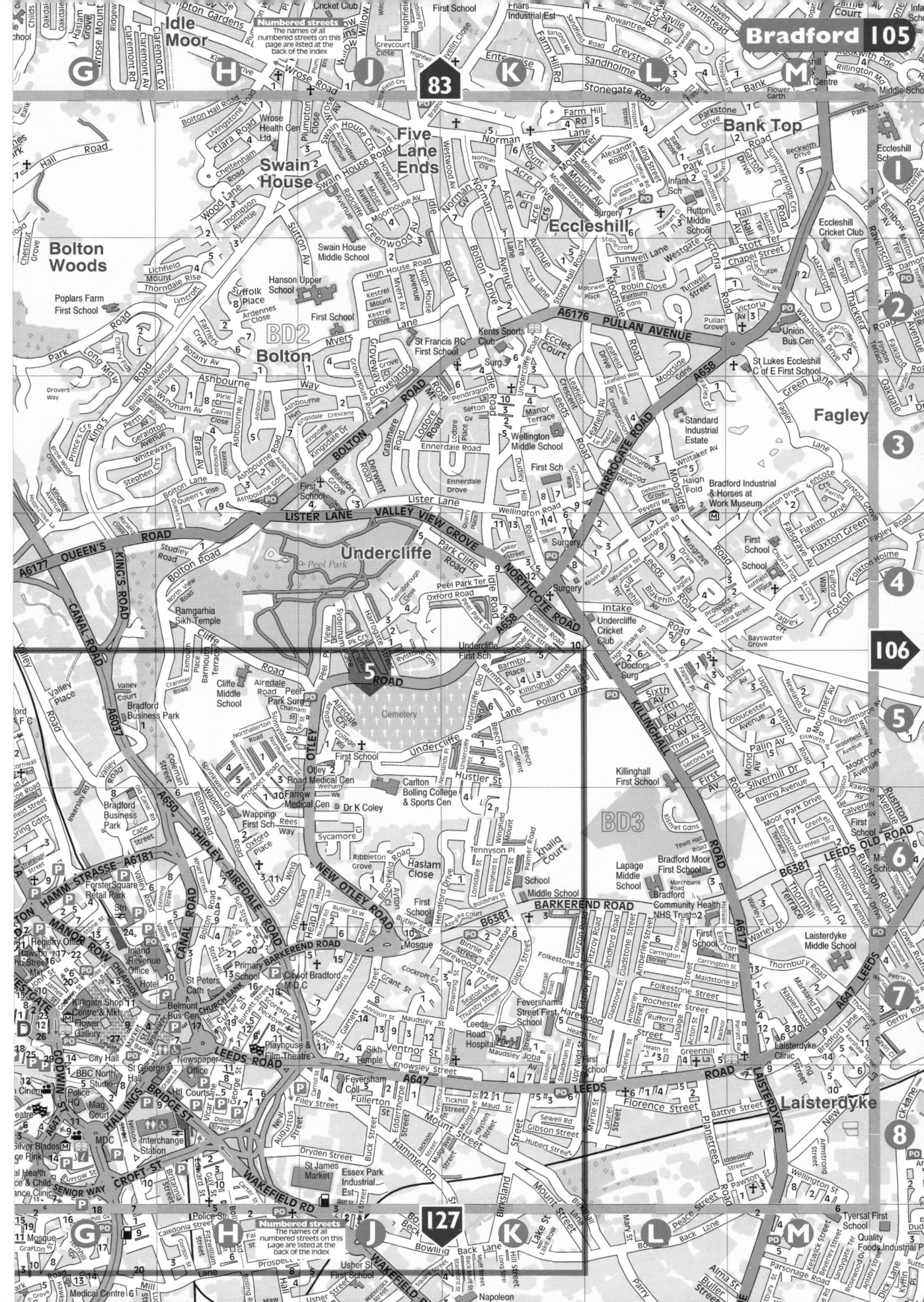

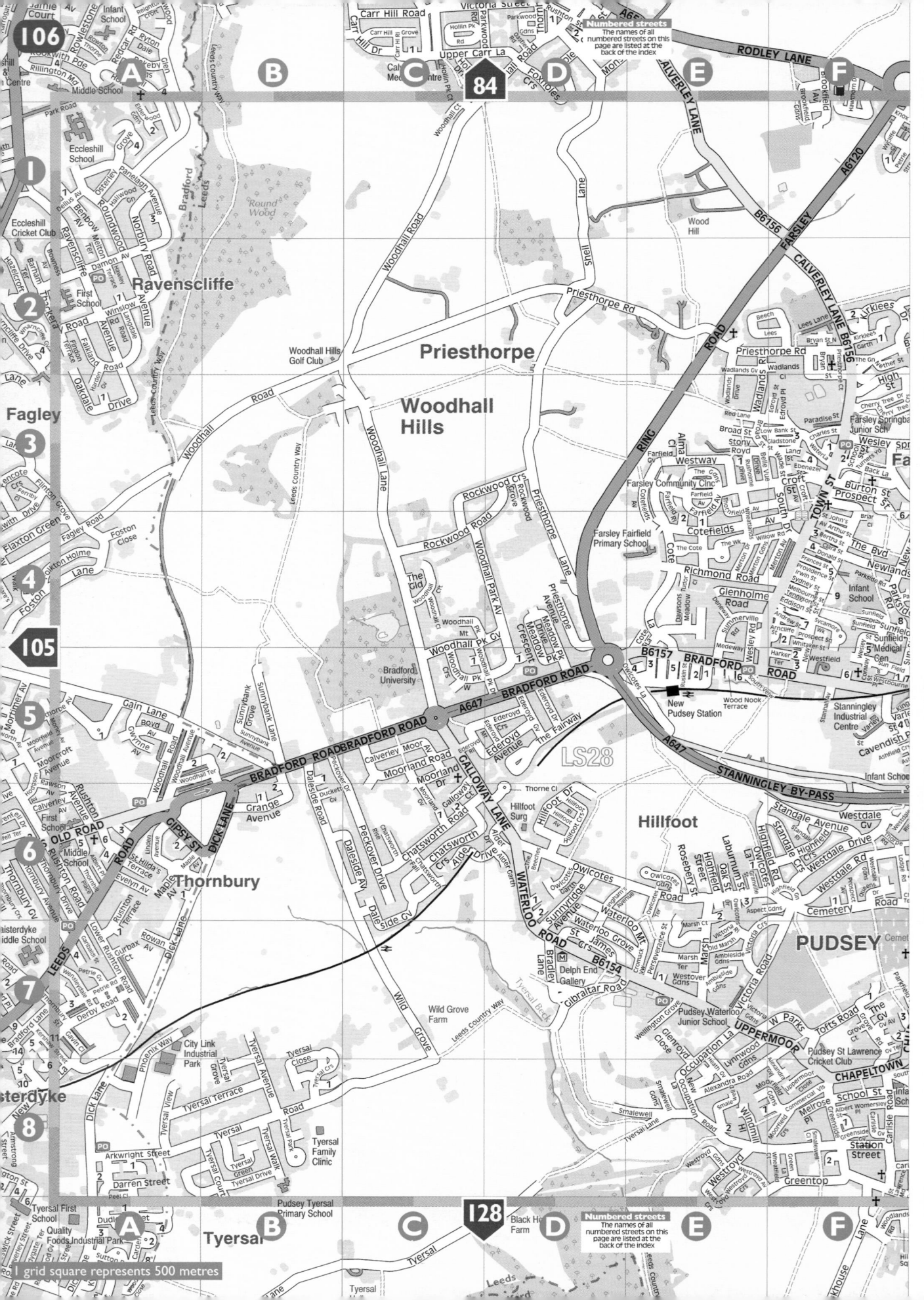

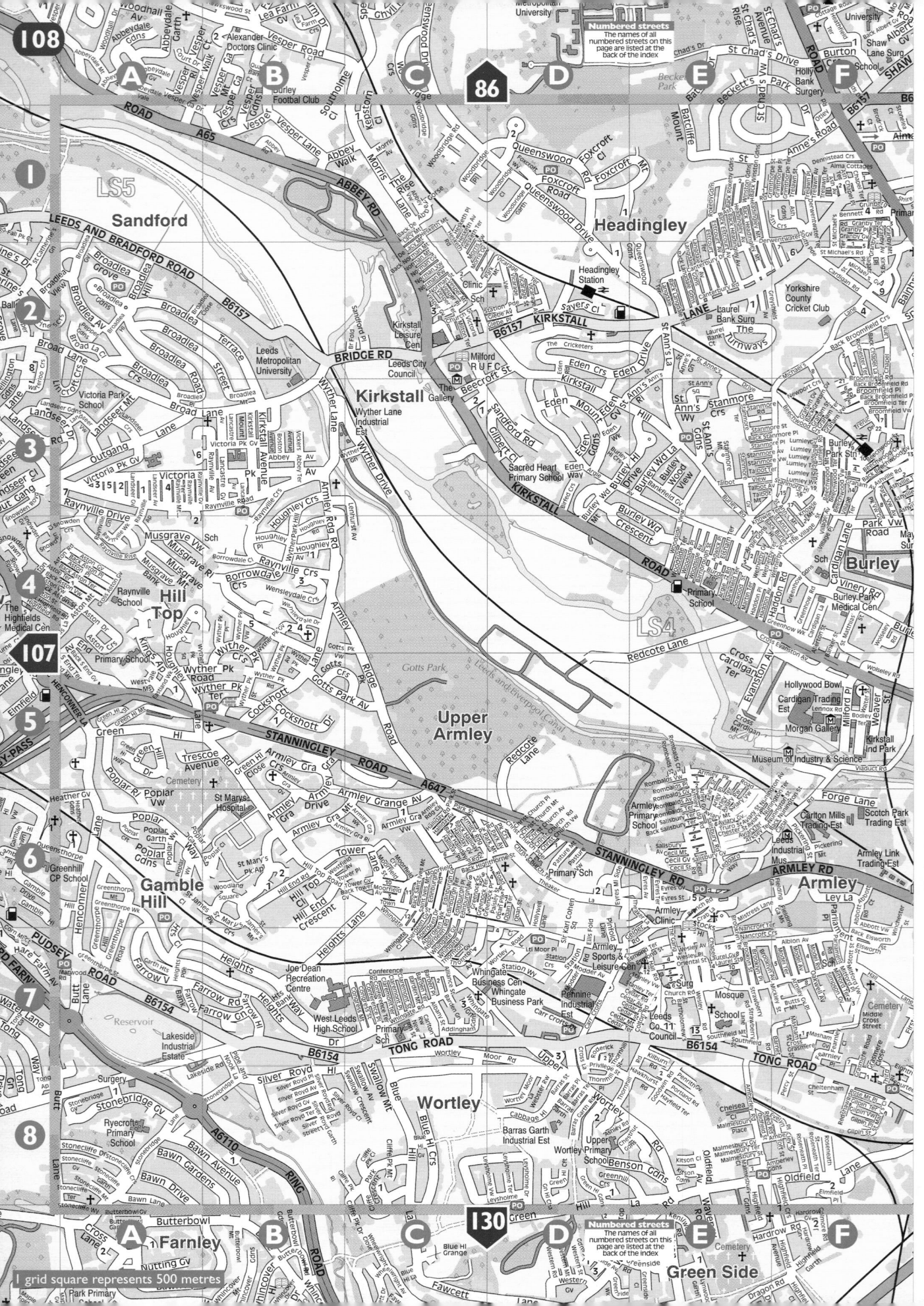

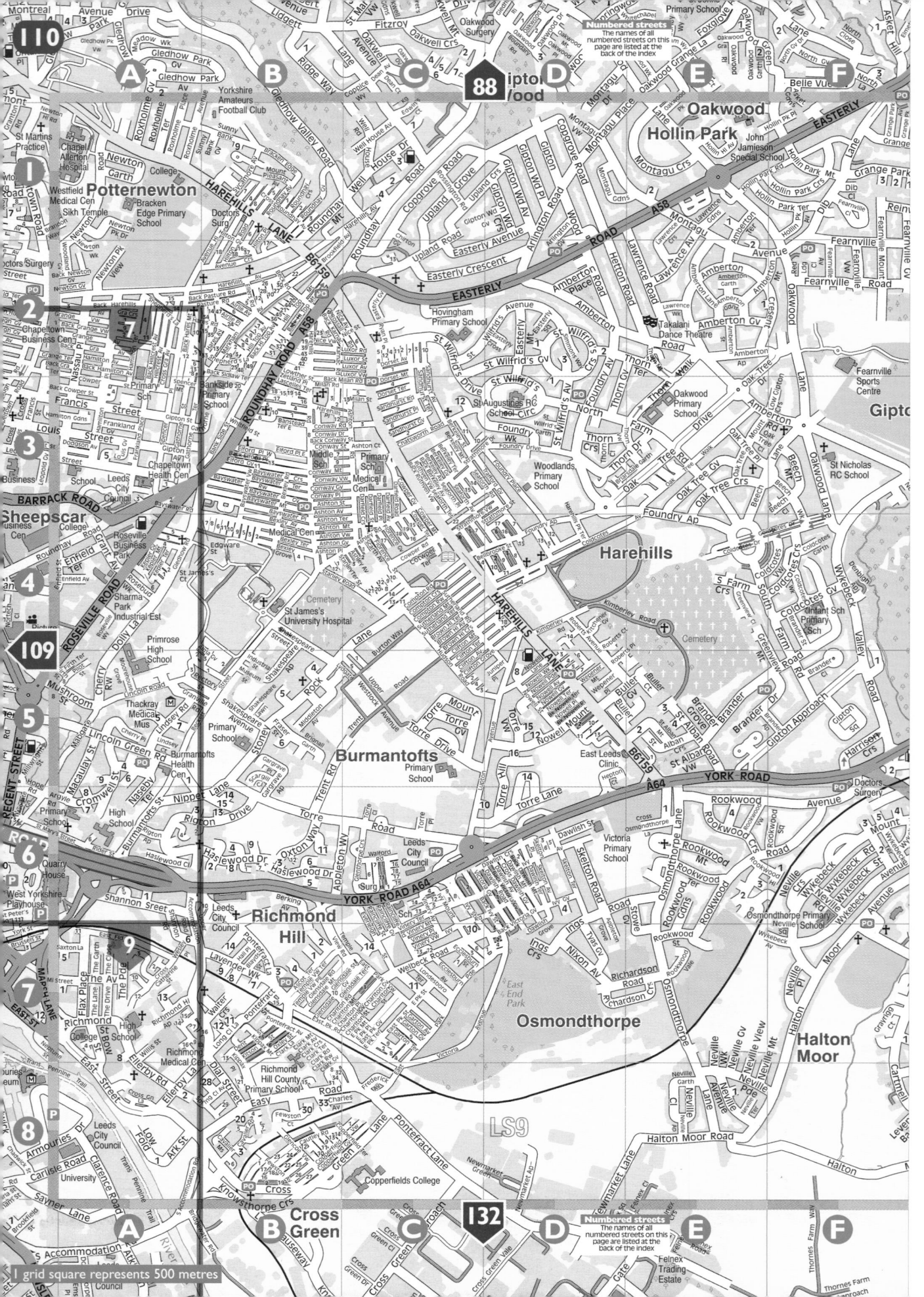

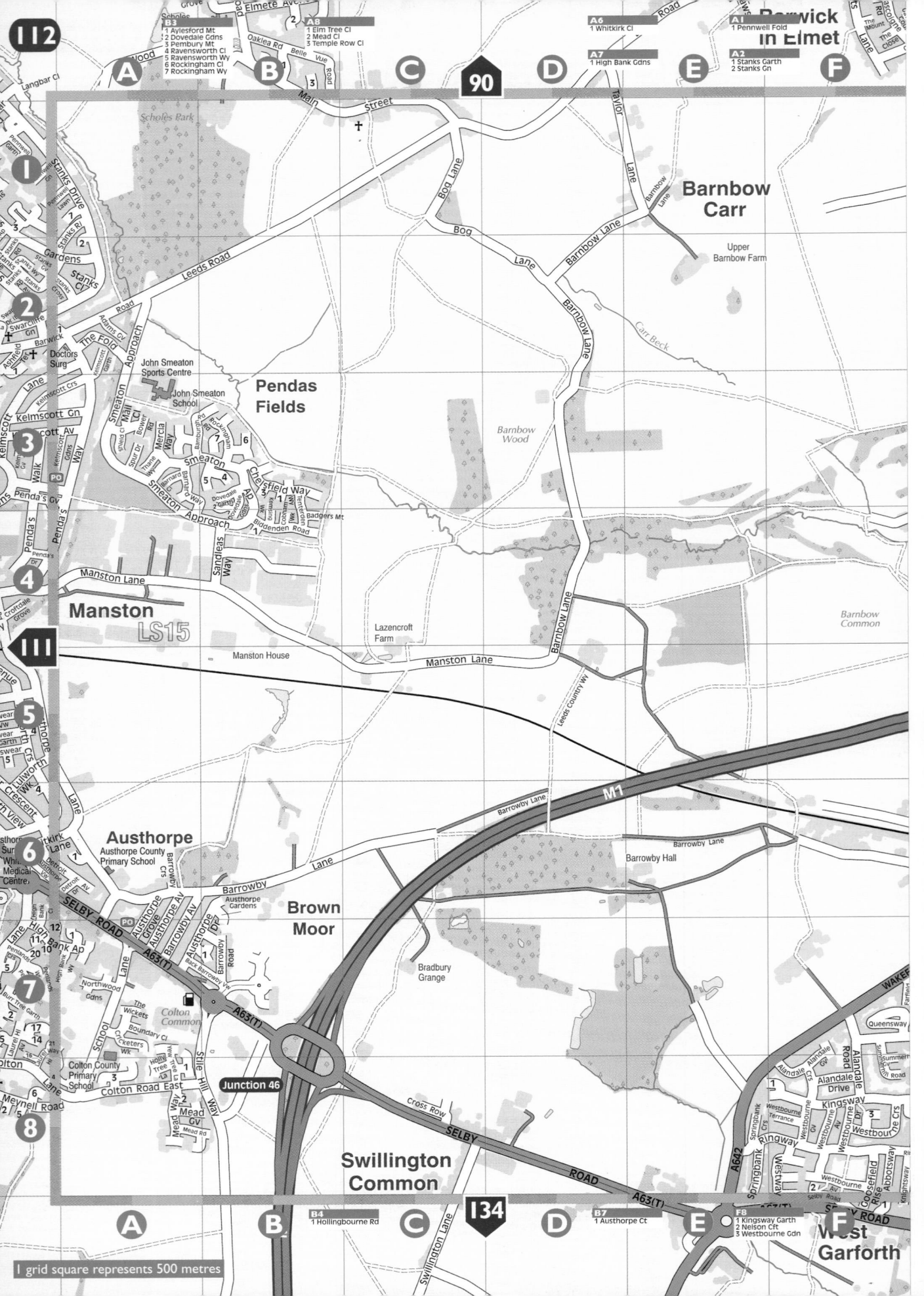

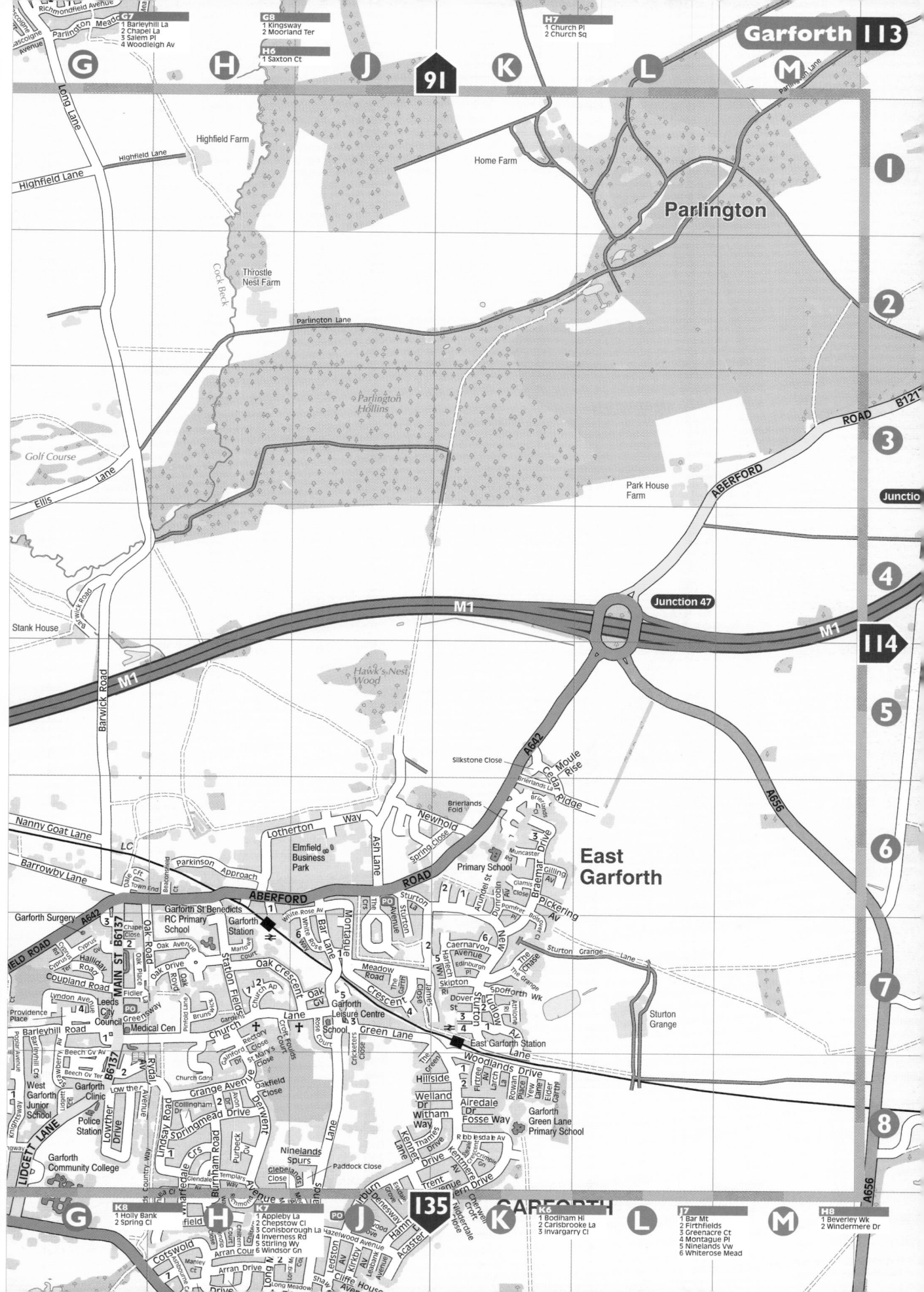

Saxton

G   H   J   93   K   L   M

Saxton C of E
Primary School
PO
Main Street

Headwell Lane

Coldhill Lane

Barkston Ash

Orchard C
Ash Tree
Garth
Main Street
Church Street

Orchard Lane

Back

2

Garlic
Flats

Oldgate Lane

A162

3

Coldhill Farm

Coldhill Lane

Stream Dike   Stream Farm

4

116

5

**SHERBURN
IN ELME**

Elizabeth
Court

Sir John's Lane

6

KIRKG

B1222

Beech
Th
C

Orchard

Chu

Crick

Laith Staid Lane

†

Foster
Wk

Garde
Cl
Tomlinson

Carr A

Garden Lane

Park

Avenue

Eversle
Deighton
Avenue
Ev

7

Huddleston
Old Wood

LS25

Low
Grange

Sherburn
High
School

Mill Dike

New

8

Lane

West
View

Highfield
Green

Highfield
VG

G   Mill Dike   H   J   137   K   L   M

Hall   Lane

Gorse Lane

LC

Nowthorpe

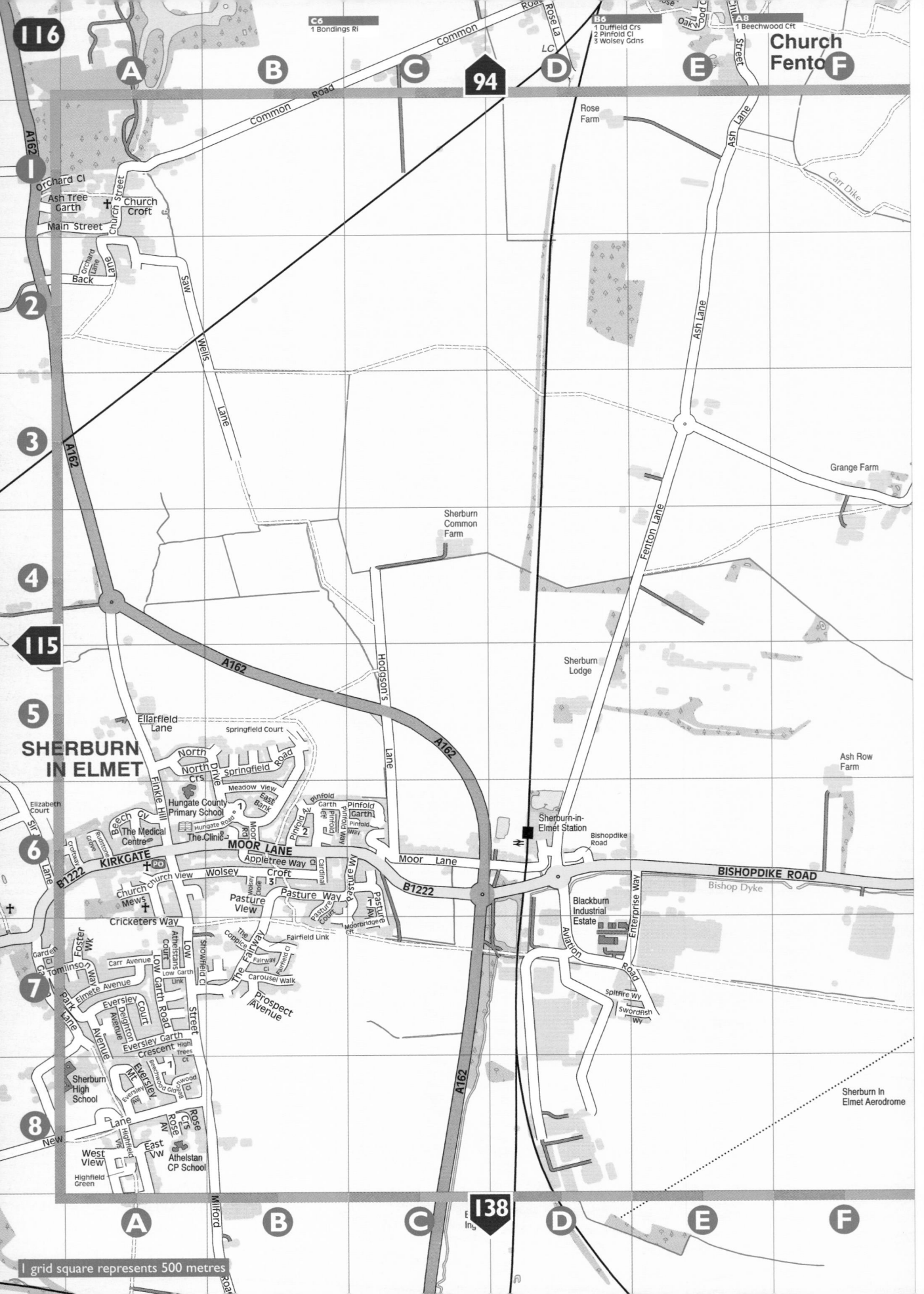

G H J **95** K L M

Sunny Lane
Partridge Hill Farm
Oxmoor Lane
Hall La
Cav
Hall Farm
Broad Lane
Meeke Wood
Lodge Farm
Broad Lane
I
Lane
2
Pickrowfield Lane
Oxmoor Lane
3
Biggin Lane
Little Fenton Lodge
Spring Well House
BISHO
Little Fenton
Biggin Lane
Biggin
4
Ash La
Sweeming Lane
B1222
5
Mattram Hall
B1222
North Sweeming
6
Lennerton Lane
Low Hall Farm
Rest Park
7
New
Lennerton Lane
8
Lennerton Lane
Lennerton Farm
Low Rest Park Farm
Melton Leys

Milford Hagg Farm
Habholme

A B C 96 D E F

I

2

3

4

5

6

7

8

A B C 140 D E F

Gorple Road

Hame...

Burnley Way

...rstwood ...servoir

Cant Clough Reservoir

Worsthorne Moor

Burnley Way

Far Pasture

Lo... ...useway

Burnley Way

Limestone Trail

Stiperden Moor

Stiperden Bar House

Lancashire County Calderdale

The Long Caus...

Coal Clou... Wind Farm

G   H   J   **97**   K   L   M

I

2

PH

3

4

120

5

6

7

8

Reservoir

Flask

Black Moor

Gorple Upper
Reservoir

Gorple Lower
Reservoir

Pennine Way

Raistrick
Greave

*Heptonstall
Moor*

*Hoar Side
Moor*

Egypt

Colden Water

Noah Dale

Greenland

Greenland   Road

Four
Gates End

G   H   J   **141**   K   L   M

*Stansfield
Moor*

Earnshaw
Hole

Moorcock   Road

Moorhall
Farm

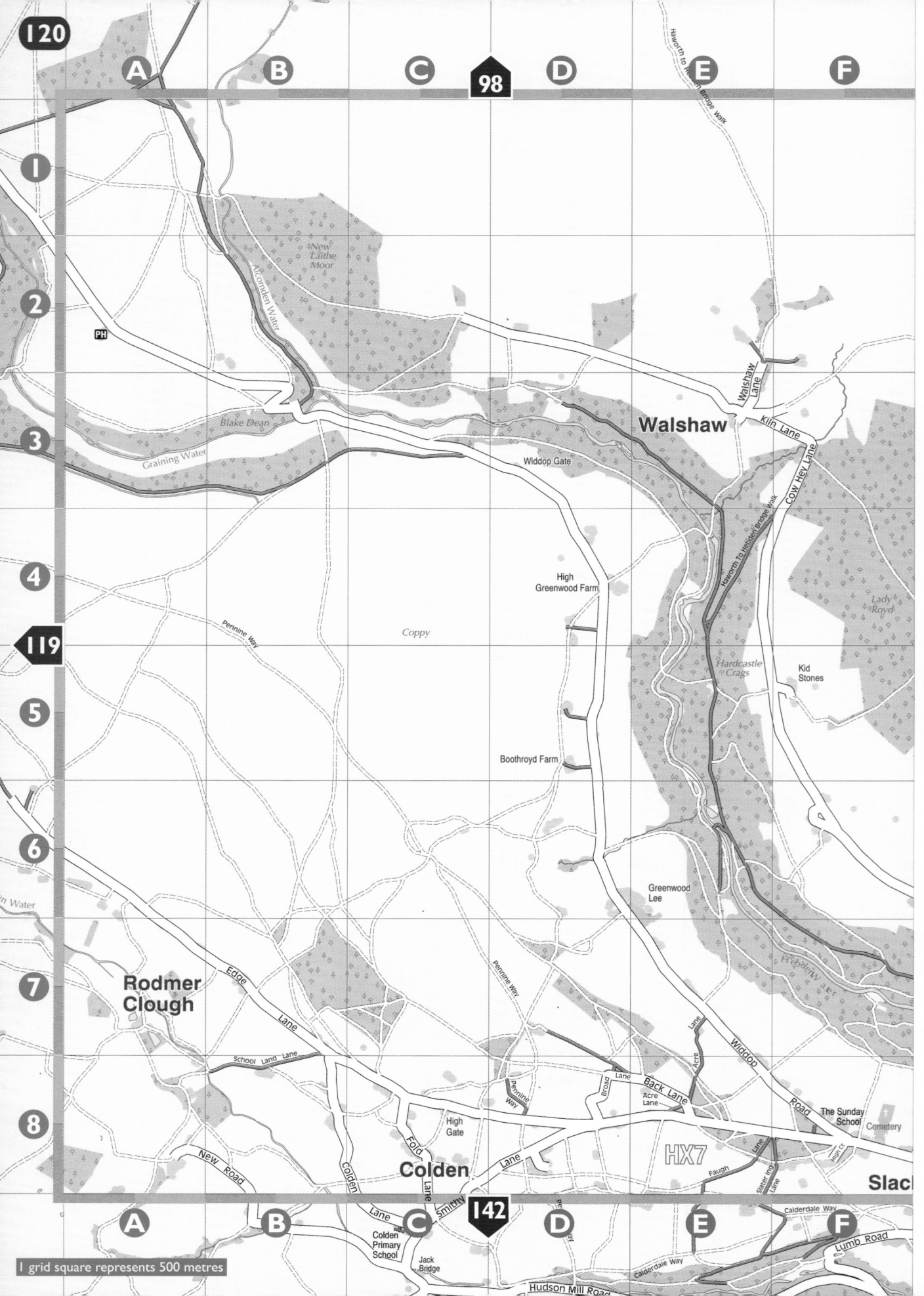

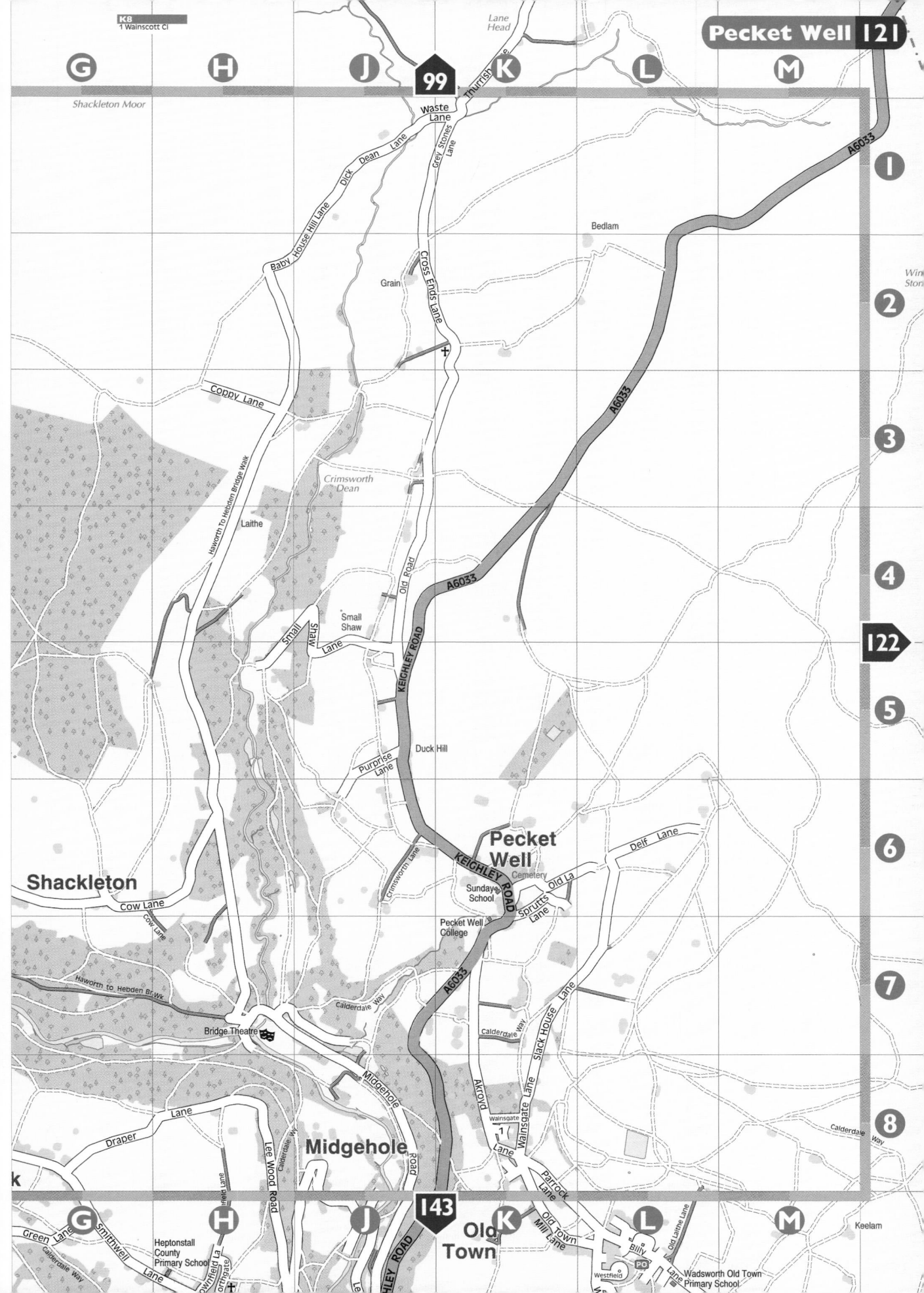

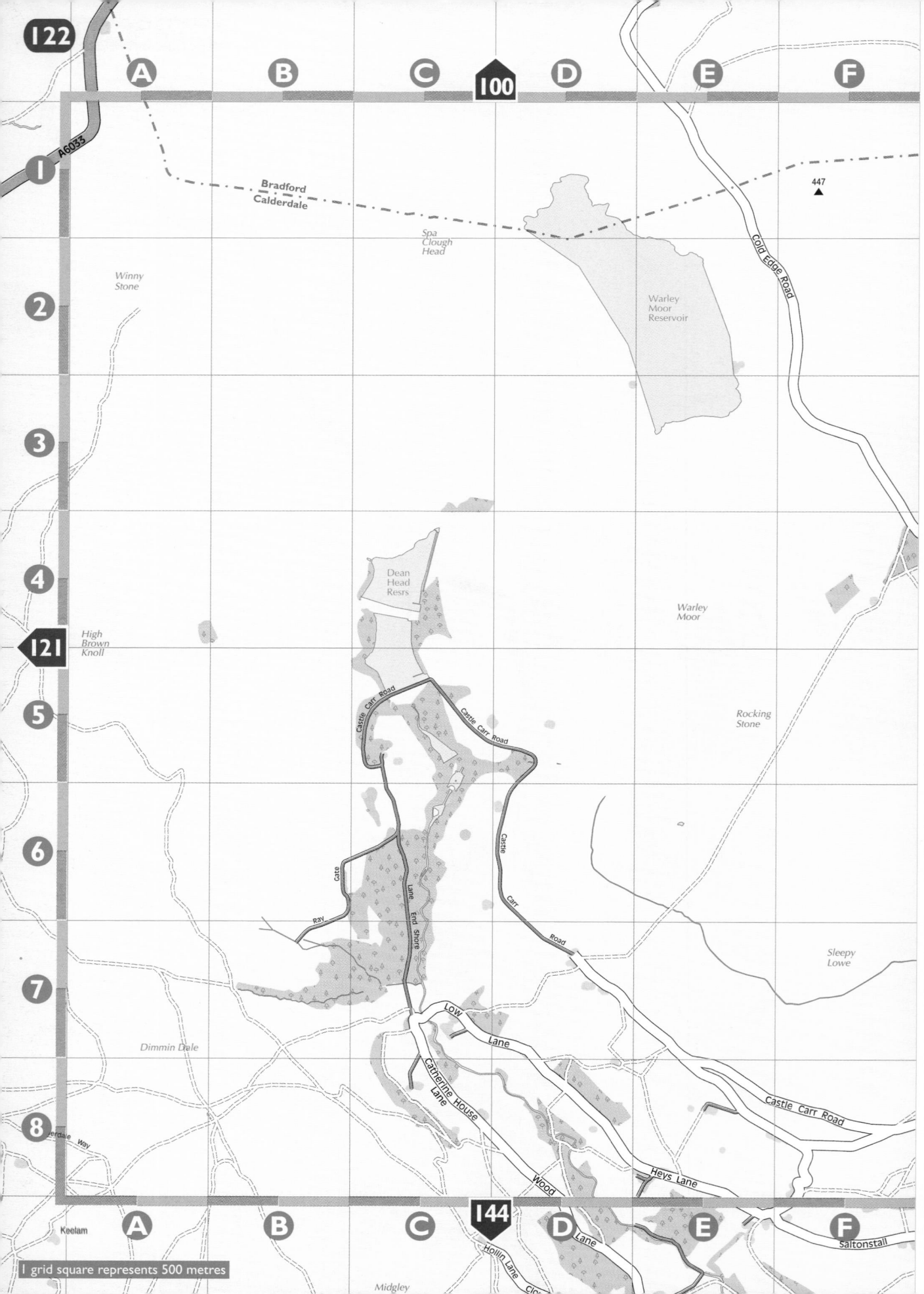

A   B   C   100   D   E   F

I   A6033

Bradford
Calderdale

Spa
Clough
Head

Winny
Stone

2

Warley
Moor
Reservoir

Cold Edge Road

447
▲

3

4   Dean
Head
Resrs

Warley
Moor

High
Brown
Knoll

5   Castle Carr Road   Castle Carr Road

Rocking
Stone

Castle

6   Gate   Lane End Shore   Carr

Ray   Road

Sleepy
Lowe

7   Dimmin Dale   LOW
Lane

Catherine House Lane

Castle Carr Road

8   erdale Way   Heys Lane

Keelam   A   B   C   144   D   E   F

Wood   Lane   Saltonstall

Hollin Lane Clo

Midgley

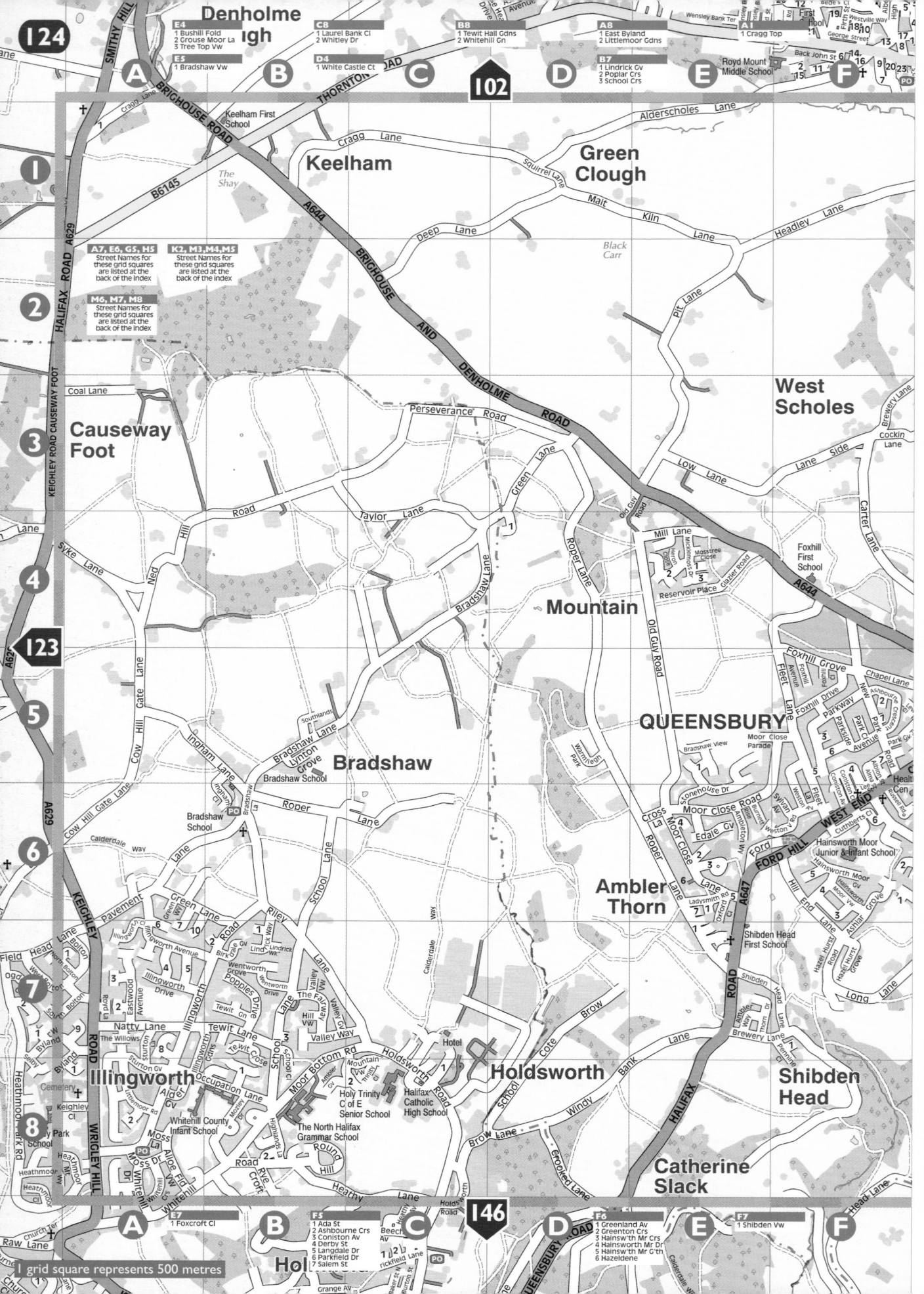

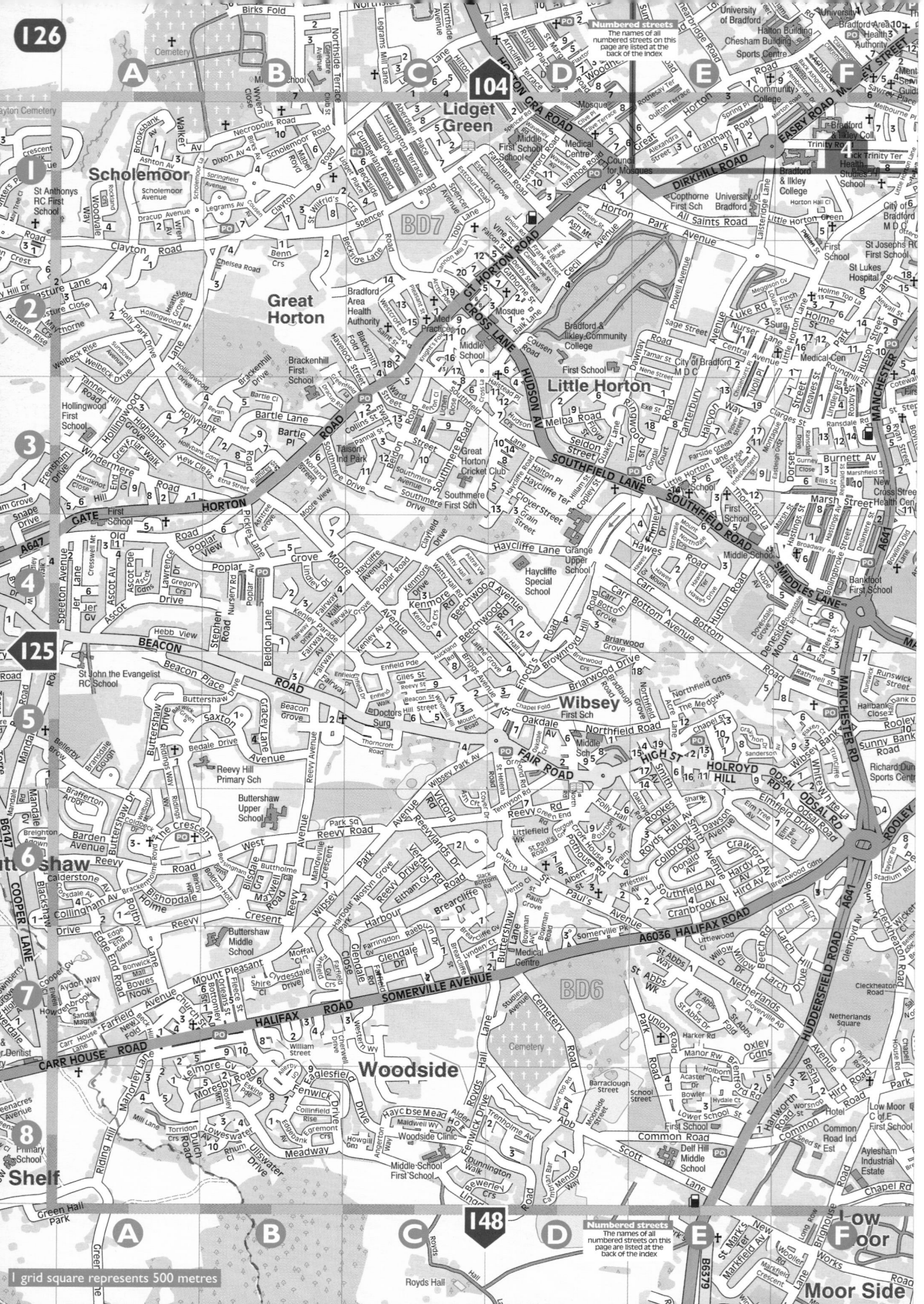

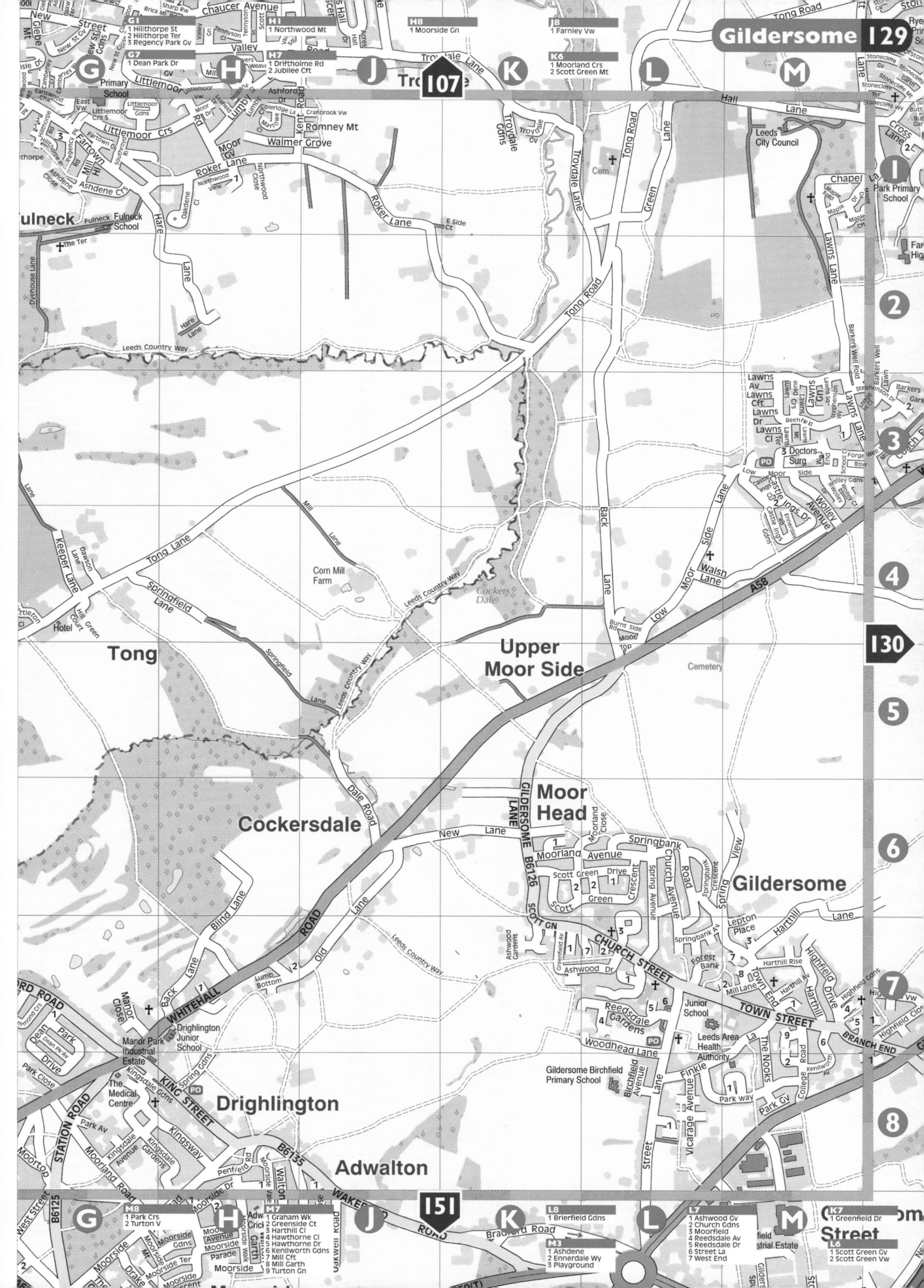

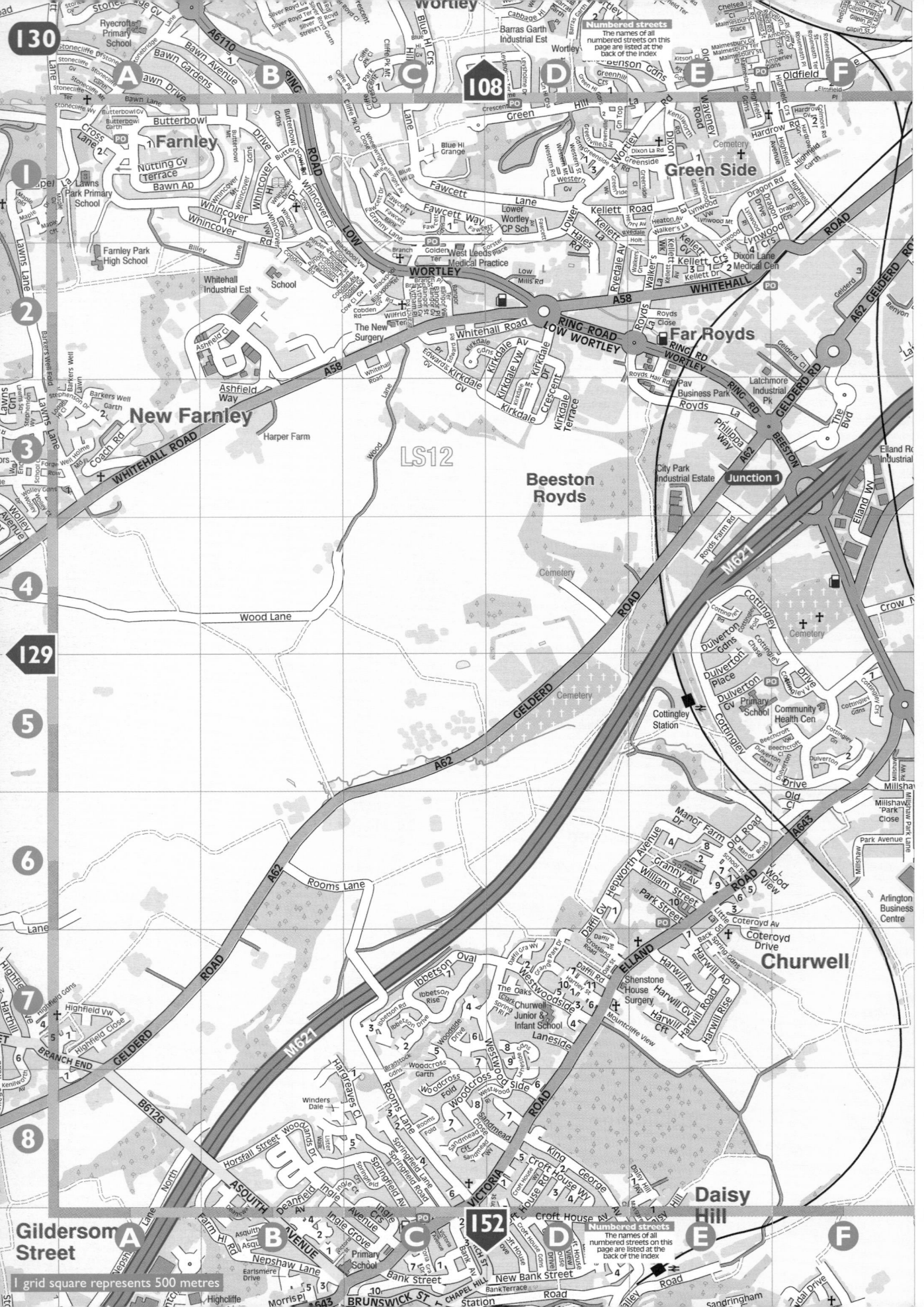

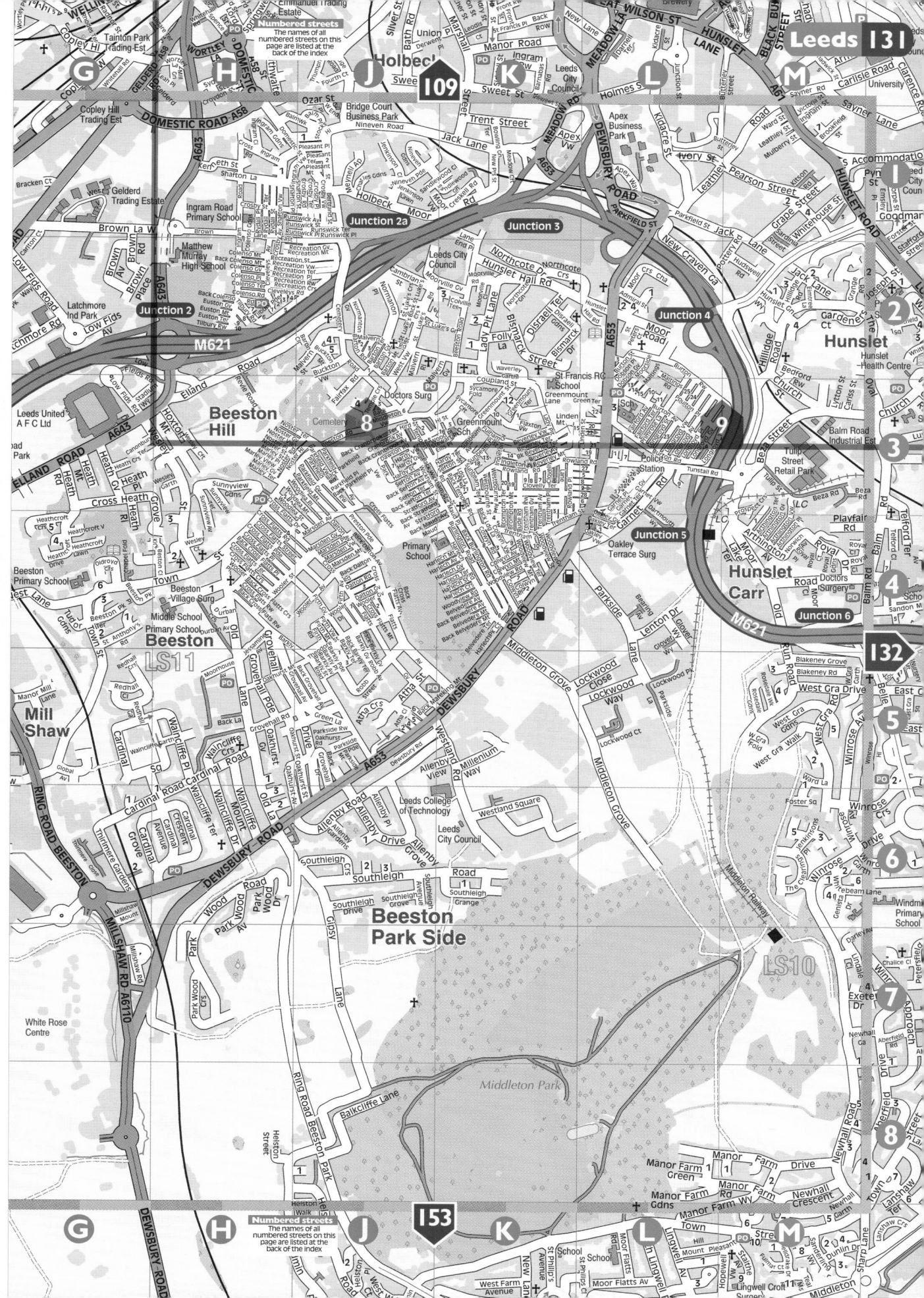

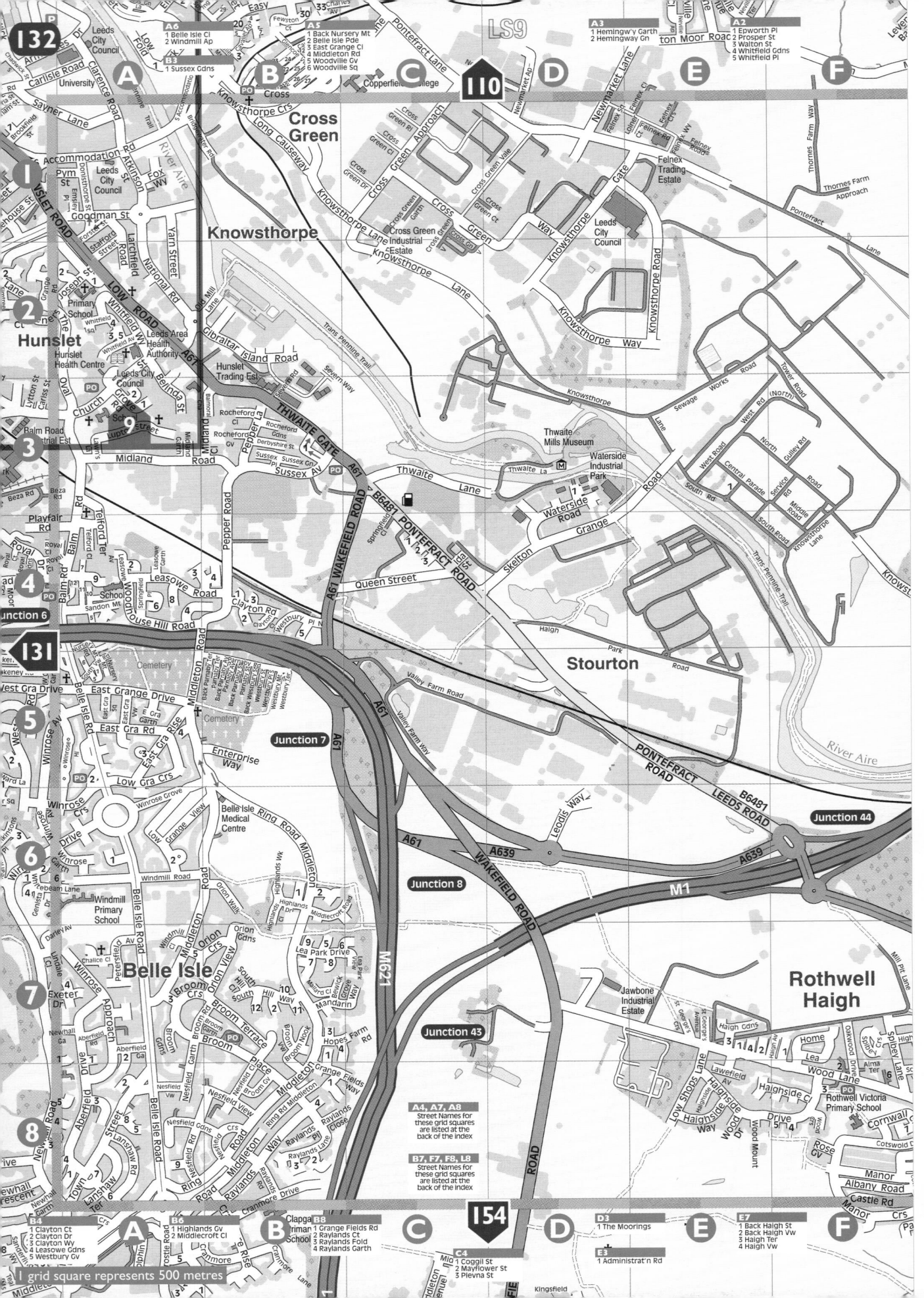

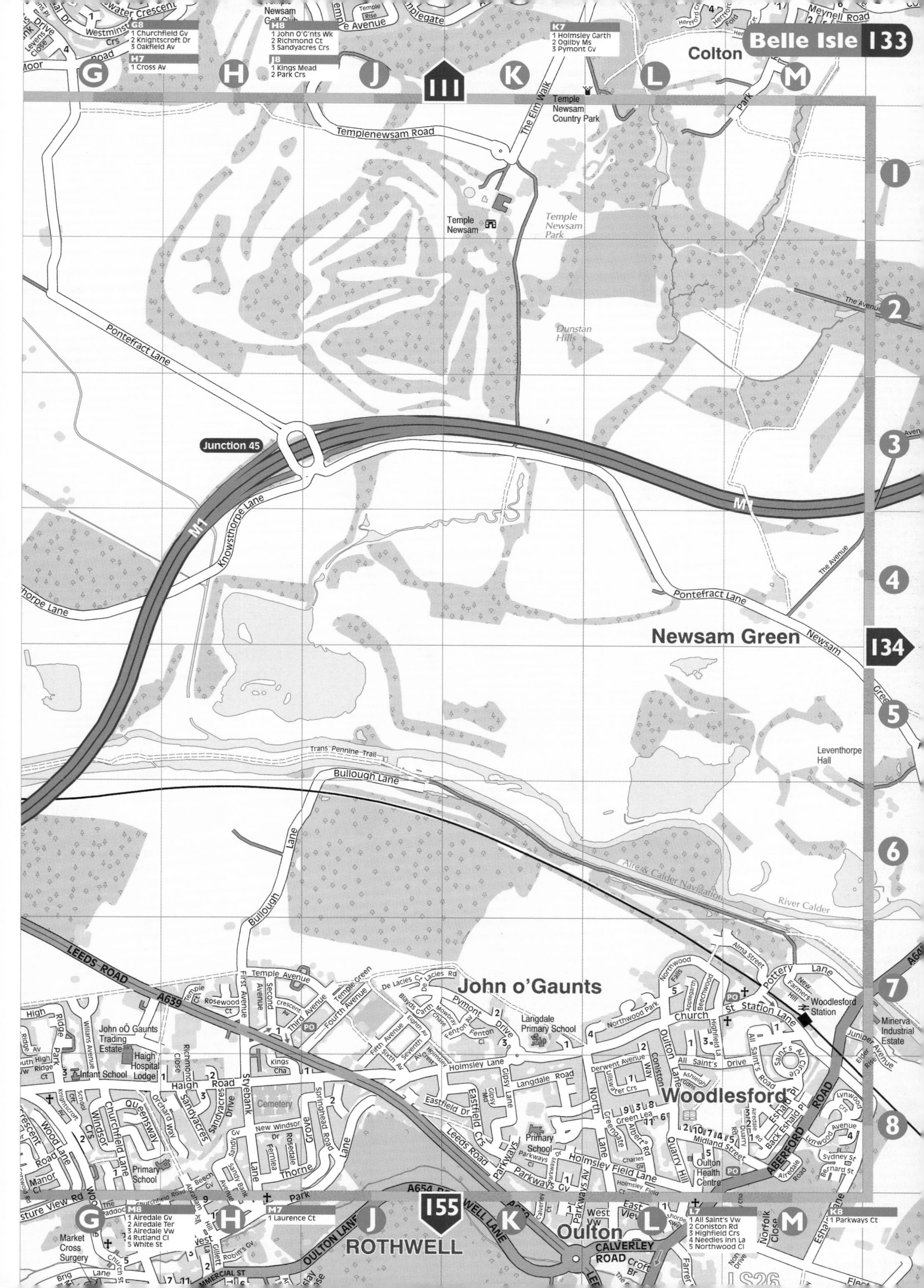
G8
1 Churchfield Gv
2 Knightscroft Dr
3 Oakfield Av
H7
1 Cross Av
H8
1 John O'G'nts Wk
2 Richmond Ct
3 Sandyacres Crs
J8
1 Kings Mead
2 Park Crs
K7
1 Holmsley Garth
2 Ogilby Ms
3 Pymont Gv
Colton
111
Temple Newsam Country Park
Templenewsam Road
The Elm Walk
Temple Newsam
Temple Newsam Park
Dunstan Hills
Pontefract Lane
Junction 45
M1
Knowsthorpe Lane
The Avenue
Newsam Green
134
Trans Pennine Trail
Bullough Lane
Leventhorpe Hall
Aire & Calder Navigation
River Calder
LEEDS ROAD
A639
John o'Gaunts
Langdale Primary School
Woodlesford Station
Minerva Industrial Estate
Woodlesford
Cemetery
Primary School
Oulton Health Centre
ABERFORD ROAD
155
M8
1 Airedale Gv
2 Airedale Ter
3 Airedale Vw
4 Rutland Cl
5 White St
M7
1 Laurence Ct
L7
1 All Saint's Vw
2 Coniston Rd
3 Highfield Crs
4 Needles Inn La
5 Northwood Cl
K8
1 Parkways Ct
ROTHWELL
Oulton
CALVERLEY ROAD
Market Cross Surgery

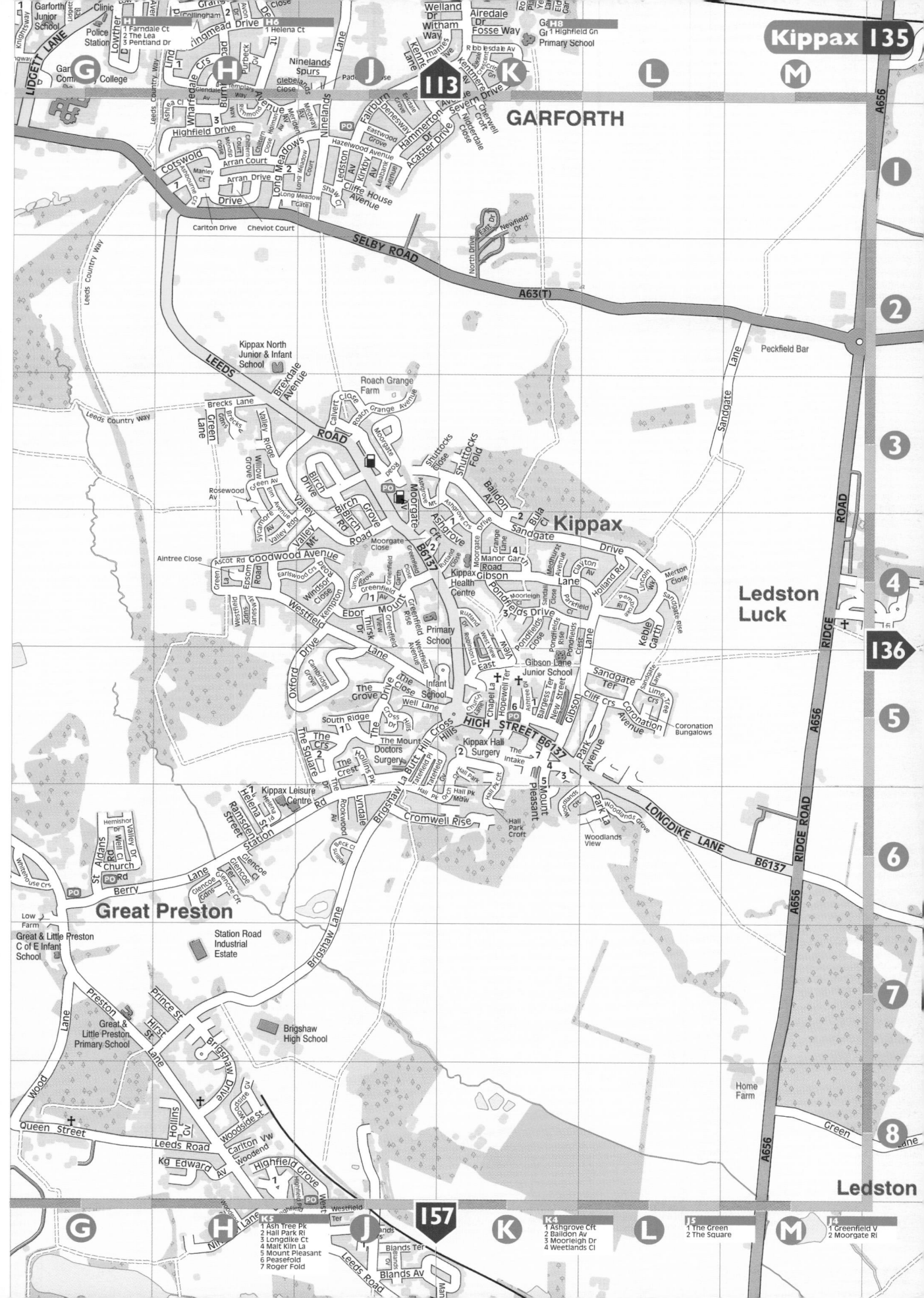

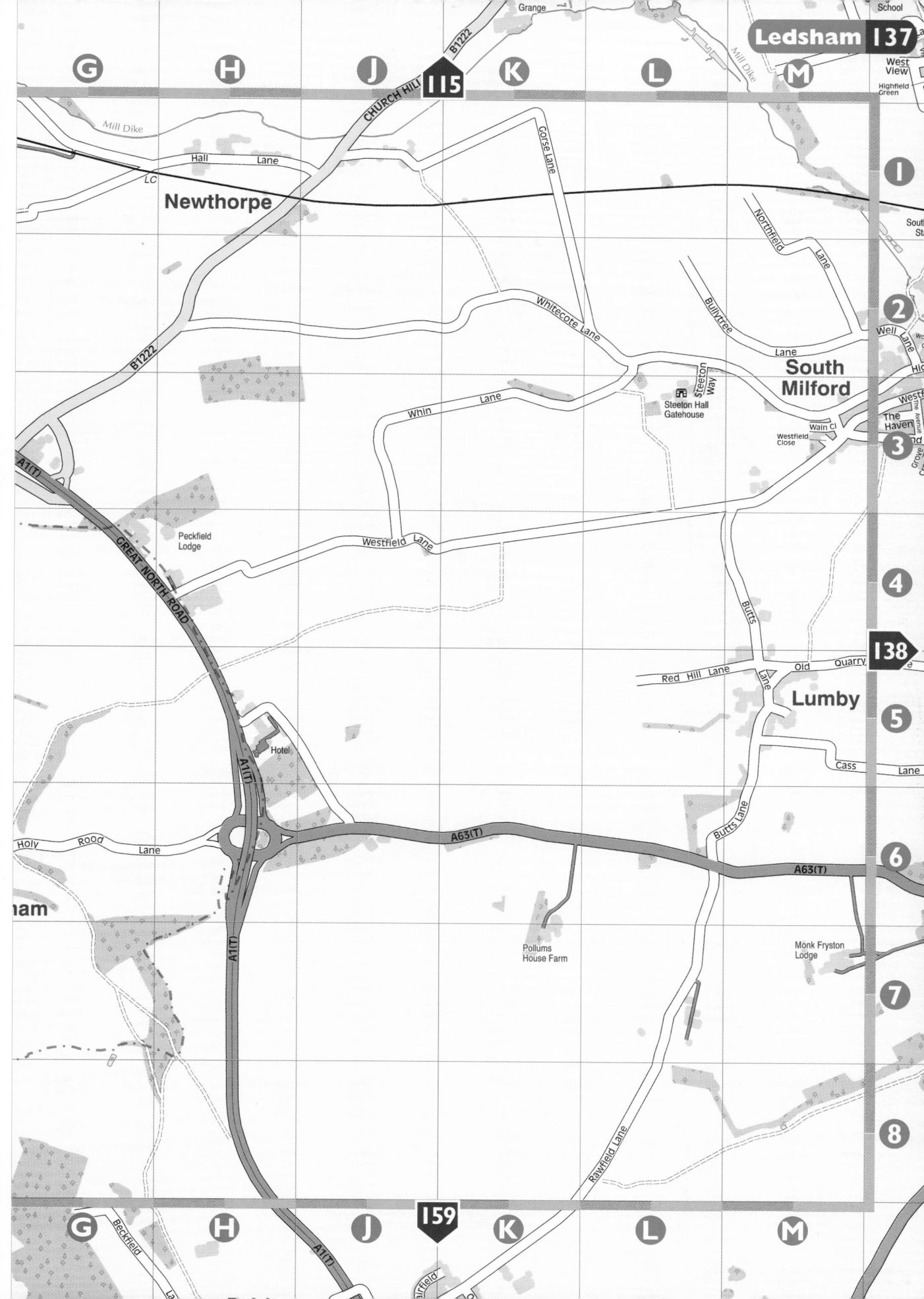

138

A B C 116 D E F

School
Everfield
Lane
Rose
Crs
Rose
Av
East
Vw
Athelstan
CP School

West
View
Highfield
Green

Milford
Road

Bond
Ings

D8
1 Hillam Hall Vw

B2
1 Beech Cl
2 Westfield Ct

Sherburn in
Elmet Aerodrome

1
I
South Milford
Station

2
South
Milford
Surgery
Bridge
Garth
Mill Lane
Mill Lane
A162

Lane

Well
Lane
Woodlands
Close
PO
Street
Common Lane
Cawdel
Ct
Cawdel
Way
Burley
Close
Common Lane
Milford
Lodge

ford
3
High
Westfield Lane
The Nook
School Lane
Orchard
The Avenue
Church
View
Maple
Close
Steincroft
Road
Beech Dr
The Row
Southlands
Close
Lund Sike Lane
Turpin Lane

Sand
Grove
Crescent
Church
Lane
The
Meadow
Lund Sike Lane
Wain Cl
The
Haven
Legion
Street

Turpin
Lane

A162

4

137
Lumby
Lane
Lane
Ingthorns
Lane
Lane
Lumby Lane
Ingthorns Lane
Ingthorns

5
A162
Lumby Lane
Long Heads Lane
Ingthorpe
Way
Ingthorpe
Lane
Cass
Lane
Ingthorns
Fryston Common Lane

6
A63(T)
MAIN STREET A63(T)
Lumby
Lane
Deer
Park Ct
A63(T)
Fryston Common Lane
Priory Park
Grove
A63(T)

A162
Church Lane
IL
Hotel
The
Meadows

Monk Fryston
lge
Old
Vicarage
Lane
Old
Vicarage
Lane
Water
Lane
PO
Orchard
Cl
Cemetery
Primary School

7
Betteras   Hill   Road
LC
Monk
Fryston
Lumby Hill
Close
Mill
Close
Hillcrest
Dunce   Mire   Road
Austfield
Lane

8
A162
Pine Tree
Lane
Rose Lea
Close
Lilac
Oval
Hillside
Cl
Bedfords
Fold
Hillam Hall
Lane
Chapel Street
Hillam
Hillam Common Lane
Hillam Hall
Close
Stocking
Lane
Woodlands Lane

A B C 160 D E F

1 grid square represents 500 metres

G　H　J　117　K　L　M

I

Low Rest
Park Farm

Lennerton
Farm

Milford Hagg
Farm

Habbolme Dike

Gascoigne Wood Mine

Hagg　Lane

Common Lane

Philip　Lane

LC

Painter Lane

Owlet
Hall

Common Lane

Church Close

Common Lane

Kingstop Dr

Orchard

Kinderton
Ct

Back
Lane

Fryston
Grange

Toll Bar Close

The
Willows

Drive

One Acre Garth

Hotel

Siddle
House

Garth
Road

Appletree Drive

Garth Lane

Chapel

Hamb
C of E
Prima

Common Lane

Bar Lane

Dunnington
Dr

Anson
Gr

Ct

Garth
View

Garth
Drive

Cherwell
Ct

Cherwell
Croft

A63(T)

Westcroft　Lane

Hambleton

Mill L

Old　Lane

Fox Lane

Stocking Lane

Lowfield　Road

Fox Lane

Hagg House

Brecks
Farm

Hillam Road

Pighill Nook Road

Bower's House
Farm

Maspin Moor Road

Gateforth
Wood

G　H　J　161　K　L　M

I
2
3
4
5
6
7
8

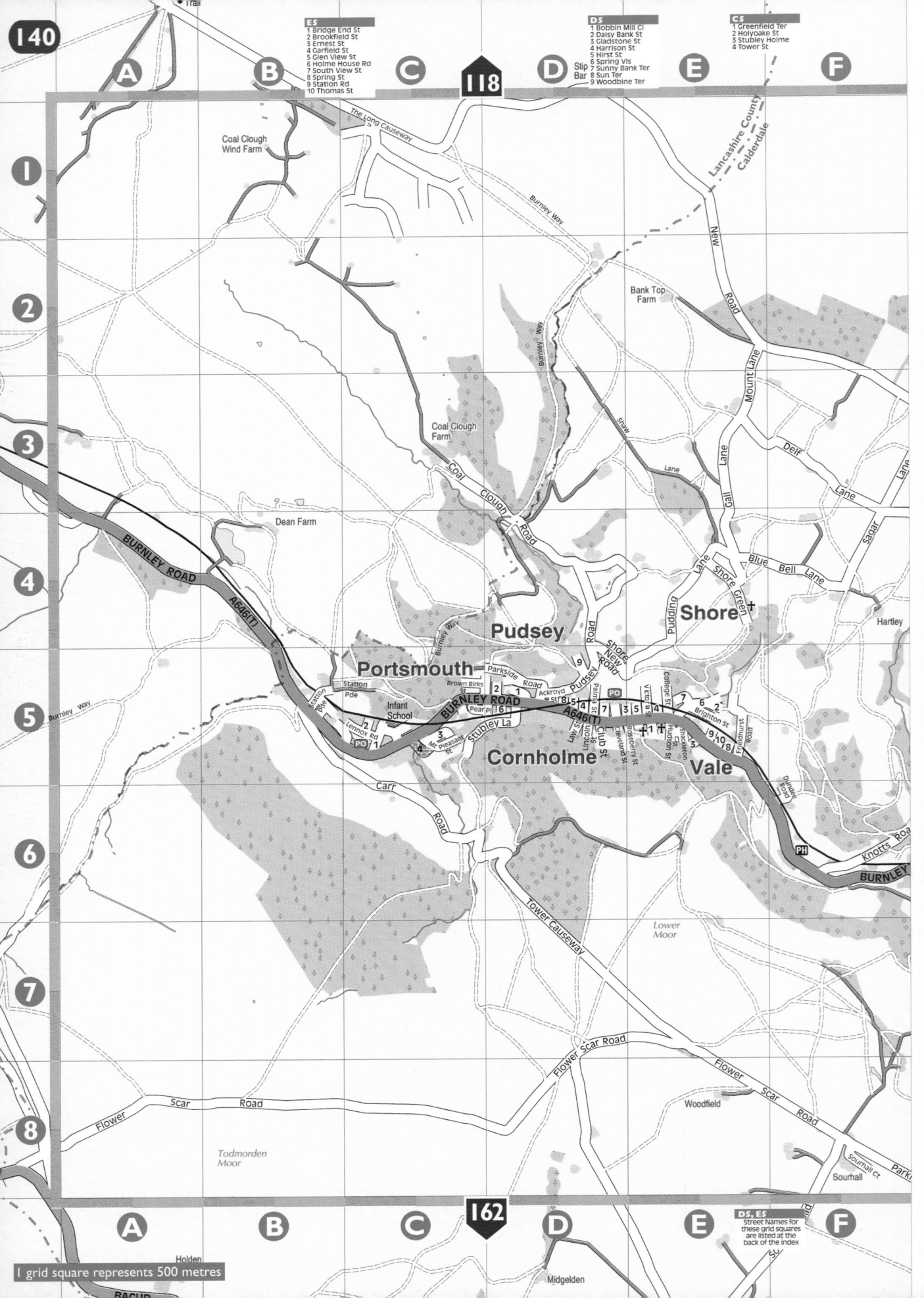

140

Ⓐ   Ⓑ   Ⓒ   Ⓓ   Ⓔ   Ⓕ

E5
1 Bridge End St
2 Brookfield St
3 Ernest St
4 Garfield St
5 Glen View St
6 Holme House Rd
7 South View St
8 Spring St
9 Station Rd
10 Thomas St

D5
1 Bobbin Mill Cl
2 Daisy Bank St
3 Gladstone St
4 Harrison St
5 Hirst St
6 Spring Vls
7 Sunny Bank Ter
8 Sun Ter
9 Woodbine Ter

C5
1 Greenfield Ter
2 Holyoake St
3 Stubley Holme
4 Tower St

118

Coal Clough Wind Farm

The Long Causeway

Burnley Way

Lancashire County
Calderdale

New Road

Bank Top Farm

Mount Lane

Coal Clough Farm

Shaw

Gall Lane

Delf Lane

Sagar Lane

Lane

Dean Farm

BURNLEY ROAD

A646(T)

Coal Clough Road

Piping Lane

Shore Green

Shore

Blue Bell Lane

Hartley

Pudsey

Shore New Road

Portsmouth

Parkside Road

Ackroyd St

PO

Victoria St

Brighton St

Friardhurst Road

Station Pde

Brown Birks St

Burnley Way

Pudsey Road

College St

Knotts Road

Burnley Way

Station Pde

Infant School

Pear Pl

BURNLEY ROAD

A646(T)

Club St

Rosebery St

Shackleton St

Hudson St

Lennox Rd

PO

Mt Pleasant St

Stubley La

Law St

Cleveland St

Cornholme

Vale

Dundee Road

Carr Road

Tower Causeway

Lower Moor

PH

BURNLEY

Flower Scar Road

Woodfield

Flower Scar Road

Flower Scar Road

Todmorden Moor

Sourhall ct

Sourhall

Park

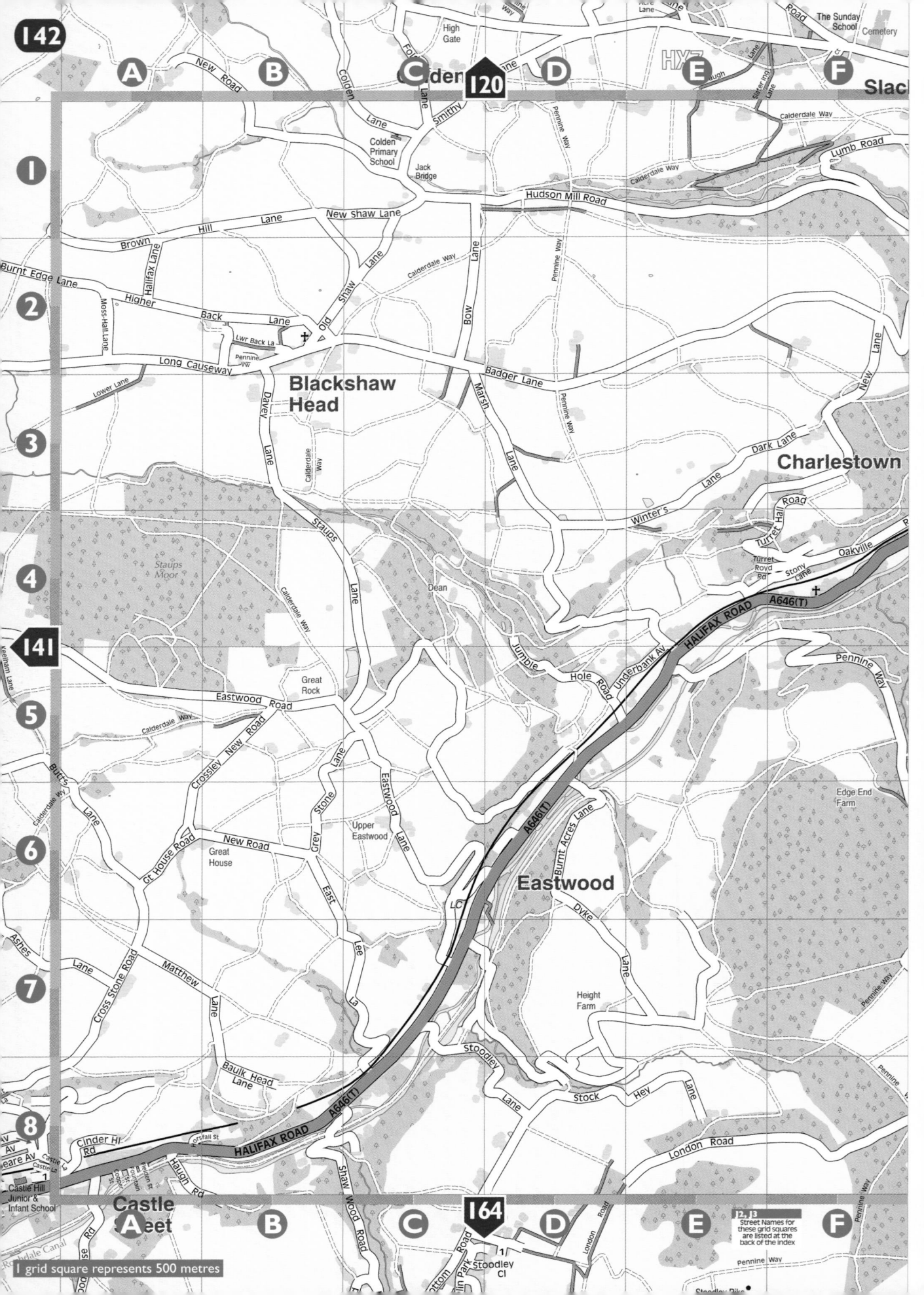

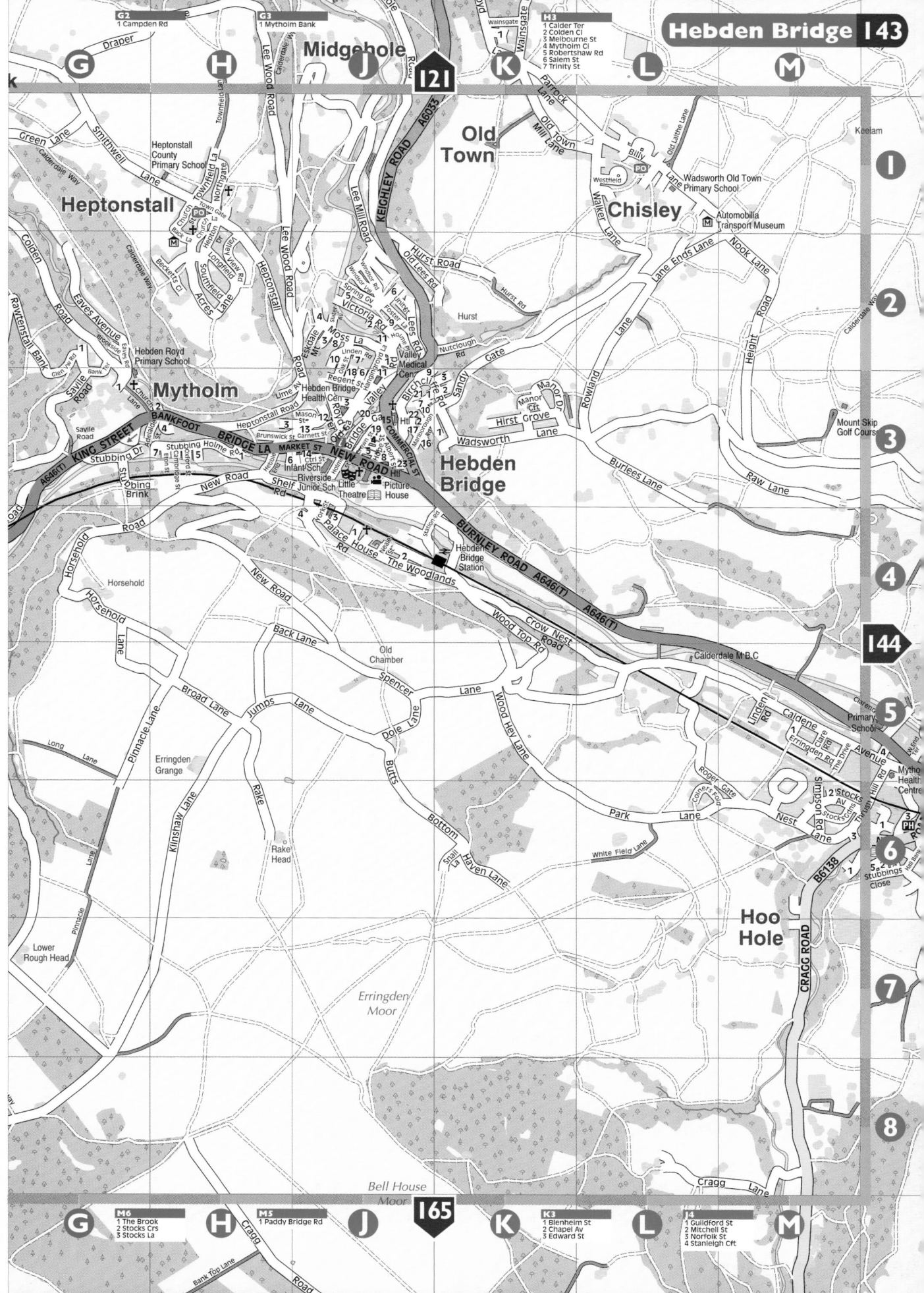

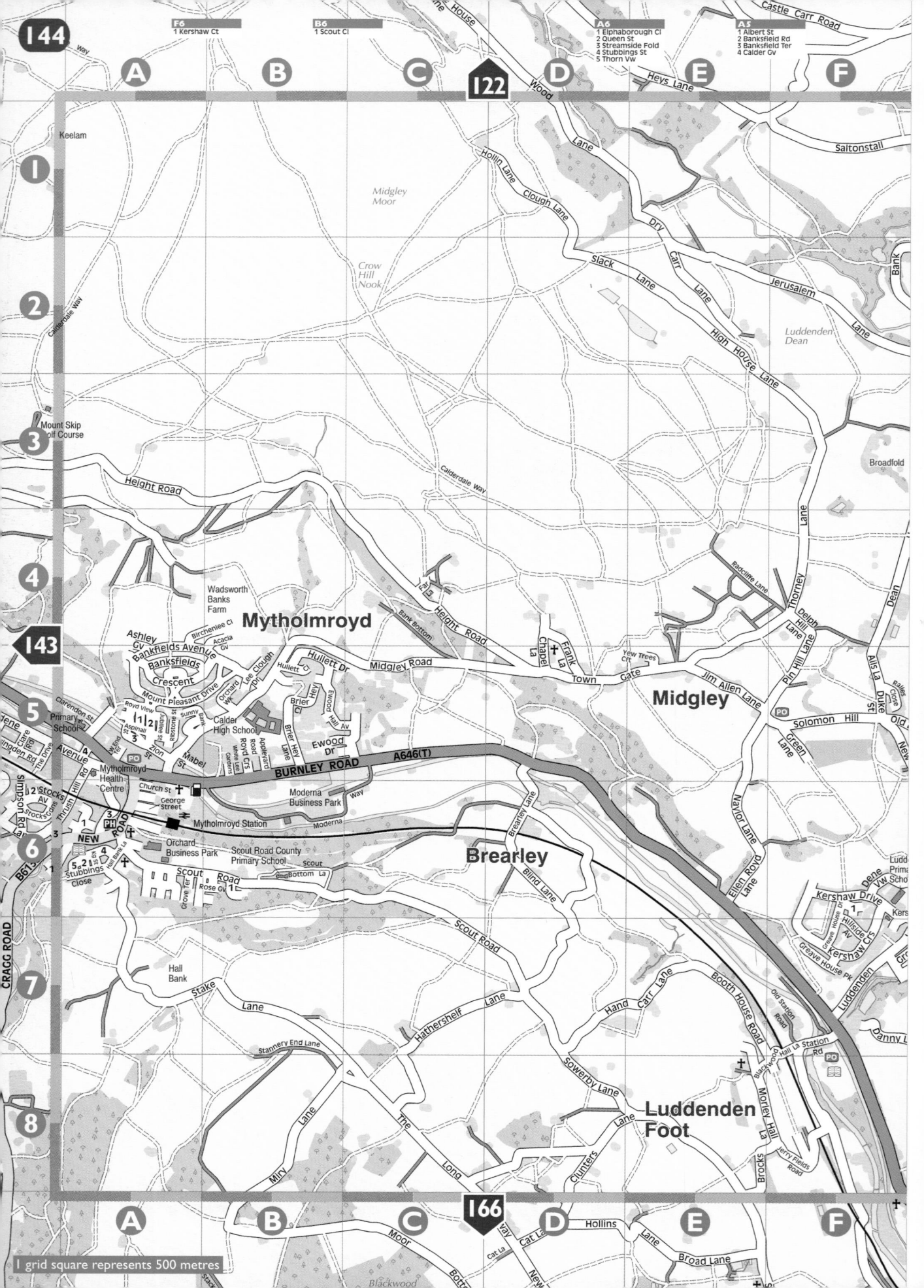

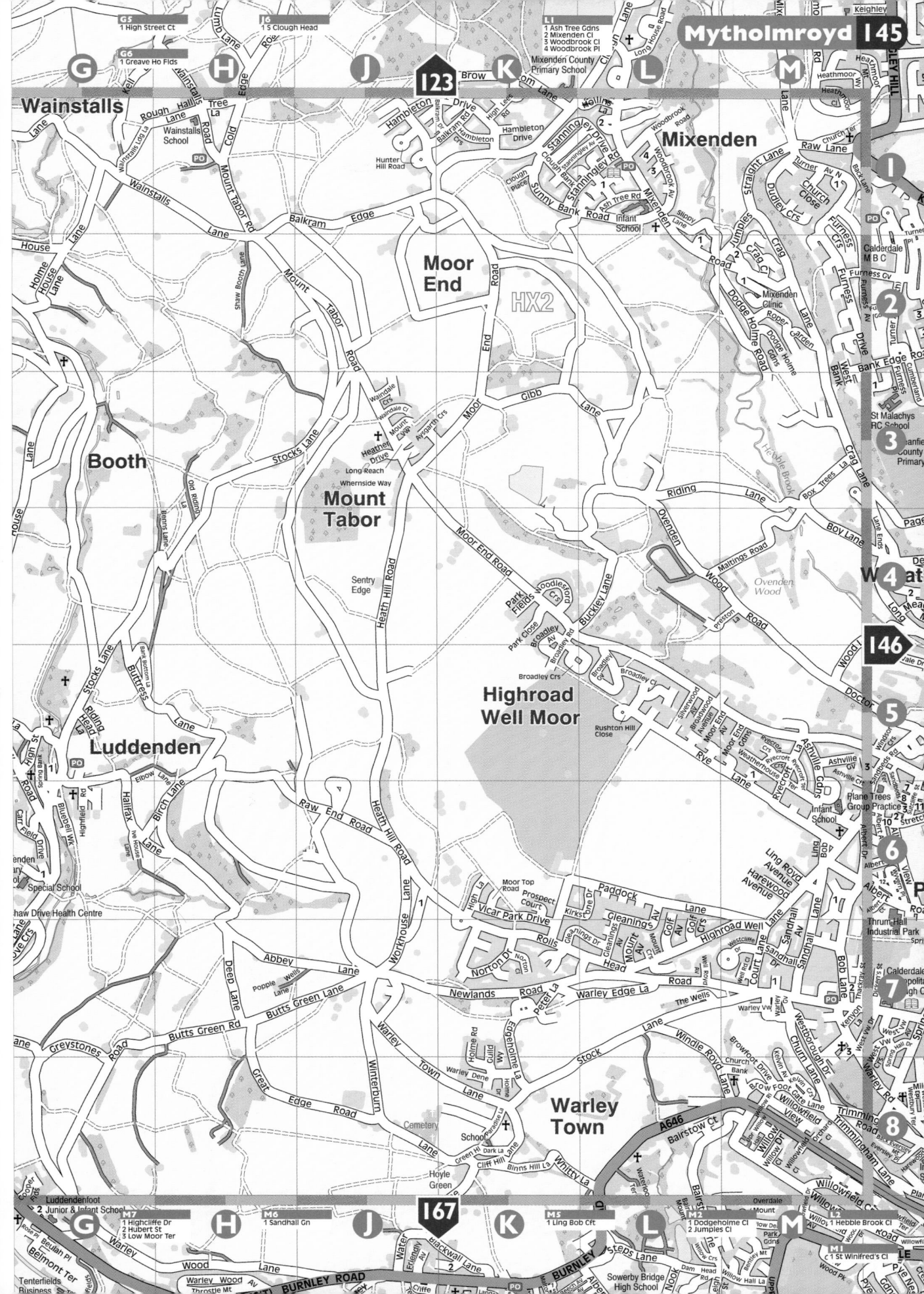

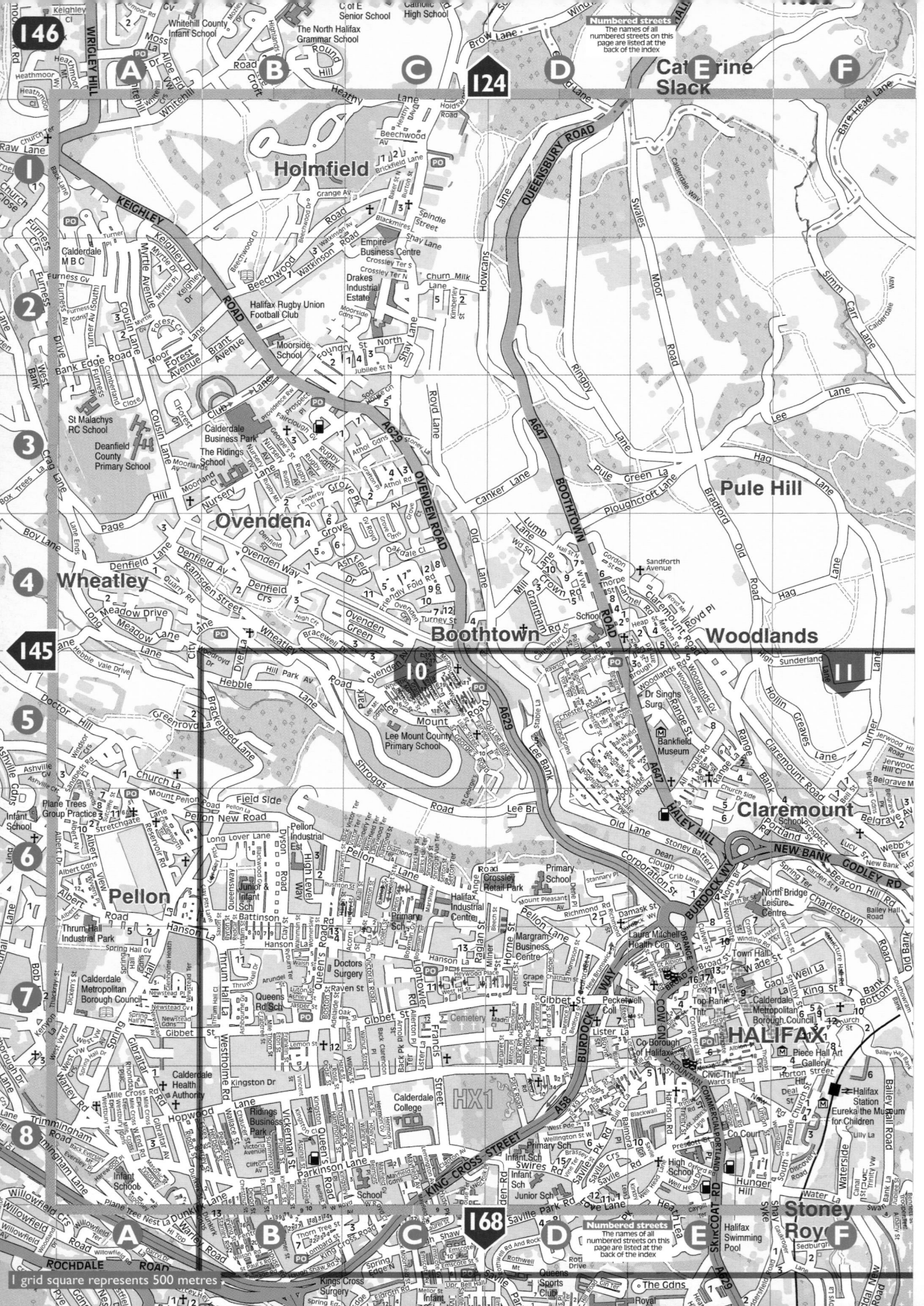

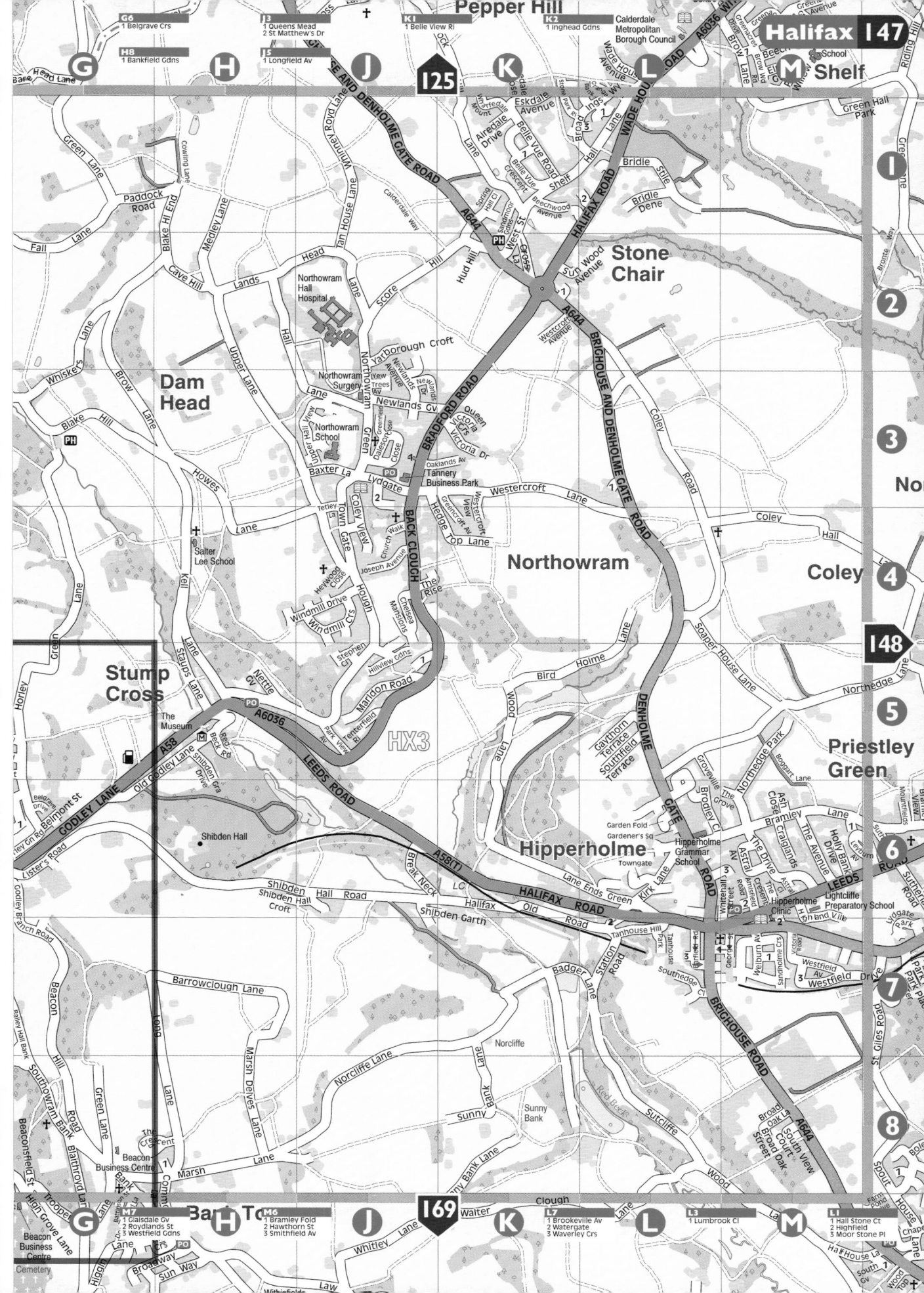

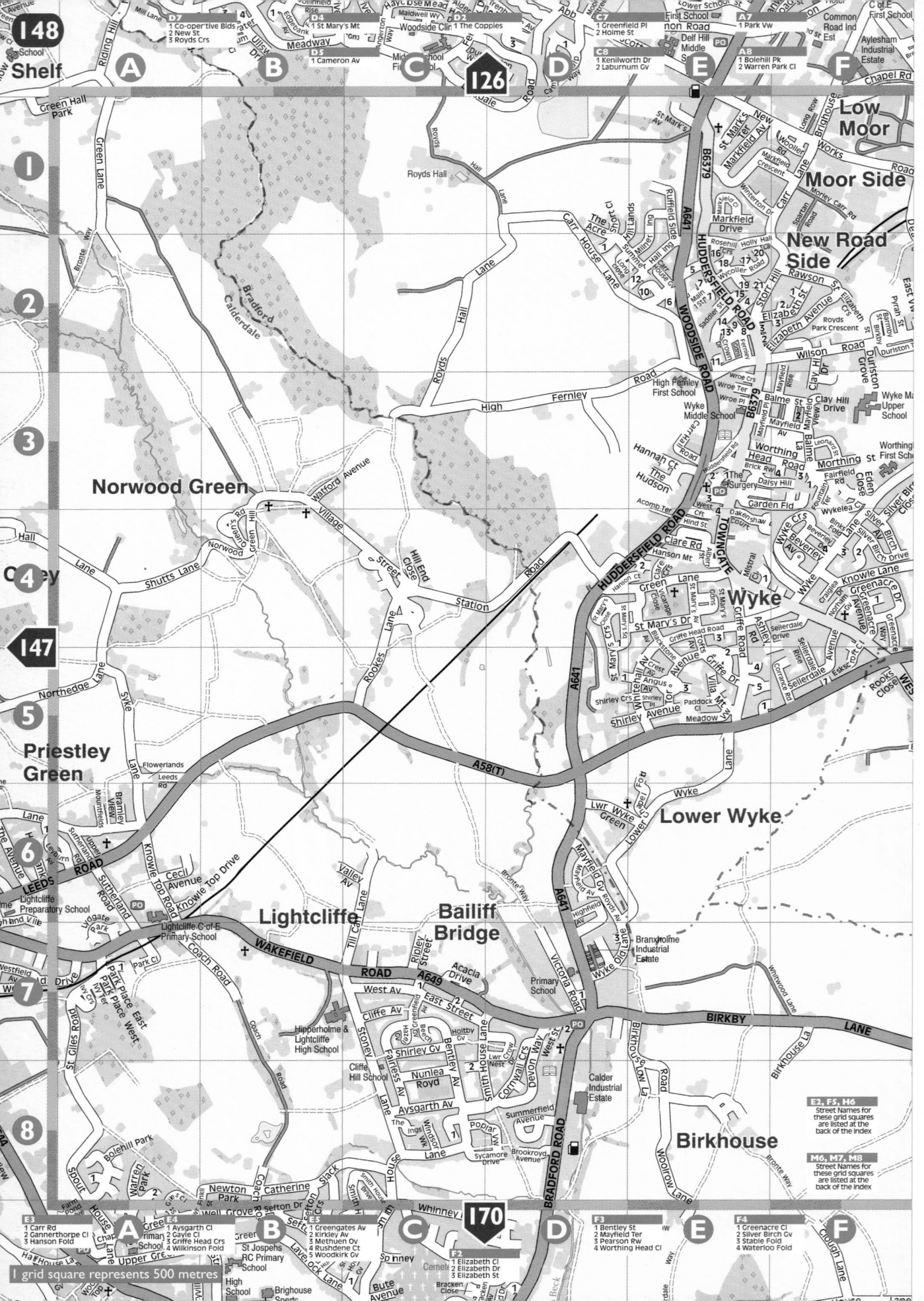

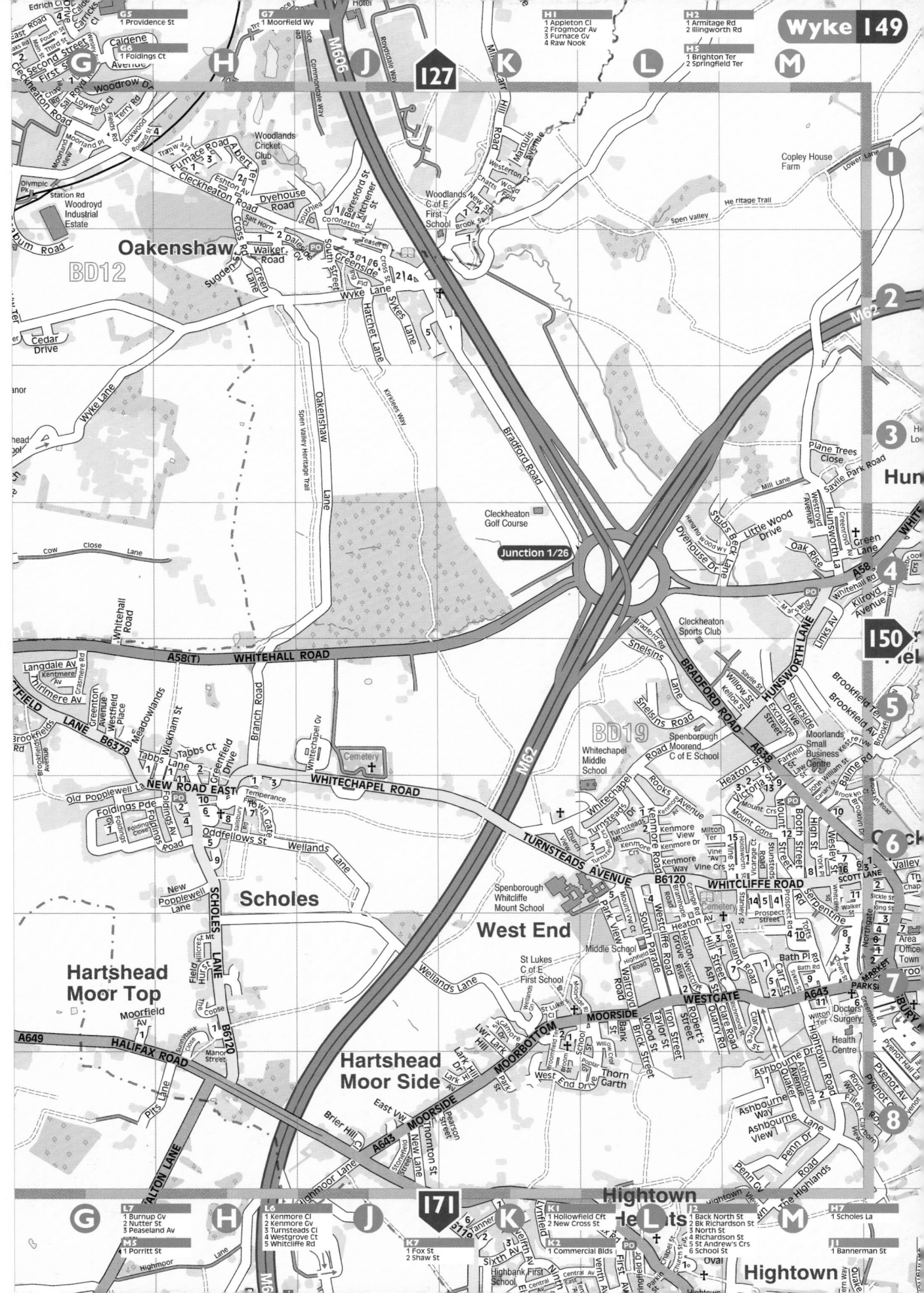

G5
1 Providence St

G6
1 Foldings Ct

G7
1 Moorfield Wy

H1
1 Appleton Cl
2 Frogmoor Av
3 Furnace Gv
4 Raw Nook

H2
1 Armitage Rd
2 Illingworth Rd

H5
1 Brighton Ter
2 Springfield Ter

127

150

171

Oakenshaw

BD12

Woodlands Cricket Club

Woodroyd Industrial Estate

Woodlands C. of E. First School

Cleckheaton Golf Course

Junction 1/26

Copley House Farm

Plane Trees Close

Cleckheaton Sports Club

BD19

Whitechapel Middle School

Spenborough Road Moorend C of E School

Whitechapel First School

A58(T) WHITEHALL ROAD

NEW ROAD EAST

WHITECHAPEL ROAD

Cemetery

Scholes

Hartshead Moor Top

TURNSTEADS AVENUE

Spenborough Whitcliffe Mount School

West End

St Lukes C.of E First School

WHITCLIFFE ROAD

WESTGATE

MOORSIDE

MOORBOTTOM

Hartshead Moor Side

HALIFAX ROAD

A649

A643

Doctors Surgery

Health Centre

Area Office Town Hall

Highbank First School

Hightown Heights

Hightown

L7
1 Burnup Gv
2 Nutter St
3 Peaseland Av

M5
1 Porritt St

L6
1 Kenmore Cl
2 Kenmore Gv
3 Turnsfields Ct
4 Westgrove Ct
5 Whitcliffe Rd

K1
1 Hollowfield Cft
2 New Cross St

K2
1 Commercial Blds

K5
1 Fox St
2 Shaw St

J2
1 Back North St
2 Bk Richardson St
3 North St
4 Richardson St
5 St Andrew's Crs
6 School St

H7
1 Scholes La

M1
1 Bannerman St

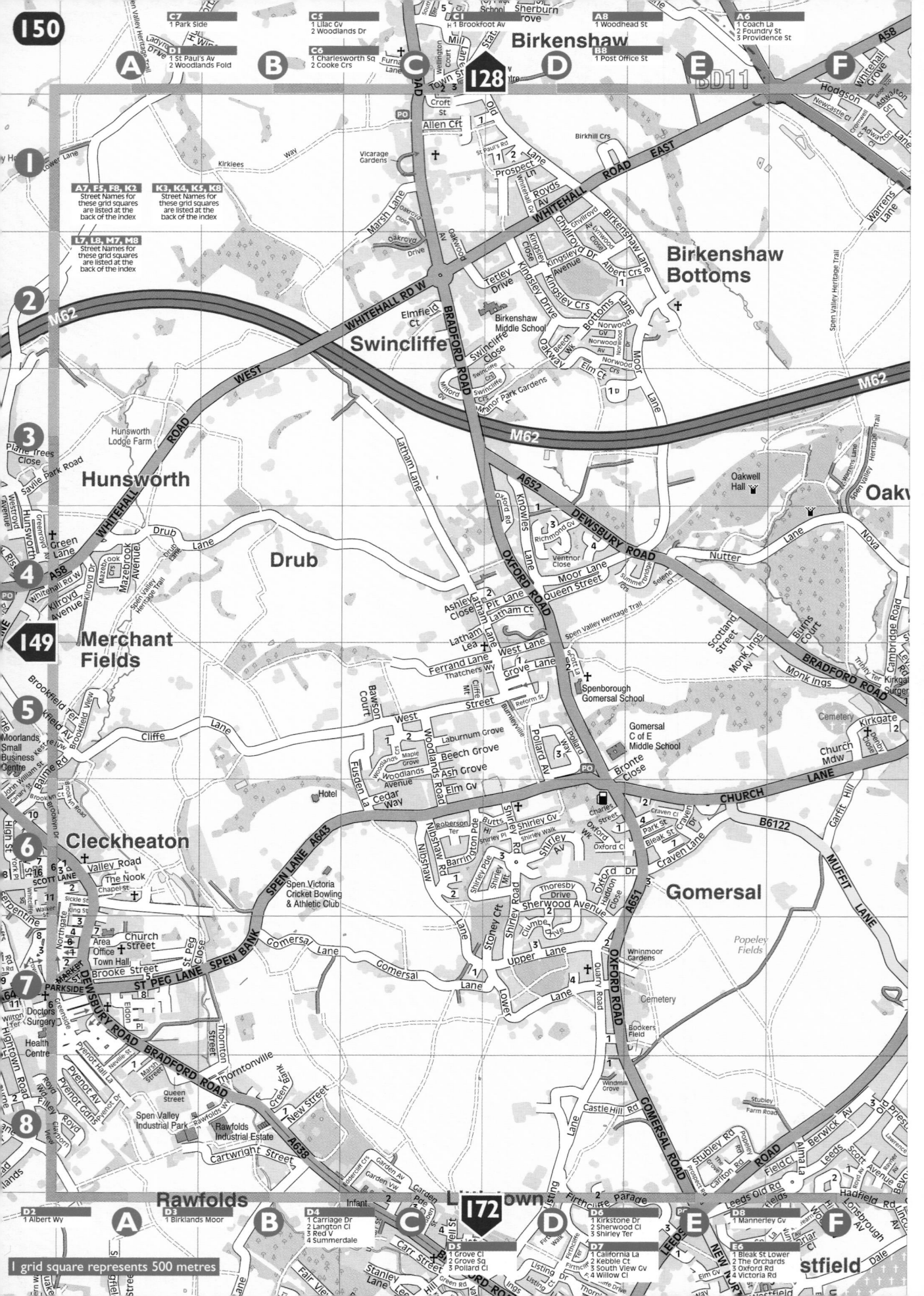

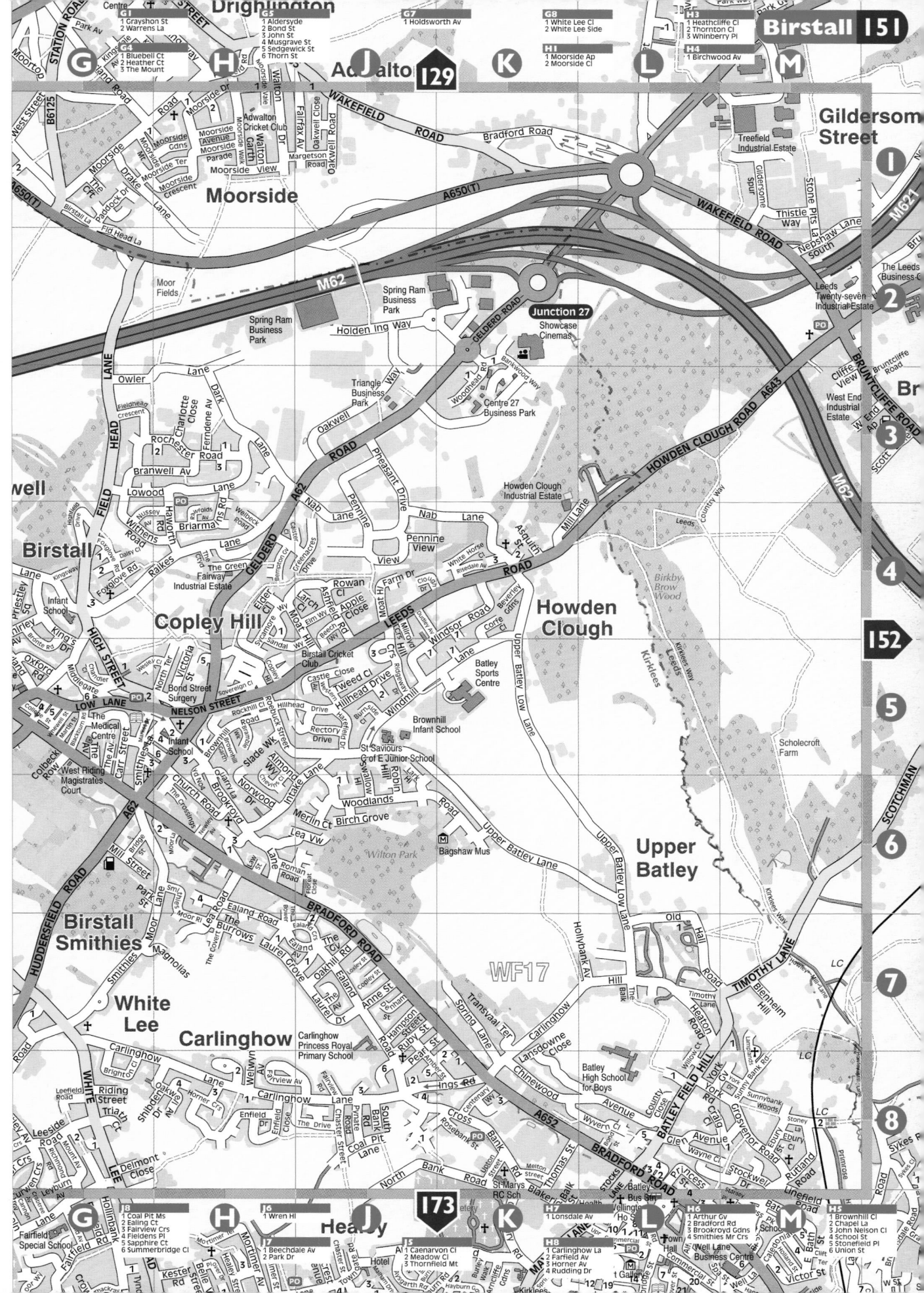

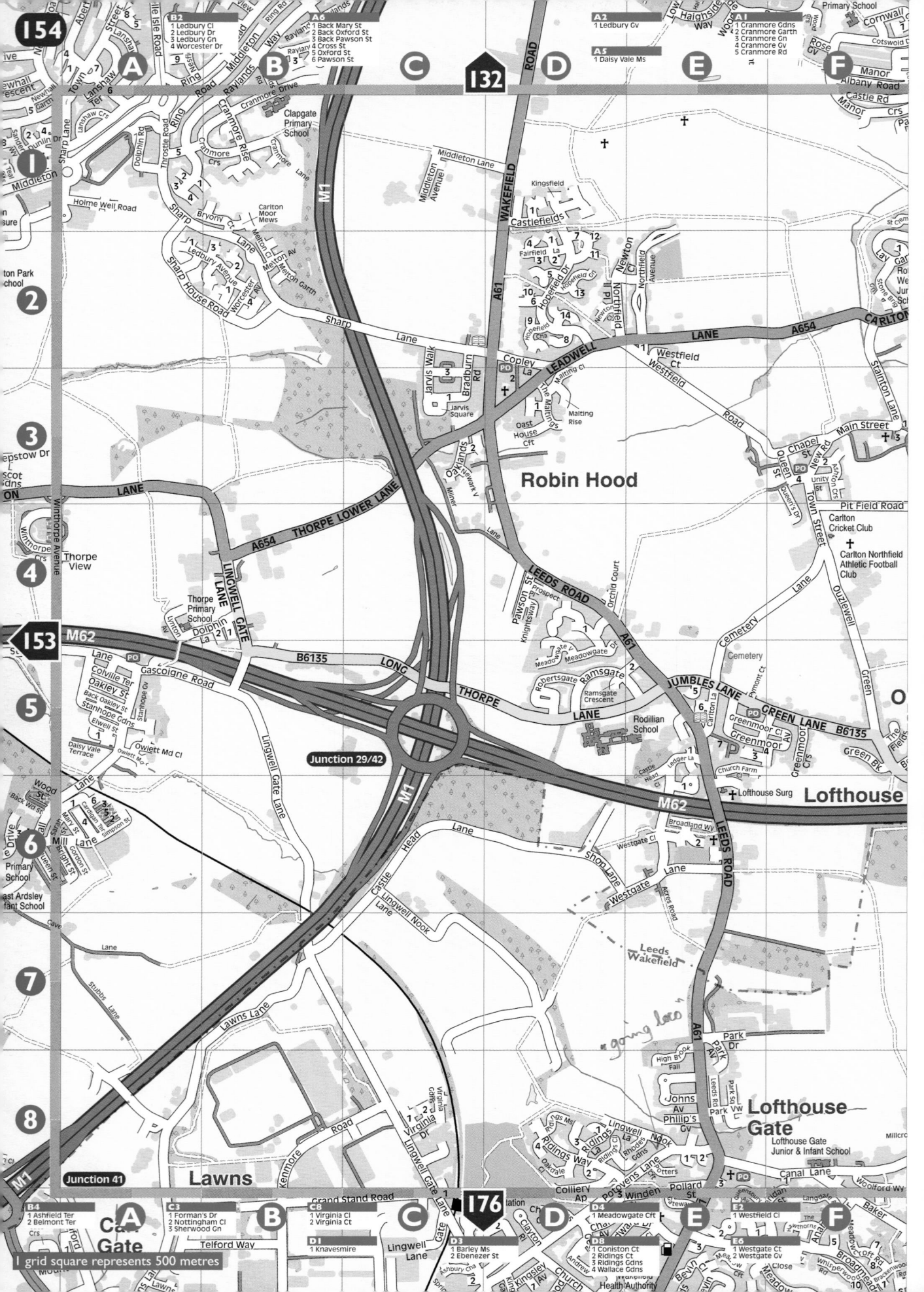

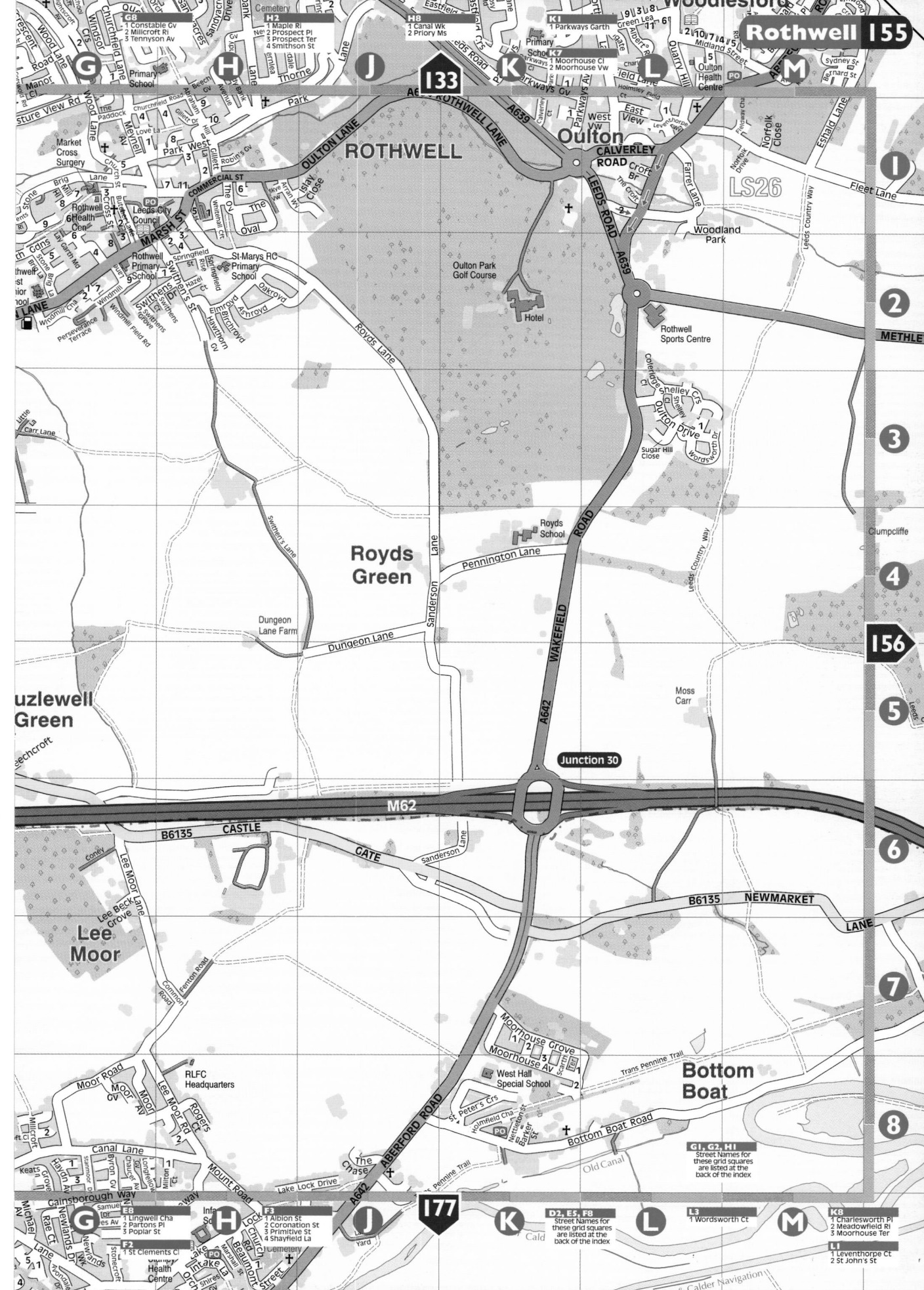

134

A   B   C   D   E   F

F6
1 Burnleys Ms

F3
1 Garden House Cl
2 St Margaret's Av
3 St Margaret's Rd
4 Woodhall Gv

E5
1 Pinders Green Ct
2 Pinders Gn Fold

E4
1 Churchside Vls
2 The Orchards

1

Leeds Country Way

Fleet Lane

Fleet Lane

Fleet Lane

2

METHLEY LANE

A639

Trans Pennine Trail

3

Methley Park Hospital

Woodrow Crs

Station Rd

Wood Row

LEEDS ROAD

The Hollings

Mickletown Rd

Mill La

Pit Lane

PO

Hicks Lane

Street

2

Main Road

3

1

Savile

4

Oaksfield

Summer Hill

Clumpcliffe

Mulberry Gdns

Church Lane

1

2

Methley C of E Infant School

Methley

155

Little Church La

Rothwell Methley CP Infant School

+

+

4

CHURCH SIDE

5

Leeds Country Way

Park Lane

WATERGATE

BARNSDALE ROAD A639

Embleton Rd

Hazell

Pinders Gn

1

2

1

2

Green Row

Burnleys VW

Burnleys Dr

Burnleys Court

Hungate

Hungate Lane

B6135

6

M62

Scholey Hill

Methley Junction

7

Methley Lanes

Trans Pennine Trail

Leeds Wakefield

8

Kings Road

Lock

Lower Altofts

Express Way

Altofts Lane

LANE

ET

178

Pope Street

California Drive

A   B   C   D   E   F

Fernley Hill Dr

Rose Farm

1

Pearson St

Yard St

PO

Kings Av

Altofts

Poplar

Express Way

Gilcar Way

1 grid square represents 500 metres

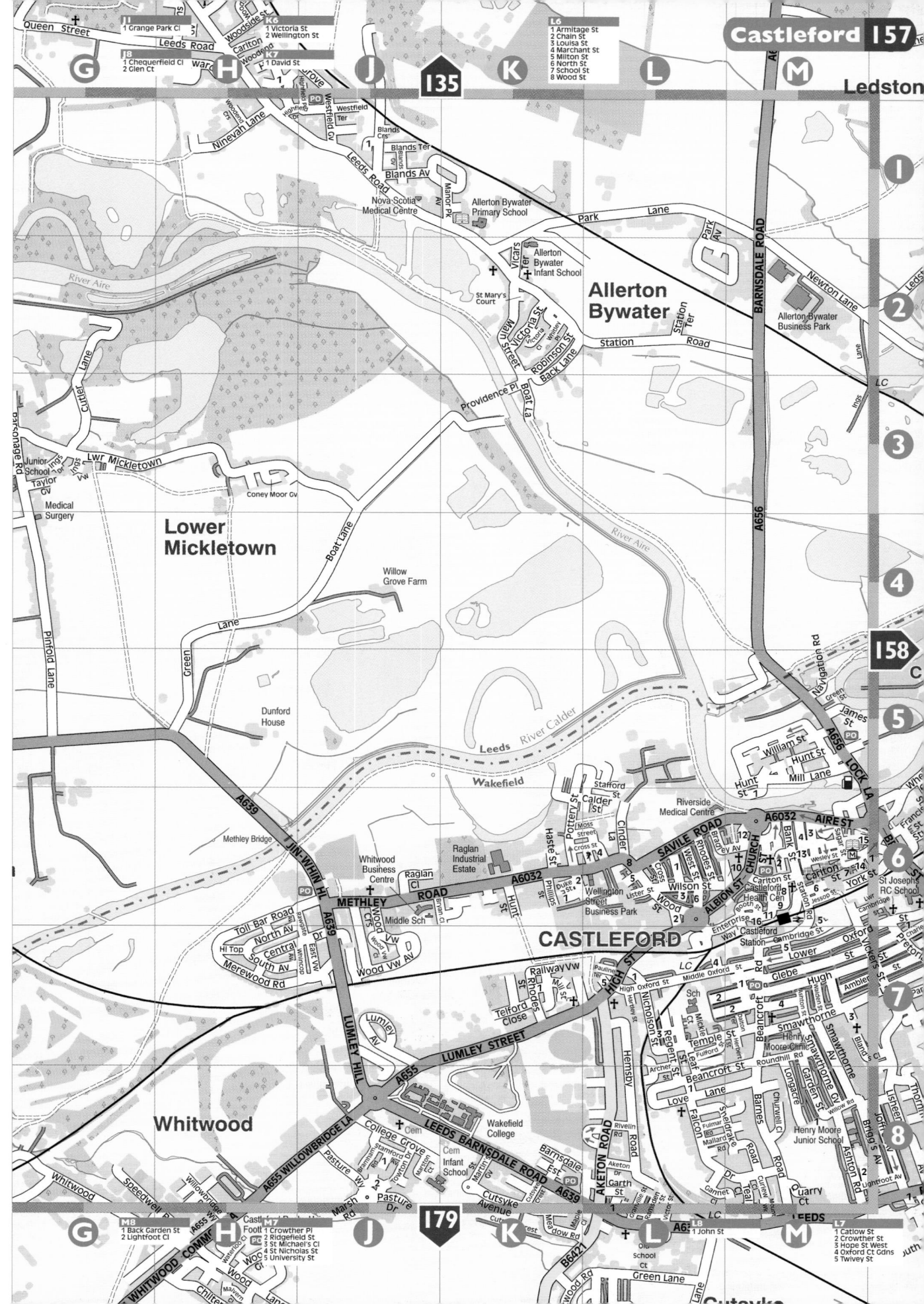

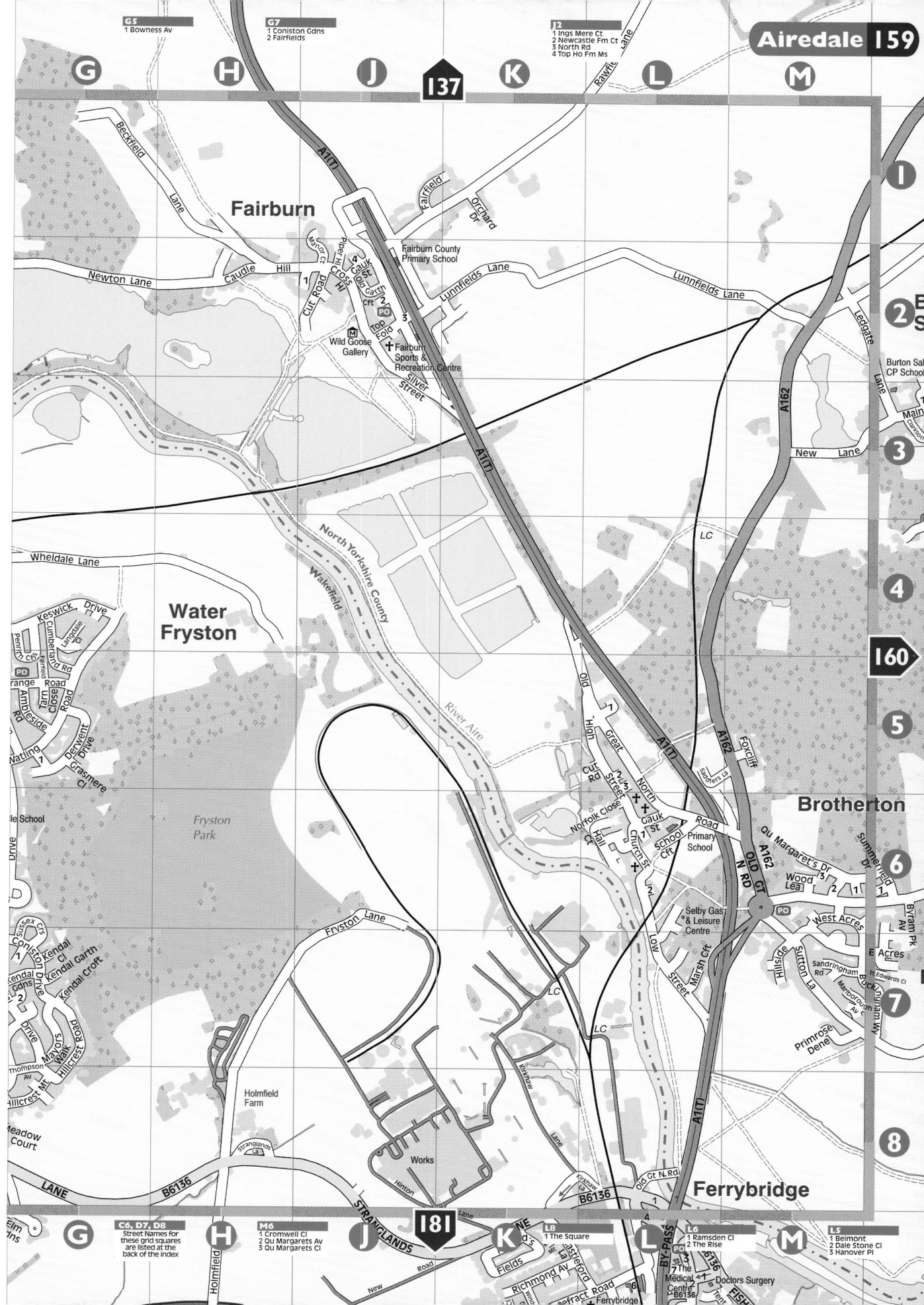

G   H   J   **137**   K   L   M

1

Fairburn

2   B S

3

Newton Lane

Fairburn County
Primary School

Caudle   Hill

Beckfield Lane

Manor Ct
Piper Hl Cross Hl
Cut Rope
Gauk St
Old Garth
Cft

Orchard Dr

Fairfield

Lunnfields Lane

Lunnfields Lane

Leggate Lane

A162

New Lane

Burton Salr
CP School

Main   Claxton

Wild Goose
Gallery

Top Fold
PO

Fairburn
Sports &
Recreation Centre

Silver Street

A1(T)

LC

4

Wheldale Lane

North Yorkshire County

Water
Fryston

Wakefield

River Aire

Old High

Great Street

A1(T)

A162

Foxcliff

160

5

Keswick Drive
Cumberland Rd
Penrith Cfs
Lapgate
Orange Road
Ambleside Rd
Watling
Grasmere Cl
Derwent Drive

PO

Fryston
Park

Cut Rd
North Street
Norfolk Close
Hall Ct
Church St
Gauk St
School Cft

Primary
School

Road

Old Ct
N RD

Qu Margaret's Dr
Wood Lea

Brotherton

Summerfield Dr

6

Selby Gas
& Leisure
Centre

A162

Low Street

Marsh Cft

PO

West Acres

Hillside
Sutton La
Sandringham Rd

Byram Pk Av
E Acres
St Edwards Cl

7

Fryston Lane

Kirkhaw Lane

LC

LC

Primrose Dene

Marlborough Av
Buckingham Wy

Sussex Crs
Coniston Drive
Kendal Cl
Kendal Drive
Kendal Garth
Kendal Croft
Kendal Gdns

Drive

Mayors Walk
Hillcrest Mt
Hillcrest Road

Thompson Av
Hillcrest Road

Holmfield
Farm

Stranglands La

8

Meadow
Court

B6136

LANE

Stranglands

181

Works

Hinton

Kirkhaw Lane

Old Gt N Rd

B6136

Ferrybridge

Kirkhaw

G   Holmfield   H   Richmond Av   J   NE   K   Fields   L   BY-PASS   M   The Medical Centre   Doctors Surgery

Ferrybridge

A   B   C   **138**   D   E   F

Pine Tree
Lane
Rose Lea
Close

Chapel Street

A6
1 Summerfield Cl

Hillam Hall Lane

A3
1 Beech Gv

Hillam Hall
Close

I

Hillam Lane

Hillam Lane

Woodlands   Lane

Fairfield Lane

Stocking Lane

2

**Burton
Salmon**

Ledgate Lane

Burton   Common   Lane

Burton Common
Farm

Burton Salmon
CP School   The Paddock

Main St

Clareton Dry Stone Cl

Poole   Lane

3

4

◀ **159**

5

Byram
Hall

Byram Farm

Brotherton

Summerfield Dr

6

Byram Park Road

Byram Park Road

Sutton   Lane

Birkin Lane

West Acres

Byram Pk Av

E Acres

Tiphaby Lane

Smeathalls
Farm

Sandringham
Rd

St Edwards Cl

Buckingham Av

Marlborough Av

Byram

Sutton   Lane

Sutton

7

Primrose
Dene

Marsh   La

8

River Aire

A   B   C   **182**   D   E   F

West Ings Crescent

West Ings
Mews

West Ings
Way

West Ings
Lane

Croftlands   Aire St

River Aire

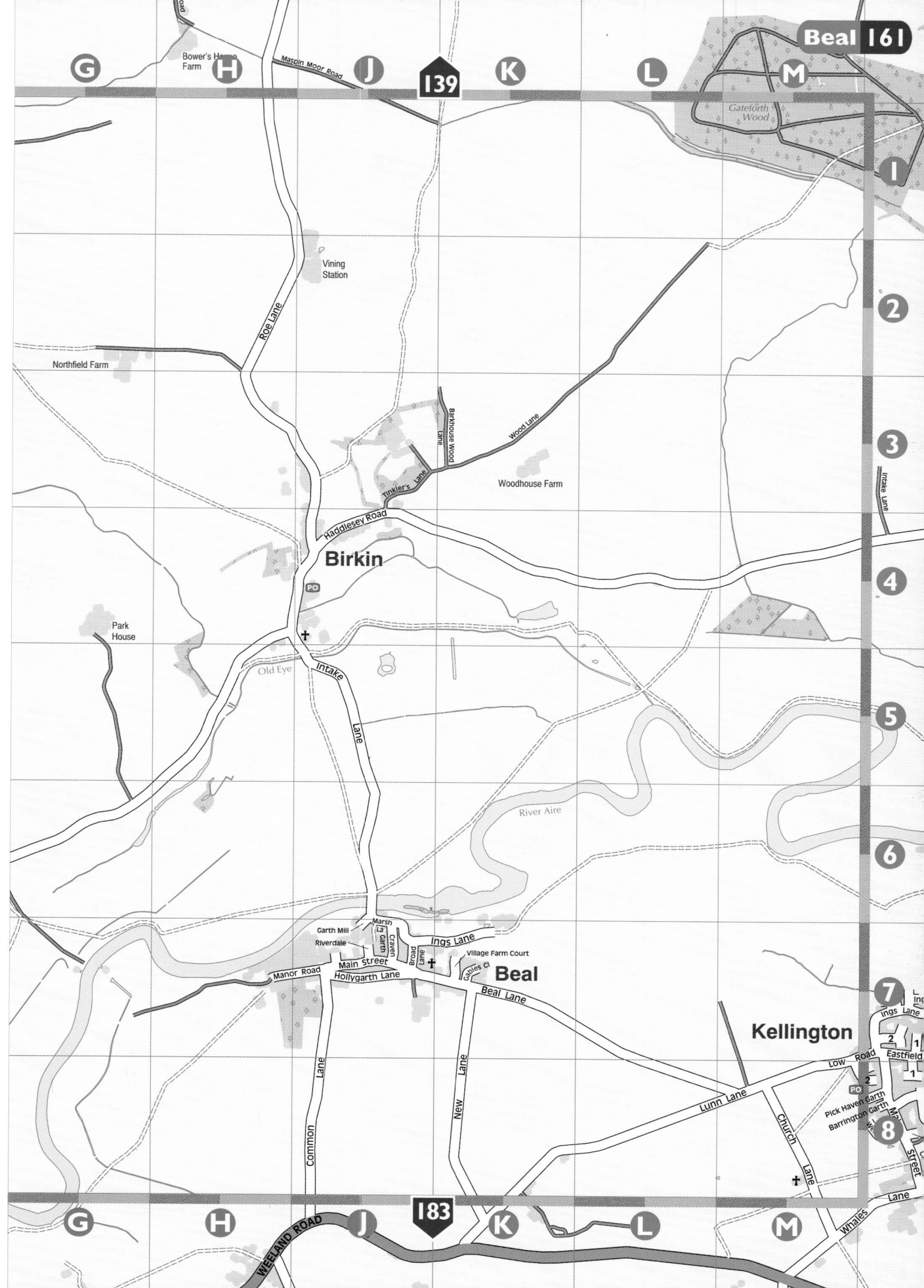

G H J **139** K L M

I

2

3

4

5

6

7

8

Bower's Home Farm

Maspin Moor Road

Gateforth Wood

Vining Station

Roe Lane

Northfield Farm

Barkhouse Wood Lane

Wood Lane

Tinkler's Lane

Woodhouse Farm

Intake Lane

Haddlesey Road

Birkin

PO

Park House

Old Eye

Intake Lane

River Aire

Garth Mill

Riverdale

Marsh La Garth

Craven Lane

Broad Lane

Ings Lane

Village Farm Court

Main Street

Hollygarth Lane

Manor Road

Cables Ct

Beal

Beal Lane

Kellington

Common Lane

New Lane

Ings Lane

Eastfield

Low Road

PO

Pick Haven Garth

Barrington Garth

Lunn Lane

Church Lane

Whales Lane

G H **183** J K L M

WEELAND ROAD

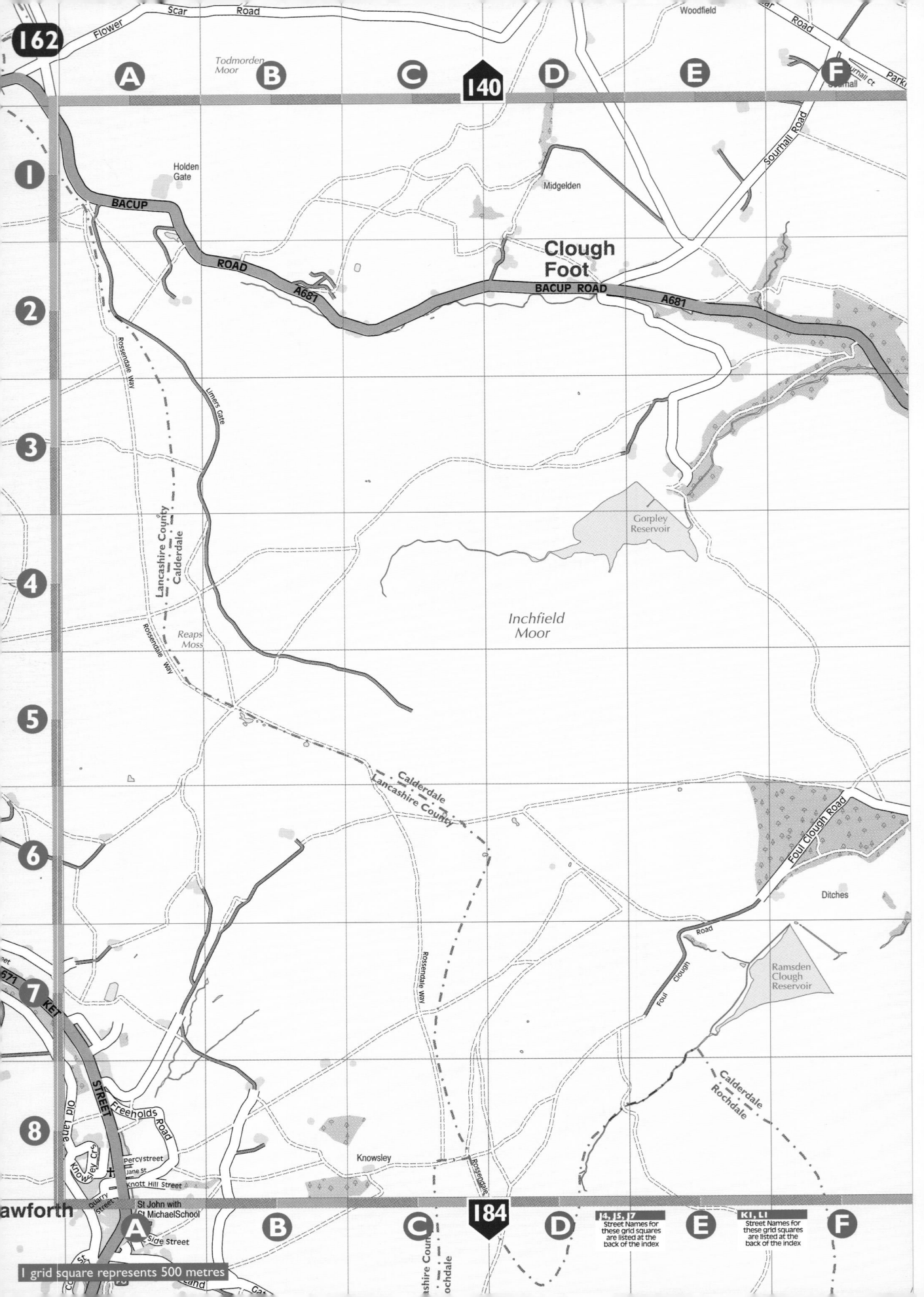

A   B   C   140   D   E   F
Sournall Parki

Woodfield

Scar   Road
Flower
Todmorden
Moor

Holden
Gate
1

BACUP   Midgelden

ROAD   Clough
Foot
A681   BACUP ROAD   A681

2

Rossendale Way
Limers Gate

3
Gorpley
Reservoir

Lancashire County
Calderdale

4
Reaps
Moss   Inchfield
Moor
Rossendale Way

5
Calderdale
Lancashire County

Foul Clough Road

6
Ditches

Rossendale Way
Foul Clough Road
7
KEY
STREET   Ramsden
Clough
Reservoir
Freeholds Road
Calderdale
Rochdale

Old Lane
8   Percy street
Jane St   Rossendale
Knott Hill Street

awforth   St John with
St MichaelSchool
A   B   C   184   D   E   F
Side Street
J4, J5, J7   K1, L1
Street Names for   Street Names for
these grid squares   these grid squares
are listed at the   are listed at the
back of the index   back of the index

1 grid square represents 500 metres

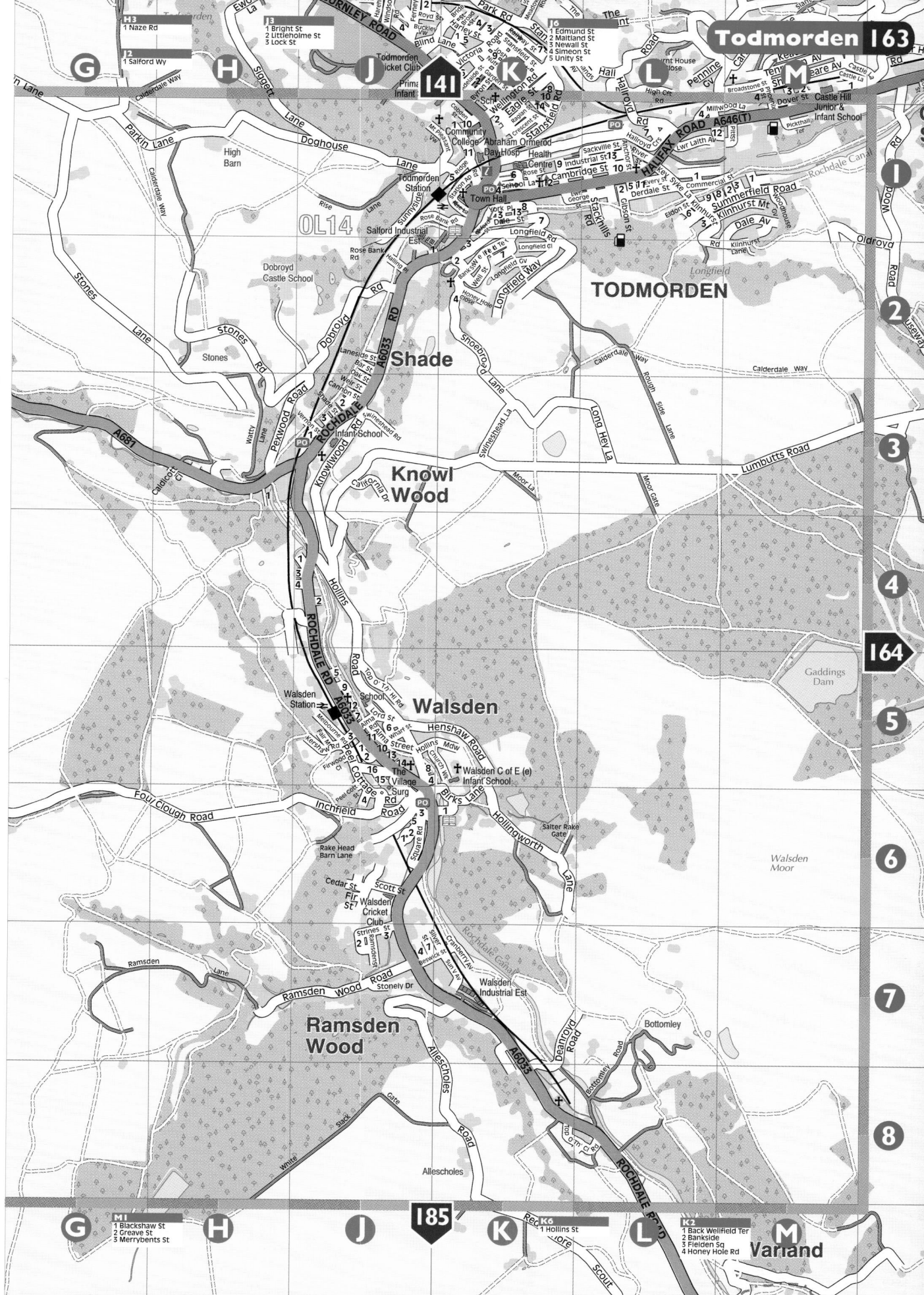

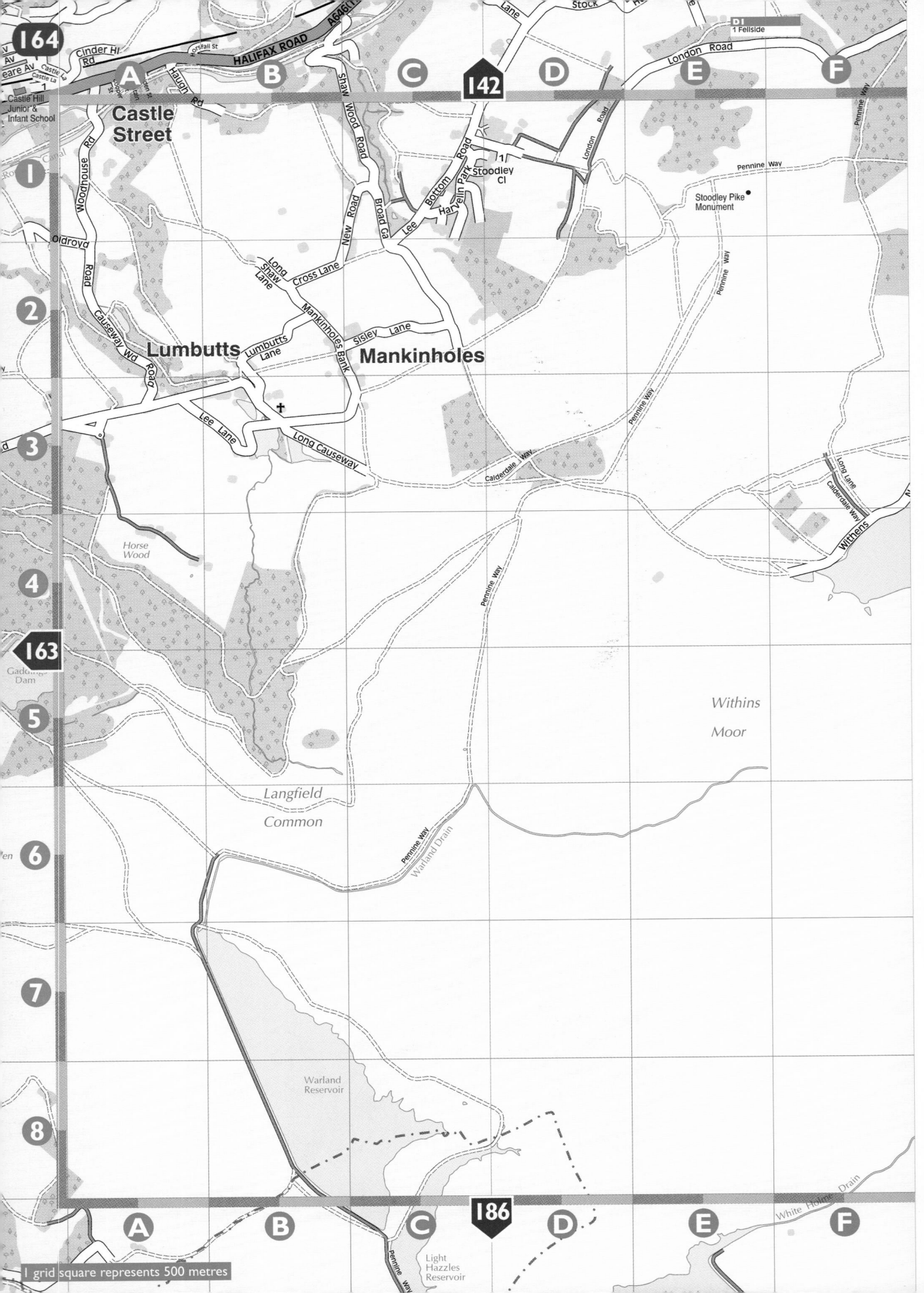

L3
1 Church Bank La

G   H   J   **143**   K   L   M

Bell Ho
Moor

Cragg Lane

I

Cragg Road

Bank Top Lane

Blaith Royd Lane

Stony Royd Lane

Lane

CRAGG ROAD

New La

2

Sunny Bank La

Heseltine

Field Head Lane

Hill Top Lane

Castle Gate

B6138

Cragg Vale

New Lane

Coppy

Lane

3

Swine Lane

Withens Lane

Market Lane

Rud Lane

Kirby Cote Lane

Calderdale Way

High Lane

Bent Cl La

Bent Cl La

Folly Hall La

High

Calderdale Way

Road

† 1

Hebden Royd Cragg Vale County Primary School

Clattering

4

Withins Clough Reservoir

Turley Holes Edge

B6138

166

5

New Road

Water Stalls Road

6

Turley Holes and Higher House Moor

Sykes Gate

Cald le Way

7

Blake Moor

Washfold Road

BLACKSTONE EDGE ROAD

Turvin Clough

8

G   H   **187**   J   K   L   M

B6138

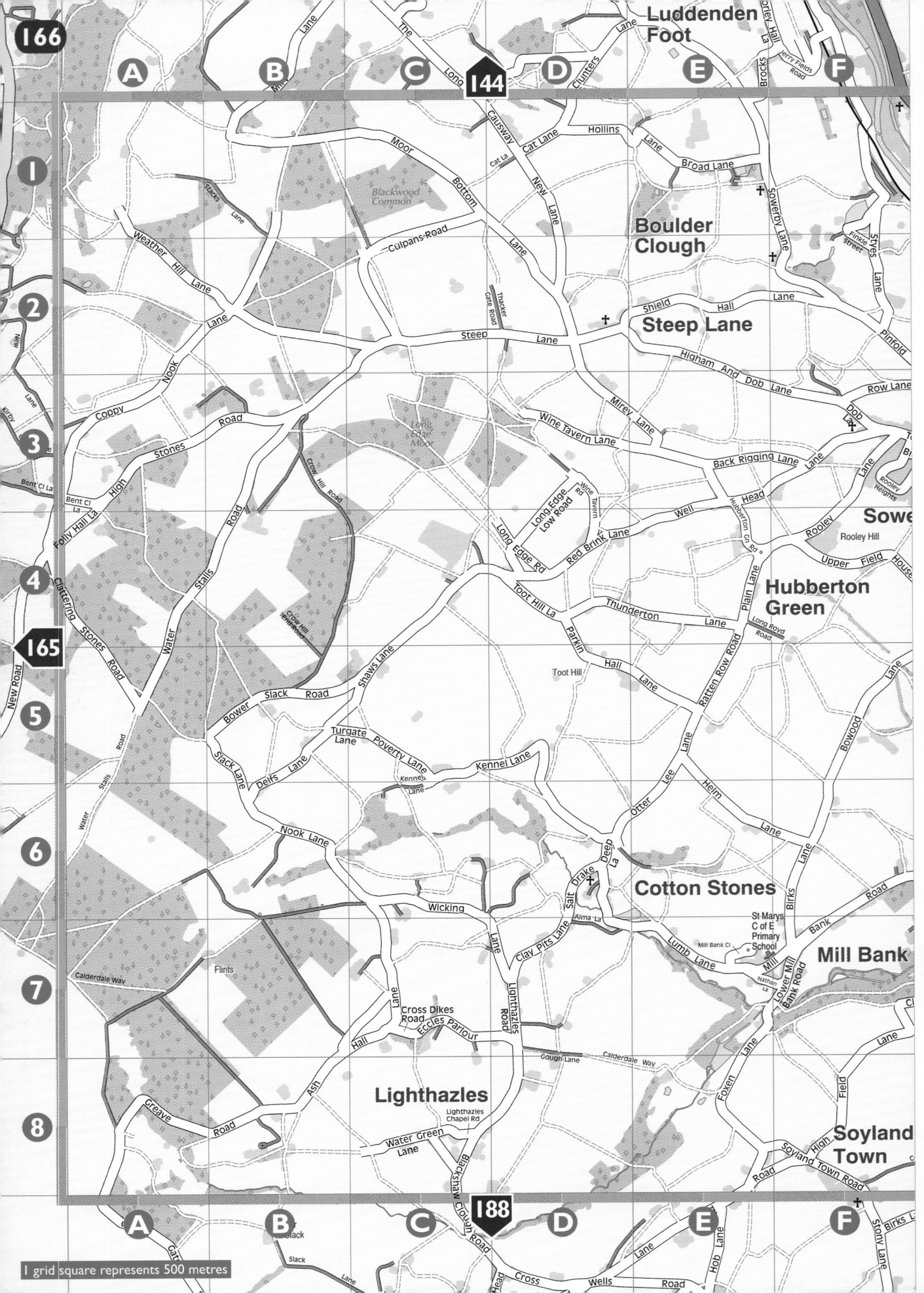

G1
1 John Naylor La
2 Victoria Ter

G3
1 King St
2 Longbottom Av
3 Rooley Banks

G7
1 Overdale

G8
1 Hillside Av

G H J 145 K L M

Warley
1 Daisy Mt

Luddendenfoot
2 Junior & Infant School

Belmont Ter
Beulah Pl
Tenterfields Business Park
Rose Grove La

Wood Lane
Warley Wood Av
Throstle Mt
BURNLEY ROAD A646(T)
Woodroyd Gdns

Rochdale Canal
River Calder

Friendly

Hollins
Hollins Lane
Primary School

Cemetery

Sowerby Bridge Cricket Club
Walton St

Cemetery Lane

Sowerby New Road

Sowerby New Road
Beechwood Av
Pollit Av
Fore La Av
Whiteley Av
Maude Crs
Eastwood Dr
Kingsley
Bates Av
Peter's St

Queen St
Infant School
Junior School
Ryburn County Secondary School
Orchard Rl

Bentley Royd Close
Fore Lane
Brockwell Gardens

Hgr Brockwell
Brock Well Lea
Lower Brock Well La
Brock Willow
Haugh End Lane
Brock Well La
A58

Parkfield Dr
Rochdale Road
Mill House La
Woodlands

ROCHDALE ROAD

Sowerby New Road
Ogden St
Boston St
Margate St
George St
Salisbury
The Nook
Sowerby Royd
Quarry Hill
Syke La
WEST STREET
TOWN HALL ST
A6139

Tuel La
Church Vw
The Surgery
Surg
Surg
Victoria Rd
Norland Road
Sowerby Bridge Clinic
Sowerby Bridge Station
Station Rd
Calder Trading Estate

Calderdale M B C
Holmes

BURNLEY ROAD
Water
Blackwall Lane
Friendly
Cliffe Ter
Bright St
Height St
Mill
PO
Langton St
Regent St
Denby
Perseverance St
Recreation Rd
Industrial St
Corporation St
WHARF ST
Back Whf St
St Anns Sq
Bolton Brow
A58 BOLTON BROW
Chapel La
The Bolton Brow Gallery
Mearclough Road

Sowerby Bridge High School
ALBERT RD
Wood Nook Rd
Willow Hall La
Dam Head
Willow Hall Dr
Christ Church Junior School
A6142 PYE NEST ROAD
A6026
School Walke
Gas Works Road

Overdale Mount
Willow Dene Rd
Park Gdns
Bairstow Mount
Crow Wood Pk
Pye Nest Gdns
Pye Nest Cr
Arlington Av
Prospect Av
High Fields
Atalanta Ter

ROCHDALE
I
2

Sowerby Bridge

Bank
Boggart
Scar Head Road
Sowerby
House
Spark
Harper Royd Lane
Allan Ter
Hope St

Parkfield Lane
London Road
Fall Lane

3

Mill Lane
Long Lane
Goose West Lane
Hob Lane
Hollin Lane
Shaw Lane
Bottom Lane
Lane
Croft
Spring Terrace
New Clough Road
Stormer Hill Lane
Kitson Lane
Dye House Lane

Norland C of E Junior & Infant School
Berry Moor Rd
PO
Clough

Clough Head

Norland
168
Pickwell Lane
4
5

Triangle C.of E Primary School
PO
Stansfield Lane
Stansfield Mill Lane
Stansfield Mill Lane
Butterworth La
Union St
Middle St

Triangle

Longley

Longley Lane
Longley Lane
Moor Bottom Lane
New Longley Lane
Butterworth End Lane

Calderdale Way
Norland Moor

Norland Road
Calderdale Way
Turbury
6

Oak Lane
Sandy Dyke
Dean Lane
River Ryburn
Stubbing Lane
Oak Hill

Dean Lane

Garden Lane
B6113
Lightcliffe Royd Lane
Barsey Green Lane
High Trees La
Dog Lane
Greetland Wall Nook
7
8

Kebroyd
Parkdale Dr
Kebroyd La
Higher Park Royd Dr
Parkfields
Kenworthy Lane
Jubilee Ter
Coronation Ter

HALIFAX ROAD

Meadowcroft Ln
Haigh Ln
Scammonden Road
Calderdale Way
B6114
189
B6113
Greetland

L2
1 Belmont St
2 Church Bank
3 Croft St
4 Exeter St
5 Lower Clifton St
6 Stanley St

L1
1 Claremont St

K3
1 Foundry St
2 Lower Clyde St
3 Stansfield Ct

H3, J3, K1, K2
Street Names for these grid squares are listed at the back of the index

G H J K L M

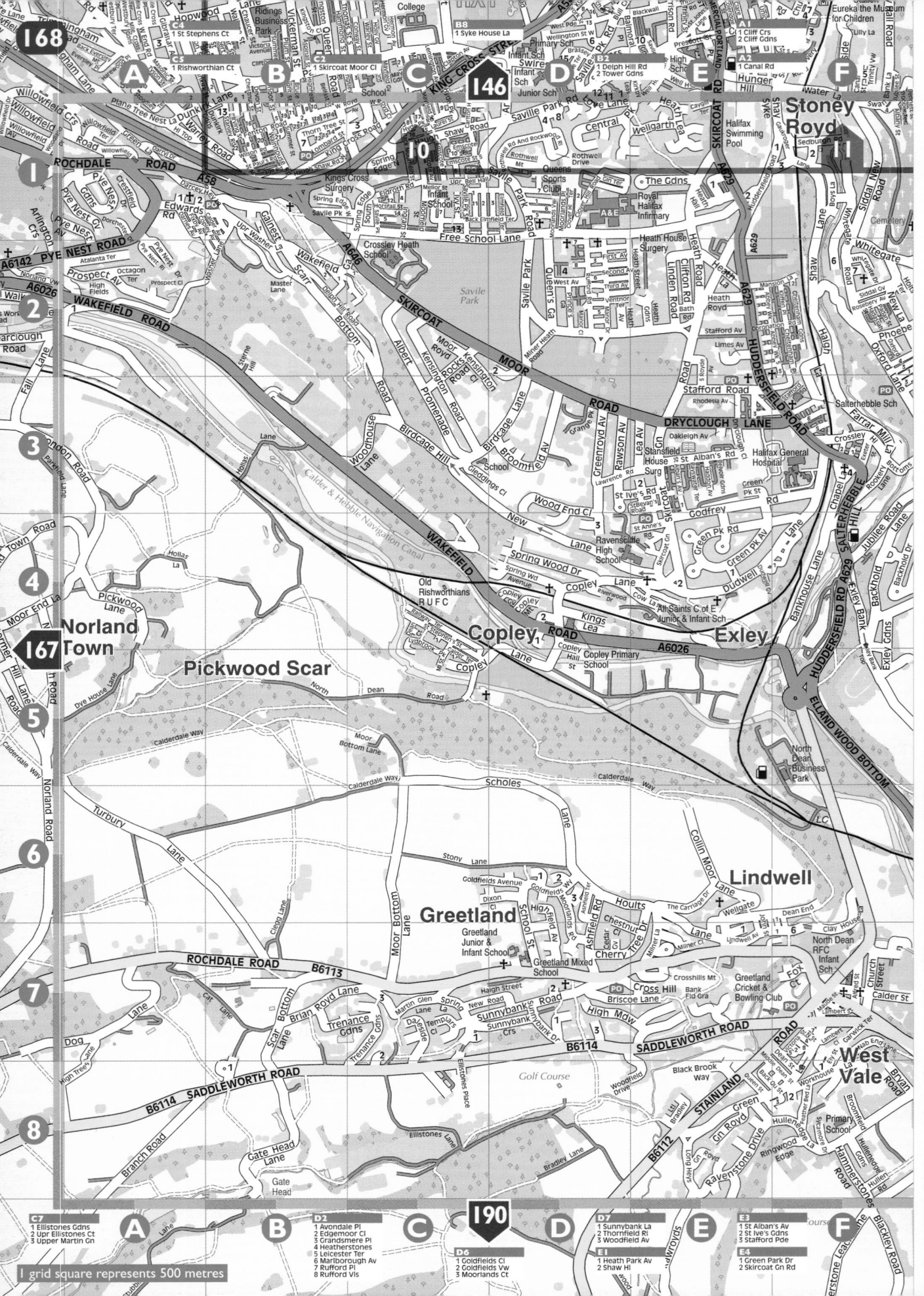

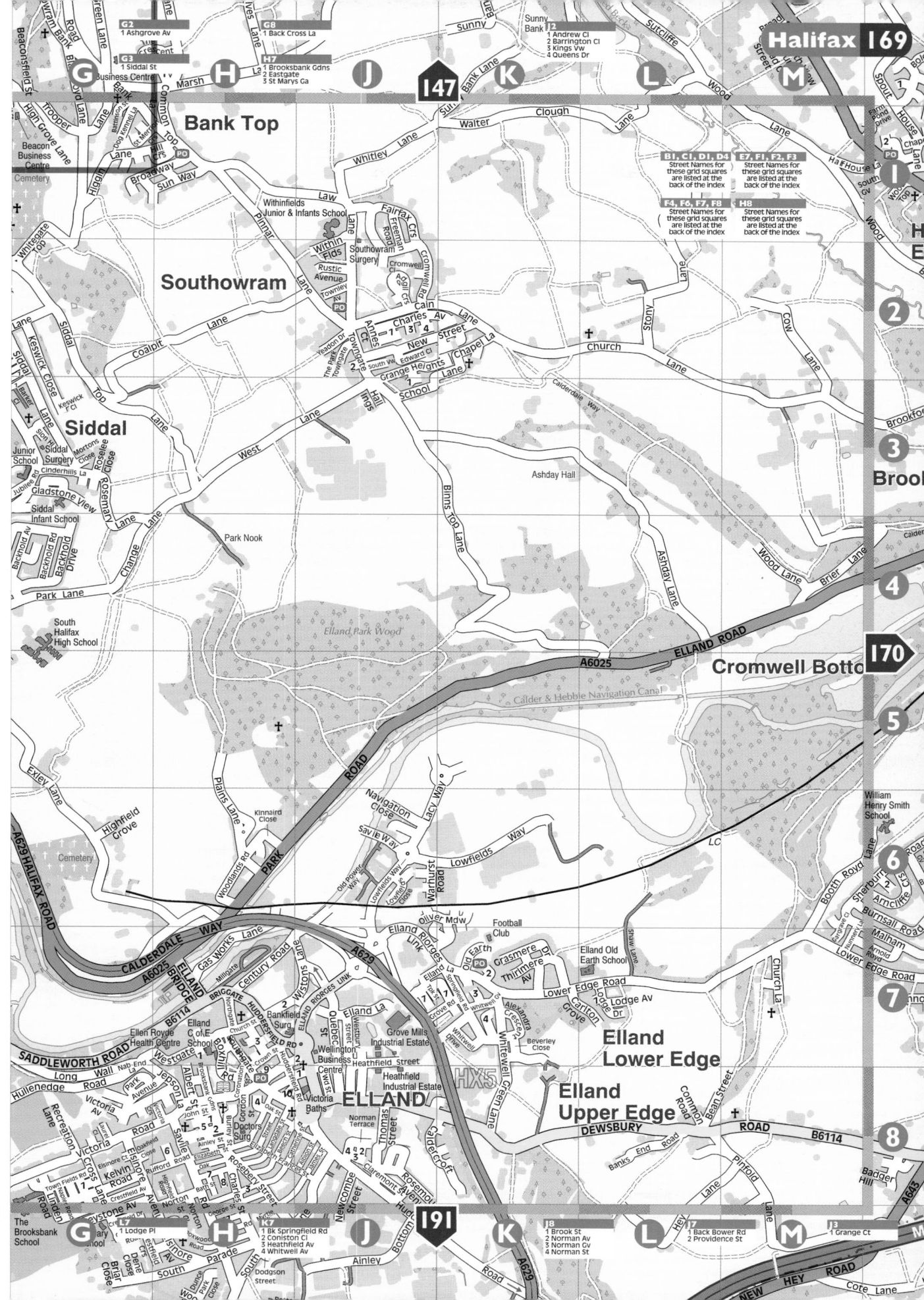

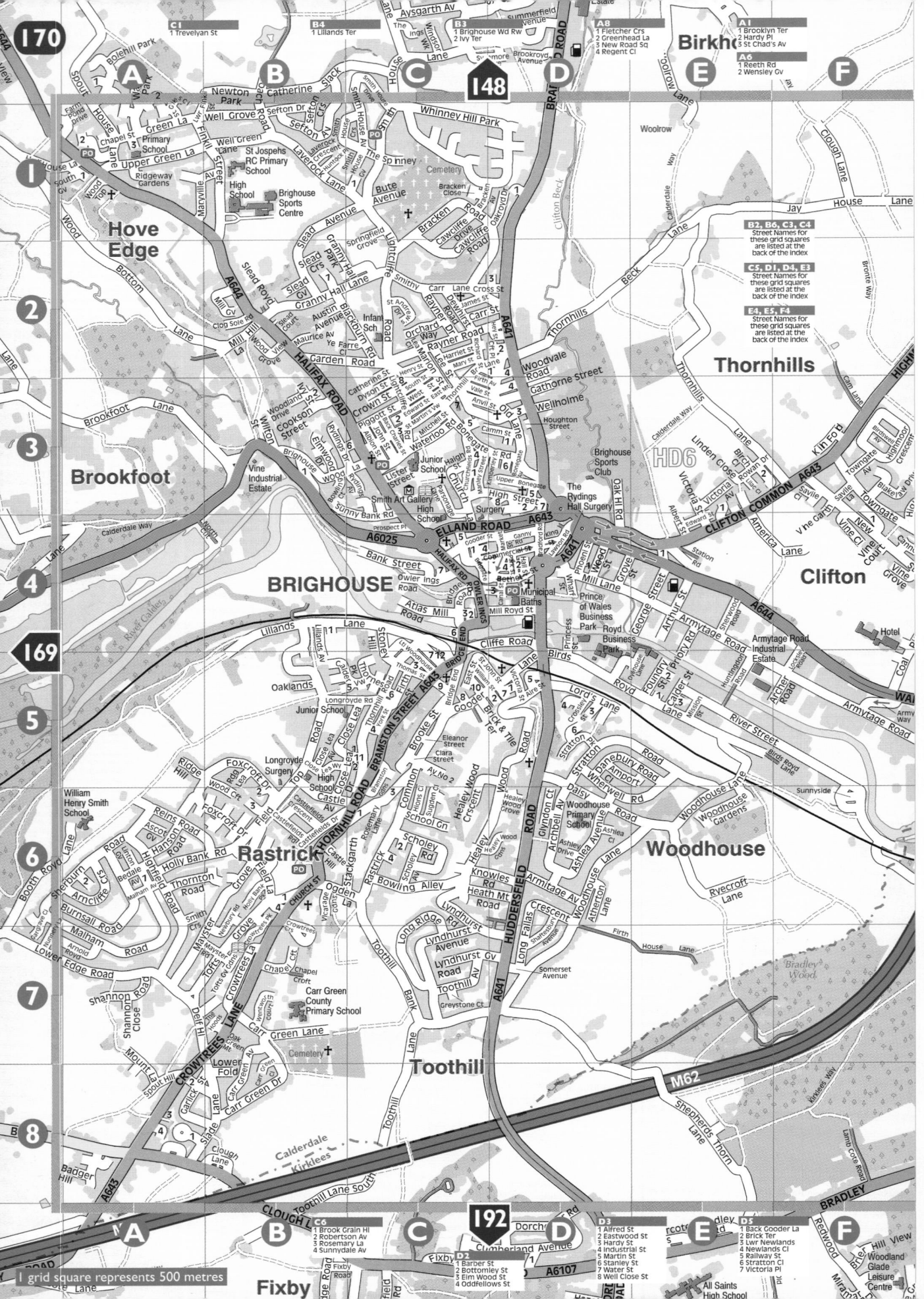

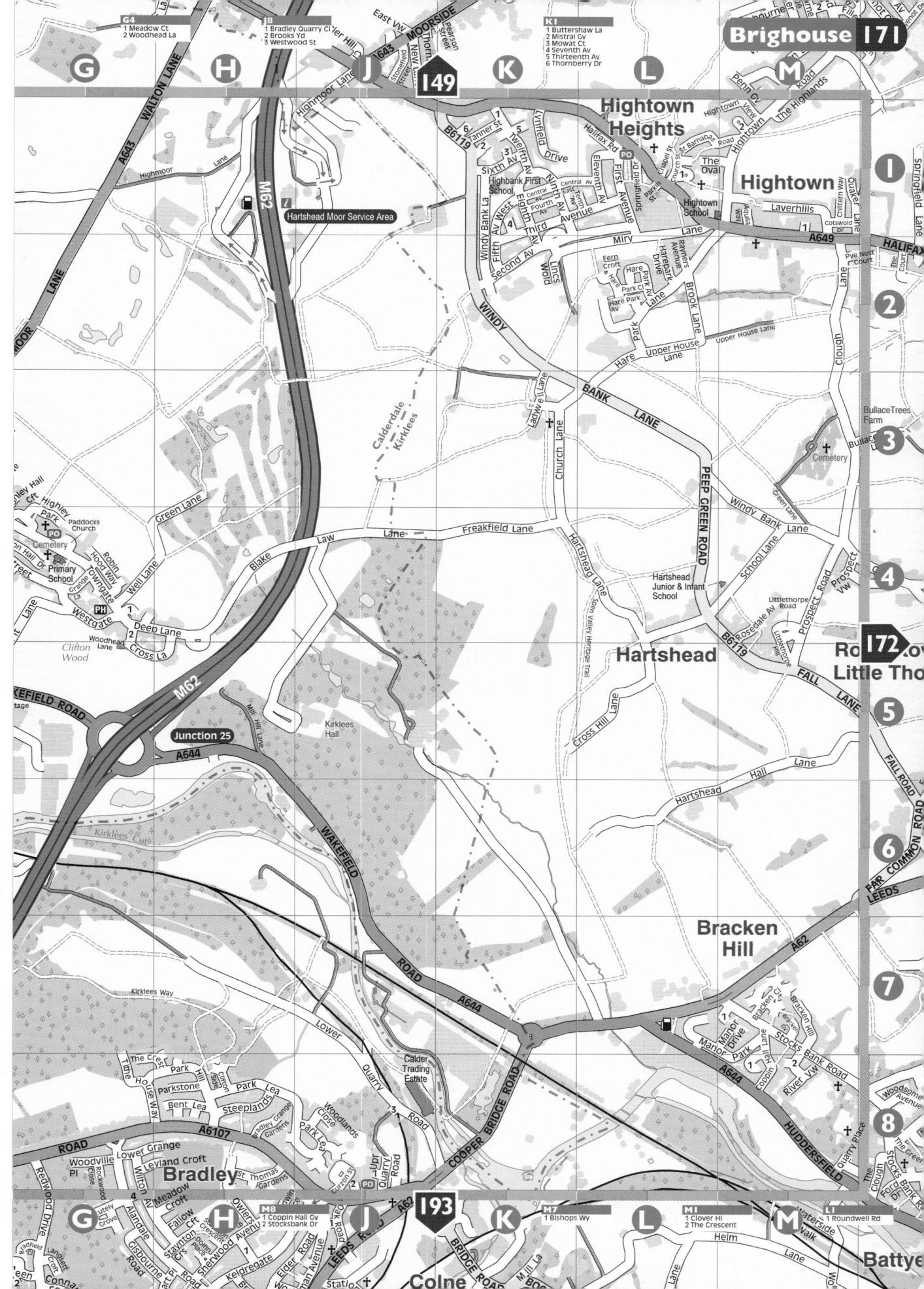

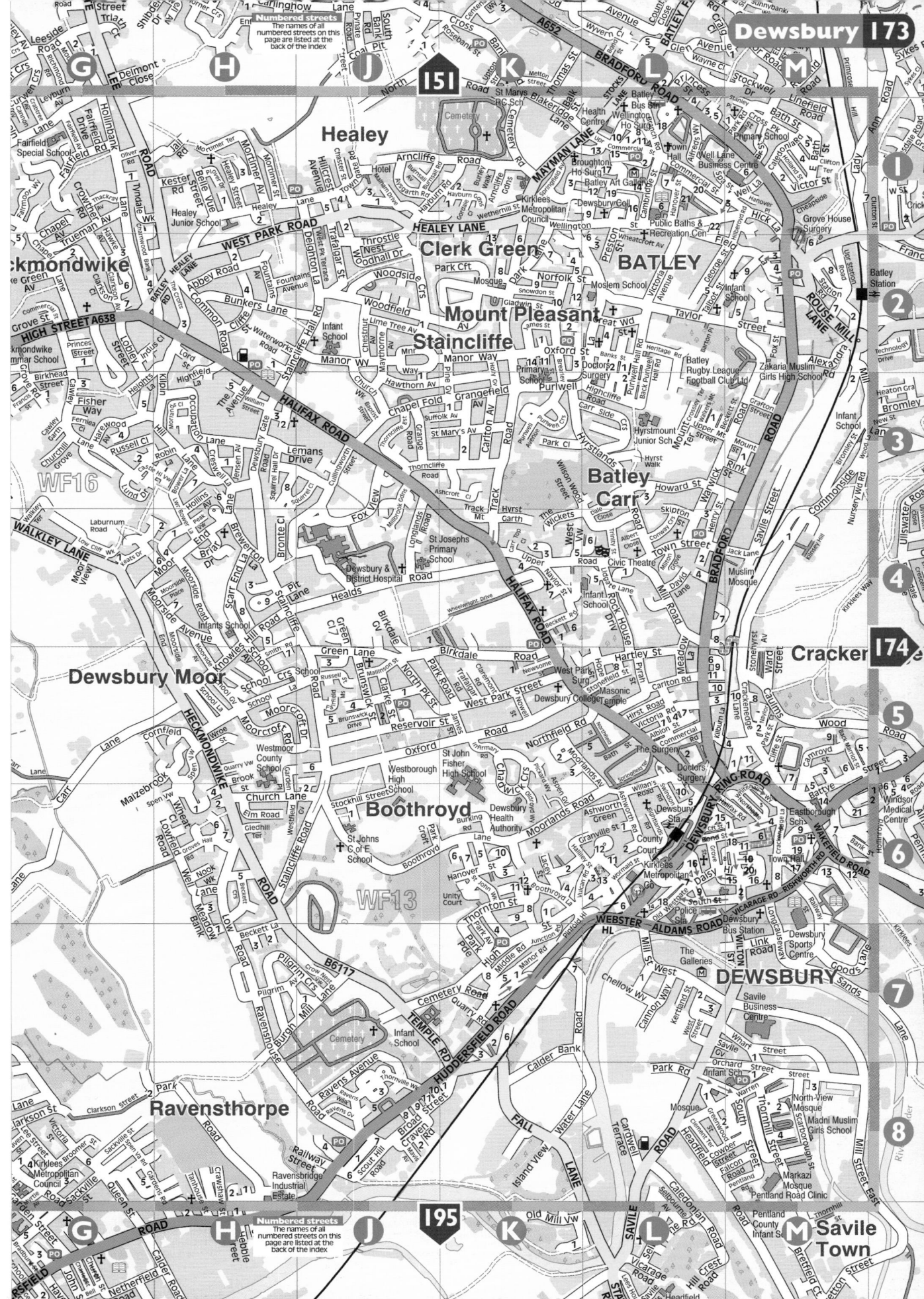

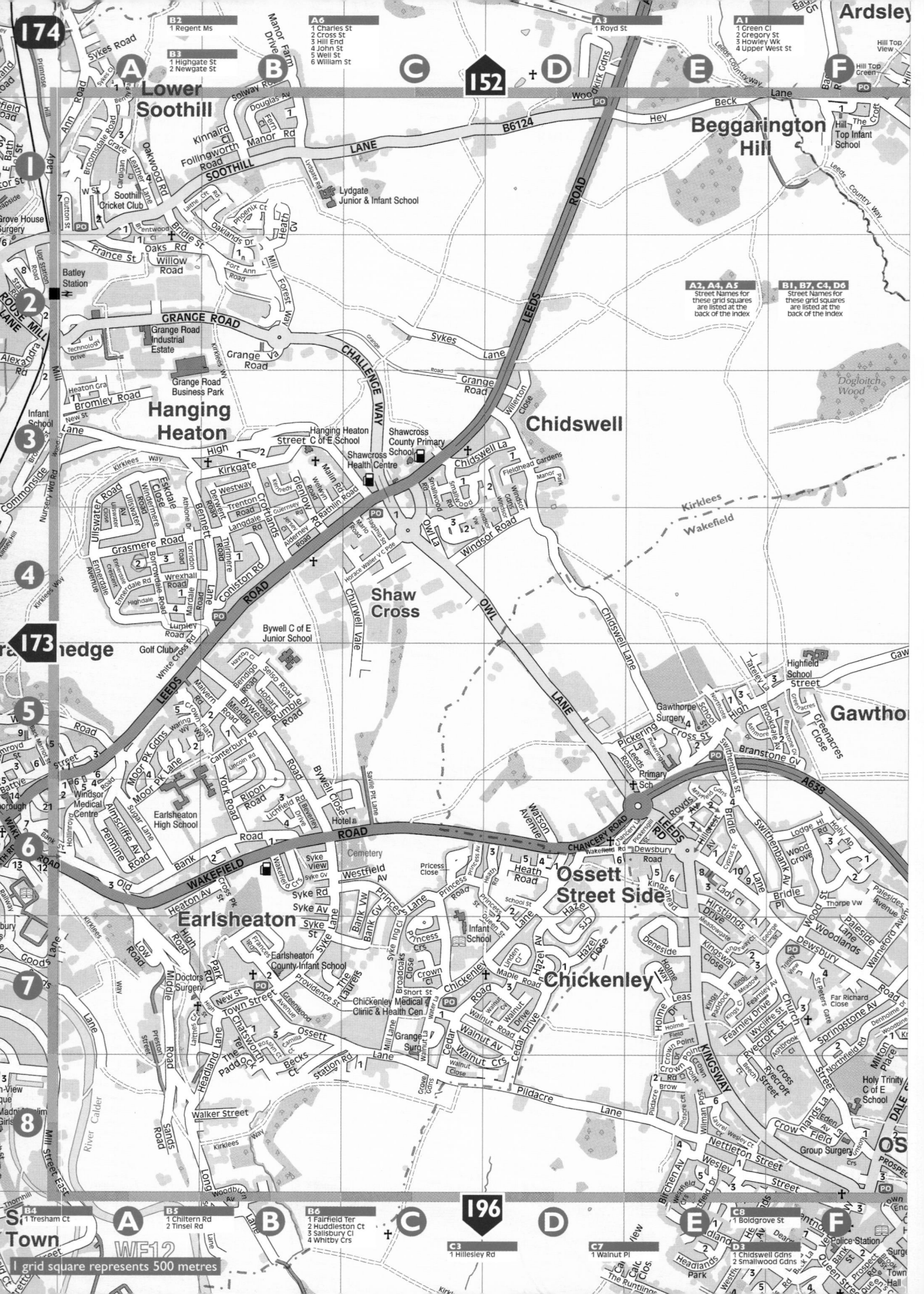

G7
1 Cromwell Pl
2 St Oswalds Pl

G8
1 Littlefield Gv
2 Townfold

H8
1 Spring Vw

East Ardsley United
Cricket & Athletic Club

G **H** **J** 153 **K** **L** **M** **I**

Junction 4

Haigh
Moor

Hill Top
Grove

Woodlin Crs
Woodlin Av

Holly
Ct

Redhill Av
Redhill Dr
Redhill Cl

Pump Lane

Clarke La

Batley Road

Blind Lane

Woodhouse
Hall Farm

Woodhouse Lane

Stoney

Carr
Gate Crs

Carr Gate
Mount

Bradford Road

A650

C
Ga

Melbo

2

D7, E5, E6, E7
Street Names for
these grid squares
are listed at the
back of the index

E8, F1, F5, F6
Street Names for
these grid squares
are listed at the
back of the index

F7, F8
Street Names for
these grid squares
are listed at the
back of the index

Jaw
Hill

**Brandy
Carr**

Brandy Carr Road

3

Leeds
Wakefield

Red Lo

M1

Westfield
Pl

Hawthorn
Ct

Brandy Carr Road

Infant
School

West
View

Caledonia
Court

Pippins
Green
Avenue

The
Pound

Beck
Bottom

Lindale Gth

Jerry Clay Lane

**Beck
Bottom**

Lindale
Lane

Jerry Clay Lane
Junior & Infant School

4

Kirkhamgate

Cawthorpe Lane

PO

Greenlay
Drive

New
Row

Sunr
Cft

Sunr

176

5

Queens

Sunnyhill Crs

Lower
Park Farm

-thorpe   Lane

Leeds Country Way

Batley Road

Park Mill Lane

Wrenthorpe Lane

Lindale Gv

Harewood
Dr

The Mount

Toll Bar

Silcoates

Silcoates Ct

Childs Rd

Canning Av

Marion Av

Marion Gv

Alverth

Pau
Aided Junior & Infa

6

-rpe

Leeds Country Way

Lodge
Hill

M1

Mill   Lane

Park

Leeds Country Way

Flushdyke

Eldon Street

A638

B6129

Primary
School

WAKEFIELD   ROAD

Cross Keys

Geary
Cl
Gelder
Court

Geary Dr

St Clare
St
Billingham
Cl

Gelder Cft

Allan
Haigh
Cl

St Paul's Dr

Batley Road

Highfield
Green

Wellingto

Laithes
W

Willow Ms

Willow Road

Laithes
Drive

Willow Cdns

Laithes Fold

Willow
Brick La

Willow
La

Tyrrell
Ct

7

Leeds Country   Way

Flanshaw   Way

Oakes St

Harrap

Flanshaw Crs

Flans

Jacksons
Estate

Albion
Cft

Longlands Trading
Estate

Smith
Way

Mortimer
Rise

Milner
Way

Milner

Ashley
Industrial Estate

Towngate
J & I
School

WF5

Spring Mill Lane

Whitley

Spring
Close

Spring
Road

Shepherd Hill

A638   WAKEFIELD   ROAD

Hotel

Spout
Fold

Eagle Av

Springfield
Gra

Beechwood
Av

Woodland Road

Woodland Rise

Oakwood

8

-SETT

Ingfield
Avenue

Longlands
Close

Greatfield
Cl

Atholm

Queen's

197

Towngate

Hinchcliffe

Woodland Rd

Teall Parks

Sunnyd

DEWSBURY   ROAD

Town

A638

Ashleigh

G **H** **J** **K** **L** **M** **I**

M8
1 Huntsman Fold
2 Pinewood Av

M7
1 Laithes Cha
2 Laithes Cl
3 Laithes Crs
4 Laithes Ct
5 Willow Ct
6 Willow Mt

M6
1 Armitage Rd
2 Charles Cotton Cl
3 Gelder Cft
4 Pacaholme Rd
5 St Paul's Wk

M5
1 Winchester Cl

K4
1 Kirkham Av
2 Westfield Crs

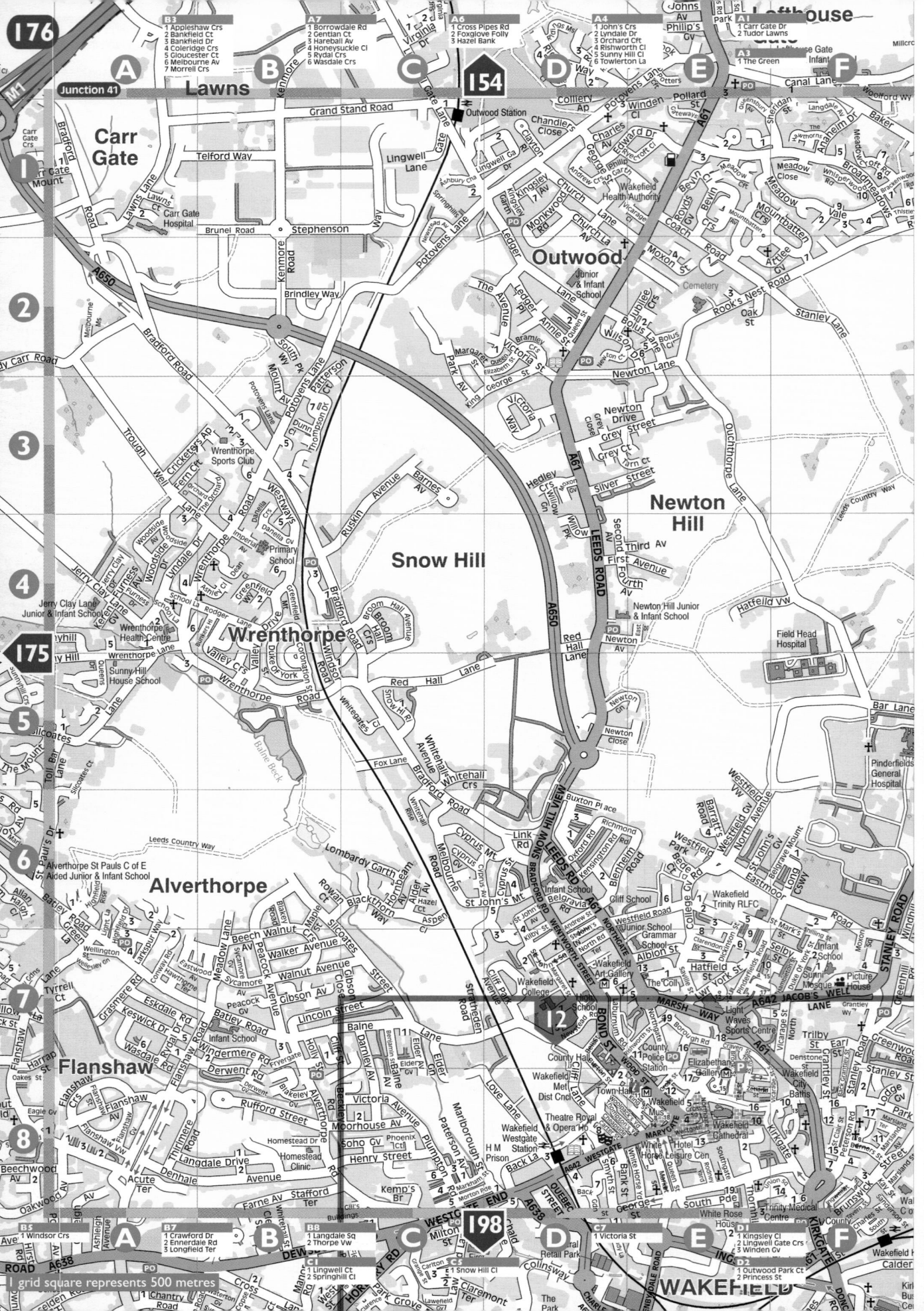

climacteric

By the *climacteric system*, seven years was declared to be the termination of childhood; fourteen the term of puberty; twenty-one of adult age; thirty-five as the height of physical and bodily strength. At forty-nine the person . . . reached the height of his mental strength or intellectual powers; at sixty-three he was said to have reached the *grand climacteric*.

—T. Ellwood Zell's *Popular Encyclopedia of Knowledge and Language*, 1871

Death of Joanna Southcott (1750–1814),

English religious prophet. Chambers's *Book of Days* (1864) related her story: "When about forty years old, she assumed the pretensions of a prophetess, and declared herself the woman mentioned in the twelfth Book of Revelation. She asserted that [she had] received a divine appointment to be the mother of the Messiah, who was to be miraculously born of her [on October 19, 1814] . . . after she had passed her *grand climacteric*." A steadfast group of followers awaited her resurrection for nearly a century after she died.

Bank Holiday (U.K.)

© JEFFREY KACIRK

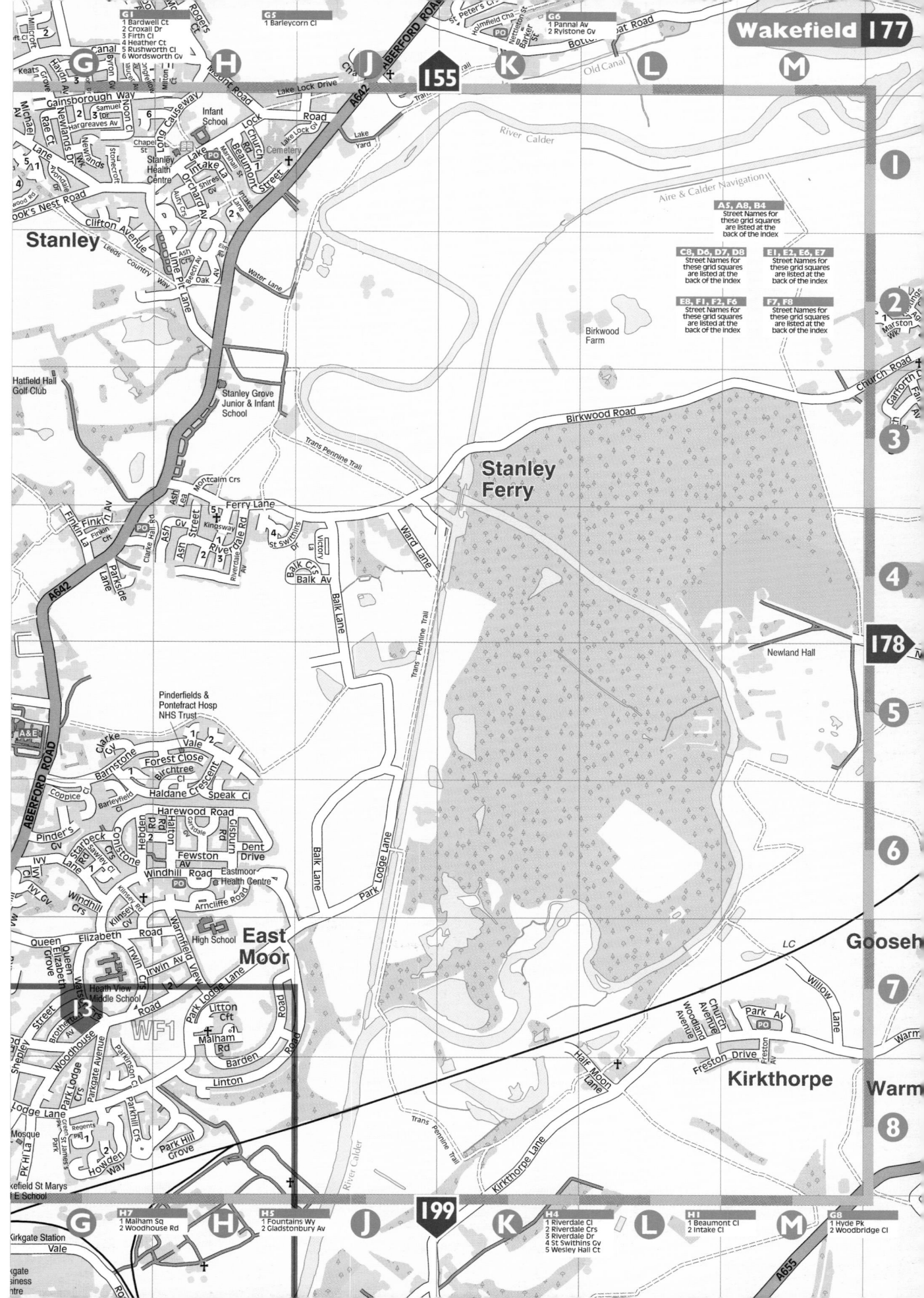

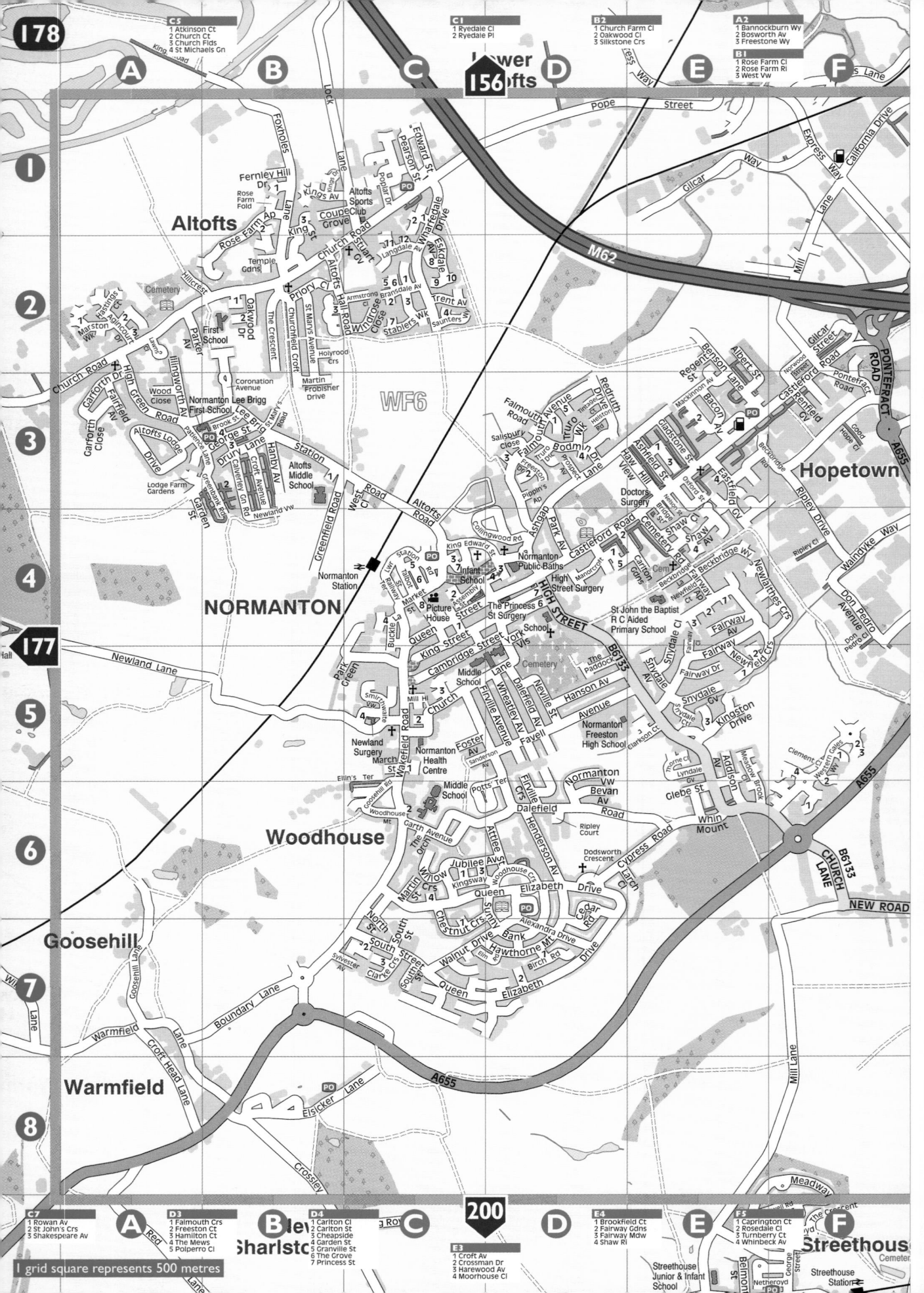

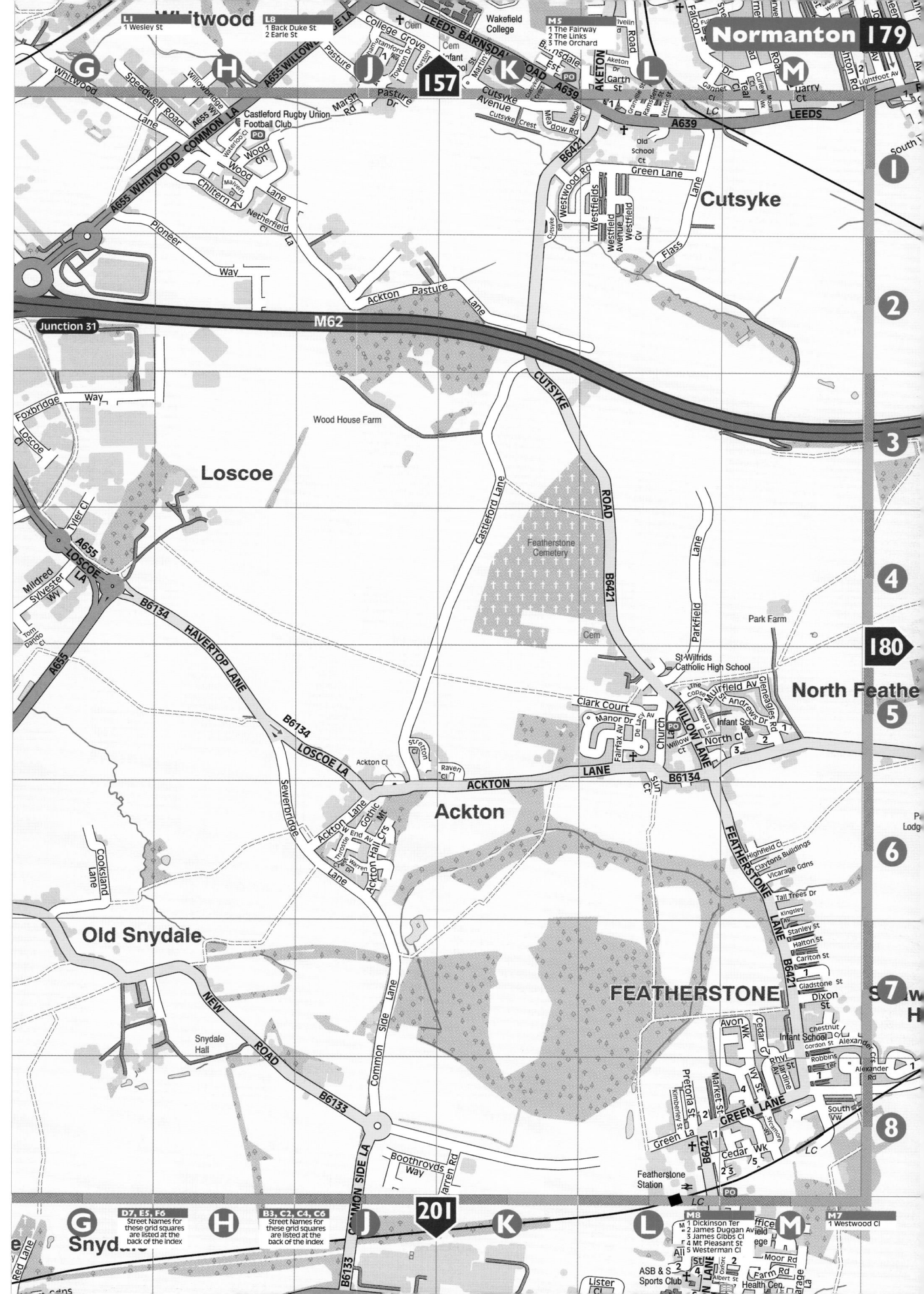

Whitwood
L1 1 Wesley St
L8 1 Back Duke St 2 Earle St
M5 1 The Fairway 2 The Links 3 The Orchard

G H J K L M

157

I

Cutsyke

Castleford Rugby Union Football Club

LEEDS BARNSDALE ROAD A639

Wakefield College

Westwood Rd
Westfields
Westfield Avenue
Westfield Gv
Green Lane
Flass

2

M62

Junction 31

CUTSYKE ROAD B6421

3

Wood House Farm

Loscoe

Featherstone Cemetery

Foxbridge Way
Loscoe
Tyler Cl
A655 LOSCOE LA
Mildred Sylvester Wy
Tom Dando Cl
A655

HAVERTOP LANE

B6134

Cem

4

180

St Wilfrids Catholic High School

North Feathe

5

B6134 LOSCOE LA

Ackton Cl

Stretton

Raven Cl

Clark Court

Manor Dr
Fairfax Av
De Lacy Av
Church
WILLOW LANE
North Cl
Infant Sch

ACKTON LANE

B6134

Ackton

6

Ackton Lane
Gothic Mt
Throstle End Av
Warren Cres
Ackton Hall

Old Snydale

FEATHERSTONE LANE B6421

Highfield Cl
Claytons Buildings
Vicarage Gdns
Tall Trees Dr
Kingsley
Stanley St
Halton St
Carlton St

FEATHERSTONE

7

S
H

Snydale Hall

NEW ROAD B6133

Common Side Lane

Gladstone St
Dixon St
Avon Wk
Cedar Wk
Infant School
Gordon St
Alexander
Robbins Ter
Alexander Rd

8

Cookland Lane

Boothroyds Way
Warren Rd

COMMON SIDE LA
B6133

201

Pretoria St
Kimberley St
Market St
Rhyl
Ivy St
Jardine Av
GREEN LANE
Green
Sycamore
Cedar Wk
B6421

Featherstone Station

LC

G **D7, E5, F6** Street Names for these grid squares are listed at the back of the index

H **B3, C2, C4, C6** Street Names for these grid squares are listed at the back of the index

L **M8** 1 Dickinson Ter 2 James Duggan Av 3 James Gibbs Cl 4 Mt Pleasant St 5 Westerman Cl

M **M7** 1 Westwood Cl

Red Lane
Lister
ASB & S Sports Club
Moor Rd
Health Cen

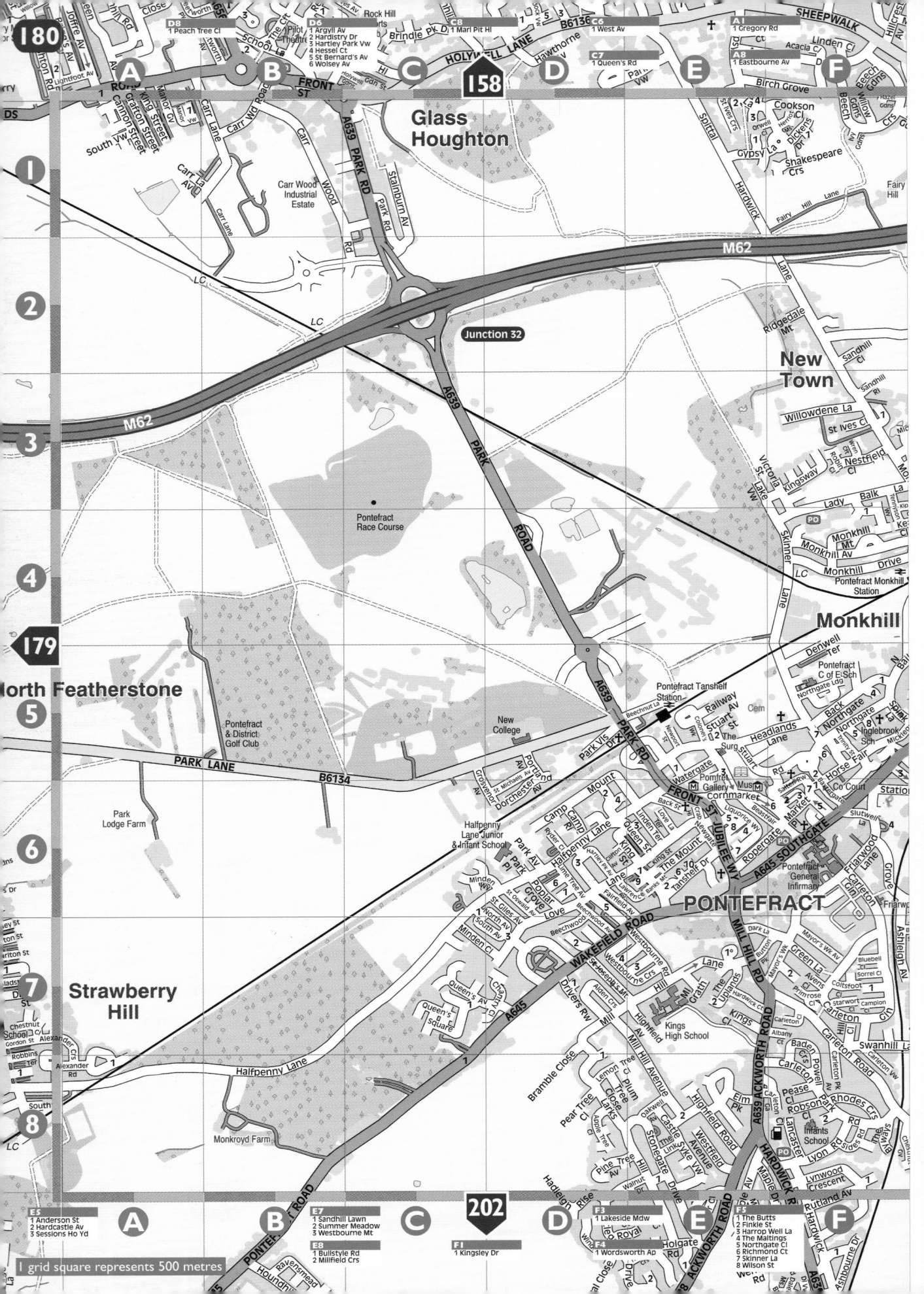

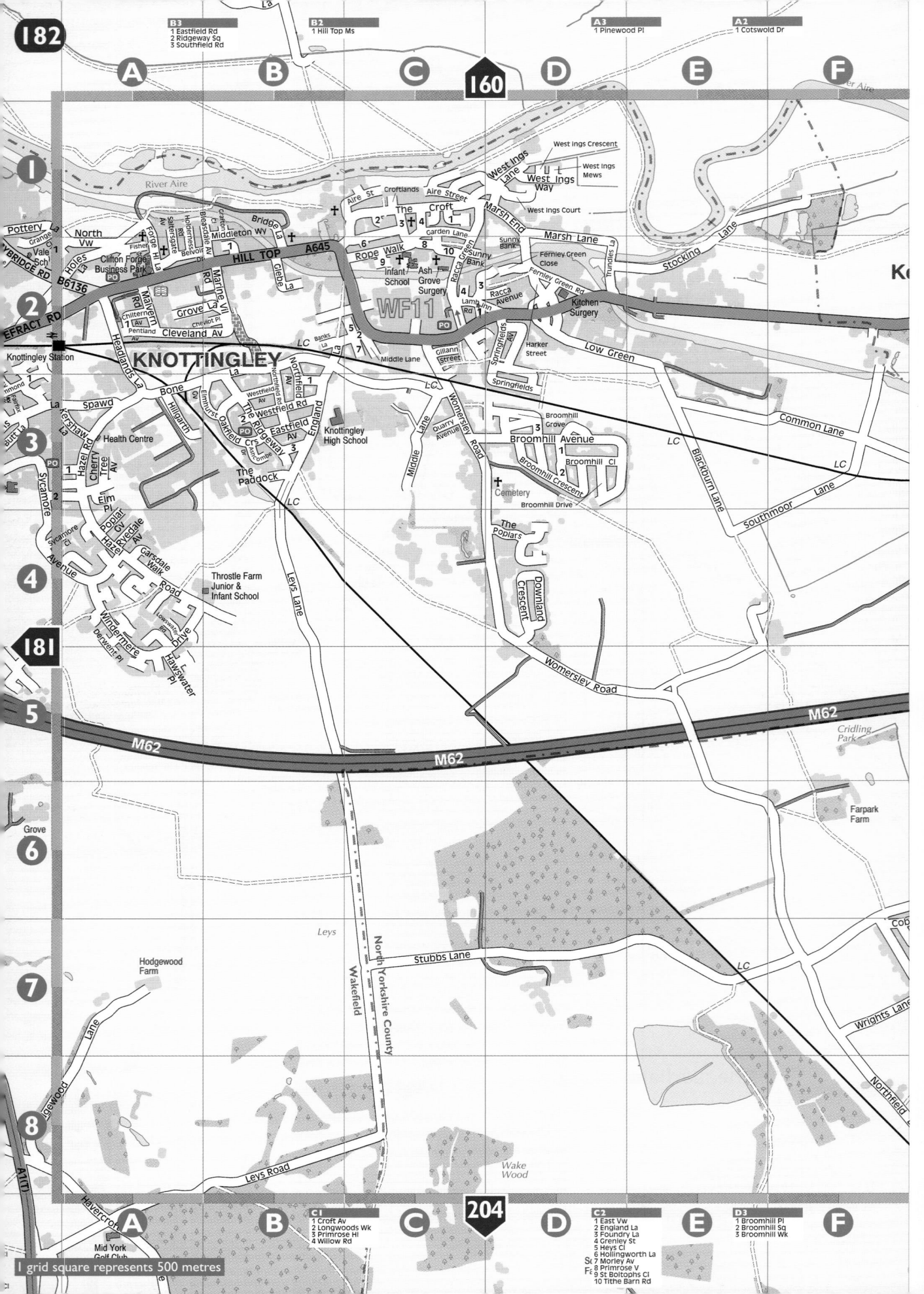

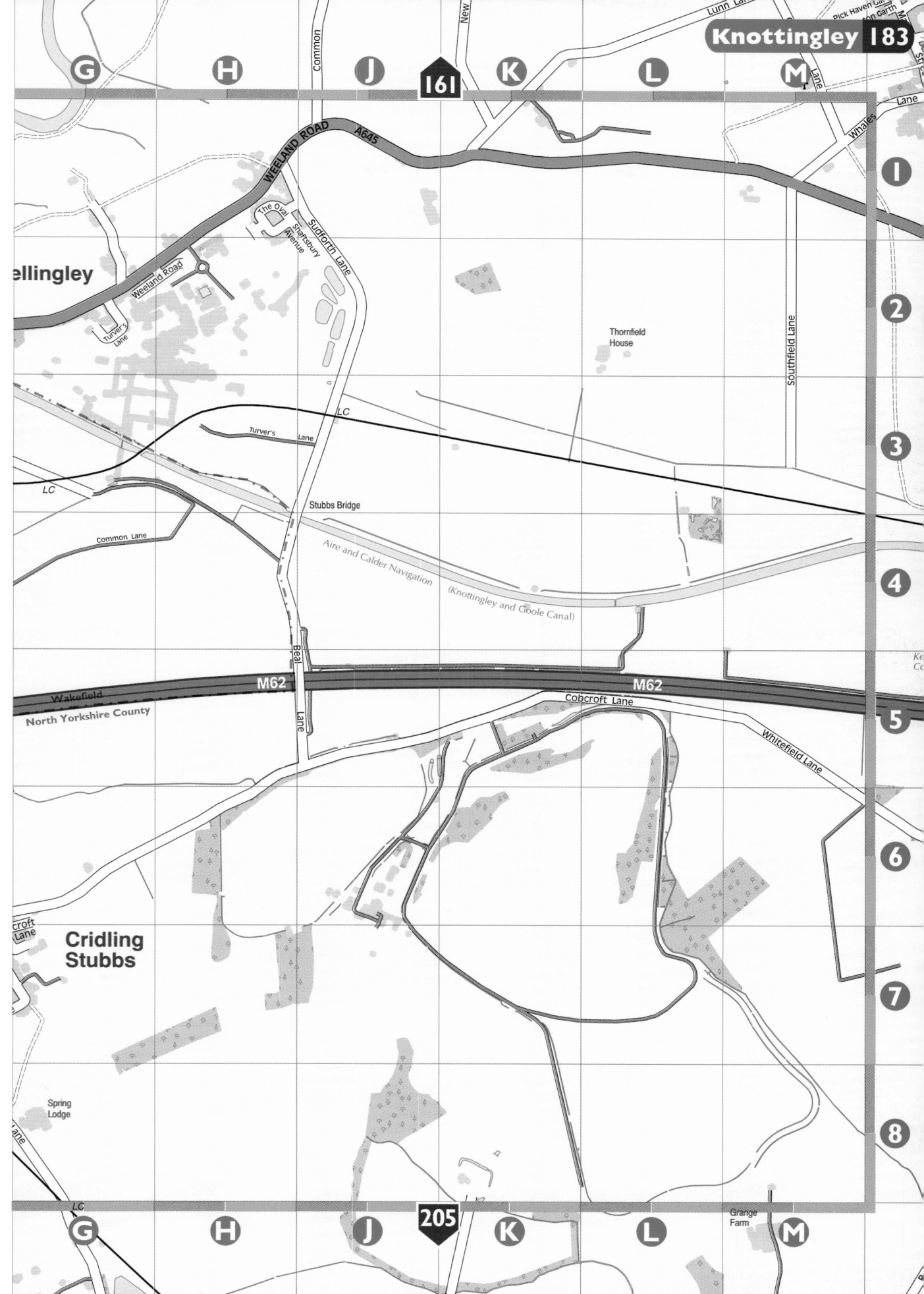

G   H   J   161   K   L   M

I

2

3

4

5

6

7

8

WEELAND ROAD   A645

The Oval

Common

New

Lunn Lane

Pick Haven Garth

ton Garth

Whales

Lane

Lane

ellingley

Weeland Road

Turver's Lane

Shaftsbury Avenue

Sudforth Lane

Thornfield House

Southfield Lane

LC

Turver's Lane

LC

Common Lane

Stubbs Bridge

Aire and Calder Navigation

(Knottingley and Goole Canal)

Beal Lane

M62

M62

Wakefield

North Yorkshire County

Cobcroft Lane

Whitefield Lane

Ke

Co

Cridling Stubbs

croft Lane

Spring Lodge

Lane

LC

Grange Farm

G   H   J   205   K   L   M

wforth

A B Knowsley C **162** D E F

F8
1 Ashbourne Cl

E8
1 Birch St
2 Brook St
3 Hartley St
4 Jackson St
5 Lodge St

E7
1 Back Chapel St
2 Crossfield Cl

Freeholds Road

Knowley Crs

Knowl Hill Street

St John with
St MichaelSchool

Moss Side Street

Cowm St

PO

Land Gate

1

Oak St
Oak Cl
Side
Oak
ET cross
EET

2

Lancashire County
Rochdale

Rossendale way

3

Cemetery

Facit

Edward St

Long Acres

Council

street

A671

thel St

4

5

Lancashire County
Rochdale

Rossendale Way

Slack Gate

HWORTH

Rake

6

Hard Lane

Watergove
Reservoir

Bent La

Old

Barn Field Lane

Lower House Lane

Ramsden

Alderbank

Wardle Fold

Bank Lane

Bank Barn Lane

Knowl Syke St

Vineyard Close

7

Clough House Lane

Hey Bottom Lane

Chapel St

PO

Primary School

Aldine Drive

Pennine

Crossfield Road

Fern St

Holly

East St

Clough Street

Heath Road

Hilbson

Newhouse Close

Haymaker Dr

Dovedale Drive

Shaftesbury
Drive

Woodend Lane

Birch

Hill

Lane

8

Dirty Leech

Linnet La

Hey Bottom Lane

Rydings Lane

206

Wardle Road

Corn brook Close

Fir Grove

Warehouse Close

Lawflat

Westmorland

Wardle

A B C **206** D E F

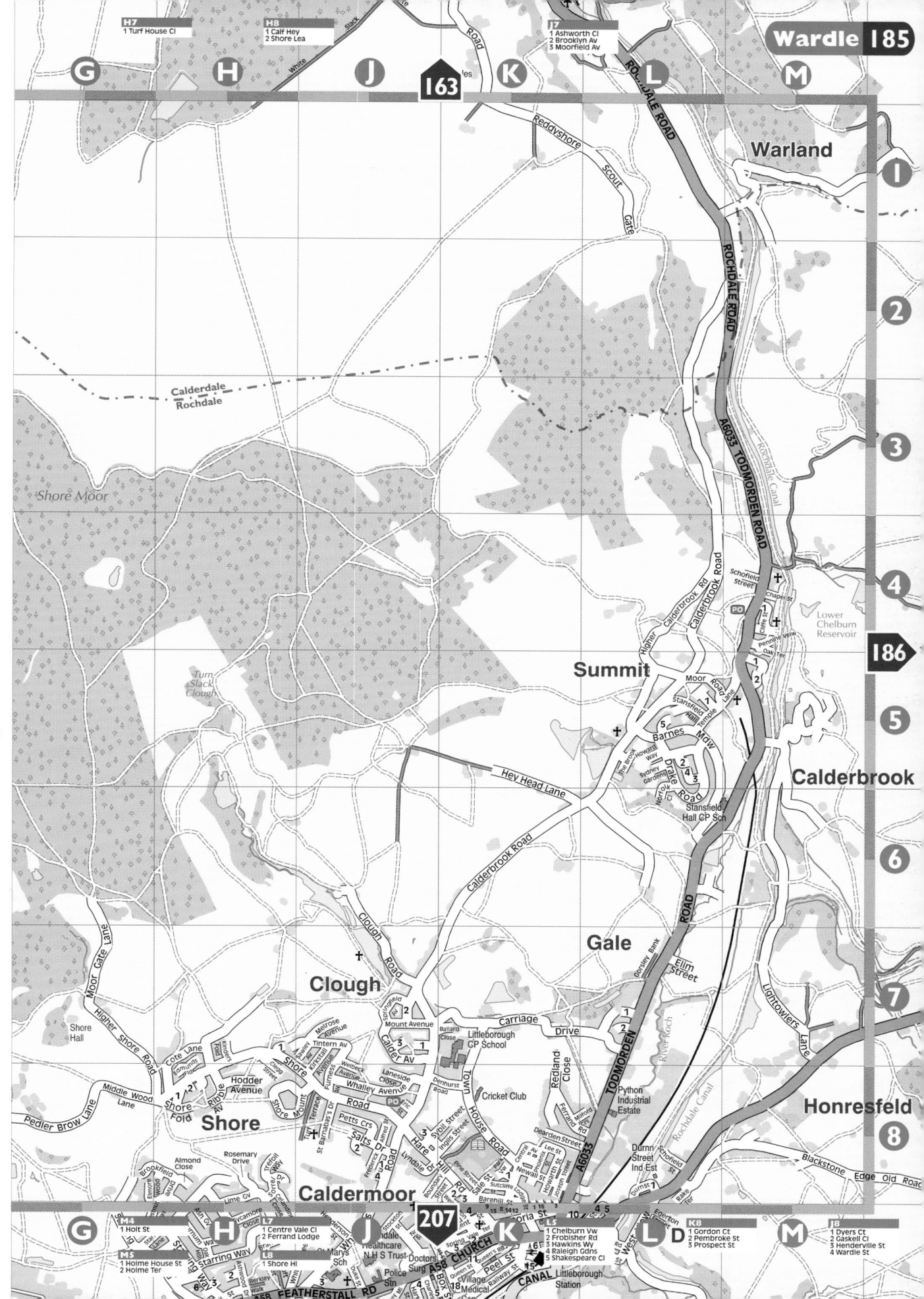

G H J **163** K L M

H7
1 Turf House Cl

H8
1 Calf Hey
2 Shore Lea

J7
1 Ashworth Cl
2 Brooklyn Av
3 Moorfield Av

I

2

3

Warland

Reddyshore

Scout

Cafe

ROCHDALE ROAD

A6033 TODMORDEN ROAD

Rochdale Canal

Calderdale
Rochdale

Shore Moor

Turn
Slack
Clough

4

186

5

6

Calderbrook Rd

Calderbrook Road

Schofield
Street

PO

Cliffe St

Chapel St

Pennine View

Oak Ter

Lower
Chelburn
Reservoir

Higher

Moor Road St

Summit

Stansfield
Hall

Barnes

The Brook

Norfolk

Drake Road

Maw

Howard
Way

Sydney
Gardens

Stansfield
Hall CP Sch

Calderbrook

Hey Head Lane

Calderbrook Road

Clough Road

Clough

Springfield

Mount Avenue

Melrose
Avenue

Tintern Av

Calder Av

Ballard
Close

Littleborough
CP School

Gale

Crenley Bank

Elim
Street

Carriage
Drive

TODMORDEN

7

Shore
Hall

Higher Shore Road

Cote Lane

Edmunds
Fold

Kirkgate
Street

Welbeck
Avenue

Laneside
Close

Denhurst
Road

Cricket Club

Redland
Close

Ferrand Rd

Python
Industrial
Estate

River Roch

Rochdale Canal

Lightowlers Lane

Honresfield

8

Middle Wood
Lane

Pedler Brow Lane

Hodder
Avenue

Shore
Fold

Ribble
St

Shore Mount

Furness
Avenue

Whalley Avenue

Road

PO

Town House Road

Dearden Street

ROAD

A6033

Dunn
Street
Ind Est

Durns St

Schofield
St

Blackstone
Edge Old Road

Shore

Almond
Close

Brookfield
Road

Rosemary
Drive

Sawley
Fold

Clegg
Street

St Barnabas's Dr

Salts Dr

Petts Crs

Hare
Hill

Lyndale Dr

Ingliss Street

Sybil Street

Village

Newall St

Joseph St

Howarth St

Egerton St

Rake
St

Caldermoor

207

Lime Gv

Sycamore
Close

St
Marys
Sch

Healthcare
NHS Trust

Doctors
Surg

Police
Stn

A58 CHURCH

Medical

CANAL

Railway

Littleborough
Station

FEATHERSTALL RD

M4
1 Holt St

L7
1 Centre Vale Cl
2 Ferrand Lodge

L8
1 Shore Hl

M5
1 Holme House St
2 Holme Ter

L5
1 Chelburn Vw
2 Frobisher Rd
3 Hawkins Wy
4 Raleigh Gdns
5 Shakespeare Cl

K8
1 Gordon Ct
2 Pembroke St
3 Prospect St

J8
1 Dyers Ct
2 Gaskell Cl
3 Henderville St
4 Wardle St

Starring Way

Ⓐ Ⓑ Ⓒ 164 Ⓓ Ⓔ Ⓕ

Ⓘ

White Holme Drain

Pennine Way

Light
Hazzles
Reservoir

White Holme
Reservoir

⓶

White Holme
Reservoir

⓷

Chelburn Moor

River Roch

TURVIN

⓸

Lower
Chelburn
Res

185

Head Drain

Higher
Chelburn Reservoir

Blackstone Edge
Reservoir

⓹

alderbrook

HALIFAX ROAD   A58

⓺

Dick
Slack

⓻

Swaindrod Lane

A58   HALIFAX ROAD

Pennine Way

Honresfeld

Blackstone Edge

Ⓧ

Blackstone   Edge Old Road

Ⓐ Ⓑ Lydgate Ⓒ 208 Ⓓ Ⓔ Ⓕ

Edge Fold

Broad Head Drain

G H J 165 K L M

I
2
3
188
5
6
7
8

Turvin Clough

BLACKSTONE

B6138

BLACKSTONE EDGE ROAD

B6138

Soyland Moor

Manshead End

Baitings Pasture

Blue Ball Road

A58 ROCHDALE ROAD

Baitings Reservoir

Back O' Th' Height

ROCHDALE ROAD

A58

Rishworth Drain

Cat Stones

Rishworth Moor

Rishworth Moor

Joiner Stones

G H J 209 K L M

Green Withens Reservoir

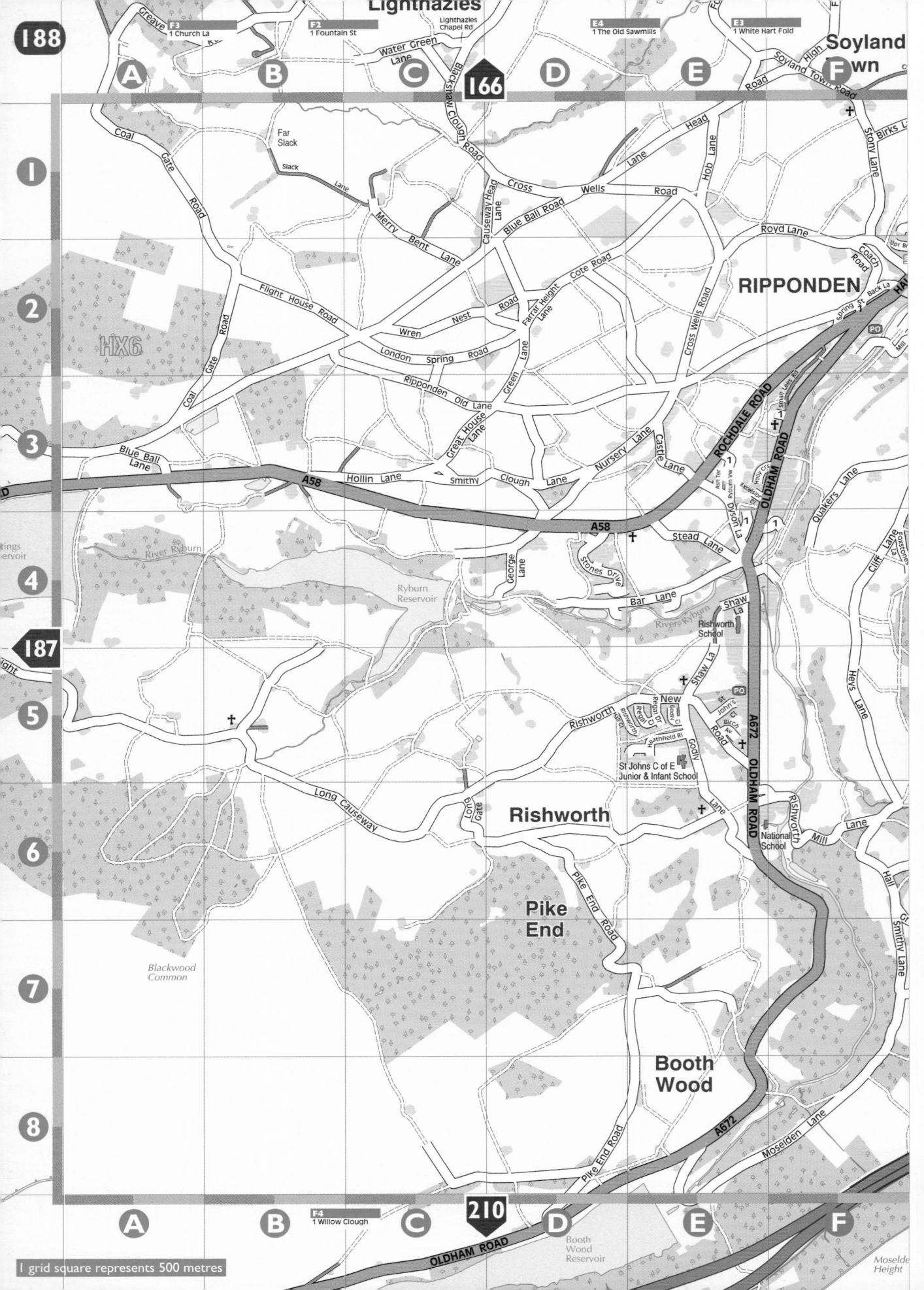

Lighthazies

High **Soyland Twn**

A   B   C   D   E   F

F3 1 Church La
F2 1 Fountain St
Lighthazies Chapel Rd
E4 1 The Old Sawmills
E3 1 White Hart Fold

166

Water Green Lane

Coal Gate Road

Far Slack

Slack

Merry Bent Lane

Blackshaw Clough Road

Causeway Head Lane

Cross Wells Road

Hob Lane

Head Lane

Birks L

Stony Lane

Soyland Town Road

Coach Road

Royd Lane

RIPPONDEN

HX6

Flight House Road

Coal Gate Road

Wren

Nest Road

London Spring Road

Ripponden Old Lane

Great House Lane

Green Lane

Farrar Height Lane

Cote Road

Cross Wells Road

Nursery Lane

Castle Lane

ROCHDALE ROAD

OLDHAM ROAD

Spring St

PO

Small Lees Rd

Quakers Lane

Cliff Lane

Heys Lane

Blue Ball Lane

A58

Hollin Lane

Smithy

Clough Lane

A58

George Lane

Stones Drive

Stead Lane

Dyson La

Ash Ter

Ryburn Vw

Excelsior

River Ryburn

Ryburn Reservoir

Bar Lane

River Ryburn

Shaw La

Rishworth School

187

Long Causeway

Rishworth

Shaw La

New

PO

St John's

Regal Dr

Birca

Heathfield Ri

St Johns C of E Junior & Infant School

Godly Lane

A672

OLDHAM ROAD

Rishworth Lane

Mill Lane

National School

Pike End

Godly Gate

Pike End Road

Hall Lane

Smithy Lane

Blackwood Common

Booth Wood

A672

Moselden Lane

A   B   C   D   E   F

F4 1 Willow Clough

210

OLDHAM ROAD

Booth Wood Reservoir

Moselden Height

I grid square represents 500 metres

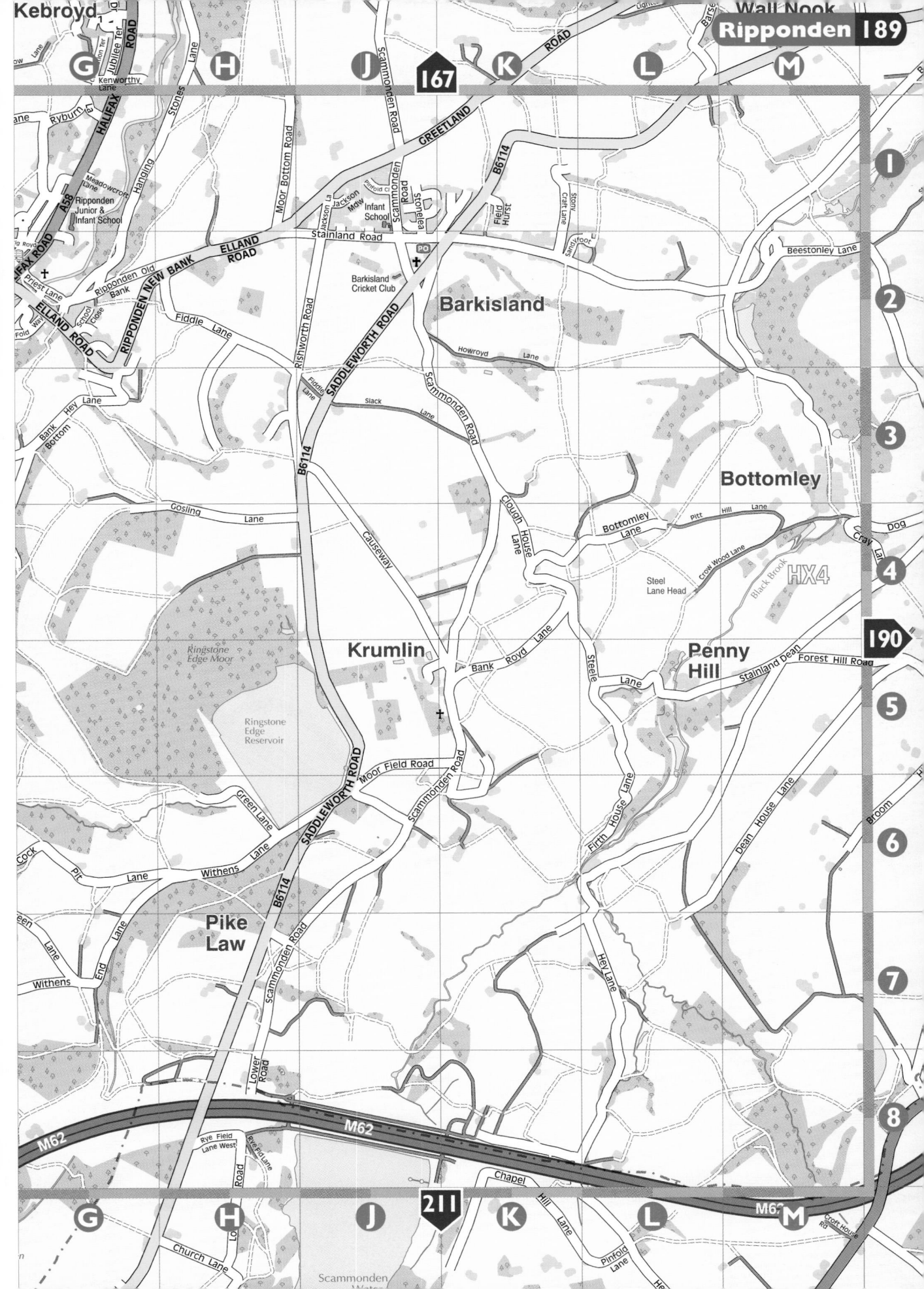

Kebroyd

G   H   J   **167**   K   L   M

Kenworthy Lane
Jubilee Ter
HALIFAX ROAD
Ryburn
Lane
Stones
Lane
Hanging
Meadowcroft
Lane
Ripponden Junior & Infant School
A58
HALIFAX ROAD
Priest Lane
School Close
ELLAND ROAD
Fold Way
Ripponden Old Bank
RIPPONDEN NEW BANK
Fiddle Lane
ELLAND ROAD
Moor Bottom Road
Stainland Road
Jackson La
Jackson Mdw
Pinfold Cl
Steelea
Scammonden Road
GREETLAND ROAD
B6114
Stony Croft Lane
Ryfoot
Field Hurst
I
Beestonley Lane
2
Infant School
PO
Barkisland Cricket Club
Barkisland
Howroyd Lane
Rishworth Road
SADDLEWORTH ROAD
Fiddle Lane
Slack Lane
Scammonden Road
3
Bottomley
B6114
Gosling Lane
Causeway
Clough House Lane
Bottomley Lane
Pitt Hill Lane
Crow Wood Lane
Black Brook
Dog Lane
Cray La
HX4
4
Steel Lane Head
Ringstone Edge Moor
Krumlin
Bank Royd Lane
Steele Lane
Penny Hill
Stainland Dean
Forest Hill Road
190
Ringstone Edge Reservoir
Green Lane
SADDLEWORTH ROAD
Moor Field Road
Scammonden Road
5
Broom
6
COCK
Pitt Lane
Withens Lane
Lane
End
Withens
B6114
Scammonden Road
Pike Law
Firth House Lane
Dean House Lane
Hey Lane
7
Green
Lane
M62
Lower Road
Rye Field Lane West
Rye Fld Lane
M62
Chapel
Hill Lane
M62
Croft House Rd
8

Church Lane
Long
Scammonden Water
Pinfold Lane
He

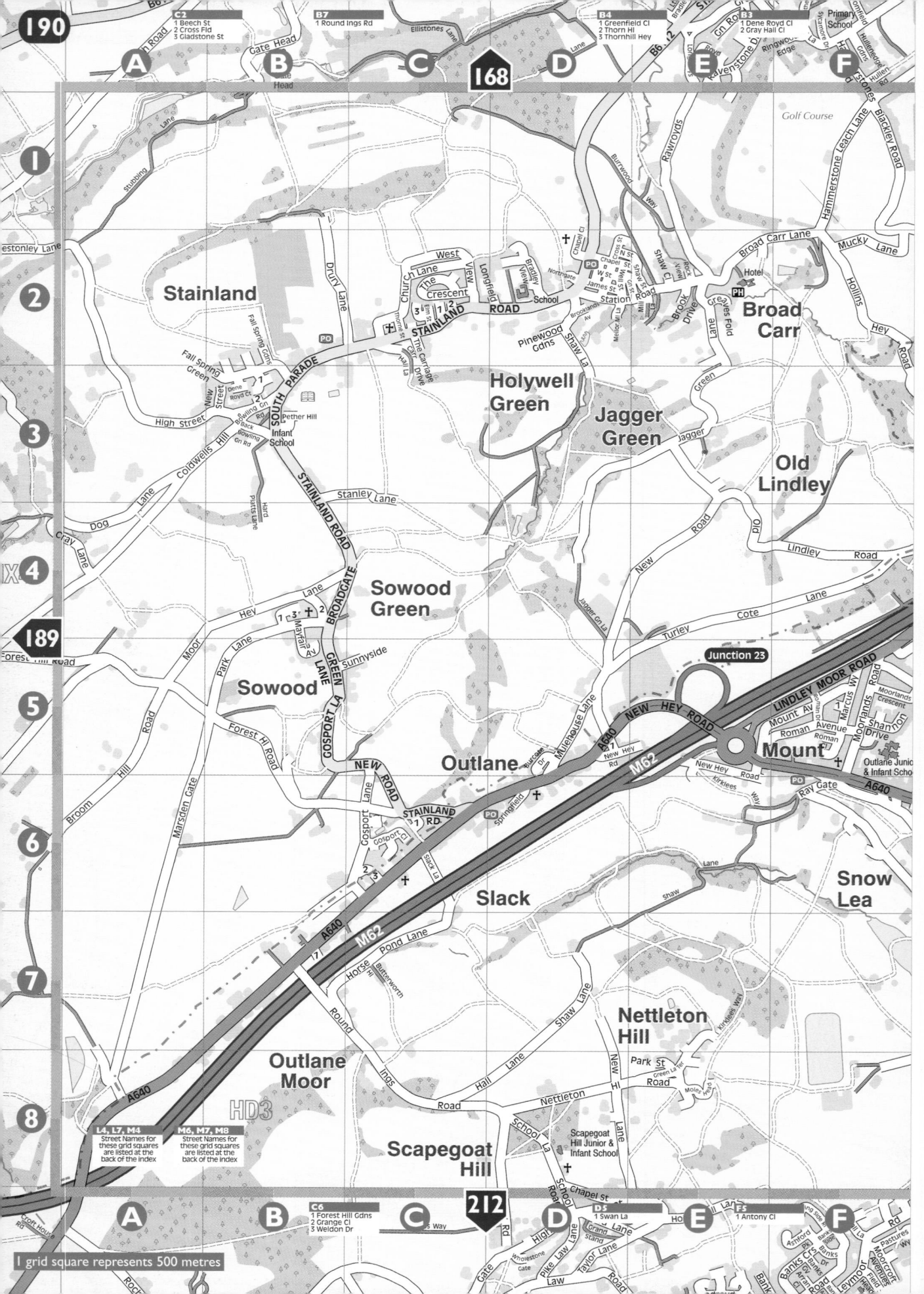

Stainland

Gate Head
Head

A   B   C   D   E   F

Golf Course

C2
1 Beech St
2 Cross Fld
3 Gladstone St

B7
1 Round Ings Rd

B4
1 Greenfield Cl
2 Thorn Hl
3 Thornhill Hey

B3
1 Dene Royd Cl
2 Gray Hall Cl

Primary
School

Ellistones Lane

Broad Carr Lane

Mucky Lane

estonley Lane

Church Lane
West
View
The
Crescent
Longfield
ROAD
School
STAINLAND
Elm La
Thorne La
Car Drive
The Carriage
Drive
Hall La

Drury Lane

Chapel Cl
W St
Chapel St
Northgate
James St
Station
Broadlands Av
Mellor Mll La
Shaw Cl
Rock
Shaw Rd
Mill Royd
Brook
Hotel
PH
Greaves Fold
Brook
Drive
Broad
Carr
Hey
Hollins
Road

Fall Spring Gdns
PO

Fall Spring
Green
New
Street
High street
Dene
Royd Cl
Swilling Gn
Back
Bowling Gn Rd
SOUTH PARADE
Pether Hill
Infant
School
Bowling Gn Rd

Pinewood
Gdns
Shaw La
Green

**Holywell
Green**

**Jagger
Green**
Jagger

**Broad
Carr**

Coldwells Hill
Dog
Lane
Cray Lane
Lane

STANLAND ROAD
Stanley Lane
Platts Lane
Hard

**Sowood
Green**

Jagger Gn La
New
Road
Lindley
Road
Old
Lane

**Old
Lindley**

X4

Forest Hill Road

Hey
Lane
BROADGATE
Mayfair
Av
Sunnyside
GREEN LANE
GOSPORT LA

Moor
Lane
Park Lane

Sowood
Forest Hl Road

Cote
Lane
Turley
Lane

Junction 23
LINDLEY MOOR ROAD
M62
NEW HEY ROAD
A640

Moorlands
crescent
Mount Av
Roman
Roman
Avenue
Shannon
Drive
Marcus Wy
Moorlands
Drive

Mount
Outlane Junior
& Infant Scho
A640
PO

Broom Hill Road
Marsden Gate
Road
Forest Hl Road

NEW ROAD
Gosport
Lane
Gosport Cl
Gosport

STAINLAND RD.
Slack La
Millenhouse Lane
Burcombe
Dr
New Hey
Rd
New Hey
Road

Outlane
PO Springfield
M62
Kirklees
Way
Ray Gate
New Hey
Road

A640
M62
Pond Lane
Horse
Butterworth

Slack
Lane
Shaw
Shaw Lane

**Snow
Lea**

Round
Ings
Road
Horse
Hall
Lane

**Nettleton
Hill**
Park St
Green La Ter
New Hl
Road
Kinder Wy
Mole

HD3

A640

**Outlane
Moor**

Nettleton
School La
Road

Scapegoat
Hill Junior &
Infant School

**Scapegoat
Hill**

Chapel St
High
School La
Wholestone
Gate
Pike Law Lane
Taylor Lane
Pike
Law
Road
Gate

A   B   C   D   E   F

C6
1 Forest Hill Gdns
2 Grange Cl
3 Weldon Dr

D5
1 Swan La
2 Grand
Stand

F5
1 Antony Cl

Ashford
PK
Banks
CFS
Banks
Levmoor
Road
Moorcroft
Croft House
Rd
Pastures

1 grid square represents 500 metres

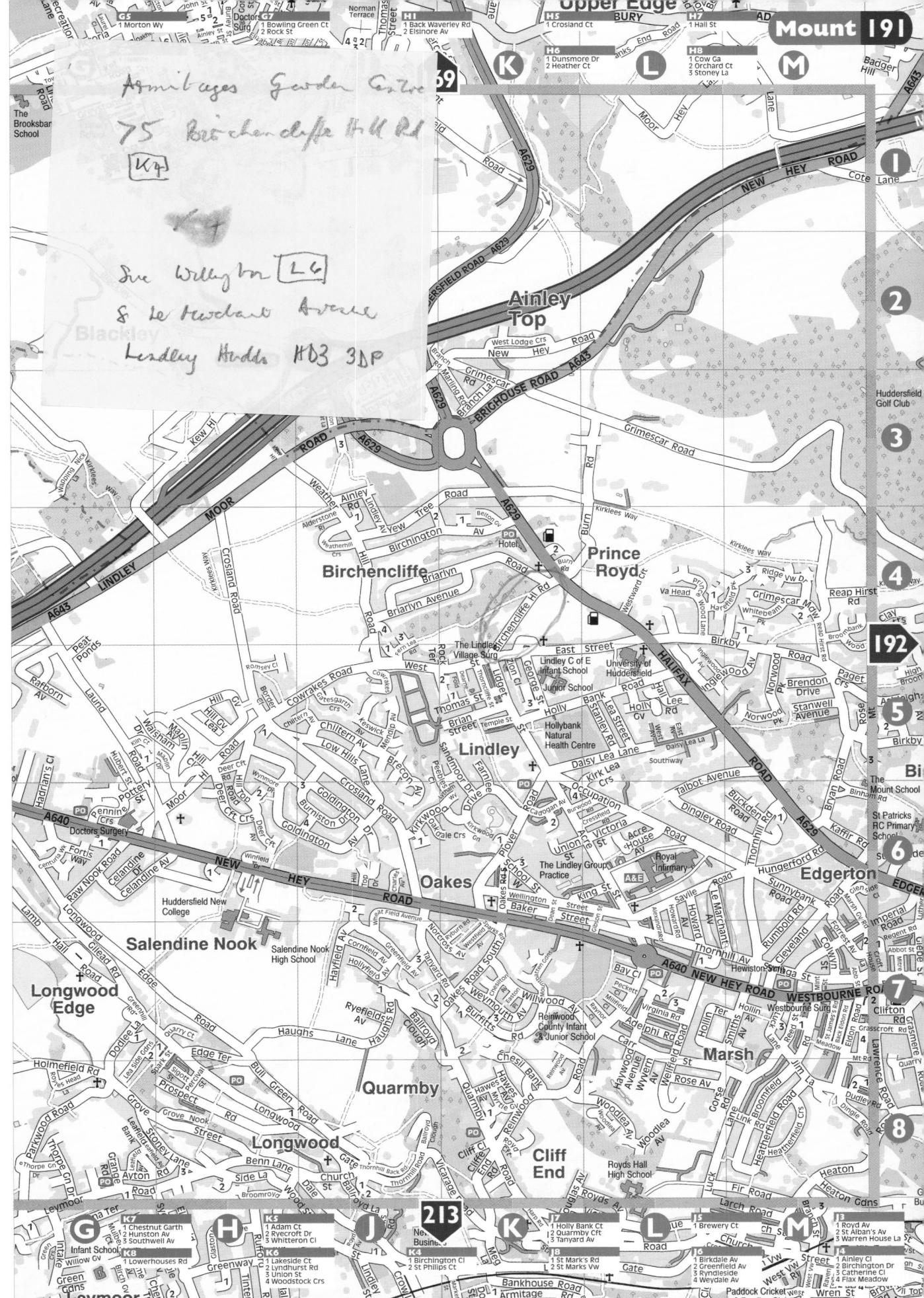

Handwritten note:
Armitages Garden Centre
75 Birchencliffe Hill Rd
K7

Sue Wellington L6
8 La Newland Avenue
Lindley Hudds HD3 3DP

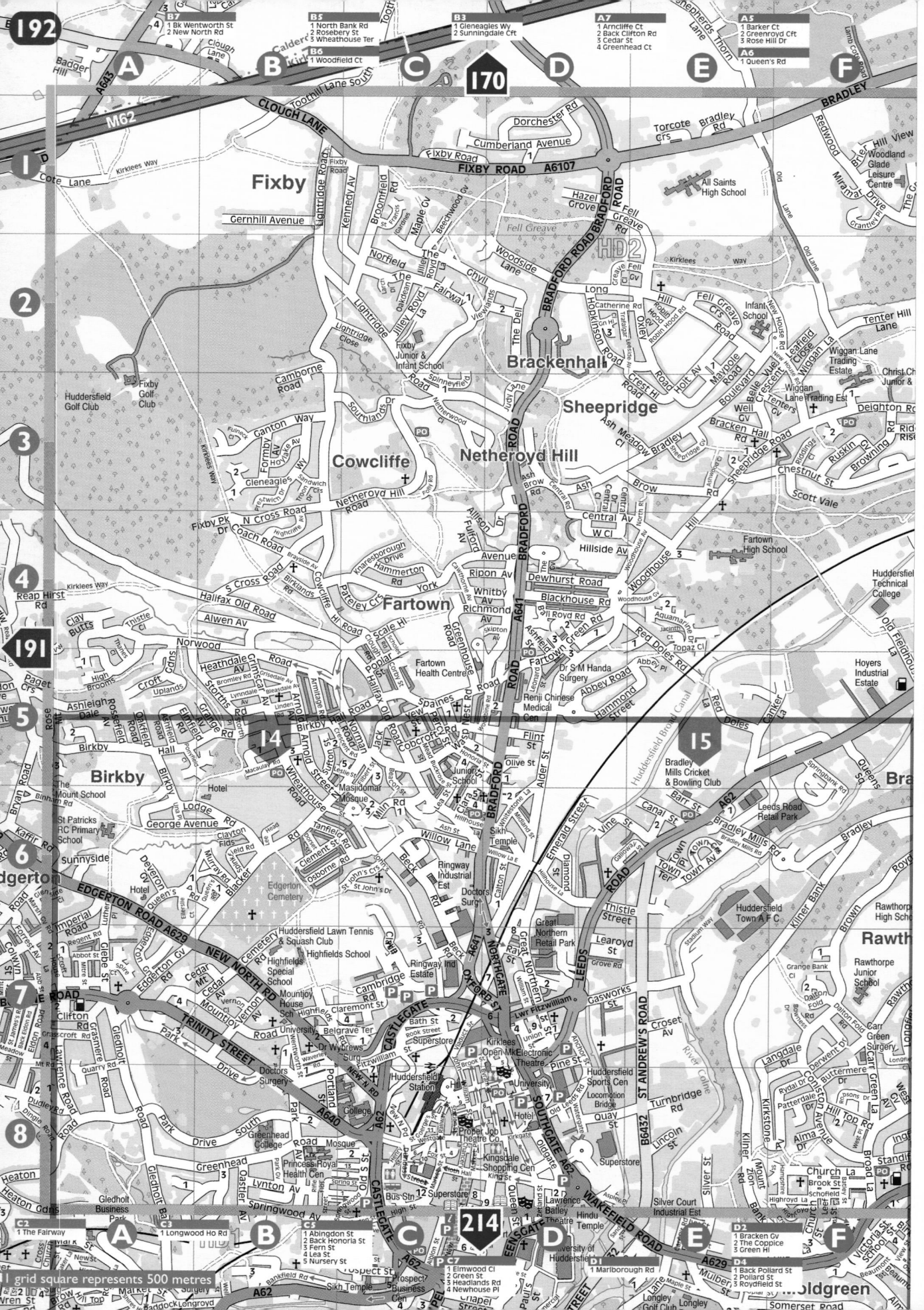

G1
1 The Muirlands
2 Sandringham
3 Sickleholme Ct
4 White Cross

G6
1 Nether Crs
2 Rawthorpe La

G7
1 Dalton Clowes

G8
1 Carmine Cl

H1
1 Copthorne Gdns

H3
1 Churchfields

171

A8, B8, C6, C8
Street Names for these grid squares are listed at the back of the index

D5, D6, D7, D8
Street Names for these grid squares are listed at the back of the index

E2, E3, E4, E6
Street Names for these grid squares are listed at the back of the index

F3, F7, F8, G2
Street Names for these grid squares are listed at the back of the index

H4, H7
Street Names for these grid squares are listed at the back of the index

Bradley

Deighton

Colne Bridge

Upper Heaton

Nab Hill

Kirkheaton

Hill Side

Dalton

Gawthor

Cockley

194

215

G
L6
1 Furnbrook Gdns
2 St Andrews Dr

H
K8
1 Woburn Dr

J

K
J8
1 Cranwood Dr

L
J2
1 Brooklands

M
H8
1 Marlow Cl

K5
1 Glendore Dr

K5
1 Larch Cl
2 Stoney Ford La
3 Willowbank Gv

K4
1 Medway

J7
1 Hever Gv
2 Higson Ct
3 Lincoln Ct
4 Picton Wy

J1
1 Elder La

Greenside

Cow

HD5

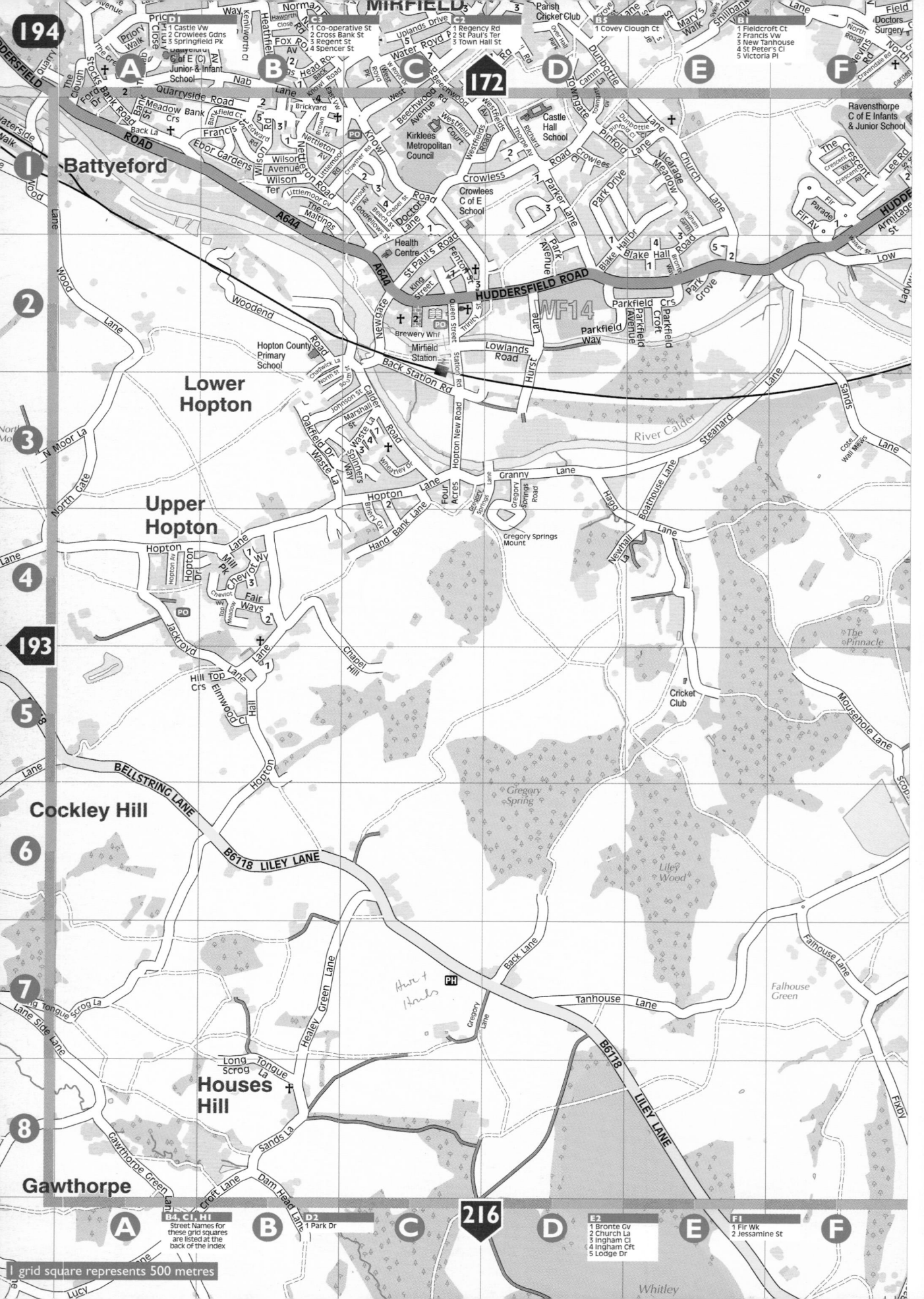

194

MIRFIELD

172

193

216

Battyeford

Lower Hopton

Upper Hopton

Cockley Hill

Houses Hill

Gawthorpe

D1
1 Castle Vw
2 Crowlees Gdns
3 Springfield Pk

C3
1 Co-operative St
2 Cross Bank St
3 Regent St
4 Spencer St

C2
1 Regency Rd
2 St Paul's Ter
3 Town Hall St

B5
1 Covey Clough Ct

B1
1 Fieldcroft Ct
2 Francis Vw
3 New Tanhouse
4 St Peter's Cl
5 Victoria Pl

B4, C1, H1 Street Names for these grid squares are listed at the back of the index

D2
1 Park Dr

E2
1 Bronte Gv
2 Church La
3 Ingham Cl
4 Ingham Cft
5 Lodge Dr

F1
1 Fir Wk
2 Jessamine St

Parish Cricket Club

Kirklees Metropolitan Council

Crowlees C of E School

Castle Hall School

Ravensthorpe C of E Infants & Junior School

Hopton County Primary School

Mirfield Station

River Calder

Gregory Springs Mount

The Pinnacle

Cricket Club

Gregory Spring

Liley Wood

Falhouse Green

WF14

HUDDERSFIELD ROAD

A644

ROAD

Quarryside Road

BELLSTRING LANE

B6718 LILEY LANE

B6718 LILEY LANE

Whitley

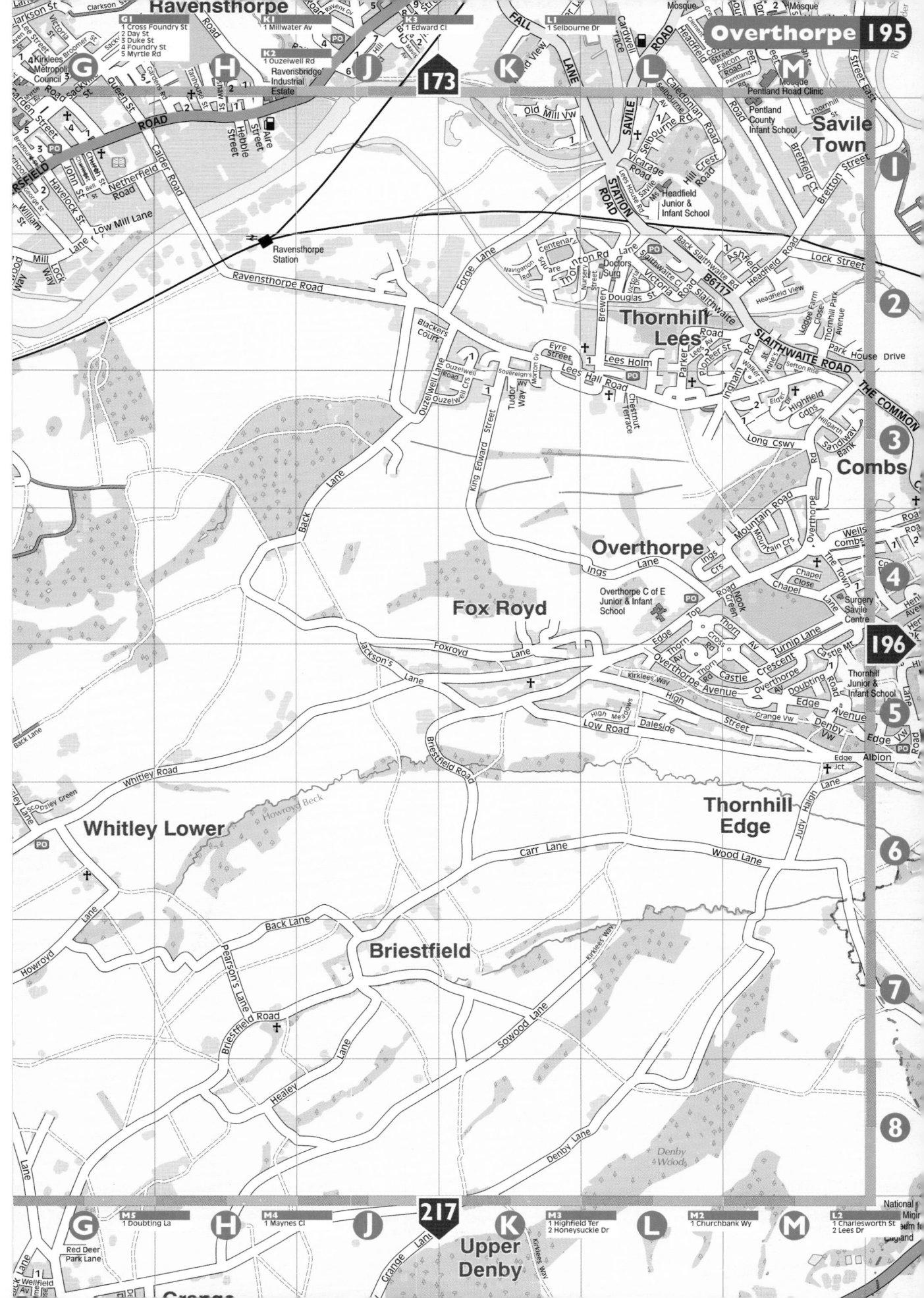

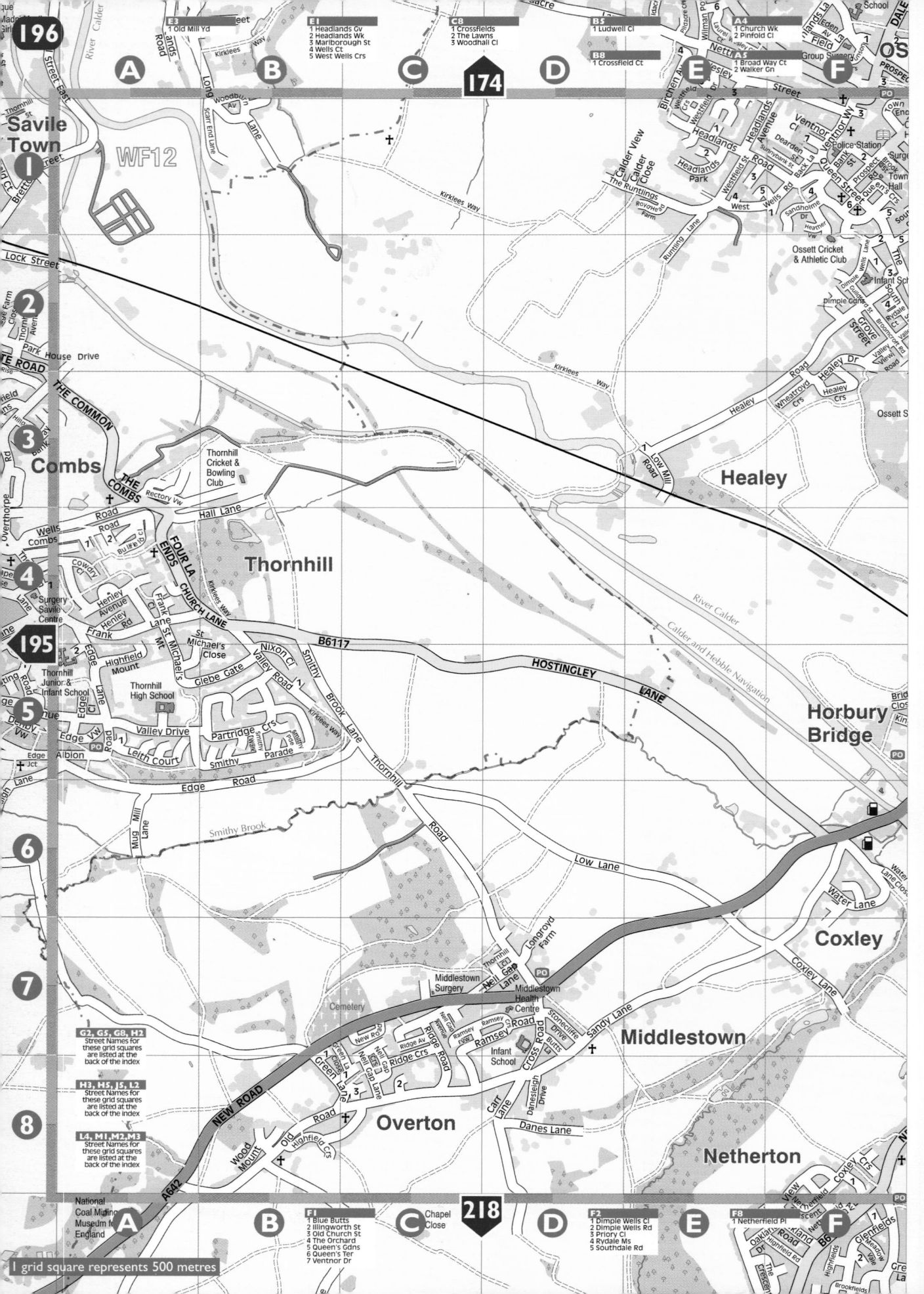

196

174

A   B   C   D   E   F

E3
1 Old Mill Yd

E1
1 Headlands Gv
2 Headlands Wk
3 Marlborough St
4 Wells Ct
5 West Wells Crs

C8
1 Crossfields
2 The Lawns
3 Woodhall Cl

B5
1 Ludwell Cl

B8
1 Crossfield Ct

A4
1 Church Wk
2 Pinfold Cl

A5
1 Broad Way Ct
2 Walker Gn

Savile Town

WF12

1

Lock Street

2

THE COMMON

Combs

3

THE COMBS

Thornhill

4

195

CHURCH LANE

B6117

HOSTINGLEY LANE

Horbury Bridge

Thornhill High School

Thornhill Junior & Infant School

5

Partridge Crs

Edge Road

Smithy Brook

Thornhill Road

Coxley

6

Low Lane

Water Lane

7

G2, G5, G8, H2
Street Names for these grid squares are listed at the back of the index

H3, H5, J5, L2
Street Names for these grid squares are listed at the back of the index

L4, M1, M2, M3
Street Names for these grid squares are listed at the back of the index

Middlestown

Overton

8

NEW ROAD

A642

Netherton

National Coal Mining Museum for England

218

A   B   C   D   E   F

F1
1 Blue Butts
2 Illingworth St
3 Old Church St
4 The Orchard
5 Queen's Gdns
6 Queen's Ter
7 Ventnor Dr

F2
1 Dimple Wells Cl
2 Dimple Wells Rd
3 Priory Cl
4 Rydale Ms
5 Southdale Rd

F8
1 Netherfield Pl

1 grid square represents 500 metres

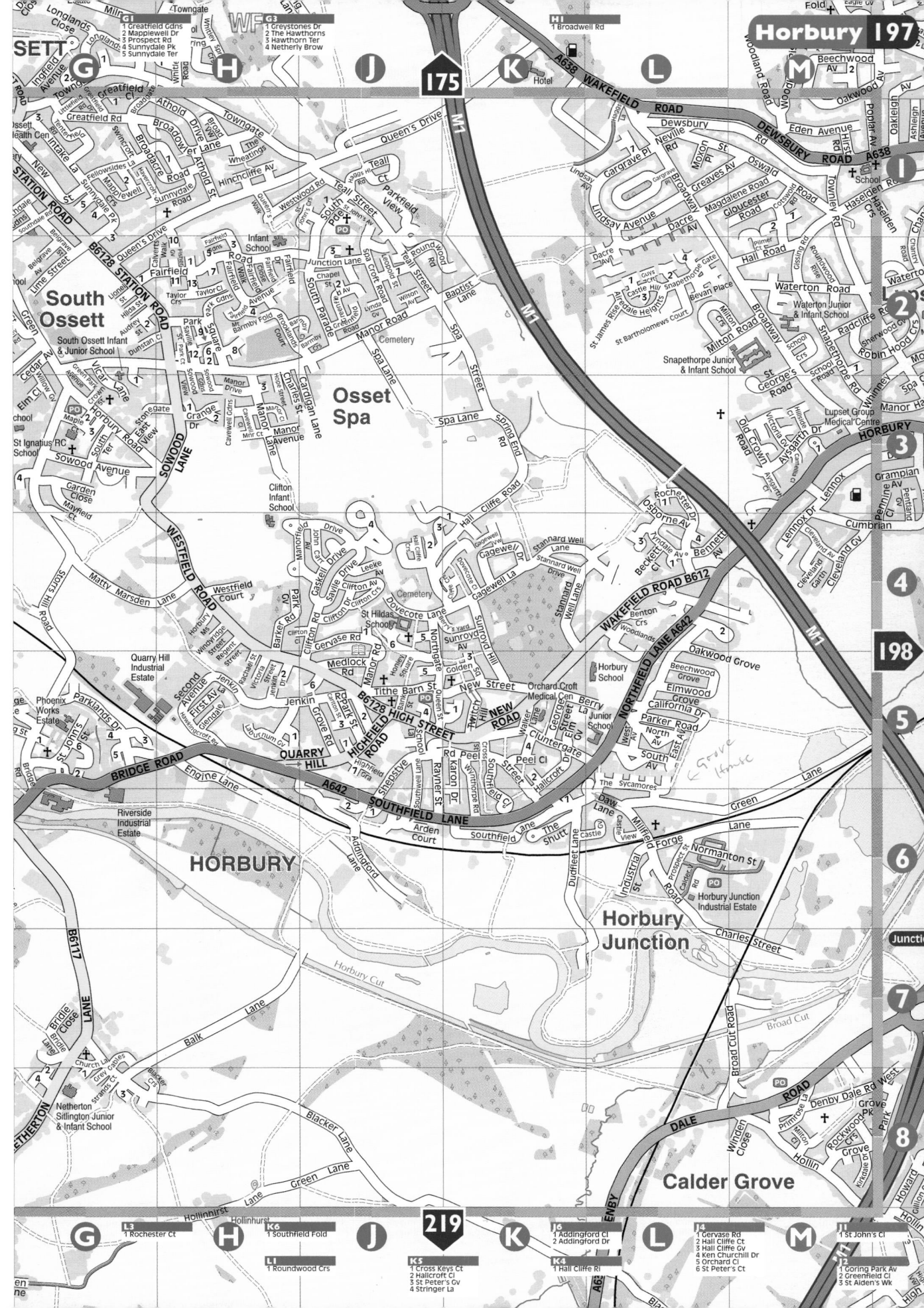

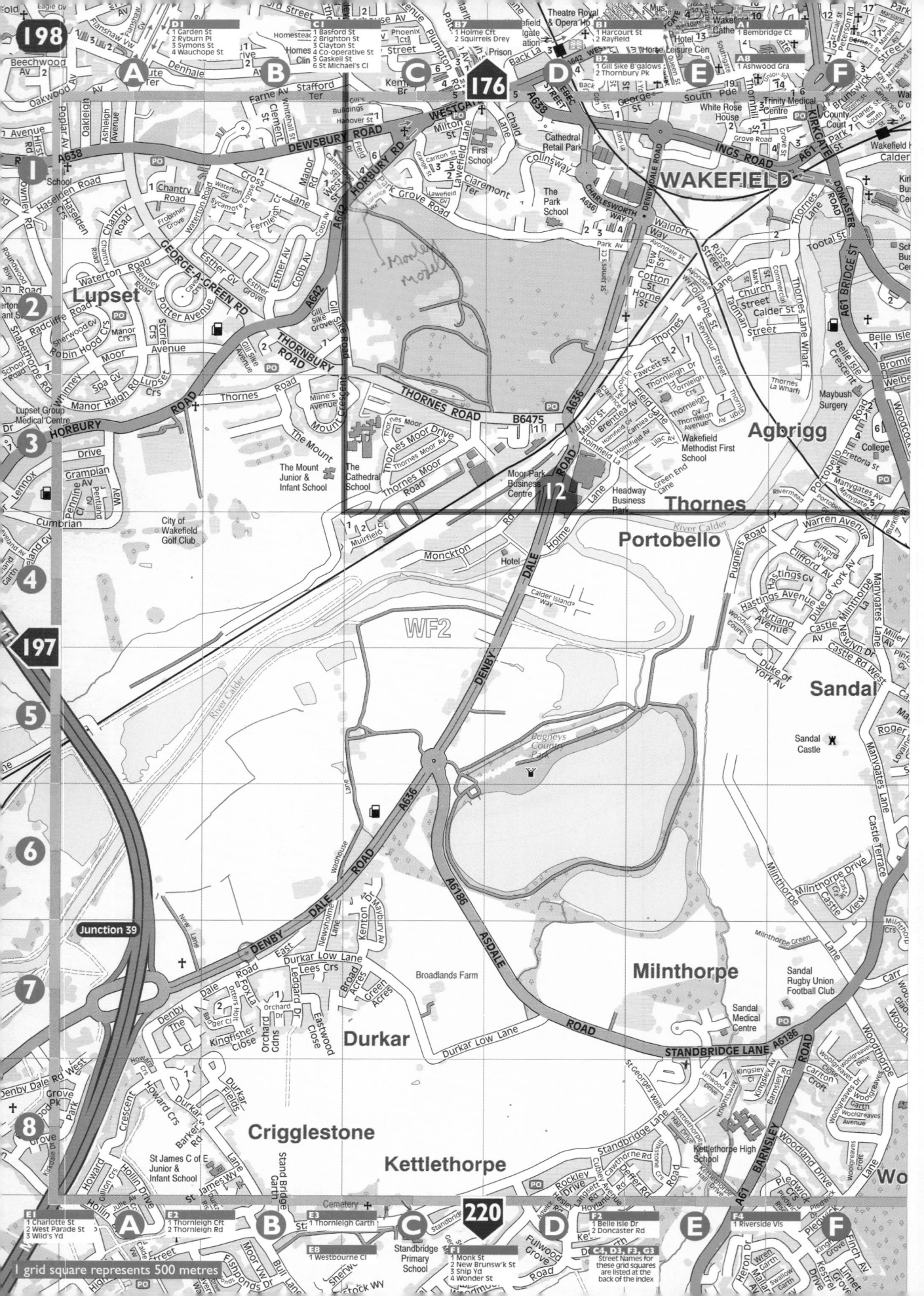

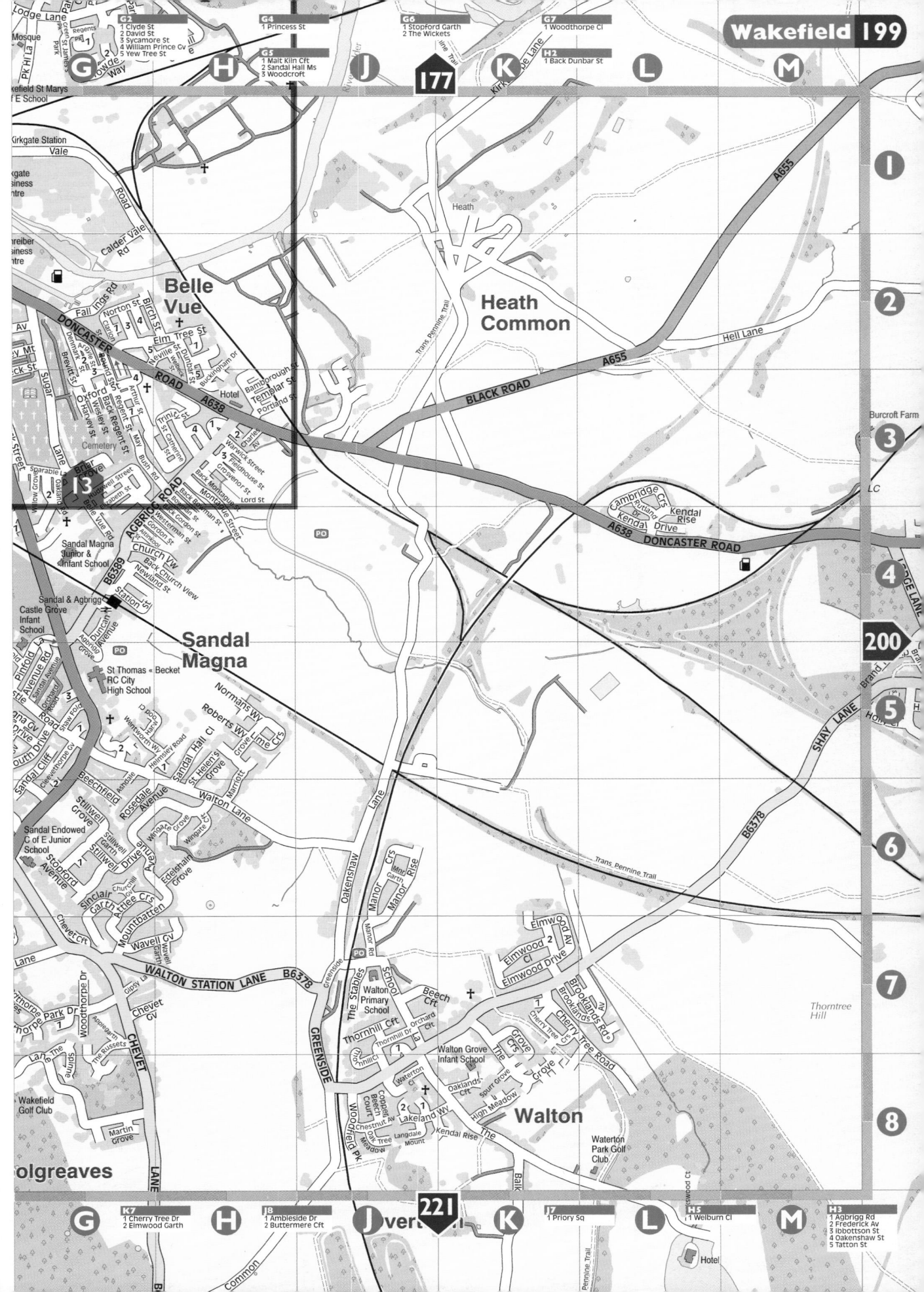

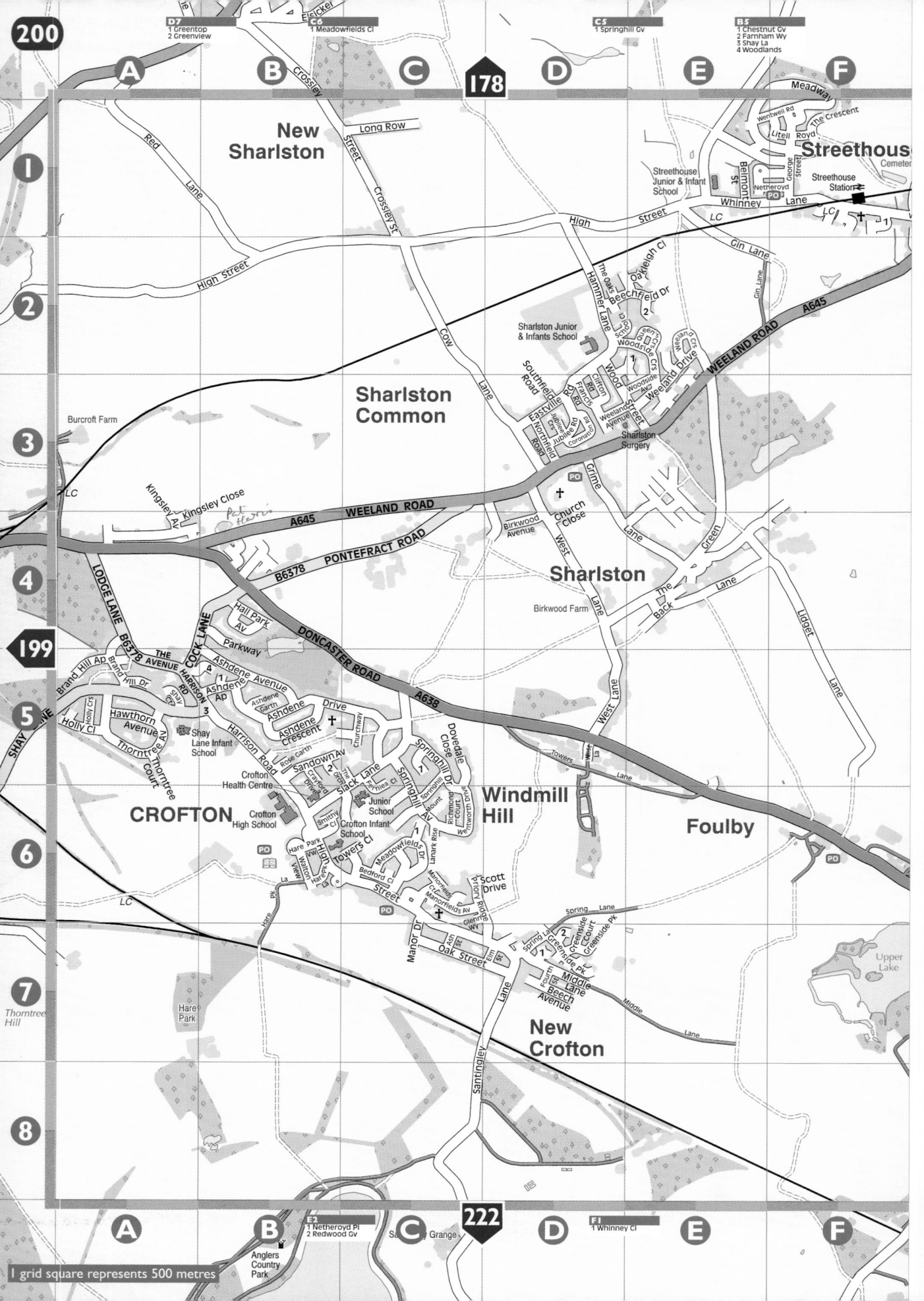

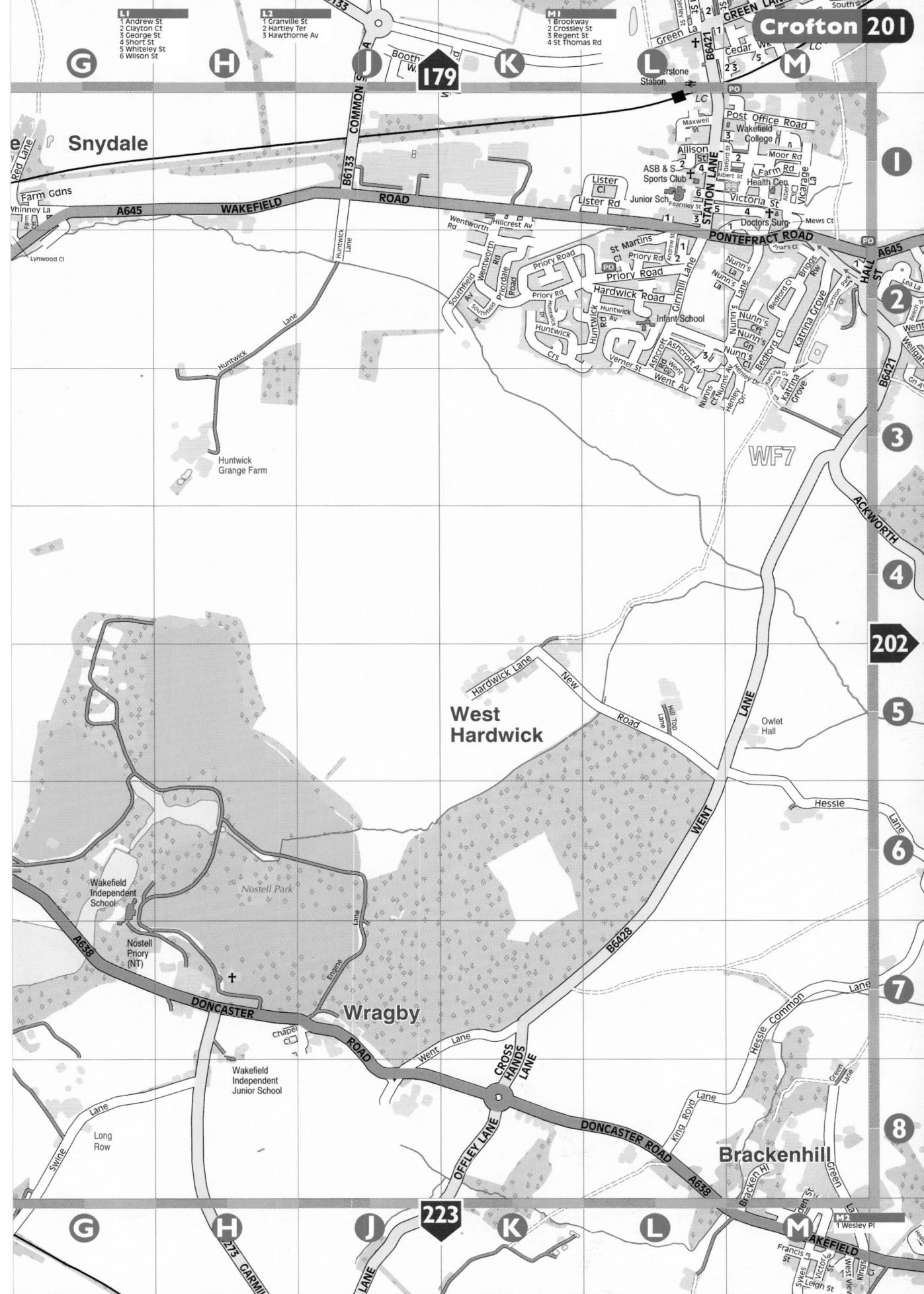

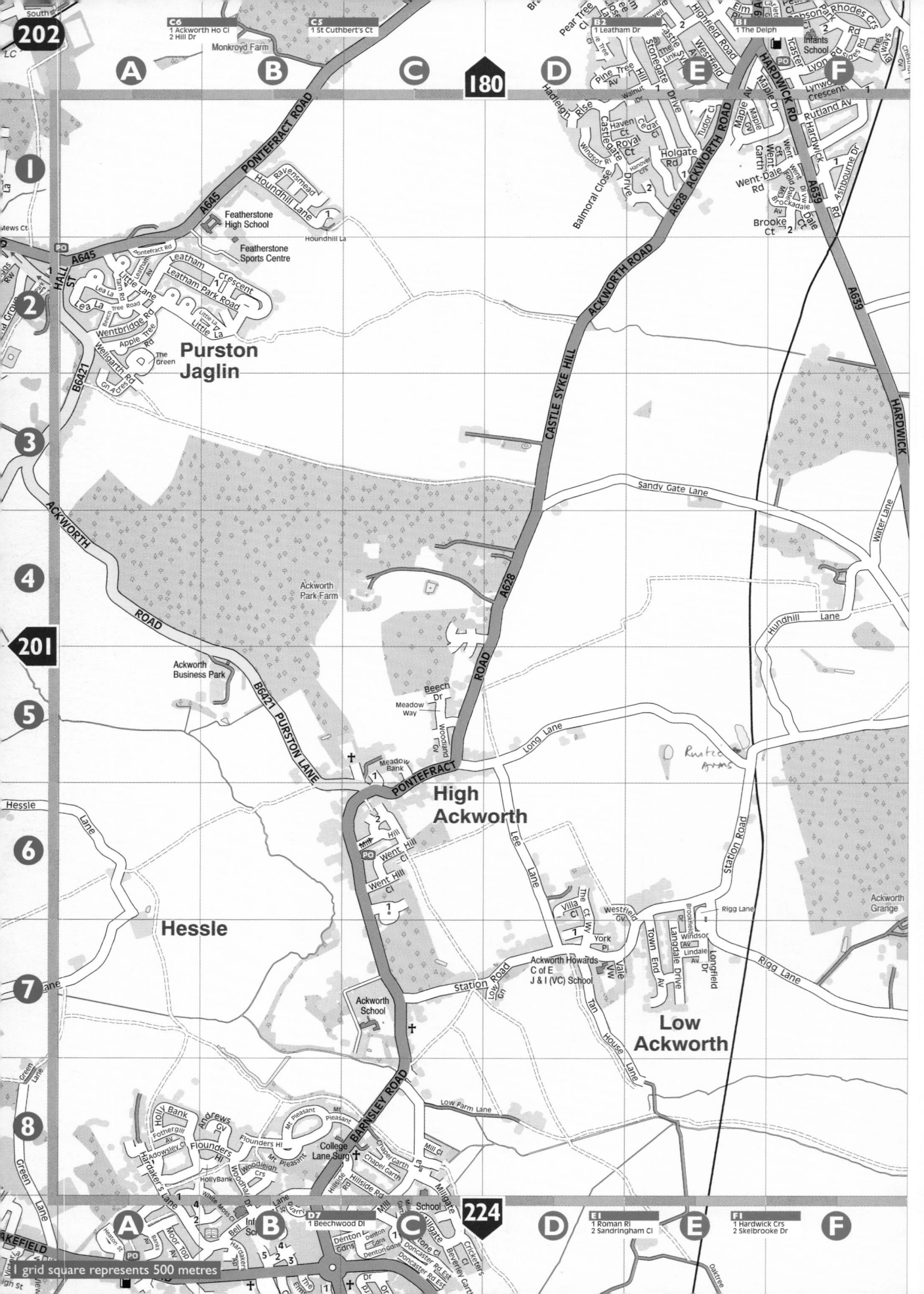

A B C D E F

Wake Wood

Havercroft

Mid York Golf Club

Scrombeck Farm

I

Valley Road

Bank Wood Road

North Lodge Lane

2

Bank Wood

†

3

Stapleton Park Farm

◇

New Road

4

Stapleton Park

Castle Farm

North Yorkshire County
Wakefield

5

A1(T)

6

Jackson's Lane

Leys Lane

Hotel

†

7

River Went

WENT EDGE ROAD B6474   West Edge Road

West Edge Road

A1(T)

8

▽

Kirk Smeaton

Main Street

PO

Pinfold Lane

Kirk Smeaton
C of E
Primary School

Manor Close

A B C D E F

Norton

1 grid square represents 500 metres

G H J K L M

1
2
3
4
5
6
7
8

Spring
Lodge

LC

Grange
Farm

Northfield Lane

Road

Woodhall Lane

Womersley C of E
Primary School

Northfield Close

Cow Lane

Womersley

Cemetery

Main Street

Park Lane

Station Road

LC

Highfield Lane

Fulham Lane

Stocking Green
Farm

Wormesley Park

Churchfield Lane

Smeatley's Lane

Churchfield Lane

Little Lane

Willowbridge Road

Wentdale

stan Valley

Chapel
Lane

Hodge
Lane

**Little
Smeaton**

Water Lane

Springfield Crts

Smeaton Cem

LC

LC

LC

Wentbank House

Tan Lane

G H J K L M

Stubbs 227 Road

183

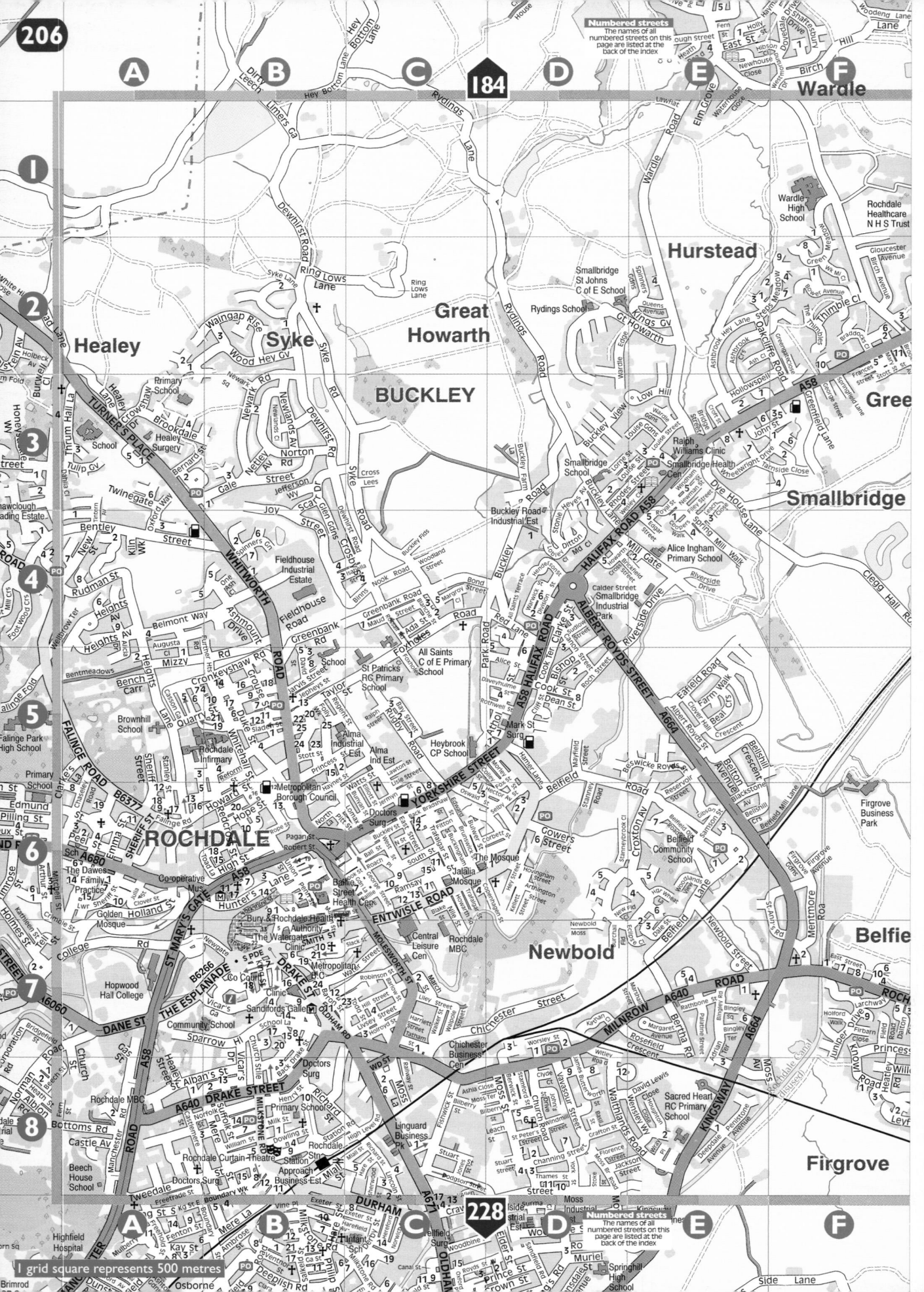

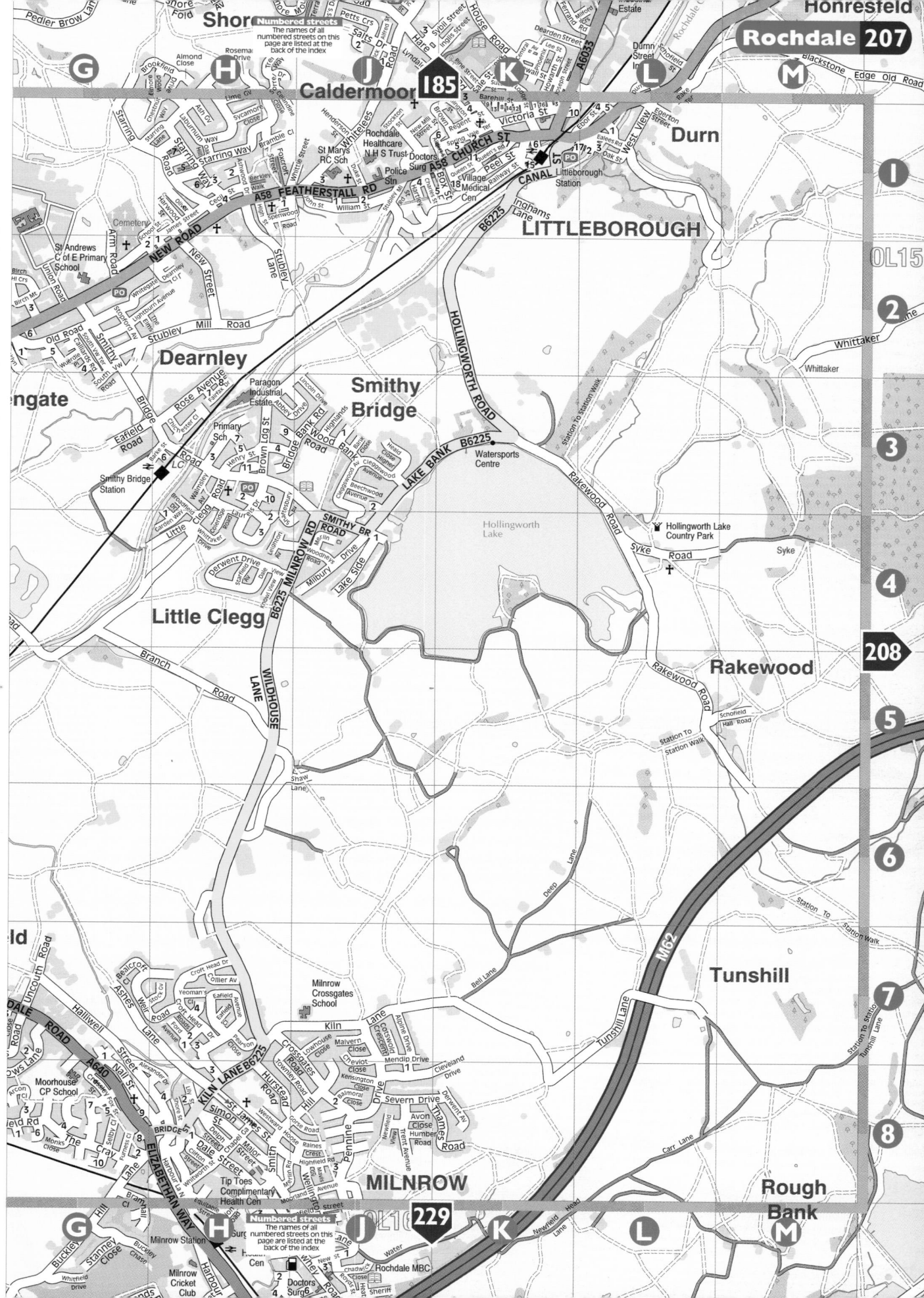

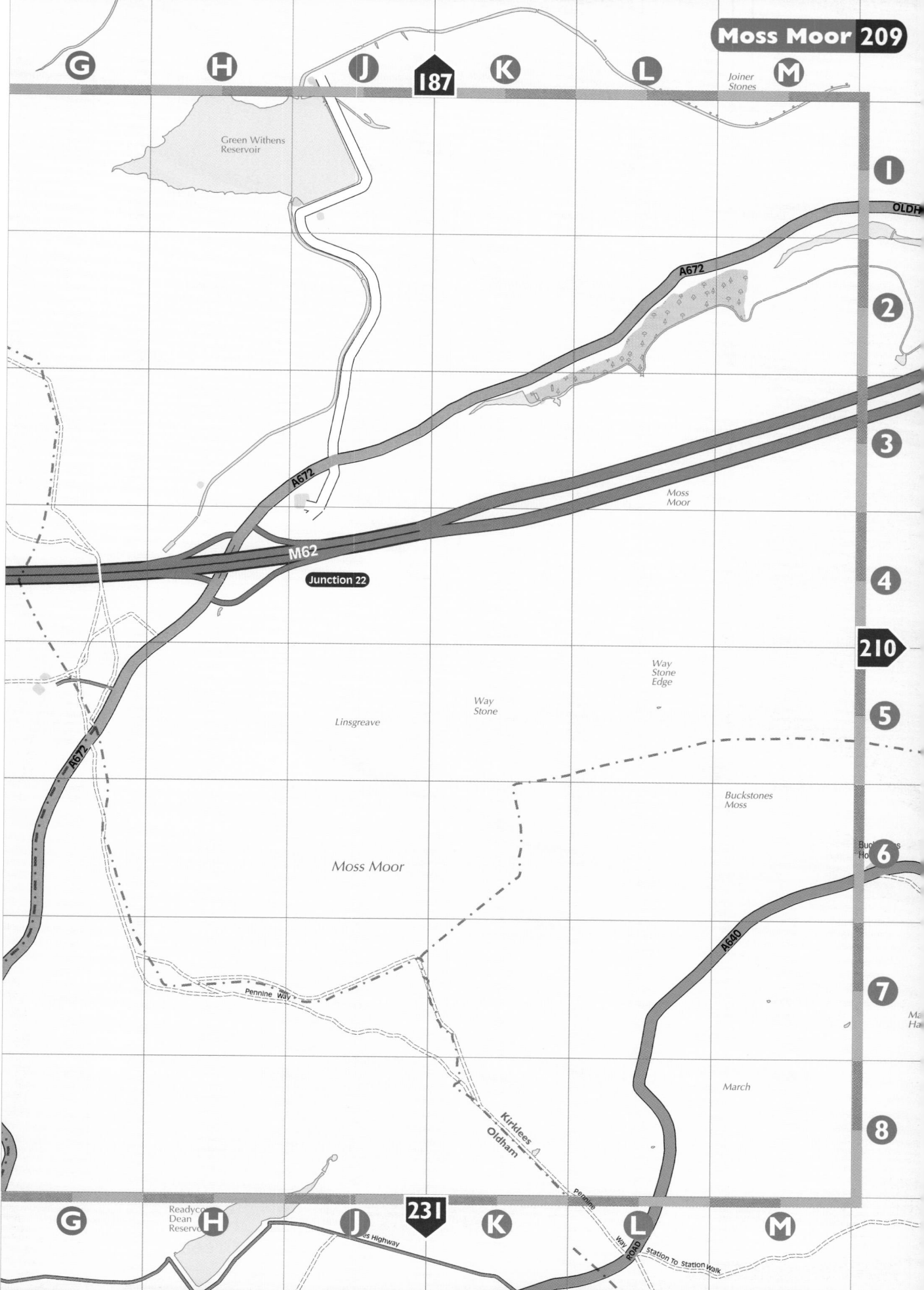

G H J 187 K L M

Joiner
Stones

I

OLDH

A672

2

3

Moss
Moor

4

210

5

Way
Stone
Edge

Way
Stone

Linsgreave

Buckstones
Moss

Buckstones
Ho

6

Moss Moor

A672

A640

Pennine Way

7

Ma
Ha

March

Green Withens
Reservoir

A672

M62

Junction 22

Kirklees
Oldham

Pennine

8

Readyco
Dean
Reservo

G H 231 J K L M

s Highway

WAY ROAD station To Station Walk

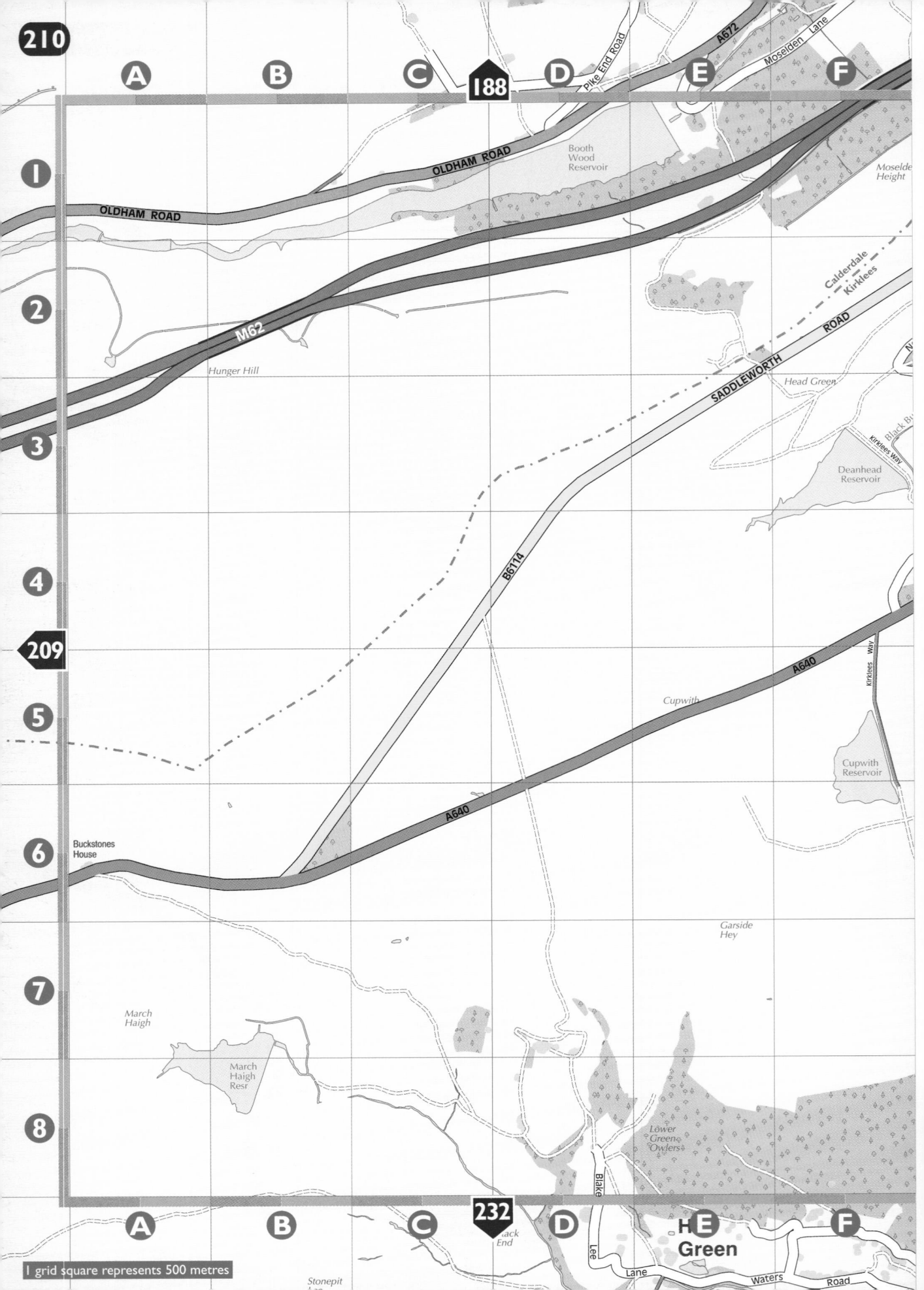

Ⓐ Ⓑ Ⓒ 188 Ⓓ Ⓔ Ⓕ

A672

Pike End Road

Moselden Lane

1

OLDHAM ROAD

Booth Wood Reservoir

Moselden Height

2

OLDHAM ROAD

M62

Hunger Hill

Calderdale

Kirklees

SADDLEWORTH ROAD

Head Green

3

Deanhead Reservoir

Kirklees Way

Black B

N

4

B6114

209

A640

Cupwith

Kirklees Way

5

Cupwith Reservoir

6

Buckstones House

A640

Garside Hey

7

March Haigh

March Haigh Resr

8

Lower Green Owlers

Blake

Ⓐ Ⓑ Ⓒ 232 Ⓓ Ⓔ Ⓕ

ack End

Green

Lee Lane

Waters Road

1 grid square represents 500 metres

Stonepit

Map labels:

M62
M62
M62
189
Chapel
G H J K L M

Croft House Rd
1

Rye Field Lane
Lane West
Rye Rd Lane

Hill Lane
Pinfold Lane
Hey Lane

Church Lane
Lower
Road

Scammonden Water
Cemetery
Pole Gate
Pole Moor
2

Deanhead
A640 NEW HEY ROAD
Pole Gate Branch
Pole
Worts Hill Side
Worts Hill
Worts Hi Lane

B6114
Lane
Kirklees Way
Crimea Lane
3
Moor

Kirklees Way
Scammonden Sailing Club
Laund Road
Side
Sledge Gate
Back
A640
O'wall

Tiding Field Lane
Lane
Burnt Plats Lane
Laund Road
Intake Road
Wilberlee
4
West
Carr Lane
Goat Hill
Colne Valley Circular Wk
Tyas Lane
Wilberlee Junior & Infant School
Lane
212

Bradshaw Lane
Bradshaw
Clough House Lane
Ilfra Head Lon
Longl
5

Slaithwaite Moor
Coal Gate
Scout Lane
North Lane
Follingworth Lane

Colne Valley Circular Walk
New Cl Lane
Scout Lane
Slacks La
Cop Hill
Side
Row La
Lane
Hoime
6
Old Ground
Cop Hill Lane

Shaw Lane
Marsden Lane
Shaw Fields Lane

Drop Clough
Green Lane
Booth Bank
White Hill
Old Lane
MANCHESTER ROAD
7

Marsden Lane
Crow Trees Road
W Slaithwaite Road
Lane

Lingards Wood
Kettle Lane
School Lane
Hollins
8

Park Gate Road
River Colne
A62
Colne Va Circular Wk.
Lingards
B6107

TER ROAD (MAR..

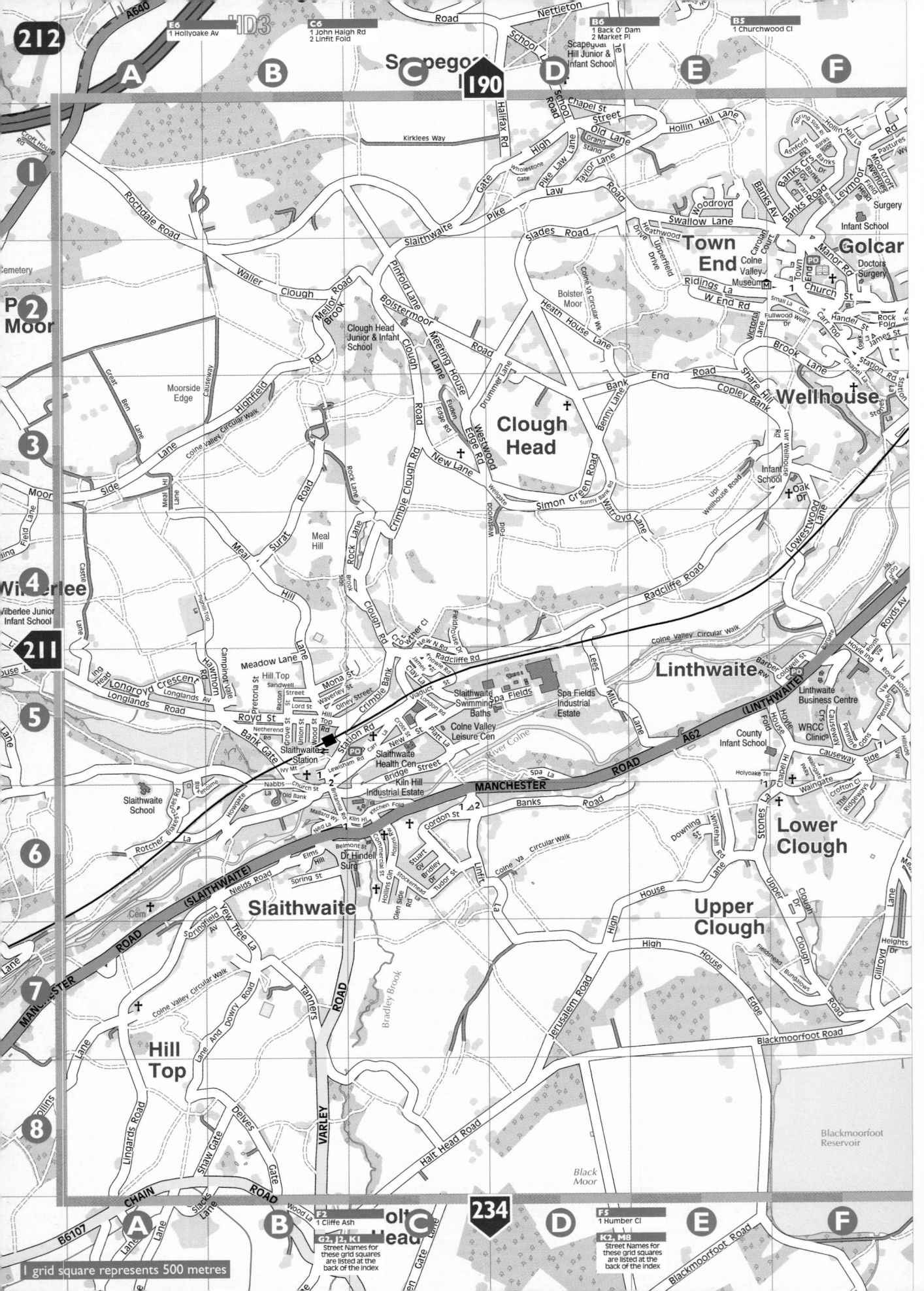

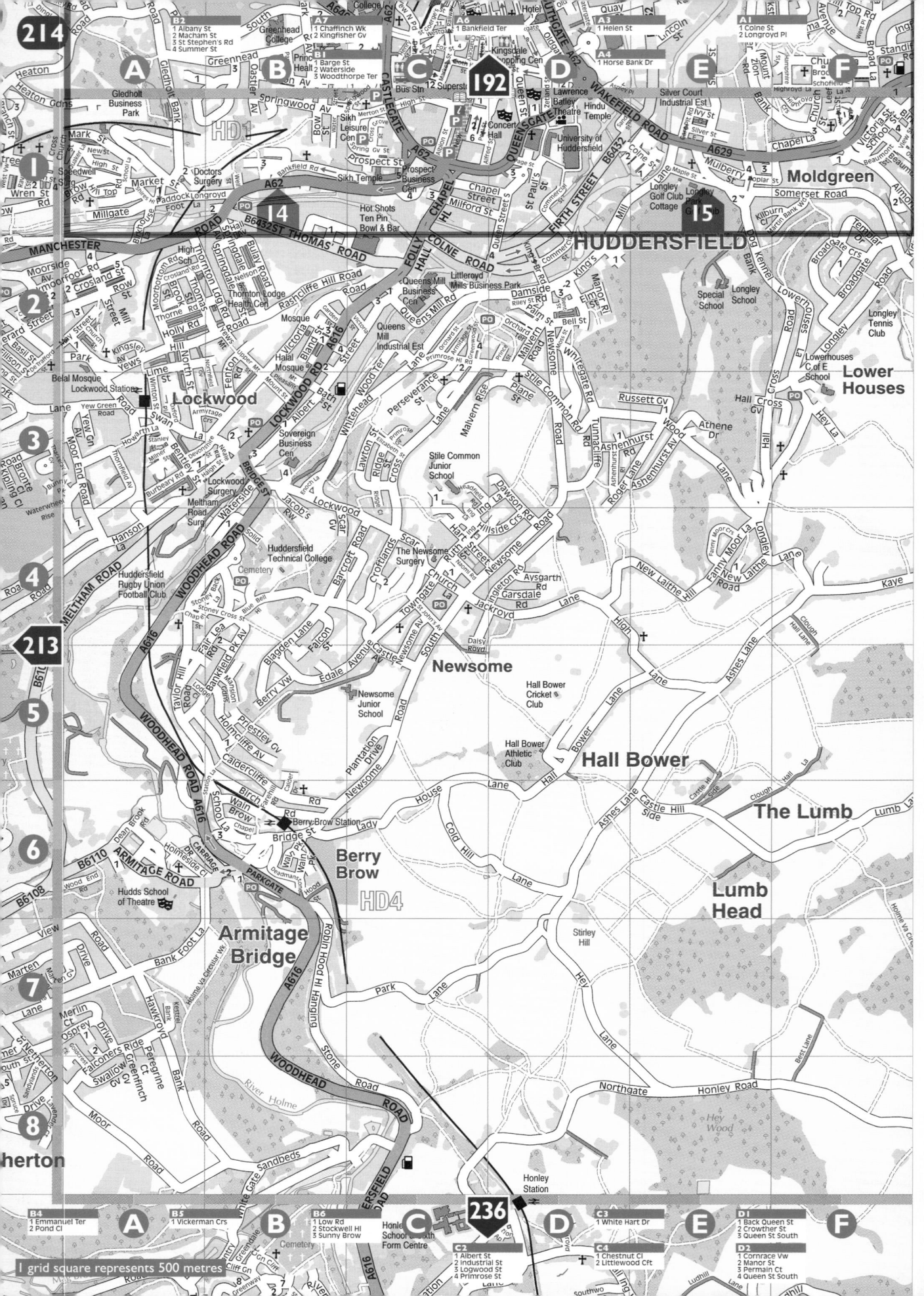

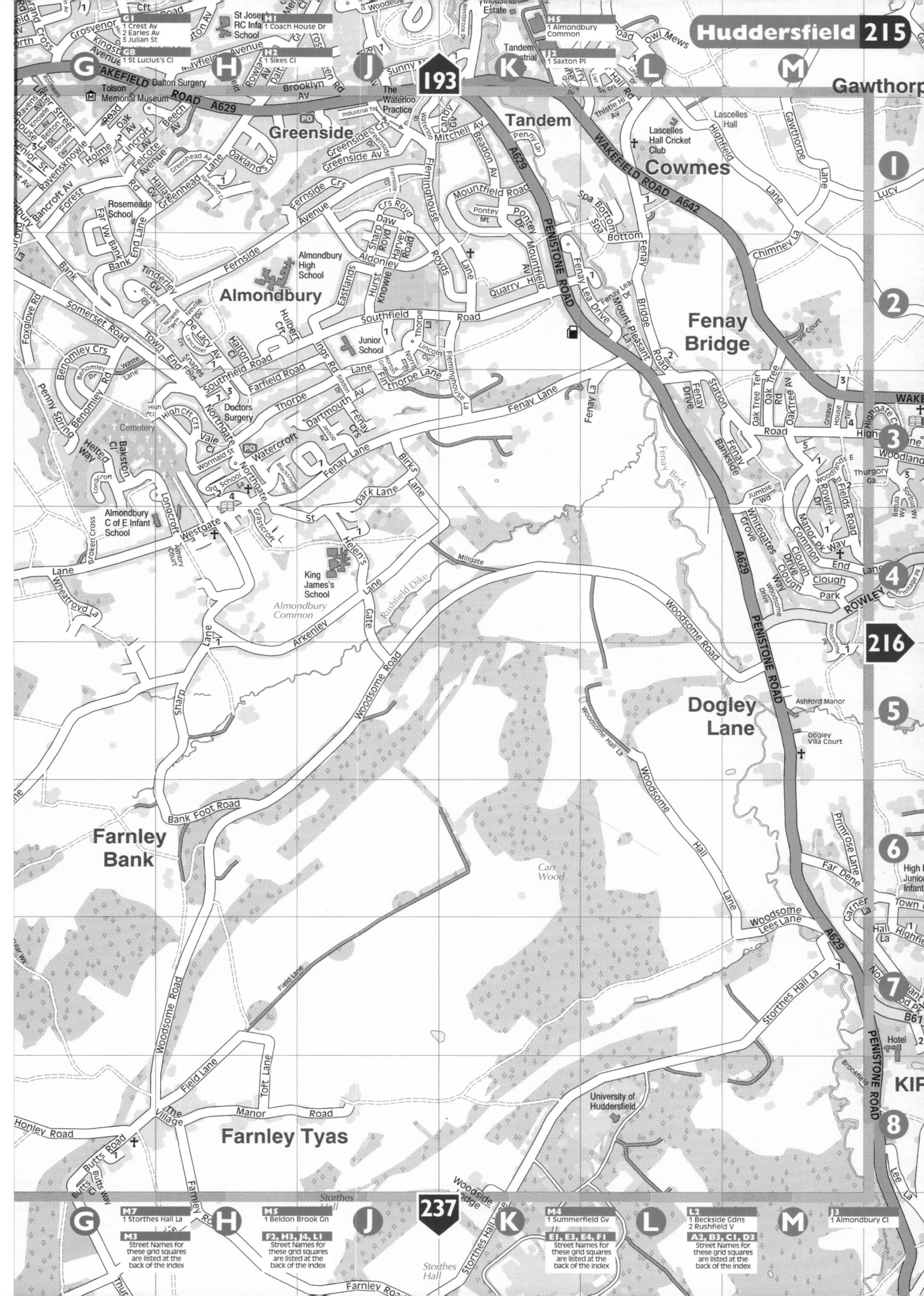

G
1 Crest Av
2 Earles Av
3 Julian St

G8
1 St Lucius's Cl

H1
1 Coach House Dr

H2
1 Sikes Cl

H5
1 Almondbury Common

J2
1 Saxton Pl

G   H   J   193   K   L   M

WAKEFIELD Dalton Surgery
Tolson
Memorial Museum
ROAD A629

The Waterloo
Practice

Greenside

Tandem

Cowmes
Lascelles
Hall Cricket
Club

I

Rosemeade
School

Almondbury
High
School

Almondbury

Fenay
Bridge

2

Junior
School

Cemetery

Doctors
Surgery

Watercroft

PO

3

Almondbury
C of E Infant
School

Rowley

4

King
James's
School

Almondbury
Common

216

Dogley
Lane

Ashford Manor

5

Dogley
Villa Court

Farnley
Bank

Carr
Wood

6

High E
Junior
Infant
Town

7

Hotel

KIF

University of
Huddersfield

Farnley Tyas

8

M7
1 Storthes Hall La

M3
Street Names for
these grid squares
are listed at the
back of the index

M5
1 Beldon Brook Gn

F2, H3, J4, L1
Street Names for
these grid squares
are listed at the
back of the index

M4
1 Summerfield Gv

E1, E3, E4, F1
Street Names for
these grid squares
are listed at the
back of the index

L2
1 Beckside Gdns
2 Rushfield V

A2, B3, C1, D3
Street Names for
these grid squares
are listed at the
back of the index

J3
1 Almondbury Cl

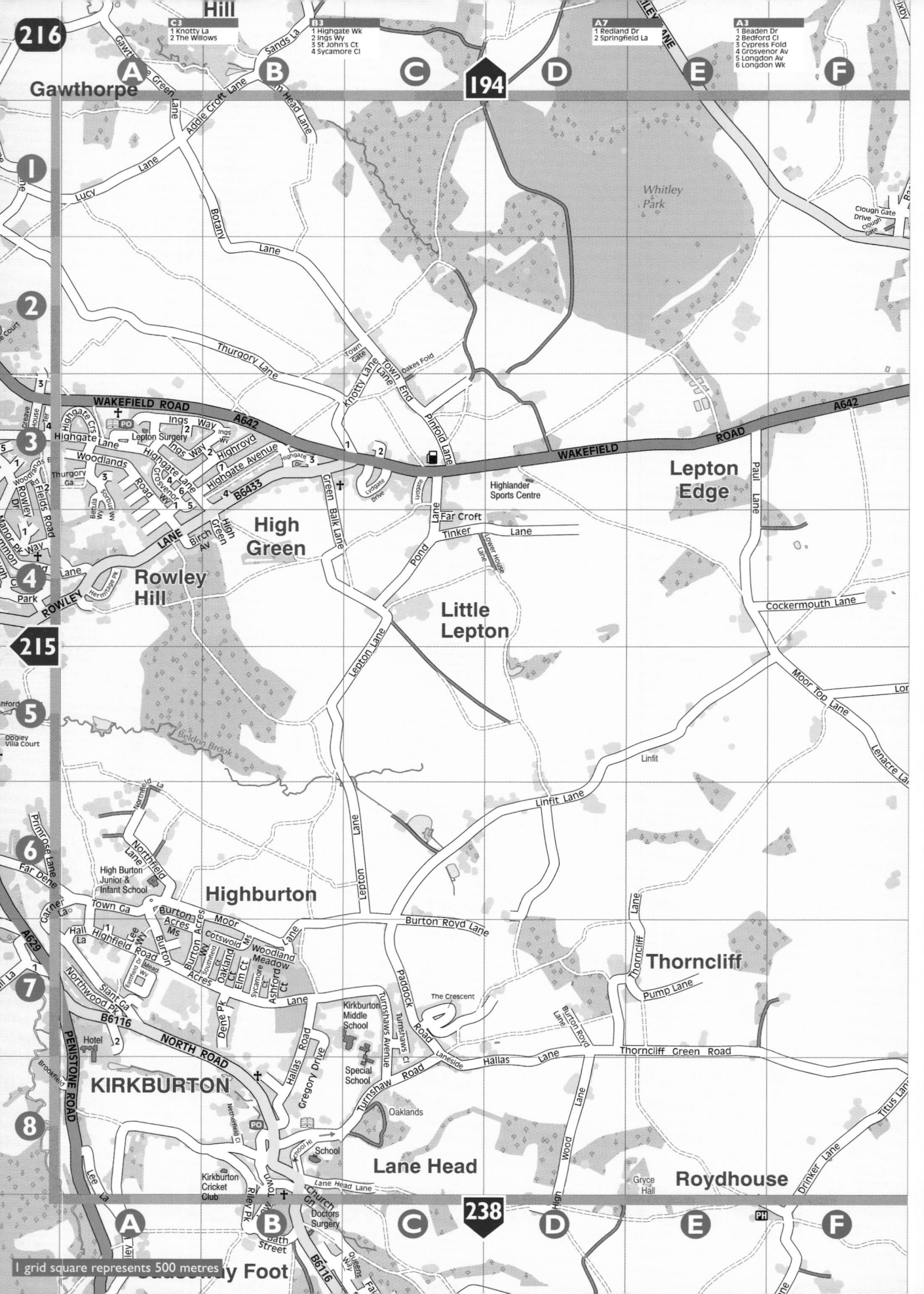

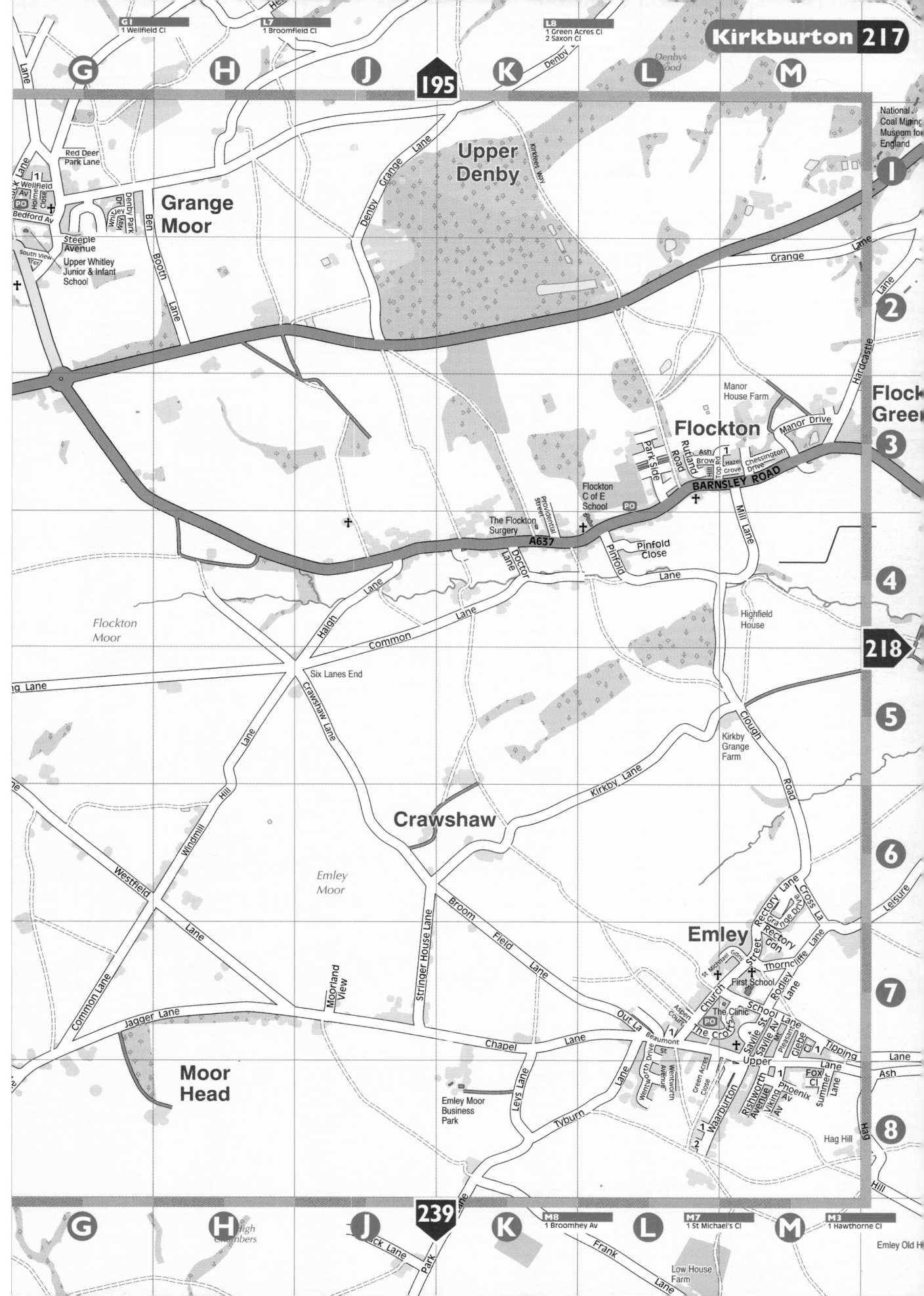

G
H
J
195
K
L
M

National
Coal Mining
Museum for
England

1

Denby

Denby
Wood

**Upper
Denby**

Kirklees Way

Grange Lane

2

**Grange
Moor**

Red Deer
Park Lane

Denby Park

Denby
View

Bedford Av

Steeple
Avenue

Upper Whitley
Junior & Infant
School

South View
Terr

Booth Lane

Ben

Manor
House Farm

Flock
Gree

Flockton

Manor Drive

3

Park Side

Rutland Road

Ash
Brow

Hazel
Grove

Chessington
Drive

Hardcastle

Providential Street

Flockton
C of E
School

PO

BARNSLEY ROAD

Mill Lane

The Flockton
Surgery

A637

Pinfold

Pinfold
Close

Lane

4

Doctor Lane

Highfield
House

**Flockton
Moor**

Haigh Lane

Common

Lane

Six Lanes End

218

Clough Road

Kirby
Grange
Farm

5

Crawshaw Lane

ng Lane

Hill

Kirkby Lane

6

Windmill

Leisure

Westfield

Crawshaw

**Emley
Moor**

Rectory Lane

Cross La

Emley

Grange Dr

Rectory
Gdn

St Michael

Cres

Thorncliffe

First School

Lane

7

Lane

Common Lane

Jagger Lane

Stringer House Lane

Broom

Field

Lane

Moorland
View

Moorland
View

Church Street

School Lane

Rodley Lane

The Clinic

Aspen
Court

The Croft

PO

Savile St

Savile Av

Glebe Cl

Pleasant

Tipping
Lane

Lane

Ash

**Moor
Head**

Chapel

Lane

Levs Lane

Out La

Beaumont
St

Wentworth Drive

Wentworth
Avenue

Green Acres
Close

1

Upper

Waarburton

Rishworth
Avenue

Viking Av

Fox
Cl

Phoenix
Av

Summer
Lane

Hill

Emley Moor
Business
Park

Tyburn

1
2

Hag Hill

8

G
H
High
Chambers
J
239
Jack Lane
K
L
M

Park

Frank

Lane

Low House
Farm

Emley Old H

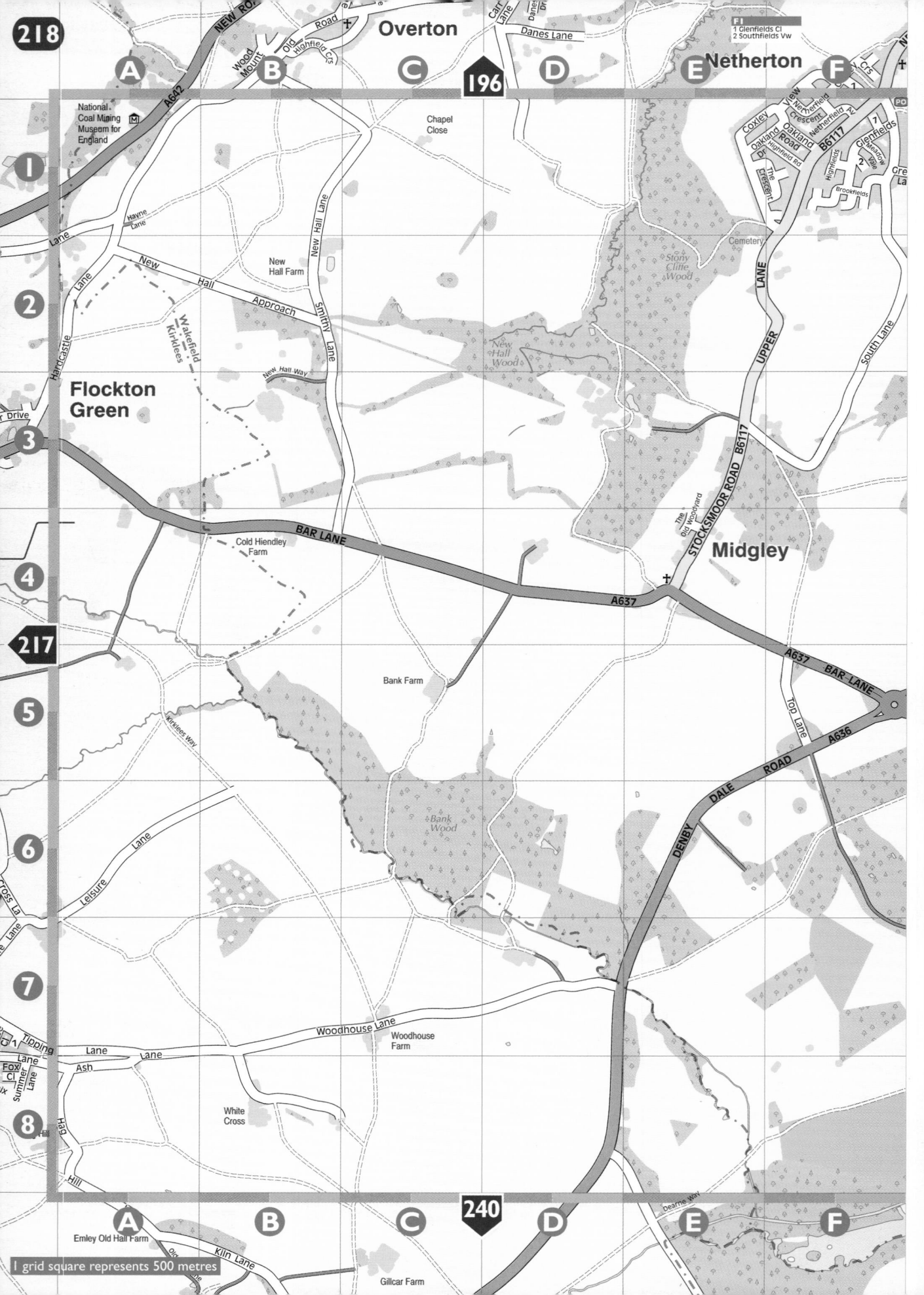

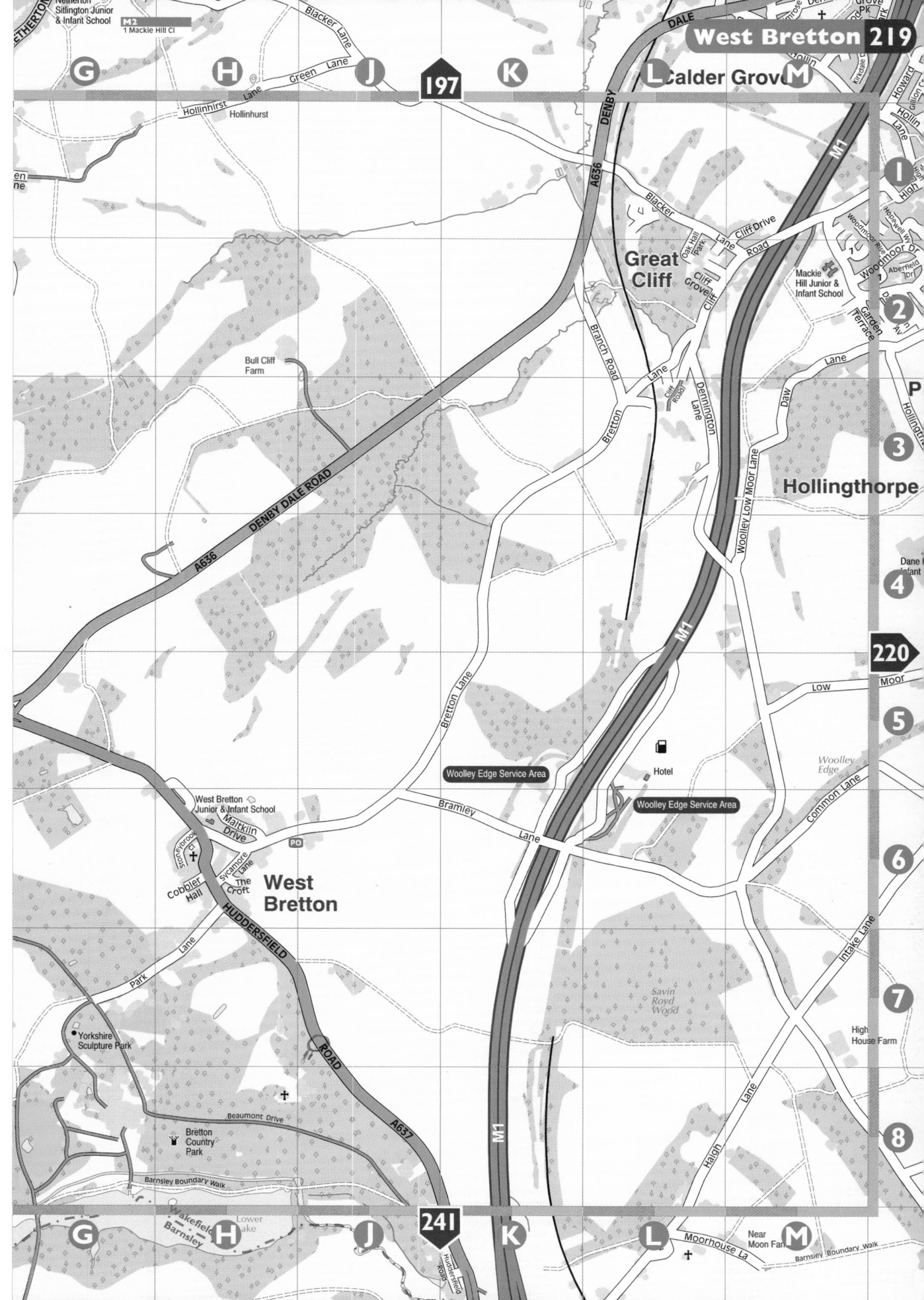

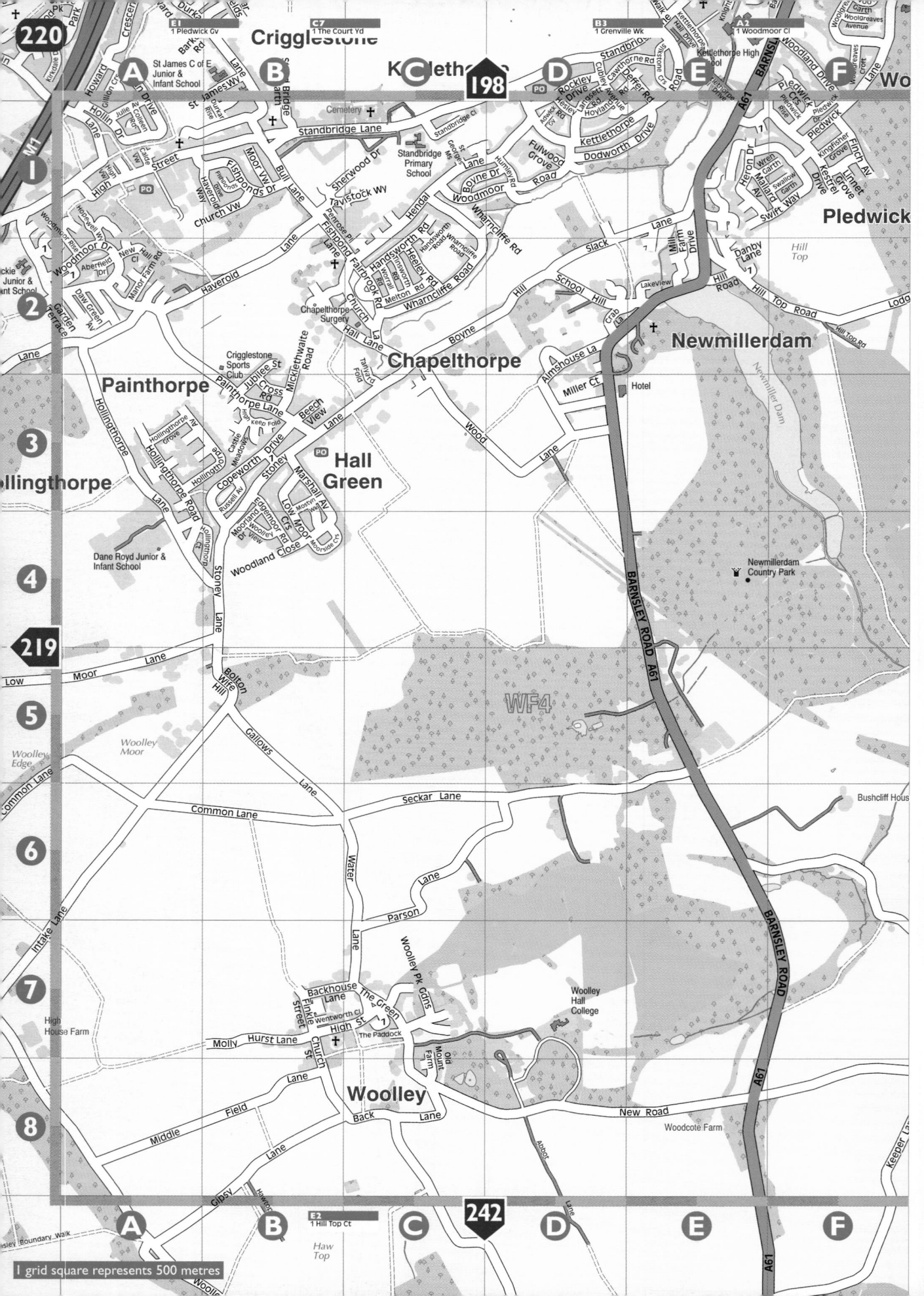

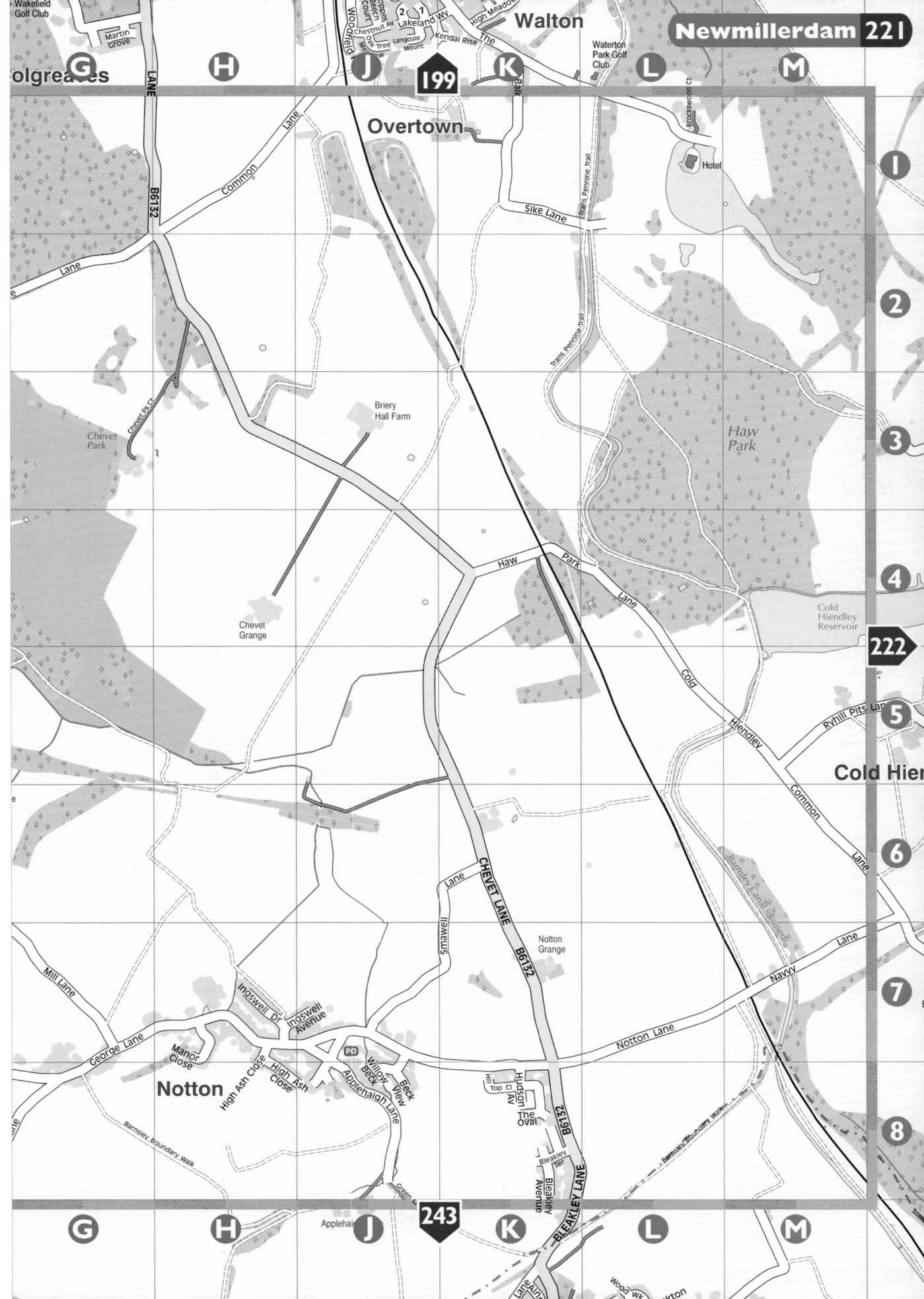

Wakefield
Golf Club

Martin
Grove

olgreaves

G

H

J

199

K

L

M

I

2

3

4

222

5

6

7

8

Walton

Waterton
Park Golf
Club

Brockswood Ct

Hotel

Lakeland Wy

Kendal Rise

The

Balk

High Meadow

Overtown

Sike Lane

Trans Pennine Trail

Trans Pennine Trail

Haw
Park

Cold
Hiendley
Reservoir

Ryhill Pits Lane

Cold Hien

Chevet
Park

Chevet Pk Ct

Briery
Hall Farm

Haw

Park

Lane

Cold

Hiendley

Common

Lane

Cold Hier

Chevet
Grange

B6132

Common

Lane

Lane

Lane

Barnsley Canal (disused)

Navvy

Lane

Mill Lane

Smawell

Lane

CHEVET LANE

B6132

Notton
Grange

Notton Lane

George Lane

Ingswell Dr

Ingswell
Avenue

Manor
Close

High Ash Close

High Ash
Close

PO

Willow
View

Beck

Applehaigh Lane

Back

Hill
Top Cl

Hudson
Av

The
Oval

B6132

Bleakley
Ter

Bleakley
Avenue

Barnsley Boundary Walk

Notton

Barnsley Boundary Walk

Green La

Applehai

G

H

J

243

K

BLEAKLEY LANE

Lane

L

M

Wood Wk

kton

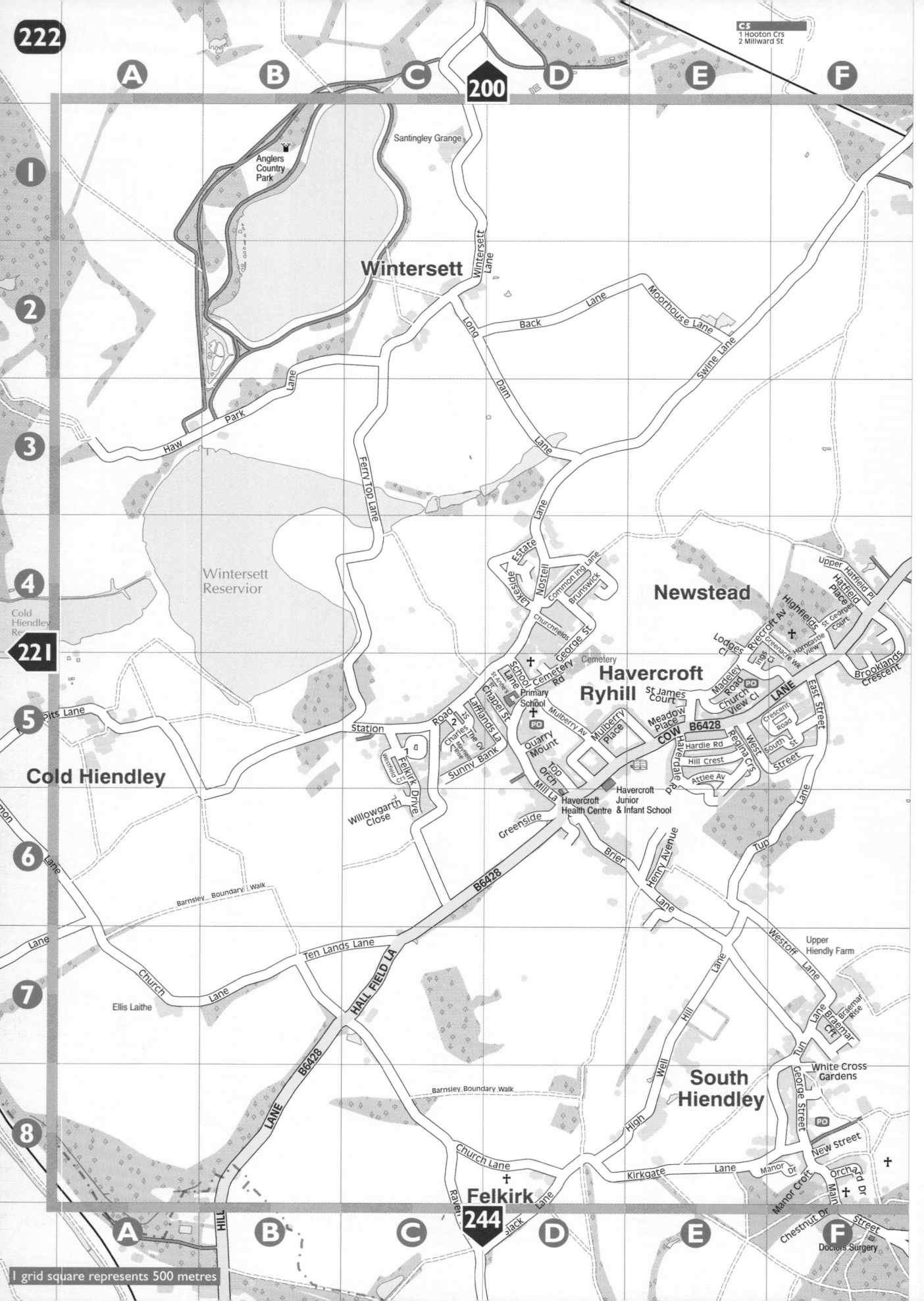

C.5
1 Hooton Crs
2 Millward St

A   B   C   200   D   E   F

I

Santingley Grange

Anglers
Country
Park

Wintersett

Wintersett Lane

2   Back   Lane   Moorhouse Lane

Long   Dam   Swine Lane

3   Haw   Park   Lane   Lane

Ferry Top Lane

Wintersett
Reservior

4   Newstead
Cold
Hiendley   Highfields   Hatfield
Re   Place
221
                                    Cemetery   Ryecroft Av   St Georges
                                                   Lodges   Court
                          Churchfields   Ct   Greenacre Hornsastle
5   Pits Lane   George St   View
Cold Hiendley   Station   Road   Havercroft   Madeley   Church   Crescent   East Street
                                  Laithlands La   Ryhill   Place   View Cl   Road   Brooklands
                        Felkirk Drive   St James   B6428   South   Street   Crescent
                        Westfield Cl Sunny Bank   Court   Meadow   Hardie Rd   West   St
                                  Charles The Cl   Mulberry Av Place COW   Hill Crest   Regina Ct
                                  St   Quarry   Mulberry   Haverdale   Attlee Av
                        Willowgarth   Mount   Place
                        Close   Top   Mill La   Havercroft
                                        Orch   Health Centre   Havercroft
6   Greenside   Junior
                                                              & Infant School   Tup
                    Barnsley Boundary Walk   B6428   Brier   Henry Avenue   Lane
                                                                      Lane
Lane   Westoff   Upper
                    Ten Lands Lane   Hill   Lane   Hiendly Farm
7   Lane   Braemar
    Lane   Church   Lane   Well   Ct   Braemar
    Ellis Laithe   High   George   Rise
                    HALL FIELD LA   South   Street   White Cross
                                                                                         Hiendley   Gardens
                    B6428   PO   New Street
8   Manor Croft
                    LANE   Kirkgate   Lane   Manor Dr   Orchard Dr
                    HILL   Church Lane   Main   Chestnut Dr   Street
                                    Felkirk   Doctors Surgery
A   B   C   244   D   E   F

G H J 201 K L M

1 Farmfield Dr
2 Hill Top
3 Meadowfield Cl

J4
1 West Moor Rd

K3
1 Hill Top Cl
2 Rockingham St

Long
Row
Swine Lane

B6273 GARMIL HEAD LANE
HEMSWORTH LANE

LANE Ends CI

WAKEFIELD
A638

King Royd
STER ROAD

Francis St
Sykes
Dicky
Victor's
Leigh St
West View
West St
Carden La
Heaton St
Bracken Hi
Green
Lane

1

ACKW
MOO

2

B6428

NEWSTEAD LANE

Second Avenue
Central Av
First Av
Ella St
Catherine St
Elward Av
Annie St

Hemsworth
Fitzwilliam
School

Priory
Business
Park

Rose Lane

3

Fitzwilliam

PO

Lynwood Crs
Newall Crs
Newstead Tce
Albion St
Newstead Dr
Sunny Bank
Newstead Av

Railway Terrace
Duke St
Earl St
Wentworth Terrace

Athletic
Club

4

NEWSTEAD LANE

Carr Lane

WAKEFIELD ROAD

Fitzwilliam Station

Kinsley
Common

Hoyle Road

Mill Road

224

Forrester Cl
Farm Lane
Common Rd
Common Cft
Kinsley House Crs
Oakwell Cl
Wood Cl
Briar Bank
Beech Grove
Chantry
Carrgate
Mont Cl
Kinsley Close
Fieldhead Road
Milton Dr
Redland Crs

Ashmount
Ind Park

Mill Road

5

Kinsley

Brownhill
Crs
Tombridge Crs
Kinsley St
Gorton Street
Fitzwilliam St
Vale Rd
Park Rd
Inns Rd
Kings Ct
PO
Ford St
New St

Hoyle
Kinsley
Industrial
Estate

B6273

6

WAKEFIELD ROAD

Springvale
North Wk
Rise
Hegford
Dorset
Sussex
Woodla

Cemetery

Cemetery Road
St Helen's Av
Lodge St
Centre
Holly
Mayfair Pl

Wakefield Metropolitan
District Council

Garth Rectory
Cross

7

HEMSWORTH

Sandygate Lane
Holgate Pl
Wortley Pl
Westgate
Holgate Crs
Top St
Town St
West St
Regent St
Westcroft Rd
Westfield Road
Barnsley Rd
Hollins Mt
Orangeway
Grove Rd
Marton Av
Beechwood Crs
Beck St
Plimsoll St
Lilley St
Hemsworth
Town Council
PO
Hemsworth
Infant
School

Becca
House
Surg

Springstone Av
Ridgestone Av
Valestone Av
Cottam

MARKET ST

Everdale Mt
Bronte Dv
Mill Vw
Gargrave
Moorhutt Road
Moorfield
Highfield
Clifton Street
Ferndale Pl
Craven Rd
Hamel Rise
Roselili Road
Bullenshaw Rd

Grove

8

PO

Vissitt
Manor

Vissitt La

Northgate
Southgate
Wood Street
Havercroft Rd
James St
High Street
Street
East St
Bridle La
Nelly
Regent St
West St

ROBIN Lane

245

SOUTH ROAD
B6273
Carr Road
Moor Field Road
Greenfield Rd
Willow Cl
Burntwood Bank
Meadow Croft

G H J 245 K L M

G
M7
1 Pear Tree La
M8
1 Beechwood Mt
2 Hawthorne Av

H
L8
1 Hawthorne Crs
2 Highfield Pl
3 Lime Tree Ct Ct
4 Marton Av

J

K
L7
1 Brettegate
2 Lacy St
3 Old Mill Cl

L
K5
1 Hazelwood Rd
2 Tombridge Crs

M
K4
1 Green Cft

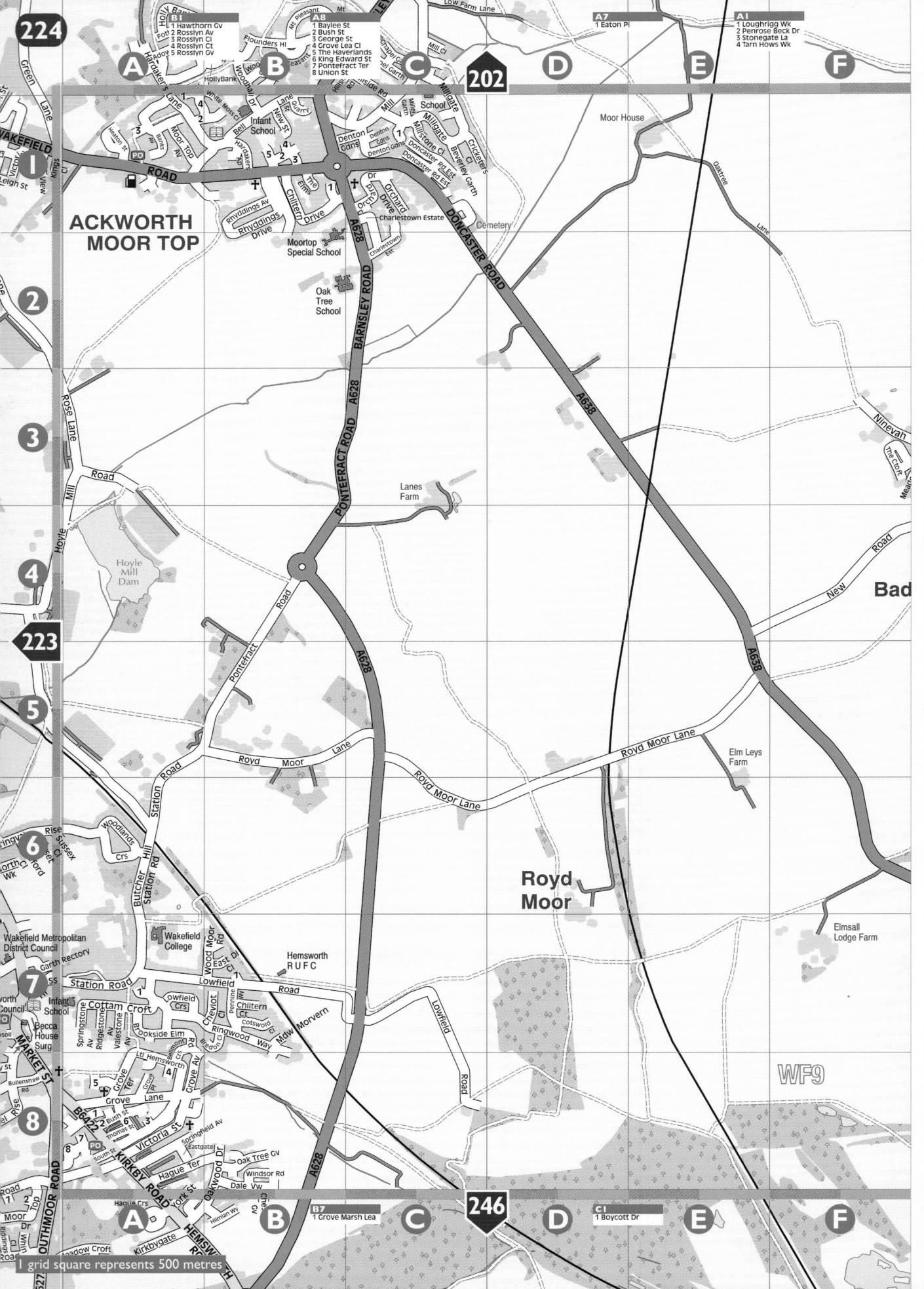

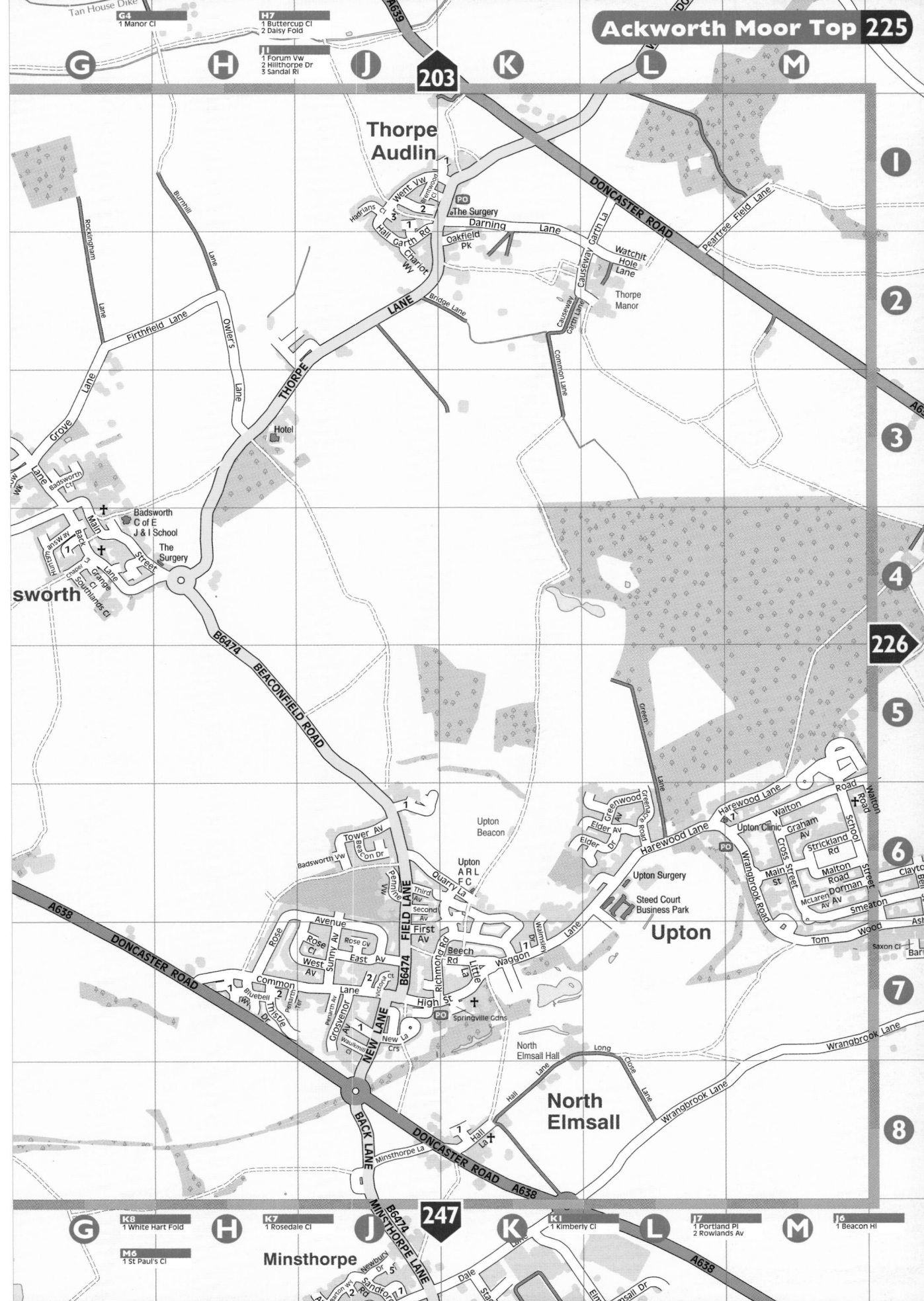

G H J **203** K L M

I
2
3
226
5
6
7
8

G4
1 Manor Cl

H7
1 Buttercup Cl
2 Daisy Fold

J1
1 Forum Vw
2 Hillthorpe Dr
3 Sandal Ri

Thorpe
Audlin

Tan House Dike

A639

DONCASTER ROAD

Peartree Field Lane

A63

Went Vw
Greenwod Cl
PO
The Surgery
Hadrians Cl
Hall Garth Rd
Chariot Vw
Darning   Lane
Oakfield
PK
Garth La
Causeway
Watchit
Hole
Lane
Thorpe
Manor
Causeway Garth La

Burnhill

Rockingham

Lane

Firthfield Lane

Owler's

Lane

THORPE

LANE

Bridge Lane

Common Lane

Grove

Lane

Badsworth Cl

Main

Street

answay

Back

Chapel   Grange

Southlands Cl

Badsworth
C of E
J & I School

The
Surgery

Westfield

sworth

Hotel

B6474

BEACONFIELD ROAD

Green

Lane

Upton
Beacon

A638

DONCASTER ROAD

Tower Av
Beacon Dr
Badsworth Vw

FIELD LANE

Quarry La
Third
Av
Second
Av
First
Av
Upton
A R L
F C

Pennine

Avenue
Rose
Cl
Rose Gv
Sunny Av
East Av
West
Av
B6474
Richmond Rd
Beech
Rd
Little
St
Waggon
Victoria Ct
Common
Lane
Bluebell
Thistle
Penmthorpe
Pentrich Av
Grosvenor Av
High St
New La
Crs
Waulkmill
NEW LANE
PO
Springville Gdns

Greenwood
Elder
Av
Elder
Dr
Greenyard Road
Harewood Lane
Harewood Lane
Upton Clinic
Walton
Av
Walton
Road
School Street
Graham
Av
Strickland
Rd
Malton
Road
McLaren Dorman
Av Av
Smeaton

Upton Surgery
Steed Court
Business Park
Walmsley
Dr
Walmsley
Lane
PO
Wrangbrook Road
Cross Street
Main
St

Upton

Tom   Wood
Saxon Cl
Bar
Clayto

Ash

North
Elmsall Hall

Long
Close
Lane

Hall
Lane

Wrangbrook Lane

Wrangbrook Lane

**North
Elmsall**

Hall
La

Minsthorpe La

BACK LANE

MINSTHORPE LANE

B6474

247

DONCASTER ROAD   A638

A638

G H J K L M

K8
1 White Hart Fold

M6
1 St Paul's Cl

K7
1 Rosedale Cl

K1
1 Kimberly Cl

J7
1 Portland Pl
2 Rowlands Av

J6
1 Beacon Hi

Minsthorpe

Newbold
Dr
Sandford
Rd
Dale
Stac
Beacon Wk
Elmsall Dr

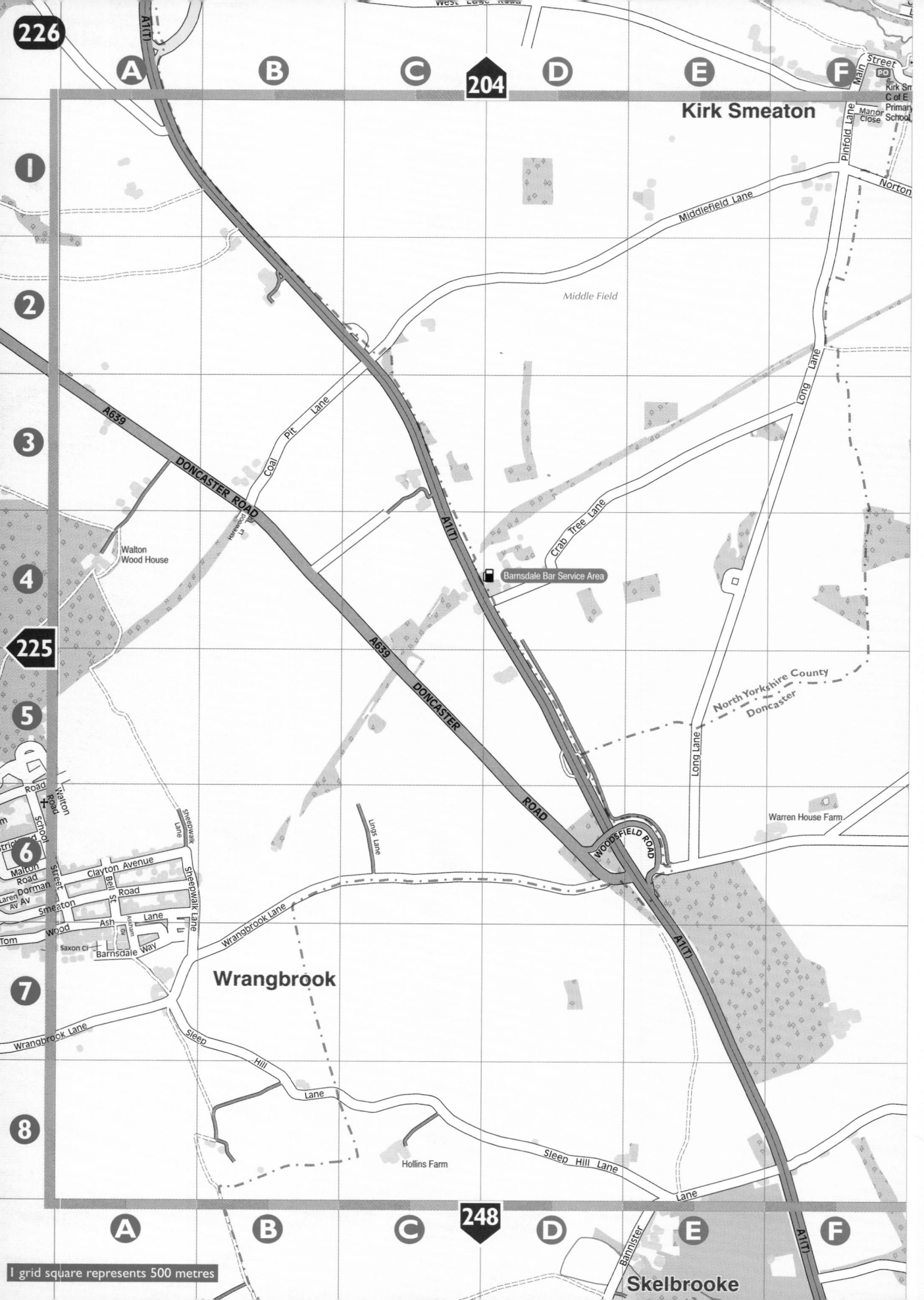

Little Smeaton

Norton

Campsall

Sutton

L5
1 Byron Av
2 Sherwood Cl

L6
1 Campsmount

M3
1 Linkway
2 Orchard Cl

M5
1 Langleys Rd

G H J 205 K L M

G H J 249 K L M

I 2 3 4 5 6 7 8

Wentbank House

Stubbs Road

North Yorkshire County
Doncaster

River Went

Spittlerush Lane

Norton And Kirk Smeaton Road

And Kirk Smeaton Road

Westfield Lane

Cliff Hill Road
Cliff Hill

Ryecroft
Ryecroft Av
West End

Back Lane
Broc-O-Bank
Barnsdale Rd
Newthorpe Rd
Forester's Cbse

Norton Mill Lane
Norton Priory

Walden Stubbs Road

Priory Road Or Hall Lane

Trafford Rd
Adelaide Rd
Arundel Close
Orchard Dr
Headingley Rd
The Close
PO
High Street

Lyndhurst Close
Lyndhurst Dr
Lyn Rise
Den

Pinfold Lane

Common Lane

Fir Tree Drive
Manor Close

Norton

Norton County
Junior &
Infant School

Greengate Road

Fox Covert Rd
Or Whin Covert La

White Ley Road

Windmill Lane
Stygate Lane

Balk

Campsall

Campsmount
School

Campsmount
Home Farm

Woodlands Rise
Tennyson Av
Shakespeare Av
Wordsworth Av

The Avenue
Welling Lana Rd
Drive

Church

Glebe Road
Park
East View
1

Grange Road

Field

Willow Road
Beech Road

Drive

Cemetery
Brayton Gdns
Cedar
Loxley Mount
Campsall Park Road

Campsall Park
Road
Vaughan Road

Campsall

Campsall Hall Road

Church View

Askern
Swimming
Pool

Road

Woodfield Road

New Road

High Street
The Orchard
Barnsdale Lane
Cherry Garth
Bone Lane

Mews

Back Lane
PO

Sutton Road
Woodgarth Road

Woodfield Farm

New Close Lane

Burghwallis Road

Sixroad

The Abbe's
Close

Burghwallis Lane
Gap

Lady

Lane

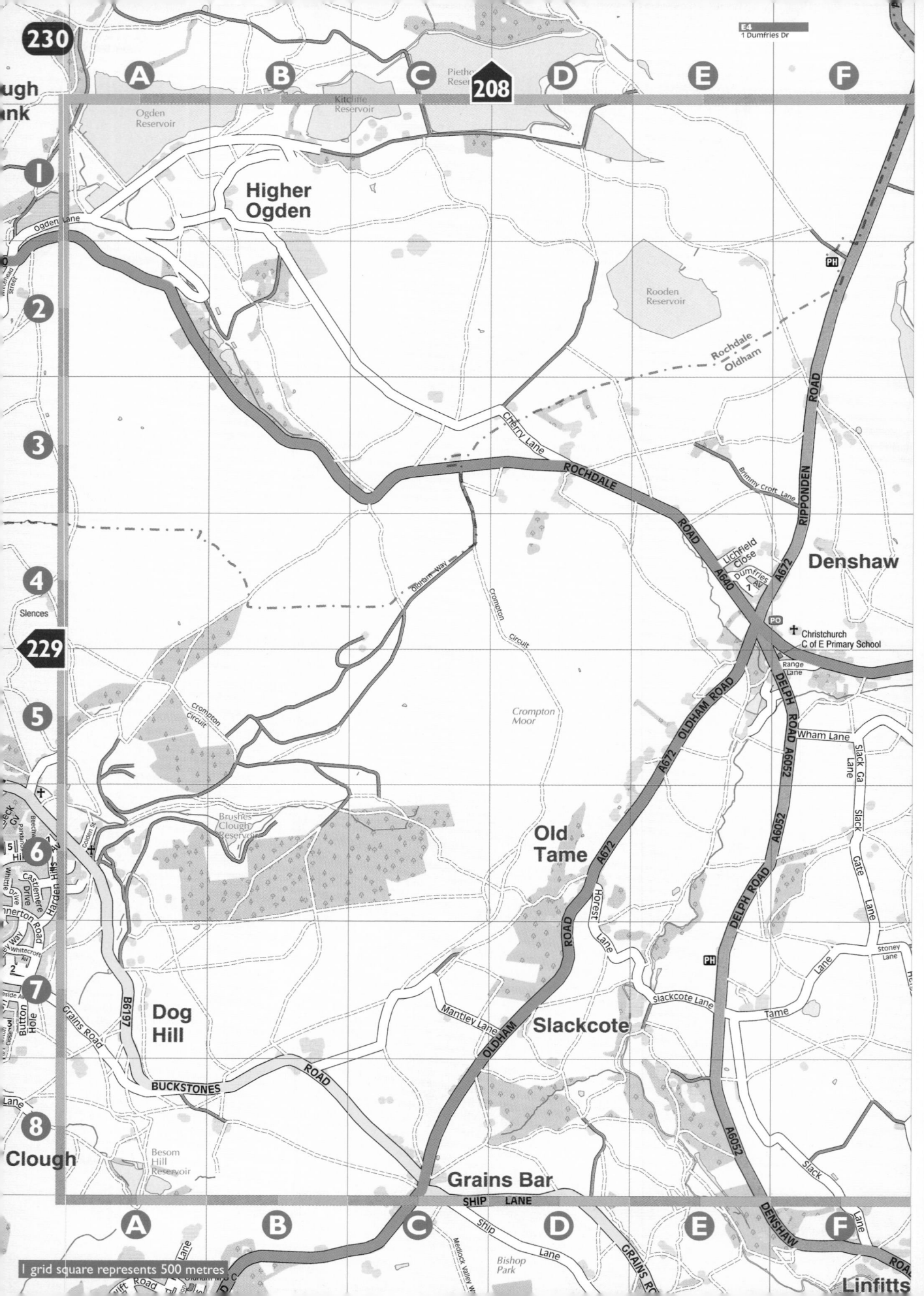

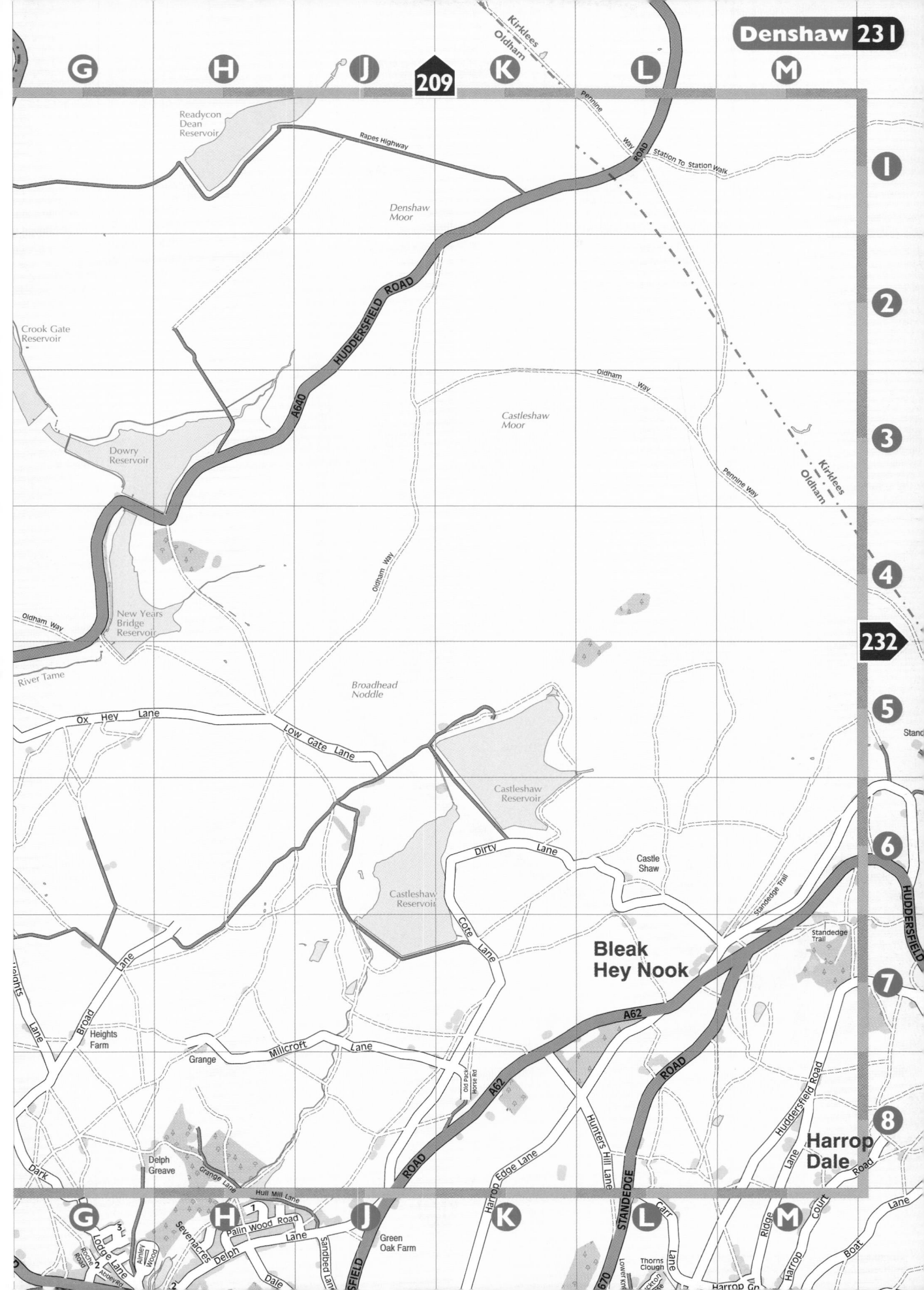

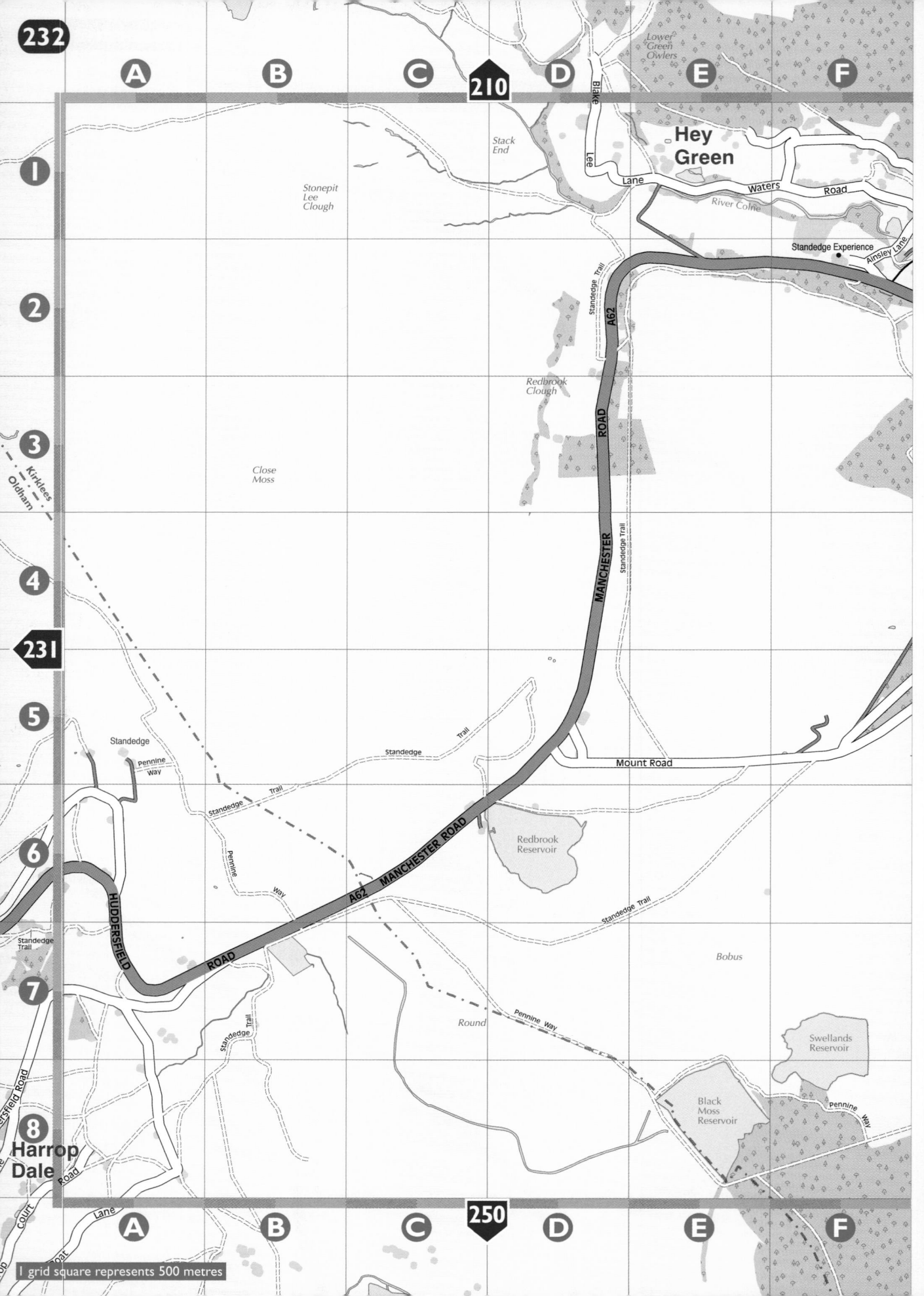

232

A   B   C   210   D   E   F

I

Stonepit
Lee
Clough

Stack
End

Lower
Green
Owlers

Hey
Green

Lane

Waters   Road

River Colne

Standedge Experience

Ainsley Lane

2

Redbrook
Clough

Standedge Trail

A62

MANCHESTER   ROAD

231

Kirklees
Oldham

Close
Moss

3

4

Standedge Trail

5

Standedge

Pennine

Way

Trail

Standedge

Mount Road

Standedge   Trail

Standedge   Trail

6

HUDDERSFIELD

Pennine

A62   MANCHESTER ROAD

Way

Redbrook
Reservoir

Standedge Trail

Bobus

Standedge
Trail

ROAD

7

Standedge Trail

Round

Pennine   Way

Swellands
Reservoir

Pennine   Way

Black
Moss
Reservoir

8
Harrop
Dale

ersfield Road

Road

Lane

Court

Oat

A   B   C   250   D   E   F

1 grid square represents 500 metres

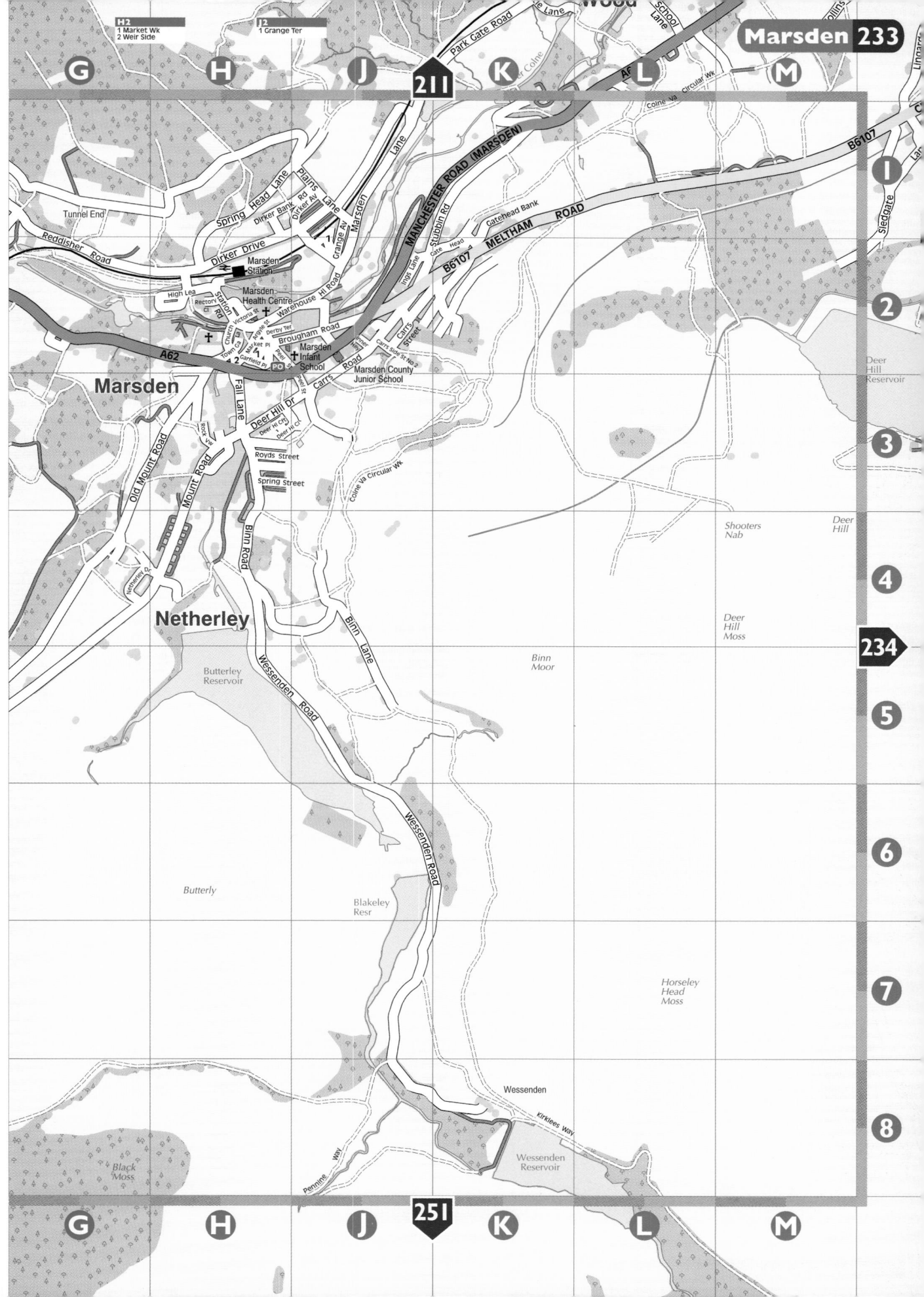

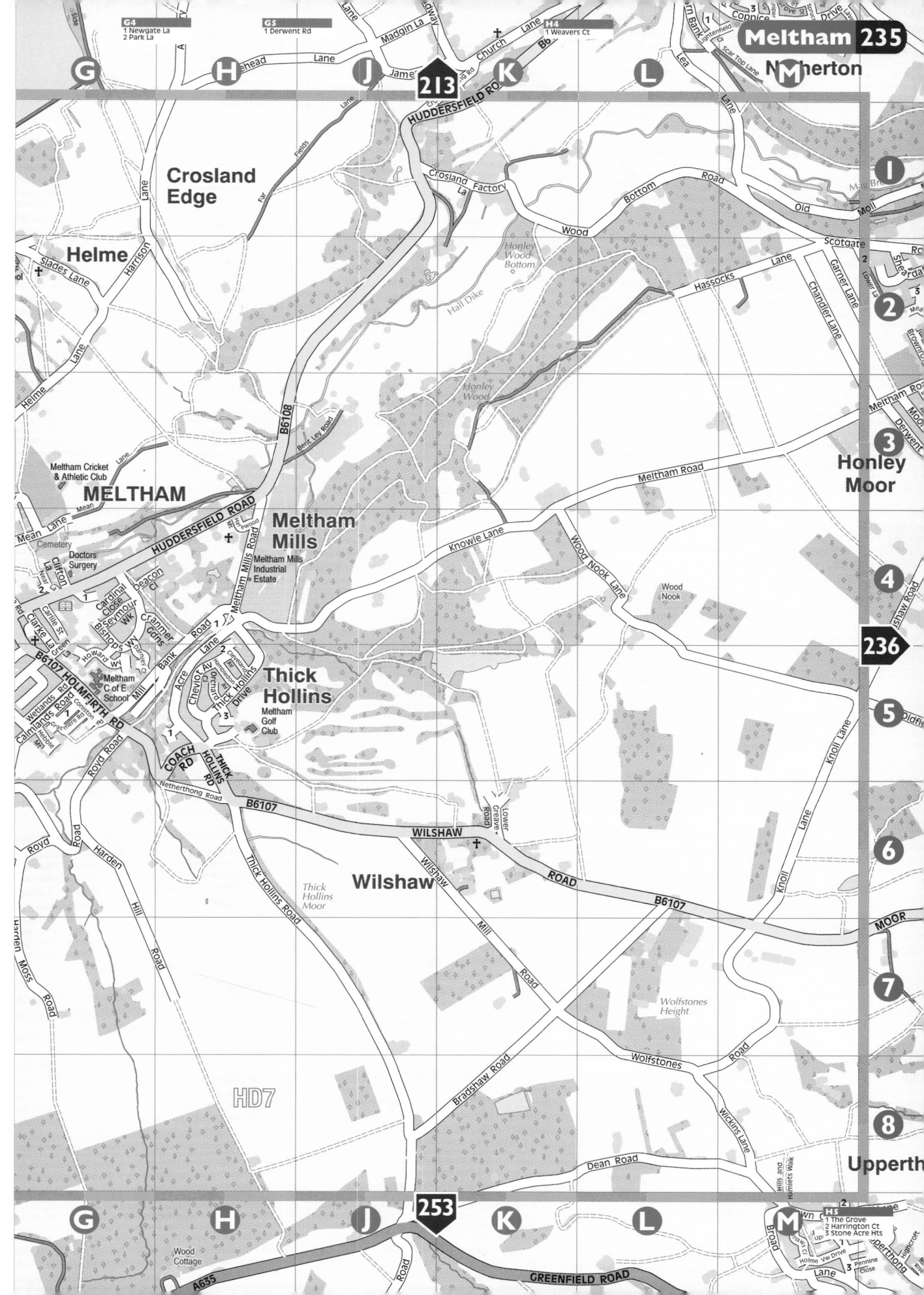

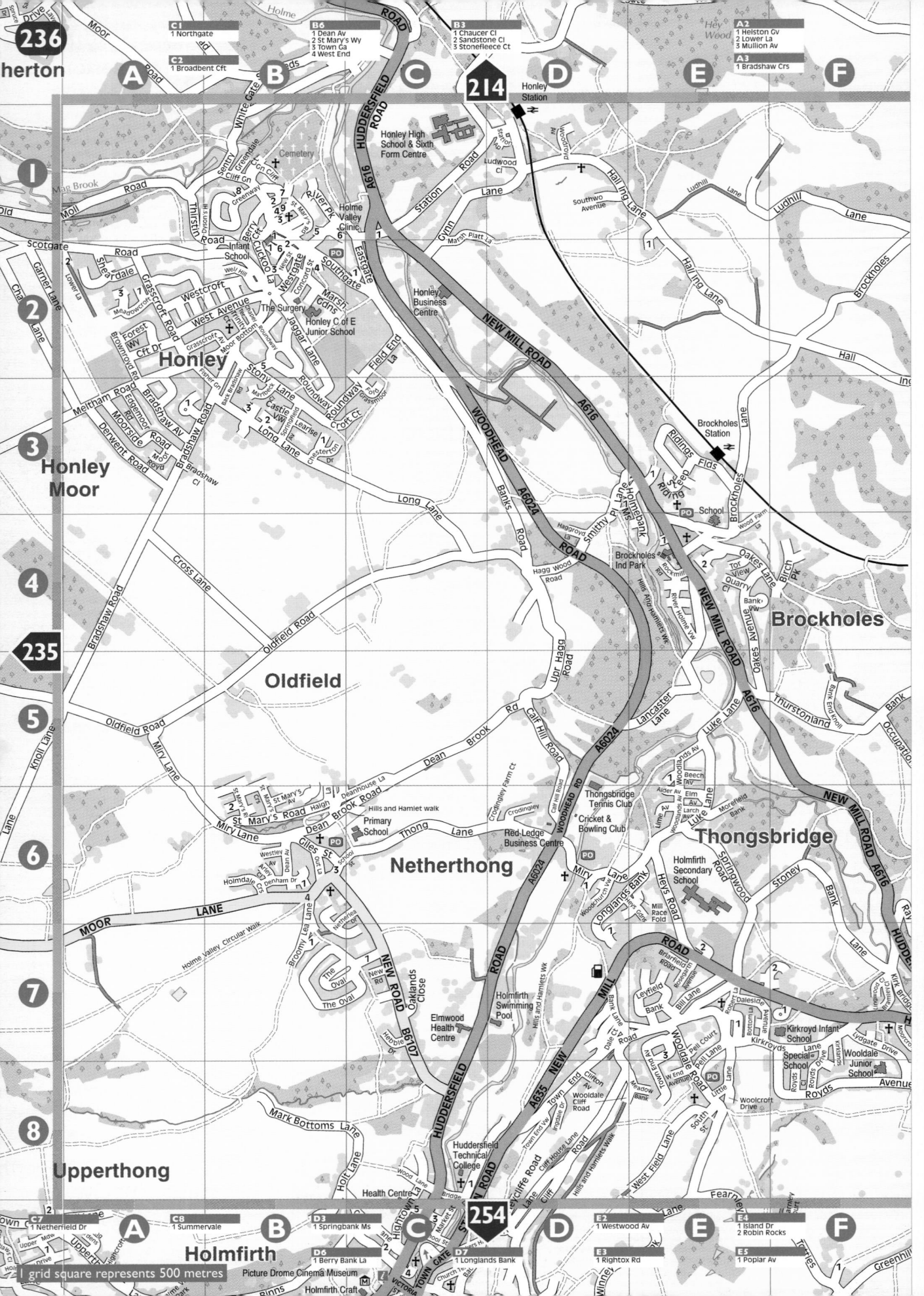

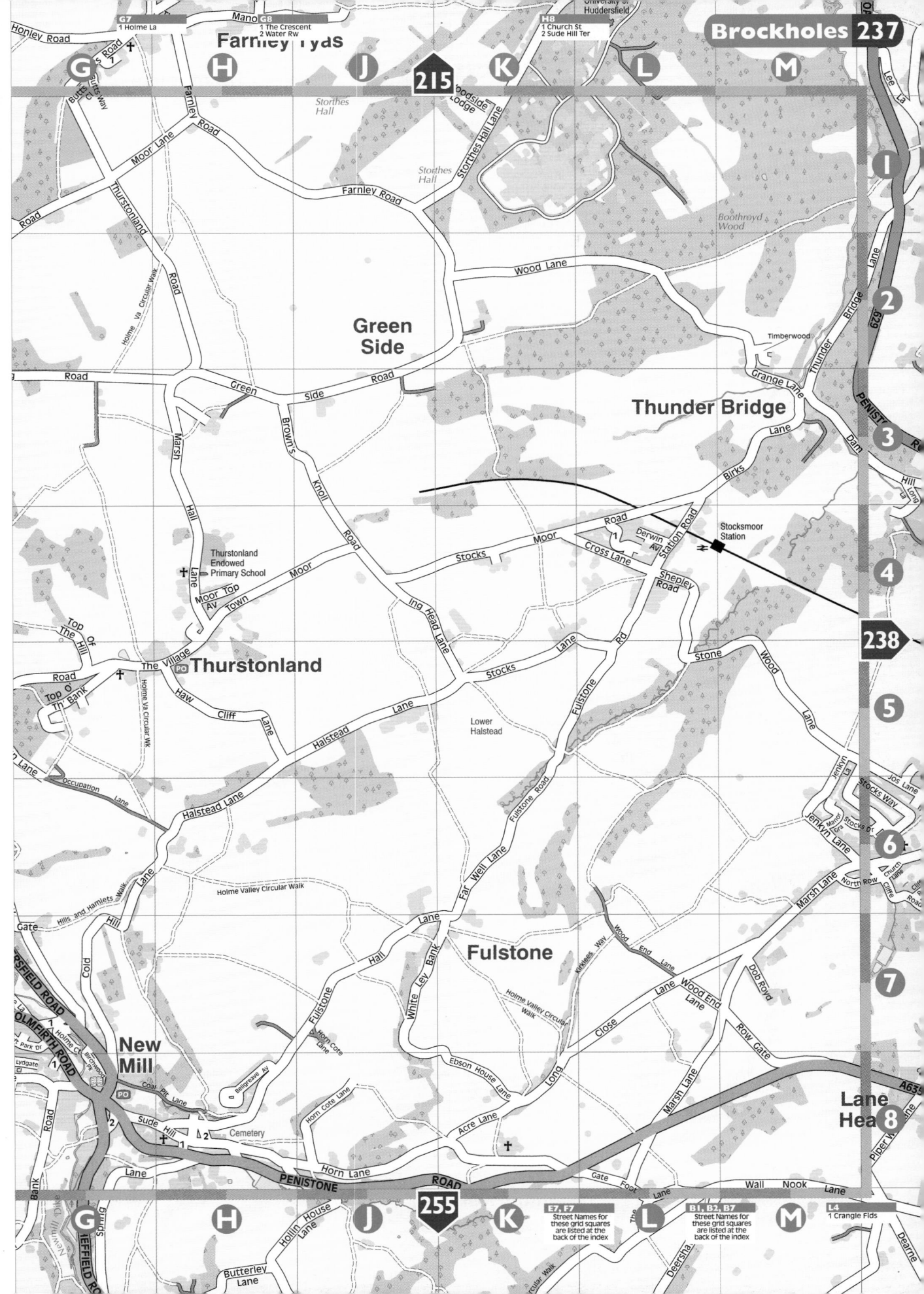

Honley Road

Mano G8
1 The Crescent
2 Water Rw

Farnley Tyas

University of
Huddersfield

H8
1 Church St
2 Sude Hill Ter

215

Butts Way

G7
1 Holme La

Woodside
Lodge

Storthes
Hall

Storthes
Hall Lane

Lee La

Moor Lane

Farnley Road

Farnley Road

Wood Lane

Boothroyd
Wood

Timberwood

Grange Lane

Thunder Bridge

PENIST RD

Thunder Bridge

Thurstonland Road

Moor Lane

Road

Green Side Road

Green Side

Brown's Knoll Road

Marsh Hall Lane

Lane

Birks

Dam

Hill Lane

Thurstonland
Endowed
Primary School

Moor

Ing Head Lane

Stocks Road

Moor Road

Cross Lane

Derwin Av

Station Rd

Stocksmoor
Station

Top Av

Town

Shepley Road

Moor Top

Top Of
The Hill
Road

The Village

PO **Thurstonland**

Haw Cliff Lane

Halstead Lane

Stocks Lane

Stone Lane

238

Top O
Th Bank

Holme Va Circular Wk

Lower
Halstead

Fulstone Lane

Wood Lane

Jenkyn La

Stocks Way

Jos Lane

Lane

Occupation Lane

Halstead Lane

Holme Valley Circular Walk

Fulstone Road

Far Well Lane

Jenkyn Lane

Marsh Lane

North Row

Cliffe Road

Church Lane

Hills and Hamlets Walk

Cold Hill

Lane

Fulstone

Knirkles Way

Wood End Lane

Marsh Lane

Dod Roya

Gate

Fulstone Hall Lane

White Ley Bank

Holme Valley Circular Walk

Close

Long

Wood End Lane

Row Gate

A635

New Mill

Belgrave Av

Horn Cote Lane

Ebson House Lane

Lane Hea

Piper W

Lydgate Cl

Coal Pit Lane

PO

Horn Cote Lane

Acre Lane

Marsh Lane

Sude Hill

Cemetery

Gate Foot Lane

Wall Nook Lane

Bank Lane

Horn Lane

255

PENISTONE ROAD

Hollin House Lane

E7, F7
Street Names for
these grid squares
are listed at the
back of the index

B1, B2, B7
Street Names for
these grid squares
are listed at the
back of the index

L4
1 Crangle Flds

Butterley Lane

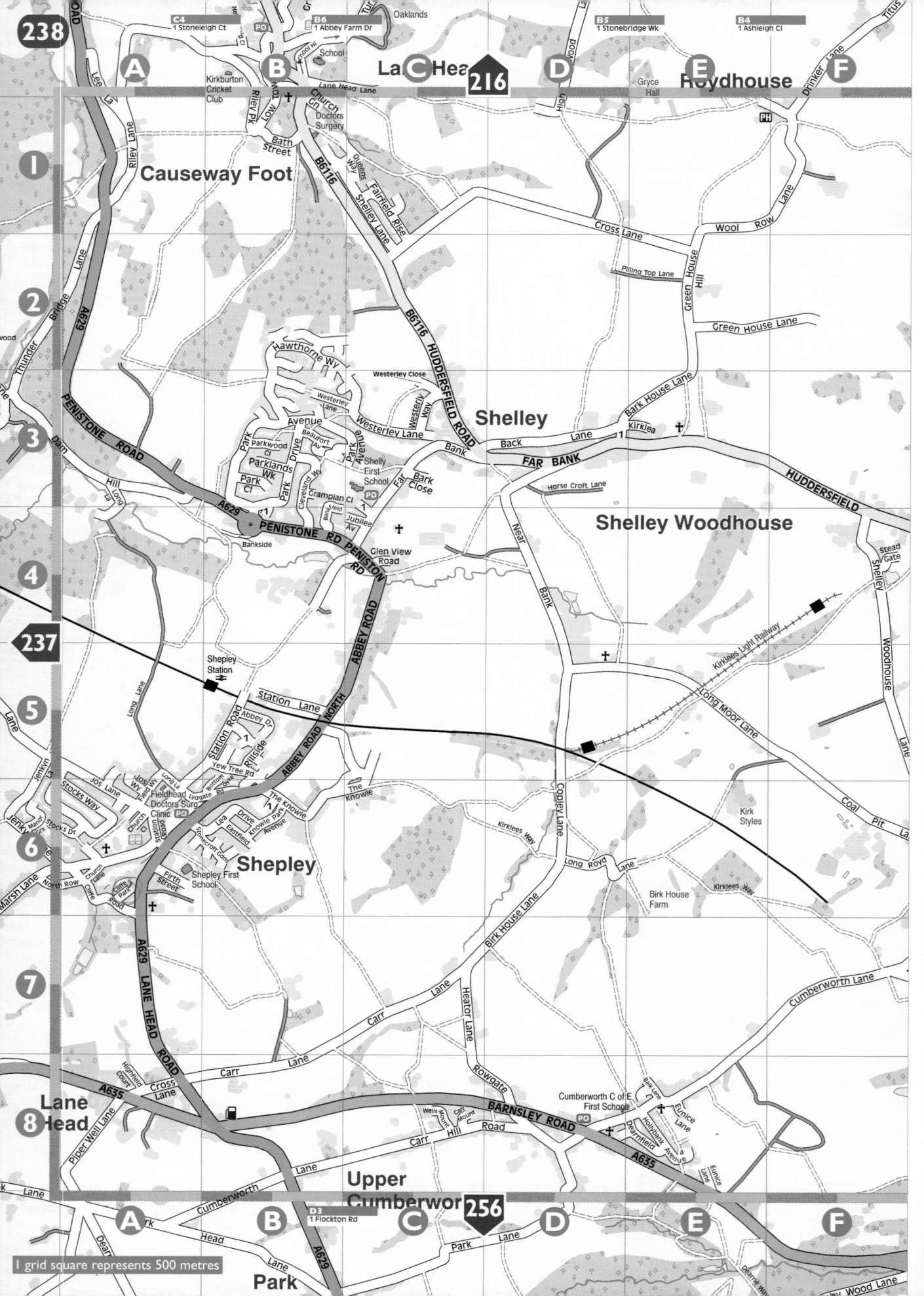

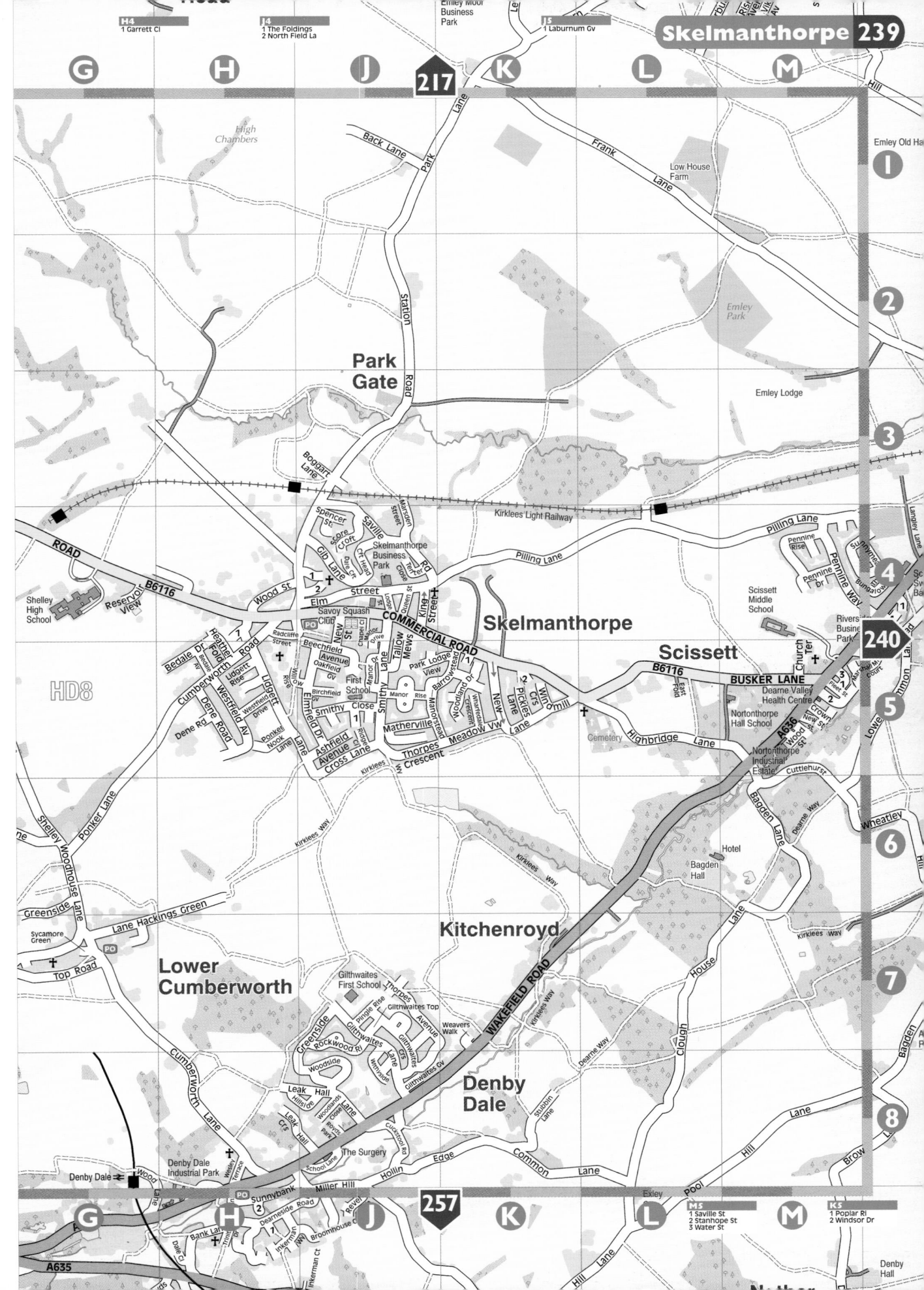

217

H4
1 Garrett Cl

J4
1 The Foldings
2 North Field La

Emley Moor
Business
Park

J5
1 Laburnum Gv

1

Emley Old Ha

Low House
Farm

Frank   Lane

High
Chambers

Back Lane

Park   Lane

2

Emley
Park

Station   Road

Emley Lodge

Park
Gate

3

Boggart Lane

Kirklees Light Railway

Pilling Lane

ROAD

B6116

Spencer St
Score
Croft
Gib Lane
Dale St
Saville
Marsden   Street

Street

Skelmanthorpe
Business
Park

Pilling Lane

Pennine
Rise

Langley

Pennine Way

4

240

Shelley
High
School

Reservoir
View

Wood St

Elm   Street

King St
Lodge   High   Street

Savoy Squash
PO
New St
Chapel St
Tallow Mews

COMMERCIAL ROAD

Skelmanthorpe

Scissett
Middle
School

Church Ter

Riversi
Busine
Park

Bedale Dr
Heather Ford Rd
Cumberworth Road
Westfield AV
Lidgett Rise
Lidgett
Emfield Dr
Dene Rd
Dene Road

Radcliffe
Street
Beechfield
Avenue
Willow Rise
Oakfield
GV
Birchfield
First
School
Smithy
Close

Manor Drive
Park Lodge
View

Woodland Dr
Barrowstead
Manor Rise
Wharfedale
Crescent
Pickles Crs
Windmill

Scissett

B6116

BUSKER LANE

East
Fold

Dearne Valley
Health Centre

Nortonthorpe
Hall School

Crown

Low

Wood St
New St

5

HD8

Ponker Nook Lane

Ashfield
Avenue
Kirklees Cross Lane
Smith Lane
Matherville
Thorpes
Crescent

New   Lane
Meadow Vw

Cemetery

Highbridge   Lane

Nortonthorpe
Industrial
Estate

A636

Cuttlehurst

Bagden Lane

Wheatley

Shelley Woodhouse Lane

Ponker Lane

Kirklees Way

Kirklees   Way

Dearne Way

Hotel

Bagden
Hall

Kirklees Way

6

Greenside

Lane Hackings Green

Kitchenroyd

WAKEFIELD ROAD

Kirklees Way

Clough   House   Lane

7

Sycamore
Green
PO
Top Road

Lower
Cumberworth

Gilthwaites
First School

Greenside
Pingle Rise
Gilthwaites
Rockwood Ri
Woodside
Thorpes
Avenue
Gilthwaites Top
Gilthwaites
Lane
Wimvade
Gilthwaites GV

Weavers
Walk

Dearne Way

8

Cumberworth Lane

Leak Hall
Hillside
Leak
Crs
Leak
Hall
Lane
Woodlands

Woodlands
Capel La
Roydfield

Denby
Dale

Stubbin Lane

Common
Lane

Hill

Pool

Brow

Denby Dale

Wood Lane

Denby Dale
Industrial Park

PO
Sunnybank
2
Dearneside Road
Revel
Bank Lane
Tinker La
Inkerman St
Broomhouse La
Inkerman Ct

Miller   Hill
School Lane
Clucksford Rd

Hollin   Edge   Lane

Common   Lane

Exley

257

M5
1 Saville St
2 Stanhope St
3 Water St

K5
1 Poplar Ri
2 Windsor Dr

A635

Denby
Hall

A
B
C
D
E
F

I
2
3
4
5
6
7
8

White Cross

Emley Old Hall Farm

Kiln Lane
Old Hall Lane

Hill
Lane

Gillcar Farm

River Dearne
A636

Park Mill

Dearne Way

Barnsley Boundary Walk

Colliers Way

Manor Road

Pack Horse Close

Langley Lane
Lane

Wakefield Road

Deane Way

Park Road
Long Lane
Back Lane
The Royds

Kirklees Way

Clayton Hall Farm

Church Lane

Kirklees Barnsley

Park Mill Way
Ings Mill Av

A636
Riverside

Ings Ml
Vinery Cl
Scott Hill
Church Lane
First School
PO

Clayton West

Bilham Road
Bilham Grange

Albert Rd
Victoria St
Dearne Park
Grove Drive
Hill
Cliffe Vw
Newlands
Holmfield Rd
High Street
Moorland View
Ash Av

Scissett Swimming Baths
Chapel
Duke
Wood
Springfield Road
Cliffe Street

Holmfield Cl
Oldfield Lane

Church Ter
E

Pennine Way
Perseverance
Bungalows
Busker Way

Marshall Mill Court
Kirklees Way

Barnsley Road
Lower Common Lane

Bank End Lane

High Hoyland

Upper Lane

Wheatley Hill

Wheatley Hill Farm
Hill Lane
Kirklees Way

Kirklees Way
Upper Common Lane
Hollin
House
Lane

High Hoyland
High

Dean Hill

Bagden Lane
Ackin Royd

Defier Wood

Kirklees Barnsley
New Road

Brow Lane

A
B
C
D
E
F

Cannon Hall Museum & Country Park

Cannon Hall Country Park

Hall

I grid square represents 500 metres

K6
1 Oakwood Sq

L6
1 Churchfield Av
2 Highwood Cl
3 Jacobs Hall Ct
4 Lambe Flatt
5 Rushworth Cl

M5
1 High Cl
2 Sike Cl

G **H** **J** **219** **K** **L** **M**

Bretton
Country
Park

Beaumont Drive

A637

M1

1

Barnsley Boundary F

Wakefield
Barnsley

Lower
Lake

Moorhouse La

Near
Moon Farm

Barnsley Boundary Walk

Haigh

Junction 38

Huddersfield Road

Haigh Lane

2

Jebb Lane

SWITHEN HILL

River Dearne

Dearne Way

Longsides

3

Woolley
Colliery Rd

High
Wood

PARK HILL

WALK ROYD

A637

M1

4

Dearne Way

Birthwaite
Hall

242

Ballfield
Lane

A637

HUDDERSFIELD ROAD

5

PO

Field
Lane

Windsor
Avenue

Bretton
Close

Swallow Cl

Bretton
Road

Allendale Road

Barnsley
MBC

CHURCH ST

Upper Field Lane

Home View
Road

Highfields
Road

Brookhill Rd

Birthwaite Rd

Ballfield Lane

Priestley
Av

Stratford
St

Airedale Rd

Alan
Rd

Agnes

6

Darton
High School

Hawthorne Ct

Cooper Rd

Wentworth Road

Lane

Richard Rd

Lansdowne Crs

BARNS

Upper
Field
Lane

Junior
School

Kexbrough

Churchfield

Kexbrough Dr

Roman Rd

Hedge Lane

Meyrick
Dr

Thivydale

Bence

PO

Infant
School

Uplands Av

Beaumont Rd

Kilbroyd Dr

Churchfield Lane

Bence Lane

Cawthorne
Park

Churchfield Close

7

Chedworth
Close

Barnsley Boundary Walk

8

Cinder
Hill

Barnsley Boundary Walk

Bar

Cawthorne Lane

G **H** **J** **259** **K** **L** **M7**
1 Richmond Av **M** **M6**
1 Carrfield Cl
2 Daykin Cl
3 Hedge La
4 Oak Tree Cl
5 Quarry Cl

Cliff Hill

Horn Cft

Love Acres

Barnby

G H J 221 K L M

I
2
3
4
244
5 Carlton
6
7
8

ROYSTON

Athersley North

Athersley South

New Lodge

Carlton Industrial Estate

St Helen's

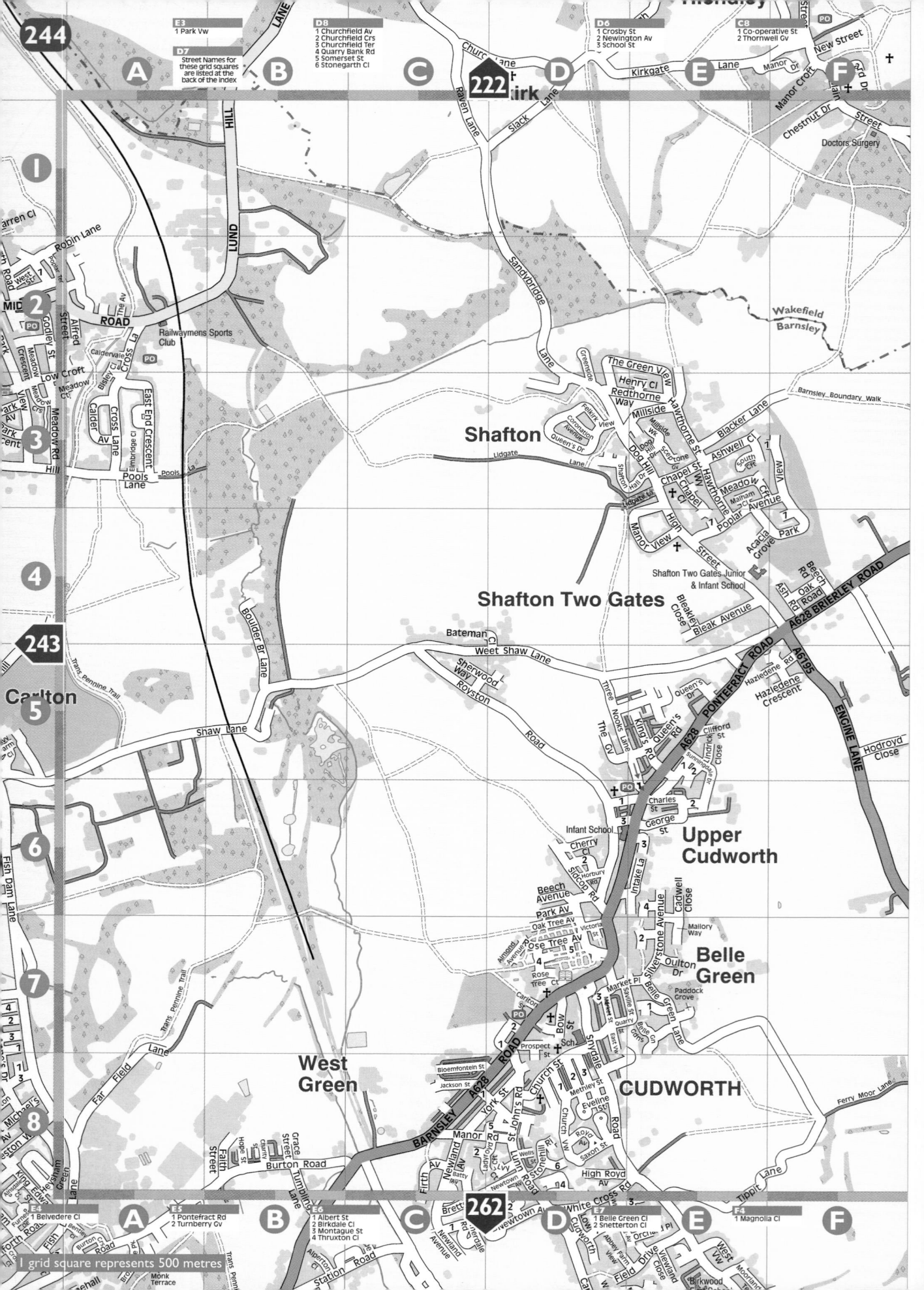

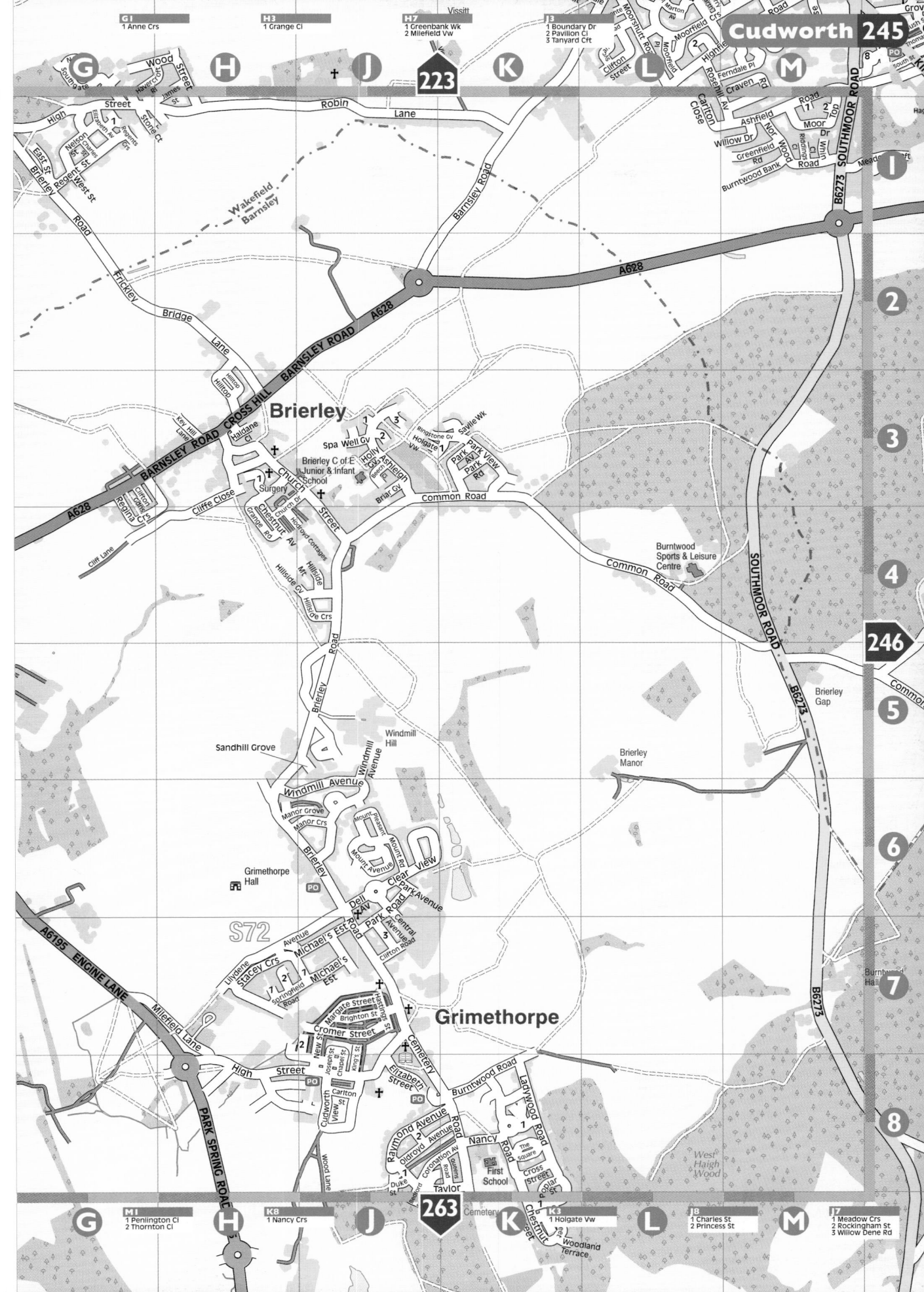

G1
1 Anne Crs

H3
1 Grange Cl

H7
1 Greenbank Wk
2 Milefield Vw

J3
1 Boundary Dr
2 Pavilion Cl
3 Tanyard Cft

G **H** **J** **223** **K** **L** **M**

I

Vissitt

Wood Street

High Street

Southgate

James St

Stone Ct

Elizabeth Wk

Charles Crs

Nelson St

Regent St

West St

East St

Brierley Road

Frickley Bridge Lane

Robin Lane

Barnsley Road

A628

Wakefield Barnsley

Marton Av

Moorshutt Rd

Moorfield

Clifton Street

Highfie

Ferndale Pl

Rosemil Av

Craven Rd

Carlton Close

Ashfield Rd

Willow Dr

Greenfield Road

Burntwood Bank

Road

Moor Dr

Moor Top

SOUTHMOOR ROAD

B6273

2

A628

Hillside

Key Hill Lane

BARNSLEY ROAD CROSS HILL

BARNSLEY ROAD

Brierley

Spa Well Gv

Haldane Cl

Clifton Gdns

Regina Crs

Cliff Lane

Cliffe Close

Church Street

Surgery

Grange Rd

Chestnut Av

Church Dr

Holroyd Cottages

Brierley C of E Junior & Infant School

Holly

Beech

Ashleigh

Briar Gv

Ringstone Gv

Holgate Vw

Savile Wk

Park Av

Park View

Park View Rd

Common Road

Common Road

Burntwood Sports & Leisure Centre

SOUTHMOOR ROAD

3

4

246

Brierley Gap

B6273

5

Hillside Gv

Mt Hillside

Hillside Crs

Brierley Road

Sandhill Grove

Windmill Hill

Windmill Avenue

Windmill Avenue

Brierley Manor

Manor Grove

Manor Crs

Mount Grove

Mount Av

Mount Avenue

Mount Rd

6

S72

Grimethorpe Hall

PO

Brierley Road

Dell

X AV

Clear View

Park Road

Park Avenue

Central Avenue

Clifton Road

A6195 ENGINE LANE

Milefield Lane

Michael's Est

Avenue

Lilydene Stacey Crs

Springfield Road

Michael's Est

Michael's Est

Margate Street

Brighton St

Hastings St

Cromer Street

New St

Joseph St

Chapel St

St King St

Grimethorpe

Cemetery

Elizabeth Street

Burntwood Road

Ladywood Road

Burntwood Hall

7

West Haigh Wood

PARK SPRING ROAD

High Street

Wood Lane

Cudworth View

Carlton St

PO

Raymond Avenue

Oldroyd Avenue

Coronation Av

Brierley Road

Nancy Road

Duke St

Taylor

First School

The Square

Cross Street

Poplar St

Cemetery

8

B6273

G M1
1 Penlington Cl
2 Thornton Cl **H** K8
1 Nancy Crs **J** **263** **K** K3
1 Holgate Vw **L** J8
1 Charles St
2 Princess St **M** J7
1 Meadow Crs
2 Rockingham St
3 Willow Dene Rd

Woodland Terrace

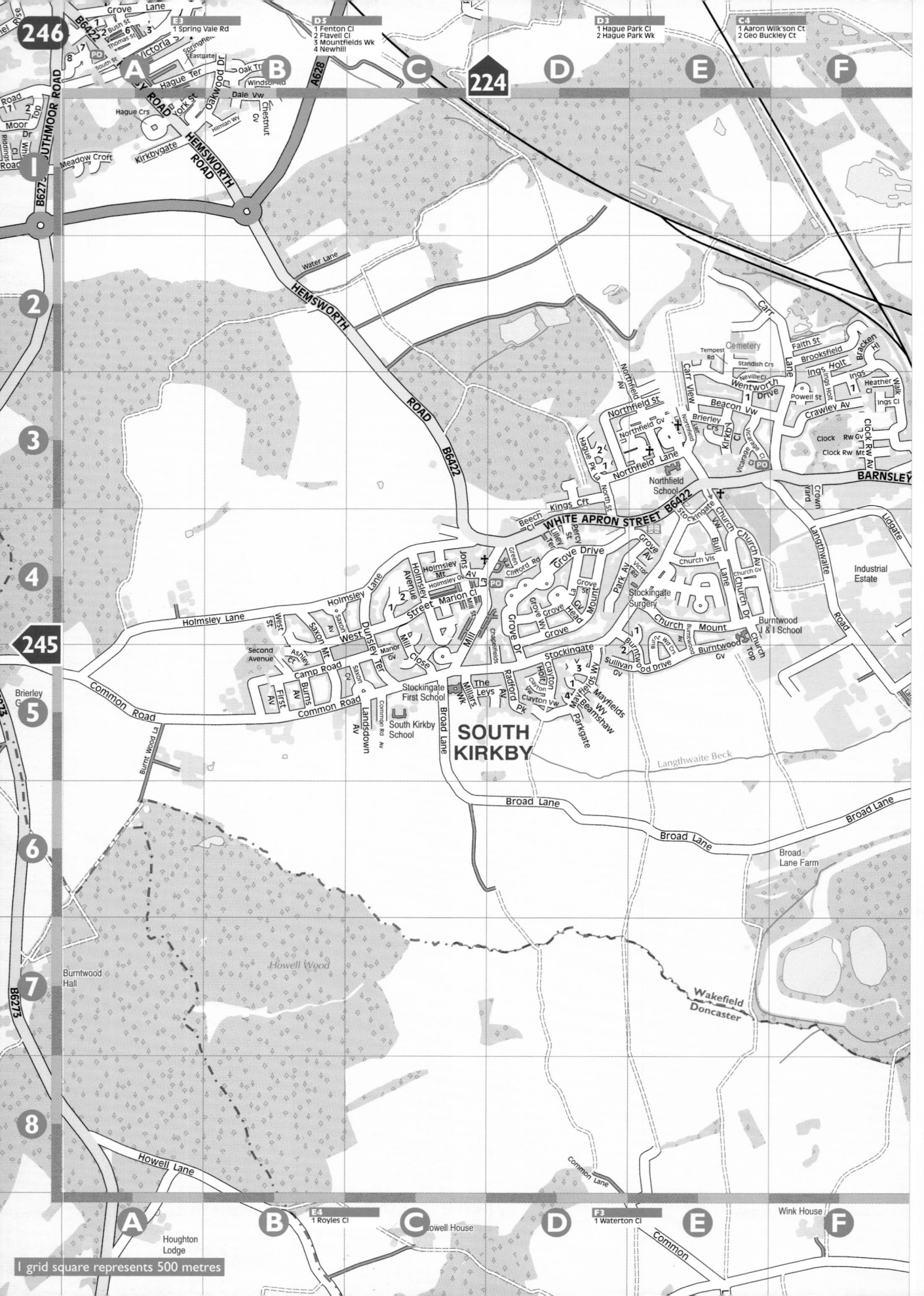

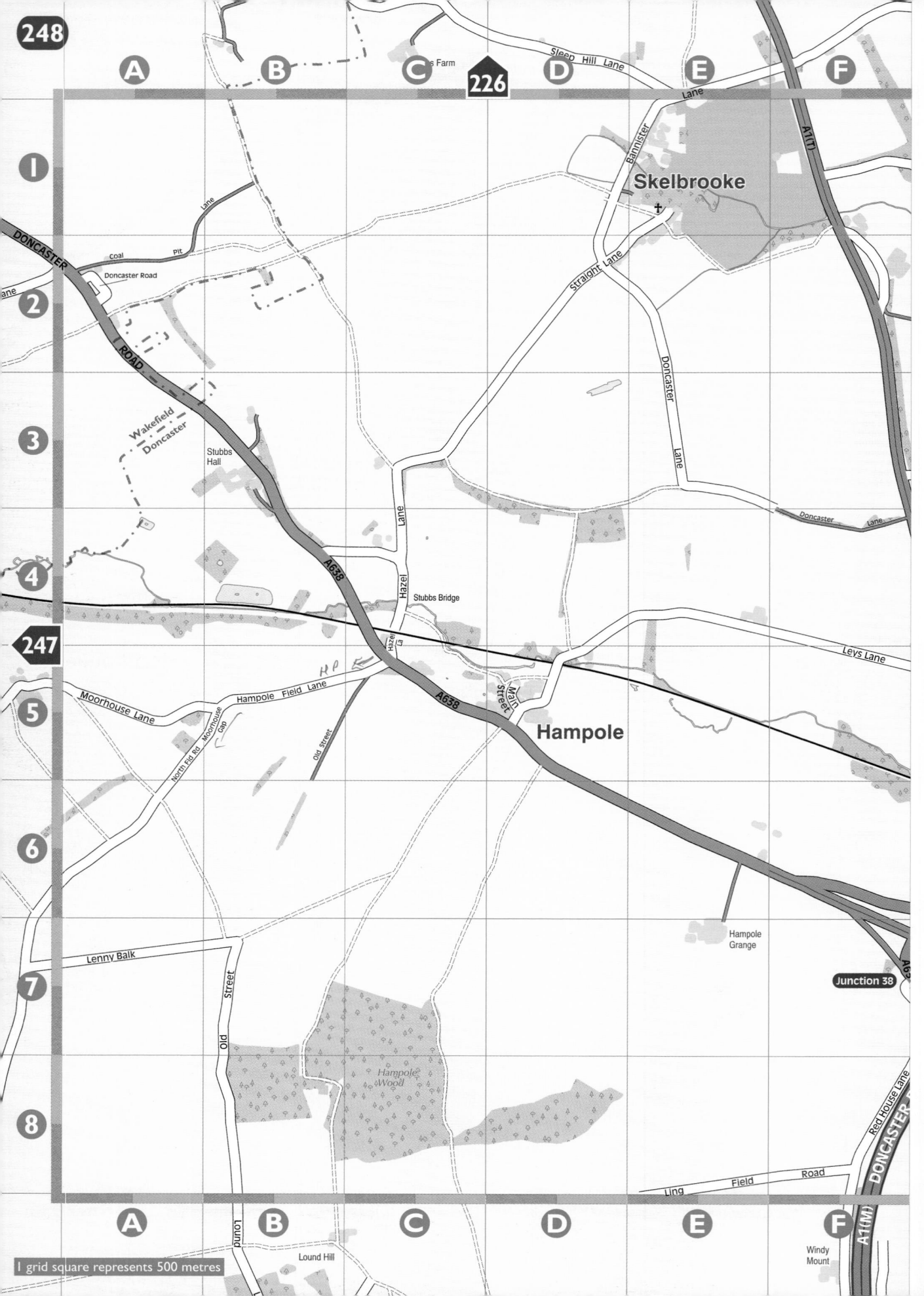

A B C D E F

226

1

Skelbrooke

Sleep Hill Lane

Lane

Bannister

Straight Lane

Doncaster Lane

2

DONCASTER

Coal Pit

Doncaster Road

ROAD

3

Wakefield
Doncaster

Stubbs
Hall

Lane

Doncaster Lane

4

A658

Hazel

Stubbs Bridge

247

Leys Lane

HP

Moorhouse Lane

Hampole Field Lane

Hazel

A658

Main Street

Hampole

5

North Eld Rd

Moorhouse Cap

Old Street

6

Hampole
Grange

Lenny Balk

A1(M)

7

Old Street

Junction 38

8

Hampole
Wood

Ling Field Road

DONCASTER

Red House Lane

A1(M)

Windy
Mount

A B C D E F

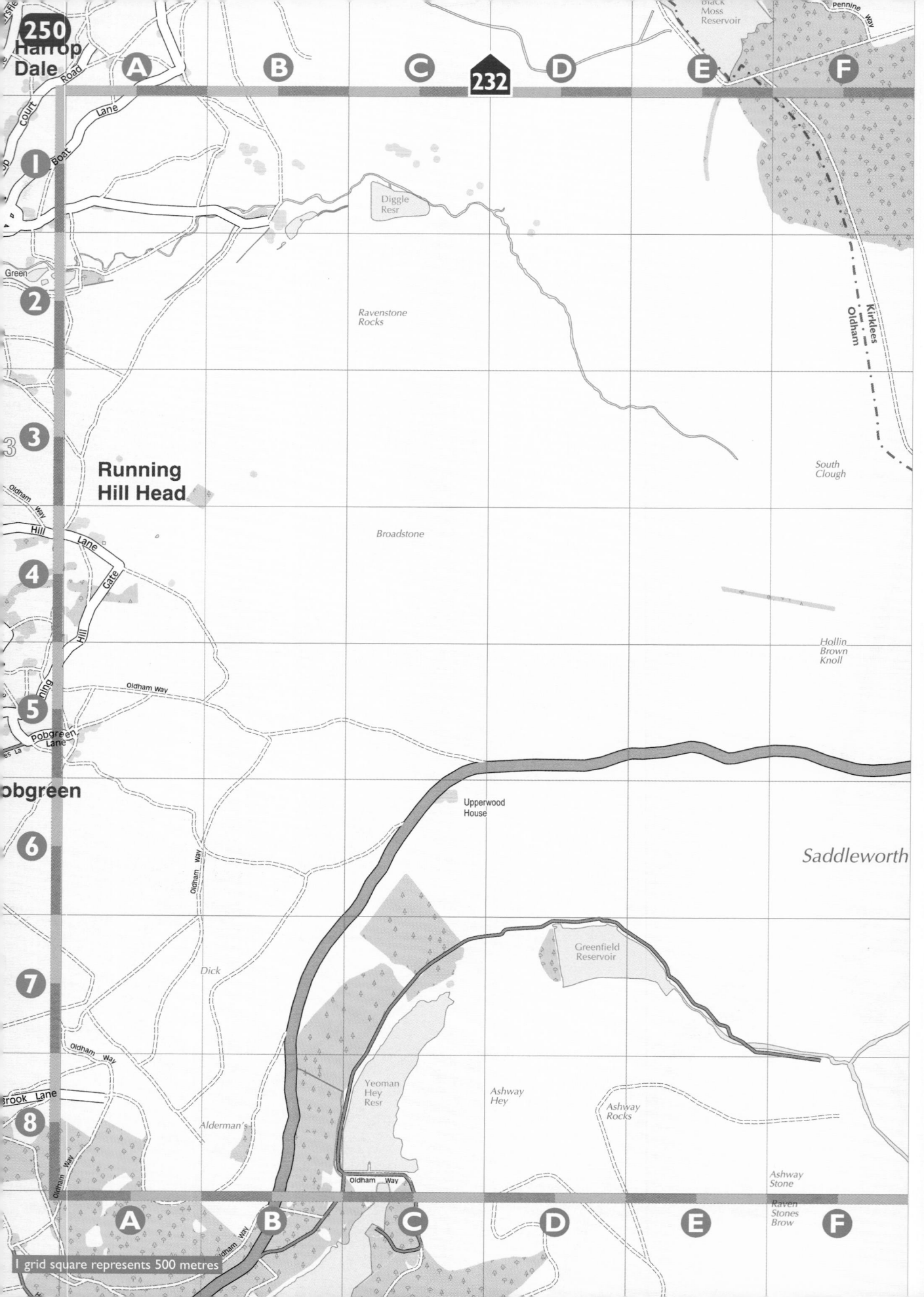

232

A B C D E F

I

2

3

4

5

6

7

8

Diggle Resr

Ravenstone Rocks

Running Hill Head

Broadstone

South Clough

Hollin Brown Knoll

Black Moss Reservoir

Pennine Way

Kirklees
Oldham

Oldham Way

Hill Lane

Gate Hill

Pobgreen Lane

ning

Pobgreen

Green

Court

Boat

Road

Castle

Lane

Oldham Way

Oldham Way

Dick

Alderman's

Oldham Way

brook Lane

Upperwood House

Saddleworth

Yeoman Hey Resr

Greenfield Reservoir

Ashway Hey

Ashway Rocks

Ashway Stone

Raven Stones Brow

Oldham Way

A B C D E F

I grid square represents 500 metres

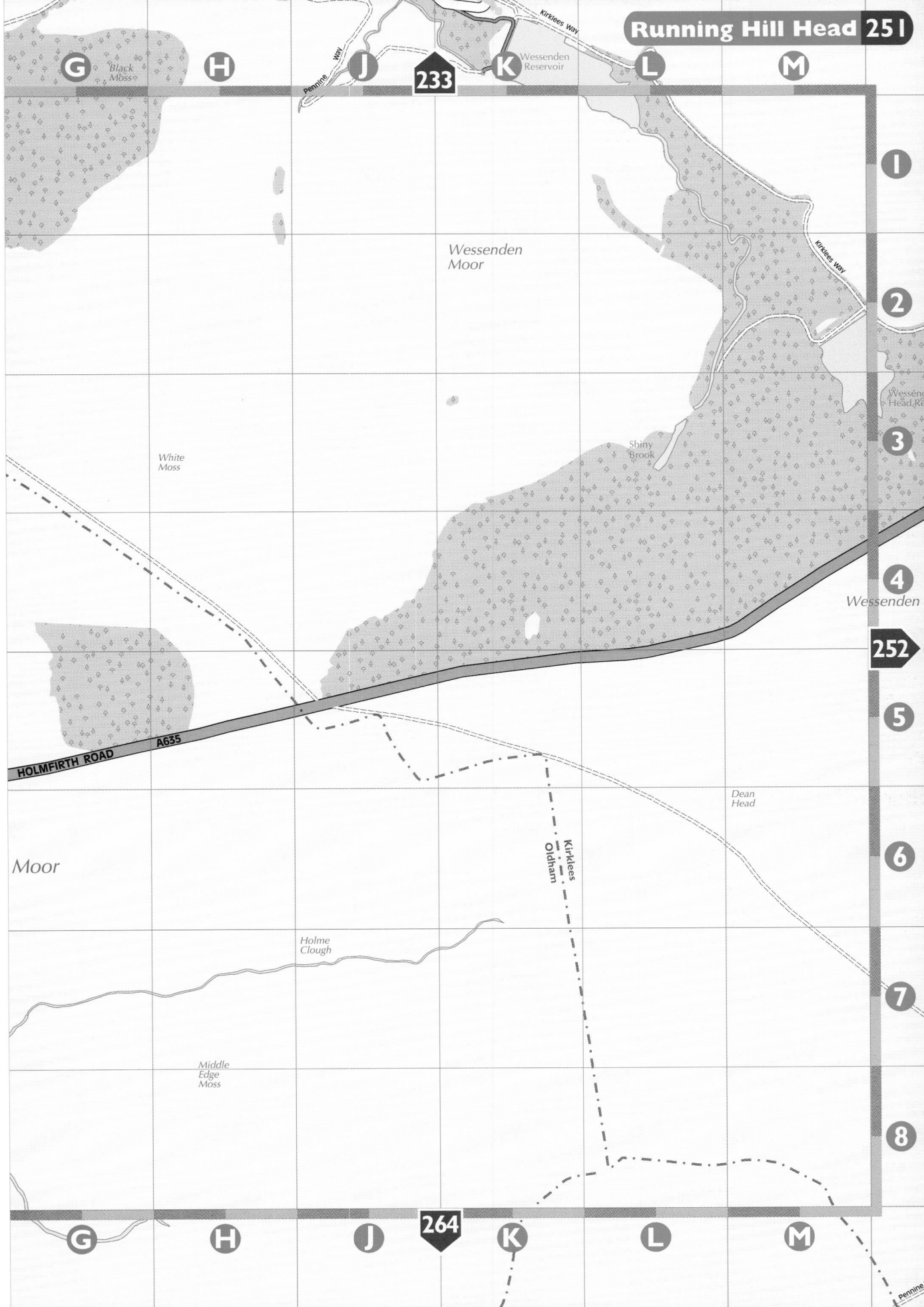

G H J 233 K L M

Kirklees Way

Pennine Way

Wessenden Reservoir

I

Wessenden Moor

2

White Moss

Wessende Head, Re

3

Shiny Brook

4

Wessenden

252

5

HOLMFIRTH ROAD A635

Dean Head

Moor

6

Holme Clough

Kirklees
Oldham

7

Middle Edge Moss

8

Black Moss

G H J 264 K L M

Pennine

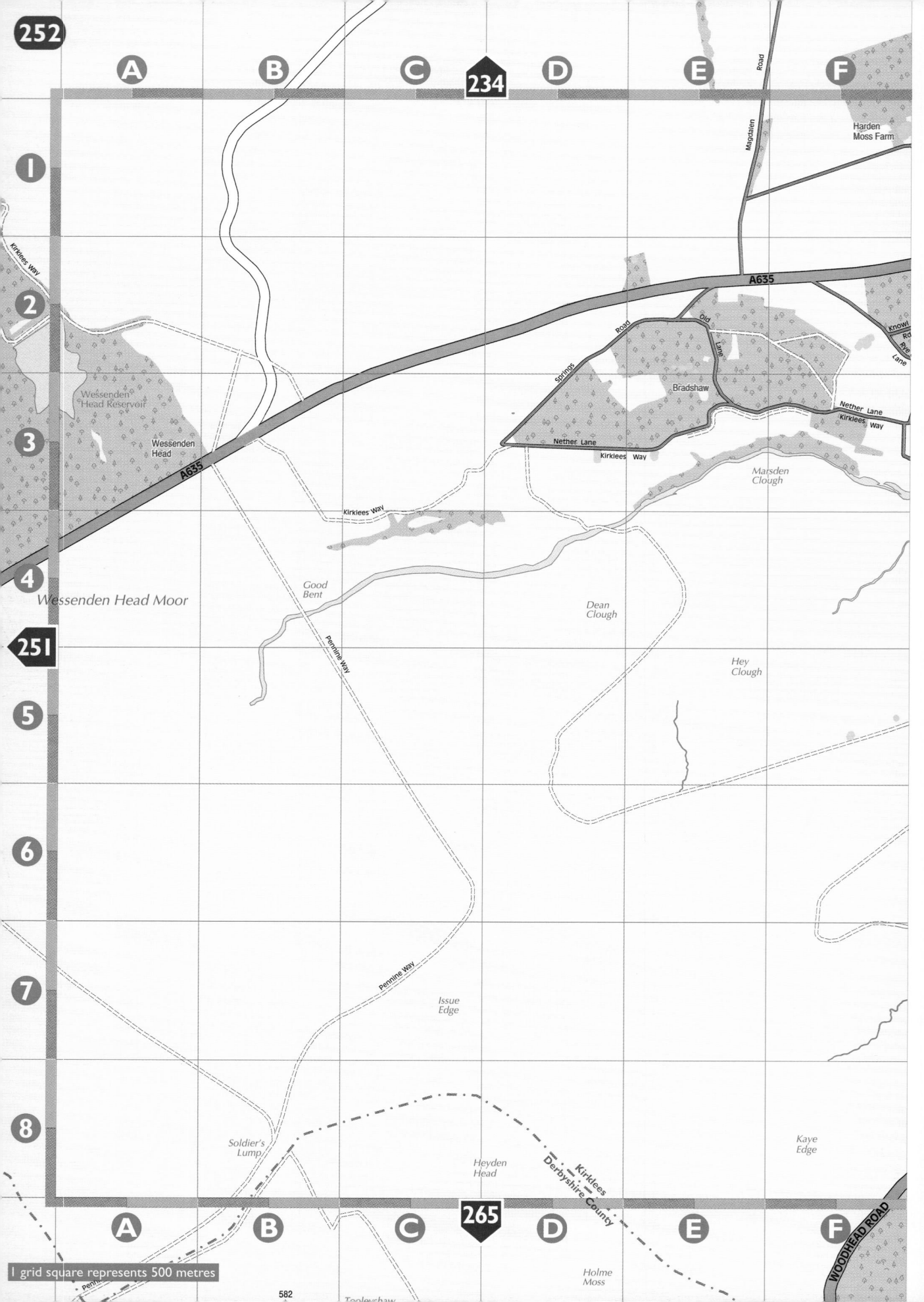

A
B
234
C
D
E
F

I

Kirklees Way

Magdalen Road

Harden Moss Farm

2

A635

Springs Road

Old Lane

Knowl Lane
Rye Lane

Bradshaw

3

Wessenden Head Reservoir

Wessenden Head

A635

Nether Lane

Nether Lane

Kirklees Way

Kirklees Way

Marsden Clough

Kirklees Way

4

Good Bent

Wessenden Head Moor

Dean Clough

Pennine Way

Hey Clough

5

6

7

Pennine Way

Issue Edge

8

Soldier's Lump

Heyden Head

Kirklees
Derbyshire County

Kaye Edge

A
B
265
C
D
E
F

WOODHEAD ROAD

Holme Moss

Pennine

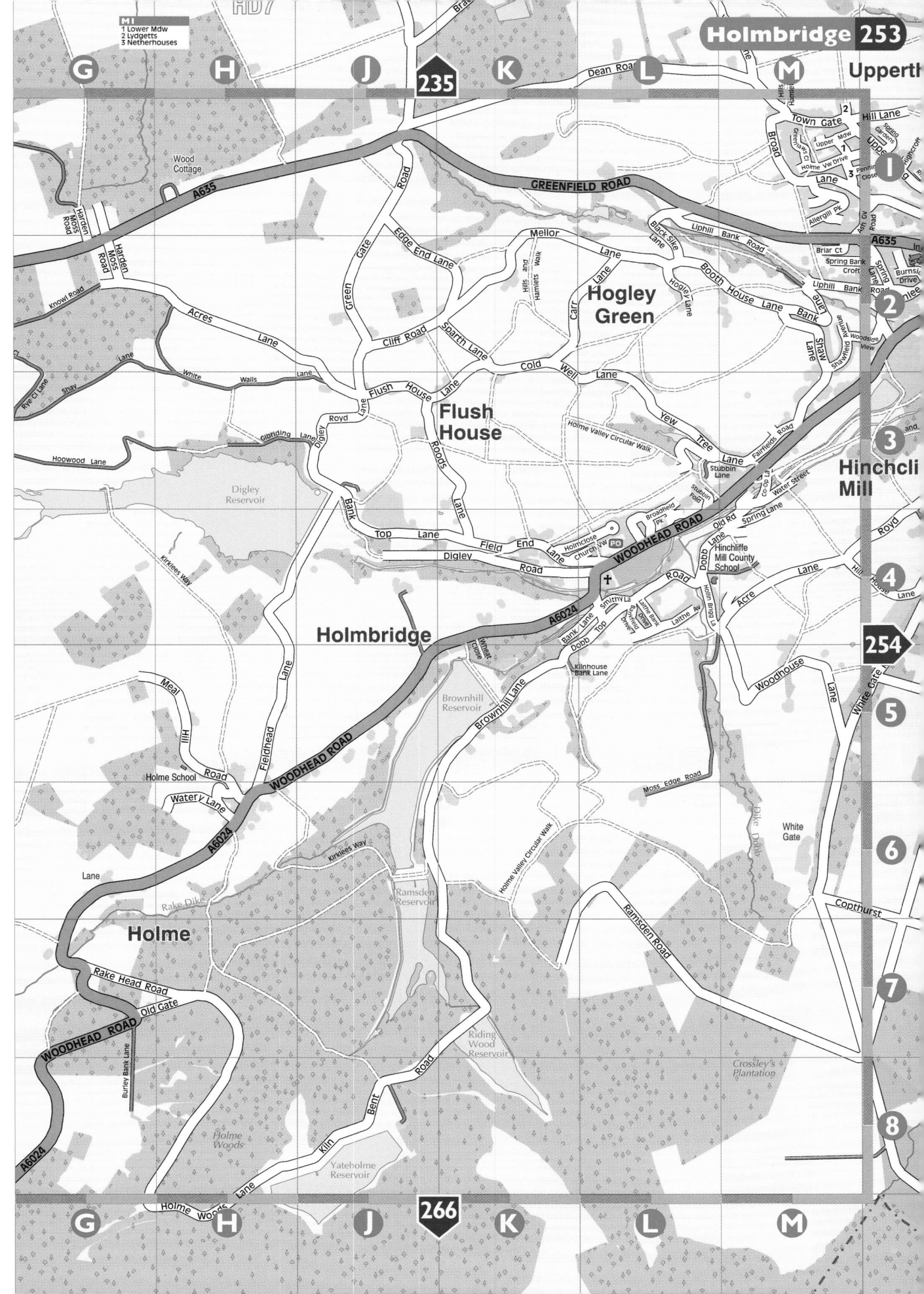

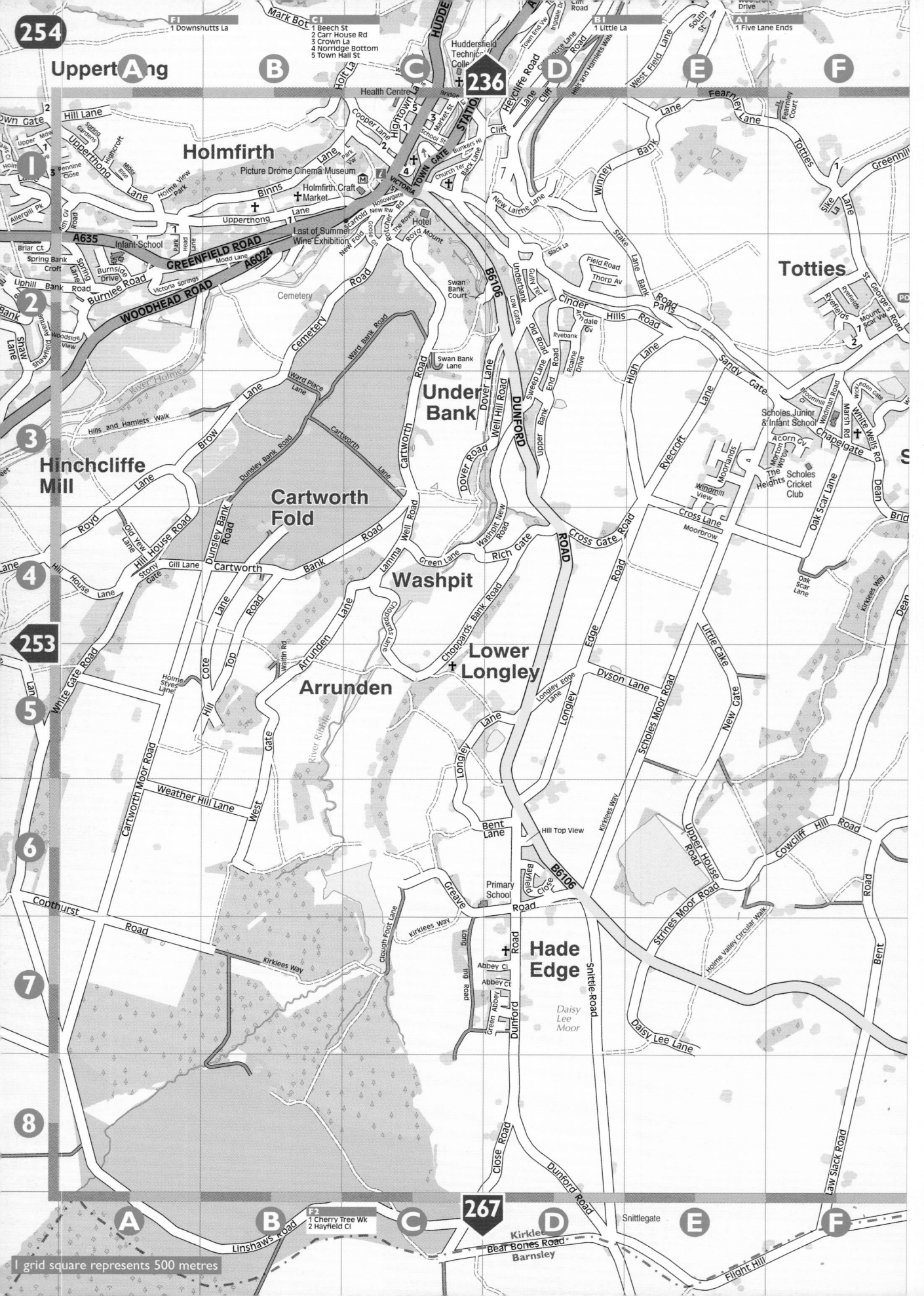

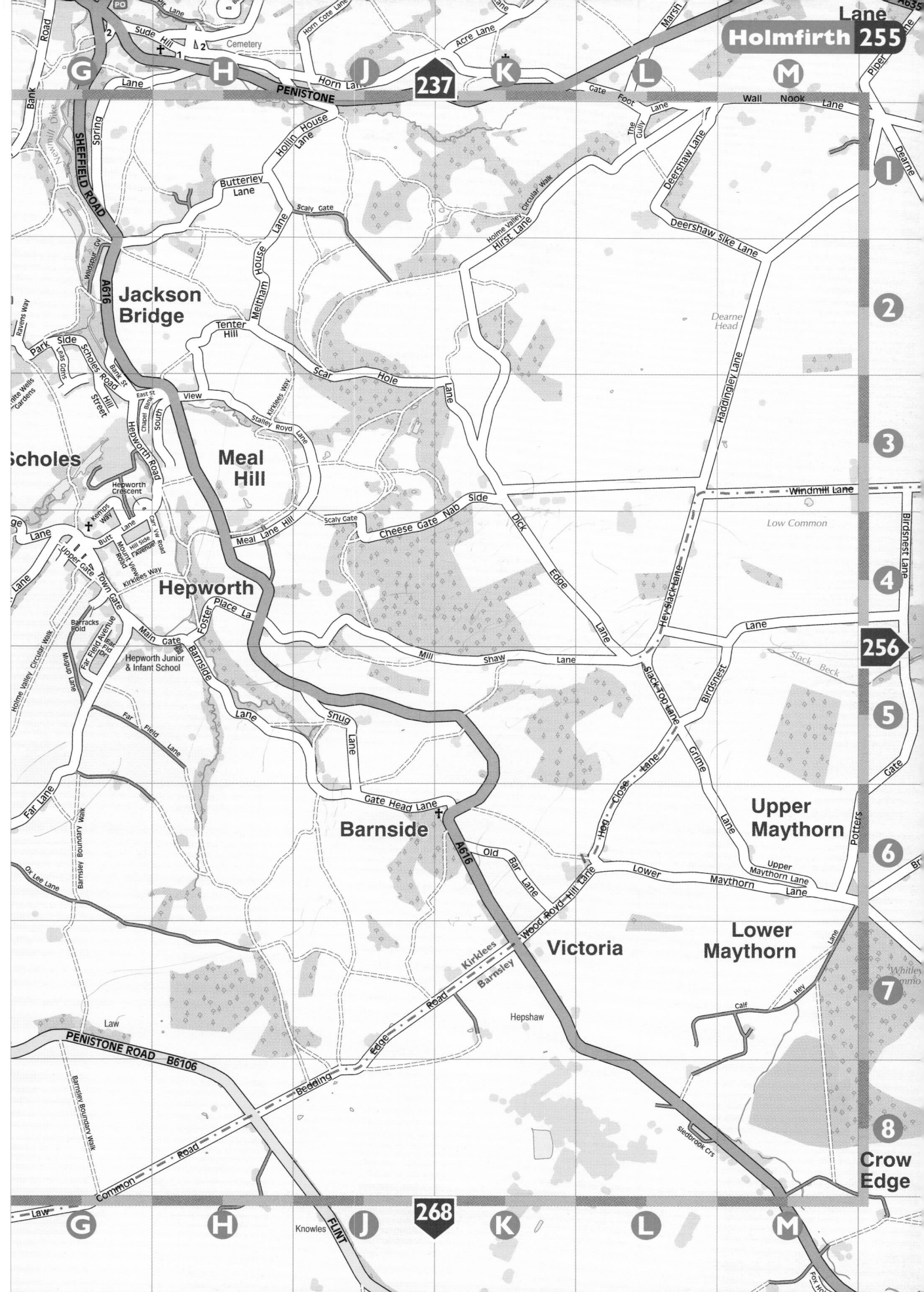

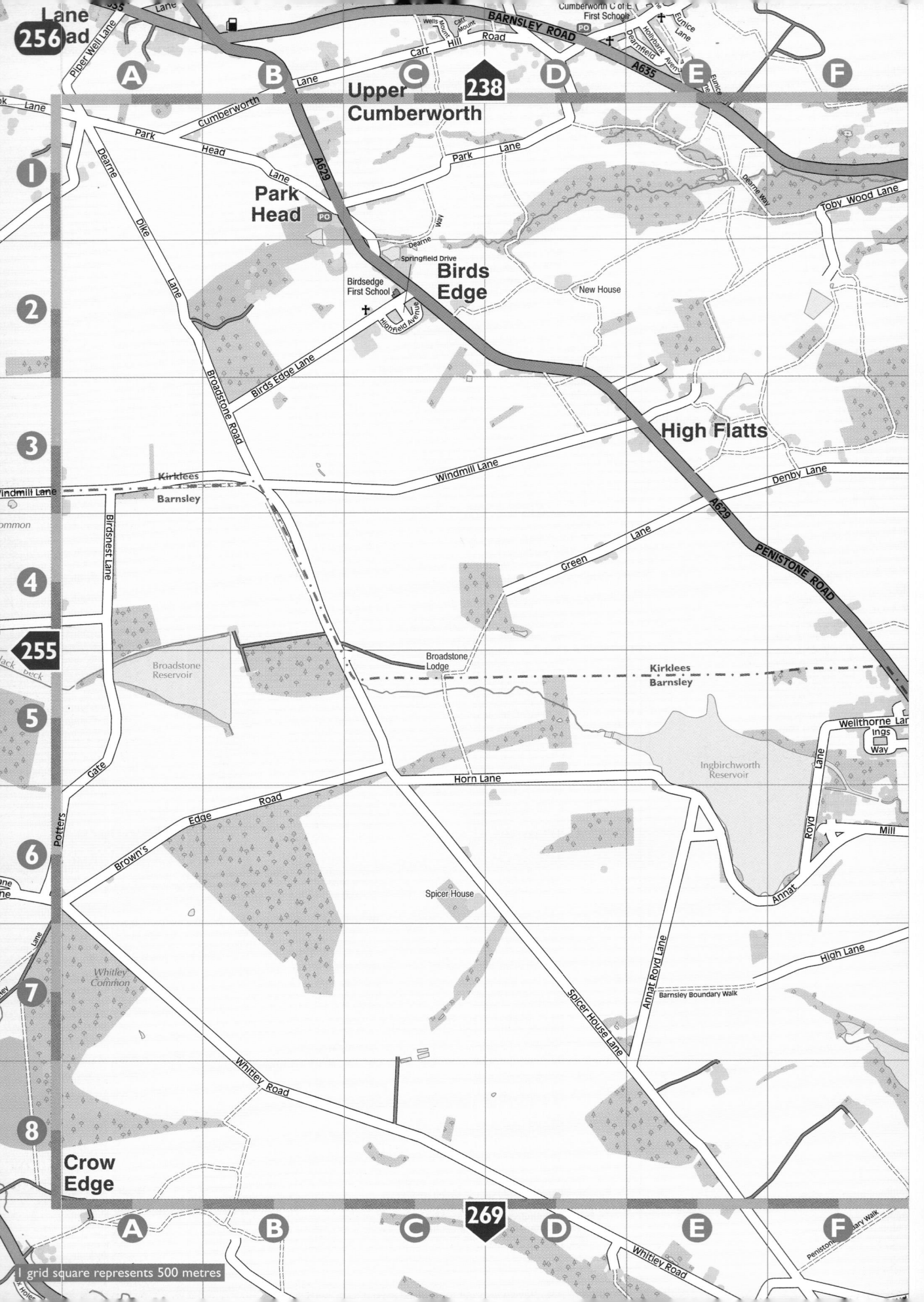

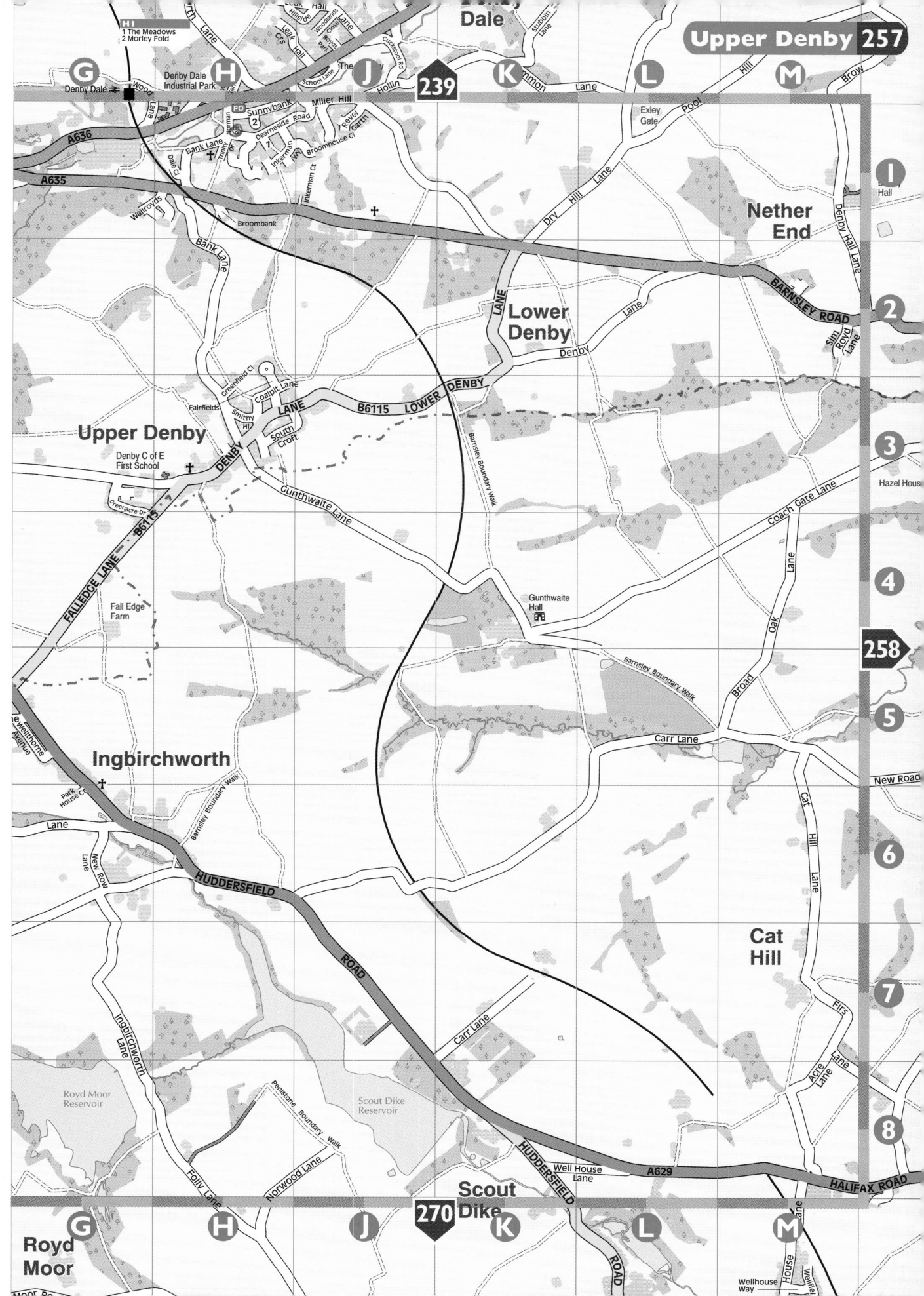

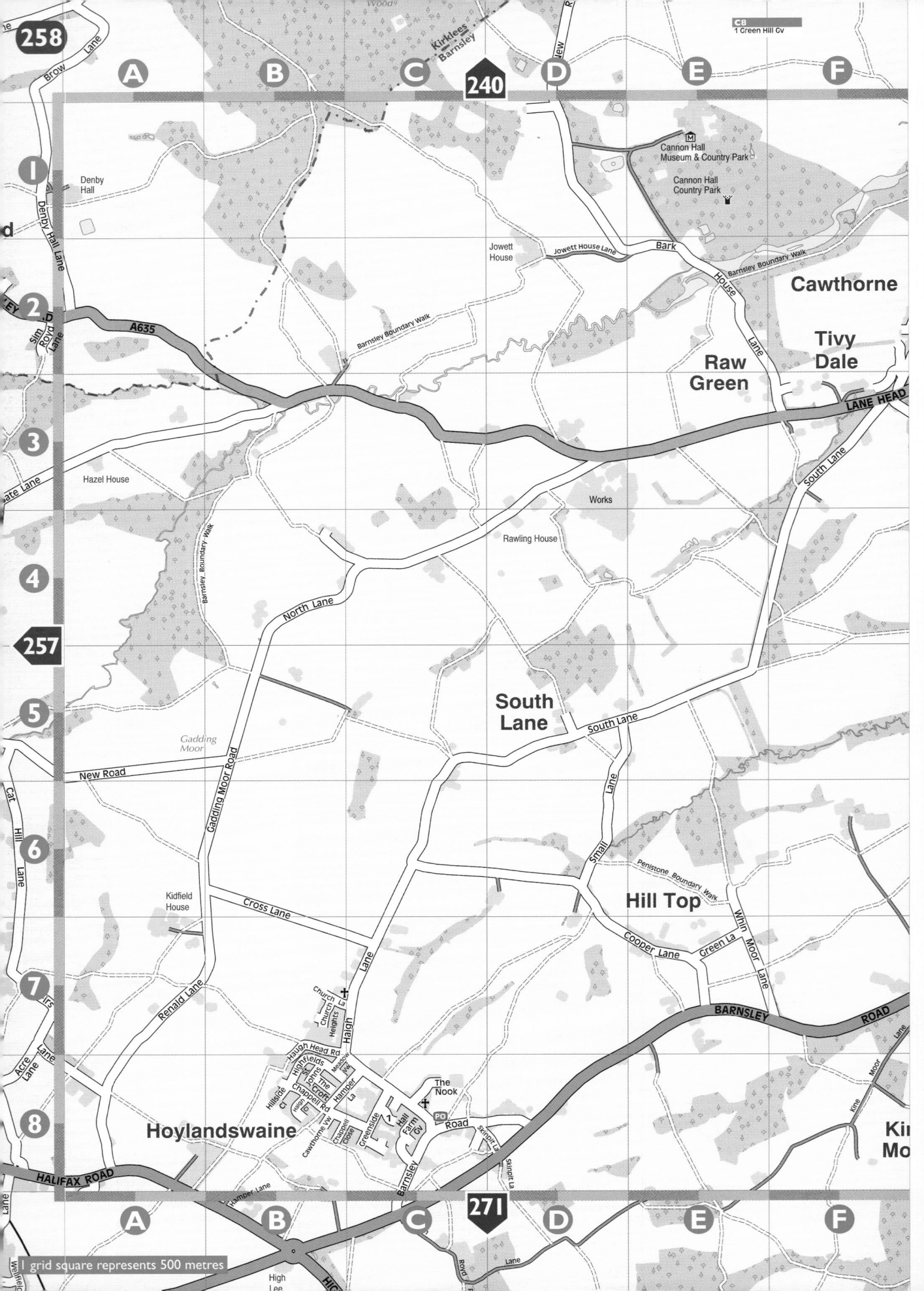

A   B   C   240   D   E   F

C8
1 Green Hill Gv

1

Denby
Hall

d

Denby Hall Lane

2   A635

Sim Royd Lane

Jowett
House

Jowett House Lane

Bark

Cannon Hall
Museum & Country Park

Cannon Hall
Country Park

House

Barnsley Boundary Walk

Cawthorne

Raw
Green

Tivy
Dale

LANE HEAD

Barnsley Boundary Walk

3

Hazel House

gate Lane

Works

South Lane

4

Barnsley Boundary Walk

North Lane

Rawling House

257

5

Gadding
Moor

Gadding Moor Road

South
Lane

South Lane

Lane

New Road

Cat Hill Lane

6

Kidfield
House

Cross Lane

Small Lane

Penistone Boundary Walk

Hill Top

Cooper Lane

Green La

Whin Moor Lane

7

rs

Renald Lane

Church La

Church
Heights

Haigh

Lane

BARNSLEY   ROAD

Acre Lane

Haigh Head Rd

Highfields

Hillside Cl

Chappell Rd

Cawthorne Vw   Chappell Close   Greenside

Hamper La

Hall Farm Gv

The Nook

PO

Road

Skiplt La

Kine Moor

8

Hoylandswaine

Barnsley

Skiplt La

Kir
Mo

HALIFAX ROAD

Weinfield

Hamper Lane

High
Lee

271

HIC

Royd

A   B   C   D   E   F

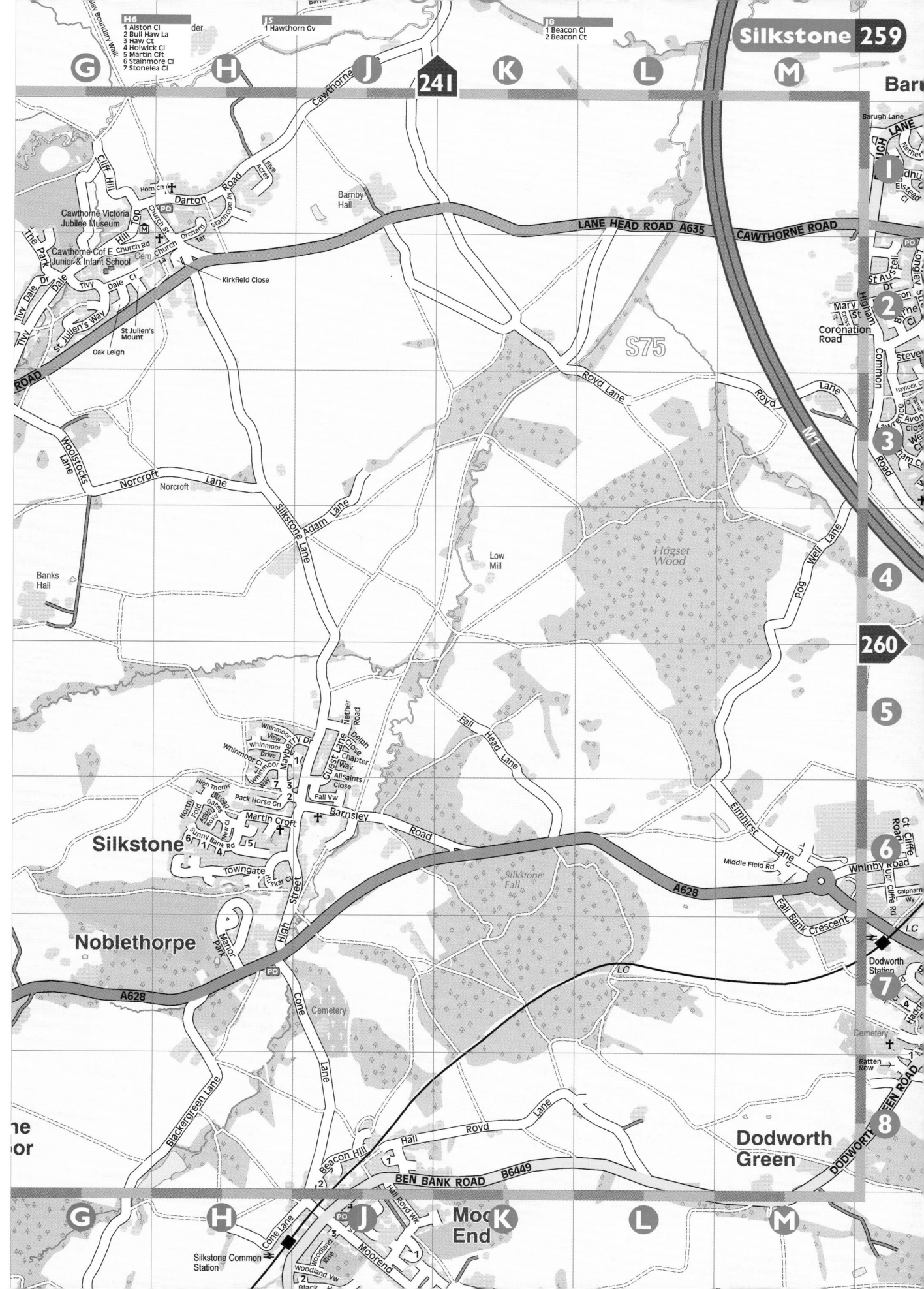

Bar

G H J K L M I

Map labels

H6
1 Alston Cl
2 Bull Haw La
3 Haw Ct
4 Holwick Cl
5 Martin Crft
6 Stainmore Cl
7 Stonelea Cl

J5
1 Hawthorn Gv

J8
1 Beacon Cl
2 Beacon Ct

241

260

Place names and roads

Barugh Lane

LANE HEAD ROAD A635 CAWTHORNE ROAD

Darton

Cawthorne Victoria Jubilee Museum

Cawthorne Cof E Church Rd Junior & Infant School

Kirkfield Close

Barnby Hall

St Julien's Way

St Julien's Mount

Oak Leigh

Woolstocks Lane

Norcroft Lane

Norcroft

Silkstone Lane

Adam Lane

Banks Hall

Low Mill

Hugset Wood

S75

Royd Lane

Royd

Pog Well Lane

Coronation Road

Mary Cross

Higham Common Road

Whinmoor
Whinmoor View
Whinmoor Cl
Whinmoor Drive
Whinmoor Way

Nether Road

Delph Close

Guest Lane

Chapter Way

All Saints Close

Pack Horse Gn

High Thorns

Fall Vw

Barnsley Road

Martin Croft

Sunny Bank Rd

Silkstone

Towngate

High Street

Manor Park

Cone Lane

Cemetery

Noblethorpe

A628

Silkstone Fall

Elmhirst Lane

Middle Field Rd

Fall Bank Crescent

A628

Whinby Road

Gt Cliffe Road

Galpharm Wy

Upr Cliffe Rd

LC

Dodworth Station

Cemetery

Ratten Row

DODWORTH GREEN ROAD

Dodworth Green

Blackergreen Lane

Beacon Hill

Hall Royd Wk

Royd

Lane

Hall Royd Wk

BEN BANK ROAD B6449

Silkstone Common Station

Cone Lane

Woodland Rise

Woodland Vw

Moorend

Moor End

G H J K L M

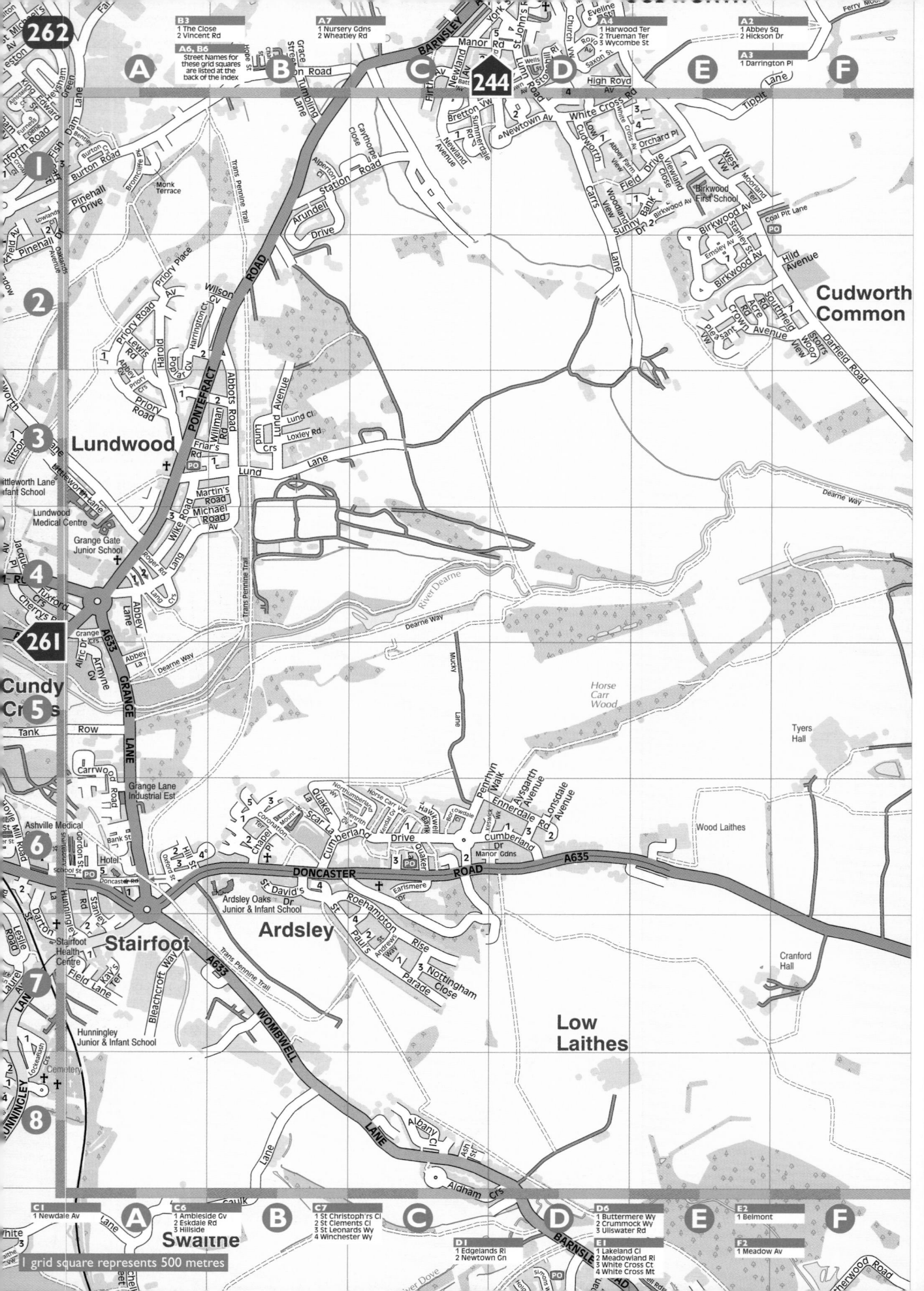

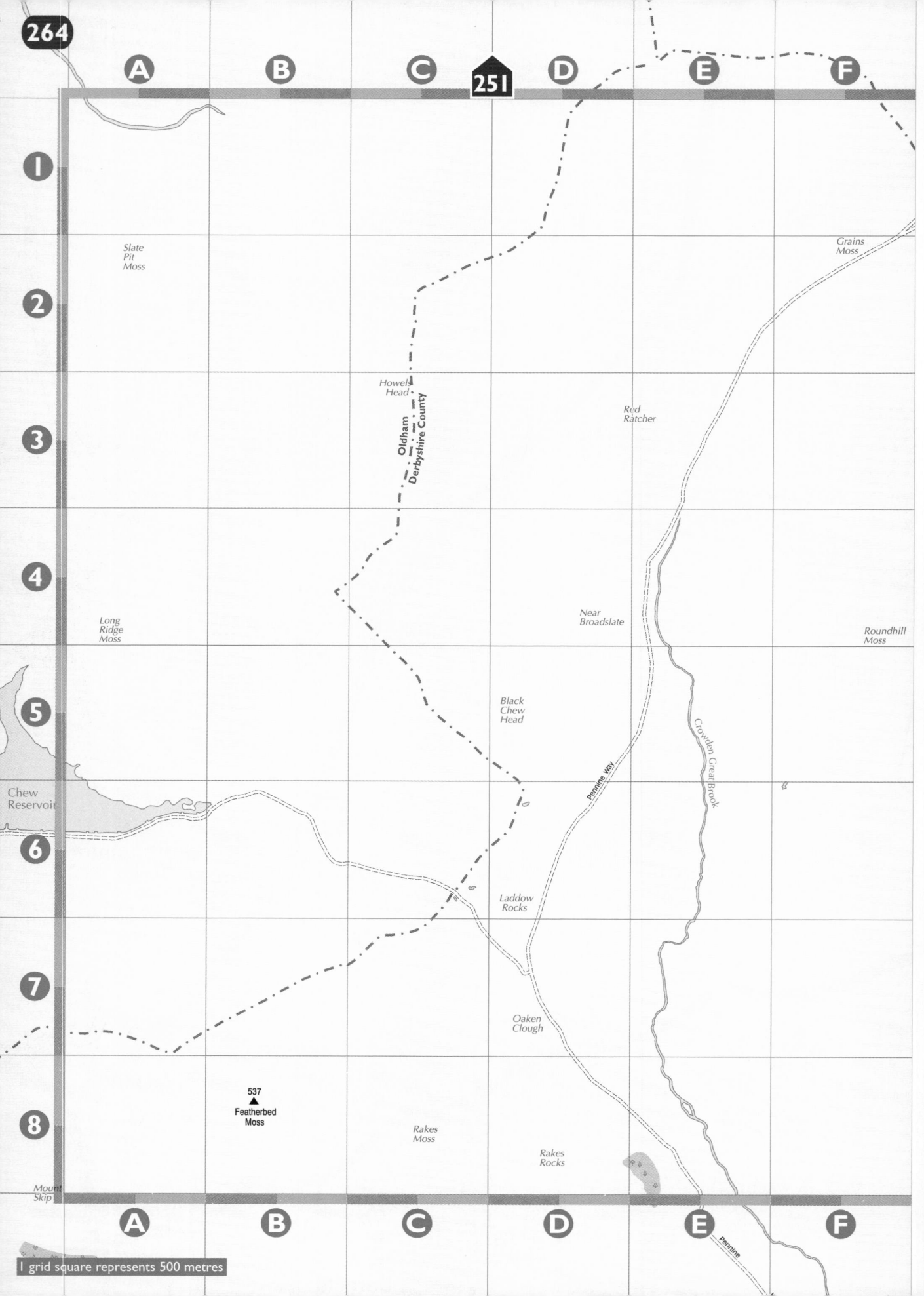

251

A B C D E F

1

Slate
Pit
Moss

2

Grains
Moss

Howels
Head

3

Oldham
Derbyshire County

Red
Ratcher

4

Long
Ridge
Moss

Near
Broadslate

Roundhill
Moss

5

Black
Chew
Head

Crowden Great Brook

Chew
Reservoir

6

Pennine Way

Laddow
Rocks

7

Oaken
Clough

537
▲
Featherbed
Moss

8

Rakes
Moss

Rakes
Rocks

Mount
Skip

A B C D E F

Pennine

Pennine

I grid square represents 500 metres

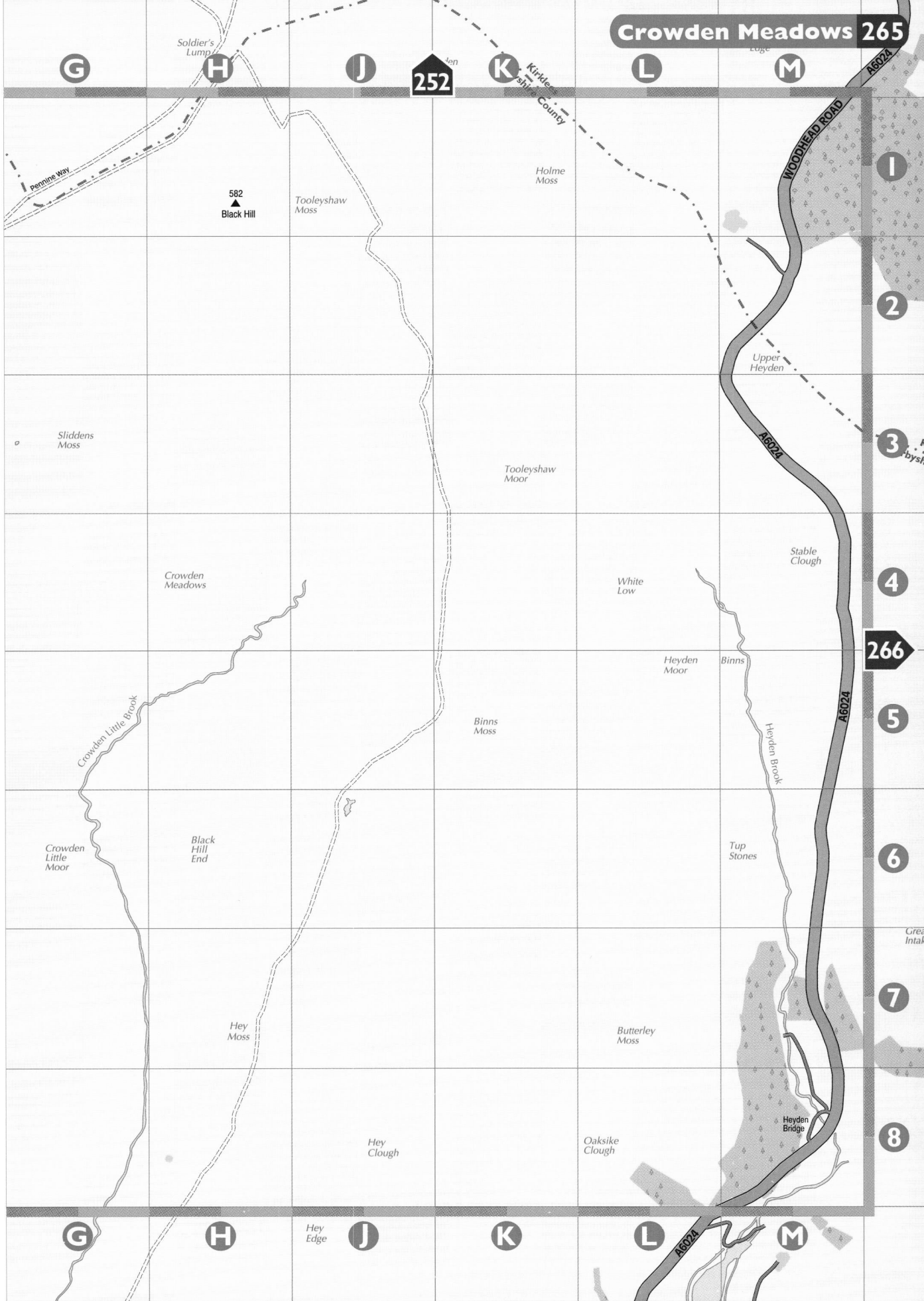

Soldier's Lump

Pennine Way

G   H   252   K   L   M

582 ▲
Black Hill

Tooleyshaw Moss

Holme Moss

Kirklees
shire County

1

Woodhead Road

A6024

2

Upper Heyden

Sliddens Moss

3   K
byshi

Tooleyshaw Moor

A6024

Stable Clough

Crowden Meadows

White Low

4

266

Crowden Little Brook

Heyden Moor

Binns

5

A6024

Binns Moss

Heyden Brook

Crowden Little Moor

Black Hill End

Tup Stones

6

Grea
Intake

7

Hey Moss

Butterley Moss

Heyden Bridge

8

Hey Clough

Oaksike Clough

G   H   Hey Edge   J   K   L   A6024   M

253

265

A6024

A B C D E F

1

2

3

4

5

6

7

8

ROHEAD ROAD
A6024

Holme
Woods

Holme Woods Lane

Kiln

Bent

Yateh
Reserv

Ramsden
Clough

Twizle
Head
Moss

Kirklees
Derbyshire County

Kirklees
Barnsley

West
Withens
Clough

Great
Grains
Clough

Withens
Edge

Grains
Moss

Dewhill
Naze

Withens
Moor

Barnsley
Derbyshire County

Great
Intake

Cat
Clough

Little
Intake

Stone
Low

Pikenaze
Moor

able
ough

en

Hawthorn
Clough

A B C D E F

1 grid square represents 500 metres

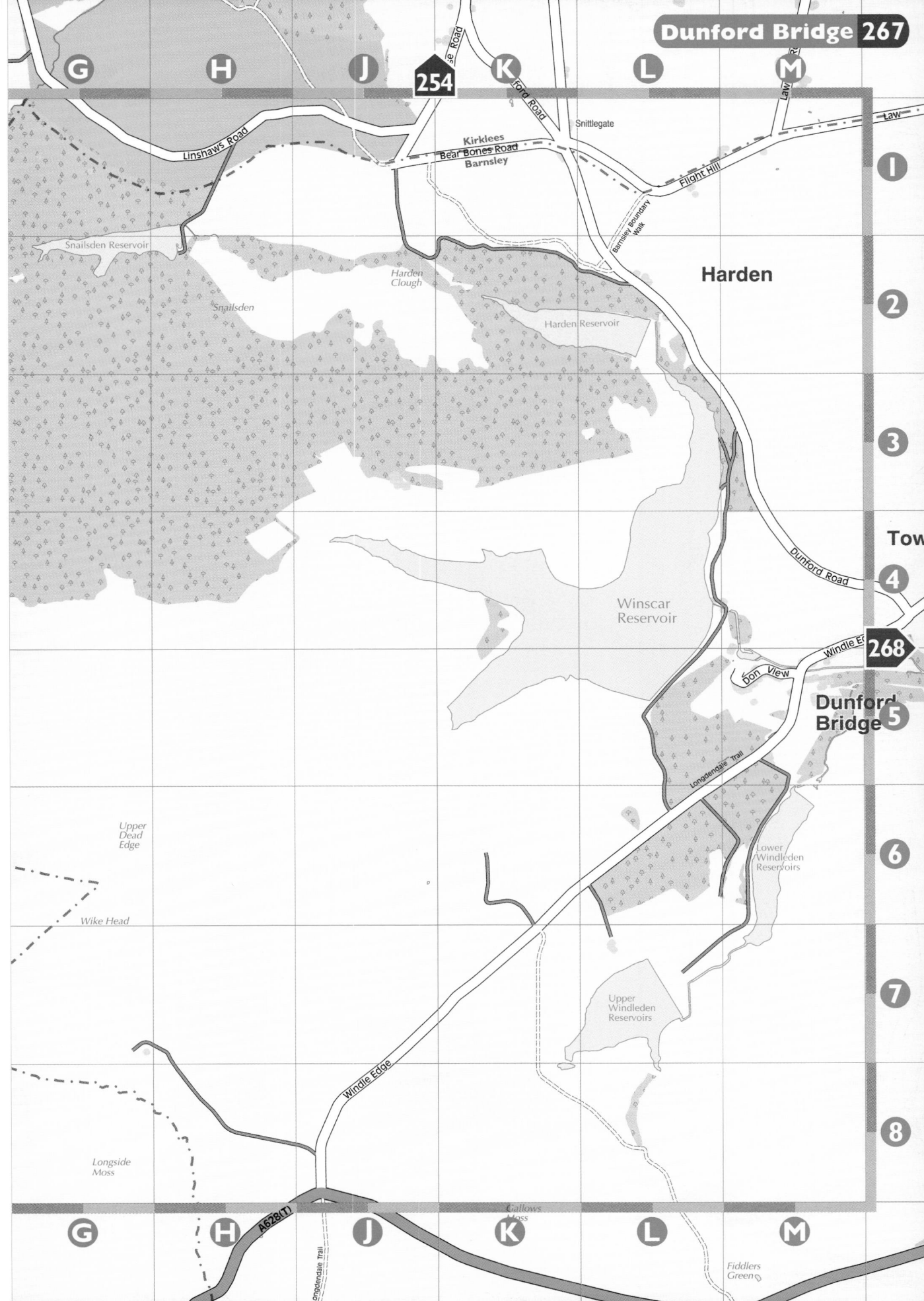

G H J 254 K L M

I

Law

Linshaws Road

Kirklees
Bear Bones Road
Barnsley

Snittlegate

Flight Hill

Barnsley Boundary Walk

Harden

Snailsden Reservoir

Snailsden

Harden
Clough

Harden Reservoir

2

3

Dunford Road

Tow

4

Winscar
Reservoir

Windle E

268

Don View

**Dunford
Bridge**

5

Upper
Dead
Edge

Longdendale Trail

Lower
Windleden
Reservoirs

6

Wike Head

7

Upper
Windleden
Reservoirs

Windle Edge

8

Longside
Moss

Windle Edge

Longdendale Trail

G H A628(T) J K L M

Gallows
Moss

Fiddlers
Green

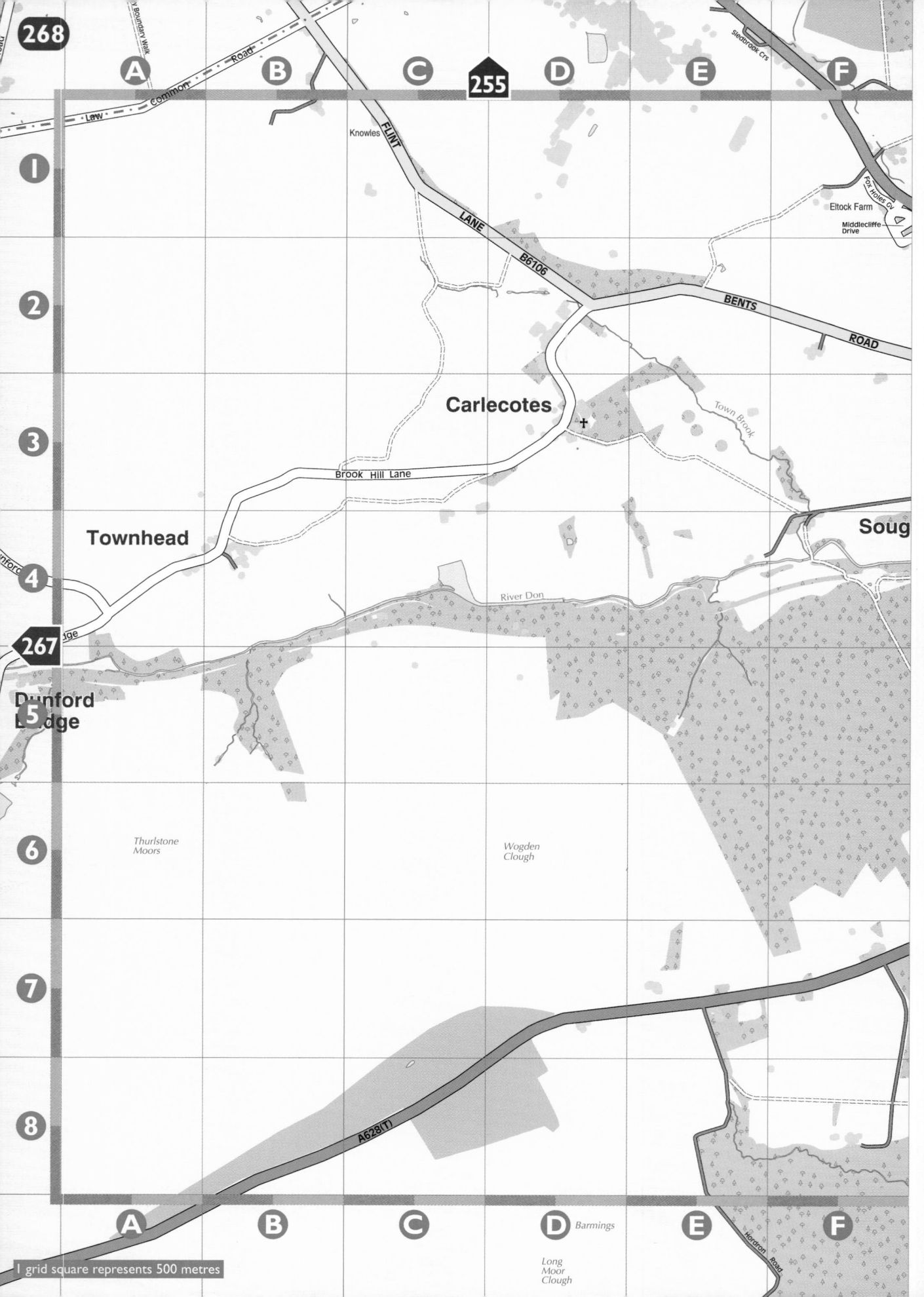

A B C **255** D E F

I

Law Common Road

Boundary Walk

Knowles

FLINT

Sledbrook Crs

LANE

B6106

Fox Holes Cv

Eltock Farm

Middlecliffe
Drive

2

BENTS

ROAD

Carlecotes

Town Brook

3

Brook Hill Lane

Townhead

Soug

4

River Don

5

Dunford
Lodge

Thurlstone
Moors

Wogden
Clough

6

7

A628(T)

8

A B C D Barmings E F

Hordron Road

Long
Moor
Clough

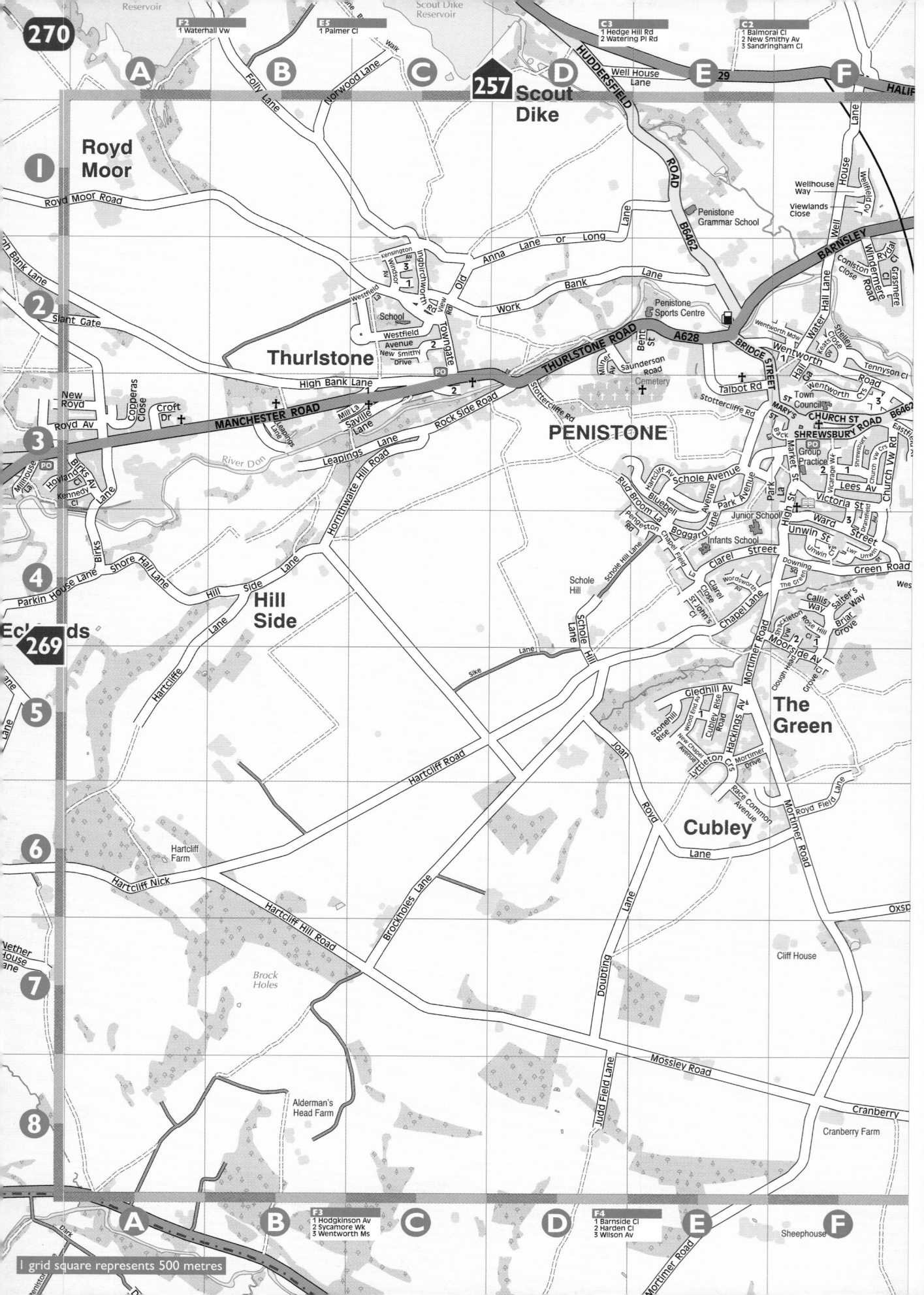

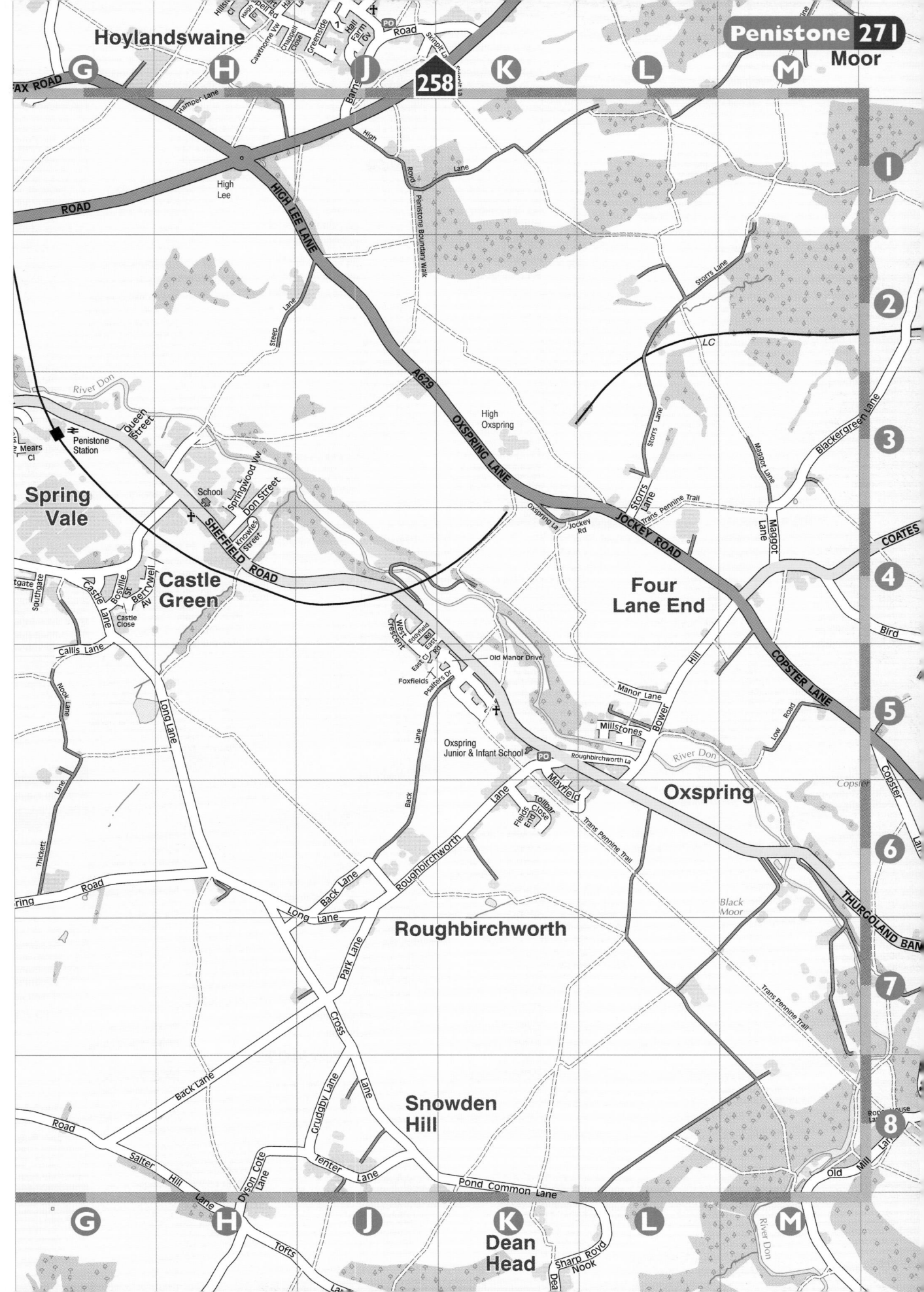

Hoylandswaine

G H J 258 K L M

1

2

LC

3

High
Oxspring

COATES

Spring
Vale

Penistone
Station

River Don

Mears
Cl

Queen
Street

School

Don Street

Knowles Street

SHEFFIELD ROAD

Castle
Green

Castle
Lane

Castle
Close

Bosville

Berrywell
Av

Southgate

Callis Lane

Nook Lane

Long Lane

HIGH LEE LANE

High
Lee

ROAD

Steep Lane

Lane

A629

Penistone Boundary Walk

High Royd

OXSPRING LANE

Oxspring La

Storrs Lane

Storrs Lane

Storrs Lane

Jockey Rd

Maggot Lane

JOCKEY ROAD

Maggot Lane

Blackergreen Lane

Four
Lane End

COPSTER LANE

Bird

4

5

West
Crescent

Oxyfield

East Cl

Foxfields

Psalters Dr

Old Manor Drive

Manor Lane

Bower
Hill

Millstones

Roughbirchworth La

River Don

Low
Road

Copster

Copster

THURGOLAND BAN

6

Oxspring
Junior & Infant School

PO

Back Lane

Lane

Mayfield

Tollbar
Close

Fields
End

Trans Pennine Trail

Oxspring

Black
Moor

7

Thickett Lane

Spring
Road

Long Lane

Back Lane

Park Lane

Cross Lane

Roughbirchworth

Roughbirchworth

Trans Pennine Trail

Road

Back Lane

Cruddaby Lane

Snowden
Hill

Salter Hill Lane

Dyson Cote Lane

Tenter Lane

Pond Common Lane

Old Mill Lane

Rond House
Lane

8

G H J K L M

Dean
Head

Toffs

Sharp Royd
Nook

River Don

Aberford 91 M7
Ackton 179 J6
Ackworth Moor Top 224 A1
Addingham 19 C6
Addingham Moorside 36 F2
Adel 86 E2
Adwalton 129 J8
Agbrigg 13 K9
Ainley Top 191 K2
Airedale 158 D7
Aire View 34 B4
Allerton 103 L6
Allerton Bywater 157 L2
Almondbury 215 H2
Altofts 178 A1
Alverthorpe 176 A6
Alwoodley 87 L1
Alwoodley Gates 66 A8
Alwoodley Park 65 H8
Ambler Thorn 124 D6
Angram 33 M8
Apperley Bridge 84 A5
Appleton Roebuck 73 M4
Ardsley 262 B4
Armitage Bridge 214 B7
Armley 108 F6
Arrunden 254 B5
Arthington 43 M8
Arthursdale 90 B6
Askwith 40 B1
Athersley North 243 H6
Athersley South 243 J7
Austhorpe 112 A6
Badsworth 224 F4
Bagley 107 G2
Baildon 82 F3
Baildon Green 82 C4
Bailiff Bridge 148 C6
Balderstone 228 D4
Bank Top 105 L1
Bank Top 169 H1
Bantam Grove 152 F2
Barcroft 79 H6
Bardsey 67 L2
Barkisland 189 K2
Barkston Ash 115 L1
Barnbow Carr 112 E1
Barnside 255 J6
Barnsley 261 J7
Barugh 242 A8
Barugh Green 260 A2
Barwick in Elmet 90 E8
Batley 173 L2
Batley Carr 173 L3
Battyeford 194 A1
Beal 161 K7
Beamsley 19 G1
Beck Bottom 175 L3
Beck Foot 81 G5
Beechcliffe 57 M5
Beechwood 89 G8
Beeston 131 G4
Beeston Hill 8 C9
Beeston Park Side 131 J6
Beeston Royds 130 D3
Beggarington Hill 174 E1
Belfield 206 F7
Belle Green 244 E7
Belle Isle 132 A7
Belle Vue 13 K7
Ben Rhydding 39 G3
Bentgate 229 J2
Berry Brow 214 B6
Bickerton 31 L4
Bierley 127 K5
Biggin 117 M4
Bilton in Ainst 32 C5
Bingley 81 G3
Birchencliffe 191 J4
Birds Edge 256 C2
Birkby 14 A1
Birkenshaw 128 D8
Birkenshaw Bottoms 150 E2
Birkhouse 148 E8
Birkin 161 J4
Birks 152 C4
Birstall 151 G4
Birstall Smithies 151 G7
Blacker 242 E7
Black Hill 2 A2
Blackley 191 G2
Black Moor 87 J2
Blackmoorfoot 213 G7
Blackshaw Head 142 B3
Bleak Hey Nook 231 L7
Bogthorn 79 G2
Bolton 105 H2
Bolton Percy 73 H7
Bolton Woods 105 G2
Booth 145 G3
Boothroyd 173 J6
Boothtown 146 C4
Booth Wood 188 E8
Boston Spa 48 E7
Bottom Boat 155 L8
Bottomley 189 M3
Boulder Clough 166 E1
Bowling 127 K2
Bracken Bank 79 H3
Brackenhall 192 D2
Bracken Hill 171 L7
Bracken Park 67 H7
Brackenthwaite 26 A3
Bradford 4 D6
Bradley 171 H8
Bradley Mills 15 M1
Bradshaw 124 B5
Bradshaw 211 J5
Braithwaite 56 F6
Brakenhill 201 L8
Bramham 69 M3
Bramhope 63 L3
Bramley 107 L5
Brandy Carr 175 M2
Braythorn 24 E7
Brearley 144 C6
Brierley 245 H3
Briestfield 195 J7

Brighouse 170 B4
Briscoerigg 25 G4
Broad Carr 190 B2
Brockholes 236 F4
Brookfoot 170 A3
Brookhouse 123 K6
Brooklands 111 L1
Brotherton 159 M6
Brown Moor 112 B6
Bruntcliffe 152 A3
Brunthwaite 36 C5
Buckley 206 C3
Buersil Head 228 E5
Burley 108 F4
Burley in Wharfedale 39 L5
Burley Woodhead 39 L8
Burmantofts 110 B5
Burn Bridge 26 E2
Burnedge 229 G5
Burton Salmon 160 A2
Buttershaw 125 M6
Byram 160 A7
Cackleshaw 78 F4
Calderbrook 185 M5
Calder Grove 197 L8
Caldermoor 185 J8
Calverley 84 E8
Cambridge 41 L7
Campsall 227 M6
Camp Town 87 K3
Carcroft 249 L4
Carlecotes 268 C3
Carleton 203 H1
Carlinghow 151 K7
Carlton 243 M5
Carr Gate 176 A1
Cartworth Fold 254 B3
Castleford 157 K7
Castleford Ings 158 A5
Castle Green 271 H4
Castle Street 164 A1
Castley 43 K6
Catherine Slack 124 E8
Cat Hill 257 M7
Catshaw 269 K3
Catterton 51 L6
Causeway Foot 124 A3
Causeway Foot 238 A1
Cawthorne 258 F2
Chapel Allerton 87 L7
Chapelthorpe 220 C2
Chapeltown 87 L6
Charlestown 83 G4
Charlestown 142 E4
Chat Hill 125 J1
Chequerfield 181 H8
Chevin End 61 M1
Chickenley 174 D7
Chidswell 174 D3
Chiserley 143 L1
Church Clough 74 A3
Church Fenton 94 F8
Churwell 130 E7
Claremount 11 H3
Clayton 125 L2
Clayton Heights 125 L4
Clayton West 240 C4
Cleckheaton 173 J2
Clerk Green 173 J2
Cliff End 191 K8
Clifford 69 M1
Clifton 41 G1
Clifton 170 F4
Clough 185 J7
Clough 229 M8
Clough Foot 162 D2
Clough Head 167 L5
Clough Head 212 D3
Cockersdale 129 H6
Cockley Hill 193 M6
Colden 120 C8
Cold Hiendley 221 M5
Coley 147 M4
Collingham 47 J7
Colne Bridge 193 J1
Colton 111 L8
Combs 195 M3
Compton 47 M8
Cononley 34 A3
Cookridge 63 M8
Copley 168 C4
Copley Hill 151 H4
Cornholme 140 D5
Cottingley 81 J7
Cotton Stones 166 E6
Cowcliffe 192 B3
Cowling 54 E4
Cowmes 215 L1
Cowthorpe 30 F1
Coxley 196 F7
Crackenedge 173 M5
Cragg Hill 85 L6
Cragg Vale 165 M2
Crawshaw 217 J6
Cridling Stubbs 183 G7
Cringles 18 B8
Crofton 200 A6
Crompton Fold 229 L5
Cromwell Bottom 169 L5
Crosland Edge 235 H1
Crosland Hill 213 J4
Crosland Moor 213 L3
Crossflatts 59 G8
Cross Gates 111 J5
Cross Green 132 B1
Cross Hills 34 F8
Crossley 172 D6
Crossley Hall 104 A7
Cross Roads 79 G5
Crow Edge 256 A8
Crow Nest 81 K3
Cubley 270 E6
Cudworth 244 D8
Cudworth Common 262 F2
Cullingworth 79 K8
Cundy Cross 261 M5

Cutsyke 179 L1
Daisy Hill 103 H4
Daisy Hill 130 E8
Dalton 193 H8
Damems 79 H4
Dam Head 147 H3
Darrington 203 L1
Darton 242 A6
Daw Cross 26 C2
Dearnley 207 H2
Deighton 193 H2
Denby Dale 239 K8
Denholme 101 L6
Denholme Clough 102 A8
Denholme Edge 101 L5
Denholme Gate 123 M1
Denshaw 230 F4
Denton 21 J8
Dewsbury 173 L7
Dewsbury Moor 173 G5
Dockroyd 78 E5
Dodworth 260 B7
Dodworth Bottom 260 A8
Dodworth Green 259 M8
Dog Hill 230 A7
Dogley Lane 215 L5
Draughton 17 M1
Drighlington 129 H8
Drub 150 B4
Dudley Hill 127 L4
Dunford Bridge 267 M5
Dunkeswick 44 E4
Durkar 198 C7
Durn 207 L1
Earlsheaton 174 A7
East Ardsley 153 J7
East Bierley 128 B7
Eastburn 35 J8
East Carlton 63 C3
East Garforth 113 L6
East Hardwick 203 H4
East Keswick 46 E8
East Moor 177 H7
East Morton 59 C5
East Rigton 68 A1
Eastwood 142 D6
Eccleshill 105 K1
Eccup 65 J5
Ecklands 269 M4
Edgerton 191 M6
Egypt 102 D6
Eldwick 81 M1
Elland 169 J8
Elland Lower Edge 169 L7
Elland Upper Edge 169 K8
Emley 217 L7
Esholt 83 L1
Exley 168 E4
Facit 184 A4
Fagley 105 M3
Fairburn 159 H1
The Fall 153 M6
Farnhill 34 E5
Farnley 41 M2
Farnley 130 A1
Farnley Bank 215 G6
Farnley Tyas 215 H8
Far Royds 130 E2
Farsley 106 F3
Farsley Beck Bottom 107 C3
Fartown 192 C4
Fearnville 111 G2
Featherstone 179 L2
Felkirk 222 C8
Fell Lane 2 A6
Fell Lane 57 J2
Fenay Bridge 215 L2
Ferrybridge 159 L8
Firgrove 206 F8
Fishpool 42 C2
Fitzwilliam 223 J2
Five Lane Ends 105 J1
Fixby 192 B1
Flanshaw 176 A8
Flockton 217 L3
Flockton Green 218 A3
Flushdyke 175 H7
Flush House 253 K3
Follifoot 28 A1
Foulby 200 E6
Foulridge 52 A5
Four Lane End 271 L4
Four Lane Ends 104 A6
Fox Royd 195 K4
Friendly 167 J1
Frizinghall 104 C1
Fullshaw 269 K7
Fulneck 128 F1
Fulstone 237 K7
Gale 185 L2
Gamble Hill 108 A6
Garden Village 114 B8
Garforth 135 K1
Gawber 260 C3
Gawthorpe 174 F5
Gawthorpe 193 M8
Gildersome 129 M6
Gildersome Street 151 M1
Gill 54 C3
Gilstead 81 L3
Gipton 110 F3
Gipton Wood 88 D8
Girlington 104 C5
Glass Houghton 180 C1
Gledhow 88 C7
Golcar 212 F2
Gomersal 150 E6
Goose Eye 56 D8
Goosehill 177 M7
Grains Bar 230 D8
Grange Moor 217 H1
Gravel Hole 228 F7
Great Cliff 219 L2
Great Horton 126 B2
Great Howarth 206 C2
Great Preston 135 G6
Green Clough 124 D1
Greengate 206 F3

Greengates 83 M8
Green Hill 92 B6
Green Side 130 E1
Green Side 237 J2
Greenside 215 H1
The Green 270 F5
Greetland 168 C6
Greetland Wall Nook 167 M8
Grimethorpe 245 J7
Grove Town 181 J7
Guard House 57 G7
Guiseley 61 L6
Hade Edge 254 D7
Haigh 241 J2
Haigh Moor 153 H8
Hainworth 79 L3
Hainworth Shaw 79 M3
Halifax 11 H6
Hall Bower 214 D5
Hall Green 220 B3
Halton 111 G6
Halton Moor 110 F7
Hambleton 139 M5
Hampole 248 D5
Hanging Heaton 174 A3
Harden 80 D5
Harden 267 L2
Hare Croft 102 B2
Harehills 110 D4
Harewood 45 J7
Harewood Hill 79 G4
Harrop Dale 231 M8
Hartshead 171 L5
Hartshead Moor Side 149 J8
Hartshead Moor Top 149 G7
Haugh 229 L3
Havercroft 222 D5
Hawks Stones 141 G3
Hawksworth 61 H6
Hawksworth 85 M7
Haworth 78 D7
Hazlehead 269 G4
Headingley 108 C3
Healaugh 51 H2
Healey 173 J1
Healey 196 E3
Healey 206 A2
Heath Common 199 K2
Heaton 104 B3
Heaton Royds 104 A2
Heaton Shay 104 B1
Hebden Bridge 143 K3
Heckmondwike 172 F2
Helme 235 G2
Hemsworth 223 K7
Henshaw 84 C1
Heptonstall 143 G1
Hepworth 255 H4
Hessle 202 A7
Hey Green 232 E1
High Ackworth 202 C6
Higham 260 A3
Higham Common 260 A4
High Bradley 16 E6
Highburton 216 B6
High Crompton 229 G7
Higher Ogden 230 B1
High Flatts 256 E3
High Green 216 B4
High Hoyland 240 F5
Highroad Well Moor 145 K5
Hightown 171 M1
Hightown Heights 171 L1
Hilam 138 E8
Hillfoot 106 E6
Hill Side 193 L7
Hill Side 270 B4
Hill Top 102 F7
Hill Top 108 A4
Hill Top 212 A7
Hill Top 258 D6
Hinchliffe Mill 253 M3
Hipperholme 147 K6
Hogley Green 253 L2
Holbeck 8 D4
Holdsworth 124 D8
Hole 78 D8
Hole Bottom 141 K7
Hollingthorpe 219 M3
Hollin Hall 74 B7
Hollin Park 110 E1
Hollinthorpe 134 C2
Holmbridge 253 J4
Holme 128 B2
Holme 253 G7
Holme Wood 128 B3
Holmfield 146 B1
Holmfirth 254 A1
Holt Head 234 C1
Holt Park 86 B1
Holywell Green 190 D3
Honley 236 A2
Honley Moor 235 M3
Honresfeld 185 M8
Hoo Hole 143 M7
Hopetown 178 F3
Horbury 197 G5
Horbury Bridge 196 F5
Horbury Junction 197 G6
Horsforth 85 H4
Horsforth Woodside 85 L6
Hough Side 107 K6
Houses Hill 194 A8
Howden Clough 151 K4
Hoylandswaine 258 A8
Hoyle Mill 261 L5
Hubberton Green 166 E4
Huby 43 L2
Huddersfield 15 H7
Huddersfield 214 D2
Hungate 156 B6
Hunslet 9 K8
Hunslet Carr 131 M4
Hunsworth 150 A3
Hurstead 206 E2
Hutton Wandesley 33 J4
Ickornshaw 54 C3

Idle 83 K6
Idle Moor 83 H8
Ilkley 38 C2
Illingworth 124 A8
Ingbirchworth 257 G5
Ingmanthorpe 30 D4
Ingrow 79 J2
Intake 107 H3
Ireland Wood 86 B4
Jackson Bridge 255 G2
Jagger Green 190 D3
Jaw Hill 175 J2
John O'Gaunts 133 K7
Jubilee 229 K4
Junction 35 G7
Kearby Town End 46 B3
Kebroyd 166 F8
Keelham 124 B1
Keighley 3 J2
Kelbrook 52 C1
Kelcliffe 61 M4
Kellingley 182 F2
Kellington 161 M7
Kendray 261 L7
Keresforth Hill 260 E7
Kettlethorpe 198 C8
Kexbrough 241 L6
Kiddal Lane End 91 G2
Kildwick 35 G6
Killingbeck 111 G4
Kine Moor 258 F8
Kingstone 260 F7
Kinsley 223 J4
Kippax 135 K4
Kirkburton 216 A8
Kirkby Overblow 27 K7
Kirkby Wharfe 72 C8
Kirk Deighton 29 L5
Kirkhamgate 175 J4
Kirkheaton 193 L5
Kirkholt 228 A3
Kirk Smeaton 226 E1
Kirkstall 108 C3
Kirkthorpe 177 M8
Kitchenroyd 239 J7
Knottingley 182 A2
Knowle Park 2 D8
Knowl Wood 163 J3
Knowsthorpe 9 M6
Knowsthorpe 132 B1
Krumlin 189 J5
Lady House 229 G2
Lady Wood 88 E7
Laisterdyke 105 M8
Lane Bottom 101 K4
Lane End 78 C4
Lane Ends 55 G2
Lane Ends 85 H3
Lane Head 216 C8
Lane Head 237 M8
Laneshaw Bridge 53 G7
Langbar 19 L3
Langsett 269 L8
Larkfield 84 F2
Lawns 154 A8
Lawnswood 86 C4
Laycock 56 D7
Leathley 42 C3
Ledsham 136 F6
Ledston 135 M8
Ledston Luck 135 M4
Leeds 6 E7
Leeming 100 F5
Lee Moor 155 G7
Lees 79 G6
Lepton Edge 216 E3
Leventhorpe 103 L8
Leymoor 213 G1
Lidget Green 126 C1
Lidgett Park 88 C6
Lightcliffe 148 B7
Lighthazles 166 C8
Lindley 24 A7
Lindley 191 K5
Lindwell 168 E6
Lingards Wood 211 L8
Lingbob 102 F2
Linthwaite 212 E5
Linton 47 J4
Littleborough 207 K1
Little Clegg 207 H4
Little Fenton 117 G3
Little Horton 126 D3
Little Houghton 263 M6
Little Lepton 216 C4
Little London 84 C3
Little Preston 134 E5
Little Smeaton 205 H8
Little Thorpe 171 M5
Littletown 172 C1
Liversedge 172 C2
Lockwood 214 A3
Lofthouse 154 F6
Lofthouse Gate 154 E8
Long Lee 3 L8
Longley 167 H5
Long Marston 33 J3
Longwood 191 H8
Longwood Edge 191 G7
Loscoe 179 H3
Low Ackworth 202 E7
Low Barugh 242 B8
Low Bradley 34 F1
Low Compton 229 G8
Lower Altofts 156 C8
Lower Clough 212 F6
Lower Cumberworth 239 H7
Lower Denby 257 K2
Lower Grange 103 L7
Lower Hopton 194 A3
Lower Houses 214 F3
Lower Longley 254 C5
Lower Maythorn 255 M7
Lower Mickletown 157 H4
Lower Place 228 C2
Lower Soothill 152 A8
Lower Town 100 F4
Lower Wyke 148 E6

Low Fold 85 H6
Low Green 84 E3
Low Laithes 262 D7
Low Moor 148 F1
Low Snaygill 16 C6
Luddenden 145 G5
Luddenden Foot 144 E8
Lumb Foot 78 B6
Lumb Head 214 E6
The Lumb 214 E6
Lumbutts 164 A2
Lumby 137 M5
Lundwood 262 A3
Lupset 198 A2
Lydgate 141 G7
Mankinholes 164 C2
Manningham 104 E4
Manor Park 39 M3
Manston 112 A4
Mapplewell 242 E5
Marsden 233 G3
Marsh 100 D2
Marsh 191 L8
Meal Hill 255 H3
Meanwood 87 G6
Measborough Dike 261 K6
Meltham 235 C3
Meltham Mills 235 H4
Menston 61 H3
Merchant Fields 150 A5
Methley 156 E4
Methley Junction 156 F6
Methley Lanes 156 A7
Micklefield 114 B8
Micklethwaite 59 G7
Middlecliffe 263 L8
Middlestown 196 D7
Middleton 20 D7
Middleton 54 C3
Middleton 153 M2
Midgehole 121 J8
Midgley 144 E5
Midgley 218 E4
Miles Hill 87 J8
Mill Bank 166 F7
Millhouse Green 269 L3
Mill Shaw 131 G5
Milnrow 207 J8
Milnsbridge 213 H2
Milnthorpe 198 E7
Minsthorpe 247 H1
Mirfield 172 C8
Mixenden 145 L1
Moldgreen 15 K8
Monk Bretton 261 K2
Monk Fryston 138 C7
Monkhill 180 F4
Monkswood 89 H7
Moor Allerton 87 M4
Moor End 48 D6
Moor End 145 J2
Moor Head 129 K6
Moor Head 217 H8
Moorhead 82 A7
Moorhouse 247 M5
Moor Side 100 B2
Moor Side 148 F1
Moorside 107 L2
Moorside 151 H1
Moorthorpe 247 H3
Moor Top 172 A6
Moortown 87 L4
Morley 152 D3
Mount 190 E5
Mountain 124 D4
Mount Pleasant 173 K2
Mount Tabor 145 J3
Mytholm 143 H3
Mytholmes 78 F6
Mytholmroyd 144 B4
Nab Hill 193 J5
Nab Wood 81 M6
Netherby 45 M4
Nether End 257 M1
Netherley 233 H4
Netheroyd Hill 192 C3
Netherthong 236 C6
Netherton 196 E8
Netherton 213 M8
Nether Yeadon 84 C1
Nettleton Hill 190 D7
Newall 41 J5
Newbold 206 D7
New Brighton 81 L8
New Brighton 152 B2
Newby 43 K3
New Crofton 200 D7
New Farnley 130 A3
New Fryston 158 F3
Newhey 229 H3
New Holland 102 E3
New Lodge 242 F7
New Micklefield 114 D8
New Mill 237 G2
Newmillerdam 220 E2
New Road Side 54 F3

New Road Side 148 F2
Newsam Green 133 L4
New Scarbro 107 M4
New Sharlston 200 B1
Newsholme 78 C2
Newsome 214 C5
Newstead 222 E4
Newthorpe 137 H1
Newton Hill 176 E3
Newton Kyme 50 A7
New Town 180 F2
New Wortley 109 G7
Noblethorpe 259 G7
Noon Nick 103 K2
Norland Town 167 M4
Normanton 178 B4
Norr 102 F1
Norristhorpe 172 D4
North Deighton 29 L2
North Elmsall 225 K8
North Featherstone 179 M5
Northorpe 172 F7
Northowram 147 K4
North Rigton 26 A7
Norton 227 L3
Norton 148 A3
Norwood Green 148 A3
Notton 221 H8
Oakenshaw 149 G2
Oakes 191 J6
Oakwell 150 F3
Oakwood 110 E1
Oakworth 78 D5
Odsal 127 G6
Ogden 123 M4
Old Bramhope 63 K3
Old Dolphin 125 J4
Oldfield 77 M6
Oldfield 236 B5
Old Lindley 190 F3
Old Micklefield 114 A6
Old Snydale 179 G7
Old Tame 230 D6
Old Town 143 K1
Osmondthorpe 110 D7
Osset Spa 197 J3
Ossett 174 F8
Ossett Street Side 174 D6
Otley 41 K5
Oulton 155 K1
Ousel Hole 59 G4
Outlane 190 C5
Outlane Moor 190 B8
Outwood 176 D2
Ouzlewell Green 154 F5
Ovenden 146 B4
Overthorpe 195 L4
Overton 196 C8
Overtown 221 J1
Owlet 104 E1
Oxenhope 100 E4
Oxspring 271 L6
Oxton 72 C3
Paddock 213 M1
Painthorpe 220 A3
Pannal 26 E3
Pannal Ash 26 C1
Park Gate 239 J2
Park Head 256 B1
Parklands 111 H2
Park Mill 240 C2
Park Villas 88 C5
Parlington 113 L1
Peas Acre 59 G6
Pecket Well 121 K6
Pellon 146 A6
Pendas Fields 112 B3
Penistone 270 D3
Penny Hill 189 L5
Pepper Hill 125 K8
Pickles Hill 78 B5
Pickwood Scar 168 A5
Pike End 188 D6
Pike Law 189 H7
Pledwick 220 F1
Pogmoor 260 C4
Pole Moor 211 M2
Pontefract 180 E6
Pool 42 E7
Portobello 198 D4
Portsmouth 140 C5
Potternewton 110 A1
Potterton 91 G3
Pottery Field 9 J5
Priest Hill 29 L6
Priesthorpe 106 C2
Priestley Green 147 M5
Priestthorpe 81 J2
Prince Royd 191 L4
Pudsey 106 F7
Pudsey 140 D4
Pule Hill 146 E3
Purston Jaglin 202 A2
Quarmby 191 J8
Queensbury 124 E5
Rakewood 207 L5
Ramsden Wood 163 H7

Rastrick 170 B6
Ravenscliffe 106 A2
Ravensthorpe 173 G8
Rawdon 84 E3
Rawdon Carrs 84 F4
Rawfolds 172 A1
Raw Green 258 E2
Rawthorpe 15 M4
Red Hill 158 C7
Richmond Hill 110 B6
Riddlesden 58 C5
Ripponden 188 E2
Rishworth 188 D6
Robertown 171 M5
Robin Hood 154 D3
Rochdale 206 A6
Rodley 107 G1
Rodmer Clough 120 A7
Rothwell 155 J1
Rothwell Haigh 132 F7
Rough Bank 207 M8
Roughbirchworth 271 J7
Roundhay 88 F6
Rowley Hill 216 A4
Royd 269 M2
Roydhouse 216 E8
Royd Moor 224 D6
Royd Moor 270 A1
Royds Green 155 J4
Royston 243 J4
Ryhill 222 D5
Ryecroft 80 A5
Ryther 95 M3
St Helen's 261 L1
St John's 92 A5
Salendine Nook 191 G7
Saltaire 82 C5
Sandal 198 F5
Sandal Magna 199 H5
Sandford 108 A1
Sandhill 263 M5
Sandhills 90 A3
Sandy Lane 103 H3
Savile Park 168 C2
Savile Town 195 M1
Sawood 101 H6
Saxton 93 J8
Scapegoat Hill 190 C8
Scarcroft 67 L5
Scarthingwell 94 A7
Scholemoor 126 A1
Scholes 90 B7
Scholes 149 H6
Scholes 254 F3
Scholey Hill 156 C6
School Green 103 J8
Scissett 239 L5
Scout Dike 257 K8
Seacroft 111 J1
Shackleton 121 G6
Shade 163 J2
Shadwell 89 H2
Shafton 244 C3
Shafton Two Gates 244 C4
Sharlston 200 D4
Sharlston Common 200 C3
Shaw 100 D4
Shaw 229 J6
Shaw Cross 174 C4
Shawfield Head 25 J1
Shaw Green 25 J1
Shaw Lands 260 E5
Shay Gate 103 G2
Sheepridge 192 D3
Sheepscar 7 K4
Shelf 125 M8
Shelley 238 C3
Shelley Woodhouse 238 D4
Shepherd Hill 175 H8
Shepley 238 B6
Sherburn in Elmet 115 M5
Shibden Head 124 F8
Shipley 82 C7
Shore 140 E4
Shore 185 H8
Sicklinghall 28 E8
Siddal 169 G3
Silkstone 259 G6
Silsden 36 A5
Skelbrooke 248 E1
Skellow 249 J4
Skelmanthorpe 239 K4
Skipton 16 A4
Slack 120 F8
Slack 190 C6
Slackcote 230 D7
Slaithwaite 212 B6
Slippery Ford 55 L8
Smallbridge 206 F3
Smithies 261 H1
Smithy Bridge 207 J3
Snowden Hill 271 J8
Snow Hill 176 C4
Snow Lea 190 F6
Snydale 201 G1

Soughley 268 F4
South Crosland 213 K8
South Elmsall 247 K3
South Hiendley 222 E8
South Kirkby 246 C5
South Lane 258 D5
South Milford 137 M2
South Ossett 197 G2
Southowram 169 H2
Sowerby 166 F4
Sowerby Bridge 167 L3
Sowood 190 B5
Sowood Green 190 C4
Soyland Town 166 F8
Spacey Houses 26 F3
Spofforth 28 F4
Spring Green 53 J3
Spring Vale 271 G3
Stainburn 25 G8
Staincliffe 173 J2
Staincross 242 D4
Stainland 190 A2
Stairfoot 262 A7
Stanbury 77 L7
Stanks 111 M3
Stanley 177 G2
Stanley Ferry 177 K3
Stanningley 107 H5
Stead 39 J5
Steep Lane 166 E2
Steeton 56 F1
Stockbridge 57 M4
Stone Chair 147 L2
Stone Head 53 M3
Stoneyfield 228 B2
Stoney Royd 11 H8
Stourton 132 D5
Strawberry Hill 180 A7
Streethouse 200 F1
Stutton 71 L7
Summit 185 K5
Summit 228 D7
Sutton 160 B7
Sutton 227 M8
Sutton-in-Craven 56 A1
Sutton Mill 56 A1
Swain House 105 H1
Swallow Hill 242 C7
Swarcliffe 111 L2
Swartha 36 B4
Swillington 134 C4
Swillington Common 112 B8
Swincliffe 150 C2
Swinnow Moor 107 K6
Syke 206 B2
Sympson Green 83 L5
Tadcaster 71 L2
Tandem 215 K1
Tarn 83 G2
Thackley 83 J5
Thackley End 83 H4
Thick Hollins 235 H5
Thongsbridge 236 E6
Thornbury 106 A6
Thorncliff 216 E7
Thorner 90 B1
Thornes 12 E9
Thornham Fold 228 C7
Thornhill 196 B4
Thornhill Edge 195 L6
Thornhill Lees 195 L2
Thornhills 170 E2
Thornton 103 G8
Thorp Arch 49 G6
Thorpe Audlin 225 J1
Thorpe Edge 83 K8
Thorpe on The Hill 153 L4
Thunder Bridge 237 L3
Thurlstone 270 B2
Thurstonland 237 H5
Thwaites 58 B7
Thwaites Brow 58 B8
Tingley 153 G5
Tinshill 86 A3
Tivy Dale 258 F2
Todmorden 163 L2
Toftshaw 127 L6
Tong 129 G5
Tong Park 83 H2
Tong Street 127 M5
Toothill 170 C8
Totties 254 F7
Toulston 70 E1
Town End 212 E2
Town Head 36 B4
Townhead 268 A4
Towton 93 M2
Trawden 74 E4
Triangle 167 G5
Troydale 107 J8
Tunshill 207 L7
Turf Hill 228 F2
Tyersal 128 B1
Tyersal 94 E2
Under Bank 254 C3
Undercliffe 105 J4

Upper Armley 108 C5
Upper Batley 151 L6
Upper Brockholes 123 L6
Upper Clough 212 E6
Upper Cudworth 244 E6
Upper Cumberworth 238 C8
Upper Denby 217 K1
Upper Denby 257 G3
Upper Green 153 G7
Upper Heaton 193 J3
Upper Hopton 194 A4
Upper Marsh 100 C2
Upper Maythorn 255 M8
Upper Moor Side 129 K5
Upperthong 235 M8
Upper Town 100 D4
Upton 225 L7
Utley 57 K4
Vale 140 E5
Victoria 255 K7
Wainstalls 145 G1
Wakefield 12 E2
Walsden 163 H5
Walshaw 120 E3
Walton 49 J2
Walton 199 K8
Wardle 184 F8
Warland 185 M1
Warley Town 145 K8
Warmfield 178 A8
Washpit 254 C4
Water Fryston 159 H4
Wayside Gardens 67 L5
Weardley 44 D8
Weeton 44 B4
Weetwood 86 E6
Well Heads 102 C7
Wellhouse 212 F3
Wellington Hill 89 G5
Wellroyd 84 F5
Wentbridge 203 L7
Wescoe Hill 43 L4
West Ardsley 152 F8
West Bowling 127 H3
West Bretton 219 H6
West Carlton 62 D3
West End 85 G4
West End 94 E1
West End 149 K7
Westfield 84 A1
Westfield 172 F1
West Garforth 134 F1
Westgate Hill 128 C6
West Green 244 B8
West Hardwick 201 K5
West Morton 58 C4
Weston 40 D3
West Park 86 D6
West Royd 82 F6
West Scholes 124 F3
West Vale 168 F8
Wetherby 48 B1
Wheatley 145 M4
Wheldale 158 D5
Whinmoor 89 L6
Whins Wood 79 J5
Whitecote 107 L1
White Hill 77 M1
White Lee 151 G7
Whitkirk 111 L7
Whitley Head 56 E2
Whitley Lower 195 G6
Whitwood 157 G8
Wibsey 126 D5
Wighill 50 C4
Wike 66 F5
Wilberlee 211 M4
Wilsden 102 D1
Wilshaw 235 J6
Wilthorpe 260 E2
Windhill 82 F7
Windmill Hill 200 C6
Winewall 74 E2
Wintersett 222 C2
Womersley 205 J3
Woodhall Hills 106 C3
Woodhouse 3 H9
Woodhouse 6 E2
Woodhouse 170 E6
Woodhouse 178 B6
Woodkirk 152 E7
Woodlands 11 H1
Woodlesford 133 L8
Wood Row 156 D3
Woodside 126 C8
Woolgreaves 198 F8
Woolley 220 C8
Worsbrough Common 261 G8
Wortley 108 C8
Wragby 201 J7
Wrangbrook 226 B7
Wrenthorpe 176 B4
Wrose 83 G8
Wycoller 75 H3
Wyke 148 E4
Yeadon 84 D1

USING THE STREET INDEX

Street names are listed alphabetically. Each street name is followed by its postal town or area locality, the Postcode District, the page number, and the reference to the square in which the name is found.

Aaron Wilkinson Ct *HEM/SK/SE* WF9 .... 246 C4 🔲

Some entries are followed by a number in a blue box. This number indicates the location of the street within the referenced grid square. The full street name is listed at the side of the map page.

GENERAL ABBREVIATIONS

ACC ...ACCESS	CTYD ...COURTYARD	HLS ...HILLS	MWY ...MOTORWAY	SE ...SOUTH EAST
ALY ...ALLEY	CUTT ...CUTTINGS	HO ...HOUSE	N ...NORTH	SER ...SERVICE AREA
AP ...APPROACH	CV ...COVE	HOL ...HOLLOW	NE ...NORTH EAST	SH ...SHORE
AR ...ARCADE	CYN ...CANYON	HOSP ...HOSPITAL	NW ...NORTH WEST	SHOP ...SHOPPING
ASS ...ASSOCIATION	DEPT ...DEPARTMENT	HRB ...HARBOUR	O/P ...OVERPASS	SKWY ...SKYWAY
AV ...AVENUE	DL ...DALE	HTH ...HEATH	OFF ...OFFICE	SMT ...SUMMIT
BCH ...BEACH	DM ...DAM	HTS ...HEIGHTS	ORCH ...ORCHARD	SOC ...SOCIETY
BLDS ...BUILDINGS	DR ...DRIVE	HVN ...HAVEN	OV ...OVAL	SP ...SPUR
BND ...BEND	DRO ...DROVE	HWY ...HIGHWAY	PAL ...PALACE	SPR ...SPRING
BR ...BRIDGE	DRY ...DRIVEWAY	IMP ...IMPERIAL	PAS ...PASSAGE	SQ ...SQUARE
BRK ...BROOK	DWGS ...DWELLINGS	IN ...INLET	PAV ...PAVILION	ST ...STREET
BTM ...BOTTOM	E ...EAST	IND EST ...INDUSTRIAL ESTATE	PDE ...PARADE	STN ...STATION
BUS ...BUSINESS	EMB ...EMBANKMENT	INF ...INFIRMARY	PH ...PUBLIC HOUSE	STR ...STREAM
BVD ...BOULEVARD	EMBY ...EMBASSY	INFO ...INFORMATION	PK ...PARK	STRD ...STRAND
BY ...BYPASS	ESP ...ESPLANADE	INT ...INTERCHANGE	PKWY ...PARKWAY	SW ...SOUTH WEST
CATH ...CATHEDRAL	EST ...ESTATE	IS ...ISLAND	PL ...PLACE	TDG ...TRADING
CEM ...CEMETERY	EX ...EXCHANGE	JCT ...JUNCTION	PLN ...PLAIN	TER ...TERRACE
CEN ...CENTRE	EXPY ...EXPRESSWAY	JTY ...JETTY	PLNS ...PLAINS	THWY ...THROUGHWAY
CFT ...CROFT	EXT ...EXTENSION	KG ...KING	PLZ ...PLAZA	TNL ...TUNNEL
CH ...CHURCH	F/O ...FLYOVER	KNL ...KNOLL	POL ...POLICE STATION	TOLL ...TOLLWAY
CHA ...CHASE	FC ...FOOTBALL CLUB	L ...LAKE	PR ...PRINCE	TPK ...TURNPIKE
CHYD ...CHURCHYARD	FK ...FORK	LA ...LANE	PREC ...PRECINCT	TR ...TRACK
CIR ...CIRCLE	FLD ...FIELD	LDG ...LODGE	PREP ...PREPARATORY	TRL ...TRAIL
CIRC ...CIRCUS	FLDS ...FIELDS	LGT ...LIGHT	PRIM ...PRIMARY	TWR ...TOWER
CL ...CLOSE	FLS ...FALLS	LK ...LOCK	PROM ...PROMENADE	U/P ...UNDERPASS
CLFS ...CLIFFS	FLS ...FLATS	LKS ...LAKES	PRS ...PRINCESS	UNI ...UNIVERSITY
CMP ...CAMP	FM ...FARM	LNDG ...LANDING	PRT ...PORT	UPR ...UPPER
CNR ...CORNER	FT ...FORT	LTL ...LITTLE	PT ...POINT	VA ...VALE
CO ...COUNTY	FWY ...FREEWAY	LWR ...LOWER	PTH ...PATH	...VALLEY
COLL ...COLLEGE	FY ...FERRY	MAG ...MAGISTRATE	PZ ...PIAZZA	VIAD ...VIADUCT
COM ...COMMON	GA ...GATE	MAN ...MANSIONS	QD ...QUADRANT	VIL ...VILLA
COMM ...COMMISSION	GAL ...GALLERY	MD ...MEAD	QU ...QUEEN	VIS ...VISTA
CON ...CONVENT	GDN ...GARDEN	MDW ...MEADOWS	QY ...QUAY	VLG ...VILLAGE
COT ...COTTAGE	GDNS ...GARDENS	MEM ...MEMORIAL	R ...RIVER	VLS ...VILLAS
COTS ...COTTAGES	GLD ...GLADE	MKT ...MARKET	RBT ...ROUNDABOUT	VW ...VIEW
CP ...CAPE	GLN ...GLEN	MKTS ...MARKETS	RD ...ROAD	W ...WEST
CPS ...COPSE	GN ...GREEN	ML ...MALL	RDG ...RIDGE	WD ...WOOD
CR ...CREEK	GND ...GROUND	ML ...MILL	REP ...REPUBLIC	WHF ...WHARF
CREM ...CREMATORIUM	GRA ...GRANGE	MNR ...MANOR	RES ...RESERVOIR	WK ...WALK
CRS ...CRESCENT	GRG ...GARAGE	MS ...MEWS	RFC ...RUGBY FOOTBALL CLUB	WKS ...WALKS
CSWY ...CAUSEWAY	GT ...GREAT	MSN ...MISSION	RI ...RISE	WLS ...WELLS
CT ...COURT	GTWY ...GATEWAY	MT ...MOUNT	RP ...RAMP	WY ...WAY
CTRL ...CENTRAL	GV ...GROVE	MTN ...MOUNTAIN	RW ...ROW	YD ...YARD
CTS ...COURTS	HGR ...HIGHER	MTS ...MOUNTAINS	S ...SOUTH	YHA ...YOUTH HOSTEL
	HL ...HILL	MUS ...MUSEUM	SCH ...SCHOOL	

POSTCODE TOWNS AND AREA ABBREVIATIONS

AIRE ...Airedale	CLAY ...Clayton	HBR ...Hebden Bridge	LDS ...Leeds	RPDN/SBR ...Ripponden/Sowerby Bridge
AL/HA/HU ...Alwoodley/Harewood/Huby	CLECK ...Cleckheaton	HDGY ...Headingley	LDSU ...Leeds University	RTHW ...Rothwell
AWLS/ASK ...Adwick le Street/Askern	COL ...Colne	HECK ...Heckmondwike	LIT ...Littleborough	RYKW ...Rural York west
BAIL ...Baildon	COP/BISH ...Copmanthorpe/Bishopthorpe	HEM/SK/SE ...Hemsworth/South Kirby/South Elmsall	LM/WK ...Low Moor/Wyke	SCFT ...Seacroft
BCUP ...Bacup	CUD/GR ...Cudworth/Grimethorpe	HFAX ...Halifax	LUD/ILL ...Luddenden/Illingworth	SEL ...Selby
BEE/HOL ...Beeston-Holbeck	CUL/QBY ...Cullingworth/Queensbury	HIPP ...Hipperholme	LVSG ...Liversedge	SHPY ...Shipley
BFD ...Bradford	DEWS ...Dewsbury	HOLM/MEL ...Holmfirth/Meltham	MDTN ...Middleton (Gtr.Man)	SKP/WHF ...Skipton/Wharfedale
BFDE ...Bradford east	DOD/DAR ...Dodworth/Darton	HOR/CROF ...Horbury/Crofton	MID ...Middleton (W.Yorks)	STKB/PEN ...Stocksbridge/Penistone
BGLY ...Bingley	EARD/LOFT ...East Ardley/Lofthouse	HORS ...Horsforth	MILN ...Milnrow	TAD ...Tadcaster
BHP/TINH ...Bramhope/Tinshill	EARL ...Earlsheaton	HTON ...Heaton	MIRF ...Mirfield	TOD ...Todmorden
BIRK/DRI ...Birkenshaw/Drighlington	ECHL ...Eccleshill	HUD ...Huddersfield	MOR ...Morley	UPML ...Uppermill
BOW ...Bowling	ELL ...Elland	HUDE ...Huddersfield east	MSTN/BAR ...Manston/Barwick in Elmet	WBOW ...West Bowling
BRAM ...Bramley	FEA/AMT ...Featherstone/Ackworth Moor Top	HUDN ...Huddersfield north	NORM ...Normanton	WBSY ...Wibsey
BRFD/BLYE ...Brierfield/Burnley east	GFTH/SHER ...Garforth/Sherburn in Elmet	HUDS ...Huddersfield south	OLD ...Oldham	WBY ...Wetherby
BRIG ...Brighouse	GIR ...Girlington	HUDW ...Huddersfield west	OSM ...Osmandthorpe	WHIT ...Whitworth
BSLY ...Barnsley	GLE ...Goole	HWTH ...Haworth	OSS ...Ossett	WIL/AL ...Wilsden/Allerton
BSLYN/ROY ...Barnsley north/Royston	GLSP ...Glossop	IDLE ...Idle	OT ...Otley	WKFDE ...Wakefield east
BTLY ...Bentley	GSLY ...Guiseley	ILK ...Ilkley	PBR ...Pateley Bridge	WKFDW/WTN ...Wakefield west/Walton
BULY ...Burley	GTHN ...Great Horton	KBTN ...Kirkburton	PDSY/CALV ...Pudsey/Calverley	WMB/DAR ...Wombwell/Darfield
BVRD ...Belle Vue Road	GTL/HWG ...Greetland/Holywell Green	KGHY ...Keighley	PONT ...Pontefract	WOR/ARM ...Wortley/Armley
BWCK/EAR ...Barnoldswick/Earby	HARS ...Harrogate south	KNA ...Knaresborough	RHAY ...Roundhay	YEA ...Yeadon
CAS ...Castleford		KNOT ...Knottingley	ROCH ...Rochdale	
CHAL ...Chapel Allerton		KSTL ...Kirkstall	ROY/SHW ...Royton/Shaw	

A

Aachen Wy HFAX HX1 ...10 C9
Aaron Wilkinson Ct
  HEM/SK/SE WF9 ...246 C4 □
Abaseen Cl BFDE BD3 ...5 M6
Abber La TAD LS24 ...51 J3
The Abbe's Cl AWLS/ASK DN6 ...249 K1
The Abbe's Wk AWLS/ASK DN6 ...249 M2
Abbey Av KSTL LS5 ...108 B3
Abbey Cl HOLM/MEL HD7 ...254 C1
  ILK LS29 ...19 J6
Abbey Ct HOLM/MEL HD7 ...254 C1
  HORS LS18 ...85 K8
Abbeydale Gdns KSTL LS5 ...86 A8
Abbeydale Garth KSTL LS5 ...86 A8
Abbeydale Gv KSTL LS5 ...86 A8
Abbeydale Mt KSTL LS5 ...86 A8
Abbeydale V KSTL LS5 ...86 A8
Abbeydale Wy KSTL LS5 ...86 A8
Abbey Dr KBTN HD8 ...238 B5
  LIT OL15 ...207 H3
Abbey Farm Dr KBTN HD8 ...238 B6 □
Abbey Farm Vw CUD/GR S72 ...262 D1
Abbey Gorse KSTL LS5 ...108 C1
Abbey Gv BSLYN/ROY S71 ...262 A1
Abbey La BSLYN/ROY S71 ...262 A4
  LUD/ILL HX2 ...145 H7
Abbey Lea WIL/AL BD15 ...103 L6
Abbey Pl HUDN HD2 ...192 E5
Abbey Rd BTLY WF17 ...173 H2
  HUDN HD2 ...192 D5
  KBTN HD8 ...238 C5
  KSTL LS5 ...108 B1
Abbey Rd North KBTN HD8 ...238 B5
Abbey Sq BSLYN/ROY S71 ...262 A2 □
Abbey St KSTL LS3 ...6 B8
Abbey Ter KSTL LS5 ...108 B3
Abbey V KSTL LS5 ...108 C1
Abbey Wk HIPP HX3 ...168 C1
  KSTL LS5 ...108 B3
Abbey Wk South HIPP HX3 ...168 C1
Abbot La HOR/CROF WF4 ...220 D8
Abbotside Cl IDLE BD10 ...83 L8 □
Abbots Rd BSLYN/ROY S71 ...262 B3

Abbot St HUDW HD3 ...14 A4
Abbotsway GFTH/SHER LS25 ...112 F8
Abbott Ct WOR/ARM LS12 ...108 F6
Abbott Rd WOR/ARM LS12 ...108 F6
Abbotts Cl GFTH/SHER LS25 ...92 A6
Abbott Ter WKFDE WF1 ...13 H8
Abbott Vw WOR/ARM LS12 ...108 F6
Abb Scott La LM/WK BD12 ...126 D8
Abb St HUDW HD3 ...191 M7
Abelia Mt GTHN BD7 ...104 A8 □
Abel St LM/WK BD12 ...148 E2 □
Aberdeen Dr WOR/ARM LS12 ...108 C7
Aberdeen Gv WOR/ARM LS12 ...108 C7
Aberdeen Pl GTHN BD7 ...126 C1
Aberdeen Rd WOR/ARM LS12 ...108 C7
Aberdeen Ter CLAY BD14 ...125 M2
  GTHN BD7 ...104 C8 □
Aberdeen Wk WOR/ARM LS12 ...108 C7
Aberfield Bank MID LS10 ...132 A8 □
Aberfield Cl MID LS10 ...132 A7 □
Aberfield Crest MID LS10 ...132 A8 □
Aberfield Dr HOR/CROF WF4 ...220 A2
  MID LS10 ...132 A8
Aberfield Ga MID LS10 ...132 A7
Aberfield Mt MID LS10 ...132 A8 □
Aberfield Ri MID LS10 ...132 A7 □
Aberfield Rd MID LS10 ...132 A7
Aberfield Wk MID LS10 ...132 A8 □
Aberford Rd BSPA/BRAM LS23 ...69 M5
  GFTH/SHER LS25 ...113 H6
  GIR BD8 ...104 D5
  MSTN/BAR LS15 ...91 G7
  RTHW LS26 ...133 M8
  WKFDE WF1 ...177 G6
Abingdon Cl ROCH OL11 ...228 A2
Abingdon St GIR BD8 ...104 D5
  HUDN HD2 ...192 C5 □
Aboukir St MILN OL16 ...206 D6 □
Abraham Hl RTHW LS26 ...133 H8
Acacia Cl CAS WF10 ...158 F8
Acacia Dr BRIC HD6 ...148 C7
  CAS WF10 ...158 E8
  WIL/AL BD15 ...103 J2
Acacia Gv CUD/GR S72 ...244 E4
  HBR HX7 ...144 B4
Acacia Park Crs IDLE BD10 ...84 B4
Acacia Park Dr IDLE BD10 ...84 B4

Acacia Park Ter IDLE BD10 ...84 B4
Acacia Rd AWLS/ASK DN6 ...249 J4
Acaster Dr GFTH/SHER LS25 ...135 J1
  LM/WK BD12 ...126 E8
Accommodation Rd OSM LS9 ...7 M7
Acer Wy CLECK BD19 ...149 H6 □
Ackroyd Ct CUL/QBY BD13 ...102 F8 □
Ackroyd St MOR LS27 ...152 D2
  TOD OL14 ...140 D5
Ackton Cl FEA/AMT WF7 ...179 J5
Ackton Hall Crs FEA/AMT WF7 ...179 J6
Ackton La FEA/AMT WF7 ...179 J6
Ackton Pasture La CAS WF10 ...179 J2
Ackworth Av YEA LS19 ...62 E8 □
Ackworth Bridle Rd
  PONT WF8 ...203 G7
Ackworth Crs YEA LS19 ...62 E8 □
Ackworth Dr YEA LS19 ...62 F8 □
Ackworth House Cl
  FEA/AMT WF7 ...202 C6 □
Ackworth Rd FEA/AMT WF7 ...201 M3
  PONT WF8 ...202 D2
Ackworth St WBOW BD5 ...127 G2
Acme Ter WKFDE WF1 ...13 H8
Acorn Cl WBSY BD6 ...126 A8 □
Acorn Dr SCFT LS14 ...89 L6
Acorn Gv HOLM/MEL HD7 ...254 F3
Acorn Pk BAIL BD17 ...83 G4
Acorn St HFAX HX1 ...10 C5
Acre Av ECHL BD2 ...105 K1
Acre Barn ROY/SHW OL2 ...229 G6 □
Acre Cl ECHL BD2 ...105 K1
Acre Crs ECHL BD2 ...105 K1
  MID LS10 ...153 L2
Acre Dr ECHL BD2 ...105 K1
Acre Fold ILK LS29 ...19 G6 □
Acre Gv ECHL BD2 ...105 K1 □
  MID LS10 ...153 L2
Acre House Av HUDW HD3 ...191 L6
Acrehowe Ri BAIL BD17 ...83 G2 □
Acre La ECHL BD2 ...105 K2
  HBR HX7 ...120 E8
  HOLM/MEL HD7 ...235 H5
  HOLM/MEL HD7 ...237 K8
  HOLM/MEL HD7 ...253 M4
  HWTH BD22 ...78 E7
  STKB/PEN S36 ...257 M8

  WBSY BD6 ...126 E5
Acre Meadow HWTH BD22 ...54 E3
Acre Mt MID LS10 ...153 L2
Acre Pl MID LS10 ...153 L2
Acre Ri BAIL BD17 ...82 E2
Acre Rd CUD/GR S72 ...262 E2
  HWTH BD22 ...54 E3
  MID LS10 ...153 L2
Acresfield COL BB8 ...74 C1 □
Acres Hall Av PDSY/CALV LS28 ...107 J8
Acres Hall Crs PDSY/CALV LS28 ...107 J8
Acres Hall Dr PDSY/CALV LS28 ...107 J8
Acres La HBR HX7 ...143 H2
  HOLM/MEL HD7 ...253 H2
Acre Sq MID LS10 ...153 L2
Acres Rd EARD/LOFT WF3 ...154 E6
The Acres AIRE BD20 ...55 L2
  ILK LS29 ...19 H5 □
Acre St HUDW HD3 ...191 K6
  MID LS10 ...153 L2
Acre Ter MID LS10 ...153 M2
Acton Flat La HUDW HD3 ...191 J1
Acton St BFDE BD3 ...105 L7
  WHIT OL12 ...206 C5 □
Acute Ter WKFDW/WTN WF2 ...176 A8
Adam Ct HUDW HD3 ...191 K5 □
Adam La DOD/DAR S75 ...259 J4
Adams Gv MSTN/BAR LS15 ...112 A2
Adam St TOD OL14 ...141 K8 □
  WBSY BD6 ...126 D5 □
Ada's Pl PDSY/CALV LS28 ...107 G4
Ada St BAIL BD17 ...83 G4 □
  CUL/QBY BD13 ...124 F5 □
  HIPP HX3 ...11 J2
  KGHY BD21 ...2 D5
  SHPY BD18 ...82 B6 □
  WHIT OL12 ...206 C4
Addingford Cl
  HOR/CROF WF4 ...197 J6 □
Addingford Dr
  HOR/CROF WF4 ...197 J6 □
Addingford La HOR/CROF WF4 ...197 J6
Addingham Gdns
  WOR/ARM LS12 ...108 C7

Addingham Wharfedale Rd
  ILK LS29 ...18 F6
Addison Av BFDE BD3 ...105 M5 □
  NORM WF6 ...178 E5
Addison Ct HOR/CROF WF4 ...197 L4 □
  MSTN/BAR LS15 ...111 M8 □
Addison Dr HWTH BD22 ...78 E8 □
Addi St BOW BD4 ...127 L3
Addle Croft La HUDE HD5 ...216 A1
Addlethorpe La WBY LS22 ...46 B1
Addy Crs HEM/SK/SE WF9 ...247 H3
Adelaide Rd AWLS/ASK DN6 ...227 M3
Adelaide St HFAX HX7 ...143 G3
  HFAX HX1 ...10 B6
  TOD OL14 ...141 K8
  WBOW BD5 ...4 F7
Adel Garth BHP/TINH LS16 ...86 F1
Adel Grange Cl BHP/TINH LS16 ...86 E4
Adel Grange Cft
  BHP/TINH LS16 ...86 E4 □
Adel Grange Ms
  BHP/TINH LS16 ...86 E4 □
Adel Gn BHP/TINH LS16 ...86 F2
Adel La BHP/TINH LS16 ...86 F2
Adel Md BHP/TINH LS16 ...86 F2
Adel Ml BHP/TINH LS16 ...64 F8
Adel Park Cl BHP/TINH LS16 ...86 E3
Adel Park Ct BHP/TINH LS16 ...86 E3
Adel Park Cft BHP/TINH LS16 ...86 E3
Adel Park Dr BHP/TINH LS16 ...86 E3
Adel Park Gdns BHP/TINH LS16 ...86 E3
Adel Pasture BHP/TINH LS16 ...86 E3
Adelphi Rd HUDW HD8 ...191 L7
Adel Towers Ct BHP/TINH LS16 ...86 F3
Adel V BHP/TINH LS16 ...86 F2
Adel Wood Dr BHP/TINH LS16 ...86 F3
Adel Wood Gv BHP/TINH LS16 ...86 F3
Adel Wood Pl BHP/TINH LS16 ...86 F3 □
Adel Wood Rd BHP/TINH LS16 ...86 F3 □
Aden St WHIT OL12 ...206 C5 □
Adgil Crs HIPP HX3 ...169 J2
Adkin Royd DOD/DAR S75 ...259 H6
Administration Rd OSM LS9 ...132 E3 □
Admiral St BEE/HOL LS11 ...9 G7
Adolphus St BFD BD1 ...5 H7
Adowsley Cl FEA/AMT WF7 ...202 A8
Adrian Ter MILN OL16 ...206 E4

Adwalton Cl BIRK/DRI BD11 150 F1
Adwalton Gn BIRK/DRI BD11 150 F1
Adwalton Gv CUL/QBY BD13 125 H5
Adwick Gv WKFDW/WTN WF2 220 D1
Adwick Pl BULY LS4 108 E4
Agar St GIR BD8 104 B6
Agar Ter GIR BD8 104 B6 1
Agbrigg Gv WKFDW/WTN WF2 199 G4
Agbrigg Rd WKFDE WF1 13 L9 1
Agincourt Dr NORM WF6 178 A2
Agnes Rd BSLY S70 261 G6
DOD/DAR S75 241 M6
Agnes St KGHY BD21 57 L5
Ails La LUD/ILL HX2 144 F5
Aimbry Ct HUDE HD5 215 H4
Ainley Bottom ELL HX5 191 H1
Ainley Cl HUDW HD3 191 J4 1
Ainley Pk HOLM/MEL HD7 213 G2 1
Ainley Rd HUDW HD3 191 J3
Ainley St ELL HX5 169 H8
Ainsbury Av IDLE BD10 83 K3
Ainsdale Ct BSLYN/ROY S71 261 M1
Ainsdale Gv CUL/QBY BD13 80 A8
Ainsdale Rd BSLYN/ROY S71 243 K1
Ainsley La HOLM/MEL HD7 232 F2
Ainsty Crs WBY LS22 30 A7
Ainsty Dr WBY LS22 30 A7
Ainsty Garth WBY LS22 30 A7
Ainsty Rd WBY LS22 29 M7 1
Ainsty Vw WBY LS22 30 A7
Ainsworth St MILN OL16 206 C8 1
Aintree Cl GFTH/SHER LS25 135 H4
Airebank BGLY BD16 81 H3
Aire Cl BAIL BD17 82 D5
Aire Crs AIRE BD20 34 F8
Airedale Av BGLY BD16 81 J8
SKP/WHF BD23 16 D2
Airedale College Rd BFDE BD3 5 J1
Airedale College Ter BFDE BD3 5 J2
Airedale Ct SCFT LS14 111 H1 1
Airedale Crs BFDE BD3 5 J1
Airedale Cft BRAM LS13 107 H2 1
Airedale Dr CAS WF10 158 E4
GFTH/SHER LS25 113 K8
HIPP HX3 147 K1
HORS LS18 85 H6
Airedale Gdns BRAM LS13 107 H2
Airedale Gv HORS LS18 85 H6
RTHW LS26 133 M8 1
Airedale Hts
WKFDW/WTN WF2 197 L2
Airedale Ms AIRE BD20 36 A5
SKP/WHF BD23 16 B3 1
Airedale Mt AIRE BD20 58 E6
Airedale Pl BAIL BD17 83 G4
Airedale Quay BRAM LS13 107 J2
Airedale Rd BFDE BD3 5 H1
CAS WF10 158 D7
DOD/DAR S75 241 L6
KGHY BD21 58 B6
RTHW LS26 133 M8
Airedale St BGLY BD16 81 H3 1
ECHL BD2 105 K3 1
KGHY BD21 3 M3
Airedale Ter MOR LS27 152 D2 1
RTHW LS26 133 M8 2
Airedale Vw AIRE BD20 34 F7
RTHW LS26 133 M8 3
Airedale Whf BRAM LS13 107 H1
Aire Gv YEA LS19 62 E8
Aire Mt WBY LS22 29 M7
Aire Pl BVRD LS3 109 G5
Aire Rd WBY LS22 29 M7
Aireside Av AIRE BD20 34 D4
Aireside Ter AIRE BD20 34 C3
Aire St AIRE BD20 35 G8
BGLY BD16 81 G1
BRIG HD6 170 D5
CAS WF10 157 M6
DEWS WF13 195 H1
HWTH BD22 78 F7 1
IDLE BD10 83 J5 1
KGHY BD21 3 K3
KNOT WF11 182 C1
LDS LS1 8 E1
Aire Ter CAS WF10 157 M6 1
Aireton Rd BSLY S70 261 G4 1
Aire Valley Dr AIRE BD20 34 E1 1
Airevalley Rd KGHY BD21 3 L2
Aire Vw AIRE BD20 35 M5
AIRE BD20 58 B4
YEA LS19 62 E8
Aire View Av BGLY BD16 81 K6
SHPY BD18 82 C6 1
Aireview Crs BAIL BD17 82 C5
Aire View Dr AIRE BD20 58 E7
Aireville Av SHPY BD18 104 D1
Aireville Cl AIRE BD20 57 J4
SHPY BD18 104 D1 1
Aireville Crs AIRE BD20 36 B5
HTON BD9 104 D1
Aireville Dr AIRE BD20 36 B5
HTON BD9 104 D1 2
Aireville Gra SHPY BD18 104 D1 3
Aireville Gv HTON BD9 104 D1 4
Aireville Mt AIRE BD20 58 E7
Aireville Mouny AIRE BD20 36 B5
Aireville Ri HTON BD9 104 D2
Aireville Rd HTON BD9 104 E1
Aireville St AIRE BD20 57 J4 1
Aireville Ter ILK LS29 40 A5
Aire Wy BAIL BD17 82 C5
Aireworth Cl KGHY BD21 3 M2
Aireworth Gv KGHY BD21 3 M3
Aireworth Rd KGHY BD21 3 M2
Aireworth St KGHY BD21 2 F6
Airey St KGHY BD21 2 D4
Airlie Av RHAY LS8 110 B2
Airlie Pl RHAY LS8 110 B2
Akam Rd BFD BD1 4 C5
Aked's Rd HFAX HX1 10 E7
Aked St BFD BD1 5 H6 1
Aketon Dr CAS WF10 157 L8
Aketon Rd CAS WF10 157 L8
Akroyd La HBR HX7 121 K8
Akroyd Pl HFAX HX1 11 G4
Akroyd Ter LUD/ILL HX2 168 B1 1
Alabama St HFAX HX1 10 B5 1
Alan Crs MSTN/BAR LS15 111 J7
Alandale Crs GFTH/SHER LS25 112 F8
Alandale Dr GFTH/SHER LS25 112 F8
Alandale Gv GFTH/SHER LS25 112 F8
Alandale Rd GFTH/SHER LS25 112 F7
HUDN HD2 193 G1
Alan Rd DOD/DAR S75 241 M6
Alaska Pl CHAL LS7 88 A8
Alba Cl WMB/DAR S73 263 G8
Albans Cl AL/HA/HU LS17 47 G8
Alban St BOW BD4 127 K2 1
Albany Cl WMB/DAR S73 262 C8
Albany Ct KGHY BD21 2 D3
PONT WF8 180 F7
Albany Crs HEM/SK/SE WF9 247 H4
Albany Dr HUDE HD5 193 J8
Albany Rd HUDE HD5 193 J8
RTHW LS26 132 F8
Albany St HEM/SK/SE WF9 247 H4
HIPP HX3 11 K9
HUD HD1 214 B2 1
ROCH OL11 228 C1 1
WBOW BD5 127 G2 1
WBSY BD6 126 E5 1
WOR/ARM LS12 108 C7
Albany Ter WOR/ARM LS12 108 C7 1
Alberta Av CHAL LS7 88 A8
Albert Av IDLE BD10 83 L6
LUD/ILL HX2 146 A6
SHPY BD18 82 A5
Albert Cl BTLY WF17 173 L4
Albert Ct LUD/ILL HX2 146 A6
Albert Crs BIRK/DRI BD11 150 D2
CUL/QBY BD13 125 G5 1
Albert Dr LUD/ILL HX2 145 M6
MOR LS27 152 F1
Albert Gdns LUD/ILL HX2 146 A6
Albert Gv HDGY LS6 86 F8
Albert Pl BFDE BD3 106 A6
HORS LS18 85 L5
Albert Prom HIPP HX3 168 C2
Albert Rd AIRE BD20 34 F8
CUL/QBY BD13 124 F4
KBTN HD8 240 A3
LUD/ILL HX2 146 A6
MOR LS27 152 D1 1
RPDN/SBR HX6 167 L1
RTHW LS26 133 L8
SHPY BD18 82 B6
Albert Royds St MILN OL16 206 E5
Albert Sq AIRE BD20 36 A5 1
Albert St AIRE BD20 55 M1
BAIL BD17 82 E5 1
BRIG HD6 170 E3
BSLY S70 261 H5
CAS WF10 158 A6 1
CLECK BD19 149 M6 1
CUD/GR S72 244 E6 1
CUL/QBY BD13 102 F8
CUL/QBY BD13 125 H5 1
ELL HX5 169 H8
FEA/AMT WF7 201 M1
HBR HX7 143 J3
HBR HX7 144 A5 1
HFAX HX1 10 E5
HUD HD1 214 C2 1
HWTH BD22 79 H6 1
IDLE BD10 83 K8
KGHY BD21 2 F4
LIT OL15 207 J1
LM/WK BD12 148 E4
LVSG WF15 172 E3 1
MILN OL16 229 H1
NORM WF6 178 E2
PDSY/CALV LS28 106 F8
ROY/SHW OL2 229 J7 1
WBSY BD6 126 D6
WIL/AL BD15 102 E2
Albert Ter LM/WK BD12 149 H1
SHPY BD18 82 B5
SKP/WHF BD23 16 B2 1
Albert Vw LUD/ILL HX2 146 A6
Albert Wk SHPY BD18 82 A6
Albert Wy BIRK/DRI BD11 150 D2 1
Albert Yd HUD HD1 14 F8
Albion Av WOR/ARM LS12 108 F7
Albion Cl BSPA/BRAM LS23 69 M1 1
Albion Ct WKFDE WF1 12 E3
Albion Cft OSS WF5 175 G8
Albion Fold WIL/AL BD15 102 E1
Albion Pl HEM/SK/SE WF9 247 J3
LDS LS1 7 G9
Albion Rd BSLYN/ROY S71 243 L7
EARL WF12 195 M5
IDLE BD10 83 L6
PDSY/CALV LS28 107 G4
Albion St BRIG HD6 170 C3
BSPA/BRAM LS23 69 M1
BTLY WF17 173 M2 1
CAS WF10 157 L6
CLECK BD19 150 A7 1
CUL/QBY BD13 102 A6
CUL/QBY BD13 124 F5
DEWS WF13 195 H1 1
EARD/LOFT WF3 154 F3 1
ELL HX5 169 J8
HECK WF16 172 E2
HEM/SK/SE WF9 223 H3
HFAX HX1 11 H6
HUD HD1 14 F8
HWTH BD22 79 G6
LDS LS1 7 G9
LIT OL15 207 J1 1
LVSG WF15 172 C2 1
MOR LS27 152 C2 1
OT LS21 41 K7
PDSY/CALV LS28 107 H2
WBSY BD6 126 B7 1
WKFDE WF1 176 E7
Albion Ter BSPA/BRAM LS23 48 F8
Albion Wy WOR/ARM LS12 109 G6
Alcester Garth BFDE BD3 5 L4
Alcester Pl RHAY LS8 110 B2 1
Alcester Rd RHAY LS8 110 B2 2
Alcester St RHAY LS8 110 B2 3
Alcester Ter RHAY LS8 110 B2 4
Aldams Rd EARL WF12 173 L7
Aldbury Cl BSLYN/ROY S71 243 K8
Alden Av MOR LS27 152 C4
Alden Cl MOR LS27 152 C4 1
Alden Ct MOR LS27 152 C4 2
Alden Crs PONT WF8 180 D7
Alden Fold MOR LS27 152 C4 3
Alder Av HOLM/MEL HD7 236 E6
KGHY BD21 3 K8
WKFDW/WTN WF2 176 C6
Alderbank WHIT OL12 184 E7
Alder Carr BAIL BD17 82 D3
Alder Cl DOD/DAR S75 242 C5
Alder Dr PDSY/CALV LS28 106 C6
Alder Garth PDSY/CALV LS28 106 D6
Alder Gv LUD/ILL HX2 124 A8
NORM WF6 178 D7 1
Alder Hill Av CHAL LS7 87 J7
Alder Hill Gv CHAL LS7 87 J7
Alder Holt Dr WBSY BD6 126 C8
Aldermanbury BFD BD1 4 E7
Alderney Rd EARL WF12 174 B4
Alderscholes Cl
CUL/QBY BD13 102 F8 2
Alderscholes La
CUL/QBY BD13 124 E1
Aldersley Av SKP/WHF BD23 16 D3
Alderson Dr BSLYN/ROY S71 243 J8
Alderson St WBSY BD6 126 A7 1
Alderstone Ri HUDW HD3 191 J4
Alder St HUD HD1 15 G3
Aldersyde BTLY WF17 151 G5 1
Alderton Bank AL/HA/HU LS17 87 H4
Alderton Crs AL/HA/HU LS17 87 H4
Alderton Mt AL/HA/HU LS17 87 H4 1
Alderton Pl AL/HA/HU LS17 87 H4 2
Alderton Ri AL/HA/HU LS17 87 H4
Aldham Crs WMB/DAR S73 262 C8
Aldonley HUDE HD5 215 J2
Aldwych ROCH OL11 228 B3
Alegar St BRIG HD6 170 E4 1
Alexander Av MSTN/BAR LS15 111 H7
Alexander Crs FEA/AMT WF7 179 M7
Alexander Dr MILN OL16 207 G8
Alexander Rd FEA/AMT WF7 179 M8
Alexander Sq CLAY BD14 125 K2 1
Alexander St LDS LS1 6 F8 1
WBSY BD6 126 D6 1
Alexander Ter HFAX HX1 10 B5
Alexandra Cl RPDN/SBR HX6 167 L2
Alexandra Ct SKP/WHF BD23 16 B4
Alexandra Crs ELL HX5 169 K7
ILK LS29 38 C2
Alexandra Dr NORM WF6 178 D7
Alexandra Gv HDGY LS6 109 G4 1
PDSY/CALV LS28 106 E7
Alexandra Rd AWLS/ASK DN6 249 M8
BTLY WF17 173 M2
ECHL BD2 105 L1
HBR HX7 143 J3 1
HDGY LS6 109 G4 2
HORS LS18 85 L5
HUDW HD3 191 L6
PDSY/CALV LS28 106 E8
SHPY BD18 82 C7 1
Alexandra St CUL/QBY BD13 125 G5 2
GTHN BD7 4 A9
HFAX HX1 11 G7
LVSG WF15 172 C2 2
Alexandra Ter
BSLYN/ROY S71 262 B6 1
ECHL BD2 105 L4
YEA LS19 62 E7 1
Alford Ter GTHN BD7 104 C7
Alfred St East HFAX HX1 11 J6 1
Alfred St BRIG HD6 170 D3 1
BSLYN/ROY S71 244 A2
BTLY WF17 173 K2 1
EARL WF12 174 A5 1
GTL/HWG HX4 168 F7
HECK WF16 172 F3 1
HFAX HX1 10 B5
HUD HD1 14 F8
LIT OL15 185 J8
LVSG WF15 172 D2 1
MOR LS27 130 E6 1
ROY/SHW OL2 229 J7
Alfreds Wy BTLY WF17 173 L1
Alice St CLECK BD19 149 M6 2
GIR BD8 4 C3
HWTH BD22 78 E8 2
KGHY BD21 3 G4
WHIT OL12 206 D5
Alicia Dr WHIT OL12 206 A4
Alison St ROY/SHW OL2 229 J6
Alkincote St KGHY BD21 2 F6
All Alone Rd IDLE BD10 83 H7
Allanbridge Cl IDLE BD10 83 L7 1
Allandale Av WBSY BD6 126 C7 1
Allandale Rd WBSY BD6 126 C7 2
Allan Haigh Cl
WKFDW/WTN WF2 175 M6
Allan St BFDE BD3 5 L7
Allan Ter RPDN/SBR HX6 167 L3
Allatt Cl BSLY S70 261 H6
Allenby Crs BEE/HOL LS11 131 J6 1
Allenby Dr BEE/HOL LS11 131 J6
Allenby Gdns BEE/HOL LS11 131 J6
Allenby Gv BEE/HOL LS11 131 J6
Allenby Pl BEE/HOL LS11 131 J6
Allenby Rd BEE/HOL LS11 131 J6
Allenby St ROY/SHW OL2 229 J7 2
Allenby Vw BEE/HOL LS11 131 J5
Allen Cl ROY/SHW OL2 229 J8
Allen Cft BIRK/DRI BD11 150 C1
Allendale Rd DOD/DAR S75 241 M6
DOD/DAR S75 261 G2
Allendale St COL BB8 74 B1 1
Allen St MILN OL16 228 C1
Allerby Gn WBSY BD6 126 B8
Allergill Pk HOLM/MEL HD7 253 M1
Allerton Cl WIL/AL BD15 103 K5
Allerton Dr AL/HA/HU LS17 46 E7
Allerton Grange Av
AL/HA/HU LS17 88 A5
Allerton Grange Cl
AL/HA/HU LS17 87 L6 1
Allerton Grange Crs
AL/HA/HU LS17 87 M6
Allerton Grange Cft
RHAY LS8 88 A6 1
Allerton Grange Dr
AL/HA/HU LS17 87 M6
WIL/AL BD15 103 K5
Allerton Grange Gdns
AL/HA/HU LS17 87 M6
Allerton Grange Ri
AL/HA/HU LS17 87 M6
Allerton Grange V
AL/HA/HU LS17 87 M6
Allerton Grange Wk
AL/HA/HU LS17 87 M6 1
Allerton Grange Wy RHAY LS8 87 M6
Allerton Gv AL/HA/HU LS17 87 M4
Allerton Hl CHAL LS7 87 L7
Allerton La WIL/AL BD15 103 J7
Allerton Pk CHAL LS7 87 M7
Allerton Pl AL/HA/HU LS17 87 M4 1
HFAX HX1 10 C6
Allerton Rd GIR BD8 103 M5
WIL/AL BD15 102 F5
Allerton St BULY LS4 108 F5
Allescholes Rd TOD OL14 163 J7
Alliance St WOR/ARM LS12 108 C7
Allinson St WOR/ARM LS12 109 G8 1
Allison Dr HUDN HD2 192 C3
Allison Gv COL BB8 52 B8
Allison La ECHL BD2 104 F2
Allison St FEA/AMT WF7 201 L1
Alloe Field Vw LUD/ILL HX2 124 A8
Allott Cl HEM/SK/SE WF9 247 H3
All Saint's Cir RTHW LS26 133 M7
All Saints Cl DOD/DAR S75 259 J6
All Saint's Dr RTHW LS26 133 L8
All Saints Rd GTHN BD7 126 E1
RTHW LS26 133 M7
All Saints Ter WHIT OL12 206 D4
All Saint's Vw RTHW LS26 133 L7 1
All Souls' Rd HIPP HX3 11 G2
All Souls' St HIPP HX3 11 G2 1
All Souls' Ter HIPP HX3 11 G2
Allums La OT LS21 65 G2
Alma Cl PDSY/CALV LS28 106 E3
Alma Cottages HDGY LS6 108 F1
Alma Dr HUDE HD5 15 L7
Alma Gv OSM LS9 7 M5
Alma La HECK WF16 150 F8
RPDN/SBR HX6 166 D7
Alma Pl KGHY BD21 3 G9 1
OSM LS9 7 M5
Alma Rd COL BB8 52 F8
HDGY LS6 108 F1
TOD OL14 163 J5
Alma St BOW BD4 127 L1
BSLY S70 260 F5
CUL/QBY BD13 124 F5
HWTH BD22 78 E6
KGHY BD21 79 L2
OSM LS9 7 M6
OSM LS9 110 B5 1
RTHW LS26 133 M7
SHPY BD18 82 F6
TOD OL14 163 J5
WHIT OL12 206 B5 1
YEA LS19 62 E7 2
Alma Ter KGHY BD21 79 L2
RTHW LS26 132 F8
Almond Av CUD/GR S72 244 D7
Almondbury Bank HUDE HD5 15 M9
Almondbury Cl HUDE HD5 215 J3 1
Almondbury Common
HUDS HD4 215 H5 1
Almond Cl HEM/SK/SE WF9 247 J1
LIT OL15 185 H8
Almondroyd HECK WF16 172 E1 1
Almond St BFDE BD3 105 L8 1
Almond Wy BTLY WF17 151 H5
Almscliffe Av EARL WF12 174 A6
Almscliffe Dr AL/HA/HU LS17 43 K2
Almscliffe Garth
AL/HA/HU LS17 25 M7
Almshouse Hl BSPA/BRAM LS23 69 M4
Almshouse La WKFDE WF1 12 F3
WKFDW/WTN WF2 220 D3
Alperton Cl BSLYN/ROY S71 262 B1
Alpha St KGHY BD21 3 J5
Alpine Cl BTLY WF17 173 K2 2
Alpine Dr MILN OL16 207 J7
WHIT OL12 184 E8
Alpine Ri CUL/QBY BD13 102 F7
Alric Dr BSLYN/ROY S71 262 A5
Alston Av ROY/SHW OL2 229 K6
Alston Cl DOD/DAR S75 259 H6 1
HTON BD9 103 M5
Alston La SCFT LS14 111 J3
Alston Rd KGHY BD21 3 K1
Altar Dr AIRE BD20 58 C5
HTON BD9 104 C3
Altar La BGLY BD16 80 C2
Althorpe Gv IDLE BD10 83 J8
Altinkool St WKFDE WF1 199 G4
Altofts Hall Rd NORM WF6 178 B2
Altofts La CAS WF10 156 F8
Altofts Lodge Dr NORM WF6 178 A3
Altofts Rd NORM WF6 178 C3
Alton Av HUDE HD5 193 H7
Alton Gv HTON BD9 104 B3
SHPY BD18 104 D1 1
Alton Wy DOD/DAR S75 242 C5
Alum Ct HTON BD9 104 C3 1
Alum Dr HTON BD9 104 C3
Alvanley Ct GIR BD8 103 M6
Alverthorpe Rd
WKFDW/WTN WF2 176 B8
Alwen Av HUDN HD2 192 B4
Alwin Rd ROY/SHW OL2 229 J6
Alwoodley Cha AL/HA/HU LS17 88 A1
Alwoodley Court Gdns
AL/HA/HU LS17 65 J8
Alwoodley Gdns
AL/HA/HU LS17 87 J1
Alwoodley La AL/HA/HU LS17 65 H8
Amberley Gdns
WOR/ARM LS12 108 E8
Amberley Ri AWLS/ASK DN6 249 H4
Amberley Rd WOR/ARM LS12 108 E8
Amberley St BFDE BD3 105 L8
WOR/ARM LS12 108 E8
Amber St BTLY WF17 151 J8
Amberton Ap RHAY LS8 110 E2
Amberton Cl RHAY LS8 110 E1 1
Amberton Crs RHAY LS8 110 E2 1
Amberton Gdns RHAY LS8 110 E2
Amberton Garth RHAY LS8 110 E2
Amberton Gv RHAY LS8 110 E2
Amberton La RHAY LS8 110 E2
Amberton Mt RHAY LS8 110 E2
Amberton Pl RHAY LS8 110 D2
Amberton Rd OSM LS9 110 E3
RHAY LS8 110 D2
Amberton St RHAY LS8 110 E2
Amberton Ter RHAY LS8 110 E2
Ambler Gv LUD/ILL HX2 124 B8
Amblers Ct PDSY/CALV LS28 107 G8
Amblers Cft IDLE BD10 83 K4
Amblers Ter HIPP HX3 11 H2
Ambler St CAS WF10 157 M7
GIR BD8 104 E4
KGHY BD21 3 K5
Ambler Wy CUL/QBY BD13 124 E7
Ambleside Av HTON BD9 104 B4
Ambleside Dr
WKFDW/WTN WF2 199 J8 1
Ambleside Gdns
PDSY/CALV LS28 106 E7
Ambleside Gv
BSLYN/ROY S71 262 C6 1
RTHW LS26 133 L8 1
Ambleside Rd CAS WF10 159 G5
Ambleside Wk WBY LS22 29 K8
Ambleton Wy CUL/QBY BD13 124 E6
Ambrose St ROCH OL11 228 B1
Amelia St SHPY BD18 82 B5 1
America La AIRE BD20 56 A6
BRIG HD6 170 E4
America Moor La MOR LS27 152 C4
Amisfield Rd HIPP HX3 147 M6
Amos St HFAX HX1 10 B5
Amport Cl BRIG HD6 170 D5
Amundsen Av ECHL BD2 105 J1
Amyroyce Dr SHPY BD18 83 G7
Amy St BGLY BD16 81 J3 1
HIPP HX3 146 C4 1
Anaheim Dr WKFDE WF1 176 F1
Ancaster Crs BHP/TINH LS16 86 D7
Ancaster Rd BHP/TINH LS16 86 D7
Ancaster Vw BHP/TINH LS16 86 D7
The Anchorage BGLY BD16 81 H2 1
Anchor Bridge Wy
EARL WF12 173 L7 1
Anchor St HUD HD1 15 H6
TOD OL14 163 L1
Ancote Cl DOD/DAR S75 260 C5 1
Andersen Ct CAS WF10 180 E1 1
Anderson Av RHAY LS8 7 M4
Anderson Mt RHAY LS8 7 M4
Anderson St GIR BD8 4 A1
PONT WF8 180 E5 1
WKFDW/WTN WF2 12 B3 1
Anderton St AIRE BD20 34 F7 1
WKFDE WF1 13 K8 1
Andover Gn BOW BD4 128 A2 1
Andrew Cl HIPP HX3 169 J2 1
Andrew Crs HUDS HD4 213 J5
WKFDE WF1 176 D1
Andrews Gv FEA/AMT WF7 202 B8
Andrew St FEA/AMT WF7 201 L1 1
PDSY/CALV LS28 106 F3 1
WKFDE WF1 176 D7
Angel Rd HFAX HX1 10 D4
Angel St BAIL BD17 82 F2 1
Angel Wy BFD BD1 4 C6
Angerton Wy WBSY BD6 126 C8
Angram Rd RYKW YO26 33 J4
Angus Av LM/WK BD12 148 E5
Anlaby St BOW BD4 127 M1
Annan Cl DOD/DAR S75 260 A1
Annat Royd La STKB/PEN S36 256 E7
Anne Crs CUD/GR S72 245 G1 1
Annersley Av ROY/SHW OL2 229 J8
Annes Ct HIPP HX3 169 J2
Anne St BTLY WF17 151 J7
GTHN BD7 126 B3 1
Annie St HEM/SK/SE WF9 223 J2
KGHY BD21 3 G1 1
MOR LS27 152 D2
RPDN/SBR HX6 167 K2 1
SHPY BD18 82 E8
WKFDE WF1 176 D2
Annison St BFDE BD3 5 J6
Annotes Cft HUDE HD5 193 H7
Ann Pl WBOW BD5 4 E9
Ann St CUL/QBY BD13 101 M5 1
KGHY BD21 2 E6
ROCH OL11 206 B8 1
Anroyd St DEWS WF13 173 J5 1
Ansdell Rd MILN OL16 228 D2
Anson Cft SEL YO8 139 M5
Anson Gv GTHN BD7 126 B4 1
Anston Dr HEM/SK/SE WF9 247 J1
Anthony La BGLY BD16 80 D4
Antony Cl HUDW HD3 190 F5 1
Anvil St BRIG HD6 170 C3
GIR BD8 104 D5 1
Apex Vw BEE/HOL LS11 8 F5
Apex Wy BEE/HOL LS11 9 G6
Apperley Gdns IDLE BD10 84 A6
Apperley La IDLE BD10 84 B4
YEA LS19 84 C2
Apperley Rd IDLE BD10 83 M6
Appleby Cl DOD/DAR S75 242 B5
Appleby La GFTH/SHER LS25 113 K7 1
Appleby Pl AWLS/ASK DN6 249 H4
MSTN/BAR LS15 111 G6
Appleby Wk MSTN/BAR LS15 111 G6
Appleby Wy MOR LS27 152 D1
WBY LS22 30 A7
Apple Cl BTLY WF17 151 J4
Applegarth RTHW LS26 133 L7
WKFDW/WTN WF2 199 G7
Applehaigh Gv BSLYN/ROY S71 243 J2
Applehaigh La HOR/CROF WF4 221 J8
Applehaigh Vw
BSLYN/ROY S71 243 J2
Applehurst Bank BSLY S70 261 K6 1

Appleshaw Crs
WKFDW/WTN WF2 176 B3 1
Apple St HWTH BD22 79 J3 1
HWTH BD22 100 E4 1
Appleton Cl BGLY BD16 81 K1
LM/WK BD12 149 H1 1
Appleton Gv OSM LS9 110 D6
Appleton Wy OSM LS9 110 B6
Appletree Cl BSPA/BRAM LS23 48 F7 1
Apple Tree Cl EARD/LOFT WF3 153 L6
PONT WF8 180 D8
Apple Tree Ct
EARD/LOFT WF3 153 L7 1
Appletree Dr SEL YO8 139 M4
Apple Tree Gdns ILK LS29 38 B2
Apple Tree Rd FEA/AMT WF7 202 A2
Appletree Wy
GFTH/SHER LS25 116 B6
Appleyard Rd HBR HX7 144 B5
The Approach MSTN/BAR LS15 90 B7
SCFT LS14 89 K6 1
April Cl BSLYN/ROY S71 261 L2
April Ct LVSG WF15 172 C4
April Dr BSLYN/ROY S71 261 M2
Apsley Crs GIR BD8 4 B1
Apsley St HWTH BD22 78 F3
KGHY BD21 2 F8
Aquamarine Dr HUDN HD2 192 E4
Aqueduct St BSLYN/ROY S71 261 H3
Aquila Wy LVSG WF15 171 M1
Arborary La HOLM/MEL HD7 213 H8
The Arbour AIRE BD20 34 F5 1
ILK LS29 20 C8
Arcadia St KGHY BD21 2 F8
Archbell Av BRIG HD6 170 D6
Archer Rd BRIG HD6 170 F5
Archer St CAS WF10 157 L8
Archery Pl LDSU LS2 6 E5
Archery Rd LDSU LS2 6 E4 1
Archery St LDSU LS2 6 F5
Archery Ter LDSU LS2 6 E5
Arches St HFAX HX1 10 F7
Archibald St GTHN BD7 4 A6
Arcon Cl MILN OL16 207 G8
Arctic Pde GTHN BD7 126 C2
Arctic St HWTH BD22 79 G6 1
KGHY BD21 57 K5
Arden Ct HOR/CROF WF4 197 J6
HUDE HD5 193 L7
Ardennes Cl ECHL BD2 105 H2
Arden Rd GIR BD8 103 L7
HFAX HX1 10 E9
Ardsley Cl BOW BD4 128 B4 1
Argent Wy BOW BD4 128 B4
Argie Av BULY LS4 108 D3
Argie Gdns BULY LS4 108 E4
Argie Rd BULY LS4 108 E4
Argie Ter BULY LS4 108 E4 1
Argyle Ms AL/HA/HU LS17 67 L1
Argyle Rd KNOT WF11 181 L1 1
OSM LS9 7 K8
Argyle St BOW BD4 127 K2 2
HOLM/MEL HD7 233 H2
KGHY BD21 2 E4
MILN OL16 228 C2 1
SHPY BD18 82 D8 1
WKFDE WF1 13 J7
Argyll Av PONT WF8 180 D6 1
Argyll Cl BAIL BD17 83 G4
HORS LS18 85 K2
Arkendale Ms GTHN BD7 126 A3 1
Arkenley La HUDS HD4 215 H5
Arkenmore HUDE HD5 193 H7
Arksey Pl WOR/ARM LS12 108 E6 1
Arksey Ter WOR/ARM LS12 108 E6
Ark St OSM LS9 9 M4
Arkwright St BOW BD4 106 A8
CLAY BD14 125 K2 2
Arkwright Wk MOR LS27 130 C8 1
Arlesford Rd BOW BD4 128 A4 1
Arley Cl HOLM/MEL HD7 236 B6
Arley Dr ROY/SHW OL2 229 L6
Arley Gv WOR/ARM LS12 108 E5
Arley Pl WOR/ARM LS12 108 E6
Arley St WOR/ARM LS12 108 E6
Arley Ter WOR/ARM LS12 108 E6
Arlington Crs LUD/ILL HX2 167 M1
Arlington Gv CAS WF10 158 B7 1
RHAY LS8 110 D2
Arlington Rd RHAY LS8 110 D2
Arlington St WKFDE WF1 176 D6 1
Arlington Wy HUDE HD5 193 J7
Armadale Av BOW BD4 127 K6 1
Armgill La SHPY BD18 104 F2
Armidale Wy ECHL BD2 105 H3 1
Armitage Av BRIG HD6 170 D6
Armitage Rd HFAX HX1 10 A9
HUDN HD2 192 B5
HUDS HD4 214 A6
HUDW HD3 213 K1
LM/WK BD12 149 H2 1
WKFDW/WTN WF2 175 M6 1
Armitage Sq PDSY/CALV LS28 106 F8 1
Armitage St CAS WF10 157 L6 1
DEWS WF13 194 F1
HUDS HD4 214 C2
RTHW LS26 155 G2 1
Armley Gra WOR/ARM LS12 108 B6
Armley Grange Av
WOR/ARM LS12 108 B6
Armley Grange Crs
WOR/ARM LS12 108 B5
Armley Grange Dr
WOR/ARM LS12 108 B6
Armley Grange Mt
WOR/ARM LS12 108 B6
Armley Grange Ov
WOR/ARM LS12 108 B5
Armley Grange Ri
WOR/ARM LS12 108 B6
Armley Grange Vw
WOR/ARM LS12 108 C6 1
Armley Grange Wk
WOR/ARM LS12 108 C6
Armley Grove Pl
WOR/ARM LS12 108 F7
Armley Lodge Rd
WOR/ARM LS12 108 E5
Armley Park Rd
WOR/ARM LS12 108 E5
Armley Ridge Cl
WOR/ARM LS12 108 C6
Armley Ridge Rd
WOR/ARM LS12 108 C6
Armley Rd WOR/ARM LS12 108 F6
Armouries Dr MID LS10 9 K4
Armouries Wy MID LS10 9 J2
Armoury Av MIRF WF14 194 C1
Arm Rd WHIT OL12 207 G1
Armstrong Cl NORM WF6 178 C2
Armstrong Hurst Cl
WHIT OL12 206 D3 1
Armstrong St BOW BD4 105 M8
PDSY/CALV LS28 106 F4 1
Armstrong Ter PONT WF8 180 D7 1
Armyne Gv BSLYN/ROY S71 262 A5
Armytage Crs HUD HD1 214 A3
Armytage Rd BRIG HD6 170 E4
Armytage Wy BRIG HD6 170 F5
Arncliffe Av HWTH BD22 2 C7 1
Arncliffe Ct HUDW HD3 14 A4
Arncliffe Crs BRIG HD6 170 A6
MOR LS27 152 E4
Arncliffe Dr BSLY S70 260 D5
KNOT WF11 181 K2
Arncliffe Gdns BTLY WF17 173 K1
Arncliffe Garth
PDSY/CALV LS28 106 F4 2
Arncliffe Gra AL/HA/HU LS17 87 M4 2
Arncliffe Gv HWTH BD22 2 C8
Arncliffe Rd BHP/TINH LS16 86 C6
BTLY WF17 173 J1
HWTH BD22 2 C8
WKFDE WF1 177 H6
Arncliffe St PDSY/CALV LS28 106 F4
Arncliffe Ter GTHN BD7 104 D8
Arndale Gv HOLM/MEL HD7 254 D2
Arnford Cl BFDE BD3 5 H3
Arnold Av BSLYN/ROY S71 243 H6
HUDN HD2 192 B5
Arnold Pl GIR BD8 4 A3
Arnold Royd BRIG HD6 170 A7
Arnold St GIR BD8 4 A2
HFAX HX1 10 C6
HUDN HD2 14 D1
LVSG WF15 172 C2
RPDN/SBR HX6 167 K2 2
Arnside Av AIRE BD20 58 A5 1
Arnside Cl CAS WF10 158 F6
ROY/SHW OL2 229 M7
Arnside Crs CAS WF10 158 F6
Arnside Rd WBOW BD5 126 F4
Arran Cl HOLM/MEL HD7 212 F1
Arran Ct GFTH/SHER LS25 135 H1
Arran Dr GFTH/SHER LS25 135 H1
HORS LS18 85 K2
Arran Wy RTHW LS26 155 H1
Arrunden La HOLM/MEL HD7 254 B5
Arthington Av MID LS10 131 M4
Arthington Cl EARD/LOFT WF3 152 F7
Arthington Garth OT LS21 43 H8
Arthington Gv MID LS10 131 M4
Arthington La OT LS21 43 G7
Arthington Lawns OT LS21 43 G8
Arthington Pl MID LS10 131 M4
Arthington Rd BHP/TINH LS16 64 E5
Arthington St GIR BD8 4 A3
MID LS10 131 M4 1
MILN OL16 206 D6
Arthington Ter MID LS10 131 M4
Arthington Vw MID LS10 131 M4
Arthur Av GIR BD8 103 M7 1
Arthur Gv BTLY WF17 151 H6 1
Arthursdale Cl
MSTN/BAR LS15 90 B7
Arthursdale Dr MSTN/BAR LS15 90 B7
Arthursdale Gra
MSTN/BAR LS15 90 B7
Arthur St BGLY BD16 81 H3 2
BRIG HD6 170 E4
HOLM/MEL HD7 213 G2
HWTH BD22 78 D4
IDLE BD10 83 K8 1
PDSY/CALV LS28 106 F4
ROY/SHW OL2 229 J7
WKFDE WF1 13 K8
Artillery St HECK WF16 172 F3
Artist St WOR/ARM LS12 109 G7
Arum St WBOW BD5 126 E3 1
Arundel Av ROCH OL11 228 A2
Arundel Cl BTLY WF17 151 K4 1
Arundell Dr BSLYN/ROY S71 262 B2
Arundel Rd AWLS/ASK DN6 227 M3
Arundel St GFTH/SHER LS25 113 K6
HFAX HX1 10 B5 2
PDSY/CALV LS28 107 G6
ROCH OL11 228 A2
WKFDE WF1 176 E7 1
Arundel Wk BTLY WF17 151 K5 1
Ascot Av GTHN BD7 126 A4
Ascot Dr WBSY BD6 126 A4
Ascot Gdns EARD/LOFT WF3 153 M3
GTHN BD7 126 A4
Ascot Gv BRIG HD6 170 A6
Ascot Pde GTHN BD7 126 A4
Ascot Rd GFTH/SHER LS25 135 H4
Ascot Ter OSM LS9 110 B7
Asdale Rd HOR/CROF WF4 198 C7
Ash Av HDGY LS6 108 F1
Ashbourne Av CLECK BD19 149 M8
ECHL BD2 105 H3
Ashbourne Bank ECHL BD2 105 H3 2
Ashbourne Cl ECHL BD2 105 H2 1
WHIT OL12 184 F8 1
Ashbourne Crs
CUL/QBY BD13 124 F5 2
ECHL BD2 105 H3
GFTH/SHER LS25 135 H1
Ashbourne Cft CLECK BD19 149 M8 1
Ashbourne Dr CLECK BD19 149 M8
ECHL BD2 105 H3
PONT WF8 202 F1
Ashbourne Gdns
CLECK BD19 149 M8 2
ECHL BD2 105 H3
Ashbourne Garth ECHL BD2 105 J2 1
Ashbourne Gv ECHL BD2 105 H3 3
HFAX HX1 10 A6
Ashbourne Hvn ECHL BD2 105 H3
Ashbourne Mt ECHL BD2 105 H3 4
Ashbourne Ov ECHL BD2 105 H3
Ashbourne Ri ECHL BD2 105 H3 5
Ashbourne Rd BSLYN/ROY S71 243 J7
ECHL BD2 105 H3
HWTH BD22 79 J2
Ashbourne Vw CLECK BD19 149 M8
Ashbourne Wy CLECK BD19 149 M8
ECHL BD2 105 H3
Ashbrook Cl OSS WF5 174 F8
Ashbrook Crs WHIT OL12 206 E2
Ashbrook Hey La WHIT OL12 206 E2
Ash Brow HOR/CROF WF4 217 L3
Ash Brow Rd HUDN HD2 192 D3
Ashburn Cl WBY LS22 29 M7 2
Ashburn Cft WBY LS22 29 M7
Ashburn Dr WBY LS22 29 M7
Ashburn Gv BAIL BD17 82 E2 1
WBY LS22 29 M8
Ashburnham Gv HTON BD9 104 D3
Ashburn Pl ILK LS29 38 C3
Ashburn Wy WBY LS22 29 M7
Ashburton Cl AWLS/ASK DN6 249 J8
Ashbury Cha WKFDE WF1 176 C1
Ashby Av BRAM LS13 107 M4
Ashby Cl LVSG WF15 172 B5 1
Ashby Ct BSLY S70 260 F6
Ashby Crs BRAM LS13 107 M4
Ashby Mt BRAM LS13 107 M4
Ashby Sq BRAM LS13 107 M4 1
Ashby St BOW BD4 127 J2 1
Ashby Ter BRAM LS13 107 M4
Ashby Vw BRAM LS13 107 M4 2
Ash Cl HIPP HX3 147 M6
ILK LS29 38 A2
WHIT OL12 206 E2
Ashcombe Dr KNOT WF11 182 B3
Ash Ct CLECK BD19 149 H6 2
Ash Crs EARD/LOFT WF3 177 H2
HDGY LS6 108 E1
Ash Cft WBSY BD6 126 C6
Ashcroft Av FEA/AMT WF7 201 L2
Ashcroft Cl BTLY WF17 173 J3
Ashcroft Rd FEA/AMT WF7 201 L3
Ashdale WKFDW/WTN WF2 199 G6
Ashdale La WBY LS22 29 M6
Ashday La HIPP HX3 169 L4
Ashdene WOR/ARM LS12 129 M3 1
Ashdene Ap HOR/CROF WF4 200 B5
Ashdene Av HOR/CROF WF4 200 B5
Ashdene Cl PDSY/CALV LS28 129 G1
Ashdene Ct CUL/QBY BD13 79 M8
Ashdene Crs HOR/CROF WF4 200 B5
PDSY/CALV LS28 129 G1
Ashdene Dr HOR/CROF WF4 200 B5
Ashdene Garth
HOR/CROF WF4 200 B5
Ashdene Gv PONT WF8 181 H2
Ashdown Cl HWTH BD22 78 F5
Ashdown St BRAM LS13 107 L4 1
Ashdown Wy ROY/SHW OL2 229 G6
Ash Dyke Cl DOD/DAR S75 241 M7
Ashenhurst Av HUDS HD4 214 E3
Ashenhurst Cl HUDS HD4 214 D3 1
TOD OL14 141 J7
Ashenhurst Ri HUDS HD4 214 D3
Ashenhurst Rd HUDS HD4 214 D3
TOD OL14 141 H7 1
Ashes La HUDS HD4 214 D6
MILN OL16 207 G7
TOD OL14 141 M7
Ashfield BOW BD4 127 M5
EARL WF12 195 M2
WBY LS22 30 B8
Ashfield Av KBTN HD8 239 J5
MOR LS27 152 B4 1
ROCH OL11 228 B1
SHPY BD18 104 D1
Ashfield Cl DOD/DAR S75 260 E3
HIPP HX3 146 B4 1
MSTN/BAR LS15 111 M2 1
WOR/ARM LS12 130 A2
Ashfield Crs BGLY BD16 81 J4
PDSY/CALV LS28 106 F5
Ashfield Dr BAIL BD17 82 F2
HIPP HX3 146 B4
SHPY BD18 104 D1 6
Ashfield Gv PDSY/CALV LS28 107 G5 1
SHPY BD18 104 C1
Ashfield La MILN OL16 229 H2
Ashfield Pl ECHL BD2 105 M4
Ashfield Rd BTLY WF17 151 J4
CUL/QBY BD13 102 F8
GTL/HWG HX4 168 D7
HEM/SK/SE WF9 245 M1
HUDN HD2 14 B1
IDLE BD10 83 K5 1
IDLE BD10 83 L5 1
MOR LS27 152 B4 2
PDSY/CALV LS28 106 F5
ROCH OL11 228 B1
SHPY BD18 82 A7
Ashfield St HUDN HD2 192 D4
NORM WF6 178 E3
Ashfield Ter EARD/LOFT WF3 154 B4 1
GTL/HWG HX4 168 D6
HWTH BD22 78 E8 3
MSTN/BAR LS15 111 M2
Ashfield Wy WOR/ARM LS12 130 B3
Ashford Ct KBTN HD8 216 B7
Ashford Dr PDSY/CALV LS28 107 H8
Ash Ford Gn WBSY BD6 126 B5 1
Ashford Mnr KBTN HD8 215 M5
Ashford Pk HOLM/MEL HD7 212 F1
Ashgap La NORM WF6 178 D4
Ash Gdns HDGY LS6 108 F1
Ash Ghyll Gdns BGLY BD16 81 H2 2
Ash Gv AIRE BD20 55 L1
AIRE BD20 56 F1 1
BIRK/DRI BD11 128 C8 1
BRIG HD6 170 E3 1
BSLY S70 261 M7
CLECK BD19 150 C5
EARD/LOFT WF3 177 H4
HDGY LS6 6 A2
HEM/SK/SE WF9 247 J2
HWTH BD22 79 K2 1
ILK LS29 38 E1
LIT OL15 207 H1
MILN OL16 229 J3
OT LS21 41 H7
PDSY/CALV LS28 107 G8
PONT WF8 203 L1
ROY/SHW OL2 228 F8
BGLY BD16 81 J5
Ashgrove ECHL BD2 105 L3
GTHN BD7 4 C8
IDLE BD10 84 A7
MILN OL16 228 D5 1
Ashgrove Av HIPP HX3 169 G2 1
Ashgrove Crs GFTH/SHER LS25 135 K3
Ashgrove Cft
GFTH/SHER LS25 135 K4 1
Ashgrove Ms BRAM LS13 107 H2
Ashgrove Mt GFTH/SHER LS25 135 J3
Ashgrove Rd AIRE BD20 57 J4 2
Ash Grove Rd HOLM/MEL HD7 254 A1
Ashgrove Rd HUDE HD5 193 H4
Ash Hall La RPDN/SBR HX6 166 B8
Ash Hill Dr AL/HA/HU LS17 89 H2
Ash Hill Gdns AL/HA/HU LS17 89 H2
Ash Hill La AL/HA/HU LS17 89 H2
Ashia Cl MILN OL16 206 C8
Ashington Cl ECHL BD2 105 M3 1
Ashlands Rd ILK LS29 38 E1
Ash La GFTH/SHER LS25 113 J6
GFTH/SHER LS25 117 G4
KBTN HD8 218 A8
TAD LS24 116 E2
Ashlar Cl HWTH BD22 78 F7 2
Ashlar Gv CAS WF10 158 B8 1
CUL/QBY BD13 124 F7
Ash Lea EARD/LOFT WF3 177 H4
Ashlea Av BRIG HD6 170 D6
Ashlea Cl BRIG HD6 170 D6
GFTH/SHER LS25 135 H1
Ashlea Dr BRIG HD6 170 D6
Ashlea Ga BRAM LS13 107 L2
Ashlea Gn BRAM LS13 107 L3
Ashleigh CUD/GR S72 245 J3
Ashleigh Av PONT WF8 180 F7
WKFDW/WTN WF2 198 A1
Ashleigh Cl KBTN HD8 238 B4 1
Ashleigh Dl HUDN HD2 192 A5
Ashleigh Gdns OSS WF5 174 E6 1
RTHW LS26 133 L8
Ashleigh Rd BHP/TINH LS16 86 C6
Ashleigh St KGHY BD21 3 G2
Ashley Av OSM LS9 110 C4
Ashley Cl CLECK BD19 150 C4
WKFDW/WTN WF2 176 B4
Ashley Ct HEM/SK/SE WF9 246 B5
Ashley Cft BSLYN/ROY S71 243 K2
Ashley Gv HBR HX7 144 A4
Ashley La BAIL BD17 82 C6
Ashley Rd BGLY BD16 81 J4 1
LM/WK BD12 148 E4
OSM LS9 110 C4
WOR/ARM LS12 108 D8
Ashley St HFAX HX1 10 B6
SHPY BD18 82 D6 1
Ashley Ter OSM LS9 110 C4 1
Ashmead BSPA/BRAM LS23 69 M1 2
BTLY WF17 173 J3 1
Ash Meadow Cl HUDN HD2 192 D3
Ashmere Gv HUDN HD2 192 E4 1
Ashmews IDLE BD10 84 A7 1
Ashmore Dr OSS WF5 174 E5
Ashmore Gdns BOW BD4 127 K6 2
Ashmount CLAY BD14 125 M2 1
Ash Mt GTHN BD7 126 D1
KGHY BD21 2 C9
Ashmount Dr WHIT OL12 206 B4
Ash Rd AWLS/ASK DN6 249 K4
CUD/GR S72 244 F4
HDGY LS6 108 E1
Ashroyd RTHW LS26 155 H2
Ash St AIRE BD20 34 F8 1
CLECK BD19 149 L7
COL BB8 74 E4
EARD/LOFT WF3 177 H4
HOR/CROF WF4 200 C7
HUD HD1 14 E2
HWTH BD22 100 E3
WMB/DAR S73 262 C8
Ash Ter BGLY BD16 81 H4
HDGY LS6 108 F1
RPDN/SBR HX6 188 E3
Ashtofts Mt GSLY LS20 62 A5
Ashton Av GTHN BD7 126 A1
RHAY LS8 110 B4
Ashton Clough Rd
LVSG WF15 172 C2 3
Ashton Ct RHAY LS8 110 C3
Ashton Crs EARD/LOFT WF3 154 F3
Ashton Gdns ROCH OL11 228 A1
Ashton Gv OSM LS9 110 B4
Ashton Mt OSM LS9 110 B4
Ashton Pl OSM LS9 110 B4
Ashton Rd CAS WF10 157 M8
RHAY LS8 110 C3
Ashton St BFD BD1 4 C5
CAS WF10 157 M7
RHAY LS8 110 B3
ROCH OL11 228 A1 1
Ashton Ter RHAY LS8 110 B4
Ashton Vw OSM LS9 110 B4
Ashton Wk IDLE BD10 83 J7
Ash Tree Ap SCFT LS14 111 M2
Ash Tree Av CUL/QBY BD13 102 D8
Ash Tree Bank SCFT LS14 111 M1 1
Ash Tree Cl SCFT LS14 111 M1 2
Ash Tree Gdns LUD/ILL HX2 145 L1 1
NORM WF6 178 B3 1
SCFT LS14 111 M1
Ash Tree Garth TAD LS24 115 M1
Ashtree Gv GFTH/SHER LS25 135 K5
GTHN BD7 126 B4
Ash Tree Gv SCFT LS14 111 M1 3
Ash Tree Pk GFTH/SHER LS25 135 K5 1
Ash Tree Rd LUD/ILL HX2 145 L1
Ash Tree Wk ILK LS29 40 A5 1
Ash Vw EARD/LOFT WF3 153 L7
Ashville Av HDGY LS6 108 F3
Ashville Cft LUD/ILL HX2 145 M5
Ashville Gdns LUD/ILL HX2 145 M5
Ashville Gv HDGY LS6 108 F3
LUD/ILL HX2 145 M5
Ashville Rd HDGY LS6 108 F3
Ashville St HIPP HX3 10 D1 1
Ashville Ter HDGY LS6 108 F3
Ashville Vw HDGY LS6 109 G4
Ashwell Cl CUD/GR S72 244 E3
Ashwell Rd GIR BD8 104 D5
HTON BD9 104 C2
Ashwell St GIR BD8 104 D5 2
Ashwood SCFT LS14 89 K5
Ashwood Cl HUDN HD2 192 E3
Ashwood Dr AIRE BD20 58 C5
LIT OL15 207 H1
MOR LS27 129 K7
Ashwood Gdns MOR LS27 129 K7
Ashwood Gra
HOR/CROF WF4 198 A8 1
Ashwood Gv CUD/GR S72 263 M3
HOR/CROF WF4 197 L4 2
MOR LS27 129 L7 1
Ashwood St BOW BD4 127 M5
Ashwood Ter HDGY LS6 109 H2
Ashwood Vls HDGY LS6 6 A1
Ashworth Cl DEWS WF13 173 L6 1
LIT OL15 185 J7 1
Ashworth Gdns DEWS WF13 173 L6 2
Ashworth Gn DEWS WF13 173 L6
Ashworth Pl WBSY BD6 126 F5 1
Ashworth Rd DEWS WF13 173 L6
Ashworth St WHIT OL12 206 A6 1
Askam Av PONT WF8 181 H2
Asket Av SCFT LS14 111 G1
Asket Cl SCFT LS14 89 G8
Asket Crs SCFT LS14 111 G1
Asket Dr SCFT LS14 89 G8 1
Asket Gdns RHAY LS8 88 F8
Asket Garth SCFT LS14 111 G1
Asket Gn SCFT LS14 89 G8
Asket Hl RHAY LS8 88 F8
Asket Pl SCFT LS14 111 G1
Asket Wk SCFT LS14 111 G1
Askey Av MOR LS27 152 D4
Askey Crs MOR LS27 152 D4
Askham Gv HEM/SK/SE WF9 226 A6
Askham Rd CAS WF10 158 F5 1
Askwith La OT LS21 22 C8
Askwith Moor Rd OT LS21 22 B1
Aspden St TOD OL14 141 K8
Aspect Gdns PDSY/CALV LS28 106 E6
Aspen Cl KGHY BD21 3 L8
WKFDW/WTN WF2 176 C6
Aspen Ct EARD/LOFT WF3 152 E5
KBTN HD8 217 L7
Aspen Mt BHP/TINH LS16 86 A4
Aspen Ri WIL/AL BD15 103 H2 1
Aspen Wy TAD LS24 71 K3
Aspinall St HBR HX7 144 A5
HFAX HX1 10 B8
Aspley Pl HUD HD1 15 H7
Asprey Dr WIL/AL BD15 103 K6
Asquith Av MOR LS27 130 B8
Asquith Cl MOR LS27 152 B1
Asquith Dr MOR LS27 152 B1
Asquith St BTLY WF17 151 K4
Assembly St LDSU LS2 9 H1
NORM WF6 178 C4
Assheton Rd ROY/SHW OL2 229 H7
Astley Av RTHW LS26 134 C5
Astley Cl ROY/SHW OL2 229 H7 1
Astley La RTHW LS26 134 D6
Astley Wy RTHW LS26 134 D6
Aston Av BRAM LS13 108 A4 1
Aston Cl LVSG WF15 172 B4
Aston Crs BRAM LS13 108 A4
Aston Dr BRAM LS13 108 A4
BSLYN/ROY S71 243 J8
Aston Gv BRAM LS13 108 A4
Aston Mt BRAM LS13 108 A4
Aston Pl BRAM LS13 108 A4
Aston Rd BRAM LS13 107 M4
WBOW BD5 127 G3
Aston St BRAM LS13 107 M4
Aston Ter BRAM LS13 107 M4
Aston Vw BRAM LS13 107 M4
Astor Gv BRAM LS13 107 J4
Astor St BRAM LS13 107 J4
Astral Av HIPP HX3 147 M6
Astral Cl HIPP HX3 147 M6
Astral Vw WBSY BD6 126 C4
Atalanta Ter LUD/ILL HX2 168 A2
Atha Cl BEE/HOL LS11 131 J5
Atha Crs BEE/HOL LS11 131 J5
Atha St BEE/HOL LS11 131 J5
Athelstan La OT LS21 41 J4
Athelstans Ct GFTH/SHER LS25 116 A7
Athene Dr HUDS HD4 214 E3
Athersley Crs BSLYN/ROY S71 243 J8
Athersley Rd BSLYN/ROY S71 243 J8
Atherstone Rd WIL/AL BD15 103 K7 1
Atherton La BRIG HD6 170 D6
Athlone Dr EARL WF12 174 A3
Athlone Gv WOR/ARM LS12 108 E7 1
Athlone Ri GFTH/SHER LS25 113 K7
Athlone St WOR/ARM LS12 108 E7 2
Athlone Ter WOR/ARM LS12 108 E7 3
Athol Crs HIPP HX3 146 C3 1
Athold Dr OSS WF5 197 H1
Athold St OSS WF5 197 H1
Athol Gdns HIPP HX3 146 C3
Athol Gn HIPP HX3 146 C3 2
Athol Rd HIPP HX3 146 C3
HTON BD9 104 D4
Athol St HIPP HX3 146 C3 3
KGHY BD21 3 M1 1
WHIT OL12 206 D5
Atkinson Ct NORM WF6 178 C5 1
Atkinson La PONT WF8 181 H4
Atkinson St MID LS10 9 L5
SHPY BD18 82 D6 2
Atlanta St BRAM LS13 107 J4
Atlas Mill Rd BRIG HD6 170 C4
Atlas St GIR BD8 104 D5 3
Atterwith La RYKW YO26 33 H1
Attlee Av HOR/CROF WF4 222 E5
Attlee Crs WKFDW/WTN WF2 199 G7

Attlee Gv WKFDE WF1 176 E2
Attlee St NORM WF6 178 D6
Aubrey St ROCH OL11 228 B1 1
Auckland Rd WBSY BD6 126 C5
Audby Ct WBY LS22 30 B8
Audby La WBY LS22 30 B7
Audrey St OSS WF5 197 G2
Audsley's Yd
HOR/CROF WF4 197 G5 1
Augusta Cl WHIT OL12 206 A5
Augusta Dr NORM WF6 178 F6 1
Augusta St WHIT OL12 206 A5 1
Auster Bank Av TAD LS24 72 A2 1
Auster Bank Crs TAD LS24 72 A2
Auster Bank Rd TAD LS24 72 A1
Auster Bank Vw TAD LS24 72 A1
Austfield La GFTH/SHER LS25 138 E7
Austhorpe Av MSTN/BAR LS15 112 A7
Austhorpe Ct
MSTN/BAR LS15 112 B7 1
Austhorpe Dr MSTN/BAR LS15 112 A7
Austhorpe Gdns
MSTN/BAR LS15 112 B6
Austhorpe Gv MSTN/BAR LS15 112 A7
Austhorpe La MSTN/BAR LS15 111 M5
Austhorpe Rd MSTN/BAR LS15 111 M4
Austhorpe Vw
MSTN/BAR LS15 111 M6
Austin Av BRIG HD6 170 B2
Austin Rd CAS WF10 158 F6
Austin St KGHY BD21 3 J3
Austwick Cl DOD/DAR S75 242 C4
Authorpe Rd CHAL LS7 87 H8 1
Autumn Av HDGY LS6 109 G4
WBY LS22 30 A6 1
Autumn Crs HORS LS18 85 M7
Autumn Gv HDGY LS6 109 G4
Autumn Pl HDGY LS6 109 G4
Autumn St HDGY LS6 109 G4
HFAX HX1 10 B9 1
Autumn Ter HDGY LS6 109 G4 1
Auty Crs EARD/LOFT WF3 177 H1
Auty Sq MOR LS27 152 D3 1
Avenel Rd WIL/AL BD15 103 K6
Avenel Ter WIL/AL BD15 103 K6 1
Avenham Wy BFDE BD3 5 J4
Avens Cl PONT WF8 180 F7
Avenue A BSPA/BRAM LS23 49 K3
Avenue B BSPA/BRAM LS23 49 J5
Avenue C East
BSPA/BRAM LS23 49 L4
Avenue Crs RHAY LS8 110 B2
Avenue C West
BSPA/BRAM LS23 49 K5
Avenue D BSPA/BRAM LS23 49 K6
Avenue Des Hirondelles OT LS21 42 F8
Avenue E East BSPA/BRAM LS23 49 L5
Avenue E West BSPA/BRAM LS23 49 K6
Avenue F BSPA/BRAM LS23 49 L5
Avenue G BSPA/BRAM LS23 49 M4
Avenue Gdns AL/HA/HU LS17 87 H1
Avenue Hl RHAY LS8 110 B2
Avenue No 2 BRIG HD6 170 C5
Avenue Rd WBOW BD5 127 H3
WKFDW/WTN WF2 199 G5
Avenue St BOW BD4 127 M5
The Avenue AL/HA/HU LS17 45 J8
AL/HA/HU LS17 87 J1
AWLS/ASK DN6 227 L5
BGLY BD16 81 K6 1
BSLYN/ROY S71 244 A2
BTLY WF17 151 G5
BTLY WF17 151 J7
CLAY BD14 125 K2
DEWS WF13 173 H3
EARD/LOFT WF3 153 J6
GFTH/SHER LS25 138 A3
HIPP HX3 147 M6
HOR/CROF WF4 200 A5
HORS LS18 85 H5
HUDE HD5 15 L8
IDLE BD10 84 A5
MSTN/BAR LS15 90 B6
MSTN/BAR LS15 111 M3
MSTN/BAR LS15 133 M2
OSM LS9 9 L1
RHAY LS8 88 C6
ROY/SHW OL2 229 J8
TAD LS24 50 C1
WBY LS22 47 J5
WKFDE WF1 176 C2
Avenue Victoria RHAY LS8 88 C6
Averingcliffe Rd IDLE BD10 83 M8
Aviary Gv WOR/ARM LS12 108 E6
Aviary Mt WOR/ARM LS12 108 E6
Aviary Pl WOR/ARM LS12 108 E6
Aviary Rd WOR/ARM LS12 108 E6 2
Aviary Rw WOR/ARM LS12 108 E6
Aviary St WOR/ARM LS12 108 E6
Aviary Ter WOR/ARM LS12 108 E6
Aviary Vw WOR/ARM LS12 108 E6
Aviation Rd GFTH/SHER LS25 116 D7
Avison Rd HUDS HD4 213 J3
Avison Yd WKFDE WF1 13 G3
Avis St ROY/SHW OL2 229 J7
Avocet Garth MID LS10 153 M1 1
Avon Cl AL/HA/HU LS17 89 H2
DOD/DAR S75 260 A3
MILN OL16 207 J8
Avon Ct AL/HA/HU LS17 89 G1
Avondale KGHY BD21 2 C3
Avondale Crs SHPY BD18 82 C7
Avondale Dr BSLYN/ROY S71 243 L5
EARD/LOFT WF3 177 G1
Avondale Gv SHPY BD18 82 C7 2
Avondale Mt SHPY BD18 82 C7
Avondale Pl HIPP HX3 168 D2 1
Avondale Rd SHPY BD18 82 B7
Avondale St BRAM LS13 107 L5 1
COL BB8 74 C1
WKFDW/WTN WF2 12 E6
Avondale Wy WKFDW/WTN WF2 12 E6
Avon Dr GFTH/SHER LS25 113 H8
Avon Garth WBY LS22 47 L1
Avon Rd ROY/SHW OL2 229 K6
Avon St BSLYN/ROY S71 261 J5
Avon Wk FEA/AMT WF7 179 M7
Aydon Wy WBSY BD6 126 A7
Aygill Av HTON BD9 103 M3
Aylesbury St HWTH BD22 79 J2 1
Aylesford Cl BSLYN/ROY S71 261 H3 1
Aylesford Mt
MSTN/BAR LS15 112 B3 1
Aynholme Dr ILK LS29 19 H6
Aynsley Gv WIL/AL BD15 103 K5
Ayres Dr HUDS HD4 213 J3
Ayresome Av RHAY LS8 88 C4
Ayresome Ov WIL/AL BD15 103 J7
Ayresome Ter RHAY LS8 88 B4
Ayrton St COL BB8 74 A1 1
Aysgarth Av BRIG HD6 148 C8
BSLYN/ROY S71 262 D6
Aysgarth Cl LM/WK BD12 148 E4 1
OSM LS9 110 B7 1
WKFDW/WTN WF2 197 M3
Aysgarth Crs LUD/ILL HX2 145 J3
Aysgarth Dr OSM LS9 110 B7 2
WKFDW/WTN WF2 197 M3
Aysgarth Fold MID LS10 153 L2 1
Aysgarth Pl OSM LS9 110 B7 3
Aysgarth Rd BTLY WF17 173 J1
HUDS HD4 214 D4
Aysgarth Wk OSM LS9 110 B7 4
Ayton Cl BFDE BD3 5 K4
Ayton Rd HUDW HD3 191 G8
Azealea Ct BFDE BD3 5 L4

B

Baby House Hill La HBR HX7 121 H2
Bachelor La HORS LS18 85 L4 1
Back Ada St KGHY BD21 2 D5
Back Aireview Ter KGHY BD21 3 M6 1
Back Aireville St AIRE BD20 57 J4 3
Back Airlie Av RHAY LS8 110 B2 5
Back Airlie Pl RHAY LS8 110 B2 6
Back Albert Gv HDGY LS6 86 F8
Back Albert Ter HDGY LS6 109 G4 1
Back Alcester Pl RHAY LS8 110 B2 7
Back Alcester Rd RHAY LS8 110 B2 8
Back Alcester Ter RHAY LS8 110 B2 9
Back Anderton St
WKFDE WF1 13 K8 2
Back Ann St CUL/QBY BD13 101 M5 1
Back Archery Pl LDSU LS2 6 E4
Back Archery Rd LDSU LS2 6 F5
Back Archery St LDSU LS2 6 F5
Back Archery Ter LDSU LS2 6 E5
Back Ash Gv HDGY LS6 6 A2
Back Ashgrove (West)
GTHN BD7 4 C8
Back Ashley Av OSM LS9 110 C4 2
Back Ashley St OSM LS9 110 C4 3
Back Ashville Av HDGY LS6 109 G3 1
Back Ashville Gv HDGY LS6 108 F3 1
Back Ashville Rd HDGY LS6 108 F3 2
Back Ashville Ter HDGY LS6 108 F3 3
Back Ashwood Ter HDGY LS6 109 H2
Back Aston Pl BRAM LS13 108 A4
Back Aston St BRAM LS13 107 M4
Back Aston Ter BRAM LS13 107 M4
Back Aston Vw BRAM LS13 107 M4
Back Athlone Av
WOR/ARM LS12 108 E7 4
Back Athlone Gv
WOR/ARM LS12 108 E7 5
Back Athlone Ter
WOR/ARM LS12 108 E7 6
Back Atlanta St BRAM LS13 107 J4 1
Back Austhorpe Rd
MSTN/BAR LS15 111 L4 1
MSTN/BAR LS15 111 M4 1
Back Autumn Rd HDGY LS6 109 G4 5
Back Aylesbury St
HWTH BD22 79 J2 2
Back Baker St SHPY BD18 82 C6 2
Back Baldovan Ter
RHAY LS8 110 B2 10
Back Balfour St BGLY BD16 81 H4 1
KGHY BD21 2 E7 1
Back Bank St CAS WF10 157 M6 2
Back Bank Ter
PDSY/CALV LS28 107 G4
Back Banstead St RHAY LS8 110 B3 1
Back Barden Pl
WOR/ARM LS12 108 C7 2
Back Barkly Gv BEE/HOL LS11 131 J4
Back Barkly Pde
BEE/HOL LS11 131 J5 1
Back Barkly Ter BEE/HOL LS11 131 J4
Back Barrowby Vw
MSTN/BAR LS15 112 A7
Back Bath Rd BRAM LS13 107 L4 5
Back Beamsley Gv HDGY LS6 109 G4 6
Back Beamsley Mt HDGY LS6 109 G4 7
Back Beamsley Ter
HDGY LS6 109 G4 8
Back Beaumont St
BTLY WF17 173 L2 1
Back Beck La ILK LS29 19 H5
Back Beech St BGLY BD16 81 H4 2
Back Beech Ter HUD HD1 15 G1
Back Beechwood Gv BULY LS4 108 F3
Back Beechwood Rd
BULY LS4 108 F3 4
Back Bellbrooke Gv
OSM LS9 110 D4 1
Back Bellbrooke Pl OSM LS9 110 D4 2
Back Bellbrooke Ter
OSM LS9 110 C4 4
Back Belvedere Av
BEE/HOL LS11 131 K4
Back Belvedere Mt
BEE/HOL LS11 131 K4
Back Bentley Av HDGY LS6 87 H8 1
Back Bentley Gv HDGY LS6 87 H8
Back Berkeley Av RHAY LS8 110 C3
Back Berkeley Ter RHAY LS8 110 C3 1
Back Beverley Ter
BEE/HOL LS11 131 K3
Back Blackwood Gv
HFAX HX1 10 A3 1
Back Blenheim Av LDSU LS2 6 F4 1
Back Blenheim Mt GIR BD8 104 E4 1
Back Blenheim Ter LDSU LS2 6 E5
Back Boundary Ter BVRD LS3 109 G5 1
Back Bower Rd ELL HX5 169 J7 1
Back Bowling Green Rd
GTL/HWG HX4 190 B3
Back Bowman St WKFDE WF1 13 L9
Back Bradshaw Rd
HOLM/MEL HD7 236 B3
Back Bradshaw St MILN OL16 206 C6
Back Breary Av HORS LS18 85 M5
Back Breary Ter HORS LS18 85 M5
Back Bridge St SKP/WHF BD23 16 B2 2
Back Briggate AIRE BD20 36 A4 1
Back Broad La BRAM LS13 107 M2 1
Back Broomfield Crs
HDGY LS6 108 F2
Back Broomfield Pl HDGY LS6 108 F3
Back Broomfield Rd HDGY LS6 108 F3
KGHY BD21 2 F4 1
Back Broomfield St
KGHY BD21 2 F4 2
Back Broughton Av
OSM LS9 110 C4 5
Back Broughton Ter
OSM LS9 110 C4 6
Back Brudenell Gv HDGY LS6 6 A4
Back Brudenell Mt HDGY LS6 109 G4
Back Brudenell Rd HDGY LS6 109 G3 2
Back Brunswick St
DEWS WF13 173 J5 2
LDSU LS2 7 H7
Back Burchett Gv HDGY LS6 6 D1
Back Burchett Pl HDGY LS6 6 D1
Back Burley Hl BULY LS4 108 E4
Back Burley Lodge Rd
HDGY LS6 109 G4
Back Burley Lodge Ter
HDGY LS6 109 G5
Back Burley St BVRD LS3 6 C8 1
Back Burlington Pl
BEE/HOL LS11 131 K4 1
Back Burlington Rd
BEE/HOL LS11 131 K4
Back Burton Crs HDGY LS6 86 F8 1
Back Burton Ter
BEE/HOL LS11 131 L3 1
Back Buxton St KGHY BD21 3 J4
Back Byrl St KGHY BD21 3 H1 1
Back Byrom St TOD OL14 141 K8 2
Back Caister St KGHY BD21 79 K2 2
Back Caledonia Rd KGHY BD21 3 J1 1
Back Camberley St
BEE/HOL LS11 131 L3 2
Back Carberry Pl HDGY LS6 109 G4
Back Carberry Rd HDGY LS6 109 G4
Back Carberry Ter HDGY LS6 109 G4
Back Carter Ter
MSTN/BAR LS15 111 L5 1
Back Cartmel Rd KGHY BD21 2 D5 1
Back Castle Rd KGHY BD21 2 F2
Back Cavendish Rd IDLE BD10 83 K7 1
Back Cavendish St KGHY BD21 3 H4
Back Cavendish Ter
HFAX HX1 10 D5 1
Back Cecil St HUD HD1 14 D7
Back Chapel La HDGY LS6 108 F2
Back Chapel St WHIT OL12 184 E7 1
Back Charles St BRIG HD6 170 C3
Back Charlton Rd OSM LS9 110 C7 1
Back Chatsworth Rd
RHAY LS8 110 C3 2
Back Chestnut Av HDGY LS6 109 G3
MSTN/BAR LS15 111 M4 3
MSTN/BAR LS15 111 M4 2
Back Chiswick Ter HDGY LS6 109 G4 9
Back Christ Church Vw
WOR/ARM LS12 108 D6 1
Back Church La BHP/TINH LS16 86 E1
KSTL LS5 108 C2 1
Back Church Vw WKFDE WF1 199 G4
Back Claremont Av BVRD LS3 6 C7 1
Back Clarence Rd HORS LS18 85 K7 1
Back Clarence St HFAX HX1 10 E6
Back Clarendon Pl HFAX HX1 10 C6
Back Clarkson Vw HDGY LS6 6 D1
Back Clayton St RTHW LS26 155 H1 1
Back Cliff Mt HDGY LS6 6 C1
Back Clifton Rd HUD HD1 14 A5
Back Clifton Ter OSM LS9 110 D4 3
Back Clipston Av HDGY LS6 87 H8 3
Back Clock View St
KGHY BD21 57 K4 1
Back Close Lea BRIG HD6 170 C5 1
Back Close Lea Dr BRIG HD6 170 C5 2
Back Clough HIPP HX3 147 J4
Back Coldcotes Av OSM LS9 110 D4 4
Back Colenso Mt BEE/HOL LS11 8 B7
Back Colenso Rd BEE/HOL LS11 8 A7
KGHY BD21 3 M1
Back Colne Rd AIRE BD20 34 E8
Back Colton Rd
WOR/ARM LS12 108 E7 7
Back Colwyn Pl
BEE/HOL LS11 131 K4 2
Back Colwyn Vw
BEE/HOL LS11 131 K4 3
Back Commerical St
TOD OL14 163 L1 1
Back Compton St KGHY BD21 3 J3 1
Back Conway St RHAY LS8 110 B3
Back Cowper Gv RHAY LS8 110 C3 3
Back Cowper St CHAL LS7 7 K2
Back Cranbrook Av
BEE/HOL LS11 131 J3
Back Cranbrook Ter
BEE/HOL LS11 131 J3
Back Croft House La
AIRE BD20 57 J4 4
Back Cromer Ter LDSU LS2 6 D5
Back Cromwell Ter HFAX HX1 10 E5 1
Back Cross Flats Rw
BEE/HOL LS11 131 H4
Back Cross Flatts Av
BEE/HOL LS11 131 J4
Back Cross Flatts Crs
BEE/HOL LS11 131 H4
Back Cross Flatts Gv
BEE/HOL LS11 131 J4 1
Back Cross Flatts Mt
BEE/HOL LS11 131 J4 2
Back Cross Flatts Pl
BEE/HOL LS11 131 H4
Back Cross Green Crs OSM LS9 110 B8 1
Back Cross Green La OSM LS9 110 B8 2
Back Crossland Ter BEE/HOL LS11 8 F9
Back Cross La ELL HX5 169 G8 1
Back Dalton Av BEE/HOL LS11 131 J4
Back Dalton Gv BEE/HOL LS11 131 J4 3
Back Dalton Rd BEE/HOL LS11 131 J4
Back Dargai St CHAL LS7 7 G2
Back Dawlish Mt OSM LS9 110 D6
Back De Lacy Mt KSTL LS5 108 C1
Back Delph Mt HDGY LS6 6 D1
Back Dent St OSM LS9 110 B7 5
Back Der St TOD OL14 163 L1 2
Back Devonshire La RHAY LS8 88 C4
Back Dorset Mt RHAY LS8 110 C2 1
Back Dorset Rd RHAY LS8 110 C2 2
Back Dorset Ter RHAY LS8 110 C3 4
Back Drake St MILN OL16 206 B8
Back Dudley Hill Rd
ECHL BD2 105 K4 1
Back Duke of York St
WKFDE WF1 176 F7 1
Back Duke St FEA/AMT WF7 179 L8 1
Back Dunbar St WKFDE WF1 13 L7
Back Durham St ROCH OL11 228 C1 1
Back East Park Rd OSM LS9 110 C7 2
Back Eaton St HWTH BD22 79 J2 3
Back Ecclesburn Gv
OSM LS9 110 D7 1
Back Ecclesburn St OSM LS9 110 C7 3
Back Edensor Rd KGHY BD21 2 D5 2
Back Eldon Rd HUD HD1 191 M7
Back Elford Pl RHAY LS8 110 B3
Back Elizabeth St WBOW BD5 4 E9
Back Ellers Gv RHAY LS8 110 B2 11
Back Ellers Rd RHAY LS8 110 B2 12
Back Elmfield Ter HFAX HX1 168 C1
Back Elsworth St
WOR/ARM LS12 108 F7
Back Eric St BRAM LS13 107 L1
KGHY BD21 3 H2
Back Eshald Pl RTHW LS26 133 M8
Back Esmond Ter
WOR/ARM LS12 108 D7 1
Back Estcourt Av HDGY LS6 108 E1
Back Eversley Mt LUD/ILL HX2 146 A8
Back Fairford Pl BEE/HOL LS11 9 G9
Back Ferguson St HFAX HX1 11 G7 1
Back Fld CUL/QBY BD13 102 F8 3
Back Field Ct CUL/QBY BD13 102 F8 4
Back Fitzwilliam St HUD HD1 14 D6
Back Florist St KGHY BD21 3 M1
Back Fold CLAY BD14 125 K1 1
Back Foster Rd KGHY BD21 2 E9 1
KGHY BD21 79 K2 3
Back Garden St CAS WF10 157 M8 1
WKFDE WF1 12 D3
Back Garton Rd OSM LS9 110 C7 4
Back Garton Ter OSM LS9 110 C7 5
Back Gathorne St RHAY LS8 7 M3
Back Gerrard St HFAX HX1 10 E6
Back Giles St South
WBOW BD5 126 F1 2
Back Gillett La RTHW LS26 155 H1 2
Back Girlington Rd GIR BD8 104 C6 1
Back Gladstone St BGLY BD16 81 H4 3
Back Glenthorpe Ter OSM LS9 110 C6 1
Back Glossop St HDGY LS6 6 E1
Back Gooder La BRIG HD6 170 D5 1
Back Gordon St WKFDE WF1 13 L9
Back Gordon Ter HDGY LS6 87 H8 4
Back Graham Gv BULY LS4 108 F3
Back Granby Gv HDGY LS6 108 F2 1
Back Grange Av CHAL LS7 7 K1
Back Grange Crs CHAL LS7 7 L1
Back Grange Ter CHAL LS7 7 K1
Back Grange Vw CHAL LS7 7 K1
Back Grantley St WKFDE WF1 13 G2
Back Grant St HWTH BD22 2 C5
Back Graveley St
MSTN/BAR LS15 111 J6 1
Back Great Russell St GTHN BD7 4 A6
Back Greaves Streen
WBOW BD5 126 F3 1
Back Gn MOR LS27 130 E7
Back Greenhead Rd HUD HD1 14 D7
Back Greenmount Ter
BEE/HOL LS11 8 F9 1
Back Greenwood Mt
HDGY LS6 87 G7 1
Back Grosvenor Ter HDGY LS6 109 H2
HFAX HX1 10 D6
Back Grouse St KGHY BD21 3 J3 2
Back Grovehall Av
BEE/HOL LS11 131 J5
Back Grovehall Dr
BEE/HOL LS11 131 J5
Back Grove Rd ILK LS29 38 D2
Back Haigh Av RTHW LS26 132 F7 1
Back Haigh St RTHW LS26 132 E7 1
Back Haigh Vw RTHW LS26 132 E7 2
Back Halliday Gv
WOR/ARM LS12 108 C6
Back Halliday Pl
WOR/ARM LS12 108 C6
Back Hambleton St
WKFDE WF1 12 F1
Back Hamilton Av CHAL LS7 7 L1
Back Hamilton Vw CHAL LS7 7 L1
Back Harehills Av CHAL LS7 110 A2 3
Back Harehills Park Vw
OSM LS9 110 D4 5
Back Harehills Pl RHAY LS8 110 B3 2
Back Hares Av RHAY LS8 110 B2 13
Back Hares Mt RHAY LS8 7 M1
Back Hares Ter RHAY LS8 110 B2 14
Back Hares Vw RHAY LS8 110 B2 15
Back Harold Gv HDGY LS6 109 G4
Back Hartley Av HDGY LS6 6 E1
Back Hartley Gv HDGY LS6 6 D1
Back Hartley St MOR LS27 152 D3
Back Hatfeild St WKFDE WF1 176 E7 3
Back Headingley Av HDGY LS6 108 E1
Back Headingley Mt HDGY LS6 108 E1
Back Heddon St HDGY LS6 87 G8
Back Heights Rd CUL/QBY BD13 102 D7
Back Henrietta St BTLY WF17 173 L1 1
Back Hessle Av HDGY LS6 109 G3 3
Back Hessle Mt HDGY LS6 109 G3 4
Back Hessle Ter HDGY LS6 109 G3 5
Back Hessle Vw HDGY LS6 109 G3 6
Back Highbury Ter HDGY LS6 87 G8
Back Highfield Rd BRAM LS13 107 M4
Back High St CUL/QBY BD13 102 F8 5
Back Highthorne Gv
WOR/ARM LS12 108 C6 2
Back Highthorne St
WOR/ARM LS12 108 C6
Back Hillcrest Av CHAL LS7 7 M1
Back Hillcrest Vw CHAL LS7 7 M1
Back Hill Top Av RHAY LS8 110 B2
Back Hill Top Mt RHAY LS8 110 B2
Back Hilton Gv RHAY LS8 110 B2 16
Back Hilton Pl RHAY LS8 110 B2 17
Back Hilton Rd RHAY LS8 110 B2 18
Back Hird St KGHY BD21 2 E7 2
Backhold Av HIPP HX3 169 G4
Backhold Dr HIPP HX3 168 F4
Backhold La HIPP HX3 168 F4
Backhold Rd HIPP HX3 169 G4
Back Hollyshaw Ter
MSTN/BAR LS15 111 L6 1
Back Holywell La
AL/HA/HU LS17 88 F1
Back Honoria St HUDN HD2 14 F1
Backhouse La HOR/CROF WF4 220 B7
Back Hovingham Gv
RHAY LS8 110 C2 3
Back Hovingham Mt
RHAY LS8 110 C2 4
Back Hovingham Ter
RHAY LS8 110 C2 5
Back Hyde Ter LDSU LS2 6 C6
Back Ibbetson Pl LDSU LS2 6 E6
Back Ingledew Crs RHAY LS8 88 D4 1
Back Irwell St BOW BD4 127 J1 1
Back Ivy Av OSM LS9 110 C6 2
Back Ivy Gv OSM LS9 110 D7 2
Back Ivy Mt OSM LS9 110 C6 3
Back Ivy St OSM LS9 110 D7 3
Back John St CUL/QBY BD13 102 F8
Back Karnac Rd RHAY LS8 110 B2
Back Kelso Rd LDSU LS2 6 B5
Back Kendal La BVRD LS3 6 C7 2
Back Kennerleigh Wk
MSTN/BAR LS15 111 L5 2
Back Kensington St GIR BD8 104 C6 2
Back Kensington Ter HDGY LS6 6 A2
Back Kirby St KGHY BD21 3 J2
Back Kirkgate SHPY BD18 82 C7 3
Back Kitson St OSM LS9 110 B7 6
Back Knowl Rd MIRF WF14 172 B8
Back Laisteridge La GTHN BD7 4 B8 1
Back Lambton Gv
RHAY LS8 110 B2 19
Back Landseer Av
BRAM LS13 108 A3 1
Back Landseer Gv
BRAM LS13 108 A3 2
Back Landseer Ter
BRAM LS13 108 A3 3
Back La AIRE BD20 16 E7
AIRE BD20 36 A4 2
AIRE BD20 58 F5 1
AL/HA/HU LS17 44 B3
AWLS/ASK DN6 227 L2
AWLS/ASK DN6 227 L6
BEE/HOL LS11 131 H5
BIRK/DRI BD11 129 H7
BRAM LS13 107 M5
BRFD/BLYE BB10 74 A6
BRFD/BLYE BB10 96 C1
BSLYN/ROY S71 261 L1
BSPA/BRAM LS23 69 M3
CAS WF10 157 K3
COL BB8 74 D4
CUL/QBY BD13 103 G7
CUL/QBY BD13 125 K4
EARL WF12 195 G5
EARL WF12 195 H7
EARL WF12 195 J4
GSLY LS20 61 M5
HBR HX7 99 J8
HBR HX7 120 E8
HBR HX7 143 H1
HBR HX7 143 H4
HECK WF16 172 F2 1
HEM/SK/SE WF9 225 G4
HEM/SK/SE WF9 225 J8
HOLM/MEL HD7 254 C1
HOR/CROF WF4 200 E4
HOR/CROF WF4 216 F1
HOR/CROF WF4 220 C8
HOR/CROF WF4 222 D2
HORS LS18 85 K6
HTON BD9 104 C2 1
HWTH BD22 56 D7
HWTH BD22 77 L8
IDLE BD10 83 J6
ILK LS29 40 B5
KBTN HD8 238 D3
KBTN HD8 239 J1
KBTN HD8 240 C3
LUD/ILL HX2 145 M1
MIRF WF14 194 A1
MIRF WF14 194 D7
OSS WF5 196 F1
PDSY/CALV LS28 106 F3
RPDN/SBR HX6 188 F2
RYKW YO26 33 J3
STKB/PEN S36 270 F3
STKB/PEN S36 271 H8
TAD LS24 116 A2
WBY LS22 46 D1
WIL/AL BD15 103 G2
WKFDE WF1 12 D3
WOR/ARM LS12 129 L3
YEA LS19 84 C1
Back La West BSLYN/ROY S71 243 J2
Back Langdale Gdns HDGY LS6 108 E2
Back Langdale Ter HDGY LS6 108 E2

Back Leatham St DEWS WF13 — 173 J5
Back Leeming HWTH BD22 — 100 F5
Back Lime St KGHY BD21 — 79 K3
Back Linden Gv BEE/HOL LS11 — 8 F9
Back Lindum St GIR BD8 — 104 E4
Back Lodge La BEE/HOL LS11 — 131 K3
Back Lombard St YEA LS19 — 84 C2
Back Longroyd Ter BSLY LS10 — 131 L3
Back Lord St HFAX HX1 — 10 F6
Back Lucas St HDGY LS6 — 6 D1
Back Lunan Pl RHAY LS8 — 110 B2
Back Lunan Ter RHAY LS8 — 110 B2
Back Lune Ct COL BB8 — 74 A2
Back Lyon St CUL/QBY BD13 — 125 H5
Back Mafeking Av BEE/HOL LS11 — 131 J5
Back Mafeking Mt BEE/HOL LS11 — 131 J5
Back Malt St HWTH BD22 — 79 J2
Back Mannville Rd KGHY BD21 — 2 D7
Back Manor Dr HDGY LS6 — 109 G3
Back Manor Gv CHAL LS7 — 87 M8
Back Manor Ter ECHL BD2 — 105 K3
Back Manor Ter HDGY LS6 — 109 G2
Back Market St WBSY BD6 — 126 E5
Back Markham Av RHAY LS8 — 110 B2
Back Marriot St DEWS WF13 — 173 M5
Back Marshall St MSTN/BAR LS15 — 111 L4
Back Marshall Ter MSTN/BAR LS15 — 111 L4
Back Mary St AIRE BD20 — 34 F6
Back Mary St EARD/LOFT WF3 — 154 A6
Back Masham St WOR/ARM LS12 — 108 F7
Back Maud Av BEE/HOL LS11 — 131 J4
Back Mayville Av HDGY LS6 — 109 G3
Back Mayville Pl HDGY LS6 — 109 G3
Back Mayville Ter HDGY LS6 — 109 G3
Back Meadow Vw HDGY LS6 — 109 G3
Back Melbourne Gv BRAM LS13 — 107 L4
Back Methley Dr CHAL LS7 — 87 M8
Back Mexborough Av CHAL LS7 — 7 J1
Back Mexborough Dr CHAL LS7 — 7 J1
Back Mexborough Gv CHAL LS7 — 7 J1
Back Mexborough Gv CHAL LS7 — 7 J1
Back Meynell Av RTHW LS26 — 155 G1
Back Middle Cross St WOR/ARM LS12 — 108 F7
Back Middleton Vw BEE/HOL LS11 — 8 D9
Back Midland Rd HDGY LS6 — 6 A2
Back Milan Av RHAY LS8 — 110 B3
Back Milan Rd RHAY LS8 — 110 B3
Back Milan St RHAY LS8 — 110 C3
Back Minnie St KGHY BD21 — 2 E7
Back Mitchell Ter BGLY BD16 — 81 H4
Back Mitford Rd WOR/ARM LS12 — 108 F7
Back Model Rd WOR/ARM LS12 — 108 F7
Back Model Ter WOR/ARM LS12 — 108 F7
Back Model Vw WOR/ARM LS12 — 108 F7
Back Monk Bridge Dr HDGY LS6 — 87 H8
Back Montague St WKFDE WF1 — 13 L9
Back Moorfield St HFAX HX1 — 10 C9
Back Moorfield Ter WOR/ARM LS12 — 108 C6
Back Moorland Ter LDSU LS2 — 6 C4
Back Moor La HUDS HD4 — 213 M7
Back Morning St KGHY BD21 — 79 K2
Back Morritt Dr MSTN/BAR LS15 — 111 H6
Back Mount Pleasant MID LS10 — 153 L1
Back Mount Pleasant WKFDE WF1 — 13 H2
Back Mount Vw HDGY LS6 — 6 B1
Back Muff St BOW BD4 — 5 L9
Back Myrtle Av BGLY BD16 — 81 H4
Back Nansen St BRAM LS13 — 107 J4
Back Newport Gdns HDGY LS6 — 108 F3
Back Newport Mt HDGY LS6 — 108 F3
Back Newport Pl HDGY LS6 — 108 F3
Back Newton Gv CHAL LS7 — 109 M2
Back Newton La CAS WF10 — 136 C7
Back New York St LDSU LS2 — 9 H1
Back Nice Vw RHAY LS8 — 110 B2
Back Norman Mt KSTL LS5 — 108 C2
Back Norman Pl RHAY LS8 — 88 C4
Back Norman Ter RHAY LS8 — 88 C4
Back Northbrook St CHAL LS7 — 87 M7
Back Northgate PONT WF8 — 180 F5
Back North St LM/WK BD12 — 149 J2
Back Norwood Gv HDGY LS6 — 109 G3
Back Norwood Pl HDGY LS6 — 109 G3
Back Norwood Rd HDGY LS6 — 109 G3
Back Nowell Crs OSM LS9 — 110 D5
Back Nowell Mt OSM LS9 — 110 D5
Back Nowell Pl OSM LS9 — 110 D5
Back Nowell Ter OSM LS9 — 110 D5
Back Nunington St WOR/ARM LS12 — 108 F6
Back Nunington Vw WOR/ARM LS12 — 108 E5
Back Nunroyd Rd AL/HA/HU LS17 — 87 M5
Back Nursery Mt MID LS10 — 132 A5
Back Oak Av BGLY BD16 — 81 H5
Back Oakfield Ter HDGY LS6 — 87 G8
Back Oakley St EARD/LOFT WF3 — 154 A4
Back Oakley Ter BEE/HOL LS11 — 131 L4
Back Oak Rd CHAL LS7 — 109 M1
Back Oakwood Av RHAY LS8 — 88 D3
Back Oakwood Dr RHAY LS8 — 88 D2
Back O' Dam HOLM/MEL HD7 — 212 B6
Back of the Beck SKP/WHF BD23 — 16 B2
Back Oldham Rd MILN OL16 — 206 C8

Back Osmondthorpe La OSM LS9 — 110 E6
Back O' the MI BGLY BD16 — 80 C5
Back O' Th' Height RPDN/SBR HX6 — 187 L4
Back Otterburn St KGHY BD21 — 3 G2
Back Outwood La HORS LS18 — 85 L7
Back Overdale Ter MSTN/BAR LS15 — 111 J6
Back O'wall HUDW HD3 — 211 K3
Back Oxford Pl LDS LS1 — 6 E8
Back Oxford St EARD/LOFT WF3 — 154 A6
Back Paget St KGHY BD21 — 2 D5
Back Parish Ghyll Rd ILK LS29 — 38 D3
Back Park Crs RHAY LS8 — 88 D4
Back Parkfield Pl BEE/HOL LS11 — 131 J3
Back Parkfield Rd BEE/HOL LS11 — 131 J3
Back Park La HFAX HX1 — 10 C6
Back Park Vw BEE/HOL LS11 — 131 J3
Back Park View Av BULY LS4 — 108 F3
Back Parkville Rd BRAM LS13 — 107 L3
Back Parnaby Av MID LS10 — 132 B5
Back Parnaby St MID LS10 — 132 B5
Back Parnaby Ter MID LS10 — 132 B5
Back Pasture Gv CHAL LS7 — 87 M7
Back Pasture Rd RHAY LS8 — 110 A2
Back Pawson St EARD/LOFT WF3 — 154 A6
Back Pleasant St RPDN/SBR HX6 — 167 L1
Back Pollard La BRAM LS13 — 107 L1
Back Pollard St HUDN HD2 — 192 D4
Back Poplar Av MSTN/BAR LS15 — 111 M4
Back Potternewton La CHAL LS7 — 87 L8
Back Potters St CHAL LS7 — 87 M8
Back Prospect Pl KGHY BD21 — 2 F6
Back Prospect Ter HDGY LS6 — 110 B7
Back Providence Av HDGY LS6 — 6 D1
Back Providence St BTLY WF17 — 173 L1
Back Purlwell Hall Rd BTLY WF17 — 173 L3
Back Quarry Mount Ter HDGY LS6 — 6 D1
Back Queen St GTL/HWG HX4 — 168 E8
Back Queen St HUD HD1 — 15 G7
Back Ravenscar Av RHAY LS8 — 88 C8
Back Raynville Mt BRAM LS13 — 108 A3
Back Regent Park Ter HDGY LS6 — 6 B1
Back Regent St WKFDE WF1 — 13 K8
Back Regent Ter HDGY LS6 — 6 A4
Back Reginald Mt CHAL LS7 — 109 M2
Back Reginald Pl CHAL LS7 — 109 M2
Back Reginald St CHAL LS7 — 109 M2
Back Rhodes St HFAX HX1 — 10 E6
Back Ribble St KGHY BD21 — 58 B6
Back Richardson St LM/WK BD12 — 149 J2
Back Richmond Mt HDGY LS6 — 109 G3
Back Ridge Mount Ter HDGY LS6 — 109 J2
Back Ridge St TOD OL14 — 163 K1
Back Ridge Vw CHAL LS7 — 109 J1
Back Rigging La RPDN/SBR HX6 — 166 E3
Back Ripley St AIRE BD20 — 58 B5
Back Ripon Ter HIPP HX3 — 10 F1
Back River St HWTH BD22 — 78 F2
Back Rd LM/WK BD12 — 148 E2
Back Roberts St RTHW LS26 — 133 L8
Back Rochester Ter HDGY LS6 — 108 F2
Back Rokeby Gdns HDGY LS6 — 108 E1
Back Roman Av RHAY LS8 — 88 C4
Back Roman Pl RHAY LS8 — 88 D4
Back Roman St RHAY LS8 — 88 D4
Back Rosebank Crs HDGY LS6 — 6 A5
Back Rosemont Wk BRAM LS13 — 107 L4
Back Rossall Rd RHAY LS8 — 110 C2
Back Rossington Gv RHAY LS8 — 7 M1
Back Rossington Pl RHAY LS8 — 7 M1
Back Rossington Rd RHAY LS8 — 7 M2
Back Roundhay Av RHAY LS8 — 110 B1
Back Roundhay Crs RHAY LS8 — 110 B1
Back Roundhay Gv RHAY LS8 — 110 B1
Back Roundhay Pl RHAY LS8 — 110 B1
Back Roundhay Vw RHAY LS8 — 110 B1
Back Rw BEE/HOL LS11 — 8 F3
Back Rowland Ter BEE/HOL LS11 — 131 L3
Back Royds St MILN OL16 — 228 C1
Back Rupert St KGHY BD21 — 3 H2
Back Russell St WBOW BD5 — 4 D9
Back Ruthven Vw RHAY LS8 — 110 C3
Back Rydal St KGHY BD21 — 3 K2
Back Rylstone St KGHY BD21 — 3 K2
Back St Alban Crs OSM LS9 — 110 C6
Back St Elmo Gv OSM LS9 — 110 C6
Back Saint Ives Mt WOR/ARM LS12 — 108 C6
Back St Luke's Crs BEE/HOL LS11 — 8 D8
Back St Mary's Rd CHAL LS7 — 109 M1
Back St Paul's Rd SHPY BD18 — 82 C7
Back Salisbury Gv WOR/ARM LS12 — 108 E6
Back Salisbury Ter WOR/ARM LS12 — 108 E6
Back Salisbury Vw WOR/ARM LS12 — 108 E6
Back Saltaire Rd North SHPY BD18 — 82 C6
Back Sandhurst Gv RHAY LS8 — 110 C3
Back Sandhurst Pl RHAY LS8 — 110 C3
Back Sandhurst Rd RHAY LS8 — 110 C3
Back Savile Gn HFAX HX1 — 168 D1
Back Savile Pde HFAX HX1 — 7 J2
Back Savile Rd CHAL LS7 — 7 J2
Back School Vw HDGY LS6 — 109 G3
Back Seaforth Av OSM LS9 — 110 D4

Back Seaforth Ter OSM LS9 — 110 C3
Back Sefton Av BEE/HOL LS11 — 131 J3
Back Sefton Ter BEE/HOL LS11 — 131 J4
Back Shaftesbury Av RHAY LS8 — 88 C5
Back Shaw La KGHY BD21 — 79 M3
Back Shepherd's La CHAL LS7 — 110 A2
Back Shepherd's Pl RHAY LS8 — 110 B2
Back Sholebroke Av CHAL LS7 — 109 M1
Back Sholebroke Mt CHAL LS7 — 109 M2
Back Sholebroke Pl CHAL LS7 — 109 M2
Back Sholebroke Rw CHAL LS7 — 109 M1
Back Sholebroke Ter CHAL LS7 — 109 M1
Back Sholebroke Vw CHAL LS7 — 109 M2
Back Sidlaw Ter RHAY LS8 — 110 B2
Back Simpson St KGHY BD21 — 2 D4
Back Sladen St KGHY BD21 — 2 D5
Back Slaithwaite Rd EARL WF12 — 195 L2
Back Smith Rw WBOW BD5 — 126 E3
Back South End Gv BRAM LS13 — 108 A4
Back Spencer Mt RHAY LS8 — 7 M2
Back Springfield Mt WOR/ARM LS12 — 108 C6
Back Springfield Rd ELL HX5 — 169 K7
Back Spring Grove Wk HDGY LS6 — 109 G4
Back Spring St HUD HD1 — 14 D7
Back Stanley St OSM LS9 — 110 B4
Back Stanmore Pl BULY LS4 — 108 E3
Back Stanmore St BULY LS4 — 108 E3
Back Station Rd AIRE BD20 — 34 F7
Back Station Rd BTLY WF17 — 173 M2
Back Station Rd MIRF WF14 — 194 C2
Backstone Gill La AL/HA/HU LS17 — 66 F5
Back Stone Hill Rd ECHL BD2 — 105 K2
Backstone La ILK LS29 — 38 E5
Backstone Wy ILK LS29 — 38 E2
Back Storey Pl SCFT LS14 — 111 G5
Back Stratford Av BEE/HOL LS11 — 131 J4
Back Stratford St BEE/HOL LS11 — 131 L3
Back Stratford Ter BEE/HOL LS11 — 131 K3
Back St BSPA/BRAM LS23 — 69 L3
Back St PONT WF8 — 180 E6
Back Sunnydene SCFT LS14 — 111 H5
Back Sutton Ap SCFT LS14 — 111 G5
Back Swinton St HFAX HX1 — 10 A8
Back Sycamore Av BGLY BD16 — 81 H4
Back Tamworth St BOW BD4 — 106 A8
Back Temple Vw BEE/HOL LS11 — 8 D9
Back Thornhill St PDSY/CALV LS28 — 84 D8
Back Thornville Rw HDGY LS6 — 109 G4
Back Trafford Av OSM LS9 — 110 D4
Back Trentham Pl BEE/HOL LS11 — 131 K3
Back Trinity Ter WBOW BD5 — 4 D7
Back Union St HUD HD1 — 15 G5
Back Unity St North BGLY BD16 — 81 H4
Back Unity St South BGLY BD16 — 81 H4
Back Vicars Rd RHAY LS8 — 110 B2
Back Victoria Av OSM LS9 — 110 D6
Back Victoria Gv OSM LS9 — 110 D7
Back Victoria St HFAX HX1 — 11 G5
Back Victor Ter HFAX HX1 — 10 C3
Back Walmsley Rd HDGY LS6 — 109 G3
Back Walnut St KGHY BD21 — 79 K3
Back Waverley Rd ELL HX5 — 191 H1
Back Webster St DEWS WF13 — 173 L6
Back Wellfield Ter TOD OL14 — 163 K2
Back Welton Gv HDGY LS6 — 109 G3
Back Welton Mt HDGY LS6 — 109 G3
Back Welton Pl HDGY LS6 — 109 G3
Back Wentworth St HUD HD1 — 14 D6
Back Wesley St CAS WF10 — 157 M6
Back Westbourne Ter LDSU LS2 — 6 C5
Back Westbury St MID LS10 — 132 B5
Back Westlock Av OSM LS9 — 110 C5
Back Westover Rd BRAM LS13 — 107 L3
Back West St RPDN/SBR HX6 — 167 K3
Back Wetherby Gv BULY LS4 — 108 E4
Back Wetherby Rd RHAY LS8 — 88 D8
Back Wharf St RPDN/SBR HX6 — 167 L2
Back Wickham St BEE/HOL LS11 — 131 J3
Back William Av MSTN/BAR LS15 — 111 G6
Back Wilton Gv HDGY LS6 — 87 G8
Back Winfield Gv LDSU LS2 — 6 F4
Back Winston Gdns HDGY LS6 — 108 F1
Back Winterburn St KGHY BD21 — 3 G2
Back Woodbine Ter HDGY LS6 — 87 G8
Back Woodland Park Rd HDGY LS6 — 109 G1
Back Wood St EARD/LOFT WF3 — 153 M6
Back Wright Av HWTH BD22 — 78 F3
Back York Pl LDS LS1 — 8 E1
Back York St LDSU LS2 — 9 J1
Bacon Av NORM WF6 — 178 E3
Bacon St GSLY LS20 — 62 B6
Bacup Rd TOD OL14 — 162 A1
Baddeley Gdns IDLE BD10 — 83 J5
Baden Powell Crs PONT WF8 — 180 F7
Baden St HWTH BD22 — 78 E6
Badger Brow HOLM/MEL HD7 — 234 F4
Badger Cl HOR/CROF WF4 — 198 B7
Badger Cl MILN OL16 — 228 D5
Badger Ga HOLM/MEL HD7 — 234 F4
Badgergate Av WIL/AL BD15 — 102 E2
Badger Hl BRIG HD6 — 169 M8
Badger La HBR HX7 — 142 C2
Badger La HIPP HX3 — 147 K7

Badgers Ga ILK LS29 — 20 A2
Badgers Mt MSTN/BAR LS15 — 112 B4
Badgers Wk HECK WF16 — 173 G3
Badger Wood Gld WBY LS22 — 30 A6
Badsworth Ct HEM/SK/SE WF9 — 225 G3
Badsworth Vw HEM/SK/SE WF9 — 225 J6
Bagden La KBTN HD8 — 240 C2
Baghill Ct PONT WF8 — 181 H6
Baghill Gn EARD/LOFT WF3 — 152 B3
Baghill La PONT WF8 — 181 G5
Baghill Rd EARD/LOFT WF3 — 152 B3
Bagley La PDSY/CALV LS28 — 106 F2
Bagnall Ter WBSY BD6 — 126 D5
Baildon Av GFTH/SHER LS25 — 135 K4
Baildon Cl SCFT LS14 — 89 L8
Baildon Dr SCFT LS14 — 89 L8
Baildon Gn SCFT LS14 — 89 L8
Baildon Holmes BAIL BD17 — 82 E5
Baildon Pl SCFT LS14 — 89 L8
Baildon Rd BAIL BD17 — 82 C4
Baildon Rd SCFT LS14 — 89 L7
Baildon Wood Ct BAIL BD17 — 82 E5
Bailey Crs HEM/SK/SE WF9 — 247 J1
Bailey Hall Bank HIPP HX3 — 11 K6
Bailey Hall Rd HIPP HX3 — 11 K4
Bailey Hills Rd BGLY BD16 — 81 G2
Bailey's Ct SCFT LS14 — 111 J1
Bailey's Hl SCFT LS14 — 111 J1
Bailey's La SCFT LS14 — 111 J1
Baileys Lawn SCFT LS14 — 111 J1
Baillie St BOW BD4 — 127 H1
Baillie St MILN OL16 — 206 B7
Baillie St East MILN OL16 — 206 C6
Bainbrigge Rd HDGY LS6 — 108 F2
Baines St HFAX HX1 — 10 C4
Baines St RTHW LS26 — 155 G1
Bainton Dr BSLY S70 — 260 F7
Baird St WBOW BD5 — 127 G2
Bairstow La LUD/ILL HX2 — 145 L8
Bairstow La LUD/ILL HX2 — 145 L6
Bairstow Mt LUD/ILL HX2 — 167 L1
Bairstow St WIL/AL BD15 — 103 J5
Bakehouse La DOD/DAR S75 — 260 C3
Baker Crs MOR LS27 — 152 C3
Baker La EARD/LOFT WF3 — 176 F1
Baker Rd MOR LS27 — 152 C3
Baker's St HBR HX7 — 143 J2
Baker St ECHL BD2 — 105 K4
Baker St HUDW HD3 — 191 K6
Baker St MOR LS27 — 152 C3
Baker St SHPY BD18 — 82 C6
Baker St North LUD/ILL HX2 — 146 C1
Bakes St GTHN BD7 — 126 C2
Bakewell Rd BSLYN/ROY S71 — 243 J8
Bakston Cl HUDE HD5 — 215 G3
Bala St BSLYN/ROY S71 — 261 H5
Balbec Av HDGY LS6 — 109 G1
Balbec St HDGY LS6 — 109 G1
Balderstone Hall La MIRF WF14 — 172 E8
Balderstone Rd ROCH OL11 — 228 B4
Baldovan Mt RHAY LS8 — 110 B2
Baldovan Pl RHAY LS8 — 110 B2
Baldovan Ter RHAY LS8 — 110 B2
Baldwin La CLAY BD14 — 125 L2
Balfour St BGLY BD16 — 81 H4
Balfour St BOW BD4 — 127 J2
Balfour St KGHY BD21 — 2 E7
Balfour St ROY/SHW OL2 — 229 K6
Balk Av EARD/LOFT WF3 — 177 H3
Balkcliffe La MID LS10 — 131 J8
Balk Crs EARD/LOFT WF3 — 177 H4
Balk La EARD/LOFT WF3 — 177 H4
Balk La GTHN BD7 — 126 C2
Balk La HEM/SK/SE WF9 — 247 M2
Balk La HOR/CROF WF4 — 197 H7
Balk La HUDE HD5 — 193 K7
Balk La KBTN HD8 — 238 E8
Balk La WKFDE WF1 — 177 J6
Balkram Dr LUD/ILL HX2 — 145 J1
Balkram Edge LUD/ILL HX2 — 145 H1
Balkram Rd LUD/ILL HX2 — 145 K1
Balks LVSG WF15 — 172 B2
Balk St BTLY WF17 — 173 K1
The Balk BTLY WF17 — 151 L7
The Balk DOD/DAR S75 — 242 E4
The Balk WKFDW/WTN WF2 — 199 K8
Ballantyne Rd IDLE BD10 — 83 J3
Ballard Cl LIT OL15 — 185 K7
Ballard Wy ROY/SHW OL2 — 229 L7
Ballater Av HUDS HD4 — 213 L4
Ballfield La DOD/DAR S75 — 241 L6
Ball Grove Dr COL BB8 — 74 D1
Ballroyd Clough HUDW HD3 — 191 J7
Ballroyd La HUDW HD3 — 191 J7
Ball Royd Rd HUDN HD2 — 192 D4
Ball St CUL/QBY BD13 — 103 G3
Ball St MILN OL16 — 206 C6
Balme La LM/WK BD12 — 148 F3
Balme Rd CLECK BD19 — 149 M6
Balme St BFD BD1 — 5 G5
Balme St LM/WK BD12 — 148 E3
Balmfield LVSG WF15 — 172 C4
Balmfield Crs LVSG WF15 — 172 C4
Balmoral Av HUDS HD4 — 213 L4
Balmoral Cha MID LS10 — 132 B3
Balmoral Cl MILN OL16 — 207 L8
Balmoral Cl PONT WF8 — 202 D1
Balmoral Cl STKB/PEN S36 — 270 C2
Balmoral Pl HFAX HX1 — 10 F1
Balmoral St HBR HX7 — 143 J3
Balmoral Wy YEA LS19 — 62 F2
Balm Pl BEE/HOL LS11 — 8 C5
Balm Rd MID LS10 — 132 A4
Balm Wk BEE/HOL LS11 — 8 B5
Balne La WKFDW/WTN WF2 — 12 A1
Balne La WKFDW/WTN WF2 — 12 A1
Bamborough St WKFDE WF1 — 13 M8
Bamburgh Rd MSTN/BAR LS15 — 112 A3
Bamford Av BSLYN/ROY S71 — 243 J8
Bamford Cl DOD/DAR S75 — 260 D1

Bamford St LIT OL15 — 207 H1
Bamlett Brow HWTH BD22 — 78 F6
Banbury Rd PONT WF8 — 181 G3
Bancroft Av HUDE HD5 — 215 G1
Bangor Gv WOR/ARM LS12 — 130 C2
Bangor Pl WOR/ARM LS12 — 130 C2
Bangor St WOR/ARM LS12 — 206 D8
Bangor St WOR/ARM LS12 — 130 C2
Bangor Ter WOR/ARM LS12 — 130 C2
Bangor Vw WOR/ARM LS12 — 130 C2
Bank IDLE BD10 — 83 M8
Bank Av HORS LS18 — 85 K6
Bank Av MOR LS27 — 152 C1
Bank Barn La WHIT OL12 — 184 F7
Bank Bottom HBR HX7 — 144 C3
Bank Bottom HFAX HX1 — 11 K6
Bank Bottom La LUD/ILL HX2 — 145 G8
Bank Cl IDLE BD10 — 105 L1
Bank Cl LIT OL15 — 207 J3
Bank Crest BAIL BD17 — 82 E3
Bank Crest Ri SHPY BD18 — 81 M7
Bank Dr WBSY BD6 — 126 F5
Bank Edge Gdns LUD/ILL HX2 — 146 A3
Bank Edge Rd LUD/ILL HX2 — 145 M3
Bank End Knoll HOLM/MEL HD7 — 236 F5
Bank End La HUDE HD5 — 215 G2
Bank End La KBTN HD8 — 240 C5
Bank End Rd HOLM/MEL HD7 — 212 D3
Banker St BULY LS4 — 108 F5
Bankfield AL/HA/HU LS17 — 67 M2
Bankfield KBTN HD8 — 238 B4
Bankfield Av HUDE HD5 — 193 K6
Bankfield Av SHPY BD18 — 81 M7
Bankfield Cl OSS WF5 — 197 L2
Bankfield Dr HUDE HD5 — 15 M9
Bankfield Dr MIRF WF14 — 194 B1
Bankfield Dr WKFDW/WTN WF2 — 176 B3
Bankfield Dr HOLM/MEL HD7 — 253 L4
Bankfield Dr HWTH BD22 — 57 G7
Bankfield Dr SHPY BD18 — 81 M7
Bankfield Dr WKFDW/WTN WF2 — 176 B3
Bankfield Gdns BULY LS4 — 108 E4
Bankfield Gdns HIPP HX3 — 147 H8
Bank Field Gra GTL/HWG HX4 — 168 E7
Bankfield Gv BULY LS4 — 108 E3
Bankfield La HUDE HD5 — 193 K6
Bankfield Mt HWTH BD22 — 57 G7
Bankfield Park Av HUDS HD4 — 214 B5
Back Field Rd BTLY WF17 — 173 L1
Bankfield Rd BULY LS4 — 108 E4
Bankfield Rd HUD HD1 — 14 D9
Bankfield Rd HWTH BD22 — 57 G6
Bankfield Rd SHPY BD18 — 81 M7
Bankfields St COL BB8 — 74 D2
Bankfield Ter BAIL BD17 — 82 F4
Bankfield Ter BULY LS4 — 108 E4
Bankfield Ter HUD HD4 — 214 A6
Bankfield Wk HWTH BD22 — 57 G7
Bankfoot HBR HX7 — 143 H3
Bank Foot La HUDS HD4 — 214 A7
Bank Foot Pl BTLY WF17 — 173 L1
Bank Foot Rd HUDS HD4 — 215 H6
Bank Foot St BTLY WF17 — 173 L1
Bank Gdns HORS LS18 — 85 K6
Bank Ga HOLM/MEL HD7 — 212 B5
Bank Gv EARL WF12 — 174 C7
Bank Hey Bottom La RPDN/SBR HX6 — 189 G3
Bankholme Ct BOW BD4 — 128 B4
Bankhouse PDSY/CALV LS28 — 128 F1
Bank House Cl MOR LS27 — 152 C1
Bankhouse La HIPP HX3 — 168 F4
Bankhouse La HUDW HD3 — 213 K1
Bank House La LUD/ILL HX2 — 144 F2
Bankhouse La PDSY/CALV LS28 — 128 F1
Bank House Rd HUDW HD3 — 213 K1
Banklands AIRE BD20 — 36 A4
Banklands Av AIRE BD20 — 36 B4
Banklands La AIRE BD20 — 36 B4
Bank La HBR HX7 — 18 A6
Bank La HOLM/MEL HD7 — 236 D7
Bank La HOLM/MEL HD7 — 253 M2
Bank La KBTN HD8 — 257 H2
Bank La WHIT OL12 — 184 E7
Bank Pde OT LS21 — 41 H7
Bank Rd AIRE BD20 — 34 F7
Bank Rd RPDN/SBR HX6 — 167 K3
Bank Royd La GTL/HWG HX4 — 189 K5
Banks Ap HOLM/MEL HD7 — 212 F1
Banks Av FEA/AMT WF7 — 224 A1
Banks Av HOLM/MEL HD7 — 212 E1
Banks Av PONT WF8 — 180 E6
Banks Crs HOLM/MEL HD7 — 212 F1
Banks Dr HOLM/MEL HD7 — 212 F1
Banks End Rd ELL HX5 — 169 L8
Banksfield Av YEA LS19 — 62 D6
Banksfield Cl YEA LS19 — 62 D6
Banksfield Crs YEA LS19 — 62 D6
Banksfield Gv YEA LS19 — 62 D6
Banksfield Ri YEA LS19 — 62 D6
Banksfield Rd HBR HX7 — 144 A5
Banksfields Crs HBR HX7 — 144 A5
Banksfield Ter HBR HX7 — 144 A5
Banks Gv HOLM/MEL HD7 — 212 F1
Bankside TOD OL14 — 163 K2
Bank Side St RHAY LS8 — 110 B3
Banks La AIRE BD20 — 58 B4
Banks La AIRE BD20 — 58 B4
Banks La KNOT WF11 — 182 B2
Banks Mt PONT WF8 — 180 E6
Bank Sq MOR LS27 — 152 C1
Banks Rd HOLM/MEL HD7 — 212 D6
Banks Rd HOLM/MEL HD7 — 236 D3
Banks Side HOLM/MEL HD7 — 212 F1
Banks St BTLY WF17 — 173 L2
Bank St BFD BD1 — 4 F6
Bank St BRIG HD6 — 170 C4
Bank St BSLY S70 — 261 H7
Bank St BSLYN/ROY S71 — 262 A6
Bank St CAS WF10 — 157 M6
Bank St CLECK BD19 — 149 L7

COL BB8 ... 74 E5
CUD/GR S72 ... 244 D7
EARL WF12 ... 173 M6
HOLM/MEL HD7 ... 255 G2
HOR/CROF WF4 ... 197 J5
LDS LS1 ... 9 G1
MIRF WF14 ... 194 A1
MOR LS27 ... 152 C1
OSS WF5 ... 196 F1
ROCH OL11 ... 228 C2
SHPY BD18 ... 82 D7
TOD OL14 ... 163 K2
WBSY BD6 ... 126 E5
WBY LS22 ... 48 A1
WKFDE WF1 ... 12 E3
Bank Ter HBR HX7 ... 143 G3
MOR LS27 ... 152 C1
Bank Top HIPP HX3 ... 11 M9
Bank Top Dr AIRE BD20 ... 58 B4
Bank Top La HBR HX7 ... 165 H1
HOLM/MEL HD7 ... 253 J3
OT LS21 ... 64 F3
Bank Top Wy KGHY BD21 ... 58 B8
Bank Vw BAIL BD17 ... 82 D4
EARL WF12 ... 174 C7
HOLM/MEL HD7 ... 236 C6
Bank View Ter CHAL LS7 ... 87 K7
Bank Wk BAIL BD17 ... 82 E5
Bankwell Fold WBSY BD6 ... 126 F5
Bankwell Rd HUDS HD4 ... 213 K2
Bankwood BTLY WF17 ... 151 K2
Bank Wood Rd AWLS/ASK DN6 ... 204 C7
PONT WF8 ... 204 B2
Bankwood Wy BTLY WF17 ... 151 K2
Bannerman St LM/WK BD12 ... 149 J1
Banner St BFDE BD3 ... 5 L7
Bannister Cl COL BB8 ... 74 D3
Bannister La AWLS/ASK DN6 ... 248 C1
Bannister Wk HWTH BD22 ... 54 F2
Bannockburn Dr BOW BD4 ... 127 K5
Bannockburn Wy NORM WF6 ... 178 A2
Banstead St East RHAY LS8 ... 110 B3
Banstead St West RHAY LS8 ... 110 B3
Banstead Ter East RHAY LS8 ... 110 B3
Banstead Ter West RHAY LS8 ... 110 B3
Bantam Cl MOR LS27 ... 152 F2
Bantam Grove La MOR LS27 ... 152 F2
Bantree Ct IDLE BD10 ... 83 J5
Baptist Fold CUL/QBY BD13 ... 125 G5
Baptist La OSS WF5 ... 197 K2
Baptist Pl BFD BD1 ... 4 D5
Baptist St BTLY WF17 ... 173 J3
Bar Av DOD/DAR S75 ... 242 F6
Barber Rw HOLM/MEL HD7 ... 212 C5
Barberry Av BFDE BD3 ... 106 A6
Barber Sq HECK WF16 ... 172 E2
Barber St BRIG HD6 ... 170 D2
Barclay Cl CUL/QBY BD13 ... 102 A1
Barclay St ROCH OL11 ... 228 A3
Barclyde St ROCH OL11 ... 7 J6
Barcroft DOD/DAR S75 ... 260 C2
Bar Cft HUDE HD5 ... 193 K5
Barcroft HWTH BD22 ... 79 J4
Barcroft Gv YEA LS19 ... 62 C3
Barcroft Rd HUDS HD4 ... 214 B4
Barden Av WBSY BD6 ... 125 M5
Barden Cl BTLY WF17 ... 173 K1
WOR/ARM LS12 ... 108 C7
Barden Dr BGLY BD16 ... 81 L2
DOD/DAR S75 ... 260 D3
Barden Gn WOR/ARM LS12 ... 108 C7
Barden Mt WOR/ARM LS12 ... 108 C7
Barden Pl WOR/ARM LS12 ... 108 C7
Barden Rd WKFDE WF1 ... 13 M2
Barden St GIR BD8 ... 104 C6
Barden Ter WOR/ARM LS12 ... 108 C7
Bardsey Crs BFDE BD3 ... 5 K6
Bardwell Ct EARD/LOFT WF3 ... 177 G1
Bare Head La HIPP HX3 ... 124 F8
Barehill St LIT OL15 ... 185 K8
Barfield Av YEA LS19 ... 62 C3
Barfield Crs AL/HA/HU LS17 ... 88 B1
Barfield Dr YEA LS19 ... 62 C3
Barfield Gv AL/HA/HU LS17 ... 88 C1
Barfield Mt AL/HA/HU LS17 ... 88 C1
Barfield Rd HIPP HX3 ... 147 L7
Bargate HOLM/MEL HD7 ... 212 F5
Bargess Ter GFTH/SHER LS25 ... 135 K5
Bargrange Av SHPY BD18 ... 82 D8
Bargreen HUDE HD5 ... 193 K5
Barham Ter IDLE BD10 ... 105 M2
Bari Cl WMB/DAR S73 ... 263 C8
Baring Av BFDE BD3 ... 105 M6
Bark Cl KBTN HD8 ... 238 C3
Barker Cl HIPP HX3 ... 169 C8
Barker St HUDN HD2 ... 192 A5
Barkerend Rd BFDE BD3 ... 5 H5
Barker Pl BRAM LS13 ... 107 H3
Barker Rd HOR/CROF WF4 ... 197 H4
Barker St EARD/LOFT WF3 ... 155 K8
LVSG WF15 ... 172 D2
TOD OL14 ... 141 K8
Barkers Well Fold
WOR/ARM LS12 ... 129 M2
Barkers Well Garth
WOR/ARM LS12 ... 130 A3
Barkers Well Lawn
WOR/ARM LS12 ... 130 A3
Barke St MILN OL16 ... 207 G3
Bark House La DOD/DAR S75 ... 258 C2
KBTN HD8 ... 238 D3
Barkhouse Wood La
KNOT WF11 ... 161 K3
Bark La ILK LS29 ... 19 J6
Barkly Av BEE/HOL LS11 ... 131 J5
Barkly Dr BEE/HOL LS11 ... 131 J5
Barkly Gv BEE/HOL LS11 ... 131 J4
Barkly Pde BEE/HOL LS11 ... 131 J5
Barkly Pl BEE/HOL LS11 ... 131 J5
Barkly Rd BEE/HOL LS11 ... 131 H4
Barkly St BEE/HOL LS11 ... 131 J5
Barkly Ter BEE/HOL LS11 ... 131 J4
Bark Mdw DOD/DAR S75 ... 260 C7
Barkston Rd BSLYN/ROY S71 ... 243 L8
Bar La AIRE BD20 ... 58 B5
BSPA/BRAM LS23 ... 49 J8

DOD/DAR S75 ... 242 F6
GFTH/SHER LS25 ... 113 J7
HOR/CROF WF4 ... 218 B4
HORS LS18 ... 85 G6
RPDN/SBR HX6 ... 188 E4
SEL YO8 ... 139 M5
WKFDE WF1 ... 176 F5
Barlbro' Pl HUDW HD3 ... 213 J2
Barlby Wy RHAY LS8 ... 88 B4
Barleycorn Cl WKFDE WF1 ... 177 G5
Barley Cote Av AIRE BD20 ... 58 B4
Barley Cote Gv AIRE BD20 ... 58 C4
Barley Cote Rd AIRE BD20 ... 58 B4
Barley Cft DEWS WF13 ... 173 H6
Barleyfield Cl WKFDE WF1 ... 177 G6
Barley Field Ct
MSTN/BAR LS15 ... 111 J6
Barleyfields Cl WBY LS22 ... 30 A7
Barleyfields La WBY LS22 ... 30 A8
Barleyfields Ms WBY LS22 ... 30 A8
Barleyfields Rd WBY LS22 ... 30 A8
Barleyfields Ter WBY LS22 ... 30 A8
Barley Hill WHTH BD22 ... 79 J2
Barleyhill Crs GFTH/SHER LS25 ... 113 G7
Barleyhill La GFTH/SHER LS25 ... 113 G7
Barleyhill Rd GFTH/SHER LS25 ... 113 G7
Barley Horn Rd TAD LS24 ... 94 F2
Barley Ms EARD/LOFT WF3 ... 154 D3
Barley St HWTH BD22 ... 79 J2
Barlow Rd KGHY BD21 ... 2 E1
Barlow St BFDE BD3 ... 5 L5
MILN OL16 ... 206 F1
Barmby Cl OSS WF5 ... 197 H2
Barmby Crs OSS WF5 ... 197 J2
Barmby Fold OSS WF5 ... 197 H2
Barmby Pl ECHL BD2 ... 5 L1
Barmby Rd ECHL BD2 ... 5 L1
Barmby St LM/WK BD12 ... 148 F2
Barmouth Ter BFDE BD3 ... 5 L1
Barnaby Rd BGLY BD16 ... 81 L2
Barnard Cl MSTN/BAR LS15 ... 112 A3
Barnard Rd BOW BD4 ... 127 J1
Barnard Wy MSTN/BAR LS15 ... 112 A3
Barnbow La MSTN/BAR LS15 ... 112 D2
Barnbrough St BULY LS4 ... 108 A4
Barnby Av GIR BD8 ... 103 L7
Barnby Royd HUDE HD5 ... 193 G7
Barncroft Cl SCFT LS14 ... 89 H7
Barncroft Dr SCFT LS14 ... 89 H8
Barncroft Gdns SCFT LS14 ... 89 H8
Barncroft Mt SCFT LS14 ... 89 H8
Barncroft Ri SCFT LS14 ... 89 H8
Barncroft Rd SCFT LS14 ... 89 H8
Barnes Av WKFDE WF1 ... 176 B3
Barnes Mdw LIT OL15 ... 185 L5
Barnes Rd CAS WF10 ... 157 M8
GIR BD8 ... 104 B7
Barnes St TOD OL14 ... 163 J5
Barnet Gv MOR LS27 ... 152 C4
Barnet Rd WOR/ARM LS12 ... 108 C7
Barn Field Cl COL BB8 ... 74 C1
Barn Field La WHIT OL12 ... 184 C7
Barnfield Ri ROY/SHW OL2 ... 229 J5
Barnfield St WHIT OL12 ... 206 B4
Barnsdale Est CAS WF10 ... 157 K8
Barnsdale Ms AWLS/ASK DN6 ... 227 L6
Barnsdale Rd CAS WF10 ... 157 M2
RTHW LS26 ... 156 E5
Barnsdale Vw AWLS/ASK DN6 ... 227 K2
Barnsdale Wy HEM/SK/SE WF9 ... 226 F4
Barnside Cl STKB/PEN S36 ... 270 F4
Barnside La HOLM/MEL HD7 ... 255 H5
Barnsley Beck Gv BAIL BD17 ... 82 F3
Barnsley Boundary Wk
DOD/DAR S75 ... 258 E2
HOLM/MEL HD7 ... 255 J8
HOR/CROF WF4 ... 222 A6
KBTN HD8 ... 257 K3
STKB/PEN S36 ... 256 E7
Barnsley Rd CUD/GR S72 ... 244 C8
DOD/DAR S75 ... 242 A6
DOD/DAR S75 ... 258 D8
DOD/DAR S75 ... 260 A7
FEA/AMT WF7 ... 224 C2
HEM/SK/SE WF9 ... 246 F3
HOR/CROF WF4 ... 217 L3
KBTN HD8 ... 238 E8
KBTN HD8 ... 240 A5
STKB/PEN S36 ... 270 F2
WKFDE WF1 ... 13 H7
WKFDW/WTN WF2 ... 198 B3
WKFDW/WTN WF2 ... 220 B4
WMB/DAR S73 ... 263 H1
Barnstone V WKFDE WF1 ... 177 C6
Barn St HWTH BD22 ... 100 A4
Barnswick Cl PONT WF8 ... 180 F8
Barnswick Vw BHP/TINH LS16 ... 86 A2
The Barn LM/WK BD12 ... 127 G8
Baron Cl BEE/HOL LS11 ... 8 B8
Baronscourt MSTN/BAR LS15 ... 111 M6
Baronsmead MSTN/BAR LS15 ... 111 L6
Baron St MILN OL16 ... 206 B7
Baronsway MSTN/BAR LS15 ... 111 L6
Barrack Rd CHAL LS7 ... 7 K3
Barracks Fold HOLM/MEL HD7 ... 255 C4
Barracks St HECK WF16 ... 172 E2
Barrack St CHAL LS7 ... 7 K3
Barraclough Sq LM/WK BD12 ... 148 E2
Barraclough St LM/WK BD12 ... 126 D8
Barran St BGLY BD16 ... 81 J3
Barras Garth Pl WOR/ARM LS12 .. 108 C7
Barras Garth Rd
WOR/ARM LS12 ... 108 C8
Barras Pl WOR/ARM LS12 ... 108 C8
Barras St WOR/ARM LS12 ... 108 C8
Barras Ter WOR/ARM LS12 ... 108 C8
Barratt's Rd WKFDE WF1 ... 176 E6
Barrett St AIRE BD20 ... 35 M5
Barrington Cl HIPP HX3 ... 169 J2
Barrington Garth GLE DN14 ... 161 M8
Barrington Pde CLECK BD19 ... 150 C6
Barrowby Av MSTN/BAR LS15 ... 112 A7
Barrowby Crs MSTN/BAR LS15 ... 112 A6
Barrowby La GFTH/SHER LS25 ... 113 G6
MSTN/BAR LS15 ... 112 B6
PBR HG3 ... 27 K8
Barrowby Rd MSTN/BAR LS15 ... 112 B7

Barrowclough La HIPP HX3 ... 147 H7
Barrows La AIRE BD20 ... 56 E2
Barrowstead KBTN HD8 ... 239 J5
Barr St HUD HD1 ... 15 J2
Barry St BFD BD1 ... 4 E6
Barsey Green La
GTL/HWG HX4 ... 167 L8
Barstow Sq WKFDE WF1 ... 12 E2
Bar St BTLY WF17 ... 173 M2
TOD OL14 ... 163 J2
Barthorpe Cl BOW BD4 ... 128 B4
Barthorpe Crs CHAL LS7 ... 87 L6
Bartle Cl GTHN BD7 ... 126 B3
Bartle Fold GTHN BD7 ... 126 C2
Bartle Gill Dr BAIL BD17 ... 83 C2
Bartle Gill Ri BAIL BD17 ... 83 G2
Bartle Gill Vw BAIL BD17 ... 83 G2
Bartle La GTHN BD7 ... 126 B3
Bartle Pl GTHN BD7 ... 126 B3
Bartle Sq GTHN BD7 ... 126 C2
Bartlett Rd ROY/SHW OL2 ... 229 J8
Barton Ct MSTN/BAR LS15 ... 111 L7
Barton Gv BEE/HOL LS11 ... 8 C8
Barton Hl BEE/HOL LS11 ... 8 C8
Barton Manor Cl HUDS HD4 ... 213 K4
Barton Mt BEE/HOL LS11 ... 8 C8
Barton Pl BEE/HOL LS11 ... 8 C8
BTLY WF17 ... 173 L2
Barton Rd BEE/HOL LS11 ... 8 C8
Barton St BRIG HD6 ... 170 C3
WBOW BD5 ... 126 D3
Barton Ter BEE/HOL LS11 ... 8 C8
Barton Vw BEE/HOL LS11 ... 8 C8
Barton Wy HEM/SK/SE WF9 ... 247 J5
Barugh Green Rd DOD/DAR S75 .. 260 A2
Barugh La DOD/DAR S75 ... 260 A1
Barwick Gn WBSY BD6 ... 126 A5
Barwick Rd GFTH/SHER LS25 ... 113 C6
MSTN/BAR LS15 ... 111 M2
SCFT LS14 ... 111 K3
Basford Ct WKFDW/WTN WF2 ... 12 A4
Basford St WKFDW/WTN WF2 ... 12 A4
Basil St HUDS HD4 ... 213 M2
MILN OL16 ... 206 D8
WBOW BD5 ... 126 D5
Baslow Crs DOD/DAR S75 ... 260 A7
Baslow Gv HTON BD9 ... 104 B4
Baslow Rd BSLYN/ROY S71 ... 243 K7
Bassett Wy WHIT OL12 ... 206 A4
Bateman Cl CUD/GR S72 ... 244 C4
Bateman St GIR BD8 ... 4 D1
Bates Av RPDN/SBR HX6 ... 167 H3
Bates La PONT WF8 ... 203 H1
Bateson St IDLE BD10 ... 84 A7
Bath Cl BRAM LS13 ... 107 L4
Bath Gv BRAM LS13 ... 107 L4
Bath La BRAM LS13 ... 107 L4
Bath Pl CLECK BD19 ... 149 M7
HIPP HX3 ... 10 F2
Bath Rd BEE/HOL LS11 ... 8 D4
BRAM LS13 ... 107 L4
CLECK BD19 ... 149 M7
HECK WF16 ... 172 F2
HIPP HX3 ... 168 F2
Bath St BFDE BD3 ... 5 J6
BTLY WF17 ... 173 M1
COL BB8 ... 74 A1
DEWS WF13 ... 173 L5
ELL HX5 ... 169 H8
HFAX HX1 ... 11 J7
HUD HD1 ... 14 E5
HUD HD1 ... 214 B3
ILK LS29 ... 38 E1
KBTN HD8 ... 238 B1
KGHY BD21 ... 2 F4
TOD OL14 ... 163 K1
WHIT OL12 ... 206 D5
Batley Av HUD HD1 ... 191 M8
Batley Ct BAIL BD17 ... 82 F2
Batley Field Hl BTLY WF17 ... 151 L8
Batley Rd EARD/LOFT WF3 ... 175 C1
HECK WF16 ... 173 H2
WKFDW/WTN WF2 ... 175 L5
Batley St HUDE HD5 ... 15 M7
Batter La YEA LS19 ... 84 E2
Battinson Rd HFAX HX1 ... 10 A4
Battinson St HIPP HX3 ... 11 M9
Batty Av CUD/GR S72 ... 244 D8
Battye Av HUDS HD4 ... 213 K3
Battye St BOW BD4 ... 105 L8
EARL WF12 ... 173 M6
Baulk Head La TOD OL14 ... 142 B8
Bavaria Pl GIR BD8 ... 104 D5
Bawn Ap WOR/ARM LS12 ... 130 A1
Bawn Av WOR/ARM LS12 ... 108 A3
Bawn Dr WOR/ARM LS12 ... 108 A3
Bawn Gdns WOR/ARM LS12 ... 108 A3
Bawn La WOR/ARM LS12 ... 108 A3
Bawson Ct CLECK BD19 ... 150 C5
Baxandall St WBOW BD5 ... 126 F3
Baxtergate PONT WF8 ... 180 F6
Baxter La HIPP HX3 ... 147 J3
Baxter Wd AIRE BD20 ... 34 E7
Baycliff Rd BSLYN/ROY S71 ... 243 M7
Bay Cl HUDW HD3 ... 191 L7
Bayfield Cl HOLM/MEL HD7 ... 254 D6
Bay Hall Common Rd HUDN HD2.. 14 E1
Bay Horse La AL/HA/HU LS17 ... 89 J2
Bay Horse Yd SKP/WHF BD23 ... 16 E2
Bayldons Pl BTLY WF17 ... 173 L1
Baylee St HEM/SK/SE WF9 ... 224 A8
Bayne Dr BOW BD4 ... 127 K6
Bay of Biscay WIL/AL BD15 ... 103 K2
Bayswater Crs RHAY LS8 ... 110 B3
Bayswater Gv ECHL BD2 ... 105 M4
RHAY LS8 ... 110 B3
Bayswater Mt RHAY LS8 ... 110 B3
Bayswater Pl RHAY LS8 ... 110 B3
Bayswater Rw RHAY LS8 ... 110 B3
Bayswater Ter HIPP HX3 ... 168 E3
RHAY LS8 ... 110 B3
Bayswater Vw RHAY LS8 ... 110 B3
Bayton La HORS LS18 ... 85 H2

YEA LS19 ... 63 G8
Beacon Av MOR LS27 ... 152 D4
Beacon Brow WBSY BD6 ... 125 M4
Beacon Cl BGLY BD16 ... 81 K3
DOD/DAR S75 ... 259 J8
Beacon Ct DOD/DAR S75 ... 259 J8
Beacon Hl HEM/SK/SE WF9 ... 225 J6
Beaconfield Rd
HEM/SK/SE WF9 ... 225 H5
Beacon Rd MOR LS27 ... 152 D4
WBSY BD6 ... 126 B5
Beacon St DEWS WF13 ... 173 G8
GTHN BD7 ... 126 A4
HUDN HD2 ... 14 E1
ILK LS29 ... 19 J6
WBSY BD6 ... 126 C5
Beacon Vw HEM/SK/SE WF9 ... 246 E3
Beaden Dr KBTN HD8 ... 216 A3
Beadon Av HUDE HD5 ... 215 K1
Beagle Av HUDS HD4 ... 213 L5
Bealbank Cl MILN OL16 ... 229 J3
Beal Crs MILN OL16 ... 206 E5
Bealcroft Cl MILN OL16 ... 207 G7
Bealcroft Wk MILN OL16 ... 207 G7
Beal La GLE DN14 ... 161 K7
KNOT WF11 ... 183 H4
ROY/SHW OL2 ... 229 L8
Beamshaw HEM/SK/SE WF9 ... 246 D5
Beamsley St SKP/WHF BD23 ... 16 C4
Beamsley Gv BGLY BD16 ... 81 K3
HDGY LS6 ... 109 G4
Beamsley Mt HDGY LS6 ... 109 G4 11
Beamsley Pl HDGY LS6 ... 109 G4
Beamsley Rd HTON BD9 ... 104 D4
Beamsley Ter HDGY LS6 ... 109 G4
Beamsley Vw ILK LS29 ... 38 A2
Beancroft Rd CAS WF10 ... 157 M7
Beancroft St CAS WF10 ... 157 M8
Beanlands Dr AIRE BD20 ... 34 E8
Beanlands Pde ILK LS29 ... 38 E1
Beanlands St GIR BD8 ... 34 E8
Bean St ELL HX5 ... 169 J8
Bear Bones Rd HOLM/MEL HD7 .. 267 K1
Bearing Av BEE/HOL LS11 ... 131 K4
Beastfair PONT WF8 ... 180 E6
Beast Market HUD HD1 ... 15 G6
Beatrice St CLECK BD19 ... 149 M6
HWTH BD22 ... 100 A4
KGHY BD21 ... 57 L3
Beaufort Av KBTN HD8 ... 238 B3
Beaufort Gv ECHL BD2 ... 105 J3
Beaulieu Cl DOD/DAR S75 ... 242 E6
Beaulieu Vw DOD/DAR S75 ... 242 E6
Beaumont Av AWLS/ASK DN6 ... 249 H8
BSLY S70 ... 260 D5
HEM/SK/SE WF9 ... 247 H3
HUDE HD5 ... 15 M8
Beaumont Cl EARD/LOFT WF3 ... 177 H1
LIT OL15 ... 207 H1
Beaumont Dr HOR/CROF WF4 ... 219 H8
Beaumont Park Rd HUDS HD4 ... 213 M5
Beaumont Rd DOD/DAR S75 ... 241 L7
GIR BD8 ... 104 D5
Beaumont St BTLY WF17 ... 173 L2
EARD/LOFT WF3 ... 177 H1
HUD HD1 ... 15 G4
HUDE HD5 ... 15 M8
HUDS HD4 ... 213 L7
KBTN HD8 ... 217 L7
TOD OL14 ... 141 J8
Beaver Dr DEWS WF13 ... 173 H7
Becca La GFTH/SHER LS25 ... 91 M6
Beck Bottom PDSY/CALV LS28 ... 84 A8
WKFDW/WTN WF2 ... 175 L3
Beckbridge La NORM WF6 ... 178 E3
Beckbridge Rd NORM WF6 ... 178 E3
Beckbridge Wy NORM WF6 ... 178 E4
Beckbury Pl PDSY/CALV LS28 ... 106 F4
Beckbury St PDSY/CALV LS28 ... 106 F4
Beckenham Pl HFAX HX1 ... 146 A6
Beckett Cl HOR/CROF WF4 ... 197 L4
Beckett Crs DEWS WF13 ... 173 H6
Beckett Gv DEWS WF13 ... 173 H7
Beckett La DEWS WF13 ... 173 K4
Becketts Cl HBR HX7 ... 143 H2
Beckett's Park Dr HDGY LS6 ... 108 E1
Beckett St BSLYN/ROY S71 ... 261 H4
BTLY WF17 ... 173 L3
OSM LS9 ... 7 M7
Beckett Ter OSM LS9 ... 110 B5
Beckett Wk DEWS WF13 ... 173 H7
Beckfield La KNOT WF11 ... 159 G1
Beckfield Rd BGLY BD16 ... 81 H7
Beckfoot La BGLY BD16 ... 81 H5
Beck Gv ROY/SHW OL2 ... 229 M6
Beck Hl WBSY BD6 ... 126 B5
Beckhill Ap CHAL LS7 ... 87 J8
Beckhill Av CHAL LS7 ... 87 J8
Beckhill Cl CHAL LS7 ... 87 J8
Beckhill Dr CHAL LS7 ... 87 J8
Beckhill Gdns CHAL LS7 ... 87 J8
Beckhill Garth CHAL LS7 ... 87 J8
Beckhill Ga CHAL LS7 ... 87 J8
Beckhill Gn CHAL LS7 ... 87 K8
Beckhill Gv CHAL LS7 ... 87 J8
Beckhill Lawn CHAL LS7 ... 87 J8
Beckhill Pl CHAL LS7 ... 87 J7
Beckhill Rw CHAL LS7 ... 87 J8
Beckhill Vw CHAL LS7 ... 87 J8
Beck La BGLY BD16 ... 81 H2
LVSG WF15 ... 172 E3
WBY LS22 ... 47 K5
Beckley Rd WKFDW/WTN WF2 ... 176 B5

Beck Meadow MSTN/BAR LS15 ... 91 G8
Beck Ri HEM/SK/SE WF9 ... 223 M7
Beck Rd BGLY BD16 ... 59 G6
HUD HD1 ... 14 F4
RHAY LS8 ... 110 B2
Becks Ct EARL WF12 ... 174 B8
Beck Side KGHY BD21 ... 3 G6
Beck Side AIRE BD20 ... 34 C4
Beckside Cl ILK LS29 ... 19 H6
ILK LS29 ... 40 B5
Beckside Gdns HUDE HD5 ... 215 L2
Beckside Rd GTHN BD7 ... 126 B3
Beckside Rd GTHN BD7 ... 126 C1
Becks Rd HWTH BD22 ... 2 C6
Beck St KGHY BD21 ... 3 G6
Beck Vw HOR/CROF WF4 ... 221 J8
Beckwith Dr IDLE BD10 ... 105 M1
Bedale Av BRIG HD6 ... 170 A6
KBTN HD8 ... 239 H5
Bedale Dr KBTN HD8 ... 239 H5
WBSY BD6 ... 126 A5
Bedding Edge Rd
HOLM/MEL HD7 ... 255 J8
Bede St WKFDE WF1 ... 176 E6
Bede's Cl CUL/QBY BD13 ... 102 F3
Bedford Av HOR/CROF WF4 ... 217 G1
ROY/SHW OL2 ... 229 H7
Bedford Cl BHP/TINH LS16 ... 86 A3
FEA/AMT WF7 ... 201 M3
HOR/CROF WF4 ... 200 C6
KBTN HD8 ... 216 A3
Bedford Dr BHP/TINH LS16 ... 86 A3
Bedford Gdns BHP/TINH LS16 ... 86 A3
Bedford Garth BHP/TINH LS16 ... 86 A3
Bedford Gn BHP/TINH LS16 ... 86 A3
Bedford Gv BHP/TINH LS16 ... 86 A4
Bedford Mt BHP/TINH LS16 ... 86 A4
Bedford Rw MID LS10 ... 9 J8
Bedfords Fold GFTH/SHER LS25 .. 138 D8
Bedford St BOW BD4 ... 5 G8
BSLY S70 ... 261 H7
CUD/GR S72 ... 263 J1
ELL HX5 ... 169 H8
HFAX HX1 ... 10 F6
KGHY BD21 ... 2 E5
LDS LS1 ... 6 F9
TOD OL14 ... 141 G7
Bedford St North HFAX HX1 ... 10 F6
Bedford Ter BSLYN/ROY S71 ... 261 J1
Bedford Vw BHP/TINH LS16 ... 86 A3
Bedivere Rd GIR BD8 ... 103 M7
Bedlam La OT LS21 ... 65 H1
Beech Av CUD/GR S72 ... 244 D6
CUL/QBY BD13 ... 101 L3
EARD/LOFT WF3 ... 177 H1
HOLM/MEL HD7 ... 213 G1
HOLM/MEL HD7 ... 236 E5
HOR/CROF WF4 ... 200 D7
HORS LS18 ... 85 L7
HUDE HD5 ... 215 H1
RPDN/SBR HX6 ... 167 K1
TOD OL14 ... 141 J8
WKFDW/WTN WF2 ... 176 B7
Beech Cl CUD/GR S72 ... 245 G3
GFTH/SHER LS25 ... 138 B2
HEM/SK/SE WF9 ... 246 D4
HIPP HX3 ... 125 M8
IDLE BD10 ... 83 K4
ILK LS29 ... 40 C8
OSM LS9 ... 110 F3
PONT WF8 ... 181 G3
TAD LS24 ... 72 A3
Beech Ct OSS WF5 ... 174 B8
Beech Crs BAIL BD17 ... 82 B5
BFDE BD3 ... 5 M2
CAS WF10 ... 158 F8
PONT WF8 ... 203 L1
Beechcroft EARD/LOFT WF3 ... 154 F3
WKFDW/WTN WF2 ... 199 J7
Beechcroft Cl BEE/HOL LS11 ... 130 F5
Beechcroft Md AL/HA/HU LS17 ... 88 C2
Beechcroft Vw BEE/HOL LS11 ... 130 F5
Beechdale Av BTLY WF17 ... 151 J7
Beech Dr CUL/QBY BD13 ... 101 L3
FEA/AMT WF7 ... 202 C5
GFTH/SHER LS25 ... 138 B2
WOR/ARM LS12 ... 108 E6
Beecher St HIPP HX3 ... 146 D4
KGHY BD21 ... 3 L1
Beeches End BSPA/BRAM LS23 ... 49 J3
Beeches Rd KGHY BD21 ... 3 K3
The Beeches BAIL BD17 ... 82 F2
GSLY LS20 ... 62 A4
PDSY/CALV LS28 ... 106 D6
WBY LS22 ... 30 B8
Beechfield WKFDW/WTN WF2 ... 199 G5
WOR/ARM LS12 ... 129 M3
Beechfield Av HUDE HD5 ... 239 J5
Beechfield Dr HOR/CROF WF4 ... 200 D2
Beechfield Rd MILN OL16 ... 229 G1
Beech Gdns CAS WF10 ... 158 F8
Beech Gv AIRE BD20 ... 35 M5
BFDE BD3 ... 5 L2
BGLY BD16 ... 81 L1
BSLY S70 ... 260 F7
CLAY BD14 ... 125 L2
CLECK BD19 ... 150 C5
GFTH/SHER LS25 ... 116 A6
GFTH/SHER LS25 ... 160 A3
HEM/SK/SE WF9 ... 223 J4
HIPP HX3 ... 148 C7
NORM WF6 ... 178 C4
RTHW LS26 ... 133 H8
Beech Grove Av
GFTH/SHER LS25 ... 113 G8
Beech Grove Ter
GFTH/SHER LS25 ... 113 G8
Beech Hl OT LS21 ... 41 J6
PONT WF8 ... 181 G5
Beech La OSM LS9 ... 110 F3
ILK LS29 ... 28 E3
Beech Lees PDSY/CALV LS28 ... 106 C2
Beech Mt OSM LS9 ... 110 F3
Beechmount Cl BAIL BD17 ... 82 F2
Beechnut La PONT WF8 ... 180 E5
Beech Rd AWLS/ASK DN6 ... 227 M5

AWLS/ASK DN6 .... 249 J5
BSPA/BRAM LS23 .... 48 E6
CUD/GR S72 .... 244 F4
HEM/SK/SE WF9 ...... 225 K7
RPDN/SBR HX6 .... 167 L2
WBSY BD6 .... 126 E7
Beech Spinney WBY LS22 ...... 30 B6
Beech Sq CLAY BD14 ...... 125 L2
Beech St AIRE BD20 ...... 34 F8
AIRE BD20 ...... 56 E1
BGLY BD16 ...... 81 H4
BSLY S70 ...... 261 H6
EARD/LOFT WF5 ...... 153 C5
ELL HX5 ...... 169 H8
GTL/HWG HX4 ...... 190 C2
HEM/SK/SE WF9 ...... 247 C5
HFAX HX1 ...... 10 E5
HOLM/MEL HD7 ...... 254 C1
HUD HD1 ...... 213 M1
KGHY BD21 ...... 3 L3
MILN OL16 ...... 229 J2
MIRF WF14 ...... 194 C1
PONT WF8 ...... 180 F7
Beech Ter BFDE BD3 ...... 5 L3
Beechtree Ct BAIL BD17 .... 82 C4
Beech Tree Rd FEA/AMT WF7 .... 202 A2
Beechtree Rd TAD LS24 ...... 71 K4
Beech Vw GFTH/SHER LS25 ...... 91 M7
HOR/CROF WF4 ...... 220 B3
RPDN/SBR HX6 ...... 167 K1
Beech Wk BHP/TINH LS16 ...... 86 F4
CLECK BD19 ...... 150 D2
OSM LS9 ...... 110 F3
TAD LS24 ...... 71 K3
Beech Wy BTLY WF17 ...... 151 J6
Beechwood PONT WF8 ...... 180 D7
ROY/SHW OL2 ...... 229 M6
RTHW LS26 ...... 133 L7
Beechwood Av AIRE BD20 ...... 58 B5
BIRK/DRI BD11 ...... 128 F7
HIPP HX3 ...... 147 K1
LIT OL15 ...... 207 J3
LUD/ILL HX2 ...... 146 C1
MIRF WF14 ...... 194 C1
PONT WF8 ...... 180 D7
RPDN/SBR HX6 ...... 167 H3
SHPY BD18 ...... 82 A7
WBSY BD6 ...... 126 C4
WKFDW/WTN WF2 ...... 175 M8
Beechwood Ct GFTH/SHER LS25.. 116 J3
HORS LS18 ...... 85 J3
LUD/ILL HX2 ...... 146 B2
SCFT LS14 ...... 89 G8
Beechwood Crs BULY LS4 ...... 108 F3
HEM/SK/SE WF9 ...... 223 L8
PONT WF8 ...... 180 D7
RPDN/SBR HX6 ...... 167 H3
Beechwood Cft
GFTH/SHER LS25 ...... 116 A8
Beechwood Dl FEA/AMT WF7 .... 202 D7
Beechwood Dr LUD/ILL HX2 ...... 146 B2
ROY/SHW OL2 ...... 228 E8
RPDN/SBR HX6 ...... 167 H3
WBSY BD6 ...... 126 D4
Beechwood Gld
GFTH/SHER LS25 ...... 116 A8
Beechwood Gv
BIRK/DRI BD11 ...... 128 F7
BULY LS4 ...... 108 F3
HOR/CROF WF4 ...... 197 L5
HUDN HD2 ...... 192 C1
ILK LS29 ...... 38 B2
LUD/ILL HX2 ...... 146 B2
SHPY BD18 ...... 82 A7
WBSY BD6 ...... 126 D4
Beechwood Mt BULY LS4 ...... 108 F3
HEM/SK/SE WF9 ...... 223 M8
Beechwood Pl BULY LS4 ...... 108 F3
Beechwood Ri WBY LS22 ...... 30 A7
Beechwood Rd BULY LS4 ...... 108 F3
LUD/ILL HX2 ...... 146 B2
MIRF WF14 ...... 172 C8
WBSY BD6 ...... 126 C4
Beechwood Rw BULY LS4 ...... 108 F3
Beechwood St HDGY LS6 ...... 108 F3
PDSY/CALV LS28 ...... 106 E5
Beechwood Ter BULY LS4 ...... 108 F3
Beechwood Vw BULY LS4 ...... 108 F3
Beecroft Cl BRAM LS13 ...... 107 L3
Beecroft Crs BRAM LS13...... 107 K3
Beecroft Gdns BRAM LS13 ...... 107 L3
Beecroft Mt BRAM LS13 ...... 107 J3
Beecroft St KGHY BD21 ...... 3 K4
KSTL LS5 ...... 108 C3
Beehive St WBSY BD6 ...... 126 B7
Beehive Yd WBSY BD6 ...... 126 B7
Beestonley La GTL/HWG HX4 ...... 189 M2
Beeston Park Cft
BEE/HOL LS11 ...... 131 G4
Beeston Park Garth
BEE/HOL LS11 ...... 131 G4
Beeston Park Pl BEE/HOL LS11... 131 G4
Beeston Park Ter
BEE/HOL LS11 ...... 131 G4
Beeston Rd BEE/HOL LS11 ...... 131 J3
Beeston's La AL/HA/HU LS17 ...... 25 M7
Beeston Sq BSLYN/ROY S71 ...... 243 H6
Beever La DOD/DAR S75...... 260 D5
Beevor Cl BSLYN/ROY S71 ...... 261 J5
Beevor St BSLYN/ROY S71 ...... 261 K5
Bela Av BOW BD4 ...... 127 L3
Belcross Dr HIPP HX3 ...... 11 J3
Beldon Brook Gn KBTN HD8 .... 215 M5
Beldon La WBSY BD6 ...... 126 B5
Beldon Park Av GTHN BD7 ...... 126 B4
Beldon Park Cl GTHN BD7 ...... 126 B4
Beldon Pl ECHL BD2 ...... 105 K4
Beldon Rd GTHN BD7 ...... 126 C3
Belfast St HFAX HX1 ...... 10 B8
Belfield Cl MILN OL16 ...... 206 E6
Belfield La MILN OL16 ...... 206 F7
Belfield Mill La MILN OL16...... 206 E6
Belfield Old Rd MILN OL16...... 206 E6
Belfield Rd MILN OL16 ...... 206 E6
Belfry Ct WKFDE WF1...... 176 L1
The Belfry YEA LS19 ...... 62 E8
Belgrave Av HIPP HX3 ...... 11 K3

OSS WF5 ...... 197 G2
Belgrave Cl HIPP HX3 ...... 11 K3
Belgrave Crs HIPP HX3 ...... 11 L3
Belgrave Dr HIPP HX3 ...... 11 L3
Belgrave Gdns HIPP HX3 ...... 11 K3
Belgrave Gv HIPP HX3 ...... 11 K3
Belgrave Ms YEA LS19 ...... 84 C2
WKFDE WF1 ...... 176 F6
Belgrave Mt HIPP HX3 ...... 11 K2
WKFDE WF1 ...... 176 F6
Belgrave Pk HIPP HX3 ...... 11 K3
Belgrave Rd BGLY BD16 ...... 81 J3
BSLYN/ROY S71 ...... 261 J5
KGHY BD21 ...... 2 E3
Belgrave St LDSU LS2 ...... 7 H7
OSS WF5 ...... 197 G2
RPDN/SBR HX6 ...... 167 K2
SKP/WHF BD23 ...... 16 B2
Belgrave Ter HUD HD1 ...... 14 D5
WKFDE WF1 ...... 176 F6
Belgravia Ms ROY/SHW OL2 ...... 229 L7
Belgravia Rd WKFDE WF1 ...... 176 D6
Belinda St MID LS10 ...... 9 M8
Bell Bank Vw AIRE BD20 ...... 81 G2
Bellbrooke Av OSM LS9 ...... 110 D4
WMB/DAR S73 ...... 263 H7
Bellbrooke Gv OSM LS9 ...... 110 D4
Bellbrooke Pl OSM LS9 ...... 110 D4
Bellbrooke St OSM LS9 ...... 110 C4
Bell Dean Rd WIL/AL BD15 ...... 103 K6
Belle Green Cl CUD/GR S72 .... 244 E7
Belle Green Gdns CUD/GR S72... 244 E7
Belle Green La CUD/GR S72 .... 244 E7
Belle Isle Av WKFDE WF1 ...... 13 K7
Belle Isle Cl MID LS10 ...... 132 A6
Belle Isle Crs WKFDE WF1 ...... 13 K7
Belle Isle Pde MID LS10 ...... 132 A5
MID LS10 ...... 132 A5
Bellerby Brow WBSY BD6 ...... 125 M5
Bellerby Pl AWLS/ASK DN6 .... 249 H6
Bellerby Rd AWLS/ASK DN6 .... 249 H6
Belle View Ri HIPP HX3 ...... 147 K1
Belle Vue CUL/QBY BD13 ...... 125 C2
GIR BD8 ...... 4 C2
ILK LS29 ...... 38 E3
Belle Vue Av MSTN/BAR LS15 .... 90 B7
RHAY LS8 ...... 88 F8
Belle Vue Crs HIPP HX3 ...... 147 K1
HUDN HD2 ...... 192 E3
Belle Vue Dr PDSY/CALV LS28 .... 106 E3
Belle Vue Est MSTN/BAR LS15.... 90 B8
Belle Vue Rd BVRD LS3 ...... 6 B7
HIPP HX3 ...... 147 K1
LDSU LS2 ...... 6 B5
MSTN/BAR LS15 ...... 90 B8
WKFDE WF1 ...... 13 K9
Belle Vue St BTLY WF17 ...... 173 H1
Bellgreave Av HOLM/MEL HD7 .... 237 H8
Bell Hall HFAX HX1 ...... 168 C1
Bell Hall Ter HFAX HX1 ...... 168 C1
Bell House Av BOW BD4 ...... 127 K5
Bellhouse Crs BOW BD4 ...... 127 K6
Bellingham Cl ROY/SHW OL2 .... 229 K6
Bell La AIRE BD13 ...... 107 L3
FEA/AMT WF7 ...... 224 B1
MILN OL16 ...... 207 K7
TAD LS24 ...... 95 G2
Bellmont Crs HEM/SK/SE WF9.... 224 A4
Bellmount Cl BRAM LS13 ...... 107 M3
Bellmount Gdns BRAM LS13 .... 107 L2
Bellmount Gn BRAM LS13 ...... 107 M3
Bellmount Pl BRAM LS13 ...... 107 L2
Bellmount Vw BRAM LS13 ...... 107 M3
Belloe St WBOW BD5 ...... 126 F2
Bell Rd BRAM LS13 ...... 107 L3
Bellshaw St GIR BD8 ...... 104 A7
Bell Sq DEWS WF13 ...... 195 C1
HEM/SK/SE WF9 ...... 226 A6
HIPP HX3 ...... 11 J3
HUD5 HD4 ...... 214 D2
LM/WK BD12 ...... 148 E2
MILN OL16 ...... 206 B6
OSM LS9 ...... 7 K8
WKFDE WF1 ...... 12 D1
Bellstring La HUDE HD5 ...... 194 A5
Bellwood Av BSPA/BRAM LS23 .... 48 E8
Belmont CUD/GR S72 ...... 262 E2
KNOT WF11 ...... 159 L5
Belmont Av BAIL BD17 ...... 82 D3
BSLYN/ROY S71 ...... 261 K1
LM/WK BD12 ...... 127 G7
OT LS21 ...... 41 H5
Belmont Cl BAIL BD17 ...... 82 D3
Belmont Crs LM/WK BD12 ...... 127 G7
SHPY BD18 ...... 82 C6
Belmont Gdns WBSY BD6 ...... 126 F7
Belmont Gv LDSU LS2 ...... 6 D7
WBSY BD6 ...... 126 F7
YEA LS19 ...... 84 E1
Belmont Pl HFAX HX1 ...... 10 C8
Belmont Ri BAIL BD17 ...... 82 D3
LM/WK BD12 ...... 127 G7
Belmont St ECHL BD2 ...... 105 L1
FEA/AMT WF7 ...... 200 E1
HIPP HX3 ...... 11 L3
HOLM/MEL HD7 ...... 212 B6
HUD HD1 ...... 14 D5
RPDN/SBR HX6 ...... 167 L2
SKP/WHF BD23 ...... 16 B2
WKFDE WF1 ...... 12 D1
Belmont Ter EARD/LOFT WF3 .... 154 B4
LUD/ILL HX2 ...... 167 G1
SHPY BD18 ...... 82 C6
Belmont Wy HEM/SK/SE WF9.... 247 K3
WHIT OL12 ...... 206 A4
Belmont Whf SKP/WHF BD23 .... 16 B2
Belridge Cl DOD/DAR S75 ...... 260 D2
Belton Av MILN OL16 ...... 206 E5
Belton Cl GTHN BD7 ...... 126 B4
Belton Gv HUDW HD3 ...... 191 K4
Belton Rd AIRE BD20 ...... 36 A6
Belton St HUDE HD5 ...... 215 G1
Belvedere Av AL/HA/HU LS17 ...... 87 M2
BEE/HOL LS11 ...... 131 K4

Belvedere Cl CUD/GR S72 .... 244 E4
Belvedere Dr WMB/DAR S73... 263 G7
Belvedere Gv AL/HA/HU LS17... 87 M2
Belvedere Mt BEE/HOL LS11 .... 131 K4
Belvedere Rd AL/HA/HU LS17 .... 87 M2
BTLY WF17 ...... 173 K2
Belvedere Ter BEE/HOL LS11 .... 131 K5
GIR BD8 ...... 104 D6
Belvedere Vw AL/HA/HU LS17 .... 88 A2
Belvoir Dr WKF WF11 ...... 182 A2
Belvoir Gdns HIPP HX3 ...... 168 E3
Belvoir Mdw MILN OL16 ...... 207 G2
Bembridge Ct
WKFDW/WTN WF2 ...... 198 A1
Bempton Ct GTHN BD7 ...... 126 D2
Bempton Gv BTLY WF17 ...... 151 H4
Bempton Pl GTHN BD7 ...... 126 D2
Ben Bank Rd HOR/CROF WF4 .... 217 C1
Ben Booth La HOR/CROF WF4 .... 217 G1
Benbow Av IDLE BD10 ...... 106 A1
Bence Cl DOD/DAR S75 ...... 242 A7
Bence La DOD/DAR S75 ...... 241 L7
Bence St COL HX8 ...... 74 A1
Bench Carr WHIT OL12 ...... 206 A5
Bendigo Rd EARL WF12 ...... 174 B5
Benjamin Cl LVSG WF15 ...... 172 D3
WKFDW/WTN WF2 ...... 12 A1
Benjamin Sykes Wy
WKFDW/WTN WF2 ...... 197 L2
Benn Av GTHN BD7 ...... 126 B2
Benn Crs GTHN BD7 ...... 126 B2
Bennet Ct MSTN/BAR LS15 .... 111 M6
Bennett Av HOR/CROF WF4.... 197 L4
Bennett La EARL WF12 ...... 174 A3
Bennett Rd HDGY LS6 ...... 108 F1
Bennett St HIPP HX3 ...... 11 K8
LVSG WF15 ...... 172 D2
SKP/WHF BD23 ...... 16 B3
Benns La HUDW HD3 ...... 191 H8
Benns La HOLM/MEL HD7 ...... 212 D3
Benny Parr Cl BTLY WF17 ...... 174 A1
Benomley Crs HUDE HD5 ...... 215 G3
Benomley Dr HUDE HD5 ...... 215 G3
Benomley Rd HUDE HD5 ...... 215 G3
Ben Rhydding Dr ILK LS29 ...... 39 H3
Ben Rhydding Rd ILK LS29 ...... 38 E3
Benson Gdns WOR/ARM LS12 .... 108 D8
Benson La NORM WF6 ...... 178 D2
Benson St CHAL LS7 ...... 7 K5
Bentcliffe Cl AL/HA/HU LS17 .... 88 A4
Bentcliffe Ct AL/HA/HU LS17 .... 88 A5
Bentcliffe Dr AL/HA/HU LS17 .... 88 A4
Bentcliffe Gdns AL/HA/HU LS17... 88 A5
Bentcliffe Gv AL/HA/HU LS17 .... 88 A5
Bentcliffe La AL/HA/HU LS17 .... 88 A4
Bentcliffe Mt AL/HA/HU LS17 .... 88 A5
Bent Close La WHIT OL12 ...... 165 M3
Bentfield Cottages CLAY BD14.. 125 L1
Bentfield Crs MILN OL16 ...... 229 J2
Bentgate Cl MILN OL16 ...... 229 J2
Bentgate St MILN OL16 ...... 229 J3
Bentham Dr BSLYN/ROY S71 .... 261 M2
Bentham Wy DOD/DAR S75 ...... 242 C4
Bent La AIRE BD20 ...... 55 L1
COL BB8 ...... 52 D8
HOLM/MEL HD7 ...... 254 C6
Bent Lea HUDN HD2 ...... 171 H8
Bentley Av BRIG HD6 ...... 148 C7
Bentley Cl BAIL BD17 ...... 82 D3
BSLYN/ROY S71 ...... 262 A1
Bentley Gdns CHAL LS7 ...... 87 H8
Bentley Gv HDGY LS6 ...... 87 H8
Bentley La HDGY LS6 ...... 87 H8
Bentley Moor La
AWLS/ASK DN6 ...... 249 M7
Bentley Mt HDGY LS6 ...... 87 H8
RPDN/SBR HX6 ...... 167 M1
Bentley Pde HDGY LS6 ...... 87 H8
Bent Ley Rd HOLM/MEL HD7 .... 235 J3
Bentley Rd WKFDW/WTN WF2 .... 198 A2
Bentley Royd Cl RPDN/SBR HX6.. 167 J3
Bentley St HUD5 HD4 ...... 214 A3
LM/WK BD12 ...... 148 F3
WHIT OL12 ...... 206 A4
Bentmeadows WHIT OL12 ...... 206 A5
Benton Crs HOR/CROF WF4 .... 197 L4
Benton Park Av YEA LS19 ...... 84 E1
Benton Park Crs YEA LS19 ...... 84 E1
Benton Park Dr YEA LS19 ...... 84 E1
Benton Park Rd YEA LS19 ...... 84 E1
Bent Rd HOLM/MEL HD7 ...... 254 F7
Bents Farm Cl LIT OL15 ...... 207 H1
Bents La HOLM/MEL HD7 ...... 211 K7
WIL/AL BD15 ...... 80 C8
Bents Rd STKB/PEN S36 ...... 268 C3
Bent St HUDS HD4 ...... 214 D2
STKB/PEN S36 ...... 270 E2
Benyon Park Wy
WOR/ARM LS12 ...... 130 F2
Beresford Rd WBSY BD6 ...... 126 D7
Beresford St LM/WK BD12 ...... 149 J1
MILN OL16 ...... 229 K2
Berkeley Av RHAY LS8 ...... 110 C3
Berkeley Crs RHAY LS8 ...... 110 C3
Berkeley Cft BSLYN/ROY S71 .... 243 K2
Berkeley Dr MILN OL16 ...... 228 D2
Berkeley Gv RHAY LS8 ...... 110 C3
Berkeley Mt RHAY LS8 ...... 110 C3
Berkeley Rd RHAY LS8 ...... 110 C3
Berkeley Ter RHAY LS8 ...... 110 C3
Berkeley Vw RHAY LS8 ...... 110 C3
Berking Av OSM LS9 ...... 110 B6
Berkley Wk LIT OL15 ...... 207 H1
Bermondsey Ms OT LS21 ...... 41 K7
Bermondsey St OT LS21 ...... 41 K7
Bernard St HUDN HD2 ...... 193 G3
RTHW LS26 ...... 133 M8
WHIT OL12 ...... 206 A3
Berne Gv WKFDE WF1 ...... 176 F7
Berners St WKFDE WF1 ...... 13 H3
Berneslai Cl BSLY S70 ...... 261 G4
Berrington Wy HWTH BD22 ...... 78 D3
Berry Bank La
HOLM/MEL HD7 ...... 236 D6
Berry Cft HOLM/MEL HD7 ...... 236 B2
Berryfield Garth OSS WF5...... 174 F6
Berry La HFAX HX1 ...... 11 K6

HOR/CROF WF4 ...... 197 K5
KGHY BD21 ...... 2 F8
RTHW LS26 ...... 135 G6
Berry Moor Rd RPDN/SBR HX6.. 167 M4
Berry Rd HOLM/MEL HD7 ...... 234 E3
Berry St KGHY BD21 ...... 3 J4
Berry's Yd HOR/CROF WF4 ...... 197 J4
Berry Vw HUDS HD4 ...... 214 B5
Berrywell Av STKB/PEN S36 .... 271 G4
Bertha St MILN OL16 ...... 206 F7
Bertha St PDSY/CALV LS28 ...... 106 F4
Bertie St BOW BD4 ...... 127 L3
Bertram Dr BAIL BD17 ...... 82 D4
Bertram Rd GIR BD8 ...... 104 E4
Bertrand St LM/WK BD12 ...... 8 C5
Berwick Av HECK WF16 ...... 150 F4
Berwick St HFAX HX1 ...... 11 J6
MILN OL16 ...... 206 D8
Bescaby Gv BAIL BD17 ...... 83 G3
Besha Av LM/WK BD12 ...... 126 F7
Besha Gv LM/WK BD12 ...... 126 F8
Bessingham Gdns WBSY BD6 .... 126 B6
Best La HUDS HD4 ...... 214 F8
HWTH BD22 ...... 100 A3
Beswick Cl BFDE BD3 ...... 105 M7
Beswick Royds St MILN OL16 .... 206 D5
Beswicke St LIT OL15 ...... 207 L1
WHIT OL12 ...... 206 A6
Beswick St TOD OL14 ...... 163 J7
Bethany La MILN OL16 ...... 229 L2
Bethel Rd SHPY BD18 ...... 82 F6
Bethel St AIRE BD20 ...... 58 F6
BRIG HD6 ...... 170 D4
HIPP HX3 ...... 146 C4
Betjeman Pl ROY/SHW OL2 .... 229 M7
Betteras Hill Rd
GFTH/SHER LS25 ...... 138 A7
Betula Wy KBTN HD8 ...... 216 A4
Beulah Gv HDGY LS6 ...... 6 E2
Beulah Mt HDGY LS6 ...... 6 E2
Beulah Pl LUD/ILL HX2 ...... 167 G1
Beulah St HDGY LS6 ...... 6 E2
Beulah Ter HDGY LS6 ...... 6 E2
Beulah Vw HDGY LS6 ...... 6 E2
Bevan Av NORM WF6 ...... 178 D6
Bevan Ct GTHN BD7 ...... 126 B3
Bevan Pl WKFDW/WTN WF2 .... 197 L8
Bevedere Gdns AL/HA/HU LS17... 88 A2
Beverley Av BEE/HOL LS11 ...... 131 K3
BSLY S70 ...... 261 H8
LM/WK BD12 ...... 148 F4
Beverley Cl BSLYN/ROY S71 .... 243 G7
ELL HX5 ...... 169 K2
LM/WK BD12 ...... 148 F4
Beverley Dr EARL WF12 ...... 174 B6
Beverley Gdns BTLY WF17 ...... 151 K4
Beverley Garth FEA/AMT WF7.... 224 C1
Beverley Mt BEE/HOL LS11 ...... 131 K3
Beverley Pl HIPP HX3 ...... 10 F1
HIPP HX3 ...... 146 C4
MILN OL16 ...... 206 C6
Beverley Ri ILK LS29 ...... 38 A2
Beverley Rd BOW BD4 ...... 127 M1
Beverley Ter BEE/HOL LS11 ...... 131 K3
HIPP HX3 ...... 10 F1
Beverley Vw BEE/HOL LS11 ...... 8 F9
Beverley Wk GFTH/SHER LS25... 113 H8
Bevin Cl WKFDE WF1 ...... 176 E1
Bevin Crs WKFDE WF1 ...... 176 E1
Bevor Crs HECK WF16 ...... 172 F1
Bewerley Crs LM/WK BD12 ...... 126 C8
Bewick Gv RTHW LS26 ...... 132 B7
Bexhill Cl PONT WF8 ...... 181 H4
Bexley Av RHAY LS8 ...... 110 B4
Bexley Gv OSM LS9 ...... 110 B4
Bexley Mt RHAY LS8 ...... 110 B4
Bexley Pl RHAY LS8 ...... 110 B4
Bexley Rd RHAY LS8 ...... 110 B4
Bexley Ter OSM LS9 ...... 110 B4
Bexley Vw OSM LS9 ...... 110 B4
Beza Rd MID LS10 ...... 131 M3
Beza St MID LS10 ...... 131 M3
Bickerton Wy OT LS21 ...... 41 C5
Biddenden Rd MSTN/BAR LS15... 112 B4
Bidder Dr EARD/LOFT WF3 ...... 153 L5
Bideford Av RHAY LS8 ...... 88 B3
Bidston Cl ROY/SHW OL2 ...... 229 M8
Bierley Hall Gv BOW BD4 ...... 127 K6
Bierley House Av BOW BD4 .... 127 K5
Bierley La BOW BD4 ...... 127 K5
Bierley Vw BOW BD4 ...... 127 L5
Biggin La GFTH/SHER LS25 .... 117 H3
Big Meadow Dr ILK LS29 ...... 18 F6
Bilberry Ri HWTH BD22 ...... 78 F3
Bilberry St MILN OL16 ...... 206 C8
Bilham Rd KBTN HD8 ...... 240 C4
Billams Hl OT LS21 ...... 41 H5
Billey La WOR/ARM LS12 ...... 130 A2
Billing Ct YEA LS19 ...... 84 F3
Billing Dr YEA LS19 ...... 85 C3
Billingbauk Dr BRAM LS13 ...... 107 M5
Billingham Cl
WKFDW/WTN WF2 ...... 175 M6
Billing Vw IDLE BD10 ...... 83 L7
YEA LS19 ...... 84 F3
Bill La HOLM/MEL HD7 ...... 236 F7
Billy La HBR HX7 ...... 143 L1
Bilsdale Gra WBSY BD6 ...... 126 B6
Bilsdale Wy BAIL BD17 ...... 82 B4
Bilton Pl GIR BD8 ...... 4 B3
Bingley Bank AL/HA/HU LS17 .... 67 L4
CUL/QBY BD13 ...... 79 M7
HTON BD9 ...... 103 M2
ILK LS29 ...... 60 D4
KGHY BD21 ...... 79 K5
MILN OL16 ...... 206 E7
SHPY BD18 ...... 81 M6
Bingley Sq BVRD LS3 ...... 6 B7
Bingley St BVRD LS3 ...... 6 B7
DOD/DAR S75 ...... 260 F4
GIR BD8 ...... 104 D3
Bingley Ter MILN OL16 ...... 206 E7
Binham Rd HUDN HD2 ...... 191 H6
Binks Fold LM/WK BD12 ...... 148 F4
Binks St WKFDE WF1 ...... 176 E2
Binnie St BFDE BD3 ...... 5 L5

Binn La HOLM/MEL HD7 ...... 233 J4
Binn Rd HOLM/MEL HD7 ...... 233 H4
Binns Hill La LUD/ILL HX2 ...... 145 K8
Binns La AIRE BD20 ...... 34 C8
GTHN BD7 ...... 126 B1
HOLM/MEL HD7 ...... 254 B1
Binns Nook Rd WHIT OL12 ...... 206 C4
Binns St BGLY BD16 ...... 81 J3
Binns Top La HPP HX3 ...... 169 K3
Birch Av AWLS/ASK DN6 ...... 249 J5
KBTN HD8 ...... 216 A4
MSTN/BAR LS15 ...... 111 J6
RPDN/SBR HX6 ...... 188 C5
TOD OL14 ...... 141 J7
WBOW BD5 ...... 127 H4
WHIT OL12 ...... 206 F2
Birch Cliff BAIL BD17 ...... 82 D4
Birchcliffe Rd HBR HX7 ...... 143 H5
Birch Cl BRIG HD6 ...... 170 E3
WBOW BD5 ...... 127 H4
Birch Close La BGLY BD16 ...... 60 B6
Birch Crs MILN OL16 ...... 229 J3
MSTN/BAR LS15 ...... 111 J6
Birchdale BGLY BD16 ...... 59 H8
Birch Dr GFTH/SHER LS25 ...... 135 J3
Birchen Av OSS WF5 ...... 196 E1
Birchencliffe Hill Rd HUDW HD3... 191 K5
Birchenlee Cl HBR HX7 ...... 144 A4
The Birches BHP/TINH LS16 .... 64 B4
GSLY LS20 ...... 62 A4
Birchfield Av MOR LS27 ...... 129 L8
Birchfield Crs DOD/DAR S75 .... 260 C6
Birchfield Garth SCFT LS14 ...... 89 L7
Birchfields Av SCFT LS14 ...... 89 L6
Birchfields Cl SCFT LS14 ...... 89 L7
Birchfields Ct SCFT LS14 ...... 89 L7
Birchfields Ri SCFT LS14 ...... 89 L6
Birch Gv BTLY WF17 ...... 151 J6
CAS WF10 ...... 158 E8
GFTH/SHER LS25 ...... 135 J4
HOLM/MEL HD7 ...... 213 G1
HWTH BD22 ...... 79 K2
WBOW BD5 ...... 127 G5
Birch Hey Cl WHIT OL12 ...... 206 E2
Birch Hill Crs WHIT OL12 ...... 207 G2
Birch Hill La WHIT OL12 ...... 184 F8
Birch Hill Ri HORS LS18 ...... 86 A6
Birchington Av HUDW HD3 ...... 191 J4
Birchington Cl HUDW HD3 ...... 191 K4
Birchington Dr HUDW HD3 ...... 191 J4
Birchlands Av WIL/AL BD15 ...... 80 D8
Birchlands Gv WIL/AL BD15 ...... 80 D8
Birch La LUD/ILL HX2 ...... 145 H6
WBOW BD5 ...... 127 H3
Birch Ms BHP/TINH LS16 ...... 86 F4
Birch Mt WHIT OL12 ...... 207 G2
Birch Pk HOLM/MEL HD7 ...... 236 F4
Birch Rd BSLY S70 ...... 261 M7
GFTH/SHER LS25 ...... 135 J4
HUDS HD4 ...... 214 B6
NORM WF6 ...... 178 D7
Birchroyd RTHW LS26 ...... 155 H2
Birchroyd Cl HUDN HD2 ...... 191 M4
Birch St GIR BD8 ...... 104 C3
MOR LS27 ...... 152 D4
WHIT OL12 ...... 184 E8
WKFDE WF1 ...... 13 K7
Birchtree Cl WKFDE WF1 ...... 177 H6
Birch Tree Gdns KGHY BD21 ...... 3 L7
Birchtree Wy BHP/TINH LS16 .... 86 A4
Birch Wy WBOW BD5 ...... 127 H4
Birchwood Av AIRE BD20 ...... 57 K4
AL/HA/HU LS17 ...... 88 C3
BTLY WF17 ...... 151 H4
Birchwood Ct ILK LS29 ...... 38 C2
LVSG WF15 ...... 172 D3
Birchwood Dr AIRE BD20 ...... 57 J4
Birchwood Hl AL/HA/HU LS17 .... 88 C2
Birchwood Mt AL/HA/HU LS17... 88 C2
Birchwood Pk HOLM/MEL HD7... 237 G8
Birchwood Rd AIRE BD20 ...... 57 J4
Birdale Field La WBY LS22 ...... 47 M6
Birdcage Hl HIPP HX3 ...... 168 C3
Birdcage La HIPP HX3 ...... 168 C3
Birdcage Wk OT LS21 ...... 41 J8
Bird Holme La HIPP HX3 ...... 147 K5
Birds Edge La KBTN HD8 ...... 256 B3
Birdsnest La HOLM/MEL HD7 .... 255 L5
KBTN HD8 ...... 256 A4
Birds Royd La BRIG HD6 ...... 170 D5
Birdswell Av BRIG HD6 ...... 170 F4
Birdwell Rd DOD/DAR S75 ...... 260 C8
Birfed Crs BULY LS4 ...... 108 D3
Birk Av BSLY S70 ...... 261 L7
Birkby Brow Crs BTLY WF17 .... 151 K4
Birkby Fold HUDN HD2 ...... 14 B2
Birkby Hall Rd HUDN HD2 ...... 191 L4
Birkby Hvn WBSY BD6 ...... 126 A6
Birk By Rd HUDW HD3 ...... 14 B1
Birkby St LM/WK BD12 ...... 148 F2
Birk Crs BSLY S70 ...... 261 L7
Birkdale Av HUDW HD3 ...... 191 J6
Birkdale Cl AL/HA/HU LS17 ...... 87 K2
CUD/GR S72 ...... 244 E6
CUL/QBY BD13 ...... 123 J3
Birkdale Ct AIRE BD20 ...... 57 J3
Birkdale Gn AL/HA/HU LS17 .... 87 K2
Birkdale Gv AL/HA/HU LS17 .... 87 K2
DEWS WF13 ...... 173 J4
LUD/ILL HX2 ...... 124 B7
Birkdale Mt AL/HA/HU LS17 .... 87 K2
Birkdale Pl AL/HA/HU LS17 ...... 87 J2
Birkdale Ri AL/HA/HU LS17 ...... 87 J2
Birkdale Rd BSLYN/ROY S71 .... 243 K1
DEWS WF13 ...... 173 K5
MILN OL16 ...... 228 E2
Birkdale Wk AL/HA/HU LS17 .... 87 J2
Birkenshaw La BIRK/DRI BD11 .... 150 D1
Birkett St CLECK BD19 ...... 149 M6
Birkhead St HECK WF16 ...... 173 G3
Birkhill CAS WF10 ...... 158 E6

Birkhill Crs *BIRK/DRI* BD11 ...... 150 D1
Birkhouse La *BRIG* HD6 ...... 148 F8
Birk House La *BSLY* S70 ...... 261 M7
Birkhouse La *HUDE* HD5 ...... 15 M8
  HUDS HD4 ...... 14 B9
  HUDS HD4 ...... 214 A2
Birk House La *KBTN* HD8 ...... 238 D7
Birkin La *KNOT* WF11 ...... 160 F6
Birklands Moor *CLECK* BD19 ...... 150 D3 [1]
Birklands Rd *HUDN* HD2 ...... 192 B4
  SHPY BD18 ...... 82 C7
Birklands Ter *SHPY* BD18 ...... 82 D7 [1]
Birk La *MOR* LS27 ...... 152 A2
Birk Lea St *WBOW* BD5 ...... 127 H2 [1]
Birk Rd *BSLY* S70 ...... 261 L7
Birks Av *GTHN* BD7 ...... 126 B1
  STKB/PEN S36 ...... 270 A3
Birks Fold *GTHN* BD7 ...... 104 B8
Birkshall La *BFDE* BD3 ...... 5 M8
Birks Hall St *HFAX* HX1 ...... 10 C4
Birks Hall Ter *HFAX* HX1 ...... 10 A3
Birksland St *BOW* BD4 ...... 5 L9
Birks La *HUDE* HD5 ...... 215 J3
  KBTN HD8 ...... 237 M3
  RPDN/SBR HX6 ...... 166 F6
  STKB/PEN S36 ...... 270 A4
  TOD OL14 ...... 163 K6
Birks Rd *HUDW* HD3 ...... 213 J1
Birk Ter *BSLY* S70 ...... 261 L7
Birkwith Cl *SCFT* LS14 ...... 89 K6 [2]
Birkwood Av *CUD/GR* S72 ...... 262 L1
  HOR/CROF WF4 ...... 200 D4
Birkwood Rd *NORM* WF6 ...... 177 K3
Birley St *WHIT* OL12 ...... 206 C1
Birmingham La
  HOLM/MEL HD7 ...... 234 E3
Birnam Gv *BOW* BD4 ...... 127 J2
Birr Rd *HTON* BD9 ...... 104 D3
Birstall La *BIRK/DRI* BD11 ...... 151 G1
Birthwaite Rd *DOD/DAR* S75 ...... 241 K6
Birtwistle Cl *COL* BB8 ...... 74 A1
Bishopdale Dr *WBY* LS22 ...... 47 J5
Bishopdale Holme *WBSY* BD6 ...... 126 A6
Bishopdike Rd
  GFTH/SHER LS25 ...... 116 D6
Bishopgate St *LDS* LS1 ...... 8 F1
Bishopsgate St *MILN* OL16 ...... 228 E2 [1]
Bishop St *HTON* BD9 ...... 104 D3
  MILN OL16 ...... 206 D5
Bishops Wy *BSLYN/ROY* S71 ...... 261 L3
  HOLM/MEL HD7 ...... 235 G4
  MIRF WF14 ...... 171 M7 [1]
Bishop Wy *EARD/LOFT* WF3 ...... 153 H6
Bisley Cl *BSLYN/ROY* S71 ...... 244 A3
Bismarck Dr *BEE/HOL* LS11 ...... 8 E7
Bismarck St *BEE/HOL* LS11 ...... 8 F8
  BSLY S70 ...... 261 H7
Bittern Ri *MOR* LS27 ...... 152 E3 [1]
Black Abbey La *AIRE* BD20 ...... 34 E8
Black Aston Rd *BRAM* LS13 ...... 107 K7 [1]
Blackbird Gdns *GIR* BD8 ...... 103 K7 [1]
Black Brook Wy *GTL/HWG* HX4 ...... 168 B5 [1]
Black Bull St *MID* LS10 ...... 9 J4
Blackburn Cl *GIR* BD8 ...... 103 M7 [1]
  HIPP HX3 ...... 146 B3 [1]
Blackburn Ct *RTHW* LS26 ...... 155 H1 [1]
  KNOT WF11 ...... 182 E3
Blackburn La *DOD/DAR* S75 ...... 260 F4
Blackburn Pl *BTLY* WF17 ...... 173 M1 [1]
Blackburn Rd *BRIG* HD6 ...... 170 B2
  BTLY WF17 ...... 151 G5
Blackchapel Dr *MILN* OL16 ...... 228 D3
Black Dyke La *CUL/QBY* BD13 ...... 102 D5
Black Edge La *CUL/QBY* BD13 ...... 101 L8
Blacker Crs *HOR/CROF* WF4 ...... 197 J8
Blackergreen La *STKB/PEN* S36 ...... 271 M3
Blacker La *CUD/GR* S72 ...... 244 E3
  HOR/CROF WF4 ...... 197 J8
Blacker Rd *DOD/DAR* S75 ...... 242 E6
Blacker Rd North *HUDW* HD3 ...... 14 C3
Blackers Ct *EARL* WF12 ...... 195 L1
Blackett St *PDSY/CALV* LS28 ...... 84 D7
Black Gates Ct
  EARD/LOFT WF3 ...... 153 H6 [1]
Blackgates Crs
  EARD/LOFT WF3 ...... 153 G6
Blackgates Dr
  EARD/LOFT WF3 ...... 153 H6
Blackgates Fold
  EARD/LOFT WF3 ...... 153 H6 [2]
Black Gates Ri
  EARD/LOFT WF3 ...... 153 H6 [3]
Blackheath Cl *BSLYN/ROY* S71 ...... 243 K7 [1]
Blackheath Rd *BSLYN/ROY* S71 ...... 243 K7
Blackheath Wk *BSLYN/ROY* S71 ...... 243 K7
Black Hill La *AIRE* BD20 ...... 56 D5
  BHP/TINH BD16 ...... 64 F5
Black Hill Rd *OT* LS21 ...... 64 E1
Blackhouse Rd *HUDN* HD2 ...... 192 D4
Black La *HOLM/MEL* HD7 ...... 213 L10
Blackledge *HFAX* HX1 ...... 11 J7
Blackley Rd *ELL* HX5 ...... 191 G4
Blackman La *LDSU* LS2 ...... 6 C5
Blackmires *LUD/ILL* HX2 ...... 146 C1
Blackmoorfoot Rd
  HOLM/MEL HD7 ...... 234 E1
Blackmoor La *AL/HA/HU* LS17 ...... 67 K4
Black Moor Rd *AL/HA/HU* LS17 ...... 87 H5
  HWTH BD22 ...... 78 F8
Blackpool Gv *WOR/ARM* LS12 ...... 130 C2
Blackpool Pl *WOR/ARM* LS12 ...... 130 C2 [1]
Blackpool Ter *WOR/ARM* LS12 ...... 130 C2
Blackpool Vw *WOR/ARM* LS12 ...... 130 B2
Black Rd *WKFDE* WF1 ...... 199 K3
Blackshaw Beck La *HIPP* HX3 ...... 125 J7
Blackshaw Clough Rd
  RPDN/SBR HX6 ...... 166 C8
Blackshaw Dr *WBSY* BD6 ...... 125 M6
Blackshaw St *TOD* OL14 ...... 163 M1 [1]
Black Sike La *HOLM/MEL* HD7 ...... 253 L1
Blacksmith *GTHN* BD7 ...... 126 C2 [1]
Blacksmith Fold *GTHN* BD7 ...... 126 C2
Blacksmith La *BHP/TINH* LS16 ...... 65 M5
Blacksmiths Fold *HUDE* HD5 ...... 215 H3
Blackstone Av *LM/WK* BD12 ...... 148 E4
  MILN OL16 ...... 206 E6

Blackstone Edge Old Rd
  LIT OL15 ...... 185 M8
Blackstone Edge Rd *HBR* HX7 ...... 165 L4 [1]
  RPDN/SBR HX6 ...... 187 G2
Blackthorn Cl *WHIT* OL12 ...... 206 A4 [1]
Blackthorn La *MID* LS10 ...... 131 M6 [1]
Blackthorn PBR HG3 ...... 26 D2
Blackthorn Wy
  WKFDW/WTN WF2 ...... 176 C6
Black Wk *PONT* WF8 ...... 181 G4
Blackwall *HFAX* HX1 ...... 10 F7
Blackwall La *RPDN/SBR* HX6 ...... 167 J1
Blackwall Ri *RPDN/SBR* HX6 ...... 167 K1 [1]
Black Wood Gv *BHP/TINH* LS16 ...... 85 M3
Blackwood Av *BHP/TINH* LS16 ...... 85 M3
Blackwood Gdns *BHP/TINH* LS16 ...... 85 M3
Black Wood Gv *BHP/TINH* LS16 ...... 85 M3
Blackwood Hall La *LUD/ILL* HX2 ...... 144 E8
Black Wood Mt *BHP/TINH* LS16 ...... 85 M3
Black Wood Ri *BHP/TINH* LS16 ...... 85 M3
Blacup Moor Vw *CLECK* BD19 ...... 149 M7 [1]
Blagden La *HUDS* HD4 ...... 214 B5
Blair Cl *ROY/SHW* OL2 ...... 229 K7
Blairsville Gdns *BRAM* LS13 ...... 107 L2
Blairsville Gv *BRAM* LS13 ...... 107 L2 [1]
Blaith Royd La *HBR* HX7 ...... 165 H1
Blaithroyd La *HIPP* HX3 ...... 11 L8
Blake Crs *GSLY* LS20 ...... 62 B6
Blake Gv *CHAL* LS7 ...... 87 M8
Blake Hall Dr *MIRF* WF14 ...... 194 D2
Blake Hall Rd *MIRF* WF14 ...... 194 D2
Blake Hi *HIPP* HX3 ...... 147 G3
Blakehill Av *ECHL* BD2 ...... 105 L4
Blake Hill End *HIPP* HX3 ...... 147 H2
Blakehill Ter *ECHL* BD2 ...... 105 L4
Blakeholme Cl *HOLM/MEL* HD7 ...... 212 A5
Blakelaw Dr *BRIG* HD6 ...... 170 F3
Blake Law La *BRIG* HD6 ...... 171 H4
Blake Lee La *HOLM/MEL* HD7 ...... 210 D8
Blakeley Cl *BSLYN/ROY* S71 ...... 243 K7
Blakeley Gv *WKFDW/WTN* WF2 ...... 176 B8
Blakelock St *ROY/SHW* OL2 ...... 229 J7
Blakeney Gv *MID* LS10 ...... 131 M5
Blakeney Rd *MID* LS10 ...... 131 M5
Blakeridge La *BTLY* WF17 ...... 173 K1
Blakestones Rd
  HOLM/MEL HD7 ...... 212 A6
Blake St *HOLM/MEL* HD7 ...... 206 C6
Blakey Rd *WKFDW/WTN* WF2 ...... 176 B6
Blamires Pl *GTHN* BD7 ...... 126 B3 [1]
Blamires St *GTHN* BD7 ...... 126 B3
Blanche St *BOW* BD4 ...... 105 M8 [1]
  WHIT OL12 ...... 206 C4
Blandford Gdns *LDSU* LS2 ...... 6 E5
Blandford Gv *LDSU* LS2 ...... 6 E5
Blands Av *CAS* WF10 ...... 157 J1
Bland's Cl *CAS* WF10 ...... 157 M7
Blands Crs *CAS* WF10 ...... 157 J1
Blands Gv *CAS* WF10 ...... 157 J1
Blands Ter *CAS* WF10 ...... 157 J1
Bland St *HFAX* HX1 ...... 10 F6 [1]
  HUD HD1 ...... 214 B2
Blantyre Ct *CUL/QBY* BD13 ...... 79 M8 [1]
Blayds Garth *RTHW* LS26 ...... 133 J7
Blayd's Ms *LDS* LS1 ...... 9 G2 [1]
Blayds St *OSM* LS9 ...... 110 B7
Blayds's Yd *LDS* LS1 ...... 9 G2
Bleachcroft Wy *BSLY* S70 ...... 262 A7
Bleach Mill La *ILK* LS29 ...... 61 C1
Bleak Av *CUD/GR* S72 ...... 244 E4
Bleakley Av *HOR/CROF* WF4 ...... 221 K8
Bleakley Cl *CUD/GR* S72 ...... 244 E4
Bleakley La *BSLYN/ROY* S71 ...... 243 K1
Bleakley Ter *HOR/CROF* WF4 ...... 221 K8
Bleak St *CLECK* BD19 ...... 150 E6
Bleak Street Lower
  CLECK BD19 ...... 150 E6 [1]
Bleasdale Av *HUDN* HD2 ...... 192 B5
  KNOT WF11 ...... 182 A1
Bleasdale Gv *BSLYN/ROY* S71 ...... 261 J2
Blencarn Cl *SCFT* LS14 ...... 111 H2
Blencarn Garth *SCFT* LS14 ...... 111 H2
Blencarn Rd *SCFT* LS14 ...... 111 H2
Blencarn Vw *SCFT* LS14 ...... 111 H2
Blenheim Av *BSLY* S70 ...... 261 C6
  LDSU LS2 ...... 6 F4 [1]
Blenheim Cl *KNOT* WF11 ...... 181 L2 [1]
Blenheim Dr *BTLY* WF17 ...... 151 L8 [1]
  DEWS WF13 ...... 173 J5 [1]
Blenheim Gv *LDSU* LS2 ...... 6 F5
Blenheim Hi *BTLY* WF17 ...... 151 M7
Blenheim Mt *GIR* BD8 ...... 104 E4 [1]
Blenheim Pl *IDLE* BD10 ...... 83 K5 [1]
Blenheim Rd *BSLY* S70 ...... 260 F7
  GIR BD8 ...... 4 B1
  WKFDE WF1 ...... 176 D6
Blenheim Sq *LDSU* LS2 ...... 6 F4
Blenheim St *COL* BB8 ...... 74 C1 [1]
  HBR HX7 ...... 143 K3 [1]
Blenheim Vw *LDSU* LS2 ...... 6 E5
Blenheim Wk *LDSU* LS2 ...... 6 E5
Blind La *AL/HA/HU* LS17 ...... 89 G2
  BGLY BD16 ...... 80 F3
  BIRK/DRI BD11 ...... 129 H7
  EARD/LOFT WF3 ...... 175 J1
  LUD/ILL HX2 ...... 144 D6
  TOD OL14 ...... 141 J8
Bloemfontein St *CUD/GR* S72 ...... 244 C8
Bloomfield Ri *DOD/DAR* S75 ...... 242 C5 [1]
Bloomfield Rd *DOD/DAR* S75 ...... 242 B4
Bloomhouse La *DOD/DAR* S75 ...... 242 A4
Blossom Pl *MILN* OL16 ...... 206 B6 [1]
Blucher St *BOW* BD4 ...... 105 M8 [1]
  BSLY S70 ...... 261 G5
  COL BB8 ...... 74 A2 [1]
  COL BB8 ...... 74 A2 [2]
Blue Ball La *RPDN/SBR* HX6 ...... 188 A3
Blue Ball Rd *RPDN/SBR* HX6 ...... 187 L4
Bluebell Av *STKB/PEN* S36 ...... 270 E3
Bluebell Cl *PONT* WF8 ...... 180 F7
  WIL/AL BD15 ...... 103 K6 [1]
Bluebell Ct *BTLY* WF17 ...... 151 C4 [1]
Blue Bell Hi *HUDS* HD4 ...... 214 B4
Blue Bell La *TOD* OL14 ...... 140 E4
Bluebell Rd *DOD/DAR* S75 ...... 242 A3
Bluebell Wk *LUD/ILL* HX2 ...... 145 G6
Bluebell Wy *HEM/SK/SE* WF9 ...... 225 F7 [1]
Blueberry Dr *ROY/SHW* OL2 ...... 229 M7 [2]

Blue Butts *OSS* WF5 ...... 196 F1 [1]
Bluefields *ROY/SHW* OL2 ...... 229 M6 [1]
Blue Hill Crs *WOR/ARM* LS12 ...... 108 C8
Blue Hill Gra *WOR/ARM* LS12 ...... 130 C1
Blue Hill Gv *WOR/ARM* LS12 ...... 108 C8
Blue Hill La *WOR/ARM* LS12 ...... 108 C8
Blundell Ct *BSLYN/ROY* S71 ...... 261 M1 [1]
Blundell St *HEM/SK/SE* WF9 ...... 247 G3 [1]
  LDS LS1 ...... 6 E7
Bly Rd *WMB/DAR* S73 ...... 263 H8
Blyth Av *LIT* OL15 ...... 207 H3 [1]
Blythe Av *GIR* BD8 ...... 104 C6
Blythe St *GTHN* BD7 ...... 4 B6
Boardman St *TOD* OL14 ...... 141 K8 [1]
Boar La *LDS* LS1 ...... 9 G1
Boathouse La *MIRF* WF14 ...... 194 B4
Boat La *CAS* WF10 ...... 157 K3
  RTHW LS26 ...... 157 J4
Bobbin Mill Cl *TOD* OL14 ...... 140 D5 [1]
Bobbin Mill Ct *AIRE* BD20 ...... 56 E1
Bob La *LUD/ILL* HX2 ...... 146 A3
Bodiham Hi *GFTH/SHER* LS25 ...... 113 K6 [1]
Bodkin La *HWTH* BD22 ...... 100 A3
Bodley Ter *BULY* LS4 ...... 108 C5
Bodmin Ap *MID* LS10 ...... 153 J1
Bodmin Av *SHPY* BD18 ...... 83 G7
Bodmin Crs *BSLYN/ROY* S71 ...... 261 L3
Bodmin Crs *MID* LS10 ...... 153 J1
Bodmin Cft *MID* LS10 ...... 153 K2 [1]
Bodmin Dr *NORM* WF6 ...... 178 D3
Bodmin Gdns *MID* LS10 ...... 153 J2
Bodmin Garth *MID* LS10 ...... 153 J2
Bodmin Pl *MID* LS10 ...... 153 K2 [2]
Bodmin Rd *MID* LS10 ...... 153 H1
Bodmin St *MID* LS10 ...... 153 J2
Boggard La *STKB/PEN* S36 ...... 270 E4
Boggart Hi *SCFT* LS14 ...... 89 G8
Boggart Hill Crs *SCFT* LS14 ...... 89 G8
Boggart Hill Dr *SCFT* LS14 ...... 89 G8
Boggart Hill Gdns *SCFT* LS14 ...... 89 G8
Boggart Hill Rd *SCFT* LS14 ...... 89 G8
Boggart La *HIPP* HX3 ...... 147 M5 [1]
  KBTN HD8 ...... 239 J3
  RPDN/SBR HX6 ...... 167 K3
  TAD LS24 ...... 95 H2
Bog Green La *HUDE* HD5 ...... 193 K3
  HUDN HD2 ...... 193 J1
Bog La *MSTN/BAR* LS15 ...... 112 C1
Boland Crs *HWTH* BD22 ...... 79 G3
Boldgrove St *EARL* WF12 ...... 174 C8 [1]
Boldmere Rd *MSTN/BAR* LS15 ...... 111 H6 [1]
Boldron Holt *WBSY* BD6 ...... 126 B6
Boldshay St *BFDE* BD3 ...... 5 L4
Bold St *COL* BB8 ...... 74 A2
Bold Venture St *SKP/WHF* BD23 ...... 16 E4 [1]
Bolehill Pk *BRIC* HD6 ...... 148 A8 [1]
Bolingbroke St *WBOW* BD5 ...... 126 F4
Bolland St *LM/WK* BD12 ...... 149 G1
Bolling Rd *BOW* BD4 ...... 5 H8
  ILK LS29 ...... 38 F2
Bolsover Cl *GFTH/SHER* LS25 ...... 113 K7
Bolstermoor Rd
  HOLM/MEL HD7 ...... 212 C2
Boltby La *WBSY* BD6 ...... 126 A6
Bolton Av *WH ROCH* OL11 ...... 228 B1
Bolton Brow *RPDN/SBR* HX6 ...... 167 L2
Bolton Dr *ECHL* BD2 ...... 105 K2
Bolton Gra *YEA* LS19 ...... 62 E8
Bolton Gv *ECHL* BD2 ...... 105 K2 [1]
  SHPY BD18 ...... 83 G5
Bolton La *ECHL* BD2 ...... 105 H1
Bolton Rd *AIRE* BD20 ...... 36 A4
  BFD BD1 ...... 5 L1
  BFDE BD3 ...... 5 J5
  ECHL BD2 ...... 105 J3 [1]
  ILK LS29 ...... 19 H6
  SKP/WHF BD23 ...... 19 G1
  YEA LS19 ...... 62 E8
Bolton St *BFDE* BD3 ...... 5 J5
  LM/WK BD12 ...... 126 E8 [1]
Bolton Ter *AIRE* BD20 ...... 36 A4
Bolton Wy *BSPA/BRAM* LS23 ...... 48 E7
Bolton Wife Hi *HOR/CROF* WF4 ...... 220 B5
Bolus Cl *WKFDE* WF1 ...... 176 E2
Bolus La *WKFDE* WF1 ...... 176 E2
Bondage *AL/HA/HU* LS17 ...... 45 J7
  OT LS21 ...... 41 J7
  PONT WF8 ...... 181 H4
Bondings Ri *GFTH/SHER* LS25 ...... 116 C6 [1]
Bond Rd *DOD/DAR* S75 ...... 260 F3
Bond St *BRIG* HD6 ...... 170 C3 [1]
  BTLY WF17 ...... 151 G5 [1]
  DEWS WF13 ...... 173 L6
  HBR HX7 ...... 143 J3 [1]
  HFAX HX1 ...... 10 F7 [1]
  LDS LS1 ...... 7 G9
  PONT WF8 ...... 181 G4
  TOD OL14 ...... 163 K1 [1]
  WHIT OL12 ...... 206 C4
  WKFDE WF1 ...... 12 D1
Bonegate Av *BRIG* HD6 ...... 170 D3
Bonegate Rd *BRIG* HD6 ...... 170 D3
Bone La *AWLS/ASK* DN6 ...... 227 K6
Bonn Rd *HTON* BD9 ...... 104 C4
Bonwick MI *WBSY* BD6 ...... 126 A7
Boocock St *PDSY/CALV* LS28 ...... 107 G5 [1]
Bookers Fld *CLECK* BD19 ...... 150 E7
Bootham Pk *HTON* BD9 ...... 103 M4
Booth House La
  HOLM/MEL HD7 ...... 253 L2
Booth House Rd *LUD/ILL* HX2 ...... 144 E7
Boothman Wk *KGHY* BD21 ...... 2 D9
Booth Royd *IDLE* BD10 ...... 83 K5 [1]
Boothroyd Dr *HDGY* LS6 ...... 109 H1
  HUDS HD4 ...... 213 K3 [1]
Booth Royd Dr *IDLE* BD10 ...... 83 K5 [2]
Boothroyd Gn *DEWS* WF13 ...... 173 K6 [1]
Booth Royd La *BRIG* HD6 ...... 169 M6 [1]
Boothroyd La *DEWS* WF13 ...... 173 J6
Boothroyds Wy *FEA/AMT* WF7 ...... 179 J8
Booth St *CAS* WF10 ...... 157 M6
  CLECK BD19 ...... 149 M6
  IDLE BD10 ...... 83 K7 [1]
  ILK LS29 ...... 40 A4
  SHPY BD18 ...... 82 F7 [1]
Boothtown Rd *HIPP* HX3 ...... 146 D3
Border Cl *HUDW* HD3 ...... 191 H5

Boroughgate *OT* LS21 ...... 41 J6
Borough Rd *WKFDE* WF1 ...... 12 E1
Borrins Wy *BAIL* BD17 ...... 82 F3
Borrough Av *RHAY* LS8 ...... 88 A6
Borrough Vw *RHAY* LS8 ...... 88 A6 [1]
Borrowdale Cl *AWLS/ASK* DN6 ...... 249 L5
  BSLYN/ROY S71 ...... 262 C6
  ROY/SHW OL2 ...... 228 F8
  WOR/ARM LS12 ...... 108 B4
Borrowdale Crs *WOR/ARM* LS12 ...... 108 A4
Borrowdale Cft *YEA* LS19 ...... 62 D7 [1]
Borrowdale Dr *CAS* WF10 ...... 158 F5
Borrowdale Rd *EARL* WF12 ...... 174 A4
  WKFDW/WTN WF2 ...... 176 A7 [1]
Borrowdale Ter *SCFT* LS14 ...... 111 H3
Boston Av *KSTL* LS5 ...... 108 B3
Boston Rd *BSPA/BRAM* LS23 ...... 48 F7
  WBY LS22 ...... 48 A3
Boston St *CAS* WF10 ...... 158 A6
  HFAX HX1 ...... 10 B6
  RPDN/SBR HX6 ...... 167 J3
Boston Wk *WBSY* BD6 ...... 126 B6 [1]
Bosville St *STKB/PEN* S36 ...... 271 C4
Bosville Cl *BSLYN/ROY* S71 ...... 243 K2 [1]
Bosworth Av *NORM* WF6 ...... 178 A2 [2]
Bosworth Cl *WIL/AL* BD15 ...... 103 K5
Bosworth Rd *AWLS/ASK* DN6 ...... 249 G4
Botany Av *ECHL* BD2 ...... 105 H2
Botany La *KBTN* HD8 ...... 216 B1
Botany Wy *ECHL* BD2 ...... 105 H2 [1]
Botham Flds *HOLM/MEL* HD7 ...... 213 H1
Botham Hall Rd *HUDW* HD3 ...... 213 H3
Botheby Wd *SKP/WHF* BD23 ...... 16 A1
Bottom Boat Rd
  EARD/LOFT WF3 ...... 155 K8
Bottom Dyke *KBTN* HD8 ...... 238 B6
Bottom La *HOLM/MEL* HD7 ...... 236 E7
Bottomley La *GTL/HWG* HX4 ...... 189 L4
Bottomley Rd *TOD* OL14 ...... 163 L8
Bottomley St *BRIG* HD6 ...... 170 D2 [2]
  WBOW BD5 ...... 126 F2 [2]
Bottoms *HIPP* HX3 ...... 168 F3
Bottoms La *BIRK/DRI* BD11 ...... 150 D2
Boulder Bridge La *CUD/GR* S72 ...... 244 B4
The Boulevard *BEE/HOL* LS11 ...... 130 F3
  PDSY/CALV LS28 ...... 106 F4
Boulsworth Dr *COL* BB8 ...... 74 C1
Boulsworth Gv *COL* BB8 ...... 74 C1 [1]
Boulview Ter *COL* BB8 ...... 74 C1 [2]
Boundary Av *AIRE* BD20 ...... 34 C8
Boundary Cl *MSTN/BAR* LS15 ...... 112 A7 [1]
Boundary Dr *CUD/GR* S72 ...... 245 J3 [1]
Boundary Farm Rd
  AL/HA/HU LS17 ...... 87 J3
Boundary La *WKFDE* WF1 ...... 178 D7
Boundary Pl *CHAL* LS7 ...... 7 L4
Boundary St *DEWS* WF13 ...... 173 H4 [1]
Boundary St *BSLY* S70 ...... 261 K6
  CHAL LS7 ...... 7 L4 [1]
  LIT OL15 ...... 185 J8
  LVSG WF15 ...... 172 E3
  ROCH OL11 ...... 228 A1
The Boundary *GIR* BD8 ...... 104 A5
Bourbon Cl *WBSY* BD6 ...... 126 D6
Bourne Ct *DOD/DAR* S75 ...... 242 E4
Bourne La *ROY/SHW* OL2 ...... 229 J6 [1]
Bourne St *IDLE* BD10 ...... 83 K5 [1]
Bourne Wk *DOD/DAR* S75 ...... 242 D4
Bourn View Rd *HUDS* HD4 ...... 213 M7
Bowater Ct *BOW* BD4 ...... 128 B4 [1]
Bow Beck *BOW* BD4 ...... 5 K9
Bowbridge Rd *WBOW* BD5 ...... 127 C3 [1]
Bow Bridge Vw *TAD* LS24 ...... 71 L5
Bowcliffe Rd *BSPA/BRAM* LS23 ...... 69 L4
Bowden Gv *DOD/DAR* S75 ...... 260 B7
Bower Av *WHIT* OL12 ...... 206 C5
Bower La *DEWS* WF13 ...... 173 H3
Bower Rd *MSTN/BAR* LS15 ...... 112 A3
Bower Slack Rd *RPDN/SBR* HX6 ...... 166 B5
Bowers La *GTL/HWG* HX4 ...... 167 M8 [1]
Bower St *WBOW* BD5 ...... 4 E9
The Bower *BTLY* WF17 ...... 151 H6
Bowes Nook *WBSY* BD6 ...... 126 A7
Bowfell Cl *SCFT* LS14 ...... 111 J2
Bowfell Vw *BSLYN/ROY* S71 ...... 261 J2
Bow Gn *CLAY* BD14 ...... 125 M2 [1]
Bowland Cl *MSTN/BAR* LS15 ...... 111 G7
  ROY/SHW OL2 ...... 229 G2 [1]
Bowland Gv *MILN* OL16 ...... 229 H2 [1]
Bowlan St *GIR* BD8 ...... 4 C3
Bow La *HBR* HX7 ...... 142 C2
Bowler Cl *LM/WK* BD12 ...... 126 E8
Bowler St *ROY/SHW* OL2 ...... 229 K7
Bowlers Wk *WHIT* OL12 ...... 206 B4 [1]
Bowling Aly *BRIG* HD6 ...... 170 C6
Bowling Av *WKFDE* WF1 ...... 176 B4 [1]
Bowling Back La *BOW* BD4 ...... 5 K9
Bowling Ct *BRIG* HD6 ...... 170 B3
Bowling Dyke *HFAX* HX1 ...... 11 H4
Bowling Green Ct *HUDW* HD3 ...... 191 G7 [1]
Bowling Green Rd
  GTL/HWG HX4 ...... 190 B3
Bowling Green Ter
  BEE/HOL LS11 ...... 8 E5
Bowling Hall Rd *BOW* BD4 ...... 127 L3
Bowling Old La *WBOW* BD5 ...... 127 G3 [1]
Bowling Park Cl *BOW* BD4 ...... 127 H2
Bowling Park Dr *WBOW* BD5 ...... 127 H2
Bowling Rd *HUDS* HD4 ...... 213 J2 [1]
Bowman Gv *HFAX* HX1 ...... 10 D7
Bowman La *LDS* LS1 ...... 9 J2
Bowman Pl *HFAX* HX1 ...... 10 C5 [1]
Bowman Rd *WBSY* BD6 ...... 126 D7
Bowman St *HFAX* HX1 ...... 10 C5 [2]
Bowman Ter *HFAX* HX1 ...... 10 C5 [3]
Bowness Av *BSPA/BRAM* LS23 ...... 48 E6
Bowness Av *CAS* WF10 ...... 159 G5 [1]
  IDLE BD10 ...... 105 M2
Bowood Av *CHAL* LS7 ...... 87 J7
Bowood Crs *CHAL* LS7 ...... 87 J7
Bowood Gv *CHAL* LS7 ...... 87 J7 [1]

Bowood La *RPDN/SBR* HX6 ...... 166 F5
Bow St *CUD/GR* S72 ...... 244 D7
  HUD HD1 ...... 14 D8
  KGHY BD21 ...... 3 G5
  OSM LS9 ...... 9 L2
Bowwood Dr *AIRE* BD20 ...... 58 D6 [1]
Boxhill Rd *ELL* HX5 ...... 169 H7
Box La *PONT* WF8 ...... 181 G4
Box St *LIT* OL15 ...... 207 J3
Box Tree Cl *GIR* BD8 ...... 104 A5 [1]
Box Trees La *LUD/ILL* HX2 ...... 145 M3
Boxwood Rd *ELL* HX5 ...... 191 H1
Boycott Dr *FEA/AMT* WF7 ...... 224 C1 [1]
Boyd Av *BFDE* BD3 ...... 106 A5
Boy La *BOW* BD4 ...... 127 K7
  HIPP HX3 ...... 145 M4
The Boyle *MSTN/BAR* LS15 ...... 90 F6
Boyne Dr *WKFDW/WTN* WF2 ...... 220 C1
Boyne HI *HOR/CROF* WF4 ...... 220 C2
Boyne St *HFAX* HX1 ...... 10 F6
Boynton St *WBOW* BD5 ...... 126 F5
Boynton Ter *WBOW* BD5 ...... 127 C3 [3]
Boys La *HIPP* HX3 ...... 168 F1
Bracewell Av *WIL/AL* BD15 ...... 103 J6
Bracewell Bank *HIPP* HX3 ...... 146 C4 [1]
Bracewell Dr *HIPP* HX3 ...... 146 B4
Bracewell Gv *HIPP* HX3 ...... 10 C1
Bracewell Rd *HOLM/MEL* HD7 ...... 234 E5
Bracken Av *BRIG* HD6 ...... 170 C5
Bracken Bank Av *HWTH* BD22 ...... 79 H3
Bracken Bank Crs *HWTH* BD22 ...... 79 H3
Bracken Bank Gv *HWTH* BD22 ...... 79 H3
Bracken Bank Wk *HWTH* BD22 ...... 79 H4 [1]
Bracken Bank Wy *HWTH* BD22 ...... 79 H3
Brackenbeck Rd *GTHN* BD7 ...... 126 B2 [2]
Brackenbed La *HFAX* HX1 ...... 10 A1
Bracken Cl *BRIG* HD6 ...... 170 C5
  MIRF WF14 ...... 171 M7 [1]
Bracken Ct *AL/HA/HU* LS17 ...... 87 L5
  WOR/ARM LS12 ...... 131 G1 [1]
Brackendale *IDLE* BD10 ...... 83 J4 [1]
Brackendale Av *IDLE* BD10 ...... 83 J4 [2]
Brackendale Dr *IDLE* BD10 ...... 83 H4
Brackendale Gv *IDLE* BD10 ...... 83 H4
Brackendale Pde *IDLE* BD10 ...... 83 H4
Bracken Edge *IDLE* BD10 ...... 83 L7 [1]
  RHAY LS8 ...... 110 B1
Bracken Ghyll Dr *AIRE* BD20 ...... 35 M4
Bracken Gv *HUDN* HD2 ...... 192 D3 [1]
  MIRF WF14 ...... 171 M7
Bracken Hall Rd *HUDN* HD2 ...... 192 D3
Bracken HI *AL/HA/HU* LS17 ...... 87 L5
  FEA/AMT WF7 ...... 223 M1
  HEM/SK/SE WF9 ...... 246 F2
  MIRF WF14 ...... 171 M7
Brackenhill Dr *GTHN* BD7 ...... 126 B3 [1]
Brackenhill La *TAD* LS24 ...... 95 H7
Brackenholme Royd *WBSY* BD6 ...... 126 A6
Bracken Mt *BGLY* BD16 ...... 81 L3
  SCFT LS14 ...... 67 J6
Bracken Pk *BGLY* BD16 ...... 81 L3
Brackens La *HIPP* HX3 ...... 125 K7
Bracken Sq *HUDN* HD2 ...... 192 E2 [1]
Bracken St *KGHY* BD21 ...... 79 K2
Brackenthwaite La *PBR* HG3 ...... 25 L3
Brackenwell La *AL/HA/HU* LS17 ...... 25 M7
Brackenwood Cl *ILK* LS29 ...... 39 G2 [1]
  RHAY LS8 ...... 88 A7
Brackenwood Ct *WKFDE* WF1 ...... 176 F1 [1]
Brackenwood Dr *RHAY* LS8 ...... 88 A6
Brackenwood Gn *RHAY* LS8 ...... 88 A6 [1]
Brackenwood Rd *WKFDE* WF1 ...... 176 F1
Bradbeck Rd *GTHN* BD7 ...... 104 B7
Bradburn Rd *EARD/LOFT* WF3 ...... 154 C3
Bradbury St *BSLY* S70 ...... 260 F5
  DEWS WF13 ...... 173 J6
Bradd Cl *LVSG* WF15 ...... 172 D1 [1]
Braddocks Cl *WHIT* OL12 ...... 206 F2 [1]
Bradfield Cl *HUDN* HD2 ...... 193 G1
Bradford & Wakefield Rd
  BOW BD4 ...... 128 C2
Bradford La *BFDE* BD3 ...... 105 M7
Bradford Old Rd *BGLY* BD16 ...... 81 K7
  HIPP HX3 ...... 146 E3
Bradford Rd *BFDE* BD3 ...... 106 C5
  BGLY BD16 ...... 81 J5
  BIRK/DRI BD11 ...... 150 C2
  BOW BD4 ...... 128 B6
  BRIG HD6 ...... 170 C2
  BTLY WF17 ...... 151 H6 [1]
  CLAY BD14 ...... 125 M1
  CLECK BD19 ...... 149 K3
  DEWS WF13 ...... 173 L4
  EARD/LOFT WF3 ...... 153 G5
  GSLY LS20 ...... 61 L5
  HIPP HX3 ...... 147 L5
  HUD HD1 ...... 14 F3
  HUDN HD2 ...... 192 D2
  IDLE BD10 ...... 83 K8
  IDLE BD10 ...... 105 J3
  ILK LS29 ...... 40 B6
  KGHY BD21 ...... 3 M1
  PDSY/CALV LS28 ...... 106 D5
  SHPY BD18 ...... 82 D8
  WKFDE WF1 ...... 176 D6
  WKFDW/WTN WF2 ...... 176 A2
Bradfords Cl *BSPA/BRAM* LS23 ...... 69 L3 [1]
Bradford St *DEWS* WF13 ...... 173 M5 [1]
  KGHY BD21 ...... 3 H5
Bradlaugh Rd *WBSY* BD6 ...... 126 D5
Bradlaugh Ter *WBSY* BD6 ...... 126 E5 [1]
Bradley Av *AIRE* BD20 ...... 35 M4
  CAS WF10 ...... 157 L6
Bradley Bvd *HUDN* HD2 ...... 192 E3
Bradley Carr Ter
  HEM/SK/SE WF9 ...... 247 G3
Bradley Dr *AIRE* BD20 ...... 35 M4
Bradley Grange Gdns
  HUDN HD2 ...... 171 H8
Bradley La *GTL/HWG* HX4 ...... 168 D8
  MILN OL16 ...... 229 J2
  PDSY/CALV LS28 ...... 106 D7
Bradley Mills Rd *HUD* HD1 ...... 15 M2
  HUDE HD5 ...... 193 G6
Bradley Quarry Cl *HUDN* HD2 ...... 171 J8 [1]

Bradley Ri *AIRE* BD20 .... 35 M4
Bradley Rd *AIRE* BD20 .... 35 M3
  HUDN HD2 .... 192 F1
Bradley Smithy Cl *WHIT* OL12 .. 206 A4
Bradley St *BGLY* BD16 .... 81 H3
  CAS WF10 .... 157 M6
  COL BB8 .... 74 B1
  HTON BD9 .... 104 E2
  HUD HD1 .... 15 H8
  MILN OL16 .... 229 K2
Bradley Vw *GTL/HWG* HX4 .... 190 D2
Bradshaw Av *HOLM/MEL* HD7 .. 236 A3
Bradshaw Cl *DOD/DAR* S75 .. 260 C4
  HOLM/MEL HD7 .... 236 A3
Bradshaw Crs *HOLM/MEL* HD7.. 236 A3
  LUD/ILL HX2 .... 124 B5
Bradshaw La *HOLM/MEL* HD7.. 211 J5
Bradshaw Rd *HOLM/MEL* HD7.. 235 K8
Bradshaw St *MILN* OL16 .... 206 C8
Bradstock Gdns *MOR* LS27 .. 130 C8
Brae Av *ECHL* BD2 .... 105 H3
Braegate La *TAD* LS24 .... 73 K1
Braemar Cft *CUD/GR* S72 .... 222 F7
Braemar Dr *GFTH/SHER* LS25 .. 113 K6
Braemar Ri *CUD/GR* S72 .... 222 F7
Braemore Cl *ROY/SHW* OL2 .. 229 G6
Brafferton Arbor *WBSY* BD6 .. 126 A6
Braine Rd *WBY* LS22 .... 30 B8
Braithwaite Av *HWTH* BD22 .. 57 G7
Braithwaite Crs *HWTH* BD22 .. 2 B4
Braithwaite Dr *HWTH* BD22 ... 2 A4
Braithwaite Edge Rd
  HWTH BD22 .... 56 F1
Braithwaite Gv *HWTH* BD22 ... 2 A4
Braithwaite Rd *HWTH* BD22 .. 56 F7
Braithwaite Rw *MID* LS10 .. 132 M4
Braithwaite St *BEE/HOL* LS11 ... 8 A4
Braithwaite Wk *HWTH* BD22 ... 2 A4
Braithwaite Wy *HWTH* BD22 ... 2 A4
Brakehouse Cl *MILN* OL16 .. 207 G8
Bramah St *BSLYN/ROY* S71 .. 243 L5
Bramble Av *BSPA/BRAM* LS23 .. 48 D7
Bramble Cl *CLAY* BD14 .... 125 K3
  LIT OL15 .... 207 H1
  PONT WF8 .... 180 D8
Bramble Ct *HWTH* BD22 .... 78 F8
The Brambles *ILK* LS29 .... 38 B2
Bramble Wk *BTLY* WF17 .... 151 H5
Brambling Ms *MOR* LS27 .. 152 E2
Bramcote Av *BSLYN/ROY* S71 .. 243 G6
Bramhall Cl *MILN* OL16 .... 207 G8
Bramham Dr *BAIL* BD17 .... 82 F2
Bramham La *BSPA/BRAM* LS23 .. 68 C2
Bramham Rd *BGLY* BD16 .... 81 J2
  BSPA/BRAM LS23 .... 69 M1
  CAS WF10 .... 157 J8
  SCFT LS14 .... 68 D8
Bramhope Old La *OT* LS21 .... 63 G2
Bramhope Rd *CLECK* BD19 .. 149 L6
Bramleigh Dr *MOR* LS27 .. 130 C8
Bramleigh Gv *MOR* LS27 .. 130 C8
Bramley Cl *HOLM/MEL* HD7 .. 236 F7
  HWTH BD22 .... 78 D3
Bramley Crs *WKFDE* WF1 .. 176 D2
Bramley Fold *HIPP* HX3 .. 147 M6
Bramley La *HIPP* HX3 .... 147 M6
  HOR/CROF WF4 .... 219 J6
Bramley St *BRAM* LS13 .... 107 G1
  WBOW BD5 .... 127 G1
Bramley Vw *HIPP* HX3 .... 148 A6
Brampton Ct *HEM/SK/SE* WF9 .. 247 J1
Bramston St *BRAM* LS13 .... 107 J3
Bramston Cl *BRAM* LS13 .. 107 J3
Bramston Gdns *BRIG* HD6 .. 170 C6
Bramston Gdns *BRIG* HD6 .. 170 C6
Bramston St *BRIG* HD6 .... 170 C5
Brancepeth Pl *WOR/ARM* LS12 .. 109 J7
Branch Cl *WOR/ARM* LS12 .. 130 C2
Branch End *MOR* LS27 .... 129 M7
Branch La *HUDW* HD3 .... 191 M4
Branch Pl *WOR/ARM* LS12 .. 130 C2
Branch Rd *BTLY* WF17 .... 173 L1
  CLECK BD19 .... 149 H5
  DEWS WF13 .... 173 M6
  GTL/HWG HX4 .... 168 B4
  HUDW HD3 .... 191 J7
  LIT OL15 .... 207 G5
  SKP/WHF BD23 .... 16 E1
  WOR/ARM LS12 .... 108 E6
Branch St *HUD* HD1 .... 213 M1
  WOR/ARM LS12 .... 130 C2
Brander Ap *OSM* LS9 .... 110 E5
Brander Cl *OSM* LS9 .... 110 F5
Brander Dr *OSM* LS9 .... 110 E5
Brander Gv *OSM* LS9 .... 110 E5
Brander Rd *OSM* LS9 .... 110 E5
Brander St *OSM* LS9 .... 110 F4
Brandfort St *GTHN* BD7 .... 126 C1
Brand Hill Ap *HOR/CROF* WF4 .. 200 A5
Brand Hill Dr *HOR/CROF* WF4 .. 200 A5
Brandon Ct *AL/HA/HU* LS17 .... 88 D1
Brandon Crs *AL/HA/HU* LS17 .... 67 H8
  ROY/SHW OL2 228
Brandon Rd *BVRD* LS3 .... 6 C1
Brandon St *WOR/ARM* LS12 .... 8 A1
Brandon Wy *CHAL* LS7 .... 109 M1
Brandy Carr Rd
  WKFDW/WTN WF2 .. 175 K4
Branksome Av *BSLY* S70 .. 260 E5
Branksome Ct *HTON* BD9 .. 104 B4
Branksome Crs *HTON* BD9 .. 104 B4
Branksome Dr *SHPY* BD18 .... 81 M6
Branksome Gv *BGLY* BD16 .... 81 K1
Branksome Pl *HDGY* LS6 .. 109 G4
Branksome St *HDGY* LS6 .. 109 G4
Branksome Ter *HDGY* LS6 .. 109 G4
Bransby Cl *PDSY/CALV* LS28 .. 107 G4
Bransby Ri *PDSY/CALV* LS28 .. 107 G4
Bransdale Av *GSLY* LS20 .... 62 A6
  NORM WF6 .... 178 C1
Bransdale Cl *BAIL* BD17 .... 82 C4
  GSLY LS20 .... 62 A6
  NORM WF6 .... 178 C2
Bransdale Clough *WBSY* BD6 .. 126 A5
Bransdale Garth *GSLY* LS20 .. 62 A6

Bransdale Ms *NORM* WF6 .. 178 C2
Bransdale Wk *NORM* WF6 .. 178 C2
Branshaw Gv *HWTH* BD22 .... 79 G1
Branshaw Mt *HWTH* BD22 .... 79 G1
Branstone Gv *OSS* WF5 .. 174 F5
Bran St *HWTH* BD22 .... 79 J2
Brant Av *LUD/ILL* HX2 .. 146 B2
Brant Bank La *ILK* LS29 .... 19 L8
Brantcliffe Dr *BAIL* BD17 .... 82 D2
Brantcliffe Wy *BAIL* BD17 .... 82 D2
Brantdale Cl *HTON* BD9 .. 103 L2
Brantdale Rd *HTON* BD9 .. 103 L2
Brantford St *CHAL* LS7 .... 87 M8
Brant La *TAD* LS24 .... 71 J7
Brantwood Av *HTON* BD9 .. 103 L2
Brantwood Cl *HTON* BD9 .. 103 L2
Brantwood Crs *HTON* BD9 .. 103 K2
Brantwood Dr *HTON* BD9 .. 103 K2
Brantwood Gv *HTON* BD9 .. 103 K2
Brantwood Ov *HTON* BD9 .. 103 K2
Brantwood Rd *HTON* BD9 .. 103 K2
Brantwood Vls *HTON* BD9 .. 103 L2
Branwell Av *BTLY* WF17 .. 151 G3
Branwell Dr *HWTH* BD22 .... 78 E6
Brassey Rd *BOW* BD4 .... 127 J2
Brassey St *HFAX* HX1 .... 10 F8
Brassey Ter *BOW* BD4 .... 127 J2
Brathay Gdns *SCFT* LS14 .. 111 J3
Brat La *OT* LS21 .... 23 J1
Braybrook Ct *GIR* BD8 .... 104 E3
Bray Cl *WBSY* BD6 .. 125 M4
Brayshaw Dr *CTHN* BD7 .. 126 A4
Brayshaw Rd *EARD/LOFT* WF3 .. 153 L7
Brayside Av *HUDN* HD2 .. 192 B4
Braythorne La *OT* LS21 .... 24 F7
Brayton Ap *SCFT* LS14 .. 111 L1
Brayton Cl *SCFT* LS14 .. 111 L1
Brayton Gdns *AWLS/ASK* DN6 .. 227 L5
Brayton Gn *SCFT* LS14 .. 111 M1
Brayton Gv *SCFT* LS14 .. 111 L1
Brazil St *CAS* WF10 .. 158 A6
Breakmoor Av *AIRE* BD20 .... 36 A4
Break Neck *HIPP* HX3 .. 147 J6
Breaks Rd *LM/WK* BD12 .. 126 F8
Brearcliffe Cl *WBSY* BD6 .. 126 C6
Brearcliffe Dr *WBSY* BD6 .. 126 C6
Brearcliffe Gv *WBSY* BD6 .. 126 C6
Brearcliffe Rd *WBSY* BD6 .. 126 D7
Brearcliffe St *WBSY* BD6 .. 126 C6
Brearley Gdns *LVSG* WF15 .. 172 C3
Brearley La *LUD/ILL* HX2 .. 144 D6
Brearley St *BTLY* WF17 .. 173 K2
Brearton St *BFD* BD1 .... 4 E3
Breary Av *HORS* LS18 .... 85 M5
Breary Ct *BHP/TINH* LS16 .... 64 B3
Breary La *BHP/TINH* LS16 .... 64 B3
Breary La East *BHP/TINH* LS16 .. 64 B3
Breary Ri *BHP/TINH* LS16 .... 64 A4
Breary Ter *HORS* LS18 .... 85 M5
Breary Wk *HORS* LS18 .... 85 M5
Breck Lea *RPDN/SBR* HX6 .. 167 J4
Brecks Gdns *GFTH/SHER* LS25 .. 135 J4
Brecks La *GFTH/SHER* LS25 .. 135 J1
  RTHW LS26 .... 134 E2
Brecks Rd *CLAY* BD14 .. 125 M1
Breck Willows *RPDN/SBR* HX6 .. 167 H4
Brecon Ap *OSM* LS9 .. 110 F5
Brecon Av *HUDW* HD3 .. 191 J5
Brecon Cl *IDLE* BD10 .... 83 K7
  ROY/SHW OL2 .. 228 E8
Bredon Av *SHPY* BD18 .... 83 H7
Bredon Cl *HEM/SK/SE* WF9 .. 224 A7
Breeze Cl *COL* BB8 .... 52 A5
Breighton Adown *WBSY* BD6 .. 125 M6
Brellafield Dr *ROY/SHW* OL2 .. 229 H5
Bremner St *OT* LS21 .... 41 K6
Brendon Ct *BOW* BD4 .. 127 M3
  MIRF WF14 .. 194 B4
Brendon Dr *HUDN* HD2 .. 191 M5
Brendon Wk *BOW* BD4 .. 127 M4
Brentford St *WOR/ARM* LS12 .. 108 E7
Brentford Rd *LM/WK* BD12 .. 126 E8
  WBSY BD6 .. 126 E7
Brentlea Av *WKFDW/WTN* WF2 .. 12 D8
Brentwood Cl *BTLY* WF17 .. 174 A1
  LIT OL15 .. 207 H3
  PONT WF8 .. 225 J1
Brentwood Gdns *WBSY* BD6 .. 126 E6
Brentwood St *WOR/ARM* LS12 .. 108 E7
Brentwood Ter
  WOR/ARM LS12 .. 108 E7
Bretfield Ct *EARL* WF12 .. 195 M1
Brettegate *HEM/SK/SE* WF9 .. 223 L7
Bretton Cl *DOD/DAR* S75 .. 241 L6
Bretton La *HOR/CROF* WF4 .. 219 K5
Bretton Rd *DOD/DAR* S75 .. 241 M6
Bretton St *EARL* WF12 .. 195 M1
Bretton Vw *CUD/GR* S72 .. 262 C1
Brevitt St *WKFDE* WF1 .... 13 J8
Brewerton La *DEWS* WF13 .. 173 H4
Brewery Ct *HUDW* HD3 .. 191 J5
  EARL WF12 .. 195 L2
  SKP/WHF BD23 .. 16 B2
Brewery Dr *HWTH* BD22 .... 79 J3
  ILK LS29 .. 38 E2
Brewery St *HECK* WF16 .. 172 F3
  HIPP HX3 .. 146 E4
  KGHY BD21 .... 3 K4
  TOD OL14 .. 141 G6
Brewery Whf *MIRF* WF14 .. 194 C2
Brexdale Av *GFTH/SHER* LS25 .. 135 H3
Brian Crs *MSTN/BAR* LS15 .. 111 K4
Brian Pl *MSTN/BAR* LS15 .. 111 K3
Brian Royd La *GTL/HWG* HX4 .. 168 B7
Brian St *HUDW* HD3 .. 191 K5
Brian Vw *MSTN/BAR* LS15 .. 111 K3
Briar Av *HOLM/MEL* HD7 .. 234 E3
Briar Bank *HEM/SK/SE* WF9 .. 223 J4
Briar Cl *ELL* HX5 .. 191 H1
  HECK WF16 .. 172 D1
  PDSY/CALV LS28 .. 106 F4
Briar Ct *HOLM/MEL* HD7 .. 253 M2
Briardale Rd *HTON* BD9 .. 103 K2
Briar Dr *DEWS* WF13 .. 173 H4
Briarfield Cl *IDLE* BD10 .... 83 J7

  ILK LS29 .... 38 F3
Briarfield Gdns *SHPY* BD18 .... 82 D8
Briarfield Gv *IDLE* BD10 .... 83 J7
Briarfield Rd *HOLM/MEL* HD7 .. 236 E7
  SHPY BD18 .... 82 E8
Briar Ga *WBY* LS22 .... 30 A1
Briar Gv *CUD/GR* S72 .. 245 J3
  STKB/PEN S36 .. 270 F4
  WKFDE WF1 .... 13 K9
Briarlea Cl *YEA* LS19 .... 62 B8
Briarlyn Av *HUDW* HD3 .. 191 J4
Briarlyn Rd *HUDW* HD3 .. 191 J4
Briarmains Rd *BTLY* WF17 .. 151 H4
Briar Rhydding *BAIL* BD17 .... 83 G4
Briar Rd *AWLS/ASK* DN6 .. 249 J5
Briars Ct *COP/BISH* YO23 .... 73 M5
Briarsdale Garth *RHAY* LS8 .. 110 D3
Briars Dr *COP/BISH* YO23 .... 73 M5
Briar Wd *SHPY* BD18 .... 83 G7
Briarwood Av *KGHY* BD21 .... 58 B5
Briarwood Cl *WKFDE* WF1 .. 176 F1
Briarwood Crs *WBSY* BD6 .. 126 C5
Briarwood Dr *WBSY* BD6 .. 126 C5
Briarwood Gv *WBSY* BD6 .. 126 C5
Brick And Tile Ter *BRIG* HD6 .. 170 C5
Brickbank *HUDE* HD5 .. 215 H3
Brickfield Cl *LUD/ILL* HX2 .. 146 C1
Brickfield La *LUD/ILL* HX2 .. 146 C1
Brickfield St *MILN* OL16 .. 206 D4
Brickfield Ter *LUD/ILL* HX2 .. 146 C1
Brick Mill Rd *PDSY/CALV* LS28 .. 107 G8
Brick Rw *LM/WK* BD12 .. 148 E3
Brick St *CLECK* BD19 .. 149 L7
  OSM LS9 .... 9 K1
  WKFDW/WTN WF2 .. 175 M7
Brick Ter *TOD* OL14 .. 140 E5
Brickyard *MIRF* WF14 .. 194 B1
Bride St *TOD* OL14 .. 141 K8
Bridge Bank Rd *LIT* OL15 .. 207 H3
Bridge Cl *BSPA/BRAM* LS23 .... 49 G6
  HOR/CROF WF4 .. 196 F5
  KBTN HD8 .. 240 A4
Bridge Ct *HEM/SK/SE* WF9 .. 223 J4
  MOR LS27 .. 152 D3
Bridge Cft *HUDW* HD3 .. 213 K2
  LDS LS1 .... 9 H7
Bridge End *BRIG* HD6 .. 170 C5
Bridge Fold *KSTL* LS5 .. 108 C2
Bridge Foot *BSPA/BRAM* LS23 .... 49 G6
Bridge Garth *BSPA/BRAM* LS23 .. 48 F8
  GFTH/SHER LS25 .. 138 B2
Bridge Gv *HBR* HX7 .. 143 J3
Bridgegate Wy *IDLE* BD10 .. 105 M1
Bridgehouse La *HWTH* BD22 .... 78 E8
Bridge La *HIPP* HX3 .. 125 K7
  HOLM/MEL HD7 .. 236 C6
  ILK LS29 .... 38 C1
  KNOT WF11 .. 182 B1
  PONT WF8 .. 225 J2
  HBR HX7 .. 143 H3
Bridgenorth Dr *LIT* OL15 .. 207 H3
Bridge Rd *AIRE* BD20 .... 55 M1
  BEE/HOL LS11 .... 8 C4
  BRAM LS13 .. 107 G1
  BRIG HD6 .. 170 C4
  BSPA/BRAM LS23 .... 49 G6
  HOR/CROF WF4 .. 197 G5
  HUDN HD2 .. 193 K1
Bridge St *AIRE* BD20 .... 36 A4
  BFD BD1 .... 4 F5
  BSLY S70 .. 262 A6
  BSLYN/ROY S71 .. 261 H4
  BTLY WF17 .. 151 G6
  BTLY WF17 .. 173 M1
  CAS WF10 .. 158 A4
  DOD/DAR S75 .. 242 A5
  HECK WF16 .. 172 E2
  HOLM/MEL HD7 .. 212 C5
  HUD HD1 .. 214 B3
  HUDS HD4 .. 214 B6
  HWTH BD22 .... 78 D4
  KGHY BD21 .... 2 F6
  LDSU LS2 .... 7 J8
  MILN OL16 .. 207 H8
  MOR LS27 .. 152 D4
  NORM WF6 .. 178 E4
  OT LS21 .... 41 J6
  PONT WF8 .. 225 J2
  ROY/SHW OL2 .. 229 L6
  SKP/WHF BD23 .. 16 B2
  STKB/PEN S36 .. 270 E2
  TAD LS24 .... 71 M3
  TOD OL14 .. 163 K1
  WHIT OL12 .. 206 E3
  WKFDE WF1 .... 13 H6
Bridge Vw *BRAM* LS13 .. 107 G1
Bridge View Ct *HORS* LS18 .... 85 M4
Bridgewater Park Dr
  AWLS/ASK DN6 .. 249 H4
Bridgewater Rd *HTON* BD9 .. 104 C4
Bridgeway *BOW* BD4 .. 127 L4
Bridgland Av *ILK* LS29 .... 61 J1
Bridgwater Rd *HTON* BD9 .. 104 C4
Bridle Av *OSS* WF5 .. 174 E6
Bridle Cl *HOR/CROF* WF4 .. 197 G5
Bridle Dene *HIPP* HX3 .. 147 L1
Bridle La *HOR/CROF* WF4 .. 197 G5
  OSS WF5 .. 174 E6
Bridle Pth *MSTN/BAR* LS15 .. 111 J3
Bridle Path Rd *AL/HA/HU* LS17 .... 88 F1
Bridle Path Wk
  MSTN/BAR LS15 .. 111 J4
Bridle Pl *OSS* WF5 .. 174 E6
Bridle Stile *HIPP* HX3 .. 147 L1
Bridle Stile La *CUL/OBY* BD13 .. 125 G4
Bridle St *BTLY* WF17 .. 174 A1
Bridley Dr *HOLM/MEL* HD7 .. 212 C6
Brierdene *ELL* HX5 .. 191 H1
Brierey Cl *DOD/DAR* S75 .. 242 C6
Brierfield Cl *DOD/DAR* S75 .. 242 C6
Brierfield Gdns *MOR* LS27 .. 129 L8
Brier Hey Cl *HBR* HX7 .. 144 B5
Brier Hey La *HBR* HX7 .. 144 B5
Brier Hill Cl *CLECK* BD19 .. 149 J8
Brier Hill Vw *HUDN* HD2 .. 192 F1
Brierlands Fold *GFTH/SHER* LS25 .. 113 K6

Brierlands Fold
  GFTH/SHER LS25 .. 113 K6
Brier La *ELL* HX5 .. 169 M4
  HOR/CROF WF4 .. 222 D6
Brierley Cl *SHPY* BD18 .... 82 E8
Brierley Crs *HEM/SK/SE* WF9 .. 246 E3
Brierley Rd *CUD/GR* S72 .. 244 F4
  CUD/GR S72 .. 245 C1
Brier St *HIPP* HX3 .. 146 D4
  KGHY BD21 .... 79 K2
Briery Cl *ILK* LS29 .... 38 C3
Briery Fld *SHPY* BD18 .. 104 D1
Briery Gv *MIRF* WF14 .. 194 C3
Briestfield Rd *EARL* WF12 .. 195 H7
Briggate *AIRE* BD20 .... 36 A4
  BAIL BD17 .... 82 D6
  BRIG HD6 .. 170 C4
  ELL HX5 .. 169 H7
  LDS LS1 .... 9 G1
  SHPY BD18 .... 82 D8
Briggland Ct *WIL/AL* BD15 .. 102 E1
Brigg's Av *CAS* WF10 .. 157 M8
  WBSY BD6 .. 126 C5
Briggs Gv *WBSY* BD6 .. 126 C5
Briggs Pl *WBSY* BD6 .. 126 C5
Briggs Rd *BSLYN/ROY* S71 .. 243 C5
Briggs Rw *FEA/AMT* WF7 .. 201 M2
Briggs St *CUL/OBY* BD13 .. 125 G5
Briggs Ter *HUDE* HD5 .. 15 L1
Brighouse & Denholme Gate Rd
  HIPP HX3 .. 147 L2
Brighouse & Denholme Rd
  CUL/OBY BD13 .. 124 C2
Brighouse Rd *CUL/OBY* BD13 .. 102 A8
  CUL/OBY BD13 .. 125 C5
  HIPP HX3 .. 147 L2
  HUDW HD3 .. 191 K3
  LM/WK BD12 .. 148 F1
Brighouse Wood La *BRIG* HD6 .. 170 B3
Brighouse Wood Rw
  BRIG HD6 .. 170 B3
Brighton Av *MOR* LS27 .. 152 B1
Brighton Cliff *BRAM* LS13 .. 107 L4
Brighton Cl *BTLY* WF17 .. 151 L4
Brighton Gv *BRAM* LS13 .. 107 M5
Brighton Rd *ILK* LS29 .... 39 G3
Brighton St *BAIL* BD17 .... 82 D6
  CUD/GR S72 .. 245 J7
  HECK WF16 .. 172 F1
  HIPP HX3 .. 10 D1
  IDLE BD10 .. 84 F5
  TOD OL14 .. 140 E5
  WKFDW/WTN WF2 .. 12 B5
Brighton Ter *CLECK* BD19 .. 149 H5
Bright St *AIRE* BD20 .... 34 F5
  CLAY BD14 .. 125 K2
  COL BB8 .... 74 D1
  CUL/OBY BD13 .. 125 H5
  DEWS WF13 .. 173 L5
  EARD/LOFT WF3 .. 153 M6
  MILN OL16 .. 228 C1
  MIRF WF14 .. 172 B6
  MOR LS27 .. 152 B2
  PDSY/CALV LS28 .. 107 H4
  RPDN/SBR HX6 .. 167 K1
  SKP/WHF BD23 .. 16 A2
  TOD OL14 .. 163 J3
  WIL/AL BD15 .. 103 K5
Brignall Garth *OSM* LS9 .. 110 B5
Brignall Wy *OSM* LS9 .. 110 B5
Brigshaw Dr *CAS* WF10 .. 135 M4
Brigshaw La *CAS* WF10 .. 135 J5
  GFTH/SHER LS25 .. 135 J6
Brimmy Croft La *UPML* OL3 .. 230 E3
Brinckman St *BSLY* S70 .. 261 H6
Brindle Park Dr *CAS* WF10 .. 158 C8
Brindley Gv *GIR* BD8 .. 103 L7
Brindley Rd *BIRK/DRI* BD11 .... 36 B6
Brindley Wy *WKFDW/WTN* WF2 .. 176 B2
Brisbane Av *ECHL* BD2 .. 105 C3
Briscoe La *GTL/HWG* HX4 .. 168 D7
Briscoe Ridge La *PBR* HG3 .... 25 J4
Bristol Av *AIRE* BD20 .... 58 D6
Bristol St *CHAL* LS7 .... 7 K6
  COL BB8 .... 52 A8
  HIPP HX3 .. 168 F5
Britannia Av *ROY/SHW* OL2 .. 229 L8
Britannia Cl *BSLY* S70 .. 261 H6
  PDSY/CALV LS28 .. 107 H4
Britannia Ct *BRAM* LS13 .. 107 J6
Britannia Rd *HOLM/MEL* HD7 .. 212 B6
  HOLM/MEL HD7 .. 212 B6
  MOR LS27 .. 152 B4
Britannia St *BGLY* BD16 .... 81 J3
  LDS LS1 .... 8 E1
  PDSY/CALV LS28 .. 107 H4
  WBOW BD5 .... 5 C8
Britannia Ter *CLECK* BD19 .. 149 M6
Britland Cl *DOD/DAR* S75 .. 260 C4
Broadacre Rd *OSS* WF5 .. 197 C1
Broad Acres *HOR/CROF* WF4 .. 198 C7
Broadbent Cft
  HOLM/MEL HD7 .. 236 C2
Broad Carr La *GTL/HWG* HX4 .. 190 E2
Broadcroft Cha
  EARD/LOFT WF3 .. 153 C7
Broadcroft Dr *EARD/LOFT* WF3 .. 153 C6
Broadcroft Gv *EARD/LOFT* WF3 .. 153 C6
Broadcroft Wy *EARD/LOFT* WF3 .. 153 C6
Broad Cut Rd *HOR/CROF* WF4 .. 197 M8
Broadfield Cl *BOW* BD4 .. 128 A5
Broadfield Pk *HOLM/MEL* HD7 .. 253 L4
Broadfield Stile *MILN* OL16 .. 206 A8
Broadfield St *MILN* OL16 .. 206 B8
Broadfolds *CLAY* BD14 .. 125 L2
Broadgate *GTL/HWG* HX4 .. 190 B4
  HUDE HD5 .. 214 F2
Broad Ga *TOD* OL14 .. 141 H8
  TOD OL14 .. 164 C5
Broadgate Av *HORS* LS18 .... 85 M5
Broadgate Crs *HORS* LS18 .... 85 L6
Broadgate Dr *HORS* LS18 .... 85 L5

Broadgate La *HORS* LS18 .... 85 L5
Broadgate Ri *HORS* LS18 .... 85 M6
Broad Gates *DOD/DAR* S75 .. 259 H6
Broadgate Wk *HORS* LS18 .... 85 L6
Broad Head La *HWTH* BD22 .... 78 A2
Broad Ings Wy *HIPP* HX3 .. 147 L1
Broadlands *KGHY* BD21 .... 2 C2
Broadlands Rd *HOLM/MEL* HD7 .. 234 F3
Broadlands St *BOW* BD4 .. 127 J2
Broadland Wy *EARD/LOFT* WF3 .. 154 E6
Broad La *BOW* BD4 .. 127 M1
  BRAM LS13 .. 107 J4
  GLE DN14 .. 161 J7
  HBR HX7 .. 120 D8
  HBR HX7 .. 143 H5
  HEM/SK/SE WF9 .. 246 C5
  HOLM/MEL HD7 .. 253 M1
  HUDE HD5 .. 15 M7
  LUD/ILL HX2 .. 166 E1
  MILN OL16 .. 228 E3
  PDSY/CALV LS28 .. 107 H4
  TAD LS24 .. 117 H1
  TOD OL14 .. 141 M4
  UPML OL3 .. 231 G7
Broad Lane Cl *BRAM* LS13 .. 108 A2
Broadlea Av *BRAM* LS13 .. 108 A2
Broadlea Cl *BRAM* LS13 .. 108 A2
  WBOW BD5 .. 127 H3
Broadlea Gdns *BRAM* LS13 .. 108 A2
Broadlea Gv *BRAM* LS13 .. 108 A2
Broadlea Hl *BRAM* LS13 .. 108 A2
Broadlea Mt *BRAM* LS13 .. 108 B3
Broadlea Pl *BRAM* LS13 .. 108 A2
Broadlea Rd *BRAM* LS13 .. 108 A2
Broadlea St *BRAM* LS13 .. 108 A2
Broadlea Ter *BRAM* LS13 .. 108 A2
Broadlea Vw *BRAM* LS13 .. 108 A2
Broadley Av *LUD/ILL* HX2 .. 145 K5
Broadley Cl *LUD/ILL* HX2 .. 145 K5
Broadley Gv *LUD/ILL* HX2 .. 145 K5
Broadmead *CAS* WF10 .. 158 B6
Broadmeadows *WKFDE* WF1 .. 176 F1
  STKB/PEN S36 .. 257 M5
Broadoaks Cl *EARL* WF12 .. 174 C7
Broad Oak St *HIPP* HX3 .. 147 M8
Broadowler La *OSS* WF5 .. 197 C1
Broad Shaw La *MILN* OL16 .. 228 F4
Broadstone Rd *KBTN* HD8 .. 256 B2
Broadstone St *TOD* OL14 .. 141 M8
Broadstone Wy *BOW* BD4 .. 128 A2
  BOW BD4 .. 128 A5
Broad St *BFD* BD1 .... 4 F5
  DEWS WF13 .. 173 J8
  HFAX HX1 .. 11 H5
  PDSY/CALV LS28 .. 106 E3
  TOD OL14 .. 141 K8
Broad Tree Rd *HIPP* HX3 .. 146 C4
Broad Vw *OSS* WF5 .. 197 H4
Broadway *BFD* BD1 .... 4 F6
  BGLY BD16 .... 81 J3
  BSLY S70 .. 260 D6
  DOD/DAR S75 .. 242 D5
  GSLY LS20 .... 61 L6
  HEM/SK/SE WF9 .. 247 C5
  HIPP HX3 .. 169 G1
  HORS LS18 .. 85 H7
  HORS LS18 .. 85 L6
  HUD HD1 .. 15 C5
  KSTL LS5 .. 86 A7
  MSTN/BAR LS15 .. 111 H8
  PONT WF8 .. 181 G7
  RPDN/SBR HX6 .. 166 F3
  WKFDW/WTN WF2 .. 197 M2
Broadway Cl *WBOW* BD5 .. 126 F4
Broad Way Ct *EARL* WF12 .. 196 A5
Broadway Dr *HORS* LS18 .... 85 K6
Broadwell Rd *OSS* WF5 .. 197 H1
Broadwood Av *LUD/ILL* HX2 .. 145 K5
Brockadale Av *PONT* WF8 .. 202 F1
Brock Bank *HUDE* HD5 .. 193 H7
Brockholes La *HOLM/MEL* HD7 .. 236 F4
  STKB/PEN S36 .. 270 C4
Brockholes Rd *HOLM/MEL* HD7 .. 236 F2
Brocklebank Rd *MILN* OL16 .. 206 F7
Brocklehurst Av *BSLY* S70 .. 261 M8
Brocklesby Dr *WIL/AL* BD15 .. 103 K5
Brockley Cl *TAD* LS24 .... 94 E8
Brocks *LUD/ILL* HX2 .. 144 E8
Brockswood Ct
  WKFDW/WTN WF2 .. 221 L1
Brockway *MILN* OL16 .. 228 E3
Brockwell Gdns *RPDN/SBR* HX6 .. 167 J3
Brock Well La *RPDN/SBR* HX6 .. 167 H4
Broc-o-bank *AWLS/ASK* DN6 .. 227 L3
Brodley Cl *HIPP* HX3 .. 147 L6
Brodrick Ct *HDGY* LS6 .. 108 F1
Broken Banks *COL* BB8 .... 74 A2
Broken Cross *HUDE* HD5 .. 215 G4
Broken Wy *WBOW* BD5 .. 126 F4
Bromcliffe Pk *BSLYN/ROY* S71 .. 262 A1
Bromet Pl *ECHL* BD2 .. 105 K2
Bromford Rd *BOW* BD4 .. 127 J2
  ROY/SHW OL2 .. 228 D8
Bromley Av *HOLM/MEL* HD7 .. 236 F7
  ROY/SHW OL2 .. 228 D8
Bromley Gv *HWTH* BD22 .... 79 G1
Bromley Mt *WKFDE* WF1 .. 13 H7
Bromley Rd *BGLY* BD16 .... 81 J3
  BTLY WF17 .. 174 A3
  HUDN HD2 .. 192 B5
  SHPY BD18 .... 82 A6
Bromley St *BTLY* WF17 .. 173 M3
Brompton Av *BOW* BD4 .. 127 J2
Brompton Gv *BEE/HOL* LS11 .. 131 K4
Brompton Mt *BEE/HOL* LS11 .. 131 K4
Brompton Rd *BOW* BD4 .. 127 J2
Brompton Rw *BEE/HOL* LS11 .. 131 K3
Brompton Ter *BEE/HOL* LS11 .. 131 K4
Bronshill Gv *WIL/AL* BD15 .. 103 L5
Bronte Av *KNOT* WF11 .. 181 K2
Bronte Cl *BSLYN/ROY* S71 .. 261 K3
  CLECK BD19 .. 150 D5
  DEWS WF13 .. 173 H4
  HTON BD9 .. 104 A4

HUDS HD4 .... 213 M3
Bronte Dr HWTH BD22 ...... 79 G3
Bronte Gv HEM/SK/SE WF9 ... 223 L8
　MIRF WF14 .... 194 E2
Bronte Old Rd CUL/QBY BD13 ... 103 C8
Bronte Pl CUL/QBY BD13 ... 103 C8
Bronte Rd BTLY WF17 ..... 151 G4
Bronte St HWTH BD22 ..... 78 D7
　KGHY BD21 .... 3 K3
Bronte Vls HWTH BD22 ..... 79 H6
Bronte Wy BRFD/BLYE BB10 ... 96 D2
　BRIG HD6 .... 170 F2
　COL BB8 .... 75 H2
　CUL/QBY BD13 ...... 103 H8
　CUL/QBY BD13 ...... 125 K6
　HIPP HX3 .... 125 K6
　HWTH BD22 .... 99 K2
　MIRF WF14 .... 194 E2
Brook Av ROY/SHW OL2 ..... 229 K6
Brook Cl OSS WF5 ..... 197 H3
Brookdale WHIT OL12 ..... 206 A3
Brookdale Av OSS WF5 .... 174 A3
Brookdale Bank HUDW HD8 ... 213 J1
Brook Dr GTL/HWG HX4 ..... 190 D2
Brooke Ct PONT WF8 ..... 202 E1
Brooke Fold HOLM/MEL HD7 ... 236 B1
Brooke St BRIG HD6 ..... 170 C5
　CLECK BD19 .... 150 A7
　HECK WF16 .... 172 F3
Brookeville Av HIPP HX3 .... 147 L7
Brook Fld MIRF WF14 ..... 194 B4
Brookfield KBTN HD8 ..... 215 M8
　ROY/SHW OL2 .... 229 J3
Brookfield Av BRAM LS13 .... 84 F8
　CAS WF10 .... 158 B7
　CLECK BD19 .... 149 M5
　RHAY LS8 .... 110 B2
　SHPY BD18 .... 82 F6
Brookfield Ct NORM WF6 .... 178 E4
Brookfield Dr FEA/AMT WF7 ... 202 E6
　LIT OL15 .... 185 G8
Brookfield Gdns BRAM LS13 ... 84 F8
　HDGY LS6 .... 87 G3
　SHPY BD18 .... 82 F6
Brookfields HOR/CROF WF4 ... 218 F1
Brookfields Av CLECK BD19 ... 149 G6
Brookfields Rd LM/WK BD12 ... 148 F5
Brookfield St MID LS10 ..... 9 K5
　TOD OL14 .... 140 E5
Brookfield Ter CLECK BD19 ... 149 M5
　MID LS10 .... 9 K5
Brookfield Vw CLECK BD19 ... 150 A5
Brookfoot Av BIRK/DRI BD11 ... 150 C1
Brook Gdns HOLM/MEL HD7 ... 234 F3
Brook Hey Cl WHIT OL12 ..... 206 F2
Brookhill Av AL/HA/HU LS17 ... 88 A2
Brookhill Cl AL/HA/HU LS17 ... 88 A2
Brookhill Crs AL/HA/HU LS17 ... 88 A2
Brookhill Dr AL/HA/HU LS17 ... 88 A2
Brook Hill La STKB/PEN S36 ... 268 B3
Brookhill Rd DOD/DAR S75 ... 241 K6
Brookhouse Gdns IDLE BD10 ... 84 B6
Brook House La STKB/PEN S36 ... 269 H1
Brooklands HUDN HD3 ..... 193 J2
Brooklands Av GTL/HWG HX4 ... 190 D2
　SCFT LS14 .... 111 H2
　WKFDW/WTN WF2 ...... 199 K7
Brooklands Cl SCFT LS14 ... 111 G2
Brooklands Cl OSS WF5 .... 197 H2
　SCFT LS14 .... 111 H2
Brooklands Crs HOR/CROF WF4 ... 222 F1
　SCFT LS14 .... 111 G2
　YEA LS19 .... 62 D8
Brooklands Dr SCFT LS14 ... 111 G2
　YEA LS19 .... 62 D8
Brooklands Garth SCFT LS14 ... 111 G2
Brooklands La ILK LS29 ..... 61 J1
　SCFT LS14 .... 111 H2
Brooklands Rd AWLS/ASK DN6 ... 249 L1
　WKFDW/WTN WF2 ...... 199 K7
Brooklands Ter SKP/WHF BD23 ... 16 B3
Brookland Vw SCFT LS14 .... 111 H2
Brooklands Vw ILK LS29 ..... 61 K1
Brooklands Wy ILK LS29 ..... 61 J1
Brook La AL/HA/HU LS17 ..... 44 B3
　HOLM/MEL HD7 .... 212 F2
　LVSG WF15 .... 171 L2
　MILN OL16 .... 228 D3
Brooklyn Av HUDE HD5 ..... 193 H8
　LIT OL15 .... 185 J7
　MILN OL16 .... 206 E7
　WOR/ARM LS12 .... 108 E7
Brooklyn Ct CLECK BD19 .... 149 M6
Brooklyn Dr CLECK BD19 .... 149 M6
Brooklyn Pl WOR/ARM LS12 ... 108 E7
Brooklyn Rd CLECK BD19 .... 150 A6
Brooklyn St AIRE BD20 ..... 57 J3
　WOR/ARM LS12 .... 108 E7
Brooklyn Ter BRIG HD6 ..... 170 A1
　WOR/ARM LS12 .... 108 E6
Brook Rd DEWS WF13 ..... 173 K7
Brookroyd Av BRIG HD6 .... 148 D8
Brookroyd Gdns BTLY WF17 ... 151 H6
Brookroyd La BTLY WF17 .... 151 H6
Brooksbank WKFDW/WTN WF2 ... 12 C2
Brooksbank Av GTHN BD7 .... 126 A1
Brooksbank Dr
　MSTN/BAR LS15 .... 111 J6
Brooksbank Gdns ELL HX5 ... 169 H7
Brooksfield HEM/SK/SE WF9 ... 246 F2
Brook Side HOLM/MEL HD7 ... 212 C4
Brookside AL/HA/HU LS17 ... 88 A1
　HBR HX7 .... 143 G2
　HEM/SK/SE WF9 .... 224 A7
　WBY LS22 .... 47 K6
Brookside Dr BSLY S70 ..... 261 M8
Brookside Fold HWTH BD22 ... 79 C1
Brookside St HEM/SK/SE WF9 ... 247 H3
Brook's Pl WHIT OL12 ..... 206 A6
Brooks Ter CUL/QBY BD13 ... 125 K4
Brook St CAS WF10 ..... 158 E3
　DEWS WF13 .... 173 H6
　ELL HX5 .... 169 J8

　HBR HX7 .... 143 J2
　HUD HD1 .... 14 F5
　HUD HD1 .... 214 A2
　HUDE HD5 .... 15 L7
　ILK LS29 .... 38 D2
　KGHY BD21 .... 2 F8
　LIT OL15 .... 207 L1
　LM/WK BD12 .... 149 K2
　NORM WF6 .... 178 B3
　OSS WF5 .... 196 F1
　SKP/WHF BD23 .... 16 B2
　WHIT OL12 .... 184 E8
　WKFDE WF1 .... 13 H1
Brooks Yd DEWS WF13 .... 173 K7
　HUD HD1 .... 14 F7
　HUDN HD2 .... 171 J8
The Brook HBR HX7 .... 143 H6
　LIT OL15 .... 185 L5
Brookvale BSLYN/ROY S71 ... 261 M3
Brookway FEA/AMT WF7 ... 201 M1
Broombank HUDN HD2 ..... 191 M4
　KBTN HD8 .... 257 J1
Broom Cl BSLY S70 ..... 261 M8
　DOD/DAR S75 .... 242 C3
Broom Crs MID LS10 .... 132 A7
Broomcroft CLAY BD14 .... 125 L2
Broomcroft Rd OSS WF5 ... 196 F2
Broome Av ECHL BD2 .... 105 G3
Broome Cl NORM WF6 .... 178 C2
Broomer St DEWS WF13 ... 173 G8
Broomfield BHP/TINH LS16 ... 86 D2
　CLAY BD14 .... 125 J3
　GTL/HWG HX4 .... 168 D3
Broomfield Av HIPP HX3 ... 168 D3
Broomfield Cl BSLY S70 .... 260 D6
　KBTN HD8 .... 217 L7
Broomfield Crs HDGY LS6 ... 108 F2
　HDGY LS6 .... 108 F3
　KGHY BD21 .... 2 F4
Broomfield Pl CLAY BD14 ... 125 J3
　HDGY LS6 .... 108 F3
　HUD HD1 .... 191 M8
　HUDN HD2 .... 192 C1
　KGHY BD21 .... 2 F3
Broomfield Rd HDGY LS6 ... 108 F3
　HUD HD1 .... 191 M8
　HUDN HD2 .... 192 C1
　KGHY BD21 .... 2 F3
Broomfield Sq ROCH OL11 ... 228 B1
Broomfield St CUL/QBY BD13 ... 125 G5
　HDGY LS6 .... 108 F3
　KGHY BD21 .... 2 F4
Broomfield Ter CLECK BD19 ... 149 K8
　HDGY LS6 .... 108 F3
　HUD HD1 .... 191 M7
　MILN OL16 .... 229 K2
Broomfield Vw HDGY LS6 ... 108 F3
Broom Gdns MID LS10 .... 132 A7
Broom Garth MID LS10 .... 132 B7
Broom Gv MID LS10 ..... 132 B8
Broom Hall Av WKFDE WF1 ... 176 C4
Broom Hall Crs WKFDE WF1 ... 176 C4
Broomhead Ct DOD/DAR S75 ... 242 D6
Broomhey Av KBTN HD8 ... 217 M8
Broomhill CAS WF10 ..... 158 C4
Broomhill Av AL/HA/HU LS17 ... 87 M4
　KGHY BD21 .... 2 D9
　KGHY BD21 .... 79 J2
　KNOT WF11 .... 182 D3
Broomhill Cl HOLM/MEL HD7 ... 254 F3
　KNOT WF11 .... 182 D3
Broomhill Crs AL/HA/HU LS17 ... 87 M4
　KGHY BD21 .... 2 D9
　KNOT WF11 .... 182 D3
Broomhill Dr AL/HA/HU LS17 ... 87 L5
　KGHY BD21 .... 2 D9
　KNOT WF11 .... 182 D3
Broomhill Gv KGHY BD21 ... 2 D9
　KNOT WF11 .... 182 D3
Broomhill Mt KGHY BD21 ... 2 D9
Broomhill Pl KNOT WF11 ... 182 D3
Broom Hill Rd GTL/HWG HX4 ... 190 A6
Broomhill Sq KGHY BD21 ... 2 D9
Broomhill St KGHY BD21 ... 79 J2
Broomhill Wk KGHY BD21 ... 2 D9
　KNOT WF11 .... 182 D3
Broomhill Wy KGHY BD21 ... 2 D9
Broomhouse Cl KBTN HD8 ... 257 J1
Broom Nook MID LS10 .... 132 A7
Broom Pl MID LS10 ..... 132 A7
Broom Rd MID LS10 ..... 132 A7
　TAD LS24 .... 71 K4
Broomroyd HUDW HD3 ..... 191 M8
Broomsdale Rd BTLY WF17 ... 174 A1
Broom St BOW BD4 ..... 5 C8
　CLECK BD19 .... 149 K8
　KGHY BD21 .... 3 H1
　MILN OL16 .... 229 K2
Broom Ter MID LS10 .... 132 B7
Broom Vw MID LS10 .... 132 B7
Broomy Lea La HOLM/MEL HD7 ... 236 B7
Broster Av HWTH BD22 ... 2 B4
Brotherton Av WKFDE WF1 ... 13 J1
Brougham Rd HIPP HX3 ... 10 F1
　HOLM/MEL HD7 .... 233 H2
Brougham St HIPP HX3 ... 11 G1
　SKP/WHF BD23 .... 16 C3
Broughton Av BOW BD4 ... 127 K5
　OSS WF5 .... 110 C4
Broughton Rd HUDS HD4 ... 213 K3
　SKP/WHF BD23 .... 16 B2
Broughton Ter PDSY/CALV LS28 ... 107 C6
Brow Bottom La LUD/ILL HX2 ... 124 B8
Browcliff AIRE BD20 ..... 36 A4
Brow Cl BSLY S70 ..... 261 M8
Browfield Vw HWTH BD22 ... 79 C1
Browfoot SHPY BD18 .... 82 F7
Browfoot Dr LUD/ILL HX2 ... 145 K7
Brow Foot Gate La LUD/ILL HX2 ... 145 M8
Browgate BAIL BD17 .... 82 E5
Brow Grains Rd
　HOLM/MEL HD7 .... 234 C5
Brow La CLAY BD14 ..... 125 J3
　HIPP HX3 .... 125 M8
　HIPP HX3 .... 147 G3
　HOLM/MEL HD7 .... 254 A3
　KBTN HD8 .... 239 M8
　LUD/ILL HX2 .... 124 C8
Brown Av BEE/HOL LS11 ... 131 G2
Brown Bank La AIRE BD20 ... 36 B3
Brown Bank Rd LIT OL15 ... 207 H3

Brownberrie Av HORS LS18 ... 85 L3
Brownberrie Crs HORS LS18 ... 85 K3
Brownberrie Dr HORS LS18 ... 85 L3
Brownberrie Gdns HORS LS18 ... 85 K3
Brownberrie La HORS LS18 ... 85 J3
Brownberrie Wk HORS LS18 ... 85 J3
Brownberry Gv HIPP HX3 ... 125 M7
Brown Birks St TOD OL14 ... 140 C5
Brown Hill Av OSM LS9 ... 110 C4
Brown Hill Cl BIRK/DRI BD11 ... 128 C8
Brownhill Cl BTLY WF17 ... 151 H5
Brown Hill Crs HEM/SK/SE WF9 ... 223 J4
Brown Hill Crs OSM LS9 ... 110 C5
Brown Hill Dr BIRK/DRI BD11 ... 128 C8
Brownhill Garth BTLY WF17 ... 151 H5
Brown Hill La COL BB8 ... 52 B7
　HBR HX7 .... 142 A2
Brown Hill La HOLM/MEL HD7 ... 253 K5
Brownhill Rd BTLY WF17 ... 151 H5
　OSM LS9 .... 110 C4
Browning Av HIPP HX3 ... 168 F2
Browning Cl BSLYN/ROY S71 ... 261 K1
Browning Rd HUDN HD2 ... 192 F3
Browning St BFDE BD3 ... 5 L6
Brown La East BEE/HOL LS11 ... 8 A4
Brown La West WOR/ARM LS12 ... 131 J5
Brown Lee La WIL/AL BD15 ... 102 C2
Brown Lodge St LIT OL15 ... 207 H3
Brown Pl BEE/HOL LS11 ... 131 G2
Brown Rd BEE/HOL LS11 ... 131 G2
Brownroyd Av BSLYN/ROY S71 ... 243 L4
Brownroyd Hill Rd WBSY BD6 ... 126 D5
Brownroyd Rd HOLM/MEL HD7 ... 236 A2
Brownroyd St GIR BD8 ... 104 D7
　GTHN BD7 .... 104 D8
Brownroyd Wk WBSY BD6 ... 126 D4
Browns Ct AIRE BD20 ... 34 E1
Brown's Edge La
　STKB/PEN S36 .... 269 L3
Brown's Edge Rd
　STKB/PEN S36 .... 256 A6
Brownside Cl MILN OL16 ... 206 F3
Brown's Knoll Rd HUDS HD4 ... 237 H3
Brown's Pl BTLY WF17 ... 173 K2
Brown St BTLY WF17 ... 173 K2
Brown St KGHY BD21 ... 3 J6
　LIT OL15 .... 207 J1
　MIRF WF14 .... 194 B1
Brow Rd HWTH BD22 ... 78 E8
Browroyd Rd ILK LS29 ... 18 F6
Browsholme St KGHY BD21 ... 2 F7
Brow St KGHY BD21 ... 3 J6
　ROCH OL11 .... 228 C2
Brow Top Rd HWTH BD22 ... 79 G7
Brow Wood Crs ECHL BD2 ... 105 G3
Brow Wood Ri HIPP HX3 ... 125 M8
Brow Wood Rd HWTH BD22 ... 79 G7
Browwood Ter WBSY BD6 ... 126 D7
Broe Av BSLY S70 ..... 261 H8
Bruce Gdns WOR/ARM LS12 ... 109 J7
Bruce Lawn WOR/ARM LS12 ... 109 G7
Bruce St HFAX HX1 ..... 10 B8
Brudenell Gv HDGY LS6 ... 6 A3
Brudenell Mt HDGY LS6 ... 6 A3
Brudenell Rd HDGY LS6 ... 109 G3
Brudenell St HDGY LS6 ... 6 A3
Brudenell Vw HDGY LS6 ... 6 A3
Brunel Cl HTON BD9 ..... 104 C4
Brunel Rd WKFDW/WTN WF2 ... 176 B1
Brunswick HOR/CROF WF4 ... 222 D4
Brunswick Cl BSLYN/ROY S71 ... 243 H8
Brunswick Ct LDSU LS2 ... 7 J7
Brunswick Dr DEWS WF13 ... 173 J5
Brunswick
　GFTH/SHER LS25 ...... 113 H7
Brunswick Gv WKFDE WF1 ... 13 H1
Brunswick Pl IDLE BD10 ... 83 M7
Brunswick Rd IDLE BD10 ... 83 M7
　PDSY/CALV LS28 ...... 107 G6
Brunswick Rw LDSU LS2 ... 7 J7
Brunswick St BGLY BD16 ... 81 K3
　BTLY WF17 .... 173 L1
　CUL/QBY BD13 .... 80 A8
　CUL/QBY BD13 .... 125 H5
　DEWS WF13 .... 173 J5
　HBR HX7 .... 143 H3
　HECK WF16 .... 172 F3
　HUD HD1 .... 14 E6
　MILN OL16 .... 206 C6
　MOR LS27 .... 152 C1
　ROY/SHW OL2 .... 229 K7
　WKFDE WF1 .... 13 G4
Brunswick Ter LDSU LS2 ... 7 G7
Bruntcliffe Av MOR LS27 ... 152 A1
Bruntcliffe Cl MOR LS27 ... 152 B2
Bruntcliffe Dr MOR LS27 ... 152 A2
Bruntcliffe La MOR LS27 ... 152 A2
Bruntcliffe Rd MOR LS27 ... 151 M2
Bruntcliffe Wy MOR LS27 ... 152 A2
Brunthwaite Br AIRE BD20 ... 36 C7
Brunthwaite Bridge La
　AIRE BD20 .... 36 B7
Brunthwaite La AIRE BD20 ... 36 C5
Brussels St OSM LS9 ... 9 K1
Bryan Cl CAS WF10 .... 110 C4
Bryan Rd GTL/HWG HX4 ... 168 F8
　HUDW HD3 .... 191 H6
Bryanstone Rd BOW BD4 ... 127 M1
Bryan St BRIG HD6 ..... 170 C5
　PDSY/CALV LS28 ...... 106 F2
Bryan St North PDSY/CALV LS28 ... 106 F2
Bryan Ter HUDW HD3 ... 191 H3
Bryer St DEWS WF13 ... 173 L5
Bryngate RTHW LS26 ... 133 L8
Bryony Ct EARD/LOFT WF3 ... 164 A4
Buckden Cl AIRE BD20 ... 36 A4
Buckden Rd BSLY S70 ... 260 F4
　HUDN HD3 .... 191 H6
Buckfast Ct IDLE BD10 ... 83 K7
Buckingham Av HDGY LS6 ... 109 G3
Buckingham Dr HDGY LS6 ... 109 G2
　WKFDE WF1 .... 13 L8
Buckingham Gv HDGY LS6 ... 109 G2
Buckingham Mt HDGY LS6 ... 109 G3
Buckingham Park Cl
　ROY/SHW OL2 .... 229 K6

Buckingham Rd HDGY LS6 ... 109 G3
Buckingham St MILN OL16 ... 206 C6
Buckingham Wy
　BSLYN/ROY S71 ...... 243 K2
　KNOT WF11 .... 159 M7
Buckland Pl HFAX HX1 ... 146 A8
Buck La BAIL BD17 ..... 83 H3
Buckle La ILK LS29 ..... 61 L2
　NORM WF6 .... 178 C5
Buckley Brook St WHIT OL12 ... 206 D4
Buckley Cha MILN OL16 ... 229 G1
Buckley Ct BSLY S70 ... 261 H6
Buckley Farm La WHIT OL12 ... 206 D3
Buckley Hill La MILN OL16 ... 229 G1
Buckley La LUD/ILL HX2 ... 145 L4
　WHIT OL12 .... 206 D3
Buckley Rd WHIT OL12 ... 206 D4
Buckley St MILN OL16 ... 206 C6
　ROY/SHW OL2 .... 229 L7
Buckley Vw TOD OL14 ... 141 J8
　WHIT OL12 .... 206 D3
Buckley Wood Bottom
　TOD OL14 .... 163 K1
Buck Mill La IDLE BD10 ... 83 J3
Buckrose St HUD HD1 ... 14 F1
Buck Stone Av AL/HA/HU LS17 ... 87 H2
Buck Stone Crs AL/HA/HU LS17 ... 87 H2
Buckstone Dr YEA LS19 ... 84 C3
Buck Stone Gdns AL/HA/HU LS17 ... 87 H2
Buck Stone Gn AL/HA/HU LS17 ... 87 H2
Buck Stone Gv AL/HA/HU LS17 ... 87 H2
Buck Stone La HWTH BD22 ... 55 G4
Buck Stone Mt AL/HA/HU LS17 ... 87 H2
Buck Stone Oval AL/HA/HU LS17 ... 87 H2
Buck Stone Ri AL/HA/HU LS17 ... 87 H2
Buckstones Rd OLD OL1 ... 230 A8
　ROY/SHW OL2 .... 229 L5
Buck Stone Rd AL/HA/HU LS17 ... 87 H2
Buck Stone Vw AL/HA/HU LS17 ... 87 H2
Buck Stone Wy AL/HA/HU LS17 ... 87 H2
Buck St BFDE BD3 ..... 5 K8
　COL BB8 .... 74 A1
　CUL/QBY BD13 .... 102 A6
Buckthorne Cl
　EARD/LOFT WF3 ...... 153 M6
Buckthorne Ct
　EARD/LOFT WF3 ...... 153 M6
Buckthorne Dr
　EARD/LOFT WF3 ...... 153 M6
Buckthorne Fold
　EARD/LOFT WF3 ...... 153 M6
Buckton Cl BEE/HOL LS11 ... 8 C8
Buckton Mt BEE/HOL LS11 ... 8 C8
Buckton Vw BEE/HOL LS11 ... 8 C8
Bude Cl BSLYN/ROY S71 ... 261 L3
Bude Rd BEE/HOL LS11 ... 131 K4
　WBOW BD5 .... 127 H5
Buersil Av MILN OL16 ... 228 D2
Buersil St MILN OL16 ... 228 D3
Bula Cl GFTH/SHER LS25 ... 135 K4
Bulay Rd HUD HD1 ..... 214 B2
Bullace Trees La LVSG WF15 ... 171 M3
Bull Close La HFAX HX1 ... 10 F3
Bullcroft Cl AWLS/ASK DN6 ... 249 L5
Bullenshaw Rd
　HEM/SK/SE WF9 ...... 223 M8
Buller Cl OSM LS9 ..... 110 D5
Buller Ct OSM LS9 ..... 110 E5
Buller Gv OSM LS9 ..... 110 D5
Buller St BOW BD4 ..... 127 L1
　RTHW LS26 .... 133 L8
Bullerthorpe La RTHW LS26 ... 154 A6
Bullfields Cl EARL WF12 ... 196 A4
Bull Gn HFAX HX1 ..... 11 G7
Bull Green Rd HUDW HD3 ... 191 G7
Bull Haw La DOD/DAR S75 ... 259 H6
Bullhouse La STKB/PEN S36 ... 269 L4
Bull La HEM/SK/SE WF9 ... 246 E4
　HOR/CROF WF4 .... 220 B1
Bullough La RTHW LS26 ... 133 H7
Bull Ring WKFDE WF1 ... 12 E2
Bull Royd Av GIR BD8 ... 104 A6
Bull Royd Crs GIR BD8 ... 104 A6
Bull Royd Dr GIR BD8 ... 104 A6
Bull Royd La GIR BD8 ... 104 A6
Bullstyle Rd PONT WF8 ... 180 E8
Bullytree La GFTH/SHER LS25 ... 137 L2
Bulwer St MILN OL16 ... 206 C6
Bungalow Rd AIRE BD20 ... 34 D8
The Bungalows KBTN HD8 ... 240 A4
Bunkers Hl GFTH/SHER LS25 ... 114 A1
　HOLM/MEL HD7 .... 254 C1
　SKP/WHF BD23 .... 16 C2
　WKFDW/WTN WF2 ...... 176 B4
Bunker's Hill La HWTH BD22 ... 78 F1
Bunkers La BTLY WF17 ... 173 H2
Bunny Pk HUDS HD4 ... 213 M3
Bunyan St WHIT OL12 ... 206 B5
Burbeary Rd HUDS HD4 ... 214 A3
Burberry Cl BOW BD4 ... 127 L6
Burchall Fld MILN OL16 ... 206 D7
Burchett Gv HDGY LS6 ... 6 D1
Burchett Pl HDGY LS6 ... 6 D1
Burchett Ter HDGY LS6 ... 6 D1
Burcote Dr HUDW HD3 ... 190 D5
Burdale Pl GTHN BD7 ... 104 D8
Burdett Ter BULY LS4 ... 108 E4
Burdock Wy HFAX HX1 ... 10 E5
Burfitts Rd HUDW HD3 ... 191 K7
Burgh Mill La DEWS WF13 ... 173 J7
Burghwallis La AWLS/ASK DN6 ... 249 L1
Burghwallis Rd AWLS/ASK DN6 ... 227 L7
Burkill St WKFDE WF1 ... 198 F4
Burking Rd DEWS WF13 ... 173 K6
Burlees La HBR HX7 ... 143 L3
Burleigh Ct BSLY S70 ... 261 H5
Burleigh St BSLY S70 ... 261 H5
　HFAX HX1 .... 10 B9
Burley Bank La HOLM/MEL HD7 ... 253 C8
Burley Cl GFTH/SHER LS25 ... 138 B2
Burley Ct AIRE BD20 ... 56 E1
Burley Hill Crs BULY LS4 ... 108 D3
Burley Hill Dr BULY LS4 ... 108 D3
Burley Hill La HORS LS18 ... 85 K7
　ILK LS29 .... 61 H1

Burley Lodge Pl HDGY LS6 ... 109 C5
Burley Lodge Rd HDGY LS6 ... 109 G4
Burley Lodge Ter HDGY LS6 ... 109 G4
Burley Ms AIRE BD20 ... 56 E1
Burley Rd BULY LS4 ... 108 E3
　BVRD LS3 .... 6 A7
　ILK LS29 .... 40 C8
Burley St BVRD LS3 ... 6 B8
　ECHL BD2 .... 104 F2
　ELL HX5 .... 169 H8
Burley Wk BTLY WF17 ... 173 K1
Burley Wood Crs BULY LS4 ... 108 D4
Burley Wood La BULY LS4 ... 108 E3
Burley Wood Mt BULY LS4 ... 108 E3
Burley Wood Vw BULY LS4 ... 108 E3
Burlington Ar BSLY S70 ... 261 H5
Burlington Av BRFD BD3 ... 106 A5
Burlington Pl BEE/HOL LS11 ... 131 K4
Burlington Rd BEE/HOL LS11 ... 131 K4
Burlington St GIR BD8 ... 4 D2
　HFAX HX1 .... 10 B5
　ROCH OL11 .... 228 C3
Burmantofts St LDSU LS9 ... 7 L8
Burn Bridge La PBR HG3 ... 26 C3
Burn Bridge Ov PBR HG3 ... 26 D2
Burn Bridge Rd PBR HG3 ... 26 D2
Burned Gv HIPP HX3 ... 125 L7
Burned Rd HIPP HX3 ... 125 M7
Burneston Gdns WBSY BD6 ... 126 A6
Burnet Cl MILN OL16 ... 228 E2
Burnett Av WBOW BD5 ... 126 F3
Burnett Pl WBOW BD5 ... 126 F3
Burnett Ri CUL/QBY BD13 ... 124 E6
Burnett St BFD BD1 ... 5 H6
Burnham Av BOW BD4 ... 127 K5
　DOD/DAR S75 .... 242 D5
Burnham Ct WBY LS22 ... 29 L8
Burnham Rd GFTH/SHER LS25 ... 135 H1
Burniston Cl WIL/AL BD15 ... 102 E2
Burniston Dr HUDW HD3 ... 191 J6
Burnlee Rd HOLM/MEL HD7 ... 254 A2
Burnley Rd COL BB8 ... 74 D5
　HBR HX7 .... 143 K4
　RPDN/SBR HX6 .... 167 K1
　TOD OL14 .... 140 C5
Burnleys Ct RTHW LS26 ... 156 F5
Burnleys Dr RTHW LS26 ... 156 F5
Burnleys Ms RTHW LS26 ... 156 F6
Burnleys Vw RTHW LS26 ... 156 F5
Burnleyville CLECK BD19 ... 150 D5
Burnley Wy BRFD/BLYE BB10 ... 118 A7
　HBR HX7 .... 118 F1
　TOD OL14 .... 140 D1
Burns Av HEM/SK/SE WF9 ... 246 B5
Burns Ct BTLY WF17 ... 150 F4
Burnsdale WIL/AL BD15 ... 103 J3
Burnshaw Ms EARD/LOFT WF3 ... 153 L3
Burns Hl ILK LS29 ..... 19 G6
Burnside Av SKP/WHF BD23 ... 16 B4
Burnside Cl BTLY WF17 ... 151 J5
Burnside Crs SKP/WHF BD23 ... 16 B4
Burnside Dr HOLM/MEL HD7 ... 254 A2
Burnside Rd MILN OL16 ... 206 E8
Burns St LUD/ILL HX2 ... 146 C2
Burns Wy BSPA/BRAM LS23 ... 48 F3
Burnt Acres La TOD OL14 ... 142 D6
Burnt Edge La HBR HX7 ... 141 M2
Burnt House Cl TOD OL14 ... 141 J8
Burnt Plats La HOLM/MEL HD7 ... 211 J4
Burnt Side Rd WOR/ARM LS12 ... 129 L4
Burntwood Av HEM/SK/SE WF9 ... 246 E4
Burntwood Bank
　HEM/SK/SE WF9 ...... 245 M1
Burnt Wood Crs
　HEM/SK/SE WF9 ...... 246 E5
Burntwood Dr HEM/SK/SE WF9 ... 246 E4
Burntwood Gv
　HEM/SK/SE WF9 ...... 246 E5
Burnt Wood La CUD/GR S72 ... 246 A5
Burntwood Rd CUD/GR S72 ... 245 K8
Burnup Gv CLECK BD19 ... 149 L2
Burnwells Av IDLE BD10 ... 83 J4
Burrage St BGLY BD16 ... 81 H3
Burras Av OT LS21 ..... 41 H7
Burras Dr OT LS21 ..... 41 H7
Burras La OT LS21 ..... 41 H7
Burras Rd BOW BD4 ... 127 K4
Burrel Cl WBY LS22 ... 48 C1
Burrell St WKFDE WF1 ... 13 H3
The Burrows BTLY WF17 ... 151 H7
Burrow St WBOW BD5 ... 4 E8
Burr Tree Dr MSTN/BAR LS15 ... 111 M7
Burr Tree Garth
　MSTN/BAR LS15 ...... 111 M7
Burr Tree V MSTN/BAR LS15 ... 111 M7
Burrwood Wy GTL/HWG HX4 ... 190 D1
Burton Acres La KBTN HD8 ... 216 A6
Burton Acres Ms KBTN HD8 ... 216 A6
Burton Acres Wy KBTN HD8 ... 216 A7
Burton Av BEE/HOL LS11 ... 9 G9
　BSLYN/ROY S71 ...... 261 M2
Burton Bank Rd
　BSLYN/ROY S71 ...... 261 J3
Burton Common La
　GFTH/SHER LS25 ...... 160 C2
Burton Crs BSLYN/ROY S71 ... 262 A1
　HDGY LS6 .... 86 F3
Burton Ms AL/HA/HU LS17 ... 87 M1
Burton Rd BEE/HOL LS11 ... 9 G9
　BSLYN/ROY S71 ...... 261 L3
Burton Rw BEE/HOL LS11 ... 9 H8
Burton Royd La KBTN HD8 ... 216 D7
Burton St BEE/HOL LS11 ... 9 G8
　BOW BD4 .... 127 J2
　BSLYN/ROY S71 ...... 261 G3
　HEM/SK/SE WF9 ...... 247 G3

KGHY BD21 .... 57 K5
LUD/ILL HX2 .... 146 C1
PDSY/CALV LS28 .... 106 F3
WKFDE WF1 .... 12 D1
Burton Ter *BEE/HOL* LS11 .... 131 L3 7
Burton Wy *OSM* LS9 .... 110 C5
Burwood Rd *HUDW* HD3 .... 191 K6
Busely Ct *MOR* LS27 .... 152 B1 1
Busfield St *BGLY* BD16 .... 81 H3
BOW BD4 .... 127 K3
Bushill Fold *CUL/QBY* BD13 .... 124 E4 1
Bush St *HEM/SK/SE* WF9 .... 224 A8 2
Busker La *KBTN* HD8 .... 239 M5
Busk La *TAD* LS24 .... 95 G7
Buslingthorpe Gn *CHAL* LS7 .... 7 G2
Buslingthorpe La *CHAL* LS7 .... 7 H2
Bussey Ct *HDGY* LS6 .... 6 D2
Busy La *SHPY* BD18 .... 83 G5
Butcher Hl *BHP/TINH* LS16 .... 86 B6
Butcher Hill Station Rd
HEM/SK/SE WF9 .... 224 A6
Butcher La *RTHW* LS26 .... 155 G1
Butcher St *BEE/HOL* LS11 .... 8 E3
BFD BD1 .... 4 C7
Bute Av *BRIG* HD6 .... 170 C1
Bute St *SHPY* BD18 .... 104 F2 1
Butler La *BAIL* BD17 .... 82 F2
Butler St East *BFDE* BD3 .... 5 K4
Butler St West *BFDE* BD3 .... 5 J4
Butterbowl Dr *WOR/ARM* LS12 .... 130 A1
Butterbowl Gdns
WOR/ARM LS12 .... 130 B1
Butterbowl Garth
WOR/ARM LS12 .... 130 A1
Butterbowl Gv *WOR/ARM* LS12 .. 130 A1
Butterbowl Lawn
WOR/ARM LS12 .... 130 A1 1
Butterbowl Mt *WOR/ARM* LS12 .. 130 B1
Butterbowl Rd *WOR/ARM* LS12 .. 130 B1
Buttercross *AWLS/ASK* DN6 .... 249 J5 1
Buttercross Cl *AWLS/ASK* DN6 .... 249 J4 1
Buttercross Dr *CUD/GR* S72 .... 263 L6
Buttercup Cl *HEM/SK/SE* WF9 .... 225 H7 1
Butterfield St *OSM* LS9 .... 110 B7 8
Butterley Dr *BSLY* S70 .... 261 M8 2
Butterley La *HOLM/MEL* HD7 .... 255 H5
Butterleys *DOD/DAR* S75 .... 260 C7
Butterley St *MID* LS10 .... 9 H5
Buttermeade Cl *WBSY* BD6 .... 126 C7 3
Buttermere Av *COL* BB8 .... 52 B8 1
WBY LS22 .... 29 L8
Buttermere Cl *AWLS/ASK* DN6 .... 249 K5
Buttermere Cft
WKFDW/WTN WF2 .... 199 J8 2
Buttermere Dr *HUDE* HD5 .... 15 L6
Buttermere Gv *ROY/SHW* OL2 .... 228 F7 1
Buttermere Wy
BSLYN/ROY S71 .... 262 D6 1
Butternab Rdg *HUDS* HD4 .... 213 M6
Butternab Rd *HUDS* HD4 .... 213 M7
Buttershaw Dr *WBSY* BD6 .... 126 A5
Buttershaw La *LVSG* WF15 .... 171 K1 1
WBSY BD6 .... 126 D7
Butterton Cl *DOD/DAR* S75 .... 242 E5 1
Butterwick Gdns *WBY* LS22 .... 47 L1
Butterwood Cl *HUDS* HD4 .... 213 M6 1
Butterworth End La
RPDN/SBR HX6 .... 167 J7
Butterworth Hall *MILN* OL16 .... 229 J1 1
Butterworth Hl *HUDW* HD3 .... 190 C7
Butterworth La *RPDN/SBR* HX6 .. 167 G5
Butterworth St *LIT* OL15 .... 207 J1 2
Butt Hedge *RYKW* YO26 .... 33 J4
Butt Hl *GFTH/SHER* LS25 .... 135 J5
Buttholme Ga *WBSY* BD6 .... 126 B6
Butt La *HOLM/MEL* HD7 .... 255 G4
HWTH BD22 .... 78 E7
IDLE BD10 .... 83 K6
WOR/ARM LS12 .... 107 M8
Button Hole *ROY/SHW* OL2 .... 229 M7
Button Pk *PONT* WF8 .... 180 E7
Buttress La *LUD/ILL* HX2 .... 145 G5
The Butts Av *MILN* OL16 .... 206 B7 2
Butts Bottom *HBR* HX7 .... 143 J5
Butts Cl *HUDS* HD4 .... 237 G1
Butts Ct *LDS* LS1 .... 6 F9
Butts Garth *SCFT* LS14 .... 90 B1
Butts Green La *LUD/ILL* HX2 .... 145 H7
Butts Green Rd *LUD/ILL* HX2 .... 145 H7
Butts Hl *CLECK* BD19 .... 150 C6
Butts La *GFTH/SHER* LS25 .... 137 L6
HOR/CROF WF4 .... 196 D7
TOD OL14 .... 141 M5
Butts Mt *WOR/ARM* LS12 .... 108 F7
Butts Rd *HUDS* HD4 .... 215 G8
The Butts *PONT* WF8 .... 180 F5 1
Butts Wy *HUDS* HD4 .... 215 G8
Butts Yd *CLECK* BD19 .... 149 M7 2
Buxton Av *HTON* BD9 .... 104 E2 2
Buxton Crs *MILN* OL16 .... 228 D2
Buxton La *HTON* BD9 .... 104 E2 3
Buxton Pl *WKFDE* WF1 .... 176 D6
Buxton Rd *BSLYN/ROY* S71 .... 243 J7
Buxton St *HIPP* HX3 .... 10 C1 1
HTON BD9 .... 104 D4
KGHY BD21 .... 3 J4
Buxton Wy *HIPP* HX3 .... 146 B3 2
Byeway *GSLY* LS20 .... 61 L5
Byland *LUD/ILL* HX2 .... 123 M8
Byland Cl *BSPA/BRAM* LS23 .... 48 E7
Byland Gv *WIL/AL* BD15 .... 103 H4
Byland Wy *BSLYN/ROY* S71 .... 261 L4
Byram Park Av *KNOT* WF11 .... 160 A6
Byram Park Rd *KNOT* WF11 .... 160 A6
Byram St *HUD* HD1 .... 14 F6
Byrl St *KGHY* BD21 .... 3 H2
Byrne Cl *DOD/DAR* S75 .... 260 A2
Byron Av *AWLS/ASK* DN6 .... 227 L5 1
RPDN/SBR HX6 .... 167 K1 3
Byron Dr *BSLYN/ROY* S71 .... 261 K2
Byron Gv *DEWS* WF13 .... 173 H4 2
EARD/LOFT WF3 .... 155 G8
Byron Ms *BGLY* BD16 .... 81 J1 2
Byron Rd *COL* BB8 .... 74 B1
Byron St *BFDE* BD3 .... 5 L4
HFAX HX1 .... 10 A5
LDSU LS2 .... 7 J5
RPDN/SBR HX6 .... 167 K1 4
SKP/WHF BD23 .... 16 C3
TOD OL14 .... 163 K1
The Byways *PONT* WF8 .... 180 F8
Bywell Cl *EARL* WF12 .... 174 B5
Bywell Rd *EARL* WF12 .... 174 B5

C

Cabbage Hl *WOR/ARM* LS12 .... 108 D8
Cabin Rd *OT* LS21 .... 63 K1
Cad Beeston Ms *BEE/HOL* LS11 .... 8 C9 1
Cadney Cft *HFAX* HX1 .... 11 G7
Cadogan Av *HUDW* HD3 .... 191 K6
Cadwell Cl *CUD/GR* S72 .... 244 E6
Caenarvon Cl *BTLY* WF17 .... 151 J5 1
Caernarvon Av
GFTH/SHER LS25 .... 113 K7
Caesar St *ROCH* OL11 .... 228 C4
Cain La *HIPP* HX3 .... 169 J2
Cairns Cl *ECHL* BD2 .... 105 H3
Caister Cl *BTLY* WF17 .... 151 H4
Caister St *KGHY* BD21 .... 79 K2 7
Caister Wy *KGHY* BD21 .... 79 K2
Caistor Av *BSLY* S70 .... 260 E7
Calcaria Crs *TAD* LS24 .... 71 K4
Calcaria Rd *TAD* LS24 .... 71 K4
Calde Ct *LM/WK* BD12 .... 127 G8
Caldene Av *HBR* HX7 .... 143 M5
LM/WK BD12 .... 127 G8
Calder Av *BSLYN/ROY* S71 .... 244 A3
LIT OL15 .... 185 J7
LUD/ILL HX2 .... 168 B1
Calder Bank Rd *EARL* WF12 .... 173 K8
Calder Banks *CUL/QBY* BD13 .... 125 J5
Calderbrook Rd *LIT* OL15 .... 185 K6
Caldercliffe Rd *HUDS* HD4 .... 214 B5
Calder Cl *OSS* WF5 .... 196 E1
WBY LS22 .... 29 M6
Calder Crs *BSLY* S70 .... 261 M7
Caldercroft *ELL* HX5 .... 169 J8
Calderdale Wy *BRIG* HD6 .... 170 E1
ELL HX5 .... 169 G7
GTL/HWG HX4 .... 168 C6
HBR HX7 .... 164 F3
HIPP HX3 .... 147 J1
Calder Dr *HUDS* HD4 .... 214 B6
Calder Gv *HBR* HX7 .... 144 A5 4
ROY/SHW OL2 .... 229 J6
Calder Island Wy
WKFDW/WTN WF2 .... 198 D4
Calder Rd *DEWS* WF13 .... 195 G1
MIRF WF14 .... 194 C3
Calderstone Av *WBSY* BD6 .... 125 M6
Calder St *BRIG* HD6 .... 170 E5
CAS WF10 .... 157 K6
GTL/HWG HX4 .... 168 F7
MILN OL16 .... 206 D4
TOD OL14 .... 163 K1 6
WKFDE WF1 .... 12 F7
Calder Ter *HBR* HX7 .... 143 H3 1
HIPP HX3 .... 168 C5
Caldervale *BSLYN/ROY* S71 .... 244 A2
Calder Vale Rd *HOR/CROF* WF4 .... 197 L6
WKFDE WF1 .... 13 H4
Calder Vw *BRIG* HD6 .... 170 B5
HOR/CROF WF4 .... 220 A1
OSS WF5 .... 196 D1
Calder Wy *HUDW* HD3 .... 190 C7
Caldicott Cl *TOD* OL14 .... 163 H3
Caledonia Ct *WKFDW/WTN* WF2 .. 175 K4
Caledonian Rd *EARL* WF12 .... 173 L8
Caledonia Rd *BTLY* WF17 .... 173 M1
KGHY BD21 .... 3 H2
Caledonia St *BOW* BD4 .... 5 H9
WBOW BD5 .... 4 F9
Calf Hey *LIT* OL15 .... 185 H8 1
Calf Hey La *STKB/PEN* S36 .... 255 M7
Calf Hey North *ROCH* OL11 .... 228 C2 4
Calf Hey Rd *ROY/SHW* OL2 .... 229 M6
Calf Hey South *ROCH* OL11 .... 228 C2 5
Calf Hill Rd *HOLM/MEL* HD7 .... 236 D6
Calgary Crs *EARD/LOFT* WF3 .... 153 H7
Calgary Pl *CHAL* LS7 .... 87 M8
California Crs *BSLY* S70 .... 261 H7 1
California Dr *CAS* WF10 .... 178 F1
HOR/CROF WF4 .... 197 L5
TOD OL14 .... 163 J3
California La *CLECK* BD19 .... 150 D7 1
California Ms *MOR* LS27 .... 130 D8 1
California St *BSLY* S70 .... 261 G7
MOR LS27 .... 152 D2 2
California Ter *BSLY* S70 .... 261 G7 1
Calliards Rd *MILN* OL16 .... 207 G2
Callis La *STKB/PEN* S36 .... 271 G5
Callis Wy *STKB/PEN* S36 .... 270 F4
Call La *LDS* LS1 .... 9 H1
The Calls *LDSU* LS2 .... 9 J1
Calmlands Rd *HOLM/MEL* HD7 .... 234 F5
Calpin Cl *IDLE* BD10 .... 83 K6 1
Calton Gv *KGHY* BD21 .... 58 B8 1
Calton St *HUD* HD1 .... 15 G3
KGHY BD21 .... 2 E8
Calver Av *HWTH* BD22 .... 2 B3
Calver Gv *KGHY* BD21 .... 2 B3
Calverley Av *BFDE* BD3 .... 105 M6
BRAM LS13 .... 107 K3
Calverley Ct *BRAM* LS13 .... 107 K3 1
RTHW LS26 .... 155 K1
Calverley Cutting *IDLE* BD10 .... 84 B6
Calverley Dr *BRAM* LS13 .... 107 K3
Calverley Gdns *BRAM* LS13 .... 107 J2 1
Calverley Garth *BRAM* LS13 .... 107 K3
Calverley Green Rd *NORM* WF6 .... 178 B3
Calverley Gv *BRAM* LS13 .... 107 K3 2
Calverley La *BRAM* LS13 .... 107 J3
HORS LS18 .... 85 H6
PDSY/CALV LS28 .... 84 E8
Calverley Moor Av
PDSY/CALV LS28 .... 106 C5
Calverley Rd *RTHW* LS26 .... 155 L1
Calverley St *LDS* LS1 .... 6 F7
Calverley Ter *BRAM* LS13 .... 107 K3 3
Calverley Wy *WHIT* OL12 .... 206 A2 1
Calver Rd *HWTH* BD22 .... 2 B4
Calversyke St *HWTH* BD22 .... 2 A5
Calvert Cl *GFTH/SHER* LS25 .... 135 J3
Calverts Wk *OSS* WF5 .... 197 H2
Camargue Fold *ECHL* BD2 .... 105 H2 2
Camberley Cl *PDSY/CALV* LS28 .... 107 G8
Camberley Mt *BOW* BD4 .... 128 A2
Camberley St *BEE/HOL* LS11 .... 131 L3 8
Camborne Rd *HUDN* HD2 .... 192 B3
Camborne Wy *BSLYN/ROY* S71 .... 261 L3
HWTH BD22 .... 79 G1
Cambourne Cl *AWLS/ASK* DN6 .... 249 K8
Cambrian Bar *LM/WK* BD12 .... 126 D8
Cambrian Dr *MILN* OL16 .... 207 J8 1
Cambrian St *BEE/HOL* LS11 .... 8 D7
Cambridge Cl *MOR* LS27 .... 152 D1 2
Cambridge Ct *MOR* LS27 .... 152 D1 3
Cambridge Crs *HOR/CROF* WF4 .... 199 L4
Cambridge Dr *BRAM* LS13 .... 107 K3
OT LS21 .... 41 K7
Cambridge Gdns *BRAM* LS13 .... 107 K3
Cambridge Gv *GFTH/SHER* LS25 .... 135 J5
OT LS21 .... 41 K7
Cambridge Pl *BFDE* BD3 .... 5 H3
CUL/QBY BD13 .... 125 G5 6
Cambridge Rd *BTLY* WF17 .... 150 F5
CHAL LS7 .... 6 F3
HUD HD1 .... 14 E4
Cambridge St *BTLY* WF17 .... 173 L1
CAS WF10 .... 157 M7
CLAY BD14 .... 125 K2 4
CUL/QBY BD13 .... 125 H5 2
GTHN BD7 .... 126 D2
HBR HX7 .... 143 H3
HECK WF16 .... 173 G2 1
HEM/SK/SE WF9 .... 247 G3
NORM WF6 .... 178 C5
OT LS21 .... 41 J7
TOD OL14 .... 163 K1
WKFDW/WTN WF2 .... 198 B1
Cambridge Wy *OT* LS21 .... 41 K7
Camden Rd *CAS* WF10 .... 158 F6
Camellia Cl *WKFDW/WTN* WF2 .... 197 M3
Camellia Mt *GTHN* BD7 .... 104 A8 2
Cameron Av *LM/WK* BD12 .... 148 D5 1
Cameron Ct *ROY/SHW* OL2 .... 228 F8 1
Camilla Ct *EARL* WF12 .... 174 B7
Cam La *BRIG* HD6 .... 170 F3
Camm La *MIRF* WF14 .... 172 D8
Camm St *BRIG* HD6 .... 170 C3
Campbell St *AIRE* BD20 .... 34 F7 3
CUL/QBY BD13 .... 125 H5 3
KGHY BD21 .... 3 G4 1
WHIT OL12 .... 206 A4 4
Campden Rd *HBR* HX7 .... 143 G2 1
Campinot V *HOLM/MEL* HD7 .... 212 B4
Campion Cl *PONT* WF8 .... 180 F7
Camp Mt *PONT* WF8 .... 180 D6
Camp Ri *PONT* WF8 .... 180 D6
Camp Rd *BHP/TINH* LS16 .... 63 M5
HEM/SK/SE WF9 .... 246 B5
Campsall Balk *AWLS/ASK* DN6 .... 227 M4
Campsall Hall Rd
AWLS/ASK DN6 .... 227 M5
Campsall Park Rd
AWLS/ASK DN6 .... 227 L5
Campsmount *AWLS/ASK* DN6 .... 227 L6 1
Campus Rd *GTHN* BD7 .... 4 A7
Camroyd St *DEWS* WF13 .... 173 M5
Canada Crs *YEA* LS19 .... 84 E2
Canada Dr *YEA* LS19 .... 84 E1 1
Canada Rd *YEA* LS19 .... 84 E1
Canada St *BSLY* S70 .... 261 G7
Canada Ter *YEA* LS19 .... 84 E2
Canal Ct *EARD/LOFT* WF3 .... 154 F8 1
Canal La *AIRE* BD20 .... 36 C7
EARD/LOFT WF3 .... 154 F8
Canal Pl *WOR/ARM* LS12 .... 8 B1
Canal Rd *AIRE* BD20 .... 58 A4
BFD BD1 .... 5 G5
BFDE BD3 .... 5 G3
BGLY BD16 .... 81 H1
BRAM LS13 .... 107 G1
ECHL BD2 .... 104 E2
RPDN/SBR HX6 .... 168 A2 1
WOR/ARM LS12 .... 108 F6
Canal St *BRIG* HD6 .... 170 D4
BSLYN/ROY S71 .... 261 H3
HIPP HX3 .... 11 K8
HUD HD1 .... 15 J2
LIT OL15 .... 207 K1
ROCH OL11 .... 228 C1
SKP/WHF BD23 .... 16 B2
WOR/ARM LS12 .... 109 G6
Canal Wk *EARD/LOFT* WF3 .... 155 H8 1
Canal Whf *BEE/HOL* LS11 .... 8 E2
Canal Yd *SKP/WHF* BD23 .... 16 B2 5
Canary St *CLECK* BD19 .... 149 M6
Canberra Cl *HWTH* BD22 .... 79 H6 2
Canberra Dr *HWTH* BD22 .... 79 H6
Canby Gv *HUDE* HD5 .... 215 K1
Canby La *PBR* HG3 .... 28 E3
Cancel St *MID* LS10 .... 9 J6
Canford Dr *WIL/AL* BD15 .... 103 K5
Canford Gv *WIL/AL* BD15 .... 103 L5
Canford Rd *WIL/AL* BD15 .... 103 K5 1
Canker La *HIPP* HX3 .... 146 C3
HUD HD1 .... 15 K1
Canning Av *WKFDW/WTN* WF2 .... 175 M6
Cannon Gv *HECK* WF16 .... 173 G1
Cannon Hall Cl *BRIG* HD6 .... 170 F4 1
Cannon Hall Dr *BRIG* HD6 .... 170 F4
Cannon Mill La *GTHN* BD7 .... 126 C2
Cannon St *BGLY* BD16 .... 81 J4 2
CAS WF10 .... 158 A8
HFAX HX1 .... 10 B9 2
TOD OL14 .... 163 J3
Cannon Wy *DOD/DAR* S75 .... 260 B1
EARL WF12 .... 173 L7
Canonbury Ter *BEE/HOL* LS11 .... 131 G3
Canon Flynn Ct *MILN* OL16 .... 206 E7 1
Canon St *MILN* OL16 .... 206 D4
Canons Wy *BSLYN/ROY* S71 .... 261 L3
Canterbury Av *WBOW* BD5 .... 126 E3
Canterbury Crs *HIPP* HX3 .... 10 E1
Canterbury Dr *HDGY* LS6 .... 108 E2
Canterbury Rd *EARL* WF12 .... 174 B5
HDGY LS6 .... 108 E2
The Canter *EARD/LOFT* WF3 .... 153 M3
Capas Heights Wy *HECK* WF16 .. 173 G3 2
Capel Ct *PDSY/CALV* LS28 .... 84 D8 2
Capel St *BRIG* HD6 .... 170 C5 4
PDSY/CALV LS28 .... 84 D8
Capesthorne Dr *ROY/SHW* OL2 .... 229 H7
Cape St *BFD* BD1 .... 4 F3
Capri Ct *WMB/DAR* S73 .... 263 G8
Caprington Ct *NORM* WF6 .... 178 F5 1
Captain St *BFD* BD1 .... 5 G5
Carberry Pl *HDGY* LS6 .... 109 G4
Carberry Rd *HDGY* LS6 .... 109 G4
Carberry Ter *HDGY* LS6 .... 109 G4
Carbis Cl *BSLYN/ROY* S71 .... 261 K3 1
Cardan Dr *ILK* LS29 .... 39 G2
Carden Av *MSTN/BAR* LS15 .... 111 G6
Carden Rd *BOW* BD4 .... 128 A1
Cardigan Av *MOR* LS27 .... 152 C4
Cardigan Cl *BTLY* WF17 .... 174 A1
Cardigan Ct *HDGY* LS6 .... 109 G2
Cardigan La *BULY* LS4 .... 108 F4
HDGY LS6 .... 108 F3 13
OSS WF5 .... 197 H3
Cardigan Rd *HDGY* LS6 .... 108 F2
Cardigan St *CUL/QBY* BD13 .... 125 H5 4
WHIT OL12 .... 206 A3 1
Cardigan Ter *EARD/LOFT* WF3 .... 154 A6
WKFDE WF1 .... 12 D1
WKFDE WF1 .... 176 E7 3
Cardinal Av *BEE/HOL* LS11 .... 131 H6
Cardinal Cl *GFTH/SHER* LS25 .... 116 B6
HOLM/MEL HD7 .... 235 G4
Cardinal Crs *BEE/HOL* LS11 .... 131 H6
Cardinal Gdns *BEE/HOL* LS11 .... 131 G6 1
Cardinal Gv *BEE/HOL* LS11 .... 131 G6
Cardinal Rd *BEE/HOL* LS11 .... 131 G6
Cardinal Sq *BEE/HOL* LS11 .... 131 G5
Cardinal Wk *BEE/HOL* LS11 .... 131 H6 1
Cardwell Ter *EARL* WF12 .... 173 L8
Carey Av *BSLYN/ROY* S71 .... 261 J5
Carforth St *HUD* HD1 .... 15 H9
Carisbrooke Crs *WBSY* BD6 .... 126 D6 2
Carisbrooke La
GFTH/SHER LS25 .... 113 K6 2
Cariss St *MID* LS10 .... 9 K9
Cark Rd *KGHY* BD21 .... 3 G2
Carlby St *HWTH* BD22 .... 2 D6
Carleton Av *SKP/WHF* BD23 .... 16 A3 1
Carleton Br *SKP/WHF* BD23 .... 16 A5
Carleton Cl *BSPA/BRAM* LS23 .... 48 D6
PONT WF8 .... 180 F7
Carleton Crest *PONT* WF8 .... 181 G8
Carleton Dr *BSPA/BRAM* LS23 .... 48 D7
Carleton Ga *PONT* WF8 .... 180 E8
Carleton Gln *PONT* WF8 .... 180 F6
Carleton Green Cl *PONT* WF8 .... 181 G8
Carleton New Rd *SKP/WHF* BD23 .. 16 A3
Carleton Park Av *PONT* WF8 .... 180 F7
Carleton Park Rd *PONT* WF8 .... 180 E8
Carleton Rd *PONT* WF8 .... 180 F7
SKP/WHF BD23 .... 16 A4
Carleton St *KGHY* BD21 .... 57 L5 4
SKP/WHF BD23 .... 16 B3
Carleton Vw *PONT* WF8 .... 180 F8
Carlile St *HOLM/MEL* HD7 .... 235 G4
Carling Cl *GTHN* BD7 .... 126 B3 5
Carlinghow Hl *BTLY* WF17 .... 151 K7
Carlinghow La *BTLY* WF17 .... 151 H8 1
Carlisle Av *YEA* LS19 .... 62 E8
Carlisle Cl *DEWS* WF13 .... 173 L4 1
Carlisle Dr *PDSY/CALV* LS28 .... 106 F8
Carlisle Gv *PDSY/CALV* LS28 .... 106 F8
Carlisle Pl *GIR* BD8 .... 4 A1
Carlisle Rd *GIR* BD8 .... 104 D5
MID LS10 .... 9 K4
PDSY/CALV LS28 .... 106 F8
Carlisle St *GIR* BD8 .... 4 A1
KGHY BD21 .... 3 K5
LUD/ILL HX2 .... 146 A6 2
PDSY/CALV LS28 .... 106 E5 1
WHIT OL12 .... 206 B3 1
Carlisle Ter *GIR* BD8 .... 4 B1
Carlton Ap *WBY* LS22 .... 29 L8
Carlton Av *BTLY* WF17 .... 173 K3
CAS WF10 .... 158 B7
PDSY/CALV LS28 .... 107 G7
SHPY BD18 .... 82 B6
Carlton Carr *CHAL* LS7 .... 7 H5
Carlton Cl *HEM/SK/SE* WF9 .... 223 L8
NORM WF6 .... 178 D4 1
Carlton Ct *OSS* WF5 .... 174 F8 1
WOR/ARM LS12 .... 131 G2
Carlton Cft *WKFDW/WTN* WF2 .... 198 F8
Carlton Dr *BAIL* BD17 .... 82 E2 2
GFTH/SHER LS25 .... 135 H1
GSLY LS20 .... 62 B4
HTON BD9 .... 104 C2
SHPY BD18 .... 104 C1
Carlton Gdns *CHAL* LS7 .... 7 H4
HEM/SK/SE WF9 .... 247 H3
NORM WF6 .... 178 E4
Carlton Garth *AL/HA/HU* LS17 .... 88 C1
Carlton Ga *CHAL* LS7 .... 7 G5
Carlton Gv *CHAL* LS7 .... 7 G4
ELL HX5 .... 169 K7
SHPY BD18 .... 104 D1 3
WBOW BD5 .... 126 F3 4
Carlton Hl *CHAL* LS7 .... 7 G5
Carlton House Ter *HFAX* HX1 .... 10 D9
Carlton La *EARD/LOFT* WF3 .... 154 E5
GSLY LS20 .... 62 B4
RTHW LS26 .... 154 F2
Carlton Moor Ms
EARD/LOFT WF3 .... 154 B1
Carlton Mt *YEA* LS19 .... 62 E6
Carlton Pl *CHAL* LS7 .... 7 G4
HFAX HX1 .... 11 G7 2
Carlton Ri *CHAL* LS7 .... 7 G5
PDSY/CALV LS28 .... 107 G7
Carlton Rd *BSLYN/ROY* S71 .... 243 K7 2
DEWS WF13 .... 173 L5
HECK WF16 .... 150 E8
HEM/SK/SE WF9 .... 247 H4 1
LVSG WF15 .... 172 C3
SHPY BD18 .... 82 A6
Carlton Rw *WOR/ARM* LS12 .... 108 C7
Carlton St *BSLYN/ROY* S71 .... 261 G2
CAS WF10 .... 157 M6
CUD/GR S72 .... 244 D7
CUD/GR S72 .... 245 J8
FEA/AMT WF7 .... 179 M7
GTHN BD7 .... 4 D7
HBR HX7 .... 143 J3 4
HFAX HX1 .... 11 G7
HOR/CROF WF4 .... 197 J5
HWTH BD22 .... 78 F7 4
NORM WF6 .... 178 D4 2
OT LS21 .... 41 K7
WKFDW/WTN WF2 .... 12 B4
Carlton Ter *HFAX* HX1 .... 11 G7 3
Carlton Vw *CAS* WF10 .... 135 H8
CHAL LS7 .... 7 G4
Carlton Wk *SHPY* BD18 .... 82 B6 2
Carlyle Crs *CAS* WF10 .... 158 C7
Carlyle Rd *CAS* WF10 .... 158 C7
Carmel Rd *HIPP* HX3 .... 146 D4
Carmine Cl *HUDE* HD5 .... 193 G8 1
Carmona Av *SHPY* BD18 .... 104 D1 3
Carmona Gdns *SHPY* BD18 .... 104 D1
Carnaby Rd *GTHN* BD7 .... 126 A4 2
Carnegie Dr *SHPY* BD18 .... 82 E6 1
Carnforth Rd *BSLYN/ROY* S71 .... 261 M1
Carnlea Gv *WKFDW/WTN* WF2 .... 12 E8
Carnoustie Gv *BGLY* BD16 .... 81 K7 1
Carolan Ct *HOLM/MEL* HD7 .... 212 E2
Caroline St *CLECK* BD19 .... 149 M6 8
SHPY BD18 .... 82 B6
Carousel Wk *GFTH/SHER* LS25 .... 116 B7
Carpenters Wy *MILN* OL16 .... 228 D2 1
Carperley Crs *CUL/QBY* BD13 .... 102 A6 1
Carr Av *GFTH/SHER* LS25 .... 116 A7
Carr Bank *AIRE* BD20 .... 58 D5
Carr Bottom Av *WBOW* BD5 .... 126 E4 1
Carr Bottom Fold *WBSY* BD6 .... 126 E5 5
Carr Bottom Gv *WBSY* BD6 .... 126 D4
Carr Bottom Rd *IDLE* BD10 .... 84 A8 2
WBOW BD5 .... 126 E4
Carr Bridge Av *BHP/TINH* LS16 .... 85 M3
Carr Bridge Cl *BHP/TINH* LS16 .... 85 M3
Carr Bridge Dr *BHP/TINH* LS16 .... 85 M3
Carr Bridge Vw *BHP/TINH* LS16 .... 85 M3
Carr Cl *YEA* LS19 .... 84 F3
Carr Crofts *WOR/ARM* LS12 .... 108 D7
Carr Crofts Dr *WOR/ARM* LS12 .... 108 D7
Carrfield Cl *DOD/DAR* S75 .... 241 M6 1
Carr Field Dr *LUD/ILL* HX2 .... 145 G6
Carrfield Dr *MSTN/BAR* LS15 .... 90 F7
Carrfield La *MSTN/BAR* LS15 .... 90 F7
Carrfield Rd *MSTN/BAR* LS15 .... 90 F7
Carr Furlong *BSLYN/ROY* S71 .... 243 H5 1
Carrgate *HEM/SK/SE* WF9 .... 223 K4
Carr Gate Crs
WKFDW/WTN WF2 .... 175 M1
Carr Gate Dr
WKFDW/WTN WF2 .... 176 A1 1
Carr Gate Mt *WKFDW/WTN* WF2 .. 175 M1
Carr Green Av *BRIG* HD6 .... 170 B8
Carr Green Cl *BRIG* HD6 .... 170 B8
Carr Green Dr *BRIG* HD6 .... 170 B8
Carr Green La *BRIG* HD6 .... 170 B7
DOD/DAR S75 .... 242 E6 2
HUDE HD5 .... 15 M5
Carr Gv *AIRE* BD20 .... 58 C5
Carr Hall La *GTL/HWG* HX4 .... 190 C2
Carr Hall Rd *LM/WK* BD12 .... 148 E3
Carr Hill Av *PDSY/CALV* LS28 .... 84 C8
Carr Hill Dr *PDSY/CALV* LS28 .... 84 C8
Carr Hill Gv *PDSY/CALV* LS28 .... 84 C8
Carr Hill Nook *PDSY/CALV* LS28 .. 84 C8 1
Carr Hill Ri *PDSY/CALV* LS28 .... 84 C8
Carr Hill Rd *KBTN* HD8 .... 238 C8
PDSY/CALV LS28 .... 84 C8
Carrholm Crs *CHAL* LS7 .... 87 K7
Carrholm Dr *CHAL* LS7 .... 87 K7
Carrholm Gv *CHAL* LS7 .... 87 K7
Carrholm Mt *CHAL* LS7 .... 87 K7
Carrholm Rd *CHAL* LS7 .... 87 K7
Carrholm Vw *CHAL* LS7 .... 87 K7
Carr House Gv *LM/WK* BD12 .... 148 E2
Carr House La *HIPP* HX3 .... 126 A7
LM/WK BD12 .... 148 E2 5
TOD OL14 .... 141 M8
Carr House Mt *LM/WK* BD12 .... 148 E2 6
Carr House Rd *HIPP* HX3 .... 125 M8
HOLM/MEL HD7 .... 254 C1 2
Carriage Dr *CLECK* BD19 .... 150 D4 1
HUDS HD4 .... 214 A6
LIT OL15 .... 185 K7
The Carriage Dr *GTL/HWG* HX4 .... 190 C2
RHAY LS8 .... 88 E5
Carricks Cl *LM/WK* BD12 .... 127 G8
Carrier's Rw *COL* BB8 .... 53 G8
Carrington Av *DOD/DAR* S75 .... 261 G2
Carrington Cl *MILN* OL16 .... 206 F3 2
Carrington St *BFDE* BD3 .... 105 L7
DOD/DAR S75 .... 260 F3 1
Carrington Ter *GSLY* LS20 .... 61 M6 1
Carr La *AIRE* BD20 .... 58 C5
AL/HA/HU LS17 .... 89 J2
BGLY BD16 .... 59 G6
CAS WF10 .... 180 A1
CUL/QBY BD13 .... 102 A4
DEWS WF13 .... 173 G6
EARD/LOFT WF3 .... 155 G3
EARL WF12 .... 195 K6
HECK WF16 .... 172 F5
HEM/SK/SE WF9 .... 223 H3
HEM/SK/SE WF9 .... 246 E2
HOLM/MEL HD7 .... 212 C5
HOLM/MEL HD7 .... 253 K2
HOR/CROF WF4 .... 196 D8
KBTN HD8 .... 238 B8
LM/WK BD12 .... 148 F1
MILN OL16 .... 207 L8
SCFT LS14 .... 89 L2
SHPY BD18 .... 82 F7
STKB/PEN S36 .... 257 K7
WBY LS22 .... 30 C8
WKFDW/WTN WF2 .... 198 F7
YEA LS19 .... 84 F3
Carr Lane Av *CAS* WF10 .... 180 A1
Carr Manor Av *AL/HA/HU* LS17 .... 87 K6
Carr Manor Cft *CHAL* LS7 .... 87 K7
Carr Manor Cr *AL/HA/HU* LS17 .... 87 K6
Carr Manor Gdns
AL/HA/HU LS17 .... 87 K6 1
Carr Manor Garth
AL/HA/HU LS17 .... 87 K5
Carr Manor Gv *AL/HA/HU* LS17 .... 87 K6

Carr Manor Mt AL/HA/HU LS17 87 K6
Carr Manor Pde AL/HA/HU LS17 87 K6
Carr Manor Pl CHAL LS7 87 K6 2
Carr Manor Rd AL/HA/HU LS17 87 K6
Carr Manor Vw AL/HA/HU LS17 87 K5
CHAL LS7 87 L6 2
Carr Manor Wk CHAL LS7 87 K6
Carr Mill Ms HWTH BD22 54 E4
Carr Moor Side BEE/HOL LS11 131 L3 6
Carr Mt KBTN HD8 238 C8
Carroll Ct HEM/SK/SE WF9 247 G3
Carroll St BFDE BD3 5 J7
Carron Dr DOD/DAR S75 242 E6
Carr Pit Rd HUD HD1 15 J8
Carr Rd COL BB8 52 A8
LM/WK BD12 148 E3 1
PDSY/CALV LS28 84 B7
TOD OL14 140 C6
Carr Side Crs BTLY WF17 173 K3
Carrs La CUD/GR S72 262 D1
Carrs Rd HOLM/MEL HD7 233 J3
Carrs Side Street No 2
HOLM/MEL HD7 233 J2
Carrs St HOLM/MEL HD7 233 J2
Carr St BRIG HD6 170 C2
BSLYN/ROY S71 261 M1
BTLY WF17 151 G6
CLECK BD19 149 M7
DEWS WF13 173 L4 2
HECK WF16 172 E2 1
HUDW HD3 191 L7
KGHY BD21 3 G5
LVSG WF15 172 C1
WBOW BD5 126 F4 3
Carr Top Cl DEWS WF13 173 K4
Carr Top La HOLM/MEL HD7 212 F2
Carr Vw HEM/SK/SE WF9 246 E2
Carr View Rd HOLM/MEL HD7 255 G4
Carr Wood Gdns
PDSY/CALV LS28 84 C8
Carrwood Rd BSLY S70 262 A5
Carr Wood Rd CAS WF10 180 B1
Carry La COL BB8 74 A1
Carter Av MSTN/BAR LS15 111 L6
Carter La CUL/QBY BD13 124 F3
MSTN/BAR LS15 111 L5
Carter Mt MSTN/BAR LS15 111 L6
Carter's La ILK LS29 21 G8
Carter St BFD BD1 5 H8
WKFDE WF1 12 D2
Carter Ter MSTN/BAR LS15 111 L5 3
Cartmel Av MILN OL16 229 H2 2
Cartmel Ct BSLYN/ROY S71 243 M7 2
Cartmell Dr MSTN/BAR LS15 110 F8
Cartmel Rd KGHY BD21 2 D4
Cartworth Bank Rd
HOLM/MEL HD7 254 B4
Cartworth La HOLM/MEL HD7 254 B3
Cartworth Moor Rd
HOLM/MEL HD7 254 A6
Cartworth Rd HOLM/MEL HD7 254 C3
Cartwright Gdns HUDS HD4 213 L3 1
Cartwright St CLECK BD19 150 B8
Carver St CLECK BD19 149 M6 7
Caryl Rd BOW BD4 127 J3
Cashmere St HWTH BD22 2 D5
Casserley Rd COL BB8 52 B8
Cass La GFTH/SHER LS25 137 M5
Casson Av EARD/LOFT WF3 153 K5
Casson Dr EARD/LOFT WF3 153 K5
Casson Ga WHIT OL12 206 A5
Casson Gv EARD/LOFT WF3 153 K5 1
Casterton Gdns SCFT LS14 111 J3 2
Castle Av BRIG HD6 170 B6
HUDS HD4 214 C5
ROCH OL11 206 A8
WKFDW/WTN WF2 198 F4
Castle Carr Rd HBR HX7 122 D6
LUD/ILL HX2 122 E8
Castle Cl AL/HA/HU LS17 67 M3
BSLYN/ROY S71 261 K3
BTLY WF17 151 J5
COL BB8 52 A8
PBR HG3 28 E3
STKB/PEN S36 271 G4
Castle Crs EARL WF12 195 L5
WKFDW/WTN WF2 198 F6
Castle Cft BGLY BD16 80 C5 2
Castlefield Ct CAS WF10 157 M6 3
Castlefields RTHW LS26 154 D1
Castlefields Crs BRIG HD6 170 B6
Castlefields Dr BRIG HD6 170 B6
Castlefields La BGLY BD16 81 G1
Castlefields Rd BGLY BD16 80 F1
BRIG HD6 170 B6
Castleford La FEA/AMT WF7 179 K4
KNOT WF11 181 K1
Castleford Rd NORM WF6 178 D4
Castle Garth PONT WF8 181 G5
Castle Ga HBR HX7 165 L3
Castlegate HUD HD1 14 F5
Castle Ga RTHW LS26 155 H6
WBY LS22 48 A1 1
Castlegate Dr IDLE BD10 83 L8
PONT WF8 202 D1
Castlegate Slip HUD HD1 14 E5
Castle Gv AL/HA/HU LS17 67 M3
BGLY BD16 80 C5 3
HOR/CROF WF4 197 K6
Castle Grove Av HDGY LS6 86 F7
Castle Grove Dr HDGY LS6 86 F8
Castle Head Cl EARD/LOFT WF3 154 E5
Castle Head La EARD/LOFT WF3 154 C6
Castle Hl BRIG HD6 170 B6
WKFDW/WTN WF2 197 L2
Castle Hill Crs ROCH OL11 206 A8 2
Castle Hill Rd CLECK BD19 150 D8
Castle Hill Side HUDS HD4 214 E6
Castle Hill Vw HECK WF16 173 G3
Castle Ings Cl WOR/ARM LS12 129 M3
Castle Ings Dr WOR/ARM LS12 129 M3
Castle Ings Gdns
WOR/ARM LS12 129 M4
Castle La HOLM/MEL HD7 212 A4
RPDN/SBR HX6 188 E3
STKB/PEN S36 271 G4
TOD OL14 141 M8
Castle Lane Cl TOD OL14 141 M8 1
Castle Mdw HOR/CROF WF4 220 B3
Castlemere Dr ROY/SHW OL2 229 M6
Castlemere St ROCH OL11 206 A8
Castlemere Ter ROCH OL11 206 A8 1
Castlemore Rd BAIL BD17 82 F4
Castle Mt EARL WF12 195 M5
Castle Pde CAS WF10 158 B8 2
Castlereagh St BSLY S70 261 G5
Castlerigg Dr ROY/SHW OL2 228 E8 1
Castle Rd COL BB8 52 A8
ILK LS29 38 D2
KGHY BD21 2 F7
RTHW LS26 154 F1
SHPY BD18 82 C7
WKFDW/WTN WF2 198 F5
Castle Rd West
WKFDW/WTN WF2 198 F4
Castle St BSLY S70 261 G6
LDS LS1 6 D9
PBR HG3 28 E3
SKP/WHF BD23 16 C3
WBOW BD5 127 G1 6
Castle Syke Hl FEA/AMT WF7 202 D3
Castle Syke Vw PONT WF8 180 E8
Castle Ter WKFDW/WTN WF2 198 F6
Castleton Cl WOR/ARM LS12 8 A1
Castleton Rd ROY/SHW OL2 228 E6
WOR/ARM LS12 109 G6
Castle Vw AL/HA/HU LS17 87 K5
HOLM/MEL HD7 236 B3
HOR/CROF WF4 197 L6
MIRF WF14 194 D1 1
WKFDW/WTN WF2 198 F6
Castle View Ter SKP/WHF BD23 16 B2 6
Castle Wood Ct AL/HA/HU LS17 45 J7
Castley La AL/HA/HU LS17 43 K4
OT LS21 43 G6
Catania Ri WMB/DAR S73 263 G8
Cater St BFD BD1 5 H6
Cathcart St HDGY LS6 6 C2
Cathedral Cl WKFDE WF1 12 D1
Catherine Cl HUDW HD3 191 J4 3
Catherine Gv BEE/HOL LS11 131 K3 6
Catherine House La HBR HX7 122 C8
Catherine Rd HUDN HD2 192 D2
Catherine Slack BRIG HD6 148 B8
Catherine St BRIG HD6 170 C3
ELL HX5 169 H8
HEM/SK/SE WF9 223 J2
KGHY BD21 2 F8 1
Cat Hill La STKB/PEN S36 257 M6
Cat La GTL/HWG HX4 168 A7
LUD/ILL HX2 166 D1
Catlow St CAS WF10 157 L7 1
Caton St MILN OL16 206 B8 3
Catshaw La STKB/PEN S36 269 K3
Catterton La TAD LS24 51 J3
TAD LS24 72 D1
Cattlelaith La KNOT WF11 181 L3
Cattle La GFTH/SHER LS25 92 A7
Cattle Market St OT LS21 41 J6 2
Caudle Hl KNOT WF11 159 H2
Cauldwell Gdns WBOW BD5 127 G2 3
Caulms Wood Rd DEWS WF13 173 M5
Causeway GTL/HWG HX4 189 J4
HFAX HX1 11 J6
HOLM/MEL HD7 212 B3
Causeway Crs HOLM/MEL HD7 212 F5
Causeway Garth La PONT WF8 225 K2
Causeway Head La
RPDN/SBR HX6 188 D2
Causeway Side HOLM/MEL HD7 212 F5
Causeway Wood Rd TOD OL14 164 A2
Cautley Rd OSM LS9 110 B8
Cavalier Ap OSM LS9 110 B8
Cavalier Cl OSM LS9 110 B8 3
Cavalier Ct OSM LS9 110 B8 4
Cavalier Dr IDLE BD10 83 M7
Cavalier Gdns OSM LS9 110 B8 5
Cavalier Ga OSM LS9 110 B8 6
Cavalier Ms OSM LS9 110 B8
Cavalier Vw OSM LS9 110 B8 7
Cave Crs WKFDW/WTN WF2 198 A2
Cave Hl HIPP HX3 147 H2
Cave La EARD/LOFT WF3 153 M7
Cavendish Dr BGLY BD16 81 K2
GSLY LS20 61 M6 2
Cavendish Gv GSLY LS20 61 M6
Cavendish Ms AL/HA/HU LS17 87 M2
Cavendish Pl PDSY/CALV LS28 106 F5
Cavendish Ri PDSY/CALV LS28 107 J7 1
Cavendish Rd DOD/DAR S75 261 C3 3
GSLY LS20 61 M6
IDLE BD10 83 K7
IDLE BD10 105 L1
LDS LS1 6 E5
ROCH OL11 228 A3
Cavendish St BVRD LS3 109 G5
HFAX HX1 10 D5
KGHY BD21 3 G4
PDSY/CALV LS28 107 J7 2
SKP/WHF BD23 16 B2
YEA LS19 62 E7
Cavendish Ter HFAX HX1 10 D5 2
HFAX HX1 10 D6 1
Cavewell Cl OSS WF5 197 H3
Cavewell Gdns OSS WF5 197 H3
Cawcliffe Dr BRIG HD6 170 C2
Cawcliffe Rd BRIG HD6 170 C2
Cawdel Cl GFTH/SHER LS25 138 B2
Cawdel Wy GFTH/SHER LS25 138 B2
Cawder Ghyll SKP/WHF BD23 16 C5
Cawder La SKP/WHF BD23 16 C5
Cawder Rd SKP/WHF BD23 16 C5
Cawley Garth HECK WF16 173 G3
Cawley La HECK WF16 173 G3
Cawley Pl BSLYN/ROY S71 261 J2
Cawood Crs TAD LS24 95 G5
Cawood Hvn WBSY BD6 126 A6 2
Cawthorne Av HUDN HD2 192 C4
Cawthorne La DOD/DAR S75 259 J1
Cawthorne Rd DOD/DAR S75 259 M2
WKFDW/WTN WF2 198 D8
Cawthorne Vw STKB/PEN S36 258 B8
Caxton Rd OT LS21 41 G8
Caxton St BSLY S70 261 G3
WBY LS22 48 A1
Caygill Ter HFAX HX1 11 G9
Cayley St MILN OL16 206 D7 1
Caythorne Wk IDLE BD10 105 L1 1
Caythorpe Cl BSLYN/ROY S71 262 C1
Caythorpe Rd BHP/TINH LS16 86 D7
Cayton Cl BSLYN/ROY S71 243 G7 2
Cecil Av BAIL BD17 82 E2
GTHN BD7 126 D2
HIPP HX3 148 A6
Cecil Gv WOR/ARM LS12 108 E6
Cecil Mt WOR/ARM LS12 108 E6
Cecil Rd WOR/ARM LS12 108 E6
Cecil St HUD HD1 14 D7
HWTH BD22 79 G6 2
LIT OL15 207 H1
ROCH OL11 228 B1
WOR/ARM LS12 108 E6
Cedar Av HUD HD1 14 C4
OSS WF5 197 G3
Cedar Cl BSLYN/ROY S71 243 J2
PONT WF8 202 E1
WOR/ARM LS12 108 E7 11
Cedar Covert WBY LS22 30 A6 2
Cedar Crs BSLY S70 261 K7
Cedar Dr EARL WF12 174 D8
LM/WK BD12 149 G2
TAD LS24 71 K3
Cedar Gv AIRE BD20 55 L1
FEA/AMT WF7 179 M7
GTL/HWG HX4 168 D7
ROY/SHW OL2 228 F8
ROY/SHW OL2 229 K8 1
Cedar La MILN OL16 229 J3
Cedar Mt HUDW HD3 14 B4
WOR/ARM LS12 108 D7
Cedar Pl WOR/ARM LS12 108 D7
Cedar Rdg GFTH/SHER LS25 113 K5
Cedar Rd EARL WF12 174 C8
NORM WF6 178 D7
The Cedars BHP/TINH LS16 64 B5
Cedar St HFAX HX1 10 B6
HUD HD1 14 B5
KGHY BD21 79 K2
TOD OL14 163 J6
WHIT OL12 206 B5 3
WOR/ARM LS12 108 D7
Cedar Ter WOR/ARM LS12 108 D7
Cedar Wk AWLS/ASK DN6 227 L6
FEA/AMT WF7 179 M8
Cedar Wy CLECK BD19 150 C6
Celandine Av HUDW HD3 191 G6
Celandine Cl LIT OL15 185 H8
PONT WF8 180 F7 1
Celandine Dr HUDW HD3 191 G6
Cemetery La AIRE BD20 57 K4
EARD/LOFT WF3 154 E5
RPDN/SBR HX6 167 J2
Cemetery Rd BEE/HOL LS11 8 C8
BGLY BD16 81 G2
BSLY S70 261 H6
BTLY WF17 173 K1
CUD/GR S72 245 J7
DEWS WF13 173 J7
GIR BD8 104 B7
HECK WF16 172 F2
HEM/SK/SE WF9 223 L7
HOLM/MEL HD7 254 B2
HOR/CROF WF4 222 D5
HUD HD1 14 C4
HWTH BD22 78 C7
NORM WF6 178 E4
PDSY/CALV LS28 106 F6
WBSY BD6 126 D7
YEA LS19 62 E7
Centenary Rd BAIL BD17 83 H2
Centenary Sq EARL WF12 195 K2
Centenary Wy BTLY WF17 151 K8
Central Av BAIL BD17 82 D4
CUD/GR S72 245 J7
HEM/SK/SE WF9 223 J2
HEM/SK/SE WF9 247 H4 2
HUDN HD2 192 D4
HWTH BD22 79 H3
LIT OL15 185 K8
LVSG WF15 171 K1
SHPY BD18 82 D7 5
WBOW BD5 126 E2
Central Av East LVSG WF15 171 K1
Central Cl HUDN HD2 192 D3
Central Dr BSLYN/ROY S71 243 L3
CAS WF10 157 H7
HUDN HD2 192 D3
HWTH BD22 79 H3
Central Pde OSM LS9 132 E3
Central Pk HFAX HX1 10 F9
Central Rd HUDN HD2 192 D3
LDS LS1 9 H1
Central St DEWS WF13 173 L6 4
HBR HX7 143 J3
HFAX HX1 11 G6
LDS LS1 6 E9
Centre La TAD LS24 71 M3
Centre St HECK WF16 172 E2 2
HEM/SK/SE WF9 223 M7
HEM/SK/SE WF9 247 J3 1
WBOW BD5 126 E3 4
Centre Vale Cl LIT OL15 185 L7 1
Centuria Wk HUDW HD3 191 G6
Century Pl GIR BD8 4 A1
Century Rd ELL HX5 169 H7
Ceres Rd WBY LS22 48 B1
Chaddlewood Cl HORS LS18 85 L5 1
Chadwell Springs BGLY BD16 81 J7
Chadwick Cl MILN OL16 229 J1
Chadwick Crs DEWS WF13 173 K5
Chadwick La MILN OL16 228 E4
MIRF WF14 194 B3
Chadwick St MID LS10 9 K3
MILN OL16 206 F7 3
Chadwick St South MID LS10 9 K4
Chaffinch Rd GIR BD8 103 L7
Chaffinch Wk HUDS HD4 214 A7 1
Chain Rd HOLM/MEL HD7 234 A1
Chain St BFD BD1 4 D5
CAS WF10 157 L6 2
Chalcroft Cl HECK WF16 173 G1 1
Chald La WKFDW/WTN WF2 12 C4
Chalfont Rd BHP/TINH LS16 86 D6 1
Chalice Cl MID LS10 132 A7
Challenge Wy BOW BD4 127 M2
BTLY WF17 174 B2
Challis Gv WBOW BD5 127 G3
Chalner Av MOR LS27 152 B4
Chalner Cl MOR LS27 152 B4
Chalwood HUDN HD2 193 G2
Chamber Rd ROY/SHW OL2 229 J7
Chancellor St HDGY LS6 7 G2
Chancel Pl MILN OL16 206 B7 3
Chancel Wy BSLYN/ROY S71 261 L3
Chancery Cl HUD HD1 14 F7 1
Chancery La HUD HD1 14 F7
OSS WF5 174 D6
ROY/SHW OL2 229 L7 3
WKFDE WF1 12 E2 2
Chancery Rd EARL WF12 174 D6
Chandler Cl BTLY WF17 151 G5
Chandler La HOLM/MEL HD7 235 M2
Chandlers Cl WKFDE WF1 176 D1
The Chandlers MID LS10 9 J2
Chandos Av RHAY LS8 88 A6
Chandos Gdns RHAY LS8 88 A6
Chandos Garth RHAY LS8 88 A6 4
Chandos Gn RHAY LS8 88 A6
Chandos Pl RHAY LS8 88 B6
Chandos St BOW BD4 5 G8
KGHY BD21 2 F8
ROY/SHW OL2 229 L7
Chandos Ter RHAY LS8 88 B6 1
Changegate HWTH BD22 78 D6
Changegate Ct HWTH BD22 78 D7 2
Change La HIPP HX3 169 G4
Channing Sq MILN OL16 206 D8 2
Channing St MILN OL16 206 D8
Channing Wy BFD BD1 4 E7
Chantry Cl PONT WF8 180 D7
Chantry Cft MSTN/BAR LS15 111 M7 3
Chantry Garth MSTN/BAR LS15 111 M7
Chantry Gv BSLYN/ROY S71 243 L3
Chantry La TAD LS24 92 E2
Chantry Rd WKFDW/WTN WF2 198 A2
Chapel Av BSLYN/ROY S71 243 L5
HBR HX7 143 K3 2
HECK WF16 173 G2
Chapel Bank HOLM/MEL HD7 255 G3
Chapel Cl CUD/GR S72 244 E3
EARL WF12 195 M4
GFTH/SHER LS25 113 G7
GTL/HWG HX4 190 D2
HOR/CROF WF4 201 H7
HUDS HD4 214 B6
WBY LS22 31 L5
Chapel Ct MSTN/BAR LS15 111 J6 5
Chapel Cft BRIG HD6 170 B7
Chapel Field La STKB/PEN S36 270 E4
Chapelfields HEM/SK/SE WF9 246 D4
Chapel Fold BEE/HOL LS11 131 G4
BTLY WF17 173 J3
LM/WK BD12 148 E6
MSTN/BAR LS15 111 J6 6
WBSY BD6 126 D5
Chapel Garth FEA/AMT WF7 202 C8
Chapelgate HOLM/MEL HD7 254 F3
Chapel Ga MILN OL16 207 H8
Chapel Gv BGLY BD16 81 G1
Chapel Hl HOLM/MEL HD7 212 F6
KBTN HD8 240 A4
LIT OL15 207 K1 1
MIRF WF14 194 C5
MOR LS27 152 C1
SKP/WHF BD23 16 B1
WBY LS22 45 M4
YEA LS19 62 D7 2
Chapel Hill La HUDW HD3 189 K8
OT LS21 43 K6
Chapel House Rd LM/WK BD12 126 F7
Chapel La BAIL BD17 83 K1
BSLYN/ROY S71 243 L6
BSPA/BRAM LS23 48 F8
BTLY WF17 151 H5 2
CUD/GR S72 263 M5
CUL/QBY BD13 125 K4
EARL WF12 195 M4
GFTH/SHER LS25 113 G7 2
GFTH/SHER LS25 135 K5
HBR HX7 144 D4
HDGY LS6 108 F2
HECK WF16 173 G2
HEM/SK/SE WF9 225 G4
HEM/SK/SE WF9 247 K3
HIPP HX3 168 F3
HOLM/MEL HD7 212 F2
HUDE HD5 15 L8
HWTH BD22 56 E7
KBTN HD8 217 K7
KGHY BD21 2 F5
MSTN/BAR LS15 91 G7
PONT WF8 204 F8
RPDN/SBR HX6 167 M2
STKB/PEN S36 270 E4
WIL/AL BD15 103 L6
WOR/ARM LS12 108 E7
WOR/ARM LS12 129 M1
YEA LS19 62 D7
Chapel Pl BSLYN/ROY S71 262 B6
HDGY LS6 108 F1
Chapel Rd AIRE BD20 56 E1
BGLY BD16 81 G1
CHAL LS7 109 M1 6
LM/WK BD12 126 F8
Chapel Rw WIL/AL BD15 80 E8
Chapel St South TOD OL14 163 J5 2
Chapel St AIRE BD20 36 A4 5
AWLS/ASK DN6 249 K6
BFD BD1 5 H6
BRIG HD6 170 A1
BSLYN/ROY S71 262 B6 2
CLECK BD19 150 A6
COL BB8 52 A5 3
CUD/GR S72 244 E3
CUD/GR S72 245 J8
CUL/QBY BD13 101 M6
CUL/QBY BD13 102 F8 6
CUL/QBY BD13 124 F5
EARD/LOFT WF3 153 H5
EARD/LOFT WF3 177 G1
EARL WF12 173 L8 1
ECHL BD2 105 M2
GFTH/SHER LS25 138 E8
GTL/HWG HX4 190 D2
HDGY LS6 108 F1 1
HOLM/MEL HD7 212 D1
HOR/CROF WF4 222 C5
HUDE HD5 15 L8
HUDS HD4 213 L7
HUDS HD4 214 A4
ILK LS29 19 H6
LIT OL15 185 M4
LUD/ILL HX2 146 A6 3
LVSG WF15 171 L1
LVSG WF15 172 E2 3
MIRF WF14 194 C1
MSTN/BAR LS15 111 J6
OSS WF5 197 J2
PDSY/CALV LS28 84 D7
PDSY/CALV LS28 107 G5
ROCH OL11 228 C2 5
ROY/SHW OL2 229 K7 1
TAD LS24 71 L3
WBOW BD5 126 F2 5
WBSY BD6 126 E5
WHIT OL12 184 E7
YEA LS19 84 D2 1
Chapel St North HIPP HX3 146 B3 3
Chapel Ter HDGY LS6 108 F1
HOLM/MEL HD7 236 B2
HUDS HD4 213 M2
WIL/AL BD15 103 K5 2
Chapeltown HFAX HX1 10 F5
PDSY/CALV LS28 106 F8
Chapeltown Rd CHAL LS7 7 J3
Chapel Wk BGLY BD16 81 H3
ECHL BD2 105 M2
Chapelway Gdns
ROY/SHW OL2 228 F8 2
Chapel Yd MSTN/BAR LS15 111 M8
Chapman St BOW BD4 105 M8 3
OSM LS9 7 M6
Chappell Cl STKB/PEN S36 258 B8
Chappell Rd STKB/PEN S36 258 B8
Chapter Wy BSLYN/ROY S71 261 L3 2
DOD/DAR S75 259 J5
Chariot St LDS LS1 6 E8
Chariot Wy PONT WF8 225 J2
Charity St BSLYN/ROY S71 244 B8
Charles Av BFDE BD3 105 M7 2
HIPP HX3 169 J2
HUDW HD3 191 J6
OSM LS9 110 B8
WKFDE WF1 13 M9
Charles Cotton Cl
WKFDW/WTN WF2 175 M6 2
Charles Gdns BEE/HOL LS11 8 C6
Charles Gv RTHW LS26 133 L8
Charles La MILN OL16 229 J1
Charles St AWLS/ASK DN6 249 K4
BAIL BD17 82 D6
BGLY BD16 81 H3
BSLY S70 261 G6
BTLY WF17 173 L2 3
CAS WF10 158 A7
CLECK BD19 150 D6
COL BB8 74 B1 2
CUD/GR S72 244 E6
CUD/GR S72 245 G1
CUD/GR S72 245 J8 1
CUD/GR S72 263 M7
DEWS WF13 173 H6 2
EARL WF12 174 A6 1
ELL HX5 169 H8
HFAX HX1 11 J6
HOR/CROF WF4 197 L7
HOR/CROF WF4 222 C5
HORS LS18 85 K6
HUDS HD4 213 M2 1
LIT OL15 207 J1
OSS WF5 197 H2
OT LS21 41 J7
PDSY/CALV LS28 106 F3
RPDN/SBR HX6 167 K2 4
WKFDE WF1 13 H4
Charlestown Est FEA/AMT WF7 224 C2
Charlestown Rd HIPP HX3 11 J4
Charlesworth Gv LUD/ILL HX2 146 A6 4
Charlesworth Pl
EARD/LOFT WF3 155 K8 1
Charlesworth Sq CLECK BD19 150 C6 1
Charlesworth St EARL WF12 195 L2 1
Charlesworth Ter LUD/ILL HX2 146 A6
Charlesworth Wy
WKFDW/WTN WF2 12 D5
Charlotte Cl BTLY WF17 151 H3
Charlotte Ct HWTH BD22 78 F6 1
Charlotte Gv OSS WF5 197 H2 2
Charlotte St ROCH OL11 228 C2
WKFDE WF1 12 F4
Charlton Gv AIRE BD20 36 B6
OSM LS9 110 C7
Charlton Mt OSM LS9 110 B7
Charlton Pl OSM LS9 110 B7
Charlton Rd OSM LS9 110 B7
Charlton St OSM LS9 110 C7
Charnwood Bank HECK WF16 173 G1
Charnwood Cl ECHL BD2 105 L4 1
ROY/SHW OL2 229 G6
Charnwood Gv ECHL BD2 105 L4 2
Charnwood Rd ECHL BD2 105 L4 3
Charterhouse Rd IDLE BD10 83 K5 6
Charteris Rd GIR BD8 103 L7
Charter St MILN OL16 228 D2
Chartists Wy MOR LS27 152 C3
Charville Gdns AL/HA/HU LS17 89 H3
Chaseley Rd WHIT OL12 206 A6
The Chase EARD/LOFT WF3 155 J8
GFTH/SHER LS25 113 K7
KGHY BD21 2 B2
WBY LS22 30 B8
YEA LS19 84 C2
Chase Wy WBOW BD5 127 G4
Chassum Gv HTON BD9 104 C4
Chaster St BTLY WF17 173 J1
Chatham Crs COL BB8 52 A8 2
Chatham St BFDE BD3 5 H1
COL BB8 52 A8
HFAX HX1 10 E5
RPDN/SBR HX6 167 K1 5

Chat Hill Rd CUL/QBY BD13 125 H1
Chatswood Av BEE/HOL LS11 131 H6 2
Chatswood Crs BEE/HOL LS11 131 H6 3
Chatswood Dr BEE/HOL LS11 131 H5 1
Chatsworth Av
PDSY/CALV LS28 106 C6 1
Chatsworth Cl HUDE HD5 214 F2 1
RHAY LS8 110 C3 12
ROY/SHW OL2 229 L6
Chatsworth Ct EARL WF12 174 B7 1
Chatsworth Crs
PDSY/CALV LS28 106 C6
Chatsworth Dr
PDSY/CALV LS28 106 C6 2
WBY LS22 29 L8
Chatsworth Fall
PDSY/CALV LS28 106 C6
Chatsworth Ms MOR LS27 152 E3 2
Chatsworth Pl GIR BD8 104 D4 1
Chatsworth Ri DOD/DAR S75 260 B8 1
PDSY/CALV LS28 106 C6
Chatsworth Rd BSLYN/ROY S71 243 J8
PDSY/CALV LS28 106 C6
RHAY LS8 110 C3
Chatsworth St KGHY BD21 3 K4
WHIT OL12 206 A3 2
Chatsworth Ter EARL WF12 174 B7
Chatts Wood Fold LM/WK BD12 149 K1
Chaucer Av EARD/LOFT WF3 155 G8
PDSY/CALV LS28 107 H8
Chaucer Cl HOLM/MEL HD7 236 B3 1
Chaucer Gdns PDSY/CALV LS28 107 H8
Chaucer Gv PDSY/CALV LS28 107 H8
Chaucer St HFAX HX1 10 A7
Cheapside BFD BD1 4 F5
BSLY S70 261 H5 3
BTLY WF17 173 M1
CLECK BD19 150 A7 2
HIPP HX3 125 L8
NORM WF6 178 D4 3
WKFDE WF1 12 D2
Cheddington Gv WIL/AL BD15 103 K6
Chedworth Cl DOD/DAR S75 242 A7
Cheese Gate Nab Side
HOLM/MEL HD7 255 J4
Cheetham Hl ROY/SHW OL2 229 K8 2
Cheetham St HBR HX7 143 J3 5
MILN OL16 206 B6 3
ROY/SHW OL2 229 L8
Chelburn Vw LIT OL15 185 L5 1
Chellow Grange Rd HTON BD9 103 L3
Chellow La HTON BD9 103 L4
Chellow St WBOW BD5 126 F4 4
Chellow Wy EARL WF12 173 L7
Chelmsford Rd BFDE BD3 105 L6 1
Chelmsford Ter BFDE BD3 105 L7
Chelsea Cl ROY/SHW OL2 229 K7
WOR/ARM LS12 108 E8
Chelsea Man HIPP HX3 147 J4
Chelsea Rd GTHN BD7 126 B2
Chelsea St KGHY BD21 2 E8
Chelsfield Wy MSTN/BAR LS15 112 B3
Cheltenham Av ILK LS29 39 G2
Cheltenham Ct HIPP HX3 168 F2 2
Cheltenham Gdns HIPP HX3 168 F2
Cheltenham Pl HIPP HX3 168 F2 1
Cheltenham Rd ECHL BD2 105 H1
Cheltenham St WOR/ARM LS12 108 F8
Chelwood Av RHAY LS8 88 A3
Chelwood Crs RHAY LS8 88 B4
Chelwood Dr RHAY LS8 88 B4
WIL/AL BD15 103 K7
Chelwood Gv RHAY LS8 88 B3
Chelwood Mt RHAY LS8 88 B3
Chelwood Pl RHAY LS8 88 A3 1
Chenies Cl SCFT LS14 111 G5 1
Chepstow Cl GFTH/SHER LS25 113 K7 2
Chepstow Dr EARD/LOFT WF3 153 M3
Chequerfield Av PONT WF8 181 H6 1
Chequerfield Cl CAS WF10 157 J8 1
Chequerfield Dr PONT WF8 181 G7
Chequerfield La PONT WF8 181 H6
Chequerfield Mt PONT WF8 181 H7
Chequerfield Rd PONT WF8 181 G7
Chequers Cl PONT WF8 181 H7
Chequers Ct PONT WF8 181 H6 2
Cheriton Av AWLS/ASK DN6 249 J8
Cheriton Dr CUL/QBY BD13 125 H5
Cherry Cl BSLYN/ROY S71 243 J2
CUD/GR S72 244 D6
Cherry Flds ECHL BD2 105 G2
Cherry Garth AWLS/ASK DN6 227 L6
HEM/SK/SE WF9 223 L8
Cherry Gv ILK LS29 38 B2
ROY/SHW OL2 228 E8
Cherry Hall Dr ROY/SHW OL2 229 G7 2
Cherry Hills DOD/DAR S75 242 C5
Cherry La KBTN HD8 240 B4 1
LIT OL15 230 D3
Cherry Lea Ct YEA LS19 84 D1
Cherry Nook Rd HUDN HD2 193 G3
Cherry Pl OSM LS9 7 L7
Cherry Ri SCFT LS14 89 L6
Cherry Rw OSM LS9 7 L6
Cherrys Rd BSLYN/ROY S71 261 M4
Cherry St HWTH BD22 79 G6 3
KGHY BD21 3 L3
Cherry Tree Av IDLE BD10 83 M7 2
KNOT WF11 182 A3
Cherry Tree Cl DOD/DAR S75 242 E5 2
HOLM/MEL HD7 213 G1
Cherry Tree Ct
EARD/LOFT WF3 153 L7 3
Cherry Tree Crs
PDSY/CALV LS28 106 F3
WKFDW/WTN WF2 199 K7
Cherry Tree Dr GTL/HWG HX4 168 D7
PDSY/CALV LS28 106 F3
WKFDW/WTN WF2 199 K7 1
Cherry Tree Gdns SHPY BD18 83 H5
Cherry Tree Ri KGHY BD21 3 K8
Cherry Tree Rd
WKFDW/WTN WF2 199 K7
Cherry Tree Rw BGLY BD16 80 D7
Cherry Tree Wk
EARD/LOFT WF3 153 L7
HOLM/MEL HD7 254 F2 1
Cherrywood Cl SCFT LS14 89 K5
Cherrywood Gdns SCFT LS14 89 K5 1
Chertsey Cl ROY/SHW OL2 229 K6 3
Chervana Ct BOW BD4 128 A2 3
Cherwell Cft GFTH/SHER LS25 135 K1
SEL YO8 139 M5
Cherwell Dr WBSY BD6 126 B7
Chesham Rd BSLY S70 260 F5
Chesham St KGHY BD21 3 K4
Chesil Bank HUDW HD3 191 K8
Chesilton Av HUDW HD3 191 K7
Chesney Av MID LS10 9 J7 1
Chesnut End BSPA/BRAM LS23 49 G7
Chessington Dr HOR/CROF WF4 217 M3
Chester Cl HIPP HX3 10 F1
Chester Gv HIPP HX3 10 F1 1
Chester Pl HIPP HX3 10 F1
Chester Rd HIPP HX3 10 F1
Chester St GTHN BD7 4 D7
HIPP HX3 10 F1
RPDN/SBR HX6 167 K2 5
WOR/ARM LS12 108 E6
Chester Ter HIPP HX3 10 F1
Chesterton Ct HOR/CROF WF4 197 L4 3
MSTN/BAR LS15 111 M8 2
Chesterton Dr HOLM/MEL HD7 236 B3
Chestnut Av AWLS/ASK DN6 249 K5
BSPA/BRAM LS23 48 E6
BTLY WF17 173 J2
CUD/GR S72 245 H3
HDGY LS6 109 G3
MSTN/BAR LS15 111 M4
TOD OL14 141 J7
WBY LS22 29 M8
WKFDW/WTN WF2 199 J8
Chestnut Cl FEA/AMT WF7 179 M7
GTL/HWG HX4 168 D6
HUDS HD4 214 C4 1
HWTH BD22 2 B7 1
ILK LS29 39 G3 1
Chestnut Ct BSLY S70 261 H7 2
SHPY BD18 82 A7
Chestnut Crs BSLY S70 261 K7
NORM WF6 178 C6
Chestnut Dr BHP/TINH LS16 86 D1
CUD/GR S72 244 F1
Chestnut Garth HUDW HD3 191 K7 1
Chestnut Gv BSPA/BRAM LS23 48 E6
ECHL BD2 105 G2
HDGY LS6 109 G3 13
HEM/SK/SE WF9 246 B1
HOR/CROF WF4 200 B5 1
PDSY/CALV LS28 84 D8 3
PONT WF8 180 F8
Chestnut Mdw MIRF WF14 172 B7
Chestnut Pl HDGY LS6 109 G3 14
Chestnut Rd HDGY LS6 109 G3
The Chestnuts PONT WF8 181 H2
Chestnut St CUD/GR S72 263 K1
HDGY LS6 109 G3 15
HEM/SK/SE WF9 247 H5
HFAX HX1 10 A8
HUDN HD2 192 F3
Chestnut Ter EARL WF12 195 L3
Chestnut Wy BHP/TINH LS16 86 D1
LIT OL15 207 G1
Chevet Cft WKFDW/WTN WF2 199 G6
Chevet Gv WKFDW/WTN WF2 199 G7
Chevet La HOR/CROF WF4 221 K6
WKFDW/WTN WF2 199 G7
Chevet Mt WIL/AL BD15 103 J7
Chevet Park Ct
WKFDW/WTN WF2 221 G3
Chevet Ri BSLYN/ROY S71 243 J2
Chevet Vw BSLYN/ROY S71 243 J2
Chevin Av ILK LS29 61 J1
OT LS21 41 K8
Chevin End Rd ILK LS29 61 L2
Chevington Ct YEA LS19 84 C3 1
Chevins Cl BTLY WF17 151 H6
Chevin Side OT LS21 41 J8
Cheviot Av HOLM/MEL HD7 235 H5
Cheviot Cl HEM/SK/SE WF9 224 B7
MILN OL16 207 J7
Cheviot Ct GFTH/SHER LS25 135 H1
Cheviot Ga LM/WK BD12 126 D8 1
Cheviot Pl KNOT WF11 182 A2
Cheviots Rd ROY/SHW OL2 229 J6
Cheviot Wy MIRF WF14 194 B4
Cheyne Wk KGHY BD21 2 D7 2
Chichester Cl LIT OL15 207 H3
Chichester St MILN OL16 206 C7
WOR/ARM LS12 108 E6 6
Chickenley La EARL WF12 174 C7
Chidswell Gdns EARL WF12 174 D3 1
Chidswell La EARL WF12 174 C3
OSS WF5 174 D4
Child La LVSG WF15 172 B4
Childs La SHPY BD18 83 G8
Childs Rd WKFDW/WTN WF2 175 M6
Chiltern Av CAS WF10 179 H1
HUDW HD3 191 J5
KNOT WF11 182 A2
Chiltern Cl GFTH/SHER LS25 135 H1
ROY/SHW OL2 229 H6
Chiltern Ct BRAM LS13 107 G1
GFTH/SHER LS25 135 H1
HEM/SK/SE WF9 224 B7
Chiltern Dr FEA/AMT WF7 224 B1
MIRF WF14 194 B4 3
Chiltern Rd EARL WF12 174 B5 1
Chiltern Wy LVSG WF15 171 M1
Chilton St BSLY S70 261 J6
Chilwell Cl BSLYN/ROY S71 243 H5 2
Chilwell Gdns BSLYN/ROY S71 243 H5 3
Chimney La KBTN HD8 215 M2
Chinewood Av BTLY WF17 151 K8
Chippendale Ri GIR BD8 103 M6
OT LS21 41 J4
Chipping Fold MILN OL16 229 H1 1
Chirton Gv RHAY LS8 110 C1
Chislehurst Pl WBOW BD5 126 E3
Chiswick St HDGY LS6 109 G5
Chiswick Ter HDGY LS6 109 G4
Choppards Bank Rd
HOLM/MEL HD7 254 C5
Choppards La HOLM/MEL HD7 254 C4
Chorley La BVRD LS3 6 D8
LDSU LS2 6 D7
Chrisharben Pk CLAY BD14 125 L2 3
Chrismoor IDLE BD10 83 J7 3
Christ Church Av
WOR/ARM LS12 108 D6
Christ Church Mt
WOR/ARM LS12 108 D6
Christ Church Pde
WOR/ARM LS12 108 D6
Christ Church Pl
WOR/ARM LS12 108 D6
Christ Church Rd
WOR/ARM LS12 108 D6
Christ Church Ter
WOR/ARM LS12 108 D6
Christ Church Vw
WOR/ARM LS12 108 D6
Christine St ROY/SHW OL2 229 K7
Christopher Rd HDGY LS6 6 D2
Christopher St WBOW BD5 126 E3 5
Christopher Ter WBOW BD5 126 E3 6
Church Ap GFTH/SHER LS25 113 H7
Church Av HDGY LS6 87 H7
HEM/SK/SE WF9 246 E4
HOLM/MEL HD7 213 G4 1
HORS LS18 85 K5
HUDS HD4 214 A2 1
MOR LS27 129 L6
RTHW LS26 134 C4
WKFDE WF1 177 L7
Churchbalk Dr PONT WF8 181 G8
Churchbalk La PONT WF8 181 G7
Church Bank BFD BD1 5 G6
LUD/ILL HX2 145 M8
RPDN/SBR HX6 167 L2 2
Church Bank La HBR HX7 165 L3 1
Churchbank Wy EARL WF12 195 M2 1
Church Cswy BSPA/BRAM LS23 49 H5
Church Cl DOD/DAR S75 242 A6
HOR/CROF WF4 200 D4
KBTN HD8 238 A6
LUD/ILL HX2 145 M1
OT LS21 42 E7
RTHW LS26 134 C4
SCFT LS14 111 K2
Church Ct GTHN BD7 126 B1 2
NORM WF6 178 C5 2
YEA LS19 62 D8
Church Crs AL/HA/HU LS17 87 L3
HOR/CROF WF4 197 G8 1
RTHW LS26 134 D5
TAD LS24 71 K7
YEA LS19 62 C8
Church Cft TAD LS24 116 A1
Church Dr AL/HA/HU LS17 67 K1
CUD/GR S72 245 H4
HEM/SK/SE WF9 246 E4
Church Farm SCFT LS14 68 B8
Church Farm Cl
EARD/LOFT WF3 154 E5
NORM WF6 178 B2 1
Churchfarm Garth
AL/HA/HU LS17 89 H2
Church Farm Vw
MSTN/BAR LS15 91 G7 1
Church Fenton La TAD LS24 94 F1 1
Churchfield BSLY S70 261 G4 2
Churchfield Av CUD/GR S72 244 D8 1
DOD/DAR S75 241 L6 1
Churchfield Cl DOD/DAR S75 241 K6
LVSG WF15 172 C2 1
Churchfield Crs CUD/GR S72 244 D8 2
Churchfield Cft NORM WF6 178 B2
RTHW LS26 155 H1 1
Churchfield Gv RTHW LS26 133 G8 1
Churchfield La AWLS/ASK DN6 205 K4
CAS WF10 158 B8
DOD/DAR S75 241 K6
RTHW LS26 133 G8
Church Field Rd AWLS/ASK DN6 227 M5
Churchfield Rd RTHW LS26 155 G1
Church Flds ECHL BD2 105 M4
NORM WF6 178 C5 3
Churchfields HOR/CROF WF4 222 D4
HUDN HD2 193 H3 1
Churchfields Rd BRIG HD6 170 C3
Churchfield St BTLY WF17 173 L1 3
Churchfield Ter CUD/GR S72 244 D8 3
Church Gdns AL/HA/HU LS17 87 M3
GFTH/SHER LS25 113 H8
MOR LS27 129 L7 2
Church Garth CAS WF10 158 B8 3
OT LS21 42 E7
Churchgate BHP/TINH LS16 63 M3
Church Ga HORS LS18 85 K5
Church Gn KBTN HD8 216 B8
LUD/ILL HX2 146 A5 1
Church Gv BSLYN/ROY S71 261 L2
HEM/SK/SE WF9 246 E4
HORS LS18 85 K5
Church Hts STKB/PEN S36 258 B7
Church Hl AL/HA/HU LS17 25 M8
BAIL BD17 82 F2 4
BHP/TINH LS16 63 M3
BSLYN/ROY S71 243 M3
BSPA/BRAM LS23 69 M3
GFTH/SHER LS25 137 J1
PBR HG3 28 E3
SCFT LS14 68 C8
Church Hill Gdns
PDSY/CALV LS28 107 H4
Church Hill Gn PDSY/CALV LS28 107 H4
Church Hill Mt PDSY/CALV LS28 107 H4
Churchill Gdns LDSU LS2 6 E5
Churchill Gv HECK WF16 173 G3
WKFDW/WTN WF2 199 G6
Churchill Rd CUL/QBY BD13 103 H8
Churchill St TOD OL14 141 G6 2
Churchill Wy AIRE BD20 35 G7
Church La AL/HA/HU LS17 45 H7
AWLS/ASK DN6 249 L8 1
BAIL BD17 83 L1
BHP/TINH LS16 86 E2
BRIG HD6 170 C4 1
BSLY S70 261 G4 2
BSLY S70 261 G4 3
CHAL LS7 87 M8
CLECK BD19 150 E6
COP/BISH YO23 73 K6
CUD/GR S72 222 C8
DEWS WF13 173 H6
DOD/DAR S75 240 F3
DOD/DAR S75 259 H2
EARD/LOFT WF3 152 F7
EARL WF12 196 A4
ELL HX5 169 M7
FEA/AMT WF7 178 F6
GFTH/SHER LS25 113 H7
GFTH/SHER LS25 135 K5
GFTH/SHER LS25 138 D6
GLE DN14 161 M8
GTL/HWG HX4 190 C2
HBR HX7 143 H2
HDGY LS6 87 G7
HECK WF16 172 F2
HIPP HX3 169 L2
HOLM/MEL HD7 213 G5
HOLM/MEL HD7 233 H2
HOR/CROF WF4 197 G7
HOR/CROF WF4 220 C2
HOR/CROF WF4 222 A7
HORS LS18 85 K5
HUDE HD5 15 K7
HUDS HD4 213 K8
HUDS HD4 214 C4
HUDW HD3 211 H1
KBTN HD8 238 A6
KBTN HD8 240 B4
LUD/ILL HX2 146 A5
LVSG WF15 171 K3
LVSG WF15 172 C1
MILN OL16 206 B7 4
MIRF WF14 194 E2 2
MSTN/BAR LS15 111 L4
NORM WF6 178 C5
OT LS21 24 F8
OT LS21 40 D4
PBR HG3 28 E3
PDSY/CALV LS28 107 G7
PONT WF8 180 F6 2
PONT WF8 203 M1
RPDN/SBR HX6 188 F3 1
RTHW LS26 134 C5
RTHW LS26 156 E4
STKB/PEN S36 258 B7
TAD LS24 50 C4
TAD LS24 71 K6
WBSY BD6 126 D6
WBY LS22 47 K5
WKFDE WF1 176 D1
Church Lane Av WKFDE WF1 176 D1
Church Mdw BSPA/BRAM LS23 69 M3 1
BTLY WF17 150 F5
Church Ms BSPA/BRAM LS23 48 F6 1
GFTH/SHER LS25 116 A6
Church Mt HEM/SK/SE WF9 246 E4
HORS LS18 85 K5
Church Pk LVSG WF15 172 A4
Church Pl GFTH/SHER LS25 113 H7 1
HFAX HX1 10 E7
Church Rd AIRE BD20 55 M1
BTLY WF17 151 H6
DOD/DAR S75 259 G2
EARD/LOFT WF3 177 H1
HORS LS18 85 K6
LVSG WF15 172 A4
MILN OL16 206 D8
NORM WF6 177 M3
OSM LS9 9 L2
ROY/SHW OL2 229 K8
RTHW LS26 135 G6
TOD OL14 141 G6
WBSY BD6 126 D6 3
WOR/ARM LS12 108 E7
Church Rw LDSU LS2 9 J1
Church Side RTHW LS26 156 E4
Church Side Cl HIPP HX3 11 H2
Church Side Dr HIPP HX3 11 H2
Churchside Vls RTHW LS26 156 E4 1
Church Sq GFTH/SHER LS25 113 H7 2
Church Stile MILN OL16 206 B7
Church St AIRE BD20 34 F7 4
BGLY BD16 81 J4
BRIG HD6 170 B6
BSLY S70 261 G4 4
BSLYN/ROY S71 243 L3
BSLYN/ROY S71 243 M5
BSPA/BRAM LS23 48 F7
CAS WF10 157 M6
CLECK BD19 150 A7
COL BB8 74 E4
CUD/GR S72 244 D8
CUD/GR S72 245 H3
CUL/QBY BD13 79 M8 3
DEWS WF13 195 G1
DOD/DAR S75 242 A6
DOD/DAR S75 242 E5 3
DOD/DAR S75 259 G1
DOD/DAR S75 260 C3
EARL WF12 173 M6 2
ELL HX5 169 H7
GIR BD8 104 D5
GSLY LS20 62 A5
GTL/HWG HX4 168 F7
HBR HX7 143 H1
HBR HX7 144 A6
HECK WF16 172 F3
HEM/SK/SE WF9 247 J4
HFAX HX1 11 J6
HOLM/MEL HD7 212 B6
HOLM/MEL HD7 212 F2
HOLM/MEL HD7 237 H8 1
HOR/CROF WF4 220 B7
HUD HD1 14 F6
HUDE HD5 15 L8
HUDS HD4 214 A2
HUDW HD3 191 J8
HUDW HD3 213 L1
HWTH BD22 78 D7
HWTH BD22 100 E4
ILK LS29 19 J6
KBTN HD8 217 L7
KGHY BD21 2 F6
KGHY BD21 3 J4
KNOT WF11 159 L6
KSTL LS5 108 C2
LIT OL15 207 K1
LVSG WF15 171 L1
LVSG WF15 172 C1
MID LS10 9 L9
MILN OL16 206 F3 3
MILN OL16 229 K2
MOR LS27 129 L7
MOR LS27 152 C1
OSS WF5 174 F7
ROCH OL11 206 A7
RTHW LS26 133 L7
RTHW LS26 155 G1
RYKW YO26 32 D5
SHPY BD18 82 F6
SKP/WHF BD23 16 B3
STKB/PEN S36 270 F3
TAD LS24 94 E8
TAD LS24 95 G1 1
TAD LS24 116 A1
TOD OL14 141 H6
WBSY BD6 126 A7
WBY LS22 48 A1 2
WKFDE WF1 12 F6
YEA LS19 62 C8
Church Ter HOLM/MEL HD7 254 C1
KBTN HD8 239 M5
LUD/ILL HX2 145 M1
MILN OL16 229 J1 2
Church Top HEM/SK/SE WF9 246 E4
Church Vw AWLS/ASK DN6 227 L6
CLECK BD19 149 K6
CUD/GR S72 244 D8
DOD/DAR S75 260 E3
GFTH/SHER LS25 116 A6
GFTH/SHER LS25 136 A4
GFTH/SHER LS25 138 A3
HEM/SK/SE WF9 246 E3
HOLM/MEL HD7 253 K4
HOR/CROF WF4 220 A1
RPDN/SBR HX6 167 L2
WKFDE WF1 199 G4
Church View Cl HOR/CROF WF4 222 E5
Church View Crs STKB/PEN S36 270 F3
Church View Ms
BSPA/BRAM LS23 69 M1 3
Church View Rd STKB/PEN S36 270 F3
Church Vls HEM/SK/SE WF9 246 E4
Churchville GFTH/SHER LS25 114 C7
Churchville Av GFTH/SHER LS25 114 B7
Churchville Dr GFTH/SHER LS25 114 C7
Churchville Ter
GFTH/SHER LS25 114 B6
Church Wk BTLY WF17 173 J3
EARL WF12 196 A4 1
HIPP HX3 147 J4
LDSU LS2 9 J1
TOD OL14 163 J5
Churchway HOR/CROF WF4 200 C5
Church Wy KGHY BD21 3 G6
MOR LS27 152 C1 3
Church Wood Av BHP/TINH LS16 86 E8
Churchwood Cl
HOLM/MEL HD7 212 B5 1
Church Wood Mt BHP/TINH LS16 86 E8
Church Wood Rd BHP/TINH LS16 86 E8
Churn La LUD/ILL HX2 145 M7
Churn Milk La HIPP HX3 146 C2
Churwell Av DEWS WF13 173 H3 1
Churwell Cl CAS WF10 157 M8
Churwell V EARL WF12 174 C4
Cinder Hill Rd TOD OL14 142 A8
Cinderhills La HIPP HX3 169 G3
Cinder Hills Rd HOLM/MEL HD7 254 D2
Cinder Hills Wy DOD/DAR S75 260 C7 1
Cinder La BSPA/BRAM LS23 49 G8
CAS WF10 157 L6
OT LS21 42 B1
The Circle PONT WF8 181 G7
The Circuit AWLS/ASK DN6 249 H8
City La HIPP HX3 146 A5
City Rd GIR BD8 4 B4
City Sq LDS LS1 8 F1
Clanricarde St BSLYN/ROY S71 261 G3
Clapgate OT LS21 41 J6 3
Clapgate La RPDN/SBR HX6 166 F7
Clapham Dene Rd
MSTN/BAR LS15 111 K5 1
Clapham St CUL/QBY BD13 102 A6 3
Clapton Av HFAX HX1 10 D8
Clara Dr PDSY/CALV LS28 84 B7
Clara Rd ECHL BD2 105 H1
Clara St BRIG HD6 170 C5
HUD HD1 14 F2
HUDS HD4 213 J2
PDSY/CALV LS28 106 F4
ROCH OL11 228 B1
Clare Crs LM/WK BD12 148 E4
Clare Hall La HFAX HX1 11 H8
Clare Hl HUD HD1 14 E3
Clarehurst Rd WMB/DAR S73 263 J8 1
Clarel Cl STKB/PEN S36 270 E4
Clarel St STKB/PEN S36 270 E4
Claremont GTHN BD7 4 C8
HECK WF16 172 F2
PDSY/CALV LS28 107 H7
Claremont Av BVRD LS3 6 C7
SHPY BD18 83 G8
Claremont Ct HDGY LS6 87 G8
Claremont Crs HDGY LS6 109 H1
SHPY BD18 83 G8 1
Claremont Dr HDGY LS6 87 G8
Claremont Gdns BGLY BD16 81 J2 2
Claremont Gv BVRD LS3 6 C7 3
PDSY/CALV LS28 107 G7
SHPY BD18 83 G8
Claremont Pl WOR/ARM LS12 108 C7
Claremont Rd DEWS WF13 173 K5
HDGY LS6 87 G8
MILN OL16 229 G1
SHPY BD18 83 G8
Claremont St CLECK BD19 149 M6 3
ELL HX5 169 J8
HUD HD1 14 E4
RPDN/SBR HX6 167 L1 1
RTHW LS26 133 L8 3
WKFDE WF1 13 K7
WOR/ARM LS12 108 C7
Claremont Ter
WKFDW/WTN WF2 12 B5

Cla - Col 287

WOR/ARM LS12 108 C7
Claremont Vw BVRD LS3 6 C7 4
Claremount Rd HIPP HX3 146 E4
Clarence Dr HORS LS18 85 K7
ILK LS29 40 B8
Clarence Gdns HORS LS18 85 K7 2
Clarence Rd BSLYN/ROY S71 261 K2
HORS LS18 85 K7
MID LS10 9 L4
SHPY BD18 82 B6 3
WKFDW/WTN WF2 12 D8 1
Clarence St BRAM LS13 107 L5 2
BTLY WF17 173 M1 2
CLECK BD19 149 M7
COL BB8 74 C1
COL BB8 74 E4
HFAX HX1 10 F6
Clarence Ter PDSY/CALV LS28 106 F6
Clarence Wk WKFDW/WTN WF2 12 A5
Clarendon Ct WKFDE WF1 176 E7 6
Clarendon Pl CUL/QBY BD13 124 E6 1
LDSU LS2 6 C5
Clarendon Rd BGLY BD16 81 K2
BSPA/BRAM LS23 48 E6
BVRD LS3 6 C7
LDSU LS2 6 C4
Clarendon St BSLY S70 260 F5
COL BB8 74 D1 2
HWTH BD22 78 E8 4
MILN OL16 228 D2
WKFDE WF1 176 E7 7
Clarendon Ter PDSY/CALV LS28 107 G8
Clarendon Wy LDSU LS2 6 D7
Clare Rd CLECK BD19 149 L7
HBR HX7 143 M5
HFAX HX1 11 H7
LM/WK BD12 148 E4
Clare St HFAX HX1 11 H7
Clarges St WBOW BD5 126 E3
Clarion St WKFDE WF1 13 K7
Clark Av OSM LS9 110 B7
Clark Ct FEA/AMT WF7 179 K5
Clark Crs OSM LS9 110 B7
Clarke Crs NORM WF6 178 C7
Clarke Gv WKFDE WF1 177 G5
Clarke Hall Rd EARD/LOFT WF3 177 G4
Clarke La HOLM/MEL HD7 235 G4
Clarke Rd EARD/LOFT WF3 175 G1
Clarke St DEWS WF13 173 J5
DOD/DAR S75 260 F3
MILN OL16 206 D4
PDSY/CALV LS28 84 D8
Clark Gv OSM LS9 110 B8
Clark La OSM LS9 110 B7
Clark Mt OSM LS9 110 B7
Clark Rd OSM LS9 110 B8
Clark Rw OSM LS9 110 B8
Clarks Ct AWLS/ASK DN6 249 K8
Clarkson Av HECK WF16 173 G2
Clarkson Cl HECK WF16 173 G2
Clarkson Ct NORM WF6 178 E5
Clarkson Dr GFTH/SHER LS25 160 A3
Clarkson St DEWS WF13 173 G8 2
Clarkson Vw HDGY LS6 6 D1
Clark Spring Ri MOR LS27 130 D7
Clark Ter OSM LS9 110 B7
Clark Vw OSM LS9 110 B8 3
Clarney Av WMB/DAR S73 263 H8
Clarney Pl WMB/DAR S73 263 H8
Clattering Stones Rd HBR HX7 165 M4
Clayborn Vw CLECK BD19 149 M8
Clay Butts HUDN HD2 192 A4
Claycliffe Av DOD/DAR S75 260 B2
Claycliffe Rd DOD/DAR S75 260 B1
Clayfield Dr GTHN BD7 126 C4
Clay Hill Dr LM/WK BD12 148 F3
Clay House La GTL/HWG HX4 168 F7 1
Clay La HOLM/MEL HD7 212 C5
Claymore Ri AIRE BD20 36 B6
Claypit La CAS WF10 136 D7
Clay Pit La LDSU LS2 7 H6
Claypit La SCFT LS14 90 B1
Clay Pits La HFAX HX1 10 A4
RPDN/SBR HX6 166 D7
Clay St HFAX HX1 10 B5
LIT OL15 207 H1 4
RPDN/SBR HX6 167 L2
Clayton Av GFTH/SHER LS25 135 K4
HEM/SK/SE WF9 226 A6
Clayton Cl MID LS10 132 B4
Clayton Ct FEA/AMT WF7 201 L1 2
MID LS10 132 B4 1
Clayton Dr MID LS10 132 B4 2
Clayton Flds HUDN HD2 14 C2
Clayton Gv YEA LS19 62 D7
Clayton Hall Rd AIRE BD20 35 G8
Clayton Holt HEM/SK/SE WF9 246 D5
Clayton La CLAY BD14 125 K3
WBOW BD5 127 G2 4
Clayton Ms NORM WF6 178 C2 5
Clayton Pl NORM WF6 178 C2 6
Clayton Ri KGHY BD21 2 D2
WKFDE WF1 176 D1
Clayton Rd GTHN BD7 126 A2
MID LS10 132 B4
Claytons Buildings
FEA/AMT WF7 179 M6
Clayton St COL BB8 74 A2 4
RTHW LS26 155 H1 5
WHIT OL12 206 D4 2
WKFDW/WTN WF2 12 B4 1
Clayton Vw HEM/SK/SE WF9 246 D5
Clayton Wy MID LS10 132 B4 3
Clayton Wood Cl BHP/TINH LS16 86 B5
Clayton Wood Ct BHP/TINH LS16 86 B5
Clayton Wood Ri BHP/TINH LS16 86 B5
Clayton Wood Rd
BHP/TINH LS16 86 B5
Clay Well HOLM/MEL HD7 212 F2
The Clearings MID LS10 131 M6
Clear Vw CUD/GR S72 245 J6
Cleasby Rd ILK LS29 61 J3
Cleavesty La AL/HA/HU LS17 46 D7
Cleckheaton Rd WBSY BD6 126 F6
Cleeve Hl YEA LS19 84 D2
Cleevethorpe Gv
WKFDW/WTN WF2 199 G6
Clegg Hall Rd MILN OL16 206 F4
Clegg La GTL/HWG HX4 168 B7
Clegg St LIT OL15 185 H7
MILN OL16 229 J1 3
ROY/SHW OL2 229 H6
Cleggswood Av LIT OL15 207 J3
Clement Cl NORM WF6 178 F5
Clementina St WHIT OL12 206 B5 4
WHIT OL12 206 B5 4
Clement Royds St WHIT OL12 206 A6 4
Clement St GIR BD8 104 B6 2
HUD HD1 14 D3
HUDS HD4 213 M2 2
RPDN/SBR HX6 167 K2 6
WKFDW/WTN WF2 198 B1
Clement Ter EARL WF12 173 L8
RTHW LS26 155 G2 2
Clerk Green St BTLY WF17 173 K2 6
Clevedon Pl HIPP HX3 146 C4 5
Clevedon Wy BSLYN/ROY S71 243 K2 2
Cleveland Av HIPP HX3 168 F2 3
HOLM/MEL HD7 235 H5
KNOT WF11 182 A2
WKFDW/WTN WF2 197 M4
Cleveland Dr MILN OL16 207 K8
Cleveland Garth
WKFDW/WTN WF2 197 M4
Cleveland Gv
WKFDW/WTN WF2 197 M4
Cleveland Pl HBR HX7 143 J3 6
Cleveland Rd HTON BD9 104 D3
HUDW HD3 191 M7
Cleveland St COL BB8 52 B8
TOD OL14 140 D5
Cleveland Wy KBTN HD8 238 B4
Cleveleys Av BEE/HOL LS11 8 B7
MILN OL16 228 D3
Cleveleys Ct BEE/HOL LS11 8 B8 1
Cleveleys Mt BEE/HOL LS11 8 B7 1
Cleveleys Rd BEE/HOL LS11 8 B7
Cleveleys St BEE/HOL LS11 8 B7 2
Cleveleys Ter BEE/HOL LS11 8 B7 3
Clevlands Cl ROY/SHW OL2 229 J6 2
Cliff Cl HUDW HD3 191 K8
Cliff Ct LVSG WF15 172 C3
Cliff Crs GFTH/SHER LS25 135 L5
LUD/ILL HX2 168 A1 1
Cliffdale Rd CHAL LS7 109 K2
Cliff Dr HOR/CROF WF4 219 M1
Cliffe Ash HOLM/MEL HD7 212 F2 1
Cliffe Av BAIL BD17 82 E3
BGLY BD16 80 C5
HIPP HX3 148 C7
Cliffe Cl CUD/GR S72 245 H4
Cliffe Ct BSLYN/ROY S71 261 L3
Cliffe Crs AIRE BD20 58 D6
DOD/DAR S75 260 A7 2
Cliffe Crest HOR/CROF WF4 197 K4
Cliffedale Crs BSLY S70 261 K8
Cliffe End Rd HUDW HD3 191 K8
Cliffe House Av
GFTH/SHER LS25 135 J1
Cliffe La BAIL BD17 82 E5
BSLYN/ROY S71 261 L3 3
CLECK BD19 150 A5
CUL/QBY BD13 103 G7
YEA LS19 84 E3
Cliffe La South BAIL BD17 82 E5
Cliffe La West BAIL BD17 82 E4
Cliffe Mill Fold AIRE BD20 59 G6
Cliffe Mt CLECK BD19 150 C5
Cliffe Pk KBTN HD8 238 A6
Cliffe Park Cha
WOR/ARM LS12 108 C8 1
Cliffe Park Cl WOR/ARM LS12 108 C8
Cliffe Park Crs WOR/ARM LS12 130 C1
Cliffe Park Dr WOR/ARM LS12 108 C8
Cliffe Park Mt WOR/ARM LS12 108 C8
Cliffe Park Ri WOR/ARM LS12 108 B8
Cliffe Rd BFDE BD3 105 H4
BRIG HD6 170 C4
KBTN HD8 238 A6
KGHY BD21 79 L2
Cliffestone Dr AIRE BD20 58 F6
Cliffe St BTLY WF17 173 H2
CUL/QBY BD13 102 E7 1
DEWS WF13 173 M5
HBR HX7 143 J3 7
KBTN HD8 240 B4
LIT OL15 185 M4
Cliffe Ter BAIL BD17 82 E5
GIR BD8 4 D1
KGHY BD21 79 L2
RPDN/SBR HX6 167 J1
Cliffe Vw KBTN HD8 240 B4
MOR LS27 151 M3
WIL/AL BD15 103 H4
Cliffe Wood Cl HTON BD9 104 A3
Cliffewood Ri KBTN HD8 240 A4 2
Cliff Gdns LUD/ILL HX2 168 A1 2
Cliff Gv HOR/CROF WF4 219 L2
Cliff Hl DOD/DAR S75 259 G1
Cliff Hill La LUD/ILL HX2 145 K8
Cliff Hill Rd AWLS/ASK DN6 227 K3
ROY/SHW OL2 229 L5
Cliff Hollins La LM/WK BD12 127 M8
Cliff House La HOLM/MEL HD7 236 D8
Cliff La CUD/GR S72 245 G4
HDGY LS6 6 B1
HOLM/MEL HD7 254 D1
RPDN/SBR HX6 188 F4
WKFDE WF1 12 D1
Cliff Mt HDGY LS6 6 C1
Cliff Mount St HDGY LS6 6 C1
Cliff Mount Ter HDGY LS6 6 C1
Clifford Av ILK LS29 38 C1
WKFDW/WTN WF2 198 F4
Clifford Hodgson Pl MOR LS27 130 D7 1
Clifford Moor Rd
BSPA/BRAM LS23 48 D7
Clifford Rd BAIL BD17 82 E4
BSPA/BRAM LS23 69 M3
HEM/SK/SE WF9 246 D4
ILK LS29 20 C8
Clifford St AIRE BD20 35 M4
COL BB8 74 A1
CUD/GR S72 244 E5
HEM/SK/SE WF9 247 H4 3
ROCH OL11 228 B1
SKP/WHF BD23 16 B3
WBOW BD5 4 F9
Clifford Vw WKFDW/WTN WF2 198 F4
Cliff Pde WKFDE WF1 12 D2
Cliff Park Av WKFDE WF1 176 D7
Cliff Rd HDGY LS6 6 C1
HOLM/MEL HD7 253 J2
HOLM/MEL HD7 254 D1
HOR/CROF WF4 219 L3
Cliff Side Gdns HDGY LS6 109 J2
Cliff St HWTH BD22 78 F7
MILN OL16 206 D5
PONT WF8 180 E6 2
WKFDW/WTN WF2 176 B7
Cliff Ter HDGY LS6 6 C1
Cliff Vale Rd SHPY BD18 104 D1 10
Cliff Wood Av SHPY BD18 82 D8
Clifton Av BSLYN/ROY S71 243 G6
EARD/LOFT WF3 177 G1
HFAX HX1 10 A8
HOLM/MEL HD7 236 D8
HOR/CROF WF4 197 J4
OSM LS9 110 C5
PONT WF8 180 D6
Clifton Cl BSLYN/ROY S71 243 G6
HOR/CROF WF4 197 H4
Clifton Common BRIG HD6 170 E4
Clifton Ct DEWS WF13 173 H5 1
Clifton Crs BSLYN/ROY S71 243 H5
HOR/CROF WF4 197 J4
Clifton Dr HOR/CROF WF4 197 J4
PDSY/CALV LS28 107 G6
Clifton Gdns CUD/GR S72 245 G3
Clifton Gv OSM LS9 110 C5
Clifton Hl PDSY/CALV LS28 107 G6
Clifton La HOLM/MEL HD7 235 G4
OT LS21 41 G2
Clifton Mt OSM LS9 110 C5
Clifton Pl PDSY/CALV LS28 107 G6
SHPY BD18 82 D8
WKFDE WF1 176 D6 3
Clifton Rd CUD/GR S72 245 J7
HIPP HX3 168 E2
HOR/CROF WF4 197 J5
HOR/CROF WF4 200 D3
HUD HD1 14 A5
ILK LS29 38 F3
PDSY/CALV LS28 107 G6
Clifton Side HUDN HD2 171 H8
Clifton St BSLY S70 261 J6 1
COL BB8 74 D4
GIR BD8 4 C1
HEM/SK/SE WF9 223 L8
HIPP HX3 10 C1
HWTH BD22 2 C7
MILN OL16 207 H8
ROCH OL11 228 C1 5
RPDN/SBR HX6 167 L2
Clifton Ter BTLY WF17 173 M1
OSM LS9 110 C5
Clifton Vw KBTN HD8 240 B4 2
Clifton Vls GIR BD8 4 C1
Cliftonville Rd MILN OL16 228 E6
Clipston Av HDGY LS6 87 H8
Clipstone Av BSLYN/ROY S71 243 H6
Clipstone St WBOW BD5 127 G4 1
Clipston St HDGY LS6 87 H8
Clipston Ter HDGY LS6 87 H8 9
Clive Pl GTHN BD7 126 D1
Clive Rd PBR HG3 28 E3
Clive Ter GTHN BD7 126 D1
Cloberry St LDSU LS2 6 C5
Clock La CUL/QBY BD13 101 M5
Clock Row Av HEM/SK/SE WF9 246 F3
Clock Row Gv HEM/SK/SE WF9 246 F3
Clock Row Mt HEM/SK/SE WF9 246 F3
Clock View St KGHY BD21 57 K5
Clog Br AIRE BD20 36 A5 2
Clog Sole Rd BRIG HD6 170 B2
The Cloisters MILN OL16 206 D5 2
Cloisters Wy BSLYN/ROY S71 261 M4
Close Head Dr CUL/QBY BD13 102 C8
Close Head La CUL/QBY BD13 102 D7
Close La HWTH BD22 54 E5
Close Lea BRIG HD6 170 B5
Close Lea Av BRIG HD6 170 B5
Close Lea Dr BRIG HD6 170 B6
Close Lea Wy BRIG HD6 170 B5
Close Rd CAS WF10 158 B7
Closes Rd BRIG HD6 170 C5 3
Close St HEM/SK/SE WF9 223 L7
The Close AL/HA/HU LS17 67 L1
AL/HA/HU LS17 87 J1
AWLS/ASK DN6 227 M3
BSLYN/ROY S71 243 L5
BSLYN/ROY S71 262 B3 1
BSPA/BRAM LS23 48 F6
EARD/LOFT WF3 153 M7
GFTH/SHER LS25 135 J5
GSLY LS20 61 L6
HOR/CROF WF4 198 A7
KBTN HD8 240 A4 3
MSTN/BAR LS15 90 F8
OSM LS9 9 L1
PONT WF8 181 H7
SCFT LS14 68 C8
SKP/WHF BD23 16 B3
TAD LS24 93 M3
WBY LS22 47 K6 1
Cloth Hall St DEWS WF13 173 M6 3
HUD HD1 14 F7
LDS LS1 9 H1
Cloudberry Wy DOD/DAR S75 242 F6
Cloudsdale Av WBOW BD5 127 G2
Clough Av AIRE BD20 56 E1
Clough Bank LUD/ILL HX2 145 K1
Clough Bank La HWTH BD22 56 D8
Clough Dr BTLY WF17 151 J4
HOLM/MEL HD7 212 F6
KBTN HD8 215 M4
Clough Foot La HOLM/MEL HD7 254 C7
Clough Ga HOR/CROF WF4 216 F1
HWTH BD22 78 F4 1
Clough Gate Dr HOR/CROF WF4 216 F1
Clough Hall La HUDE HD5 214 F4
HUDS HD4 214 E6
Clough Head STKB/PEN S36 270 F5
Clough House La GTL/HWG HX4 189 K3
HOLM/MEL HD7 211 M5
KBTN HD8 239 L8
WHIT OL12 184 D8
Clough La BRIG HD6 170 B8
BRIG HD6 170 F1
HBR HX7 144 D1
HUDN HD2 192 B1
HUDW HD3 213 L1
HWTH BD22 78 E3
LUD/ILL HX2 123 L8
LVSG WF15 171 M2
Clough Pk KBTN HD8 215 M4
Clough Pl LUD/ILL HX2 145 K1
Clough Rd HOLM/MEL HD7 212 C2
HOR/CROF WF4 217 M5
HUDN HD2 192 C4
LIT OL15 185 J6
ROY/SHW OL2 229 M8
RPDN/SBR HX6 167 M4
TOD OL14 163 J5 3
Clough St MOR LS27 152 D2
WBOW BD5 127 G3 4
WHIT OL12 184 E8
The Clough KBTN HD8 215 M3 1
MIRF WF14 172 A8
Clough Wy KBTN HD8 215 M4
Clovelly Av BEE/HOL LS11 131 K3 7
Clovelly Gv BEE/HOL LS11 131 K3 8
Clovelly Pl BEE/HOL LS11 131 K3
Clovelly Rw BEE/HOL LS11 131 K3 9
Clovelly Ter BEE/HOL LS11 131 K3
Clover Ct PDSY/CALV LS28 84 C8
Clover Crs PDSY/CALV LS28 84 C7
Cloverdale HIPP HX3 125 M7
Clover Hall Crs MILN OL16 206 E5
Clover Hl LVSG WF15 171 M1 1
SKP/WHF BD23 16 D1
Clover Hill Cl HFAX HX1 10 F8
Clover Hill Rd HFAX HX1 168 D1
Clover Hill Ter HFAX HX1 168 D1
Clover Hill Vw HFAX HX1 168 D1 2
Cloverlands Dr DOD/DAR S75 242 E6
Clover St GTHN BD7 126 D3
WHIT OL12 206 A6
Clover Vw MILN OL16 206 E7 2
Cloverville Ap WBSY BD6 126 E7
Clubhouses Cft
HOR/CROF WF4 197 J5 1
Club La BRAM LS13 107 G1
LUD/ILL HX2 146 B3
Club Rw CHAL LS7 87 L7
YEA LS19 62 E7
Club St BSLYN/ROY S71 261 L2
GTHN BD7 104 B8
TOD OL14 140 D5
Clumber Dr CLECK BD19 150 D7
Clumber St DOD/DAR S75 260 F4
Cluntergate HOR/CROF WF4 197 K5
Clunters La LUD/ILL HX2 144 D8
Clutton St BTLY WF17 174 A1
Clyde Ap WOR/ARM LS12 109 G8 2
Clyde Ct MILN OL16 206 D8
Clyde Gdns WOR/ARM LS12 109 G7
Clydesdale Dr WBSY BD6 126 B7
Clyde St BGLY BD16 81 H3
BSLYN/ROY S71 261 H5
RPDN/SBR HX6 167 K3
WKFDE WF1 13 K7
Clyde Vw WOR/ARM LS12 109 G8 3
Coach Gate La STKB/PEN S36 257 M4
Coach House Dr HUDE HD5 215 H1 1
Coach House La BSLY S70 261 H8 1
Coach La CLECK BD19 150 A6 1
CUL/QBY BD13 103 H8 1
OT LS21 24 B8
Coach Rd BRIG HD6 148 B8
GSLY LS20 61 M7
HIPP HX3 148 A7
HOLM/MEL HD7 235 H5
HUDN HD2 192 B4
RPDN/SBR HX6 188 F2
WKFDE WF1 176 E1
WOR/ARM LS12 130 A3
Coach St SKP/WHF BD23 16 B2
Coach Street Yd
SKP/WHF BD23 16 B2 7
Coal Clough Rd TOD OL14 140 C3
Coal Ga HOLM/MEL HD7 211 H5
Coal Gate Rd RPDN/SBR HX6 188 A3
Coal Hill Dr BRAM LS13 107 H2
Coal Hill Fold BRAM LS13 107 H2
Coal Hill Gdns BRAM LS13 107 H2
Coal Hill Gn BRAM LS13 107 H2
Coal Hill La PDSY/CALV LS28 107 G2
Coal La LUD/ILL HX2 124 A3
Coal Pit La BRIG HD6 170 F5
BTLY WF17 151 J8
COL BB8 74 B2
CUD/GR S72 262 E1
HEM/SK/SE WF9 248 A2
HOLM/MEL HD7 237 G8
KBTN HD8 238 F6
PONT WF8 226 B3
Coalpit La HIPP HX3 169 G2
KBTN HD8 257 H3
Coal Pit Ms BTLY WF17 151 J8 1
Coal Rd AL/HA/HU LS17 89 J2
SCFT LS14 89 K8
Coates Cl EARL WF12 174 A5 2
Coate's La AIRE BD20 35 H2
Coates St WBOW BD5 126 F2 4
Coates Ter WBOW BD5 126 F2 5
Cobb Av WKFDW/WTN WF2 198 B2
Cobbler Hall HOR/CROF WF4 219 H6
Cobblers La PONT WF8 181 H4
PONT WF8 181 H5
Cobcroft La KNOT WF11 182 F7
Cobcroft Rd HUDN HD2 14 F1
Cobden Av WOR/ARM LS12 130 B2
Cobden Ms MOR LS27 152 C2 2
Cobden Pl WOR/ARM LS12 130 B2
Cobden Rd WOR/ARM LS12 130 C2
Cobden St CLAY BD14 125 K2
CUL/QBY BD13 125 H5
IDLE BD10 83 K7 5
MOR LS27 152 C2 3
TOD OL14 163 K1
WIL/AL BD15 103 K5 3
WOR/ARM LS12 130 B2 1
Cobden Ter WOR/ARM LS12 130 B2
Cobham Wk MSTN/BAR LS15 112 B4
Cob La BWCK/EAR BB18 52 C1
Cockburn Cl BEE/HOL LS11 9 G9
Cockburn Wy BEE/HOL LS11 9 H9
Cockerham Av DOD/DAR S75 261 G3
Cockerham La DOD/DAR S75 261 G3
Cockermouth La
HOR/CROF WF4 216 E4
Cockhill La COL BB8 52 D6
Cock Hill La HIPP HX3 125 J8
Cocking La ILK LS29 36 E1
Cockin La CLAY BD14 125 G3
CUL/QBY BD13 124 F3
Cock La HOR/CROF WF4 200 A5
Cockley Hill La HUDE HD5 193 L5
Cockley Mdw HUDE HD5 193 L5
Cock Pit La GTL/HWG HX4 189 G6
Cockroft Gv BFDE BD3 5 K5
Cockshott Cl WOR/ARM LS12 108 B5 1
Cockshott Dr WOR/ARM LS12 108 B5
Cockshott La IDLE BD10 83 J6
WOR/ARM LS12 108 B5
Cockshott Pl ILK LS29 19 G6
Coggil St MID LS10 132 C4 1
Coiners Fold HBR HX7 143 L6
Colbeck Rw BTLY WF17 151 G6
Colbert Av ILK LS29 39 G1
Colby Ri MSTN/BAR LS15 111 G7
Coldbeck Dr WBSY BD6 126 A6
Coldcotes Av OSM LS9 110 D4
Coldcotes Crs OSM LS9 110 F4
Coldcotes Dr OSM LS9 110 E4
Coldcotes Garth OSM LS9 110 F4
Coldcotes Gv OSM LS9 110 F4
Coldcotes Vw OSM LS9 110 E4
Coldcotes Wk OSM LS9 110 F4
Cold Edge Rd LUD/ILL HX2 122 E1
LUD/ILL HX2 145 H1
Colden Cl HBR HX7 143 H3 2
Colden La HBR HX7 120 B8
Colden Rd HBR HX7 143 G2
Colders Dr HOLM/MEL HD7 234 F5
Colders Gn HOLM/MEL HD7 234 F4
Cold Greave Cl MILN OL16 229 L2
Cold Hiendley Common La
HOR/CROF WF4 221 L5
Coldhill La GFTH/SHER LS25 115 H1
Cold Hill La HOLM/MEL HD7 237 G7
HUDS HD4 214 C6
Cold Royd La HUDE HD5 193 J7
Coldshaw Top HWTH BD22 100 E1
Cold St HWTH BD22 78 E8
Cold Well La HOLM/MEL HD7 253 K2
Cold Well Rd MSTN/BAR LS15 111 K5
Coldwells Hl GTL/HWG HX4 190 A3
Cold Well Sq MSTN/BAR LS15 111 K5 2
Coldwell St HOLM/MEL HD7 212 F5
Coleman St BFDE BD3 5 G2
WOR/ARM LS12 8 A3
Colenso Gdns BEE/HOL LS11 8 B7
Colenso Gv BEE/HOL LS11 8 B7
Colenso Mt BEE/HOL LS11 8 B7
Colenso Pl BEE/HOL LS11 8 B7
Colenso Rd BEE/HOL LS11 8 B7
Colenso Ter BEE/HOL LS11 8 B7
Coleridge Av BSLYN/ROY S71 261 K2
Coleridge Cl RTHW LS26 155 L2
Coleridge Crs
WKFDW/WTN WF2 176 B3 4
Coleridge Gdns IDLE BD10 83 L6 1
Coleridge La PDSY/CALV LS28 129 H1
Coleridge Rd LIT OL15 207 H4
Coleridge St HFAX HX1 11 H7
Coles Wy AIRE BD20 57 M4
Coley Hall La HIPP HX3 147 M4
Coley Rd HIPP HX3 147 L3
Coley Vw HIPP HX3 147 J3
Colinsway WKFDW/WTN WF2 12 C4
Collbrook Av WBSY BD6 126 E6
Colleen Rd HOR/CROF WF4 220 A1
College Ct AIRE BD20 34 E1 3
College Farm La WBY LS22 47 K3
College Gv CAS WF10 157 J8
WKFDE WF1 176 E7 8
College Grove Cl WKFDE WF1 176 E6 1
College Grove Rd WKFDE WF1 176 E7
College Grove Vw WKFDE WF1 176 E6 2
College La AIRE BD20 16 F8
College Rd AIRE BD20 34 F1
BGLY BD16 59 J8
CAS WF10 158 D7
MOR LS27 129 M8
College St BTLY WF17 151 G5
HUDS HD4 213 M2
TOD OL14 140 E5
College St East HUDS HD4 213 M2
Colley Av BSLY S70 261 L8
Colley Crs BSLY S70 261 L8
Colley Pl BSLY S70 261 L7 1
Colley St MILN OL16 206 C5
Collier Av MILN OL16 207 H7
Collier Hag La COP/BISH YO23 33 M8
Collier La BAIL BD17 82 D2
GFTH/SHER LS25 114 B2
Colliers Cl SHPY BD18 82 A7 3
Colliers La AL/HA/HU LS17 89 G2
Colliers Wy KBTN HD8 240 B2
Colliery Ap WKFDE WF1 176 D1
Collindale Cl IDLE BD10 84 A8 3
Collinfield Ri WBSY BD6 126 B8
Collinge Rd HWTH BD22 54 F3
Collinge St ROY/SHW OL2 229 K7 2
Collingham Av WBSY BD6 125 M6
Collingham Dr GFTH/SHER LS25 113 H8
Collingwood Rd NORM WF6 178 C4
Collin Moor La GTL/HWG HX4 168 E6
Collin Rd SCFT LS14 111 H5
Collins Cl DOD/DAR S75 260 A7
HWTH BD22 79 G6 4
Collinson St CLECK BD19 149 M6 9
Collins St BOW BD4 127 K1
GTHN BD7 126 C3
Colmore Gv WOR/ARM LS12 130 F1 1
Colmore Rd WOR/ARM LS12 130 F1
Colne Hurst HUDN HD2 193 G2
Colne La COL BB8 74 A2

Colne Rd *AIRE* BD20 .... 34 E8
AIRE BD20 .... 55 H1
BWCK/EAR BB18 .... 52 B2
COL BE8 .... 74 C4
HUD HD1 .... 214 C2
HWTH BD22 .... 54 C4
Colne Rd (Goodley) *HWTH* BD22 .. 78 D4
HUD HD1 .... 14 B9
HUD HD1 .... 15 J8
Colne Vale Rd *HUDS* HD4 ... 213 J2
HOLM/MEL HD7 .... 211 H6
Colne Valley Circular Wk
HOLM/MEL HD7 .... 211 H6
Colonel's Wk *PONT* WF8 ...... 180 E5
Colster Cl *DOD/DAR* S75 ..... 260 E4
Colston Cl *GIR* BD8 .... 104 A5
Colton Br *TAD* LS24 .... 73 K3
Colton Ct *MSTN/BAR* LS15 .. 111 M7 ⑤
Colton Cft *MSTN/BAR* LS15 .. 111 M7 ⑦
Colton Garth *MSTN/BAR* LS15 111 M7 ⑧
Colton La *COP/BISH* YO23 ..... 73 M4
MSTN/BAR LS15 .... 111 M8
Colton Rd *MSTN/BAR* LS15 .. 111 L7
WOR/ARM LS12 .... 108 C7
Colton Rd East *MSTN/BAR* LS12 .. 108 E7 ⑫
Colton St *WOR/ARM* LS12 .... 108 C7 ⑥
Coltsfoot Cl *PONT* WF8 .... 180 L4
Columbia St *BSLY* S70 .... 261 G7
Columbus St *HIPP* HX3 .... 10 D1 ④
Colville Ter *HOL/MEL* LS11 ...... 8 E7
EARD/LOFT WF3 .... 154 A1
Colwyn Av *BEE/HOL* LS11 .... 131 K4
Colwyn Mt *BEE/HOL* LS11 .... 131 K4
Colwyn Pl *BEE/HOL* LS11 ..... 131 K4
Colwyn Rd *BEE/HOL* LS11 .... 131 K4
Colwyn St *HUDW* HD3 .... 191 M7
Colwyn Ter *BEE/HOL* LS11 .. 131 K4 ⑤
Colwyn Vw *BEE/HOL* LS11 ... 131 K4
Colyton Mt *WIL/AL* BD15 ...... 103 J5 ⑨
Combs Rd *EARL* WF12 .... 195 M4
The Combs *EARL* WF12 .... 196 A3
Commerce Ct *BOW* BD4 .... 127 M2 ⑨
Commercial Buildings
LM/WK BD12 .... 149 K2 ⑪
KBTN HD8 .... 239 J4
Commercial Rd *DEWS* WF13 .. 173 L5
KBTN HD8 .... 239 J4
Commercial St *BRIG* HD6 ..... 170 C4
BSLY S70 .... 261 J6
BTLY WF17 .... 173 L1
CAS WF10 .... 157 M6 ⑥
CLECK BD19 .... 150 A7 ③
CUL/QBY BD13 .... 101 M6 ⑪
CUL/QBY BD13 .... 101 M6 ③
DEWS WF13 .... 173 H8 ⑪
EARL WF12 .... 174 B7 ②
HBR HX7 .... 143 J3
HECK WF16 .... 173 G2
HFAX HX1 .... 11 C6 ⑪
HFAX HX1 .... 11 C6 ⑫
HOLM/MEL HD7 .... 212 C6
HUD HD1 .... 14 C2
LDS LS1 .... 7 C9
MOR LS27 .... 152 C2
RTHW LS26 .... 155 C1 ⑤
SHPY BD18 .... 82 D6
TAD LS24 .... 71 M3
TOD OL14 .... 163 L1
WKFDE WF1 .... 13 G6
Commercial Vls
PDSY/CALV LS28 .... 106 F8
Commondale Wy *BOW* BD4 .. 127 J8
Common End La *KBTN* HD8 .. 215 M4
Common Holme La *ILK* LS29 .. 20 A8
Common Ing La
HOR/CROF WF4 .... 222 C4
Common La *AWLS/ASK* DN6 .. 227 M3
BSLYN/ROY S71 .... 243 L2
BTLY DN5 .... 246 D8
EARD/LOFT WF3 .... 153 L5
GFTH/SHER LS25 .... 138 B2
GLE DN14 .... 161 J8
HEM/SK/SE WF9 .... 225 H7
HIPP HX3 .... 147 H8
HOR/CROF WF4 .... 217 J5
KBTN HD8 .... 217 C2
KBTN HD8 .... 239 K8
KNOT WF11 .... 182 F3
PONT WF8 .... 225 K2
SEL YO8 .... 139 K4
TAD LS24 .... 95 G2
WKFDW/WTN WF2 .... 221 H1
Common Rd *BTLY* WF17 ...... 173 H2
CUD/GR S72 .... 245 J3
CUD/GR S72 .... 246 A5
EARD/LOFT WF3 .... 155 H7
ELL HX5 .... 169 L8
HEM/SK/SE WF9 .... 223 J4
HUD HD1 .... 14 E2
LM/WK BD12 .... 126 E8
TAD LS24 .... 116 B1
Common Road Av
HEM/SK/SE WF9 .... 246 C5
Commonside Wy *BTLY* WF17 .. 173 M4
LVSG WF15 .... 172 A4
Common Side La *FEA/AMT* WF7 .. 201 J1
The Common *EARL* WF12 .... 195 M3
Como Av *GIR* BD8 .... 104 B5
Como Dr *GIR* BD8 .... 104 B5
Como Gdns *GIR* BD8 .... 104 B6 ④
Como Gv *GIR* BD8 .... 104 B5
Compeigne Av *AIRE* BD20 ..... 55 B3 ⑤
Compton Av *OSM* LS9 .... 110 C4 ⑤
Compton Crs *OSM* LS9 .... 110 C4
Compton Gv *OSM* LS9 .... 110 C4 ⑥
Compton La *AL/HA/HU* LS17 .. 68 B1
WBY LS22 .... 48 A1
Compton Mt *OSM* LS9 .... 110 C4 ⑩
Compton Pl *OSM* LS9 .... 110 C4 ⑭
Compton Rd *OSM* LS9 .... 110 C4
Compton Rw *OSM* LS9 .... 110 C4
Compton St *BOW* BD4 .... 127 L4
OSM LS9 .... 110 C4 ⑫
Compton Ter *OSM* LS9 .... 110 C4 ⑬
Compton Wy *ROY/SHW* OL2 .. 229 K8
Concordia St *LDS* LS1 .... 9 C2
Concord St *HOLM/MEL* HD7 .. 236 D2
LDSU LS2 .... 7 J7

Concrete St *HIPP* HX3 .... 10 D1
Conduit St *GIR* BD8 .... 4 A1
Cone La *DOD/DAR* S75 .... 259 J7
Coney La *KGHY* BD21 .... 3 H6
Coney Moor Gv *RTHW* LS26 .. 157 H3
Coney Wk *DEWS* WF13 .... 173 H6 ⑧
Coney Warren La
EARD/LOFT WF3 .... 155 G6
Conference Pl *WOR/ARM* LS12 .. 108 C7
Conference Rd *WOR/ARM* LS12 .. 108 C7
Conference Ter *WOR/ARM* LS12 .. 108 C7
Congress Mt *WOR/ARM* LS12 .. 108 C7
Congress St *WOR/ARM* LS12 .. 108 C7
Congreve Ap *AL/HA/HU* LS17 .. 68 A1
Congreve Wy *AL/HA/HU* LS17 .. 47 C2
Conisborough La
GFTH/SHER LS25 .... 113 K7 ⑤
Coniston Av *CUL/QBY* BD13 .. 124 F5 ⑤
DOD/DAR S75 .... 242 C4
HDGY LS6 .... 109 G1
HUDE HD5 .... 15 L6
Coniston Cl *CUL/QBY* BD13 .. 124 F5
ELL HX5 .... 169 K7 ②
STKB/PEN S36 .... 270 C7
Coniston Ct *EARD/LOFT* WF3 .. 154 D8 ①
Coniston Crs *WKFDE* WF1 .... 177 G6
Coniston Gdns *CAS* WF10 .... 159 G7 ②
MSTN/BAR LS15 .... 111 G8 ①
Coniston Gv *COL* BB8 .... 52 B7 ③
HTON BD9 .... 104 B4
ROY/SHW OL2 .... 228 F8
Coniston Rd *BSLYN/ROY* S71 .. 261 J5
EARL WF12 .... 174 B4
GTHN BD7 .... 126 A3 ⑧
HOLM/MEL HD7 .... 235 C5
RTHW LS26 .... 133 L7 ②
Coniston Wy *RTHW* LS26 .... 133 L7
WBY LS22 .... 29 K8
Connaught Av *MILN* OL16 .... 228 D5 ⑤
Connaught Fold *HUDN* HD2 .. 193 G1
Cononley La *AIRE* BD20 .... 34 C4
Cononley Rd *AIRE* BD20 .... 34 D6
Consort Av *ROY/SHW* OL2 .... 228 E8
Consort Gv *BVRD* LS3 .... 6 B7
SKP/WHF BD23 .... 16 D2
Consort St *BVRD* LS3 .... 6 B7
Consort Vw *BVRD* LS3 .... 6 B7
Consort Wk *BVRD* LS3 .... 6 B7
Constable Gv *EARD/LOFT* WF3 .. 155 G8 ①
Constable Rd *EARD/LOFT* WF3 .. 153 H7
ILK LS29 .... 38 F3
Constance Gdns *CHAL* LS7 ..... 6 F4
Constance St *SHPY* BD18 ...... 82 B6 ①
Constance Wy *CHAL* LS7 .... 6 F4
Constantine La *MILN* OL16 .. 206 B7 ①
Constitutional St *HFAX* HX1 .. 10 B9
Conway Av *BSLY* S70 .... 261 J4
HOLM/MEL HD7 .... 234 F5 ①
Conway Crs *BTLY* WF17 .... 173 L4
Conway Dr *RHAY* LS8 .... 110 B3
Conway Gv *RHAY* LS8 .... 110 B3
Conway Mt *RHAY* LS8 .... 110 B3
Conway Pl *RHAY* LS8 .... 110 B3
Conway Rd *RHAY* LS8 .... 110 B3
WKFDW/WTN WF2 .... 178 A7
Conway St *BSLY* S70 .... 261 J4
HFAX HX1 .... 10 C7
PDSY/CALV LS28 .... 106 F5
RHAY LS8 .... 110 B3
Conway Ter *RHAY* LS8 .... 110 B3
Conway Vw *RHAY* LS8 .... 110 B3
Cooke Crs *CLECK* BD19 .... 150 C6 ②
Cooke La *KGHY* BD21 .... 3 G5
Cooke St *KGHY* BD21 .... 3 G4
Cook House Rd *COL* BB8 .... 52 A8
Cook La *HECK* WF16 .... 172 E2
Cookridge Av *BHP/TINH* LS16 .. 64 A8
Cookridge Dr *BHP/TINH* LS16 .. 63 M8
Cookridge Gv *BHP/TINH* LS16 .. 64 A8
Cookridge La *BHP/TINH* LS16 .. 64 A7
Cookridge St *LDSU* LS2 .... 6 F7
Cooksland La *FEA/AMT* WF7 .. 179 C6
Cookson Cl *CAS* WF10 .... 180 F1
Cookson St *BRIG* HD6 .... 170 B3
Cook St *MILN* OL16 .... 206 D5
Cook Ter *MILN* OL16 .... 206 D5
Coombe Hi *CUL/QBY* BD13 .. 125 K4
Coombe Rd *HOLM/MEL* HD7 .. 213 H1 ①
Co-operative Buildings
BRIG HD6 .... 148 D7 ①
Co-operative St *CUD/GR* S72 .. 244 C8 ①
EARD/LOFT WF3 .... 154 E5 ①
EARL WF12 .... 174 D6 ①
HOR/CROF WF4 .... 197 J5 ③
MIRF WF14 .... 194 C3 ①
MOR LS27 .... 152 C2 ②
ROY/SHW OL2 .... 229 K7 ③
Cooperative St *TOD* OL14 .... 163 J7 ①
Co-operative St
WKFDW/WTN WF2 .... 12 A4 ③
Co-operative Ter
HOLM/MEL HD7 .... 236 E7 ①
Cooper Bridge Rd *HUDN* HD2 .. 171 K8 ①
Cooper Cl *BGLY* BD16 .... 81 J1
Cooper Flds *LUD/ILL* HX2 .... 167 C1
Cooper Gv *WBSY* BD6 .... 125 M7
Cooper La *HIPP* HX3 .... 125 M6
HOLM/MEL HD7 .... 254 C1
STKB/PEN S36 .... 258 D7
WBSY BD6 .... 125 M5
Cooper Rd *DOD/DAR* S75 .... 241 L6
Cooper St *MILN* OL16 .... 206 F2 ②
TOD OL14 .... 142 A8
Coopers Wk *MILN* OL16 ...... 206 E4
Co-op La *HOLM/MEL* HD7 ... 253 M5
Copeland St *BOW* BD4 .... 127 M1
Copenhagen Sq *MILN* OL16 .. 206 C6 ④
Copenhagen St *MILN* OL16 .. 206 C6
Cope St *BSLY* S70 .... 261 H7
Copeworth Dr *HOR/CROF* WF4 .. 220 B3
Copgrove Cl *BOW* BD4 .... 128 A3 ②
Copgrove Rd *BOW* BD4 .... 128 A3 ②
RHAY LS8 .... 110 C1
Cop Hill La *HOLM/MEL* HD7 .. 211 K6

Cop Hill Side *HOLM/MEL* HD7 .. 211 K6
Copley Av *HOLM/MEL* HD7 .. 234 E4
LUD/ILL HX2 .... 168 A1
Copley Bank Rd
HOLM/MEL HD7 .... 212 E3
Copley Gln *HIPP* HX3 .... 168 D4 ①
Copley Hall St *HIPP* HX3 ..... 168 D4
Copley Hall St *HIPP* HX3 ..... 168 D4
Copley Hi *BTLY* WF17 .... 151 H5
WOR/ARM LS12 .... 109 G8
Copley Hill Wy *WOR/ARM* LS12 .. 131 G1
Copley La *EARD/LOFT* WF3 .. 154 D2
GFTH/SHER LS25 .... 114 E1
HIPP HX3 .... 168 D4
KBTN HD8 .... 238 D6
Copley Mt *HIPP* HX3 .... 168 D4
Copley St *BTLY* WF17 .... 151 J7
ROY/SHW OL2 .... 229 L6 ②
WBOW BD5 .... 126 D3
WOR/ARM LS12 .... 109 G8 ④
Copley Ter *HIPP* HX3 .... 168 D4 ②
Copley Yd *WOR/ARM* LS12 .. 109 G8 ⑤
Coplowe La *WIL/AL* BD15 ..... 80 F7
Copmanroyd *OT* LS21 .... 41 J3
Copperas St *STKB/PEN* S36 .. 270 A3
Copperas House Ter *TOD* OL14 .. 163 J4 ①
Copper Beech Ct
WKFDW/WTN WF2 .... 199 J8
Copper Cl *OSM* LS9 .... 261 H6 ⑤
Copperfield Av *OSM* LS9 ..... 110 B8 ⑤
Copperfield Cl *OSM* LS9 ...... 110 B8 ⑩
Copperfield Dr *OSM* LS9 ..... 110 B8 ⑪
Copperfield Gv *OSM* LS9 ..... 110 B8
Copperfield Mt *OSM* LS9 ..... 110 C8 ⑥
Copperfield Pl *OSM* LS9 ...... 110 B8 ⑫
Copperfield Rw *OSM* LS9 .... 110 B8 ⑬
Copperfield Ter *OSM* LS9 .... 110 B8
Copperfield Vw *OSM* LS9 .... 110 B8
Copperfield Wk *OSM* LS9 ... 110 B8 ⑭
Coppice Av *DOD/DAR* S75 ... 260 D2
Coppice Cl *WKFDE* WF1 ..... 177 G6
Coppice Dr *HUDS* HD4 .... 213 M8
Coppice Head *RTHW* LS26 .. 155 H1 ⑤
The Coppice *AIRE* BD20 .... 34 E8
GFTH/SHER LS25 .... 116 B7
HUDN HD2 .... 192 D2 ②
ILK LS29 .... 20 C8
MIRF WF14 .... 172 C6 ①
MSTN/BAR LS15 .... 90 F8 ①
YEA LS19 .... 62 D6 ②
Coppice Vw *IDLE* BD10 .... 83 J6
Coppice Wy *RHAY* LS8 .... 88 C8
Coppice Wood Av *GSLY* LS20 .. 62 C5
GTHN BD7 .... 104 C8 ②
Coppice Wood Cl *GSLY* LS20 .. 62 C5
Coppice Wood Crs *YEA* LS19 .. 62 C6
Coppice Wood Gv *GSLY* LS20 .. 62 C6
GTHN BD7 .... 104 C8 ③
Coppice Wood Ri *YEA* LS19 .. 62 D6 ③
The Coppies *LM/WK* BD12 .. 148 D2 ③
Coppin Hall Gv *MIRF* WF14 .. 171 M8
Coppin Hall La *MIRF* WF14 .. 171 M8
Coppy Cl *BGLY* BD16 .... 81 J8 ①
Coppy La *AIRE* BD20 .... 34 B2
BRAM LS13 .... 107 L2
HBR HX7 .... 121 H3
HWTH BD22 .... 55 L7
Coppy Nook La *HBR* HX7 .... 166 A3
Coppy Rd *AIRE* BD20 .... 56 D1
ILK LS29 .... 19 G6
Coppy Wood Dr *ILK* LS29 ...... 20 D7
The Copse *BGLY* BD16 .... 81 M3
CLECK BD19 .... 149 H7
FEA/AMT WF7 .... 179 L5
ILK LS29 .... 40 A6
Copster La *STKB/PEN* S36 ... 271 M5
Copthorne Gdns *HUDN* HD2 .. 193 H1 ①
Copthurst Rd *HOLM/MEL* HD7 .. 253 M6
Coptrod Head Cl *WHIT* OL12 .. 206 A2 ②
Copt Royd Gv *YEA* LS19 .... 62 C7
Corban St *BOW* BD4 .... 127 L3 ①
Corbett St *HUDN* HD2 .... 192 C5
Corby St *HUDN* HD2 .... 192 C5
Cordingley Cl *BOW* BD4 ...... 128 A5 ①
Cordingley St *BOW* BD4 ...... 128 A5
Corfe Cl *BTLY* WF17 .... 151 K4
Corn Bank *HUDS* HD4 .... 213 L8
Cornbrook St *WHIT* OL12 .... 184 E8
Cornfield *DEWS* WF13 .... 173 G5
Cornfield St *HUDW* HD3 ..... 191 J7
Cornfield St *MILN* OL16 ...... 229 H1
TOD OL14 .... 141 M8 ②
Cornmarket *PONT* WF8 .... 180 E6
Corn Ml *ILK* LS29 .... 61 L2
Cornmill Cl *AL/HA/HU* LS17 .. 67 M3
Corn Mill Ct *WOR/ARM* LS12 .. 107 M7
Cornmill Crs *LVSG* WF15 .... 172 D3
Cornmill Dr *LVSG* WF15 ...... 172 D3
Cornmill La *AL/HA/HU* LS17 .. 67 M5 ①
Corn Mill La *CLAY* BD14 ...... 125 H1
ILK LS29 .... 40 C5
Cornmill La *LVSG* WF15 ...... 172 D3
Cornrace Vw *HUD* HD1 .... 214 D2 ①
Corn St *HWTH* BD22 .... 79 J2
Cornus Gdns *MID* LS10 .... 131 M6 ⑤
Cornwall Av *AIRE* BD20 .... 35 L5
Cornwall Cl *BSLYN/ROY* S71 .. 261 K2
RTHW LS26 .... 132 F8 ④
Cornwall Crs *BAIL* BD17 .... 82 D2
BRIG HD6 .... 148 D3
RTHW LS26 .... 132 F8
Cornwall Pl *GIR* BD8 .... 4 D1
Cornwall Rd *BGLY* BD16 .... 81 K4
GIR BD8 .... 4 D2
KGHY BD21 .... 3 M1
Cornwall Ter *GIR* BD8 .... 4 D2
Coronation Av *CUD/GR* S72 .. 244 D3
CUD/GR S72 .... 245 J8
GFTH/SHER LS25 .... 135 L5
IDLE BD10 .... 83 M2
NORM WF6 .... 178 B3
Coronation Bungalows
GFTH/SHER LS25 .... 135 L5
Coronation Mt *HWTH* BD22 .... 2 B4
Coronation Pde
MSTN/BAR LS15 .... 111 G7 ①
Coronation Rd *DOD/DAR* S75 .. 259 M2

HIPP HX3 .... 168 E2
HOR/CROF WF4 .... 200 D3
Coronation St *BSLYN/ROY* S71 .. 261 L2
CAS WF10 .... 158 B5 ①
CAS WF10 .... 158 C8 ①
EARD/LOFT WF3 .... 154 F3 ②
ELL HX5 .... 169 H8
GTL/HWG HX4 .... 168 F6 ①
LM/WK BD12 .... 149 J1 ①
WKFDW/WTN WF2 .... 176 B4
WMB/DAR S73 .... 263 K8
Coronation Ter *BSLYN/ROY* S71 .. 262 B6
CAS WF10 .... 158 C8 ②
RPDN/SBR HX6 .... 167 C8
Coronation Wk *HWTH* BD22 .... 2 B3
Coronation Wy *HWTH* BD22 .. 57 G6
Corporal La *CUL/QBY* BD13 .. 125 C8
Corporation St *BSLY* S70 ..... 261 J7
DEWS WF13 .... 173 M6 ①
ECHL BD2 .... 105 L3
HFAX HX1 .... 11 G4
HUD HD1 .... 14 F7
MOR LS27 .... 152 C2 ①
RPDN/SBR HX6 .... 167 K2
Corrance Rd *LM/WK* BD12 .. 148 F5
Corrie St *CUL/QBY* BD13 .... 103 G8 ①
Cortina Ri *WMB/DAR* S73 ... 263 G8 ①
Cotchers La *TAD* LS24 .... 93 K6
Cote Farm La *SHPY* BD18 ..... 83 H5 ①
Cotefields Av *PDSY/CALV* LS28 .. 106 E3
Cote La *HOLM/MEL* HD7 .... 254 C6
HUDN HD2 .... 191 M1
LIT OL15 .... 185 H8
PDSY/CALV LS28 .... 106 E4
UPML OL3 .... 231 K7
WIL/AL BD15 .... 103 J5 ②
Cote Rd *RPDN/SBR* HX6 .... 188 D2
Coteroyd Av *MOR* LS27 .... 130 E6
Coteroyd Dr *MOR* LS27 .... 130 E6
The Cote *PDSY/CALV* LS28 .. 106 E4
Cotewall Rd *WBOW* BD5 .... 126 C3
SHPY BD18 .... 83 G7
Cotswold Av *ROY/SHW* OL2 .. 229 H6
Cotswold Cl *DOD/DAR* S75 .. 260 D4 ②
HEM/SK/SE WF9 .... 224 B7
Cotswold Crs *MILN* OL16 .... 207 J7
Cotswold Dr *GFTH/SHER* LS25 .. 135 H1
KNOT WF11 .... 182 A2 ②
LVSG WF15 .... 171 M1
RTHW LS26 .... 132 F8
Cotswold Ms *KBTN* HD8 ..... 216 B7 ①
Cotswold Rd *RTHW* LS26 .... 132 F8
WKFDW/WTN WF2 .... 197 M1
Cottage Rd *HDGY* LS6 .... 86 F8
IDLE BD10 .... 83 M7
Cottam Av *GTHN* BD7 .... 104 D8 ③
Cottam Cft *HEM/SK/SE* WF9 .. 224 A7
Cottam Ter *GTHN* BD7 .... 104 D8 ⑤
Cotterdale *WIL/AL* BD15 ..... 103 J3 ④
Cotterdale Holt *WBY* LS22 .... 47 J5
Cotterdale Vw *MSTN/BAR* LS15 .. 111 G8 ④
Cotterill Rd *KNOT* WF11 ..... 199 M6
Cottesmore Cl *DOD/DAR* S75 .. 260 E3 ①
Cottingley Cha *DEWS* WF13 .. 130 E4
Cottingley Cliffe Rd *BGLY* BD16 .. 81 J8
Cottingley Crs *BEE/HOL* LS11 .. 130 F5
Cottingley Dr *BEE/HOL* LS11 .. 130 F5
BGLY BD16 .... 81 J6
Cottingley Fold *BEE/HOL* LS11 .. 130 F5
Cottingley Gdns *BEE/HOL* LS11 .. 130 F5
Cottingley Gn *BEE/HOL* LS11 .. 130 F5
Cottingley Gv *BEE/HOL* LS11 .. 130 F5 ①
Cottingley Manor Pk
BGLY BD16 .... 81 K7 ③
Cottingley Moor Rd *BGLY* BD16 .. 103 J1
Cottingley New Rd *BGLY* BD16 .. 81 K7
WIL/AL BD15 .... 103 J3
Cottingley Ter *GIR* BD8 .... 4 D1 ③
Cottingley V *BEE/HOL* LS11 .. 130 F5
Cotton Fold *MILN* OL16 ...... 206 E8 ②
Cotton St *OSM* LS9 .... 9 K2
WKFDW/WTN WF2 .... 12 E6
Cotton Tree La *COL* BB8 .... 74 C1
Couford Gv *HUDN* HD2 .... 193 H2
Coule Royd *HUDE* HD5 .... 193 J1
Coultas Cl *ILK* LS29 .... 61 K2
Counting House Ms
SKP/WHF BD23 .... 16 B2
Count St *MILN* OL16 .... 228 C2
County Cl *BTLY* WF17 .... 151 L8
County Wy *BSLY* S70 .... 261 H4
Coupe Gv *NORM* WF6 .... 178 B3
Coupland Pl *BEE/HOL* LS11 ... 8 C8
Coupland Rd *BEE/HOL* LS11 ... 8 C8
GFTH/SHER LS25 .... 113 C7
Coupland St *BEE/HOL* LS11 ... 8 C9
Court Dr *KSTL* LS5 .... 86 A7
Courtenay Cl *BFDE* BD3 ...... 106 A7 ①
Courtenays *SCFT* LS14 .... 111 K2 ①
Courthouse St *OT* LS21 .... 41 J6
Court La *LUD/ILL* HX2 .... 145 M7
SKP/WHF BD23 .... 16 C2
Courts Leet *LM/WK* BD12 ... 148 E2 ②
The Court *AL/HA/HU* LS17 .... 87 H1 ①
LVSG WF15 .... 172 A2
The Courtyard *BTLY* WF17 .. 151 H4
The Court Wy *FEA/AMT* WF7 .. 202 B4
The Court Yd *HOR/CROF* WF4 .. 220 C7
The Courtyard *HUDS* HD4 ... 213 M2
Cousen Av *GTHN* BD7 .... 126 B1
Cousen Rd *GTHN* BD7 .... 126 C2
Cousin La *LUD/ILL* HX2 ...... 146 A2
Coutances Wy *ILK* LS29 .... 39 J2
Coventry St *BOW* BD4 .... 127 K2 ④
HFAX HX1 .... 146 A7 ①
ROCH OL11 .... 206 B8 ①
Coverdale Garth *WBY* LS22 .. 47 J6
Coverdale Wy *BAIL* BD17 ..... 83 C2
Cover Dr *WBSY* BD6 .... 126 C6
WMB/DAR S73 .... 263 K8
Coverley Ri *YEA* LS19 .... 62 B7
The Covet *BTLY* WF17 .... 151 H7
The Covet *IDLE* BD10 .... 83 M6 ①
Covey Clough Ct *MIRF* WF14 .. 194 B5 ④
Cowcliffe Hill Rd *HUDN* HD2 .. 192 B4
Cowcliff Hill Rd *HOLM/MEL* HD7 .. 254 F6
Cow Close La *LM/WK* BD12 .. 149 G4

Cow Close Rd *WOR/ARM* LS12 .. 130 B1
Cowdray Dr *CLECK* BD19 .... 149 H6 ③
Cowdry Cl *EARL* WF12 .... 196 A4
Cowfold St *TOD* OL14 .... 141 K8 ②
Cow Ga *HUDW* HD3 .... 191 H8 ①
Cowgill St *GIR* BD8 .... 4 A1 ①
Cow Gn *HFAX* HX1 .... 11 G6
Cow Hey La *HBR* HX7 .... 120 F3
Cow Heys *HUDE* HD5 .... 193 G7
Cow Hill Gate La *LUD/ILL* HX2 .. 124 A6
Cowhurst Av *TOD* OL14 ...... 141 H7
Cowie St *ROY/SHW* OL2 ..... 229 K6
Cow La *AWLS/ASK* DN6 ...... 205 J3
HBR HX7 .... 121 C6
HIPP HX3 .... 168 E4
HOR/CROF WF4 .... 200 C2
HOR/CROF WF4 .... 222 E5
HWTH BD22 .... 54 D1
HWTH BD22 .... 54 F3
RPDN/SBR HX6 .... 166 F3
Cowlersley La *HOLM/MEL* HD7 .. 213 C4
Cowley Crs *HOR/CROF* WF4 .. 196 F7
Cowley Rd *BRAM* LS13 .... 107 H1
Cowling Br *AIRE* BD20 .... 35 L6
Cowling Hill La *HWTH* BD22 .. 54 C1
Cowling La *HIPP* HX3 .... 147 H1
Cowmbes Av *OSM* LS9 .... 110 C4 ③
Cowper Crs *OSM* LS9 .... 110 C4 ⑥
Cowper Gv *RHAY* LS8 .... 110 C3
Cowper Mt *OSM* LS9 .... 110 C4
Cowper Rd *OSM* LS9 .... 110 C4
Cowper St *CHAL* LS7 .... 7 L2
EARL WF12 .... 173 L8 ②
SKP/WHF BD23 .... 16 C3
Cowper Ter *OSM* LS9 .... 110 C3
Cowrakes Cl *HUDW* HD3 .... 191 J5
Cowrakes Rd *HUDW* HD3 ... 191 H5
Cowroyd Pl *HIPP* HX3 .... 11 J3
Cowslip St *HUD* HD1 .... 213 M1 ②
Coxley Crs *HOR/CROF* WF4 .. 196 F7
Coxley La *HOR/CROF* WF4 .. 196 F7
Coxley Vw *HOR/CROF* WF4 .. 218 E1
Coxwold Hi *WBY* LS22 .... 30 A7
Coxwold Vw *WBY* LS22 .... 30 A8
Crabgate Dr *AWLS/ASK* DN6 .. 249 G4
Crabgate La *AWLS/ASK* DN6 .. 249 G4
Crab Hi *PONT* WF8 .... 180 E6
Crab La *WKFDW/WTN* WF2 .. 220 D2
WOR/ARM LS12 .... 108 C6
Crabtree Av *HECK* WF16 ..... 173 G1
Crabtree Dr *CUD/GR* S72 .... 263 M3
Crabtree Gn *WBY* LS22 .... 47 J3
Crabtree Hi *WBY* LS22 .... 47 K6
Crabtree La *AL/HA/HU* LS17 .. 46 E7
Crab Tree La *PONT* WF8 ...... 226 D4
Crabtree Pl *GTHN* BD7 .... 126 C2 ⑧
Crabtree St *GTHN* BD7 .... 126 C2 ②
HFAX HX1 .... 10 A6
Crabtree Wy *EARD/LOFT* WF3 .. 153 H7 ①
Crackenedge La *DEWS* WF13 .. 173 M6
Crackenedge Ter *DEWS* WF13 173 M5 ②
Crack La *WIL/AL* BD15 .... 102 F1
Craddock Rd *COL* BB8 .... 74 A1
Crag Cl *AIRE* BD20 .... 55 L2
LUD/ILL HX2 .... 145 M4
Crag Gdns *BSPA/BRAM* LS23 .. 69 M4
Cragg Av *HORS* LS18 .... 85 K6
Cragg Bottom Rd *HWTH* BD22 .. 76 F6
Cragg Dr *ILK* LS29 .... 39 H3
Cragg La *CUL/QBY* BD13 .... 124 A1 ①
GTHN BD7 .... 126 C3 ②
HBR HX7 .... 143 L8
Cragg Rd *HBR* HX7 .... 165 H1
HBR HX7 .... 165 M2
HORS LS18 .... 85 L6
Cragg Ter *GTHN* BD7 .... 126 C3 ②
HORS LS18 .... 85 K6
Cragg Top *CUL/QBY* BD13 .. 124 A1 ①
Cragg Vw *AIRE* BD20 .... 36 A4 ②
Cragg Wood Dr *YEA* LS19 ..... 84 C3
Craggwood Rd *HORS* LS18 .... 85 L7
Crag Hill Av *BHP/TINH* LS16 .. 64 A7
Crag Hill Rd *IDLE* BD10 .... 83 J4
Crag Hill Vw *BHP/TINH* LS16 .. 64 A8
Crag La *AIRE* BD20 .... 34 E2
AIRE BD20 .... 55 L1
AL/HA/HU LS17 .... 25 L8
AL/HA/HU LS17 .... 43 L2
AL/HA/HU LS17 .... 87 H1
LUD/ILL HX2 .... 145 M2
Crag Mt *PONT* WF8 .... 180 E6 ③
Crag Pl *KGHY* BD21 .... 79 L2
Crag Rd *SHPY* BD18 .... 82 E8
Cragside Cl *KSTL* LS5 .... 86 A7
Cragside Crs *KSTL* LS5 .... 86 A7
Cragside Gdns *KSTL* LS5 ...... 85 M7
Cragside Gv *KSTL* LS5 .... 85 M7
Cragside Mt *KSTL* LS5 .... 85 M7
Cragside Pl *KSTL* LS5 .... 86 A7
Cragside Wk *KSTL* LS5 .... 86 A7
The Crag *BSPA/BRAM* LS23 .. 69 M4
Crag Vw *AIRE* BD20 .... 34 C5
AL/HA/HU LS17 .... 43 K2
IDLE BD10 .... 83 L7
Crag View Rd *SKP/WHF* BD23 .. 16 D3
Craig Cl *BTLY* WF17 .... 151 L8
Craiglands *HIPP* HX3 .... 147 M6
MILN OL16 .... 228 D4
Craiglands Pk *ILK* LS29 .... 38 E3
Craiglands Ri *ILK* LS29 .... 38 E3
Craiglea Dr *LM/WK* BD12 ... 148 F4
Craigmore Ct *BOW* BD4 ...... 128 B4 ①
Craigmore Dr *ILK* LS29 .... 39 G2
Cramlands *DOD/DAR* S75 ... 260 C7 ③
Cranberry Av *TOD* OL14 ...... 163 K7
Cranberry Rd *STKB/PEN* S36 .. 270 C4
Cranborne Dr *DOD/DAR* S75 .. 242 B5 ①
Cranbourne Rd *HTON* BD9 .. 103 M4
Cranbrook Av *BEE/HOL* LS11 .. 131 J3
WBSY BD6 .... 126 E6
Cranbrook Pl *WBOW* BD5 ... 127 G3 ⑧
Cranbrook Rd *BSLY* S70 ...... 260 F6 ①
CLAY BD14 .... 125 K2 ③
WBOW BD5 .... 127 G3 ⑧

Cranbrook Vw *PDSY/CALV* LS28 .. **129** J1
Cranewells Dr
  MSTN/BAR LS15 .... **111** M7 7
Cranewells Gn
  MSTN/BAR LS15 .... **111** L8 8
Cranewells Ri *MSTN/BAR* LS15 **111** L8 8
Cranewells V *MSTN/BAR* LS15 .. **111** L8 8
Cranewells Vw *MSTN/BAR* LS15 . **111** L7
Cranfield Dr *AWLS/ASK* DN6 ...... **249** H4
Cranford Gdns *BSLYN/ROY* S71 .. **243** K2
Cranford Pl *WIL/AL* BD15 .... **102** E1 1
Crangle Flds *HUDS* HD4 .... **237** L4 1
Cranleigh Mt *KGHY* BD21 .... **2** C9
Cranmer Bank *AL/HA/HU* LS17 .... **87** J3
Cranmer Cl *AL/HA/HU* LS17 .... **87** J3
Cranmer Gdns *AL/HA/HU* LS17 .... **87** J3
  HOLM/MEL HD7 .... **235** G4
Cranmer Ri *AL/HA/HU* LS17 .... **87** J3
Cranmer Rd *AL/HA/HU* LS17 .... **87** J3
  BFDE BD3 .... **5** G1
Cranmore Crs *MID* LS10 .... **154** A1
Cranmore Dr *MID* LS10 .... **154** B1
Cranmore Gdns
  EARD/LOFT WF3 .... **154** A1 1
Cranmore Garth *MID* LS10 .... **154** A1 2
Cranmore Gn *MID* LS10 .... **154** A1 3
Cranmore Gv *EARD/LOFT* WF3 .. **154** A1 4
Cranmore Ri *MID* LS10 .... **154** B1
Cranmore Rd *MID* LS10 .... **154** B1
Cranston Cl *BSLYN/ROY* S71 .... **261** M2
Cranwood Dr *HUDE* HD5 .... **193** J8 8
Craven Cl *AIRE* BD20 .... **36** A5
  CUL/QBY BD13 .... **103** C8 4
Craven Crs *BSLYN/ROY* S71 ...... **243** K2
  CLECK BD19 .... **150** B5
Craven Ct *AIRE* BD20 .... **36** B5
  HWTH BD22 .... **54** F2 1
Craven Crs *ILK* LS29 .... **19** C6 3
Craven Dr *AIRE* BD20 .... **36** A5
  CLECK BD19 .... **150** B5
Cravendale Rd *DEWS* WF13 ...... **172** F8
Craven Dr *AIRE* BD20 .... **36** A5
Craven Garth *GLE* DN14 .... **161** J7
Craven Gv *AIRE* BD20 .... **36** B5 1
Craven La *CLECK* BD19 .... **150** L6
Craven Pk *ILK* LS29 .... **61** H1
Craven Rd *DEWS* WF13 .... **173** J8
  HDGY LS6 .... **6** F3
  HEM/SK/SE WF9 .... **223** M8
  KGHY BD21 .... **3** L2
Craven St *BFDE* BD3 .... **5** H4 1
  COL BB8 .... **74** C1
  DEWS WF13 .... **172** F8
  HUDS HD4 .... **213** J2
  OT LS21 .... **41** K7 1
  SKP/WHF BD23 .... **16** B3
  WKFDE WF1 .... **12** F1
Craven Wood Cl *DOD/DAR* S75 .. **260** C3
Crawford Av *WBSY* BD6 .... **126** E6
Crawford Dr
  WKFDW/WTN WF2 .... **176** B7 1
Crawford St *BOW* BD4 .... **127** J2 6
  MILN OL16 .... **228** C1
Crawley Av *HEM/SK/SE* WF9 .... **246** F1
Crawshaw Av *PDSY/CALV* LS28 .. **107** H7
Crawshaw Gdns
  PDSY/CALV LS28 .... **107** G7
Crawshaw Hl *PDSY/CALV* LS28 .. **107** G7
Crawshaw La *HOR/CROF* WF4 .... **217** C3
Crawshaw Pk *PDSY/CALV* LS28 .. **107** G7
Crawshaw Ri *PDSY/CALV* LS28 .. **107** G8
Crawshaw Rd *PDSY/CALV* LS28 .. **107** G8
Crawshaw St *DEWS* WF13 .... **173** H8
Crawthorne Crs *HUDN* HD2 ...... **193** G2
Crayford Dr *HOR/CROF* WF4 ...... **200** B5
Cray La *GTL/HWG* HX4 .... **189** M4
The Cray *MILN* OL16 .... **207** G8
Crediton Av *WIL/AL* BD15 .... **103** K6
Crescent Av *DEWS* WF13 .... **194** F1
  RTHW LS26 .... **133** H7
Crescent Gdns *AL/HA/HU* LS17 .. **87** M2
Crescent Rd *HOR/CROF* WF4 .... **222** E5
  HUDN HD2 .... **14** D1
  HUDS HD4 .... **213** M7
Crescent Royd *HUDE* HD5 .... **215** J1
Crescent St *TOD* OL14 .... **163** K1
The Crescent *AL/HA/HU* LS17 .... **25** M8
  AL/HA/HU LS17 .... **65** H8
  BAIL BD17 .... **82** E4
  BGLY BD16 .... **59** G8
  BHP/TINH LS16 .... **86** C2
  BIRK/DRI BD11 .... **128** C7
  CAS WF10 .... **158** B8 8
  DEWS WF13 .... **194** F1
  DOD/DAR S75 .... **260** D2
  EARD/LOFT WF3 .... **153** L4
  FEA/AMT WF7 .... **200** F1
  GFTH/SHER LS25 .... **113** J6
  GFTH/SHER LS25 .... **135** J5
  GSLY LS20 .... **61** L6
  GTL/HWG HX4 .... **190** C4
  HOLM/MEL HD7 .... **237** C8 8
  HOR/CROF WF4 .... **218** F1
  ILK LS29 .... **39** G1
  ILK LS29 .... **40** A6
  KBTN HD8 .... **216** C7
  LVSG WF15 .... **171** M1 8
  MSTN/BAR LS15 .... **111** K6
  NORM WF6 .... **178** B2
  OT LS21 .... **41** J4
  PDSY/CALV LS28 .... **107** H6
  ROY/SHW OL2 .... **229** L2
  WBSY BD6 .... **126** A6
  WBY LS22 .... **46** E1
Crescent Vw *AL/HA/HU* LS17 .... **65** H8
  HWTH BD22 .... **79** J3
Crescent Wk *CLAY* BD14 .... **125** M1
  DEWS WF13 .... **194** F1
The Cresent *HIPP* HX3 .... **147** M6
Creskeld Crs *BHP/TINH* LS16 .... **64** A3
Creskeld Dr *BHP/TINH* LS16 ...... **64** A3
Creskeld Gdns *BHP/TINH* LS16 .. **64** A3
Creskeld Garth *BHP/TINH* LS16 .. **64** B3
Creskeld La *BHP/TINH* LS16 ...... **64** B3
Creskeld Pk *BHP/TINH* LS16 ...... **64** B3
Creskeld Wy *WIL/AL* BD15 .... **103** H4
Creskell Rd *BEE/HOL* LS11 .... **8** E6

Cressfield Rd *HUDW* HD3 .... **191** L6
Cresswell Mt *GTHN* BD7 .... **126** A4
Cresswell Pl *GTHN* BD7 .... **126** A4 3
Cresswell St *DOD/DAR* S75 ...... **260** E4
Cresswell Ter *GTHN* BD7 .... **126** A4 1
Crest Av *HUDE* HD5 .... **215** G1 8
  LM/WK BD12 .... **148** E5
Crest Dr *PONT* WF8 .... **181** G8
Crestfield Av *ELL* HX5 .... **169** C8
Crestfield Crs *ELL* HX5 .... **191** G1
Crestfield Dr *ELL* HX5 .... **191** C1
  LUD/ILL HX2 .... **168** A1
Crestfield Rd *ELL* HX5 .... **191** C1
Crest Hill Rd *HUDN* HD2 .... **192** D3
Crest Mt *PONT* WF8 .... **181** G8
Crest Rd *HUDW* HD3 .... **191** J2
The Crest *GFTH/SHER* LS25 ...... **135** J5
  HUDN HD2 .... **171** G8
  RTHW LS26 .... **134** C5
Crestville Cl *CLAY* BD14 .... **125** M1 3
Crestville Rd *CLAY* BD14 .... **125** L1
Crestville Ter *CLAY* BD14 .... **125** M1
Crestwood Cl *BOW* BD4 .... **127** K5 5
Creswell La *DEWS* WF13 .... **173** H3
Crewe Av *KNOT* WF11 .... **181** K2
Crewe Rd *CAS* WF10 .... **158** F2
Crib La *HFAX* HX1 .... **11** C4
Crich Av *BSLYN/ROY* S71 .... **243** J7
Cricketers Ap
  WKFDW/WTN WF2 .... **176** A3
Cricketers Cl *FEA/AMT* WF7 .... **224** C1
  GFTH/SHER LS25 .... **113** J8
Cricketers Gn *YEA* LS19 .... **62** D8
Cricketers Ter
  WOR/ARM LS12 .... **108** E7 13
The Cricketers *BULY* LS4 .... **108** D2
Cricketers Wk *AIRE* BD20 .... **56** F1
  MSTN/BAR LS15 .... **112** A7
Cricketers Wy *GFTH/SHER* LS25 . **116** A7
Cricket Vw *MILN* OL16 .... **229** H1
Cricklegate *MSTN/BAR* LS15 .... **111** K6 8
Crimble Bank *HOLM/MEL* HD7 .. **212** C5
Crimble Clough Rd
  HOLM/MEL HD7 .... **212** C4
Crimbles Ct *PDSY/CALV* LS28 .. **107** H7
Crimbles Pl *PDSY/CALV* LS28 .. **107** H7
Crimbles Rd *PDSY/CALV* LS28 .. **107** H7
Crimbles Ter *PDSY/CALV* LS28 .. **107** H7
Crimea La *HUDW* HD3 .... **211** M3
Crimple Gn *GFTH/SHER* LS25 .... **113** K8
Crimple Mdw *PBR* HG3 .... **26** E2
Crimshaw La *SHPY* BD18 .... **82** F8
Crimsworth La *HBR* HX7 .... **121** J6
Crinan St *NORM* WF6 .... **178** C2 7
Cringles La *AIRE* BD20 .... **18** A7
Cripplegate *HFAX* HX1 .... **11** K5
Cripple Gate La *ROCH* OL11 .... **228** A5
Croasdale Gdns
  AWLS/ASK DN6 .... **249** L6 8
Crodingley Gv *HOLM/MEL* HD7 .. **236** D6
Crodingley Farm Ct
  HOLM/MEL HD7 .... **236** D6
Croft Av *BGLY* BD16 .... **58** F8
  BSLYN/ROY S71 .... **243** K3
  EARD/LOFT WF3 .... **153** M7
  KNOT WF11 .... **182** C1 1
  NORM WF6 .... **178** B3
  NORM WF6 .... **178** E3 8
  OT LS21 .... **41** H5
  PDSY/CALV LS28 .... **106** D3
Croft Br *RTHW* LS26 .... **133** M4
Croft Chantry *HEM/SK/SE* WF9 . **223** J4
Croft Ct *DOD/DAR* S75 .... **242** C5
  ILK LS29 .... **61** H2
Croft Ct *HOLM/MEL* HD7 .... **236** B3
  HORS LS18 .... **85** K5
Croftdale Gv *MSTN/BAR* LS15 .. **111** M4
Croft Dr *BSLYN/ROY* S71 .... **243** H7 1
  BSPA/BRAM LS23 .... **69** M3
  DOD/DAR S75 .... **242** D1
  HOLM/MEL HD7 .... **236** A2
  ILK LS29 .... **61** J2
  STKB/PEN S36 .... **270** A3
Croft End *WBY* LS22 .... **47** L1
Croft Foulds Ct
  GFTH/SHER LS25 .... **113** H7
Croft Gdns *HUDN* HD2 .... **192** A5
Croft Head *KBTN* HD8 .... **239** J8
Croft Head Rd *MILN* OL16 ...... **207** H7
Croft Head La *WKFDE* WF1 ...... **178** A7
Croft Hill *AIRE* BD20 .... **34** E8 8
Croft House Av *MOR* LS27 ...... **152** D1
Croft House Cl *MOR* LS27 ...... **152** D1 8
  WBSY BD6 .... **126** D6 4
Croft House Ct
  PDSY/CALV LS28 .... **107** G6 8
Croft House Dr *MOR* LS27 ...... **152** D1
Croft House Fold *ILK* LS29 ...... **19** J6 8
Croft House Gdns *MOR* LS27 .. **152** D1
Croft House Gv *MOR* LS27 ...... **152** D1
Croft House La *AIRE* BD20 ...... **57** J4 8
  MOR LS27 .... **152** D1
  WBSY BD6 .... **126** D6
Croft House Ms *MOR* LS27 ...... **152** D1
Croft House Mt *MOR* LS27 ...... **130** D8 8
Croft House Ri *MOR* LS27 ...... **130** D8 8
Croft House Rd *HUDW* HD3 .... **211** M1
  MOR LS27 .... **152** D1
  WBSY BD6 .... **126** D6
Croft House Vw *MOR* LS27 ...... **152** D1
Croft House Wk *MOR* LS27 ...... **130** D8 8
Croft House Wy *MOR* LS27 ...... **130** D8
Croftlands *BTLY* WF17 .... **174** B3
  HUDS HD4 .... **214** C4
  IDLE BD10 .... **83** J6
  KNOT WF11 .... **182** C1
Croft La *BSPA/BRAM* LS23 ...... **49** J2
  TAD LS24 .... **51** K8
Crofton Cl *HOLM/MEL* HD7 ...... **212** F6
Crofton Ri *AL/HA/HU* LS17 ...... **87** J2
Crofton Rd *HTON* BD9 .... **104** C3
Croft Pk *ILK* LS29 .... **61** H2
Croft Pl *BRIG* HD6 .... **170** D2

Croft Ri *ILK* LS29 .... **61** J2
Croft Rd *AIRE* BD20 .... **58** F5 8
  BSLY S70 .... **261** L7
  BSPA/BRAM LS23 .... **69** M3 8
Croft's Ct *LDS* LS1 .... **6** F9
Croftside Cl *SCFT* LS14 .... **111** K3 8
Cromack Vw *PDSY/CALV* LS28 .. **106** E7
Cromarty Av *HUDS* HD4 .... **213** L4
Cromarty Dr *HUDS* HD4 .... **213** L4
Cromer Pl *LDSU* LS2 .... **6** C5
Cromer Rd *KGHY* BD21 .... **2** E9
  LDSU LS2 .... **6** C5
Cromer St *CUD/GR* S72 .... **245** J7
  HFAX HX1 .... **10** A9 1
  LDSU LS2 .... **6** C5
  ROY/SHW OL2 .... **229** K7 8
  WHIT OL12 .... **206** A6 8
Cromer Ter *LDSU* LS2 .... **6** C5
Cromford Av *BSLYN/ROY* S71 .. **243** K8
Crompton Av *BSLY* S70 .... **260** F6
  ROCH OL11 .... **228** D3
Crompton Circuit
  ROY/SHW OL2 .... **230** C4
Crompton St *ROY/SHW* OL2 .... **229** K7 8
Cromwell Cl *HIPP* HX3 .... **169** J2
  KNOT WF11 .... **159** M1 8
Cromwell Ct *AWLS/ASK* DN6 .... **249** H5 1
  BGLY BD16 .... **103** K2
  BIRK/DRI BD11 .... **150** F2
Cromwell Crs *PONT* WF8 .... **181** G6
Cromwell Gv *AWLS/ASK* DN6 .... **249** J4 2
Cromwell Mt *BSLY* S70 .... **261** M6 8
  MID LS10 .... **131** M6 8
  OSM LS9 .... **7** L7
Cromwell Pl *OSS* WF5 .... **175** G7 8
Cromwell Ri *GFTH/SHER* LS25 .. **135** J6
Cromwell Rd *CAS* WF10 .... **158** F7
  HIPP HX3 .... **169** J2
  ROY/SHW OL2 .... **228** E8
Cromwell St *OSM* LS9 .... **7** L8
  SKP/WHF BD23 .... **16** C3
Cromwell Ter *HFAX* HX1 .... **10** E6 1
Cronkeyshaw Rd *WHIT* OL12 .... **206** A5
Cronkhill La *BSLYN/ROY* S71 .... **243** M5
Crooked La *HIPP* HX3 .... **124** D8
  IDLE BD10 .... **83** H5
Crooke House La
  BSLYN/ROY S71 .... **263** H5
Crooke La *WIL/AL* BD15 .... **102** E2
Crookes La *BSLYN/ROY* S71 .... **243** L5
Crookes St *BSLY* S70 .... **260** F5
Crook St *MILN* OL16 .... **206** B6
Cropper Ga *LDS* LS1 .... **6** C9
Cropredy Cl *CUL/QBY* BD13 .... **125** H5
Cropstones *BSPA/BRAM* LS23 .. **69** M4 8
Cropton Rd *BSLYN/ROY* S71 .... **243** K3
Crosby Av *BEE/HOL* LS11 .... **8** B7
Crosby Ct *BSLYN/ROY* S71 ...... **261** M5
Crosby Pl *BEE/HOL* LS11 .... **8** C6
Crosby Rd *BEE/HOL* LS11 .... **8** C6
Crosby St *BEE/HOL* LS11 .... **8** C6
  CUD/GR S72 .... **244** D6 8
  KGHY BD21 .... **2** E3
  WHIT OL12 .... **206** B4
Crosby Ter *BEE/HOL* LS11 .... **8** C6
Crosby Vw *BEE/HOL* LS11 .... **8** C6
Croscombe Wk *WBOW* BD5 ...... **4** E9 8
Croset Av *HUDE* HD5 .... **15** C1 8
Crosland Ct *HUDW* HD3 .... **191** H5 8
Crosland Factory La *HUDS* HD4 .. **235** J1 8
Crosland Hill Rd *HUDS* HD4 .... **213** K3
Crosland Rd *HUD* HD1 .... **214** A2
  HUDW HD3 .... **191** H4
Crosland Spring Rd *HUDS* HD4 . **235** J1 8
Crosland St *HUDS* HD4 .... **214** A2
Crosley Vw *BGLY* BD16 .... **81** K4
Crosley Wood Rd *BGLY* BD16.... **81** K4
Cross Albert Pl
  WOR/ARM LS12 .... **108** F8 1
Cross Alcester Rd *RHAY* LS8 .... **110** B2 8
Cross Alma St *OSM* LS9 .... **110** B5 8
Cross Aston Gv *BRAM* LS13 .... **108** A4
Cross Av *RTHW* LS26.............. **133** H7 1
Cross Bank Rd *BTLY* WF17 ...... **151** K8
Cross Banks *SHPY* BD18 .... **82** D7
Cross Bank St *MIRF* WF14 ...... **194** C3 8
Cross Banstead St *RHAY* LS8 .. **110** B3 8
Cross Barstow St *BEE/HOL* LS11.. **9** G4

Cross Bath Rd *BRAM* LS13 ...... **107** L4
Crossbeck Cl *ILK* LS29 .... **38** C3 8
Crossbeck Rd *ILK* LS29 .... **38** D3
Cross Beck Rd *RHAY* LS8 .... **110** B2 8
Cross Belgrave St *LDSU* LS2 .... **7** H8 1
Cross Bellbrooke Av
  OSM LS9 .... **110** D4 8
Cross Bell St *OSM* LS9 .... **7** K8 8
Cross Bentley La *HDGY* LS6 .... **87** H8
Cross Burley Lodge Rd
  HDGY LS6 .... **109** C4 17
Cross Cardigan Mt *BULY* LS4 .. **108** E5
Cross Cardigan Ter *BULY* LS4 .. **108** E5
Cross Catherine St *OSM* LS9 .... **9** M1
Cross Chancellor St *HDGY* LS6.. **6** F2
Cross Chapel St *HDGY* LS6 .... **108** F1 2
Cross Church St *HUD* HD1 ...... **15** G7 8
  HUD HD1 .... **213** M1
Cross Cliff Rd *HDGY* LS6 .... **3** H3 8
Cross Cowper St *CHAL* LS7 ...... **7** K2
Cross Crown St *CLECK* BD19 .. **149** M7 8
Crossdale Av *WBSY* BD6 .... **125** M6
Cross Dawlish Gv *OSM* LS9 .... **110** B5 8
Cross Dikes Rd *RPDN/SBR* HX6 .. **166** C7
Cross Easy Rd *OSM* LS9 .... **110** B8 8
Cross Elford St *RHAY* LS8 ...... **110** B3 8
Cross Emily St *KGHY* BD21 ...... **3** H3 8
Cross End Fold *ILK* LS29 .... **19** J6 2
Cross Ends La *HBR* HX7 .... **121** J2
Cross Evanston Av *BULY* LS4 .. **108** E4
Cross Farm Ct *HWTH* BD22 .... **100** D3
Cross Fld *GTL/HWG* HX4 .... **190** C2 8
Crossfield Cl *HWTH* BD22 ...... **100** D3
Crossfield Ct *HWTH* BD22 ...... **100** D3
Cross Field La *AWLS/ASK* DN6 .. **249** J5
Crossfield Pl *ROCH* OL11 .... **228** C3
Crossfield Rd *HWTH* BD22 ...... **100** D3
Crossfield House Cl
  AWLS/ASK DN6 .... **249** J4 8
Crossfields *HOR/CROF* WF4 .... **196** C8 8
Cross Flds *HUDE* HD5 .... **193** G2
Crossfield St *LDSU* LS2 .... **6** D3
Cross Firs St *HUD* HD1 .... **213** K1
Cross Flats Rw *BEE/HOL* LS11.. **131** H4
Cross Flatts Av *BEE/HOL* LS11 .. **131** J3
Cross Flatts Crs *BEE/HOL* LS11 . **131** H3
Cross Flatts Dr *BEE/HOL* LS11 .. **131** H3
Cross Flatts Gv *BEE/HOL* LS11 .. **131** H3
Cross Flatts Mt *BEE/HOL* LS11 .. **131** J3
Cross Flatts Pde *BEE/HOL* LS11 . **131** H4
Cross Flatts Pl *BEE/HOL* LS11 .. **131** H4
Cross Flatts Rd *BEE/HOL* LS11 .. **131** H4
Cross Flatts Rw *BEE/HOL* LS11 .. **131** H4
Cross Flatts St *BEE/HOL* LS11 .. **131** H4
Cross Flatts Ter *BEE/HOL* LS11 .. **131** H4
Cross Foundry St *DEWS* WF13 . **195** G1 8
Cross Fountaine St *LDS* LS1 .... **6** F9 8
Cross Francis St *CHAL* LS7 ...... **7** K2
Crossgate *DOD/DAR* S75 .... **242** D5
  OT LS21 .... **41** J4
Cross Gate Rd *HOLM/MEL* HD7.. **254** D4
Cross Gates Av *MSTN/BAR* LS15 . **111** J3
Cross Gates La *BGLY* BD16 ...... **80** E3
  MSTN/BAR LS15............ **111** K3
Crossgates Rd *MILN* OL16 ...... **207** H7
Cross Gates Rd *MSTN/BAR* LS15 . **111** J4
Cross Glen Rd *BHP/TINH* LS16 .. **86** E7
Cross Granby Ter *HDGY* LS6 .... **108** F1 3
Cross Grange Av *RHAY* LS8 ...... **7** M2
Cross Grasmere St
  WOR/ARM LS12 .... **108** F7
Cross Gn *OT* LS21 .... **41** K6
Cross Green Ap *OSM* LS9 ...... **132** C1
Cross Green Cl *OSM* LS9 .... **132** C1
Cross Green Ct *OSM* LS9 .... **132** D1
Cross Green Crs *OSM* LS9 ...... **110** B8 8
Cross Green Garth *OSM* LS9 .... **132** C1
Cross Green Gv *OSM* LS9 ...... **110** B8 8
Cross Green La *MSTN/BAR* LS15 . **111** K6
  OSM LS9 .... **9** J3
Cross Green Rd *HUDE* HD5 .... **193** J8
  OSM LS9 .... **110** B8 8
Cross Green Rw *HDGY* LS6 ...... **87** G7
Cross Green V *OSM* LS9 .... **132** C1
Cross Green Wy *OSM* LS9 ...... **132** C1
Cross Grove St *HUD* HD1 .... **14** B5 8
Cross Hands La *HOR/CROF* WF4.. **201** K8
Cross Hartley Av *RHAY* LS8 ...... **6** D1
Cross Heath Gv *BEE/HOL* LS11 .. **131** C4
Cross Henley Rd *BRAM* LS13 .. **107** L4
The Crossings *BTLY* WF17 ...... **151** H6
Cross Hilton Gv *RHAY* LS8 ...... **110** B1 8
Cross Ingleby Ter *BULY* LS4 .... **88** D4 8
Cross Ingram Rd *BEE/HOL* LS11.. **8** B5
Cross Ivy Mt *OSM* LS9 .... **110** C6 8
Cross Kelso Rd *LDSU* LS2 ...... **6** B6
Cross Keys *OSS* WF5 .... **175** J7
Cross Keys Ct *HOR/CROF* WF4 .. **197** K5 8
Crossland Ct *MOR* LS27 .... **130** D7
Cross Land Ter *BEE/HOL* LS11 .. **8** H3
Cross La *BGLY* BD16 .... **81** H5
  BIRK/DRI BD11 .... **128** D7
  BRIG HD6 .... **171** C5
  BSLYN/ROY S71 .... **244** A3
  CUL/QBY BD13 .... **124** C6
  ELL HX5 .... **169** C8
  GSLY LS20 .... **62** B3
  GTHN BD7 .... **4** C8
  HIPP HX3 .... **147** K2
  HOLM/MEL HD7 .... **236** A4
  HOLM/MEL HD7 .... **254** A4
  HUDS HD4 .... **214** C3

  HUDS HD4 .... **237** L4
  HWTH BD22 .... **100** C3 8
  KBTN HD8 .... **217** M6
  KBTN HD8 .... **238** A8
  KBTN HD8 .... **238** D1
  KBTN HD8 .... **239** J5
  STKB/PEN S36 .... **258** B6
  STKB/PEN S36 .... **271** J2
  TOD OL14 .... **164** B2
  WIL/AL BD15 .... **80** F7
  WKFDW/WTN WF2 .... **198** B1
  WOR/ARM LS12 .... **108** D7
  WOR/ARM LS12 .... **130** A1
Cross Lea Farm Rd *KSTL* LS5 .. **86** B7
Cross Lee *TOD* OL14 .... **141** H7
Cross Leeds St *KGHY* BD21 .... **2** F5 8
Cross Lee Ga *TOD* OL14 .... **141** H7
Cross Lee Rd *TOD* OL14 .... **141** H7
Cross Lees *WHIT* OL12 .... **206** C3
Crossley Cl *MIRF* WF14 .... **172** C6
Crossley Gv *MIRF* WF14 .... **172** C6
Crossley Hall Ms *GIR* BD8 ...... **104** A7 2
Crossley Hall St *GIR* BD8 ...... **103** M7 3
Crossley Hl *HIPP* HX3 .... **168** F1
Crossley La *HUDE* HD5 .... **193** J7
  MIRF WF14 .... **172** C6
Crossley New Rd *TOD* OL14 .... **142** A6
Crossley Pl *SKP/WHF* BD23 .... **16** B2 8
Crossley St *BRIG* HD6 .... **170** D5
  CUL/QBY BD13 .... **125** H5
  FEA/AMT WF7 .... **201** M1 2
  GTHN BD7 .... **126** D1
  HFAX HX1 .... **11** H5
  HOR/CROF WF4 .... **200** C1
  MILN OL16 .... **207** G8
  ROY/SHW OL2 .... **229** L7
  TOD OL14 .... **163** K1 7
  WBY LS22 .... **48** A1 8
  WKFDE WF1 .... **178** B8
Crossley Ter *BTLY* WF17 .... **173** L3
Crossley Ter North *LUD/ILL* HX2 . **146** C2
Crossley Ter South *LUD/ILL* HX2 . **146** C2
Cross Lidget Pl *RHAY* LS8 ...... **88** B6
Cross Louis St *CHAL* LS7 .... **7** K3
Crossman Dr *NORM* WF6 .... **178** E3 2
Cross Maude St *LDSU* LS2 ...... **9** J1 8
Crossmoor Cl *AIRE* BD20 .... **35** L5
Crossmount St *BTLY* WF17 ...... **173** L3 8
Cross Park Av *CAS* WF10 .... **158** B7
Cross Park St *BTLY* WF17 ...... **173** M1
  EARL WF12 .... **174** B6
  HOR/CROF WF4 .... **197** J5 8
  MSTN/BAR LS15 .... **111** J6 2
Cross Peel St *MOR* LS27 .... **152** D2 8
Cross Pipes Rd
  WKFDW/WTN WF2 .... **176** A6 1
Cross Quarry St *HDGY* LS6 ...... **6** D1
Cross Queen St *NORM* WF6 .... **178** C4 1
Cross Reginald Mt *CHAL* LS7 .... **7** J1 8
Cross Rink St *BTLY* WF17 ...... **173** M3 8
Cross River St *KGHY* BD21 ...... **3** L1 8
Cross Rd *EARL* WF12 .... **195** L4
  GIR BD8 .... **104** D5 8
  HOR/CROF WF4 .... **196** D8
  HOR/CROF WF4 .... **220** B3
  HORS LS18 .... **85** J6 8
  IDLE BD10 .... **83** L6
  LM/WK BD12 .... **149** H1
Cross Roseville Rd *RHAY* LS8 .. **7** M3
Cross Rosse St *SHPY* BD18...... **82** D6 3
Cross Roundhay Av *RHAY* LS8 .. **110** B1
Cross Row *MSTN/BAR* LS15 .... **112** C8
Cross Ryecroft St *OSS* WF5 .... **174** F3 8
Cross St *BRIG* HD6 .... **170** C2
  BSLYN/ROY S71 .... **261** L2
  BTLY WF17 .... **173** M1 8
  CAS WF10 .... **157** K6
  CLAY BD14 .... **125** L2 8
  CUD/GR S72 .... **245** K8
  DOD/DAR S75 .... **259** M2
  DOD/DAR S75 .... **260** D5
  EARD/LOFT WF3 .... **154** A6 8
  EARL WF12 .... **173** M7 1
  EARL WF12 .... **174** A4 2
  GTL/HWG HX4 .... **168** F7 2
  GTL/HWG HX4 .... **190** C2 8
  HEM/SK/SE WF9 .... **223** L7
  HEM/SK/SE WF9 .... **225** M6
  HFAX HX1 .... **11** J7 2
  HOLM/MEL HD7 .... **212** C5
  HOLM/MEL HD7 .... **236** B2 8
  HOR/CROF WF4 .... **197** K5
  HWTH BD22 .... **54** E3
  LM/WK BD12 .... **149** J2
  LVSG WF15 .... **172** C4
  MILN OL16 .... **206** F7 8
  MSTN/BAR LS15 .... **111** J6 5
  OSS WF5 .... **174** F5
  PONT WF8 .... **180** F6 5
  RTHW LS26 .... **155** G1
  SKP/WHF BD23 .... **16** B3
  WBSY BD6 .... **126** B7 8
  WBY LS22 .... **48** A1 8
  WKFDE WF1 .... **12** E2 8
Cross St West *LUD/ILL* HX2 .... **146** A6 2
Cross Sun St *BFD* BD1 .... **5** G4
The Cross *MSTN/BAR* LS15 .... **91** C7 8
Cross Union St *LDSU* LS2 ...... **7** J9
Cross Valley Dr *MSTN/BAR* LS15 . **111** J3
Crossway *BGLY* BD16 .... **81** H7 8
The Crossways *OT* LS21 .... **41** J4
Cross Wells Rd *RPDN/SBR* HX6 .. **188** C2
Cross Westfield Rd *BVRD* LS3 .. **6** B7 8
Cross Wingham St *CHAL* LS7 .. **7** J1 8
Cross Woodstock St *LDSU* LS2.. **6** E4 8
Cross York St *LDSU* LS2 .... **9** J1
Crowden Wk *DOD/DAR* S75 .... **260** C5 8
Crowgill Rd *SHPY* BD18 .... **82** D6
Crow Hill End Rd
  RPDN/SBR HX6 .... **166** B4

Crow Hill Rd HBR HX7 ... 166 B3
Crow La HUDW HD3 ... 213 J1
 OT LS21 ... 41 J7
Crowlees Cl MIRF WF14 ... 194 D1
Crowlees Gdns MIRF WF14 ... 194 D1
Crowless Rd MIRF WF14 ... 194 C1
Crown & Anchor Yd PONT WF8 . 180 E6
Crown Av BSLY S70 ... 261 J7
 CUD/GR S72 ... 262 E2
Crown Cl BSLY S70 ... 261 H7
 EARL WF12 ... 174 C7
Crown Dr LM/WK BD12 ... 148 E3
Crow Nest La BEE/HOL LS11 ... 130 F4
Crownest La BGLY BD16 ... 81 J2
Crownest Rd BGLY BD16 ... 81 J3
Crown Nest Vw DEWS WF13 ... 173 J7
Crown Flatt Wy EARL WF12 ... 174 A5
Crown Gdns MILN OL16 ... 228 D1
Crown Gn HUDS HD4 ... 213 J3
Crown Hill Rd DOD/DAR S75 ... 260 C5
Crownlands La OSS WF5 ... 174 D1
Crown La HOLM/MEL HD7 ... 254 C1
Crown Point Cl OSS WF5 ... 174 E8
Crown Point Dr OSS WF5 ... 174 E8
Crown Point Rd MID LS10 ... 9 J3
 OSM LS9 ... 9 K2
 OSS WF5 ... 174 E8
Crown Rd HIPP HX3 ... 146 D4
Crown St BFD BD1 ... 4 B5
 BRIG HD6 ... 170 C3
 BSLY S70 ... 261 J7
 CLECK BD19 ... 149 M7
 ELL HX5 ... 169 H8
 HBR HX7 ... 143 J3
 HFAX HX1 ... 11 G6
 HOLM/MEL HD7 ... 236 B1
 ILK LS29 ... 40 B5
 KBTN HD8 ... 239 M5
 LDS LS1 ... 9 H1
 LM/WK BD12 ... 148 E2
 LVSG WF15 ... 172 D2
 MILN OL16 ... 228 C1
 OSS WF5 ... 197 G3
 ROY/SHW OL2 ... 229 K7
Crown Well HI BSLYN/ROY S71 . 262 B6
Crown Yd HEM/SK/SE WF9 ... 246 F3
Crowshaw Dr WHIT OL12 ... 206 A3
Crowther Av PDSY/CALV LS28 ... 84 B8
Crowther Fold BGLY BD16 ... 80 D5
Crowther Pl CAS WF10 ... 157 M7
 HDGY LS6 ... 6 F2
Crowther Rd HECK WF16 ... 173 C1
 MIRF WF14 ... 194 C1
Crowther St BTLY WF17 ... 173 H1
 CAS WF10 ... 157 L7
 CLECK BD19 ... 149 M6
 HUD HD1 ... 15 H8
 HUD HD1 ... 214 B3
 IDLE BD10 ... 83 M7
 LIT OL15 ... 207 G2
 LM/WK BD12 ... 148 E2
 MILN OL16 ... 228 C1
Crow Tree Cl BAIL BD17 ... 82 F3
Crow Tree La GIR BD8 ... 104 A5
Crowtrees Ct YEA LS19 ... 84 D3
Crowtrees Crs BRIG HD6 ... 170 B6
Crowtrees La BRIG HD6 ... 170 B7
Crowtrees Pk BRIG HD6 ... 170 B7
Crow Trees Pk YEA LS19 ... 84 D3
Crow Trees Rd HOLM/MEL HD7 . 211 K8
Crow Wood La GTL/HWG HX4 ... 189 L4
Crow Wood Pk LUD/ILL HX2 ... 142 A3
Croxall Dr EARD/LOFT WF3 ... 177 C1
Croxton Av MILN OL16 ... 206 C6
Croydon Av ROY/SHW OL2 ... 228 D3
Croydon St GTHN BD7 ... 126 E2
Croydon St BEE/HOL LS11 ... 8 A4
Crumack La HWTH BD22 ... 101 C3
Crummock Wy
 BSLYN/ROY S71 ... 262 D6
Crystal Pl WKFDE WF1 ... 13 H3
Crystal Ter BOW BD4 ... 127 L3
Cubley Av WKFDW/WTN WF2 ... 198 D8
Cubley Rise Rd STKB/PEN S36 ... 270 E5
Cuckoo La HOLM/MEL HD7 ... 236 B2
Cuckstool Rd KBTN HD8 ... 239 L8
Cudbear St MID LS10 ... 9 J3
Cudworth Vw CUD/GR S72 ... 245 J6
Cullingworth Rd
 CUL/QBY BD13 ... 101 M1
Cullingworth St DEWS WF13 ... 173 J3
Culpans Rd HBR HX7 ... 166 C2
Culver St HFAX HX1 ... 11 G5
Culvert St MILN OL16 ... 228 C1
Cumberland Cl LUD/ILL HX2 ... 146 A1
Cumberland Dr BSLYN/ROY S71 . 262 B6
Cumberland Rd CAS WF10 ... 159 G4
 GTHN BD7 ... 126 C1
 ROCH OL11 ... 228 B4
Cumberland St SKP/WHF BD23 .. 16 B3
Cumberworth La KBTN HD8 ... 238 F7
 KBTN HD8 ... 256 A1
Cumberworth Rd KBTN HD8 ... 239 H5
Cumbrian Wy ROY/SHW OL2 ... 229 H6
Cumbrian Wy
 WKFDW/WTN WF2 . 197 M4
Cuncliffe Dr ROY/SHW OL2 ... 229 M7
Cunliffe La BAIL BD17 ... 83 K1
Cunliffe Rd GIR BD8 ... 104 E4
 ILK LS29 ... 38 C3
Cunliffe Ter GIR BD8 ... 104 F3
Cunliffe Vis HTON BD9 ... 104 F3
Cure HI HWTH BD22 ... 78 D3
Curlew Cl CAS WF10 ... 157 M8
 ILK LS29 ... 38 A2
Curlew Ct AIRE BD20 ... 35 K8
Curlew Ri MOR LS27 ... 152 F3
Curlew St WBOW BD5 ... 126 E3
Curly Hl ILK LS29 ... 20 D8
Currer Av BOW BD4 ... 127 K5
Currer La ILK LS29 ... 19 L2
Currer St BFD BD1 ... 5 G6
Currer Wk AIRE BD20 ... 35 K8
Curwen Crs HECK WF16 ... 172 F1

ROCH OL11 ... 228 B4
Curzon Rd BFDE BD3 ... 5 M5
Curzon St HUDN HD2 ... 193 J1
Cuthberts Cl CUL/QBY BD13 ... 124 F6
Cutler Heights La BOW BD4 ... 127 L3
Cutler La RTHW LS26 ... 157 G3
Cutler Pl BOW BD4 ... 127 M2
Cutlers Av BSLY S70 ... 260 F6
Cut Rd KNOT WF11 ... 159 L5
Cutsyke Av CAS WF10 ... 157 K8
Cutsyke Crest WF10 ... 157 K8
Cutsyke Rd CAS WF10 ... 157 K8
 FEA/AMT WF7 ... 179 K3
Cuttlehurst KBTN HD8 ... 239 M5
Cutts Field Vw
 BSLYN/ROY S71 ... 243 K1
Cutty La DOD/DAR S75 ... 260 F3
Cypress Fold KBTN HD8 ... 216 A3
Cypress Rd BSLY S70 ... 261 K7
 NORM WF6 ... 178 D6
Cyprus Av IDLE BD10 ... 83 H5
 WKFDE WF1 ... 176 C6
Cyprus Crs MIRF WF14 ... 172 F7
Cyprus Dr IDLE BD10 ... 83 H5
Cyprus Gv GFTH/SHER LS25 ... 113 G7
 WKFDE WF1 ... 176 D6
Cyprus Mt WKFDE WF1 ... 176 C6
Cyprus Rd GFTH/SHER LS25 ... 113 G7
Cyprus St OSS WF5 ... 174 E6
 WKFDE WF1 ... 176 D6
Cyprus Ter GFTH/SHER LS25 ... 113 G7
Cyril St ROY/SHW OL2 ... 229 L7

D

Dacre Av WKFDW/WTN WF2 ... 197 L2
Dacre Cl LVSG WF15 ... 172 B1
Dacre Ct TAD LS24 ... 93 J8
Dacre Rd ROCH OL11 ... 228 B2
Daffels Wood Cl BOW BD4 ... 127 K6
Daffil Av MOR LS27 ... 130 D7
Daffil Grange Ms MOR LS27 ... 130 D7
Daffil Grange Wy MOR LS27 ... 130 D7
Daffil Gv MOR LS27 ... 130 D7
Daffil Rd MOR LS27 ... 130 D7
Daffodil Cl WHIT OL12 ... 206 A3
Daffodil Ct WIL/AL BD15 ... 103 K6
Dagenham Rd BOW BD4 ... 127 L3
Daisy Bank St TOD OL14 ... 140 D5
Daisy Cl BTLY WF17 ... 151 G4
Daisy Cft AIRE BD20 ... 36 B3
Daisyfield Rd BRAM LS13 ... 107 M4
Daisy Fold HEM/SK/SE WF9 ... 225 H7
Daisy HI AIRE BD20 ... 36 B3
 EARL WF12 ... 173 L6
 LM/WK BD12 ... 148 E3
 MOR LS27 ... 152 E1
Daisy Hill Av MOR LS27 ... 130 E8
Daisy Hill Back La HTON BD9 ... 104 A4
Daisy Hill Cl MOR LS27 ... 130 E8
Daisy Hill Gv HTON BD9 ... 104 A4
Daisy Hill La HTON BD9 ... 104 A4
Daisy Lea La HUDW HD3 ... 191 L5
Daisy Lee Gv HOLM/MEL HD7 .. 254 E7
Daisy Mt RPDN/SBR HX6 ... 167 J1
Daisy Royd HUDS HD4 ... 214 C4
Daisy St BRIG HD6 ... 170 C4
 GTHN BD7 ... 126 C3
 HFAX HX1 ... 10 E7
 HWTH BD22 ... 79 G6
 WHIT OL12 ... 206 A6
Daisy Vale Ms EARD/LOFT WF3 . 154 A5
Daisy Vale Ter EARD/LOFT WF3 . 154 A5
Dalby Av BFDE BD3 ... 105 M5
Dalby St BFDE BD3 ... 105 L6
Dalcross Gv WBOW BD5 ... 127 H2
Dalcross St WBOW BD5 ... 127 C2
Dale Av TOD OL14 ... 163 M1
Dale Cl BSLYN/ROY S71 ... 243 J7
 BTLY WF17 ... 173 J1
 GSLY LS20 ... 61 K6
 KBTN HD8 ... 257 H1
 OSS WF5 ... 175 G8
Dale Crs AIRE BD20 ... 56 E1
Dale Cft GFTH/SHER LS25 ... 113 G6
 ILK LS29 ... 38 A2
 KBTN HD8 ... 239 J4
Dale Croft Ri WIL/AL BD15 ... 103 J4
Dalecroft Rd AWLS/ASK DN6 ... 249 K6
Dalefield Av NORM WF6 ... 178 D5
Dalefield Rd NORM WF6 ... 178 D5
Dale Garth BAIL BD17 ... 82 D3
Dale Gv SHPY BD18 ... 83 G5
Dalehead Dr ROY/SHW OL2 ... 229 M7
Dale La HECK WF16 ... 172 F1
 HEM/SK/SE WF9 ... 247 K1
Dale Ms PONT WF8 ... 202 F1
Dale Park Av BHP/TINH LS16 ... 85 M2
Dale Park Cl BHP/TINH LS16 ... 85 M2
Dale Park Gdns BHP/TINH LS16 . 85 M2
Dale Park Ri BHP/TINH LS16 ... 85 M2
Dale Park Vw BHP/TINH LS16 ... 85 M2
Dale Park Wk BHP/TINH LS16 ... 85 M2
Dale Rd BIRK/DRI BD11 ... 129 J6
Dales Dr GSLY LS20 ... 61 K6
Daleside EARL WF12 ... 195 L5
 GTL/HWG HX4 ... 168 C7
Daleside Av HOLM/MEL HD7 ... 236 C7
 PDSY/CALV LS28 ... 106 C6
Daleside Cl PDSY/CALV LS28 ... 106 B5
Daleside Gv LM/WK BD12 ... 149 H2
 PDSY/CALV LS28 ... 106 C6
Daleside Rd AIRE BD20 ... 58 C5
 BFDE BD3 ... 106 B5
 SHPY BD18 ... 83 G5
Daleside Wk WBOW BD5 ... 127 H4
Daleson Cl HIPP HX3 ... 147 J3
Dale Stone Cl KNOT WF11 ... 159 L5
Dale St BFD BD1 ... 4 F5
 HUDW HD3 ... 191 J8
 KGHY BD21 ... 3 L1
 MILN OL16 ... 206 D7
 OSS WF5 ... 174 F8
 ROY/SHW OL2 ... 229 K8

RPDN/SBR HX6 ... 167 K2
 SHPY BD18 ... 82 D7
 TOD OL14 ... 163 K1
Dalesway BGLY BD16 ... 81 K1
Dales Wy BHP/TINH LS16 ... 65 G8
 GSLY LS20 ... 61 K6
 ILK LS29 ... 37 M1
Dales Way Link BAIL BD17 ... 82 A1
 BHP/TINH LS16 ... 63 J3
 HDGY LS6 ... 87 G7
 OT LS21 ... 41 K6
Daleswood Av BSLY S70 ... 260 D5
The Dale GFTH/SHER LS25 ... 92 A6
Dale Vw AIRE BD20 ... 36 A4
 AIRE BD20 ... 56 E1
 HEM/SK/SE WF9 ... 224 B8
 ILK LS29 ... 38 A2
 LIT OL15 ... 207 H4
 PONT WF8 ... 202 F1
Dale View Cl BAIL BD17 ... 82 C4
Daleview Ct BAIL BD17 ... 82 C4
Dale View Gv KGHY BD21 ... 3 M6
Dale View Rd KGHY BD21 ... 3 L8
Dallam Av SHPY BD18 ... 82 A6
Dallam Rd SHPY BD18 ... 82 A6
Dallam Wk SHPY BD18 ... 82 B6
Dalmeny Av HUDS HD4 ... 213 L4
Dalmeny Cl HUDS HD4 ... 213 L3
Dalmeny Ter ROCH OL11 ... 228 B2
Dalton Av BEE/HOL LS11 ... 131 J4
 MILN OL16 ... 206 F7
Dalton Bank Rd HUDE HD5 ... 193 K1
 HUDE HD5 ... 193 K1
Dalton Cl MILN OL16 ... 206 F7
Dalton Clowes HUDE HD5 ... 193 C2
Dalton Fold Rd HUDE HD5 ... 15 L1
Dalton Green La HUDE HD5 ... 193 H8
Dalton Gv BEE/HOL LS11 ... 131 J4
 HUDE HD5 ... 193 G7
Dalton La BSPA/BRAM LS23 ... 69 J3
 KGHY BD21 ... 3 K4
Dalton Rd BEE/HOL LS11 ... 131 J4
Dalton St RPDN/SBR HX6 ... 167 K3
Dalton Ter CAS WF10 ... 157 M7
 GIR BD8 ... 104 D6
Damask St HFAX HX1 ... 10 F4
Dam Br CRP/BISH YO23 ... 33 L7
Damems La HWTH BD22 ... 79 J3
Damems Rd HWTH BD22 ... 79 J3
Dames La HWTH BD22 ... 79 J4
Dam Head La HUDE HD5 ... 194 B8
Dam Head Rd RPDN/SBR HX6 .. 167 L1
Dam HI CRP/BISH YO23 ... 33 M7
 KBTN HD8 ... 237 M3
Dam La TAD LS24 ... 93 J8
 YEA LS19 ... 62 F7
Damon Av IDLE BD10 ... 163 J5
Dampier St TOD OL14 ... 163 J5
Damside KGHY BD21 ... 2 F6
Damside Rd HUDS HD4 ... 214 D2
Damsteads DOD/DAR S75 ... 260 C7
Danby Av BOW BD4 ... 127 K6
Danby La WKFDW/WTN WF2 ... 220 C2
Danby Wk OSM LS9 ... 110 B7
Dandy Mill Cft PONT WF8 ... 181 H4
Dandy Mill Vw PONT WF8 ... 181 H4
Danebury Rd BRIG HD6 ... 170 C5
Danecourt Rd BOW BD4 ... 128 A3
Danefield Ter OT LS21 ... 41 K6
Dane Hill Dr BOW BD4 ... 128 A2
Danella Crs WKFDW/WTN WF2 . 176 B4
Danella Gv WKFDW/WTN WF2 .. 176 B4
Danes La HOR/CROF WF4 ... 196 D8
Danesleigh Dr HOR/CROF WF4 . 196 D8
Dane St ROCH OL11 ... 206 A7
Daniel Ct BOW BD4 ... 128 B4
Dan La CUL/QBY BD13 ... 125 L4
Danny La LUD/ILL HX2 ... 144 F7
Dansk Wy ILK LS29 ... 38 F1
Danum Dr BAIL BD17 ... 82 E4
Darcey Hey La LUD/ILL HX2 ... 168 A1
Darfield Av RHAY LS8 ... 110 C3
Darfield Crs RHAY LS8 ... 110 C3
Darfield Gv RHAY LS8 ... 110 B3
Darfield Pl RHAY LS8 ... 110 C3
Darfield Rd CUD/GR S72 ... 262 F2
 RHAY LS8 ... 110 C3
Darfield St GIR BD8 ... 4 D4
 RHAY LS8 ... 110 C3
Darkfield La PONT WF8 ... 181 G7
Dark La BSLY S70 ... 260 D7
 BTLY WF17 ... 151 H3
 BTLY WF17 ... 173 K2
 HBR HX7 ... 142 K2
 HUDE HD5 ... 215 J3
 HWTH BD22 ... 78 B5
 HWTH BD22 ... 100 E3
 LUD/ILL HX2 ... 145 K8
 OT LS21 ... 42 F1
 PBR HG3 ... 29 G1
 PONT WF8 ... 180 E7
 UPML OL3 ... 231 C8
Darkwood Cl AL/HA/HU LS17 ... 88 C2
Darkwood Wy AL/HA/HU LS17 .. 88 C2
Darley Av BSLY S70 ... 261 G8
 BSLYN/ROY S71 ... 243 J8
 MID LS10 ... 131 M7
Darley Cl BSLYN/ROY S71 ... 243 J8
Darley Rd LVSG WF15 ... 172 B1
 ROCH OL11 ... 228 B2
Darley St BFD BD1 ... 4 F5
 HECK WF16 ... 172 F2
 KGHY BD21 ... 57 K5
Darley Ter DOD/DAR S75 ... 260 F4
Darnell Ter BEE/HOL LS11 ... 9 G5
Darnes Av LUD/ILL HX2 ... 168 A1
Darning La WKFDW/WTN WF2 ... 225 K1
Darnley Av WKFDW/WTN WF2 .. 12 A1
Darnley Cl HOLM/MEL HD7 ... 253 J8
Darnley La MSTN/BAR LS15 ... 111 L8
Darren St BFD BD4 ... 128 A1
Darrington Pl BSLYN/ROY S71 .. 262 A3
Darrington Rd PONT WF8 ... 203 G4
Darryl Dr LUD/ILL HX2 ... 168 A1
Dartmouth Av HUDE HD5 ... 215 J3

MOR LS27 ... 152 C4
Dartmouth Ms MOR LS27 ... 152 B3
Dartmouth Ter GIR BD8 ... 104 E4
Dartmouth Wy BEE/HOL LS11 .. 131 L3
Darton Hall Cl DOD/DAR S75 ... 242 C6
Darton La DOD/DAR S75 ... 242 C6
Darton Rd DOD/DAR S75 ... 259 H1
Darton St BSLY S70 ... 261 M6
Dartree Cl WMB/DAR S73 ... 263 H8
Dartree Wk WMB/DAR S73 ... 263 H8
Darwin St WBOW BD5 ... 126 E3
Datchett Ter ROCH OL11 ... 228 B3
Daventry Rd ROCH OL11 ... 228 B3
Daveyhulme St WHIT OL12 ... 206 C6
Davey La HBR HX7 ... 142 B3
David La DEWS WF13 ... 173 L4
David Lewis Cl MILN OL16 ... 206 D8
David St BEE/HOL LS11 ... 8 C7
 CAS WF10 ... 157 K7
 WHIT OL12 ... 206 B5
 WKFDE WF1 ... 13 K7
Davies Av RHAY LS8 ... 88 C6
Davies Ct CAS WF10 ... 158 C6
Dawcross Ri PBR HG3 ... 26 C2
Dawes Av CAS WF10 ... 158 B8
Daw Green Av HOR/CROF WF4 .. 220 A2
Daw La HOR/CROF WF4 ... 197 H3
 HOR/CROF WF4 ... 219 M3
Dawlish Av OSM LS9 ... 110 C6
Dawlish Crs OSM LS9 ... 110 C6
Dawlish Gv OSM LS9 ... 110 C6
Dawlish Mt OSM LS9 ... 110 C6
Dawlish Pl OSM LS9 ... 110 D6
Dawlish Rd OSM LS9 ... 110 C6
Dawlish Rw OSM LS9 ... 110 D6
Dawlish St OSM LS9 ... 110 C6
Dawlish Ter OSM LS9 ... 110 C6
Dawnay Rd WBOW BD5 ... 126 D4
Dawn St ROY/SHW OL2 ... 229 K8
Daw Royds HUDE HD5 ... 215 J1
Daw Rw WBSY BD6 ... 126 E6
Dawson HI MOR LS27 ... 152 C1
Dawson La BOW BD4 ... 127 L5
 BOW BD4 ... 129 G4
Dawson Mt BOW BD4 ... 127 L5
Dawson Pl BOW BD4 ... 127 L5
 KGHY BD21 ... 3 H9
Dawson Rd BEE/HOL LS11 ... 8 D9
 HUDS HD4 ... 214 D3
 KGHY BD21 ... 3 H8
Dawsons Meadow
 PDSY/CALV LS28 ... 106 E4
Dawson St BOW BD4 ... 127 L4
 IDLE BD10 ... 83 K5
 PDSY/CALV LS28 ... 106 C5
 SKP/WHF BD23 ... 16 C3
Dawson Ter BOW BD4 ... 127 L5
Dawson Wy KGHY BD21 ... 3 H9
Dawtrie Cl CAS WF10 ... 158 F6
Dawtrie St CAS WF10 ... 158 F6
Daykin Cl DOD/DAR S75 ... 241 M6
Day St BSLY S70 ... 261 G6
 DEWS WF13 ... 195 G1
Deacon Cl HOLM/MEL HD7 ... 235 H4
Deacon St MILN OL16 ... 206 D5
Deacons Wy BSLYN/ROY S71 ... 261 L2
Deadmanstone HUDS HD4 ... 214 B6
Dealburn Rd LM/WK BD12 ... 148 E1
Deal St HFAX HX1 ... 11 J7
 KGHY BD21 ... 3 J1
Dean Av HOLM/MEL HD7 ... 236 B6
 RHAY LS8 ... 88 C6
Dean Bank Dr ROCH OL11 ... 228 D5
Dean Beck Av WBSY BD6 ... 127 G6
Dean Beck Ct WBSY BD6 ... 127 H6
Dean Bridge La HOLM/MEL HD7. 254 C1
Dean Brook Rd HOLM/MEL HD7. 236 B6
 HUDS HD4 ... 214 A6
Dean Cl GIR BD8 ... 103 M5
 WKFDW/WTN WF2 ... 176 B4
Dean Clough HFAX HX1 ... 11 C4
Dean Ct HIPP HX3 ... 168 C4
 RHAY LS8 ... 88 C6
Deancourt ROCH OL11 ... 228 A2
Dean Edge Rd HWTH BD22 ... 77 H5
Dean End GTL/HWG HX4 ... 168 B6
Deanery Gdns IDLE BD10 ... 105 L1
Deanfield Av MOR LS27 ... 152 B1
Dean Hall Cl MOR LS27 ... 152 B2
Dean Head LS18 ... 63 J6
Dean House La GTL/HWG HX4 .. 189 H6
Deanhouse La LUD/ILL HX2 ... 144 F4
Deanhurst Gdns MOR LS27 ... 130 A8
Dean La CUL/QBY BD13 ... 102 C5
 GSLY LS20 ... 61 H6
 HOLM/MEL HD7 ... 254 C1
 HORS LS18 ... 63 J6
 HWTH BD22 ... 56 A8
 RPDN/SBR HX6 ... 167 G4
Dean Park Av BIRK/DRI BD11 ... 129 C7
Dean Park Dr BIRK/DRI BD11 ... 129 G7
Dean Rd HOLM/MEL HD7 ... 235 L8
 WBSY BD6 ... 126 F6
Deanroyd Rd TOD OL14 ... 163 K7
Deanstones Crs CUL/QBY BD13 . 125 C6
Deanstones La CUL/QBY BD13 .. 125 C6
Dean St BSLY S70 ... 260 F5
 COL BB8 ... 74 D4
 ELL HX5 ... 169 H4
 GTL/HWG HX4 ... 168 C7
 HUDW HD3 ... 191 K7
 HWTH BD22 ... 78 F7
 ILK LS29 ... 38 C3
 MILN OL16 ... 206 D6
Deans Wy BSLYN/ROY S71 ... 261 L2
Deansway MOR LS27 ... 130 B8
Deanswood Cl AL/HA/HU LS17 .. 87 H3
Deanswood Dr AL/HA/HU LS17 . 87 H3
Deanswood Gn AL/HA/HU LS17 . 87 H3
Deanswood HI AL/HA/HU LS17 .. 87 H3
Deanswood Pl AL/HA/HU LS17 .. 87 H3
Deanswood Ri AL/HA/HU LS17 .. 87 H3
Deanswood Vw AL/HA/HU LS17 . 87 H3

Deanwood Crs WIL/AL BD15 ... 103 J4
Deanwood Wk WIL/AL BD15 ... 103 J4
Dearden St LIT OL15 ... 185 K8
 OSS WF5 ... 196 F1
 RPDN/SBR HX6 ... 167 K1
Dearne Cft WBY LS22 ... 30 A6
Dearne Dike La KBTN HD8 ... 256 A1
Dearne Fold HUDN HD2 ... 191 K5
Dearne Hall Fold DOD/DAR S75 . 242 B8
Dearne Hall Rd DOD/DAR S75 .. 242 B8
Dearne Pk KBTN HD8 ... 240 A4
Dearne Royd KBTN HD8 ... 240 A4
Dearneside Rd KBTN HD8 ... 257 H1
Dearne St DOD/DAR S75 ... 242 A5
 HEM/SK/SE WF9 ... 247 H3
Dearne Wy DOD/DAR S75 ... 241 L3
 DOD/DAR S75 ... 242 D7
 KBTN HD8 ... 239 L8
 KBTN HD8 ... 240 A3
 KBTN HD8 ... 256 C2
Dearnfield KBTN HD8 ... 238 E8
Dearnley Cl LIT OL15 ... 207 H2
Dearnley St DEWS WF13 ... 173 G3
Dearnly Vw DOD/DAR S75 ... 260 F2
Dee Ct HWTH BD22 ... 78 E4
Deepcar La HUDW HD3 ... 191 H6
Deep Dl BSPA/BRAM LS23 ... 48 E5
Deepdale Av MILN OL16 ... 206 D6
 ROY/SHW OL2 ... 228 E6
Deepdale Cl BAIL BD17 ... 82 C4
Deepdale La BSPA/BRAM LS23 .. 48 F4
Deep La BRIG HD6 ... 171 G4
 CLAY BD14 ... 125 L1
 CUL/QBY BD13 ... 124 C2
 HUDS HD4 ... 213 K3
 LIT OL15 ... 207 K6
 LUD/ILL HX2 ... 145 H7
 RPDN/SBR HX6 ... 166 D6
Deeplish Rd ROCH OL11 ... 228 C2
Deeplish St ROCH OL11 ... 228 B1
Deer Croft Av HUDW HD3 ... 191 H6
Deer Croft Crs HUDW HD3 ... 191 H6
Deer Croft Rd HUDW HD3 ... 191 H5
Deer Hill Cl HOLM/MEL HD7 ... 233 H3
Deer Hill Cft HOLM/MEL HD7 .. 233 H3
Deer Hill Dr HOLM/MEL HD7 ... 233 H3
Deer Hill End Rd
 HOLM/MEL HD7 ... 234 B3
Deer Park Ct GFTH/SHER LS25 . 138 C4
Deershaw La KBTN HD8 ... 255 L1
Deershaw Sike La KBTN HD8 ... 255 L1
Deerstone Rdg WBY LS22 ... 30 A6
Defarge Ct WBOW BD5 ... 127 G3
Deffer Rd WKFDW/WTN WF2 ... 198 D8
Deganwy Dr HUDN HD2 ... 193 L4
Deighton Av GFTH/SHER LS25 .. 116 A7
Deighton Cl WBY LS22 ... 30 B8
Deighton La BTLY WF17 ... 173 J1
Deighton Rd HUDN HD2 ... 192 F3
 PBR HG3 ... 29 G3
 WBY LS22 ... 30 A6
De Lacey Ms BOW BD4 ... 127 L4
De Lacies Ct RTHW LS26 ... 133 J7
De Lacies Rd RTHW LS26 ... 133 J7
De Lacy Av BOW BD4 ... 127 K6
 FEA/AMT WF7 ... 179 L5
Delacy Crs CAS WF10 ... 158 F5
De Lacy Mt KSTL LS5 ... 108 C2
De Lacy Ter PONT WF8 ... 181 G6
Delamere Av ROY/SHW OL2 ... 229 M6
Delamere St MILN OL16 ... 228 C2
Delamere St WBOW BD5 ... 127 G5
Delaware Ct BOW BD4 ... 127 K6
Delf HI BRIG HD6 ... 170 A7
Delf La HBR HX7 ... 121 L6
 TOD OL14 ... 140 F3
Delfs La RPDN/SBR HX6 ... 166 B6
Delius Av IDLE BD10 ... 105 M1
Della Av BSLY S70 ... 260 F6
Dell Av CUD/GR S72 ... 245 J6
Dell Cft AIRE BD20 ... 35 L4
Dellside Fold CUL/QBY BD13 ... 79 M8
The Dell AL/HA/HU LS17 ... 67 M3
 CUL/QBY BD13 ... 80 A8
 HUDN HD2 ... 192 D2
Delmont Cl BTLY WF17 ... 151 G8
Delph Cl DOD/DAR S75 ... 259 J5
Delph Crs CLAY BD14 ... 125 K2
Delph Croft Vw KGHY BD21 ... 3 K7
Delph Dr CLAY BD14 ... 125 J2
Delph Gv CLAY BD14 ... 125 K2
Delph HI BAIL BD17 ... 82 E2
 PDSY/CALV LS28 ... 107 G6
Delph Hill La LUD/ILL HX2 ... 144 F4
Delph Hill Rd LUD/ILL HX2 ... 168 B2
Delph La HDGY LS6 ... 6 D1
 HUDS HD4 ... 213 M7
Delph Mt HDGY LS6 ... 6 D1
Delph Rd UPML OL3 ... 230 E7
Delph St HFAX HX1 ... 10 F7
 MILN OL16 ... 207 H8
Delph Ter CLAY BD14 ... 125 K2
The Delph FEA/AMT WF7 ... 202 B1
Delph Vw HDGY LS6 ... 6 C2
Delph Wood Cl BGLY BD16 ... 81 L3
Delverne Gv ECHL BD2 ... 105 L3
Delves Ga HOLM/MEL HD7 ... 212 B8
Delves Wood Rd HUDS HD4 ... 213 L5
Denbigh Ap OSM LS9 ... 110 F4
Denbigh Dr ROY/SHW OL2 ... 229 H8
Denbrook Av BOW BD4 ... 128 B6
Denbrook Cl BOW BD4 ... 128 B5
Denbrook Crs BOW BD4 ... 128 B5
Denbrook Wk BOW BD4 ... 128 B5
Denbrook Wy BOW BD4 ... 128 B5
Denbury Mt BOW BD4 ... 128 B5
Denby Cl BTLY WF17 ... 150 F5
 LVSG WF15 ... 172 B1
Denby Ct HWTH BD22 ... 78 D4
Denby Crest PONT WF8 ... 181 G6
Denby Dale Rd HOR/CROF WF4 . 218 E6
 HOR/CROF WF4 ... 219 L1
 WKFDE WF1 ... 12 E4
 WKFDE WF1 ... 12 D7
Denby Dale Rd East
 HOR/CROF WF4 ... 198 A7

Denby Dale Rd West
  HOR/CROF WF4 .... 197 M8
Denby Dr *BAIL* BD17 .... 82 D5
Denby Grange La
  HOR/CROF WF4 .... 217 J1
Denby Hall La *KBTN* HD8 .... 257 M1
Denby Hill Rd *HWTH* BD22 .... 78 D4
Denby La *HOR/CROF* WF4 .... 195 K8
  KBTN HD8 .... 256 F3
  WIL/AL BD15 .... 103 K5
Denby Mt *HWTH* BD22 .... 100 E4
Denby Park Dr *HOR/CROF* WF4 .. 217 G1
Denby Pl *RPDN/SBR* HX6 ...... 167 K1
Denby Rd *BSLYN/ROY* S71 .... 243 H7
  KGHY BD21 .... 3 G1
  PONT WF8 .... 203 L1
Denby St *GIR* BD8 .... 4 B3
Denby Vw *EARL* WF12 .... 195 M5
Dence Gn *BOW* BD4 .... 128 A1 ₪
Dence Pl *MSTN/BAR* LS15 ...... 111 G6 ₪
Dene Bank *BGLY* BD16 .... 59 J4
Dene Cl *ELL* HX5 .... 191 G1
Dene Crs *GTHN* BD7 .... 126 A2 ₪
Dene Gv *AIRE* BD20 .... 36 A4
Dene Hl *BAIL* BD17 .... 82 B3
Denehill *HTON* BD9 .... 103 M4
Dene House Ct *LDSU* LS2 ...... 6 F4
Dene Mt *WIL/AL* BD15 .... 103 L5 ₪
Dene Pk *KBTN* HD8 .... 216 B7
Dene Pl *HFAX* HX1 .... 10 F4
Dene Rd *KBTN* HD8 .... 239 H5
  WBSY BD6 .... 125 M5
Dene Royd Cl *GTL/HWG* HX4 .. 190 B3 ₪
Dene Royd Ct *GTL/HWG* HX4 .. 190 B3
Deneside *OSS* WF5 .... 174 E7
Deneside Mt *WBOW* BD5 ...... 126 E5
Deneside Ter *WBOW* BD5 ...... 126 F4 ₪
Denesway *GFTH/SHER* LS25 .. 135 J1
Dene Vw *LUD/ILL* HX2 .... 144 F6
Deneway *PDSY/CALV* LS28 .... 106 E4
Denfield Av *HIPP* HX3 .... 146 A4
Denfield Crs *HIPP* HX3 .... 146 B4
Denfield Edge *HIPP* HX3 ...... 146 B4 ₪
Denfield Gdns *HIPP* HX3 ...... 146 B4 ₪
Denfield La *HIPP* HX3 .... 146 A4
Denfield Sq *HIPP* HX3 .... 146 B4
Denhale Av *WKFDW/WTN* WF2 .. 176 A3
Denham Av *MOR* LS27 .... 152 C4
Denham Dr *HOLM/MEL* HD7 .. 236 B6
Denham St *BRIG* HD6 .... 170 C5 ₪
  BTLY WF17 .... 151 J7
Denholme Dr *OSS* WF5 .... 174 F7
Denholme Gate Rd *HIPP* HX3 .. 147 L5
Denholme Meadow
  HEM/SK/SE WF9 .... 247 H2
Denholme Rd *HWTH* BD22 ...... 100 F5
  ROCH OL11 .... 228 B2
Denhurst Rd *LIT* OL15 .... 185 J8
Denison Ct *BSLY* S70 .... 261 H6 ₪
Denison Rd *BVRD* LS3 .... 6 C3 ₪
Denison St *BTLY* WF17 .... 173 L2 ₪
  YEA LS19 .... 62 D7 ₪
Denmark St *MILN* OL16 .... 206 C6 ₪
  WKFDE WF1 .... 13 J7
Dennil Crs *MSTN/BAR* LS15 .... 111 M4
Dennil Rd *MSTN/BAR* LS15 .... 111 M3
Dennington La *HOR/CROF* WF4 .. 219 L3
Dennis La *AIRE* BD20 .... 35 J3
Dennis Rd *AIRE* BD20 .... 35 J3
Dennison Fold *BOW* BD4 ...... 128 A1 ₪
Dennison Hl *OT* LS21 .... 41 K6 ₪
Dennistead Crs *HDGY* LS6 .... 108 F1
Denshaw Dr *MOR* LS27 .... 152 E2
Denshaw Gv *MOR* LS27 .... 152 E2
Denshaw La *EARD/LOFT* WF3 .. 153 L3
Denstone St *WKFDE* WF1 ...... 13 G1
Dent Dr *WKFDE* WF1 .... 177 H6
Denton Av *RHAY* LS8 .... 88 B4
Denton Dr *BGLY* BD16 .... 81 G2
Denton Gdns *FEA/AMT* WF7 .. 224 B1
Denton Gv *RHAY* LS8 .... 88 B6 ₪
Denton Rd *ILK* LS29 .... 38 C1
  WHIT OL12 .... 206 B5 ₪
Denton Ter *CAS* WF10 .... 158 A6
Dent St *OSM* LS9 .... 110 B7
Denver Rd *ROCH* OL11 .... 228 B2
Denwell Ter *PONT* WF8 .... 180 F5
Derby Rd *BFDE* BD3 .... 106 A7
  YEA LS19 .... 84 D2
Derbyshire St *MID* LS10 ...... 132 B3
Derby St *BSLY* S70 .... 260 F5
  CLAY BD14 .... 125 K2 ₪
  CUL/QBY BD13 .... 124 F5 ₪
  GTHN BD7 .... 126 D2
  ROCH OL11 .... 228 C1
  RPDN/SBR HX6 .... 167 L1
Derby Ter *HOLM/MEL* HD7 .... 233 H2
Derdale St *TOD* OL14 .... 163 L1
Derry Hl *ILK* LS29 .... 61 H3
Derry Hill Gdns *ILK* LS29 ...... 61 H2
Derry La *ILK* LS29 .... 61 H2
Der St *TOD* OL14 .... 163 L1 ₪
Derwent Av *GFTH/SHER* LS25 .. 113 G4
  MILN OL16 .... 207 K8
  RTHW LS26 .... 133 L8
  WIL/AL BD15 .... 102 C2
Derwent Cl *BSLYN/ROY* S71 .. 243 K7 ₪
  COL BB8 .... 52 C8 ₪
  HBR HX7 .... 143 J2 ₪
Derwent Crs *BSLYN/ROY* S71 .. 243 K7
Derwent Dr *BHP/TINH* LS16 .. 86 D2
  CAS WF10 .... 159 G5
  HUDE HD5 .... 15 C4
  LIT OL15 .... 207 H4
  ROY/SHW OL2 .... 229 J6
Derwent Gv *WKFDW/WTN* WF2 .. 176 B3
  KNOT WF11 .... 182 A4
Derwent Pl *BEE/HOL* LS11 .... 8 D4
Derwent Ri *WBY* LS22 .... 29 M6
Derwent Rd *BSLYN/ROY* S71 .. 243 J7
  EARL WF12 .... 174 B3
  ECHL BD2 .... 105 J3
  HOLM/MEL HD7 .... 235 G5 ₪
  HOLM/MEL HD7 .... 236 A3
  WKFDW/WTN WF2 .... 176 B8
Derwent St *WHIT* OL12 .... 206 B5 ₪
Derwentwater Gv *HDGY* LS6 .. 108 E2
Derwentwater Ter *HDGY* LS6 .. 108 F1

Derwin Av *HUDS* HD4 .... 237 L4
De Trafford St *HUDS* HD4 ...... 213 M3
Detroit Av *MSTN/BAR* LS15 .... 111 M6
Detroit Dr *MSTN/BAR* LS15 .... 112 A6
Deveron Gv *HUDW* HD3 .... 14 B3
Devine Cl *ROY/SHW* OL2 ...... 228 F8 ₪
Devon Cl *LDSU* LS2 .... 6 E4
  ROY/SHW OL2 .... 229 H7
Devon Rd *CHAL* LS7 .... 6 E4
  LDSU LS2 .... 6 E4
Devonshire Av *RHAY* LS8 ...... 88 C4
Devonshire Cl *RHAY* LS8 ...... 88 C4 ₪
  RHAY LS8 .... 88 C4 ₪
Devonshire Crs *RHAY* LS8 .... 88 B5
Devonshire Dr *DOD/DAR* S75 .. 260 F2
Devonshire Gdns *LDSU* LS2 .. 6 E3
Devonshire La *RHAY* LS8 ...... 88 C4 ₪
Devonshire Pl *SKP/WHF* WF3 .. 16 B2 ₪
Devonshire Rd *ROCH* OL11 .... 228 B4
  KGHY BD21 .... 2 E4
  SKP/WHF BD23 .... 16 C3
Devonshire St West *KGHY* BD21 .. 2 D5
Devonshire Ter *GIR* BD8 ...... 104 E4 ₪
  WHIT OL12 .... 206 B8 ₪
Devon Wy *BRIG* HD6 .... 148 D8
Dew Meadow Cl *WHIT* OL12 .. 206 A4 ₪
Dewsbury Gate Rd *DEWS* WF13 .. 173 H4
Dewsbury Ring Rd *DEWS* WF13 .. 173 L6
Dewsbury Rd *BEE/HOL* LS11 .. 9 G7
  CLECK BD19 .... 150 A3
  CLECK BD19 .... 150 D4
  EARD/LOFT WF3 .... 152 F6
  EARL WF12 .... 152 F7
  ELL HX5 .... 169 L8
  MOR LS27 .... 153 C1
  OSS WF5 .... 174 E6
  WKFDW/WTN WF2 .... 197 L1
Deyne Rd *HUDS* HD4 .... 213 L7
Diadem Dr *SCFT* LS14 .... 111 C5
Dial St *OSM* LS9 .... 110 B8
Diamond Av *HEM/SK/SE* WF9 .. 247 G3 ₪
Diamond St *BFD* BD1 .... 5 J2
  BTLY WF17 .... 151 K8 ₪
  HFAX HX1 .... 10 C4
  HUD HD1 .... 15 H3
  HUDE HD5 .... 15 M8
  HWTH BD22 .... 79 J2 ₪
Diamond Ter *HFAX* HX1 ...... 10 C4
Dibb La *YEA* LS19 .... 62 B7
Dib Cl *RHAY* LS8 .... 110 F1
Dib La *RHAY* LS8 .... 110 F1
Dick Dean La *HBR* HX7 .... 121 J1
Dick Edge La *HOLM/MEL* HD7 .. 255 K4
Dicken Gn *ROCH* OL11 .... 228 B2
Dicken Green La *ROCH* OL11 .. 228 B2
Dickens Dr *CAS* WF10 .... 180 F1
Dicken's St *LUD/ILL* HX2 ...... 146 A7
  WBOW BD5 .... 127 C3
Dickinson St *WKFDE* WF1 .... 176 E6 ₪
Dickinson Pl *BSLY* S70 .... 261 H7 ₪
Dickinson Rd *BSLY* S70 .... 261 H7 ₪
Dickinson St *HORS* LS18 ...... 85 L4 ₪
  WKFDE WF1 .... 176 E7
Dickinson Ter *FEA/AMT* WF7 .. 179 M8 ₪
Dick La *BFDE* BD3 .... 106 B6
  BOW BD4 .... 128 A1
  HWTH BD22 .... 54 F2
Dick's Garth Rd *ILK* LS29 ...... 61 H2
Dickson St *COL* BB8 .... 74 A1
Dicky Sykes La *FEA/AMT* WF7 .. 223 M1
Digby Rd *ILK* LS29 .... 61 J2
  ROCH OL11 .... 228 B2
Dig Gate La *MILN* OL16 .... 229 G3
Diggle St *ROY/SHW* OL2 ...... 229 K8 ₪
Digley Rd *HOLM/MEL* HD7 .... 253 K4
Digley Royd La *HOLM/MEL* HD7 .. 253 J3
Dillington Rd *BSLY* S70 .... 261 H1 ₪
Dillington Sq *BSLY* S70 .... 261 H7
Dimple Gdns *OSS* WF5 .... 196 F2
Dimple Wells Cl *OSS* WF5 .... 196 F2 ₪
Dimple Wells La *OSS* WF5 .... 196 F2
Dimple Well Rd *OSS* WF5 ...... 196 F2 ₪
Dineley Av *TOD* OL14 .... 141 H7
Dingle Av *ROY/SHW* OL2 ...... 229 L5
Dingle Rd *HUDW* HD3 .... 191 M8
Dingle Rd *HUD* HD1 .... 191 M8
Dingley Rd *HUDW* HD3 .... 191 L6
Dirker Av *HOLM/MEL* HD7 .... 233 H1
Dirker Bank Rd *HOLM/MEL* HD7 .. 233 H1
Dirker Dr *HOLM/MEL* HD7 .... 233 H2
Dirkhill Rd *GTHN* BD7 .... 126 E1
Dirkhill St *GTHN* BD7 .... 126 D1 ₪
Dirty La *UPML* OL3 .... 231 K6
Dirty Leech *WHIT* OL12 .... 184 B8
Discovery Rd *HFAX* HX1 .... 11 J6
Disney Cl *HUDS* HD4 .... 213 M3
Dispensary Wk *HFAX* HX1 .... 11 J6
Disraeli Gdns *BEE/HOL* LS11 .. 8 F8
Disraeli Ter *BEE/HOL* LS11 .... 8 F8
Ditton Mead Cl *WHIT* OL12 .. 206 D4
Division St *GTHN* BD7 .... 126 B1
Dixon Av *GTHN* BD7 .... 126 B3
Dixon Cl *AIRE* BD20 .... 56 E1 ₪
  GTL/HWG HX4 .... 168 C6
Dixon La *WOR/ARM* LS12 ...... 130 E1
Dixon Lane Rd *WOR/ARM* LS12 .. 130 E1
Dixon St *AIRE* BD20 .... 56 A1 ₪
  FEA/AMT WF7 .... 179 M7
Dixon's Yd *WKFDE* WF1 .... 13 G3 ₪
Dobbin Dr *ROCH* OL11 .... 228 B3
Dobb La *HOLM/MEL* HD7 ...... 253 L4
Dobb Top Rd *HOLM/MEL* HD7 .. 253 K5
Dobie St *BSLY* S70 .... 261 J6
Dob La *RPDN/SBR* HX6 .... 166 F3
Dob Park Rd *OT* LS21 .... 23 H7
Dob Royd *KBTN* HD8 .... 237 M7

Dobroyd Rd *TOD* OL14 .... 163 J2
Dobson Av *BEE/HOL* LS11 .... 9 G9
Dobson Gv *BEE/HOL* LS11 .... 9 G9
Dobson Pl *BEE/HOL* LS11 ...... 9 G9
Dobson Ter *BEE/HOL* LS11 .... 9 G9
Dobson Vw *BEE/HOL* LS11 .... 9 G9
Dockery *HUD* HD1 .... 214 B3 ₪
Dockfield Pl *BAIL* BD17 .... 82 E5
Dockfield Rd *BAIL* BD17 .... 82 E6
Dockfield Ter *BAIL* BD17 ...... 82 E5
Dock La *BAIL* BD17 .... 82 E6 ₪
Dockray St *COL* BB8 .... 74 A1
Dockroyd La *HWTH* BD22 ...... 78 E4
Dock St *MID* LS10 .... 9 H2
Doctor Fold *HOLM/MEL* HD7 .. 236 B1 ₪
Doctor Hl *IDLE* BD10 .... 83 K7
  LUD/ILL HX2 .... 145 M5
Doctor La *HOR/CROF* WF4 .... 217 K4
  IDLE BD10 .... 83 K5
  MIRF WF14 .... 194 C1
Dodd Cft *MILN* OL16 .... 229 G3
Dodgeholme Cl *LUD/ILL* HX2 .. 145 M2 ₪
Dodge Holme Gdns
  LUD/ILL HX2 .... 145 M1
Dodge Holme Rd *LUD/ILL* HX2 .. 145 M2
Dodgson Av *CHAL* LS7 .... 7 L2
Dodgson St *ELL* HX5 .... 191 H1
  MILN OL16 .... 206 C8
Dodlee La *HUDW* HD3 .... 191 G7
Dodsworth Crs *NORM* WF6 .. 178 D6
Dodworth Dr
  WKFDW/WTN WF2 .... 220 D1
Dodworth Green Rd
  DOD/DAR S75 .... 259 M8
Dodworth Rd *BSLY* S70 .... 260 E5
Dog Hl *CUD/GR* S72 .... 244 E3
Dog Hill Dr *CUD/GR* S72 ...... 244 E3
Doghouse La *TOD* OL14 .... 163 J1
Dog Kennel Bank *HUDE* HD5 .. 15 K9
Dog Kennel La *HIPP* HX3 ...... 11 M9
Dog La *GTL/HWG* HX4 .... 190 A4
Dogley Villa Ct *KBTN* HD8 .... 215 M5
Doldram La *RPDN/SBR* HX6 .. 167 J5
Dole La *HBR* HX7 .... 143 J5
Doles Av *BSLYN/ROY* S71 ...... 243 K3
Doles Crs *BSLYN/ROY* S71 .... 243 K3
Dole St *CUL/QBY* BD13 .... 103 J3
Dolfin Pl *HUDN* HD2 .... 193 H1
Doll La *CUL/QBY* BD13 .... 102 A1
Dolly La *OSM* LS9 .... 7 L6
Dolphin La *EARD/LOFT* WF3 .. 154 A4
Dolphin Rd *MID* LS10 .... 154 A1
Dolphin St *OSM* LS9 .... 9 M1
Dolphin Ct *BRAM* LS13 .... 107 K5
Dombey St *HFAX* HX1 .... 10 D6
Domestic Rd *BEE/HOL* LS11 .. 131 G5
Domestic St *BEE/HOL* LS11 .. 8 B5
Dominion Av *CHAL* LS7 .... 87 M8
Donald Av *WBSY* BD6 .... 126 E6
Donald St *PDSY/CALV* LS28 .. 106 F4
Don Av *WBY* LS22 .... 29 M6
Doncaster La *AWLS/ASK* DN6 .. 248 E3
Doncaster Rd *BSLY* S70 .... 261 K6
  BSLY S70 .... 261 M6 ₪
  BSLYN/ROY S71 .... 262 A6
  FEA/AMT WF7 .... 224 C1
  HEM/SK/SE WF9 .... 225 J8
  HOR/CROF WF4 .... 199 L4
  KNOT WF11 .... 181 L1 ₪
  PONT WF8 .... 203 H6
  WMB/DAR S73 .... 263 K8
Doncaster Road Est
  FEA/AMT WF7 .... 224 C1
Doncaster St *HFAX* HX3 ...... 168 F3 ₪
Don Ct *AIRE* BD20 .... 36 A5 ₪
Don Dr *BSLY* S70 .... 261 M7
Donisthorpe St *MID* LS10 ...... 9 L5
  WBOW BD5 .... 127 G3 ₪
Don Pedro Av *NORM* WF6 .... 178 F4
Don Pedro Cl *NORM* WF6 ...... 178 F4
Don St *KGHY* BD21 .... 2 E3
  STKB/PEN S36 .... 271 H4
Don Vw *STKB/PEN* S36 .... 267 M5
Dorchester Av *PONT* WF8 .... 180 D6
Dorchester Crs *BAIL* BD17 .... 83 H7
  BOW BD4 .... 128 A3 ₪
Dorchester Dr *LUD/ILL* HX2 .. 168 A1
  YEA LS19 .... 62 E8
Dorchester Rd *HUDN* HD2 .... 192 D1
  TAD LS24 .... 50 C5
Dorian Cl *IDLE* BD10 .... 83 M8 ₪
Dorman Av *HEM/SK/SE* WF9 .. 225 M6
Dorothy St *KGHY* BD21 .... 79 J3
Dorset Av *RHAY* LS8 .... 110 C2
  ROY/SHW OL2 .... 229 H7
Dorset Cl *HEM/SK/SE* WF9 .... 223 M6
  WBOW BD5 .... 126 E3 ₪
Dorset Gv *PDSY/CALV* LS28 .. 107 G6 ₪
Dorset Mt *RHAY* LS8 .... 110 C2 ₪
Dorset Rd *RHAY* LS8 .... 110 C2 ₪
Dorset St *HUD* HD1 .... 14 D2
  RHAY LS8 .... 110 C2 ₪
  ROCH OL11 .... 206 B8 ₪
  SKP/WHF BD23 .... 16 C3
  WBOW BD5 .... 126 F3
Dorset Ter *RHAY* LS8 .... 110 C3
Dorts Crs *TAD* LS24 .... 95 G5
Dotterel Gln *MOR* LS27 ...... 152 E3
Doubting La *EARL* WF12 ...... 195 M5 ₪
  STKB/PEN S36 .... 270 D7
Doubting Rd *EARL* WF12 ...... 195 M5
Douglas Av *BTLY* WF17 .... 174 B1
  HUDE HD5 .... 215 G1
  HUDW HD3 .... 213 K1
Douglas Crs *SHPY* BD18 .... 82 F9
Douglas Rd *BOW* BD4 .... 127 L2 ₪
Douglas St *COL* BB8 .... 52 A8 ₪
  EARL WF12 .... 175 J2
  HIPP HX3 .... 146 D4 ₪
  HWTH BD22 .... 79 G6 ₪

Dovedale Cl *HIPP* HX3 .... 125 K8
  HOR/CROF WF4 .... 200 C5
Dovedale Dr *WHIT* OL12 ...... 184 F8
Dovedale Gdns
  MSTN/BAR LS15 .... 112 B3 ₪
Dovedale Garth
  MSTN/BAR LS15 .... 112 B3
Dovelands *AIRE* BD20 .... 55 M2
Dover Ln *HOLM/MEL* HD7 .... 254 D3
Dover Rd *HOLM/MEL* HD7 .... 254 C5
Dover St *BFDE* BD3 .... 5 K2
  GFTH/SHER LS25 .... 113 K7
  MILN OL16 .... 206 D4 ₪
  TOD OL14 .... 163 M1
Dovesdale Gv *WBOW* BD5 .... 126 E4
Dovesdale Rd *WBOW* BD5 .... 126 F4
Dove St *SHPY* BD18 .... 82 B6 ₪
  HUDW HD3 .... 213 K1
Dowley Gap La *BGLY* BD16 .... 81 K5
Dowling St *ROCH* OL11 .... 206 B8
Downes Crs *DOD/DAR* S75 .... 260 D3
Downham St *BFDE* BD3 .... 5 K7
Downing Cl *BFDE* BD3 .... 5 L5
Downing Sq *STKB/PEN* S36 .. 270 F4
Downing St *HOLM/MEL* HD7 .. 212 E6
  MILN OL16 .... 206 D4 ₪
Downland Crs *KNOT* WF11 .... 182 C5
Downshutts La
  HOLM/MEL HD7 .... 254 F1 ₪
Downside Crs *WIL/AL* BD15 .. 103 J5
Dracup Av *GTHN* BD7 .... 126 A1
Dracup Rd *GTHN* BD7 .... 126 B3
Dradishaw Rd *AIRE* BD20 ...... 35 M5
Dragon Crs *WOR/ARM* LS12 .. 130 F1
Dragon Dr *WOR/ARM* LS12 .... 130 E1
Dragon Rd *WOR/ARM* LS12 .. 130 E1
Drake La *BIRK/DRI* BD11 ...... 151 G1
Drake Rd *LIT* OL15 .... 185 L5
Drake St *KGHY* BD21 .... 3 G3
  MILN OL16 .... 206 B7
  ROCH OL11 .... 228 C1
Dransfield Av *STKB/PEN* S36 .. 270 F4
Draper La *HBR* HX7 .... 121 G8
Draughton Gv *WBOW* BD5 .... 126 F5 ₪
Draughton St *WBOW* BD5 .... 126 F5 ₪
Drayton Manor Yd
  BEE/HOL LS11 .... 9 G7 ₪
Dray Vw *DEWS* WF13 .... 173 H4 ₪
Drewry Rd *KGHY* BD21 .... 2 D4
Drewton Rd *BFD* BD1 .... 4 D5
Driftholme Rd *BIRK/DRI* BD11 .. 129 H7 ₪
Drill Pde *GIR* BD8 .... 4 C2
Drill St *HWTH* BD22 .... 78 E8 ₪
  KGHY BD21 .... 3 G4
Drinker La *KBTN* HD8 .... 216 F8
Driver Pl *WOR/ARM* LS12 ...... 109 G8 ₪
Drivers Rw *PONT* WF8 .... 180 D7
Driver Ter *AIRE* BD20 .... 36 B4
  WOR/ARM LS12 .... 109 G8
The Drive *AL/HA/HU* LS17 .... 65 J8
  AL/HA/HU LS17 .... 67 M1
  BGLY BD16 .... 59 G8
  BHP/TINH LS16 .... 86 C2
  BTLY WF17 .... 151 J8
  GFTH/SHER LS25 .... 135 J5
  HBR HX7 .... 143 M5
  HEM/SK/SE WF9 .... 147 M6
  IDLE BD10 .... 83 M8 ₪
  ILK LS29 .... 40 A6
  MSTN/BAR LS15 .... 111 M4
  OSM LS9 .... 9 L2
  RHAY LS8 .... 88 B4
  RTHW LS26 .... 134 C5
Drovers Wy *ECHL* BD2 .... 105 G3
Drub La *CLECK* BD19 .... 150 A4
Druggist La *ILK* LS29 .... 19 H6 ₪
Druids St *CLAY* BD14 .... 125 K2
Drummer La *HOLM/MEL* HD7 .. 212 C5
Drummond Av *HDGY* LS6 ...... 86 E8
Drummond Ct *HDGY* LS6 ...... 86 E8 ₪
Drummond Rd *BHP/TINH* LS16 .. 86 E7
  GIR BD8 .... 4 A2 ₪
Drury Av *HORS* LS18 .... 85 K6
Drury Cl *HORS* LS18 .... 85 K6
  PBR HG3 .... 27 C3
Drury Farm Ct *DOD/DAR* S75 .. 260 C5 ₪
Drury La *GTL/HWG* HX4 .... 190 B2
  HORS LS18 .... 85 K6
  NORM WF6 .... 178 B3
  PBR HG3 .... 27 C3
  WKFDE WF1 .... 12 D3
Dry Carr La *LUD/ILL* HX2 ...... 144 E1
Dryclough Av *HUDS* HD4 ...... 213 L4
Dryclough Cl *HIPP* HX3 .... 168 E3
Dryclough La *HIPP* HX3 .... 168 E3
Dryclough Rd *HUDS* HD4 ...... 213 L3
Dryden Rd *BSLYN/ROY* S71 .. 261 J4
Dryden St *BFD* BD1 .... 5 M1
  BGLY BD16 .... 81 H3 ₪
Dry Hill La *KBTN* HD8 .... 257 K1
Dubb La *BGLY* BD16 .... 81 J3
Duchess Park Cl *ROY/SHW* OL2 .. 229 K6
Duchess St *ROY/SHW* OL2 .... 229 J6
Duchy Av *HTON* BD9 .... 104 A3
Duchy Crs *HTON* BD9 .... 104 A3
Duchy Dr *HTON* BD9 .... 104 A4
Duchy Gv *HTON* BD9 .... 104 A4
Duchy Vls *HTON* BD9 .... 104 A3 ₪
Duchywood *HTON* BD9 .... 104 A3 ₪
Ducie St *IDLE* BD10 .... 83 K5
Duckett Gv *PDSY/CALV* LS28 .. 106 B6
Duckett St *SKP/WHF* BD23 .... 16 C3
Duckworth Gv *HTON* BD9 .... 104 B4
Duckworth La *HTON* BD9 ...... 104 A3
Duckworth St *ROY/SHW* OL2 .. 229 L7
Duckworth Ter *HTON* BD9 .... 104 B4
Dudfleet La *HOR/CROF* WF4 .. 197 K6
Dudley Av *BTLY* WF17 .... 151 J4
  HUD HD1 .... 191 M8 ₪
Dudley Crs *LUD/ILL* HX2 ...... 145 M1
Dudley Gv *BOW* BD4 .... 128 A1 ₪
Dudley Hill Rd *ECHL* BD2 ...... 105 K3
Dudley Rd *HUD* HD1 .... 191 M8
Dudley St *BOW* BD4 .... 127 L3 ₪
  BOW BD4 .... 128 A1
  COL BB8 .... 74 B1

Dudwell Gv *HIPP* HX3 .... 168 E4
Dudwell La *HIPP* HX3 .... 168 E4
Duffield Crs *GFTH/SHER* LS25 .. 116 B6 ₪
Dufton Ap *SCFT* LS14 .... 111 J3
Duich Rd *WBOW* BD5 .... 126 A8
Duinen St *WBOW* BD5 .... 5 C9
Duke Crs *BSLY* S70 .... 261 H6 ₪
Duke of York Av
  WKFDW/WTN WF2 .... 198 E5
Duke of York St *WKFDE* WF1 .. 176 F7
  WKFDW/WTN WF2 .... 176 B4
Duke St *BFD* BD1 .... 4 F5
  BSLY S70 .... 261 H6 ₪
  CAS WF10 .... 157 K6
  CUD/GR S72 .... 244 F2
  DEWS WF13 .... 195 G1 ₪
  ELL HX5 .... 169 H8 ₪
  HEM/SK/SE WF9 .... 223 J3
  HWTH BD22 .... 78 F7 ₪
  KGHY BD21 .... 57 K5
  LIT OL15 .... 207 J1
  LUD/ILL HX2 .... 144 F5
  OSM LS9 .... 9 K1
  ROY/SHW OL2 .... 229 L8
  SKP/WHF BD23 .... 16 C2
  WHIT OL12 .... 206 B5
Duke Wood Rd *KBTN* HD8 .... 240 A4
Dulverton Cl *BEE/HOL* LS11 .. 130 F5
  PONT WF8 .... 181 H5
Dulverton Gdns *BEE/HOL* LS11 .. 130 E4
Dulverton Garth *BEE/HOL* LS11 .. 130 E5
Dulverton Gn *BEE/HOL* LS11 .. 130 F5 ₪
Dulverton Gv *BEE/HOL* LS11 .. 130 E5
  BOW BD4 .... 127 M3
Dulverton Pl *BEE/HOL* LS11 .. 130 E5
Dulverton Ri *PONT* WF8 ...... 181 H5
Dulverton Sq *BEE/HOL* LS11 .. 130 F5
Dulverton Wy *PONT* WF8 .... 181 H5
Dumfries Av *UPML* OL3 ...... 230 E4
Dumfries Dr *UPML* OL3 ...... 230 E4 ₪
Dunbar Cft *CUL/QBY* BD13 .. 125 H5 ₪
Dunbar St *WKFDE* WF1 .... 13 L7
Dunbottle Cl *MIRF* WF14 ...... 194 D1
Dunbottle La *MIRF* WF14 .... 172 B8
Dunbottle Wy *MIRF* WF14 .... 194 D1
Duncan Av *OT* LS21 .... 40 F8
  WKFDW/WTN WF2 .... 199 C4
Duncan St *LDS* LS1 .... 9 G1
  WBOW BD5 .... 5 C9
Dunce Mire Rd *GFTH/SHER* LS25 .. 138 C3
Dunce Park Cl *ELL* HX5 .... 191 H1
Duncombe Rd *GIR* BD8 .... 104 C7
Duncombe St *GIR* BD8 .... 104 C7
  LDS LS1 .... 6 C8
Duncombe Wy *GTHN* BD7 .... 104 C7
Dundas St *HFAX* HX1 .... 10 B9
  HUD HD1 .... 14 E7
  KGHY BD21 .... 3 J6
Dundee Rd *TOD* OL14 .... 140 F6
Dunderdale Crs *CAS* WF10 .... 158 F5
Dunford Rd *HOLM/MEL* HD7 .. 254 D7
Dungeon La *RTHW* LS26 ...... 155 J5
Dunhill Crs *OSM* LS9 .... 111 C6 ₪
Dunhill Ri *OSM* LS9 .... 111 G6
Dunkeswick La *AL/HA/HU* LS17 .. 26 C7
Dunkhill Cft *IDLE* BD10 .... 83 K7 ₪
Dunkirk Crs *HFAX* HX1 .... 146 A8 ₪
Dunkirk La *HFAX* HX1 .... 168 A1
Dunkirk Ri *AIRE* BD20 .... 58 A4
Dunkirk St *HFAX* HX1 .... 146 A8
Dunkirk Ter *HFAX* HX1 .... 10 A8
Dunlin Cl *MOR* LS27 .... 152 F3
Dunlin Ct *MID* LS10 .... 153 M1 ₪
Dunlin Cft *MID* LS10 .... 153 M1 ₪
Dunlin Dr *MID* LS10 .... 153 M1
Dunlin Fold *MID* LS10 .... 153 M1
Dunlin Wy *GIR* BD8 .... 103 L7 ₪
Dunlop Av *ROCH* OL11 .... 228 A3
Dunmere Cl *BSLYN/ROY* S71 .. 261 J1
Dunn Cl *WKFDW/WTN* WF2 .. 176 B3
Dunningley La *EARD/LOFT* WF3 .. 153 G3
Dunningley La *EARD/LOFT* WF3 .. 153 H4
Dunnington Dr *SEL* YO8 .... 139 M5
Dunnington Wk *LM/WK* BD12 .. 126 C8
Dunnock Cft *MOR* LS27 .... 152 E3
Dunrobin Av *GFTH/SHER* LS25 .. 113 K7
Dunsford Av *BOW* BD4 .... 127 K6
Dunsley Bank Rd
  HOLM/MEL HD7 .... 254 B4
Dunsley Ter *HEM/SK/SE* WF9 .. 246 C4
Dunsmore Dr *HUDW* HD3 .... 191 H6 ₪
Dunstan Cl *OSS* WF5 .... 197 C2
Dunstarn Dr *BHP/TINH* LS16 .. 86 F3
Dunstarn Gdns *BHP/TINH* LS16 .. 87 G3
Dunstarn La *BHP/TINH* LS16 .. 86 F3
Dunster Av *ROCH* OL11 .... 228 A1
Dunsterville Ter *ROCH* OL11 .. 228 A1 ₪
Dunwood Av *ROY/SHW* OL2 .. 229 L6 ₪
Dunwoods Park Cts
  ROY/SHW OL2 .... 229 L5
Durban Av *BEE/HOL* LS11 .... 131 H4
Durban Cl *ROY/SHW* OL2 ...... 229 J8
Durban Crs *BEE/HOL* LS11 .... 131 H4
Durden Ms *ROY/SHW* OL2 .... 229 K8 ₪
Durham Rd *GIR* BD8 .... 104 B7
Durham St *CAS* WF10 .... 158 A8 ₪
  HFAX HX1 .... 146 A7 ₪
  ROCH OL11 .... 206 A1
  ROCH OL11 .... 228 C1
Durham Ter *GIR* BD8 .... 104 C5
Durkar Flds *HOR/CROF* WF4 .. 198 B8
Durkar La *HOR/CROF* WF4 .... 198 A8
Durkar Low La *HOR/CROF* WF4 .. 198 B7
Durkar Ri *HOR/CROF* WF4 .... 198 B7
Durley Av *HTON* BD9 .... 104 B3
Durling Dr *SHPY* BD18 .... 83 G7 ₪
Durlston Gv *LM/WK* BD12 .... 148 F2
Durlston Ter *LM/WK* BD12 .... 148 F2
Durn St *LIT* OL15 .... 185 L8
Durrance Rd *HWTH* BD22 ...... 2 A7
Durrant Cl *WBY* LS22 .... 48 B1
Dutton Gn *SCFT* LS14 .... 89 J6 ₪
Dutton Wy *SCFT* LS14 .... 89 J7
Duxbury Ri *CHAL* LS7 .... 6 F4
Dyehouse Dr *CLECK* BD19 .... 149 L4
Dyehouse La *BRIG* HD6 .... 170 B7
Dye House La *MILN* OL16 ...... 206 E3
Dyehouse La *PDSY/CALV* LS28 .. 129 G2
Dye House La *RPDN/SBR* HX6 .. 168 A5

WIL/AL BD15 .... **102** C1
Dyehouse Rd *LM/WK* BD12 .. **149** H1
Dyer La *HIPP* HX3 .... **10** A1
Dyer St *LDSU* LS2 .... **7** J9
Dyke Cl *MIRF* WF14 .... **172** C6
Dyke La *TOD* OL14 .... **142** D6
Dymond Gv *LVSG* WF15 .. **172** C3 🗓
Dymond Rd *LVSG* WF15 .. **172** C3 🗓
Dymond Vw *LVSG* WF15 .. **172** C3 🗓
Dyson La *HOLM/MEL* HD7 .. **254** D5
  RPDN/SBR HX3 .... **188** E3
Dyson Pl *HIPP* HX3 .... **168** F3 🗓
Dyson Rd *HFAX* HX1 .... **10** B4
Dyson's Hl *HOLM/MEL* HD7 .. **236** D1
Dyson St *BFD* BD1 .... **4** C7
  BRIG HD6 .... **170** C3
  BSLY S70 .... **260** F7 🗓
  HTON BD9 .... **104** C2 🗓
  HUDE HD5 .... **193** C8

E

Eafield Av *MILN* OL16 .... **207** H7
Eafield Cl *MILN* OL16 .... **207** H7
Eafield Rd *MILN* OL16 ...... **206** E5
  MILN OL16 .... **207** G3
Eagle Gv *WKFDW/WTN* WF2 .. **175** M8
Eaglesfield Dr *WBSY* BD6 .. **126** B8
Eagle St *HWTH* BD22 .... **79** G7 🗓
  KGHY BD21 .... **2** F4
  TOD OL14 .... **163** K1
Ealand Av *BTLY* WF17 .... **151** H7
Ealand Crs *BTLY* WF17 ...... **151** H7
Ealand Rd *BTLY* WF17 .... **151** H6
Ealees Rd *LIT* OL15 .... **207** L1
Ealing Ct *BTLY* WF17 .... **151** J8 🗓
Eaming Vw *BSLYN/ROY* S71 .. **261** J3
Earles Av *HUDE* HD5 .... **215** G1 🗓
Earle St *FEA/AMT* WF7 ...... **179** L8
Earlsmere Dr *BSLYN/ROY* S71 .. **262** C6
  MOR LS27 .... **152** B1
Earl St *EARL* WF12 .... **174** D6 🗓
  HEM/SK/SE WF9 .... **223** J4
  HWTH BD22 .... **78** E8 🗓
  KGHY BD21 .... **2** F2
  WKFDE WF1 .... **13** C1
Earls Vw *AIRE* BD20 .... **55** L2 🗓
Earlswood Av *RHAY* LS8 .... **88** B4
Earlswood Cha *PDSY/CALV* LS28 .. **107** C8
Earlswood Crs *GFTH/SHER* LS25 .. **135** K5
Earlswood Md *PDSY/CALV* LS28 .. **129** C1
Earl Ter *HIPP* HX3 .... **146** C4 🗓
Earnshaw Av *WHIT* OL12 .... **206** A3 🗓
Earnshaw Ter *DOD/DAR* S75 .. **260** F3
Easby Av *BTLY* WF17 .... **173** H2 🗓
Easby Cl *ILK* LS29 .... **38** B2
Easby Dr *ILK* LS29 .... **38** B2
Easby Rd *WBOW* BD5 .... **4** C9
Easdale Cl *SCFT* LS14 .... **111** H2
Easdale Crs *SCFT* LS14 ...... **111** J1
Easdale Mt *SCFT* LS14 ...... **111** H2
Easdale Rd *SCFT* LS14 ...... **111** H2
Easingwood Dr *HUDE* HD5 .. **193** K5
East Acres *KNOT* WF11 ...... **160** A7
East Av *AIRE* BD20 .... **34** F8 🗓
  HEM/SK/SE WF9 .... **225** J7
  HEM/SK/SE WF9 .... **247** K2
  HOR/CROF WF4 .... **197** L2
  HUDW HD3 .... **191** L5
  KGHY BD21 .... **3** C2
  PONT WF8 .... **180** D7 🗓
East Bank *GFTH/SHER* LS25 .. **116** B6
East Bath St *BTLY* WF17 .... **173** M1
East Beck Ct *OT* LS21 .... **40** B1
East Bolton *LUD/ILL* HX2 .... **124** A7 🗓
Eastborough Crs *DEWS* WF13 .. **173** M5 🗓
Eastbourne Av *FEA/AMT* WF7 .. **180** A8 🗓
Eastbourne Cl *PONT* WF8 .. **181** J7 🗓
Eastbourne Crs *PONT* WF8 .. **181** J7 🗓
Eastbourne Dr *PONT* WF8 .. **181** J6
Eastbourne Rd *HTON* BD9 .. **104** D1 🗓
Eastbourne St *ROCH* OL11 .. **228** E1 🗓
Eastbourne Ter *PONT* WF8 .. **181** H6
Eastbourne Vw *PONT* WF8 .. **181** H6
Eastburn Br *AIRE* BD20 ...... **35** H3
Eastbury Av *WBSY* BD6 ...... **125** M5
East Busk La *OT* LS21 .... **41** L6
East Byland *LUD/ILL* HX2 .... **124** A8 🗓
East Cswy *BHP/TINH* LS16 .. **86** F1
East Causeway Cl
  BHP/TINH LS16 .... **86** F1 🗓
East Causeway Crs
  BHP/TINH LS16 .... **86** F1 🗓
East Causeway V
  BHP/TINH LS16 .... **87** G2
East Chevin Rd *OT* LS21 .... **62** F1
East Cl *PONT* WF8 .... **203** G1
  STKB/PEN S36 .... **271** J5
East Dale *HEM/SK/SE* WF9 .. **224** B7
Eastdean Bank *SCFT* LS14 .. **89** J8
Eastdean Gdns *SCFT* LS14 .. **89** K8
Eastdean Ga *SCFT* LS14 .... **111** K1 🗓
Eastdean Gv *SCFT* LS14 .... **89** K8
Eastdean Ri *SCFT* LS14 ...... **89** K3 🗓
Eastdean Rd *SCFT* LS14 .... **89** J8
East Dene *AIRE* BD20 .... **36** A4
East Down *CAS* WF10 .... **158** C6
East Dr *GFTH/SHER* LS25 .... **135** K1
  PONT WF8 .... **181** H7
East End Crs *BSLYN/ROY* S71 .. **244** A3
Easterly Av *RHAY* LS8 .... **110** C3
Easterly Cl *RHAY* LS8 .... **110** D5 🗓
Easterly Crs *RHAY* LS8 ...... **110** C3 🗓
Easterly Cross *RHAY* LS8 .. **110** C2
Easterly Garth *RHAY* LS8 .. **110** D2 🗓
Easterly Gv *RHAY* LS8 .... **110** C2
Easterly Mt *RHAY* LS8 .... **110** D2 🗓
Easterly Rd *RHAY* LS8 .... **110** F1
Easterly Sq *RHAY* LS8 .... **110** D2 🗓
Easterly Vw *RHAY* LS8 .... **110** D2 🗓
Eastfield *KBTN* HD8 .... **238** B6
Eastfield Av *KNOT* WF11 .... **182** B3 🗓
  STKB/PEN S36 .... **270** F3 🗓
Eastfield Cl *DOD/DAR* S75 .. **242** F6

TAD LS24 .... **72** B1 🗓
Eastfield Crs *DOD/DAR* S75 .. **242** F6
  RTHW LS26 .... **133** K8
Eastfield Dr *KBTN* HD8 ...... **216** A7
  PONT WF8 .... **181** H6
  RTHW LS26 .... **133** J8
Eastfield Gdns *BOW* BD4 .. **128** A3 🗓
Eastfield Gv *NORM* WF6 .... **178** E3
Eastfield La *CAS* WF10 ...... **158** A6
  MIRF WF14 .... **172** F8
East Field St *OSM* LS9 .... **9** M1
East Fold *KBTN* HD8 .... **239** L5
Eastgate *BHP/TINH* LS16 .... **63** M3
  BSLY S70 .... **261** G4 🗓
  ELL HX5 .... **169** H7 🗓
  HEM/SK/SE WF9 .... **224** A8
  HOLM/MEL HD7 .... **236** C2
  LDSU LS2 .... **7** H9
  OSM LS9 .... **7** J9
Eastgate Cl *BHP/TINH* LS16 .. **63** M3
East Gate St *WHIT* OL12 .... **206** B6 🗓
East Grange Cl *MID* LS10 .. **132** A5 🗓
East Grange Dr *MID* LS10 .. **132** A5
East Grange Garth *MID* LS10 .. **132** A5
East Grange Ri *MID* LS10 .. **132** A5
East Grange Rd *MID* LS10 .. **132** A5
East Grange Sq *MID* LS10 .. **132** A5
East Grange Vw *MID* LS10 .. **132** A5
East King St *OSM* LS9 .... **9** L2
Eastlands *HUDE* HD5 .... **215** J2
Eastlands Wk *BRAM* LS13 .. **108** A5
East Lee La *TOD* OL14 .... **142** B6
Eastleigh Ct *EARD/LOFT* WF3 .. **153** J6 🗓
Eastleigh Gv *WBOW* BD5 .. **126** F3
East Moor Crs *RHAY* LS8 .... **88** B4
East Moor Dr *RHAY* LS8 ...... **88** C5
East Moor La *BHP/TINH* LS16 .. **86** F2
East Moor Rd *RHAY* LS8 .... **88** B4
Eastmoor Rd *WKFDE* WF1 .. **176** E6
East Mt *BRIG* HD6 .... **170** C3
East Neville St *SKP/WHF* BD23 .. **16** E6 🗓
Easton Pl *HUDW* HD3 .... **191** K7
East Pde *AIRE* BD20 .... **56** F1
  BAIL BD17 .... **82** F2
  BFDE BD3 .... **5** H5
  ILK LS29 .... **38** E2
  ILK LS29 .... **61** J2
  KGHY BD21 .... **3** H5
  LDS LS1 .... **6** F9
  RPDN/SBR HX6 .... **167** M1
East Parade Wk *LDS* LS1 .. **6** F9
East Park Dr *OSM* LS9 .... **110** B7 🗓
East Park Gv *OSM* LS9 ...... **110** C7
East Park Mt *OSM* LS9 ...... **110** C7
East Park Pde *OSM* LS9 .... **110** C7
East Park Rd *HIPP* HX3 ...... **146** C3
East Park St *MOR* LS27 .... **152** B3 🗓
  OSM LS9 .... **110** C7
East Park Ter *OSM* LS9 .... **110** C7
East Park Vw *OSM* LS9 ...... **110** C7
East Pinfold *BSLYN/ROY* S71 .. **243** L3
East Royd *HWTH* BD22 .... **78** F4 🗓
East Side *PDSY/CALV* LS28 .. **129** K1
East Squire La *GIR* BD8 ...... **104** E4
East St *BRIG* HD6 .... **170** C5
  BTLY WF17 .... **173** L1 🗓
  CUD/GR S72 .... **245** G1
  HEM/SK/SE WF9 .... **247** K2
  HIPP HX3 .... **148** C7
  HOLM/MEL HD7 .... **213** G1
  HOLM/MEL HD7 .... **255** G3
  HOR/CROF WF4 .... **222** F5
  HUDW HD3 .... **191** K5
  LIT OL15 .... **207** L1 🗓
  MILN OL16 .... **206** C6
  MILN OL16 .... **206** F7 🗓
  OSM LS9 .... **9** K2
  RPDN/SBR HX6 .... **167** G6
  WHIT OL12 .... **184** E8
  WKFDE WF1 .... **176** E4
  WMB/DAR S73 .... **263** J8
East Ter *HWTH* BD22 .... **79** G6 🗓
East Vw *AIRE* BD20 .... **36** A4
  AWLS/ASK DN6 .... **227** M5
  CAS WF10 .... **157** J7
  CLECK BD19 .... **149** J8
  COL BB8 .... **74** E4
  CUD/GR S72 .... **244** D7
  GFTH/SHER LS25 .... **116** A8
  GFTH/SHER LS25 .... **135** K5
  KNOT WF11 .... **182** C3 🗓
  MIRF WF14 .... **172** B8
  MSTN/BAR LS15 .... **111** L4 🗓
  OSS WF5 .... **197** G3
  PDSY/CALV LS28 .... **129** C1
  RTHW LS26 .... **155** L1
  WBSY BD6 .... **125** L4 🗓
  YEA LS19 .... **62** E8
East View Rd *YEA* LS19 ...... **62** E8
East View Ter *LM/WK* BD12 .. **148** F2
Eastville Rd *LM/WK* BD12 .. **148** F2
Eastway *MIRF* WF14 .... **172** C7
  ROY/SHW OL2 .... **229** K8
Eastway Pk *MIRF* WF14 .... **172** C7 🗓
Eastwood Av *LUD/ILL* HX2 .. **124** A7
  RPDN/SBR HX6 .... **167** H3
  WKFDW/WTN WF2 .... **176** D1
Eastwood Dr *SCFT* LS14 .... **111** M2
Eastwood Gdns *SCFT* LS14 .. **111** L2
Eastwood Garth *SCFT* LS14 .. **111** M2
Eastwood Gv *GFTH/SHER* LS25 .. **135** J1
  LUD/ILL HX2 .... **124** A7 🗓
Eastwood La *SCFT* LS14 .... **111** M2
  TOD OL14 .... **142** C4
Eastwood Nook *SCFT* LS14 .. **111** M2
Eastwood Rd *TOD* OL14 .... **141** J3
Eastwood St *BOW* BD4 ...... **127** H1 🗓

BRIG HD6 .... **170** D3 🗓
  HIPP HX3 .... **146** C4 🗓
  HUDE HD5 .... **193** K8
  LIT OL15 .... **207** K1 🗓
Easy Rd *OSM* LS9 .... **110** B8
Eaton Hl *BHP/TINH* LS16 .... **86** B3
Eaton Ms *MID* LS10 .... **153** L1 🗓
Eaton Pl *HEM/SK/SE* WF9 .. **224** F7 🗓
Eaton Rd *ILK* LS29 .... **38** C3
Eaton Sq *MID* LS10 .... **153** L2
Eaton St *KGHY* BD21 .... **79** J2 🗓
Eaton Wk *HEM/SK/SE* WF9 .. **247** J1 🗓
Eaves Av *HBR* HX7 .... **143** G2
Eaves Rd *HBR* HX7 .... **143** G2
Ebberston Gv *HDGY* LS6 .... **6** A2
Ebberston Pl *HDGY* LS6 .... **6** A2
Ebberston Ter *HDGY* LS6 .. **6** A2
Ebenezer Pl *GTHN* BD7 .... **126** D2 🗓
Ebenezer St *BFD* BD1 .... **5** G7
  EARD/LOFT WF3 .... **154** D3 🗓
  PDSY/CALV LS28 .... **106** F3
Ebor Cl *ROY/SHW* OL2 ...... **229** J6
Ebor Gdns *MIRF* WF14 ...... **194** A1
Ebor La *HWTH* BD22 .... **78** F6
Ebor Mt *GFTH/SHER* LS25 .. **135** J4
  HDGY LS6 .... **6** A4
Ebor Pl *HDGY* LS6 .... **6** A4
Ebor St *HDGY* LS6 .... **6** A4
  LIT OL15 .... **207** L1
Ebor Wy *AL/HA/HU* LS17 .. **44** F7
  AL/HA/HU LS17 .... **65** K2
  ILK LS29 .... **39** M8
  OT LS21 .... **62** C1
Ebson House La
  HOLM/MEL HD7 .... **237** K8
Ebury Cl *BTLY* WF17 .... **151** M8
Ebury St *BTLY* WF17 .... **151** M8
Eccleaburn Rd *OSM* LS9 .... **110** C7 🗓
Eccleaburn St *OSM* LS9 .... **110** C7 🗓
Eccleaburn Ter *OSM* LS9 .. **110** C7 🗓
Eccles Cl *ECHL* BD2 .... **105** K2
Eccles Parlour *RPDN/SBR* HX6 .. **166** C7 🗓
Eccup La *BHP/TINH* LS16 .... **66** F7 🗓
Eccup Moor Rd *BHP/TINH* LS16 .. **65** H4 🗓
Echo St *WKFDE* WF15 .... **172** B4
Ecklands Long La
  STKB/PEN S36 .... **269** M6
Eclipse Cl *MILN* OL16 .... **206** D7 🗓
Edale Av *HUDE* HD4 .... **214** B5
Edale Cl *HUDE* HD5 .... **193** K6
Edale Gv *CUL/QBY* BD13 .... **124** L6
Edale Ri *DOD/DAR* S75 ...... **260** A7 🗓
Edale Wy *BHP/TINH* LS16 .. **86** B3 🗓
Edderciff Crs *CLECK* BD19 .. **150** C3 🗓
Edderthorpe La *WMB/DAR* S73 .. **263** J2
Edderthorpe St *BFDE* BD3 .. **5** K7
Eddison Cl *BHP/TINH* LS16 .. **86** F1
Eddison Pl *PDSY/CALV* LS28 .. **106** F4
Eddyfield Rd *STKB/PEN* S36 .. **271** J5
Eddystone Ri *KNOT* WF11 .. **181** M3 🗓
Edelshain Gv *WKFDW/WTN* WF2 .. **199** H6
Eden Av *OSS* WF5 .... **174** F8
  WKFDW/WTN WF2 .... **197** M1
Eden Cl *DOD/DAR* S75 ...... **260** A1
  LM/WK BD12 .... **148** F3
Eden Crs *BULY* LS4 .... **108** D2
Edendale *CAS* WF10 .... **158** B6
Eden Dr *BULY* LS4 .... **108** D2
Edenfield Cl *BSLYN/ROY* S71 .. **243** M8 🗓
Eden Gdns *BULY* LS4 .... **108** D3
Eden Gv *BULY* LS4 .... **108** D3
Eden Mt *BULY* LS4 .... **108** D3
Eden Rd *BULY* LS4 .... **108** D2
Edensor Rd *KGHY* BD21 ...... **2** D4
Eden Wk *BULY* LS4 .... **108** D3
Eden Wy *BULY* LS4 .... **108** D3
  ROY/SHW OL2 .... **229** J6
Ederoyd Av *PDSY/CALV* LS28 .. **106** D5
Ederoyd Crs *PDSY/CALV* LS28 .. **106** D5
Ederoyd Dr *PDSY/CALV* LS28 .. **106** C5
Ederoyd Gv *PDSY/CALV* LS28 .. **106** C5
Ederoyd Mt *PDSY/CALV* LS28 .. **106** C5
Ederoyd Ri *PDSY/CALV* LS28 .. **106** C5
Edgar St *CLAY* BD14 .... **125** M2
  MILN OL16 .... **206** D2
Edgbaston Cl *AL/HA/HU* LS17 .. **65** J8
Edgbaston Wk *AL/HA/HU* LS17 .. **65** J8
Edge Av *RTHW* LS26 .... **133** M8
Edgebank Av *WBSY* BD6 .... **126** B8
Edgecliffe Pl *BSLYN/ROY* S71 .. **261** J3
Edge Cl *EARL* WF12 .... **196** F1
  HOLM/MEL HD7 .... **213** G2
Edge End Gdns *WBSY* BD6 .. **126** A7
Edge End La *HOLM/MEL* HD7 .. **253** J1
Edge End Rd *WBSY* BD6 .... **126** A7
Edgehill Cl *CUL/QBY* BD13 .. **125** H5 🗓
Edge Hill Cl *HUDE* HD5 ...... **15** L4
Edgehill Rd *DOD/DAR* S75 .. **242** C4
Edgeholme La *LUD/ILL* HX2 .. **145** K7
Edge Jct *EARL* WF12 .... **195** M5
Edge La *EARL* WF12 .... **196** A5
  HBR HX7 .... **120** B7
Edgemoor Cl *BOW* BD4 .... **128** A6
  HIPP HX3 .... **168** D2 🗓
Edgemoor Rd *HOLM/MEL* HD7 .. **236** A3
  HOR/CROF WF4 .... **220** B3
Edge Rd *EARL* WF12 .... **196** A6
Edgerton Cl *TAD* LS24 .... **71** K3
Edgerton Dr *TAD* LS24 ...... **71** K3
Edgerton Garth *TAD* LS24 .. **71** K3
Edgerton Gn *HUD* HD1 ...... **14** A4
Edgerton Grove Rd *HUD* HD1 .. **14** A4
Edgerton La *HUDW* HD3 .... **14** A4
Edgerton Rd *BHP/TINH* LS16 .. **86** D3
  HUDW HD3 .... **14** A4
Edge Ter *HUDW* HD3 .... **191** H7
Edge Top Rd *EARL* WF12 .. **195** L5
Edge Vw *EARL* WF12 .... **196** A5
  HOLM/MEL HD7 .... **213** G2
Edgeware Rd *HUDE* HD5 .. **193** J8
Edgware Av *RHAY* LS8 ...... **110** B4 🗓
Edgware Gv *RHAY* LS8 ...... **110** B4 🗓
Edgware Mt *RHAY* LS8 ...... **110** B4 🗓
Edgware Pl *RHAY* LS8 .... **110** B4 🗓
Edgware Rw *RHAY* LS8 ...... **110** B4 🗓

Edgware St *RHAY* LS8 .... **7** M4
Edgware Ter *RHAY* LS8 .... **110** B4 🗓
Edgware Vw *RHAY* LS8 .... **110** B4 🗓
Edinburgh Av *WOR/ARM* LS12 .. **108** C5
Edinburgh Cl *BSLYN/ROY* S71 .. **261** K2 🗓
Edinburgh Gv *WOR/ARM* LS12 .. **108** C6
Edinburgh Pl *GFTH/SHER* LS25 .. **113** K7
  WOR/ARM LS12 .... **108** C6
Edinburgh Rd *WOR/ARM* LS12 .. **108** C6
Edinburgh Ter *WOR/ARM* LS12 .. **108** C6
Edlington Cl *BOW* BD4 ...... **128** A3 🗓
Edmonton Cl *DOD/DAR* S75 .. **260** C4 🗓
Edmonton Pl *CHAL* LS7 ...... **87** M8 🗓
Edmund St *GTHN* BD7 .... **5** G6
  ROY/SHW OL2 .... **229** L7 🗓
Edmund St *TOD* OL14 .... **163** J6 🗓
Edrich Cl *LM/WK* BD12 ...... **127** C8 🗓
Edroyd Pl *PDSY/CALV* LS28 .. **106** F3
Edroyd St *PDSY/CALV* LS28 .. **106** F3
Eduard St *CHAL* LS7 .... **7** H3
Edward Av *LIT* OL15 .... **207** K1 🗓
Edward Cl *BSLY* S70 .... **261** L7
  EARL WF12 .... **195** K3 🗓
  HIPP HX3 .... **169** J2
Edward Dr *WKFDE* WF1 ...... **176** D1
Edward Rd *AWLS/ASK* DN6 .. **249** K5
  AWLS/ASK DN6 .... **249** M8
  MIRF WF14 .... **194** B1
  ROY/SHW OL2 .... **229** J8
Edwards Rd *LUD/ILL* HX2 .. **168** A1
Edwards St *BOW* BD4 .... **5** G8
  BRIG HD6 .... **170** C3
  CLECK BD19 .... **172** C1 🗓
  DOD/DAR S75 .... **242** F6 🗓
  HBR HX7 .... **143** K3 🗓
  LDSU LS2 .... **7** H9
  LVSG WF15 .... **172** C2
  MILN OL16 .... **206** C6
  NORM WF6 .... **178** C1
  RPDN/SBR HX6 .... **167** K2
  SHPY BD18 .... **82** B5 🗓
  WHIT OL12 .... **206** F2 🗓
  WHIT OL12 .... **176** F7 🗓
Edward Turner Cl
  LM/WK BD12 .... **126** E8 🗓
Edwin Rd *HDGY* LS6 .... **6** A4
Eel Holme View St *KGHY* BD21 .. **57** K3 🗓
Eel Mires Garth *WBY* LS22 .. **30** B8
Effingham Rd *BGLY* BD16 .. **80** C5
Egerton Gv *WIL/AL* BD15 .... **103** H5
Egerton Pl *ROY/SHW* OL2 .. **229** J8 🗓
Egerton St *LIT* OL15 .... **207** L1
  RPDN/SBR HX6 .... **167** K2 🗓
Eggleston Dr *BOW* BD4 .... **128** A3
Eggleston Sq *BSPA/BRAM* LS23 .. **48** E7
Eggleston St *BRAM* LS13 .. **107** H1
Egmanton Rd *BSLYN/ROY* S71 .. **243** H5 🗓
Egremont Crs *WBSY* BD6 .. **126** B8
Egremont Rd *MILN* OL16 .. **229** G2
Egremont St *RPDN/SBR* HX6 .. **167** J3 🗓
Egypt Rd *CUL/QBY* BD13 .... **102** E8
Eiffel Buildings *HBR* HX7 .. **143** J3 🗓
Eighth Av *LVSG* WF15 .... **171** K1
  RTHW LS26 .... **133** J7
  WOR/ARM LS12 .... **108** B8
Eightlands Av *BRAM* LS13 .. **107** M4 🗓
Eightlands La *BRAM* LS13 .. **107** M4
Eightlands Rd *DEWS* WF13 .. **173** L6 🗓
Ekota Pl *RHAY* LS8 .... **110** B2 🗓
Elam Wood Rd *AIRE* BD20 .. **57** L3
Elbow La *ECHL* BD2 .... **105** K4 🗓
  LUD/ILL HX2 .... **145** G6
Elder Av *HEM/SK/SE* WF9 .. **225** L6
  WKFDW/WTN WF2 .... **12** H1
Elder Cl *BTLY* WF17 .... **151** H4
Elder Cft *BRAM* LS13 .... **107** L5
Elder Dr *EARL* WF12 .... **195** M3
  HEM/SK/SE WF9 .... **225** K6
Elder Garth *GFTH/SHER* LS25 .. **113** K8
Elder Gn *WKFDW/WTN* WF2 .. **12** H1
Elder Gv *HUDS* HD4 .... **213** M8
Elder Grove Ms *HUDS* HD4 .. **213** M8 🗓
Elder La *HUDN* HD2 .... **193** J1 🗓
Elder Mt *BRAM* LS13 .... **107** L5 🗓
Elder Pl *BRAM* LS13 .... **107** L5
Elder Ri *RTHW* LS26 .... **133** M8
Elder Rd *BRAM* LS13 .... **107** L5
  HUDN HD2 .... **193** H1
Elder St *AIRE* BD20 .... **35** M3
  BRAM LS13 .... **107** L5
  IDLE BD10 .... **84** A7
  MILN OL16 .... **228** D1
Elderwood Gdns *IDLE* BD10 .. **106** A1
Eldon Pl *BFD* BD1 .... **4** D4
  CLECK BD19 .... **150** A7
Eldon Rd *HUD* HD1 .... **191** M7
Eldon St *BSLY* S70 .... **261** G5
  HECK WF16 .... **172** E2
  HIPP HX3 .... **11** H3
  OSS WF5 .... **175** H7
  TOD OL14 .... **163** L1
Eldon St North *BSLYN/ROY* S71 .. **261** H4
Eldroth Mt *HFAX* HX1 .... **168** C1 🗓
Eldroth Rd *HFAX* HX1 .... **168** C1
Eleanor Dr *PDSY/CALV* LS28 .. **84** B7
Eleanor St *BRIG* HD6 .... **170** C5
  HUD HD1 .... **14** F2
Eleventh Av *LVSG* WF15 .... **171** L1
Elford Gv *RHAY* LS8 .... **110** B3 🗓
Elford Pl East *RHAY* LS8 .... **110** B4 🗓
Elford Pl West *RHAY* LS8 .. **110** B4 🗓
Elford Rd *RHAY* LS8 .... **110** B3 🗓
Elgin Cl *HUDS* HD4 .... **213** L4
Elia St *KGHY* BD21 .... **3** K3
Elim St *LIT* OL15 .... **185** L2
Eliot Gv *GSLY* LS20 .... **62** B6
Eliots Cl *CAS* WF10 .... **180** E3 🗓
Eli St *WBOW* BD5 .... **127** H3 🗓
Elizabethan Ct *PONT* WF8 .. **181** G4 🗓
Elizabeth Av *CUD/GR* S72 .. **245** G1
  LM/WK BD12 .... **148** F2 🗓
Elizabeth Cl *LM/WK* BD12 .. **148** F2 🗓
Elizabeth Crs *LM/WK* BD12 .. **148** F2

Elizabeth Dr *CAS* WF10 .... **158** E5
  KNOT WF11 .... **181** L2
  LM/WK BD12 .... **148** F2 🗓
Elizabeth Frances St *ELL* HX5 .. **169** H8
Elizabeth Gdns *WKFDE* WF1 .. **176** E6 🗓
Elizabeth Gv *MOR* LS27 .... **152** E1 🗓
  ROY/SHW OL2 .... **229** K7
Elizabeth Pl *SCFT* LS14 ...... **111** J1 🗓
Elizabeth St *BGLY* BD16 .... **81** J3 🗓
  CUD/GR S72 .... **245** J8
  ELL HX5 .... **169** H8
  GTL/HWG HX4 .... **168** F7 🗓
  HDGY LS6 .... **109** G3
  HUDS HD4 .... **214** C3
  LM/WK BD12 .... **148** F2 🗓
  LVSG WF15 .... **172** A2
  WBOW BD5 .... **4** E9
  WKFDE WF1 .... **199** G4
Elland Br *ELL* HX5 .... **169** H7
Elland Cl *BSLYN/ROY* S71 .. **243** G7
Elland La *ELL* HX5 .... **169** J7
Elland Riorges Link *ELL* HX5 .. **169** J7
Elland Rd *BEE/HOL* LS11 .... **8** B8
  BRIG HD6 .... **170** C4
  ELL HX5 .... **169** L5
  MOR LS27 .... **130** D7
  RPDN/SBR HX6 .... **189** C2
Elland St *CAS* WF10 .... **158** A5
Elland Wy *BEE/HOL* LS11 .... **130** F4
Elland Wood Bottom *ELL* HX5 .. **168** F5
Ellar Carr Rd *CUL/QBY* BD13 .. **79** L7
  IDLE BD10 .... **83** L4
Ellarfield La *GFTH/SHER* LS25 .. **116** A3
Ellar Gdns *ILK* LS29 .... **61** K1
Ella St *HEM/SK/SE* WF9 ...... **223** J2
Ellenroad Ap *MILN* OL16 .. **229** J2
Ellenroad St *MILN* OL16 .... **229** J2
Ellen Royd La *LUD/ILL* HX2 .. **144** E6
Ellen Royd St *HIPP* HX3 .... **11** H3
Ellen St *BGLY* BD16 .... **81** J3 🗓
Ellenthorpe Rd *BAIL* BD17 .. **82** A4 🗓
Ellerby La *OSM* LS9 .... **9** M3
Ellerby Rd *OSM* LS9 .... **9** L2
Ellercroft Av *GTHN* BD7 .... **104** C8 🗓
Ellercroft Rd *GTHN* BD7 .... **104** C8 🗓
Ellercroft Ter *GTHN* BD7 .... **104** C8 🗓
Ellerker La *SCFT* LS14 .... **90** D1
Ellerker Rd *SCFT* LS14 ...... **68** C8
Eller Ms *SKP/WHF* BD23 .... **16** A3 🗓
Ellers Gv *RHAY* LS8 .... **110** B2 🗓
Ellerslie Gv *HUDW* HD3 .... **14** B3
Ellers Rd *AIRE* BD20 .... **55** M2
  RHAY LS8 .... **110** B2
Ellerton St *BFDE* BD3 .... **105** L7
Ellesmere Av *COL* BB8 ...... **74** B1
Ellesmere St *ROCH* OL11 .. **228** B1 🗓
Ellington Ct *BSLY* S70 .... **260** F7 🗓
Ellin's Ter *NORM* WF6 .... **178** B5
Ellinthorpe St *BOW* BD4 .... **127** K1 🗓
Elliot St *SKP/WHF* BD23 ...... **16** B2 🗓
Elliott St *AIRE* BD20 .... **35** M5
  SHPY BD18 .... **82** C6
  WHIT OL12 .... **206** C6
Ellis Fold *WOR/ARM* LS12 .. **108** D7
Ellison St *HUDS* HD4 .... **213** M2
Ellis Pl *BEE/HOL* LS11 .... **131** J5
Ellis St *WBOW* BD5 .... **126** F3
Elliston Av *DOD/DAR* S75 .. **242** E5
Ellistones Gdns *GTL/HWG* HX4 .. **168** C7 🗓
Ellistones La *GTL/HWG* HX4 .. **168** C8
Ellistones Pl *GTL/HWG* HX4 .. **168** C7
Ellmont Av *KBTN* HD8 .... **217** G8
Elmont Gv *WBSY* BD6 .... **126** C5 🗓
Elm Av *EARD/LOFT* WF3 .... **177** K2
  GFTH/SHER LS25 .... **135** H3
  HOLM/MEL HD7 .... **236** E6
  RPDN/SBR HX6 .... **167** K1
  TOD OL14 .... **141** K7
Elmbridge *BSLYN/ROY* S71 .. **244** A3
Elm Cl *OSS* WF5 .... **197** G3
  PONT WF8 .... **203** L1
Elm Ct *CLECK* BD19 .... **150** D2
  KBTN HD8 .... **216** B7
Elm Crs *AIRE* BD20 .... **58** F6
Elm Cft *SCFT* LS14 .... **89** L6 🗓
Elmet Dr *MSTN/BAR* LS15 .. **91** J7
Elmete Av *GFTH/SHER* LS25 .. **116** A7
  MSTN/BAR LS15 .... **90** B8
  RHAY LS8 .... **88** B8
Elmete Cl *RHAY* LS8 .... **88** F8
Elmete Ct *RHAY* LS8 .... **88** F8
Elmete Cft *MSTN/BAR* LS15 .. **90** B8 🗓
Elmete Dr *RHAY* LS8 .... **88** F7
Elmete Gv *RHAY* LS8 .... **88** E7
Elmete Hl *RHAY* LS8 .... **88** F8
Elmete La *AL/HA/HU* LS17 .. **89** C4
  RHAY LS8 .... **88** F6
Elmete Mt *RHAY* LS8 .... **88** F8
Elmete Rd *CAS* WF10 .... **158** F5
Elmete Wk *RHAY* LS8 .... **88** E8
Elmete Wy *RHAY* LS8 .... **89** G8
Elmfield *BAIL* BD17 .... **82** F2
Elmfield Av *HUDW* HD3 ...... **213** H1
Elmfield Ct *BIRK/DRI* BD11 .. **150** C2
  MOR LS27 .... **152** C3
Elmfield Dr *KBTN* HD8 .... **239** J5
  WBSY BD6 .... **126** C5
Elmfield Gv *WOR/ARM* LS12 .. **108** F2 🗓
Elmfield Pl *WOR/ARM* LS12 .. **108** F8
Elmfield Rd *AIRE* BD20 ...... **35** G3
  HUDN HD2 .... **192** A5
  MOR LS27 .... **152** D4
Elmfield Ter *HFAX* HX1 ...... **168** D1
Elmfield Wy *BRAM* LS13 .. **107** M5
Elm Gdns *CAS* WF10 .... **180** F1
Elm Gv *AIRE* BD20 .... **35** M5
  AIRE BD20 .... **58** F6
  CLECK BD19 .... **150** C6
  HECK WF16 .... **172** E1
  HEM/SK/SE WF9 .... **247** H3
  HIPP HX3 .... **125** M8
  HOR/CROF WF4 .... **197** K5
  HWTH BD22 .... **79** J2
  ILK LS29 .... **40** B6
  MILN OL16 .... **229** J3

ROCH OL11 228 A1
SHPY BD18 83 J7
WHIT OL12 206 D2
Elmhirst La DOD/DAR S75 259 N6
Elmhurst Cl AL/HA/HU LS17 88 C2
Elmhurst Gdns AL/HA/HU LS17 88 C2
Elmore Wd LIT OL15 185 G8
Elm Pk PONT WF8 180 E8
Elm Pl BSLYN/ROY S71 261 M1
  KNOT WF11 182 A3
  RPDN/SBR HX6 167 K1
Elm Rd AIRE BD20 55 L1
  AWLS/ASK DN6 249 J4
  DEWS WF13 173 H6
  HEM/SK/SE WF9 224 D5
  NORM WF6 178 C7
  SHPY BD18 82 F7
Elm Rw BSLYN/ROY S71 261 K5
Elmroyd RTHW LS26 155 H5
Elmsall Dr HEM/SK/SE WF9 247 L5
Elmsall La AWLS/ASK DN6 247 K6
Elmsall St GIR BD8 4 D3
Elmsall Wy HEM/SK/SE WF9 247 L1
Elmsdale Cl HEM/SK/SE WF9 247 K4
Elms Hl HOLM/MEL HD7 212 B6
Elmsley St AIRE BD20 56 E1
The Elms FEA/AMT WF7 224 B1
  GSLY LS20 62 A5
  LIT OL15 207 G2
Elm St COL BB8 74 A1
  GTL/HWG HX4 190 C2
  HDGY LS6 6 C1
  HOR/CROF WF4 200 D7
  HUDS HD4 214 D2
  HWTH BD22 100 E4
  KBTN HD8 239 J4
  WHIT OL12 206 B5
Elm Ter PONT WF8 180 E6
Elm Tree Av WBSY BD6 126 E6
Elm Tree Cl KGHY BD21 3 K7
  LVSG WF15 172 E4
  MSTN/BAR LS15 112 A8
  WBSY BD6 126 F6
Elm Tree Gdns WBSY BD6 126 E6
Elmtree La MID LS10 9 K7
Elm Tree St WKFDE WF1 13 K7
Elm Vw AIRE BD20 35 K8
The Elm Wk MSTN/BAR LS15 133 K1
Elm Wy BTLY WF17 151 J4
Elmwood Av AWLS/ASK DN6 249 H8
  HUD HD1 14 E5
  MSTN/BAR LS15 90 F7
  WKFDW/WTN WF2 199 K7
Elmwood Cha MSTN/BAR LS15 90 F7
Elmwood Cl HUD HD1 14 E5
  MIRF WF14 194 D3
  WKFDW/WTN WF2 199 K7
Elmwood Dr BRIG HD6 170 D8
  HWTH BD22 79 H2
  WKFDW/WTN WF2 199 K7
Elmwood Garth
  WKFDW/WTN WF2 199 K7
Elmwood Gv HOR/CROF WF4 197 L5
  MSTN/BAR LS15 90 F7
Elmwood Rd HWTH BD22 79 H3
  LDSU LS2 7 G6
Elm Wood St BRIG HD6 170 D2
Elmwood St HFAX HX1 168 C1
Elmwood Ter HWTH BD22 79 H2
Elphaborough Cl HBR HX7 144 A6
Elsdon Gv WBOW BD5 127 G1
Elsham Ter BULY LS4 108 E4
Elsicker La WKFDE WF1 178 B8
Elsie St HWTH BD22 79 H6
  KGHY BD21 57 K4
Elsinore Av ELL HX5 191 H1
Elsinore Ct ELL HX5 169 G8
Elstead Cl DOD/DAR S75 260 A1
Elsworth Av BFDE BD3 105 M5
Elsworth St WOR/ARM LS12 108 F7
Eltham Cl HDGY LS6 6 C2
Eltham Dr HDGY LS6 6 C2
Eltham Gdns HDGY LS6 6 C2
Eltham Gv WBSY BD6 126 C6
Eltham Ri HDGY LS6 6 C2
Elvaston Rd MOR LS27 152 C2
Elvey Cl ECHL BD2 105 M2
Elvey St WKFDE WF1 176 E7
Elwell Cl WBSY BD6 125 M7
Elwell St GTL/HWG HX4 168 F8
Elwyn Gv WBOW BD5 127 G3
Elwyn Rd WBOW BD5 127 H1
Ely St GTL/HWG HX4 168 F8
The Embankment MIRF WF14 194 C1
Emblem Ter WKFDE WF1 13 G9
Embleton Rd RTHW LS26 156 C5
Emerald St BTLY WF17 151 H1
  HUD HD1 15 G3
  HWTH BD22 79 J2
Emerson Av HTON BD9 103 M3
Emily Cl BSLYN/ROY S71 261 M4
Emily St KGHY BD21 3 H3
Emmanuel Ter HUDS HD4 214 B4
Emma St WHIT OL12 206 A6
Emmeline Cl IDLE BD10 83 K6
Emmfield Dr HTON BD9 104 C2
Emm La HTON BD9 104 C3
Emmott Dr YEA LS19 84 F3
Emmott Farm Fold HWTH BD22 78 E8
Emmott La COL BB8 52 F7
Empress St COL BB8 74 A1
Emscote Av HFAX HX1 10 D9
Emscote Gdns HFAX HX1 10 D9
  HFAX HX1 168 C1
Emscote Gv HFAX HX1 10 D9
Emscote Pl HFAX HX1 10 D9
Emscote St South HFAX HX1 10 D9
Emsley Av CUD/GR S72 262 C2
Emsley Cl BOW BD4 127 K6
Emsley Pl MID LS10 9 L6
Emville Av AL/HA/HU LS17 88 E1
Enderby Cl HIPP HX3 146 B3
Enderley Rd CUL/QBY BD13 102 F8
Endor Cl ILK LS29 40 B7
Endor Gv ILK LS29 40 B7
Endsleigh Pl CLAY BD14 125 K2

Enfield YEA LS19 62 D8
Enfield Av LS17 7 L4
Enfield Cl BTLY WF17 151 H4
Enfield Dr BTLY WF17 151 H8
  GTHN BD7 126 B5
  WBSY BD6 126 C5
Enfield Pde WBSY BD6 126 C5
Enfield Rd BAIL BD17 82 E4
Enfield Side Rd HWTH BD22 99 M1
Enfield St CHAL LS7 7 K5
  KGHY BD21 2 E1
Enfield Ter CHAL LS7 7 L4
  WBSY BD6 126 C5
Engine La CUD/GR S72 244 F5
  HOR/CROF WF4 197 H5
  HOR/CROF WF4 201 J7
England La KNOT WF11 182 C2
Englefield Cl BOW BD4 128 A4
Englefield Crs BOW BD4 128 A4
Ennerdale Av EARL WF12 174 A4
  ROY/SHW OL2 228 E7
Ennerdale Cl WBY LS22 29 L8
Ennerdale Crs EARL WF12 174 A4
Ennerdale Dr ECHL BD2 105 K3
Ennerdale Rd BSLYN/ROY S71 262 D6
  EARL WF12 174 A4
  ECHL BD2 105 J3
  WKFDW/WTN WF2 176 B7
  WOR/ARM LS12 129 M4
Ennerdale Wy
  WOR/ARM LS12 129 M3
Enoch La HUDS HD4 214 B3
Enterprise Wy AIRE BD20 16 C7
  CAS WF10 157 L7
  GFTH/SHER LS25 116 E7
  IDLE BD10 83 K8
  MID LS10 132 B5
Entwisle Rd MILN OL16 206 C7
Entwisle St MILN OL16 207 G8
Envoy St BEE/HOL LS11 9 G8
Epsom Rd GFTH/SHER LS25 135 H4
Epsom Wy HUDE HD5 193 L5
Epworth Pl HWTH BD22 78 D5
  MID LS10 9 L7
Equitable St MILN OL16 229 H1
Eric St BRAM LS13 107 L1
  HEM/SK/SE WF9 247 J3
  KGHY BD21 3 J4
  LIT OL15 185 J8
Ermysted St SKP/WHF BD23 16 C2
Ernest St DEWS WF13 173 M6
  TOD OL14 140 E5
Ernest Ter WHIT OL12 206 D5
Erringden Rd HBR HX7 143 M5
Erringden St TOD OL14 163 L1
Escroft Cl LM/WK BD12 148 F5
Eshald La BAIL BD17 83 J2
Eshald La RTHW LS26 155 M1
Eshald St RTHW LS26 133 M8
Esholt Av GSLY LS20 61 M7
Eshton Av LM/WK BD12 149 H1
  NORM WF6 178 C2
  ROY/SHW OL2 228 F7
Eshton Ct DOD/DAR S75 242 C4
  NORM WF6 178 C2
Eskdale Av HIPP HX3 147 K1
  NORM WF6 178 C2
Eskdale Cl EARL WF12 174 A3
  NORM WF6 178 C2
Eskdale Cft NORM WF6 178 C2
Eskdale Gv GFTH/SHER LS25 113 J8
Eskdale Mt HBR HX7 143 J2
  SCFT LS14 111 H2
Eskdale Ri WIL/AL BD15 103 K6
Eskdale Rd BSLYN/ROY S71 262 D6
  WKFDW/WTN WF2 176 A7
Esk Gdns WBY LS22 30 A6
Eskine Pde WBSY BD6 126 B8
Esmond St GTHN BD7 126 B5
  WOR/ARM LS12 108 E7
Esmond Ter WOR/ARM LS12 108 D7
The Esplanade MILN OL16 206 A7
Essex Cl ROY/SHW OL2 229 H7
Essex Rd BSLY S70 261 H7
Essex St BFDE BD3 5 J9
  BOW BD4 5 J9
  COL BB8 74 A2
  HFAX HX1 10 A7
  ROCH OL11 206 B8
Estcourt Av HDGY LS6 108 E1
Estcourt Dr PONT WF8 203 M2
Estcourt Gv GTHN BD7 126 C1
Estcourt Rd GTHN BD7 126 C1
  PONT WF8 203 M2
Estcourt Ter HDGY LS6 108 E1
Esther Av WKFDW/WTN WF2 198 B2
Esther Gv WKFDW/WTN WF2 198 A2
Esthwaite Gdns
  MSTN/BAR LS15 111 G8
Ethel St KGHY BD21 57 K5
Etna St GTHN BD7 126 B3
Eton Av HUDE HD5 193 G8
Eton St HBR HX7 143 H3
  HFAX HX1 10 B6
Euden Edge Rd
  HOLM/MEL HD7 212 C3
Eunice La KBTN HD8 238 E8
Euston Gv BEE/HOL LS11 8 A7
Euston Mt BEE/HOL LS11 8 A8
Euston Ter BEE/HOL LS11 8 A8
Evanston Av BULY LS4 108 C5
Eva St WHIT OL12 206 C4
Eveline St CUD/GR S72 244 D8
Evelyn Av WOR/ARM LS12 108 E8
Evelyn Pl WOR/ARM LS12 108 E8
Evelyn Ter BSLY S70 261 K6
Everard St WBOW BD5 127 G4
Everdale Mt HEM/SK/SE WF9 223 K8
  HEM/SK/SE WF9 247 G3
Everest Av SHPY BD18 83 G7
Everest St ROCH OL11 228 C4
Everleigh St OSM LS9 110 C6
Eversley Av GFTH/SHER LS25 116 A8
Eversley Ct BAIL BD17 82 D5
Eversley Dr BOW BD4 128 A2
Eversley Garth Crs
  GFTH/SHER LS25 116 A7
Eversley Mt GFTH/SHER LS25 116 A8

Eversley Pl LUD/ILL HX2 146 A8
Eversley Rd HBR HX7 143 J2
Every St TOD OL14 163 L1
Evesham Gv IDLE BD10 83 K7
Ewart Pl GTHN BD7 126 C3
Ewart St CUL/QBY BD13 125 G5
  GTHN BD7 126 C3
Ewden Wy DOD/DAR S75 260 C5
Ewood Dr HBR HX7 144 B5
Ewood Hall Av HBR HX7 144 B5
Ewood La TOD OL14 141 H8
Excelsior Cl RPDN/SBR HX6 188 E3
Excelsior Ter MILN OL16 207 H3
Exchange HOLM/MEL HD7 236 B2
Exchange St CLECK BD19 149 M5
  GTL/HWG HX4 168 F8
  HEM/SK/SE WF9 247 H3
  NORM WF6 178 C4
Exe St WBOW BD5 126 C3
Exeter Dr MID LS10 131 M7
Exeter St HIPP HX3 168 F3
  ROCH OL11 228 D4
  RPDN/SBR HX6 167 L2
Exhibition Rd SHPY BD18 82 B6
Exley Bank HIPP HX3 168 F4
Exley Bank Top HIPP HX3 168 F4
Exley Crs KGHY BD21 2 C9
Exley Dr KGHY BD21 2 D9
Exley Gdns ELL HX5 168 F5
Exley Gv KGHY BD21 79 J2
Exley La ELL HX5 168 D5
Exley Mt GTHN BD7 104 B8
  KGHY BD21 2 C9
Exley Rd KGHY BD21 2 C9
Exley St KGHY BD21 2 C9
Exley Wy KGHY BD21 79 J2
Exmoor St HFAX HX1 10 A8
Exmouth Pl BFDE BD3 5 G1
  ROCH OL11 228 C3
Exmouth Sq ROCH OL11 228 C3
Exmouth St ROCH OL11 228 C3
Express Wy NORM WF6 156 D8
Exton Pl MSTN/BAR LS15 111 H5
Eyam Cl DOD/DAR S75 260 A7
Eyres Av WOR/ARM LS12 108 E6
Eyres Gv WOR/ARM LS12 108 E6
Eyres Mill Side WOR/ARM LS12 108 D6
Eyres St WOR/ARM LS12 108 E6
Eyres Ter WOR/ARM LS12 108 E6
Eyre St BTLY WF17 173 K2
  EARL WF12 195 K2
Eyrie Ap MOR LS27 152 E3

F

Factory La BOW BD4 127 K4
Factory St BOW BD4 127 K4
Fagley Crs ECHL BD2 105 L4
Fagley Cft ECHL BD2 105 M4
Fagley Dr ECHL BD2 105 L4
Fagley La ECHL BD2 105 M3
Fagley Pl ECHL BD2 105 L5
Fagley Rd ECHL BD2 106 A4
Fagley Ter BFDE BD3 105 L5
Fair Bank SHPY BD18 82 B6
Fairbank Rd GIR BD8 104 C5
Fairbank Ter GIR BD8 104 C5
Fairbrook Rd HOR/CROF WF4 220 C2
Fairburn Dr GFTH/SHER LS25 135 J1
Fairburn Gdns ECHL BD2 105 L2
Fairclough Gv LUD/ILL HX2 146 B3
Fairfax Av BIRK/DRI BD11 151 J1
  BOW BD4 127 L5
  FEA/AMT WF7 179 L5
  KNOT WF11 181 G5
Fairfax Cl COP/BISH YO23 73 J1
  SCFT LS14 111 K3
Fairfax Crs BOW BD4 127 L5
  HIPP HX3 169 J1
Fairfax Dr LIT OL15 207 H3
Fairfax Gdns ILK LS29 61 H1
Fairfax Gv YEA LS19 62 D8
Fairfax Rd BEE/HOL LS11 8 C9
  BGLY BD16 81 H1
  CUL/QBY BD13 79 M7
  ILK LS29 61 H1
  PONT WF8 181 G6
Fairfax St AIRE BD20 35 M5
  BOW BD4 127 L5
  HWTH BD22 78 F7
  OT LS21 41 J7
  SKP/WHF BD23 16 C3
Fairfax Vw HORS LS18 85 K2
Fairfield CUL/QBY BD13 101 M6
  KNOT WF11 159 J1
Fairfield Av BRAM LS13 107 J4
  HECK WF16 173 G1
  NORM WF6 178 A3
  OSS WF5 197 H2
  PDSY/CALV LS28 107 H6
  PONT WF8 180 D6
Fairfield Cl BRAM LS13 107 K4
  CAS WF10 159 G5
  GFTH/SHER LS25 116 B7
  OSS WF5 197 H2
  RTHW LS26 154 D2
Fairfield Ct CAS WF10 158 C7
  LVSG WF15 172 B2
Fairfield Crs BRAM LS13 107 J4
  DEWS WF13 173 J5
Fairfield Dr BAIL BD17 83 G2
  HECK WF16 173 G1
  OSS WF5 197 H2
  RTHW LS26 154 D2
Fairfield Gdns OSS WF5 197 H2
  RTHW LS26 154 D2
Fairfield Gv BRAM LS13 107 K4
  RTHW LS26 154 D2
Fairfield Hl BRAM LS13 107 K4
Fairfield La GFTH/SHER LS25 160 D2
  RTHW LS26 154 D2
Fairfield Link GFTH/SHER LS25 116 B7
Fairfield Mdns DEWS WF13 173 J5
Fairfield Mt BRAM LS13 107 K4
  OSS WF5 197 H2
Fairfield Ri KBTN HD8 238 C1

Fairfield Rd BRAM LS13 107 J4
  GIR BD8 104 D5
  HECK WF16 173 G1
  LM/WK BD12 148 F3
  OSS WF5 197 G2
  TAD LS24 71 L3
Fairfields CAS WF10 159 G7
  KBTN HD8 257 H3
Fairfield Sq BRAM LS13 107 K4
Fairfields Rd HOLM/MEL HD7 253 H3
Fairfield St BOW BD4 127 M5
  BRAM LS13 107 K4
Fairfield Ter BRAM LS13 107 K4
  EARL WF12 174 B6
  OSS WF5 197 G2
Fairfield Wk OSS WF5 197 H2
Fairfield Wy TAD LS24 71 L3
Fairford Av BEE/HOL LS11 9 G9
Fairford Ter BEE/HOL LS11 9 G9
Fairhaven Gn IDLE BD10 83 L7
Fairlands St ROCH OL11 228 D4
Fairleigh Rd EARD/LOFT WF3 153 H6
Fairless Av HIPP HX3 148 C7
Fairmoor Wy HECK WF16 173 G1
Fairmount HTON BD9 104 E4
Fairmount Pk SHPY BD18 82 A7
Fairmount Ter KGHY BD21 58 B8
Fair Rd WBSY BD6 126 C5
Fair Vw LVSG WF15 172 B1
  PONT WF8 203 L1
Fairview Av BTLY WF17 151 H8
Fairview Ct BAIL BD17 82 D5
Fairview Crs BTLY WF17 151 J8
Fairview Rd BTLY WF17 151 J8
Fairview Ter HIPP HX3 10 D1
Fairway DOD/DAR S75 260 C8
  GSLY LS20 61 L5
  IDLE BD10 84 B5
  NORM WF6 178 B5
  SHPY BD18 82 B7
  WBSY BD6 126 B5
Fairway Ap NORM WF6 178 E4
Fairway Av DOD/DAR S75 242 C4
  GTHN BD7 126 B5
  NORM WF6 178 E4
Fairway Cl GFTH/SHER LS25 116 B7
  GSLY LS20 61 L6
  NORM WF6 178 E4
  WBSY BD6 126 B5
Fairway Crs HWTH BD22 78 F8
  ROY/SHW OL2 228 F8
Fairway Dr GTHN BD7 126 B4
  NORM WF6 178 E5
Fairway Gdns NORM WF6 178 E4
Fairway Gv GTHN BD7 126 B4
Fairway Mdw NORM WF6 178 E4
The Fairways AIRE BD20 57 J3
  HTON BD9 104 A1
The Fairway AL/HA/HU LS17 65 K8
  FEA/AMT WF7 179 M5
  GFTH/SHER LS25 116 B7
  HUDN HD2 192 C2
  LUD/ILL HX2 124 B7
  PDSY/CALV LS28 106 D5
  TAD LS24 71 L5
Fairway Wk GTHN BD7 126 B4
Fairweather Ms GIR BD8 104 A7
Fairy Dell BGLY BD16 81 J7
Fairy Hill La CAS WF10 180 L1
Faith St BSLYN/ROY S71 244 B8
  HEM/SK/SE WF9 246 F2
Falcon Cliffe AIRE BD20 56 E1
Falcon Cl AWLS/ASK DN6 249 K8
  OT LS21 41 J7
Falcon Dr CAS WF10 157 L8
Falconers Ride HUDS HD4 214 A8
Falcon Ms GIR BD8 103 L6
  MOR LS27 152 E3
Falcon Rd BGLY BD16 81 H1
  EARL WF12 173 L8
Falcon St BSLY S70 261 G4
  GTHN BD7 126 C1
  HIPP HX3 168 F3
  HUDS HD4 214 B5
Falhouse La EARL WF12 194 F7
Falinge Ms WHIT OL12 206 A6
Falinge Rd WHIT OL12 206 A6
Falkland Crs AL/HA/HU LS17 87 L5
Falkland Gv AL/HA/HU LS17 87 L5
Falkland Mt AL/HA/HU LS17 87 L5
Falkland Ri AL/HA/HU LS17 87 L5
Falkland Rd AL/HA/HU LS17 87 L5
  IDLE BD10 106 A2
Fall Bank Crs DOD/DAR S75 259 M6
Fall Brow Cl CLAY BD14 125 J3
Falledge La DOD/DAR S75 259 K5
Fall Head La DOD/DAR S75 259 K3
Fall Ings Rd WKFDE WF1 13 L1
Fall La EARD/LOFT WF3 153 M6
  EARL WF12 173 L8
  HIPP HX3 147 G2
  HOLM/MEL HD7 233 H2
  LVSG WF15 171 M5
  PBR HD2 26 B3
  RPDN/SBR HX6 167 M3
Fallow Cft HUDN HD2 193 H1
Fallow Fld SKP/WHF BD23 16 D1
Fallowfield Cl BOW BD4 127 L6
Fallowfield Dr BOW BD4 127 L6
Fallowfield Gdns BOW BD4 127 L5
Fallow La HWTH BD22 56 C8
Fall Park Ct BRAM LS13 107 M1
Fall Spring Gdns GTL/HWG HX4 190 A2
Fall Spring Gn GTL/HWG HX4 190 A2
Fallswood Gv BRAM LS13 107 M2
Fall Vw DOD/DAR S75 259 J6
Fall Wood St HWTH BD22 78 F8
Falmouth Av BFDE BD3 5 H2
Falmouth Cl BSLYN/ROY S71 261 M4
Falmouth Crs NORM WF6 178 D3
Falmouth Rd NORM WF6 178 D3
Falmouth St ROCH OL11 228 C1

Falsgrave Av ECHL BD2 105 M4
Faltis IDLE BD10 105 L1
Fanny La TAD LS24 71 K7
Fanny Moor Crs HUDE HD5 214 E4
Fanny Moor La HUDE HD5 214 E4
Fanny St KGHY BD21 2 E6
  SHPY BD18 82 B5
Far Bank KBTN HD8 238 C3
Farcliffe Pl GIR BD8 104 C5
Farcliffe Rd GIR BD8 104 C5
Farcliffe Ter GIR BD8 104 C5
Far Common Rd MIRF WF14 172 A6
Far Cft KBTN HD8 216 C4
Fardale ROY/SHW OL2 229 K8
Far Dene KBTN HD8 241 M6
Fardene St AIRE BD20 35 M4
Farehill Rd HUDE HD5 214 B6
Farfield Av BTLY WF17 151 H8
Far Field Av HOLM/MEL HD7 255 G5
Farfield Av PDSY/CALV LS28 106 E3
  WBSY BD6 126 A7
Farfield Ct AL/HA/HU LS17 88 A1
  GFTH/SHER LS25 112 F7
Farfield Crs WBSY BD6 126 B5
Far Field Dr HOLM/MEL HD7 255 G4
Farfield Dr PDSY/CALV LS28 106 E4
Farfield Gv PDSY/CALV LS28 106 E3
  WBSY BD6 126 B5
Far Field La BSLYN/ROY S71 244 A8
  HOLM/MEL HD7 255 G5
Farfield Ri BAIL BD17 82 F4
  HUDE HD5 215 H3
  SHPY BD18 82 C7
  WBSY BD6 126 C7
Far Fields La HOLM/MEL HD7 235 H1
Farfield St CLECK BD19 149 M5
  HTON BD9 104 C4
Farfield Ter HTON BD9 104 C4
Farlands Ri MILN OL16 228 C3
Far La HBR HX7 144 C4
  HOLM/MEL HD7 255 G6
Farlea Dr ECHL BD2 105 L3
Farleton Dr ECHL BD2 105 M4
Farley Crs HWTH BD22 78 D3
Farm Cl BSLYN/ROY S71 261 L2
Farm Ct AWLS/ASK DN6 249 L8
  MSTN/BAR LS15 111 K4
Farm Cft FEA/AMT WF7 201 G1
  SKP/WHF BD23 16 B5
Far Mead Cft ILK LS29 40 A7
Farmfield Dr HEM/SK/SE WF9 223 J3
Farm Gdns FEA/AMT WF7 201 G1
Farm Hill Crs CHAL LS7 109 J1
Farm Hl North CHAL LS7 87 J8
Farm Hill Rd IDLE BD10 105 K1
  MOR LS27 152 A1
Farm Hl South CHAL LS7 109 J1
Farm Hill Wy CHAL LS7 109 J1
Farm House La DOD/DAR S75 260 C4
Farm La HEM/SK/SE WF9 223 J4
Farm Mt MSTN/BAR LS15 111 J4
Far Moss AL/HA/HU LS17 87 J1
Farm Pond Dr BRIG HD6 170 A1
Farm Rd BSLY S70 261 L8
  FEA/AMT WF7 201 M1
  MSTN/BAR LS15 111 K4
Farmstead Rd IDLE BD10 83 L8
Farm Wk LIT OL15 207 H1
  MILN OL16 206 E5
Farm Wy WMB/DAR S73 263 J8
Farnboro St TOD OL14 163 J4
Farndale Ap SCFT LS14 111 L1
Farndale Cl SCFT LS14 111 L1
  WBY LS22 29 K8
Farndale Ct GFTH/SHER LS25 135 K1
Farndale Garth SCFT LS14 89 L8
Farndale Pl SCFT LS14 89 L8
Farndale Rd BAIL BD17 82 C4
  WIL/AL BD15 102 E2
Farne Av WKFDW/WTN WF2 198 B1
Farnham Cl BAIL BD17 82 F2
  SCFT LS14 89 K5
Farnham Cft SCFT LS14 89 K5
Farnham Rd GTHN BD7 126 C1
Farnham Wy HOR/CROF WF4 200 D3
Farnlee HUDW HD3 191 K5
Farnley Cl ILK LS29 61 J2
Farnley La OT LS21 23 L8
Farnley Pk OT LS21 42 A3
Farnley Rd HUDS HD4 215 H8
  ILK LS29 61 K2
Farnley Vw BIRK/DRI BD11 129 J8
Farrar Av MIRF WF14 172 B8
Farrar Ct BRAM LS13 107 L3
Farrar Cft BHP/TINH LS16 86 C2
Farrar Dr MIRF WF14 172 A7
Farrar Gv BHP/TINH LS16 86 C2
Farrar Height La
  RPDN/SBR HX6 188 D2
Farrar La BHP/TINH LS16 86 C2
Farrar Mill La HIPP HX3 168 F3
Far Reef Cl HORS LS18 85 L4
Farrer La RTHW LS26 155 L1
Far Richard Cl OSS WF5 174 F7
Farriers Cft ECHL BD2 105 H2
Farriers Pl CAS WF10 158 D8
Farringdon Cl BOW BD4 128 A2
Farringdon Dr BOW BD4 128 A3
Farringdon Gv WBSY BD6 126 C7
Farrow Bank WOR/ARM LS12 108 A7
Farrow Cl DOD/DAR S75 260 C4
Farrowdale Av ROY/SHW OL2 229 K8
Farrow Gn WOR/ARM LS12 108 A7
Farrow Hl WOR/ARM LS12 108 A7
Farrow Rd WOR/ARM LS12 108 B7
Farrow St ROY/SHW OL2 229 K8
Farrow St East ROY/SHW OL2 229 K8
Farrow V WOR/ARM LS12 108 A7
Farside Gn WBOW BD5 126 E3
Fartown PDSY/CALV LS28 129 L5
Fartown Cl PDSY/CALV LS28 129 L5
Far Townend DOD/DAR S75 260 C7
Fartown Green Rd HUDN HD2 192 D3
Far View Bank HUDE HD5 215 G1
Farway BOW BD4 128 A2
Far Well Fold YEA LS19 84 F3

Far Well La HOLM/MEL HD7 .... 237 K6
Faugh La HBR HX7 .... 120 E8
Faulkner St MILN OL16 .... 206 B7 3
Favell Av NORM WF6 .... 178 D5
Faversham Wk BOW BD4 .... 128 A2 3
Favordale Rd COL BB8 .... 52 C8
Fawcett Av WOR/ARM LS12 .... 130 C1
Fawcett Bank WOR/ARM LS12 .... 130 C1
Fawcett Cl WOR/ARM LS12 .... 130 C1
Fawcett Ct WOR/ARM LS12 .... 130 C1
Fawcett Gdns WOR/ARM LS12 .... 130 C1
Fawcett La WOR/ARM LS12 .... 130 C1
Fawcett Pl BOW BD4 .... 127 L6
Fawcett Rd WOR/ARM LS12 .... 130 C1 4
Fawcett V WOR/ARM LS12 .... 130 C1
Fawcett Wy WOR/ARM LS12 .... 130 C1
Fawkes Dr OT LS21 .... 40 F8
Faxfleet St WBOW BD5 .... 126 F5
Faye Gdns BOW BD4 .... 127 M5
Fearnley Av OSS WF5 .... 174 E7
Fearnley Cl HUDE HD5 .... 108 F7
Fearnley Cl HOLM/MEL HD7 .... 254 E7
Fearnley Dr OSS WF5 .... 174 E7
Fearnley La HOLM/MEL HD7 .... 254 E7
Fearnley Pl HUDE HD5 .... 108 F7
Fearnley St DEWS WF13 .... 173 K7 2
FEA/AMT WF7 .... 201 L1
Fearnside's Cl HOR/CROF WF4 .. 197 L3
Fearnsides St GIR BD8 .... 104 D6
Fearnsides Ter GIR BD8 .... 104 D6 3
Fearnville Av RHAY LS8 .... 110 F3
Fearnville Cl RHAY LS8 .... 110 F2
Fearnville Dr BOW BD4 .... 127 M1 6
RHAY LS8 .... 110 F2
Fearnville Gv BSLYN/ROY S71 .... 243 L3
RHAY LS8 .... 110 F1
Fearnville Mt RHAY LS8 .... 110 F1
Fearnville Pl RHAY LS8 .... 111 G1
Fearnville Rd RHAY LS8 .... 110 F2
Fearnville Ter RHAY LS8 .... 111 G1
Fearnville Vw RHAY LS8 .... 110 F2
Feast Fld HWTH BD22 .... 85 K5
Featherbank Av HORS LS18 .... 85 K7
Featherbank La HORS LS18 .... 85 K6 3
Featherbank Ter HORS LS18 .... 85 K7 2
Featherbank Wk HORS LS18 .... 85 K7 3
Featherbed Cl GTL/HWG HX4 .... 168 F8 3
Feather Bed La LIT HX24 .... 168 F8
Featherbed La TAD LS24 .... 31 M8
Feather Rd BFDE BD3 .... 5 L5
Featherstall Rd LIT OL15 .... 207 H1
Featherstone La FEA/AMT WF7 .. 179 M4
Federation St WBOW BD5 .... 127 H4 5
Felcote Av HUDE HD5 .... 215 C1
Felcourt Dr BOW BD4 .... 128 A4
Felcourt Fold BOW BD4 .... 128 A4 8
Felinfach CUD/GR S72 .... 244 D3
Felks Stile Rd HUDS HD4 .... 213 H4
Fell Crs HWTH BD22 .... 2 A8
Fell Greave Crs HUDN HD2 .... 192 E1
Fell Greave Rd HUDN HD2 .... 192 D1
Fell Gv HUDN HD2 .... 192 D1
HWTH BD22 .... 2 A7
Fell La HWTH BD22 .... 2 B7
Fellowsides La OSS WF5 .... 197 G1
Fellside TOD OL14 .... 164 D1 3
Fellside Cl WBOW BD5 .... 127 H4
Fellwood Av HWTH BD22 .... 79 G6
Fellwood Cl HWTH BD22 .... 79 G6 3
Felnex Cl OSM LS9 .... 132 E1
Felnex Crs OSM LS9 .... 132 E1
Felnex Rd OSM LS9 .... 132 E1
Felnex Sq OSM LS9 .... 132 E1
Fenay Bankside KBTN HD8 .... 215 M3
Fenay Bridge Rd HUDE HD5 .... 215 L2
Fenay Crs HUDE HD5 .... 215 L3
Fenay Dr KBTN HD8 .... 215 L3
Fenay La HUDE HD5 .... 215 L3
KBTN HD8 .... 215 L3
Fenay Lea Dr HUDE HD5 .... 215 L2
Fenby Av BOW BD4 .... 127 K2
Fenby Cl BOW BD4 .... 127 L3 4
Fenby Gdns BOW BD4 .... 127 L3 5
Fenby Gv BOW BD4 .... 127 L2
Fencote Crs ECHL BD2 .... 105 M3
Fender Rd WBSY BD6 .... 126 B5 2
Fennec Rd BAIL BD17 .... 57 M4
Fenton Av RTHW LS26 .... 133 K7
Fenton Cl HEM/SK/SE WF9 .... 246 D5 5
RTHW LS26 .... 133 K7
Fenton La GFTH/SHER LS25 .... 116 E4
Fenton Ms ROCH OL11 .... 228 A1 2
Fenton Rd EARD/LOFT WF3 .... 155 H7
HFAX HX1 .... 10 A9
HUD HD1 .... 214 B3
Fentonsgate EARD/LOFT WF3 .. 154 E5 3
Fenton Sq HUD HD1 .... 14 C9
Fenton St BSLY S70 .... 261 L5 2
EARD/LOFT WF3 .... 153 H5
ILK LS29 .... 40 B5
LDSU LS2 .... 6 F6
MIRF WF14 .... 194 C2
ROCH OL11 .... 228 A1
Fenwick Dr WBSY BD6 .... 126 B8
Fenwick Rd ROCH OL11 .... 206 A7 3
Ferguson St HFAX HX1 .... 11 G7
Fern Av HOLM/MEL HD7 .... 234 C3
Fern Bank AWLS/ASK DN6 .... 249 K8
Fernbank BRAM LS13 .... 107 H3
Fernbank Av HWTH BD22 .... 79 H3
Fernbank Cl BRAM LS13 .... 107 H3
Fernbank Dr BAIL BD17 .... 82 C5
BGLY BD16 .... 81 J3
BRAM LS13 .... 107 H3
Fernbank Gdns BRAM LS13 .... 107 H3
Fernbank Pl BRAM LS13 .... 107 H3
Fernbank Rd BFDE BD3 .... 5 L2
BRAM LS13 .... 107 H3
Fern Cha SCFT LS14 .... 67 J7
Ferncliffe Dr AIRE BD20 .... 57 H4
Ferncliffe Rd BGLY BD16 .... 81 J3
SHPY BD18 .... 82 B6 7

Ferncliffe Ter BRAM LS13 .... 107 K4
Fern Cl BTLY WF17 .... 174 A1
Fern Ct AIRE BD20 .... 57 J4
Fern Cft SHPY WF15 .... 171 L2
SCFT LS14 .... 67 J7
WKFDW/WTN WF2 .... 176 A3
Ferndale Av CLAY BD14 .... 125 J3
MILN OL16 .... 228 E5
Ferndale Gv HTON BD9 .... 104 E2
Ferndale Pl HEM/SK/SE WF9 .... 223 L8
Ferndene BGLY BD16 .... 81 K3
Ferndown Gn WBOW BD5 .... 126 F3 6
Ferney Lee Rd TOD OL14 .... 141 J8
Fernhill BGLY BD16 .... 81 J1
Fern Hill Av SHPY BD18 .... 82 B7
Fern Hill Gv SHPY BD18 .... 82 B7 3
Fern Hill Mt SHPY BD18 .... 82 B7
Fern Hill Rd SHPY BD18 .... 82 B7 2
Fernhurst Cl MIRF WF14 .... 172 C8 1
Fernhurst Crs MIRF WF14 .... 172 D8 8
Fernhurst Lea MIRF WF14 .... 172 D8 2
Fernhurst Rd MIRF WF14 .... 172 C8
Fernhurst Wy MIRF WF14 .... 172 C8 3
Fernlea RTHW LS26 .... 133 H8
Fernlea Cl HECK WF16 .... 173 G3
HOR/CROF WF4 .... 200 C5
Fernlea Gv HOLM/MEL HD7 .... 213 G3
Fern Lea Rd HUDW HD3 .... 191 J5
Fern Lea Gv SHPY BD18 .... 82 B7
Fern Lea Vw PDSY/CALV LS28 .... 128 C8
Fernleigh Ct WKFDW/WTN WF2 .. 198 B1
Fernley Gdns LM/WK BD12 .... 148 E2
Fernley Green Cl KNOT WF11 .... 182 D2
Fernley Green Rd KNOT WF11 .... 182 D2
Fernley Hill Dr NORM WF6 .... 178 B1
Fernside Av HUDE HD5 .... 215 H2
Fernside Cl HUDE HD5 .... 215 J1
Fernside Crs HUDE HD5 .... 215 H1
Fern St BOW BD4 .... 127 M3 2
COL BB8 .... 52 B8
HIPP HX3 .... 146 D4 6
HUDN HD2 .... 14 C2
KGHY BD21 .... 3 G2
WHIT OL12 .... 184 E8
Fern Ter PDSY/CALV LS28 .... 107 G4
Fern Wy SCFT LS14 .... 67 J7
Fernwood RHAY LS8 .... 88 C5
Ferrand Av BOW BD4 .... 127 L5
Ferrand Rd BGLY BD16 .... 81 H3
CLECK BD19 .... 150 C5
Ferrand Ldg LIT OL15 .... 185 L7 2
Ferrand Rd LIT OL15 .... 185 K8
Ferrands Park Wy BGLY BD16 .... 80 D5
Ferrand St BGLY BD16 .... 81 H3
Ferrara Cl ECHL BD2 .... 105 M3
Ferrybridge By-pass
KNOT WF11 .... 181 L2
Ferrybridge Rd CAS WF10 .... 158 A6
KNOT WF11 .... 181 M1
PONT WF8 .... 181 L3
Ferry La EARD/LOFT WF3 .... 177 H4
Ferry Moor La CUD/GR S72 .... 244 F8
Ferry Top La HOR/CROF WF4 .... 222 C3
Festival St SHPY BD18 .... 82 F8
Fewston Av OSM LS9 .... 110 B8
WKFDE WF1 .... 177 H6
Fewston Ct OSM LS9 .... 110 B8
Fiddle La GTL/HWG HX4 .... 189 J3
RPDN/SBR HX6 .... 189 H2
Fidler La GFTH/SHER LS25 .... 113 C2
Field Cl HECK WF16 .... 150 F8
WMB/DAR S73 .... 263 J8
Fieldcroft Ct MIRF WF14 .... 194 B1 3
Field Dr CUD/GR S72 .... 262 D1
TAD LS24 .... 72 B1
Fieldedge La AIRE BD20 .... 58 C4
Field End MSTN/BAR LS15 .... 111 J7
Field End Cl MSTN/BAR LS15 .... 111 J7 8
Field End Ct MSTN/BAR LS15 .... 111 J7 9
Field End Crs MSTN/BAR LS15 .... 111 J7
Field End Gdns MSTN/BAR LS15 .. 111 J7
Field End Garth
MSTN/BAR LS15 .... 111 J7
Field End Gn MSTN/BAR LS15 .... 111 J7 6
Field End Gv MSTN/BAR LS15 .... 111 K6 6
Field End La HOLM/MEL HD7 .... 236 C2
HOLM/MEL HD7 .... 253 K4
Field End Mt MSTN/BAR LS15 .... 111 J7
Field End Rd MSTN/BAR LS15 .... 111 J7
Fieldens Pl BTLY WF17 .... 151 J8 4
Fielden Sq TOD OL14 .... 163 K2 3
Fielden St TOD OL14 .... 142 A8
Fieldgate Rd IDLE BD10 .... 83 M7
Field Head HOLM/MEL HD7 .... 212 F1
Field Head La PONT WF8 .... 181 H5
Fieldhead Ct BSPA/BRAM LS23 .. 48 F7
Fieldhead Crs BTLY WF17 .... 151 G3
Fieldhead Dr AIRE BD20 .... 34 F8
CSLY LS20 .... 61 M6
MSTN/BAR LS15 .... 91 H7
Fieldhead Gdns EARL WF12 .... 174 D3
Field Head La BIRK/DRI BD11 .... 151 G2
BTLY WF17 .... 151 G4
HBR HX7 .... 165 K2
HWTH BD22 .... 100 C1
LUD/ILL HX2 .... 123 M7
Fieldhead La HOLM/MEL HD7 .... 253 H5
Fieldhead Paddock
BSPA/BRAM LS23 .... 48 E6
Fieldhead Rd CSLY LS20 .... 61 L6
Fieldhead St GTHN BD7 .... 104 D8
Fieldhead Wy LVSG WF15 .... 172 E1
Fieldhouse Cl AL/HA/HU LS17 .... 87 L4
Field House Dr WBY LS22 .... 47 L1
Fieldhouse Dr AL/HA/HU LS17 .... 87 L4
HOLM/MEL HD7 .... 212 C4
Fieldhouse Gv
PDSY/CALV LS28 .... 106 E4 2
Fieldhouse Lawn AL/HA/HU LS17.. 87 L4
Field House Rd HUD HD1 .... 15 J1
WHIT OL12 .... 206 B4
Fieldhouse St WKFDE WF1 .... 13 L9
Fieldhouse Wk AL/HA/HU LS17 .. 87 L4 1
AL/HA/HU LS17 .... 87 L4 1
Field Hurst CLECK BD19 .... 149 H7

GTL/HWG HX4 .... 189 K1
Fieldhurst Ct BOW BD4 .... 127 K6
Fielding Ga WOR/ARM LS12 .... 108 F7
Fielding Gate Ms
WOR/ARM LS12 .... 108 F6
Field La BRIG HD6 .... 170 B6
BSLY S70 .... 262 A7
BTLY WF17 .... 173 L2
DEWS WF13 .... 172 F8
GFTH/SHER LS25 .... 92 B6
HEM/SK/SE WF9 .... 225 J7
HEM/SK/SE WF9 .... 247 M2
HUDS HD4 .... 215 H8
OSS WF5 .... 174 F8
STKB/PEN S36 .... 269 M5
Field Pl WKFDW/WTN WF2 .... 12 A4
Field Rd HOLM/MEL HD7 .... 254 D2
MILN OL16 .... 206 F7
Fields End STKB/PEN S36 .... 271 K6
Fieldshead Bungalows
HOLM/MEL HD7 .... 212 C7
Fieldside CUL/QBY BD13 .... 79 M8
Field Side HFAX HX1 .... 10 A3
Fieldside Rd HEM/SK/SE WF9 .. 223 K4
Fields Ri HUDE HD5 .... 193 K5
Fields Rd KBTN HD8 .... 215 M3 2
LM/WK BD12 .... 149 G1
The Fields EARD/LOFT WF3 .... 154 F5
Field St BFD BD1 .... 5 K4
DEWS WF13 .... 173 G8 4
ROCH OL11 .... 228 C2 3
Fields Wy HUDE HD5 .... 193 K5
Field Ter MSTN/BAR LS15 .... 111 J6 3
Field Top Rd BRIG HD6 .... 170 B4
Field Wy KBTN HD8 .... 238 A6
Fieldway CLAY BD14 .... 125 K2
ILK LS29 .... 39 G2
MILN OL16 .... 228 D3
Fieldway Av BRAM LS13 .... 107 J2
Fieldway Cha RTHW LS26 .... 155 M1
Fieldway Cl BRAM LS13 .... 107 J2
Fieldway Ri BRAM LS13 .... 107 H2
Fife St BSLY S70 .... 260 F6 3
Fifth Av BFDE BD3 .... 105 L5
RTHW LS26 .... 133 J8
Fifth Av West LVSG WF15 .... 171 K2
Filbert St HUDN HD2 .... 14 E2
Filey Av BSLYN/ROY S71 .... 243 M2
Filey St BFD BD1 .... 5 H7
BFDE BD3 .... 5 H7
MILN OL16 .... 206 E4
Filley Royd CLECK BD19 .... 149 M8
Fillingfir Dr BHP/TINH S16 .... 86 B6
Fillingfir Rd BHP/TINH S16 .... 86 B6
Fillingfir Wk BHP/TINH S16 .... 86 B6
Finance St LIT OL15 .... 207 H2 1
Finch Av WKFDW/WTN WF2.. 220 F1
Finching Gv MIRF WF14 .... 172 C6 2
Finchley St WBOW BD5 .... 126 F3 8
Finchley Wy MOR LS27 .... 152 C3 1
Finch St WBOW BD5 .... 126 F2
Findon Ter IDLE BD10 .... 106 A2
Fine Garth Cl BSPA/BRAM LS23 .. 69 M3
Finghall Rd AWLS/ASK DN6 .... 249 H4
Fink Hl HORS LS18 .... 85 J6
Finkil St BRIG HD6 .... 170 A1
Finkin Av EARD/LOFT WF3 .... 177 G4
Finkin Cft EARD/LOFT WF3 .... 177 G4
Finkin La EARD/LOFT WF3 .... 177 G4
Finkle Hl GFTH/SHER LS25 .... 116 A5
Finkle La MOR LS27 .... 129 J8
Finkle St HOR/CROF WF4 .... 220 B7
LUD/ILL HX2 .... 166 F2
PONT WF8 .... 180 F5 2
Finsbury Dr ECHL BD2 .... 105 H1 3
Finsbury Rd LDS LS1 .... 6 E6
Finthorpe La HUDE HD5 .... 215 J3
Fir Av MIRF WF14 .... 194 F1
Firbank Gn ECHL BD2 .... 105 M3 2
Firbank Gv MSTN/BAR LS15 .... 111 G8
Fir Bank Rd ROY/SHW OL2 .... 228 F8
Firbarn Cl MILN OL16 .... 206 F7
Firbeck BGLY BD16 .... 80 D3
Firbeck Rd BSPA/BRAM LS23 .. 69 M3
Firethorn Cl GIR BD8 .... 104 C6 3
Firgrove Av MILN OL16 .... 206 F6
Firgrove Gdns MILN OL16 .... 206 F6
Firham Cl BSLYN/ROY S71 .... 243 J2
Fir La ROY/SHW OL2 .... 228 F8
Fir Pde DEWS WF13 .... 194 F1
Firs La HUDW HD3 .... 191 M4
Firs La STKB/PEN S36 .... 257 M7
First Av AL/HA/HU LS17 .... 68 A1
BFDE BD3 .... 105 L5
HEM/SK/SE WF9 .... 223 J2
HEM/SK/SE WF9 .... 225 J7
HIPP HX3 .... 168 D2
HOR/CROF WF4 .... 197 H5
HUDE HD5 .... 193 H7 4
KGHY BD21 .... 2 E7 3
LVSG WF15 .... 171 L1
PDSY/CALV LS28 .... 107 G5
RTHW LS26 .... 133 H7
WBY LS22 .... 48 B1
WKFDE WF1 .... 176 D4
WOR/ARM LS12 .... 108 F7
YEA LS19 .... 84 E1
The Firs BSLY S70 .... 261 L8
BSLYN/ROY S71 .... 243 J2
SCFT LS14 .... 67 L7
Fir St HWTH BD22 .... 78 E8 3
KGHY BD21 .... 79 K2
TOD OL14 .... 163 J6
Firth Av BEE/HOL LS11 .... 131 J4
BRIG HD6 .... 170 C3
CUD/GR S72 .... 262 C1
Firthcliffe Dr LVSG WF15 .... 172 D1 6
Firthcliffe Gv LVSG WF15 .... 172 D1 5
Firthcliffe La LVSG WF15 .... 172 D1
Firthcliffe Mt LVSG WF15 .... 172 D1 2
Firthcliffe Pde LVSG WF15 .... 172 D1
Firthcliffe Pl LVSG WF15 .... 172 E1 4
Firthcliffe Rd LVSG WF15 .... 172 D1
Firthcliffe Ter LVSG WF15 .... 172 D1 3
Firthcliffe Vw LVSG WF15 .... 172 D1 1
Firthcliffe Wk LVSG WF15 .... 172 D1

Firth Cl EARD/LOFT WF3 .... 177 G1 3
Firthfield La HEM/SK/SE WF9 .. 225 G2
Firthfields GFTH/SHER LS25 .... 113 J2 7
Firth Gv BEE/HOL LS11 .... 131 J4
Firth House La BRIG HD6 .... 170 D7
GTL/HWG HX4 .... 189 L6
Firth La WIL/AL BD15 .... 102 E1
Firth Mt BEE/HOL LS11 .... 131 J4
Firth Rd BEE/HOL LS11 .... 131 J4
HTON BD9 .... 104 C3 2
Firth St BRIG HD6 .... 170 C5
CHAL LS7 .... 7 K6
CUL/QBY BD13 .... 102 F8
KBTN HD8 .... 238 A6
SKP/WHF BD23 .... 16 C4
Firth Ter OSM LS9 .... 7 L6
Firth Vw BEE/HOL LS11 .... 131 J4
Fir Tree Ap AL/HA/HU LS17 .... 87 K3
Firtree Av GFTH/SHER LS25 .... 113 K8
Fir Tree Cl AL/HA/HU LS17 .... 87 L2
Firtree Crs TAD LS24 .... 71 K4
Fir Tree Dr AWLS/ASK DN6 .... 227 L3
IDLE BD10 .... 83 M8 8
Fir Tree Gn AL/HA/HU LS17 .... 87 L2
Fir Tree Gv AL/HA/HU LS17 .... 87 L3
Fir Tree La AL/HA/HU LS17 .... 87 L3
Fir Tree Ri AL/HA/HU LS17 .... 87 L3
Fir Tree Vw AL/HA/HU LS17 .... 87 L2
Firville Av NORM WF6 .... 178 C5
Firville Crs NORM WF6 .... 178 C5
Fir Wk DEWS WF13 .... 194 F1 8
Firwood Cl TOD OL14 .... 163 J3
Fishbeck La AIRE BD20 .... 36 C2
Fish Dam La BSLYN/ROY S71 .. 243 M5
Fishergate KNOT WF11 .... 181 M1
Fisher Gn HOLM/MEL HD7 .... 236 A2
Fisher Gv OSS WF5 .... 197 H2
Fisher St KNOT WF11 .... 182 A2
Fisher Wy HECK WF16 .... 173 G3
Fishponds Dr HOR/CROF WF4 .. 220 B1
Fishponds Dr HOR/CROF WF4 .. 220 B1
Fishwick St MILN OL16 .... 206 C8
Fitton St MILN OL16 .... 206 C8
ROY/SHW OL2 .... 229 H7
Fitts La AL/HA/HU LS17 .... 45 J6
Fitzroy Dr RHAY LS8 .... 88 C3
Fitzroy Rd BFDE BD3 .... 5 M6
Fitzwilliam Rd WMB/DAR S73 .. 263 L8
Fitzwilliam St BOW BD4 .... 5 G9
BSLY S70 .... 260 F5
HEM/SK/SE WF9 .... 223 K5
HUD HD1 .... 14 D6
Five Acres DOD/DAR S75 .... 259 H1
Five Lane Ends
HOLM/MEL HD7 .... 254 A1 4
Five Oaks BAIL BD17 .... 82 C4
Fixby Av LUD/ILL HX2 .... 168 A1
Fixby La EARL WF12 .... 194 F8
Fixby Park Dr HUDN HD2 .... 192 A4
Fixby Rd HUDN HD2 .... 192 B1
Flagship Sq EARL WF12 .... 174 C4
Flannel St WHIT OL12 .... 206 C6 8
Flanshaw Av WKFDW/WTN WF2.. 176 A8
Flanshaw Crs
WKFDW/WTN WF2 .... 176 A8
Flanshaw Gv WKFDW/WTN WF2.. 176 A8
Flanshaw La WKFDW/WTN WF2 .. 175 M8
Flanshaw Rd
WKFDW/WTN WF2 .... 176 A8
Flanshaw St WKFDW/WTN WF2 .. 176 A8
Flanshaw Vw
WKFDW/WTN WF2 .... 176 A8
Flanshaw Wy
WKFDW/WTN WF2 .... 175 L7
Flasby St KGHY BD21 .... 3 G2
Flash La MIRF WF14 .... 172 D8
Flass La CAS WF10 .... 179 L2
Flat Nook BGLY BD16 .... 81 K3 6
Flats La MSTN/BAR LS15 .... 90 F8
Flavell Cl HEM/SK/SE WF9 .. 246 D5 8
Flawith Dr ECHL BD2 .... 105 M4
Flaxen Ct WBSY BD6 .... 126 F5 8
Flax Meadow HUDW HD3 .... 191 J4
Flax Pl OSM LS9 .... 9 L2
Flaxton Gn ECHL BD2 .... 105 M4
Flaxton Pl GTHN BD7 .... 104 D8
Flaxton St BEE/HOL LS11 .... 8 E9
Flaxton Vw BEE/HOL LS11 .... 8 F9
Fledborough Rd WBY LS22 .... 47 L1
Fleece St BSPA/BRAM LS23 .. 48 D1
WBSY BD6 .... 126 B7
Fleet Hill Crs BSLYN/ROY S71 .. 261 J1
Fleet La CUL/QBY BD13 .... 124 F5
RTHW LS26 .... 156 C2
Fleet St KBTN HD8 .... 239 M5
Fleet Thro Rd HORS LS18 .... 85 K8
Fleetwood Av BSLYN/ROY S71 .. 261 L1
Fleminghouse La HUDE HD5 .... 215 J1
Fleming Pl BSLY S70 .... 261 G6 7
Fleming St BTLY WF17 .... 173 L1 10
Fletcher Av AIRE BD20 .... 36 A1 10
Fletcher Crs BRIG HD6 .... 170 A8 1
Fletcher La SHPY BD18 .... 104 F1
Fletcher Rd WBSY BD6 .... 126 D5 3
Fletton Ter ECHL BD2 .... 105 K4 4
Flexbury Av MOR LS27 .... 152 C3
Flight Hl HOLM/MEL HD7 .... 267 L1
Flight House Rd RPDN/SBR HX6.. 188 B2
Flint La HOLM/MEL HD7 .... 268 C1
Flintmill La BSPA/BRAM LS23 .. 48 F3
Flinton Gv ECHL BD2 .... 105 M4
Flint St HUDN HD2 .... 15 G1
Flockton Av BOW BD4 .... 127 J2 7
Flockton Cl BOW BD4 .... 127 J2
Flockton Dr BOW BD4 .... 127 J2
Flockton Gv BOW BD4 .... 127 J2 9
Flockton Rd BOW BD4 .... 127 J2
KBTN HD8 .... 238 D3 9
Floral Av CHAL LS7 .... 87 L6
Floreat Cl BTLY WF17 .... 151 G4
Florence Av OSM LS9 .... 110 C4 9
WIL/AL BD15 .... 80 D8
Florence Gv OSM LS9 .... 110 C4
Florence Mt OSM LS9 .... 110 C4 12

Florence Pl OSM LS9 .... 110 C4 13
Florence Steet MILN OL16 .... 206 D8
Florence St BFDE BD3 .... 105 L8
CAS WF10 .... 157 M6 2
HFAX HX1 .... 10 C7
OSM LS9 .... 110 C4
Florence Ter MOR LS27 .... 152 D2 6
Florida Rd WIL/AL BD15 .... 103 J2
Florist St KGHY BD21 .... 3 M1
Flounders Hl FEA/AMT WF7 .... 202 A8
Flower Acre ELL HX5 .... 169 H8 6
Flower Bank ECHL BD2 .... 105 H2 3
RPDN/SBR HX6 .... 167 H5 3
Flower Cl YEA LS19 .... 62 C7
Flower Cft HWTH BD22 .... 2 B9
Flower Garth IDLE BD10 .... 83 M8
Flower Hvn HTON BD9 .... 103 M2 6
Flower Hl HTON BD9 .... 104 D3
Flowerlands HIPP HX3 .... 148 A5
Flower Scar Rd TOD OL14 .... 140 A8
Floyd St WBOW BD5 .... 126 D3
Flush LVSG WF15 .... 172 D2
Flush House La HOLM/MEL HD7.. 253 J3
Fold Grassmoor
HOLM/MEL HD7 .... 236 C3
Foldings Av CLECK BD19 .... 149 H6
Foldings Cl CLECK BD19 .... 149 G6
Foldings Ct CLECK BD19 .... 149 G6 1
Foldings Gv CLECK BD19 .... 149 G6
Foldings Pde CLECK BD19 .... 149 G6
Foldings Rd CLECK BD19 .... 149 G6
The Foldings KBTN HD8 .... 239 J4 3
Fold La HBR HX7 .... 120 C8
HWTH BD22 .... 54 E3
The Fold MSTN/BAR LS15 .... 112 A2
Foljambe St WKFDW/WTN WF2 .. 12 F6
BFDE BD3 .... 105 L7
Folkestone St BFDE BD3 .... 5 M5 3
Folkton Holme ECHL BD2 .... 105 M4
Follett Av HUDS HD4 .... 213 L4
Follifoot La PBR HG3 .... 27 J6
Follifoot Rd PBR HG3 .... 27 G2
Follingworth La
HOLM/MEL HD7 .... 211 L5
Follingworth Rd BTLY WF17 .... 174 A1
Folly Hall Av WBSY BD6 .... 126 D6
Folly Hall Gdns WBSY BD6 .. 126 D6 1
Folly Hall La HBR HX7 .... 165 M4
Folly Hall Rd EARD/LOFT WF3 .. 153 G6
Folly Hall Wy WBSY BD6 .... 126 D6 2
Folly La BEE/HOL LS11 .... 8 E8
BSPA/BRAM LS23 .... 69 M4
STKB/PEN S36 .... 257 H8
Folly Rd HUDN HD2 .... 192 C3
Folly Vw BSPA/BRAM LS23 .... 69 M4
Folly View Rd HWTH BD22 .... 78 F4 3
Folly Wk WHIT OL12 .... 206 B5
Fontmell Cl BOW BD4 .... 128 A4 2
Football Sq LS19 .... 62 E8
Forber Gv BOW BD4 .... 128 A3 7
Forber Pl MSTN/BAR LS15 .... 111 G7
Ford CUL/QBY BD13 .... 124 E6
Ford Dr MIRF WF14 .... 194 A1
Ford Hl CUL/QBY BD13 .... 124 E6
Ford St HEM/SK/SE WF9 .... 223 K5
KGHY BD21 .... 3 L1
Fore La RPDN/SBR HX6 .... 167 J3
Fore Lane Av RPDN/SBR HX6 .. 167 H3
Foreside Bottom La
CUL/QBY BD13 .... 123 M2
Foreside La CUL/QBY BD13 .... 123 K1
Forest Av LUD/ILL HX2 .... 146 A3
Forest Bank MOR LS27 .... 129 L7
Forest Cl WKFDE WF1 .... 177 G5
Forest Crs LUD/ILL HX2 .... 146 A2
Forest Ga OT LS21 .... 41 J7
Forest Gn LUD/ILL HX2 .... 146 A3
Forest Hill Gdns HUDW HD3 .. 190 C6 3
Forest Hill Rd GTL/HWG HX4 .. 189 M5
Forest Rdg EARD/LOFT WF3 .... 153 L2
Forest Rd BSLYN/ROY S71 .... 243 H6 2
HUDE HD5 .... 215 G1
Forest Wy HOLM/MEL HD7 .... 236 A2
Forge Gn PBR HG3 .... 28 A1
Forge Hill La KNOT WF11 .... 182 A1
Forge La AL/HA/HU LS17 .... 66 F5
EARL WF12 .... 195 K2
HOR/CROF WF4 .... 197 L6
LVSG WF15 .... 172 D4
WOR/ARM LS12 .... 108 F6
Forge Rw WOR/ARM LS12 .... 129 M3
Forge Vw AIRE BD20 .... 56 E1 7
Forman's Dr EARD/LOFT WF3 .. 154 C3 1
Formby Av HUDN HD2 .... 192 D2
Formby Gv BSLYN/ROY S71 .. 243 M8 2
Forrest Av HUDW HD3 .... 191 M7
Forrester Cl HEM/SK/SE WF9 .. 223 J3
Forrester Dr ROY/SHW OL2 .. 229 M6 3
Forrester's Cl AWLS/ASK DN6 .. 227 L3
Forster Ct BFD BD1 .... 4 C5
Forster Dr HECK WF16 .... 173 G3 3
Forster Pl WOR/ARM LS12 .... 130 C2
Forster Sq BFD BD1 .... 5 G6
Forster St HUD HD1 .... 9 L6
Forsythia Av EARD/LOFT WF3 .. 153 L7
Fort Ann Rd BTLY WF17 .... 174 B2
Fortis Wy HUDW HD3 .... 191 G6
Fortshot La AL/HA/HU LS17 .... 66 D5
Forum Vw PONT WF8 .... 225 J1 1
Foss Av WBY LS22 .... 29 M7
Fosse Wy GFTH/SHER LS25 .... 113 K8
Foster Av AIRE BD20 .... 35 M4
CUL/QBY BD13 .... 103 H8
HUDS HD4 .... 213 L4
NORM WF6 .... 178 C5
Foster Cl ILK LS29 .... 40 B6
MOR LS27 .... 152 C1 5
Foster Crs MOR LS27 .... 152 C1 5
Foster La HBR HX7 .... 143 J2
Foster Park Gv CUL/QBY BD13 .. 102 A5
Foster Park Rd CUL/QBY BD13 .. 102 A5
Foster Park Vw CUL/QBY BD13 .. 102 A5
Foster Place La
HOLM/MEL HD7 .... 255 H4
Foster Rd KGHY BD21 .... 2 E9 2
KGHY BD21 .... 79 K2
Foster Sq MID LS10 .... 131 M5 4

Foster St *BSLY* S70 ... 261 M6
CUL/OBY BD13 ... 124 F5
MOR LS27 ... 152 C2 2
Foster Wk *GFTH/SHER* LS25 ... 116 A7
Foston Cl *ECHL* BD2 ... 106 A4
Foston La *ECHL* BD2 ... 105 M4
Fothergill Av *FEA/AMT* WF7 ... 202 A8
Foulcauseway La *OT* LS21 ... 41 M7
Foulds Rd *COL* BB8 ... 74 D3
Foulds' Ter *BGLY* BD16 ... 81 J2 2
Foundry Ap *OSM* LS9 ... 110 D4
Foundry Cl *RHAY* LS8 ... 110 D3
Foundry Dr *RHAY* LS8 ... 110 D3
Foundry Hl *BGLY* BD16 ... 81 H3 3
Foundry La *BOW* BD4 ... 127 K1
KNOT WF11 ... 182 C2 1
OSM LS9 ... 111 G3
PDSY/CALV LS28 ... 107 G4
Foundry Mill Crs *SCFT* LS14 ... 111 H3
Foundry Mill Dr *SCFT* LS14 ... 111 G2
Foundry Mill Gdns *SCFT* LS14 ... 111 G1 1
Foundry Mill Mt *SCFT* LS14 ... 111 H3
Foundry Mill St *SCFT* LS14 ... 111 H3
Foundry Mill Ter *SCFT* LS14 ... 111 H3
Foundry Mill Vw *SCFT* LS14 ... 111 H3
Foundry Mill Wk *SCFT* LS14 ... 111 H3
Foundry Pl *OSM* LS9 ... 110 D3
Foundry St *BEE/HOL* LS11 ... 8 E3
BRIG HD6 ... 170 F5
BSLY S70 ... 261 G6
CLECK BD19 ... 150 A6 2
DEWS WF13 ... 173 M1 1
DEWS WF13 ... 195 G1 2
HFAX HX1 ... 11 H4
OSM LS9 ... 9 L1 1
RPDN/SBR HX6 ... 167 K3 1
Foundry St North *LUD/ILL* HX2 ... 146 B2
Foundry Wk *RHAY* LS8 ... 110 D3
Fountain Cl *DOD/DAR* S75 ... 242 A5
LVSG WF15 ... 172 B5
Fountain Ct *BSLYN/ROY* S71 ... 243 G3
Fountain Gv *LVSG* WF15 ... 172 B5
Fountain Gv *HUDS* HD4 ... 213 L2
Fountains Av *BSPA/BRAM* LS23 ... 48 E1
BTLY WF17 ... 173 L5
Fountain La *CUL/OBY* BD13 ... 102 F8 2
CUL/OBY BD13 ... 125 C5 3
HECK WF16 ... 172 E1
HFAX HX1 ... 11 G6
LDS LS1 ... 6 D9
LM/WK BD12 ... 126 E8 2
LVSG WF15 ... 172 B5
MOR LS27 ... 152 B3
RPDN/SBR HX6 ... 188 F2 1
TOD OL14 ... 142 M4
Fountains Wy *BSLYN/ROY* S71 ... 261 M3
WKFDE WF1 ... 177 H5 1
Fountain Ter *LM/WK* BD12 ... 148 F4
Fountain Wy *SHPY* BD18 ... 82 E7 1
Four Acres *MIRF* WF14 ... 194 C3
Fourlands Cl *IDLE* BD10 ... 83 L6 2
Fourlands Crs *IDLE* BD10 ... 83 L6 1
Fourlands Dr *IDLE* BD10 ... 83 L6
Fourlands Gdns *IDLE* BD10 ... 83 L6 3
Fourlands Gv *IDLE* BD10 ... 83 L6 6
Fourlands Rd *IDLE* BD10 ... 83 L6
Four Lane Ends *EARL* WF12 ... 181 M3
Four Lanes Cl *DOD/DAR* S75 ... 260 A1 1
Fourteenth Av *WOR/ARM* LS12 ... 108 E6
Fourth Av *BFDE* BD3 ... 105 L5
KGHY BD21 ... 2 D7
LVSG WF15 ... 171 K4
RTHW LS26 ... 133 J7
WBY LS22 ... 48 B2
WKFDE WF1 ... 176 D4
Fourth Ct *BEE/HOL* LS11 ... 8 C4
Fourth St *HOR/CROF* WF4 ... 200 D7
LM/WK BD12 ... 127 G8
Fowler's Pl *PDSY/CALV* LS28 ... 107 G4
Fowler Rd *BOW* BD4 ... 127 K1 3
Foxbridge Wy *NORM* WF6 ... 179 G3
Foxcliff *KNOT* WF11 ... 159 M5
Fox Cl *KBTN* HD8 ... 217 M8
Fox Ct *GTL/HWG* HX4 ... 168 F7
Fox Covert Rd Or
Whin Covert La
PONT WF8 ... 227 G4
Foxcroft Cl *CUL/OBY* BD13 ... 124 E7 1
HDGY LS6 ... 108 D1
Foxcroft Dr *BRIG* HD6 ... 170 B6
Foxcroft Gn *HDGY* LS6 ... 108 D1 1
Foxcroft Mt *HDGY* LS6 ... 108 D1
Foxcroft Rd *HDGY* LS6 ... 108 D1
Foxcroft St *LIT* OL15 ... 207 H1
Foxcroft Wy *HDGY* LS6 ... 108 D1
Foxen La *RPDN/SBR* HX6 ... 166 F4
Foxfields *STKB/PEN* S36 ... 271 J5
Foxfield Wk *BSLY* S70 ... 261 H8
Foxglove Av *RHAY* LS8 ... 88 E8
Foxglove Folly
WKFDW/WTN WF2 ... 176 A6 1
Foxglove Rd *BTLY* WF17 ... 151 G4
HUDE HD5 ... 215 G2
Fox Heads La *PBR* HG3 ... 28 C6
WBY LS22 ... 28 D7
Fox Hl *ROY/SHW* OL2 ... 229 G6
Foxhill *BAIL* BD17 ... 82 C3
WBY LS22 ... 30 A8
Foxhill Av *BHP/TINH* LS16 ... 86 F5
CUL/OBY BD13 ... 124 F5
Foxhill Cl *CUL/OBY* BD13 ... 124 F5
Foxhill Cl *BHP/TINH* LS16 ... 86 F5
Foxhill Crs *BHP/TINH* LS16 ... 86 F5
CUL/OBY BD13 ... 124 F5
Foxhill Dr *BHP/TINH* LS16 ... 86 F5
CUL/OBY BD13 ... 124 F5
Foxhill Gn *BHP/TINH* LS16 ... 86 F5
Foxhill Gv *BHP/TINH* LS16 ... 86 F5
CUL/OBY BD13 ... 124 F5
The Foxhills *BHP/TINH* LS16 ... 85 M2
Foxhole La *PDSY/CALV* LS28 ... 84 D8
Foxholes Cl *WHIT* OL12 ... 206 C5
Foxholes Crs *PDSY/CALV* LS28 ... 84 D8
Fox Holes Gv *STKB/PEN* S36 ... 268 F1
Foxholes La *NORM* WF6 ... 178 B1
Fox La *GFTH/SHER* LS25 ... 139 K6
HOR/CROF WF4 ... 198 B7

WKFDW/WTN WF2 ... 176 C5
Foxlow Av *HUDE* HD5 ... 193 G6
Fox Royd Av *MIRF* WF14 ... 172 B8
Foxroyd Cl *BSLYN/ROY* S71 ... 262 B6 1
Fox Royd Dr *MIRF* WF14 ... 172 B8
Foxroyd La *EARL* WF12 ... 195 J5
Fox Royd La *MIRF* WF14 ... 172 B8 1
Foxstone Rd *BAIL* BD17 ... 83 G3
Fox St *BGLY* BD16 ... 81 H3 7
BTLY WF17 ... 173 M2
CLECK BD19 ... 149 K7 8
HUD HD1 ... 14 F7
MILN OL16 ... 206 D6
MILN OL16 ... 207 D8
WBOW BD5 ... 126 E3 10
Fox Ter *PONT* WF8 ... 181 G4
Fox Vw *DEWS* WF13 ... 173 J4
Fox Wy *MID* LS10 ... 9 M6
Fox Wood Av *RHAY* LS8 ... 111 G1 1
Fox Wood Cl *RHAY* LS8 ... 111 G1
Foxwood Farm Wy *RHAY* LS8 ... 111 G1 1
Fox Wood Gv *RHAY* LS8 ... 111 G1
Fox Wood Ri *RHAY* LS8 ... 111 G1
Fox Wood Wk *RHAY* LS8 ... 111 G1
Foxwood Wk *WBY* LS22 ... 30 B7
Frain Cl *PONT* WF8 ... 181 G7 2
France Fold *HOLM/MEL* HD7 ... 236 B1 1
Frances Av *HUDS* HD4 ... 213 K3
Frances La *EARL* WF12 ... 174 F4
Frances St *BRIG* HD6 ... 170 C3 3
KGHY BD21 ... 2 D3
MILN OL16 ... 206 F3
PDSY/CALV LS28 ... 106 F4
France St *BTLY* WF17 ... 174 A2
Francis Av *HUDS* HD4 ... 213 J2 2
Francis Gv *BEE/HOL* LS11 ... 131 K3 11
Francis Rd *HOR/CROF* WF4 ... 200 D3
Francis St *CAS* WF10 ... 158 A6
CHAL LS7 ... 7 K2
FEA/AMT WF7 ... 223 M1
HECK WF16 ... 173 G3
HFAX HX1 ... 10 D7
HUDS HD4 ... 213 J2
MIRF WF14 ... 194 B1
Francis Vw *MIRF* WF14 ... 194 B1 2
Francus Rd *BSLYN/ROY* S71 ... 243 L5
Frank Cl *EARL* WF12 ... 196 A4
Frank Dr *EARL* WF12 ... 196 A4
Frankland Gv *CHAL* LS7 ... 7 L2
Frankland Pl *CHAL* LS7 ... 7 L3
Frank La *EARL* WF12 ... 196 A4
KBTN HD8 ... 239 L1
LUD/ILL HX2 ... 144 D4
Franklin St *HFAX* HX1 ... 10 B6
MILN OL16 ... 228 D1 2
Frank Peel Cl *HECK* WF16 ... 172 F2 3
Frank Pl *GTHN* BD7 ... 126 D2
Frank St *GTHN* BD7 ... 126 D2 4
HFAX HX1 ... 10 C7
Fraser Av *HORS* LS18 ... 85 J4
Fraser Rd *PDSY/CALV* LS28 ... 84 B8
Fraser St *GIR* BD8 ... 4 B3
MILN OL16 ... 228 D2
OSM LS9 ... 110 B5
ROY/SHW OL2 ... 229 J6
Freakfield La *LVSG* WF15 ... 171 K4
Frederick Av *BSLY* S70 ... 260 F6
OSM LS9 ... 110 C8
WKFDE WF1 ... 13 L9
Frederick Cl *IDLE* BD10 ... 83 H5 7
Frederick St *BFD1* ... 5 H7
HUDS HD4 ... 213 L2
KGHY BD21 ... 3 K4
LIT OL15 ... 185 J8
LVSG WF15 ... 172 D3 1
PDSY/CALV LS28 ... 106 E3 1
WKFDE WF1 ... 12 F2
Frederic Pl *BSLY* S70 ... 261 H7 2
Fred's Pl *BOW* BD4 ... 127 L3
Fred St *KGHY* BD21 ... 2 E6
Freeholds Rd *WHIT* OL12 ... 162 A8
Freehold St *ROCH* OL11 ... 228 A1
Freely La *BSPA/BRAM* LS23 ... 69 M4
Freeman Rd *HIPP* HX3 ... 169 J1
Freeman St *BSLY* S70 ... 261 H6 7
Freemans Wy *WBY* LS22 ... 30 B8
Freemans Yd *BSLY* S70 ... 261 H5 6
Freestone Ct *NORM* WF6 ... 178 D3 2
Freeston Av *NORM* WF6 ... 178 F8
Freestone Ms *WOR/ARM* LS12 ... 107 L7
Freestone Wy *NORM* WF6 ... 178 A2 3
Freetrade St *ROCH* OL11 ... 228 A1
Fremantle Gv *BOW* BD4 ... 128 A1 8
Fremantle Pl *MSTN/BAR* LS15 ... 111 G7 2
French St *AWLS/ASK* DN6 ... 249 J5 2
Frensham Av *MOR* LS27 ... 152 B3
Frensham Dr *CAS* WF10 ... 158 F8
GTHN BD7 ... 125 M3
Frensham Gv *GTHN* BD7 ... 125 M4
Frensham Wy *GTHN* BD7 ... 125 M3 1
Freshfield Gdns *WIL/AL* BD15 ... 103 K5
Freston Av *WKFDE* WF1 ... 177 H8
Freston Dr *WKFDE* WF1 ... 177 L8
Friar Ct *IDLE* BD10 ... 83 L8 2
Friar Pl *HUDN* HD2 ... 193 H1
Friar's Cl *FEA/AMT* WF7 ... 201 M8
Friars Crs *ROCH* OL11 ... 228 B4
Friar's Rd *BSLYN/ROY* S71 ... 262 A3
Friarwood La *PONT* WF8 ... 180 F6 6
Frickley Bridge La *CUD/GR* S72 ... 245 G2
Frickley La *BTLY* DN5 ... 247 H8
Frieldhurst Rd *TOD* OL14 ... 140 E5
Friendly Av *WKFDE* WF1 ... 167 J1
Friendly Fold Rd *HIPP* HX3 ... 146 C4
Friendly St *CUL/OBY* BD13 ... 102 F8 9
HIPP HX3 ... 146 C4 8
HUD HD1 ... 15 G5
Frimley Dr *WBOW* BD5 ... 126 E4
Frith St *HWTH* BD22 ... 79 G6 8
Frizinghall Rd *ECHL* BD2 ... 104 E1
Frizley Gdns *HTON* BD9 ... 104 E2 4
Frobisher Gv *WKFDW/WTN* WF2 ... 198 A1
Frobisher Rd *LIT* OL15 ... 185 L5 2
Frogmoor Av *LM/WK* BD12 ... 149 H1 3

Front Rw *BEE/HOL* LS11 ... 8 E3
Front St *BEE/HOL* LS11 ... 8 E3
BSPA/BRAM LS23 ... 69 L1
CAS WF10 ... 158 B8
PONT WF8 ... 180 C6
Frost Hl *LVSG* WF15 ... 172 D2
Fruit St *KGHY* BD21 ... 3 L3
Fryergate *WKFDW/WTN* WF2 ... 176 B7
Fryston Common La
GFTH/SHER LS25 ... 138 D6
Fryston La *KNOT* WF11 ... 159 J7
Fryston Rd *CAS* WF10 ... 158 D8 2
Fulford Av *HUDN* HD2 ... 192 D6
Fulford St *CAS* WF10 ... 157 L7
Fulford Wk *ECHL* BD2 ... 105 M4
Fulham St *BEE/HOL* LS11 ... 8 E9
Fullerton Cl *AWLS/ASK* DN6 ... 249 H4
Fullerton St *BFDE* BD3 ... 5 J7
Fullshaw La *STKB/PEN* S36 ... 269 K7
Fullwood Dr *HOLM/MEL* HD7 ... 212 G2
Fulmar Ms *GIR* BD8 ... 103 J7 8
Fulmar Rd *CAS* WF10 ... 157 L8
Fulmer Cl *BSLYN/ROY* S71 ... 243 K8
Fulneck *PDSY/CALV* LS28 ... 129 C5
Fulneck Cl *HUDN* HD2 ... 192 B3
Fulstone Hall La
HOLM/MEL HD7 ... 237 J7
Fulstone Rd *KBTN* HD8 ... 237 K6
Fulton St *BFD1* ... 4 D6
Fulwood Gv *WKFDW/WTN* WF2 ... 220 D1
Furnace Gv *LM/WK* BD12 ... 149 H1 5
Furnace Inn St *BOW* BD4 ... 127 M1 2
Furnace La *BARN/DRI* BD11 ... 128 C8
Furnace Rd *BOW* BD4 ... 127 L3
LM/WK BD12 ... 149 H1 8
Furnbrook Gdns *HUDE* HD5 ... 193 L6 8
Furness Av *LIT* OL15 ... 185 J8
LUD/ILL HX2 ... 145 A4
WKFDW/WTN WF2 ... 176 A4
Furness Cl *MILN* OL16 ... 207 D8
Furness Crs *LUD/ILL* HX2 ... 145 M1
Furness Dene *BSLYN/ROY* S71 ... 261 M1
Furness Dr *LUD/ILL* HX2 ... 145 M2
WKFDW/WTN WF2 ... 176 A4
Furness Gdns *LUD/ILL* HX2 ... 146 A2
Furness Gv *LUD/ILL* HX2 ... 145 M2
Furness Pl *LUD/ILL* HX2 ... 146 A2
Further Heights Rd *WHIT* OL12 ... 206 A4
Furzegate *MILN* OL16 ... 228 E3
Fusden La *CLECK* BD19 ... 150 C5
Fyfe Crs *BAIL* BD17 ... 82 F4
Fyfe Gv *BAIL* BD17 ... 83 G4
Fyfe La *BAIL* BD17 ... 83 G4
Fylde Cl *BSLYN/ROY* S71 ... 243 M8

G

Gables Cl *GLE* DN14 ... 161 K7
The Gables *BAIL* BD17 ... 83 G3
The Gabriels *ROY/SHW* OL2 ... 229 H7 2
Gadding Moor Rd
STKB/PEN S36 ... 258 B6
Gagewell Dr *HOR/CROF* WF4 ... 197 K4
Gagewell La *HOR/CROF* WF4 ... 197 K4
Gagewell Vw *HOR/CROF* WF4 ... 197 K4
Gainest *LUD/ILL* HX2 ... 168 D1
Gainford Dr *GFTH/SHER* LS25 ... 113 H8
Gain La *BFDE* BD3 ... 106 A5
Gainsborough Cl *BFDE* BD3 ... 105 J4
Gainsborough Ct *SKP/WHF* BD23 ... 16 A2
Gainsborough Dr *ROCH* OL11 ... 228 A3
Gainsborough Wy
BSLYN/ROY S71 ... 261 K3
EARD/LOFT WF3 ... 177 G1
Gainsbro Av *BHP/TINH* LS16 ... 86 D1
Gainsbro Dr *BHP/TINH* LS16 ... 86 D1
Gaisby La *ECHL* BD2 ... 104 C2
SHPY BD18 ... 104 F1
Gaisby Mt *SHPY* BD18 ... 104 F1
Gaisby Pl *SHPY* BD18 ... 82 F8
Gaisby Ri *SHPY* BD18 ... 82 F8 1
Galefield Gn *WBSY* BD6 ... 126 B8 6
Gale La *OT* LS21 ... 24 D7
Gales Ter *ROCH* OL11 ... 228 A1 7
Gale St *KGHY* BD21 ... 3 G3
WHIT OL12 ... 206 B3
Gall La *TOD* OL14 ... 140 E3
Gallogate La *AL/HA/HU* LS17 ... 44 B4
Gallon Cft *HEM/SK/SE* WF9 ... 247 G3
Galloway Ct *PDSY/CALV* LS28 ... 106 C5
Galloway La *PDSY/CALV* LS28 ... 106 C5
Galloway Rd *IDLE* BD10 ... 83 M7 3
Galloway St *HUD* HD1 ... 15 H5
Gallows Hl *CAS* WF10 ... 158 E7
OT LS21 ... 41 L6
Gallows La *HOR/CROF* WF4 ... 220 D6
Galpharm Wy *DOD/DAR* S75 ... 260 A6
Galsworthy Av *HTON* BD9 ... 103 M3 1
Gamble Hl *BRAM* LS13 ... 107 M6
Gamble Hill Cl *BRAM* LS13 ... 107 M6
Gamble Hill Dr *BRAM* LS13 ... 107 M6
Gamble Hill Gn *BRAM* LS13 ... 107 M6
Gamble Hill Lawn *BRAM* LS13 ... 107 M6
Gamble Hill Pl *BRAM* LS13 ... 107 M6
Gamble Hill Ri *BRAM* LS13 ... 107 M6
Gamble Hill Vw *BRAM* LS13 ... 107 M6
Gamble La *WOR/ARM* LS12 ... 107 L8
Gamel Vw *AIRE* BD20 ... 35 K8
Game Scar La Or
Goose Eye Brow *HWTH* BD22 ... 56 D8 1
The Gang *WOR/ARM* LS12 ... 108 E6
Ganners Cl *BRAM* LS13 ... 107 L2 3
Ganners Gn *BRAM* LS13 ... 107 L2 2
Ganners Gv *BRAM* LS13 ... 107 M2
Ganners Hl *BRAM* LS13 ... 107 M2
Ganners La *BRAM* LS13 ... 107 L2
Ganners Mt *BRAM* LS13 ... 107 M2
Ganners Ri *BRAM* LS13 ... 107 M2
Ganners Rd *BRAM* LS13 ... 107 L2
Ganners Wk *BRAM* LS13 ... 107 L2 1
Ganners Wy *BRAM* LS13 ... 107 M2
Gannerthorpe Cl *LM/WK* BD12 ... 148 E3 2
Gannet Cl *CAS* WF10 ... 157 L8
Ganny Rd *BRIG* HD6 ... 170 D4

Ganton Cl *HDGY* LS6 ... 6 E1
Ganton Pl *BSLYN/ROY* S71 ... 243 G7
Ganton Wy *HUDN* HD2 ... 192 B3
Gaol La *HFAX* HX1 ... 11 H5
Garden Av *CLECK* BD19 ... 150 C8
Garden Cl *AIRE* BD20 ... 34 D8 1
CLECK BD19 ... 172 C1 3
GFTH/SHER LS25 ... 115 M7
LIT OL15 ... 207 H4 1
LM/WK BD12 ... 148 E2 10
OSS WF5 ... 197 G3
Garden Dr *DEWS* WF13 ... 173 C8 2
Gardeners Ct *MID* LS10 ... 9 K8
Gardener's Sq *HIPP* HX3 ... 147 L6
Garden Fld *LM/WK* BD12 ... 148 E3
Garden Fold *HX3* ... 147 L6
Garden House Cl
BSLYN/ROY S71 ... 261 L1
RTHW LS26 ... 156 F3 1
Garden House La
EARD/LOFT WF3 ... 153 J6
Garden La *GFTH/SHER* LS25 ... 115 M7
HTON BD9 ... 104 B3
KNOT WF11 ... 182 C1
MILN OL16 ... 206 C6
RPDN/SBR HX6 ... 167 K7
Garden Pde *CLECK* BD19 ... 150 C8
Garden Pl *DEWS* WF13 ... 173 H5
Garden Rd *BRIG* HD6 ... 170 B2
Gardens Rd *DEWS* WF13 ... 173 C8
The Gardens *BGLY* BD16 ... 81 M3 1
HFAX HX1 ... 168 E1
MID LS10 ... 153 E1
MOR LS27 ... 152 B4
PDSY/CALV LS28 ... 106 E3
Garden St *CAS* WF10 ... 157 M8
DEWS WF13 ... 172 F8
FEA/AMT WF7 ... 223 M1
HECK WF16 ... 172 F3 8
HUD HD1 ... 214 B2
HWTH BD22 ... 79 H6 8
MILN OL16 ... 229 K2
NORM WF6 ... 178 D4 8
TOD OL14 ... 141 K8
WKFDE WF1 ... 12 D1
Garden St North *HIPP* HX3 ... 11 J4
Garden Ter *HBR* HX7 ... 143 J5 10
HOR/CROF WF4 ... 219 M2
HTON BD9 ... 104 C3 3
ROY/SHW OL2 ... 228 E7
Garden Vw *BGLY* BD16 ... 81 L3
CLECK BD19 ... 150 C8
Garden Village *GFTH/SHER* LS25 ... 114 C7
Garden Wk *CLECK* BD19 ... 172 C1 8
Garden Wy *LIT* OL15 ... 207 H4
Gardiner Rw *BOW* BD4 ... 127 K4 1
Gare Forth Av *AIRE* BD20 ... 35 L8 1
Garfield Av *GIR* BD8 ... 104 D4
Garfield Rd *HOLM/MEL* HD7 ... 233 H2
Garfield St *HIPP* HX3 ... 10 D1 8
Garfit Hl *BTLY* WF17 ... 150 F6
Garforth Cl *NORM* WF6 ... 178 A3
Garforth Rd *KGHY* BD21 ... 3 M2
Garforth St *HUDS* HD4 ... 213 L7
WIL/AL BD15 ... 103 K5 8
Gargrave Ap *OSM* LS9 ... 110 B6
Gargrave Crs *HEM/SK/SE* WF9 ... 223 L8
Gargrave Pl *HEM/SK/SE* WF9 ... 223 L8
OSM LS9 ... 110 B5
WKFDW/WTN WF2 ... 197 L1
Garibaldi St *BFDE* BD3 ... 106 A7
Garland Dr *MSTN/BAR* LS15 ... 111 M7
Garlick St *BRIG* HD6 ... 170 A8
Garmil Head La
HEM/SK/SE WF9 ... 223 H1
Garmont Ms *CHAL* LS7 ... 87 M8 2
Garmont Rd *CHAL* LS7 ... 87 M8
Garner La *HOLM/MEL* HD7 ... 235 M2
KBTN HD8 ... 215 M7
Garnet Av *BEE/HOL* LS11 ... 131 L3 15
Garnet Crs *BEE/HOL* LS11 ... 131 L3 17
Garnet Gv *BEE/HOL* LS11 ... 131 L3
Garnet La *TAD* LS24 ... 71 H6
Garnet Pde *BEE/HOL* LS11 ... 131 L3 18
Garnet Pl *BEE/HOL* LS11 ... 131 L3
Garnet Rd *BEE/HOL* LS11 ... 131 L4
Garnet Ter *BEE/HOL* LS11 ... 131 L4
Garnett St *BFDE* BD3 ... 5 J6
DEWS WF13 ... 173 H3 2
HBR HX7 ... 143 J3
OT LS21 ... 41 K6 3
Garnet Vw *BEE/HOL* LS11 ... 131 L3
Garret Gv *ROY/SHW* OL2 ... 229 J7
Garrett St *KBTN* HD8 ... 239 H4 1
Garsdale Av *IDLE* BD10 ... 83 L7 8
Garsdale Crs *BAIL* BD17 ... 83 G2
Garsdale Fold *WBY* LS22 ... 47 J5
Garsdale Rd *HUDS* HD4 ... 214 D4
Garsdale Wk *KNOT* WF11 ... 182 A4
Garth Av *AL/HA/HU* LS17 ... 87 K5
NORM WF6 ... 178 C6
WBY LS22 ... 47 G5
Garth Barn Cl *HTON* BD9 ... 104 C3 3
Garth Cl *SEL* YO8 ... 139 M4
Garth Dr *AL/HA/HU* LS17 ... 87 K5
SEL YO8 ... 139 M4
Garth End *WBY* LS22 ... 47 K6
Garth Land Wy *BOW* BD4 ... 127 L3 3
Garth La *SEL* YO8 ... 139 M4
Garth Mi *GLE* DN14 ... 161 J2
Garth Rectory *HEM/SK/SE* WF9 ... 223 M7
Garth Rd *AL/HA/HU* LS17 ... 87 K5
SEL YO8 ... 139 M4
Garth St *CAS* WF10 ... 157 L8
KGHY BD21 ... 2 D5
The Garth *GFTH/SHER* LS25 ... 113 J7
OSM LS9 ... 9 L1
WBY LS22 ... 47 K6
Garth Vw *SEL* YO8 ... 139 M4
Garthwaite Mt *WIL/AL* BD15 ... 103 K4
Garth Wk *AL/HA/HU* LS17 ... 87 K5
Garth Willow *BULY* LS4 ... 109 C5

Garth Willow Av *SCFT* LS14 ... 89 K6
Garth Willow Cl *SCFT* LS14 ... 89 K6
Garton Av *OSM* LS9 ... 110 C7
Garton Dr *IDLE* BD10 ... 105 M1
Garton Gv *OSM* LS9 ... 110 C7
Garton Rd *OSM* LS9 ... 110 C7 3
Garton Ter *OSM* LS9 ... 110 C7
Garton Vw *OSM* LS9 ... 110 C7 2
Garvey Vw *WBOW* BD5 ... 127 G2 3
Garwick Ter *GTL/HWG* HX4 ... 168 F7
Gascoigne Av *MSTN/BAR* LS15 ... 90 F8
Gascoigne Ct *MSTN/BAR* LS15 ... 90 F8
Gascoigne Rd *EARD/LOFT* WF3 ... 154 A5
MSTN/BAR LS15 ... 90 F8
Gascoigne St *LDS* LS1 ... 9 C1
Gascoigne Vw *MSTN/BAR* LS15 ... 90 F8
Gashouse La *WBY* LS22 ... 48 A1 3
Gaskell Cl *LIT* OL15 ... 185 J8 2
Gaskell Dr *HOR/CROF* WF4 ... 197 A4
Gaskell St *WKFDW/WTN* WF2 ... 12 B4
Gasson St *HUDS* HD4 ... 213 J2
Gas St *HWTH* BD22 ... 78 F7 7
ROCH OL11 ... 206 A7
SKP/WHF BD23 ... 16 B3
Gas Works La *BSPA/BRAM* LS23 ... 49 H7
ELL HX5 ... 169 H7
Gas Works Rd *KGHY* BD21 ... 58 B7
RPDN/SBR HX6 ... 167 M2
Gasworks St *HUD* HD1 ... 15 H5
LVSG WF15 ... 172 D3
Gate Crs *DOD/DAR* S75 ... 260 B6
Gatefield Mt *LM/WK* BD12 ... 126 D8 2
Gate Foot La *KBTN* HD8 ... 237 L8
Gate Head *HOLM/MEL* HD7 ... 233 J2
Gatehead
HOLM/MEL HD7 ... 233 K1
Gate Head La *GTL/HWG* HX4 ... 168 B8
HOLM/MEL HD7 ... 255 J6
Gateland Dr *AL/HA/HU* LS17 ... 89 G2
Gateland La *AL/HA/HU* LS17 ... 89 G3
Gateon House La *AL/HA/HU* LS17 ... 67 J2
Gatesgarth Crs *HUDW* HD3 ... 191 J5
Gate St *ROCH* OL11 ... 228 B1
Gatesway *BGLY* BD16 ... 80 C5 3
Gate Way Dr *YEA* LS19 ... 62 C8
Gateways *WKFDE* WF1 ... 176 E1
Gathorne St *BRIG* HD6 ... 170 D3
GTHN BD7 ... 126 D2
RHAY LS8 ... 7 M3
Gathorne Ter *RHAY* LS8 ... 7 M3
RHAY LS8 ... 110 E3 3
Gaukroger La *HFAX* HX1 ... 11 J9
Gauk St *KNOT* WF11 ... 159 L6
Gavin Cl *BFDE* BD3 ... 106 A7
Gawber Rd *DOD/DAR* S75 ... 260 E3
Gawsworth Cl *ROY/SHW* OL2 ... 229 H7
Gawthorpe Dr *BGLY* BD16 ... 81 H1
Gawthorpe Green La
HUDE HD5 ... 194 D3
Gawthorpe La *KBTN* HD8 ... 215 M1
OSS WF5 ... 174 F5
WKFDW/WTN WF2 ... 175 J4
Gawthorpe St *WIL/AL* BD15 ... 80 D8 1
Gay La *OT* LS21 ... 41 J7
TAD LS24 ... 95 H3
Gayle Cl *LM/WK* BD12 ... 148 E2 3
Gaynor St *BFD1* ... 4 C5
Gaythorne Rd *ECHL* BD2 ... 105 L3 2
WBOW BD5 ... 127 G3
Gaythorne Ter *CLAY* BD14 ... 125 L2 2
Gaythorn Ter *HIPP* HX3 ... 147 L5
Geary Cl *WKFDW/WTN* WF2 ... 175 M6
Geary Dr *WKFDW/WTN* WF2 ... 175 M6
Geecroft La *WBY* LS22 ... 46 E1
Geelong Cl *ECHL* BD2 ... 105 J3
Gelder Cl *WKFDW/WTN* WF2 ... 175 M6
Gelderd Cft *WKFDW/WTN* WF2 ... 175 M6 3
Gelderd Cl *WOR/ARM* LS12 ... 130 F2
Gelderd La *WOR/ARM* LS12 ... 130 F2
Gelderd Pl *BEE/HOL* LS11 ... 8 A4
BTLY WF17 ... 151 H4
MOR LS27 ... 130 F2
WOR/ARM LS12 ... 130 F2
Gelderd Rd *WOR/ARM* LS12 ... 108 D7
Gelder Ter *HUDS* HD4 ... 15 K9
Geneva Gv *WKFDE* WF1 ... 176 E1 10
Genista Dr *MID* LS10 ... 131 M6
Genn La *BSLY* S70 ... 260 F6
Genoa Cl *WMB/DAR* S73 ... 263 G7
Gentian Ct *WKFDW/WTN* WF2 ... 176 A7 2
George-a-green Rd
WKFDW/WTN WF2 ... 198 A2
George And Crown Yd
WKFDE WF1 ... 12 E2
George Av *HUDN* HD2 ... 14 B2
George Buckley Ct
HEM/SK/SE WF9 ... 246 C4 2
George La *HOR/CROF* WF4 ... 221 C8
RPDN/SBR HX6 ... 188 D4
George Sq *BSLY* S70 ... 261 G5 2
HFAX HX1 ... 11 G6 2
George's Sq *CUL/OBY* BD13 ... 79 M8 2
KGHY BD21 ... 2 F6 1
George's St *LUD/ILL* HX2 ... 146 B3
George St *AWLS/ASK* DN6 ... 249 K4
BAIL BD17 ... 82 E5 3
BFD1 ... 5 H7
BRIG HD6 ... 170 C5 7
BSLY S70 ... 261 G5
BTLY WF17 ... 173 L2 2
CLECK BD19 ... 149 M6 13
CUD/GR S72 ... 222 F8
CUD/GR S72 ... 244 E6
CUD/GR S72 ... 263 M7
CUL/OBY BD13 ... 102 A3 3
CUL/OBY BD13 ... 102 F8 3
DEWS WF13 ... 173 H6 5
DEWS WF13 ... 195 G1 4
DOD/DAR S75 ... 242 D5
EARL WF12 ... 173 L6 6
ELL HX5 ... 191 H1
FEA/AMT WF7 ... 200 F1
FEA/AMT WF7 ... 201 L3 2
GTL/HWG HX4 ... 168 F7 2
HBR HX7 ... 144 A2
HECK WF16 ... 172 F2 5
HEM/SK/SE WF9 ... 224 A8 3

HFAX HX1 .... 11 G6
HIPP HX3 .... 147 M7
HOR/CROF WF4 .... 197 K5
HOR/CROF WF4 .... 222 D5
HUD HD1 .... 14 F7 [2]
HUDS HD4 .... 214 A2 [2]
HUDW HD3 .... 191 K5
ILK LS29 .... 19 H6 [8]
LDS LS1 .... 7 H9
LIT OL15 .... 207 K1 [8]
LVSG WF15 .... 172 C2 [8]
MILN OL16 .... 206 C6
MILN OL16 .... 206 F3
NORM WF6 .... 178 B3
OSS WF5 .... 174 E7
ROY/SHW OL2 .... 229 L6
RPDN/SBR HX6 .... 167 K3
SHPY BD18 .... 82 B6 [8]
SKP/WHF BD23 .... 16 C3
TOD OL14 .... 163 K1 [8]
WKFDE WF1 .... 12 E3
YEA LS19 .... 84 D2
George Yd BSLY S70 .... 261 G5
Georgia Ms OSS WF5 .... 197 H2 [8]
Gerald CI BSLY S70 .... 261 L7
Gerald Crs BSLY S70 .... 261 M6
Gerald PI BSLY S70 .... 261 L7
Gerald Rd BSLY S70 .... 261 L7
Geraldton La ECHL BD2 .... 105 G3
Gerald Wk BSLY S70 .... 261 L7
Gerard Av MOR LS27 .... 152 B2 [8]
Gernhill Av HUDN HD2 .... 192 B1
Gerrard St HFAX HX1 .... 10 E6
ROCH OL11 .... 228 C5
Gervase Rd HOR/CROF WF4 .... 197 J4 [8]
Ghyllbank AIRE BD20 .... 36 A4 [8]
Ghyll Beck Dr OT LS21 .... 40 F8
YEA LS19 .... 85 C3
Ghyll CI AIRE BD20 .... 36 A4
Ghyll Dr HWTH BD22 .... 78 E8 [8]
Ghyll Mt YEA LS19 .... 62 B8
Ghyll Rd HDGY LS6 .... 86 C8
Ghyll Royd GSLY LS20 .... 62 A7
Ghyllroyd Av BIRK/DRI BD11 .... 150 D1
Ghyllroyd Dr BIRK/DRI BD11 .... 150 D1
The Ghyll BGLY BD16 .... 81 J6
HUDN HD2 .... 192 C2
Ghyll Wy AIRE BD20 .... 16 C5
Ghyll Wd ILK LS29 .... 38 A3
Ghyll Wood Dr BGLY BD16 .... 81 J6
Gibbet St HFAX HX1 .... 10 E6
Gibb La LUD/ILL HX2 .... 145 K3
Gibb St HWTH BD22 .... 54 E3 [8]
Gib La WKFDW/WTN WF2 .... 239 J4
Gibraltar Av HFAX HX1 .... 146 A8 [8]
Gibraltar Island Rd MID LS10 .... 132 B2
Gibraltar Rd HFAX HX1 .... 146 A7
PDSY/CALV LS28 .... 106 D7
Gibriding La HOLM/MEL HD7 .... 253 H7
Gibside La AIRE BD20 .... 34 B4
Gibson Av WKFDW/WTN WF2 .... 176 C7
Gibson CI WKFDW/WTN WF2 .... 176 C7
Gibson Dr MSTN/BAR LS15 .... 111 L2
Gibson La GFTH/SHER LS25 .... 135 K5
Gibson St BFDE BD3 .... 5 M7
HUDW HD3 .... 191 L7
MILN OL16 .... 206 E6
TOD OL14 .... 163 L1
Gilbert Cha KSTL LS5 .... 108 C3 [8]
Gilbert CI KSTL LS5 .... 108 D3
Gilbert Gv BSLY S70 .... 261 M6
HUDS HD4 .... 213 M3
Gilbert Mt BULY LS4 .... 108 C3 [8]
Gilbert St PDSY/CALV LS28 .... 106 F4 [8]
Gilbrook Wy MILN OL16 .... 228 D4
Gilcar St NORM WF6 .... 178 F2
Gilcar Wk NORM WF6 .... 178 E1
Gilderdale CI ROY/SHW OL2 .... 229 K6 [8]
Gildersome La MOR LS27 .... 129 K6
Gildersome Sp MOR LS27 .... 151 M1
Gilead Rd HUDW HD3 .... 191 G7
Giles Hill La HIPP HX3 .... 125 J7
Giles St HOLM/MEL HD7 .... 236 B6
WBOW BD5 .... 126 F1 [8]
WBSY BD6 .... 126 C5
Gillann St KNOT WF11 .... 182 C2
Gill Bank Rd ILK LS29 .... 20 C8
Gill Beck CI BAIL BD17 .... 83 G2 [8]
Gill CI ILK LS29 .... 18 F6
Gillemere Gv ROY/SHW OL2 .... 229 L7 [8]
Gillett Dr RTHW LS26 .... 155 H1
Gillett La RTHW LS26 .... 155 H1
Gilling Av GFTH/SHER LS25 .... 113 K6
Gillingham Gn BOW BD4 .... 128 A3 [8]
Gillion Crs HOR/CROF WF4 .... 220 A1
Gill La BAIL BD17 .... 84 A2
HOLM/MEL HD7 .... 254 A4
HWTH BD22 .... 54 D3
HWTH BD22 .... 78 C2
ILK LS29 .... 19 L7
WBY LS22 .... 46 B3
YEA LS19 .... 84 C1
Gillroyd La HOLM/MEL HD7 .... 212 F7
Gillroyd PI MOR LS27 .... 152 D3 [8]
Gillroyd Ri GTHN BD7 .... 104 D7
Gill Sike Av WKFDW/WTN WF2 .... 198 B2
Gill Sike Bungalows
WKFDW/WTN WF2 .... 198 B2 [8]
Gill Sike Gv WKFDW/WTN WF2 .... 198 B2
Gill Sike Rd WKFDW/WTN WF2 .... 198 B2
The Gills OT LS21 .... 41 J4
Gillstone Dr HWTH BD22 .... 78 F8
Gill St WKFDE WF1 .... 12 E1
Gill's Yd WKFDE WF1 .... 12 E1
Gillygate PONT WF8 .... 180 F6 [8]
Gilmour St HIPP HX3 .... 10 E2
Gilpin PI WOR/ARM LS12 .... 108 F8
Gilpin St BFDE BD3 .... 5 M5
WOR/ARM LS12 .... 108 F8
Gilpin Ter WOR/ARM LS12 .... 108 F8
Gilpin Vw WOR/ARM LS12 .... 108 F8
Gilstead Ct BGLY BD16 .... 81 L3 [8]
Gilstead Dr BGLY BD16 .... 81 L3
Gilstead La BGLY BD16 .... 81 L3
Gilstead Wy ILK LS29 .... 38 C1
Gilthwaites Crs KBTN HD8 .... 239 J7
Gilthwaites Gv KBTN HD8 .... 239 J8

Gilthwaites La KBTN HD8 .... 239 J7
Gilthwaites Top KBTN HD8 .... 239 J7
Gilynda CI GIR BD8 .... 104 A7 [8]
Gindhill La OT LS21 .... 25 J7
Gin La FEA/AMT WF7 .... 200 E2
The Ginnel AL/HA/HU LS17 .... 67 L4
Gipsy La BEE/HOL LS11 .... 131 J6
DOD/DAR S75 .... 242 B1
RTHW LS26 .... 133 K8
WKFDW/WTN WF2 .... 199 C7
Gipsy Md RTHW LS26 .... 133 K8
Gipton Ap OSM LS9 .... 110 F5
Gipton Av RHAY LS8 .... 7 M3
Gipton Sq OSM LS9 .... 110 F5
Gipton St RHAY LS8 .... 7 M2
Gipton Wood Av RHAY LS8 .... 110 D1
Gipton Wood Crs RHAY LS8 .... 110 D1
Gipton Wood Gv RHAY LS8 .... 110 C1
Gipton Wood PI RHAY LS8 .... 110 D1
Gipton Wood Rd RHAY LS8 .... 110 D1
Girlington Rd GIR BD8 .... 104 C6 [8]
Girnhill La FEA/AMT WF7 .... 201 L2
Gisbourne Rd HUDN HD2 .... 193 C1
Gisburn Rd ROCH OL11 .... 228 C3
Gisburn St KGHY BD21 .... 2 E3
Gissing Rd WKFDW/WTN WF2 .... 197 M2
The Glade PDSY/CALV LS28 .... 106 C4
SCFT LS14 .... 88 F1
Gladstonbury Av WKFDE WF1 .... 177 H5 [8]
Gladstone Crs ROCH OL11 .... 228 B3
YEA LS19 .... 84 D1 [8]
Gladstone St BFDE BD3 .... 105 L7
BGLY BD16 .... 81 H4 [8]
CLECK BD19 .... 149 M7 [8]
CUL/QBY BD13 .... 125 K5
FEA/AMT WF7 .... 179 M7
GTL/HWG HX4 .... 190 C2 [8]
KGHY BD21 .... 2 E6
NORM WF6 .... 178 D4
PDSY/CALV LS28 .... 106 F3
SKP/WHF BD23 .... 16 B2
TOD OL14 .... 140 D5 [8]
WIL/AL BD15 .... 103 K5 [8]
Gladstone Ter CAS WF10 .... 158 A6 [8]
MOR LS27 .... 152 C2 [8]
Gladstone Vw HWTH BD22 .... 169 C5 [8]
Gladwin St BTLY WF17 .... 173 K2
Glaisdale Av HFAX HX1 .... 146 A3 [8]
Glaisdale Ct WIL/AL BD15 .... 103 J5
Glaisdale Gv HIPP HX3 .... 147 M7 [8]
Glamis CI GFTH/SHER LS25 .... 113 K6
Glanville Ter RTHW LS26 .... 155 G1 [8]
Glasshouse St MID LS10 .... 9 K6
Glasshouse Vw MID LS10 .... 153 K2 [8]
Glastonbury Dr HUDW HD3 .... 213 H1 [8]
Glazier Rd CUL/QBY BD13 .... 124 E4
Gleanings Av LUD/ILL HX2 .... 145 L7
Gleanings Dr LUD/ILL HX2 .... 145 K7
Glebe Av KSTL LS5 .... 108 D2
Glebe CI COP/BISH YO23 .... 73 J7
KBTN HD8 .... 217 M7
Glebe Field Cha WBY LS22 .... 29 L8
Glebe Field CI WBY LS22 .... 29 M8
Glebe Field Cft WBY LS22 .... 29 M8 [8]
Glebe Field Dr WBY LS22 .... 29 M8 [8]
Glebe Field Garth WBY LS22 .... 29 L8
Glebe Field Holt WBY LS22 .... 29 M8 [8]
Glebe Ga EARL WF12 .... 196 A5
Glebelands CI GFTH/SHER LS25 .... 113 K8 [8]
Glebelands Dr HDGY LS6 .... 86 F8
Glebe La KNOT WF11 .... 182 B2
Glebe Mt PDSY/CALV LS28 .... 107 C8
Glebe PI KSTL LS5 .... 108 D2
Glebe Rd AWLS/ASK DN6 .... 227 M5
Glebe St CAS WF10 .... 158 A7 [8]
HUDW HD3 .... 14 A4
NORM WF6 .... 178 C6
PDSY/CALV LS28 .... 107 C8
ROY/SHW OL2 .... 229 K7
Glebe Ter HDGY LS6 .... 86 F7
Gleddings CI HIPP HX3 .... 168 C3
Gledhill Av STKB/PEN S36 .... 270 E5
Gledhill CI ROY/SHW OL2 .... 229 J5
Gledhill Rd BFDE BD3 .... 5 M7
Gledhill St TOD OL14 .... 141 K8 [8]
Gledhill Ter DEWS WF13 .... 173 H6
Gledholt Bank HUD HD1 .... 14 B1
Gledholt Rd HUD HD1 .... 14 A5
Gledhow Av RHAY LS8 .... 88 B6
Gledhow Dr HWTH BD22 .... 100 E2
Gledhow Grange Vw RHAY LS8 .... 88 B7
Gledhow Grange Wk RHAY LS8 .... 88 B7 [8]
Gledhow La CHAL LS7 .... 87 M7
RHAY LS8 .... 88 D7
Gledhow Mt RHAY LS8 .... 7 M4
Gledhow Park Av CHAL LS7 .... 88 A8 [8]
Gledhow Park Crs CHAL LS7 .... 88 A8 [8]
Gledhow Park Dr CHAL LS7 .... 87 M8
Gledhow Park Gv CHAL LS7 .... 88 A8
Gledhow Park Rd CHAL LS7 .... 88 A8
Gledhow Park Vw CHAL LS7 .... 88 A8
Gledhow PI RHAY LS8 .... 7 M4
Gledhow Ri RHAY LS8 .... 88 D8
Gledhow Rd RHAY LS8 .... 7 M4
Gledhow Ter RHAY LS8 .... 7 M4
Gledhow Vale Rd CHAL LS7 .... 87 L6 [8]
Gledhow Valley Rd CHAL LS7 .... 87 M6
Gledhow Wood Av RHAY LS8 .... 88 B7
Gledhow Wood CI RHAY LS8 .... 110 C1 [8]
Gledhow Wood Gv RHAY LS8 .... 88 B7
Gledhow Wood Rd RHAY LS8 .... 88 B7
Glen Av ROY/SHW OL2 .... 229 L6 [8]
TOD OL14 .... 141 H7
Glenavon Dr ROY/SHW OL2 .... 229 H6 [8]
Glenbrook Dr GTHN BD7 .... 104 A7
Glencoe CI GFTH/SHER LS25 .... 135 H6
Glencoe Cft GFTH/SHER LS25 .... 135 H6
Glencoe Gdns GFTH/SHER LS25 .... 135 H6
Glencoe Ter GFTH/SHER LS25 .... 135 H6
LVSG WF15 .... 172 C3
Glencoe Vw OSM LS9 .... 110 B8
Glendale Av ILK LS29 .... 38 C1
Glendale CI BGLY BD16 .... 81 H7 [8]
Glendale HOR/CROF WF4 .... 197 H5

Glendale Av GFTH/SHER LS25 .... 113 H8
Glendale CI DOD/DAR S75 .... 260 D5
WBSY BD6 .... 126 C7
Glendale Dr WBSY BD6 .... 126 C7
Glendare Av GTHN BD7 .... 104 A8
Glendare Rd GTHN BD7 .... 104 A8 [8]
Glendare Ter GTHN BD7 .... 104 A8 [8]
Glen Dene BGLY BD16 .... 81 H7 [8]
ILK LS29 .... 61 K2
Glendorne Dr HUDE HD5 .... 193 L5 [8]
Glendower Pk BHP/TINH LS16 .... 86 F4
Gleneagles CI BOW BD4 .... 127 K6
Gleneagles Rd AL/HA/HU LS17 .... 87 K2
FEA/AMT WF7 .... 179 M5
Gleneagles Wy HUDN HD2 .... 192 B3 [8]
Glenfield SHPY BD18 .... 83 C5
Glen Field Av HUDN HD2 .... 193 H3
Glenfield Av WBSY BD6 .... 126 F8 [8]
WBY LS22 .... 48 B2
Glenfields HOR/CROF WF4 .... 218 F1
Glenfields CI HOR/CROF WF4 .... 218 F1 [8]
Glen Gdns WHIT OL12 .... 206 B3
Glen Garth KGHY BD21 .... 3 K9
Glen Gv MOR LS27 .... 152 D3
Glenholme SHPY BD18 .... 83 C5
Glenholme Rd GIR BD8 .... 104 D5 [8]
PDSY/CALV LS28 .... 106 C4
Glenholm Rd BAIL BD17 .... 82 E5
Glenhurst BOW BD4 .... 127 M5 [8]
Glenhurst Av KGHY BD21 .... 3 H9
Glenhurst Dr KGHY BD21 .... 3 J8
Glenhurst Gv KGHY BD21 .... 3 J8
Glenhurst Rd SHPY BD18 .... 82 A6
Glenlea CI BRAM LS13 .... 107 J3
Glenlea Gdns BRAM LS13 .... 107 J3
Glen Lee La KGHY BD21 .... 79 M2
Glenlee Rd GTHN BD7 .... 104 B8
Glenlow Rd BTLY WF17 .... 174 B3
Glenlyon Av KGHY BD21 .... 57 J5
Glenlyon Dr KGHY BD21 .... 57 J5
Glenmere Mt YEA LS19 .... 62 F7
Glenmoor Av BSLY S70 .... 260 D6 [8]
Glenmore CI ECHL BD2 .... 105 L5 [8]
Glenmore Ct BHP/TINH LS16 .... 64 A3 [8]
Glen Mt BGLY BD16 .... 81 H7 [8]
ILK LS29 .... 61 K3
MOR LS27 .... 152 D3
Glenrose Dr GTHN BD7 .... 104 A8
Glenroyd SHPY BD18 .... 83 C5
Glenroyd Av WBSY BD6 .... 126 F7
Glenroyd CI PDSY/CALV LS28 .... 106 C7
Glensdale Gv OSM LS9 .... 110 B7
Glensdale Mt OSM LS9 .... 110 B7
Glensdale Rd OSM LS9 .... 110 B7
Glensdale St OSM LS9 .... 110 B7
Glensdale Ter OSM LS9 .... 110 B7
Glenside Av SHPY BD18 .... 83 C5
Glenside CI HUDW HD3 .... 191 M6
Glen Side Rd HOLM/MEL HD7 .... 212 C7
Glenside Rd SHPY BD18 .... 83 H5 [8]
Glenstone Gv GIR BD8 .... 104 B7
Glen Ter HFAX HX1 .... 168 D1
The Glen TOD OL14 .... 141 H7 [8]
Glenthorpe Crs OSM LS9 .... 110 C6 [8]
Glenthorpe Crs OSM LS9 .... 110 C6
Glenthorpe Ter OSM LS9 .... 110 C6 [8]
Glen Vw BGLY BD16 .... 80 D5 [8]
Glenview Av BGLY BD16 .... 104 A3 [8]
Glenview CI SHPY BD18 .... 81 L7
Glenview Dr BGLY BD16 .... 81 L7
Glenview Gv SHPY BD18 .... 81 M7 [8]
Glen View Rd BGLY BD16 .... 81 L1
HBR HX7 .... 143 G3
KBTN HD8 .... 238 C4
Glenview Ter SHPY BD18 .... 81 M7
Glen Vw St TOD OL14 .... 140 E5 [8]
Glenview Ter SHPY BD18 .... 82 B6 [8]
Glen Wy BGLY BD16 .... 59 L8
Glenwood Av BAIL BD17 .... 82 A5
Global Av BEE/HOL LS11 .... 131 C5
Globe Ct LVSG WF15 .... 172 D2
Globe Fold GIR BD8 .... 4 A3
Globe Rd WOR/ARM LS12 .... 8 C2
Glossop Gv HDGY LS6 .... 6 E1
Glossop Mt HDGY LS6 .... 6 E1
Glossop St HDGY LS6 .... 6 E1
Glossop Vw HDGY LS6 .... 6 E1
Gloucester Ct
WKFDW/WTN WF2 .... 176 B3 [8]
Gloucester Gv
WKFDW/WTN WF2 .... 197 M1 [8]
Gloucester PI
WKFDW/WTN WF2 .... 197 M1 [8]
Gloucester Rd BGLY BD16 .... 81 K4
WKFDW/WTN WF2 .... 197 L1
Gloucester Ter WOR/ARM LS12 .... 109 G7
Glover St WBOW BD5 .... 127 G2 [8]
Glovershaw La BAIL BD17 .... 60 A8
Glover Wy BEE/HOL LS11 .... 131 L4
Glyndon Ct BRIG HD6 .... 170 D6
Glynn Ter GIR BD8 .... 104 D8 [8]
Glynwed Ct SKP/WHF BD23 .... 16 A3 [8]
Gobind Marg BFDE BD3 .... 5 J6
Godfrey Rd HIPP HX3 .... 168 D4
Godfrey St GIR BD8 .... 103 M7
Godley Branch Rd HIPP HX3 .... 11 H3
Godley La HIPP HX3 .... 11 M3
Godley Rd HIPP HX3 .... 11 H3
Godley St BSLYN/ROY S71 .... 243 M2
Godly CI RPDN/SBR HX6 .... 188 C5
Godly La RPDN/SBR HX6 .... 188 C5
Godwin St BFD BD1 .... 4 D9
Goff Well La KGHY BD21 .... 79 L4
Goit Stock La BGLY BD16 .... 80 D6
Goit Stock Ter BGLY BD16 .... 80 D6
Golcar Brow Rd
HOLM/MEL HD7 .... 234 E4

Goldbourne Dr ROY/SHW OL2 .... 229 K6 [8]
Goldcrest Av BGLY BD16 .... 103 K7 [8]
Goldcrest Ct HUDS HD4 .... 214 A4
Gold Cft BSLY S70 .... 261 J6 [8]
Golden Butts Rd ILK LS29 .... 38 C5
Golden Sq HOR/CROF WF4 .... 197 K5
Golden St ROY/SHW OL2 .... 230 A6
Golden Ter WOR/ARM LS12 .... 130 C2
Golden View Dr KGHY BD21 .... 58 B9
Goldfields Av GTL/HWG HX4 .... 168 C6 [8]
Goldfields CI GTL/HWG HX4 .... 168 C6 [8]
Goldfields Vw GTL/HWG HX4 .... 168 C6
Goldington Av HUDN HD2 .... 191 H6
Goldington Dr HUDN HD2 .... 191 H6
Gold St BSLY S70 .... 261 J6
Golf Av LUD/ILL HX2 .... 145 L7
Golf Crs LUD/ILL HX2 .... 145 L7
Golf La WOR/ARM LS12 .... 152 A6
Golf Links Av TAD LS24 .... 71 H4
Golf Links Ct TAD LS24 .... 71 L4
Golf Links Crs TAD LS24 .... 71 K4
Gomersal Av CLECK BD19 .... 150 B7
Gomersal Rd CLECK BD19 .... 150 B8
Gondal Ct WBOW BD5 .... 126 E5
Gooder Av BSLYN/ROY S71 .... 243 L3
Gooder La BRIG HD6 .... 170 C5
Gooder St BRIG HD6 .... 170 C4
Good Hope CI NORM WF6 .... 178 F3
Goodman St MID LS10 .... 9 M6
Goodrick La AL/HA/HU LS17 .... 65 K7
Goods La EARL WF12 .... 181 G1
Goodwin PI HUDN HD2 .... 193 H1
Goodwin Rd WOR/ARM LS12 .... 108 A8
Goodwood EARD/LOFT WF3 .... 153 M3 [8]
Goodwood Av GFTH/SHER LS25 .... 135 K4
Goody Cross La RTHW LS26 .... 134 D4
Goose Cote La HWTH BD22 .... 79 G3
Goose Cote Wy HWTH BD22 .... 79 G3
Goose Eye HWTH BD22 .... 56 D8
Goosefield Ri GFTH/SHER LS25 .... 134 F1
Goose Gn HOLM/MEL HD7 .... 254 C7
Goose Green La CGL BB8 .... 74 D4
Goose HI HECK WF16 .... 172 F2
Goosehill La WKFDE WF1 .... 178 A7
Goosehill Rd NORM WF6 .... 178 C6
Goose La GSLY LS20 .... 60 F5
WHIT OL12 .... 206 B6 [8]
Goose West La RPDN/SBR HX6 .... 167 L5
Gordale CI BTLY WF17 .... 173 K1
Gordon Av OSS WF5 .... 174 F8 [8]
Gordon Ct LIT OL15 .... 185 K8 [8]
MIRF WF14 .... 172 E8
Gordon Dr HDGY LS6 .... 87 C8
Gordon PI HEM/SK/SE WF9 .... 247 H4
Gordon St AIRE BD20 .... 55 M1
BSLY S70 .... 262 A6
CLAY BD14 .... 125 K2 [8]
COL BB8 .... 74 A1
EARD/LOFT WF3 .... 154 A6
ELL HX5 .... 169 H8
FEA/AMT WF7 .... 179 M7
HIPP HX3 .... 146 D4
HWTH BD22 .... 79 G6 [8]
IDLE BD10 .... 83 K5 [8]
ILK LS29 .... 38 F2
KGHY BD21 .... 2 E4
MILN OL16 .... 229 K3 [8]
ROCH OL11 .... 228 C1 [8]
ROY/SHW OL2 .... 229 L7
RPDN/SBR HX6 .... 167 J3
WBOW BD5 .... 5 C9
WKFDE WF1 .... 199 C4
Gordon Ter AIRE BD20 .... 34 B3 [8]
HOLM/MEL HD7 .... 212 F4
IDLE BD10 .... 83 K5 [8]
Goring Park Av OSS WF5 .... 197 J2 [8]
Gorrel St ROCH OL11 .... 228 C1 [8]
Gorse Av BAIL BD17 .... 82 A4
Gorse La GFTH/SHER LS25 .... 137 K1
Gorse Lea MID LS10 .... 131 M6 [8]
Gorse Rd HUDW HD3 .... 191 L8
MILN OL16 .... 207 H8
Gorsley Bank LIT OL15 .... 185 L7
Gorton St HEM/SK/SE WF9 .... 225 K5
Goschen St SKP/WHF BD23 .... 16 C3 [8]
Gosling La GTL/HWG HX4 .... 189 H4
Gosport CI HUDW HD3 .... 190 C6
Gosport La GTL/HWG HX4 .... 190 C6
HUDW HD3 .... 190 C6
Gothic Mt FEA/AMT WF7 .... 179 J6
Gothic St CUL/QBY BD13 .... 125 C5
Gotts Park Av WOR/ARM LS12 .... 108 B5
Gotts Park Crs WOR/ARM LS12 .... 108 B4
Gotts Park Vw WOR/ARM LS12 .... 108 B4
Gotts Rd WOR/ARM LS12 .... 8 B1
Gott's Ter AIRE BD20 .... 57 J3
Gott St HWTH BD22 .... 79 H6 [8]
Gough La RPDN/SBR HX6 .... 166 D9
Goulbourne St KGHY BD21 .... 2 F7
Governor's Yd WKFDE WF1 .... 176 F7 [8]
Gowers St MILN OL16 .... 206 D6
Gower St LDSU LS2 .... 7 J8
Gracechurch St GIR BD8 .... 4 C4
Grace Leather La BTLY WF17 .... 174 A1
Grace St BSLYN/ROY S71 .... 244 B3
KGHY BD21 .... 3 K5
LDS LS1 .... 6 D5
WHIT OL12 .... 206 C4 [8]
Gracey La WBSY BD6 .... 126 E5
Grafton CI BAIL BD17 .... 82 F2
KNOT WF11 .... 182 B1
Grafton PI HIPP HX3 .... 146 C3
Grafton Rd KGHY BD21 .... 2 F9
Grafton St BSLY S70 .... 260 F5
BTLY WF17 .... 173 M3
CAS WF10 .... 158 A4
CHAL LS7 .... 7 L1
KGHY BD21 .... 2 E9
MILN OL16 .... 206 D5
WBOW BD5 .... 4 D9
Gragwood La HORS LS18 .... 85 L6 [8]

Graham Mt BULY LS4 .... 108 F3 [14]
Graham's Orch BSLY S70 .... 261 G5 [8]
Graham St BULY LS4 .... 108 F3
HTON BD9 .... 104 C4 [8]
Graham Ter BULY LS4 .... 108 F3
Graham Vw BULY LS4 .... 108 F3
Graham Wk MOR LS27 .... 129 M7 [8]
Grains Rd ROY/SHW OL2 .... 229 L7
Grain St WBOW BD5 .... 126 D3
Gramfield Rd HUDS HD4 .... 213 K3
Grammar School St BFD BD1 .... 4 E4
Grampian Av
WKFDW/WTN WF2 .... 198 A3
Grampian CI DOD/DAR S75 .... 260 D4 [8]
KBTN HD8 .... 238 B3
Grampian Wy ROY/SHW OL2 .... 229 J6
Granary Ct ECHL BD2 .... 105 L1 [8]
Granby Av HDGY LS6 .... 108 F1
Granby Ct HEM/SK/SE WF9 .... 247 J1 [8]
Granby Gdns AIRE BD20 .... 58 B5
Granby Gv HDGY LS6 .... 108 F1
Granby La AIRE BD20 .... 58 B5
Granby Mt HDGY LS6 .... 108 F1
Granby PI HDGY LS6 .... 108 F1
Granby Rd HDGY LS6 .... 108 F2 [8]
Granby St BOW BD4 .... 5 H9
CUL/QBY BD13 .... 125 G5
Granby Ter HDGY LS6 .... 108 F1
Granby Vw HDGY LS6 .... 108 F2
Grandage Ter GIR BD8 .... 104 D6 [8]
Grand Cross Rd HUDE HD5 .... 193 G8
Grandidge St ROCH OL11 .... 228 A1 [8]
Grandsmere PI HIPP HX3 .... 168 D2 [8]
Grand Stand HOLM/MEL HD7 .... 212 D1
Grand Stand Rd
EARD/LOFT WF3 .... 176 B1
Grange Av BFDE BD3 .... 106 B6
BOW BD4 .... 128 C6 [8]
BSPA/BRAM LS23 .... 49 J3
BTLY WF17 .... 173 K5 [8]
CHAL LS7 .... 7 L1
GFTH/SHER LS25 .... 113 H8
HEM/SK/SE WF9 .... 247 J3
HOLM/MEL HD7 .... 233 J2
HUDN HD2 .... 192 B5
ILK LS29 .... 38 F2
LUD/ILL HX2 .... 146 B1
MILN OL16 .... 229 H2 [8]
PBR HG3 .... 28 E3
SHPY BD18 .... 82 A6
TAD LS24 .... 72 A2
WIL/AL BD15 .... 103 L6
YEA LS19 .... 62 E8
Grange Bank HIPP HX3 .... 125 L8
Grange Bank CI HUDE HD5 .... 15 L4
Grange Br AIRE BD20 .... 35 J6
Grange Castle YEA LS19 .... 62 F8 [8]
Grange CI AL/HA/HU LS17 .... 67 M2
CUD/GR S72 .... 245 H3 [8]
HEM/SK/SE WF9 .... 225 G4
HORS LS18 .... 85 H6 [8]
HUDW HD3 .... 190 C6 [8]
ILK LS29 .... 38 F2
KNOT WF11 .... 181 M2
MID LS10 .... 9 K7
Grange Ct AL/HA/HU LS17 .... 87 L1
BGLY BD16 .... 81 K7 [8]
HIPP HX3 .... 169 J3 [8]
MSTN/BAR LS15 .... 90 B8 [8]
Grange Crs AIRE BD20 .... 58 A5
BSLYN/ROY S71 .... 262 A4
CHAL LS7 .... 7 L1
TAD LS24 .... 71 M2
YEA LS19 .... 62 E8 [8]
Grange Cft AL/HA/HU LS17 .... 87 L1
Grange Dr GIR BD8 .... 103 L6
KBTN HD8 .... 217 M6
OSS WF5 .... 197 H3
Grange Est ILK LS29 .... 38 F2
Grangefield Av BTLY WF17 .... 173 K3
ILK LS29 .... 38 F3
Grangefield Rd PDSY/CALV LS28.. 107 G4
Grange Fields Mt MID LS10 .... 132 B7 [8]
Grange Fields Rd RTHW LS26 .... 132 B8
Grange Fields Wy RTHW LS26 .... 132 B8
Grange Gv AIRE BD20 .... 58 A5
BFDE BD3 .... 106 B6 [8]
Grange Hts HIPP HX3 .... 169 J3
Grange Holt AL/HA/HU LS17 .... 87 L1
Grange La AWLS/ASK DN6 .... 249 J2
BRIG HD6 .... 171 G4
BSLYN/ROY S71 .... 262 A5
GFTH/SHER LS25 .... 135 K4
HOR/CROF WF4 .... 217 M2
HWTH BD22 .... 78 B3
KBTN HD8 .... 237 M3
UPML OL3 .... 231 H8
Grange Mt YEA LS19 .... 62 E8
Grange Pk BAIL BD17 .... 83 G3
HIPP HX3 .... 168 D3
Grange Park Av RHAY LS8 .... 110 F1
Grange Park CI CAS WF10 .... 157 J1 [8]
MOR LS27 .... 130 D7 [8]
RHAY LS8 .... 111 G1
Grange Park Crs RHAY LS8 .... 110 F1
Grange Park Dr BGLY BD16 .... 81 J6
MOR LS27 .... 130 D7
Grange Park Gv RHAY LS8 .... 110 F1
Grange Park Ms MOR LS27 .... 130 D7 [8]
Grange Park PI RHAY LS8 .... 110 F1 [8]
Grange Park Rd BGLY BD16 .... 81 J6
RHAY LS8 .... 110 F1
Grange Park Ter RHAY LS8 .... 111 G1
Grange Park Wk RHAY LS8 .... 110 F1 [8]
Grange Park Wy MOR LS27 .... 130 D7 [8]
Grange Rd AIRE BD20 .... 34 F5
AIRE BD20 .... 56 C1
AIRE BD20 .... 58 A5
AWLS/ASK DN6 .... 227 M5
BGLY BD16 .... 81 K2
BSLYN/ROY S71 .... 243 J3
BTLY WF17 .... 173 J3
CAS WF10 .... 158 F5
CLECK BD19 .... 149 L6
CUD/GR S72 .... 245 H4
EARL WF12 .... 174 C3

HUDW HD3 .... 191 G8
ILK LS29 .... 40 A5
MID LS10 .... 9 K7
TAD LS24 .... 72 A2
WIL/AL BD15 .... 103 L6
YEA LS19 .... 62 E8
The Grange Rd BHP/TINH LS16 ... 86 D2
Grange St HIPP HX3 .... 10 C1
KGHY BD21 .... 3 H3
WKFDW/WTN WF2 .... 12 A4
Grange Ter CHAL LS7 .... 7 K1
HOLM/MEL HD7 .... 233 J2
MOR LS27 .... 130 D7
PDSY/CALV LS28 .... 107 G6
SHPY BD18 .... 82 D8
WIL/AL BD15 .... 103 L6
The Grange GFTH/SHER LS25 .. 113 K7
Grange Valley Rd BTLY WF17 ... 174 B2
Grange Vw BFDE BD3 .... 106 B6
CHAL LS7 .... 7 K1
EARL WF12 .... 195 M5
HEM/SK/SE WF9 .... 223 M8
OT LS21 .... 41 H5
PDSY/CALV LS28 .... 107 G6
TAD LS24 .... 93 M2
Grange View Gdns
AL/HA/HU LS17 .... 89 H5
Grangeway GIR BD8 .... 103 L6
HEM/SK/SE WF9 .... 223 M7
Grangewood Ct WKFDE WF1 ... 176 F1
Grangewood Gdns
BHP/TINH LS16 .... 86 D5
Granhamthorpe BRAM LS13 ... 107 L4
Granny Av MOR LS27 .... 130 E6
Granny Hall Gv BRIG HD6 ...... 170 B2
Granny Hall La BRIG HD6 ...... 170 B1
Granny Hall Pk BRIG HD6 ...... 170 B1
Granny La MIRF WF14 .... 194 D3
WOR/ARM LS12 .... 130 C1
Grant Av RHAY LS8 .... 7 L4
Grantham Pl GTHN BD7 .... 4 B9
HIPP HX3 .... 146 D3
Grantham Rd GTHN BD7 .... 4 A9
HIPP HX3 .... 146 D3
Grantham Ter GTHN BD7 .... 4 B9
Grantley Hl HUDN HD2 .... 192 F1
Grantley St WKFDE WF1 .... 13 G1
Grantley Wy WKFDE WF1 .... 13 H1
Granton Rd CHAL LS7 .... 109 M1
Granton St BFDE BD3 .... 105 L7
Grant St BFDE BD3 .... 5 K5
HWTH BD22 .... 2 C5
HWTH BD22 .... 100 E4
Granville Ct MILN OL16 .... 229 K3
Granville Mt OT LS21 .... 41 H7
Granville Pl WIL/AL BD15 ...... 103 L6
Granville Rd HTON BD9 .... 104 D1
OSM LS9 .... 7 M6
Granville St CAS WF10 .... 179 L1
CLAY BD14 .... 125 L1
COL BB8 .... 74 A1
DEWS WF13 .... 173 J4
DOD/DAR S75 .... 260 F3
ELL HX5 .... 169 H8
FEA/AMT WF7 .... 201 L2
LVSG WF15 .... 172 D3
NORM WF6 .... 178 D4
PDSY/CALV LS28 .... 106 D7
PDSY/CALV LS28 .... 107 H4
SKP/WHF BD23 .... 16 A2
TOD OL14 .... 163 J5
Granville Ter BGLY BD16 .... 81 J3
HTON BD9 .... 104 D1
YEA LS19 .... 62 E7
Grape St HFAX HX1 .... 10 E6
KGHY BD21 .... 3 J5
MID LS10 .... 9 J6
WIL/AL BD15 .... 103 L2
Grasleigh Av WIL/AL BD15 ...... 103 J4
Grasleigh Wy WIL/AL BD15 ..... 103 J3
Grasmere Av WBY LS22 .... 47 L1
Grasmere Cl CAS WF10 .... 159 G5
STKB/PEN S36 .... 270 F2
WOR/ARM LS12 .... 108 F8
Grasmere Ct WOR/ARM LS12 ... 108 F7
Grasmere Crs DOD/DAR S75 ... 242 D5
Grasmere Dr ELL HX5 .... 169 K7
WBY LS22 .... 47 L1
Grasmere Rd AWLS/ASK DN6 ... 249 H3
BSLYN/ROY S71 .... 261 J5
EARL WF12 .... 174 A4
ECHL BD2 .... 105 J3
HOLM/MEL HD7 .... 235 G5
HUD HD1 .... 14 A5
LM/WK BD12 .... 149 G5
ROY/SHW OL2 .... 228 F8
WKFDW/WTN WF2 .... 176 A2
WOR/ARM LS12 .... 108 F8
Grasmere St WHIT OL12 .... 206 B5
Grasscroft HUDE HD5 .... 215 H4
Grasscroft Av HOLM/MEL HD7 .. 236 A2
Grasscroft Rd HOLM/MEL HD7 .. 236 A2
HUD HD1 .... 191 M7
Grassington Rd SKP/WHF BD23 . 16 B1
Gratrix La RPDN/SBR HX6 ...... 167 L2
Grattan Rd BFD BD1 .... 4 D6
Graveleythorpe Ri
MSTN/BAR LS15 .... 111 K5
Graveleythorpe Rd
MSTN/BAR LS15 .... 111 K5
Gravelly Hill La AL/HA/HU LS17 . 43 J3
Gray Av SHPY BD18 .... 104 F1
Gray Ct MSTN/BAR LS15 .... 111 M6
Gray Hall Cl GTL/HWG HX4 ..... 190 B3
Grayrigg Cl MSTN/BAR LS15 ... 111 G1
Grayrigg Ct MSTN/BAR LS15 ... 110 F3
Grayshon Dr WBY BD6 .... 126 E5
Grayshon St BIRK/DRI BD11 ... 151 G1
Gray's Rd BSLYN/ROY S71 ...... 243 L5
Gray St LVSG WF15 .... 172 A4
Grayswood Crs BOW BD4 ...... 127 M3
Grayswood Dr BOW BD4 .... 127 M3
BOW BD4 .... 127 M3
Great Albion St HFAX HX1 ...... 11 G5
Great Ben La HOLM/MEL HD7 .. 212 A2
Great Bent Cl WHIT OL12 ...... 206 F2
Great Cliffe Rd DOD/DAR S75 .. 260 A6

Great Cross St BFD BD1 .... 5 G7
Great Edge Rd LUD/ILL HX2 ... 145 H8
Greatfield Cl OSS WF5 .... 197 G1
Greatfield Dr OSS WF5 .... 175 G8
Greatfield Gdns OSS WF5 ...... 197 G1
Greatfield Rd OSS WF5 .... 197 G1
Great Gates Cl ROCH OL11 ..... 228 C2
Great Gates Rd ROCH OL11 .... 228 C4
Great George St LDS LS1 .... 6 D8
MILN OL16 .... 206 F7
Great Horton Rd GTHN BD7 ...... 4 A9
GTHN BD7 .... 126 A4
Great House La RPDN/SBR HX6 . 188 C3
Great House Rd TOD OL14 ..... 142 A6
Great Howarth WHIT OL12 ..... 206 D2
Great Meadow ROY/SHW OL2 .. 229 H5
Great Northern Rd KGHY BD21 ... 3 H6
Great Northern St MOR LS27 ... 152 B3
Great North Rd AWLS/ASK DN6 . 249 H8
GFTH/SHER LS25 .... 114 A4
GFTH/SHER LS25 .... 137 G4
Great Pasture ILK LS29 .... 40 B4
Great Pond St DEWS WF13 ...... 195 H1
Great Russell Ct GTHN BD7 ...... 4 A6
Great Russell St GTHN BD7 ...... 4 A6
Great Wilson St BEE/HOL LS11 ... 8 F3
Greatwood Av SKP/WHF BD23 ... 16 C3
Great Wood St BTLY WF17 ...... 173 L2
Greave Cl HUDN HD2 .... 192 D2
Greavefield La PONT WF8 ...... 181 K6
Greave House Dr LUD/ILL HX2 .. 144 F7
Greave House Flds
LUD/ILL HX2 .... 145 G6
Greave House La KBTN HD8 ... 215 M3
Greave House Pk LUD/ILL HX2 . 144 F7
Greave House Ter KBTN HD8 ... 215 M3
Greave Rd HOLM/MEL HD7 ..... 254 C6
RPDN/SBR HX6 .... 166 A8
Greaves Av WKFDW/WTN WF2 . 197 L1
Greaves Cft KBTN HD8 .... 215 M3
Greaves Fold DOD/DAR S75 ... 260 D4
GTL/HWG HX4 .... 133 L8
Greaves Rd DEWS WF13 .... 173 M5
Greaves Smithy ILK LS29 .... 19 L7
Greaves St CAS WF10 .... 157 M6
ROY/SHW OL2 .... 229 L7
WBOW BD5 .... 126 F3
Greave St TOD OL14 .... 163 H1
Greek St CAS WF10 .... 158 A6
LDS LS1 .... 6 F9
Greenacre Av LM/WK BD12 ...... 148 E5
Green Acre Cl BAIL BD17 .... 82 F3
Greenacre Cl LM/WK BD12 ...... 148 F4
Greenacre Ct GFTH/SHER LS25 . 113 J7
Greenacre Dr KBTN HD8 .... 257 G5
LM/WK BD12 .... 148 F4
Greenacre Pk YEA LS19 .... 84 D1
Greenacre Park Av YEA LS19 ... 84 D1
Greenacre Park Ms YEA LS19 ... 84 E1
Greenacre Park Ri YEA LS19 ... 84 D1
Greenacre Rd HEM/SK/SE WF9 . 225 L6
Green Acres FEA/AMT WF7 ...... 202 A3
HOR/CROF WF4 .... 198 C7
Greenacres HIPP HX3 .... 125 M8
OSS WF5 .... 174 F5
SKP/WHF BD23 .... 16 D1
Greenacres Av HIPP HX3 .... 125 M8
Green Acres Cl KBTN HD8 ...... 217 L8
Greenacres Cl OSS WF5 .... 174 F5
Greenacres Dr BTLY WF17 ...... 151 K4
HIPP HX3 .... 125 M8
Greenacres Fold HIPP HX3 ...... 57 H5
Greenacre Gv HIPP HX3 .... 125 M8
Greenacre Wk HOR/CROF WF4 . 222 E7
Greenacre Wy LM/WK BD12 .... 148 F4
Greenaire Pl BFD BD1 .... 4 D6
Green Av AIRE BD20 .... 35 M4
GFTH/SHER LS25 .... 135 H3
HECK WF16 .... 173 G2
Green Balk La KBTN HD8 .... 216 B3
Greenbank BSLYN/ROY S71 ...... 243 H5
Green Bank CLECK BD19 .... 150 B8
EARD/LOFT WF3 .... 154 F5
Greenbank Dr LIT OL15 .... 207 H3
Greenbank Gv NORM WF6 ...... 178 B3
Greenbank Rd NORM WF6 .... 178 A3
WHIT OL12 .... 206 B4
WIL/AL BD15 .... 103 L6
Greenbanks Av HORS LS18 ...... 85 K4
Greenbanks Cl HORS LS18 ...... 85 L4
Greenbank Dr HORS LS18 ...... 85 K4
Greenbank Wk CUD/GR S72 .... 245 H7
Green Bridge Cl ROCH OL11 ... 228 B2
Green Cha HDGY LS6 .... 87 G7
Green Cliff HOLM/MEL HD7 ..... 236 B1
Greencliffe Av BAIL BD17 ...... 82 D3
Green Cl AIRE BD20 .... 16 E8
AIRE BD20 .... 35 H8
BTLY WF17 .... 174 A1
DEWS WF13 .... 173 J4
GIR BD8 .... 104 A6
HDGY LS6 .... 87 H7
Green Crs HDGY LS6 .... 87 G7
HOLM/MEL HD7 .... 213 G1
Green Cft HEM/SK/SE WF9 ...... 223 K4
Greendale Cl HIPP HX3 .... 147 K3
Greendown Cl ILK LS29 .... 38 F2
Green End BRIG HD6 .... 170 C5
CLAY BD14 .... 125 K2
Green End La WKFDW/WTN WF2 . 12 D9
Green End Rd AIRE BD20 .... 59 G5
WBSY BD6 .... 126 D6
Greenfell Cl HWTH BD22 .... 2 C7
Greenfield Av GFTH/SHER LS25 . 135 J4
GTL/HWG HX4 .... 190 B4
HIPP HX3 .... 147 J3
KBTN HD8 .... 257 H3

OSS WF5 .... 197 J2
WKFDW/WTN WF2 .... 176 B4
Greenfield Ct BHP/TINH LS16 ... 86 D2
HWTH BD22 .... 2 B7
Greenfield Crs CUL/QBY BD13 ... 80 A8
Greenfield Dr CLECK BD19 ...... 149 H6
MOR LS27 .... 129 K7
Greenfield Gdns AIRE BD20 ...... 35 H8
Greenfield Garth
GFTH/SHER LS25 .... 135 J4
Greenfield La BOW BD4 .... 127 K8
GTHN BD7 .... 126 B2
IDLE BD10 .... 83 K5
MILN OL16 .... 206 F3
ROY/SHW OL2 .... 229 K8
Greenfield Mt
WKFDW/WTN WF2 .... 176 B4
Greenfield Pl HIPP HX3 .... 148 C7
Greenfield Ri GFTH/SHER LS25 . 135 J4
Greenfield Rd HEM/SK/SE WF9 . 245 M1
HOLM/MEL HD7 .... 253 K1
NORM WF6 .... 178 B4
OSM LS9 .... 9 M1
OSS WF5 .... 197 J2
Greenfields HECK WF16 .... 172 E1
Greenfield St ROCH OL11 ...... 228 C3
Greenfields Wy ILK LS29 .... 40 B3
TOD OL14 .... 140 C5
Greenfield V GFTH/SHER LS25 .. 135 J4
Greenfield Vw GFTH/SHER LS25 . 135 J4
Greenfield Wy
WKFDW/WTN WF2 .... 176 B4
Greenfinch Gv HUDS HD4 ...... 214 B4
Greenfold La WBY LS22 .... 48 B1
Greenfoot Cl DOD/DAR S75 .... 260 F5
Greenfoot La DOD/DAR S75 .... 260 F5
Green Gdns HOLM/MEL HD7 ... 213 G1
Greengate AIRE BD20 .... 35 M4
RTHW LS26 .... 133 L8
Greengate Cl WHIT OL12 ...... 206 F2
Green Gate La HOLM/MEL HD7 . 234 C1
Green Gate Rd HOLM/MEL HD7 . 253 J2
Greengate Rd KGHY BD21 ...... 3 J2
PONT WF8 .... 227 H4
Greengates AV LM/WK BD12 ... 148 E5
Green Grove Bank MILN OL16 .. 206 F3
Green Haggs La PBR HG3 .... 28 A4
Green Hall Pk HIPP HX3 .... 147 M1
Green Head Av AIRE BD20 ...... 57 J4
Green Head Dr AIRE BD20 ...... 57 J4
Green Head La AIRE BD20 ...... 57 J4
Greenhead La BRIG HD6 .... 170 A8
HUDE HD5 .... 215 H1
Green Head Rd BHP/TINH LS16 . 86 D6
HUD HD1 .... 14 C7
Green Hl HUDN HD2 .... 192 D2
LUD/ILL HX2 .... 145 K8
Greenhill Av BSLYN/ROY S71 ... 261 G3
PONT WF8 .... 181 G8
ROY/SHW OL2 .... 229 G5
WHIT OL12 .... 206 A6
Greenhill Bank Rd
HOLM/MEL HD7 .... 254 F1
Green Hill Cha WOR/ARM LS12 . 108 D6
Green Hill Cl WOR/ARM LS12 .. 108 B5
Greenhill Crs WOR/ARM LS12 .. 108 C6
Green Hill Cft WOR/ARM LS12 . 108 D8
Greenhill Dr BGLY BD16 .... 59 G7
Green Hill Dr BRAM LS13 ...... 108 A5
Green Hill Gdns WOR/ARM LS12 . 108 D8
Green Hill Gv STKB/PEN S36 ... 258 C8
Green Hill Holt
WOR/ARM LS12 .... 108 D8
Greenhill La BFDE BD3 .... 105 L7
BGLY BD16 .... 59 H8
Green Hill La HWTH BD22 ...... 54 D5
WOR/ARM LS12 .... 130 D1
Green Hill Mt BRAM LS13 ...... 108 A5
Green Hill Mt PONT WF8 ...... 181 G8
Green Hill Pl BRAM LS13 ...... 108 A5
Greenhill Rd BRAM LS13 ...... 108 A5
Greenhill Rd HUDW HD3 .... 191 G7
WKFDE WF1 .... 13 H1
Greenhills YEA LS19 .... 84 E3
Greenhill St BFDE BD3 .... 105 L7
Green Hill Wy BRAM LS13 ...... 108 A5
Greenholme Cl ILK LS29 .... 40 B4
Greenholme Ct BOW BD4 ...... 128 B4
Green House Hl KBTN HD8 ..... 238 E2
Green House La KBTN HD8 ..... 238 E2
Greenhouse Rd HUDN HD2 .... 192 C4
Greenhow Cl BULY LS4 .... 108 F4
Greenhow Gdns BULY LS4 ...... 108 F4
Greenhow Pk ILK LS29 .... 39 M5
Greenhow Rd BULY LS4 .... 108 F4
Greenhow Wk BULY LS4 .... 108 F4
Greenland Av CUL/QBY BD13 .. 124 F6
Greenland Rd HBR HX7 .... 119 L8
Greenland Vls CUL/QBY BD13 . 125 G6
Green La AIRE BD20 .... 17 J8
AIRE BD20 .... 34 D8
AIRE BD20 .... 35 J8
AL/HA/HU LS17 .... 44 D2
AWLS/ASK DN6 .... 249 G3
BAIL BD17 .... 82 C2
BAIL BD17 .... 82 D5
BEE/HOL LS11 .... 131 J5
BHP/TINH LS16 .... 85 M2
BRIG HD6 .... 170 A1
BRIG HD6 .... 171 J4
BSPA/BRAM LS23 .... 49 G7
CAS WF10 .... 135 M8
CAS WF10 .... 158 B4
CAS WF10 .... 179 L1
CLECK BD19 .... 149 M4
CUL/QBY BD13 .... 103 G8
CUL/QBY BD13 .... 124 D3
CUL/QBY BD13 .... 125 G1
DEWS WF13 .... 173 J5
DOD/DAR S75 .... 260 D4
EARD/LOFT WF3 .... 154 E5
ECHL BD2 .... 105 M3
FEA/AMT WF7 .... 179 M8

FEA/AMT WF7 .... 201 M8
GFTH/SHER LS25 .... 113 J7
GFTH/SHER LS25 .... 135 H3
GIR BD8 .... 4 B2
GTHN BD7 .... 126 C1
GTL/HWG HX4 .... 168 E3
GTL/HWG HX4 .... 189 H6
GTL/HWG HX4 .... 190 B5
HBR HX7 .... 143 G1
HEM/SK/SE WF9 .... 225 L5
HEM/SK/SE WF9 .... 246 D4
HIPP HX3 .... 11 M7
HIPP HX3 .... 147 L1
HOLM/MEL HD7 .... 211 K6
HOLM/MEL HD7 .... 235 G5
HOLM/MEL HD7 .... 254 C4
HOR/CROF WF4 .... 196 B8
HOR/CROF WF4 .... 197 H8
HOR/CROF WF4 .... 197 M6
HOR/CROF WF4 .... 218 F1
HOR/CROF WF4 .... 221 J8
HORS LS18 .... 85 K7
HWTH BD22 .... 78 B2
HWTH BD22 .... 78 F4
IDLE BD10 .... 83 J6
IDLE BD10 .... 83 L6
ILK LS29 .... 19 G5
ILK LS29 .... 39 L8
ILK LS29 .... 40 A3
KBTN HD8 .... 256 D4
LM/WK BD12 .... 148 L4
LM/WK BD12 .... 149 H2
LUD/ILL HX2 .... 124 A6
LUD/ILL HX2 .... 144 F5
LUD/ILL HX2 .... 168 A1
LVSG WF15 .... 171 M3
MSTN/BAR LS15 .... 111 K5
OT LS21 .... 41 H5
PDSY/CALV LS28 .... 106 F8
PONT WF8 .... 180 F7
RPDN/SBR HX6 .... 188 D3
RTHW LS26 .... 157 H5
SCFT LS14 .... 89 J6
STKB/PEN S36 .... 258 E7
TAD LS24 .... 71 K7
WBY LS22 .... 47 H6
WHIT OL12 .... 206 A6
WKFDW/WTN WF2 .... 176 A6
WOR/ARM LS12 .... 129 L1
YEA LS19 .... 84 D1
Greenthorpe Hl BRAM LS13 ... 108 A7
Greenthorpe Mt BRAM LS13 ... 108 A6
Greenthorpe Rd
WOR/ARM LS12 .... 108 A7
Greenthorpe St BRAM LS13 ... 108 A7
Greenthorpe Wk BRAM LS13 ... 108 A6
Greenthwaite Cl KGHY BD21 ... 2 D1
Greenton Av CLECK BD19 ...... 149 G5
Greenton Crs CUL/QBY BD13 .. 124 F6
Greentop HOR/CROF WF4 ...... 200 D7
PDSY/CALV LS28 .... 106 F8
Green Top WOR/ARM LS12 .... 130 D1
Green Top Gdns
WOR/ARM LS12 .... 130 D1
Green Top St GIR BD8 .... 104 A7
Greenups Ter RPDN/SBR HX6 .. 167 K2
Green Vw HDGY LS6 .... 87 G3
Greenview HOR/CROF WF4 .... 200 D7
Green Vw SCFT LS14 .... 67 L6
Greenview Cl OSM LS9 .... 110 E4
Greenview Mt OSM LS9 .... 110 E4
The Green CUD/GR S72 .... 244 D2
Greenville Av WOR/ARM LS12 . 130 D1
Greenville Dr LM/WK BD12 ..... 127 J2
Greenville Gdns WOR/ARM LS12 . 130 D1
Green Wy AIRE BD20 .... 34 E7
LUD/ILL HX2 .... 124 A6
SCFT LS14 .... 67 L6
Greenway GSLY LS20 .... 61 L7
HOLM/MEL HD7 .... 213 H1
HOLM/MEL HD7 .... 236 B1
MSTN/BAR LS15 .... 111 L5
ROY/SHW OL2 .... 229 H5
Greenway Cl MSTN/BAR LS15 .. 111 L5
Greenway Dr WIL/AL BD15 ..... 103 K7
Greenway Rd WBOW BD5 ...... 127 G4
Greenwell Ct OSM LS9 .... 110 E6
Greenwell Rw CLAY BD14 ...... 125 K2
Greenwood Av EARL WF12 .... 174 D7
ECHL BD2 .... 105 J1
HEM/SK/SE WF9 .... 225 L6
Greenwood Cl NORM WF6 ...... 178 D7
Greenwood Ct HDGY LS6 ...... 87 G7
Greenwood Dr ECHL BD2 ...... 105 J2
Greenwood Mt ECHL BD2 ...... 105 J2
HDGY LS6 .... 87 G6
Green Wood Pk HDGY LS6 .... 87 G7
Greenwood Rd BAIL BD17 ...... 82 D5
EARD/LOFT WF3 .... 153 H6
WKFDE WF1 .... 13 H1
Greenwood Rw
PDSY/CALV LS28 .... 107 H7
Greenwood St DEWS WF13 .... 173 K6
EARL WF12 .... 173 L8
HBR HX7 .... 143 J3
HUDS HD4 .... 214 C1
LIT OL15 .... 207 K1
MILN OL16 .... 206 B7
Greenwood Ter BSLY S70 ...... 261 G4
Greetland Rd GTL/HWG HX4 ... 189 J1
Gregory Cl CLAY BD14 .... 125 L2
Gregory Crs GTHN BD7 .... 126 A4
Gregory Dr KBTN HD8 .... 216 B8
Gregory La HUDE HD5 .... 194 D7
Gregory Rd CAS WF10 .... 180 A1
Gregory Springs La MIRF WF14 . 194 C4
Gregory Springs Mt MIRF WF14 . 194 D4
Gregory Springs Rd MIRF WF14 . 194 D3
Gregory St BTLY WF17 .... 174 A1
Grenfell Dr BFDE BD3 .... 105 M6
Grenfell Rd BFDE BD3 .... 105 M6
Grenfell Ter BFDE BD3 .... 105 M6
Grenley St KNOT WF11 .... 182 C2
Grenville Pl DOD/DAR S75 ..... 260 E3
Grenville Wk HOR/CROF WF4 .. 220 B3
Gresham Av ECHL BD2 .... 105 H2
Gresley Rd KGHY BD21 .... 3 H5
Grey Cl WKFDE WF1 .... 176 D3
Grey Ct WKFDE WF1 .... 176 D3
Greycourt Cl ECHL BD2 .... 83 J8
HFAX HX1 .... 10 C8
Greyfriars Av HUDN HD2 ...... 193 G2
Greyfriar Wk GTHN BD7 .... 126 A3
Grey Gables HOR/CROF WF4 .. 197 G4

Grey Scar Rd HWTH BD22...... 78 C4
Greyshiels Av HDGY LS6...... 108 E2
Greyshiels Cl HDGY LS6...... 108 E2 🔢
Greystone Av ELL HX5...... 191 C1
ILK LS29...... 40 A4
Greystone Ct BRIG HD6...... 170 C7
Greystone Crs IDLE BD10...... 83 L8
Greystone La TOD OL14...... 142 B6
Greystone Mt MSTN/BAR LS15... 111 C7
Greystones Dr HWTH BD22...... 79 H3
OSS WF5...... 197 G3 🔢
Grey Stones La HBR HX7...... 121 K1
Greystones La HWTH BD22...... 55 M8
Greystones Mt HWTH BD22...... 79 H4
Greystones Ri HWTH BD22...... 79 H3
Greystones Rd LUD/ILL HX2...... 145 G7
Grey St WKFDE WF1...... 176 D3
Griffe Dr LM/WK BD12...... 148 E3
Griffe Gdns HWTH BD22...... 78 D3
Griffe Head Crs LM/WK BD12... 148 E4
Griffe Head Rd LM/WK BD12... 148 E4
Griffe Rd HWTH BD22...... 77 M6
LM/WK BD12...... 148 E4
Griff House La EARD/LOFT WF3... 153 K6
Grime La HOLM/MEL HD7...... 255 K6
HOR/CROF WF4...... 200 D3
Grimescar Mdw HUDN HD2...... 191 M4 🔢
Grimescar Rd HUDW HD3...... 191 L3
Grimethorpe St
HEM/SK/SE WF9...... 247 H4
Grimscar Av HUDN HD2...... 192 B5
Grimthorpe Av HDGY LS6...... 108 E1 🔢
Grimthorpe Pl HDGY LS6...... 108 F1
Grimthorpe St HDGY LS6...... 108 F1
Grimthorpe Ter HDGY LS6...... 108 F1
Grisedale Av HUDN HD2...... 192 B5
ROY/SHW OL2...... 228 E6 🔢
Grizedale Cl WBY LS22...... 29 K8
Grosmont Rd BRAM LS13...... 107 L4
Grosmont Ter BRAM LS13...... 107 L3
Grosvenor Av HEM/SK/SE WF9... 225 J7
KBTN HD8...... 216 A3 🔢
PONT WF8...... 180 C5
SHPY BD18...... 82 B6 🔢
Grosvenor Dr BSLY S70...... 260 E5
Grosvenor Gdns AL/HA/HU LS17... 43 L3
Grosvenor Hl CHAL LS7...... 7 G4
Grosvenor Mt HDGY LS6...... 109 H2
Grosvenor Pk CHAL LS7...... 87 L7 🔢
Grosvenor Rd BTLY WF17...... 151 M8
GIR BD8...... 4 C2
HDGY LS6...... 6 B1
HUDE HD5...... 193 C8
SHPY BD18...... 82 B7
Grosvenor St COL BB8...... 74 B1
EARL WF12...... 173 L7 🔢
ELL HX5...... 169 H8 🔢
HECK WF16...... 172 F1 🔢
WKFDE WF1...... 13 L9
Grosvenor Ter GIR BD8...... 4 C2 🔢
HDGY LS6...... 109 H2
HECK WF16...... 172 F2 🔢
HFAX HX1...... 10 D5 🔢
HFAX HX1...... 10 D6 🔢
WBY LS22...... 30 A3 🔢
Grosvenor Wy KBTN HD8...... 216 A3
Grouse Moor La
UL/QBY BD13...... 124 E4 🔢
Grouse St WHIT OL12...... 206 B5
Grove Av HDGY LS6...... 87 G8
HEM/SK/SE WF9...... 224 A8
HIPP HX3...... 146 B4
ILK LS29...... 38 B3
PDSY/CALV LS28...... 106 F7
PONT WF8...... 181 G6 🔢
SHPY BD18...... 104 D1 🔢
Grove Cl CLECK BD19...... 150 D5 🔢
ECHL BD2...... 105 J2
STKB/PEN S36...... 270 F5
Grove Ct HIPP HX3...... 146 C4
PDSY/CALV LS28...... 106 F7
Grove Crs BSPA/BRAM LS23...... 49 G7
GFTH/SHER LS25...... 138 E3
LUD/ILL HX2...... 144 F7
WKFDW/WTN WF2...... 199 K7
Grove Crs South
BSPA/BRAM LS23...... 49 G8
Grove Cft HIPP HX3...... 146 B4 🔢
Grove Dr HEM/SK/SE WF9...... 246 D4
Grove Edge HIPP HX3...... 146 B4 🔢
Grove Farm Cl BHP/TINH LS16... 86 B2
Grove Farm Crs BHP/TINH LS16... 86 A3
Grove Farm Cft BHP/TINH LS16... 86 A2
Grove Farm Dr BHP/TINH LS16... 86 A2 🔢
Grove Gdns BSPA/BRAM LS23...... 49 H7
EARL WF12...... 174 C8
HDGY LS6...... 87 G8 🔢
HIPP HX3...... 146 C4
Grovehall Av BEE/HOL LS11...... 131 H5
Grovehall Dr BEE/HOL LS11...... 131 H4
Grovehall La PONT WF8...... 181 K6
Grovehall Pde BEE/HOL LS11... 131 H5
Grovehall Rd BEE/HOL LS11...... 131 H5
Grove Head HEM/SK/SE WF9... 246 D4
Grove House Crs ECHL BD2...... 105 J3
Grove House Dr ECHL BD2...... 105 J3 🔢
Grove House Rd ECHL BD2...... 105 J2
Grovelands ECHL BD2...... 105 J3
Grove La CLECK BD19...... 150 D5
HDGY LS6...... 109 G1
HEM/SK/SE WF9...... 224 A8
HEM/SK/SE WF9...... 225 J5
HEM/SK/SE WF9...... 246 D4
KNOT WF11...... 182 A2
Grove Lea HEM/SK/SE WF9... 224 A8 🔢
Grove Lea Crs PONT WF8...... 181 G7
Grove Lea Wk PONT WF8...... 181 G7
Grove Marsh Lea
HEM/SK/SE WF9...... 224 A8 🔢
Grove Mt HEM/SK/SE WF9... 246 D4
PONT WF8...... 181 G6 🔢
Grove Nook HUDW HD3...... 191 H8
Grove Pk HIPP HX3...... 146 B3
HOR/CROF WF4...... 197 M8

Grove Pl BSPA/BRAM LS23...... 49 G7 🔢
Grove Ri AL/HA/HU LS17...... 87 H1
PONT WF8...... 181 G5 🔢
Grove Rd BSPA/BRAM LS23...... 49 G7
DOD/DAR S75...... 242 C5 🔢
ELL HX5...... 169 H8
HBR HX7...... 143 J2 🔢
HDGY LS6...... 87 G8
HECK WF16...... 173 G2
HOR/CROF WF4...... 197 J5
HORS LS18...... 85 K6 🔢
HUD HD1...... 15 H4
ILK LS29...... 38 A2
ILK LS29...... 61 J2
MID LS10...... 9 G3
MSTN/BAR LS15...... 111 J3
PDSY/CALV LS28...... 106 F7
PONT WF8...... 180 D5
SHPY BD18...... 104 D1 🔢
WKFDE WF1...... 12 F4
Grove Royd HIPP HX3...... 146 C4
Groves Hall Rd DEWS WF13... 173 H6
Grove Sq CLECK BD19...... 150 D5 🔢
HIPP HX3...... 146 B4 🔢
HIPP HX3...... 146 B4 🔢
Grove St BRIG HD6...... 170 D4
BSLYN/ROY S71...... 261 J5
DEWS WF13...... 173 L6
HECK WF16...... 173 G2
HEM/SK/SE WF9...... 246 D4
HOLM/MEL HD7...... 212 B5
HUDW HD3...... 191 G8
LDS LS1...... 6 C9
LVSG WF15...... 172 D8
MIRF WF14...... 172 D8
OSS WF5...... 196 F2
PDSY/CALV LS28...... 107 G4 🔢
ROCH OL11...... 228 A1 🔢
RPDN/SBR HX6...... 167 M2
WKFDE WF1...... 13 G4
Grove St South HFAX HX1...... 10 B6 🔢
Grove Ter HBR HX7...... 144 A6
HEM/SK/SE WF9...... 224 A8
PDSY/CALV LS28...... 106 F7
The Grove AL/HA/HU LS17...... 46 D8
AL/HA/HU LS17...... 87 H1
BAIL BD17...... 82 C2
BGLY BD16...... 59 C8
BTLY WF17...... 151 J7
CUD/GR S72...... 244 D5
EARD/LOFT WF3...... 153 K6
GFTH/SHER LS25...... 135 J5
HECK WF16...... 150 E8
HEM/SK/SE WF9...... 247 H2
HIPP HX3...... 147 L6
HOLM/MEL HD7...... 235 H5 🔢
HOR/CROF WF4...... 222 C5
HORS LS18...... 85 K6
HUDN HD2...... 192 D4
IDLE BD10...... 83 K7
IDLE BD10...... 83 M7 🔢
ILK LS29...... 38 C2
NORM WF6...... 178 D4 🔢
PDSY/CALV LS28...... 106 F7
ROY/SHW OL2...... 229 J8
RTHW LS26...... 134 D4
SHPY BD18...... 82 A7
SKP/WHF BD23...... 16 E3
WKFDW/WTN WF2...... 199 K7
YEA LS19...... 62 D8
YEA LS19...... 84 C2
Groveville HIPP HX3...... 147 L5
Groveway ECHL BD2...... 105 J2
Grove Wy HEM/SK/SE WF9... 246 D4
Grudgby La STKB/PEN S36...... 271 J8
Grunberg Rd HDGY LS6...... 108 F1
Grunberg St HDGY LS6...... 108 F1 🔢
Guard House Av HWTH BD22... 2 C5
Guard House Dr HWTH BD22... 2 C4
Guard House Gv HWTH BD22... 2 B5
Guard House Rd HWTH BD22... 2 C5
Guernsey Rd EARL WF12...... 174 B4
Guest La DOD/DAR S75...... 259 J6
Guest Rd DOD/DAR S75...... 260 F5
Guildford Rd BSLYN/ROY S71... 261 J4
Guildford St HBR HX7...... 143 J4 🔢
MILN OL16...... 206 C7 🔢
OSS WF5...... 196 F5
Guild Wy LUD/ILL HX2...... 145 K8
Guillemot Ap MOR LS27...... 152 F3 🔢
Gulley Rd OSM LS9...... 132 F3
Gully Ter HOLM/MEL HD7...... 254 D2
The Gully KBTN HD8...... 255 L1
Gunson Crs OSS WF5...... 174 F8
Gunter Rd WBY LS22...... 30 C8
Gunthwaite La KBTN HD8...... 257 H3
Gurbax Ct BFDE BD3...... 106 A7
Gurney Cl WBOW BD5...... 126 F5 🔢
Guycroft OT LS21...... 41 H6
Guys Cft WKFDW/WTN WF2... 197 L2
Guy St BOW BD4...... 5 G8
Gwynne Av BFDE BD3...... 106 A5
Gynn La HOLM/MEL HD7...... 236 C5
Gypsy Ct CAS WF10...... 158 E8
Gypsy Ter HOLM/MEL HD7... 254 D2
Gypsy Wood Cl
MSTN/BAR LS15...... 111 M7 🔢
Gypsy Wood Crest
MSTN/BAR LS15...... 111 M7 🔢

H

Hacking La HEM/SK/SE WF9... 247 K3
Hackings Av STKB/PEN S36... 270 E5
Hadassah St HIPP HX3...... 168 F2
Haddingley La KBTN HD8...... 255 M3
Haddlesey Rd KNOT WF11...... 161 J4
Haddon Av BULY LS4...... 108 E4
Haddon Cl CLECK BD19...... 150 D6
DOD/DAR S75...... 260 A7
HEM/SK/SE WF9...... 247 J1 🔢
Haddon Pl BULY LS4...... 108 E4
Haddon Rd BSLYN/ROY S71... 243 K8 🔢
BULY LS4...... 108 F4

Haddon St ROCH OL11...... 228 A2 🔢
Haddon Wy ROY/SHW OL2...... 229 L6
Hadfield Rd HECK WF16...... 172 F1
Hadleigh Ct AL/HA/HU LS17... 87 M4 🔢
Hadleigh Ri PONT WF8...... 180 D2
Hadrian Cl CAS WF10...... 158 C5
PONT WF8...... 225 J1
Hadrian's Cl HUDW HD3...... 191 G6
Hag Farm Rd ILK LS29...... 40 A7
Hagg La GFTH/SHER LS25...... 139 H2
MIRF WF14...... 194 D3
Haggroyd La HOLM/MEL HD7... 236 D4
Haggs Hill Rd OSS WF5...... 197 J1
Haggs La WKFDW/WTN WF2... 197 L1
Hagg Rd PBR HG3...... 27 L3
Hagg Wood Rd HOLM/MEL HD7.. 236 D4
Hag Hill La KBTN HD8...... 217 M8
Hag La HIPP HX3...... 146 E3
Hague Crs HEM/SK/SE WF9... 246 A1
Hague Park Cl
HEM/SK/SE WF9...... 246 D3 🔢
Hague Park La
HEM/SK/SE WF9...... 246 D3
Hague Park Wk
HEM/SK/SE WF9...... 246 D3 🔢
Hague Ter HEM/SK/SE WF9... 224 A8
Haigh Av RTHW LS26...... 132 F7
Haigh Beck Vw IDLE BD10...... 83 L7
Haigh Cl STKB/PEN S36...... 258 B8
Haigh Cnr IDLE BD10...... 83 M7
Haigh Cft BSLYN/ROY S71...... 243 K2
Haigh Fold ECHL BD2...... 105 L3
Haigh Gdns RTHW LS26...... 132 E7
Haigh Hall IDLE BD10...... 83 M7 🔢
Haigh Hall Rd IDLE BD10...... 83 M7 🔢
Haigh La DOD/DAR S75...... 241 M2
HIPP HX3...... 168 F2
HOLM/MEL HD7...... 236 B6
HOR/CROF WF4...... 217 J4
STKB/PEN S36...... 258 C7
Haigh Moor Av
EARD/LOFT WF3...... 153 G8
Haigh Moor Crs
EARD/LOFT WF3...... 153 G8
Haigh Moor Rd
EARD/LOFT WF3...... 175 G1
Haigh Moor St WKFDE WF1... 176 F6 🔢
Haigh Moor Vw
EARD/LOFT WF3...... 153 G8
Haigh Moor Wy BSLYN/ROY S71.. 243 H4
Haigh Park Rd MID LS10...... 132 D4
Haigh Rd RTHW LS26...... 133 H8
Haighside RTHW LS26...... 132 E8
Haighside Cl RTHW LS26...... 132 E8
Haighside Dr RTHW LS26...... 132 E8
Haighside Wy RTHW LS26...... 132 E8
Haigh St BOW BD4...... 127 K3
BRIG HD6...... 170 C3
GTL/HWG HX4...... 168 C3
HFAX HX1...... 10 B4
HUDS HD4...... 214 A3
ROCH OL11...... 206 C8 🔢
Haigh Ter RTHW LS26...... 132 E7 🔢
Haigh Vw RTHW LS26...... 132 F7
Haigh Wood Crs BHP/TINH LS16.. 85 M3
Haigh Wood Gn
BHP/TINH LS16...... 85 M4 🔢
Haigh Wood Rd BHP/TINH LS16.. 85 L3
Hailhead Dr PONT WF8...... 181 H6
Haincliffe Rd KGHY BD21...... 79 K2
Hainsworth Moor Crs
CUL/QBY BD13...... 124 F6 🔢
Hainsworth Moor Dr
CUL/QBY BD13...... 124 F6 🔢
Hainsworth Moor Garth
CUL/QBY BD13...... 124 F6 🔢
Hainsworth Moor Gv
CUL/QBY BD13...... 124 F6
Hainsworth Moor Vw
CUL/QBY BD13...... 124 F6
Hainsworth Rd AIRE BD20...... 36 B6
Hainsworth Sq
PDSY/CALV LS28...... 106 F3 🔢
Hainsworth St RTHW LS26...... 155 G2 🔢
WOR/ARM LS12...... 108 C7 🔢
Hainworth Crag Rd KGHY BD21.. 79 J4
Hainworth La KGHY BD21...... 79 K3
Hainworth Rd KGHY BD21...... 79 L2
Hainworth Wood Rd North
KGHY BD21...... 3 C9
Haise Mt DOD/DAR S75...... 242 C5
Halcyon Hl CHAL LS7...... 87 L6
Halcyon Wy WBOW BD5...... 126 E3
Haldane Cl CUD/GR S72...... 245 H3
Haldane Crs WKFDE WF1...... 177 G6
Hales Rd WOR/ARM LS12...... 130 D1
Halesworth Crs BOW BD4...... 128 A3
Haley Hl HFAX HX1...... 11 G3
Half Acre Rd BGLY BD16...... 55 C8
Half House La BRIG HD6...... 169 M1
Half Mile BRAM LS13...... 107 G4
Half Mile Cl PDSY/CALV LS28... 107 H4
Half Mile Gdns BRAM LS13...... 107 H4
Half Mile Gn PDSY/CALV LS28... 107 H4
Half Mile La BRAM LS13...... 107 H4
Half Moon La WKFDE WF1...... 177 K7
Half Moon St HUD HD1...... 14 F7
Halfpenny La FEA/AMT WF7... 180 B8
Half St KGHY BD21...... 2 F3
Halifax La HBR HX7...... 142 A2
LUD/ILL HX2...... 145 C6
HUDN HD2...... 192 B4
Halifax Old Rd HIPP HX3...... 147 K6
HUDN HD2...... 192 B4
Halifax Rd BRFD/BLYE BD10... 96 D5
BRIG HD6...... 170 C4
CLECK BD19...... 149 G7
CUL/QBY BD13...... 79 M8
CUL/QBY BD13...... 101 M7
DEWS WF13...... 173 H3
ELL HX5...... 169 G7
HIPP HX3...... 147 K6
HOLM/MEL HD7...... 212 D1
HUDW HD3...... 191 L5
HWTH BD22...... 79 H7
KGHY BD21...... 79 J5
LIT OL15...... 186 B7

LUD/ILL HX2...... 123 M2
LVSG WF15...... 171 L1
MILN OL16...... 206 F3
RPDN/SBR HX6...... 188 F2
STKB/PEN S36...... 257 C8
TOD OL14...... 163 L1
WBSY BD6...... 126 B7
Halifax St BSLYN/ROY S71...... 261 G2
Haliwell St LIT OL15...... 207 L1 🔢
Hallam La OT LS21...... 40 C1
Hallamshire Ms
WKFDW/WTN WF2...... 197 L2 🔢
Hallam's Yd SKP/WHF BD23... 16 B2 🔢
Hallas Gv HUDE HD5...... 215 G1
KBTN HD8...... 216 C8
Hallas La CUL/QBY BD13...... 80 B8
KBTN HD8...... 216 C8
Hallas Rd KBTN HD8...... 216 B8
Hall Av AIRE BD20...... 55 M2
HUD HD1...... 14 C9
IDLE BD10...... 105 M1
Hall Balk La DOD/DAR S75...... 260 F5
Hallbank Cl WBOW BD5...... 126 F5
Hall Bank Dr BGLY BD16...... 81 L7
Hall Bank La HBR HX7...... 144 A6
Hall Bower La HUDS HD4...... 214 D6
Hallcliffe BAIL BD17...... 82 B7
Hall Cliffe Ct HOR/CROF WF4... 197 J4 🔢
Hall Cliffe Crs HOR/CROF WF4... 197 J4
Hall Cliffe Gv HOR/CROF WF4... 197 J4
Hall Cliffe Ri HOR/CROF WF4... 197 K4 🔢
Hall Cliffe Rd HOR/CROF WF4... 197 J4
Hall Cl AIRE BD20...... 55 L2
BHP/TINH LS16...... 64 A2
ILK LS29...... 39 M5
LVSG WF15...... 172 C3
Hall Ct KNOT WF11...... 159 L6
Hall Cft HOR/CROF WF4...... 197 G8 🔢
SKP/WHF BD23...... 16 A3
Hallcroft Dr HOR/CROF WF4... 197 K5 🔢
Hallcroft Gdns MILN OL16...... 207 G8 🔢
Hallcroft Ri BSLYN/ROY S71... 243 K3 🔢
Hall Cross Gv HUDS HD4...... 214 E3
Hall Cross Rd HUDE HD5...... 214 E3
Hall Dr AIRE BD20...... 55 M2
BHP/TINH LS16...... 64 A2
ILK LS29...... 39 M5
Hall Farm Gv STKB/PEN S36... 258 C8
Hall Farm Pk GFTH/SHER LS25.. 114 B6
Hallfield Av GFTH/SHER LS25... 114 B7
Hallfield Crs WBY LS22...... 48 B1
Hallfield Dr BAIL BD17...... 82 C3
Hall Field La HOR/CROF WF4... 222 C5
Hallfield La WBY LS22...... 30 B8
Hallfield Pl BFD1...... 4 E3
Hallfield Rd GIR BD8...... 4 D4
Hallfield St BFD1...... 4 E4
Hallfield Ter GFTH/SHER LS25... 114 B7
Hall Gdns AIRE BD20...... 35 G5
Hall Garth Cl TAD LS24...... 95 C1
Hall Garth Rd PONT WF8...... 225 J1
Hall Ga STKB/PEN S36...... 270 F5
Hall Green La AL/HA/HU LS17... 26 A1
GTL/HWG HX4...... 188 F6
Hall Gv DOD/DAR S75...... 242 E5
Halliday Av WOR/ARM LS12... 108 C6
Halliday Dr WOR/ARM LS12... 108 C6 🔢
Halliday Mt WOR/ARM LS12... 108 C6
Halliday Pl WOR/ARM LS12... 108 C6
Halliday Rd GFTH/SHER LS25... 113 C7
WOR/ARM LS12...... 108 C6
Halliday St PDSY/CALV LS28... 107 G6
Halliley St DEWS WF13...... 173 K6
Hall Ing La HOLM/MEL HD7... 236 D1
Hall Ings BFD1...... 4 E7
Halling Pl TOD OL14...... 163 J2
Hall Ing Rd HOLM/MEL HD7... 236 F2
Hall Ings BFD1...... 4 E7
Halliwell St MILN OL16...... 207 G7
WHIT OL12...... 206 A6 🔢
Hall La BHP/TINH LS16...... 64 A2
BOW BD4...... 5 H9
CAS WF10...... 136 B8
CHAL LS7...... 109 M1
EARL WF12...... 196 A4
GFTH/SHER LS25...... 137 H1
HEM/SK/SE WF9...... 225 K8
HIPP HX3...... 147 K2
HOLM/MEL HD7...... 190 C8
HOR/CROF WF4...... 220 B2
HORS LS18...... 85 J5
KBTN HD8...... 216 A1
OT LS21...... 42 C4
SHPY BD18...... 82 F6 🔢
TAD LS24...... 117 C1
WOR/ARM LS12...... 107 L8
WOR/ARM LS12...... 108 C7
Hall Lee Rd HUDW HD3...... 191 L5
Hall Ms BSPA/BRAM LS23...... 49 G7
Hall Orchards Av WBY LS22... 30 C8
Hallowes Gv CUL/QBY BD13... 101 M1
Hallowes Park Rd
CUL/QBY BD13...... 101 M1
Hallows Ct HUDE HD5...... 215 H3 🔢
Hallows Rd KGHY BD21...... 3 M1
The Hallows KGHY BD21...... 2 C2
Hall Park Av HOR/CROF WF4... 200 A4
HORS LS18...... 85 J5
LVSG WF15...... 172 C4
Hall Park Cl HORS LS18...... 85 J5
Hall Park Ct GFTH/SHER LS25... 135 K5
Hall Park Cft GFTH/SHER LS25.. 135 K6
Hall Park Garth HORS LS18...... 85 J5
Hall Park Mdw
GFTH/SHER LS25...... 135 K6
Hall Park Mt HORS LS18...... 85 J5 🔢
Hall Park Orch GFTH/SHER LS25.. 135 J4
Hall Park Rd GFTH/SHER LS25.. 135 K5 🔢
HORS LS18...... 85 J5
Hall Park Rd BSPA/BRAM LS23.. 49 K2

Hall Pl BSLYN/ROY S71...... 261 L2
OSM LS9...... 110 B7
Hall Ri BHP/TINH LS16...... 64 A3
ILK LS29...... 39 M5
Hall Rise Cl BHP/TINH LS16...... 64 A3
Hall Rise Cft BHP/TINH LS16...... 64 A3
Hall Rd COL BB8...... 74 D3
IDLE BD10...... 105 M1
RTHW LS26...... 134 D5
WKFDW/WTN WF2...... 197 M2
WOR/ARM LS12...... 108 E7
Hall Royd SHPY BD18...... 82 D7
Hallroyd Crs TOD OL14...... 163 L7
Hall Royd La DOD/DAR S75... 259 J8
Hallroyd Pl TOD OL14...... 163 L7 🔢
Hall Royd Rd TOD OL14...... 141 L8
Hall Royd Wk DOD/DAR S75... 259 J8
Halls La CUL/QBY BD13...... 102 A1
Hall Stone Ct HIPP HX3...... 147 L1 🔢
Hall St AIRE BD20...... 34 F7 🔢
BRIG HD6...... 170 D4
FEA/AMT WF7...... 202 A2
HFAX HX1...... 10 F5
HUDW HD3...... 191 H7 🔢
HWTH BD22...... 78 E8 🔢
HWTH BD22...... 78 F4 🔢
WBSY BD6...... 126 E5 🔢
Hall St North HIPP HX3...... 146 D4
Hall Wy AIRE BD20...... 55 L2
Hallwood Gn IDLE BD10...... 106 A1
Halstead Dr ILK LS29...... 61 J1
ILK LS29...... 61 J1
Halstead Gv DOD/DAR S75... 242 C4
Halstead La HUDS HD4...... 237 H6
Halstead Pl GTHN BD7...... 126 C3
Halsteads Wy AIRE BD20...... 35 K8
Halt Head Rd HOLM/MEL HD7.. 212 C8
Halton Cl HUDE HD5...... 215 H1
Halton Moor Av OSM LS9...... 110 F7
Halton Moor Rd
MSTN/BAR LS15...... 111 G8
OSM LS9...... 110 E8
Halton Pl GTHN BD7...... 126 C3
Halton Rd WKFDE WF1...... 177 H6
Halton St FEA/AMT WF7...... 179 M7
Hamble Ct DOD/DAR S75...... 242 E6
Hambledon Av BOW BD4...... 127 K5
Hambleton Bank LUD/ILL HX2... 145 K1
Hambleton Cl DOD/DAR S75... 260 D4
Hambleton Crs LUD/ILL HX2... 145 K1
Hambleton St WKFDE WF1... 176 F7
Hamel Ri HEM/SK/SE WF9...... 223 M8
Hamer Hall WHIT OL12...... 206 D4 🔢
Hamer La MILN OL16...... 206 D5
Hamilton Av CHAL LS7...... 7 L1
Hamilton Ct NORM WF6...... 178 C3 🔢
Hamilton Gdns CHAL LS7...... 7 K2
Hamilton Pl CHAL LS7...... 7 L1
Hamilton Ter CHAL LS7...... 7 M2
Hamilton Vw CHAL LS7...... 7 L1
Hammer La HOR/CROF WF4... 200 D2
Hammerstone Leach La
ELL HX5...... 190 F1
Hammerstones Rd ELL HX5...... 168 F8
Hammerton Dr
GFTH/SHER LS25...... 135 J1
Hammerton Gv
PDSY/CALV LS28...... 107 H7 🔢
Hammerton Rd HUDN HD2... 192 C4
Hammerton St BFDE BD3...... 5 J7
PDSY/CALV LS28...... 107 G7
Hammond Crs BIRK/DRI BD11.. 129 J1
Hammond Rd HUDN HD2...... 192 C4
Hammond Rd HWT WF11...... 181 M3
Hammond St HFAX HX1...... 10 B7
HUDN HD2...... 192 D5
OSM LS9...... 9 M4 🔢
Hamm Strasse BFD BD1...... 4 F4
Hampden Cl KNOT WF11...... 181 K1
Hampden Pl HFAX HX1...... 10 E6
WBOW BD5...... 126 F7 🔢
Hampden Rd ROY/SHW OL2... 229 M8
Hampden St WBOW BD5...... 126 F7 🔢
Hamper La STKB/PEN S36...... 258 B8
Hampole Balk AWLS/ASK DN6.. 249 H5
Hampole Field La
AWLS/ASK DN6...... 248 B5
Hampshire Cl ILK LS29...... 38 F2
Hampshire St BTLY WF17...... 151 J7
Hampshire St IDLE BD10...... 83 K6 🔢
OSM LS9...... 110 B7 🔢
Hampton St HFAX HX1...... 10 A9
Hampton Ter OSM LS9...... 110 B7 🔢
Hamworth Dr HWTH BD22...... 78 F4 🔢
Hamza St BTLY WF17...... 173 K2 🔢
Hanbury Cl BSLYN/ROY S71... 261 M2
Hanby Av NORM WF6...... 178 B3
Hand Bank La MIRF WF14...... 194 C4
Hand Carr La LUD/ILL HX2...... 144 D7
Handel St GTHN BD7...... 4 B5
HOLM/MEL HD7...... 212 F2
Handsworth Rd
WKFDW/WTN WF2...... 220 C2
Hanging Chadder La
ROY/SHW OL2...... 228 E7
Hanging Gate La HWTH BD22.. 100 C1
Hanginground La HBR HX7...... 143 J5 🔢
Hangingroyd La HBR HX7...... 143 J3
Hanginroyd La HBR HX7...... 143 J3 🔢
Hanging Stone Rd HUDS HD4... 214 B7
Hangingstone Rd ILK LS29...... 38 F4
Hanging Stones La
RPDN/SBR HX6...... 189 G1
Hanging Wood Wy CLECK BD19.. 149 L4
Hangthwaite Rd
AWLS/ASK DN6...... 249 M7
Hanley Rd MOR LS27...... 152 C3
Hannah Ct LM/WK BD12...... 148 E3
Hannas Royd DOD/DAR S75... 260 C7 🔢
Hannerton Rd ROY/SHW OL2... 229 M6
Hanover Av BVRD LS3...... 6 B7
Hanover Cl GIR BD8...... 104 C5
Hanover Crs PONT WF8...... 202 E1

Hanover Gdns *DEWS* WF13 173 K6 3
Hanover La *BVRD* LS3 6 D8
Hanover Mt *BVRD* LS3 6 B7
Hanover Pl *BTLY* WF17 173 M1
KNOT WF11 159 L5 3
Hanover Sq *BFD* BD1 4 D3
BVRD LS3 6 C7
Hanover St *AIRE* BD20 34 F5 3
BTLY WF17 173 L1
DEWS WF13 173 K6
HFAX HX1 10 F7
KGHY BD21 3 G5
LIT OL15 207 J1 3
RPDN/SBR HX6 167 M1
WKFDW/WTN WF2 12 A4
Hanover Wy *ILK* LS29 40 A6
LDS LS1 6 C8 3
Hansby Av *SCFT* LS14 111 K1
Hansby Bank *SCFT* LS14 111 K1 2
Hansby Cl *SCFT* LS14 111 K2
Hansby Dr *SCFT* LS14 111 K1
Hansby Gdns *SCFT* LS14 111 K2
Hansby Ga *SCFT* LS14 111 K1
Hansby Pl *SCFT* LS14 111 K2
Hanson Av *NORM* WF6 178 D5
Hanson Ct *LM/WK* BD12 148 D4
Hanson Fold *LM/WK* BD12 148 E3 3
Hanson La *HFAX* HX1 10 C5
HUDS HD4 214 A4
Hanson Mt *LM/WK* BD12 148 E4
Hanson Rd *BRIG* HD6 170 A6
HOLM/MEL HD7 234 E5
Hanson St *BSLY* S70 261 H4 2
Hanworth Rd *LM/WK* BD12 126 E8
Harbeck Dr *BGLY* BD16 80 D6
Harborough Hill Rd
BSLYN/ROY S71 261 H4 3
Harbour Crs *WBSY* BD6 126 C6 2
Harbour La *MILN* OL16 229 H1
Harbour La North *MILN* OL16 207 H8
Harbour Pk *WBSY* BD6 126 B7
Harbour Rd *WBSY* BD6 126 C7
Harclo Rd *KGHY* BD21 3 L2
Harcourt Av *CUL/QBY* BD13 102 F7
Harcourt Dr *ILK* LS29 19 H5
MOR LS27 152 B1 2
Harcourt Pl *LDS* LS1 6 C9
Harcourt St *BOW* BD4 127 K3 1
WKFDW/WTN WF2 198 B1 1
Hardaker La *BAIL* BD17 82 C4
Hardakers Ap *FEA/AMT* WF7 224 B1
Hardaker's La *FEA/AMT* WF7 202 A8
Hardaker St *GIR* BD8 4 C4 1
Hardcastle Av *PONT* WF8 180 E5 2
Hardcastle La *HOR/CROF* WF4 217 M3
Harden Brow La *BGLY* BD16 80 C5 2
Harden Cl *DOD/DAR* S75 260 C4
STKB/PEN S36 270 F4 2
Harden Gv *IDLE* BD10 106 A3
KGHY BD21 3 M9
Harden Hill Rd *HOLM/MEL* HD7 235 G6
Harden Hills *ROY/SHW* OL2 229 M6
Harden La *BGLY* BD16 80 D6
Harden Moss Rd
HOLM/MEL HD7 234 F7
Harden Rd *BGLY* BD16 80 E5
KGHY BD21 3 M8
Hardgate La *HWTH* BD22 79 H8
Hardie Rd *HOR/CROF* WF4 222 E5
Hardings La *AIRE* BD20 35 G7
ILK LS29 20 C6
Hard Ings Rd *KGHY* BD21 3 G1
Hardistry Dr *PONT* WF8 180 D6 2
Hardknot Cl *GTHN* BD7 126 A3
Hard La *WHIT* OL12 184 C6
Hard Nese La *HWTH* BD22 100 B5
Hard Platts La *GTL/HWG* HX4 190 B3
Hardrow Gn *WOR/ARM* LS12 130 F1
Hardrow Gv *WOR/ARM* LS12 130 F1
Hardrow Rd *WOR/ARM* LS12 130 E1
Hardrow Ter *WOR/ARM* LS12 130 F1 2
Hardwick Ct *PONT* WF8 180 E7
Hardwick Crs *BSLYN/ROY* S71 243 J7
PONT WF8 202 F1 1
Hardwick Cft *CHAL* LS7 87 M8 6
Hardwicke St *ROCH* OL11 228 A2
Hardwick Gv *DOD/DAR* S75 260 B8 2
Hardwick La *HOR/CROF* WF4 201 K5
Hardwick Rd *FEA/AMT* WF7 201 L2
PONT WF8 202 F3
Hardwick St *KGHY* BD21 2 D7 3
Hardy Av *MOR* LS27 130 E6 2
WBSY BD6 126 E6
Hardy Cl *ROCH* OL11 228 B3
Hardy Ct *MOR* LS27 152 D2
Hardy Cft *WKFDE* WF1 13 G3
Hardy Gv *BEE/HOL* LS11 131 J3
Hardy Pl *BRIG* HD6 170 A1 2
Hardy St *BEE/HOL* LS11 131 J3
BOW BD4 5 G8
BRIG HD6 170 D3 3
MOR LS27 152 D2
Hardy Ter *BEE/HOL* LS11 131 J3
Hardy Vw *BEE/HOL* LS11 131 J3
Hareball Av *WKFDW/WTN* WF2 176 A7 3
Harecroft Rd *OT* LS21 41 J5
Hare Farm Av *WOR/ARM* LS12 107 M7
Hare Farm Cl *WOR/ARM* LS12 107 M7 1
Harefield Av *ROCH* OL11 228 B1
Harefield Cl *AIRE* BD20 56 C1 2
Harefield Dr *BTLY* WF17 151 J5
Harefield East
MSTN/BAR LS15 111 G6 4
Harefield Rd *PONT* WF8 181 H6
Harefield West
MSTN/BAR LS15 111 G6 5
Harefield Pk *HUDN* HD2 191 L4
Harehill Av *TOD* OL14 141 J8
Harehill Cl *IDLE* BD10 83 K5 3
Harehill Rd *IDLE* BD10 83 K5
Hare Hill Rd *LIT* OL15 185 J8
Harehills Av *RHAY* LS8 110 C1
Harehills La *HWTH* BD22 77 L5
OSM LS9 110 D4
Harehills Park Av *OSM* LS9 110 D4 12
Harehills Park Ter *OSM* LS9 110 D3
Harehills Park Vw *OSM* LS9 110 D4 13
Harehills Pl *RHAY* LS8 110 B3
Harehills Rd *RHAY* LS8 110 B2
Harehill St *TOD* OL14 141 J8
Hare La *PDSY/CALV* LS28 129 G1
Hare Park Av *LVSG* WF15 171 L2
Hare Park Cl *LVSG* WF15 171 L2
Harepark Dr *LVSG* WF15 171 L2
Hare Park La *HOR/CROF* WF4 200 B7
LVSG WF15 171 L2
Hare Park Mt *WOR/ARM* LS12 107 L7
Hare Park Vw *HOR/CROF* WF4 200 B6
Hares Av *RHAY* LS8 110 B2
Hares Mt *RHAY* LS8 7 M1
Hares Rd *RHAY* LS8 7 M1
Hares Ter *RHAY* LS8 110 B2 34
Hare St *HFAX* HX1 10 B6
ROCH OL11 206 C8
Hares Vw *RHAY* LS8 110 B2 35
Harewood Av *AIRE* BD20 56 C1
AL/HA/HU LS17 45 K8
BSLY S70 260 D5
HECK WF16 173 G3
LUD/ILL HX2 145 M6
NORM WF6 178 E3 3
PONT WF8 181 G6
Harewood Cl *KNOT* WF11 181 L2
Harewood Crs *HWTH* BD22 79 G3
Harewood Dr
WKFDW/WTN WF2 175 M5
Harewood Ga *AL/HA/HU* LS17 45 J7
Harewood Gv *HECK* WF16 173 G3 4
Harewood La *HEM/SK/SE* WF9 225 L6
PONT WF8 226 B4
Harewood Ms *AL/HA/HU* LS17 45 J7
Harewood Mt *HOLM/MEL* HD7 235 H4
PONT WF8 181 G6
Harewood Pl *LUD/ILL* HX2 146 A8
Harewood Ri *HWTH* BD22 79 H3
Harewood Rd *AL/HA/HU* LS17 46 D7
HWTH BD22 79 G4
ROY/SHW OL2 229 L6
SKP/WHF BD23 16 A2
WKFDE WF1 177 H6
Harewood St *BFDE* BD3 5 L5
LDSU LS2 7 H9
Harewood Vw *PONT* WF8 181 G6 4
Harewood Wy *BRAM* LS13 107 K6
Hargrave Crs *ILK* LS29 61 H2
Hargreaves Av *EARD/LOFT* WF3 177 G1
Hargreaves Cl *MOR* LS27 130 B7
Harker Rd *WBSY* BD6 126 E7
Harker St *KNOT* WF11 182 D2
Harker Ter *PDSY/CALV* LS28 106 F5
Harland Cl *ECHL* BD2 105 G4
Harland Sq *LDSU* LS2 6 D3
Harlech Av *BEE/HOL* LS11 131 K4 3
Harlech Crs *BEE/HOL* LS11 131 K4
Harlech Gv *BEE/HOL* LS11 131 J4
Harlech Mt *BEE/HOL* LS11 131 J4
Harlech Park Ct *BEE/HOL* LS11 131 K5
Harlech Rd *BEE/HOL* LS11 131 K4
Harlech St *BEE/HOL* LS11 131 K4
Harlech Ter *BEE/HOL* LS11 131 K4
Harlech Wy *GFTH/SHER* LS25 113 K7
Harley Cl *BRAM* LS13 107 J6
Harley Ct *BRAM* LS13 107 J6
Harley Dr *BRAM* LS13 107 J6
Harley Gdns *PDSY/CALV* LS28 107 J6
Harley Gn *BRAM* LS13 107 J6
Harley Ri *BRAM* LS13 107 J6
Harley Rd *BRAM* LS13 107 J6
Harley St *BRIG* HD6 170 C5 3
TOD OL14 141 K8
Harley Ter *BRAM* LS13 107 K6
Harley Vw *BRAM* LS13 107 J6
Harley Wk *BRAM* LS13 107 J6
Harley Wd *TOD* OL14 141 G6 3
Harlington Ct *MOR* LS27 152 C4 3
Harlington Rd *MOR* LS27 152 C4
Harlow Ct *RHAY* LS8 88 E7
Harlow Rd *GTHN* BD7 126 C1
Harmby Cl *AWLS/ASK* DN6 249 H4
Harmon Cl *BOW* BD4 127 L6 1
Harold Av *BSLYN/ROY* S71 262 A2
HDGY LS6 109 G4
Harold Gdns *MOR* LS27 152 E2 2
Harold Gv *HDGY* LS6 109 G4
Harold Mt *HDGY* LS6 109 G4
Harold Pl *HDGY* LS6 109 G4
Harold Rd *HDGY* LS6 109 G4
Harold St *BGLY* BD16 81 G2
HDGY LS6 109 G4
MILN OL16 206 E4 1
Harold Ter *HDGY* LS6 109 G4
Harold Vw *HDGY* LS6 109 G4
Harold Wk *HDGY* LS6 109 G4
Harpe Inge *HUDE* HD5 193 G7
Harper Av *IDLE* BD10 83 L5
Harper Crs *IDLE* BD10 83 L5
Harper Gv *AIRE* BD20 55 M2
IDLE BD10 83 K5 10
Harper La *YEA* LS19 62 D8
Harper Pl *LDSU* LS2 7 J9
Harper Royd La *RPDN/SBR* HX6 167 K4
Harper Sq *ROY/SHW* OL2 229 L7
Harpers Sq *AIRE* BD20 55 M2 2
Harper St *LDSU* LS2 9 J1
Harp Rd *HUDW* HD3 213 K1
Harrap St *WKFDW/WTN* WF2 175 M8
Harrier Cl *GIR* BD8 103 K7 4
Harrier Wy *MOR* LS27 152 F2
Harriet Cl *BSLY* S70 261 J7 3
Harriet St *BRIG* HD6 170 C2
CHAL LS7 7 K2
GIR BD8 104 D6 2
Harriett St *MILN* OL16 206 C7
Harrington Ct *BSLYN/ROY* S71 262 A2
HOLM/MEL HD7 235 H5 2
Harris Ct *GTHN* BD7 126 C3 3
Harrison Crs *OSM* LS9 110 F5
Harrison La *HOLM/MEL* HD7 235 G2
Harrison Rd *HFAX* HX1 11 G7
HOR/CROF WF4 200 A5
Harrisons Av *PDSY/CALV* LS28 107 H4 4
Harrison St *BGLY* BD16 81 J4 3
LDS LS1 7 H8
TOD OL14 140 D5 4
Harris St *BFD* BD1 5 J6
BGLY BD16 81 J4 4
Harrogate Av *BFDE* BD3 105 J4 1
Harrogate Pl *BFDE* BD3 105 J4 2
Harrogate Ringway *PBR* HG3 26 C4
Harrogate Rd *AL/HA/HU* LS17 43 L3
AL/HA/HU LS17 87 M3
CHAL LS7 87 M8 7
ECHL BD2 105 L3
IDLE BD10 83 M7
KNA HG5 28 E1
PBR HG3 26 E5
WBY LS22 29 H6
YEA LS19 84 E1
Harrogate St *BFDE* BD3 105 J4
Harrogate Ter *BFDE* BD3 105 J4 3
Harrogate Vw *AL/HA/HU* LS17 88 E1
Harrop Av *MOR* LS27 152 D4
Harrop Gv *MOR* LS27 152 D4
Harrop La *WIL/AL* BD15 102 D3
Harrop Ter *MOR* LS27 152 D4
Harrop Well La *PONT* WF8 180 F5 3
Harrowby Crs *BHP/TINH* LS16 86 D7
Harrowby Rd *BHP/TINH* LS16 86 D7
Harrow Ms *ROY/SHW* OL2 229 K7 3
Harrow St *HEM/SK/SE* WF9 247 G3
HFAX HX1 10 B6
ROCH OL11 228 D4 2
Harry La *CLAY* BD14 125 K2
HWTH BD22 100 E3
Harry Rd *DOD/DAR* S75 260 D3
Harry St *BOW* BD4 127 L3
Hartcliffe Av *STKB/PEN* S36 270 E3
Hartcliffe La *STKB/PEN* S36 270 A5
Hartcliff Hill Rd *STKB/PEN* S36 270 B6
Hartcliff Nick *STKB/PEN* S36 270 A6
Hartcliff Rd *STKB/PEN* S36 269 L6
STKB/PEN S36 270 C6
Harthill *MOR* LS27 129 M7
Harthill Av *MOR* LS27 129 M7
Harthill Cl *MOR* LS27 129 M7 3
Harthill La *MOR* LS27 129 M7
Harthill Ri *MOR* LS27 129 M7
Hartington Dr *BSLYN/ROY* S71 261 H2
Hartington St *BTLY* WF17 173 L3 2
KGHY BD21 3 G3
Hartington Ter *GTHN* BD7 126 C1
Hartland Rd *BOW* BD4 128 A2
Hartley Av *HDGY* LS6 6 E1
Hartley Ct *LVSG* WF15 172 C3
Hartley Crs *HDGY* LS6 6 E1
Hartley Gdns *HDGY* LS6 6 E1
Hartley Gv *HDGY* LS6 6 D1
Hartley Hl *LDSU* LS2 7 H7
Hartley La *ROCH* OL11 228 A3
Hartley Park Av *PONT* WF8 180 D6
Hartley Park Vw *PONT* WF8 180 D6 3
Hartley Pl *HWTH* BD22 54 F3
MOR LS27 152 D2 3
Hartley's Buildings *MOR* LS27 152 D3
Hartley's Sq *AIRE* BD20 58 F5 3
Hartleys Ter *COL* BB8 74 A2 3
Hartley St *BOW* BD4 127 K1 3
CAS WF10 157 L7
DEWS WF13 173 L5
HFAX HX1 10 C4
LIT OL15 207 J1
MILN OL16 206 F7 7
MOR LS27 130 D7
MOR LS27 152 D2
WHIT OL12 184 E8 3
Hartley Ter *FEA/AMT* WF7 201 L2 2
Hartlington Ct *BAIL* BD17 83 G3 2
Hartman Pl *HTON* BD9 104 B4 2
Harton Cl *ROY/SHW* OL2 229 J8
Hartshead Hall La *LVSG* WF15 171 L6
Hartshead La *LVSG* WF15 171 K4
Hart St *GTHN* BD7 126 D2 5
HUDS HD4 214 C4
Hartwell Rd *HDGY* LS6 109 G4
Harvard St *ROCH* OL11 228 C2 3
Harvelin Pk *TOD* OL14 164 C1
Harvey Royd *HUDE* HD5 215 J2
Harvey St *BSLY* S70 260 F6
WHIT OL12 206 D5 3
WKFDE WF1 13 K8
Harwill Ap *MOR* LS27 130 E7
Harwill Av *MOR* LS27 130 E7
Harwill Cft *MOR* LS27 130 E7
Harwill Gv *MOR* LS27 130 E7
Harwill Ri *MOR* LS27 130 E7
Harwill Rd *MOR* LS27 130 E7
Harwood Cl *HUDE* HD5 215 H1
WKFDW/WTN WF2 199 G5
Harwood St *LIT* OL15 207 H1
Harwood Ter *BSLYN/ROY* S71 262 A4 1
Haselden Crs
WKFDW/WTN WF2 197 M1
Haselden Rd *WKFDW/WTN* WF2 197 M1
Haslam Cl *BFDE* BD3 5 K4
Haslam Gv *SHPY* BD18 83 G8
Haslemere Cl *BOW* BD4 127 M3 3
Haslewood Cl *OSM* LS9 7 M9
Haslewood Ct *OSM* LS9 110 B6 1
Haslewood Dene *OSM* LS9 110 B6 3
Haslewood Dr *OSM* LS9 110 B6 3
Haslewood Gdns *OSM* LS9 110 B6 4
Haslewood Gn *OSM* LS9 110 B6 5
Haslewood Ms *OSM* LS9 110 B6 6
Haslewood Pl *OSM* LS9 110 B6 7
Haslewood Sq *OSM* LS9 110 B6 8
Haslewood Vw *OSM* LS9 110 B6 9
Hasley Rd *ILK* LS29 40 B6
Haslingden Dr *HTON* BD9 104 B4
Hassocks La *HOLM/MEL* HD7 235 L2
Hassocks Rd *HOLM/MEL* HD7 234 E3
Haste St *CAS* WF10 157 K6
Hastings Av *WBOW* BD5 126 F4
WKFDW/WTN WF2 198 E4
Hastings Ct *AL/HA/HU* LS17 89 G2
NORM WF6 178 A2
Hastings Crs *CAS* WF10 158 D7
Hastings Gv *WKFDW/WTN* WF2 198 F4
Hastings Pl *WBOW* BD5 126 F3 3
Hastings St *CUD/GR* S72 245 J7
ROCH OL11 228 B1 1
WBOW BD5 126 F4
Hastings Ter *WBOW* BD5 126 F4 6
Hastings Wk *CAS* WF10 158 D7 2
Hastings Wy *WBY* LS22 47 H6
Hatchet La *LM/WK* BD12 149 J2
Hatfeild St *WKFDE* WF1 176 E7
Hatfeild Vw *WKFDE* WF1 176 E4
Hatfield Cl *BSLYN/ROY* S71 243 G7 3
Hatfield Gdns *BSLYN/ROY* S71 243 K2
Hatfield Pl *HOR/CROF* WF4 222 F4
Hatfield Rd *ECHL* BD2 105 K4
Hathaway Av *HTON* BD9 103 M3 2
Hathaway Dr *SCFT* LS14 89 K6
Hathaway La *SCFT* LS14 89 K6 3
Hathaway Ms *SCFT* LS14 89 K5 4
Hathershelf La *LUD/ILL* HX2 144 C7
Hatton Cl *WBSY* BD6 126 F6 3
Haugh End La *RPDN/SBR* HX6 167 J4
Haugh Head Rd *STKB/PEN* S36 258 B8
Haugh La *MILN* OL16 229 L2
Haugh Rd *TOD* OL14 142 A8
Haugh Shaw Rd *HFAX* HX1 10 C9 1
Haugh Shaw Rd West
HFAX HX1 168 B1
Haughs La *HUDW* HD3 191 H7
Haughs Rd *HUDW* HD3 191 J7
Hauxley Ct *ILK* LS29 38 F1 1
Hauxwell Cl *AWLS/ASK* DN6 249 H4
Hauxwell Dr *YEA* LS19 62 D8
Havelock Sq *CUL/QBY* BD13 103 G8 2
Havelock St *BSLY* S70 260 F6 3
CUL/QBY BD13 103 G8
DEWS WF13 195 G1
GTHN BD7 126 B2
Haven Cha *BHP/TINH* LS16 86 A3
Haven Ct *BHP/TINH* LS16 86 B3
PONT WF8 202 D1
Haven Cft *BHP/TINH* LS16 86 B3
Haven Gdns *BHP/TINH* LS16 86 A3
Haven Garth *BHP/TINH* LS16 86 A3
Haven Gn *BHP/TINH* LS16 86 A3
Haven La *HBR* HX7 143 K6
Haven Mt *BHP/TINH* LS16 86 A3
Haven Ri *BHP/TINH* LS16 86 A3
Haven St *TOD* OL14 163 L1 3
The Haven *GFTH/SHER* LS25 138 A3
IDLE BD10 83 L8
MSTN/BAR LS15 111 M6
Haven Vw *BHP/TINH* LS16 86 A3
Havercroft *OSS* WF5 197 G1
WOR/ARM LS12 130 A1 2
Havercroft La *PONT* WF8 204 A1
Havercroft Ri *CUD/GR* S72 223 G8
Havercroft Wy *BTLY* WF17 173 H1 2
Haverdale Ri *DOD/DAR* S75 260 F3
Haverdale Rd *HOR/CROF* WF4 222 E5
The Haverlands
HEM/SK/SE WF9 224 A8 3
Haveroid La *HOR/CROF* WF4 220 B2
Haveroid Wy *HOR/CROF* WF4 220 A1
Haverthwaites Dr
GFTH/SHER LS25 92 A5
Havertop La *NORM* WF6 179 H4
Haw Av *YEA* LS19 62 E6
Hawber Cote Dr *AIRE* BD20 36 B4 1
Hawber La *AIRE* BD20 36 B5
Haw Cliff La *HUDS* HD4 237 H5
Haw Ct *DOD/DAR* S75 259 H6 3
Hawes Av *HUDW* HD3 191 K8
WBOW BD5 126 E4 2
Hawes Cl *CAS* WF10 158 D6
Hawes Crs *WBOW* BD5 126 E4 3
Hawes Dr *COL* BB8 52 B8 3
WBOW BD5 126 E4
Hawes Gv *WBOW* BD5 126 E4
Hawes Mt *WBOW* BD5 126 E4
Hawes Rd *WBOW* BD5 126 E4
Hawes Ter *WBOW* BD5 126 E4
Haweswater Cl *WBY* LS22 47 K1
Haw Hill Vw *NORM* WF6 178 D3
Hawkcliffe Vw *AIRE* BD20 35 L5
Hawke Av *HECK* WF16 173 G1
Hawkesworth La *GSLY* LS20 61 H6
Hawke Wy *LM/WK* BD12 127 G8
Hawkhill Av *GSLY* LS20 61 M6
MSTN/BAR LS15 111 K3
Hawkhill Dr *MSTN/BAR* LS15 111 K3
Hawkhill Gdns *MSTN/BAR* LS15 111 K3
Hawkhills *CHAL* LS7 88 A7
Hawkhurst Rd *WOR/ARM* LS12 108 E8
Hawkingcroft Rd
HOR/CROF WF4 197 H5
Hawkins Dr *CHAL* LS7 7 G4
Hawkins Wy *LIT* OL15 185 L5 3
Hawkroyd Bank Rd *HUDS* HD4 214 A7
Hawksbridge La *HWTH* BD22 100 B3
Hawkshead Cl *WBOW* BD5 127 G1 12
Hawkshead Crs *SCFT* LS14 111 H3
Hawkshead Dr *ROY/SHW* OL2 228 F8
WBOW BD5 127 G1
Hawkshead Rd *ROY/SHW* OL2 229 J6 3
Hawksmoor Dr *ROY/SHW* OL2 229 K6
Hawk's Nest Gdns East
AL/HA/HU LS17 87 M2 2
Hawk's Nest Gdns South
AL/HA/HU LS17 87 M2 3
Hawk's Nest Gdns West
AL/HA/HU LS17 87 M2 4
Hawk's Nest Ri *AL/HA/HU* LS17 87 M2
Hawkstone Av *GSLY* LS20 61 L7
Hawkstone Dr *KGHY* BD21 57 J5 1
Hawkstone Vw *GSLY* LS20 61 L7
Hawkswood Av *HTON* BD9 104 B3
KSTL LS5 86 A7
Hawkswood Crs *KSTL* LS5 86 A7
Hawkswood Gv *KSTL* LS5 86 A7
Hawkswood Mt *KSTL* LS5 86 A7
Hawkswood Pl *KSTL* LS5 86 A8
Hawkswood St *KSTL* LS5 86 B8
Hawkswood Ter *KSTL* LS5 86 B8 1
Hawksworth Av *GSLY* LS20 61 M7
Hawksworth Cl *ILK* LS29 61 J3
Hawksworth Dr *ILK* LS29 61 H2
Hawksworth Gv *KSTL* LS5 85 M8 1
Hawksworth Rd *BAIL* BD17 60 E8
HORS LS18 85 M6
Hawkwell Bank *BSLYN/ROY* S71 262 C6
Haw La *YEA* LS19 62 E6
Hawley Cl *MOR* LS27 152 B4
Hawley St *COL* BB8 74 E1
Hawley Ter *IDLE* BD10 106 A2
Hawley Wy *MOR* LS27 152 B4 4
Haworth Cl *BSLYN/ROY* S71 261 K3 2
MIRF WF14 172 B8
Haworth Gv *HTON* BD9 104 A3
Haworth La *YEA* LS19 62 D7
Haworth Rd *BTLY* WF17 151 H4
CUL/QBY BD13 79 J8
HTON BD9 104 A3
HWTH BD22 79 G6
WIL/AL BD15 102 C2
WIL/AL BD15 103 K2
Haworth to Hebden Bridge Wk
HBR HX7 99 G3
HBR HX7 121 G7
HWTH BD22 100 B2
Haw Park La *HOR/CROF* WF4 222 A3
WKFDW/WTN WF2 221 K4
Hawshaw Rd *HWTH* BD22 53 M1
Hawswater Pl *KNOT* WF11 182 A5
Hawthorn Av *BFDE* BD3 106 A6 2
BTLY WF17 173 J3
HOR/CROF WF4 200 A5
KNOT WF11 181 M3 2
TAD LS24 71 K5
YEA LS19 62 D7
Hawthorn Cl *BRIG* HD6 170 E3 2
ILK LS29 18 F6 1
TAD LS24 71 L5
WKFDW/WTN WF2 175 K3
Hawthorn Ct *EARD/LOFT* WF3 154 E5 3
Hawthorn Crs *CHAL* LS7 87 M7 3
ROY/SHW OL2 229 K8 2
YEA LS19 62 D7
Hawthorn Cft *EARD/LOFT* WF3 154 E5 4
TAD LS24 71 K5
Hawthorn Dr *BRAM* LS13 106 F1
IDLE BD10 83 L7 4
YEA LS19 62 E6
Hawthorne Av *CAS* WF10 158 D8
FEA/AMT WF7 201 L2 3
HEM/SK/SE WF9 223 M8 2
SHPY BD18 104 F1
WBY LS22 29 M7
Hawthorne Cl
HOR/CROF WF4 217 M3 1
KBTN HD8 215 M3 3
MOR LS27 129 M7 4
Hawthorne Ct *DOD/DAR* S75 241 K6
Hawthorne Crs *AWLS/ASK* DN6 249 J5
DOD/DAR S75 260 A6
HEM/SK/SE WF9 223 L8 1
Hawthorne Dr *MOR* LS27 129 M7 3
Hawthorne Gdns
BHP/TINH LS16 86 D1 1
Hawthorne La *MILN* OL16 229 J2
Hawthorne Ms *NORM* WF6 178 D7
Hawthorne Ri *SCFT* LS14 89 L6
Hawthorne St *AIRE* BD20 35 M5 4
BSLY S70 261 G6
CUD/GR S72 244 E3
Hawthorne Vw *MOR* LS27 130 A7 1
Hawthorne Wy *CUD/GR* S72 244 E3
KBTN HD8 238 B2
Hawthorn Gv *DOD/DAR* S75 259 J5 1
FEA/AMT WF7 224 B1 1
ILK LS29 40 B7
RTHW LS26 155 H2
Hawthorn La *CHAL* LS7 87 M7 4
Hawthorn Mt *CHAL* LS7 87 M7 5
Hawthorn Pl *TOD* OL14 141 K8 7
Hawthorn Rd *CHAL* LS7 87 M7 6
HOLM/MEL HD7 212 A5
YEA LS19 62 D7
The Hawthorns *AIRE* BD20 34 E8
OSS WF5 197 G3 2
WKFDE WF1 176 F1
Hawthorn St *BFDE* BD3 106 A6 3
HFAX HX1 10 C9 2
HIPP HX3 147 M6 2
Hawthorn Ter *HUDS* HD4 213 L2
OSS WF5 197 G3 3
Hawthorn V *CHAL* LS7 87 M7 7
Hawthorn Vw *BAIL* BD17 82 F3
CHAL LS7 87 M7 8
Hawthorn Wk *LIT* OL15 207 H1 6
Hawtop La *DOD/DAR* S75 220 B8
Hayburn Gdns *BTLY* WF17 173 K1 2
Hayburn Rd *BTLY* WF17 173 J1
Haycliffe Av *GTHN* BD7 126 C4
Haycliffe Dr *GTHN* BD7 126 B4 4
Haycliffe Gv *GTHN* BD7 126 C4 1
Haycliffe Hill Rd *GTHN* BD7 126 D3 3
Haycliffe La *WBSY* BD6 126 D4
Haycliffe Rd *GTHN* BD7 126 D3
Haycliffe Ter *GTHN* BD7 126 D3
Hayclose Md *WBSY* BD6 126 C8
Hayden St *BFDE* BD3 5 L8
Haydn Av *EARD/LOFT* WF3 155 G8
Haydn's Ter *PDSY/CALV* LS28 107 G4
Hayes Cft *BSLY* S70 261 H5 3
Hayfield Av *BSPA/BRAM* LS23 48 E6
HUDW HD3 191 J7
Hayfield Cl *DOD/DAR* S75 260 A7
HOLM/MEL HD7 254 F2 2
The Hayfields *HWTH* BD22 78 E6
Hayfield Ter *WOR/ARM* LS12 108 E8
Haygill Nook *SKP/WHF* BD23 17 M4
Hayhills La *AIRE* BD20 35 M2
Hayhills Rd *AIRE* BD20 36 A4
Hayleigh Av *BRAM* LS13 107 L3
Hayleigh Mt *BRAM* LS13 107 L4
Haylock Cl *DOD/DAR* S75 260 A3
Haymaker Ri *WHIT* OL12 184 E8
Hayne La *HOR/CROF* WF4 218 A1
Haynes St *KGHY* BD21 3 J5
WHIT OL12 206 B6
Hays La *LUD/ILL* HX2 123 K7
Hayson Cl *EARL* WF12 174 B5
Haythorns Av *AIRE* BD20 35 M5 3
Haythorns Mt *AIRE* BD20 35 M5 3
Hayton Dr *WBY* LS22 48 B2 1
Hayton Wood Vw
GFTH/SHER LS25 92 A6
The Haywain *ILK* LS29 38 F3
Haywood Av *HUDW* HD3 191 L8
Hazel Av *EARL* WF12 174 D7
MILN OL16 229 J3
SCFT LS14 89 L6
Hazel Bank *WKFDW/WTN* WF2 176 A6 3

Hazel Beck BGLY BD16...... 81 J6 [1]
Hazel Cl BIRK/DRI BD11...... 128 C8
　EARL WF12...... 174 D7
　PBR HG3...... 26 D2
Hazel Ct RTHW LS26...... 155 H2
　WKFDW/WTN WF2...... 176 C6
Hazel Crs EARL WF12...... 174 D6
Hazelcroft IDLE BD10...... 105 M2
Hazel Cft SHPY BD18...... 82 F7
Hazeldene CUL/QBY BD13...... 124 F6 [6]
Hazel Dr EARL WF12...... 174 D7 [7]
　PBR HG3...... 26 D2
Hazel Gdns CAS WF10...... 180 F1
Hazel Gv AIRE BD20...... 55 L1
　BTLY WF17...... 173 J2 [2]
　HIPP HX3...... 148 C7
　HOR/CROF WF4...... 217 M3
　HUDN HD2...... 192 D1
　PONT WF8...... 181 G4
Hazel Grove Rd AIRE BD20...... 55 L1
Hazelheads BAIL BD17...... 82 E1
Hazelhurst Av BGLY BD16...... 81 J6 [3]
Hazelhurst Brow HTON BD9...... 103 M4
Hazelhurst Ct BFDE BD3...... 105 L7 [4]
　PDSY/CALV LS28...... 107 H7
Hazel Hurst Gv CUL/QBY BD13...... 124 F7
Hazel Hurst Rd CUL/QBY BD13...... 124 F7
Hazelhurst Ter HTON BD9...... 103 M4
Hazel La AWLS/ASK DN6...... 248 C4
Hazelmere Av BGLY BD16...... 81 J6
Hazel Mt SHPY BD18...... 82 E7
Hazel Ri RTHW LS26...... 156 C5
Hazel Rd KNOT WF11...... 182 A3
Hazelshaw DOD/DAR S75...... 260 C8 [5]
Hazelwood Av BGLY BD16...... 58 B5 [5]
　GFTH/SHER LS25...... 135 J1
Hazelwood Ct WKFDE WF1...... 176 F1 [4]
Hazelwood Rd
　HEM/SK/SE WF9...... 223 K5 [6]
　HTON BD9...... 103 L3
　WKFDE WF1...... 176 F1 [5]
Hazelwood St TOD OL14...... 163 K1 [6]
Hazledene Crs CUD/GR S72...... 244 E5
Hazledene Rd CUD/GR S72...... 244 E5
Headfield Rd EARL WF12...... 195 M2
　HUDS HD3...... 214 C3
Headfield Vw EARL WF12...... 195 M2
Headingley Av HDGY LS6...... 108 E1
Headingley Crs HDGY LS6...... 108 F2 [8]
Headingley La HDGY LS6...... 109 G2
Headingley Mt HDGY LS6...... 108 E1
Headingley Rd AWLS/ASK DN6...... 227 M3
Headingley Vw HDGY LS6...... 108 F2 [7]
Headland Gv WBSY BD6...... 126 B5 [5]
Headland La EARL WF12...... 174 B8
Headlands Av OSS WF5...... 196 E1
Headlands Cl LVSG WF15...... 172 D3
Headlands Gv OSS WF5...... 196 E1 [1]
Headlands La KNOT WF11...... 182 A2
　PONT WF8...... 180 E5
Headlands Pk OSS WF5...... 196 E1
Headlands Rd HUD HD1...... 14 E4
　LVSG WF15...... 172 C2
　OSS WF5...... 196 E1
　WHIT OL12...... 206 A3
Headlands St LVSG WF15...... 172 C3 [3]
　WHIT OL12...... 206 A3
Headlands Wk OSS WF5...... 196 E1 [4]
Headley La BSPA/BRAM LS23...... 70 A5
　CUL/QBY BD13...... 124 F1
The Headrow LDS LS1...... 6 F8
Headwell La TAD LS24...... 115 L1
Healaugh La RYKW YO26...... 33 H7
Heald Cl LIT OL15...... 207 J3
Healdfield Rd CAS WF10...... 158 B6
Healds Av LVSG WF15...... 172 D2
Healds Rd DEWS WF13...... 173 J4
Heald St CAS WF10...... 158 B6
Healdwood Cl CAS WF10...... 158 C7
Healdwood Rd CAS WF10...... 158 C6
Healey Av BGLY BD16...... 81 J4
Healey Cl BTLY WF17...... 173 H1 [8]
Healey Crs OSS WF5...... 196 F3
Healey Croft La
　EARD/LOFT WF3...... 153 K7
Healey Dr OSS WF5...... 196 F3
Healey Green La HUDE HD5...... 194 B7
Healey La BGLY BD16...... 81 J4
　BTLY WF17...... 173 H1 [2]
　EARL WF12...... 195 H8
　WHIT OL12...... 206 A3
Healey Rd OSS WF5...... 196 E3
Healey St BTLY WF17...... 173 H1
　MILN OL16...... 206 A7
Healey Wood Crs BRIG HD6...... 170 C6
Healey Wood Gdns BRIG HD6...... 170 C6
Healey Wood Gv BRIG HD6...... 170 C6
Healey Wood Rd BRIG HD6...... 170 C6
Healing St ROCH OL11...... 228 C1 [12]
Heap La BFDE BD3...... 5 J4
Heap St BFDE BD3...... 5 J5
　HIPP HX3...... 146 E4
Heath Av HIPP HX3...... 168 D1
Heathcliff HWTH BD22...... 78 D7 [3]
Heathcliffe Cl BTLY WF17...... 151 H3 [1]
Heath Cl EARL WF12...... 174 D6 [4]
　HOLM/MEL HD7...... 213 G7
Heathcote Ri HWTH BD22...... 78 F6
Heath Crs AIRE BD20...... 16 E8
　BEE/HOL LS11...... 131 G4
Heathcroft Crs BEE/HOL LS11...... 131 G4
Heathcroft Dr BEE/HOL LS11...... 131 G4 [6]
Heathcroft Lawn
　BEE/HOL LS11...... 131 G4
Heathcroft Ri BEE/HOL LS11...... 131 G4 [3]
Heathcroft V BEE/HOL LS11...... 131 G4 [2]
Heathdale Av HUDN HD2...... 192 B5
Heath Dr AIRE BD20...... 16 E8
　BSPA/BRAM LS23...... 48 D7
Heather Av ROY/SHW OL2...... 229 M6
Heather Bank CUL/QBY BD13...... 101 J3
　HEM/SK/SE WF9...... 246 A1
　OSS WF5...... 197 H3 [2]
Heather Ct BTLY WF17...... 151 G4 [2]
　EARD/LOFT WF3...... 177 G1 [4]

HUDW HD3...... 191 H6 [2]
Heathercroft CHAL LS7...... 88 A8 [2]
Heatherdale Ct
　EARD/LOFT WF3...... 153 G6 [1]
Heatherdale Dr
　EARD/LOFT WF3...... 153 G6 [2]
Heatherdale Rd
　EARD/LOFT WF3...... 152 H6
Heatherdene TAD LS24...... 71 M2
Heatherfield Crs HUDE HD5...... 191 M8
Heatherfield Rd HUD HD1...... 191 M8
Heather Fold KGHY BD21...... 239 H4
Heather Gdns BRAM LS13...... 108 A6
　SCFT LS14...... 67 L7
Heather Gv BRAM LS13...... 107 M6
　HTON BD9...... 103 K3
　KGHY BD21...... 2 B3
Heathergrove Fold HUDE HD5...... 15 L4
Heather Knowle
　DOD/DAR S75...... 260 C7 [3]
Heatherlands Av
　CUL/QBY BD13...... 101 M4
Heather Ri ILK LS29...... 40 A4
Heather Rd BAIL BD17...... 82 F2 [3]
　HOLM/MEL HD7...... 234 F5
Heather Side BAIL BD17...... 82 D2
Heatherstones HIPP HX3...... 168 D2 [4]
Heather V SCFT LS14...... 67 L7
Heather Vw BGLY BD16...... 81 M1
　OSS WF5...... 196 F1
　SKP/WHF BD23...... 16 D3
Heathfield BHP/TINH LS16...... 86 C2
　MIRF WF14...... 172 B8
Heathfield Av ELL HX5...... 169 K7 [3]
Heathfield Cl BGLY BD16...... 81 J2
　EARD/LOFT WF3...... 153 H6 [1]
Heathfield Gv GTHN BD7...... 126 A2
Heathfield La BSPA/BRAM LS23...... 48 D6
Heathfield Ms HOLM/MEL HD7...... 213 G2 [2]
Heathfield Ri RPDN/SBR HX6...... 188 C5
Heathfield Rd HOLM/MEL HD7...... 213 G2
　OSS WF5...... 174 E6 [3]
Heathfield St ELL HX5...... 169 J8
Heathfield Ter HDGY LS6...... 86 F8
Heath Gdns HIPP HX3...... 168 E2
Heath Gv AIRE BD20...... 58 F6
　BEE/HOL LS11...... 131 G3
　BTLY WF17...... 174 B3
　PDSY/CALV LS28...... 106 E7
Heath Hall HFAX HX1...... 168 E1
Heath Hall Av BOW BD4...... 127 K5
Heath Hill Rd LUD/ILL HX2...... 145 J4
Heath House La
　HOLM/MEL HD7...... 212 D2
Heath Lea HFAX HX1...... 168 E2 [2]
Heath Mount Rd BRIG HD6...... 170 C6
Heathness Rd ILK LS29...... 18 F5
Heath Pk ILK LS29...... 38 B3
Heath Park Av HFAX HX1...... 168 E1 [1]
Heath Pl BEE/HOL LS11...... 131 G3
Heath Ri BEE/HOL LS11...... 131 G3
Heath Rd BEE/HOL LS11...... 131 G3
　BFDE BD3...... 5 L2
　EARL WF12...... 174 D6
　HFAX HX1...... 168 L1
　HOLM/MEL HD7...... 213 G6
　WHIT OL12...... 184 E8
Heath Royd HIPP HX3...... 168 E2
Heath St BFDE BD3...... 105 L7
　BGLY BD16...... 81 J3 [4]
　HIPP HX3...... 168 E2
　LVSG WF15...... 172 C4
Heath Ter BFDE BD3...... 5 M6
Heath View St HFAX HX1...... 11 H8
Heath Wk EARL WF12...... 174 D6 [4]
Heathwood Dr HOLM/MEL HD7...... 212 E1
Heathy Av LUD/ILL HX2...... 146 C1
Heathy La LUD/ILL HX2...... 124 B8
Heatley Rd MILN OL16...... 206 F8
Heaton Av AIRE BD20...... 58 E7
　CLECK BD19...... 149 L7
　EARL WF12...... 174 A6
　HUDE HD5...... 193 L5
　WOR/ARM LS12...... 130 E1
Heaton Cl BGLY BD16...... 81 K2
Heaton Crs BGLY BD16...... 81 K2 [3]
Heaton Dr BAIL BD17...... 82 D2
　BGLY BD16...... 81 K2
　HUDE HD5...... 193 L4
Heaton Fold La HUD HD1...... 213 M1 [3]
Heaton Gdns HUD HD1...... 191 M8
Heaton Gra BTLY WF17...... 174 A3
Heaton Hl WBSY BD6...... 126 B7 [8]
Heaton Moor Dr HUDE HD5...... 193 L5
Heaton Park Dr HTON BD9...... 104 B3
Heaton Park Rd HTON BD9...... 104 B3
Heaton Rd BTLY WF17...... 151 L7
　HTON BD9...... 104 C3
　HUD HD1...... 191 M8
Heaton Royds La SHPY BD18...... 104 B1
Heaton's Ct LDS LS1...... 9 G2
Heaton St BEE/HOL LS11...... 9 J9
　BOW BD4...... 5 J9
　BRIC HD6...... 170 C4 [7]
　CLECK BD19...... 149 M6
　FEA/AMT WF7...... 224 A1
　MILN OL16...... 229 J1
Heator La KBTN HD8...... 238 C7
Hebble Brook La LUD/ILL HX2...... 145 L2 [1]
Hebble Butt Cl MILN OL16...... 207 G8 [6]
Hebble Dr HOLM/MEL HD7...... 236 C5
Hebble End HBR HX7...... 143 H3
Hebble La HFAX HX1...... 10 A1
　HOLM/MEL HD7...... 234 F6
Hebble Mt HOLM/MEL HD7...... 235 G5
Hebble St DEWS WF13...... 195 H1

HUD HD1...... 15 G3
Hebble Vale Dr LUD/ILL HX2...... 146 A4
Hebb Vw WBSY BD6...... 126 A4
Hebden Ap SCFT LS14...... 89 K8
Hebden Bridge Rd HWTH BD22...... 100 A7
Hebden Cl SCFT LS14...... 89 K8 [2]
Hebden Gn SCFT LS14...... 89 K8
Hebden Pl SCFT LS14...... 89 K8
Hebden Rd HWTH BD22...... 78 F6
　WKFDE WF1...... 177 C6
Heber Cl AIRE BD20...... 36 B2 [2]
Heber Pl LIT OL15...... 207 K1 [2]
Heber's Ghyll Dr ILK LS29...... 38 A3
Heber's Gv ILK LS29...... 38 A3
Heber St KGHY BD21...... 2 F7
Heckmondwike Rd
　DEWS WF13...... 173 H5
Hector Av MILN OL16...... 206 C6
Hector Cl WBSY BD6...... 126 E5 [3]
Heddon Cl WBOW BD5...... 127 G1 [13]
Heddon Gv WBOW BD5...... 4 F9
　WBOW BD5...... 127 G1 [10]
Heddon St HDGY LS6...... 87 G8
Hedge Cl GIR BD8...... 103 M5
Hedge Hill Rd STKB/PEN S36...... 270 C3 [1]
Hedge La DOD/DAR S75...... 241 M6 [3]
Hedge Side BAIL BD17...... 82 D2
Hedge Top La HIPP HX3...... 147 J3
Hedge Wy GIR BD8...... 104 A5
Hedley Cha WKFDE WF1...... 176 D3
Hedley Crs WKFDE WF1...... 176 D3
Hedley Gn WOR/ARM LS12...... 109 G7
Heeley Rd WKFDW/WTN WF2...... 220 C2
Heelis St BSLY S70...... 261 H6
Heidelberg Rd HTON BD9...... 104 C4 [3]
Height Gn RPDN/SBR HX6...... 167 K3
Height La HWTH BD22...... 100 F4
　SKP/WHF BD23...... 17 M3
　WKFDW/WTN WF2...... 12 A3
Height Rd HBR HX7...... 143 M2
Heights Av WHIT OL12...... 206 A6
Heights Bank WOR/ARM LS12...... 108 B7
Heights Cl WHIT OL12...... 206 A4 [3]
　WOR/ARM LS12...... 108 A6
Heights Dr HOLM/MEL HD7...... 212 F7
　WOR/ARM LS12...... 108 A7
Heights Garth WOR/ARM LS12...... 108 A7
Heights Pde WOR/ARM LS12...... 108 A7
The Heights HOLM/MEL HD7...... 254 C8
Heights Wy WOR/ARM LS12...... 108 B7
Helena Cl BSLY S70...... 260 F6 [4]
Helena Ct GFTH/SHER LS25...... 135 H6 [1]
Helena Pl GFTH/SHER LS25...... 135 H6
Helena St GFTH/SHER LS25...... 135 H6
Helena Wy BOW BD4...... 127 L6
Helene Cl HUDW HD3...... 191 G6 [1]
Helensburgh Cl DOD/DAR S75...... 260 E4 [8]
Helen St HUDS HD3...... 214 A3 [1]
　SHPY BD18...... 82 B6 [1]
Hellewell St WBSY BD6...... 126 B7 [7]
Hell La WKFDE WF1...... 199 M2
Hellwood La SCFT LS14...... 67 L2
Helme La HOLM/MEL HD7...... 235 C3
Helme Pk HOLM/MEL HD7...... 234 F4
Helmet La HOLM/MEL HD7...... 234 F4
Helm La HUDE HD5...... 193 L1
　RPDN/SBR HX6...... 166 E6
Helmsley Ct MID LS10...... 153 L2 [2]
Helmsley Dr BHP/TINH LS16...... 86 D7
Helmsley Rd BHP/TINH LS16...... 86 D7
　BSPA/BRAM LS23...... 48 E7
　WKFDW/WTN WF2...... 199 G5
Helmsley St BOW BD4...... 127 J5
Helston Crs BSLYN/ROY S71...... 261 K3
Helston Cft MID LS10...... 153 J1 [1]
Helston Garth MID LS10...... 153 J1 [2]
Helston Gv HOLM/MEL HD7...... 236 A2 [7]
Helston Pl MID LS10...... 153 J1 [3]
Helston Rd MID LS10...... 131 J8
　NORM WF6...... 178 D3
Helston St MID LS10...... 131 H8
Helston Wk MID LS10...... 153 J2 [4]
Helston Wy MID LS10...... 131 J8 [7]
Helted Wy HUDE HD5...... 215 G3
Hemingway Garth MID LS10...... 9 M9
Hemingway Gn MID LS10...... 9 L9
Hemingway Rd IDLE BD10...... 83 M6
Hemishor Dr RTHW LS26...... 135 C6
Hemsby Rd CAS WF10...... 158 D7
Hemsby St KGHY BD21...... 79 J2 [3]
Hemsworth La
　HEM/SK/SE WF9...... 223 J2
Hemsworth Rd
　HEM/SK/SE WF9...... 246 A1
Henacrewood Ct
　CUL/QBY BD13...... 125 G7
Henbury St CHAL LS7...... 7 K6
Henconner Av CHAL LS7...... 87 L8
Henconner Crs CHAL LS7...... 87 L8
Henconner Dr CHAL LS7...... 87 L8
Henconner Gdns CHAL LS7...... 87 L8 [3]
Henconner Gv CHAL LS7...... 87 L8 [3]
Henconner La BRAM LS13...... 107 M5
　CHAL LS7...... 87 L8 [4]
Henconner Rd CHAL LS7...... 87 L8
Hendal La WKFDW/WTN WF2...... 220 C1
Henderson Av NORM WF6...... 178 D6
Henderson Gln BSLYN/ROY S71...... 243 J5
Henderson Pl WBSY BD6...... 126 E5 [3]
Henderson St LIT OL15...... 207 J1
　WHIT OL12...... 206 H4
Henderville St LIT OL15...... 185 K8 [3]
Hendford Dr BFDE BD3...... 5 K5
Hendriff Pl WHIT OL12...... 206 B5 [10]
Hen Holme La AIRE BD20...... 36 A7
Henley Av BRAM LS13...... 107 L4
　EARL WF12...... 196 A4
　WBOW BD5...... 127 G4
　YEA LS19...... 84 D3
Henley Cl YEA LS19...... 84 E3 [3]

Henley Ct WBOW BD5...... 127 H4 [3]
Henley Crs BRAM LS13...... 107 L4
　YEA LS19...... 84 F3
Henley Cft HOLM/MEL HD7...... 193 G8
Henley Dr FEA/AMT WF7...... 201 M3
　YEA LS19...... 84 E3
Henley Gv BRAM LS13...... 107 L4
　WBOW BD5...... 127 G4
Henley Hl YEA LS19...... 84 E3 [1]
Henley Mt YEA LS19...... 84 F3
Henley Pl BRAM LS13...... 107 L4
Henley Rd BRAM LS13...... 107 L4
　EARL WF12...... 196 A4
　WBOW BD5...... 127 G4
Henley St BRAM LS13...... 107 L4
　WHIT OL12...... 206 A5 [5]
Henley Ter BRAM LS13...... 107 L4
　YEA LS19...... 84 F3
Henley Vw BRAM LS13...... 107 L4
　ROCH OL11...... 228 A1 [10]
Henrietta St BTLY WF17...... 173 L1 [11]
Henry Av HOR/CROF WF4...... 222 K6
　WOR/ARM LS12...... 130 D1
Henry Cl CUD/GR S72...... 244 D3
Henry Frederick Av HUDS HD4...... 213 L5
Henry Moore Ct CAS WF10...... 158 D7 [2]
Henry Pl MOR LS27...... 152 C2 [3]
Henry Ralph Av HUDS HD4...... 213 L5
　BTLY WF17...... 173 L1 [9]
　CLAY BD14...... 125 L2 [9]
　CUL/QBY BD13...... 102 F8 [10]
　HFAX HX1...... 10 F7
　HUD HD1...... 14 E7
　KGHY BD21...... 3 G1
　LIT OL15...... 207 H3
　ROCH OL11...... 206 B8
　SKP/WHF BD23...... 16 B4 [1]
　WKFDW/WTN WF2...... 18 A3
Henry Ter YEA LS19...... 62 B7
Henshall St BSLY S70...... 261 J6 [3]
Henshaw Av YEA LS19...... 62 D8
Henshaw Crs YEA LS19...... 62 D8 [1]
Henshaw La YEA LS19...... 62 D8
Henshaw Ov YEA LS19...... 62 D8
Henshaw Rd TOD OL14...... 163 J5
Henson Gv CAS WF10...... 158 D8
Henthorn St ROY/SHW OL2...... 229 K8 [8]
Hepton Ct OSM LS9...... 110 D5
Hepton Dr HBR HX7...... 143 H5
Heptonstall Rd HBR HX7...... 143 H5
Hepworth Av MOR LS27...... 130 D6
Hepworth Cl MIRF WF14...... 172 D8
Hepworth Crs HOLM/MEL HD7...... 255 G5
　MOR LS27...... 130 D6 [5]
Hepworth Dr HOLM/MEL HD7...... 255 G5
Hepworth La MIRF WF14...... 172 D8
Hepworth Rd HOLM/MEL HD7...... 255 G5
Hepworth St WOR/ARM LS12...... 109 G8 [3]
Herbalist St WOR/ARM LS12...... 109 G8 [3]
Herbert Pl BGLY BD16...... 106 A6 [1]
Herbert St BGLY BD16...... 81 J3
　CAS WF10...... 157 M7
　CLAY BD14...... 125 L3 [8]
　HFAX HX1...... 10 A7
　SHPY BD18...... 82 B5 [3]
　WBOW BD5...... 126 F2 [3]
Hereford Cl HEM/SK/SE WF9...... 223 M6
　ROY/SHW OL2...... 229 H7 [3]
Hereford St ROCH OL11...... 228 C1 [1]
Heritage Pk BGLY BD16...... 59 J8
Heritage Rd BTLY WF17...... 173 L2
Heritage Wy HWTH BD22...... 78 E3 [3]
Hermitage Pk KBTN HD8...... 216 A4
Hermit La DOD/DAR S75...... 260 B4
Hermit St HWTH BD22...... 79 J4
Hermon Av HFAX HX1...... 10 C7
Hermon Gv HFAX HX1...... 10 C7
Hermon Rd MSTN/BAR LS15...... 111 K5
Hermon St MSTN/BAR LS15...... 111 K5 [6]
Heron Cl AIRE BD20...... 35 K8
　AL/HA/HU LS17...... 88 B2 [8]
　CUL/QBY BD13...... 124 E4
Heron Ct MOR LS27...... 152 F2 [2]
Heron Dr WKFDW/WTN WF2...... 220 E1
Heron Gv AL/HA/HU LS17...... 88 C2
Herriot Ms CAS WF10...... 180 F1
Herschel Rd GIR BD8...... 103 J7 [1]
Hertford Cha MSTN/BAR LS15...... 111 M8
Hertford Cl MSTN/BAR LS15...... 111 M8 [8]
Hertford Cft MSTN/BAR LS15...... 111 M8 [8]
Hertford Fold MSTN/BAR LS15...... 111 L8 [9]
Hertford Lawn
　MSTN/BAR LS15...... 111 L8 [5]
Hertford Rd
　ROY/SHW OL2...... 229 K6 [2]
Heseltine La HBR HX7...... 165 J2
Heshbon St BOW BD4...... 127 L3 [7]
Hesketh Av EARD/LOFT WF3...... 152 F5
　KSTL LS5...... 108 C2
Hesketh La EARD/LOFT WF3...... 152 F5
Hesketh Mt KSTL LS5...... 108 C1
Hesketh Pl KSTL LS5...... 108 C1
Hesketh Rd KSTL LS5...... 108 C1
　MILN OL16...... 206 E7 [3]
Hesketh Ter KSTL LS5...... 108 C2
Hesley Rd WKFDW/WTN WF2...... 198 D6
Hessel Ct PONT WF8...... 180 D6 [8]
Hessle Av HDGY LS6...... 109 G3 [3]
Hessle Common La
　HOR/CROF WF4...... 201 M7
Hessle La HOR/CROF WF4...... 201 M6
Hessle Mt HDGY LS6...... 109 G3 [1]
Hessle Pl HDGY LS6...... 109 G3 [5]
Hessle Rd HDGY LS6...... 109 G3 [6]
Hessle Ter HDGY LS6...... 109 G3 [7]
Hessle Vw HDGY LS6...... 109 G3 [8]
Hessle Wk HDGY LS6...... 109 G3 [2]
Hetchell Vw AL/HA/HU LS17...... 67 M4
Hetton Dr BFDE BD3...... 105 M8 [8]
Hetton Rd RHAY LS8...... 88 B8
Heuthwaite Av WBY LS22...... 48 B3 [9]
Hever Gv HUDE HD5...... 193 J7 [1]
Heversham Av ROY/SHW OL2...... 229 M7 [3]
New Clews GTHN BD7...... 104 C1
Hey Beck La EARL WF12...... 174 E1
Heybeck Wk BOW BD4...... 128 B4 [7]
Hey Bottom La WHIT OL12...... 184 B8
Heybrook St MILN OL16...... 206 D6 [3]

Heycliffe Rd HOLM/MEL HD7...... 254 D1
Hey Crs HOLM/MEL HD7...... 234 F4
Heyden Br GLSP SK13...... 265 M4
Heyford Ct ECHL BD2...... 104 F3
Heygate Cl BAIL BD17...... 82 F2
Heygate La BAIL BD17...... 82 F2
　BSPA/BRAM LS23...... 70 B2
Hey Head La LIT OL15...... 185 K5
　TOD OL14...... 141 M7
Hey La HUDE HD5...... 214 F3
　HUDS HD4...... 214 D7
　HUDW HD3...... 189 L7
Heys Av CUL/QBY BD13...... 103 H8
Heys Cl KNOT WF11...... 182 C2 [3]
Heys Crs CUL/QBY BD13...... 103 J8
Heys Gdns HOLM/MEL HD7...... 236 E6
Heysham Dr BSLYN/ROY S71...... 261 M1
Heysham Gn BSLYN/ROY S71...... 261 M1
Hey Slack La KBTN HD8...... 255 L4
Heys La HOLM/MEL HD7...... 211 M4
　LUD/ILL HX2...... 122 C8
　RPDN/SBR HX6...... 188 F5
Hey St BRIC HD6...... 170 D2
　GTHN BD7...... 4 C6
　MILN OL16...... 206 D6
Heywood Cl HIPP HX3...... 147 J4
Heywood Pl HFAX HX1...... 10 D5
Heywood St HFAX HX1...... 10 D5
Hibson Cl WHIT OL12...... 184 E8
Hick La BTLY WF17...... 173 M1
Hicks La RTHW LS26...... 156 F3
Hickson Dr BSLYN/ROY S71...... 262 A2 [3]
Hick St BFD BD1...... 5 H6 [2]
Higgin La HIPP HX3...... 169 G1
Higham And Dob La
　RPDN/SBR HX6...... 166 E2
Higham Common Rd
　DOD/DAR S75...... 260 A2
Higham La DOD/DAR S75...... 260 A5
Higham Vw DOD/DAR S75...... 241 M7
High Ash AL/HA/HU LS17...... 88 A1
　SHPY BD18...... 83 G7
High Ash Av AL/HA/HU LS17...... 88 B1
　KBTN HD8...... 240 B4
High Ash Cl HOR/CROF WF4...... 221 H8
High Ash Dr AL/HA/HU LS17...... 88 A1
High Ash Mt AL/HA/HU LS17...... 88 A1
High Ash Pk WIL/AL BD15...... 103 H5
High Bank AIRE BD20...... 38 A1
High Bank Ap MSTN/BAR LS15...... 111 M7
High Bank Cl KBTN HD8...... 19 H6 [3]
　MSTN/BAR LS15...... 111 M6
High Bank Gdns
　MSTN/BAR LS15...... 112 A7 [3]
High Bank Ga
　MSTN/BAR LS15...... 111 M7 [10]
High Bank La SHPY BD18...... 81 M8
　STKB/PEN S36...... 270 B3
High Bank Pl
　MSTN/BAR LS15...... 111 M7 [11]
Highbank Rd MILN OL16...... 229 L3
High Banks Cl AIRE BD20...... 58 B4 [3]
High Bank Vw
　MSTN/BAR LS15...... 111 M7 [12]
High Barn Cl ROCH OL11...... 228 A1
High Binns La HWTH BD22...... 100 F3
High Bradley La AIRE BD20...... 16 E8
Highbridge La KBTN HD8...... 239 L5
Highbridge Ter WBOW BD5...... 127 H5
High Brook Fall
　EARD/LOFT WF3...... 154 E8
High Brooms HUDN HD2...... 192 A5
High Bury Cl CUL/QBY BD13...... 124 E6 [2]
Highbury Cl HDGY LS6...... 87 G8
Highbury La HDGY LS6...... 87 G8
Highbury Pl BRAM LS13...... 107 J6
　HDGY LS6...... 87 G8
Highbury Rd HDGY LS6...... 87 G8
Highbury St HDGY LS6...... 87 G8
Highbury Ter HDGY LS6...... 87 G8
Highbury Wy ROY/SHW OL2...... 228 F3 [5]
High Busy La IDLE BD10...... 83 H6
　SHPY BD18...... 83 G6
Highcliffe Av HUDN HD2...... 192 B4
Highcliffe Dr LUD/ILL HX2...... 145 M7 [3]
Highcliffe Rd BTLY WF17...... 173 L3
　MOR LS27...... 152 B2 [3]
High Cliffe Ter WBY LS22...... 48 A1
High Cl DOD/DAR S75...... 241 M5 [3]
　GSLY LS20...... 61 K6
　HOLM/MEL HD7...... 213 G6
　HUDE HD5...... 215 G3
　OSS WF5...... 174 F5 [3]
　YEA LS19...... 84 D3
High Ct HBR HX7...... 120 F8
　LDSU LS2...... 9 J1
High Court La LDSU LS2...... 9 J2
High Crest HOLM/MEL HD7...... 213 G4
High Cft CUL/QBY BD13...... 125 C5 [3]
　HIPP HX3...... 146 B4
Highcroft HOLM/MEL HD7...... 254 A1
　WBY LS22...... 47 J6
Highcroft Cl PDSY/CALV LS28...... 106 E6 [3]
Highcroft Crs HUDS HD5...... 215 H3 [3]
Highcroft Gdns KGHY BD21...... 58 B8 [3]
High Croft Rd TOD OL14...... 141 L8
High Croft Wy AIRE BD20...... 35 G5 [2]
Highcroft Wy WHIT OL12...... 206 B2 [3]
High Cross La HIPP HX3...... 125 J7
Highdale EARL WF12...... 174 A4
Higgin La IDLE BD10...... 83 K6 [2]
Higher Ashenhurst TOD OL14...... 141 J7 [3]
Higher Bank Rd LIT OL15...... 207 J3 [3]
Higher Brockwell
　RPDN/SBR HX6...... 167 H3
Higher Calderbrook Rd
　LIT OL15...... 185 L5
Higher Cleggswood Av
　LIT OL15...... 207 J3
Higher Coach Rd BAIL BD17...... 82 A4
　BGLY BD16...... 81 L4
Higher Downs GIR BD8...... 103 M6
Higher Grange Rd
　PDSY/CALV LS28...... 107 G6

Hig - Hol 301

Higher Intake Rd ECHL BD2 105 L5
Higher Lodge St AIRE BD20 34 D8 2
Higher Park Royd Dr
RPDN/SBR HX6 167 G7
Higher Ri ROY/SHW OL2 229 J5
Higher School St SHPY BD18 82 B6 12
Higher Shore Rd WHIT OL12 185 G7
Higher Wheat La MILN OL16 206 E6
Higherwood Cl KGHY BD21 3 M5
Highfell Ri HWTH BD22 79 G1 5
High Fernley Ct
LM/WK BD12 148 E2 11
High Fernley Rd LM/WK BD12 148 C3
Highfield BOW BD4 127 M5
EARD/LOFT WF3 152 F5
HIPP HX3 147 L1 2
Highfield Av BRIG HD6 148 D6
BSLY S70 261 H8 2
BSLYN/ROY S71 243 J8
COL BB8 52 A5
GTL/HWG HX4 168 D6
HIPP HX3 125 M7
HOLM/MEL HD7 234 F3
IDLE BD10 83 J7
KBTN HD8 256 C2
PONT WF8 180 E7
PONT WF8 181 J2
WOR/ARM LS12 130 F1
Highfield Cl AIRE BD20 58 E5
FEA/AMT WF7 179 M6
MOR LS27 130 A7
WOR/ARM LS12 130 F1
Highfield Ct HWTH BD22 78 E4 3
KBTN HD8 238 A8
LVSG WF15 172 B4 1
Highfield Crs BAIL BD17 82 E2
HBR HX7 143 J2 5
HOLM/MEL HD7 234 F3
HOR/CROF WF4 196 B8
HTON BD9 103 M2
PDSY/CALV LS28 106 F6
RTHW LS26 133 L7 5
WOR/ARM LS12 108 F8
Highfield Dr BTLY WF17 151 G4
CAS WF10 157 H1
GFTH/SHER LS25 135 H1
HTON BD9 103 M2
LVSG WF15 172 A2 1
MOR LS27 129 M7
WKFDW/WTN WF2 176 A7
YEA LS19 84 E3 2
Highfield Gdns EARL WF12 195 M3
HTON BD9 103 M2 2
MOR LS27 129 M7
WOR/ARM LS12 108 E8
Highfield Garth WOR/ARM LS12 130 F1
Highfield Gra HOR/CROF WF4 197 J5
Highfield Gn CAS WF10 135 H8 1
GFTH/SHER LS25 116 A8
PDSY/CALV LS28 106 F6
Highfield Gv CAS WF10 135 H8
ELL HX5 169 G6
IDLE BD10 83 J8
High Field La HWTH BD22 78 E3
RPDN/SBR HX6 166 F8
Highfield La AIRE BD20 36 A4 12
AWLS/ASK DN6 205 K4
DEWS WF13 173 H3
GFTH/SHER LS25 136 F2
HOLM/MEL HD7 234 E3
HUDE HD5 215 L1
KGHY BD21 2 D3
MSTN/BAR LS15 113 G1
RTHW LS26 133 L7
Highfield Ms AIRE BD20 58 E5
BAIL BD17 82 E2 4
Highfield Mt EARL WF12 196 A5
RTHW LS26 133 L8 5
Highfield Pl CAS WF10 135 J8
HEM/SK/SE WF9 223 L8 2
HFAX HX1 10 B8
MOR LS27 152 D3 4
Highfield Range WMB/DAR S73 263 J7
Highfield Ri WKFDW/WTN WF2 176 A6
Highfield Rd BRAM LS13 107 M4
BRIG HD6 170 A6
CLECK BD19 149 L7
ELL HX5 169 H8
GFTH/SHER LS25 92 A6
HEM/SK/SE WF9 223 L8
HOLM/MEL HD7 212 B3
HOLM/MEL HD7 234 F3 1
HOR/CROF WF4 197 J5
HOR/CROF WF4 218 F1
HTON BD9 104 E1
IDLE BD10 83 J8
KBTN HD8 216 A7
KGHY BD21 2 C3
LUD/ILL HX2 145 G6
MILN OL16 207 J8
PDSY/CALV LS28 106 E6
PONT WF8 180 E8
WMB/DAR S73 263 J8
High Flds LUD/ILL HX2 168 A2
Highfields HOR/CROF WF4 218 F1
HOR/CROF WF4 222 F4
STKB/PEN S36 258 B8
Highfields Rd DOD/DAR S75 241 K6
HUD HD1 14 D5
Highfield St BRAM LS13 107 M4 5
KGHY BD21 2 F4 4
PDSY/CALV LS28 106 E6
Highfield Ter EARL WF12 195 M3 1
PDSY/CALV LS28 106 E6 2
SHPY BD18 82 A6 1
Highfield Vw MOR LS27 130 A7
Highfield Vls GFTH/SHER LS25 116 A8
High Fold HWTH BD22 2 B9
Highfold YEA LS19 84 C1
High Fold La AIRE BD20 57 J4
Highgate AIRE BD20 34 E7 1
HTON BD9 104 B2
Highgate Av KBTN HD8 216 B3
Highgate Cl CUL/QBY BD13 125 L4
Highgate Crs KBTN HD8 216 A3
Highgate Dr KBTN HD8 216 B3
ROY/SHW OL2 228 D7
Highgate Gv CLAY BD14 125 L4
Highgate La HUDE HD5 193 M4
KBTN HD8 215 M3
Highgate Rd CUL/QBY BD13 125 K4
EARL WF12 173 M6 7
Highgate St BTLY WF17 174 B3 1
Highgate Wk KBTN HD8 216 B3 1
High Gn KBTN HD8 216 B4
High Green Dr AIRE BD20 35 M4
High Green Rd NORM WF6 178 A2
High Grove La HIPP HX3 11 L9
High Holly Garth KGHY BD21 3 K7
High House Av ECHL BD2 105 J2
High House Edge
HOLM/MEL HD7 212 E7
High House La HOLM/MEL HD7 212 D7
LUD/ILL HX2 144 E2
High House Rd ECHL BD2 105 J2
High Hoyland La DOD/DAR S75 240 D7
High Keep Fold HOR/CROF WF4 220 B3
Highland Cl PONT WF8 181 H3
Highlands LIT OL15 207 J3
Highlands Cl GTHN BD7 126 A3 3
RTHW LS26 132 B7
Highlands Dr RTHW LS26 132 B6
Highlands Gv GTHN BD7 126 A3
RTHW LS26 132 B6 1
Highlands La LUD/ILL HX2 124 B8
Highlands Rd ROY/SHW OL2 229 H6
The Highlands LVSG WF15 171 M1
Highlands Wk RTHW LS26 132 B6
Highland Ville HIPP HX3 147 M6
High La HBR HX7 165 L3
HOLM/MEL HD7 254 E3
HUDS HD4 214 D4
HWTH BD22 54 D5
LUD/ILL HX2 145 K6
PBR HG3 28 A6
PBR HG3 28 D5
STKB/PEN S36 256 F7
High Lea HOLM/MEL HD7 233 H2
Highlea Cl YEA LS19 84 B1
Highlee La RPDN/SBR HX6 167 H7
High Lee La STKB/PEN S36 271 H1
High Lees Rd LUD/ILL HX2 145 K1
High Level Rd ROCH OL11 206 C8
High Level Wy HFAX HX1 10 B3
Highley Hall Cft BRIG HD6 170 F4
Highley Pk BRIG HD6 171 G4
High Meadow KGHY BD21 57 J5 2
High Mdw EARL WF12 195 L5
GTL/HWG HX4 168 D7
WIL/AL BD15 102 D1
WKFDW/WTN WF2 199 K8
High Mill La ILK LS29 19 J5
Highmoor BAIL BD17 82 C3
High Moor Av AL/HA/HU LS17 88 A4
High Moor Cl AL/HA/HU LS17 88 A3
High Moor Crs AL/HA/HU LS17 88 A4
Highmoor Crs BRIG HD6 170 F3
High Moor Dr AL/HA/HU LS17 88 A3
High Moor Gv AL/HA/HU LS17 88 A3
Highmoor La BRIG HD6 170 F3
CLECK BD19 171 J1
High Moor Rd AL/HA/HU LS17 25 L6
PBR HG3 25 L4
Highmoor Wk BAIL BD17 82 C4 4
Highoak Garth HWTH BD22 78 E4
High Oxford St CAS WF10 157 L7
High Park Crs HTON BD9 104 A3
High Park Dr HTON BD9 103 M3
High Park Gv HTON BD9 104 A3
High Poplars ECHL BD2 105 H2 5
High Rdg HOR/CROF WF4 197 G8 3
High Ridge Av RTHW LS26 132 F7
High Ridge Ct RTHW LS26 133 G8
High Ridge Pk RTHW LS26 133 G7
High Ridge Wy BHP/TINH LS16 64 B4
High Rd EARL WF12 174 A7
Highroad Well La LUD/ILL HX2 145 L7
Highroyd KBTN HD8 216 B3
High Royd Av CUD/GR S72 244 D8
Highroyd Crs HUDE HD5 15 L7
Highroyd La HUDE HD5 15 L7
High Royd La STKB/PEN S36 271 J1
High Spring Gardens La
KGHY BD21 2 D1
High Spring Rd KGHY BD21 58 B8
Highstone Av BSLY S70 261 G7
Highstone Crs BSLY S70 261 G7
Highstone La BSLY S70 261 H8
Highstone Rd BSLY S70 261 H7
High Stones Rd HBR HX7 166 A3
Highstone V BSLY S70 261 G7 2
High St AIRE BD20 55 M1
AIRE BD20 56 E1
AWLS/ASK DN6 227 L6
AWLS/ASK DN6 227 M3
AWLS/ASK DN6 249 L6
BRIG HD6 170 D3
BSLY S70 261 G4
BSLYN/ROY S71 243 K3
BSLYN/ROY S71 261 L2
BSPA/BRAM LS23 48 D6
BSPA/BRAM LS23 69 M4
BSPA/BRAM LS23 70 A1
BTLY WF17 151 G4
BTLY WF17 174 B3
CAS WF10 157 L7
CLECK BD19 149 M6
COL BB8 74 A1
CUD/GR S72 244 E4
CUD/GR S72 245 G1
CUD/GR S72 245 H8
CUD/GR S72 263 M4
CUL/QBY BD13 102 F8
CUL/QBY BD13 125 G5
DEWS WF13 173 K7
DOD/DAR S75 242 C4
DOD/DAR S75 259 H7
DOD/DAR S75 260 B7
EARL WF12 174 B7
EARL WF12 195 L5
GFTH/SHER LS25 135 K5
GFTH/SHER LS25 138 A2
GTL/HWG HX4 168 F7 5
GTL/HWG HX4 190 A3
HECK WF16 173 G2
HEM/SK/SE WF9 225 J7
HEM/SK/SE WF9 247 K3
HFAX HX1 10 F7
HOLM/MEL HD7 212 D1
HOLM/MEL HD7 236 B2 5
HOR/CROF WF4 197 J5
HOR/CROF WF4 200 A2
HOR/CROF WF4 200 B6
HOR/CROF WF4 220 A1
HOR/CROF WF4 220 B7
HUD HD1 14 A8
HUD HD1 14 F8
IDLE BD10 83 K6
KBTN HD8 240 B4
KGHY BD21 2 F5
KNOT WF11 159 L5
KNOT WF11 181 L1 3
LIT OL15 207 H1
LUD/ILL HX2 145 G5
MOR LS27 152 D3
NORM WF6 178 B3 5
NORM WF6 178 D4
OSS WF5 174 E5
PBR HG3 28 E4
PDSY/CALV LS28 106 F3
ROY/SHW OL2 229 K8 9
SKP/WHF BD23 16 C2
STKB/PEN S36 270 F4
TAD LS24 71 L3
WBSY BD6 126 E5
WHIT OL12 206 B6
YEA LS19 62 D7
High Street Ct LUD/ILL HX2 145 G5 1
High Sunderland La HIPP HX3 11 J1
Highthorne Ct AL/HA/HU LS17 88 B2 2
Highthorne Dr AL/HA/HU LS17 88 B2
Highthorne Gn ROY/SHW OL2 228 E6
Highthorne Gv AL/HA/HU LS17 88 C2
WOR/ARM LS12 108 C6 3
Highthorne Mt AL/HA/HU LS17 88 B2
Highthorne St WOR/ARM LS12 108 D6 3
Highthorne Vw
WOR/ARM LS12 108 C6 9
High Thorns DOD/DAR S75 259 H6
Hightown La HOLM/MEL HD7 254 C1
Hightown Rd CLECK BD19 149 M7
Hightown Vw LVSG WF15 171 L1
High Trees Ct GFTH/SHER LS25 116 A7
High Trees La GTL/HWG HX4 167 M8
High Vw BSLYN/ROY S71 243 K3
HOR/CROF WF4 220 A1
High View Cl WMB/DAR S73 263 J8
Highway GSLY LS20 61 K5
High Ways SCFT LS14 111 G5 2
High Weardley La OT LS21 44 C8
High Well Hill La CUD/GR S72 222 E8
High Wheatley ILK LS29 39 G3
High Wicken Cl CUL/QBY BD13 102 E8
High Wd ILK LS29 39 H3
Highwood Av AL/HA/HU LS17 87 L4
Highwood Cl DOD/DAR S75 241 L6 2
Highwood Crs AL/HA/HU LS17 87 L3
Highwood Gv AL/HA/HU LS17 87 L4 3
High Woodlands
EARD/LOFT WF3 153 L7 4
High Wood La KBTN HD8 238 D1
Higson Ct HUDE HD5 193 J7 2
Hilberoyd Rd BTLY WF17 173 M2
Hilda St HTON BD9 104 C2 3
OSS WF5 197 G2
Hild Av CUD/GR S72 262 F2
Hillam Common La
GFTH/SHER LS25 138 F8
Hillam Hall La GFTH/SHER LS25 138 D8
Hillam Hall Vw
GFTH/SHER LS25 138 D8 1
Hillam La GFTH/SHER LS25 160 A1
Hillam Rd ECHL BD2 104 F3
SEL YO8 139 L7
Hillam St WBOW BD5 126 D3
Hillary Pl LDSU LS2 6 E5
Hillary Rd SHPY BD18 83 G7
Hillary St DEWS WF13 173 H3 3
Hillbrook Ri ILK LS29 38 B3 1
Hill Brow Cl WIL/AL BD15 103 J5
Hill Cl BAIL BD17 82 D4
HUDW HD3 191 H5
PONT WF8 180 F7
Hill Clough Gv HWTH BD22 56 E7
Hillcote Dr WBOW BD5 127 G2 2
Hillcourt Av BRAM LS13 107 L2
Hillcourt Cft BRAM LS13 107 L2 3
Hill Court Dr BRAM LS13 107 L2
Hillcourt Gv BRAM LS13 107 L2
Hill Crs BTLY WF17 151 J5
ILK LS29 40 B7
YEA LS19 84 E1
Hill Crest HOR/CROF WF4 222 E5
WBY LS22 47 G6
Hillcrest GFTH/SHER LS25 138 D7
NORM WF6 178 A2
TAD LS24 71 K4
Hill Crest Av CUL/QBY BD13 101 M5
Hillcrest Av AIRE BD20 36 A4
BTLY WF17 173 J1
CAS WF10 158 F8
CHAL LS7 7 M2
CUL/QBY BD13 125 H6
FEA/AMT WF7 201 K1
OSS WF5 174 E6 4
Hillcrest Cl CAS WF10 158 F8
RTHW LS26 134 B5
Hillcrest Ct TAD LS24 71 K4
Hill Crest Dr CUL/QBY BD13 101 M5 3
Hillcrest Dr CAS WF10 158 F8
CUL/QBY BD13 125 H6
Hillcrest Mt BHP/TINH LS16 86 A2
CAS WF10 158 F8
CLECK BD19 149 H7
Hill Crest Mt CUL/QBY BD13 101 M5
Hillcrest Pl CHAL LS7 7 M1
Hillcrest Ri BHP/TINH LS16 86 A2
Hill Crest Rd CUL/QBY BD13 101 M5
CUL/QBY BD13 102 F7
EARL WF12 195 L1
Hillcrest Rd CAS WF10 159 C8
CUL/QBY BD13 125 H6
Hillcrest Vw CHAL LS7 7 M1
Hill Cft CUL/QBY BD13 103 C7
Hill Croft Cl PONT WF8 203 M1
Hill Dr FEA/AMT WF7 202 C6 2
Hill End EARL WF12 174 A6 3
Hill End Cl HIPP HX3 148 C4
Hill End Crs WOR/ARM LS12 108 B6
Hill End Gv GTHN BD7 126 A3
Hill End La CUL/QBY BD13 80 A6
CUL/QBY BD13 124 F6
HWTH BD22 54 A4
Hill End Rd DOD/DAR S75 242 E7
WOR/ARM LS12 108 B6
Hillesley Rd EARL WF12 174 C3 1
Hillfold HEM/SK/SE WF9 247 K3 1
Hill Foot SHPY BD18 81 M7
Hillfoot Av PDSY/CALV LS28 106 D6
Hillfoot Crs PDSY/CALV LS28 106 D6
Hillfoot Dr PDSY/CALV LS28 106 D6
Hill Foot La PBR HG3 26 C2
Hillfoot Ri PDSY/CALV LS28 106 D6
Hillgarth EARL WF12 195 M3
KNOT WF11 182 A3
Hill Green Ct BOW BD4 129 G4
Hill Gv HUDW HD3 191 H5
Hill Grove Lea HUDW HD3 191 H5
Hill Gv South MID LS10 132 B7 2
Hillhead Dr BTLY WF17 151 J5
Hill House Edge La HWTH BD22 100 D6
Hill House La HOLM/MEL HD7 253 M4
HWTH BD22 100 E5
Hillhouse La HUD HD1 14 F2
Hill House Rd HOLM/MEL HD7 254 A4
Hilliam Hall Cl GFTH/SHER LS25 138 D8
Hillidge Rd MID LS10 9 J8
Hillidge Sq MID LS10 9 J7
Hillingdon Wy AL/HA/HU LS17 87 J1
Hillings La GSLY LS20 60 F5
ILK LS29 60 F2
Hill Lands LM/WK BD12 148 D2
Hill La COL BB8 52 D8
HOLM/MEL HD7 254 A1
Hill Mount Pleasant MID LS10 153 L1
Hill Park Av HIPP HX3 10 A1
Hill Park Gv DOD/DAR S75 260 B6
Hill Ri SKP/WHF BD23 16 B1
Hill Rise Av BRAM LS13 107 L2
Hill Rise Gv BRAM LS13 107 L2
Hill Rd CAS WF10 158 B7
WKFDW/WTN WF2 220 E2
Hills & Hamlets Wk
HOLM/MEL HD7 235 M8
HOLM/MEL HD7 254 A3
Hillside BSLYN/ROY S71 262 C6 3
GFTH/SHER LS25 113 J8
KBTN HD8 239 H8
KNOT WF11 159 M7
PBR HG3 28 A1
Hill Side Av HOLM/MEL HD7 255 G4
Hillside Av GSLY LS20 61 M3
HUDN HD2 192 D4
HWTH BD22 78 D4
LUD/ILL HX2 144 F7
ROY/SHW OL2 229 M6
RPDN/SBR HX6 167 G8 1
Hillside Cl GFTH/SHER LS25 138 D7
ILK LS29 19 G6
STKB/PEN S36 258 B8
WKFDW/WTN WF2 197 M3
Hillside Ct HEM/SK/SE WF9 247 J2 1
ILK LS29 61 H2
Hillside Crs CUD/GR S72 245 J4
HUDS HD4 214 C4
SKP/WHF BD23 16 E3
Hillside Gv CUD/GR S72 245 H4
HWTH BD22 78 D4 2
PDSY/CALV LS28 107 J7 5
Hill Side La STKB/PEN S36 270 A4
Hill Side Mt PDSY/CALV LS28 107 G4
Hillside Mt CUD/GR S72 245 J4
PDSY/CALV LS28 107 J7
PONT WF8 181 G6
Hillside Ri GSLY LS20 61 M3 1
Hill Side Rd BFDE BD3 5 J5
BGLY BD16 81 H3
Hillside Rd CHAL LS7 87 M7
FEA/AMT WF7 202 B8
PBR HG3 26 F2
PONT WF8 181 G6
SHPY BD18 82 E8
Hillside Ter BAIL BD17 82 E3 1
Hillside Vw HOLM/MEL HD7 212 F5
PDSY/CALV LS28 107 H7
RPDN/SBR HX6 167 J2
Hill St BEE/HOL LS11 8 E9
BOW BD4 5 L9
BSLYN/ROY S71 262 A6
CLECK BD19 149 L7
HFAX HX1 10 F8
HOLM/MEL HD7 255 G3
HWTH BD22 78 E8
MILN OL16 206 C7 2
OSM LS9 7 M5
ROY/SHW OL2 229 L8
WBSY BD6 126 C5
Hillthorpe Ct EARD/LOFT WF3 153 L3 2
Hillthorpe Dr PONT WF8 225 J1 2
Hillthorpe Ri PDSY/CALV LS28 129 G1
Hillthorpe Rd PDSY/CALV LS28 129 G1
Hillthorpe Sq PDSY/CALV LS28 128 F1
Hillthorpe St PDSY/CALV LS28 129 G1 1
Hillthorpe Ter PDSY/CALV LS28 129 G1 2
Hilltop CUD/GR S72 245 H3
Hill Top CAS WF10 157 H7
DOD/DAR S75 259 G2
HEM/SK/SE WF9 223 J3 2
HFAX HX1 168 A1
ILK LS29 38 C4
ILK LS29 40 A5
KNOT WF11 182 B2
Hill Top Av BSLYN/ROY S71 243 G5
RHAY LS8 110 B2
Hill Top Cl EARD/LOFT WF3 153 G8
HEM/SK/SE WF9 223 K3 1
HOR/CROF WF4 221 K8
TAD LS24 71 K7
WOR/ARM LS12 108 B6
Hill Top Cottages HTON BD9 104 A4 3
Hill Top Ct EARD/LOFT WF3 153 G8
WKFDW/WTN WF2 220 E2 1
Hill Top Crs MIRF WF14 194 A5
Hill Top Cft HUDS HD4 213 L8 1
Hill Top Dr HUDW HD3 191 J6
ROCH OL11 228 B4
Hill Top Gdns EARD/LOFT WF3 153 G8 1
Hill Top Gn EARD/LOFT WF3 152 F8
Hill Top Gv EARD/LOFT WF3 153 G8
WIL/AL BD15 103 J5
Hill Top La BGLY BD16 59 H6
DOD/DAR S75 260 D3
EARD/LOFT WF3 152 F8
HBR HX7 165 K3
HOR/CROF WF4 201 L5
PBR HG3 26 B2
WIL/AL BD15 103 J5
Hill Top Ms KNOT WF11 182 B2 1
Hill Top Mt RHAY LS8 110 B2
Hill Top Pl HDGY LS6 6 A4
RHAY LS8 110 B2 36
Hill Top Rd CUL/QBY BD13 102 D7
HOLM/MEL HD7 212 B5
HOLM/MEL HD7 254 B5
HOR/CROF WF4 217 M3
HUD HD1 14 A9
HUDE HD5 15 L6
HUDW HD3 191 H5
HWTH BD22 78 D4
KGHY BD21 79 J5
WKFDW/WTN WF2 220 E2
WOR/ARM LS12 108 B6
Hill Top St HDGY LS6 6 A5
Hill Top Vw EARD/LOFT WF3 152 F8
HOLM/MEL HD7 254 D6
Hill Top Wk HWTH BD22 2 A4
Hill Top Wy HWTH BD22 2 A4
Hill Vw LUD/ILL HX2 124 B7
Hillview Gdns HIPP HX3 147 J5
Hill View Pl CHAL LS7 87 M7 9
Hill View Ter CHAL LS7 87 M7 10
Hillway GSLY LS20 61 L7
Hilmian Wy HEM/SK/SE WF9 246 B1
Hilton Av SHPY BD18 104 D1
Hilton Crs BAIL BD17 82 E4 1
Hilton Dr SHPY BD18 104 D1
Hilton Gra BHP/TINH LS16 63 J2
Hilton Gv GTHN BD7 104 C8
RHAY LS8 110 B1
SHPY BD18 104 D1 15
Hilton Pl RHAY LS8 110 B2
Hilton Rd GTHN BD7 104 C8
RHAY LS8 110 B2
SHPY BD18 104 D1
Hilton St DOD/DAR S75 260 F4 3
HBR HX7 143 J3 14
RHAY LS8 110 B2 37
Hilton Ter RHAY LS8 110 B2 38
Hinchcliffe Av OSS WF5 197 H1
Hinchcliffe St BFDE BD3 5 L3
Hinchliffe Av BAIL BD17 82 F4
Hind Ct HOLM/MEL HD7 234 E3
Hindle Pl MOR LS27 130 D7 7
Hindle St BSLY S70 260 F5 2
Hindley Rd LVSG WF15 172 C3
Hindley Wk GTHN BD7 125 M4
Hinds Crs HEM/SK/SE WF9 247 H3
Hind St LM/WK BD12 148 E4
Hinton La KNOT WF11 159 J8
Hions Cl BRIG HD6 170 C6
Hipswell St BFDE BD3 105 L6
Hird Av WBSY BD6 126 E6
Hird Rd LM/WK BD12 126 F8
Hird St BAIL BD17 82 D6
BEE/HOL LS11 8 D9
KGHY BD21 2 E8
Hirds Yd SKP/WHF BD23 16 B3
Hirst Av HECK WF16 172 F1
Hirst Gv HBR HX7 143 K3
Hirstlands Av OSS WF5 174 E7 1
Hirstlands Dr OSS WF5 174 E6
Hirst La HOLM/MEL HD7 255 K2
SHPY BD18 82 A5
Hirst Lodge Ct ECHL BD2 105 H1 2
Hirst Mill Crs SHPY BD18 82 A5
Hirst Rd DEWS WF13 173 L5
WKFDW/WTN WF2 197 M1
Hirst St CAS WF10 135 G7
TOD OL14 140 D5 5
Hirst Wood Crs SHPY BD18 82 A6
Hirst Wood Rd SHPY BD18 81 M6
Hive St HWTH BD22 2 D7
Hobart Rd CAS WF10 158 F6
EARL WF12 174 B5
Hobberley La AL/HA/HU LS17 89 H3
Hobb Nook La OT LS21 22 C7
Hob Cote La HWTH BD22 78 B5
Hobcroft Ter AWLS/ASK DN6 249 K5 1
Hob La HUDS HD4 213 K4
HWTH BD22 77 L7
RPDN/SBR HX6 167 K5
RPDN/SBR HX6 188 E1
Hockney Rd GIR BD8 104 D6
Hodder Av LIT OL15 185 H8
Hodge La PONT WF8 205 G8
Hodgewood La PONT WF8 181 M8
Hodgkinson Av STKB/PEN S36 270 F3 1
Hodgson Av AL/HA/HU LS17 88 C3
BFDE BD3 105 M6
Hodgson Crs AL/HA/HU LS17 88 C3
Hodgson Fold ILK LS29 18 F5
Hodgson La BIRK/DRI BD11 128 D7
Hodgson's La GFTH/SHER LS25 116 C5
Hodgson St MOR LS27 152 E5 1
WKFDE WF1 176 D7 2
Hodroyd Cl CUD/GR S72 244 F5
Hodroyd Cottages CUD/GR S72 245 H4
Hodster La CUD/GR S72 263 M2
Hoffman St HUDS HD4 213 J2
Hogarth Rd ROCH OL11 228 B4
Hog Close La HOLM/MEL HD7 255 L6
Hogley La HOLM/MEL HD7 253 L2
Holays HUDE HD5 193 G7
Holbeck La BEE/HOL LS11 8 B4
Holbeck Moor Rd BEE/HOL LS11 8 C6
Holborn Ap HDGY LS6 6 D2
Holborn Ct WBSY BD6 126 E8
Holborn Gdns HDGY LS6 6 D2
Holborn Gn HDGY LS6 6 D2
Holborn Gv HDGY LS6 6 D3

Holborn St *HDGY* LS6 .... 6 E2
Holborn Ter *HDGY* LS6 .... 6 E3
Holborn Vw *HDGY* LS6 .... 6 D2
Holborn Wk *HDGY* LS6 .... 6 D3
Holby Sq *WKFDW/WTN* WF2 ... 197 L2 🟦
Holden Ct *BSLY* S70 .... 261 C5 🟦
Holden La *AIRE* BD20 .... 36 D7
BAIL BD17 .... 82 F2
Holden St *WHIT* OL12 .... 206 C4 🟦
Holderness Rd *KNOT* WF11 .... 182 A1
Holderness St *TOD* OL14 .... 163 L1 🟦
Holdforth Cl *WOR/ARM* LS12 .... 109 G7
Holdforth Gdns *WOR/ARM* LS12 .... 109 G7
Holdforth Gn *WOR/ARM* LS12 .... 109 G8
Holdforth Pl *WOR/ARM* LS12 .... 109 G7
Holdsworth Av *HECK* WF16 .... 151 G7 🟦
Holdsworth Ct *CLECK* BD19 .... 149 M7 🟦
Holdsworth Rd *LUD/ILL* HX2 .... 124 C7
Holdsworth St *BFD* BD1 .... 5 C4
CLECK BD19 .... 149 M6
SHPY BD18 .... 82 E8
Hole Bottom Rd *TOD* OL14 .... 141 K8
Hole La *AIRE* BD20 .... 35 K2
Holes La *KNOT* WF11 .... 182 A2
Holford Wk *MILN* OL16 .... 206 F7
Holgate Ct *BSLY* S70 .... 261 G8 🟦
Holgate Gdns *HEM/SK/SE* WF9 .... 223 L7
Holgate Mt *BSLY* S70 .... 261 H8
Holgate Rd *PONT* WF8 .... 202 E1
Holgate Vw *CUD/GR* S72 .... 245 K3 🟦
Holker St *GIR* BD8 .... 104 D6 🟦
KGHY BD21 .... 3 C3
Holland Rd *GFTH/SHER* LS25 .... 135 L4
Holland St *BTLY* WF17 .... 173 M1
MILN OL16 .... 206 F2 🟦
WHIT OL12 .... 206 A6
Hollas La *RPDN/SBR* HX6 .... 168 A4
Hollerton La *EARD/LOFT* WF3 .... 153 H6
Hollin Av *HUDW* HD3 .... 191 M7
Hollinbank La *HECK* WF16 .... 173 G1
Hollin Brigg La *HOLM/MEL* HD7 .... 253 L4
Hollin Close La *ECHL* BD2 .... 105 C3
Hollin Ct *BHP/TINH* LS16 .... 86 F7 🟦
Hollin Crs *BHP/TINH* LS16 .... 86 F7
Hollin Cft *DOD/DAR* S75 .... 260 C6
Hollin Dr *BHP/TINH* LS16 .... 86 F7
HOR/CROF WF4 .... 220 A1
Hollin Edge *KBTN* HD8 .... 239 J8
Hollin Gdns *BHP/TINH* LS16 .... 86 E7 🟦
Hollin Ga *OT* LS21 .... 40 F5 🟦
Hollingbourne Rd
MSTN/BAR LS15 .... 112 B4 🟦
Hollin Greaves La *HIPP* HX3 .... 11 H1
Hollings Sq *GIR* BD8 .... 104 D6 🟦
Hollings St *GIR* BD8 .... 104 D6 🟦
Hollings Ter *GIR* BD8 .... 104 D6
The Hollings *RTHW* LS26 .... 156 D3
Hollingthorpe Av
HOR/CROF WF4 .... 220 A3
Hollingthorpe Ct
HOR/CROF WF4 .... 220 A4
Hollingthorpe Gv
HOR/CROF WF4 .... 220 A3
Hollingthorpe La
HOR/CROF WF4 .... 220 A3
Hollingthorpe Rd
HOR/CROF WF4 .... 220 A3
Hollington St *COL* BB8 .... 74 D1 🟦
Hollingwood Av *GTHN* BD7 .... 126 D2 🟦
Hollingwood Dr *GTHN* BD7 .... 126 A3
Hollingwood Ga *ILK* LS29 .... 38 A3
Hollingwood La *GTHN* BD7 .... 126 A3
Hollingwood Mt *GTHN* BD7 .... 126 A2
Hollingwood Ri *ILK* LS29 .... 38 A3
Hollingworth La *KNOT* WF11 .... 182 C2 🟦
TOD OL14 .... 163 K6
Hollingworth Rd *LIT* OL15 .... 207 K2
Hollin Hall Dr *ILK* LS29 .... 38 A3
Hollin Hall La *HOLM/MEL* HD7 .... 212 F1
HUDE HD5 .... 193 M4
Hollin Head *BAIL* BD17 .... 83 H2
Hollin Hill Av *RHAY* LS8 .... 110 E1
Hollinhirst La *HOR/CROF* WF4 .... 219 H1
Hollin House La
HOLM/MEL HD7 .... 255 H1
KBTN HD8 .... 240 B7
Hollin La *BHP/TINH* LS16 .... 86 F7
HBR HX7 .... 144 C1
HOR/CROF WF4 .... 197 M8
RPDN/SBR HX6 .... 167 G5
RPDN/SBR HX6 .... 188 C3
SHPY BD18 .... 82 F8
STKB/PEN S36 .... 269 J2
Hollin Mt *BHP/TINH* LS16 .... 86 F7
Hollin Park Av *RHAY* LS8 .... 110 F1
Hollin Park Ct *PDSY/CALV* LS28 .... 84 C8
Hollin Park Dr *PDSY/CALV* LS28 .... 84 C8
Hollin Park Mt *RHAY* LS8 .... 110 F1
Hollin Park Pl *RHAY* LS8 .... 110 F1
Hollin Park Ter *RHAY* LS8 .... 110 E1
Hollin Ri *SHPY* BD18 .... 82 E8 🟦
Hollin Rd *BHP/TINH* LS16 .... 86 F7
SHPY BD18 .... 82 E8
Hollinroyd Rd *EARL* WF12 .... 174 A6
Hollins Av *DEWS* WF13 .... 173 H4
Hollins Bank *RPDN/SBR* HX6 .... 167 K2 🟦
Hollins Bank La *AIRE* BD20 .... 56 F2
Hollins Beck Cl *GFTH/SHER* LS25 .... 135 J6
Hollins Cl *AIRE* BD20 .... 57 H4
Hollins Gln *HOLM/MEL* HD7 .... 212 C6
Hollins Gv *CAS* WF10 .... 135 H8
Hollins Hey Rd *GTL/HWG* HX4 .... 190 F2
Hollins Hl *BAIL* BD17 .... 61 K8
Hollins La *AIRE* BD20 .... 57 H3
HOLM/MEL HD7 .... 211 M8
LUD/ILL HX2 .... 145 L1
LUD/ILL HX2 .... 166 D1
RPDN/SBR HX6 .... 167 K1
Hollins Meadow *TOD* OL14 .... 163 J5
Hollins Mill La *RPDN/SBR* HX6 .... 167 J2
Hollins Mt *HEM/SK/SE* WF9 .... 223 L7
Hollins Pk *GFTH/SHER* LS25 .... 135 J5

Hollins Pl *HBR* HX7 .... 143 J3 🟦
TOD OL14 .... 163 J5 🟦
Hollins Rd *DEWS* WF13 .... 173 H4 🟦
TOD OL14 .... 163 J4
Hollins Rw *HOLM/MEL* HD7 .... 212 C6
Hollin St *TOD* OL14 .... 163 K6 🟦
The Hollins *TOD* OL14 .... 141 K8
Hollin St *RPDN/SBR* HX6 .... 167 G5
Hollin Ter *HUDW* HD3 .... 191 L7
SHPY BD18 .... 82 E8 🟦
Hollin Vw *BHP/TINH* LS16 .... 86 F7
Hollin Wood Cl *SHPY* BD18 .... 82 A7 🟦
Hollinwood Vw *AIRE* BD20 .... 58 F7
Hollis Pl *BVRD* LS3 .... 6 A7
Hollowdene *DOD/DAR* S75 .... 260 D3
Hollowgate *HOLM/MEL* HD7 .... 254 C1
Hollowspell *WHIT* OL12 .... 206 E3
The Hollow *HOLM/MEL* HD7 .... 234 E4
Holly Ap *OSS* WF5 .... 174 F6
Holly Av *BHP/TINH* LS16 .... 85 M3
Holly Bank *FEA/AMT* WF7 .... 202 A8
GFTH/SHER LS25 .... 113 K8 🟦
Hollybank Av *BTLY* WF17 .... 151 K7
KBTN HD8 .... 238 E8
Holly Bank Ct *HUDW* HD3 .... 191 J7 🟦
Holly Bank Dr *HIPP* HX3 .... 147 M6
Holly Bank Gdns *GTHN* BD7 .... 126 A5
Hollybank Gv *GTHN* BD7 .... 126 A3 🟦
Holly Bank Pk *BRIG* HD6 .... 170 B6
Holly Bank Rd *BRIG* HD6 .... 170 A6
Holly Bank Rd *GTHN* BD7 .... 126 A3
Holly Bank Rd *HUDW* HD3 .... 191 K5
Holly Bush La *BSPA/BRAM* LS23 .... 49 G7 🟦
HOR/CROF WF4 .... 200 A5
MID LS10 .... 153 K2
Holly Cl *EARD/LOFT* WF3 .... 153 C8
WKFDE WF1 .... 176 E1 🟦
Holly Crs *HOR/CROF* WF4 .... 200 A5
RPDN/SBR HX6 .... 188 C3
Hollycroft Ct *BHP/TINH* LS16 .... 86 C5 🟦
Holly Dene *OSS* WF5 .... 174 F6 🟦
Holly Dr *BHP/TINH* LS16 .... 85 M3
Hollyfield Av *HUDW* HD3 .... 191 J7
Hollygarth La *GLE* DN14 .... 161 J7
Holly Gv *BTLY* WF17 .... 173 K2
CUD/GR S72 .... 245 J3
HFAX HX1 .... 10 C7
HUDW HD3 .... 191 L5
Holly Hall La *LM/WK* BD12 .... 148 E2
Holly Mede *OSS* WF5 .... 174 F6 🟦
Hollynsmill *GTL/HWG* HX4 .... 168 F7 🟦
Hollyoake Av *HOLM/MEL* HD7 .... 212 C6 🟦
Holly Pk *AL/HA/HU* LS17 .... 43 L1
Holly Park Dr *GTHN* BD7 .... 126 A2
Holly Park Gv *GTHN* BD7 .... 126 A2 🟦
Holly Rd *BSPA/BRAM* LS23 .... 48 E6
HUD HD1 .... 214 A2
Holly Tree La *MSTN/BAR* LS15 .... 112 A8
Hollywell La *WOR/ARM* LS12 .... 108 D6
Holman Av *GFTH/SHER* LS25 .... 135 H1
Holmcliffe Av *HUDS* HD4 .... 214 B5
Holmclose *HOLM/MEL* HD7 .... 253 K4
Holmdale Crs *HOLM/MEL* HD7 .... 236 B6
Holmdene Dr *MIRF* WF14 .... 172 A4
Holme Av *HUDE* HD5 .... 215 G1
Holmebank Ms *HOLM/MEL* HD7 .... 236 D3
Holme Cl *AIRE* BD20 .... 34 F8
HOR/CROF WF4 .... 217 C1
Holme Ct *HOLM/MEL* HD7 .... 237 C7
Holme Cft *HOR/CROF* WF4 .... 198 B7 🟦
Holme Dr *LUD/ILL* HX2 .... 145 K8
Holme Farm *WBSY* BD6 .... 125 M5 🟦
Holme Farm La
BSPA/BRAM LS23 .... 68 B3
Holmefield Rd *AIRE* BD20 .... 55 M1
HUDW HD3 .... 191 G8
Holme Gv *ILK* LS29 .... 40 B7
Holme House La *HWTH* BD22 .... 78 D1 🟦
LUD/ILL HX2 .... 145 G2
Holme House Rd *TOD* OL14 .... 140 E5 🟦
Holme House St *LIT* OL15 .... 185 M5 🟦
Holme Ings *ILK* LS29 .... 19 L7 🟦
Holme La *AIRE* BD20 .... 55 M1
BOW BD4 .... 128 A5
HOLM/MEL HD7 .... 211 D9
HOLM/MEL HD7 .... 237 G7 🟦
WKFDW/WTN WF2 .... 198 D4
Holme Leas Dr *OSS* WF5 .... 174 E7
Holme Mill La *HWTH* BD22 .... 2 A6
Holme Pk *ILK* LS29 .... 40 B7
Holme Pl *HBR* HX7 .... 143 J3
Holme Rd *LUD/ILL* HX2 .... 145 K8
Holmeside *HUDS* HD4 .... 214 A6
Holme South *LVSG* WF15 .... 172 D2
Holmes Rd *RPDN/SBR* HX6 .... 167 L2
Holmes St *BEE/HOL* LS11 .... 9 C4
GIR BD8 .... 4 C4
WHIT OL12 .... 206 E3 🟦
Holme St *BRIG* HD6 .... 148 C7 🟦
COL BB8 .... 74 D1
HBR HX7 .... 143 J3
HWTH BD22 .... 100 E4 🟦
LVSG WF15 .... 172 D2
TOD OL14 .... 141 G7
WBOW BD5 .... 126 F2
Holme Styes La
HOLM/MEL HD7 .... 254 B6
Holme Ter *LIT* OL15 .... 185 M5 🟦
Holme Top La *WBOW* BD5 .... 126 F2 🟦
Holme Top St *WBOW* BD5 .... 126 F2 🟦
Holme Valley Circular Wk
WKFDW/WTN WF2 .... 236 A7
HOLM/MEL HD7 .... 253 K6

HUDS HD4 .... 214 A7
HUDS HD4 .... 237 G2
Holme View Dr *HOLM/MEL* HD7 .. 253 M1
Holme View Pk
HOLM/MEL HD7 .... 254 A1
Holme View Rd *DOD/DAR* S75 .... 241 K6
Holme Wy *OSS* WF5 .... 174 E7
Holme Well Rd *MID* LS10 .... 154 A1
Holme Wood Rd *BOW* BD4 .... 127 M3 🟦
HWTH BD22 .... 2 B7
Holme Woods La
HOLM/MEL HD7 .... 266 B1
Holmfield Av *KBTN* HD8 .... 240 B4 🟦
Holmfield Av *KBTN* HD8 .... 240 B4 🟦
WKFDW/WTN WF2 .... 12 D9
Holmfield Cha *EARD/LOFT* WF3 .. 155 K8
Holmfield Cl *KBTN* HD8 .... 240 B4
PONT WF8 .... 181 H3
Holmfield Dr *HOLM/MEL* HD7 .... 213 H2
RHAY LS8 .... 88 B5
Holmfield La *PONT* WF8 .... 181 H2
Holmfield Rd *KBTN* HD8 .... 240 B4
Holmfirth Rd *HOLM/MEL* HD7 .... 235 C5
Holmsley Av *HEM/SK/SE* WF9 .... 246 C4
Holmsley Crest *HEM/SK/SE* WF9 .. 133 J7
Holmsley Field Ct *RTHW* LS26 .... 133 L8
Holmsley Field La *RTHW* LS26 .... 133 K8
Holmsley Garth *RTHW* LS26 .... 133 K7 🟦
Holmsley Gv *HEM/SK/SE* WF9 .... 246 C4
Holmsley La *CUD/GR* S72 .... 246 A4
RTHW LS26 .... 133 K8
Holmsley Mt *HEM/SK/SE* WF9 .... 246 C4
Holmwood Av *HDGY* LS6 .... 87 G6
Holmwood Cl *HDGY* LS6 .... 87 G7
Holmwood Crs *HDGY* LS6 .... 87 G7
Holmwood Dr *HDGY* LS6 .... 87 G6 🟦
Holmwood Gv *HDGY* LS6 .... 87 H6 🟦
Holmwood Mt *HDGY* LS6 .... 87 H6 🟦
Holroyd Hl *WBSY* BD6 .... 126 C5
Holroyd St *CHAL* LS7 .... 7 K5
MILN OL16 .... 206 F7
Holsworthy Rd *BOW* BD4 .... 128 A3 🟦
Holt Av *BHP/TINH* LS16 .... 86 E1
HUDN HD2 .... 192 B3
Holtby Gv *BRIG* HD6 .... 148 C7
Holt Cl *BHP/TINH* LS16 .... 86 E2
Holt Crs *BHP/TINH* LS16 .... 86 B1
Holtdale Ap *BHP/TINH* LS16 .... 86 A1
Holtdale Av *BHP/TINH* LS16 .... 86 A1
Holtdale Cl *BHP/TINH* LS16 .... 86 B1
Holtdale Cft *BHP/TINH* LS16 .... 86 B1
Holtdale Dr *BHP/TINH* LS16 .... 86 A1
Holtdale Fold *BHP/TINH* LS16 .. 86 B1 🟦
Holtdale Gdns *BHP/TINH* LS16 .. 64 B8
Holtdale Garth *BHP/TINH* LS16 .. 86 B1
Holtdale Gn *BHP/TINH* LS16 .... 86 A1
Holtdale Gv *BHP/TINH* LS16 .... 86 A1
Holtdale Lawn *BHP/TINH* LS16 .. 86 B1 🟦
Holtdale Pl *BHP/TINH* LS16 .... 86 A1
Holtdale Rd *BHP/TINH* LS16 .... 86 B1
Holtdale Vw *BHP/TINH* LS16 .... 86 B1
Holtdale Wy *BHP/TINH* LS16 .... 86 C1
Holt Dr *BHP/TINH* LS16 .... 86 C1
Holt Farm Cl *BHP/TINH* LS16 .... 86 C1
Holt Farm Ri *BHP/TINH* LS16 .... 86 B1
Holt Gdns *BHP/TINH* LS16 .... 83 H6
IDLE BD10 .... 83 H6
Holt Garth *BHP/TINH* LS16 .... 86 C1 🟦
Holt La *BHP/TINH* LS16 .... 86 C1
HOLM/MEL HD7 .... 236 B8
Holt Park Ap *BHP/TINH* LS16 .. 86 C1 🟦
Holt Park Av *BHP/TINH* LS16 .. 86 C1 🟦
Holt Park Cl *BHP/TINH* LS16 .. 86 C1 🟦
Holt Park Crs *BHP/TINH* LS16 .. 86 C1
Holt Park Dr *BHP/TINH* LS16 .. 86 C1
Holt Park Gdns *BHP/TINH* LS16 .. 86 C1
Holt Park Ga *BHP/TINH* LS16 .. 86 C1 🟦
Holt Park Gn *BHP/TINH* LS16 .. 86 B1
Holt Park Gra *BHP/TINH* LS16 .. 86 B1
Holt Park La *BHP/TINH* LS16 .. 86 C1 🟦
Holt Park Ri *BHP/TINH* LS16 .. 86 C1
Holt Park Rd *BHP/TINH* LS16 .. 86 C1
Holt Park V *BHP/TINH* LS16 .. 86 C1 🟦
Holt Ri *BHP/TINH* LS16 .... 86 C1
Holt Rd *BHP/TINH* LS16 .... 86 C1
Holts La *CLAY* BD14 .... 125 K1
Holts Ter *HIPP* HX3 .... 168 F2 🟦
Holt St *LIT* OL15 .... 185 M4 🟦
MILN OL16 .... 229 J1 🟦
The Holt *SHPY* BD18 .... 82 E7
Holt Vw *BHP/TINH* LS16 .... 86 B1
Holt Wy *BHP/TINH* LS16 .... 86 B1
Holwick Cl *DOD/DAR* S75 .... 259 H6 🟦
Holybrook Av *IDLE* BD10 .... 83 M8
Holycroft St *KGHY* BD21 .... 2 D7
Holyoake Av *BGLY* BD16 .... 81 H5
BTLY WF17 .... 173 J1 🟦
Holyoake St *TOD* OL14 .... 140 C5 🟦
Holyoake Ter *HOLM/MEL* HD7 .. 212 C6
HOR/CROF WF4 .... 197 G5 🟦
Holyrood Crs *NORM* WF6 .... 178 A2
Holy Rood La *GFTH/SHER* LS25 .. 137 G6
Holy St *ROCH* OL11 .... 228 D4 🟦
Holywell Ash La *GIR* BD8 .... 4 D2
Holywell Gdns *CAS* WF10 .... 158 B8
Holywell La *AL/HA/HU* LS17 .... 88 F1
CAS WF10 .... 158 C8
Holywell Mt *CAS* WF10 .... 158 D8 🟦
Homefield Av *MOR* LS27 .... 152 C4
Home Lea *RTHW* LS26 .... 132 F7
Home Lea Dr *RTHW* LS26 .... 132 F8 🟦
Homestead Dr
WKFDW/WTN WF2 .... 176 B8
Homestead Gdns *WHIT* OL12 .. 206 F1 🟦
The Homestead *HECK* WF16 .. 173 G2 🟦
Home View Ter *GIR* BD8 .... 104 D5
Honey Hole Cl *TOD* OL14 .... 163 K2 🟦
Honey Hole Rd *TOD* OL14 .... 163 K2 🟦
Honeysuckle Cl
WKFDW/WTN WF2 .... 176 A7 🟦
Honeysuckle Dr *EARL* WF12 .. 195 M3 🟦
Honeywell Cl *BSLNY/ROY* S71 .. 261 H3
Honeywell Gv *BSLNY/ROY* S71 .. 261 H2

Honeywell La *DOD/DAR* S75 .... 261 G3
Honeywell Pl *BSLNY/ROY* S71 .... 261 H3
Honeywell St *BSLNY/ROY* S71 .... 261 H3
Honley Rd *HUDS* HD4 .... 214 B8
Honley Sq *HOR/CROF* WF4 .... 197 J5
Honoria St *HUD* HD1 .... 14 F1
The Hoods *BRIG* HD6 .... 170 B7
Hood St *HEM/SK/SE* WF9 .... 247 G6
HUDS HD4 .... 214 B6
Hooton Crs *HOR/CROF* WF4 .... 222 C5 🟦
Hoowood La *HOLM/MEL* HD7 .. 253 C3
Hopbine Av *WBOW* BD5 .... 127 G4
Hopbine Rd *WBOW* BD5 .... 127 G4
Hope Av *SHPY* BD18 .... 82 F6
WBOW BD5 .... 126 E4
Hopefield Cha *EARD/LOFT* WF3 .. 154 D3
Hopefield Cl *EARD/LOFT* WF3 .. 154 D2 🟦
EARD/LOFT WF3 .... 153 L7 🟦
Hopefield Crs *RTHW* LS26 .... 154 D2 🟦
Hopefield Dr *EARD/LOFT* WF3 .. 154 D2
Hopefield Gdns
EARD/LOFT WF3 .... 154 D2 🟦
Hopefield Gn *RTHW* LS26 .... 154 D2
Hopefield Gv *EARD/LOFT* WF3 .. 154 D2 🟦
Hopefield Ms
EARD/LOFT WF3 .... 154 D2 🟦
Hopefield Pl *RTHW* LS26 .... 154 D2 🟦
Hopefield Vw *RTHW* LS26 .... 154 D2 🟦
Hopefield Wk *RTHW* LS26 .... 154 D2 🟦
Hopefield Wy *RTHW* LS26 .... 127 K5 🟦
RTHW LS26 .... 154 D2 🟦
Hope Hall St *HFAX* HX1 .... 11 H8
Hope Hall Ter *HFAX* HX1 .... 11 H8
Hope Hill Vw *BGLY* BD16 .... 81 J7
Hope La *BAIL* BD17 .... 82 D3
Hope Pl *BGLY* BD21 .... 2 F8
Hope Rd *LDSU* LS2 .... 7 K8
Hopes Farm Mt *RTHW* LS26 .. 132 B7 🟦
Hopes Farm Rd *RTHW* LS26 .. 132 B7
Hopes Farm Vw *RTHW* LS26 .. 132 B7 🟦
Hope St *BSLNY/ROY* S71 .... 244 B8
CAS WF10 .... 158 E3
DEWS WF13 .... 173 L5
DOD/DAR S75 .... 242 A6
DOD/DAR S75 .... 260 F4
HBR HX7 .... 143 J3
HFAX HX1 .... 10 C5
HUDW HD3 .... 213 K1 🟦
MOR LS27 .... 152 C2
NORM WF6 .... 178 C6 🟦
OSS WF5 .... 197 H2
ROY/SHW OL2 .... 229 K7
RPDN/SBR HX6 .... 167 L3
WHIT OL12 .... 206 B6
Hope St East *CAS* WF10 .. 157 M6 🟦
Hope St West *CAS* WF10 .. 157 L7 🟦
Hope Vw *SHPY* BD18 .... 82 E7
Hopewell Pl *HDGY* LS6 .... 109 C4 🟦
Hopewell St *BSLY* S70 .... 261 M6
Hopewell Ter *GFTH/SHER* LS25 .. 135 K5
Hopewell Vw *MID* LS10 .... 153 M1
Hopkinson Dr *BOW* BD4 .... 127 L6 🟦
Hopkinson Rd *HUDN* HD2 .... 192 D2
Hopkinson St *COL* BB8 .... 74 D3 🟦
LUD/ILL HX2 .... 146 B2 🟦
Hopkin St *BOW* BD4 .... 128 A5 🟦
Hopps's Rd *AIRE* BD20 .... 34 E7
Hopton Av *BOW* BD4 .... 127 K5
MIRF WF14 .... 194 A4
Hopton Dr *MIRF* WF14 .... 194 A4
Hopton Hall La *HUDE* HD5 .... 194 B6
Hopton La *MIRF* WF14 .... 194 A4
Hopton New Rd *MIRF* WF14 .. 194 C3
Hopwood Bank *HORS* LS18 .. 85 L4 🟦
Hopwood Gv *CAS* WF10 .... 158 D7 🟦
Hopwood Rd *HORS* LS18 .... 85 L4
Hopwood Rd *BSLY* S70 .... 261 G4
Horace Waller V C Pde
EARL WF12 .... 174 C4
Horbury Ms *HOR/CROF* WF4 .. 197 H4
Horbury Rd *CUD/GR* S72 .... 244 D6
OSS WF5 .... 197 G3
WKFDW/WTN WF2 .... 197 H2
WKFDW/WTN WF2 .... 197 M3
Horest La *UPML* OL3 .... 230 D6
Horley Green Rd *HIPP* HX3 .... 11 L2
Hornbeam Av
WKFDW/WTN WF2 .... 176 C6
Hornbeam Cl *WIL/AL* BD15 .... 103 H2
Hornbeam Wy *SCFT* LS14 .... 89 L6
Hornby St *BSLY* S70 .... 261 H7 🟦
HFAX HX1 .... 10 C5
Horncastle St *CLECK* BD19 .. 150 A7 🟦
Horncastle Vw *HOR/CROF* WF4 .. 222 F5
Horn Cote La *HOLM/MEL* HD7 .. 237 J8
Horn Cft *DOD/DAR* S75 .... 259 C1
Horner Av *BTLY* WF17 .... 151 H8 🟦
Horner Crs *BTLY* WF17 .... 151 H8
Hornes La *DOD/DAR* S75 .... 242 E5
Horne St *HFAX* HX1 .... 10 C5
WKFDW/WTN WF2 .... 12 D6
Hornington Br *COP/BISH* YO23 .. 73 G6
Horn La *AIRE* BD20 .... 35 L1
HOLM/MEL HD7 .... 237 J8
STKB/PEN S36 .... 256 C5
Hornsea Dr *WIL/AL* BD15 .... 102 C2
Hornthwaite Hill Rd
STKB/PEN S36 .... 270 B4
Horse Bank Dr *HUDS* HD4 .... 214 A4 🟦
Horse Carr Vw *BSLNY/ROY* S71 .. 262 C6
Horse Croft La *KBTN* HD8 .... 238 D3
Horse Fair *PONT* WF8 .... 180 F6
Horsefair *WBY* LS22 .... 48 A1
Horsehold La *HBR* HX7 .... 143 G4
Horsehold Rd *HBR* HX7 .... 143 H4
Horse Pond La *HUDW* HD3 .... 190 C7
Horsewood Cl *BSLY* S70 .... 260 C6
Horsfall St *HFAX* HX1 .... 168 C1
MOR LS27 .... 152 C2
TOD OL14 .... 142 A8
Horsfield Cl *COL* BB8 .... 74 B1 🟦
Horsforth New Rd *BRAM* LS13 .. 85 G8
Horsham Cl *HWTH* BD22 .... 79 G1 🟦
Horsham Rd *BOW* BD4 .... 128 A4 🟦

Horsley St *WBSY* BD6 .... 126 E5 🟦
Horsman St *BOW* BD4 .... 128 A5 🟦
Horton Cl *BRAM* LS13 .... 107 H2
Horton Garth *BRAM* LS13 .... 107 H2 🟦
Horton Gv *BRAM* LS13 .... 107 H2
Horton Hall Cl *WBOW* BD5 .... 126 F1
Horton Park Av *GTHN* BD7 .... 126 D1
Horton Ri *BRAM* LS13 .... 107 H2
Horton St *HECK* WF16 .... 172 F3
HFAX HX1 .... 11 H7
OSS WF5 .... 174 E8 🟦
Hospital La *BHP/TINH* LS16 .... 86 B3
Hospital Rd *BSLY* S70 .... 261 G5
Hostingley La *EARL* WF12 .... 196 D5
Hothfield St *AIRE* BD20 .... 35 M5
Hough *HIPP* HX3 .... 147 L3
Hough End Av *BRAM* LS13 .... 107 M5
Hough End Cl *BRAM* LS13 .... 107 M5 🟦
Hough End Ct *BRAM* LS13 .... 107 L5
Hough End Crs *BRAM* LS13 .... 107 L5
Hough End Gdns *BRAM* LS13 .. 107 M5 🟦
Hough End Gn *BRAM* LS13 .... 107 L5
Hough End Garth *BRAM* LS13 .. 107 L5
Hough End La *BRAM* LS13 .... 107 L5
Hough Gv *BRAM* LS13 .... 107 L4
Hough La *BRAM* LS13 .... 107 L4
Houghley Av *WOR/ARM* LS12 .. 108 A4
Houghley Cl *BRAM* LS13 .... 108 A4
Houghley Crs *WOR/ARM* LS12 .. 108 A4
Houghley La *BRAM* LS13 .... 108 A4
Houghley Pl *WOR/ARM* LS12 .. 108 A4
Houghley Rd *WOR/ARM* LS12 .. 108 A4
Houghley Sq *WOR/ARM* LS12 .. 108 B4 🟦
Hough Side Cl *PDSY/CALV* LS28 .. 107 K7
Hough Side La *PDSY/CALV* LS28 .. 107 K7
Hough Side Rd *PDSY/CALV* LS28 .. 107 J7
Hough Ter *BRAM* LS13 .... 107 L4 🟦
Houghton Cl *MILN* OL16 .... 206 E8
Houghton Pl *BFD* BD1 .... 4 D4
Houghton St *BRIG* HD6 .... 170 D3
Hough Top *BRAM* LS13 .... 107 J6
Hough Tree Rd *BRAM* LS13 .... 107 L5
Hoults La *GTL/HWG* HX4 .... 168 D6
Houndhill La *FEA/AMT* WF7 .... 202 B2
House Grove Dr *KBTN* HD8 .... 240 A4
Hovingham Av *RHAY* LS8 .... 110 C2 🟦
Hovingham Gv *RHAY* LS8 .... 110 C2 🟦
Hovingham Mt *RHAY* LS8 .... 110 C2 🟦
Hovingham St *MILN* OL16 .... 206 D6
Hovingham Ter *RHAY* LS8 .... 110 C2 🟦
Howard Av *HUDW* HD3 .... 191 L6
MSTN/BAR LS15 .... 111 H7 🟦
Howard Ct *MSTN/BAR* LS15 .... 111 H7 🟦
Howard Crs *HOR/CROF* WF4 .... 198 A8
Howard Pl *BTLY* WF17 .... 173 L3 🟦
MILN OL16 .... 206 B6 🟦
Howard Rd *HUDW* HD3 .... 191 L6
Howard St *BSLY* S70 .... 261 H7 🟦
BTLY WF17 .... 173 L3
HFAX HX1 .... 10 C4
OSS WF5 .... 174 F7 🟦
ROY/SHW OL2 .... 229 J7
WBOW BD5 .... 4 D8 🟦
WKFDE WF1 .... 176 E7 🟦
Howard Wy *HOLM/MEL* HD7 .. 235 C5
LIT OL15 .... 185 L5
Howarth Av *ECHL* BD2 .... 105 J1
Howarth Crs *ECHL* BD2 .... 105 J1 🟦
Howarth Cross St *MILN* OL16 .. 206 D4
Howarth Farm Wy *WHIT* OL12 .. 206 E3 🟦
Howarth La *HUDS* HD4 .... 214 A3
Howarth Pl *CHAL* LS7 .... 7 H6
Howarth Sq *MILN* OL16 .... 206 C6
Howbeck Av *LIT* OL15 .... 185 K8
Howbeck Av *AIRE* BD20 .... 58 C5
Howbeck Dr *AIRE* BD20 .... 58 C6
Howcans La *HIPP* HX3 .... 146 C2
Howden Av *AIRE* BD20 .... 57 J4 🟦
AWLS/ASK DN6 .... 249 C5
Howdenbrook *HIPP* HX3 .... 125 M7
Howden Cl *BOW* BD4 .... 128 B4
DOD/DAR S75 .... 242 B5
HUDS HD4 .... 213 H4
Howden Clough Rd *MOR* LS27 .. 151 L3
Howden Gdns *HDGY* LS6 .... 109 G4
Howden Pl *HDGY* LS6 .... 109 G4
Howden Rd *AIRE* BD20 .... 36 B5
Howden Wy *WKFDE* WF1 .... 13 K2
Howell La *CUD/GR* S72 .... 246 A8
Howes La *HIPP* HX3 .... 147 H3
Howgate *IDLE* BD10 .... 83 L6
Howgate Rd *HOLM/MEL* HD7 .. 252 B8
Howgill Gv *WBSY* BD6 .... 126 C8
Howhill Quarry Rd *PBR* HG3 .. 25 M1
Howley Mill La *BTLY* WF17 .... 151 M7
Howley Park Cl *MOR* LS27 .... 152 B4
Howley Park Rd *MOR* LS27 .... 152 B4
Howley Park Rd East *MOR* LS27 .. 152 B5
Howley St *BTLY* WF17 .... 151 M8 🟦
Howley Wk *BTLY* WF17 .... 174 A1 🟦
Howroyd La *EARL* WF12 .... 195 G7
GTL/HWG HX4 .... 189 G2
Howroyd's Yd *OSS* WF5 .... 174 E5 🟦
Howson Cl *GSLY* LS20 .... 62 B6
Hoxton Mt *BEE/HOL* LS11 .... 8 A9
Hoxton St *GIR* BD8 .... 104 C6 🟦
Hoylake Av *HUDN* HD2 .... 192 B3
Hoyland Cl *STKB/PEN* S36 .... 269 M3
Hoyland Rd *WKFDW/WTN* WF2 .. 220 C1
Hoyle Court Av *BAIL* BD17 .... 83 G3
Hoyle Court Dr *BAIL* BD17 .... 83 G3
Hoyle Court Rd *BAIL* BD17 .... 83 G3
Hoyle Fold *HWTH* BD22 .... 2 A8
Hoyle House Fold
HOLM/MEL HD7 .... 212 F5
Hoyle Ing *HOLM/MEL* HD7 .... 212 F4
Hoyle Ing Rd *CUL/QBY* BD13 .... 103 H8
Hoyle Mill Rd *BSLY* S70 .... 261 M6
HEM/SK/SE WF9 .... 223 M4
Hoyle's Ter *MILN* OL16 .... 207 G8 🟦
Hubberton Green Rd
RPDN/SBR HX6 .... 166 E3
Hubert St *BFDE* BD3 .... 5 M8
HUDW HD3 .... 191 G5
LUD/ILL HX2 .... 145 M7 🟦
Huddersfield Rd *BRIG* HD6 .... 170 D4
BTLY WF17 .... 151 G7

DEWS WF13 ..... 194 F1
DOD/DAR S75 ..... 241 K1
DOD/DAR S75 ..... 260 E2
ELL HX5 ..... 168 F5
ELL HX1 ..... 191 J1
HFAX HX1 ..... 168 E1
HIPP HX3 ..... 168 E2
HOLM/MEL HD7 ..... 235 G4
HOR/CROF 219 H6
HUDW HD3 ..... 191 J2
KBTN HD8 ..... 238 F3
LM/WK BD12 ..... 148 E3
LVSG WF15 ..... 172 C4
MILN OL16 ..... 229 L2
MIRF WF14 ..... 171 M8
MIRF WF14 ..... 194 C2
STKB/PEN S36 ..... 257 K8
UPML OL3 ..... 231 M8
Huddleston Ct EARL WF12 ..... 174 B6
Hud Hl HIPP HX3 ..... 147 K2
Hudroyd HUDE HD5 ..... 215 H3
Hudson Av GTHN BD7 ..... 126 D2
HOR/CROF WF4 ..... 221 K8
Hudson Cl GTHN BD7 ..... 126 D3
TAD LS24 ..... 71 M2
WBY LS22 ..... 48 A1
Hudson Crs GTHN BD7 ..... 126 D3
Hudson Gdns GTHN BD7 ..... 126 D2
Hudson Gv OSM LS9 ..... 110 C5
Hudson Ms BSPA/BRAM LS23 ..... 49 G7
Hudson Mill Rd HBR HX7 ..... 142 D1
Hudson Pl OSM LS9 ..... 110 C5
Hudson Rd OSM LS9 ..... 110 C5
Hudson St BFDE BD3 ..... 105 M7
OSM LS9 ..... 110 C5
PDSY/CALV LS28 ..... 106 F5
TOD OL14 ..... 140 E5
The Hudson LM/WK BD12 ..... 148 E3
Hudson Vw TAD LS24 ..... 71 M2
Hudson Wy TAD LS24 ..... 71 M1
Hudswell Rd MID LS10 ..... 9 J7
Hughenden Vw MOR LS27 ..... 130 C8
Hughendon Dr CUL/QBY BD13 ..... 103 J8
Hughendon Wk CUL/QBY BD13 ..... 103 J8
Hugh St CAS WF10 ..... 157 M7
MILN OL16 ..... 206 C6
Hughtrede St MILN OL16 ..... 228 D3
Hugill St CUL/QBY BD13 ..... 102 F8
Hulbert Cft HUDE HD5 ..... 215 H2
Hulbert St BGLY BD16 ..... 81 J4
Hullenedge Gdns ELL HX5 ..... 168 F8
Hullenedge La GTL/HWG HX4 ..... 168 F8
Hullenedge Rd ELL HX5 ..... 169 G8
Hullen Rd ELL HX5 ..... 168 F8
Hullett Cl HBR HX7 ..... 144 B5
Hullett Dr HBR HX7 ..... 144 B5
Hull St MOR LS27 ..... 152 D2
Hulme Sq CAS WF10 ..... 158 F5
Humber Av AWLS/ASK DN6 ..... 249 J5
HOLM/MEL HD7 ..... 212 F5
Humber Ct AWLS/ASK DN6 ..... 249 J5
Humber Rd MILN OL16 ..... 207 J8
Humberside Wy
BSLYN/ROY S71 ..... 243 M8
Humboldt St BFD BD1 ..... 5 J3
Hume Crest BTLY WF17 ..... 173 L1
Hume St MILN OL16 ..... 228 C1
Humley Rd WKFDW/WTN WF2 ..... 220 D1
Hundhill La PONT WF8 ..... 202 F4
Hungate Cl TAD LS24 ..... 93 J8
Hungate La RTHW LS26 ..... 156 B5
Hungate Rd GFTH/SHER LS25 ..... 116 A6
Hungerford Rd HUDW HD3 ..... 191 H6
Hunger Hl HFAX HX1 ..... 11 H8
ILK LS29 ..... 20 E7
MOR LS27 ..... 152 C3
Hunger Hills Av HORS LS18 ..... 85 J5
Hunger Hills Dr HORS LS18 ..... 85 J5
Hunningley La BSLY S70 ..... 261 M7
Hunslet Green Wy MID LS10 ..... 9 J7
Hunslet Hall Rd BEE/HOL LS11 ..... 8 E7
Hunslet La MID LS10 ..... 9 H3
Hunslet Rd MID LS10 ..... 9 H2
Hunston Av HUDW HD3 ..... 191 K7
Hunsworth La BIRK/DRI BD11 ..... 128 A8
CLECK BD19 ..... 149 M4
Hunt Cl BSLYN/ROY S71 ..... 261 L2
Hunter Hill Rd LUD/ILL HX2 ..... 145 J1
Hunter's Av BSLY S70 ..... 260 C6
Hunters Ct HTON BD9 ..... 103 L2
Hunters Gn CUL/QBY BD13 ..... 79 M7
Hunters Hill La OL3 ..... 231 L8
Hunter's La MILN OL16 ..... 206 B6
Hunters Meadow AIRE BD20 ..... 36 A4
Hunters Park Av CLAY BD14 ..... 125 M1
Hunters Ri DOD/DAR S75 ..... 260 C5
Hunters Wk WBY LS22 ..... 30 A7
Huntingdon Av HUDN HD2 ..... 193 H1
Huntingdon Rd BRIG HD6 ..... 170 C5
Huntock Pl BRIG HD6 ..... 170 B1
Huntsman Fold
WKFDW/WTN WF2 ..... 175 M8
Huntsmans Cl BGLY BD16 ..... 81 L1
HUDS HD4 ..... 213 M6
KGHY BD21 ..... 2 D3
Huntsmans Wy
HEM/SK/SE WF9 ..... 225 C4
CAS WF10 ..... 157 M5
Huntwick Av FEA/AMT WF7 ..... 201 K2
Huntwick Crs FEA/AMT WF7 ..... 201 K2
Huntwick Dr FEA/AMT WF7 ..... 201 K2
Huntwick La FEA/AMT WF7 ..... 201 H3
Huntwick Rd FEA/AMT WF7 ..... 201 K2
Hurrs Rd SKP/WHF BD23 ..... 16 D2
Hurstead Gn WHIT OL12 ..... 206 F2
Hurstead Rd MILN OL16 ..... 207 H8
Hurst Knowle HUDE HD5 ..... 215 J1
Hurst La HBR HX7 ..... 143 J2
Hurst Meadow MILN OL16 ..... 228 D4
Hurst Rd HBR HX7 ..... 143 J2
Hurst St ROCH OL11 ..... 228 C1
Hurstville Av BIRK/DRI BD11 ..... 128 B8
Hurstwood HUDN HD2 ..... 193 G2
Huskar Cl DOD/DAR S75 ..... 259 H4
Husler Gv CHAL LS7 ..... 7 J3
Husler Pl CHAL LS7 ..... 7 J3

The Hustings LVSG WF15 ..... 172 C2
Hustlergate BFD BD1 ..... 4 F6
Hustler St BFDE BD3 ..... 5 K2
Hutchinson's Pl KSTL LS5 ..... 108 C3
Hutson St WBOW BD5 ..... 126 F2
Hutton Dr HECK WF16 ..... 173 C2
HEM/SK/SE WF9 ..... 247 J2
Hutton Rd WBOW BD5 ..... 126 E4
Hutton St RYKW YO26 ..... 33 K4
Hutton Ter IDLE BD10 ..... 105 M1
Hydale Ct LM/WK BD12 ..... 126 E8
Hyde Pk HFAX HX1 ..... 10 D8
WKFDE WF1 ..... 13 K3
Hyde Park La HDGY LS6 ..... 6 A4
Hyde Park Pl HDGY LS6 ..... 6 A4
Hyde Park Rd HDGY LS6 ..... 6 A4
HFAX HX1 ..... 10 C9
Hyde Park St HFAX HX1 ..... 10 D8
Hyde Park Ter HDGY LS6 ..... 6 A4
Hyde Pl LDSU LS2 ..... 6 A4
Hyde St IDLE BD10 ..... 83 K5
LDSU LS2 ..... 6 A4
Hyde Ter LDSU LS2 ..... 6 A4
Hydro Cl ILK LS29 ..... 39 H3
Hyne Av BOW BD4 ..... 127 L5
Hyrst Garth BTLY WF17 ..... 173 K4
Hyrstlands Rd BTLY WF17 ..... 173 L3
Hyrst Wk BTLY WF17 ..... 173 L3

I

Ibberson Av DOD/DAR S75 ..... 242 C6
Ibbetson Cl MOR LS27 ..... 130 C7
Ibbetson Ct MOR LS27 ..... 130 C7
Ibbetson Cft MOR LS27 ..... 130 C7
Ibbetson Dr MOR LS27 ..... 130 C7
Ibbetson Ms MOR LS27 ..... 130 C7
Ibbetson Ri MOR LS27 ..... 130 C7
Ibbetson Rd MOR LS27 ..... 130 C7
Ibbotroyd Av TOD OL14 ..... 141 J7
Ibbottson St WKFDE WF1 ..... 13 L9
Ida St MID LS10 ..... 132 C4
WBOW BD5 ..... 126 E3
Iddesleigh St BOW BD4 ..... 105 L8
Idlecroft Rd IDLE BD10 ..... 83 K6
Idle Rd ECHL BD2 ..... 105 K2
Idlethorp Wy IDLE BD10 ..... 83 L7
Ilbert Av BOW BD4 ..... 127 L5
Ilford St MOR LS27 ..... 152 D2
Ilkley Hall Ms ILK LS29 ..... 38 D3
Ilkley Hall Pk ILK LS29 ..... 38 D3
Ilkley Rd AIRE BD20 ..... 58 D3
ILK LS29 ..... 19 K7
ILK LS29 ..... 40 A4
OT LS21 ..... 41 G7
Illingworth Av LUD/ILL HX2 ..... 124 A7
NORM WF6 ..... 178 A2
Illingworth Cl LUD/ILL HX2 ..... 124 A7
YEA LS19 ..... 84 E1
Illingworth Crs LUD/ILL HX2 ..... 124 A7
Illingworth Dr LUD/ILL HX2 ..... 124 A7
Illingworth Gdns LUD/ILL HX2 ..... 124 A8
Illingworth Gv LUD/ILL HX2 ..... 124 A7
Illingworth Rd LM/WK BD12 ..... 149 H2
LUD/ILL HX2 ..... 124 A7
Illingworth St OSS WF5 ..... 196 F1
Illingworth Wy LUD/ILL HX2 ..... 124 A7
Ilsley Rd WMB/DAR S73 ..... 263 K5
Imperial Av WKFDW/WTN WF2 ..... 176 B4
Inchfield Rd TOD OL14 ..... 163 J6
The Incline HIPP HX3 ..... 11 K4
Independent St WBOW BD5 ..... 126 E3
Indus Cl HECK WF16 ..... 173 G2
Industrial Av BTLY WF17 ..... 150 F5
Industrial Rd RPDN/SBR HX6 ..... 167 K2
Industrial St BGLY BD16 ..... 81 H3
BRIG HD6 ..... 170 D3
CLECK BD19 ..... 149 H6
HOR/CROF WF4 ..... 197 L6
HUDS HD4 ..... 214 C2
HWTH BD22 ..... 2 C7
LVSG WF15 ..... 172 A2
OSM LS9 ..... 110 D3
TOD OL14 ..... 163 K1
WKFDE WF1 ..... 12 F1
Industrial Ter HFAX HX1 ..... 168 D1
HUDE HD5 ..... 215 J1
Industry Rd BSLYN/ROY S71 ..... 243 L7
WHIT OL12 ..... 206 B5
Industry St LIT OL15 ..... 207 K1
TOD OL14 ..... 163 J5
Infirmary Rd DEWS WF13 ..... 173 K5
Infirmary St BFD BD1 ..... 4 D5
LDS LS1 ..... 6 F9
Ingbirchworth La
STKB/PEN S36 ..... 257 G7
Ingbirchworth Rd
STKB/PEN S36 ..... 270 C2
Ingdale Dr HOLM/MEL HD7 ..... 236 D8
Ing Fld LM/WK BD12 ..... 149 J2
Ingfield Av HUDE HD5 ..... 15 M7
OSS WF5 ..... 175 G8
Ingham Cl LUD/ILL HX2 ..... 124 B6
MIRF WF14 ..... 194 E2
Ingham Cft MIRF WF14 ..... 194 E2
Ingham Garth MIRF WF14 ..... 194 E1
Ingham La LUD/ILL HX2 ..... 124 B5
Ingham Rd EARL WF12 ..... 195 M3
Ingham's Av PDSY/CALV LS28 ..... 106 D6
Inghams Ct LIT OL15 ..... 207 K1
Inghams La LIT OL15 ..... 207 K1
Inghams Ter PDSY/CALV LS28 ..... 106 D6
Ingham St WID LS10 ..... 9 K5
Ingham's Vw PDSY/CALV LS28 ..... 106 D6
Ing Head HOLM/MEL HD7 ..... 212 A5
Ing Head La HUDS HD4 ..... 237 J4
Ing La HUDS HD4 ..... 214 C4
Ingle Av MOR LS27 ..... 130 D8
Ingleborough Cl BOW BD4 ..... 128 A3
Ingleborough Dr MOR LS27 ..... 152 E4
Ingleby Cl ROY/SHW OL2 ..... 229 J6
Ingleby Pl GTHN BD7 ..... 104 C8
Ingleby Rd GIR BD8 ..... 104 C7

Ingleby St GIR BD8 ..... 104 C7
Ingleby Wy MID LS10 ..... 132 A7
ROY/SHW OL2 ..... 229 J6
Ingle Ct KBTN HD8 ..... 215 M2
MOR LS27 ..... 130 D8
Ingledew Cl AL/HA/HU LS17 ..... 87 M2
Ingledew Crs RHAY LS8 ..... 88 D4
Ingledew Dr RHAY LS8 ..... 88 D5
Ingle Gv MOR LS27 ..... 152 D8
Ingle Rw CHAL LS7 ..... 87 L8
Ingleton Cl BEE/HOL LS11 ..... 131 K3
Ingleton Dr MSTN/BAR LS15 ..... 111 K3
Ingleton Gv BEE/HOL LS11 ..... 131 K3
Ingleton Pl BEE/HOL LS11 ..... 131 K3
Ingleton Rd HUDS HD4 ..... 214 D4
Ingleton St BEE/HOL LS11 ..... 131 K3
Inglewood DOD/DAR S75 ..... 242 B5
Inglewood Av HUDW HD3 ..... 191 L5
Inglewood Dr OT LS21 ..... 41 H7
SCFT LS14 ..... 111 K3
Inglewood Pl SCFT LS14 ..... 111 K3
Inglis St HIT OL15 ..... 185 K8
Ingram Cl BEE/HOL LS11 ..... 8 B5
Ingram Crs WKFDW/WTN WF11 ..... 181 M3
Ingram Gdns BEE/HOL LS11 ..... 8 B5
Ingram Pde HEM/SK/SE WF26 ..... 155 G1
Ingram Rd BEE/HOL LS11 ..... 8 B5
Ingram Rw BEE/HOL LS11 ..... 8 F4
Ingram St BEE/HOL LS11 ..... 8 F4
HFAX HX1 ..... 168 C1
KGHY BD21 ..... 79 K3
Ingram Vw BEE/HOL LS11 ..... 8 B5
Ingrow La HWTH BD22 ..... 79 H2
Ings Av GSLY LS20 ..... 61 M4
Ings Cl HEM/SK/SE WF9 ..... 246 F5
HOR/CROF WF4 ..... 222 E5
Ings Ct GSLY LS20 ..... 61 L4
Ings Crs EARL WF12 ..... 195 L4
GSLY LS20 ..... 61 L5
LVSG WF15 ..... 172 D2
OSM LS9 ..... 110 D7
Ings Dr AIRE BD20 ..... 16 E8
RTHW LS26 ..... 157 G3
Ings Holt HEM/SK/SE WF9 ..... 246 F5
Ings La AIRE BD20 ..... 34 C2
AWLS/ASK DN6 ..... 249 J5
BSPA/BRAM LS23 ..... 49 J6
CAS WF10 ..... 157 M3
CUD/OR S72 ..... 263 K7
EARL WF12 ..... 195 L4
GLE DN14 ..... 161 J7
GSLY LS20 ..... 61 L4
HOLM/MEL HD7 ..... 233 J2
TAD LS24 ..... 50 C6
Ings Mere Ct KNOT WF11 ..... 159 J2
Ings Mill Av KBTN HD8 ..... 240 B4
Ings Mill Dr KBTN HD8 ..... 240 B4
Ings Rd AIRE BD20 ..... 35 K7
BTLY WF17 ..... 151 K8
EARL WF12 ..... 174 A5
HECK WF16 ..... 172 F2
HEM/SK/SE WF9 ..... 223 K5
HUDE HD5 ..... 215 J2
LVSG WF15 ..... 172 D1
OSM LS9 ..... 110 D7
TAD LS24 ..... 95 C1
WKFDE WF1 ..... 12 D4
The Ings BRIG HD6 ..... 148 C8
KBTN HD8 ..... 240 B4
Ings Vw CAS WF10 ..... 158 D6
RTHW LS26 ..... 157 G3
Ings Vil LVSG WF15 ..... 172 E4
Ings Wk HEM/SK/SE WF9 ..... 246 F5
Ings Wy AIRE BD20 ..... 36 A6
GIR BD8 ..... 104 A6
KBTN HD8 ..... 216 B3
STKB/PEN S36 ..... 256 F5
Ingswell Av HOR/CROF WF4 ..... 221 H7
Ingswell Dr HOR/CROF WF4 ..... 221 H7
Ingthorns La GFTH/SHER LS25 ..... 138 C6
Ingthorpe La GFTH/SHER LS25 ..... 138 C6
Ingthorpe Wy GFTH/SHER LS25 ..... 138 C5
Ingwell St WKFDE WF1 ..... 13 G3
Ingwell Ter CLECK BD19 ..... 150 A7
Inholmes La TAD LS24 ..... 49 L2
TAD LS24 ..... 71 K3
Inkerman St BOW BD4 ..... 127 M2
ECHL BD2 ..... 105 M2
WHIT OL12 ..... 206 B5
Inkerman Wy KBTN HD8 ..... 257 H1
Inkersley Rd BFD BD1 ..... 4 E3
Ink St MILN OL16 ..... 206 B7
Inner Hey HOLM/MEL HD7 ..... 233 J2
The Innings IDLE BD10 ..... 83 J6
Innovation Wy DOD/DAR S75 ..... 260 E2
Institute Rd ECHL BD2 ..... 105 L4
Institute St AIRE BD20 ..... 34 E8
Intake Crs COL BB8 ..... 52 B5
DOD/DAR S75 ..... 260 B8
Intake Gv ECHL BD2 ..... 105 L4
BRAM LS13 ..... 107 H3
BTLY WF17 ..... 151 H6
CUD/GR S72 ..... 244 E6
DOD/DAR S75 ..... 260 B8
EARD/LOFT WF3 ..... 177 H1
HOLM/MEL HD7 ..... 234 B2
HOR/CROF WF4 ..... 219 M7
HUDS HD4 ..... 213 H7
KNOT WF11 ..... 161 L5
MID LS10 ..... 153 L3
OSS WF5 ..... 197 G1
SCFT LS14 ..... 89 M3
YEA LS19 ..... 84 F3
Intake Mt MID LS10 ..... 153 L3
Intake Rd ECHL BD2 ..... 105 L4
HOLM/MEL HD7 ..... 211 M4
PDSY/CALV LS28 ..... 107 J6
Intake Sq MID LS10 ..... 153 L3
Intake Ter ECHL BD2 ..... 105 L4
The Intake GFTH/SHER LS25 ..... 135 K5
Intake Vw MID LS10 ..... 153 L3
Intercity Wy PDSY/CALV LS28 ..... 107 J2
Invargarry Cl GFTH/SHER LS25 ..... 113 K6

Inverness Rd GFTH/SHER LS25 ..... 113 K7
Invertrees Av YEA LS19 ..... 84 E2
Iona Pl HIPP HX3 ..... 146 E4
Iona St HIPP HX3 ..... 10 F1
HIPP HX3 ..... 146 E4
Ipswich St ROCH OL11 ..... 228 B1
Iqbal Ct BOW BD4 ..... 105 M8
Ireland Crs BHP/TINH LS16 ..... 86 B3
Ireland St BGLY BD16 ..... 81 G3
Ireland Ter BGLY BD16 ..... 81 G3
Ireton St GTHN BD7 ..... 104 D8
Iron Rw ILK LS29 ..... 40 B5
Iron St CLECK BD19 ..... 149 L7
Ironwood Ap SCFT LS14 ..... 111 J3
Ironwood Crs SCFT LS14 ..... 111 J3
Ironwood Vw SCFT LS14 ..... 111 J2
Irving St HFAX HX1 ..... 10 A9
Irving Ter CLAY BD14 ..... 125 L3
Irwell St BOW BD4 ..... 127 J1
Irwin Ap MSTN/BAR LS15 ..... 111 H7
Irwin Av WKFDE WF1 ..... 177 G7
Irwin Crs WKFDE WF1 ..... 177 G7
Irwin St PDSY/CALV LS28 ..... 106 F4
Isaac St GIR BD8 ..... 104 D6
Isabella St WHIT OL12 ..... 206 B4
Isherwood St ROCH OL11 ..... 228 C1
Island Dr HOLM/MEL HD7 ..... 236 E4
Island Vw EARL WF12 ..... 173 K8
Islay Cl RTHW LS26 ..... 155 J1
Isles St GIR BD8 ..... 104 B6
Issott St BSLYN/ROY S71 ..... 261 H3
Ivanhoe Rd GTHN BD7 ..... 126 D1
Ivegate BFD BD1 ..... 4 F6
COL BB8 ..... 52 A5
YEA LS19 ..... 62 D8
Ive House La LUD/ILL HX2 ..... 145 J6
Iver Wy SHPY BD18 ..... 82 C7
Iveson Av BHP/TINH LS16 ..... 86 B4
Iveson Cl BHP/TINH LS16 ..... 86 B4
Iveson Crs BHP/TINH LS16 ..... 86 B4
Iveson Dr BHP/TINH LS16 ..... 86 B4
Iveson Gdns BHP/TINH LS16 ..... 86 B4
Iveson Garth BHP/TINH LS16 ..... 86 B4
Iveson Gn BHP/TINH LS16 ..... 86 B4
Iveson Gv BHP/TINH LS16 ..... 86 B4
Iveson Lawn BHP/TINH LS16 ..... 86 C4
Iveson Ri BHP/TINH LS16 ..... 86 B4
Iveson Rd BHP/TINH LS16 ..... 86 B4
Ives St BAIL BD17 ..... 82 D6
Ivory St BEE/HOL LS11 ..... 9 H5
Ivy Av OSM LS9 ..... 110 C6
Ivy Bank La HWTH BD22 ..... 78 E8
Ivy Cha BRAM LS13 ..... 107 K7
Ivy Cl HEM/SK/SE WF9 ..... 247 K7
PBR HG3 ..... 28 A1
ROY/SHW OL2 ..... 229 K7
WKFDE WF1 ..... 177 G6
Ivy Crs HIPP HX3 ..... 148 A7
OSM LS9 ..... 110 C6
OSM LS9 ..... 110 C7
Ivy Farm Cl BSLYN/ROY S71 ..... 243 M5
Ivy Gdns BRAM LS13 ..... 107 M2
CAS WF10 ..... 180 F1
Ivy Garth CHAL LS7 ..... 87 M8
Ivy Gv OSM LS9 ..... 110 C6
SHPY BD18 ..... 82 A7
Ivy House Rd WBOW BD5 ..... 127 G4
Ivy La BSPA/BRAM LS23 ..... 48 E6
LUD/ILL HX2 ..... 123 M8
WIL/AL BD15 ..... 103 J5
WKFDE WF1 ..... 177 G6
Ivy Mt HOLM/MEL HD7 ..... 212 B5
OSM LS9 ..... 110 C6
Ivy Pl AIRE BD20 ..... 34 F7
BRAM LS13 ..... 107 M2
Ivy Rd KGHY BD21 ..... 3 M6
OSM LS9 ..... 110 C7
SHPY BD18 ..... 82 A7
Ivy St BRIG HD6 ..... 170 B3
FEA/AMT WF7 ..... 179 M8
HFAX HX1 ..... 168 C1
HUD HD1 ..... 15 J1
HUDS HD4 ..... 213 L2
KGHY BD21 ..... 2 F1
OSM LS9 ..... 110 C6
Ivy Ter BRIG HD6 ..... 170 B3
HEM/SK/SE WF9 ..... 247 J3
HIPP HX3 ..... 148 A7
KGHY BD21 ..... 58 B8
Ivy Vw OSM LS9 ..... 110 C6

J

Jacinth Ct HUDN HD2 ..... 192 E4
Jack Br HBR HX7 ..... 142 C1
Jack Close Orch
BSLYN/ROY S71 ..... 243 L2
Jackdaw La BSPA/BRAM LS23 ..... 48 E6
Jack Field La AIRE BD20 ..... 55 J2
Jack Hl HUDW HD3 ..... 14 E1
Jack Hill La OT LS21 ..... 23 H7
Jackie Smart Ct CHAL LS7 ..... 7 L2
Jackie Smart Rd WBOW BD5 ..... 127 G2
Jack La BEE/HOL LS11 ..... 8 E5
MID LS10 ..... 9 J6
Jackman Dr HORS LS18 ..... 85 M7
Jackroyd La HUDS HD4 ..... 214 C4
MIRF WF14 ..... 194 A4
Jackson Av RHAY LS8 ..... 88 B7
Jackson Hill La CUL/QBY BD13 ..... 125 H7
Jackson La GTL/HWG HX4 ..... 189 J1
Jackson Mdw GTL/HWG HX4 ..... 189 J1
Jackson Rd CHAL LS7 ..... 7 G3
Jackson's La AIRE BD20 ..... 35 G1
EARL WF12 ..... 195 J4
PONT WF8 ..... 204 A7
Jackson St AIRE BD20 ..... 55 M1
BFDE BD3 ..... 5 K8
CUD/GR S72 ..... 244 C8
MILN OL16 ..... 206 D8
WHIT OL12 ..... 184 M1
Jacky La HWTH BD22 ..... 78 E8
Jacobs Hall Ct DOD/DAR S75 ..... 241 L6

Jacob's Rw HUDS HD4 ..... 214 B3
Jacob St LDSU LS2 ..... 7 H7
WBOW BD5 ..... 126 F2
Jacques Gv AIRE BD20 ..... 36 B5
Jacques Pl BSLYN/ROY S71 ..... 261 M4
Jaggar La HOLM/MEL HD7 ..... 236 B2
HUDW HD3 ..... 190 D4
Jagger La HUDE HD5 ..... 193 J6
KBTN HD8 ..... 217 G2
Jail Rd BTLY WF17 ..... 173 H1
Jail Yd RTHW LS26 ..... 155 H1
Jakeman Cl EARD/LOFT WF3 ..... 153 C6
Jakeman Ct EARD/LOFT WF3 ..... 153 C6
Jakeman Dr EARD/LOFT WF3 ..... 153 C6
James Av AIRE BD20 ..... 56 C1
RHAY LS8 ..... 88 B3
James Butterworth St
MILN OL16 ..... 206 D7
James Cl GFTH/SHER LS25 ..... 113 J7
James Ct WBY LS22 ..... 47 K6
James Duggan Av
FEA/AMT WF7 ..... 179 M8
James Ga BFD BD1 ..... 4 E6
James Gibbs Cl FEA/AMT WF7 ..... 179 M8
James Hill St LIT OL15 ..... 207 K1
James La HUDS HD4 ..... 213 J8
James Rd AWLS/ASK DN6 ..... 249 M7
ROY/SHW OL2 ..... 229 K6
James St AIRE BD20 ..... 34 F7
BFD BD1 ..... 4 E5
BIRK/DRI BD11 ..... 128 C8
BRIG HD6 ..... 170 C2
BSLYN/ROY S71 ..... 261 H4
BTLY WF17 ..... 173 K2
CAS WF10 ..... 157 M5
COL BB8 ..... 74 A2
CUD/OR S72 ..... 245 H1
CUL/OBY BD13 ..... 102 F7
DEWS WF13 ..... 173 K5
ELL HX5 ..... 169 J8
GTL/HWG HX4 ..... 190 D2
HOLM/MEL HD7 ..... 212 F2
HWTH BD22 ..... 78 D4
LIT OL15 ..... 207 H1
LVSG WF15 ..... 172 C3
MIRF WF14 ..... 172 C7
WHIT OL12 ..... 206 A6
WIL/AL BD15 ..... 103 L5
YEA LS19 ..... 84 D2
Jamie Ct IDLE BD10 ..... 83 M8
Jane St CUL/QBY BD13 ..... 101 M5
SHPY BD18 ..... 82 B6
WHIT OL12 ..... 206 A6
Janesway GFTH/SHER LS25 ..... 135 H4
Janet St HWTH BD22 ..... 79 C6
Jardine Av FEA/AMT WF7 ..... 179 M8
Jardine Rd BGLY BD16 ..... 81 J3
Jarratt St GIR BD8 ..... 104 D5
Jarratt St (East) GIR BD8 ..... 104 D5
Jarrom Cl BOW BD4 ..... 127 M2
Jarvis Sq EARD/LOFT WF3 ..... 154 C3
Jarvis St WHIT OL12 ..... 206 B5
Jarvis Wk EARD/LOFT WF3 ..... 154 C3
Jasmin Ter GIR BD8 ..... 4 A3
Jasper La PBR HG3 ..... 27 K8
Jasper St HFAX HX1 ..... 168 C1
IDLE BD10 ..... 83 K6
Javelin Cl IDLE BD10 ..... 83 K8
Jay House La BRIG HD6 ..... 170 F1
Jay St HWTH BD22 ..... 78 F8
Jean Av MSTN/BAR LS15 ..... 111 J7
Jebb La DOD/DAR S75 ..... 241 H2
Jefferson Wy WHIT OL12 ..... 206 B3
Jenkin Dr HOR/CROF WF4 ..... 197 H5
Jenkin La HOR/CROF WF4 ..... 197 H5
Jenkin Rd HOR/CROF WF4 ..... 197 H5
Jenkinson Cl BEE/HOL LS11 ..... 8 D5
Jenkinson Lawn BEE/HOL LS11 ..... 8 D6
Jenkinsons Pl MID LS10 ..... 131 M6
Jenkinson St BTLY WF17 ..... 173 L8
Jenkyn La KBTN HD8 ..... 237 M6
Jennetts Crs OT LS21 ..... 41 H7
Jennings Cl AIRE BD20 ..... 36 A6
Jennings Pl GTHN BD7 ..... 126 C2
Jennings St GTHN BD7 ..... 126 C2
Jenny Gill Crs SKP/WHF BD23 ..... 16 D3
Jenny La BAIL BD17 ..... 82 F2
MIRF WF14 ..... 172 C7
Jensen Av DEWS WF13 ..... 173 K5
Jepheys Pl WHIT OL12 ..... 206 B5
Jepheys St WHIT OL12 ..... 206 B5
Jepson La ELL HX5 ..... 169 H8
Jeremy La HECK WF16 ..... 172 F2
Jer Gv WBSY BD6 ..... 126 A4
Jer La WBSY BD6 ..... 126 A4
Jermyn Cft DOD/DAR S75 ..... 260 B8
Jermyn St BFDE BD3 ..... 5 G5
WHIT OL12 ..... 206 C5
Jerrold St LIT OL15 ..... 207 K1
Jerry Clay Dr WKFDW/WTN WF2 ..... 176 A4
Jerry Clay La WKFDW/WTN WF2 ..... 175 M3
Jerry Cft SKP/WHF BD23 ..... 16 C2
Jerry Fields Rd LUD/ILL HX2 ..... 144 F8
Jerry La AIRE BD20 ..... 37 H5
RPDN/SBR HX6 ..... 167 J3
Jersey Cl EARL WF12 ..... 174 B4
Jerusalem La LUD/ILL HX2 ..... 144 F2
Jerusalem Rd HOLM/MEL HD7 ..... 212 D7
Jervaulx Cl BSPA/BRAM LS23 ..... 48 F1
Jervaulx Crs GIR BD8 ..... 4 B3
Jerwood Hill Cl HIPP HX3 ..... 11 K2
Jerwood Hill Rd HIPP HX3 ..... 11 K2
Jesmond Av BSLYN/ROY S71 ..... 243 K3
HTON BD9 ..... 104 B4
Jesmond Gv DEWS WF13 ..... 173 K5
HTON BD9 ..... 104 B4
Jessamine Av BEE/HOL LS11 ..... 131 H5
Jessamine St DEWS WF13 ..... 194 H3
Jesse St GIR BD8 ..... 103 M7
WBOW BD5 ..... 127 G2
Jessop Av HUDE HD5 ..... 215 J3
Jessop Fold HOLM/MEL HD7 ..... 236 B1
Jessop St CAS WF10 ..... 157 M6
WKFDW/WTN WF2 ..... 12 E7
Jewitt La WBY LS22 ..... 47 J3
Jew La HWTH BD22 ..... 100 E4

Jew Leys La COP/BISH YO23 ...... 73 M8
  COP/BISH YO23 .... 95 M2
Jilley Royd La HUDN HD2 ... 192 C2
Jill La MIRF WF14 ... 172 E7
Jim La HUD HD1 ... 191 M8
Jim Allen La LUD/ILL HX2 ... 144 E5
Jin-whin HI CAS WF10 ... 157 H6
Jinny Moor La RTHW LS26 ... 134 A6
Joan Royd HECK WF16 ... 150 F8 1
Joan Royd La STKB/PEN S36 ... 270 D5
Joba Av BFDE BD3 ... 5 M6
Jockey Rd STKB/PEN S36 ... 271 L4
Joffre Av CAS WF10 ... 158 A9
John Ashworth St WHIT OL12 ... 206 D5 2
John Booth CI LVSG WF15 ... 172 E4
John Carr Av HOR/CROF WF4 ... 197 J4
John Escritt Rd BGLY BD16 ... 81 J4
John Haigh Rd
  HOLM/MEL HD7 ... 212 C6 2
John Naylor La LUD/ILL HX2 ... 167 G1 1
John Nelson Ct BTLY WF17 ... 151 H5 3
Johnny La OT LS21 ... 41 J8
John O'gaunts Wk
  RTHW LS26 ... 133 H8 1
John Ormsby V C Wy
  EARL WF12 ... 174 C4 3
John Roberts CI ROCH OL11 ... 228 A3 1
Johns Av EARD/LOFT WF3 ... 154 E8
John's Crs
  WKFDW/WTN WF2 ... 176 A4 1
Johns La ELL HX5 ... 191 H2
Johnson St BFDE BD3 ... 105 M7 4
  BGLY BD16 ... 81 H3
  DOD/DAR S75 ... 260 F4 4
  MIRF WF14 ... 194 B3
Johnson Ter MOR LS27 ... 152 D2 7
Johnston Av LIT OL15 ... 207 H3 5
Johnston St HDGY LS6 ... 6 L2
  WKFDE WF1 ... 13 H2 4
John St AWLS/ASK DN6 ... 249 L8
  BAIL BD17 ... 82 E5
  BFD BD1 ... 4 E5
  BOW BD4 ... 128 A5
  BRIC HD6 ... 170 C3
  BSLY S70 ... 261 G6
  BTLY WF17 ... 151 C5 3
  CAS WF10 ... 157 L8 11
  CLAY BD14 ... 125 J2
  CUD/GR S72 ... 263 M7
  CUL/QBY BD13 ... 101 M6
  CUL/QBY BD13 ... 102 F8
  DEWS WF13 ... 173 L4 4
  DEWS WF13 ... 195 G1
  EARL WF12 ... 174 A6 3
  ELL HX5 ... 169 H8
  GTL/HWG HX4 ... 168 E6
  HDGY LS6 ... 109 G3
  HECK WF16 ... 172 F3 7
  HEM/SK/SE WF9 ... 247 H1
  HFAX HX1 ... 11 H6
  HUDS HD4 ... 213 K2 2
  HWTH BD22 ... 78 F4
  LIT OL15 ... 207 J1
  MILN OL16 ... 206 E3
  SHPY BD18 ... 82 C6
  WKFDE WF1 ... 13 H3
  YEA LS19 ... 84 D2
John St West RPDN/SBR HX6 ... 167 K2 1
John William St CLECK BD19 ... 149 M6
  ELL HX5 ... 169 H8 7
  HUD HD1 ... 14 F5
  LVSG WF15 ... 172 D3 4
  LVSG WF15 ... 172 E2 5
Jonathan Garth ILK LS29 ... 19 G6 5
Jones St MILN OL16 ... 206 C8
Jons Av HEM/SK/SE WF9 ... 246 C4
Jordan Av ROY/SHW OL2 ... 229 L5 2
Joseph Av HIPP HX3 ... 147 J4
Josephine Rd HUDS HD4 ... 213 J3
Joseph St BFD BD1 ... 5 J6
  BOW BD4 ... 128 A5 9
  BSLY S70 ... 261 G6
  CUD/QBY S72 ... 245 J8
  LIT OL15 ... 185 K8
  MID LS10 ... 9 L7
Joshua St TOD OL14 ... 141 K8
Jos La KBTN HD8 ... 238 A4
Jos Wy KBTN HD8 ... 238 C4
Jowett House La DOD/DAR S75 ... 258 D2 2
Jowett Park Crs IDLE BD10 ... 83 J4
Jowett's La AIRE BD20 ... 17 M6
Jowett St BFD BD1 ... 4 B5
Joy St WHIT OL12 ... 206 B4
Jubilee Av KBTN HD8 ... 238 C4
  NORM WF6 ... 178 C6
  WKFDE WF1 ... 176 E2 2
Jubilee Crs HOR/CROF WF4 ... 200 D3
  WKFDE WF1 ... 176 E2
Jubilee Cft BIRK/DRI BD11 ... 129 H7 2
Jubilee Dr KGHY BD21 ... 2 C9
Jubilee La HUDS HD4 ... 213 H3
Jubilee PI MOR LS27 ... 152 D2 2
Jubilee Rd HIPP HX3 ... 168 F4
  HOR/CROF WF4 ... 200 D3
Jubilee St HBR HX7 ... 144 A5
  HIPP HX3 ... 11 K8
  HOR/CROF WF4 ... 200 B3
  MOR LS27 ... 152 D2 2
  ROY/SHW OL2 ... 229 L7
Jubilee St North HIPP HX3 ... 146 C2
Jubilee Ter MOR LS27 ... 152 D2
  RPDN/SBR HX6 ... 167 G3
Jubilee Trees ILK LS29 ... 39 L7
Jubilee Wy PONT WF8 ... 180 E6
  SHPY BD18 ... 82 F6
Judd Field La STKB/PEN S36 ... 270 D8
Judy Haigh La EARL WF12 ... 195 M6
Judy La HUDN HD2 ... 192 D3
Judy Rw BSLYN/ROY S71 ... 261 J2
Julian Ct CUL/QBY BD13 ... 125 L4
Julian St HUDE HD5 ... 215 G1 1
Julia St WHIT OL12 ... 206 A6
Julie Av HOR/CROF WF4 ... 220 A1
Jumb Beck CI KGHY BD21 ... 40 D6
Jumble Dyke BRIC HD6 ... 170 B6 1
Jumble Hole Rd TOD OL14 ... 142 D4
Jumbles Ct EARD/LOFT WF3 ... 154 E5 1
Jumbles La EARD/LOFT WF3 ... 154 E5

Jumble Wd KBTN HD8 ... 215 M3
Jumples La MILN OL16 ... 145 M2
Jumples CI LUD/ILL HX2 ... 145 M2 2
Jumps La HBR HX7 ... 143 H5
  TOD OL14 ... 141 G5
Junction Aly MILN OL16 ... 206 B7 11
Junction CI OSS WF5 ... J2
Junction Rd BAIL BD17 ... 82 E6 5
  DEWS ... 173 K7
  MID LS10 ... 9 H4
Junction St BSLY S70 ... 261 K6
  MID LS10 ... 9 H4
June St KGHY BD21 ... 3 H2
Juniper Av RTHW LS26 ... 133 M7
Juniper Dr MILN OL16 ... 206 F8
Juniper Gv HUDS HD4 ... 213 M8
Juniper PI OSM LS9 ... 110 D5
Justin Wy HUDS HD4 ... 213 J5

K

Kaffir Rd HUDW HD3 ... 191 M6
Karnac Rd RHAY LS8 ... 110 B2
Karon Dr HOR/CROF WF4 ... 197 K5
Kathan CI MILN OL16 ... 206 D7
Katherine St SHPY BD18 ... 82 B6 11
Katrina Gv FEA/AMT WF7 ... 201 M3
Kaycell St BOW BD4 ... 127 K4
Kaye La HUDE HD5 ... 214 F4
Kaye St EARL WF12 ... 173 M8 2
  HECK WF16 ... 172 F3 5
Kay's Ter BSLY S70 ... 262 A7
Kay St EARL WF12 ... 104 E1
  ROCH OL11 ... 228 A1
  WKFDE WF1 ... 13 H3
Kearby Cliff WBY LS22 ... 45 M4
Keats Av TOD OL14 ... 141 M8
Keats CI PONT WF8 ... 180 F4
Keats Dr HECK WF16 ... 172 G4
Keats Gv EARD/LOFT WF3 ... 155 G8
  STKB/PEN S36 ... 270 F2
Keat St HUDS HD4 ... 214 A2 3
Kebble Ct CLECK BD19 ... 150 D7 2
Keble Garth GFTH/SHER LS25 ... 135 L5
Kebroyd La RPDN/SBR HX6 ... 167 G3
Kebroyd Mt RPDN/SBR HX6 ... 167 G7
Kebs Rd HBR HX7 ... 141 K3
Kedleston Rd RHAY LS8 ... 88 B3
Keelddar CI GTHN BD7 ... 126 D3 5
Keelham La AIRE BD20 ... 57 J4
  TOD OL14 ... 141 M4
Keel Moorings BRAM LS13 ... 107 H1
Keenan Av CLECK BD19 ... 149 L6
Keeper La BOW BD4 ... 129 G4
  HOR/CROF WF4 ... 220 F8
Keeton St OSM LS9 ... 110 B6 10
Keighley CI LUD/ILL HX2 ... 123 M8
Keighley Dr LUD/ILL HX2 ... 146 A1
Keighley PI PDSY/CALV LS28 ... 107 G4
Keighley Rd AIRE BD20 ... 16 C8
  AIRE BD20 ... 34 E3
  AIRE BD20 ... 34 F7
  AIRE BD20 ... 35 G8 3
  AIRE BD20 ... 35 M7
  AIRE BD20 ... 58 F7 1
  BGLY BD16 ... 80 C3
  COL BB8 ... 53 K7
  COL BB8 ... 74 D3
  COL BB8 ... 74 E3
  COL BB8 ... 74 F1
  CUL/QBY BD13 ... 79 M6
  HBR HX7 ... 143 J1
  HTON BD9 ... 104 E3
  HWTH BD22 ... 54 E3
  HWTH BD22 ... 79 G3
  HWTH BD22 ... 100 E3
  ILK LS29 ... 38 A6
  LUD/ILL HX2 ... 123 M3
  LUD/ILL HX2 ... 146 A1
  SKP/WHF BD23 ... 16 C6
Keighley Road Causeway Foot
  LUD/ILL HX2 ... 123 M3
Keir Hardy CI LVSG WF15 ... 172 D2 3
Keir St BSLY S70 ... 260 F4
Keir Ter BSLY S70 ... 260 F4 2
Kelburn Gv HWTH BD22 ... 78 D3
Kelcbar CI TAD LS24 ... 71 K2
Kelcbar HI TAD LS24 ... 71 J2
Kelcbar Wy TAD LS24 ... 71 K2
Kelcliffe Av GSLY LS20 ... 62 A5 1
Kelcliffe La GSLY LS20 ... 61 M4
Keldholme CI BRAM LS13 ... 107 G1
Keldholme Rd BRAM LS13 ... 107 H1 1
Keldregate HUDN HD2 ... 193 G2
Kell Beck OT LS21 ... 41 H4
Kellett Av WOR/ARM LS12 ... 130 E2
Kellett Crs WOR/ARM LS12 ... 130 E2
Kellett Dr WOR/ARM LS12 ... 130 E2
Kellett Gv WOR/ARM LS12 ... 130 E1
Kellett La WOR/ARM LS12 ... 130 D1
Kellett Mt WOR/ARM LS12 ... 130 E2 2
Kellett PI WOR/ARM LS12 ... 130 E2 3
Kellett Rd WOR/ARM LS12 ... 130 E2
Kellett St MILN OL16 ... 206 D6
Kellett Ter WOR/ARM LS12 ... 130 E2 3
Kellett Wk WOR/ARM LS12 ... 130 E1
Kell La HIPP HX3 ... 147 H4
  LUD/ILL HX2 ... 123 G8
Kelloe St CLECK BD19 ... 149 L5
Kell St BGLY BD16 ... 81 J3 8
Kelloe St WBSY BD6 ... 126 A8
Kelmscott Av MSTN/BAR LS15 ... 111 M3
Kelmscott Crs MSTN/BAR LS15 ... 111 M3
Kelmscott Gdns
  MSTN/BAR LS15 ... 112 A3
Kelmscott Garth
  MSTN/BAR LS15 ... 112 A3
Kelmscott Gn MSTN/BAR LS15 ... 111 M3
Kelmscott Gv MSTN/BAR LS15 ... 111 M3
Kelmscott La MSTN/BAR LS15 ... 111 M3
Kelsall Av HDGY LS6 ... 109 G4
Kelsall Gv HDGY LS6 ... 109 G5
Kelsall PI HDGY LS6 ... 109 G4
Kelsall Rd HDGY LS6 ... 109 G4
Kelsall St MILN OL16 ... 206 B6
Kelsall Ter HDGY LS6 ... 109 G4

Kelsey St HFAX HX1 ... 10 B4
Kelsey Ter BSLY S70 ... 261 H7 6
Kelso Gdns LDSU LS2 ... 6 B6
Kelso PI LDSU LS2 ... 6 B5
Kelso Rd LDSU LS2 ... 6 B5
Kelso St LDSU LS2 ... 6 B6
Kelvin Av HUDE HD5 ... 193 G8
Kelvin Crs LUD/ILL HX2 ... 145 M8
Kelvin Rd ELL HX5 ... 169 G8
Kelvin Wy ECHL BD2 ... 105 L4
Kemp's Br WKFDW/WTN WF2 ... 12 A4
Kemps Wy HOLM/MEL HD7 ... 255 C4
Kempton Rd GFTH/SHER LS25 ... 135 J4
Kemsing Rd MSTN/BAR LS15 ... 112 B3
Ken Churchill Dr
  HOR/CROF WF4 ... 197 J4 4
Kendal Bank BVRD LS3 ... 6 B7
Kendal CI BVRD LS3 ... 6 B7
  CAS WF10 ... 159 G7
Kendal Cft CAS WF10 ... 159 G7
Kendal Dr CAS WF10 ... 158 F6
  HOR/CROF WF4 ... 199 L4
  MSTN/BAR LS15 ... 111 G8
  ROY/SHW OL2 ... 229 M7
Kendal Gdns CAS WF10 ... 158 F7
  RYKW YO26 ... 32 C1
Kendal Garth CAS WF10 ... 159 G7
Kendal Gv BSLYN/ROY S71 ... 262 C6
  BVRD LS3 ... 6 B7
Kendal La BVRD LS3 ... 6 B7
  HOR/CROF WF4 ... 199 L4
  ROY/SHW OL2 ... 229 M7
Kendal Mellor Ct KGHY BD21 ... 2 F4 8
Kendal Ri KGHY BD21 ... 3 J6
Kendal Rd BVRD LS3 ... 6 B7 2
  KGHY BD21 ... 3
Kendal Wk BVRD LS3 ... 6 B7 2
Kendell St MID LS10 ... 9 H2
Kendray St BSLY S70 ... 261 H5
Kenilworth Av MOR LS27 ... 129 M8
Kenilworth Dr BRIC HD6 ... 148 C8 5
Kenilworth Gdns MOR LS27 ... 129 M7 8
  WOR/ARM LS12 ... 130 E1
Kenilworth Rd MILN OL16 ... 228 E5
Kenilworth St BOW BD4 ... 127 K2 8
Kenion St MILN OL16 ... 206 B7 17
Kenley Av WBSY BD6 ... 126 C5
Kenley Mt WBSY BD6 ... 126 C4 3
Kenley Pde GTHN BD7 ... 126 B4
Kenmore Av CLECK BD19 ... 149 L6
Kenmore CI CLECK BD19 ... 149 L6 6
Kenmore Crs CLECK BD19 ... 149 L6
  WBSY BD6 ... 126 C4
Kenmore Dr CLECK BD19 ... 149 L6
  WBSY BD6 ... 126 C4
Kenmore Gv CLECK BD19 ... 149 L6 2
  WBSY BD6 ... 126 C4 3
Kenmore Rd CLECK BD19 ... 149 L6
Kenmore Vw CLECK BD19 ... 149 L6
Kenmore Wk WBSY BD6 ... 126 C4 2
Kenmore Wy CLECK BD19 ... 149 L6
Kennedy Av HUDN HD2 ... 192 C1
Kennedy CI BTLY WF17 ... 174 B3
  STKB/PEN S36 ... 269 M3
Kennel La HWTH BD22 ... 100 A4
  RPDN/SBR HX6 ... 166 C5
Kennels La SCFT LS14 ... 68 B6
Kennerleigh Av
  MSTN/BAR LS15 ... 111 L5
Kennerleigh Crs
  MSTN/BAR LS15 ... 111 L5
Kennerleigh Dr MSTN/BAR LS15 .. 111 L5
Kennerleigh Garth
  MSTN/BAR LS15 ... 111 L5
Kennerleigh Gln
  MSTN/BAR LS15 ... 111 L5 3
Kennerleigh Gv
  MSTN/BAR LS15 ... 111 M5 1
Kennerleigh Ri
  MSTN/BAR LS15 ... 111 M5 2
Kennerleigh Wk
  MSTN/BAR LS15 ... 111 L5 2
Kenneth St BEE/HOL LS11 ... 8 A6
Kennet La GFTH/SHER LS25 ... 113 J8
Kennion St WBOW BD5 ... 126 F1 8
Kensington Av ROY/SHW OL2 ... 228 E8
  SCFT LS14 ... 68 C8
  STKB/PEN S36 ... 270 C2
Kensington CI BTLY WF17 ... 173 K2 8
  HIPP HX3 ... 168 C4
  MILN OL16 ... 207 J8
Kensington Rd DOD/DAR S75 ... 260 F3
  HIPP HX3 ... 168 C2
  WKFDE WF1 ... 176 D6
Kensington St GIR BD8 ... 104 C5
  KGHY BD21 ... 2 E7
  ROCH OL11 ... 228 A2
Kensington Ter HDGY LS6 ... 6 A2
Kenstone Crs IDLE BD10 ... 83 J7
Kent Av AIRE BD20 ... 35 M5
  PDSY/CALV LS28 ... 107 J7
Kent CI BSLYN/ROY S71 ... 243 L2 1
  PDSY/CALV LS28 ... 107 J7
Kent Crs PDSY/CALV LS28 ... 107 J7
Kent Dr PDSY/CALV LS28 ... 107 J7
Kentmere Ap SCFT LS14 ... 111 G1
Kentmere Av GFTH/SHER LS25 ... 113 K8
  LM/WK BD12 ... 149 G5
  SCFT LS14 ... 89 H7
  WHIT OL12 ... 206 D3 8
Kentmere Crs SCFT LS14 ... 111 H1
Kentmere CI SCFT LS14 ... 89 H8
Kentmere Gdns SCFT LS14 ... 89 H8
Kentmere Ga SCFT LS14 ... 89 H7 1
Kentmere Ga SCFT LS14 ... 89 H8
Kentmere Gn SCFT LS14 ... 89 H7
Kentmere Ri SCFT LS14 ... 111 J1
Kent Ms BGLY BD16 ... 81 K4
Kenton Dr HOR/CROF WF4 ... 198 C2 9
Kenton Wy BOW BD4 ... 128 A3 10
Kent Rd BGLY BD16 ... 81 K3
  PDSY/CALV LS28 ... 107 H7

Kent St HFAX HX1 ... 10 F7
  ROCH OL11 ... 206 B8 13
Kenwood CI BSLY S70 ... 261 M6 2
Kenworthy CI BHP/TINH LS16 ... 86 C1
Kenworthy Gdns BHP/TINH LS16 .. 86 C1
Kenworthy Garth
  BHP/TINH LS16 ... 86 C1
Kenworthy Ga BHP/TINH LS16 ... 86 C1 1
Kenworthy Ri RPDN/SBR HX6 ... 167 G3
Kenworthy Ri BHP/TINH LS16 ... 86 C1 10
Kenworthy Rd BSLY S70 ... 261 H7 7
Kenworthy St MILN OL16 ... 206 E7 2
Kenworthy Ter MILN OL16 ... 206 E7 2
Kenworthy V BHP/TINH LS16 ... 86 C1
Kenya Mt HWTH BD22 ... 2 A3
Kenyon La LUD/ILL HX2 ... 145 M7
Kenyon St HEM/SK/SE WF9 ... 247 J3
Kepler Gv RHAY LS8 ... 7 M4
Kepler Mt RHAY LS8 ... 7 M4
Kepler Ter RHAY LS8 ... 7 M4
Kepstorn CI KSTL LS5 ... 108 C1
Kepstorn Ri KSTL LS5 ... 108 C1 1
Kepstorn Rd BHP/TINH LS16 ... 86 D7
  HOR/CROF WF4 ... 199 L4
  ROY/SHW OL2 ... 229 M7
Keren Gv WKFDW/WTN WF2 ... 176 A4 3
Keresforth Ct BSLY S70 ... 260 E6
Keresforth Hall Rd BSLY S70 ... 260 E5
Keresforth Hill Rd BSLY S70 ... 260 E7 5
Keresforth Rd DOD/DAR S75 ... 260 D8
Kerry Garth HORS LS18 ... 85 K5
Kerry HI HORS LS18 ... 85 L5
Kerry St HORS LS18 ... 85 K5
Kershaw Av EARL WF12 ... 173 L7
Kershaw Ct LUD/ILL HX2 ... 144 F6 8
Kershaw Crs LUD/ILL HX2 ... 144 F7
Kershaw Dr LUD/ILL HX2 ... 144 F6
Kershaw La KNOT WF11 ... 181 M3
Kershaw Rd TOD OL14 ... 163 J5
Kershaw St BFDE BD3 ... 105 M7
  ROY/SHW OL2 ... 229 K7
Kershaw St East
  ROY/SHW OL2 ... 229 K7 3
Kertland St EARL WF12 ... 173 L7
Kester Rd BTLY WF17 ... 173 H1
Kesteven Ct BOW BD4 ... 128 B4 3
Kesteven Rd BOW BD4 ... 128 A4
Kestrel Bank HUDS HD4 ... 214 A7
Kestrel Ct AL/HA/HU LS17 ... 88 B2 3
Kestrel Dr AWLS/ASK DN6 ... 249 K8
  ECHL BD2 ... 105 J2
  WKFDW/WTN WF2 ... 220 F1
Kestrel Garth MOR LS27 ... 152 F2 2
Kestrel Gv AL/HA/HU LS17 ... 88 B2
Kestrel Mt ECHL BD2 ... 105 J2
Kestrel Vw CLECK BD19 ... 149 M5
Kettle La HOLM/MEL HD7 ... 211 K8
Kettlethorpe Hall Dr
  WKFDW/WTN WF2 ... 198 D3
Kettlethorpe Rd
  WKFDW/WTN WF2 ... 220 D1
Kettlewell Dr WBOW BD5 ... 126 D3 3
Ketton Wk DOD/DAR S75 ... 260 E3 3
Kew HI HUDW HD3 ... 191 H3
Kew Rd ROCH OL11 ... 228 C3
Kexbrough Dr DOD/DAR S75 ... 241 L6
Key Syke La TOD OL14 ... 163 L1
Khaliq Ct BFDE BD3 ... 5 M4
Khus Wk KGHY BD21 ... 79 L2 1
Kibroyd Dr DOD/DAR S75 ... 241 L7
Kidacre St BEE/HOL LS11 ... 9 H5
  MID LS10 ... 9 H4
Kiddal La MSTN/BAR LS15 ... 91 G3
Kidroyd La HUDE HD5 ... 214 D7
Kilburn HI HUDE HD5 ... 15 K9
Kilburn La DEWS WF13 ... 173 J3
Kilburn Rd WOR/ARM LS12 ... 108 E7
Kilby St WKFDE WF1 ... 176 D1
Kildare Crs ROCH OL11 ... 228 B4
  WIL/AL BD15 ... 103 J5
Kildare Ter WOR/ARM LS12 ... 109 G8
Killingbeck Br SCFT LS14 ... 111 G5
Killingbeck Dr SCFT LS14 ... 111 G5
Killinghall Av ECHL BD2 ... 5 M1
Killinghall Dr ECHL BD2 ... 105 M1
Killinghall Gv ECHL BD2 ... 5 L1
Killinghall Rd BFDE BD3 ... 105 L5
  ECHL BD2 ... 105 M1
Kiln Bent Rd HOLM/MEL HD7 ... 253 M8
Kiln Ct HUDW HD3 ... 191 G5
Kilner Bank HUDE HD5 ... 15 K7
Kiln Fold BRIC HD6 ... 170 F3
Kiln HI HOLM/MEL HD7 ... 212 C6
Kiln Hill La AIRE BD20 ... 17 J8
Kilnhouse Bank La
  HOLM/MEL HD7 ... 253 K5
Kilnhurst Av TOD OL14 ... 163 M2
Kilnhurst Mt TOD OL14 ... 163 L1
Kilnhurst Rd TOD OL14 ... 163 L1
Kiln La HBR HX7 ... 120 C3
  KBTN HD8 ... 240 B1
  MILN OL16 ... 207 H8 11
  MILN OL16 ... 207 H8
Kilnsea Mt BOW BD4 ... 128 A3
Kilnsey Fold AIRE BD20 ... 35 M4 3
Kilnsey Ms BAIL BD17 ... 82 D3
Kilnsey Rd WKFDE WF1 ... 177 G6
Kilnshaw La HBR HX7 ... 143 G6
Kilpin Hill La DEWS WF13 ... 173 H2 3
Kilroyd Av CLECK BD19 ... 149 M4
Kilroyd Dr CLECK BD19 ... 150 A4
Kimberley PI HIPP HX3 ... 146 C2 7
  OSM LS9 ... 110 D4 13
Kimberley Rd OSM LS9 ... 110 D4

Kimberley St BFDE BD3 ... 105 L8 2
  BRIG HD6 ... 170 D3
  FEA/AMT WF7 ... 179 L5
  HIPP HX3 ... 146 C2
  WKFDE WF1 ... 13 H8
Kimberley Vw OSM LS9 ... 110 D5 3
Kimberly CI PONT WF8 ... 225 K1 1
Kinder Av HUDN HD2 ... 213 H4
Kineholme Dr OT LS21 ... 40 F8
Kine Moor La STKB/PEN S36 ... 258 F8
King Albert St STKB/PEN S36 ... 270 C7
King Alfred's Dr HDGY LS6 ... 87 J5
King Alfred's Gn HDGY LS6 ... 87 J5
King Alfred's Vw HDGY LS6 ... 87 J5
King Cliff Rd HUDN HD2 ... 14 E1
King CI AL/HA/HU LS17 ... 87 H2
King Cross Rd HFAX HX1 ... 10 C7
King Cross St HFAX HX1 ... 10 C7
King Edward Av CAS WF10 ... 135 H8
  HORS LS18 ... 85 L5
King Edward Crs HORS LS18 ... 85 L5
King Edward Rd
  CUL/QBY BD13 ... 102 F8 12
King Edward St AIRE BD20 ... 55 M1
  BSLYN/ROY S71 ... 243 M8
  EARL WF12 ... 195 K3
  HEM/SK/SE WF9 ... 224 A8 3
  HFAX HX1 ... 11 H6 1
  LDS LS1 ... 7 H9
  NORM WF6 ... 178 C4
King Edwin's Ct RHAY LS8 ... 110 C1
Kingfield GSLY LS20 ... 62 B4
Kingfisher CI AL/HA/HU LS17 ... 88 B2 3
  HOR/CROF WF4 ... 198 D3
Kingfisher Gv GIR BD8 ... 103 J5
  HUDS HD4 ... 214 A7 2
  WKFDW/WTN WF2 ... 220 F1
Kingfisher Ms HOR/CROF WF4 ... 152 E3 3
Kingfisher Reach WBY LS22 ... 47 J5
Kingfisher Rd AWLS/ASK DN6 ... 249 K8
Kingfisher Wy AL/HA/HU LS17 ... 88 B2 2
King George Av CHAL LS7 ... 87 M7
  HORS LS18 ... 85 L5
  MOR LS27 ... 130 D8
King George Cft MOR LS27 ... 152 D1 6
King George Gdns CHAL LS7 ... 87 M7 5
King George Rd HORS LS18 ... 85 L5
King George St WKFDE WF1 ... 176 C3
King La AL/HA/HU LS17 ... 65 G7
  AL/HA/HU LS17 ... 87 K4
King Royd La HOR/CROF WF4 ... 201 J3
Kings Ap BRAM LS13 ... 108 A4
Kings Av CAS WF10 ... 158 C7
  HDGY LS6 ... 109 G5
  ILK LS29 ... 38 C2
  NORM WF6 ... 178 B1
King's Bridge Rd HUD HD1 ... 214 D2
Kingsbury PI HFAX HX1 ... 10 B6 2
Kings Cha RTHW LS26 ... 133 H8
Kings CI FEA/AMT WF7 ... 223 M1
  OSS WF5 ... 174 C7
  OT LS21 ... 41 J7
  PONT WF8 ... 180 E7
Kings Ct HEM/SK/SE WF9 ... 223 K5
King's Crs PONT WF8 ... 181 G7
Kings Cft HEM/SK/SE WF9 ... 246 D4
  OSS WF5 ... 174 E6 3
King's Croft Gdns
  AL/HA/HU LS17 ... 87 M5
Kingsdale Av BIRK/DRI BD11 ... 129 G8
  ECHL BD2 ... 105 J3
Kingsdale Ct SCFT LS14 ... 89 G8 3
  SCFT LS14 ... 89 H8 1
Kingsdale Crs ECHL BD2 ... 105 J3
Kingsdale Dr ECHL BD2 ... 105 J3
Kingsdale Gdns BIRK/DRI BD11 ... 129 G8
Kingsdale Gv ECHL BD2 ... 105 J3 2
Kingsfield RTHW LS26 ... 154 D1
Kings Gv BGLY BD16 ... 81 J2
  WHIT OL12 ... 206 E2
Kings Head Dr MIRF WF14 ... 172 B8 2
Kings Head Rd MIRF WF14 ... 172 B8
Kings Lea HIPP HX3 ... 168 D4
  LVSG WF15 ... 172 E4
  OSS WF5 ... 174 E6 3
Kingsley Av BHP/TINH LS16 ... 86 D1
  BIRK/DRI BD11 ... 150 D2
  ECHL BD2 ... 105 G3
  FEA/AMT WF7 ... 179 M6
  HOR/CROF WF4 ... 200 A3
  HUDS HD4 ... 214 A2
  KNOT WF11 ... 181 L1
  RPDN/SBR HX6 ... 167 H3
  WKFDE WF1 ... 176 D1
  WKFDW/WTN WF2 ... 198 E8
Kingsley CI BIRK/DRI BD11 ... 150 D2
  BSLYN/ROY S71 ... 243 J8 3
  HOR/CROF WF4 ... 200 A4
  WKFDE WF1 ... 176 D1 3
  WKFDW/WTN WF2 ... 198 E8
Kingsley Crs BAIL BD17 ... 82 E4 2
  BIRK/DRI BD11 ... 150 D2
Kingsley Dr BHP/TINH LS16 ... 86 D1
  BIRK/DRI BD11 ... 150 D2
  CAS WF10 ... 180 F1 1
Kingsley Garth WKFDE WF1 ... 176 D1
Kingsley PI HFAX HX1 ... 10 B8
  COL BB8 ... 52 F8 3
Kingsley Rd BHP/TINH LS16 ... 86 D1
Kingsmead OSS WF5 ... 174 E6
Kings Md RTHW LS26 ... 133 J8 8
Kingsmead SCFT LS14 ... 89 J6 2
Kingsmead Dr SCFT LS14 ... 89 H5
Kings Meadow CI WBY LS22 ... 29 M7
Kings Meadow Dr WBY LS22 ... 29 M7
Kings Meadow Gv WBY LS22 ... 29 M7
Kings Meadow Ms WBY LS22 ... 29 M7 8
Kings Meadow Vw WBY LS22 ... 29 M7
Kingsmill CI MOR LS27 ... 152 B1 8
King's Mill La HUDS HD4 ... 214 D2
King's Mt CHAL LS7 ... 87 L6
  KNOT WF11 ... 181 K1

Kings Paddock OSS WF5 .... 174 E7
King's Pl HDGY LS6 .... 108 F2
King's Rd BGLY BD16 .... 81 G1
  BHP/TINH LS16 .... 64 C5
  CUD/GR S72 .... 244 E5
  ECHL BD2 .... 83 H8
  ECHL BD2 .... 105 G3
  HDGY LS6 .... 109 G3
  ILK LS29 .... 38 B2
  MILN OL16 .... 228 D1
  NORM WF6 .... 156 A8
  ROY/SHW OL2 .... 229 J8
King's St CUD/GR S72 .... 245 J8
  SKP/WHF BD23 .... 16 D2 🔢
Kingston Cl HFAX HX1 .... 10 B7
  ROY/SHW OL2 .... 229 K6 🔢
  WIL/AL BD15 .... 102 E2 🔢
Kingston Ct HFAX HX1 .... 10 B7 🔢
  HFAX HX1 .... 10 B8 🔢
Kingston Crs SEL YO8 .... 139 M4
Kingston Dr HFAX HX1 .... 10 A7
  NORM WF6 .... 178 E5
  ROY/SHW OL2 .... 228 E8 🔢
  SEL YO8 .... 139 M4
Kingstone Pl BSLY S70 .... 260 F7 🔢
Kingston Gdns MSTN/BAR LS15 .. 111 G3
Kingston Gv IDLE BD10 .... 83 K5
Kingston Rd IDLE BD10 .... 83 K5
Kingston St HFAX HX1 .... 10 B7
Kingston Ter LDSU LS2 .... 6 E4
King St AIRE BD20 .... 36 A5 🔢
  BIRK/DRI BD11 .... 129 H3
  BRIG HD6 .... 170 D4
  BSLY S70 .... 261 H6
  CAS WF10 .... 158 A8
  CLECK BD19 .... 150 A6
  COL BB8 .... 74 A1
  HBR HX7 .... 143 G3
  HECK WF16 .... 172 F2
  HEM/SK/SE WF9 .... 223 K5
  HFAX HX1 .... 11 J5
  HOR/CROF WF4 .... 196 F5
  HUD HD1 .... 15 G7
  HUDW HD3 .... 191 K6
  IDLE BD10 .... 105 L1
  KBTN HD8 .... 239 J4
  KGHY BD21 .... 2 F7
  LDS LS1 .... 8 E1
  MILN OL16 .... 206 B7
  MIRF WF14 .... 194 C2
  MOR LS27 .... 152 C3
  NORM WF6 .... 178 C5
  OSS WF5 .... 197 G2 🔢
  PDSY/CALV LS28 .... 106 C3
  PONT WF8 .... 180 E6
  RPDN/SBR HX6 .... 167 G3 🔢
  TOD OL14 .... 141 M8 🔢
  WKFDE WF1 .... 12 E2
  YEA LS19 .... 62 E7
  YEA LS19 .... 84 C2
King St East ROCH OL11 .... 228 A1
King St South ROCH OL11 .... 228 A1
Kings Vw HIPP HX3 .... 169 J2 🔢
Kingsway AIRE BD20 .... 58 B5
  AL/HA/HU LS17 .... 43 M2
  BGLY BD16 .... 81 J4
  BIRK/DRI BD11 .... 129 H8
  BTLY WF17 .... 151 G4
  DOD/DAR S75 .... 242 B5
  EARD/LOFT WF3 .... 177 H4
  ECHL BD2 .... 83 H8
  GFTH/SHER LS25 .... 113 G8 🔢
  MILN OL16 .... 206 E8
  MSTN/BAR LS15 .... 111 L6
  NORM WF6 .... 178 C6
  OSS WF5 .... 174 E7
  PONT WF8 .... 180 E5
  SKP/WHF BD23 .... 16 D1 🔢
Kingsway Cl OSS WF5 .... 174 E7
Kingsway Ct OSS WF5 .... 174 E7
Kingsway Dr ILK LS29 .... 38 C2
Kingsway Garth
  GFTH/SHER LS25 .... 112 F8 🔢
Kingswear Cl MSTN/BAR LS15 .. 111 M5 🔢
Kingswear Crs MSTN/BAR LS15 .. 111 M5
Kingswear Garth
  MSTN/BAR LS15 .... 111 M5
Kingswear Gln
  MSTN/BAR LS15 .... 111 M5 🔢
Kingswear Gv MSTN/BAR LS15 .. 111 M5
Kingswear Pde MSTN/BAR LS15.. 111 M5
Kingswear Ri MSTN/BAR LS15 .. 111 M5 🔢
Kingswear Vw MSTN/BAR LS15 .. 111 M5
Kingswell Av WKFDE WF1 .... 176 E2 🔢
  ELL HX5 .... 169 H6
Kingswood Av RHAY LS8 .... 88 B3
Kingswood Crs RHAY LS8 .... 88 B3
Kingswood Dr RHAY LS8 .... 88 B3
Kingswood Gdns RHAY LS8 .... 88 B3
Kingswood Gv RHAY LS8 .... 88 C3
Kingswood Pl GTHN BD7 .... 126 C2 🔢
Kingswood St GTHN BD7 .... 126 C2 🔢
Kingswood Ter GTHN BD7 .... 126 C2 🔢
Kingwell Crs BSLY S70 .... 261 H6 🔢
Kinnaird Cl BTLY WF17 .... 174 A1
  ELL HX5 .... 169 H6
Kinsley House Crs
  HEM/SK/SE WF9 .... 223 J4
Kinsley St HEM/SK/SE WF9 .... 223 K5
Kipling Cl HUDS HD4 .... 213 M3
Kipling Ct IDLE BD10 .... 83 M7
Kipling Gv PONT WF8 .... 180 F4
Kippax Mt OSM LS9 .... 110 D7 🔢
Kippax Pl OSM LS9 .... 110 D7
Kipping La CUL/QBY BD13 .... 102 F8 🔢
Kipping Pl CUL/QBY BD13 .... 102 F8 🔢
Kirby Cote La HBR HX7 .... 165 M3 🔢
Kirby St KGHY BD21 .... 3 J1
Kirk Beston La BEE/HOL LS11 .. 131 G4
Kirkbourne Gv BAIL BD17 .... 83 G4
Kirk Bridge La HOLM/MEL HD7 .. 236 F7
Kirkbride Wy
  HEM/SK/SE WF9 .... 247 H3 🔢
Kirkburn Pl GTHN BD7 .... 104 D8 🔢
Kirkby Av BSLYN/ROY S71 .... 243 J6
  GFTH/SHER LS25 .... 135 J1
Kirkby Cl HEM/SK/SE WF9 .... 246 E3
Kirkbygate HEM/SK/SE WF9 .... 246 A1

Kirkby La HOR/CROF WF4 .... 217 L6
  PBR HG3 .... 45 M2
Kirkby Leas HFAX HX1 .... 11 G8
Kirkby Rd HEM/SK/SE WF9 .... 224 A8
Kirk Cl EARL WF12 .... 174 D6 🔢
Kirk Cross Crs BSLYN/ROY S71 .. 243 L4
Kirkdale CAS WF10 .... 158 D7
Kirkdale Av WOR/ARM LS12 .... 130 C3
Kirkdale Crs WOR/ARM LS12 .... 130 D3
Kirkdale Dr HOR/CROF WF4 .... 197 M8
  WOR/ARM LS12 .... 130 D2
Kirkdale Gdns WOR/ARM LS12 .. 130 C2
Kirkdale Mt WOR/ARM LS12 .... 130 D3
Kirkdale Ter WOR/ARM LS12 .... 130 D3
Kirkdale Vw WOR/ARM LS12 .... 130 D3
Kirk Dr BAIL BD17 .... 82 F2
Kirkfield Av SCFT LS14 .... 68 C8
Kirkfield Cl DOD/DAR S75 .... 259 H2
Kirkfield Crs SCFT LS14 .... 68 C8
Kirkfield Dr MSTN/BAR LS15 .... 111 L7
Kirkfield Gdns
  MSTN/BAR LS15 .... 111 M7 🔢
Kirkfields BAIL BD17 .... 83 G3
Kirkfield Vw MSTN/BAR LS15 .... 111 M7
Kirkfield Wy BSLYN/ROY S71 .... 243 L4
Kirkgate AIRE BD20 .... 35 G6 🔢
  AIRE BD20 .... 36 A5
  BFD BD1 .... 4 E6
  BTLY WF17 .... 150 F5
  BTLY WF17 .... 174 B3
  GFTH/SHER LS25 .... 116 A6
  HUD HD1 .... 15 G7
  LDS LS1 .... 7 H9
  LDSU LS2 .... 9 J1
  OT LS21 .... 41 J6 🔢
  SHPY BD18 .... 82 C7
  TAD LS24 .... 71 M3
  WKFDE WF1 .... 12 F2
Kirkgate La CUD/GR S72 .... 222 E8
Kirkham Av WKFDW/WTN WF2.. 175 K4 🔢
Kirkham Cl BSLYN/ROY S71 .... 261 L3
Kirkham Pl BSLYN/ROY S71 .... 243 M7 🔢
Kirkham Rd GTHN BD7 .... 126 D1 🔢
Kirkham St BRAM LS13 .... 107 H1
Kirkhaw La KNOT WF11 .... 159 K7
Kirk Ings Yd LDSU LS2 .... 9 J1 🔢
Kirklands HOLM/MEL HD7 .... 236 F7
  LVSG WF15 .... 172 C1
Kirklands Av BAIL BD17 .... 83 G3
  YEA LS19 .... 62 C7
Kirklands Cl BAIL BD17 .... 83 G4 🔢
Kirklands Gdns BAIL BD17 .... 83 G3 🔢
Kirklands La BAIL BD17 .... 83 G3
Kirklands Rd BAIL BD17 .... 82 F3
Kirk La HIPP HX3 .... 147 L6
  RYKW YO26 .... 32 B1
  YEA LS19 .... 62 C7
Kirklea KBTN HD8 .... 238 E3
Kirk Lea Crs HUDW HD3 .... 191 L6
Kirklees Cl PDSY/CALV LS28 .... 107 G2
Kirklees Cft PDSY/CALV LS28 .. 106 F2 🔢
Kirklees Dr PDSY/CALV LS28.. 106 F2 🔢
Kirklees Garth PDSY/CALV LS28 .. 106 F2 🔢
Kirklees Ri PDSY/CALV LS28 .. 106 F2 🔢
Kirklees Rd WIL/AL BD15 .... 103 K7 🔢
Kirklees Wy BIRK/DRI BD11 .... 150 B1
  BTLY WF17 .... 151 L5
  CLECK BD19 .... 149 J3
  EARL WF12 .... 174 A7
  HOLM/MEL HD7 .... 210 F5
  HOLM/MEL HD7 .... 255 H3
  HUDN HD2 .... 192 B3
  KBTN HD8 .... 237 L7
  OSS WF5 .... 196 D2
Kirkley Av LM/WK BD12 .... 148 E5 🔢
Kirkroyds La HOLM/MEL HD7 .... 236 F7
Kirkstall Av KSTL LS5 .... 108 B3
  LIT OL15 .... 185 J8
Kirkstall Gv GIR BD8 .... 103 M7
Kirkstall Hl BULY LS4 .... 108 D3
Kirkstall La KSTL LS5 .... 108 D2
Kirkstall Mt KSTL LS5 .... 108 B3
Kirkstall Rd BSLYN/ROY S71 .... 243 J5
  BULY LS4 .... 108 D3
  BVRD LS3 .... 109 C5
Kirkstone Av HUDE HD5 .... 15 K6
Kirkstone Dr CLECK BD19 .... 150 D6 🔢
  LUD/ILL HX2 .... 145 K6
  ROY/SHW OL2 .... 228 E8
Kirkthorpe La WKFDE WF1 .... 177 K8
Kirkwall Av OSM LS9 .... 110 D7 🔢
Kirkwall Dr BOW BD4 .... 128 A3
Kirk Wy BSLYN/ROY S71 .... 261 M3
Kirkway ROCH OL11 .... 228 B4
Kirkwood Av BHP/TINH LS16 .... 85 M2
Kirkwood Cl BHP/TINH LS16 .... 85 M1
Kirkwood Crs BHP/TINH LS16 .... 85 M1
Kirkwood Dr BHP/TINH LS16 .... 85 M1
  HUDW HD3 .... 191 K6
Kirkwood Gdns BHP/TINH LS16 .. 86 A1
Kirkwood Gn HUDW HD3 .... 191 K6
Kirkwood Gv BHP/TINH LS16 .... 85 M1
  EARD/LOFT WF3 .... 153 H6 🔢
Kirkwood La BHP/TINH LS16 .... 85 M1
Kirkwood Ri BHP/TINH LS16 .... 86 A1 🔢
Kirkwood Vw BHP/TINH LS16 .. 86 A1
Kirkwood Wy BHP/TINH LS16 .. 86 A1 🔢
Kismet Gdns BFDE BD3 .... 105 L6
Kistyaen Gdns HOLM/MEL HD7 .. 234 D3
Kitchener Av OSM LS9 .... 110 D5 🔢
Kitchener Gv OSM LS9 .... 110 D4
Kitchener Mt OSM LS9 .... 110 D5 🔢
Kitchener Pl OSM LS9 .... 110 D5 🔢
Kitchener St LM/WK BD12 .... 149 J1
  OSM LS9 .... 110 D5 🔢
  RTHW LS26 .... 133 L8 🔢
Kitchen Fold HOLM/MEL HD7 .. 212 C6 🔢
Kitchen St MILN OL16 .... 206 C6 🔢
Kite Ms GIR BD8 .... 103 L7 🔢
Kit La AIRE BD20 .... 17 L8
Kitson Dr WOR/ARM LS12 .... 108 B8
Kitson Dr BSLYN/ROY S71 .... 261 M3
Kitson Gdns WOR/ARM LS12 .... 108 B8
Kitson Hill Crs MIRF WF14 .... 172 B8
Kitson Hill Rd MIRF WF14 .... 172 A8
Kitson La RPDN/SBR HX6 .... 167 M5
Kitson Rd MID LS10 .... 9 J6

Kitson St EARD/LOFT WF3 .... 152 F5
  OSM LS9 .... 110 B7
  SHPY BD18 .... 82 E7 🔢
Kitson Wood Rd TOD OL14 .... 141 G6
Kliffen Pl HIPP HX3 .... 168 F2 🔢
Knaresborough Dr HUDN HD2 .. 192 C4
Knaresborough Rd WBY LS22 .... 29 L1
Knavesmire RTHW LS26 .... 154 D1 🔢
Knightsbridge Wk BOW BD4 .... 127 K6
Knightsclose MSTN/BAR LS15 .. 111 L6
Knights Cft WBY LS22 .... 30 B7
Knightscroft Av RTHW LS26 .... 133 G8
Knightscroft Dr RTHW LS26 .... 133 G8 🔢
Knightscroft Pde
  HEM/SK/SE WF9 .... 247 J4
Knight's Fold GTHN BD7 .... 126 C2 🔢
Knightshill MSTN/BAR LS15 .. 111 M6 🔢
Knight St HFAX HX1 .... 10 B9 🔢
  HUD HD1 .... 15 G5
Knightsway EARD/LOFT WF3 .... 154 D5
  GFTH/SHER LS25 .... 113 G8
  MSTN/BAR LS15 .... 111 L6
  WKFDW/WTN WF2 .... 198 B5
Knoll Cl WBOW BD5 .... 127 G3 🔢
Knoll La LVSG WF15 .... 171 K3
Knoll Wood Gra RHAY LS8 .... 88 F8 🔢
The Knoll BSPA/BRAM LS23 .... 69 L3
  ROY/SHW OL2 .... 229 L8 🔢
Knoll Wood Pk HORS LS18 .... 85 M6
Knott Hill St WHIT OL12 .... 162 A8
Knottingley Rd PONT WF8 .... 181 J4
Knott La AIRE BD20 .... 56 B1
  YEA LS19 .... 85 G5
Knotts Rd TOD OL14 .... 140 F6
Knotty La KBTN HD8 .... 216 C3 🔢
Knowle Av BULY LS4 .... 108 F3 🔢
  HUDE HD5 .... 215 H1
Knowle Gv BULY LS4 .... 108 F3 🔢
Knowle La HOLM/MEL HD7 .... 235 L4
  LM/WK BD12 .... 148 F4
Knowle Mt BULY LS4 .... 108 F4
Knowle Park Av KBTN HD8 .... 238 B6
Knowle Pl BULY LS4 .... 108 F3 🔢
Knowler Cl LVSG WF15 .... 172 C1
Knowler Hl LVSG WF15 .... 172 C2
Knowle Rd BSLY S70 .... 261 K8
  BULY LS4 .... 108 F4 🔢
  HOLM/MEL HD7 .... 212 C5
Knowler Wy LVSG WF15 .... 172 C1
Knowles Av BOW BD4 .... 127 M4
Knowles Hl DEWS WF13 .... 173 H4 🔢
Knowles Hill Rd DEWS WF13 .... 173 H5
Knowles La BOW BD4 .... 127 M4
  BTLY WF17 .... 173 K2 🔢
  CLECK BD19 .... 150 D3
Knowle Spring Rd KGHY BD21 .. 2 E8 🔢
Knowles Rd BRIG HD6 .... 170 C6
  BTLY WF17 .... 173 K2 🔢
Knowles St BOW BD4 .... 127 L5
  CUL/QBY BD13 .... 101 M6 🔢
  STKB/PEN S36 .... 271 H4
Knowles Ter BULY LS4 .... 108 E4
The Knowle KBTN HD8 .... 238 B6
Knowle Top Dr HIPP HX3 .... 148 A6
Knowle Top Rd HIPP HX3 .... 148 A6
Knowl Gv MIRF WF14 .... 194 C1 🔢
Knowl Rd HOLM/MEL HD7 .... 213 G2
  HOLM/MEL HD7 .... 252 F2
  MILN OL16 .... 206 F8 🔢
  MIRF WF14 .... 194 C1
  ROY/SHW OL2 .... 229 L8
Knowl Syke St WHIT OL12 .... 184 C7
Knowl Vw LIT OL15 .... 207 H4
Knowlwood Rd TOD OL14 .... 163 J3
Knowsley Av TOD OL14 .... 163 J5 🔢
Knowsley Crs WHIT OL12 .... 162 A8
Knowsley St BFDE BD3 .... 5 K7
  BSLY S70 .... 260 F5 🔢
  WHIT OL12 .... 206 A6 🔢
Knowsthorpe Crs OSM LS9 .... 110 B8
Knowsthorpe Ga OSM LS9 .... 132 B1
Knowsthorpe La OSM LS9 .... 132 B1
Knowsthorpe Rd OSM LS9 .... 132 C2
Knox St BRAM LS13 .... 106 F1
Knutsford Gv BOW BD4 .... 128 A4 🔢
Knutsford Ms BOW BD4 .... 128 A4 🔢
Krive La HOLM/MEL HD7 .... 234 C1
Kyffin Av MSTN/BAR LS15 .... 111 G7
Kyffin Pl BOW BD4 .... 128 A1

L

Laburnum Av ROY/SHW OL2 .... 229 K8
Laburnum Cl EARD/LOFT WF3.. 153 L7 🔢
Laburnum Ct HOR/CROF WF4.. 197 H5 🔢
Laburnum Dr BAIL BD17 .... 82 F2
Laburnum Gv BRIG HD6 .... 148 C8 🔢
  CLECK BD19 .... 150 C5
  HOLM/MEL HD7 .... 213 H1 🔢
  HOR/CROF WF4 .... 197 H5
  HWTH BD22 .... 79 G6
  KBTN HD8 .... 239 J3 🔢
Laburnum La MILN OL16 .... 229 J3
Laburnum Pl GIR BD8 .... 4 A3
  IDLE BD10 .... 84 A6
Laburnum Rd DEWS WF13 .... 173 H4 🔢
  HECK WF16 .... 173 G4
  SHPY BD18 .... 104 F1 🔢
  WKFDE WF1 .... 12 D1
Laburnum St GIR BD8 .... 4 B3
  PDSY/CALV LS28 .... 107 G2
Laburnum Ter ROCH OL11 .... 228 A2 🔢
Laburnum Wy LIT OL15 .... 207 H1
Laceby Cl BSLY S70 .... 260 F7
Lacey St DEWS WF13 .... 173 K6
Lachman Rd COL BB8 .... 74 A1
Lacy Av TOD OL14 .... 163 J5 🔢
Lacy Gv WBY LS22 .... 48 B2
Lacy St HEM/SK/SE WF9 .... 223 L7 🔢
Lacy Wy ELL HX5 .... 169 J6
Ladbroke Gv BOW BD4 .... 128 A5 🔢
Ladderbanks La BAIL BD17 .... 82 F2
Ladock Pl BSLYN/ROY S71 .... 261 K3

Lady Ann Rd BTLY WF17 .... 173 M1
Lady Balk La PONT WF8 .... 180 F4
Lady Beck Cl LDSU LS2 .... 7 J3
Ladybower Av HUDS HD4 .... 213 G4
Lady Cl OSM LS9 .... 174 E6
Lady Gap La AWLS/ASK DN6 .... 249 L1
Lady Heton Av MIRF WF14 .... 172 B8
Lady Heton Cl MIRF WF14 .... 172 A8 🔢
Lady Heton Dr MIRF WF14 .... 172 A8
Lady Heton Gv MIRF WF14 .... 172 A8
Ladyhouse La MILN OL16 .... 229 J2
Ladyhouse La MILN OL16 .... 229 H1
Lady La BGLY BD16 .... 59 J8
  LDSU LS2 .... 7 H9
  WKFDE WF1 .... 12 D4
Lady Pk AL/HA/HU LS17 .... 88 B2
Lady Park Av BGLY BD16 .... 59 J8
Lady Pit La BEE/HOL LS11 .... 8 F9
Ladyroyd Cft CUD/GR S72 .... 244 E5
Ladyroyd Dr BIRK/DRI BD11 .... 128 A8
Ladysmith Rd CUL/QBY BD13 .. 124 E6
Ladywell Cl WBOW BD5 .... 127 G3 🔢
Ladywell La LVSG WF15 .... 171 K3
Ladywood Gra RHAY LS8 .... 88 F8 🔢
Ladywood Md RHAY LS8 .... 88 F8
Ladywood Rd CUD/GR S72 .... 245 K8
Lady Wood Rd RHAY LS8 .... 88 D7
Ladywood Ter HFAX HX1 .... 10 C3
Ladywood Wy DEWS WF13 .... 194 F2 🔢
Lafflands La HOR/CROF WF4 .... 222 C5
Lairum Ri BSPA/BRAM LS23 .... 69 M1
Laisterdyke BFDE BD3 .... 105 M8
Laisteridge La GTHN BD7 .... 4 B3
  WBOW BD5 .... 126 E1
Laith Cl BHP/TINH LS16 .... 86 B3
Laith Gdns BHP/TINH LS16 .... 86 B3
Laith Garth BHP/TINH LS16 .... 86 B3
Laith Gn BHP/TINH LS16 .... 86 B3 🔢
Laith Rd BHP/TINH LS16 .... 86 B3
Laith Staid La GFTH/SHER LS25 .. 115 K6
Lake Bank LIT OL15 .... 207 J3
Lakeland Cl CUD/GR S72 .... 262 C1 🔢
Lakeland Crs AL/HA/HU LS17 .... 65 J8
Lakeland Dr AL/HA/HU LS17 .... 65 K8
  ROY/SHW OL2 .... 228 E6 🔢
Lakeland Wy
  WKFDW/WTN WF2 .... 199 J8
Lake Lock Dr EARD/LOFT WF3.. 177 H1
Lake Lock Rd EARD/LOFT WF3 .. 177 H1
Lake Rw BOW BD4 .... 5 M9
Lakeside AIRE BD20 .... 59 G4
Lake Side LIT OL15 .... 207 H4
Lakeside Cha YEA LS19 .... 84 E2 🔢
Lakeside Cl ILK LS29 .... 38 C1
Lakeside Ct MID LS10 .... 130 D7 🔢
Lakeside Est HOR/CROF WF4 .... 222 D4
Lakeside Gdns YEA LS19 .... 84 E2
Lakeside Mdw PONT WF8 .... 180 F3 🔢
Lakeside Rd WOR/ARM LS12 .... 108 A8
Lakeside Ter YEA LS19 .... 84 E2 🔢
Lakeside Vw YEA LS19 .... 84 E2
Lake St BOW BD4 .... 5 M9
  KGHY BD21 .... 3 J4
Lake Ter MID LS10 .... 131 M4
Lake Vw HFAX HX1 .... 10 F3
  PONT WF8 .... 180 E3
  WKFDW/WTN WF2 .... 220 E2
Lake Yd EARD/LOFT WF3 .... 177 J1
Lamb Cote Rd HUDN HD2 .... 170 F8
Lambecroft BSLYN/ROY S71 .... 243 L5 🔢
Lambe Flatt DOD/DAR S75 .... 241 L6 🔢
Lambert Av RHAY LS8 .... 88 F7
  COL BB8 .... 74 E4 🔢
  GTL/HWG HX4 .... 168 F7
  SKP/WHF BD23 .... 16 E5 🔢
Lambert Dr RHAY LS8 .... 88 F7
Lambert Fold DOD/DAR S75 .... 260 C7 🔢
Lambert Rd BSLY S70 .... 261 H5
Lambeth St COL BB8 .... 74 D1 🔢
Lambourne Av IDLE BD10 .... 106 A1 🔢
Lambourne Gv MILN OL16 .... 229 H1 🔢
Lambra Gv BSLY S70 .... 261 H5
Lambrigg Crs SCFT LS14 .... 111 J2
Lambton Gv RHAY LS8 .... 110 B2 🔢
Lambton Pl RHAY LS8 .... 110 B2 🔢
Lambton St RHAY LS8 .... 110 B2 🔢
Lambton Ter RHAY LS8 .... 110 B2 🔢
Lambton Vw RHAY LS8 .... 110 B2 🔢
Lamma Well Rd
  HOLM/MEL HD7 .... 254 C4
Lampards Cl WIL/AL BD15 .... 103 J4
Lamplands BTLY WF17 .... 151 M7
Lanark Dr HORS LS18 .... 85 J2
Lanark Ri HOR/CROF WF4 .... 200 C5 🔢
Lancaster Crs HUDE HD5 .... 215 H2
Lancaster Ga HOLM/MEL HD7 .. 236 C5
Lancaster St BSLY S70 .... 260 F5
  CAS WF10 .... 158 A8 🔢

Lancastre Gv KSTL LS5 .... 108 B3
Land Ga WHIT OL12 .... 184 A3
Landor St BSLYN/ROY S71 .... 3 K3 🔢
Lands Beck Wy LVSG WF15 .... 172 B2
Landscove Av BOW BD4 .... 128 A4
Landsdown Av
  HEM/SK/SE WF9 .... 246 C5
Landseer Av BRAM LS13 .... 108 A3
  EARD/LOFT WF3 .... 153 C6
Landseer Cl BRAM LS13 .... 107 M3
Landseer Crs BRAM LS13 .... 108 A3
Landseer Dr BRAM LS13 .... 107 M3
Landseer Gdns BRAM LS13 .... 107 M3
Landseer Gn BRAM LS13 .... 107 M3
Landseer Gv BRAM LS13 .... 108 A3
Landseer Mt BRAM LS13 .... 108 A3
Landseer Ri BRAM LS13 .... 107 M3 🔢
Landseer Rd BRAM LS13 .... 107 M3
Landseer Ter BRAM LS13 .... 108 A3 🔢
Landseer Vw BRAM LS13 .... 108 A3
Lands Head La HIPP HX3 .... 147 K2
Landsholme Ct BOW BD4 .... 128 B4 🔢
Lands La GSLY LS20 .... 62 A5 🔢
  IDLE BD10 .... 105 L1 🔢
  LDS LS1 .... 7 C9
Landsmoor Gv BGLY BD16 .... 81 K1
Land St PDSY/CALV LS28 .... 106 F3 🔢
Lane And Dowry Rd
  HOLM/MEL HD7 .... 253 L1
  PDSY/CALV LS28 .... 107 H6
Lane End CUL/QBY BD13 .... 102 F8 🔢
  PDSY/CALV LS28 .... 107 H6
Lane End Av AL/HA/HU LS17 .... 87 H1
Lane End Cft AL/HA/HU LS17 .... 87 H1
Lane End Fold PDSY/CALV LS28 .. 107 H6
Lane End Mt PDSY/CALV LS28 .. 107 H6
Lane End Pl BEE/HOL LS11 .... 8 E6
Lane Ends LUD/ILL HX2 .... 146 A4
Lane Ends Cl GIR BD8 .... 104 A6
  HEM/SK/SE WF9 .... 223 H2
Lane Ends Gn HIPP HX3 .... 147 K6
Lane Ends La HBR HX7 .... 143 L2
  HWTH BD22 .... 54 F2
Lane Hackings Gn KBTN HD8 .... 239 G7
Lane Head La KBTN HD8 .... 216 B8
  LUD/ILL HX2 .... 125 L6
Lane Head Rd DOD/DAR S75 .... 242 C4
  KBTN HD8 .... 238 A7
  RPDN/SBR HX6 .... 188 E1
Lane House La COL BB8 .... 74 E4
Lane House Rd HWTH BD22 .... 54 B2
Lane Side CUL/QBY BD13 .... 124 F3
  MOR LS27 .... 130 D7
Laneside WIL/AL BD15 .... 102 D2
Laneside Av ROY/SHW OL2 .... 229 M7
Laneside Cl LIT OL15 .... 185 J8
Lane Side Cl LM/WK BD12 .... 148 E2 🔢
Laneside Fold MOR LS27 .... 130 D7 🔢
Laneside Gdns MOR LS27 .... 130 D8
Lane Side La HUDE HD5 .... 193 L7
Laneside St TOD OL14 .... 163 J2
The Lanes PDSY/CALV LS28 .... 107 H6
The Lane AL/HA/HU LS17 .... 87 H1
  OSM LS9 .... 9 L2
Lang Av BSLYN/ROY S71 .... 262 A4
Langbar Ap SCFT LS14 .... 111 M1
Langbar Av HTON BD9 .... 103 M3
Langbar Cl SCFT LS14 .... 89 M8
Langbar Garth SCFT LS14 .... 89 M8 🔢
Langbar Gn SCFT LS14 .... 89 M8 🔢
Langbar Gv SCFT LS14 .... 111 M1
Langbar Rd ILK LS29 .... 20 C8
  SCFT LS14 .... 111 M1
Langcliffe Cl DOD/DAR S75 .... 242 C4 🔢
Lang Crs BSLYN/ROY S71 .... 262 A4
Langdale Av EARD/LOFT WF3 .. 176 F1
  GIR BD8 .... 104 A3
  HDGY LS6 .... 108 E1
  LM/WK BD12 .... 149 G3
  MILN OL16 .... 228 E6 🔢
  NORM WF6 .... 178 C2
Langdale Cl CAS WF10 .... 159 C4
  WBY LS22 .... 29 M8
Langdale Ct BGLY BD16 .... 81 J2
Langdale Crs LUD/ILL HX2 .... 146 A3 🔢
Langdale Dr CUL/QBY BD13 .... 124 F5 🔢
  FEA/AMT WF7 .... 202 E7
  HUDE HD5 .... 15 K5
  NORM WF6 .... 178 C2 🔢
  WKFDW/WTN WF2 .... 176 A3
Langdale Gdns HDGY LS6 .... 108 E2
Langdale Ms NORM WF6 .... 178 C2 🔢
Langdale Mt WKFDW/WTN WF2.. 199 J8
Langdale Ri BGLY BD16 .... 52 B8 🔢
Langdale Rd AWLS/ASK DN6 .... 249 K5
  BSLYN/ROY S71 .... 261 H5
  DOD/DAR S75 .... 260 A3
  EARL WF12 .... 174 B4
  IDLE BD10 .... 106 A2
  RTHW LS26 .... 133 K8
Langdale Sq
  WKFDW/WTN WF2 .... 176 B8 🔢
Langdale St ELL HX5 .... 169 H8
Langdale Ter HDGY LS6 .... 108 E2
Langden Cl ROY/SHW OL2 .... 229 J6
Langford Cl DOD/DAR S75 .... 260 C7
Langford La ILK LS29 .... 40 B5
Langford Rd ILK LS29 .... 40 A5
Lang Kirk Cl AIRE BD20 .... 35 G3 🔢
Langlands Rd BGLY BD16 .... 81 J7
Lang La ECHL BD2 .... 104 F2 🔢
  BOW BD4 .... 127 L5
  BRAM LS13 .... 107 J2
Langley Av BGLY BD16 .... 81 J2
  BOW BD4 .... 127 L5
  BRAM LS13 .... 107 J2
Langley Cl BRAM LS13 .... 107 J2 🔢
Langley Crs BAIL BD17 .... 83 C3
  BRAM LS13 .... 107 K3
Langley Garth BRAM LS13 .... 107 J2 🔢
Langley Gv BGLY BD16 .... 81 J2 🔢
Langley La BAIL BD17 .... 83 C2
  KBTN HD8 .... 240 A4
Langley Mt BRAM LS13 .... 107 J2
Langley Pl BRAM LS13 .... 107 J2 🔢
Langley Rd BGLY BD16 .... 81 J2
  BRAM LS13 .... 107 J2
Langleys Rd AWLS/ASK DN6 .... 227 M5 🔢

Langport Cl CUL/QBY BD13 ... 125 H5 7
Langroyd Rd COL BB8 ... 52 A8
COL BB8 ... 74 A1
Langsett Cft HUDN HD2 ... 193 G1
Langsett Rd BSLYN/ROY S71 ... 243 G7
WKFDW/WTN WF2 ... 220 D1
Langthorne Ct MOR LS27 ... 152 E4 1
Langthwaite La
HEM/SK/SE WF9 ... 247 G4
Langthwaite Rd
HEM/SK/SE WF9 ... 246 F4
Langton Av BOW BD4 ... 127 K5
Langton Cl CLECK BD19 ... 150 D4 2
Langton St RPDN/SBR HX6 ... 167 K1
Langton Ter ROCH OL11 ... 228 A2 3
Langwith Av WBY LS22 ... 47 J6
Langwith Dr WBY LS22 ... 47 G6
Langwith Valley Rd WBY LS22 ... 47 G6
Lansdale Ct BOW BD4 ... 128 B4 10
Lansdowne Av CAS WF10 ... 158 B7
Lansdowne Cl BAIL BD17 ... 83 H3
BTLY WF17 ... 151 K8
Lansdowne Crs DOD/DAR S75 ... 241 M7
Lansdowne St WOR/ARM LS12 .. 108 E7 1
Lanshaw Bank SKP/WHF BD23 ... 19 K1
Lanshaw Cl MID LS10 ... 132 A8 5
Lanshaw Crs MID LS10 ... 154 A1
Lanshaw Pl MID LS10 ... 132 A8 6
Lanshaw Rd MID LS10 ... 132 A8
Lanshaw Ter MID LS10 ... 154 A1
Lanshaw Vw MID LS10 ... 132 A8 7
Lanshaw Wk MID LS10 ... 132 A8 8
Lanyon Wy BSLYN/ROY S71 ... 261 K3
Lapage St BFDE BD3 ... 105 L7
Lapage Ter BFDE BD3 ... 105 L8 3
Lapwing Cl GIR BD8 ... 103 K6
Larch Av HOLM/MEL HD7 ... 236 E6
Larch Cl BTLY WF17 ... 151 J4
HUDE HD5 ... 193 K5 1
HWTH BD22 ... 78 F4 6
LVSG WF15 ... 172 E3
NORM WF6 ... 178 D6
Larch Dl HUDN HD2 ... 192 C2
Larch Dr WBSY BD6 ... 126 E7
Larchfield Pl BSLYN/ROY S71 ... 261 M1 2
Larchfield Rd MID LS10 ... 9 L7
Larch Gv BGLY BD16 ... 81 H1
Larch Hl WBSY BD6 ... 126 F7
Larch Hill Crs WBSY BD6 ... 126 F6
Larch La GFTH/SHER LS25 ... 113 K8
Larchmont CLAY BD14 ... 125 L2 3
Larch Pl BSLY S70 ... 261 L8
Larch Rd HUDW HD3 ... 213 L1
Larch St KGHY BD21 ... 79 K2
Larchway MILN OL16 ... 206 F7
Larch Wd SCFT LS14 ... 67 L7
Larkfield Av YEA LS19 ... 84 E2
Larkfield Crs YEA LS19 ... 84 E2
Larkfield Dr YEA LS19 ... 84 E2
Larkfield Mt YEA LS19 ... 84 E2
Larkfield Rd PDSY/CALV LS28 ... 107 G6
YEA LS19 ... 84 E2
Lark Hl BTLY WF17 ... 151 J8
Lark Hill Av CLECK BD19 ... 149 K8
Larkhill Cl RHAY LS8 ... 88 A6
Lark Hill Dr CLECK BD19 ... 149 K7
Larkhill Gn AL/HA/HU LS17 ... 88 A5
Larkhill Rd AL/HA/HU LS17 ... 88 A5
Larkhill Vw RHAY LS8 ... 88 A6
Larkhill Wk RHAY LS8 ... 88 A5
Larkhill Wy AL/HA/HU LS17 ... 88 A5
Larks Hl PONT WF8 ... 180 D8
Larkspur Wy WKFDW/WTN WF2 .. 176 A7
Lark St BGLY BD16 ... 81 H3 9
COL BB8 ... 52 A8 5
HWTH BD22 ... 78 F4 7
HWTH BD22 ... 78 F7 8
KGHY BD21 ... 2 E4
Larwood Av IDLE BD10 ... 106 A2 1
Lascelles Hall Rd HUDE HD5 ... 193 K7
Lascelles Mt RHAY LS8 ... 110 B3 14
Lascelles Pl RHAY LS8 ... 110 B3 15
Lascelles Rd HECK WF16 ... 173 G3 5
Lascelles Rd East RHAY LS8 ... 110 B3 16
Lascelles Rd West RHAY LS8 ... 110 B3 17
Lascelles St RHAY LS8 ... 110 B3 18
Lascelles Ter RHAY LS8 ... 110 B3
Lascelles Vw RHAY LS8 ... 110 B3 19
Lastingham Gn WBSY BD6 ... 126 A5 1
Latchmere Av BHP/TINH LS16 ... 86 B6
Latchmere Cl BHP/TINH LS16 ... 86 C6 1
Latchmere Crest
BHP/TINH LS16 ... 86 B6 1
Latchmere Cross BHP/TINH LS16 .. 86 B6
Latchmere Dr BHP/TINH LS16 ... 86 B6
Latchmere Rd BHP/TINH LS16 ... 86 B6
Latchmere Vw BHP/TINH LS16 ... 86 B5
Latchmere Wk BHP/TINH LS16 ... 86 C5
Latchmore Rd WOR/ARM LS12 ... 130 F2
Latham Ct CLECK BD19 ... 150 D4
Latham La CLECK BD19 ... 150 C3
Latham Lea CLECK BD19 ... 150 C5
Latimer St BFDE BD3 ... 105 M8 7
Launceston Dr BOW BD4 ... 128 A4 8
Laund Rd HOLM/MEL HD7 ... 211 L3
HUDW HD3 ... 191 G5
Launton Wy WBOW BD5 ... 126 F2 11
Laura St BRIG HD6 ... 170 C5 10
HIPP HX3 ... 11 G2
WOR/ARM LS12 ... 8 B3
Laurel Av BSLY S70 ... 261 M7
Laurel Bank Cl LUD/ILL HX2 ... 124 C8 1
Laurel Bank Ct BULY LS4 ... 108 E2
Laurel Cl AL/HA/HU LS17 ... 67 L1
ELL HX5 ... 169 G8
HIPP HX3 ... 125 L7
Laurel Ct OSS WF5 ... 174 E8
Laurel Dr BTLY WF17 ... 151 J7
Laurel Fold WOR/ARM LS12 ... 108 F7 14
Laurel Gv AIRE BD20 ... 35 M5
BGLY BD16 ... 81 G1
BTLY WF17 ... 151 H7
WOR/ARM LS12 ... 108 E7
Laurel Hill Av MSTN/BAR LS15 ... 111 M7
Laurel Hill Cft
MSTN/BAR LS15 ... 111 M7 14
Laurel Hill Gdns
MSTN/BAR LS15 ... 111 M7 15
Laurel Hill Gv
MSTN/BAR LS15 ... 111 M7 16
Laurel Hill Vw
MSTN/BAR LS15 ... 111 M7 17
Laurel Hill Wy
MSTN/BAR LS15 ... 111 M8 4
Laurel Mt CHAL LS7 ... 109 M1 5
HFAX HX1 ... 10 D9 2
PDSY/CALV LS28 ... 107 G6
Laurel Pk WIL/AL BD15 ... 102 E2
Laurel Pl MID LS10 ... 153 K3
WOR/ARM LS12 ... 108 E7 15
Laurels Dr LIT OL15 ... 207 H4
The Laurels EARL WF12 ... 174 C7
RHAY LS8 ... 88 B8
Laurel St BFDE BD3 ... 105 L8
HFAX HX1 ... 10 C9
WOR/ARM LS12 ... 108 E7
Laurel Ter AWLS/ASK DN6 ... 249 J4
PDSY/CALV LS28 ... 107 G6
Laurence Ct RTHW LS26 ... 133 M7 1
Laurie Pl WHIT OL12 ... 206 B5 14
Lavender Ct HUDS HD4 ... 213 M8
Lavender Cft HECK WF16 ... 173 G2 4
Lavender Hl IDLE BD10 ... 105 L1 5
Lavender Wk OSM LS9 ... 110 B7
Lavenham Pl AWLS/ASK DN6 ... 249 G4
Laverhills LVSG WF15 ... 171 M1
Laverock Crs BRIG HD6 ... 170 B1
Laverock La BRIG HD6 ... 170 B1
Laverton Rd BOW BD4 ... 127 K2
Lavinia Ter CLAY BD14 ... 125 M2
Lawcliffe Crs HWTH BD22 ... 78 F6 2
Law Cl WBY LS22 ... 30 B8
Law Common Rd
HOLM/MEL HD7 ... 268 A1
Lawefield Av RTHW LS26 ... 132 E8
Lawefield Gv WKFDW/WTN WF2 .. 12 B5
Lawefield La WKFDW/WTN WF2 ... 12 B5
Lawflat WHIT OL12 ... 206 E1
Lawkholme La KGHY BD21 ... 3 H2
Law La HIPP HX3 ... 169 J1
Lawn Av AWLS/ASK DN6 ... 249 H4
ILK LS29 ... 40 B5
Lawndale AWLS/ASK DN6 ... 249 H4
Lawndale Fold DOD/DAR S75 ... 242 B6 1
Lawn Rd ILK LS29 ... 40 B5
Lawns Av AL/HA/HU LS17 ... 87 H1
WOR/ARM LS12 ... 129 M3
Lawns Cl NORM WF6 ... 178 A2
WOR/ARM LS12 ... 129 M3
Lawns Ct WKFDW/WTN WF2 ... 176 A1
Lawns Crs WOR/ARM LS12 ... 129 M3
Lawns Cft WOR/ARM LS12 ... 129 M3
Lawns Dene WOR/ARM LS12 ... 129 M3
Lawns Dr WOR/ARM LS12 ... 129 M3
Lawns Gn WOR/ARM LS12 ... 129 M3
Lawns Hall Cl BHP/TINH LS16 ... 86 D3
Lawn's La MID LS10 ... 9 L9
WKFDW/WTN WF2 ... 176 A1
WOR/ARM LS12 ... 129 M2
Lawns Mt WOR/ARM LS12 ... 129 M3
Lawns Sq WOR/ARM LS12 ... 129 M3
Lawns Ter EARD/LOFT WF3 ... 153 M7
WOR/ARM LS12 ... 129 M3
The Lawns HOR/CROF WF4 ... 196 C8 2
Lawnswood Gdns
BHP/TINH LS16 ... 86 D4 1
Lawnswood Rd KGHY BD21 ... 2 C8
Lawrence Av PONT WF8 ... 180 D6
RHAY LS8 ... 110 E1
Lawrence Cl DOD/DAR S75 ... 260 A3
Lawrence Crs HECK WF16 ... 150 F8
RHAY LS8 ... 110 E2
Lawrence Dr GTHN BD7 ... 126 A4
Lawrence Gdns RHAY LS8 ... 110 E1
Lawrence Rd HIPP HX3 ... 168 D3
HUD HD1 ... 14 A5
RHAY LS8 ... 110 E2
Lawrence St HIPP HX3 ... 10 D1 7
Lawrence Wk RHAY LS8 ... 110 E2
Law Slack Rd HOLM/MEL HD7 ... 267 M1
Lawson Rd BRIG HD6 ... 170 D4
Lawson St BFDE BD3 ... 5 G3
WOR/ARM LS12 ... 108 D7 2
Law St BOW BD4 ... 127 L4
BTLY WF17 ... 151 H6
CLECK BD19 ... 149 M5
TOD OL14 ... 140 D5
Lawton St HUDS HD4 ... 214 C3
WHIT OL12 ... 206 C5
Laxton Rd BSLYN/ROY S71 ... 243 H6
Laycock La HWTH BD22 ... 56 E8
Laycock Pl CHAL LS7 ... 7 J3
Laycock St MILN OL16 ... 206 F3 5
Lay Garth Cl RTHW LS26 ... 155 G1 6
Laygarth Dr HUDE HD5 ... 193 L8
Lay Garth Gdns RTHW LS26 ... 154 F2
Lay Garth Gn RTHW LS26 ... 155 G2 4
Lay Garth Md RTHW LS26 ... 155 C2
Lay Garth Pl RTHW LS26 ... 155 G2 5
Lay Garth Sq RTHW LS26 ... 155 G2 6
Laythe Barn Cl MILN OL16 ... 207 G8 6
Layton Av YEA LS19 ... 85 G3
Layton Cl YEA LS19 ... 85 G4
Layton Crs YEA LS19 ... 84 F3
Layton Dr YEA LS19 ... 85 F3
Layton La YEA LS19 ... 85 G4
Layton Mt YEA LS19 ... 84 F3
Layton Park Av YEA LS19 ... 85 G4
Layton Park Cl YEA LS19 ... 84 F3
Layton Park Cft YEA LS19 ... 85 G4 1
Layton Park Dr YEA LS19 ... 85 G4
Layton Ri HORS LS18 ... 85 H3
Layton Rd YEA LS19 ... 85 G3
Lazenby Dr WBY LS22 ... 29 M8
Lazenby Fold WBY LS22 ... 29 M8
Lea Av HIPP HX3 ... 168 E3
Leabank Av GFTH/SHER LS25 ... 135 J1
Leach Cl MILN OL16 ... 206 E4
Leach Crs AIRE BD20 ... 58 A4 1
Leache's Br AIRE BD20 ... 57 M4
Leach Ri AIRE BD20 ... 58 A4
Leach Rd AIRE BD20 ... 57 M4
Leach St MILN OL16 ... 206 D8
MILN OL16 ... 229 H1 5
ROY/SHW OL2 ... 229 L8
Leach Wy AIRE BD20 ... 58 A4
Lea Cl BRIG HD6 ... 170 C2
Lea Ct GTHN BD7 ... 126 A4 5
Lea Cft BSPA/BRAM LS23 ... 69 M1
OT LS21 ... 41 J7
Leadenhall St HFAX HX1 ... 10 B9 6
Lea Dr KBTN HD8 ... 238 B6
Leadwell La EARD/LOFT WF3 ... 154 D3
RTHW LS26 ... 154 F2
Lea Farm Crs KSTL LS5 ... 86 B8
Lea Farm Dr KSTL LS5 ... 86 B8
Lea Farm Gv KSTL LS5 ... 86 B8
Lea Farm Mt KSTL LS5 ... 86 A7
Lea Farm Pl KSTL LS5 ... 86 B8
Lea Farm Rd KSTL LS5 ... 86 A7
Lea Farm Rw KSTL LS5 ... 86 B8
Lea Farm Wk KSTL LS5 ... 86 B7
Leafield Av ECHL BD2 ... 105 L3
HUDW HD3 ... 191 G8
Leafield Bank HUDW HD3 ... 191 G8
Leafield Cl AL/HA/HU LS17 ... 87 K4
HUDN HD2 ... 192 F2
Leafield Crs ECHL BD2 ... 105 K3
Leafield Dr AL/HA/HU LS17 ... 87 K4
ECHL BD2 ... 105 L2
PDSY/CALV LS28 ... 107 H8
Leafield Gra AL/HA/HU LS17 ... 87 K4
Leafield Gv ECHL BD2 ... 105 L3
Leafield Ter ECHL BD2 ... 105 L3
Leafield Wy ECHL BD2 ... 105 L3
Leafland St HFAX HX1 ... 10 C6
Leaf St CAS WF10 ... 157 L7
HWTH BD22 ... 79 G6 12
Leafsway WBSY BD6 ... 126 B8 2
Leah Pl WOR/ARM LS12 ... 8 A4
Leah St LIT OL15 ... 207 K1 9
Leake St CAS WF10 ... 158 A7
Leak Hall Crs KBTN HD8 ... 239 H8
Leak Hall La KBTN HD8 ... 239 H8
Lea La FEA/AMT WF7 ... 202 A2
HUDS HD4 ... 213 L8
Lea Mill Park Cl YEA LS19 ... 62 C7
Lea Mill Park Dr YEA LS19 ... 62 C7
Leamington Dr IDLE BD10 ... 83 L6
Leamington St HTON BD9 ... 104 D4
WHIT OL12 ... 206 A6 13
Leamside Wk BOW BD4 ... 128 A4 9
Lea Park Cl RTHW LS26 ... 132 B7 5
Lea Park Cft RTHW LS26 ... 132 B7 6
Lea Park Dr RTHW LS26 ... 132 B7
Lea Park Gdns RTHW LS26 ... 132 B7 7
Lea Park Garth RTHW LS26 ... 132 B7 8
Lea Park Gv RTHW LS26 ... 132 B7 9
Lea Park V RTHW LS26 ... 132 C7
Leapings La STKB/PEN S36 ... 270 B3
Learise HOLM/MEL HD7 ... 236 B3
Lea Rd BSLYN/ROY S71 ... 243 K7
BTLY WF17 ... 151 H7
Learoyd St HUD HD1 ... 15 H4
Leas Gdns HOLM/MEL HD7 ... 255 G2
Leaside Dr CUL/QBY BD13 ... 102 F7
Lea Side Gdns HUDW HD3 ... 191 G8
Leasowe Av MID LS10 ... 132 A4
Leasowe Cl MID LS10 ... 132 A4 2
Leasowe Gdns MID LS10 ... 132 A4 3
MID LS10 ... 132 B4 4
Leasowe Garth MID LS10 ... 132 A4
Leasowe Rd MID LS10 ... 132 A4
Lea St HUD HD1 ... 14 F1
HUDW HD3 ... 191 L5
Leatham Av FEA/AMT WF7 ... 202 A2
Leatham Crs FEA/AMT WF7 ... 202 A2
Leatham Dr FEA/AMT WF7 ... 202 B2 1
Leatham Park Rd
FEA/AMT WF7 ... 202 A2
The Lea GFTH/SHER LS25 ... 135 H1 2
Leather Bank ILK LS29 ... 40 A3
Leathley Av ILK LS29 ... 61 K3
Leathley Br OT LS21 ... 42 C5
Leathley Crs ILK LS29 ... 61 K3
Leathley La ILK LS29 ... 61 K2 1
OT LS21 ... 42 C3
Leathley Rd ILK LS29 ... 61 K2
MID LS10 ... 9 H6
Leathley St MID LS10 ... 9 J5
The Leavens IDLE BD10 ... 83 M6
Leaventhorpe Av GIR BD8 ... 103 L7
Leaventhorpe Cl GIR BD8 ... 103 M7 4
Leaventhorpe Gv
CUL/QBY BD13 ... 103 L8
Leaventhorpe La
CUL/QBY BD13 ... 103 L8
Leaventhorpe Wy GIR BD8 ... 103 M7
Lea Vw BTLY WF17 ... 151 H6
Leavington Cl LM/WK BD12 ... 126 D8 3
Ledbury Av MID LS10 ... 154 A2
Ledbury Cl EARD/LOFT WF3 ... 154 B2 1
Ledbury Dr EARD/LOFT WF3 ... 154 B2 2
Ledbury Gn EARD/LOFT WF3 ... 154 B2 3
Ledbury Gv MID LS10 ... 154 A2 1
Ledbury Rd BSLYN/ROY S71 ... 243 H8 1
Ledgard Dr HOR/CROF WF4 ... 198 B7
Ledgard Wy WOR/ARM LS12 ... 108 E6
Ledgate La GFTH/SHER LS25 ... 159 M2
Ledger La EARD/LOFT WF3 ... 154 E5
WKFDE WF1 ... 176 D1
Ledger Pl WKFDE WF1 ... 176 D2
Ledston Av GFTH/SHER LS25 ... 135 J1
Ledston Mill La CAS WF10 ... 158 A2
Lee Bank HIPP HX3 ... 10 E1
Lee Beck Gv EARD/LOFT WF3 ... 155 G7
Lee Bottom Rd TOD OL14 ... 164 C1
Lee Br HFAX HX1 ... 10 F3
Lee Brig NORM WF6 ... 178 B3
Leech La BGLY BD16 ... 80 B6
Lee Cl WIL/AL BD15 ... 80 E8
Lee Clough Dr HBR HX7 ... 144 B5
Lee Ct KGHY BD21 ... 58 B8
OSS WF5 ... 197 H2 6
Leeds & Bradford Rd
BRAM LS13 ... 107 J3
PDSY/CALV LS28 ... 107 H4
Leeds Barnsdale Rd CAS WF10 ... 157 J8
Leeds Country Wy
AL/HA/HU LS17 ... 65 M2
BHP/TINH LS16 ... 63 L8
HORS LS18 ... 85 J1
MOR LS27 ... 129 J7
OSS WF5 ... 175 L7
PDSY/CALV LS28 ... 84 C5
RTHW LS26 ... 134 C6
SCFT LS14 ... 68 A7
WKFDE WF1 ... 176 F4
Leeds La RTHW LS26 ... 134 D1
Leeds Old Rd BFDE BD3 ... 105 M6
HECK WF16 ... 172 E1
Leeds Rd AL/HA/HU LS17 ... 67 M3
BFD BD1 ... 5 H6
BFDE BD3 ... 5 M7
BHP/TINH LS16 ... 64 C5
BTLY WF17 ... 151 J4
CAS WF10 ... 135 H8
CAS WF10 ... 179 M1
EARD/LOFT WF3 ... 154 D4
EARL WF12 ... 174 A5
ECHL BD2 ... 105 K3
GFTH/SHER LS25 ... 135 H2
GSLY LS20 ... 62 A6
HIPP HX3 ... 147 J5
HUDE HD5 ... 193 G4
HUDN HD2 ... 193 G4
ILK LS29 ... 38 E1
LVSG WF15 ... 172 E1
MIRF WF14 ... 172 A6
MSTN/BAR LS15 ... 112 A2
OSS WF5 ... 174 E6
OT LS21 ... 41 K7
PBR HG3 ... 27 G2
RTHW LS26 ... 132 E6
SHPY BD18 ... 82 F6
TAD LS24 ... 71 L3
WBY LS22 ... 47 H7
WKFDE WF1 ... 176 D6
YEA LS19 ... 84 E3
Leeds St KGHY BD21 ... 2 E5
Leefield Rd HECK WF16 ... 151 G8
Leef St HUDE HD5 ... 15 L7
Lee Gn MIRF WF14 ... 172 C8
Lee Head HUDN HD2 ... 14 C2
Leeke Av HOR/CROF WF4 ... 197 J4
Lee La BGLY BD16 ... 103 J1
DOD/DAR S75 ... 243 G4
FEA/AMT WF7 ... 202 D6
HIPP HX3 ... 146 F3
HORS LS18 ... 85 K4
HWTH BD22 ... 100 B3
KBTN HD8 ... 216 A8
STKB/PEN S36 ... 269 H2
TOD OL14 ... 164 A3
WIL/AL BD15 ... 80 D8
Lee La East HORS LS18 ... 85 K4
Lee La West HORS LS18 ... 85 H4
Lee Mill Rd HBR HX7 ... 143 J1
Leeming St BFD BD1 ... 5 G4
Lee Moor La EARD/LOFT WF3 ... 155 G6
Lee Moor Rd EARD/LOFT WF3 ... 155 H8
Lee Mount Gdns HIPP HX3 ... 10 C1
Lee Mount Rd HIPP HX3 ... 10 C1
Lee Orchards BSPA/BRAM LS23 ... 48 F6
Lee Rd DEWS WF13 ... 194 F1
Lees Av EARL WF12 ... 195 L2
STKB/PEN S36 ... 270 F3
Lees Bank Av HWTH BD22 ... 79 G6
Lees Bank Dr HWTH BD22 ... 79 G6 13
Lees Bank Hl HWTH BD22 ... 79 G6
Lees Bank Rd HWTH BD22 ... 79 G6
Lees Cl CUL/QBY BD13 ... 79 L8
HUDE HD5 ... 193 H7
Lees Crs HOR/CROF WF4 ... 198 B7
Lees Dr EARL WF12 ... 195 L2 2
Lees Hall Rd EARL WF12 ... 195 K2
Lees Holm EARL WF12 ... 195 L2
Lees House Rd EARL WF12 ... 195 L1
Leeside Av HUDN HD2 ... 192 D2
Leeside Rd HECK WF16 ... 151 G8
Lees La HWTH BD22 ... 78 F6
PDSY/CALV LS28 ... 106 F2
Lees Mill La HOLM/MEL HD7 ... 212 D5
Lees Moor Rd CUL/QBY BD13 ... 79 L8
Lees Rd HBR HX7 ... 143 J2
Lees St ROY/SHW OL2 ... 229 K7
Lee St BFD BD1 ... 4 E7
BRIG HD6 ... 170 C2
CUL/QBY BD13 ... 124 F6
DEWS WF13 ... 173 C8
LIT OL15 ... 185 K8
LVSG WF15 ... 172 C1
WKFDE WF1 ... 12 E2
Lee Wy KBTN HD8 ... 216 A7
Lee Wood Rd HBR HX7 ... 121 H8
Legion St GFTH/SHER LS25 ... 138 A3
Legrams Av GTHN BD7 ... 126 B1
Legrams La GTHN BD7 ... 104 C8
Legrams Mill La GTHN BD7 ... 104 C8
Legrams St GTHN BD7 ... 104 D7
Legrams Ter GTHN BD7 ... 4 A6
Leicester Cl LDSU LS2 ... 6 F4
Leicester Gv LDSU LS2 ... 6 F4
Leicester Pl LDSU LS2 ... 6 F4
Leicester St BOW BD4 ... 127 J2
ROCH OL11 ... 228 C1 14
Leicester Ter HIPP HX3 ... 168 D2 5
Leigh Av EARD/LOFT WF3 ... 153 J6
Leigh Rd EARD/LOFT WF3 ... 153 J6
Leigh St FEA/AMT WF7 ... 223 M1
MILN OL16 ... 206 F7 8
RPDN/SBR HX6 ... 167 L1
Leighton Av LIT OL15 ... 207 H4
Leighton Cl BSLYN/ROY S71 ... 261 H3 2
Leighton La LDS LS1 ... 6 D8 1
Leighton Pl LDS LS1 ... 6 E8 1
Leighton St LDS LS1 ... 6 D8
Leigh Vw EARD/LOFT WF3 ... 153 H6
Leisure La KBTN HD8 ... 218 A6
Leith Ct EARL WF12 ... 196 A5
Leith St KGHY BD21 ... 2 E3
Lemans Dr DEWS WF13 ... 173 H3
Le Marchant Av HUDW HD3 ... 191 L6
Lemington Av HFAX HX1 ... 10 D8
Lemon St HFAX HX1 ... 10 B6
WBOW BD5 ... 126 E4 4
Lemon Tree Cl PONT WF8 ... 180 D8
Lenacre La KBTN HD8 ... 216 F5
Lenham Cl MOR LS27 ... 152 C4 6
Lenhurst Av WOR/ARM LS12 ... 108 C3
Lennerton La GFTH/SHER LS25 ... 117 G7
Lennie St KGHY BD21 ... 2 E7
Lennon Dr GIR BD8 ... 104 D5
Lennox Dr WKFDW/WTN WF2 ... 197 M4
Lennox Rd BULY LS4 ... 108 F5
TOD OL14 ... 140 C5
Lenny Balk AWLS/ASK DN6 ... 248 A7
Lens Dr BAIL BD17 ... 82 E2
Lentilfield St HIPP HX3 ... 146 C4 9
Lentilfield Ter HIPP HX3 ... 146 C4 10
Lenton Dr BEE/HOL LS11 ... 131 L4
Lenton Vls IDLE BD10 ... 83 K5 12
Leodis Ct BEE/HOL LS11 ... 8 E3
Leodis Wy RTHW LS26 ... 132 D6
Leonardin Cl ROY/SHW OL2 ... 229 H6 2
Leonard's Pl BGLY BD16 ... 81 J4 5
Leonard St BGLY BD16 ... 81 J4
HUDN HD2 ... 192 D5
LM/WK BD12 ... 148 F3
Leopold Gv CHAL LS7 ... 7 K3
Leopold St BSLY S70 ... 260 F6 5
CHAL LS7 ... 7 K3
OSS WF5 ... 197 J2
Lepton Gdns BSLY S70 ... 261 M8 4
Lepton La KBTN HD8 ... 216 C5
Lepton Pl MOR LS27 ... 129 M7
Lesley Wy HUDS HD4 ... 213 J5
Leslie Av YEA LS19 ... 62 D6
Leslie Rd BSLY S70 ... 261 M7
Leslie St HUDN HD2 ... 14 D1
Leslie Ter HDGY LS6 ... 6 D2
Lesmere Gv GTHN BD7 ... 126 B4 5
Letchworth Av ROCH OL11 ... 228 B1
Leven Gdns WBY LS22 ... 29 M7
Levens Bank MSTN/BAR LS15 ... 110 F8
Levens Cl MSTN/BAR LS15 ... 111 G8
Levens Garth MSTN/BAR LS15 ... 111 G8 4
Levens Pl MSTN/BAR LS15 ... 111 G8
Leventhorpe Ct RTHW LS26 ... 155 L1 1
Leventhorpe Wy RTHW LS26 ... 155 L1
Lever St WBSY BD6 ... 126 C5 5
Levita Gv BOW BD4 ... 127 M2 6
Levita Pl BOW BD4 ... 128 A1 7
MSTN/BAR LS15 ... 111 G6
Lewin Gv CAS WF10 ... 158 F6
Lewis Cl CUL/QBY BD13 ... 124 F5
Lewisham Cl ROY/SHW OL2 ... 228 E8 3
Lewisham Gv MOR LS27 ... 152 D2 10
Lewisham Rd HOLM/MEL HD7 ... 212 B5
Lewisham St MOR LS27 ... 152 A3
Lewis Rd BSLYN/ROY S71 ... 262 A2
Lewis St HFAX HX1 ... 10 C5
Lexington Cl BOW BD4 ... 127 K6
Leyburn Av HECK WF16 ... 173 G1
HIPP HX3 ... 147 M6
Leyburn Gv BGLY BD16 ... 81 J2 5
SHPY BD18 ... 82 C7
Leyburn Rd AWLS/ASK DN6 ... 249 H4
Leyden Ri WIL/AL BD15 ... 103 K6 4
Leyfield BAIL BD17 ... 82 C3
Leyfield Bank HOLM/MEL HD7 ... 236 E7
Leyfield Rd MILN OL16 ... 206 F8
Ley Fleaks Rd IDLE BD10 ... 83 K7
Leygards La HOLM/MEL HD7 ... 234 D5
Leyland Cl COL BB8 ... 74 D3
Leyland Cft HUDN HD2 ... 171 G8
Leyland Rd BTLY WF17 ... 150 F5
CAS WF10 ... 158 F6
Leylands Av HTON BD9 ... 104 B3
Leylands Gv HTON BD9 ... 104 B3
Leylands La HTON BD9 ... 104 B3
KGHY BD21 ... 3 H6
Leylands Rd LDSU LS2 ... 7 K7
Leylands Ter HTON BD9 ... 104 B3
The Leylands DOD/DAR S75 ... 260 C2
Ley La WOR/ARM LS12 ... 108 F6
Leymoor Rd HOLM/MEL HD7 ... 212 F1
Leys Cl IDLE BD10 ... 83 J5
Leysholme Crs WOR/ARM LS12 ... 108 D8
Leysholme Dr WOR/ARM LS12 ... 108 D8
Leysholme Ter WOR/ARM LS12 ... 108 D8
Leysholme Vw WOR/ARM LS12 ... 108 C8
Leyside Dr WIL/AL BD15 ... 103 K4
Leys La AWLS/ASK DN6 ... 248 F5
BSPA/BRAM LS23 ... 48 D6
KBTN HD8 ... 217 K8
KNOT WF11 ... 182 B4
PONT WF8 ... 204 E7
Leys Rd PONT WF8 ... 182 B8
The Leys HEM/SK/SE WF9 ... 246 C5
Leyton Crs IDLE BD10 ... 83 K7 7
Leyton Dr IDLE BD10 ... 83 K7
Leyton Gv IDLE BD10 ... 83 K7 8
Leyton St WHIT OL12 ... 206 B4 4
Leyton Ter IDLE BD10 ... 83 K7 9
Ley Top La WIL/AL BD15 ... 103 L6
Lichen Cl GTHN BD7 ... 126 C3
Lichfield Cl UPML OL3 ... 230 E4
Lichfield Mt ECHL BD2 ... 105 G2
Lichfield Rd EARL WF12 ... 174 B6
Lichfield Ter MILN OL16 ... 228 E2
Lickless Av HORS LS18 ... 85 M5
Lickless Dr HORS LS18 ... 85 M5
Lickless Gdns HORS LS18 ... 85 M5
Lickless Ter HORS LS18 ... 85 M5
Lidgate Cl DEWS WF13 ... 173 L4 5
Lidgate Crs HEM/SK/SE WF9 ... 246 F4
Lidgate La CUD/GR S72 ... 244 D3
DEWS WF13 ... 173 L4
Lidget Av GTHN BD7 ... 126 B1 4
Lidget Hl PDSY/CALV LS28 ... 107 G6
Lidget La HOR/CROF WF4 ... 200 F4
Lidget Pl GTHN BD7 ... 126 B1
Lidget Rd AIRE BD20 ... 34 E1
Lidget St HUDW HD3 ... 191 K5
Lidgett Av RHAY LS8 ... 88 B7
Lidgett Ct GFTH/SHER LS25 ... 113 G8
RHAY LS8 ... 88 B6
Lidgett Crs RHAY LS8 ... 88 B6
Lidget Ter CLAY BD14 ... 125 M2 5
GTHN BD7 ... 126 B1 5
Lidgett Gv RHAY LS8 ... 88 B7
Lidgett Hl RHAY LS8 ... 88 B7
Lidgett La AL/HA/HU LS17 ... 88 A5
GFTH/SHER LS25 ... 113 G8
KBTN HD8 ... 239 H5
RHAY LS8 ... 88 B8
Lidgett Mt RHAY LS8 ... 88 B5
Lidgett Park Av RHAY LS8 ... 88 B5
Lidgett Park Gdns RHAY LS8 ... 88 B6 3

Lidgett Park Gv RHAY LS8 .... 88 B6
Lidgett Park Ms RHAY LS8 .... 88 C5
Lidgett Park Rd RHAY LS8 .... 88 B5
Lidgett Park Vw RHAY LS8 .... 88 B5
Lidgett Pl RHAY LS8 .... 88 B6
Lidgett Ri KBTN HD8 .... 239 H5
Lidgett Wk RHAY LS8 .... 88 B7
Lifton Pl LDSU LS2 .... 6 C5
Light Bank La AIRE BD20 .... 36 E2
Lightburn Av LIT OL15 .... 207 G2
Lightcliffe Rd BRIG HD6 .... 170 C1
Lightcliffe Royd La
  GTL/HWG HX4 .... 167 L8
Lightenfield La HUDS HD4 .... 213 L8
Lightfoot Av CAS WF10 .... 157 M8
Lightfoot Cl CAS WF10 .... 157 M8 [2]
Lighthazles Chapel Rd
  RPDN/SBR HX6 .... 166 C8
Lighthazles Rd RPDN/SBR HX6 .. 166 D7
Light La WKFDW/WTN WF2 .... 176 A7
Lightowler Cl HFAX HX1 .... 10 D5
Lightowler Rd HFAX HX1 .... 10 D5
Lightowlers La LIT OL15 .... 185 M7
Lightowler St WBSY BD6 .... 126 E5 [1]
Lightridge Cl HUDN HD2 .... 192 B2
Lightridge Rd HUDN HD2 .... 192 B1
Lilac Av MILN OL16 .... 229 J3
  WKFDW/WTN WF2 .... 12 E8
Lilac Cl BRIG HD6 .... 170 E3
  ILK LS29 .... 19 J6 [6]
Lilac Gv BOW BD4 .... 105 M8 [6]
  CLECK BD19 .... 150 C5 [1]
  SHPY BD18 .... 104 F1
Lilac Ov GFTH/SHER LS25 .... 138 D8
Lilac Rd ROCH OL11 .... 228 B4 [1]
The Lilacs GSLY LS20 .... 62 A5
Lilac St COL BB8 .... 104 F8
  HIPP HX3 .... 10 D2
Lilac View Cl ROY/SHW OL2 .... 229 M8
Liley La HUDE HD5 .... 194 B6
  MIRF WF14 .... 194 B6
  STKB/PEN S36 .... 269 L5
Liley St MILN OL16 .... 206 C7
Lilian St BOW BD4 .... 127 L3 [3]
Lilands Av BRIG HD6 .... 170 B4
Lilands La BRIG HD6 .... 170 B4
Lilands Ter BRIG HD6 .... 170 B4 [1]
Lilley St HEM/SK/SE WF9 .... 223 M8
Lilley Ter HEM/SK/SE WF9 .... 246 D4
Lilly La HIPP HX3 .... 11 J7
Lilly St RPDN/SBR HX6 .... 167 K3
Lilycroft Rd GIR BD8 .... 104 C5
Lilycroft Wk HTON BD9 .... 104 C4
Lilydene Av CUD/GR S72 .... 245 H7
Lily St GIR BD8 .... 104 C4
  MILN OL16 .... 207 H8
  TOD OL14 .... 141 G6 [4]
Lilythorne Av IDLE BD10 .... 83 L6
Lime Av HBR HX7 .... 143 H5
  HOLM/MEL HD7 .... 236 E6
  TOD OL14 .... 141 J8
Lime Cl ILK LS29 .... 18 F6
  KGHY BD21 .... 2 C1
Lime Crs HEM/SK/SE WF9 .... 247 G5
  WKFDW/WTN WF2 .... 199 H5
Lime Gv BSLYN/ROY S71 .... 243 L5
  HEM/SK/SE WF9 .... 247 G5
  HOLM/MEL HD7 .... 213 G1
  LIT OL15 .... 207 H1
  ROY/SHW OL2 .... 228 F7
  YEA LS19 .... 84 C1 [1]
Lime Kiln La WBY LS22 .... 29 L5
Lime Pit La EARD/LOFT WF3 .... 177 L2
Limers Ga TOD OL14 .... 162 B3
  WHIT OL12 .... 206 B1
Limes Av DOD/DAR S75 .... 242 E4
  DOD/DAR S75 .... 260 D3
  HIPP HX3 .... 168 C2
Limes Cl DOD/DAR S75 .... 242 E4
Lime St BGLY BD16 .... 81 H3
  COL BB8 .... 104 F8
  GTHN BD7 .... 126 C2 [12]
  HUDS HD4 .... 214 A3
  HWTH BD22 .... 78 E8
  KGHY BD21 .... 2 D5
  OSS WF5 .... 197 G4
  TOD OL14 .... 141 J8 [2]
Limesway DOD/DAR S75 .... 260 D3
Lime Tree Av AL/HA/HU LS17 .... 88 A4
  BSPA/BRAM LS23 .... 48 F6
  BTLY WF17 .... 173 J2
  PONT WF8 .... 180 D6
Lime Tree Court Ct
  HEM/SK/SE WF9 .... 223 L8 [1]
Lime-tree Crs GFTH/SHER LS25 .. 135 L5
Lime-tree Gdns
  BSPA/BRAM LS23 .... 49 G7
Lime Tree Gv BIRK/DRI BD11 .. 128 C7 [1]
Limetrees PONT WF8 .... 181 J2
Lime Tree Sq SHPY BD18 .... 81 M6
Limewood Ap SCFT LS14 .... 89 J8
Limewood Rd SCFT LS14 .... 89 J8
Linburn Cl BSLYN/ROY S71 .... 243 J2 [1]
Linby Rd BSLYN/ROY S71 .... 243 H6
Lincoln Av HECK WF16 .... 172 F1
  LVSG WF15 .... 172 B4
Lincoln Cl ROCH OL11 .... 206 C8 [4]
Lincoln Ct HUDE HD5 .... 193 J7 [3]
Lincoln Crs HEM/SK/SE WF9 .... 247 G5
Lincoln Dr LIT OL15 .... 207 J3 [5]
  LVSG WF15 .... 172 C4 [1]
Lincoln Green Rd OSM LS9 .... 7 L7
Lincoln Leach Ct ROCH OL11 .. 228 B1 [1]
Lincoln Rd EARL WF12 .... 174 B5
  OSM LS9 .... 7 L6
Lincoln St CAS WF10 .... 158 A6
  HUD HD1 .... 15 J1 [7]
  ROCH OL11 .... 206 C8 [1]
  TOD OL14 .... 140 D5
  WKFDW/WTN WF2 .... 18 C2
Lincoln Wk GFTH/SHER LS25 .. 135 L4
Lincoln Wy HIPP HX3 .... 10 F2
Lincombe Bank RHAY LS8 .... 88 A6
Lincombe Dr RHAY LS8 .... 88 A7 [1]

Lincombe Mt RHAY LS8 .... 88 A6
Lincombe Ri RHAY LS8 .... 88 A6
Lincroft Av HUDE HD5 .... 215 G1
Lincroft Crs BRAM LS13 .... 107 M3
Lincs Wold LVSG WF15 .... 171 K2
Lindale Av FEA/AMT WF7 .... 202 E7
  ROY/SHW OL2 .... 228 E2
Lindale Cl MID LS10 .... 131 M7
Lindale Garth
  WKFDW/WTN WF2 .... 175 L4
Lindale Gv WKFDW/WTN WF2 .. 175 M5
Lindale La WKFDW/WTN WF2 .. 175 L4
Lindale Mt WKFDW/WTN WF2 .. 175 L5
Lindale Ri ROY/SHW OL2 .... 229 M7
The Lindales DOD/DAR S75 .... 260 E4 [2]
Linden Av AIRE BD20 .... 36 A4
  AL/HA/HU LS17 .... 67 M2
  BFDE BD3 .... 106 A6
  TOD OL14 .... 141 J8 [3]
Linden Cl AL/HA/HU LS17 .... 67 M2
  BRIG HD6 .... 170 E3
  CAS WF10 .... 158 F8
  EARL WF12 .... 174 D7
  KNOT WF11 .... 181 L2
Linden Ct BHP/TINH LS16 .... 86 F2 [2]
Linden Gdns BEE/HOL LS11 .. 131 L3 [3]
Linden Gv BEE/HOL LS11 .... 9 C9
Linden Mt BEE/HOL LS11 .... 8 F9 [2]
Linden Pl BEE/HOL LS11 .. 131 L3 [2]
  HBR HX7 .... 143 J2 [7]
Linden Ri KGHY BD21 .... 3 L8
Linden Rd BEE/HOL LS11 .... 8 F9 [3]
  ELL HX5 .... 169 C8
  HBR HX7 .... 143 J2
  HIPP HX3 .... 168 E2
  HUDN HD2 .... 192 B5
Linden Ter PONT WF8 .... 180 E6
Linden Wy WBY LS22 .... 29 M7
Lindhurst Rd BSLYN/ROY S71 .. 243 H6
Lindisfarne Rd SHPY BD18 .... 82 B7
Lindley Av HUDN HD3 .... 191 J3
Lindley Br OT LS21 .... 42 A1
Lindley Dr GTHN BD7 .... 126 B4
Lindley Moor Rd HUDW HD3 .... 190 F5
Lindley Rd ELL HX5 .... 191 H2
  WBOW BD5 .... 126 F3
Lindley St HUDW HD3 .... 213 J1
  SKP/WHF BD23 .... 16 B4 [2]
Lindrick Cl CUD/GR S72 .... 244 E5
Lindrick Gv LUD/ILL HX2 .... 124 B7 [1]
Lindrick St LUD/ILL HX2 .... 124 B7
Lindrick Wy LUD/ILL HX2 .... 124 B7
Lindsay Acre EARD/LOFT WF3 .. 153 J6
Lindsay Av WKFDW/WTN WF2 .. 197 L1
Lindsay Rd GFTH/SHER LS25 .. 113 H8
Lindsey Ct OSM LS9 .... 7 M7
Lindsey Gdns OSM LS9 .... 7 L7
Lindsey Rd OSM LS9 .... 7 M7
Lindwell Av GTL/HWG HX4 .... 168 K7
Lindwell Gv GTL/HWG HX4 .. 168 K7 [1]
Linefield Rd BTLY WF17 .... 173 M1
Lineham Ct LVSG WF15 .... 172 C4
Lineholme Av TOD OL14 .... 141 G7
Linfit Fold HOLM/MEL HD7 .. 212 C6 [2]
Linfit La HOLM/MEL HD7 .... 212 C6
  KBTN HD8 .... 216 D6
Lingard Ct DOD/DAR S75 .... 260 F4 [3]
Lingards Rd HOLM/MEL HD7 .. 212 A4
Lingard St DOD/DAR S75 .... 260 F3 [2]
Ling Bob LUD/ILL HX2 .... 145 M6
Ling Bob Cft LUD/ILL HX2 .. 145 M5 [1]
Lingcrag Gdns HWTH BD22 .... 54 F3
Ling Cft BSPA/BRAM LS23 .... 48 D6
Lingcroft La WBY LS22 .... 31 J3
Lingdale Rd LM/WK BD12 .... 126 C8
Lingfield Ap AL/HA/HU LS17 .... 87 K3
Lingfield Bank AL/HA/HU LS17 .... 87 J3
Lingfield Cl AL/HA/HU LS17 .... 87 L3
Lingfield Crs AL/HA/HU LS17 .. 87 K3 [1]
  CLAY BD14 .... 125 L4 [2]
Lingfield Dr AL/HA/HU LS17 .... 87 J3
  HWTH BD22 .... 79 J3
Lingfield Gdns AL/HA/HU LS17 .. 87 K3
Lingfield Ga AL/HA/HU LS17 .... 87 K3
Lingfield Gn AL/HA/HU LS17 .. 87 K3 [3]
Lingfield Gv AL/HA/HU LS17 .... 87 L3
  WIL/AL BD15 .... 102 L3
Lingfield Mt AL/HA/HU LS17 .... 87 K3
Lingfield Rd AL/HA/HU LS17 .... 87 K3
  WIL/AL BD15 .... 102 L1
Lingfield Ter WBSY BD6 .... 125 L1
Lingfield Vw AL/HA/HU LS17 .... 87 K3
Lingfield Wk AL/HA/HU LS17 .. 87 K3 [1]
Ling La AL/HA/HU LS17 .... 67 H7
Ling Park Ap WIL/AL BD15 .... 102 L3
Ling Park Av WIL/AL BD15 .... 102 L2
Ling Royd Av LUD/ILL HX2 .... 145 M6
Lings La PONT WF8 .... 226 C6
Lingthwaite DOD/DAR S75 .... 260 C7 [2]
Lingwell Ap MID LS10 .... 153 L2 [3]
Lingwell Av MID LS10 .... 153 L1
Lingwell Cha EARD/LOFT WF3 .. 154 E8 [1]
Lingwell Ct EARD/LOFT WF3 .. 176 L1 [2]
  MID LS10 .... 153 L2 [1]
Lingwell Crs MID LS10 .... 153 L1 [3]
Lingwell Gdns MID LS10 .... 153 L2 [2]
Lingwell Gate Cft WKFDE WF1 .. 176 D1 [1]
Lingwell Gate Dr WKFDE WF1 .. 176 C1
Lingwell Gate La
  EARD/LOFT WF3 .... 154 C6
  MID LS10 .... 153 L2 [8]
Lingwell Gn MID LS10 .... 153 L2
Lingwell Gv MID LS10 .... 153 L2 [7]
Lingwell Ms MID LS10 .... 153 L2 [7]
Lingwell Nook La
  EARD/LOFT WF3 .... 154 C6
Lingwell Rd MID LS10 .... 153 L1
Lingwell Vw MID LS10 .... 153 L2 [3]
Lingwell Wk MID LS10 .... 153 L2 [7]
Lingwood Av GIR BD8 .... 104 B5
Lingwood Cl HOLM/MEL HD7 .. 236 D5
Lingwood Rd GIR BD8 .... 104 B6
Lingwood Ter GIR BD8 .... 104 B6 [8]
Link Rd EARL WF12 .... 173 M7
  HUDW HD3 .... 191 M8
  WKFDE WF1 .... 176 D6
Links Av CLECK BD19 .... 149 M5
The Links FEA/AMT WF7 .... 179 M5 [2]
  TAD LS24 .... 71 L4
Links Vw DOD/DAR S75 .... 242 D4

The Link DOD/DAR S75 .... 260 C8
  PONT WF8 .... 180 C8
  ROY/SHW OL2 .... 229 H5
  RTHW LS26 .... 134 C1
Linkway AWLS/ASK DN6 .... 227 M3 [1]
  BGLY BD16 .... 81 J7 [3]
Linnet Cl GIR BD8 .... 103 L6 [5]
  MIRF WF14 .... 172 D1
Linnet Ct MOR LS27 .... 152 F3
Linnet Gv WKFDW/WTN WF2 .. 220 F1
Linnet St KGHY BD21 .... 3 H3
Linney La ROY/SHW OL2 .... 229 L7
Linnhe Av WBSY BD6 .... 126 B8 [3]
Linshaws Rd HOLM/MEL HD7 .. 267 H1
Linton Av AIRE BD20 .... 36 A4
  AL/HA/HU LS17 .... 88 A2
  BTLY WF17 .... 173 J1 [3]
  WBY LS22 .... 29 M8
Linton Cl AL/HA/HU LS17 .... 88 A2
  BSLY S70 .... 260 D1
  LVSG WF15 .... 172 B1
Linton Common WBY LS22 .... 47 L1
Linton Ct SKP/WHF BD23 .... 16 B3
Linton Crs AL/HA/HU LS17 .... 88 A2
Linton Dr AL/HA/HU LS17 .... 88 A2
  BRIG HD6 .... 170 A4
Linton Gv AL/HA/HU LS17 .... 88 A2
  BRIG HD6 .... 170 A4
Linton Hills Rd WBY LS22 .... 47 L1
Linton La WBY LS22 .... 29 H7
  WBY LS22 .... 47 L2
Linton Mdw WBY LS22 .... 47 L1
Linton Ri AL/HA/HU LS17 .... 88 A2
Linton Rd AL/HA/HU LS17 .... 88 A2
  WBY LS22 .... 47 K5
  WKFDE WF1 .... 13 M2
Linton St BOW BD4 .... 127 L1
Linton Wy AL/HA/HU LS17 .... 88 A1
Lionel St OSS WF5 .... 197 G2
Liphill Bank Rd HOLM/MEL HD7 . 253 L1
Lippersley La AIRE BD20 .... 36 D2
Lipscomb St HUDW HD3 .... 213 K1 [2]
Liquorice Wy PONT WF8 .... 180 D6
Lisbon St LDS LS1 .... 6 D9
Lisheen Av CAS WF10 .... 158 A8
Lisheen Gv CAS WF10 .... 158 A7
Lisker Av OT LS21 .... 41 K7
Lisker Dr OT LS21 .... 41 K7
Lisle St WHIT OL12 .... 206 C6
Lismore Rd KGHY BD21 .... 2 F7
Lister Av BOW BD4 .... 127 K5
Lister Cl FEA/AMT WF7 .... 201 L1
Listerdale LVSG WF15 .... 172 C1
Lister Hl AIRE BD20 .... 55 M2 [8]
  HORS LS18 .... 85 L4
Listerhills Rd GTHN BD7 .... 4 A7
Lister La ECHL BD2 .... 105 H4
  HFAX HX1 .... 10 D6
Lister Rd FEA/AMT WF7 .... 201 K1
Lister's Rd HIPP HX3 .... 11 L4
Lister St BOW BD4 .... 127 L4
  BOW BD4 .... 128 A5 [8]
  BRIG HD6 .... 170 C3
  CAS WF10 .... 157 L6
  HFAX HX1 .... 11 H5
  HUDE HD5 .... 193 J8
  ILK LS29 .... 38 C2
  KGHY BD21 .... 2 E7
Lister Vw GIR BD8 .... 104 B6
Lister Wk MOR LS27 .... 130 F5
Listing Av LVSG WF15 .... 172 D1
Listing Ct LVSG WF15 .... 172 D1
Listing Dr LVSG WF15 .... 172 D1
Listing La LVSG WF15 .... 172 D1
Litell Royd FEA/AMT WF7 .... 200 F1
Little Baines St HFAX HX1 .... 10 B9
Littlebeck Dr BGLY BD16 .... 81 L3 [2]
Little Bradley GTL/HWG HX4 .. 168 B8
Little Brunswick St HUD HD1 .. 14 E5
Little Cake HOLM/MEL HD7 .... 254 E4
Little Catterton La TAD LS24 .. 72 C1
Little Church La RTHW LS26 .. 156 E4
Little Clegg Rd LIT OL15 .... 207 H4
Little Cote IDLE BD10 .... 83 J5
Little Cross St WBOW BD5 .... 127 G4 [8]
Littledale St WHIT OL12 .... 206 A6 [18]
Littlefield Gv OSS WF5 .... 175 G8 [1]
Littlefield Rd OSS WF5 .... 197 G1
Littlefield Wk WBSY BD6 .... 126 B6
Little Fountain St MOR LS27 .. 152 C2
Little Green La HECK WF16 .... 172 E1
Little Hemsworth
  HEM/SK/SE WF9 .... 224 A8
Littleholme St TOD OL14 .... 163 J4 [8]
Little Horton Gn WBOW BD5 .. 126 E1 [1]
Little Horton La WBOW BD5 .... 4 E7
  WBOW BD5 .... 126 E3
Little Howarth Wy
  WHIT OL12 .... 206 E2 [8]
Little Ings Cl TAD LS24 .... 95 G6
Little King St LDS LS1 .... 8 F1
Littlelands BGLY BD16 .... 81 J7
Little La AIRE BD20 .... 59 G5
  AWLS/ASK DN6 .... 205 J7
  EARD/LOFT WF3 .... 155 G3
  FEA/AMT WF7 .... 202 A2
  HBR HX7 .... 99 K8
  HEM/SK/SE WF9 .... 223 M6
  HEM/SK/SE WF9 .... 247 K5
  HEM/SK/SE WF9 .... 247 K5
  HOLM/MEL HD7 .... 236 E8
  HOLM/MEL HD7 .... 254 B1 [8]
  HTON BD9 .... 104 B4
  ILK LS29 .... 38 C2
  MOR LS27 .... 130 E6
Little Lane Ct MOR LS27 .... 130 E6 [3]
Littlemoor Ct PDSY/CALV LS28 .. 107 H8 [1]
Littlemoor Crs PDSY/CALV LS28 . 129 G1
Littlemoor Crs South
  PDSY/CALV LS28 .... 129 G1
Littlemoor Gdns LUD/ILL HX2 .. 124 A8 [1]
  PDSY/CALV LS28 .... 129 G1
Littlemoor Gv MIRF WF14 .... 194 B1
Little Moor PI WOR/ARM LS12 .. 108 D7
Littlemoor Rd LUD/ILL HX2 .... 124 A8
  MIRF WF14 .... 194 B1
  PDSY/CALV LS28 .... 107 G8
Littlemoor Vw PDSY/CALV LS28 . 107 H8

Little Neville St LDS LS1 .... 8 F2
Little New Cl DOD/DAR S75 .. 260 D3 [3]
Little Pk IDLE BD10 .... 84 A5
Little Queen St LDS LS1 .... 6 D9 [3]
Littlethorpe HI LVSG WF15 .... 171 M4
Littlethorpe Rd LVSG WF15 .... 171 M4
Littlewood Cl WBSY BD6 .... 126 F7
Little Wood Dr CLECK BD19 .... 149 M4
Littlewood Cft HUDS HD4 .... 214 C4 [3]
Little Woodhouse BRIG HD6 .. 170 C4
Little Woodhouse St LDSU LS2 .. 6 D7 [9]
Littleworth La BSLYN/ROY S71 .. 261 M8
Litton Cft WKFDE WF1 .... 13 L1
Littondale Cl BAIL BD17 .... 83 G2 [8]
Litton Rd HWTH BD22 .... 2 C7
Litton Wy SCFT LS14 .... 89 K6
Liversedge Hall La LVSG WF15 .. 172 C3
Livingstone Cl ECHL BD2 .... 83 H8 [1]
Livingstone Crs BSLYN/ROY S71 . 261 K1
Livingstone Rd ECHL BD2 .... 105 H1
  SHPY BD18 .... 104 F2
Livingstone St HIPP HX3 .... 10 D1
Livingstone St North
  LUD/ILL HX2 .... 146 C1 [8]
Livinia Gv CHAL LS7 .... 6 F4
Livsey St MILN OL16 .... 206 C6
Lloyds Dr LM/WK BD12 .... 127 G8
Lloyd St TOD OL14 .... 141 K8
Lobley Cl WHIT OL12 .... 206 D4
Lobley St HECK WF16 .... 173 G2
Locarno Av HTON BD9 .... 104 A4
Locherbie Gn WIL/AL BD15 .... 103 K5 [3]
Lochy Rd WBSY BD6 .... 126 B8 [3]
Lockbridge Wy HUD HD4 .... 213 K2 [8]
Lockeaflash Crs BSLY S70 .... 261 M8
Locke Av BSLY S70 .... 261 H8 [8]
Locke Rd DOD/DAR S75 .... 260 C1
Locke St BSLY S70 .... 260 F7
Lockhart St MILN OL16 .... 228 D1 [8]
Lock La CAS WF10 .... 157 M5
  NORM WF6 .... 156 B8
Locksley Rd BRIG HD6 .... 170 F5
The Locks BGLY BD16 .... 81 H2
Lock St EARL WF12 .... 195 M2
  HIPP HX3 .... 11 K8 [8]
  TOD OL14 .... 163 J3 [8]
Lock Wy DEWS WF13 .... 195 M3
Lockwood Av MIRF WF14 .... 172 D7
Lockwood Cl BEE/HOL LS11 .. 131 L5
Lockwood Ct BEE/HOL LS11 .. 131 L5
Lockwood La BSLY S70 .... 261 H7
Lockwood Pk BEE/HOL LS11 .. 131 L5
Lockwood Scar HUDS HD4 .... 214 B3
Lockwood St LM/WK BD12 .... 149 G1
  SHPY BD18 .... 82 B6 [13]
  WBSY BD6 .... 126 E5 [13]
Lockwood's Yd HUD HD1 .... 14 F7
Lockwood Wy BEE/HOL LS11 .. 131 L5
Locomotion Br HUD HD1 .... 15 H6
Lode Pit La BGLY BD16 .... 81 M2
Lodge Av CAS WF10 .... 158 C7
  ELL HX5 .... 169 L7
Lodge Bank Rd LIT OL15 .... 207 H3 [8]
Lodge Cl HUDS HD4 .... 214 A5
Lodge Dr ELL HX5 .... 169 L7
  MIRF WF14 .... 194 E2 [8]
Lodge Farm Cl EARL WF12 .... 195 M2
Lodge Farm Gdns NORM WF6 .. 178 A3
Lodge Gate Cl CUL/QBY BD13 .. 102 A5
Lodge Gv WKFDW WF1 .... 13 H2
  BAIL BD17 .... 82 B3
Lodge Hill Cl WOR/ARM LS12 .. 129 M3
Lodge Hill Rd OSS WF5 .... 174 F6
Lodge La BEE/HOL LS11 .... 8 D9
  HOR/CROF WF4 .... 200 A4
  LVSG WF15 .... 172 F4
  WKFDW/WTN WF2 .... 220 F2
Lodge PI ELL HX5 .... 169 L7 [1]
Lodge Rd AWLS/ASK DN6 .... 249 K1 [8]
  PDSY/CALV LS28 .... 106 F6
Lodges Cl HOR/CROF WF4 .... 222 E4
Lodge St CUL/QBY BD13 .... 79 M3 [8]
  HEM/SK/SE WF9 .... 223 M6
  KBTN HD8 .... 239 J4
  LDS LS1 .... 6 E5
  LDSU LS2 .... 6 E5
  LIT OL15 .... 185 K8
  WHIT OL12 .... 184 E8 [8]
Lodge Ter BEE/HOL LS11 .... 131 K4 [3]
The Lodge HOLM/MEL HD7 .... 213 G4
Lodore PI ECHL BD2 .... 105 K3
Lodore Rd ECHL BD2 .... 105 J3
Lofthouse Ga WKFDE WF1 .... 154 A8
Lofthouse PI CHAL LS7 .... 6 F5
Lofthouse Ter CHAL LS7 .... 6 F5
Loft St GIR BD8 .... 104 B6 [3]
Logwood St HUD HD1 .... 214 C2 [3]
Lomax St WHIT OL12 .... 206 B5 [13]
Lombard Cl DOD/DAR S75 .... 261 G3 [3]
Lombardi Ct OSS WF5 .... 197 H2 [7]
Lombard St HFAX HX1 .... 10 B9
  MSTN/BAR LS15 .... 111 H7
  YEA LS19 .... 84 C2
Lomond Av HORS LS18 .... 85 K2 [3]
Lomond Ter MILN OL16 .... 228 D1 [8]
Londesboro Gv OSW LS9 .... 110 C7 [11]
Londesboro Ter OSM LS9 .... 110 C9
London La YEA LS19 .... 84 C2
London Rd HOLM/MEL HD7 .... 212 C5
  RPDN/SBR HX6 .... 167 M3
  TOD OL14 .... 142 E8
London Spring Rd
  RPDN/SBR HX6 .... 188 C2
London St YEA LS19 .... 84 C2 [3]
Longacre CAS WF10 .... 157 M8
Longacres WHIT OL12 .... 79 G6 [14]
Long Acre Wk PBR HG3 .... 26 F1
Longbottom Av AIRE BD20 .... 36 B5 [3]
Longbottom Ter HIPP HX3 .... 168 F2 [3]
Longcar La BSLY S70 .... 260 F6
Long Cswy BHP/TINH LS16 .... 86 F1
  BSLYN/ROY S71 .... 261 L3
  EARD/LOFT WF3 .... 177 H1
Longcauseway EARL WF12 .... 173 M6 [3]
Long Cswy EARL WF12 .... 195 M3
  HBR HX7 .... 142 A2
  PDSY/CALV LS28 .... 107 G8
  HWTH BD22 .... 101 J5

OSM LS9 .... 132 B1
RPDN/SBR HX6 .... 188 B5
TOD OL14 .... 164 B3
WKFDE WF1 .... 176 F6
The Long Cswy LUD/ILL HX2 .. 144 C3
Long Cl LM/WK BD12 .... 148 D2
Long Close La HEM/SK/SE WF9 .. 225 L7
  HOLM/MEL HD7 .... 237 K8
  OSM LS9 .... 110 B7
Long Crest PONT WF8 .... 181 G8
Long Cft DOD/DAR S75 .... 242 D5
Longcroft
  KGHY BD21 .... 3 H6
Longcroft PI BFD BD1 .... 4 D6
Longcroft Rd ILK LS29 .... 39 G3 [3]
Long Croft St HOLM/MEL HD7 .. 213 G2
Longdale Dr HEM/SK/SE WF9 .. 247 G2
Long Dam La HOR/CROF WF4 .. 222 C2
Longden Av HUDS HD4 .... 213 L6
Longdike Ct GFTH/SHER LS25 .. 135 K5 [3]
Longdike La GFTH/SHER LS25 .. 135 L6
Longdon Av KBTN HD8 .... 216 A3 [3]
Longdon Wk KBTN HD8 .... 216 A3 [3]
Long Edge Low Rd
  RPDN/SBR HX6 .... 166 D4
Long Edge Rd RPDN/SBR HX6 .. 166 D4
Long Fallas Crs BRIG HD6 .... 170 D7
Longfellow Gv EARD/LOFT WF3 .. 155 G8
Longfield GTL/HWG HX4 .... 190 C2
  HBR HX7 .... 143 H2
Longfield Av HIPP HX3 .... 147 J5 [3]
  HOLM/MEL HD7 .... 213 G1
  HUDE HD5 .... 15 M5
  PDSY/CALV LS28 .... 107 H7 [3]
Longfield Cl HUDE HD5 .... 15 M5
  TOD OL14 .... 163 K2
Longfield Ct HECK WF16 .... 173 G2 [3]
  PDSY/CALV LS28 .... 107 H7 [3]
Longfield Dr BOW BD4 .... 127 L3
  BRAM LS13 .... 107 H2
  DOD/DAR S75 .... 242 D5
  FEA/AMT WF7 .... 202 E7
  MSTN/BAR LS15 .... 111 J6
Longfield Garth BRAM LS13 .. 107 H7 [3]
Longfield Gv PDSY/CALV LS28 . 107 H7 [3]
  TOD OL14 .... 163 K2
Longfield Mt PDSY/CALV LS28 .. 107 H7 [3]
Longfield Rd HECK WF16 .... 172 F2
  PDSY/CALV LS28 .... 107 H7 [3]
  ROY/SHW OL2 .... 229 J8
  TOD OL14 .... 163 K1
Longfield Ter PDSY/CALV LS28 . 107 H7 [3]
  WKFDW/WTN WF2 .... 176 B7 [3]
Longfield Wy TOD OL14 .... 163 K2
Longford Ter GTHN BD7 .... 126 B1 [3]
Long Ga HWTH BD22 .... 55 L7
  RPDN/SBR HX6 .... 188 C6
Long Grove Av HUDE HD5 .... 193 G8
Long Heads La GFTH/SHER LS25 . 138 B5
Long Hey La TOD OL14 .... 163 L3
Long Heys GTL/HWG HX4 .... 168 C8
Long Hill End HWTH BD22 .... 54 E5
Long Hill Rd HUDN HD2 .... 192 D2
Longhouse Dr CUL/QBY BD13 .. 101 M6 [3]
Long House Rd LUD/ILL HX2 .. 123 L8
Long Ing Rd HOLM/MEL HD7 .. 254 C7
Longlands Av CUL/QBY BD13 .. 101 M5
  HOLM/MEL HD7 .... 212 A5
Longlands Bank
  HOLM/MEL HD7 .... 236 D7 [3]
Longlands Cl OSS WF5 .... 175 G8
Longlands Dr DOD/DAR S75 .. 242 D6 [3]
  HWTH BD22 .... 78 F6
Longlands La WBY LS22 .... 46 E1
Longlands Rd DEWS WF13 .... 173 J4
  HOLM/MEL HD7 .... 212 A5
  OSS WF5 .... 175 G8
Long La BGLY BD16 .... 80 C5
  COL BB8 .... 52 F6
  CUL/QBY BD13 .... 124 F7
  EARL WF12 .... 174 B6
  FEA/AMT WF7 .... 202 D5
  HBR HX7 .... 143 G5
  HBR HX7 .... 164 F3
  HIPP HX3 .... 146 A3
  HOLM/MEL HD7 .... 236 B3
  HOR/CROF WF4 .... 216 F5
  HTON BD9 .... 103 M1
  HUDE HD5 .... 193 G8
  HWTH BD22 .... 54 D1
  KBTN HD8 .... 238 A5
  KBTN HD8 .... 240 B3
  MSTN/BAR LS15 .... 90 F7
  PONT WF8 .... 181 M8
  PONT WF8 .... 226 E5
  RPDN/SBR HX6 .... 167 J4
  STKB/PEN S36 .... 271 M8
  WIL/AL BD15 .... 102 F5
Long Lee La KGHY BD21 .... 3 K8 [1]
Longley Cl DOD/DAR S75 .... 260 A2 [1]
Longley Edge La
  HOLM/MEL HD7 .... 254 D5
Longley Edge Rd
  HOLM/MEL HD7 .... 254 C5
Longley La HOLM/MEL HD7 .... 254 C5
  HUDE HD5 .... 214 E4
  RPDN/SBR HX6 .... 167 H6
Longley Rd HUDE HD5 .... 214 E4
Longley St DOD/DAR S75 .... 260 A2
Longman Rd BSLY S70 .... 261 G2
Long Meadow COL BB8 .... 74 C1 [3]
  SKP/WHF BD23 .... 16 D1
Long Meadow Ct
  GFTH/SHER LS25 .... 135 J1
Long Meadow Ga
  GFTH/SHER LS25 .... 135 H1
Long Mdw BHP/TINH LS16 .... 64 A4
  ECHL BD2 .... 105 G2
  GFTH/SHER LS25 .... 135 H1
  ILK LS29 .... 40 A4 [3]
Long Moor La KBTN HD8 .... 238 E5
Long Preston Cha IDLE BD10 .. 84 A7 [3]
Long Reach LUD/ILL HX2 .... 145 J3
Long Riddings ILK LS29 .... 19 C5
Long Rdg BRIG HD6 .... 170 C7
Longridge BSLYN/ROY S71 .... 243 M8 [3]
Long Rw HOR/CROF WF4 .... 200 C1

HORS LS18 .... 85 L5
LM/WK BD12 .... 148 F1
Longroyd SHPY BD18 .... 83 H6 🛭
Longroyd Av BEE/HOL LS11 .... 131 L3
Longroyd Crs AL/HA/HU LS17 .... 212 D5
Longroyd Crs North
  BEE/HOL LS11 .... 9 H9
Long Royd Dr BAIL BD17 .... 83 G2
Longroyde Cl BRIG HD6 .... 170 B6 🛭
Longroyde Gv BRIG HD6 .... 170 B6 🛭
Longroyde Rd BRIG HD6 .... 170 B5
Longroyd Farm
  HOR/CROF WF4 .... 196 D7
Longroyd Gv BEE/HOL LS11 .... 131 L3
Longroyd La HUD HD1 .... 14 B9
Long Royd La KBTN HD8 .... 238 D6
Longroyd Pl BEE/HOL LS11 .... 131 L3
Long Royd Rd RPDN/SBR HX6 .... 166 E4
  HUD HD1 .... 14 B9
Longroyd Rd RPDN/SBR HX6 .... 166 E4
Longroyd St North
  BEE/HOL LS11 .... 9 H9
Longroyd Ter BEE/HOL LS11 .... 131 L3
Longroyd Vw BEE/HOL LS11 .... 131 L3
Long Rushes ROY/SHW OL2 .... 229 H6
Longside La GTHN BD7 .... 4 B7
Longside Wy DOD/DAR S75 .... 260 C4
Longsight Rd DOD/DAR S75 .... 242 C5
Long St BOW BD4 .... 5 L9
Long Thorpe La
  EARD/LOFT WF3 .... 154 C5
Long Wall ELL HX5 .... 169 G8
Long Tongue Scrog La
  HUDE HD5 .... 193 M7
Longwood Av BGLY BD16 .... 81 G1
Longwood Cl AL/HA/HU LS17 .... 88 D1
  EARD/LOFT WF3 .... 152 F6 🛭
Longwood Crs AL/HA/HU LS17 .... 88 D1
Longwood Edge Rd
  HUDW HD3 .... 191 G6
Longwood Fold
  EARD/LOFT WF3 .... 153 G6 🛭
Longwood Garth
  EARD/LOFT WF3 .... 153 G6 🛭
Longwood Ga HUDW HD3 .... 191 H8
Longwood House Rd
  HUDN HD2 .... 192 C3 🛭
Longwood Rd EARD/LOFT WF3 .... 152 F6
  HUDW HD3 .... 213 K1
Longwoods Wk KNOT WF11 .... 182 C1 🛭
Longwood V EARD/LOFT WF3 .... 153 G6 🛭
Longwood Vw AL/HA/HU LS17 .... 81 G1
Longwood Wy AL/HA/HU LS17 .... 88 D1 🛭
Lonsbrough Av HECK WF16 .... 172 F1
Lonsdale Av BSLYN/ROY LS71 .... 262 D6
  BTLY WF17 .... 151 H7 🛭
  MILN OL16 .... 228 D1
Lonsdale Cl MID LS10 .... 131 M5 🛭
Lonsdale Mdw BSPA/BRAM LS23 .... 48 F7
Lonsdale Ri BSPA/BRAM LS23 .... 48 F7
Lonsdale Rd WKFEDE WF1 .... 176 D6 🛭
Lonsdale St BFDE BD3 .... 5 L4
Lonsdale Ter LVSG WF15 .... 172 C2 🛭
Lord La HWTH BD22 .... 78 D6
Lordsfield Pl BOW BD4 .... 127 M5
Lord's La BRIG HD6 .... 170 D5
Lord St BSLYN/ROY LS71 .... 261 L4
  DEWS WF13 .... 173 H2
  EARL WF12 .... 174 D7 🛭
  HFAX HX1 .... 10 F5
  HOLM/MEL HD7 .... 212 B1
  HUD HD1 .... 15 G6
  KGHY BD21 .... 3 G4
  RPDN/SBR HX6 .... 167 L1
  TOD OL14 .... 163 J5
  WKFDE WF1 .... 13 L9
  WOR/ARM LS12 .... 8 B3
Lord Ter WOR/ARM LS12 .... 8 B3
Loris St BOW BD4 .... 127 M5
Lorne St BOW BD4 .... 127 K3 🛭
  HWTH BD22 .... 79 H6 🛭
  KGHY BD21 .... 3 L3
  WHIT OL12 .... 206 D3
Lorry Bank CHAL LS7 .... 7 G1
Loscoe Cl NORM WF6 .... 179 G3
Loscoe La FEA/AMT WF7 .... 179 J3
  NORM WF6 .... 179 G4
Loshpot La WBY LS22 .... 30 C4
Lotherscale Rd AIRE BD20 .... 34 C7
Lotherton La GFTH/SHER LS25 .... 92 B8
Lotherton Wy GFTH/SHER LS25 .... 113 J1
Louisa St CAS WF10 .... 157 L6 🛭
  IDLE BD10 .... 83 K6 🛭
Louis Av WBOW BD5 .... 126 C2
Louise Cl WHIT OL12 .... 206 D3 🛭
Louise Gdns WHIT OL12 .... 206 D3
Louise St WHIT OL12 .... 206 D3
Louis Gv CHAL LS7 .... 7 L2
Louis St CHAL LS7 .... 7 K2
Lovaine Gv WKFDW/WTN WF2 .... 198 F5
Love La CAS WF10 .... 157 L8
  HFAX HX1 .... 10 F8
  OSS WF5 .... 174 E8 🛭
  PONT WF8 .... 180 D7
  RTHW .S26 .... 155 C1
  WKFDW/WTN WF2 .... 12 C2
Love Lane Ter PONT WF8 .... 180 E6
Lovell Park Cl CHAL LS7 .... 7 J6
Lovell Park Ga CHAL LS7 .... 7 J6
Lovell Park Hl CHAL LS7 .... 7 H6
Lovell Park Ms CHAL LS7 .... 7 J6
Lovell Park Rd CHAL LS7 .... 7 H6
Lovell Park Vw CHAL LS7 .... 7 J6
Low Ash Av SHPY BD18 .... 82 F7
Low Ash Crs SHPY BD18 .... 83 G7 🛭
Low Ash Dr SHPY BD18 .... 82 F7
Low Ash Gv SHPY BD18 .... 82 F7
Low Ash Rd SHPY BD18 .... 83 G8
Low Bank Dr HWTH BD22 .... 78 D3
Low Bank La HWTH BD22 .... 78 D3
Low Bank St PDSY/CALV LS28 .... 106 E3
Low Cliff Wk HECK WF16 .... 173 G4
Low Cl BGLY BD16 .... 81 K4 🛭

ILK LS29 .... 20 D8
Low Close St LDSU LS2 .... 6 D3
Low Cft BSLYN/ROY S71 .... 243 M3
Lowcroft WBY LS22 .... 47 J6
Low Crompton Rd
  ROY/SHW OL2 .... 228 F8
Low Cudworth CUD/GR S72 .... 262 D1
Lowdale EARL WF12 .... 174 A4 🛭
Lowell Av GTHN BD7 .... 126 B1 🛭
Lowell Gv BRAM LS13 .... 107 J5
Lowell Pl BRAM LS13 .... 107 J6
Lower Ashgrove WBOW BD5 .... 4 F5
Lower Back La HBR HX7 .... 142 B2
Lower Bankhouse
  PDSY/CALV LS28 .... 128 F2
Lower Basinghall St LDS LS1 .... 6 F9
Lower Bower La DEWS WF13 .... 173 H3
Lower Brock Well La
  RPDN/SBR HX6 .... 167 H4
Lower Brunswick St LDSU LS2 .... 7 J7
Lower Cambridge St WOR/ARM SF10 .... 157 M6
Lower Castlereagh St
  BSLY S70 .... 261 G5 🛭
Lower Clifton St
  RPDN/SBR HX6 .... 167 L2 🛭
Lower Clyde St
  RPDN/SBR HX6 .... 167 K3 🛭
Lower Common La KBTN HD8 .... 240 A5
Lower Constable Rd ILK LS29 .... 38 F3
Lower Cross St HFAX HX1 .... 11 J4
Lower Crow Nest Dr BRIG HD6 .... 148 D7
Lower Denby La KBTN HD8 .... 257 J3
Lower Edge Rd ELL HX5 .... 169 K7
Lowerfields Ri ROY/SHW OL2 .... 229 K6
Lower Finkil St BRIG HD6 .... 170 A1
Lower Fitzwilliam St HUD HD1 .... 15 C5
Lower Fold BRIG HD6 .... 170 B8
  HOLM/MEL HD7 .... 236 B1 🛭
Lower Furney Lee TOD OL14 .... 141 J8 🛭
Lower Ga HUDW HD3 .... 213 K1
Lower George St TOD OL14 .... 163 K1
  WBSY BD6 .... 126 D5 🛭
Lower Globe St GIR BD8 .... 4 A4
Lower Gra HUDN HD2 .... 171 G8
Lower Grattan Rd BFD BD1 .... 4 C6
Lower Greave Rd
  HOLM/MEL HD7 .... 235 K6
Lower Green Ter CLECK BD19 .... 149 H6 🛭
Lower Hall Cl LVSG WF15 .... 172 B3
Lower Hall Crs HUDW HD3 .... 193 L8
Lower Hall Dr LVSG WF15 .... 172 B2 🛭
Lower Hall La LVSG WF15 .... 172 B2
Lower Hall Mt LVSG WF15 .... 172 B2 🛭
Lower Hall Rd HUDW HD5 .... 193 L8
Lower Heights Rd
  CUL/QBY BD13 .... 102 E6
Lower Hey HOLM/MEL HD7 .... 234 F4
Lower High Royds
  DOD/DAR S75 .... 242 C6
Lower Holme BAIL BD17 .... 82 C5
Lower House Cl SHPY BD18 .... 83 H6
Lower House La KBTN HD8 .... 216 C4
  WHIT OL12 .... 184 D7
Lowerhouses La HUDE HD5 .... 214 F2
Lowerhouses Rd HUDW HD3 .... 191 K8 🛭
Lower Kipping La
  CUL/QBY BD13 .... 102 F8 🛭
Lower Kirkgate HFAX HX1 .... 11 K6
Lower Laith Av TOD OL14 .... 163 L1
Lower La BIRK/DRI BD11 .... 149 M1
  BOW BD4 .... 127 L2
  CLECK BD19 .... 150 D7
  HBR HX7 .... 142 A3
  HOLM/MEL HD7 .... 236 A2 🛭
  MILN OL16 .... 228 F2
Lower Langwith WBY LS22 .... 47 J6
Lower Lark Hl CLECK BD19 .... 149 K7
Lower Maythorn La
  HOLM/MEL HD7 .... 255 L6
Lower Mdw HOLM/MEL HD7 .... 253 M1 🛭
Lower Mickletown RTHW LS26 .... 157 G3
Lower Mill Bank Rd
  RPDN/SBR HX6 .... 166 F7
Lower Newlands BRIG HD6 .... 170 D5 🛭
Lower Northcroft
  HEM/SK/SE WF9 .... 247 J3
Lower Northfield La
  HEM/SK/SE WF9 .... 246 E3
Lower North St BTLY WF17 .... 173 K2 🛭
Lower Oxford St CAS WF10 .... 157 M7
Lower Park Gn AIRE BD20 .... 35 L5
Lower Park Royd Dr
  RPDN/SBR HX6 .... 167 G7
Lower Peel St DEWS WF13 .... 173 L5 🛭
Lower Quarry Rd HUDN HD2 .... 171 J7
Lower Rd HUDW HD3 .... 189 H8
  HUDW HD3 .... 211 H1
Lower Rushton Rd BFDE BD3 .... 106 A7
Lower Sandhills SCFT LS14 .... 90 A3
Lower School St LM/WK BD12 .... 126 E8
  SHPY BD18 .... 82 B6 🛭
Lower Sheriff St WHIT OL12 .... 206 A6
Lower Station Rd NORM WF6 .... 178 C4
Lower St MILN OL16 .... 228 C2
Lower Thomas St BSLY S70 .... 261 G6 🛭
Lower Tofts Rd
  PDSY/CALV LS28 .... 107 G7
Lowertown HWTH BD22 .... 100 E4
Lower Town St BRAM LS13 .... 107 M3
Lower Tweedale St
  ROCH OL11 .... 206 B8 🛭
Lower Union St SKP/WHF BD23 .... 16 B3
Lower Unwin St STKB/PEN S36 .... 270 F1
Lower Viaduct St HUD HD1 .... 15 G5
Lower Warrengate WKFDE WF1.. 12 F2 🛭
Lower Wellhouse Rd
  HOLM/MEL HD7 .... 212 F3
Lower Wellington Rd ILK LS29 .... 38 E2
Lower Westfield Rd GIR BD8.. 104 C5 🛭
Lower Wheat End MILN OL16.. 206 D6 🛭
Lower Wortley Rd
  WOR/ARM LS12 .... 130 D1
Lowestwood La
  HOLM/MEL HD7 .... 212 F4
Loweswater Av WBSY BD6 .... 126 B8
Low Farm RTHW LS26 .... 135 G6

Low Farm Cl COP/BISH YO23 .... 73 J7
Low Farm La FEA/AMT WF7 .... 202 C8
Lowfield Cl LM/WK BD12 .... 149 G1
Lowfield Crs AIRE BD20 .... 36 B6
  HEM/SK/SE WF9 .... 224 A7
Lowfield La SKP/WHF BD23 .... 19 H1
Lowfield Rd DEWS WF13 .... 173 H6
  GFTH/SHER LS25 .... 139 G6
  HEM/SK/SE WF9 .... 224 A7
Low Fields Av BEE/HOL LS11 .... 131 G3
Lowfields Cl ELL HX5 .... 169 J6
Low Fields Rd BEE/HOL LS11 .... 131 G3
  WOR/ARM LS12 .... 130 F2
Lowfields Wy ELL HX5 .... 169 J6
Low Fold AIRE BD20 .... 35 L8
  CLECK BD19 .... 149 H6 🛭
  OSM LS9 .... 9 M4
Low Garth Link
  GFTH/SHER LS25 .... 116 A7
Low Garth Rd GFTH/SHER LS25 .... 116 A7
Low Ga FEA/AMT WF7 .... 247 J3
  HOLM/MEL HD7 .... 254 D2
  LUD/ILL HD7 .... 123 H8
  LVSG WF15 .... 172 B4
  RPDN/SBR HX6 .... 166 F7
Low Gate La UPML OL3 .... 231 H5
Low Gipton Crs OSM LS9 .... 110 F3
Low Grange Crs MID LS10 .... 132 A5
Low Grange Vw MID LS10 .... 132 A6
Low Gn BD7 .... 126 C3 🛭
  GTHN BD7 .... 126 C3 🛭
  KNOT WF11 .... 182 D2
  YEA LS19 .... 84 E3
Low Green Ter GTHN BD7 .... 126 D3 🛭
Low Hall Pl BEE/HOL LS11 .... 8 B4
Low Hall Rd ILK LS29 .... 38 F4
  YEA LS19 .... 84 F6
Low HI WHIT OL12 .... 206 E3
Low Hills La HUDW HD3 .... 191 J5
Lowhouse Cl MILN OL16 .... 207 J7
Low House Dr AIRE BD20 .... 36 A6
Low House Fold LVSG WF15 .... 172 B2
Lowlands Cl BSLYN/ROY S71 .... 261 M1
Lowlands Rd MIRF WF14 .... 194 D2
Low La AIRE BD20 .... 34 A3
  AIRE BD20 .... 35 L1
  BRIG HD6 .... 36 B7
  BRIG HD6 .... 148 E8
  BTLY WF17 .... 151 G5
  CLAY BD14 .... 125 J1
  CUL/QBY BD13 .... 124 E3
  HBR HX7 .... 122 C7
  HOR/CROF WF4 .... 196 D6
  HORS LS18 .... 85 M4
  OT LS21 .... 25 H8
  PBR HG3 .... 28 B6
Low Mdw ROY/SHW OL2 .... 228 F8
Low Mill La BSLYN/ROY S71 .... 262 B3
  ILK LS29 .... 19 K6
  KGHY BD21 .... 3 J4
Low Mill Rd OSS WF5 .... 196 E3
Low Mills Rd WOR/ARM LS12 .... 130 D2
Low Moor Crs HOR/CROF WF4 .... 220 B3
Low Moor La HOR/CROF WF4 .... 219 M5
Low Moor Side WOR/ARM LS12 .. 129 M3
Low Moorside Cl
  WOR/ARM LS12 .... 130 A3 🛭
Low Moor Side La
  WOR/ARM LS12 .... 129 L4
Low Moor St LM/WK BD12 .... 126 F8 🛭
Low Moor Ter LUD/ILL HX2 .... 145 M7 🛭
Lowood La BTLY WF17 .... 151 J5
Low Park Rd ILK LS29 .... 39 K1
Low Pasture Cl DOD/DAR S75 .... 260 C2
Low Rd DEWS WF13 .... 173 H6
  EARL WF12 .... 174 A7
  EARL WF12 .... 195 L5
  GLE DN14 .... 161 M8
  HUDS HD4 .... 213 H3
  MID LS10 .... 9 M8
  STKB/PEN S36 .... 271 M5
Lowry Rd EARD/LOFT WF3 .... 153 G6
Lowry Vw KGHY BD21 .... 3 H7
Low Shops La RTHW LS26 .... 132 E8
Low's Pl WHIT OL12 .... 206 C4 🛭
Low Spring Rd KGHY BD21 .... 3 M6
Low St DEWS WF13 .... 173 L5 🛭
  DOD/DAR S75 .... 260 D8
  EARD/LOFT WF3 .... 153 G5
  GFTH/SHER LS25 .... 116 A7
  GFTH/SHER LS25 .... 138 B3
  KGHY BD21 .... 3 G5
  KNOT WF11 .... 159 L7
Lowswater Rd KNOT WF11 .... 182 A4
Lowther Av GFTH/SHER LS25 .... 113 G8
  ROY/SHW OL2 .... 228 E6
Lowther Crs RTHW LS26 .... 134 B4
Lowther Dr GFTH/SHER LS25 .... 113 G8
  RTHW LS26 .... 134 B4
Lowther Rd ROCH OL11 .... 228 A2
Lowther St RHAY LS8 .... 110 B2
Low Town KBTN HD8 .... 238 B1
Lowtown PDSY/CALV LS28 .... 107 H6
Low Wy DOD/DAR S75 .... 260 A7
Low Well Rd WBOW BD5 .... 126 F3 🛭
Low Whitehouse Rw MID LS10.. 9 K6 🛭
Low Wd WIL/AL BD15 .... 102 F2
Low Wood Av AIRE BD20 .... 57 K3 🛭
Low Wood Ri ILK LS29 .... 39 H3 🛭
Loxley Gv WBY LS22 .... 29 M6
Loxley Mt AWLS/ASK DN6.. 227 L6
Loxley Rd BSLYN/ROY S71 .... 262 B3
Loxley St BTLY WF17 .... 151 J7
Lucas Ct CHAL LS7 .... 7 G2
Lucas Gv North RYKW YO26 .... 32 A1
Lucas Gv South RYKW YO26 .... 32 A1
Lucas Pl HDGY LS6 .... 6 D1
Lucas Rd HDGY LS6 .... 6 D1
Luck La HUDW HD3 .... 191 L8
Lucknow St ROCH OL11 .... 228 B1 🛭
Lucy Av MSTN/BAR LS15 .... 111 G6
Lucy Hall Dr BAIL BD17 .... 82 A4
Lucy La KBTN HD8 .... 216 D1
Lucy St HIPP HX3 .... 11 K3
Luddenden La LUD/ILL HX2 .... 144 F7
Ludgate Rd ROCH OL11 .... 228 C4
Ludhill La HUDW HD3 .... 236 F1
Ludlam St WBOW BD5 .... 127 G1
Ludlow Av GFTH/SHER LS25 .... 113 K7

Ludolf Dr AL/HA/HU LS17 .... 89 G2
Ludwell Cl EARL WF12 .... 196 B5 🛭
Ludwood CI HOLM/MEL HD7 .... 236 C1
Lugano Gv WMB/DAR S73 .... 263 G8
Luke La HOLM/MEL HD7 .... 236 E6
Luke Rd WBOW BD5 .... 126 E2
Lulworth Av MSTN/BAR LS15 .... 111 M6
Lulworth Cl BSLY S70 .... 261 K6 🛭
  MSTN/BAR LS15 .... 111 M5 🛭
Lulworth Crs MSTN/BAR LS15 .... 111 M5
Lulworth Garth
  MSTN/BAR LS15 .... 111 M6 🛭
Lulworth Gv BOW BD4 .... 127 M4 🛭
Lulworth Vw MSTN/BAR LS15 .... 111 M5
Lulworth Wk MSTN/BAR LS15 .... 111 M6
Lumb Bottom BIRK/DRI BD11 .... 129 H7
Lumbfoot Rd HWTH BD22 .... 78 A7
Lumb Gill La ILK LS29 .... 19 K8
Lumb La GIR BD8 .... 4 B1
  HIPP HX3 .... 146 D4
  HUDS HD4 .... 214 F6
  HWTH BD22 .... 54 C5
  LUD/ILL HX2 .... 123 H8
  LVSG WF15 .... 172 B4
  RPDN/SBR HX6 .... 166 F7
Lumb Rd HBR HX7 .... 142 F1
Lumbrook Cl HIPP HX3 .... 147 L3 🛭
Lumbutts La TOD OL14 .... 164 D2
Lumbutts Rd TOD OL14 .... 163 M3
Lumby Cl PDSY/CALV LS28 .... 129 H1
Lumby HI GFTH/SHER LS25 .... 138 D7
Lumby La AL/HA/HU LS17 .... 46 C3
  GFTH/SHER LS25 .... 138 C6
  PDSY/CALV LS28 .... 129 H1
Lumby St IDLE BD10 .... 83 K6 🛭
Lumley Av BULY LS4 .... 108 F3 🛭
  CAS WF10 .... 157 J7
Lumley Gv BULY LS4 .... 108 F3
Lumley HI CAS WF10 .... 157 J7
Lumley Mt BULY LS4 .... 108 F3
Lumley Pl BULY LS4 .... 108 F3
Lumley Rd BULY LS4 .... 108 F3
Lumley St BULY LS4 .... 108 F3
  EARL WF12 .... 174 A4
Lumley St BULY LS4 .... 108 F3
  CAS WF10 .... 157 K7
Lumley Ter BULY LS4 .... 108 F3
Lumley Vw BULY LS4 .... 108 F3 🛭
Lumley Wk BULY LS4 .... 108 F3
Lunan Pl RHAY LS8 .... 110 B2 🛭
Lunan Ter RHAY LS8 .... 110 B2 🛭
Lund Av BSLYN/ROY S71 .... 262 B3
Lund Cl BSLYN/ROY S71 .... 262 B3
Lund Crs BSLYN/ROY S71 .... 262 B3
Lund Dr HECK WF16 .... 173 G3
Lund Head La PBR HG3 .... 45 L1
Lund Hill La BSLYN/ROY S71 .... 244 B2
Lund La BSLYN/ROY S71 .... 262 B3
  HWTH BD22 .... 56 D8
Lune St COL BB8 .... 74 A2
Lunnfields La KNOT WF11 .... 159 K2
Lunn La GLE DN14 .... 161 L3
Lunn Rd CUD/GR S72 .... 244 D8
Lupset Crs WKFDW/WTN WF2 .... 198 A3
Lupton Av OSM LS9 .... 110 C6
Lupton St GIR BD8 .... 4 D3
  MID LS10 .... 9 L9
Lustre St KGHY BD21 .... 2 D5
Luther St HUDW HD3 .... 4 B4
Luther Wy ECHL BD2 .... 105 H3 🛭
Luton St HFAX HX1 .... 10 B5
  HUDS HD4 .... 213 H3
  KGHY BD21 .... 2 E5
Lutterworth Dr AWLS/ASK DN6.. 249 J8
Luttrell Cl BHP/TINH LS16 .... 86 C5
Luttrell Crs BHP/TINH LS16 .... 86 C5
Luttrell Gdns BHP/TINH LS16 .... 86 C5
Luttrell Pl BHP/TINH LS16 .... 86 C4
Luttrell Rd BHP/TINH LS16 .... 86 C4
The Lutyens ILK LS29 .... 38 B2
Luxor Av RHAY LS8 .... 110 B2
Luxor Rd RHAY LS8 .... 110 B2
Luxor St RHAY LS8 .... 110 B2
Lyceum Pas MILN OL16 .... 206 B7 🛭
Lydbrook Pk HIPP HX3 .... 168 C4
Lyddon Ter LDSU LS2 .... 6 C5
Lydgate HIPP HX3 .... 147 J3
  KBTN HD8 .... 216 C3
  OSM LS9 .... 110 B5
Lydgate Cl HOLM/MEL HD7 .... 237 G8
  KBTN HD8 .... 216 C3
Lydgate Dr HOLM/MEL HD7 .... 236 F1
  KBTN HD8 .... 216 C3
Lydgate Pk HIPP HX3 .... 148 A7
Lydgate Pl PDSY/CALV LS28 .... 84 C7
  BTLY WF17 .... 174 B1
Lydgate Rd BTLY WF17 .... 174 B1
Lydgate St PDSY/CALV LS28 .... 84 C7
Lydget Ct AIRE BD20 .... 57 J4 🛭
Lydgetts HOLM/MEL HD7 .... 253 M1 🛭
Lydia St LDSU LS2 .... 7 J8
Lyme Cha SCFT LS14 .... 111 M4
Lymington Dr BOW BD4 .... 128 A2
Lynch Av GTHN BD7 .... 126 B3 🛭
Lyncroft ECHL BD2 .... 105 H2
Lynda Gv OSS WF5 .... 197 J2
Lyndale GFTH/SHER LS25 .... 135 J6
Lyndale Crs HECK WF16 .... 173 G2 🛭
Lyndale Dr LIT OL15 .... 185 J8
  SHPY BD18 .... 83 H7 🛭
  WKFDW/WTN WF2 .... 176 A4 🛭
Lyndale Gv NORM WF6 .... 178 E3
Lyndale Ms DEWS WF13 .... 173 H3 🛭
Lynden Av SHPY BD18 .... 83 G6
Lynden Ct WBSY BD6 .... 126 C7
Lyndhurst Av BRIG HD6 .... 170 C2
Lyndhurst Cl MSTN/BAR LS15 .... 90 B7
Lyndhurst Crs MSTN/BAR LS15 .... 90 B7
Lyndhurst Dr AWLS/ASK DN6.. 227 M3
Lyndhurst Gv WIL/AL BD15 .... 103 L5
Lyndhurst Grove Rd BRIG HD6 .... 170 C1
Lyndhurst Rd BRIG HD6 .... 170 C3

HUDW HD3 .... 191 K6 🛭
  MSTN/BAR LS15 .... 90 B8
Lyndhurst Vw MSTN/BAR LS15 .... 90 B8
Lyndon Av BSPA/BRAM LS23 .... 69 L3
  GFTH/SHER LS25 .... 113 G7
Lyndon Cl BSPA/BRAM LS23 .... 69 L3
Lyndon Crs BSPA/BRAM LS23 .... 69 L3 🛭
Lyndon Rd BSPA/BRAM LS23 .... 69 L3
Lyndon Sq BSPA/BRAM LS23 .... 69 L3 🛭
Lyndon Ter BGLY BD16 .... 81 J3 🛭
Lyndon Wy BSPA/BRAM LS23 .... 69 L3
Lyndum Gv GFTH/SHER LS25 .... 135 J4
Lynfield Dr HTON BD9 .... 103 L3
  LVSG WF15 .... 171 K1
Lynfield Mt SHPY BD18 .... 83 G6 🛭
Lynmoor Ct IDLE BD10 .... 83 J7
Lynndale Av AIRE BD20 .... 34 F7
  HUDN HD2 .... 192 B5
Lynnwood Gdns
  PDSY/CALV LS28 .... 106 C3
Lynsey Gdns BOW BD4 .... 127 K7
Lynthorne Rd HTON BD9 .... 104 D2
Lynton Av BSPA/BRAM LS23 .... 48 F5
  EARD/LOFT WF3 .... 154 A4
  HTON BD9 .... 104 A4
  HUD HD1 .... 14 C7
Lynton Dr AIRE BD20 .... 58 B5
  HTON BD9 .... 104 A4
  SHPY BD18 .... 82 C7
Lynton Gv CUD/ILL HX2 .... 124 B5
Lynton Pl DOD/DAR S75 .... 241 M6
Lynton Ter CLECK BD19 .... 149 M6 🛭
Lynton Vls HTON BD9 .... 104 B4
Lynwood Av RTHW LS26 .... 133 M8
  SHPY BD18 .... 83 G6 🛭
  WOR/ARM LS12 .... 130 E2
Lynwood Cl BIRK/DRI BD11 .... 150 D5
  FEA/AMT WF7 .... 201 G2
Lynwood Ct HWTH BD22 .... 79 G7
Lynwood Crs HEM/SK/SE WF9 .... 225 H3
  HFAX HX1 .... 10 A9
  PONT WF8 .... 180 F8
  RTHW LS26 .... 133 M8
  WOR/ARM LS12 .... 130 E2
Lynwood Dr BSLYN/ROY S71 .... 243 L5
Lynwood Garth WOR/ARM LS12.. 130 E2 🛭
Lynwood Ms BOW BD4 .... 128 B4 🛭
Lynwood Mt WOR/ARM LS12 .... 130 E2
Lynwood Ri WOR/ARM LS12 .... 130 E1
Lynwood Vw WOR/ARM LS12 .... 130 E1
Lyon St AIRE BD20 .... 35 H8
  PONT WF8 .... 180 F8
Lyon St CUL/QBY BD13 .... 102 F7 🛭
  CUL/QBY BD13 .... 125 H5 🛭
  ROY/SHW OL2 .... 229 K7
Lytham Av BSLYN/ROY S71 .... 261 M1
Lytham Cl SKP/WHF BD23 .... 16 E3
Lytham Dr CUL/QBY BD13 .... 125 A4
Lytham Gdns SKP/WHF BD23 .... 16 E3
Lytham Gv WOR/ARM LS12 .... 130 C2
Lytham Pl WOR/ARM LS12 .... 130 C2
Lytham St WHIT OL12 .... 206 A3 🛭
Lyttelton Crs STKB/PEN S36 .... 270 F5
Lytton Rd GIR BD8 .... 104 B6
Lytton St MID LS10 .... 9 K9

M

Mabel Royd GTHN BD7 .... 126 B1
Mabel St COL BB8 .... 74 B1
  HBR HX7 .... 144 A5
Mabgate OSM LS9 .... 7 K7
Mabgate Gn OSM LS9 .... 7 K7
Macaulay Rd HUDN HD2 .... 14 C1
Macaulay St HUD HD1 .... 7 L8
Macham St HUD HD1 .... 214 B2 🛭
Mackie Hill Cl HOR/CROF WF4.. 219 M2 🛭
Mackingstone Dr HWTH BD22.. 78 D3 🛭
Mackingstone La HWTH BD22.. 78 D3
Mackinnon Av NORM WF6 .... 178 C3
Maclure Rd ROCH OL11 .... 206 B8 🛭
Macturk Gv GIR BD8 .... 104 D5 🛭
Maddocks St SHPY BD18 .... 82 C6 🛭
Madeley Rd HOR/CROF WF4 .... 222 C6
Madeley Sq CAS WF10 .... 158 E5 🛭
Maden's Sq LIT OL15 .... 207 K1 🛭
Madgin La HUDS HD4 .... 213 J8
Madison Av BOW BD4 .... 128 A5
Madni Cl HFAX HX1 .... 10 E6
Mafeking Av BEE/HOL LS11 .... 131 J5 🛭
Mafeking Gv BEE/HOL LS11 .... 131 J5 🛭
Mafeking Mt BEE/HOL LS11 .... 131 J5 🛭
Magdalene Cl BHP/TINH LS16.. 86 C2 🛭
Magdalene Flds NORM WF6.. 178 F6 🛭
Magdalene Rd
  WKFDW/WTN WF2 .... 197 H3 🛭
Magdalen Rd HOLM/MEL HD7 .... 252 E1
Maggot La STKB/PEN S36 .... 271 M4
Magna Gv WKFDW/WTN WF2.. 198 F5
Magnolia Cl CUD/GR S72 .... 244 F1 🛭
Magnolias BTLY WF17 .... 151 G7
Magpie La MOR LS27 .... 152 D3
Maidstone St BFDE BD3 .... 105 L7
Maidwell Wy WBSY BD6 .... 126 A8
Mail Cl MSTN/BAR LS15 .... 112 A3
Main Av HUDS HD4 .... 213 H3
Main Ga HOLM/MEL HD7 .... 255 G4
Main Rd AIRE BD20 .... 35 L6
  AIRE BD20 .... 56 C1
  AIRE BD20 .... 58 F6
  CUL/QBY BD13 .... 101 M6
Mainspring Rd WIL/AL BD15 .... 102 L3
Main St AIRE BD20 .... 34 B4
  AIRE BD20 .... 34 E1
  AIRE BD20 .... 34 E4
  AIRE BD20 .... 34 E4
  AIRE BD20 .... 55 M1
  AL/HA/HU LS17 .... 66 C1
  AL/HA/HU LS17 .... 67 L1
  AL/HA/HU LS17 .... 89 G2
  AWLS/ASK DN6 .... 205 H3
  AWLS/ASK DN6 .... 248 D5

BAIL BD17 .... 83 L1
BGLY BD16 .... 81 H3
BSPA/BRAM LS23 .... 49 J2
CAS WF10 .... 158 A1
COP/BISH YO23 .... 75 M5
CUD/GR S72 .... 222 F8
EARD/LOFT WF3 .... 153 M7
EARD/LOFT WF3 .... 154 F3
GFTH/SHER LS25 .... 92 A7
GFTH/SHER LS25 .... 113 G2
GFTH/SHER LS25 .... 138 B6
GFTH/SHER LS25 .... 160 A3
GLE DN14 .... 161 J7
GSLY LS20 .... 61 G6
HEM/SK/SE WF9 .... 225 G4
HEM/SK/SE WF9 .... 225 M6
HWTH BD22 .... 77 M8
HWTH BD22 .... 78 E7
ILK LS29 .... 19 J6
ILK LS29 .... 40 A4
ILK LS29 .... 61 H2
LM/WK BD12 .... 127 G8
LM/WK BD12 .... 148 C2
MSTN/BAR LS15 .... 90 B8
OT LS21 .... 42 E7
PBR HG3 .... 26 E2
PONT WF8 .... 204 F8
RTHW LS26 .... 156 F3
SCFT LS14 .... 90 B2
TAD LS24 .... 50 A7
TAD LS24 .... 93 K8
TAD LS24 .... 94 F1
TAD LS24 .... 94 F7
TAD LS24 .... 115 M1
WBY LS22 .... 29 M5
WBY LS22 .... 31 K4
WBY LS22 .... 46 D1
WBY LS22 .... 47 K4
WBY LS22 .... 47 K6
WIL/AL BD15 .... 102 E1
Maister PI HWTH BD22 .... 78 D3
WIL/AL BD15 .... 103 K7
Maitland CI WHIT OL12 .... 206 E3
Maitland St TOD OL14 .... 163 J6
Maizebrook DEWS WF13 .... 173 G6
Maize St HWTH BD22 .... 79 J2
Major St MILN OL16 .... 207 H8
WKFDW/WTN WF2 .... 12 D8
Malais La AIRE BD20 .... 55 J1
Malcolm CI BSLY S70 .... 261 M6
Maldon St ROCH OL11 .... 228 B1
Malham Av BRIG HD6 .... 170 A6
HTON BD9 .... 103 L3
Malham CI CUD/GR S72 .... 244 E3
SCFT LS14 .... 111 J2
Malham Dr BTLY WF17 .... 173 J1
LVSG WF15 .... 172 B5
Malham Rd BRIG HD6 .... 170 A7
WKFDE WF1 .... 13 L1
Malham Sq WKFDE WF1 .... 13 M1
Maliff Rd BRFD/BLYE BB10 .... 96 D4
Malincroft DOD/DAR S75 .... 242 D6
Malin Rd EARL WF12 .... 174 B3
Mallard Av WKFDW/WTN WF2 .... 220 E1
Mallard CI IDLE BD10 .... 105 L1
RTHW LS26 .... 132 B7
Mallard Rd CAS WF10 .... 157 L8
The Mallards BD20 .... 36 A5
Mallard Vw HWTH BD22 .... 100 E4
Mallard Wy HOLM/MEL HD7 .... 212 D6
MOR LS27 .... 152 F2
Mallinson St DEWS WF13 .... 173 J3
Mallory CI GTHN BD7 .... 104 B8
Mallory Wy CUD/GR S72 .... 244 F7
Mallow Cft MILN OL16 .... 228 E2
Malmesbury CI BOW BD4 .... 128 A5
WOR/ARM LS12 .... 108 E8
Malmesbury Gv WOR/ARM LS12 .... 108 E8
Malmesbury PI WOR/ARM LS12 .... 108 E8
Malmesbury St WOR/ARM LS12 .... 108 E8
Malmesbury Ter
WOR/ARM LS12 .... 108 E8
Malsis Rd KGHY BD21 .... 2 D7
Maltby Ct MSTN/BAR LS15 .... 111 M7
Malthouse CI SCFT LS14 .... 67 L6
Malthouse La PBR HG3 .... 26 E3
Malthouse Rd BSLYN/ROY S71 .... 261 H5
Malting CI EARD/LOFT WF3 .... 154 D3
Malting Ri EARD/LOFT WF3 .... 154 D3
Maltings Rd BEE/HOL LS11 .... 9 H8
LUD/ILL HX2 .... 115 M4
The Maltings EARD/LOFT WF3 .... 154 D3
HDGY LS6 .... 109 G4
MIRF WF14 .... 194 B1
PONT WF8 .... 180 F5
Malt Kiln Cft
WKFDW/WTN WF2 .... 199 G5
Maltkiln Dr HOR/CROF WF4 .... 219 H2
Maltkiln La CAS WF10 .... 158 A6
Malt Kiln La CUL/QBY BD13 .... 124 D1
GFTH/SHER LS25 .... 135 K5
Malt Kiln Ter TAD LS24 .... 71 K7
Malton PI BSLYN/ROY S71 .... 243 G7
Malton Rd HEM/SK/SE WF9 .... 225 M6
Malton St HIPP HX3 .... 146 E4
RPDN/SBR HX6 .... 167 K1
Malt St HWTH BD22 .... 79 J2
Malvern Brow HTON BD9 .... 103 M4
Malvern CI CAS WF10 .... 179 H1
DOD/DAR S75 .... 260 D4
MILN OL16 .... 207 J7
ROY/SHW OL2 .... 229 H6
Malvern Crs AIRE BD20 .... 57 M3
Malvern Gv BEE/HOL LS11 .... 8 D8
HTON BD9 .... 103 M5
Malvern Ri BEE/HOL LS11 .... 8 D8
HUDS HD4 .... 214 C3
Malvern Rd BEE/HOL LS11 .... 8 C8
EARL WF12 .... 174 A5
HTON BD9 .... 103 M5
HUDS HD4 .... 214 D2
KNOT WF11 .... 182 A2
Malvern St BEE/HOL LS11 .... 8 C8
Malvern Vw BEE/HOL LS11 .... 8 C8
Manchester Rd HOLM/MEL HD7 .... 232 C6
HUDS HD4 .... 213 M2

HUDW HD3 .... 213 M2
ROCH OL11 .... 206 A8
STKB/PEN S36 .... 269 L5
WBOW BD5 .... 126 F3
WBSY BD6 .... 126 F6
Manchester Rd (Linthwaite)
HOLM/MEL HD7 .... 212 C6
Manchester Rd (Marsden)
HOLM/MEL HD7 .... 233 J2
Manchester Rd (Slaithwaite)
HOLM/MEL HD7 .... 211 M7
Mandale Gv WBSY BD6 .... 125 M6
Mandale Rd WBSY BD6 .... 125 M5
Mandarin Wy RTHW LS26 .... 132 B7
Mandeville Crs WBSY BD6 .... 126 B6
Mangrill La BSPA/BRAM LS23.... 68 F8
SCFT LS14 .... 68 G8
Manitoba PI CHAL LS7 .... 88 A8
Mankinholes Bank TOD OL14 .... 164 B2
Manley Ct GFTH/SHER LS25 .... 135 H1
Manley Dr WBY LS22 .... 29 K8
Manley Ri ILK LS29 .... 38 F3
Manley Rd ILK LS29 .... 38 F3
Manley St BRIG HD6 .... 170 C3
Mannerley Gv CLECK BD19 .... 150 D8
Mannheim Rd HTON BD9 .... 104 C4
Mannville Gv HWTH BD22.... 2 C1
Mannville PI HWTH BD22 .... 2 C1
Mannville Rd KGHY BD21 .... 2 C1
Mannville St HWTH BD22 .... 2 C1
Mannville Ter HWTH BD22 .... 4 D8
Mannville Wy HWTH BD22 .... 2 C7
Manor CI AL/HA/HU LS17 .... 89 H2
KNOT WF11 .... 159 J1
OSS WF5 .... 197 H3
Manor Cha WKFDW YO26 .... 33 H2
Manor CI AWLS/ASK DN6 .... 227 L3
BHP/TINH LS16 .... 63 M3
BIRK/DRI BD11 .... 129 C7
GIR BD8 .... 5 L8
HEM/SK/SE WF9 .... 225 C4
HIPP HX3 .... 168 D2
HOR/CROF WF4 .... 221 H7
OSS WF5 .... 197 H3
PONT WF8 .... 226 F1
RTHW LS26 .... 133 G8
YEA LS19 .... 62 D7
Manor Cottage Ms SCFT LS14 .... 67 L8
Manor Ct AL/HA/HU LS17 .... 89 H2
KNOT WF11 .... 159 J1
OSS WF5 .... 197 H3
Manor Crs CUD/GR S72 .... 245 H6
OT LS21 .... 42 E7
RTHW LS26 .... 154 F1
WKFDW/WTN WF2 .... 198 A2
WKFDW/WTN WF2 .... 199 J6
Manor Cft CUD/GR S72 .... 244 F1
HBR HX7 .... 143 K3
MSTN/BAR LS15 .... 111 J7
Manorcroft NORM WF6 .... 178 D4
Manor Dr BGLY BD16 .... 81 J7
CUD/GR S72 .... 222 E8
FEA/AMT WF7 .... 179 L5
HBR HX7 .... 143 K3
HDGY LS6 .... 109 G3
HIPP HX3 .... 168 D2
HOR/CROF WF4 .... 200 C7
HOR/CROF WF4 .... 217 M3
KBTN HD8 .... 239 J4
MIRF WF14 .... 171 M7
OSS WF5 .... 197 H3
Manor Farm CI AWLS/ASK DN6 .... 249 K8
BGLY BD16 .... 81 K8
BSLYN/ROY S71 .... 243 M6
MID LS10 .... 131 M8
Manor Farm Crs MOR LS27 .... 130 E6
Manor Farm Dr BTLY WF17 .... 152 B8
MID LS10 .... 131 L8
MOR LS27 .... 130 E6
Manor Farm Gdns MID LS10 .... 131 L8
Manor Farm Gn MID LS10 .... 131 L8
Manor Farm Gv MID LS10.... 131 L8
Manor Farm Ri MID LS10.... 131 M8
Manor Farm Rd
HOR/CROF WF4 .... 220 A2
MID LS10 .... 131 L8
Manor Farm Wy MID LS10 .... 153 L1
Manorfield Dr HOR/CROF WF4 .... 197 J4
Manorfields CI HOR/CROF WF4 .... 200 C6
Manorfields Ct HOR/CROF WF4 .... 200 C6
Manor Fold BGLY BD16 .... 81 K8
Manor Gdns BSLYN/ROY S71 .... 262 C6
CUL/QBY BD13.... 101 M1
EARL WF12 .... 174 C4
OT LS21 .... 42 E7
SCFT LS14 .... 68 C8
Manor Garth GFTH/SHER LS25 .... 136 F6
MSTN/BAR LS15 .... 111 J7
PBR HG3 .... 28 E3
WKFDW/WTN WF2 .... 199 J6
Manor Garth Rd EARL WF12 .... 174 B7
GFTH/SHER LS25 .... 135 K4
Manor Gra KBTN HD8 .... 237 M6
Manor Gv AIRE BD20 .... 58 C6
BSLYN/ROY S71 .... 243 K5
CAS WF10 .... 158 A8
CHAL LS7 .... 87 M8
CUD/GR S72 .... 245 H6
HEM/SK/SE WF9 .... 197 H3
OSS WF5 .... 197 H3
Manor Haigh Rd
WKFDW/WTN WF2 .... 198 A3
Manor Heath Rd HIPP HX3 .... 168 B3
Manor House Cft BHP/TINH LS16 .... 86 F3
Manor House La AL/HA/HU LS17 .... 88 F1
Manor House Rd WIL/AL BD15 .... 80 E8
Manor La OSS WF5 .... 197 H3
SHPY BD18 .... 82 D7
STKB/PEN S36 .... 271 L5
TAD LS24 .... 50 A8
Manorley La WBSY BD6 .... 126 A4
Manor Mill La BEE/HOL LS11 .... 131 G5
Manor Occupation Rd
BSLYN/ROY S71 .... 243 K2
Manor Pk CAS WF10 .... 136 A8
DOD/DAR S75 .... 259 H7
EARL WF12 .... 174 D3

GIR BD8 .... 103 M6
HWTH BD22 .... 54 E3
HWTH BD22 .... 78 E4
MIRF WF14 .... 171 L7
PONT WF8 .... 203 M1
SCFT LS14 .... 67 L7
Manor Park Av CAS WF10 .... 157 K1
PONT WF8 .... 181 H3
Manor Park Gdns CLECK BD19 .... 150 C3
Manor Park Wy KBTN HD8 .... 215 M4
Manor Ri HUD HD1 .... 214 D2
ILK LS29 .... 38 F2
KBTN HD8 .... 239 J3
WKFDW/WTN WF2 .... 199 J6
Manor Rd AIRE BD20 .... 57 J4
BEE/HOL LS11 .... 8 E4
BGLY BD16 .... 81 K7
BTLY WF17 .... 174 B1
COL BB8 .... 52 A7
DEWS WF13 .... 173 K7
GLE DN14 .... 161 H7
HOLM/MEL HD7 .... 212 F2
HOR/CROF WF4 .... 197 J5
HORS LS18 .... 85 J6
HUDS HD4 .... 215 H8
KBTN HD8 .... 240 C2
MOR LS27 .... 130 E6
OSS WF5 .... 197 J2
ROY/SHW OL2 .... 229 J1
RTHW LS26 .... 132 F8
TAD LS24 .... 71 L6
TAD LS24 .... 71 M2
WKFDW/WTN WF2 .... 198 A1
WKFDW/WTN WF2 .... 199 J7
Manor Rw BFD BD1 .... 4 E4
Manor Sq YEA LS19 .... 62 D7
Manorstead KBTN HD8 .... 239 J5
Manor St BSLYN/ROY S71 .... 243 M5
CHAL LS7 .... 7 K5
CLECK BD19 .... 149 H8
EARL WF12 .... 173 L8
ECHL BD2 .... 105 K3
HUDS HD4 .... 214 D2
OT LS21 .... 41 M8
Manor Ter ECHL BD2 .... 105 K3
HDGY LS6 .... 109 G2
Manor Vw CAS WF10 .... 180 A1
CUD/GR S72 .... 244 E4
HDGY LS6 .... 109 G2
PDSY/CALV LS28 .... 107 G7
Manor Wy AIRE BD20 .... 55 J2
BTLY WF17 .... 173 J2
Manscombe Rd WIL/AL BD15 .... 103 L5
Manse Crs ILK LS29 .... 40 A5
Manse Dr HUDS HD4 .... 213 J3
Mansel Ms BOW BD4 .... 128 A5
Manse Rd ILK LS29 .... 40 A5
Manse St BFDE BD3 .... 105 L7
Manse Wy AIRE BD20 .... 34 E8
Mansfield Av BGLY BD16 .... 81 L1
Mansfield Crs AWLS/ASK DN6 .... 249 K4
Mansfield Rd BSLYN/ROY S71 .... 243 H6
GIR BD8 .... 104 E4
ILK LS29 .... 39 M5
Mansion Gdns HUDS HD4 .... 214 B5
Mansion La HIPP HX3 .... 168 E2
RHAY LS8 .... 88 B3
Manston Ap MSTN/BAR LS15 .... 111 J3
Manston Av MSTN/BAR LS15 .... 111 J3
Manston Crs MSTN/BAR LS15 .... 111 J3
Manston Dr MSTN/BAR LS15 .... 111 J3
Manston Gdns MSTN/BAR LS15 .... 111 J3
Manston La MSTN/BAR LS15 .... 112 A4
Manston Ri MSTN/BAR LS15 .... 111 J3
Manston Wy MSTN/BAR LS15 .... 111 J3
Mantley La ROY/SHW OL2 .... 230 J2
Manygates Av WKFDE WF1 .... 13 H9
Manygates Crs WKFDE WF1 .... 13 H9
Manygates La
WKFDW/WTN WF2 .... 198 F4
Manygates Pk WKFDE WF1 .... 13 H8
Manywells Brow
CUL/QBY BD13.... 101 L2
Manywells Crs CUL/QBY BD13 .... 101 M1
Manywells La CUL/QBY BD13 .... 101 K1
Maple Av BFDE BD3 .... 106 A6
HOLM/MEL HD7 .... 213 H1
HWTH BD22 .... 78 F4
PONT WF8 .... 202 E1
Maple CI BSLY S70 .... 261 K7
CAS WF10 .... 179 K1
GFTH/SHER LS25 .... 138 A3
HUDE HD5 .... 193 J5
ROY/SHW OL2 .... 229 H6
Maple Ct OSS WF5 .... 197 G3
Maple Cft AL/HA/HU LS17 .... 88 A3
WOR/ARM LS12 .... 129 M1
Maple Dr PONT WF8 .... 180 E8
WBY LS22 .... 30 A7
WOR/ARM LS12 .... 129 M1
Maple Fold WOR/ARM LS12 .... 129 M1
Maple Gdns AL/HA/HU LS17 .... 68 A1
Maple Gv CLECK BD19 .... 150 C5
HUDN HD2 .... 192 C5
KGHY BD21 .... 2 C1
PONT WF8 .... 202 E1
WOR/ARM LS12 .... 129 M1
Maple Ri RTHW LS26 .... 155 H2
Maple Rd DOD/DAR S75 .... 242 C5
EARL WF12 .... 174 C2
Maple St HFAX HX1 .... 10 B9
HUD HD1 .... 15 J9
TOD OL14 .... 163 J7
WKFDW/WTN WF2 .... 176 B6
Maple Ter YEA LS19 .... 62 C7
Maple Wk SCFT LS14 .... 89 L6
Maple Wy EARL WF12 .... 174 D7
Maplin Av HUDW HD3 .... 191 H5
Mapplewell Crs OSS WF5 .... 197 G1
Mapplewell Dr OSS WF5 .... 197 G1
Mapbridge Ct WBSY BD6 .... 126 D4
Marchant St CAS WF10 .... 157 L6
Marchbank Rd BFDE BD3.... 5 L6
March Cote La BGLY BD16 .... 81 J8

March St MILN OL16 .... 206 C7
NORM WF6 .... 178 C5
Marchwood Gv CLAY BD14 .... 125 M1
Marcroft PI ROCH OL11 .... 228 C2
Marcus Wy HUDW HD3 .... 190 F5
Mardale Av ROY/SHW OL2 .... 228 B6
Mardale Crs SCFT LS14 .... 111 J3
Mardale Rd EARL WF12 .... 174 A4
Margaret Av AL/HA/HU LS17 .... 67 M2
MILN OL16 .... 206 E7
Margaret CI MOR LS27 .... 130 E8
Margaret St HFAX HX1 .... 10 E6
KGHY BD21 .... 2 F7
ROY/SHW OL2 .... 229 K8
WKFDE WF1 .... 176 C2
WKFDE WF1 .... 176 D7
Margate RTHW LS26 .... 133 L8
Margate Rd BOW BD4 .... 127 J2
Margate St CUD/GR S72 .... 245 J7
RPDN/SBR HX6 .... 167 J3
Margerison Crs ILK LS29 .... 39 G3
Margerison Rd ILK LS29 .... 39 G3
Margetson Rd BIRK/DRI BD11 .... 151 H1
Margroy CI WHIT OL12 .... 206 C4
Marian Gv BEE/HOL LS11 .... 131 K3
Marian Rd HDGY LS6 .... 6 C2
Marian Ter HDGY LS6 .... 6 C2
Maria St ILK LS29 .... 40 A4
Marie CI HUDE HD5 .... 193 L8
Marigold St ROCH OL11 .... 228 B1
Marina Crs MOR LS27 .... 152 B3
Marina Ter HOLM/MEL HD7 .... 213 G1
Marine Villa Rd KNOT WF11 .... 182 B2
Marion Av WKFDW/WTN WF2 .... 175 M6
Marion CI HEM/SK/SE WF9 .... 246 C4
Marion Dr SHPY BD18 .... 82 E7
Marion Gv WKFDW/WTN WF2 .... 175 M6
Marion St BGLY BD16 .... 81 J3
BRIG HD6 .... 170 C2
GTHN BD7 .... 4 A5
Marizon Gv WKFDE WF1 .... 176 E7
Mark Bottoms La
HOLM/MEL HD7 .... 236 B8
Mark CI IDLE BD10 .... 83 L6
Markenfield Dr ROY/SHW OL2 .... 229 H7
Market CI BSLYN/ROY S71 .... 261 J5
Market Ct CUL/QBY BD13 .... 103 G8
Market HI SHPY S70 .... 261 G5
Market PI CLECK BD19 .... 150 A7
COL BB8 .... 74 A1
CUD/GR S72 .... 244 A7
HOLM/MEL HD7 .... 212 B6
HUD HD1 .... 14 F7
KGHY BD21 .... 3 G5
NORM WF6 .... 178 C4
OT LS21 .... 41 M7
PDSY/CALV LS28 .... 107 G7
PONT WF8 .... 180 F6
WBY LS22 .... 48 A1
Market Sq SHPY BD18 .... 82 D6
Market St AIRE BD20 .... 56 E1
BFD BD1 .... 4 F6
BGLY BD16 .... 81 H3
BRIG HD6 .... 170 D4
BSLY S70 .... 261 G5
BTLY WF17 .... 151 G5
CLECK BD19 .... 150 A7
COL BB8 .... 74 A1
CUD/GR S72 .... 244 A7
CUL/QBY BD13 .... 102 F8
DEWS WF13 .... 173 M6
FEA/AMT WF7 .... 179 L8
HBR HX7 .... 143 H3
HECK WF16 .... 172 F3
HEM/SK/SE WF9 .... 223 M7
HFAX HX1 .... 11 H6
HOLM/MEL HD7 .... 254 C1
HUD HD1 .... 14 A9
HUDW HD3 .... 213 K1
KGHY BD21 .... 3 G6
NORM WF6 .... 178 C4
OT LS21 .... 41 J7
ROY/SHW OL2 .... 229 K8
SHPY BD18 .... 82 D7
STKB/PEN S36 .... 270 F3
WBSY BD6 .... 126 E5
WKFDE WF1 .... 12 D7
Market Wk HOLM/MEL HD7 .... 233 H2
Markfield Av LM/WK BD12 .... 148 E1
Markfield CI LM/WK BD12 .... 148 E1
Markfield Crs LM/WK BD12 .... 148 E1
Markfield Dr LM/WK BD12 .... 148 E1
Markham Av YEA LS19 .... 84 E1
Markham Cft YEA LS19 .... 84 E1
Markham St WKFDW/WTN WF2 .... 12 B8
Markington PI MID LS10 .... 153 L3
Mark La LDSU LS2 .... 7 G8
ROY/SHW OL2 .... 229 M8
TOD OL14 .... 141 H7
WBY LS22 .... 30 A5
Mark St BSLY S70 .... 261 G5
HUD HD1 .... 14 A9
LVSG WF15 .... 172 D2
WBOW BD5 .... 127 G3
WHIT OL12 .... 206 D5
WKFDE WF1 .... 12 F6
Marland Rd KGHY BD21 .... 3 M3
Marlbeck CI HOLM/MEL HD7 .... 236 B3
Marlborough Av HIPP HX3 .... 168 D2
KNOT WF11 .... 159 M7
TAD LS24 .... 71 K4
Marlborough Cft
HEM/SK/SE WF9 .... 247 H2
Marlborough Dr TAD LS24 .... 71 K4
Marlborough Gdns
DEWS WF13 .... 173 K4
LDSU LS2 .... 6 E5
Marlborough Rd GIR BD8 .... 4 B1
HUDN HD2 .... 192 D1
SHPY BD18 .... 82 C7
Marlborough Sq ILK LS29 .... 38 F3
Marlborough St KGHY BD21 .... 3 J3
LDS LS1 .... 6 C9

OSS WF5 .... 196 E1
WKFDW/WTN WF2 .... 12 B3
Marlborough Ter HBR HX7 .... 143 J5
Marldon Rd HIPP HX3 .... 147 J5
Marley Ct AIRE BD20 .... 58 F7
Marley CI GIR BD8 .... 104 A6
Marley Gv BEE/HOL LS11 .... 131 H3
Marley La CUL/QBY BD13 .... 125 G3
Marley PI BEE/HOL LS11 .... 131 H3
Marley Rd KGHY BD21 .... 58 B6
Marley St BEE/HOL LS11 .... 131 H3
BFDE BD3 .... 5 J6
KGHY BD21 .... 2 F7
Marley Ter BEE/HOL LS11 .... 131 H3
Marley Vw AIRE BD20 .... 58 F7
BEE/HOL LS11 .... 131 H3
Marlfield Rd ROY/SHW OL2 .... 229 G6
Marling Rd HUDW HD3 .... 191 K3
Marlo Rd EARL WF12 .... 174 C4
Marlott Rd SHPY BD18 .... 82 F6
Marlow CI HUDE HD5 .... 193 H6
Marlowe CI PDSY/CALV LS28 .... 129 H1
Marlowe Ct GFTH/SHER LS25 .... 113 H7
Marlow St KGHY BD21 .... 3 M3
Marl Pit HI PONT WF8 .... 180 C8
Marmion Av GIR BD8 .... 103 L7
Marne Av CLAY BD14 .... 125 L3
Marne Crs IDLE BD10 .... 83 K7
Marquis Av LM/WK BD12 .... 149 K1
Marriner Rd KGHY BD21 .... 3 G7
Marriner's Dr HTON BD9 .... 104 D3
Marriott Gv WKFDW/WTN WF2 .... 199 H6
Marsala Wk WMB/DAR S73 .... 263 H8
Marsden Av BEE/HOL LS11 .... 131 J4
Marsden Cl MILN OL16 .... 228 E6
Marsden Ga GTL/HWG HX4 .... 190 A6
Marsden Gv BEE/HOL LS11 .... 131 J4
Marsden La HOLM/MEL HD7 .... 233 J1
Marsden Mt BEE/HOL LS11 .... 131 J4
Marsden PI BEE/HOL LS11 .... 131 J4
Marsden St KBTN HD8 .... 239 J3
Marsden Vw BEE/HOL LS11 .... 131 J4
Marsett Wy SCFT LS14 .... 89 K6
Marsh HOLM/MEL HD7 .... 236 D2
PDSY/CALV LS28 .... 106 E7
Marshall Av HOR/CROF WF4 .... 220 B3
MSTN/BAR LS15 .... 111 M4
Marshall Crs MOR LS27 .... 152 C4
Marshall Dr HEM/SK/SE WF9 .... 247 G3
Marshall Mill Ct KBTN HD8 .... 239 M6
Marshall St BEE/HOL LS11 .... 8 E4
EARD/LOFT WF3 .... 177 H1
KGHY BD21 .... 57 K5
MILN OL16 .... 206 E7
MIRF WF14 .... 194 C3
MOR LS27 .... 152 C2
MSTN/BAR LS15 .... 111 L4
YEA LS19 .... 62 D7
Marshall Ter MSTN/BAR LS15 .... 111 L4
Marsham Gv HUDW HD3 .... 191 L7
Marsh Ct PDSY/CALV LS28 .... 106 E7
Marsh Cft KNOT WF11 .... 159 L7
Marsh Delves La HIPP HX3 .... 147 H7
Marsh End KNOT WF11 .... 182 C1
Marshfield PI WBOW BD5 .... 126 F3
Marsh Gdns HOLM/MEL HD7 .... 236 B2
Marsh Gv WBOW BD5 .... 126 F3
Marsh Grove Rd HUDW HD3.... 191 M7
Marsh Hall La HUDS HD4 .... 237 H3
Marsh La BIRK/DRI BD11 .... 150 C2
COP/BISH YO23 .... 73 J8
GLE DN14 .... 161 J7
HBR HX7 .... 142 C3
HIPP HX3 .... 147 H8
HWTH BD22 .... 100 E3
KBTN HD8 .... 237 L8
KNOT WF11 .... 160 B8
OSM LS9 .... 9 K1
Marsh Platt La HOLM/MEL HD7 .... 236 C2
Marsh Rd CAS WF10 .... 179 J1
HOLM/MEL HD7 .... 254 F3
Marsh St CLECK BD19 .... 150 A8
HDGY LS6 .... 6 D2
RTHW LS26 .... 155 G2
WBOW BD5 .... 126 F4
Marsh Ter PDSY/CALV LS28 .... 106 E7
Marsh V HDGY LS6 .... 6 D2
Marshway HFAX HX1 .... 10 D4
Marsh Wy WKFDE WF1 .... 12 F1
Marsland Av WKFDE WF1 .... 13 H3
Marsland Ct CLECK BD19 .... 149 M4
Marsland PI BFDE BD3 .... 105 M7
WKFDE WF1 .... 13 H3
Marsland St WKFDE WF1 .... 13 H3
Marsland Ter WKFDE WF1 .... 13 H2
Marston CI MOR LS27 .... 152 C3
Marston CI CUL/QBY BD13 .... 125 H5
Marston Ct CAS WF10 .... 157 J4
Marston Crs BSLYN/ROY S71 .... 243 H8
Marston Rd RYKW YO26 .... 32 F1
Marston Wk NORM WF6 .... 178 A2
Marston Wy WBY LS22 .... 29 L8
Marten Dr HUDS HD4 .... 213 M7
Marten Gv HUDS HD4 .... 213 M7
Marten Rd WBOW BD5 .... 126 E3
Martha's Ter MILN OL16 .... 206 E3
Martin Bank Wd HUDE HD5.... 15 J3
Martin Ct MOR LS27 .... 152 E2
Martin Ct MSTN/BAR LS15 .... 111 M6
Martin Dr DOD/DAR S75 .... 259 H6
Martindale Dr BRAM LS13 .... 108 A5
Martindale Dr AWLS/ASK DN6 .... 249 L6
Martin Frobisher Dr
NORM WF6 .... 178 B3
Martingale Dr EARD/LOFT WF3 .... 153 L3
Martin Green La GTL/HWG HX4 .... 168 C7
Martin Gv WKFDW/WTN WF2 .... 199 G3
Martin's Rd BSLYN/ROY S71 .... 262 A3
Martin St BRIG HD6 .... 170 D3
BTLY WF17 .... 151 C5
NORM WF6 .... 178 C4
Martin Ter BULY LS4 .... 108 E4
Martlett Dr WBOW BD5 .... 127 H4
Marton Av HEM/SK/SE WF9 .... 247 G3
Marton Ct BFDE BD3 .... 105 M7
Marwood Rd WOR/ARM LS12 .... 107 M7

Mary Ann Cl BSLYN/ROY S71 ...... 261 M4
Maryfield Av MSTN/BAR LS15 .... 111 J4
Maryfield Cl MSTN/BAR LS15 .... 111 J4
Maryfield Cl MSTN/BAR LS15 ... 111 K4 1
Maryfield Gdns
  MSTN/BAR LS15 .... 111 J4 2
Maryfield Gn MSTN/BAR LS15 .... 111 J4 3
Maryfield Ms MSTN/BAR LS15 ... 111 J4 4
Maryfield Wlk MSTN/BAR LS15 .... 111 J4
Marygate WKFDE WF1 ...... 12 E2
Mary's Pl PDSY/CALV S25 .... 260 D4 7
Mary St AIRE BD20 ...... 35 C5
  BOW BD4 ...... 127 L1
  BRIG HD6 ...... 170 C2
  CUL/QBY BD13 ...... 102 A5 3
  CUL/QBY BD13 ...... 102 F8 13
  DOD/DAR S75 ...... 259 M2
  EARD/LOFT WF3 ...... 154 A6
  HWTH BD22 ...... 100 E4
  LM/WK BD12 ...... 148 E2 13
  MILN OL16 ...... 206 F2
  PDSY/CALV LS28 ...... 107 G2
  SHPY BD18 ...... 82 B6 17
Maryville Av BRIG HD6 ...... 170 B1
Masefield Av HTON BD9 ...... 103 L3
Masefield St GSLY LS20 ...... 62 B6
Masham Gv WOR/ARM LS12 .... 108 F7
Masham Pl HTON BD9 ...... 104 B4 4
Masham St WOR/ARM LS12 ...... 108 F7
Masonic St HFAX HX1 ...... 146 A8
Mason St HBR HX7 ...... 143 J3
  MILN OL16 ...... 206 D7 14
Masons Wy BSLY S70 ...... 261 L8
Maspin Moor Rd
  GFTH/SHER LS25 ...... 139 H8
Master La LUD/ILL HX2 ...... 168 D3
Matherville KBTN HD8 ...... 239 L5
Matlock Rd BSLYN/ROY S71 .... 243 K8
Matlock St HIPP HX3 ...... 10 C1
  HUDS HD4 ...... 213 L2 1
Matterdale Av EARL WF12 ...... 174 A4 3
Matterdale Rd EARL WF12 ...... 174 A4 5
Matthew Cl AIRE BD20 ...... 58 A5 7
  COL BB8 ...... 74 A2
Matthew Gv HOLM/MEL HD7 .... 234 E4
Matthew La AIRE BD20 ...... 34 E1
  HOLM/MEL HD7 ...... 234 D6
  TOD OL14 ...... 142 A7
Matty Marsden La OSS WF5 .... 197 G3
Maud Av BEE/HOL LS11 ...... 131 J4
Maude Av BAIL BD17 ...... 82 E4
Maude Crs RPDN/SBR HX6 .... 167 G3
Maude St GTL/HWG HX4 ...... 168 F7
  HIPP HX3 ...... 146 C2 3
  LDSU LS2 ...... 9 J2
Maud La OT LS21 ...... 23 J2
Maud Pl BEE/HOL LS11 ...... 131 K3
Maudsley St BFDE BD3 ...... 5 K6
Maud St BFDE BD3 ...... 5 L7
  WHIT OL12 ...... 206 C4
Maufe Wy ILK LS29 ...... 38 D3
Maureen St WHIT OL12 ...... 206 C4 8
Maurice Av BRIG HD6 ...... 170 B2
Mavis Av BHP/TINH LS16 ...... 64 A8
  DEWS WF13 ...... 173 J8
Mavis Gv BHP/TINH LS16 ...... 86 A1
  MILN OL16 ...... 207 J8
Mavis La BHP/TINH LS16 ...... 64 A8
Mavis Rd DEWS WF13 ...... 173 H5 3
Mavis St BFDE BD3 ...... 5 L5
  DEWS WF13 ...... 173 J8 2
Mawcroft Cl YEA LS19 ...... 84 C1
Mawcroft Grange Dr YEA LS19 ... 84 C1
Mawfield Rd DOD/DAR S75 .... 260 D2
Mawson St SHPY BD18 ...... 82 B6 13
Maw St BOW BD4 ...... 127 H1
Maxwell Av DEWS WF13 ...... 173 G8 4
Maxwell Rd ILK LS29 ...... 38 F3
  WBSY BD6 ...... 126 B6
Maxwell St FEA/AMT WF7 ...... 201 L1
May Av CUL/QBY BD13 ...... 103 C8
Mayberry Dr DOD/DAR S75 .... 259 H5
Maybury Rd HOR/CROF WF4 .... 198 C6
May Bush Rd WKFDE WF1 ...... 13 K9
May Day St BSLY S70 ...... 261 H5 17
Mayfair WBOW BD5 ...... 126 F2 13
Mayfair Av BRIG HD6 ...... 190 B4
Mayfair Pl HEM/SK/SE WF9 .... 223 M7
Mayfair Wy HEM/SK/SE WF9 ... 127 M1 3
Mayfield BSLYN/ROY S71 ...... 261 K2
  STKB/PEN S36 ...... 271 K5
Mayfield Av BRIG HD6 ...... 148 D6
  HFAX HX1 ...... 10 C8
  HUDE HD5 ...... 193 H8
  ILK LS29 ...... 38 F2
  LM/WK BD12 ...... 148 E3
Mayfield Cl AIRE BD20 ...... 34 E8 4
  ILK LS29 ...... 38 F2 1
Mayfield Ct OSS WF5 ...... 197 G3
Mayfield Crs BSLY S70 ...... 261 C8 11
Mayfield Dr AIRE BD20 ...... 58 E6
  HFAX HX1 ...... 10 C8
Mayfield Gdns HFAX HX1 ...... 10 C8
  OSS WF5 ...... 174 E6
Mayfield Gv BAIL BD17 ...... 82 F7
  BRIG HD6 ...... 148 D6
  HFAX HX1 ...... 10 C8
  HUDE HD5 ...... 193 H8
  WIL/AL BD15 ...... 80 D8
Mayfield Mt HFAX HX1 ...... 10 C8 8
Mayfield Pl LM/WK BD12 ...... 148 E3
Mayfield Rd HOR/CROF WF4 .... 222 C5
  LM/WK BD12 ...... 148 F3
Mayfield St HFAX HX1 ...... 143 J2 7
  ILK LS29 ...... 38 E2
  KGHY BD21 ...... 3 H4
  MSTN/BAR LS15 ...... 111 K6 8
Mayfield Ter CLAY BD14 ...... 125 L2
  LM/WK BD12 ...... 148 F3 2
Mayfield Vw LM/WK BD12 ...... 148 E3
Mayfields Wy HEM/SK/SE WF9 ... 246 D5
Maylea Dr OT LS21 ...... 40 F8
Mayman Cl BTLY WF17 ...... 173 K1 3
Mayman La BTLY WF17 ...... 173 K1
Maynes Cl EARL WF12 ...... 195 M4 1

Mayo Av WBOW BD5 ...... 126 F4
Mayo Crs WBOW BD5 ...... 127 C5
Mayo Dr WBOW BD5 ...... 127 C5
Mayo Gv WBOW BD5 ...... 127 C5
Mayo Rd WBOW BD5 ...... 127 C5
Mayors Wk CAS WF10 ...... 159 G7
  PONT WF8 ...... 180 F7
Mayor's Walk Av PONT WF8 ... 180 F7 2
Maypole Rd HUDN HD2 ...... 192 B5
Mayster Gv BRIG HD6 ...... 170 A7
Mayster Rd BRIG HD6 ...... 170 A7
May St CLECK BD19 ...... 149 M6 13
  HUDS HD4 ...... 213 M2
  HWTH BD22 ...... 78 F8 5
  KGHY BD21 ...... 3 J7
May Ter BSLY S70 ...... 260 E5
  OSM LS9 ...... 110 B8 27
Maythorne Av BTLY WF17 ...... 173 J3
Maythorne Cl DOD/DAR S75 .... 242 F6
Maythorne Crs CLAY BD14 ...... 125 M2
Maythorne Dr CLAY BD14 ...... 126 A2 8
May Tree Cl CLAY BD14 ...... 125 M1
Mayville Av AIRE BD20 ...... 58 D6
  HDGY LS6 ...... 109 G3
Mayville Pl HDGY LS6 ...... 109 G3
Mayville Rd HDGY LS6 ...... 109 G3
Mayville St HDGY LS6 ...... 108 F3
Mayville Ter HDGY LS6 ...... 109 G3
Mazebrook Av CLECK BD19 .... 150 A4
Mazebrook Crs CLECK BD19 .... 150 A4
Mcbride Wy WBY LS22 ...... 48 B1
Mclaren Av HEM/SK/SE WF9 ... 225 M6
Mclaren Flds BRAM LS13 ...... 107 M4 8
Mclintock Wy BSLY S70 ...... 260 F5 5
Mcmahon Dr CUL/QBY BD13 .... 125 L4
Mc Naught St MILN OL16 ...... 206 D8 3
Mead Cl MSTN/BAR LS15 ...... 112 A8
Mead Gv MSTN/BAR LS15 ...... 112 A8
Mead Rd MSTN/BAR LS15 ...... 112 A8
Meadow Bank DEWS WF13 .... 173 H6
  FEA/AMT WF7 ...... 202 C5
  HOLM/MEL HD7 ...... 236 D6
  HOR/CROF WF4 ...... 222 E5
Meadowbank Av WIL/AL BD15 ... 103 K5
Meadow Banks Rd MIRF WF14 ... 194 A1
Meadow Bottom Rd TOD OL14 ... 141 M8
Meadow Brook Cl NORM WF6 ... 178 E5
Meadow Cl AIRE BD20 ...... 34 C4
  AL/HA/HU LS17 ...... 67 M1
  BGLY BD16 ...... 80 D5
  BSPA/BRAM LS23 ...... 48 E6 2
  BTLY WF17 ...... 151 J5 2
  HIPP HX3 ...... 146 C5 5
  LVSG WF15 ...... 172 B5
  WKFDE WF1 ...... 176 F1
Meadow Ct BRIG HD6 ...... 171 G4 4
  BSLYN/ROY S71 ...... 243 M3
  CAS WF10 ...... 158 F4
  HEM/SK/SE WF9 ...... 247 K3
  OSS WF5 ...... 174 E7 2
  WIL/AL BD15 ...... 103 J2
Meadow Crs BSLYN/ROY S71 ... 243 M3
  CUD/GR S72 ...... 245 J7 1
  HIPP HX3 ...... 146 A4 2
Meadow Cft AIRE BD20 ...... 34 B3
  AL/HA/HU LS17 ...... 67 L1
  BEE/HOL LS11 ...... 8 E5
  CUD/GR S72 ...... 244 E3
  HEM/SK/SE WF9 ...... 245 M1
Meadowcroft HOLM/MEL HD7 ... 236 D4
Meadow Cft HUDN HD2 ...... 193 H1
  HWTH BD22 ...... 57 G8
Meadowcroft ILK LS29 ...... 61 H3
Meadow Croft LDS HD10 ...... 83 H6
Meadowcroft Cl WKFDE WF1 ... 176 F1
Meadowcroft Ct WKFDE WF1 ... 176 F1 8
Meadowcroft Crs CAS WF10 ... 158 C4
Meadowcroft La
  RPDN/SBR HX6 ...... 189 G1
Meadowcroft Ms CAS WF10 ... 158 C4
  OSM LS9 ...... 9 M2 1
Meadowcroft Ri BOW BD4 ...... 127 L6
Meadowcroft Rd WKFDE WF1 ... 176 F1
Meadow Dr BSLYN/ROY S71 ... 261 M2
  HIPP HX3 ...... 146 A4
  LVSG WF15 ...... 172 A4
Meadow End BHP/TINH LS16 ... 64 A4
Meadowfield MILN OL16 ...... 228 D3
Meadowfield Cl
  HEM/SK/SE WF9 ...... 223 J3 3
Meadowfield Ri
  ARD/LOFT WF3 ...... 155 K8 2
Meadowfields Cl
  HOR/CROF WF4 ...... 200 C6 1
Meadowfields Dr
  HOR/CROF WF4 ...... 200 C6
Meadow Garth BHP/TINH LS16 ... 64 B4
  TAD LS24 ...... 72 A1
  WKFDE WF1 ...... 176 E1 3
Meadowgate Cft
  EARD/LOFT WF3 ...... 154 D4 1
Meadowgate Dr
  EARD/LOFT WF3 ...... 154 D5
Meadowgate V
  EARD/LOFT WF3 ...... 154 D5
Meadowhurst Gdns
  PDSY/CALV LS28 ...... 106 F7 1
Meadowland Ri CUD/GR S72 ... 262 E1 2
Meadowlands CLECK BD19 ...... 149 G5
Meadow La AIRE BD20 ...... 34 B3
  BEE/HOL LS11 ...... 9 G3
  DEWS WF13 ...... 173 L5
  DOD/DAR S75 ...... 242 A7
  HIPP HX3 ...... 146 A4
  HOLM/MEL HD7 ...... 212 B5
  LVSG WF15 ...... 172 B5
  ROY/SHW OL2 ...... 9 J8
  WKFDW/WTN WF2 ...... 176 B7
Meadow Lea PUDE HD5 ...... 193 K4
Meadow Park Crs
  PDSY/CALV LS28 ...... 106 D4
Meadow Park Dr
  PDSY/CALV LS28 ...... 106 D4
Meadow Ri HEM/SK/SE WF9 ... 223 L8

ROY/SHW OL2 ...... 229 J5
  SKP/WHF BD23 ...... 16 D1
Meadow Rd BEE/HOL LS11 ...... 8 F5
  BSLYN/ROY S71 ...... 243 M3
  CAS WF10 ...... 179 K1
  GFTH/SHER LS25 ...... 113 J7
  IDLE BD10 ...... 84 A6
Meadowside MILN OL16 ...... 229 L2
Meadows Morvern
  HEM/SK/SE WF9 ...... 224 B7
The Meadows BHP/TINH LS16 ... 86 E1
  GFTH/SHER LS25 ...... 138 A3
  GFTH/SHER LS25 ...... 138 D6
  KBTN HD8 ...... 257 H1 1
  WBSY BD6 ...... 126 C5
Meadow St BSLYN/ROY S71 ... 261 H4
  HUD HD1 ...... 191 M7
Meadow V HOR/CROF WF4 ... 218 F1
  WKFDE WF1 ...... 176 E1
Meadow Va AL/HA/HU LS17 ...... 87 J1
  HDGY LS6 ...... 109 G3
  HWTH BD22 ...... 78 F4 8
  KBTN HD8 ...... 239 K5
  LM/WK BD12 ...... 148 E5
  MSTN/BAR LS15 ...... 91 G6
  OSS WF5 ...... 174 E7 5
  STKB/PEN S36 ...... 258 B8
Meadow Wk CHAL LS7 ...... 88 A8
  HEM/SK/SE WF9 ...... 224 F3
  LIT OL15 ...... 207 H1 7
Meadow Wy AL/HA/HU LS17 ...... 87 J1
  CAS WF10 ...... 158 C6 1
  EARD/LOFT WF3 ...... 152 F7 1
  FEA/AMT WF7 ...... 202 C5
  TAD LS24 ...... 72 A2
Mead Rd MSTN/BAR LS15 ...... 112 A8
Meadstead Dr BSLYN/ROY S71 ... 243 K3
Mead St HUDN HD2 ...... 14 F1
Mead Vw BOW BD4 ...... 127 M3 8
Meadway FEA/AMT WF7 ...... 178 F4
Mead Wy KBTN HD8 ...... 216 A7
  MSTN/BAR LS15 ...... 112 A8
Meadway WBSY BD6 ...... 126 A8 8
Meagill Ri OT LS21 ...... 40 F4
Meal Hill La HOLM/MEL HD7 ... 212 B4
  HOLM/MEL HD7 ...... 255 H4
Meal Hill Rd HOLM/MEL HD7 ... 253 H5
Mean La HOLM/MEL HD7 ...... 235 C4
  HWTH BD22 ...... 77 M6
Meanwood Cl CHAL LS7 ...... 6 F1
Meanwood Gv HDGY LS6 ...... 87 G5
Meanwood Rd CHAL LS7 ...... 109 J1
Meanwood Valley Dr CHAL LS7 ... 87 H8
Meanwood Valley Gn CHAL LS7 ... 87 H8
Meanwood Valley Gv
  CHAL LS7 ...... 87 H8 10
Meanwood Valley Mt
  CHAL LS7 ...... 87 H8 11
Mearclough Rd RPDN/SBR HX6 ... 167 M2
Mears Cl STKB/PEN S36 ...... 271 G1
Medeway PDSY/CALV LS28 ...... 106 E4
Medhurst Av GFTH/SHER LS25 ... 135 K4
Medina Wy DOD/DAR S75 ...... 260 A1
Medley La HIPP HX3 ...... 147 H2
Medley St CAS WF10 ...... 206 B5 10
  WHIT OL12 ...... 206 B5 10
Medlock Rd HOR/CROF WF4 ... 197 J5
Medway CUL/QBY BD13 ...... 125 H6
  HUDE HD5 ...... 193 K4 2
Medway Av GFTH/SHER LS25 ... 135 J1
Medway Cl DOD/DAR S75 ...... 260 B1
Medway St ROY/SHW OL2 ...... 229 J6
Meeting House La
  HOLM/MEL HD7 ...... 212 C2
Meggison Gv WBOW BD5 ...... 126 C2
Meg La HUDW HD3 ...... 213 K1
Megnaway WBOW BD5 ...... 127 G2 10
Melba Rd GTHN BD7 ...... 126 D3
Melbourne Av
  WKFDW/WTN WF2 ...... 176 B3 8
Melbourne Cl ROCH OL11 ...... 228 C4
Melbourne Gv BFDE BD3 ...... 106 A6 3
  BRAM LS13 ...... 107 L4 7
Melbourne Ms
  WKFDW/WTN WF2 ...... 176 A2
Melbourne Pl WBOW BD5 ...... 4 D9
Melbourne Rd ROCH OL11 ...... 228 C4
  TOD OL14 ...... 163 J5
Melbourne St HBR HX7 ...... 143 H3 8
  HIPP HX3 ...... 10 D1
  LDSU LS2 ...... 7 J7
  LVSG WF15 ...... 172 D5 8
  MOR LS27 ...... 152 D2
  PDSY/CALV LS28 ...... 106 F4
  SHPY BD18 ...... 82 C6 8
Melbourne Ter WBOW BD5 ...... 4 D9
Melcombe Wk BOW BD4 ...... 128 A2 3
Melford Cl DOD/DAR S75 ...... 242 D5 1
Melford St BOW BD4 ...... 127 L4
Mellor Brook HOLM/MEL HD7 ... 212 B2
Mellor La HOLM/MEL HD7 ...... 253 K2
Mellor Mill La GTL/HWG HX4 ... 190 D2
Mellor St BRIG HD6 ...... 170 D4 1
  HFAX HX1 ...... 168 C1
Mellwood La HEM/SK/SE WF9 ... 247 C3
Melrose Av LIT OL15 ...... 185 J7
Melrose Cl HUDE HD5 ...... 193 H8
Melrose Dr ILK LS29 ...... 40 A4 8
Melrose Gv HORS LS18 ...... 86 A6
Melrose Pl HORS LS18 ...... 85 M6
  PDSY/CALV LS28 ...... 106 C8
Melrose St GTHN BD7 ...... 126 C2 13
  HIPP HX3 ...... 10 D1
Melrose Wk HORS LS18 ...... 85 M6
Melrose Wy BSLYN/ROY S71 ... 261 M4
Meltham House La
  HOLM/MEL HD7 ...... 255 H2
Meltham Mills Rd
  HOLM/MEL HD7 ...... 235 H4
Meltham Rd HOLM/MEL HD7 ... 235 J3
  HUDS HD4 ...... 213 J8
Melton Av EARD/LOFT WF3 ...... 154 B2
Melton Cl EARD/LOFT WF3 ...... 154 B1
  HEM/SK/SE WF9 ...... 247 J1 3
Melton Garth EARD/LOFT WF3 ... 154 B2
Melton Rd HOR/CROF WF4 ...... 220 C2
Melton St BTLY WF17 ...... 151 K8

Melton Ter IDLE BD10 ...... 106 A1
Melton Wy LVSG WF15 ...... 172 B5
Melville Cl HDGY LS6 ...... 6 F2
Melville Gdns HDGY LS6 ...... 6 F2
Melville Gv HDGY LS6 ...... 39 C2
Melville Pl HDGY LS6 ...... 6 F1
Melville Rd HDGY LS6 ...... 6 F2
Melville St GTHN BD7 ...... 4 A6
Melvinia Crs DOD/DAR S75 ...... 260 F2
Memorial Dr HDGY LS6 ...... 87 H7
Mendip Av HUDW HD3 ...... 191 J5
Mendip Cl DOD/DAR S75 ...... 260 D4 8
  GFTH/SHER LS25 ...... 135 H1
Mendip Dr MILN OL16 ...... 207 J8
Mendip Rd EARL WF12 ...... 174 B5
Mendips Cl ROY/SHW OL2 ...... 229 H6 8
Mendip Wy LM/WK BD12 ...... 126 D8
Menin Dr BAIL BD17 ...... 82 D1
Menston Old La ILK LS29 ...... 40 B8
Mentmore Rd MILN OL16 ...... 206 F7
Mercer Cl HUDS HD4 ...... 213 L7 2
Merchants St BOW BD4 ...... 127 J1 10
Mercia Wy MSTN/BAR LS15 ... 112 A3
Mercury Rw OT LS21 ...... 41 J7
Merefield La ROCH OL11 ...... 228 A1
Merefield St ROCH OL11 ...... 228 A1
Mere La ROCH OL11 ...... 228 B1
Mere St ROCH OL11 ...... 206 B8
Merewood Rd CAS WF10 ...... 157 H7
Meriden Av GFTH/SHER LS25 ... 135 H1
Merinall Cl MILN OL16 ...... 206 F7 8
Merlin Cl AWLS/ASK DN6 ...... 249 K8
  LIT OL15 ...... 207 J4
  MOR LS27 ...... 152 E3
Merlin Gv BTLY WF17 ...... 151 H6
  HUDS HD4 ...... 213 M7
Merlin Gv GIR BD8 ...... 103 L7
Merlin Rd MILN OL16 ...... 207 J8
Merlyn-rees Av MOR LS27 ...... 152 C2 8
Merrion Pl LDS LS2 ...... 7 H8
Merrion St LDSU LS2 ...... 7 G8
Merrion Wy LDSU LS2 ...... 7 G7
Merrivale Rd WIL/AL BD15 ...... 103 J6
Merrybank La AL/HA/HU LS17 ... 43 K1
Merrybents St TOD OL14 ...... 163 M1 8
Merrydale Rd BOW BD4 ...... 127 J8
Merryman Hall MILN OL16 ...... 206 D4 8
Merton Av GFTH/SHER LS25 ... 135 L4
Merton Cl GFTH/SHER LS25 ... 135 L4
Merton Dr PDSY/CALV LS28 ... 106 E4
Merton Fold WBOW BD5 ...... 127 G2 11
Merton Gdns PDSY/CALV LS28 ... 106 E4
Merton Rd GTHN BD7 ...... 4 C9
Merton St HUD HD1 ...... 14 D8
Merville Av BAIL BD17 ...... 82 E4
Metcalfe St BOW BD4 ...... 127 K2 8
Methley Gv CHAL LS7 ...... 87 L8
Methley La CHAL LS7 ...... 87 M8
  RTHW LS26 ...... 156 A2
Methley Mt CHAL LS7 ...... 87 M8 9
Methley Pl CHAL LS7 ...... 87 M8 10
Methley Rd CAS WF10 ...... 157 G4
Methley St CUD/GR S72 ...... 244 D8
Methley Ter CHAL LS7 ...... 87 L8
Methley Vw CHAL LS7 ...... 87 M8 11
Methuen Ov LM/WK BD12 ...... 148 E5 3
Mews FEA/AMT WF7 ...... 201 M1
The Mews NORM WF6 ...... 178 D3 8
Mexborough Av CHAL LS7 ...... 7 J1
Mexborough Dr CHAL LS7 ...... 7 J1
Mexborough Gv CHAL LS7 ...... 7 J1
Mexborough Pl CHAL LS7 ...... 7 J1
Mexborough Rd CHAL LS7 ...... 7 J1
  SHPY BD18 ...... 104 F1 8
Mexborough St CHAL LS7 ...... 7 J1
Meynell Ap BEE/HOL LS11 ...... 8 C1
Meynell Av RTHW LS26 ...... 155 K5
Meynell Ct MSTN/BAR LS15 ... 111 M7 13
Meynell Mt RTHW LS26 ...... 155 H1 8
Meynell Rd MSTN/BAR LS15 ... 111 M8
Meyrick Av WBY LS22 ...... 30 C5
Meyrick Ct MSTN/BAR LS15 ... 111 M8 8
Miall St HFAX HX1 ...... 10 C4
  ROCH OL11 ...... 206 B8
Michael Av EARD/LOFT WF3 ... 177 C1
Michael Rd BSLYN/ROY S71 ... 262 A4
Michael's Est CUD/GR S72 ...... 245 J7
Mickelden Wy DOD/DAR S75 ... 260 C5 8
Mickle Ct CAS WF10 ...... 157 G4
Mickledore Cl GTHN BD7 ...... 126 A3 8
Mickledore Rdg GTHN BD7 ...... 126 A3 8
Micklefield Ct YEA LS19 ...... 84 D2 1
Micklefield La YEA LS19 ...... 84 D2
Micklegate PONT WF8 ...... 180 F5
Micklemoss Dr CUL/QBY BD13 ... 124 E4
Mickleside RTHW LS26 ...... 132 B6 8
Micklethwaite Dr
  CUL/QBY BD13 ...... 125 C6
Micklethwaite La BGLY BD16 ... 59 C8
Micklethwaite Rd
  HOR/CROF WF4 ...... 220 B3
Micklethwaite Vw WBY LS22 ... 48 A2 3
Mickletown Rd RTHW LS26 ... 156 F1 8
Mickley St WOR/ARM LS12 ... 108 E7
Middlebrook Crs GIR BD8 ...... 104 A7 7
Middlebrook Dr GIR BD8 ...... 103 M7 8
Middlebrook Hl GIR BD8 ...... 103 M7 8
Middlebrook Ri GIR BD8 ...... 103 M7 8
Middlebrook Vw GIR BD8 ...... 104 A7
Middlebrook Wk GIR BD8 ...... 104 A7
Middlebrook Wy GIR BD8 ...... 103 M8
Middleburn Cl BSLY S70 ...... 261 J7
Middlecliffe Dr STKB/PEN S36 ... 268 E5
Middlecliff La CUD/GR S72 ...... 263 K6
Middlecroft Cl RTHW LS26 ...... 132 B6 8
Middlecroft Rd RTHW LS26 ... 132 B6
Middle Cross St WOR/ARM LS12 ... 108 F7
Middle Dean St GTL/HWG HX4 ... 168 E7
Middle Field La HOR/CROF WF4 ... 220 B4
Middlefield La PONT WF8 ...... 226 E1
Middle Field Rd DOD/DAR S75 ... 259 M6
Middlegate BTLY WF17 ...... 151 C5
Middle Hall Cl LVSG WF15 ...... 172 B8
Middleham Ct BOW BD4 ...... 128 A3 11
Middle Hl WHIT OL12 ...... 206 B2 8

Middle La CLAY BD14 ...... 125 L3
  HOR/CROF WF4 ...... 200 D7
  KNOT WF11 ...... 182 C5
  WBY LS22 ...... 47 L4
Middlemoor SCFT LS14 ...... 89 K6 8
Middle Oxford St CAS WF10 ... 157 L7
Middle Rd DEWS WF13 ...... 173 K7
  EARL WF12 ...... 174 A7
  OSM LS9 ...... 132 F3
Middleton Av EARD/LOFT WF3 ... 153 M4
  OSM LS9 ...... 110 B5
  RTHW LS26 ...... 154 C1
Middleton Cl MOR LS27 ...... 152 D2
Middleton Ct LVSG WF15 ...... 172 A2
Middleton Gv BEE/HOL LS11 ... 131 L5
  MOR LS27 ...... 152 E2 8
Middleton La EARD/LOFT WF3 ... 153 M4
  RTHW LS26 ...... 154 C1
Middleton Park Av MID LS10 ... 153 K2
Middleton Park Crs MID LS10 ... 153 K3
Middleton Park Gn MID LS10 ... 153 K2 8
Middleton Park Gv MID LS10 ... 153 K1
Middleton Park Mt MID LS10 ... 153 K1
Middleton Park Pl MID LS10 ... 153 L2 10
Middleton Park Rd MID LS10 ... 153 L1
Middleton Park Ter MID LS10 ... 153 K1
Middleton Rd ILK LS29 ...... 38 C2
  MID LS10 ...... 132 A5 8
  MOR LS27 ...... 152 D2
Middleton St GIR BD8 ...... 104 D5 8
Middleton Ter MOR LS27 ...... 152 E2 8
Middleton Wy KNOT WF11 ... 182 B2
Middleway AIRE BD20 ...... 36 B5
Middle Wood La WHIT OL12 ... 185 G8
Middlewoods DOD/DAR S75 ... 260 C2 8
Midge Hall Cl ILK LS29 ...... 40 A5 8
Midgeham Gv BGLY BD16 ...... 80 C5
Midgehole Rd HBR HX7 ...... 121 J8
Midgeley Rd BAIL BD17 ...... 82 C5
Midgley Gdns HDGY LS6 ...... 6 D2
Midgley Pl HDGY LS6 ...... 6 D2
Midgley Ri PONT WF8 ...... 180 F3
  HBR HX7 ...... 144 C5
  ILK LS29 ...... 40 A5
Midgley St COL BB8 ...... 74 A2
Midgley Ter HDGY LS6 ...... 6 E2
Midhope Wy DOD/DAR S75 ... 260 C5
Midhurst Gv DOD/DAR S75 ... 260 A1
Midhurst Rd ROCH OL11 ...... 228 D1 3
Midland Cl MID LS10 ...... 132 B3
Midland Garth MID LS10 ...... 9 M9
Midland Hl BGLY BD16 ...... 81 H3
Midland Pas HDGY LS6 ...... 6 E2
Midland Rd BAIL BD17 ...... 82 E4
  BSLYN/ROY S71 ...... 243 M2
  GIR BD8 ...... 104 F4
  HDGY LS6 ...... 6 E2
  HTON BD9 ...... 104 E1
  MID LS10 ...... 132 A3
  PONT WF8 ...... 181 G5
Midland St BSLY S70 ...... 261 H5 8
  HUD HD1 ...... 15 C2
  RTHW LS26 ...... 133 L8
  SKP/WHF BD23 ...... 16 A3
Midland Ter HTON BD9 ...... 104 E1
Midway HUDS HD4 ...... 213 J8
Midway Av BGLY BD16 ...... 81 J7 2
Milan Rd RHAY LS8 ...... 110 B3
Milan St RHAY LS8 ...... 110 C3
Milbury Dr LIT OL15 ...... 207 J4
Milden Pl BSLY S70 ...... 261 J7
Mildred Sylvester Wy
  NORM WF6 ...... 179 C4
Mile Cross Gdns HFAX HX1 ...... 146 A8
Mile Cross Gv HFAX HX1 ...... 146 A8
Mile Cross Rd HFAX HX1 ...... 146 A8
Mile Cross Ter HFAX HX1 ...... 146 A8
Mile End HOLM/MEL HD7 ...... 234 F5
Milefield La CUD/GR S72 ...... 245 G7
Miles Garth AL/HA/HU LS17 ...... 47 K8
Miles Hill Av CHAL LS7 ...... 87 K8
Miles Hill Crs BOW BD4 ...... 127 L5
  CHAL LS7 ...... 87 K8
Miles Hill Dr BOW BD4 ...... 127 L5
Miles Hill Gv CHAL LS7 ...... 87 J8
Miles Hill Mt CHAL LS7 ...... 87 J8
Miles Hill Pl CHAL LS7 ...... 87 K8
Miles Hill Rd CHAL LS7 ...... 87 K8
Miles Hill Sq CHAL LS7 ...... 87 K8
Miles Hill St CHAL LS7 ...... 87 K8
Miles Hill Ter CHAL LS7 ...... 87 K8
Miles Hill Vw CHAL LS7 ...... 87 K8
Mileswood Cl CUD/GR S72 ...... 263 M3 8
Mile Thorn St HFAX HX1 ...... 10 B6
Milford Crs LIT OL15 ...... 185 K8
Milford Gv CLECK BD19 ...... 150 C3
Milford Pl BULY LS4 ...... 108 F5
  HTON BD9 ...... 104 C3 8
Milford Rd GFTH/SHER LS25 ... 138 D1
Milford St WHIT OL12 ...... 206 B5 17
Milgate St BSLYN/ROY S71 ... 243 M2
Milkstone Pl ROCH OL11 ...... 208 B8 11
  ROCH OL11 ...... 228 B1
Milkstone Rd ROCH OL11 ...... 206 B8
  ROCH OL11 ...... 228 B1
Milk St ROCH OL11 ...... 206 B8
Millars Wk HEM/SK/SE WF9 ... 246 C5
Mill Av HUDE HD5 ...... 193 J7
Mill Bank Cl RPDN/SBR HX6 ... 166 E7
Mill Bank Ct PDSY/CALV LS28 ... 129 H1
Mill Bank Rd HOLM/MEL HD7 ... 235 C5
  RPDN/SBR HX6 ...... 166 E7
Mill Banks AIRE BD20 ...... 36 A5 8
Millbeck Cl GIR BD8 ...... 103 L8 8
Millbeck Dr BGLY BD16 ...... 80 C5 8
Millbeck Gn WBY LS22 ...... 47 J6
Millbrae Gdns ROY/SHW OL2 ... 229 H7
Mill Br SKP/WHF BD23 ...... 16 B2
Millbrook Cl ROY/SHW OL2 ... 229 P8

Millbrook Gdns *DEWS* WF13 ...... 173 J4
Mill Carr Hill Rd *BOW* BD4 .... 127 K8
Mill Cl *FEA/AMT* WF7 .... 202 C8
  GFTH/SHER LS25 .... 138 D7
  HEM/SK/SE WF9 .... 246 C4
  HOLM/MEL HD7 .... 234 F4
  PBR HG3 .... 28 E3
Mill Ct *HWTH* BD22 .... 100 E4 ☐
Millcroft *EARD/LOFT* WF3 .... 155 G8
Mill Cft *HWTH* BD22 .... 54 E3
  MOR LS27 .... 129 M7 ☐
  ROY/SHW OL2 .... 229 L8
Millcroft Cl *EARD/LOFT* WF3 .... 154 F8
Millcroft Est *OT* LS21 .... 42 F7
Millcroft La *UPML* OL3 .... 231 H8
Millcroft Ri *EARD/LOFT* WF3 .. 155 G8 ☐
Mill Dam *BSPA/BRAM* LS23 ...... 70 A1
Mill Dam La *PONT* WF8 .... 181 G4
Millenium Cl *BOW* BD4 .... 16 C6
Millenium Wy *BEE/HOL* LS11 .... 131 K5
Miller Ct *WKFDW/WTN* WF2 .... 220 D3
Miller Garth *FEA/AMT* WF7 ...... 224 C1
Miller Hl *KBTN* HD8 .... 257 J1
Miller Meadow Cl
  ROY/SHW OL2 .... 229 L6
Millers Ct *LVSG* WF15 .... 172 D4
Millersdale Cl *BOW* BD4 .... 127 J7
Mill Farm Dr *WKFDW/WTN* WF2 .. 220 E7
Millfield Cl *HUDW* HD3 .... 191 L7
Millfield Crs *PONT* WF8 .... 180 E8 ☐
Millfield Gv *MILN* OL16 .... 206 D8 ☐
Millfield Rd *HOR/CROF* WF4 .... 197 L6
Millfields *AIRE* BD20 .... 35 M5
  OSS WF5 .... 174 E8 ☐
Mill Fold Wy *RPDN/SBR* HX6 .... 188 F2
Mill Forest Wy *BTLY* WF17 ...... 174 B2
Mill Garth *MOR* LS27 .... 129 M7 ☐
Millgarth Ct *WBY* LS22 .... 47 K6
Millgarth St *LDSU* LS2 .... 7 J9
Millgate *ELL* HX5 .... 169 H7
  FEA/AMT WF7 .... 224 C1
  HUD HD1 .... 14 A9
  HUDS HD4 .... 215 K4
Mill Ga *MILN* OL16 .... 206 D4
Mill Grath *PONT* WF8 .... 180 E7
Mill Gn *BEE/HOL* LS11 .... 8 A4
Mill Green Cl *SCFT* LS14 .... 111 L1
Mill Green Gdns *SCFT* LS14 .... 111 L1
Mill Green Garth *SCFT* LS14 .. 111 L1 ☐
Mill Green Pl *SCFT* LS14 .... 111 L2
Mill Green Rd *SCFT* LS14 .... 111 L1
Mill Green Vw *SCFT* LS14 .... 111 K1
Mill Gv *BRIG* HD6 .... 170 B2
Mill Hey *HWTH* BD22 .... 78 F7
Mill Hl *FEA/AMT* WF7 .... 202 C6
  HWTH BD22 .... 78 E7 ☐
  LDS LS1 .... 9 G1
  NORM WF6 .... 178 C5
  PDSY/CALV LS28 .... 129 G1
  RTHW LS26 .... 155 G1
Mill Hill Av *PONT* WF8 .... 180 D7
Mill Hill Cl *PONT* WF8 .... 203 M1
Mill Hill Gn *RTHW* LS26 .... 155 G1 ☐
Mill Hill La *BRIG* HD6 .... 170 B2
  BRIG HD6 .... 171 H5
  PONT WF8 .... 180 D7
Mill Hill Rd *PONT* WF8 .... 180 E7
Mill Hill Sq *RTHW* LS26 .... 155 G1 ☐
Mill Hill Top *BGLY* BD16 .... 80 D6
Mill House Cl *RPDN/SBR* HX6 .. 167 H4
Millhouse La *STKB/PEN* S36 .... 269 M3
Mill House Ri *BOW* BD4 .... 127 K5 ☐
Milligan Av *ECHL* BD2 .... 105 J1 ☐
Milligan Ct *BGLY* BD16 .... 80 C5 ☐
Mill La *AIRE* BD20 .... 16 E8
  AIRE BD20 .... 56 E1
  AL/HA/HU LS17 .... 67 M3
  AWLS/ASK DN6 .... 249 H4
  AWLS/ASK DN6 .... 249 K8
  BIRK/DRI BD11 .... 128 C8
  BOW BD4 .... 129 J3
  BRAM LS13 .... 107 J3
  BRIG HD6 .... 170 D4
  BSPA/BRAM LS23 .... 49 G6
  BTLY WF17 .... 151 K4
  BTLY WF17 .... 173 M2
  CAS WF10 .... 157 M5
  CAS WF10 .... 178 F2
  CLECK BD19 .... 149 M3
  COP/BISH YO23 .... 33 M1
  CUL/QBY BD13 .... 124 E4
  DOD/DAR S75 .... 242 A5
  EARD/LOFT WF3 .... 153 M6
  EARL WF12 .... 174 C7
  FEA/AMT WF7 .... 178 F8
  FEA/AMT WF7 .... 224 C1
  GSLY LS20 .... 60 F6
  GTL/HWG HX4 .... 190 E2
  HEM/SK/SE WF9 .... 126 A4
  HEM/SK/SE WF9 .... 247 K2
  HIPP HX3 .... 146 A8
  HIPP HX3 .... 168 C5
  HOR/CROF WF4 .... 217 M3
  HOR/CROF WF4 .... 221 G7
  HOR/CROF WF4 .... 222 D5
  HUDE HD5 .... 193 K1
  HWTH BD22 .... 78 D4
  HWTH BD22 .... 100 E3
  LUD/ILL HX2 .... 123 L7
  MOR LS27 .... 129 M7
  OT LS21 .... 41 J6
  OT LS21 .... 42 E7
  PBR HG3 .... 28 E5
  PONT WF8 .... 181 H3
  RTHW LS26 .... 156 F5
  SKP/WHF BD23 .... 16 B3
  STKB/PEN S36 .... 256 D6
  STKB/PEN S36 .... 270 B3
  TAD LS24 .... 71 L6
  TAD LS24 .... 71 M4
  TAD LS24 .... 95 M4
  WBOW BD5 .... 127 G1
  WBY LS22 .... 46 A3
Millmoor Cl *HTON* BD9 .... 103 M4

Mill Moor Rd *HOLM/MEL* HD7 .... 234 E4
Mill Pk *MIRF* WF14 .... 194 B4
Mill Pit La *RTHW* LS26 .... 132 F7
Mill Pond Gv *HDGY* LS6 .... 87 G8 ☐
Mill Pond La *HDGY* LS6 .... 87 G7
Mill Race Fold *HOLM/MEL* HD7 .. 236 E6
Mill Rd *DEWS* WF13 .... 173 L4
Mill Royd St *BRIG* HD6 .... 170 D4
Mill Rw *AIRE* BD20 .... 35 H8
Mill Shaw La *HOLM/MEL* HD7 .... 255 J5
Millshaw Mt *BEE/HOL* LS11 .... 131 H5
Millshaw Park Av *MOR* LS27 .... 130 F5
Millshaw Park Cl *BEE/HOL* LS11 .. 130 F5
Millshaw Park La *BEE/HOL* LS11 .. 130 F6
Millshaw Park Wy
  BEE/HOL LS11 .... 130 F5
Millshaw Rd *BEE/HOL* LS11 .... 131 G7
Millside *CUD/GR* S72 .... 244 E3
Millside Wk *CUD/GR* S72 .... 244 E3
Millstone Cl *FEA/AMT* WF7 .... 224 C1
Millstone Ri *LVSG* WF15 .... 172 D4
Millstones *STKB/PEN* S36 ...... 271 L5
Mill St *AIRE* BD20 .... 56 A1
  BFD BD1 .... 5 G4
  BTLY WF17 .... 151 G6
  CAS WF10 .... 157 K7
  CUL/QBY BD13 .... 79 M8
  HEM/SK/SE WF9 .... 246 C4
  HIPP HX3 .... 168 C5
  HUDS HD4 .... 214 A2
  MOR LS27 .... 152 C3
  OSM LS9 .... 15 L1
  WBSY BD6 .... 126 C5 ☐
Mill St East *EARL* WF12 .... 173 M8
Mill St West *EARL* WF12 .... 173 L7
Mill Vw *HEM/SK/SE* WF9 .... 247 J1
  ILK LS29 .... 40 A4 ☐
  KNOT WF11 .... 181 K2
Millward St *HOR/CROF* WF4 .. 222 C5 ☐
Millwater Av *EARL* WF12 ...... 195 K1 ☐
Millwood La *TOD* OL14 .... 163 L1
Millwright St *LDSU* LS2 .... 7 K7
Milne Ct *MSTN/BAR* LS15 .... 111 M8 ☐
Milner Av *STKB/PEN* S36 .... 270 D3
Milner Bank *OT* LS21 .... 40 F8
Milner Cl *GTL/HWG* HX4 .... 168 D7
Milner Gdns *OSM* LS9 .... 110 B8 ☐
Milner Ing *LM/WK* BD12 .... 148 E2
Milner La *EARD/LOFT* WF3 .... 154 C3
  GTL/HWG HX4 .... 168 D7
  SCFT LS14 .... 68 B6
  TAD LS24 .... 93 J7
Milner Rd *BAIL* BD17 .... 82 D5
Milner's Av *WKFDW/WTN* WF2 .. 198 B3
Milner's La *PONT* WF8 .... 203 M2
Milner's Rd *YEA* LS19 .... 62 B7
Milner St *HFAX* HX1 .... 10 C1
  HUDS HD4 .... 214 A3
  OSS WF5 .... 174 E5 ☐
Milner Wy *OSS* WF5 .... 175 G8
Milnes Av *WKFDW/WTN* WF2 .. 198 B3
Milnes Gv *CAS* WF10 .... 157 K7
  WOR/ARM LS12 .... 109 G8
Milne St *DOD/DAR* S75 .... 260 A2
  ROY/SHW OL2 .... 229 K8 ☐☐
Milngate Cl *MILN* OL16 .... 228 E3 ☐
Miln Rd *HUD* HD1 .... 14 E2
Milnrow Rd *LIT* OL15 .... 207 H4
  MILN OL16 .... 206 D7
  ROY/SHW OL2 .... 229 K7
Milnthorpe Cl *BSPA/BRAM* LS23 .. 69 L3 ☐
Milnthorpe Crs
  WKFDW/WTN WF2 .... 198 F7
Milnthorpe Dr
  WKFDW/WTN WF2 .... 198 F6
Milnthorpe Gdns
  BSPA/BRAM LS23 .... 69 L3 ☐
Milnthorpe Garth
  BSPA/BRAM LS23 .... 69 L3 ☐
Milnthorpe Gn
  WKFDW/WTN WF2 .... 198 E7
Milnthorpe La *BSPA/BRAM* LS23 .. 69 L3
  WKFDW/WTN WF2 .... 198 F7
Milnthorpe Wy
  BSPA/BRAM LS23 .... 69 L3 ☐
Milroyd Crs *BTLY* WF17 .... 151 J4
Milton Av *LVSG* WF15 .... 172 C3
  RPDN/SBR HX6 .... 167 L1
Milton Cl *HOR/CROF* WF4 ...... 197 M8
  LVSG WF15 .... 172 C4
Milton Ct *EARD/LOFT* WF3 .... 155 H8
Milton Crs *HEM/SK/SE* WF9 .. 223 K4
  LVSG WF15 .... 172 C4
  MSTN/BAR LS15 .... 90 B7
Milton Gdns *LVSG* WF15 .... 172 C3
Milton Gv *DEWS* WF13 .... 173 L4
Milton Pl *HFAX* HX1 .... 10 E6
  OSS WF5 .... 174 E8
Milton Rd *AWLS/ASK* DN6 ...... 249 L5
  LVSG WF15 .... 172 C3
  PBR HG3 .... 26 F2
  WKFDW/WTN WF2 .... 197 L2
Milton Sq *HECK* WF16 .... 172 F2
Milton St *CAS* WF10 .... 157 L6 ☐
  CUD/GR S72 .... 263 M4
  CUL/QBY BD13 .... 101 M6
  GTHN BD7 .... 4 B6
  HECK WF16 .... 172 F1 ☐
  MILN OL16 .... 206 B6
  RPDN/SBR HX6 .... 167 K1
  SKP/WHF BD23 .... 16 C3
  WKFDW/WTN WF2 .... 12 M4
Milton Ter *CLECK* BD19 .... 149 L6
  HFAX HX1 .... 10 E6 ☐
  KSTL LS5 .... 108 C2
Minden Cl *PONT* WF8 .... 180 C7
Minden Wy *PONT* WF8 .... 180 C6
Minerva St *HUDS* HD4 .... 213 H3
Minnie St *HWTH* BD22 .... 78 E8
  KGHY BD21 .... 2 E7
Minorca Mt *CUL/QBY* BD13 .... 101 M5
Minster Wy *BSLYN/ROY* S71 .. 261 M3
Minsthorpe La *HEM/SK/SE* WF9 .. 225 J8
  HEM/SK/SE WF9 .... 247 J1
Mint St *ECHL* BD2 .... 105 K4
  HUDW HD3 .... 191 M7

Miramar *HUDN* HD2 .... 192 F1
Mire Rdg *COL* BB8 .... 74 C3
Mires La *TAD* LS24 .... 94 F4
Mirey Butt La *KNOT* WF11 ...... 181 L3
Mirey La *RPDN/SBR* HX6 .... 166 D3
Mirfield Av *ECHL* BD2 .... 105 J1 ☐
Miry La *HBR* HX7 .... 144 B8
  HOLM/MEL HD7 .... 236 A5
  LVSG WF15 .... 171 L2
  MSTN/BAR LS15 .... 91 H4
  YEA LS19 .... 62 D7
Mission St *BRIG* HD6 .... 170 C3
Mistral Cl *HOR/CROF* WF4 .... 148 E4
Mistral Gv *LVSG* WF15 .... 171 K1 ☐
Mistress La *WOR/ARM* LS12 .. 108 E6
Mitcham Dr *HTON* BD9 .... 104 C4 ☐
Mitchell Av *HUDE* HD5 .... 215 J1
Mitchell Cl *IDLE* BD10 .... 83 L5 ☐
Mitchell La *AIRE* BD20 .... 36 A3
  IDLE BD10 .... 83 L5
Mitchell Sq *WBOW* BD5 ...... 127 G2 ☐
Mitchell St *BRIG* HD6 .... 170 C3
  HBR HX7 .... 143 J4 ☐
  MILN OL16 .... 206 E3 ☐
  RPDN/SBR HX6 .... 167 L2
  TOD OL14 .... 141 G7
Mitchell Ter *BGLY* BD16 .... 81 H5
Mitchelson Av *DOD/DAR* S75 .. 260 A7
Mitchell Sq *AIRE* BD20 .... 36 A3
Mitford Pl *WOR/ARM* LS12 .... 108 F7
Mitford Rd *WOR/ARM* LS12 .... 108 F7
Mitford Ter *WOR/ARM* LS12 .. 108 F7
Mitford Vw *WOR/ARM* LS12 .. 108 F7
Mitre Ct *BOW* BD4 .... 127 M3 ☐
Mitre St *DEWS* WF13 .... 173 J6 ☐
  HUDW HD3 .... 14 A4
Mitton St *WBOW* BD5 .... 126 E3 ☐☐
Mixenden Cl *LUD/ILL* HX2 .... 145 L1 ☐
Mixenden La *LUD/ILL* HX2 .... 123 M8
Mixenden Rd *LUD/ILL* HX2 .... 145 L1
Mizzy Rd *WHIT* OL12 .... 206 A5
Moat Hl *BTLY* WF17 .... 151 H4
Moat Hill Farm Dr *BTLY* WF17 .. 151 J4
Modder Av *WOR/ARM* LS12 .... 108 A7
Modder Pl *WOR/ARM* LS12 .. 108 B7
Modd La *HOLM/MEL* HD7 ...... 254 B2
Model Av *WOR/ARM* LS12 ...... 108 F7
Model Rd *WOR/ARM* LS12 .... 108 F7
Model Ter *WOR/ARM* LS12 .... 108 F7
Modena Ct *WMB/DAR* S73 .... 263 G8
Moderna Wy *HBR* HX7 .... 144 B6
Moffat Cl *WBSY* BD6 .... 126 E8
Moles Head *HOLM/MEL* HD7 .. 190 B8
Molesworth St *MILN* OL16 .... 206 C7
Molly Hurst La *HOR/CROF* WF4 .. 220 B7
Mona St *HOLM/MEL* HD7 ...... 212 B5
  WKFDW/WTN WF2 .... 176 A8 ☐
Monckton Dr *CAS* WF10 .... 158 E8
Monckton Rd
  WKFDW/WTN WF2 .... 198 C4
Mond Av *BFDE* BD3 .... 105 M5
Monk Barn Cl *BGLY* BD16 ...... 81 J2 ☐
Monk Bridge Av *HDGY* LS6 .... 87 G8
Monk Bridge Dr *HDGY* LS6 .... 87 H8
Monk Bridge Pl *HDGY* LS6 .... 87 G8
Monk Bridge Rd *HDGY* LS6 .... 87 G8
Monk Bridge Ter *HDGY* LS6 .... 87 G8
Monkfield *MIRF* WF14 .... 172 A8 ☐
Monkhill Av *PONT* WF8 .... 180 F4
Monkhill Dr *PONT* WF8 .... 180 F4
Monkhill La *PONT* WF8 .... 180 F3
Monkhill Mt *PONT* WF8 .... 180 F4
Monk Ings *BTLY* WF17 .... 150 F5
Monk Ings Av *BTLY* WF17 ...... 150 E5
Monkmans Wharfe *AIRE* BD20 .. 35 M5 ☐
Monks Cl *MILN* OL16 .... 207 G3
Monk St *GTHN* BD7 .... 4 B6
  WKFDE WF1 .... 13 G4
Monks Wy *BSLYN/ROY* S71 .... 261 M3
Monkswood Av *SCFT* LS14 .... 89 H6
Monkswood Bank *SCFT* LS14 .. 89 H6
Monkswood Cl *SCFT* LS14 .... 89 H6 ☐
Monkswood Dr *SCFT* LS14 .... 89 H6
Monkswood Ga *SCFT* LS14 .... 89 J6 ☐
Monkswood Gn *SCFT* LS14 .... 89 H6 ☐
Monkswood Hl *SCFT* LS14 .... 89 H6
Monkswood Ri *SCFT* LS14 .... 89 H6
Monkswood Wk *SCFT* LS14 .. 89 J6 ☐
Monk Ter *BSLYN/ROY* S71 ...... 262 A1
Monkton Wy *BSLYN/ROY* S71 .. 243 L1
Monkwood Rd *WKFDE* WF1 .... 176 D1
Monmouth St *COL* BB8 .... 74 C1 ☐
  ROCH OL11 .... 206 B8 ☐
Monsal Crs *BSLYN/ROY* S71 .. 243 J7
Monson Av *PDSY/CALV* LS28 .. 84 D8
Montagu Crs *RHAY* LS8 .... 110 D1
Montagu Dr *RHAY* LS8 .... 110 D1
Montague Pl *GFTH/SHER* LS25 .. 113 J6
Montague Pl *GFTH/SHER* LS25 .. 113 J7 ☐
Montague St *COL* BB8 .... 52 A8
  CUD/GR S72 .... 244 E6 ☐
  RPDN/SBR HX6 .... 167 J3 ☐
  WBOW BD5 .... 126 E3
Montagu Gdns *RHAY* LS8 ...... 110 D1
Montagu Gv *RHAY* LS8 .... 110 E1 ☐
Montagu Pl *RHAY* LS8 .... 110 D1
Montagu Ri *RHAY* LS8 .... 110 E2 ☐
Montagu Rd *WBY* LS22 .... 30 C8
Montagu Vw *RHAY* LS8 .... 110 D1
Montcalm Crs *EARD/LOFT* WF3 .. 177 K8
  MID LS10 .... 132 A4 ☐
Montfort Cl *HORS* LS18 .... 85 K3
Montgomery St *SKP/WHF* BD23 .. 16 C3 ☐
Montreal Av *CHAL* LS7 .... 87 M8
Montreal St *TOD* OL14 .... 163 J5 ☐
Montreal Ter *BRAM* LS13 ...... 107 J6 ☐
Montrose Cl *DOD/DAR* S75 .... 242 A5
Montrose St *ECHL* BD2 .... 104 F2
Montserrat Rd *BOW* BD4 ...... 128 C5
Monument La *PONT* WF8 ...... 181 G7
Monument Ms *PONT* WF8 .... 181 G7 ☐
Moody St *BOW* BD4 .... 5 G9
Moor Allerton Av
  AL/HA/HU LS17 .... 88 A4

Moor Allerton Crs
  AL/HA/HU LS17 .... 88 A4 ☐
Moor Allerton Dr
  AL/HA/HU LS17 .... 88 B4
Moor Allerton Gdns
  AL/HA/HU LS17 .... 87 M4 ☐
Moor Av *BSPA/BRAM* LS23 .... 48 F8
  EARD/LOFT WF3 .... 155 G3
  MSTN/BAR LS15 .... 111 H7
Moor Bank La *MILN* OL16 .... 228 F2
Moorbottom *CLECK* BD19 .... 149 K8
Moor Bottom *HOLM/MEL* HD7 .. 236 B2
Moor Bottom La *BGLY* BD16 .. 81 J3
  GTL/HWG HX4 .... 168 C5
  HBR HX7 .... 166 C1
  KGHY BD21 .... 79 K4
  RPDN/SBR HX6 .... 167 J6
Moor Bottom Rd *GTL/HWG* HX4 .. 189 L1
Moorbottom Rd *HUD* HD1 .... 214 A2
Moor Bottom Rd *LUD/ILL* HX2 .. 124 B8
Moorbridge Cft
  GFTH/SHER LS25 .... 116 B7
Moorbrow *HOLM/MEL* HD7 .. 254 B4
Moor Cl *HUDS* HD4 .... 213 L5
  MID LS10 .... 131 M4
Moor Close Av *CUL/QBY* BD13 .. 124 E6 ☐
Moor Close Farm Ms
  CUL/QBY BD13 .... 124 E6 ☐
Moor Close La *CUL/QBY* BD13 .. 124 E6
Moor Close Pde *CUL/QBY* BD13 .. 124 E5
Moor Close Rd *CUL/QBY* BD13 .. 124 E6
Moorcock Rd *HBR* HX7 .... 141 L1
Moor Cottage Cl *HUDS* HD4 .. 213 M7
Moor Crs *BEE/HOL* LS11 .... 9 G7
  SKP/WHF BD23 .... 16 D2
Moor Crescent Cha
  BEE/HOL LS11 .... 9 G7
Moorcrest Ri *DOD/DAR* S75 .. 242 D4 ☐
Moor Crest Rd *HUDS* HD4 .... 213 L3
Moor Cft *BGLY* BD16 .... 81 K1
  BHP/TINH LS16 .... 86 F2
Moorcroft Av *BFDE* BD3 .... 105 M5
  HWTH BD22 .... 78 F3
Moorcroft Avenues
  HOLM/MEL HD7 .... 212 F1
Moorcroft Dr *BOW* BD4 .... 128 B5
  DEWS WF13 .... 173 H5
Moorcroft Park Dr
  HOLM/MEL HD7 .... 236 F7
Moorcroft Rd *BOW* BD4 .... 128 B5
  DEWS WF13 .... 173 H5
Moorcroft Ter *BOW* BD4 .... 128 B6
Moor Dr *HDGY* LS6 .... 87 G8
  HWTH BD22 .... 78 E3
  OT LS21 .... 41 M6
  PDSY/CALV LS28 .... 129 H1
Moore Av *BFDE* BD3 .... 105 L5 ☐
Moorehouse Gv *OSM* LS9 ...... 7 L6
Moor End Av *LUD/ILL* HX2 .... 145 L1
Moor End Gdns *LUD/ILL* HX2 .. 145 M5
Moor End La *DEWS* WF13 .... 173 H4
  RPDN/SBR HX6 .... 167 M4
Moor End Rd *HUDS* HD4 ...... 214 A3
  LUD/ILL HX2 .... 145 K3
Moore St *MILN* OL16 .... 206 B7 ☐☐
Moore Vw *GTHN* BD7 .... 126 B4
Moor Farm Gdns *CHAL* LS7 .. 87 L7 ☐
Moorfield Av *MOR* LS27 ...... 129 L7 ☐
Moorfield Av *BFDE* BD3 .... 105 M5
  CLECK BD19 .... 149 G7 ☐
  ILK LS29 .... 61 H2 ☐
  LIT OL15 .... 185 J3 ☐
  WOR/ARM LS12 .... 108 C6
Moorfield Cl *YEA* LS19 .... 62 F8
Moorfield Crs *HEM/SK/SE* WF9 .. 223 L8
  PDSY/CALV LS28 .... 106 F8
  WOR/ARM LS12 .... 108 C6
  YEA LS19 .... 62 E8
Moorfield Cft *YEA* LS19 .... 62 F8 ☐
Moorfield Dr *BAIL* BD17 .... 82 E1
  HWTH BD22 .... 78 D3
  YEA LS19 .... 62 E8
Moorfield Gdns
  PDSY/CALV LS28 .... 106 E8
Moorfield Gv *PDSY/CALV* LS28 .. 106 E8 ☐
  WOR/ARM LS12 .... 108 C6 ☐
Moorfield Hamlet
  ROY/SHW OL2 .... 229 H7 ☐
Moorfield Ms *ROY/SHW* OL2 .. 229 K7 ☐☐
Moorfield Pl *HEM/SK/SE* WF9 .. 223 L8
  IDLE BD10 .... 83 K6 ☐
  WHIT OL12 .... 206 A5 ☐
Moorfield Rd *BGLY* BD16 ...... 81 J7 ☐
Moor Field Rd *GTL/HWG* HX4 .. 189 L6
Moorfield Rd *HUDN* HD2 .... 192 D5 ☐
  ILK LS29 .... 39 G2
  WOR/ARM LS12 .... 108 C6
  YEA LS19 .... 62 F8
Moorfields *BRAM* LS13 .... 107 L3
Moorfield St *HFAX* HX1 .... 10 D9
  LDSU LS2 .... 6 D3
  WOR/ARM LS12 .... 108 C6
Moorfield Vw *LVSG* WF15 .... 172 B5 ☐
Moorfield Wy *CLECK* BD19 .. 149 G7 ☐
Moor Flatts Av *MID* LS10 ...... 153 L1
Moor Flatts Rd *MID* LS10 ...... 153 L1
Moorfoot La *AIRE* BD20 .... 34 C3
Moorgarth Av *BFDE* BD3 .... 105 M5 ☐
Moorgate *BAIL* BD17 .... 82 E2
Moor Ga *TOD* OL14 .... 163 L3
Moorgate Av *BFDE* BD3 .... 105 L5 ☐
  GFTH/SHER LS25 .... 135 J3
Moorgate Cl *GFTH/SHER* LS25 .. 135 J4
Moorgate Dr *GFTH/SHER* LS25 .. 135 K4
Moor Gate La *WHIT* OL12 .... 185 G7
Moorgate Ri *GFTH/SHER* LS25 .. 135 J4 ☐
Moorgate Rd *GFTH/SHER* LS25 .. 135 J3
Moorgate St *HFAX* HX1 .... 10 B9 ☐
Moor Grange Ri *BHP/TINH* LS16 .. 86 C6
Moor Grange Vw *BHP/TINH* LS16 .. 86 C6
Moor Green Cl *DOD/DAR* S75 .. 260 C4
Moor Gv *EARD/LOFT* WF3 .... 155 G8
  HIPP HX3 .... 125 L7

Moorhead Cl *HOLM/MEL* HD7 .. 234 F4
Moorhead Crs *SHPY* BD18 .... 82 A7 ☐
Moor Hey La *ELL* HX5 .... 191 L1
  GTL/HWG HX4 .... 190 A5
Moor Hill Rd *HUDW* HD3 ...... 191 H6
Moorhouse Av *BEE/HOL* LS11 .. 131 H5
  ECHL BD2 .... 105 J1
  WKFDW/WTN WF2 .... 176 B8
Moorhouse Cl *EARD/LOFT* WF3 .. 155 K7 ☐
  HWTH BD22 .... 100 A4 ☐
  NORM WF6 .... 178 E3 ☐
Moorhouse Ct *HEM/SK/SE* WF9 .. 247 J5
  HWTH BD22 .... 100 D2
Moorhouse Crs
  WKFDW/WTN WF2 .... 12 A2 ☐
Moorhouse Farm *MILN* OL16 .. 207 G8 ☐
Moorhouse Gap
  AWLS/ASK DN6 .... 248 B5
Moorhouse Gv *EARD/LOFT* WF3 .. 155 K7
Moorhouse La *AWLS/ASK* DN6 .. 247 L6
  DOD/DAR S75 .... 241 L1
  HOR/CROF WF4 .... 222 E2
  HWTH BD22 .... 100 D2
Moorhouse Ter
  EARD/LOFT WF3 .... 155 K8 ☐
Moorhouse Vw
  EARD/LOFT WF3 .... 155 K7 ☐
  HEM/SK/SE WF9 .... 247 K4
The Moorings *AL/HA/HU* LS17 .. 88 A1
  IDLE BD10 .... 83 M6
  MID LS10 .... 132 D3
Moor Knoll Cl *EARD/LOFT* WF3 .. 153 M6
Moor Knoll Dr *EARD/LOFT* WF3 .. 153 L6
Moor Knoll La *EARD/LOFT* WF3 .. 153 L5
Moorland Av *BAIL* BD17 .... 82 F2 ☐
  BGLY BD16 .... 59 L8
  DOD/DAR S75 .... 242 D4
  GSLY LS20 .... 62 A5
  HDGY LS6 .... 6 A4
  MILN OL16 .... 229 H1
  MOR LS27 .... 129 K6
Moorland Cl *HOLM/MEL* HD7 .. 213 G6
  LUD/ILL HX2 .... 146 A3
  MOR LS27 .... 129 L6
Moorland Crs *AL/HA/HU* LS17 .. 87 L5
  BAIL BD17 .... 82 F2
  DOD/DAR S75 .... 242 D4
  GSLY LS20 .... 62 A4
  ILK LS29 .... 61 J1
  MOR LS27 .... 129 K6 ☐
Moorland Dr *AL/HA/HU* LS17 .. 87 M5 ☐
  BIRK/DRI BD11 .... 128 D7
  GSLY LS20 .... 62 A4
  HOR/CROF WF4 .... 220 B4
  PDSY/CALV LS28 .... 106 C6
Moorland Gdns *AL/HA/HU* LS17 .. 87 L5
Moorland Garth *AL/HA/HU* LS17 .. 87 L5 ☐
Moorland Gv *AL/HA/HU* LS17 .. 87 L4
  PDSY/CALV LS28 .... 106 C6
Moorland Ings *AL/HA/HU* LS17 .. 87 L5
Moorland Pl *LM/WK* BD12 .... 149 G1
Moorland Ri *AL/HA/HU* LS17 .. 87 L5
  HOLM/MEL HD7 .... 234 E5
Moorland Rd *BHP/TINH* LS16 .. 63 A1 ☐
  BIRK/DRI BD11 .... 129 G8
  HDGY LS6 .... 6 B4
  PDSY/CALV LS28 .... 106 C5
Moorlands *HOLM/MEL* HD7 .. 254 E3
  ILK LS29 .... 38 C4
Moorlands Av *BFDE* BD3 ...... 105 M5 ☐
  BIRK/DRI BD11 .... 128 C7 ☐
  DEWS WF13 .... 173 K5 ☐
  HWTH BD22 .... 79 H2
  LUD/ILL HX2 .... 146 A3
  MIRF WF14 .... 172 B8 ☐
  OSS WF5 .... 174 E6 ☐
  YEA LS19 .... 62 F8
Moorlands Ct *GTL/HWG* HX4 .. 168 D6 ☐
Moorlands Crs *HUDW* HD3 .... 190 F5
Moorlands Dr *LUD/ILL* HX2 .. 146 A4 ☐
  YEA LS19 .... 62 F8
Moorlands Pl *HFAX* HX1 ...... 168 C1
Moorlands Rd *BIRK/DRI* BD11 .. 128 C7
  DEWS WF13 .... 173 K6
  GTL/HWG HX4 .... 168 D6
  HUDW HD3 .... 190 F5
Moorlands St *ROY/SHW* OL2 .. 229 L7 ☐
The Moorlands *AL/HA/HU* LS17 .. 88 A2 ☐
  WBY LS22 .... 48 B1
Moorland St *WHIT* OL12 ...... 206 A5 ☐
Moorlands Vw *HFAX* HX1 ...... 168 C1
Moorland Ter *CUD/GR* S72 .... 262 C1
  GFTH/SHER LS25 .... 113 G8 ☐
  KGHY BD21 .... 58 B8
Moorland Vw *AL/HA/HU* LS17 .. 87 L4
  BRAM LS13 .... 107 K2
  KBTN HD8 .... 217 J1
  KBTN HD8 .... 240 C4
  LM/WK BD12 .... 149 G1
  RPDN/SBR HX6 .... 167 H3 ☐
Moorland Wk *AL/HA/HU* LS17 .. 87 L4 ☐
Moor La *AIRE* BD20 .... 56 B1
  AL/HA/HU LS17 .... 67 J1
  BIRK/DRI BD11 .... 150 E2
  BSPA/BRAM LS23 .... 48 F1
  BTLY WF17 .... 151 H6
  CLECK BD19 .... 150 D4
  GFTH/SHER LS25 .... 116 B6
  GSLY LS20 .... 62 A4
  HOLM/MEL HD7 .... 236 A7
  HUDS HD4 .... 213 M7
  HUDS HD4 .... 237 C1
  ILK LS29 .... 18 C4
  ILK LS29 .... 18 F2
  ILK LS29 .... 39 M6
  ILK LS29 .... 61 G2
  KBTN HD8 .... 216 B7
  LUD/ILL HX2 .... 146 A2
  OT LS21 .... 22 D6
  OT LS21 .... 40 D3
  PBR HG3 .... 45 L3
  PONT WF8 .... 203 G2
  RYKW YO26 .... 32 D4

TAD LS24 ... 51 L5
TAD LS24 ... 71 H6
TAD LS24 ... 95 M4
TOD OL14 ... 163 K3
WBY LS22 ... 48 B6
Moorlea Dr BAIL BD17 ... 82 F3
Moorleigh Cl GFTH/SHER LS25 ... 135 K4
Moorleigh Dr GFTH/SHER LS25 ... 135 K4 3
Moor Park Av HDGY LS6 ... 86 F6
HUDS HD4 ... 213 L5
Moor Park Cl ILK LS29 ... 18 F6
Moor Park Ct EARL WF12 ... 174 A5 6
Moor Park Crs ILK LS29 ... 18 F6
Moor Park Dr BFDE BD3 ... 105 M6
HDGY LS6 ... 86 F8
ILK LS29 ... 18 F6
Moor Park Gv EARL WF12 ... 174 A6
Moor Park La EARL WF12 ... 174 A6
Moor Park Mt HDGY LS6 ... 86 F7
Moor Park Rd BFDE BD3 ... 105 L6 3
Moor Park Wy ILK LS29 ... 19 G6
Moor Rd BEE/HOL LS11 ... 9 G8
BHP/TINH LS16 ... 63 M4
EARD/LOFT WF3 ... 155 H6
FEA/AMT WF7 ... 201 M1
GFTH/SHER LS25 ... 116 B6
HDGY LS6 ... 86 F8
ILK LS29 ... 39 H5
LIT OL15 ... 185 L5
MID LS10 ... 131 M4
Moor Royd HIPP HX3 ... 168 C2 3
HOLM/MEL HD7 ... 236 A3
Moorroyd St OSS WF5 ... 7 J3
Moorshutt Rd HEM/SK/SE WF9 .. 223 L8
Moorside BAIL BD17 ... 82 F1
Moor Side BSPA/BRAM LS23 ... 48 D6
Moorside CLECK BD19 ... 149 J8
HTON BD9 ... 104 A4
ROCH OL11 ... 228 B3
Moorside Ap BIRK/DRI BD11 ... 151 H1 6
Moorside Av AIRE BD20 ... 56 C1
BIRK/DRI BD11 ... 128 C7
BIRK/DRI BD11 ... 151 H1
DEWS WF13 ... 173 G4
ECHL BD2 ... 105 M4 8
HUDS HD4 ... 213 M2
STKB/PEN S36 ... 270 E4
Moorside Cl BIRK/DRI BD11 ... 151 H1 6
DOD/DAR S75 ... 242 D6
ECHL BD2 ... 105 L3 8
Moorside Crs BIRK/DRI BD11 ... 151 H1
DEWS WF13 ... 173 H4 7
HOR/CROF WF4 ... 220 B4
BRAM LS13 ... 107 L2
Moorside Dr BIRK/DRI BD11 ... 151 H1
BRAM LS13 ... 107 L2
Moorside End DEWS WF13 ... 173 H4
Moorside Gdns BIRK/DRI BD11 ... 151 H1
ECHL BD2 ... 105 L3
LUD/ILL HX2 ... 146 B2
Moorside Gn BIRK/DRI BD11 ... 129 H8 6
Moor Side La HOLM/MEL HD7 ... 211 M3
HWTH BD22 ... 100 B1
Moorside La BFDE BD3 ... 105 M7 8
ILK LS29 ... 37 G2
OT LS21 ... 22 B7
Moorside Maltings
BEE/HOL LS11 ... 9 G8
Moorside Mt BIRK/DRI BD11 ... 151 G1
Moorside Pde BIRK/DRI BD11 ... 151 H1
Moorside Pl BFDE BD3 ... 105 M7 7
DEWS WF13 ... 173 H4
Moorside Ri CLECK BD19 ... 149 K7
Moorside Rd BFDE BD3 ... 105 M7 8
BIRK/DRI BD11 ... 151 G1
DEWS WF13 ... 173 H4
ECHL BD2 ... 105 L2
HOLM/MEL HD7 ... 236 A3
HUDE HD5 ... 193 L4
WIL/AL BD15 ... 102 E2 4
Moorside St BRAM LS13 ... 107 L2 4
LM/WK BD12 ... 126 D8
Moorside Ter BIRK/DRI BD11 ... 151 G1
BRAM LS13 ... 107 L2
ECHL BD2 ... 105 M4 8
Moorside V BIRK/DRI BD11 ... 129 H8
Moorside Vw BIRK/DRI BD11 ... 151 H1
Moorside Wk BIRK/DRI BD11 ... 151 H1
Moor Stone Pl HIPP HX3 ... 147 L1 8
Moor St CUL/QBY BD13 ... 125 G5 10
HWTH BD22 ... 78 F3
ROY/SHW OL2 ... 229 G5
Moorthorpe Av BFDE BD3 ... 105 M5 4
Moortop BIRK/DRI BD11 ... 128 F8
Moor Top BIRK/DRI BD11 ... 150 F1
MIRF WF14 ... 172 A8 8
OT LS21 ... 61 M1
WOR/ARM LS12 ... 129 L4
Moor Top Av FEA/AMT WF7 ... 224 A1
HUDS HD4 ... 237 H4
Moor Top Dr HEM/SK/SE WF9 .. 245 M1
Moor Top Gdns LUD/ILL HX2 ... 124 A7 7
Moor Top La HOR/CROF WF4 ... 216 F5
Moor Top Rd HUDE HD5 ... 193 L4
LM/WK BD12 ... 126 D8
LUD/ILL HX2 ... 145 K6
Moor Vw BEE/HOL LS11 ... 8 D6
HECK WF16 ... 173 G4
HOLM/MEL HD7 ... 234 E3
HOR/CROF WF4 ... 220 B1
MIRF WF14 ... 172 C5
Moor View Av SHPY BD18 ... 82 C6
Moor View Cl CAS WF10 ... 158 B7
Moorview Cft ILK LS29 ... 63 H1
Moorview Dr SHPY BD18 ... 83 H7 2
Moorview Gv KGHY BD21 ... 3 K8
Moorview Rd SKP/WHF BD23 ... 16 D3
Moorview Wy SKP/WHF BD23 ... 16 D3
Moorville Av BFDE BD3 ... 105 M5 4
Moorville Cl BEE/HOL LS11 ... 8 E8
Moorville Dr BIRK/DRI BD11 ... 128 C7
Moorville Gv BEE/HOL LS11 ... 8 D7
Moorville Rd BEE/HOL LS11 ... 8 D7
Moorway GSLY LS20 ... 61 K5
Moor Wy HWTH BD22 ... 78 F3
Moorwell Pl ECHL BD2 ... 105 K2

Moravian Pl WBOW BD5 ... 126 F2 13
Morefield Bank
HOLM/MEL HD7 ... 236 E6
Moresby Rd WBSY BD6 ... 126 A8
Moresdale La SCFT LS14 ... 111 H3
Morgan St LIT OL15 ... 207 K1 11
Morlands Cl DEWS WF13 ... 173 H3
Morley Av BFDE BD3 ... 105 M5
KNOT WF11 ... 182 C2 7
Morley Carr Rd LM/WK BD12 ... 148 F1
Morley Fold KBTN HD8 ... 257 H1 2
Morley Hall La LUD/ILL HX2 ... 144 E8
Morley La HUDS HD4 ... 213 J2
Morley St GTHN BD7 ... 4 D8
MILN OL16 ... 206 D8
Morningside GIR BD8 ... 104 D5
Morningside Cl MILN OL16 ... 206 D8 8
Morning St KGHY BD21 ... 79 K2 6
ILK LS29 ... 38 E2 7
ROCH OL11 ... 228 B4 7
Mornington Rd BGLY BD16 ... 81 J3
Mornington St KGHY BD21 ... 2 F1
Mornington Vls CUL/QBY BD8 ... 4 C1
Morpeth Pl OSM LS9 ... 9 L3
Morpeth St CUL/QBY BD13 ... 125 G5
Morphet Ter CHAL LS7 ... 7 H6 8
Morrell Crs WKFDW/WTN WF2 .. 176 B5 7
Morris Av KSTL LS5 ... 108 C1
Morris Cl HEM/SK/SE WF9 ... 223 K4
Morris Gv KSTL LS5 ... 108 C2
Morris La KSTL LS5 ... 108 C2
Morris Mt KSTL LS5 ... 108 C2 8
Morrison Rd WMB/DAR S73 ... 263 J8
Morrison St CUL/QBY BD13 ... 125 G5
Morris Vw KSTL LS5 ... 108 C2
Morritt Av MSTN/BAR LS15 ... 111 K5
Morritt Dr MSTN/BAR LS15 ... 111 H6
Mortimer Av BFDE BD3 ... 105 M5
BTLY WF17 ... 173 H1
Mortimer Dr STKB/PEN S36 ... 270 E4
Mortimer Ri OSS WF5 ... 175 G8
Mortimer Rw BFDE BD3 ... 105 M8 8
HOR/CROF WF4 ... 197 H5 8
Mortimer St BTLY WF17 ... 173 H1
CLECK BD19 ... 149 M7 8
GIR BD8 ... 104 B6
Mortimer Ter BTLY WF17 ... 173 H1
Morton Crs CAS WF10 ... 158 B7
Morton Gn HUDE HD5 ... 215 J2
Morton Gv AIRE BD20 ... 58 F6
EARL WF12 ... 195 K3
Morton La AIRE BD20 ... 58 F7
Morton Pde WKFDW/WTN WF2 .. 12 B3
Morton Rd BOW BD4 ... 127 M1 8
Mortons Cl HIPP HX3 ... 169 G3
Morton Wy HUDW HD3 ... 191 G5 11
Morton Wood Gv
HOLM/MEL HD7 ... 254 F3
Morwick Gv MSTN/BAR LS15 ... 90 A4
Moselden La RPDN/SBR HX6 ... 188 B8
Moseley Pl HDGY LS6 ... 6 F2
Moseley Wood Ap
BHP/TINH LS16 ... 85 M2
Moseley Wood Av
BHP/TINH LS16 ... 63 M8
Moseley Wood Bank
BHP/TINH LS16 ... 85 M1
Moseley Wood Cl
BHP/TINH LS16 ... 85 M2
Moseley Wood Crs
BHP/TINH LS16 ... 85 M1
Moseley Wood Cft
HORS LS18 ... 85 L2
Moseley Wood Dr
BHP/TINH LS16 ... 85 M1
Moseley Wood Gdns
BHP/TINH LS16 ... 85 M1
Moseley Wood Gn
BHP/TINH LS16 ... 85 M1
Moseley Wood Gv
BHP/TINH LS16 ... 85 M1
Moseley Wood La
BHP/TINH LS16 ... 64 A8
Moseley Wood Ri
BHP/TINH LS16 ... 85 L1
Moseley Wood Vw
BHP/TINH LS16 ... 64 A8
Moseley Wood Wk
BHP/TINH LS16 ... 85 M1
Moseley Wood Wy
BHP/TINH LS16 ... 63 M8
Moser Av ECHL BD2 ... 105 J1 3
Moser Crs ECHL BD2 ... 105 J1 3
Moss Av MILN OL16 ... 206 E8
Moss Bridge Rd BRAM LS13 ... 107 H3
MILN OL16 ... 206 D8
MILN OL16 ... 228 D1
Moss Carr Av KGHY BD21 ... 80 B1
Moss Carr Gv KGHY BD21 ... 80 B1 8
Moss Carr Rd KGHY BD21 ... 80 B1
Mossdale Av HTON BD9 ... 103 L3 8
Moss Edge Rd HOLM/MEL HD7 .. 253 G8
Moss End Rd HWTH BD22 ... 54 A4
Moss Gdns AL/HA/HU LS17 ... 87 J1
Moss Gate ROY/SHW OL2 ... 229 G5 8
Moss Gv ROY/SHW OL2 ... 229 G5 11
Moss Hall La HBR HX7 ... 142 A2
Moss Hey St ROY/SHW OL2 ... 229 K8
Moss La HBR HX7 ... 143 J2
LUD/ILL HX2 ... 124 A4 8
MILN OL16 ... 206 C8
Mossley Rd STKB/PEN S36 ... 270 E8
Moss Ri AL/HA/HU LS17 ... 87 J1
HOLM/MEL HD7 ... 254 A1
Moss Rw WIL/AL BD15 ... 80 E8
Moss Side HTON BD9 ... 104 A4 4
Moss Side La MILN OL16 ... 228 E1
Moss Side St WHIT OL12 ... 184 A1
Moss St CAS WF10 ... 157 K6
CUL/QBY BD13 ... 102 E2 7
HUDS HD4 ... 214 D2
HWTH BD22 ... 79 G6
MILN OL16 ... 206 D8
Moss Syke SCFT LS14 ... 67 L5

Moss Ter MILN OL16 ... 206 C8
Mosstree Cl CUL/QBY BD13 ... 124 E4
Moss Va AL/HA/HU LS17 ... 87 J1
Mossy Bank Cl CUL/QBY BD13... 125 G4
Mostyn Gv WBSY BD6 ... 126 C6
Mostyn Mt HIPP HX3 ... 146 C3 8
Mostyn Wk HOR/CROF WF4 ... 220 B3
Motley La GSLY LS20 ... 62 A4
Mottram St BSLYN/ROY S71 ... 261 H4
Moule Ri GFTH/SHER LS25 ... 113 K5
Moulson Ct WBOW BD5 ... 127 G3 13
Mountain Crs EARL WF12 ... 195 M4
Mountain Rd EARL WF12 ... 195 M4
Mountain Vw LUD/ILL HX2 ... 124 C8
SHPY BD18 ... 82 F8
Mountain Wy HUDE HD5 ... 193 L7
Mount Av CUD/GR S72 ... 245 J6
ECHL BD2 ... 105 K1
HECK WF16 ... 151 G8
HEM/SK/SE WF9 ... 223 M6
HUDW HD3 ... 190 E5
LIT OL15 ... 185 J7
LUD/ILL HX2 ... 145 L7
WHIT OL12 ... 207 C2 8
Mountbatten Av WKFDE WF1 ... 176 D3
Mountbatten Ct WKFDW/WTN WF2 .. 197 L1
Mountbatten Crs WKFDE WF1 ... 176 E1
Mountbatten Gdns HUDW HD3 .. 191 K7
Mountbatten Gv WKFDE WF1 ... 176 F2 8
Mountcliffe Vw MOR LS27 ... 130 D7
Mount Cl BSLY S70 ... 261 H7
Mount Crs CLECK BD19 ... 149 M6
LUD/ILL HX2 ... 145 L7
WKFDW/WTN WF2 ... 198 B3
Mount Dr AL/HA/HU LS17 ... 65 K8
Mountfield Av HUDE HD5 ... 215 K1
Mountfield Rd HUDE HD5 ... 215 K1
Mountfields HIPP HX3 ... 148 A6
Mountfields Wk
HEM/SK/SE WF9 ... 246 D5 8
Mount Gdns AL/HA/HU LS17 ... 65 K8
CLECK BD19 ... 149 M6
Mount Gv ECHL BD2 ... 105 K1
Mountjoy Rd HUD HD1 ... 14 C5
Mount La BRIG HD6 ... 170 A7
TOD OL14 ... 140 E3
Mountleigh Cl BOW BD4 ... 127 J8
Mount Pellon Rd LUD/ILL HX2 .. 146 A6
Mount Pl SHPY BD18 ... 82 D6 8
Mount Pleasant AIRE BD20 ... 58 E7
BRAM LS13 ... 107 K2
CAS WF10 ... 158 B8
CUD/GR S72 ... 245 J6
CUL/QBY BD13 ... 101 M6 8
FEA/AMT WF7 ... 202 B8
GFTH/SHER LS25 ... 135 K5 8
GSLY LS20 ... 62 A4
HUD HD1 ... 214 B3
ILK LS29 ... 19 H6
KBTN HD8 ... 217 M7
WBSY BD6 ... 126 A7
Mount Pleasant Av HFAX HX1 ... 10 C6
RHAY LS8 ... 110 B1
Mount Pleasant La HUDE HD5 .. 215 L2
Mount Pleasant Rd
PDSY/CALV LS28 ... 107 G6
Mount Pleasant St
FEA/AMT WF7 ... 179 M8 8
HUDE HD5 ... 15 L6
TOD OL14 ... 140 C5
Mount Pleasant Vw TOD OL14 .. 163 J1
Mount Preston LDSU LS2 ... 6 C1
Mount Preston St LDSU LS2 ... 6 C1
Mount Ri AL/HA/HU LS17 ... 65 K8
Mount Rd CUD/GR S72 ... 245 J6
EARD/LOFT WF3 ... 155 H8
ECHL BD2 ... 105 K1
HOLM/MEL HD7 ... 232 D5
HUD HD1 ... 191 M8
WBSY BD6 ... 126 C5
Mount Royd GIR BD8 ... 104 E4
Mount Scar Vw
HOLM/MEL HD7 ... 254 F2
Mountside Cl WHIT OL12 ... 206 B4 8
Mount St BFDE BD3 ... 5 K7
BOW BD4 ... 5 M8
BSLY S70 ... 261 G6
BSLYN/ROY S71 ... 262 B6
BTLY WF17 ... 173 M3
CLECK BD19 ... 149 M6
ECHL BD2 ... 105 K1
HFAX HX1 ... 10 F6
HUD HD1 ... 214 B3
HUDS HD4 ... 213 J2 8
HWTH BD22 ... 2 D5
RPDN/SBR HX6 ... 167 M2
WHIT OL12 ... 206 A6 13
Mount St West LUD/ILL HX2 ... 146 A6 8
Mount Tabor Rd LUD/ILL HX2 .. 145 H2
Mount Tabor St
PDSY/CALV LS28 ... 106 E7 8
Mount Ter BTLY WF17 ... 173 L3
ECHL BD2 ... 105 K1
The Mount AL/HA/HU LS17 ... 65 K8
BTLY WF17 ... 151 G4 8
CAS WF10 ... 158 E7
GFTH/SHER LS25 ... 135 J5
MSTN/BAR LS15 ... 90 F4
MSTN/BAR LS15 ... 111 K5
PONT WF8 ... 180 C5
TOD OL14 ... 141 J8
WKFDW/WTN WF2 ... 175 M5
WKFDW/WTN WF2 ... 198 B3
Mount Vernon Av BSLY S70 ... 261 H7
Mount Vernon Crs BSLY S70 ... 261 J8
Mount Vernon Rd BSLY S70 ... 261 J8
YEA LS19 ... 84 E2 3
Mount Vw HWTH BD22 ... 78 D4
LUD/ILL HX2 ... 145 J3
Mount View Ct CLECK BD19 ... 149 L6
Mount View Rd
HOLM/MEL HD7 ... 255 G4
ROY/SHW OL2 ... 229 J8
Mount Wk CAS WF10 ... 157 M8
Mount Zion Rd HUDE HD5 ... 15 K7

Mousehole La MIRF WF14 ... 194 F5
Moverley Flatts PONT WF8 ... 181 G7
Mowat Ct LVSG WF15 ... 171 K1 3
Mowbray Cha RTHW LS26 ... 133 J7
Mowbray Cl CUL/QBY BD13 ... 101 L1
Mowbray Ct SCFT LS14 ... 111 J3
Mowbray Crs SCFT LS14 ... 111 J3
Moxon Ct PONT WF8 ... 180 F8 2
Moxon Gv WKFDE WF1 ... 176 D3
Moxon Pl WKFDW/WTN WF2 ... 197 L1
Moxon Sq WKFDE WF1 ... 176 E2
Moxon St WKFDE WF1 ... 176 E2 8
Moxon Wy WKFDE WF1 ... 176 E2 8
Moynihan Cl RHAY LS8 ... 110 D2 3
Mozley Dr LUD/ILL HX2 ... 124 B8
Mucky La BSLYN/ROY S71 ... 262 C5
GTL/HWG HX4 ... 190 F2
Muddy La WBY LS22 ... 47 K3
Muffit La CLECK BD19 ... 150 F6
Muff St BOW BD4 ... 5 L9
Mug Mill La EARL WF12 ... 196 A6
Mugup La HOLM/MEL HD7 ... 255 G5
Muirfield Av FEA/AMT WF7 ... 179 L5
Muirfield Cl BOW BD4 ... 128 A4 8
Muirhead Ct BOW BD4 ... 128 A4
Muirhead Dr BOW BD4 ... 128 A4 11
Muirhead Fold BOW BD4 ... 128 A4 11
The Muirlands HUDN HD2 ... 193 G1 8
Mulberry Av BHP/TINH LS16 ... 86 F2
HOR/CROF WF4 ... 222 D5
Mulberry Cl ROCH OL11 ... 228 A1
Mulberry Ct HOLM/MEL HD7 ... 213 L3
Mulberry Garth BHP/TINH LS16 .. 86 F3
BSPA/BRAM LS23 ... 49 G6
Mulberry Pl HOR/CROF WF4 ... 222 D5
Mulberry Ri BHP/TINH LS16 ... 86 F3
WKFDW/WTN WF2 ... 198 B3
Mulberry St HUD HD1 ... 15 K8
KGHY BD21 ... 3 J3 8
MID LS10 ... 128 B8
PDSY/CALV LS28 ... 107 G7 8
Mulberry Street Sq
PDSY/CALV LS28 ... 107 G7 4
Mulberry Vw BHP/TINH LS16 ... 86 F3
Mulcture Hall Rd HFAX HX1 ... 11 J5
Mulehouse La HUDW HD3 ... 190 D5
Mulgrave St BFDE BD3 ... 5 L8
Mullberry Gdns RTHW LS26 ... 156 D4
Mullins Ct OSM LS9 ... 110 B7 13
Mullion Av HOLM/MEL HD7 ... 236 A2 8
Mumford St WBOW BD5 ... 127 G3 13
Munby St GIR BD8 ... 104 A7
Muncaster Rd GFTH/SHER LS25 .. 113 K6
Munster St BOW BD4 ... 127 K3 8
Munton Cl WBSY BD6 ... 126 E5 15
Murdoch Pl BSLYN/ROY S71 ... 243 G7 8
Murdoch St KGHY BD21 ... 58 B6
Murgatroyd St SHPY BD18 ... 82 D6 8
WBOW BD5 ... 127 G3 13
WBOW BD5 ... 127 G4 8
Muriel St MILN OL16 ... 228 D1
Murray Rd HUDN HD2 ... 14 C3
Murray St WBOW BD5 ... 126 E3 15
Murton Cl SCFT LS14 ... 111 J3
Museum Ct ECHL BD2 ... 105 L4 8
Museum St OSM LS9 ... 110 B5
Musgrave Bank BRAM LS13 ... 108 A4
Musgrave Buildings
PDSY/CALV LS28 ... 107 H6
Musgrave Dr ECHL BD2 ... 105 L4 8
Musgrave Mt BRAM LS13 ... 108 A4
ECHL BD2 ... 105 L4 8
Musgrave Ri BRAM LS13 ... 108 A4
Musgrave Rd ECHL BD2 ... 105 L4
Musgrave St BTLY WF17 ... 151 G5 4
Musgrave Vw BRAM LS13 ... 108 A4
Mushroom St CHAL LS7 ... 7 K6
Musselburgh St GTHN BD7 ... 4 A5
Mutton La WIL/AL BD15 ... 102 F4
Myers Av ECHL BD2 ... 105 J2
Myers Cft HUDE HD5 ... 193 H8 2
OT LS21 ... 41 J7
Myers La ECHL BD2 ... 105 J2
Mylor Ct BSLYN/ROY S71 ... 261 L3 4
Myrtle Av BGLY BD16 ... 81 H4 8
DEWS WF13 ... 195 G1
LUD/ILL HX2 ... 146 A2
Myrtle Ct BGLY BD16 ... 81 H4
Myrtle Dr HWTH BD22 ... 79 H5
LUD/ILL HX2 ... 146 A2
Myrtle Gdns LUD/ILL HX2 ... 146 A2 3
HUDW HD3 ... 191 K8
LUD/ILL HX2 ... 146 A2
Myrtle Gv BGLY BD16 ... 81 H4
HUDW HD3 ... 191 K8
LUD/ILL HX2 ... 146 A2
Myrtle Pl BGLY BD16 ... 81 H3
LUD/ILL HX2 ... 146 A2
Myrtle Rd DEWS WF13 ... 195 G1 8
ELL HX5 ... 191 H1
Myrtle St BFDE BD3 ... 105 L8
BGLY BD16 ... 81 J3 12
DOD/DAR S75 ... 260 E4 3
HUD HD1 ... 15 G4
Myson Av PONT WF8 ... 181 H2
Mytholm Bank HBR HX7 ... 143 G3 8
Mytholm Cl HBR HX7 ... 143 H3 8
Mytholmes La HWTH BD22 ... 78 E7

N

Nabbs La HOLM/MEL HD7 ... 212 B6
Nab Crs HOLM/MEL HD7 ... 234 E4
Nabcroft La HUDS HD4 ... 213 M3
Nabcroft Ri HUDS HD4 ... 213 M2 3
Nab End La ELL HX5 ... 169 G8
GTL/HWG HX4 ... 168 F7
Nab La BTLY WF17 ... 151 J4
MIRF WF14 ... 172 B8
WIL/AL BD15 ... 81 M1
The Nab MIRF WF14 ... 172 A8
Naburn Ap SCFT LS14 ... 89 K5
Naburn Cl SCFT LS14 ... 89 K7
Naburn Ct SCFT LS14 ... 89 K7
Naburn Dr SCFT LS14 ... 89 K7
Naburn Fold SCFT LS14 ... 89 L7
Naburn Gn SCFT LS14 ... 89 K7
Naburn Pl SCFT LS14 ... 89 K7
Naburn Rd SCFT LS14 ... 89 L6
Naburn Vw SCFT LS14 ... 89 L7

Nab Vw AIRE BD20 ... 36 B3
Nab Water La HWTH BD22 ... 100 E8
Nab Wood Bank SHPY BD18 ... 81 M7
Nab Wood Cl SHPY BD18 ... 82 A7 8
Nab Wood Crs SHPY BD18 ... 81 M7
Nab Wood Dr BGLY BD16 ... 81 M7
Nab Wood Gdns SHPY BD18 ... 82 A7 8
Nab Wood Gv SHPY BD18 ... 81 M7
Nab Wood Mt SHPY BD18 ... 81 M7 8
Nab Wood Pl SHPY BD18 ... 81 M7 8
Nab Wood Ri SHPY BD18 ... 81 M7 8
Nab Wood Rd SHPY BD18 ... 81 M8
Nab Wood Ter SHPY BD18 ... 81 M7
Nairn Cl HUDS HD4 ... 213 L4
Nall St MILN OL16 ... 207 G8
Nancroft Crs WOR/ARM LS12 .. 108 E7
Nancroft Ter WOR/ARM LS12 .. 108 E7
Nancy Crs CUD/GR S72 ... 245 K8 3
Nancy Rd CUD/GR S72 ... 245 K8
Nanny Goat La GFTH/SHER LS25.. 113 G6
Nanny La TAD LS24 ... 95 G8
Nanny Marr Rd WMB/DAR S73 .. 263 K8
Nansen Av BRAM LS13 ... 107 H5
Nansen Gv BRAM LS13 ... 107 H5
Nansen Mt BRAM LS13 ... 107 H5
Nansen Pl BRAM LS13 ... 107 H5
Nansen St BRAM LS13 ... 107 H5
Nansen Ter BRAM LS13 ... 107 K4 8
Nansen Vw BRAM LS13 ... 107 H5
Nantwich Av WHIT OL12 ... 206 B3 8
Naomi Rd HUDS HD4 ... 214 C4
Napier Mt BSLY S70 ... 261 H8
Napier Rd BFDE BD3 ... 105 M7
ELL HX5 ... 169 G8
Napier St BFDE BD3 ... 105 M7 8
CUL/QBY BD13 ... 125 H5 10
ROY/SHW OL2 ... 229 K6
Napier Ter BFDE BD3 ... 105 M7 8
Naples St BGLY BD8 ... 104 D5
Nares St HWTH BD22 ... 79 G6 8
KGHY BD21 ... 2 E4
Narrow La BGLY BD16 ... 80 D5
The Narrows BGLY BD16 ... 80 D5
Naseby Garth OSM LS9 ... 7 L8
Naseby Ri CUL/QBY BD13 ... 125 H5
Naseby Ter OSM LS9 ... 7 M8
Nashville Rd HWTH BD22 ... 2 D7
Nashville St HWTH BD22 ... 2 D7
Nassau Pl CHAL LS7 ... 7 L1
Nathan La AL/HA/HU LS17 ... 43 J1
National Rd MID LS10 ... 9 M7
Nat La AL/HA/HU LS17 ... 43 J1
Natty Fields Cl LUD/ILL HX2 ... 124 A7 8
Natty La LUD/ILL HX2 ... 124 A7
Nature Wy WBSY BD6 ... 126 A7 3
Navigation Rd CAS WF10 ... 157 M5
EARL WF12 ... 11 K7
HIPP HX3 ... 11 K7
Navigation Wk MID LS10 ... 9 H2
Navvy La BSLYN/ROY S71 ... 221 M7
Naylor Ct DEWS WF13 ... 173 M5
Naylor Gv DOD/DAR S75 ... 260 B7
Naylor St DEWS WF13 ... 173 K4
HFAX HX1 ... 10 A5
OSS WF5 ... 174 E6 8
Naze Rd TOD OL14 ... 163 H3 7
Neale Rd HUD HD1 ... 214 B3
Neale St HBR HX7 ... 143 J4
Neal St WBOW BD5 ... 4 E8
Near Bank KBTN HD8 ... 238 D4
Nearcliffe Rd HTON BD9 ... 104 C4
Near Crook SHPY BD18 ... 83 H5 3
Near La HOLM/MEL HD7 ... 235 G4
Neath Gdns OSM LS9 ... 110 F3
Necropolis Rd GTHN BD7 ... 126 B1
Ned Hill Rd LUD/ILL HX2 ... 124 A4
Ned La BOW BD4 ... 128 B2
HOLM/MEL HD7 ... 212 B6
Needles Inn La RTHW LS26 ... 133 L7 2
Needlewood DOD/DAR S75 ... 260 B8 3
Nell Gap Av HOR/CROF WF4 ... 196 C7
Nell Gap Crs HOR/CROF WF4 .. 196 C7
Nell Gap La HOR/CROF WF4 ... 196 C7
Nelson Av BSLYN/ROY S71 ... 261 J2
Nelson Cft MOR LS27 ... 152 B4
Nelson Cft GFTH/SHER LS25... 112 F8 2
Nelson Pl CUL/QBY BD13 ... 125 G5 11
MOR LS27 ... 152 C1 8
Nelson Rd ILK LS29 ... 38 D2
Nelson St BFD BD1 ... 4 F8
BSLY S70 ... 261 G5 3
BTLY WF17 ... 151 H5
BTLY WF17 ... 173 J1 8
CUD/GR S72 ... 245 G1
CUL/QBY BD13 ... 125 G5
DEWS WF13 ... 173 L6 8
HUD HD1 ... 214 B2
HWTH BD22 ... 79 G6
LIT OL15 ... 207 K1 12
LVSG WF15 ... 172 D3
MILN OL16 ... 206 D7 13
NORM WF6 ... 178 E3
OT LS21 ... 41 J7 8
RPDN/SBR HX6 ... 167 M2
SKP/WHF BD23 ... 16 C3 8
WBOW BD5 ... 4 F8
WIL/AL BD15 ... 103 L5
Nene St WBOW BD5 ... 126 C2
Nepshaw La MOR LS27 ... 152 B1
Nepshaw La North MOR LS27 .. 152 A1
Nepshaw La South MOR LS27 .. 151 M2
Neptune St OSM LS9 ... 9 K2
Nesfield Cl MID LS10 ... 132 B8
Nesfield Crs MID LS10 ... 132 A8
Nesfield Gdns MID LS10 ... 132 A8
Nesfield Garth MID LS10 ... 132 A8
Nesfield Rd ILK LS29 ... 38 B1
MID LS10 ... 132 A8
Nesfield St BFD BD1 ... 4 D5
Nesfield Vw ILK LS29 ... 38 A2 8
MID LS10 ... 132 A8
Nesfield Wk MID LS10 ... 132 A8 8
Nessfield Dr HWTH BD22 ... 2 B8
Nessfield Gv HWTH BD22 ... 2 B8
Nessfield Rd HWTH BD22 ... 2 B8
Nestfield Cl PONT WF8 ... 180 F3

Nest La *HBR* HX7 .... **143** M6
Neston Cl *ROY/SHW* OL2 .... **229** M7
Neston Rd *MILN* OL16 .... **228** E2
Neston Wy *OSS* WF5 .... **174** F5 🔟
Netherby St *BFDE* BD3 .... **5** M6
Nethercliffe Rd *GSLY* LS20 .... **61** M4
Nether Cl *HUDE* HD5 .... **193** C6
Nether Crs *HUDE* HD5 .... **193** C6 🔟
Nethercroft *DOD/DAR* S75 .... **260** A1
Netherdale Ct *WBY* LS22 .... **30** C8
Netherend Rd *HOLM/MEL* HD7 ..... **218** F5
Netherfield Av *HOR/CROF* WF4 .... **218** D1
Netherfield Cl *CAS* WF10 .... **179** H1
KBTN HD8 .... **216** B8
YEA LS19 .... **62** D7 🔟
Netherfield Crs *HOR/CROF* WF4 .... **218** F1
Netherfield Dr *GSLY* LS20 .... **61** M4
HOLM/MEL HD7 .... **236** C7 🔟
HOR/CROF WF4 .... **196** F8 🔟
Netherfield Rd *DEWS* WF13 ...... **195** G1
GSLY LS20 .... **61** M4
ILK LS29 .... **61** L3
Nethergill La *AIRE* BD20 .... **34** A4
Nether Hall Av *HUDE* HD5 .... **193** G6
Netherhall Rd *BAIL* BD17 .... **82** F3
Nether House La *STKB/PEN* S36 .. **269** M7
Netherhouse Rd *ROY/SHW* OL2 ... **229** J7
Netherhouses
  HOLM/MEL HD7 .... **253** M1 🔟
Netherlands Av *WBSY* BD6 .... **126** E7
Netherlands Sq *WBSY* BD6 .... **126** F7
Nether La *HOLM/MEL* HD7 .... **252** D3
Netherlea Dr *HOLM/MEL* HD7 ..... **236** B7
Netherley Dr *HOLM/MEL* HD7 ..... **233** D4
Netherly Brow *OSS* WF5 .... **197** G3 🔟
Nether Moor Rd *HUDS* HD4 .... **213** K6
Nether Moor Rd *WBOW* BD6 .. **81** J3 🔟
Netheroyd *FEA/AMT* WF7 .... **200** E1
Netheroyd Hill Rd *HUDN* HD2 ..... **192** B3
Netheroyd Pl *HOR/CROF* WF4 .... **200** E2 🔟
Nether St *DOD/DAR* S75 .... **259** J5
PDSY/CALV LS28 .... **106** F2
Netherthong Rd
  HOLM/MEL HD7 .... **235** H6
Netherton Fold *HUDS* HD4 .... **213** L8
Netherton Hall Gdns
  HOR/CROF WF4 .... **197** G8 🔟
Netherton La *HOR/CROF* WF4 .... **196** F8
Netherton Moor Rd *HUDS* HD4 .. **213** M7
Netherwood Cl *HUDN* HD2 .... **192** C3
Netley Av *WHIT* OL12 .... **206** M7
Nettle Gv *HIPP* HX3 .... **147** H5
Nettleton Av *MIRF* WF14 .... **194** B1
Nettleton Cha *OSS* WF5 .... **174** E5 🔟
Nettleton Cl *BOW* BD4 .... **129** C4
Nettleton Ct *MSTN/BAR* LS15 ... **111** M6 🔟
Nettleton Hill Rd
  HOLM/MEL HD7 .... **190** D8
Nettleton Rd *HUDE* HD5 .... **193** L8
MIRF WF14 .... **194** B1
Nettleton St *EARD/LOFT* WF3 ... **155** M8
OSS WF5 .... **174** F4
Neville Ap *OSM* LS9 .... **110** E8
Neville Av *BOW* BD4 .... **127** K5
BSLY S70 .... **261** L7
OSM LS9 .... **110** E8
Neville Cl *BSLY* S70 .... **261** M7 🔟
HEM/SK/SE WF9 .... **246** E3
OSM LS9 .... **110** E8
Neville Crs *BSLY* S70 .... **261** M7
OSM LS9 .... **110** F6
Neville Garth *OSM* LS9 .... **110** E8
Neville Gv *HUDE* HD5 .... **215** H2
OSM LS9 .... **110** E8
RTHW LS26 .... **134** C4
Neville Mt *OSM* LS9 .... **110** E8
Neville Pde *OSM* LS9 .... **110** E8
Neville Pl *OSM* LS9 .... **110** F7
Neville Rd *BOW* BD4 .... **127** K5
MSTN/BAR LS15 .... **111** G7
OSM LS9 .... **110** E8
OT LS21 .... **41** K7
WKFDW/WTN WF2 .... **197** L1
Neville Rw *OSM* LS9 .... **110** E8 🔟
Neville Sq *OSM* LS9 .... **110** F7
Neville St *BEE/HOL* LS11 .... **8** E1
CLECK BD19 .... **150** A4
KGHY BD21 .... **3** J3 🔟
NORM WF6 .... **178** D6
SKP/WHF BD23 .... **16** C2
WKFDE WF1 .... **13** L7
Neville Ter *OSM* LS9 .... **110** E8
Neville Vw *OSM* LS9 .... **110** E8
Neville Wk *OSM* LS9 .... **110** E8
Nevill Gv *HTON* BD9 .... **103** M3
Nevins Rd *DEWS* WF13 .... **172** F8
Nevison Av *PONT* WF8 .... **181** G3
Nevis St *ROCH* OL11 .... **228** C4
New Adel Av *BHP/TINH* LS16 ... **86** C3
Newall Carr Rd *OT* LS21 .... **23** G8
Newall Cl *ILK* LS29 .... **61** K1
OT LS21 .... **41** H5
Newall Crs *HEM/SK/SE* WF9 .... **223** J1
Newall Hall Pk *OT* LS21 .... **41** J5
Newall St *LIT* OL15 .... **185** K8
TOD OL14 .... **163** J6 🔟
WBOW BD5 .... **126** F2
Newark *DOD/DAR* S75 .... **242** D4
Newark Park Wy *ROY/SHW* OL2 . **228** F8
Newark Rd *BGLY* BD16 .... **81** G1
WHIT OL12 .... **206** B3
Newark Sq *WHIT* OL12 .... **206** B3
Newark St *BOW* BD4 .... **5** K9
BOW BD4 .... **127** K1 🔟
Newark V *EARD/LOFT* WF3 ...... **154** C1
New Augustus St *BFD* BD1 ...... **5** H8
New Av *HUDE* HD5 .... **193** K5
New Bank *HIPP* HX3 .... **11** J3
New Bank Ri *BOW* BD4 ..... **127** M3 🔟
New Bank St *MOR* LS27 .... **152** D1
Newbarn Cl *ROY/SHW* OL2 .... **229** J7 🔟
ROY/SHW OL2 .... **229** J7
New Bath St *COL* BB8 .... **52** A8 🔟

New Bbrighton *BGLY* BD16 .... **81** L8
Newbold Moss *MILN* OL16 .... **206** D7
Newbold St *MILN* OL16 .... **206** E6
New Bond St *HFAX* HX1 .... **10** F7
New Bridge Rd *HOLM/MEL* HD7 .. **234** D4 🔟
New Briggate *LDSU* LS2 ...... **7** H3 🔟
New Broad La *MILN* OL16 .... **228** E5
New Brook St *ILK* LS29 .... **38** D1
New Brunswick St *HFAX* HX1 ... **10** F5
WKFDE WF1 .... **12** F6
New Buildings Pl *MILN* OL16 .... **206** B6 🔟
Newburn Rd *GTHN* BD7 .... **126** D1 🔟
Newbury Dr *HEM/SK/SE* WF9 ... **247** J1
Newbury Rd *BRIG* HD6 .... **170** B7
Newbury Wk *HUDE* HD5 .... **193** L5
Newby Garth *AL/HA/HU* LS17 ... **88** D1
Newby Rd *AIRE* BD20 .... **34** F6
Newby St *AIRE* BD20 .... **34** F7 🔟
WBOW BD5 .... **127** G2
Newcastle Cl *BIRK/DRI* BD11 ... **150** F1
Newcastle Farm Ct
  KNOT WF11 .... **159** J2 🔟
New Chapel La *STKB/PEN* S36 .. **270** C2 🔟
New Cl *DOD/DAR* S75 .... **259** H6
SHPY BD18 .... **81** M7 🔟
New Close Av *AIRE* BD20 ...... **36** A5 🔟
New Close La *AWLS/ASK* DN6 ... **227** C7
HOLM/MEL HD7 .... **211** K5
New Close Rd *SHPY* BD18 .... **81** M7 🔟
New Clough Rd *RPDN/SBR* HX6 . **167** M4
Newcombe St *ELL* HX5 .... **191** J1
New Craven Ga *BEE/HOL* LS11 ... **9** H7
New Crs *HORS* LS18 .... **85** K6
New Cft *HORS* LS18 .... **85** K6
New Cross St *LM/WK* BD12 ... **149** K1 🔟
WBOW BD5 .... **127** C4
Newdale Av *CUD/GR* S72 ..... **262** C1 🔟
New Dales La *AIRE* BD20 .... **16** D8
New England Rd *KGHY* BD21 .... **79** K7
New Farmers Hill *RTHW* LS26 .. **133** M7
Newfield Av *BSLYN/ROY* S71 ... **261** M2
CAS WF10 .... **158** E5 🔟
NORM WF6 .... **178** E5 🔟
New Field Cl *MILN* OL16 .... **206** D6
Newfield Cl *NORM* WF6 ...... **178** E5 🔟
Newfield Ct *NORM* WF6 .... **178** E4
Newfield Crs *NORM* WF6 .... **178** E5
Newfield Dr *GFTH/SHER* LS25 .. **135** K1
ILK LS29 .... **61** J2
Newfield Head La *MILN* OL16 ... **229** K1
Newfield La *GFTH/SHER* LS25 .. **136** F5
Newfield Vw *MILN* OL16 .... **207** J8
New Fold *HOLM/MEL* HD7 .... **254** B2
WBSY BD6 .... **126** A7
Newforth Gv *WBOW* BD5 .... **126** E4 🔟
New Ga *HOLM/MEL* HD7 .... **254** E5
Newgate *MILN* OL16 .... **206** A7
MIRF WF14 .... **194** C2
PONT WF8 .... **180** E6
Newgate La *HOLM/MEL* HD7 .. **235** G4 🔟
Newgate St *BTLY* WF17 .... **174** B3 🔟
New Grove Dr *HUDS* HD4 .... **193** C7
Newhall Bank *MID* LS10 .... **153** M1 🔟
Newhall Cha *MID* LS10 ...... **131** M8 🔟
Newhall Cl *MID* LS10 .... **131** M8 🔟
Newhall Crs *MID* LS10 ...... **131** M8
Newhall Cft *MID* LS10 ...... **131** M7 🔟
Newhall Dr *WBSY* BD6 .... **127** H6
Newhall Gdns *MID* LS10 ...... **153** M1 🔟
Newhall Garth *MID* LS10 .... **153** M1
Newhall Gn *MID* LS10 .... **131** M7
Newhall Gn *MID* LS10 ...... **131** M8 🔟
New Hall La *HOR/CROF* WF4 ... **218** B2
Newhall La *MIRF* WF14 .... **194** D4
Newhall Mt *MID* LS10 .... **153** M1 🔟
WBSY BD6 .... **127** H6 🔟
Newhall Rd *BOW* BD4 ...... **127** K5 🔟
MID LS10 .... **131** M8
New Hall Rd *PONT* WF8 .... **181** G3
New Hey Rd *BOW* BD4 .... **127** J2
HUDN HD2 .... **191** M1
HUDW HD3 .... **190** E5
HUDW HD3 .... **211** L2
Newhey Rd *MILN* OL16 .... **229** J1
Newhill *HEM/SK/SE* WF9 .... **246** D5 🔟
Newhill Rd *BSLYN/ROY* S71 .... **261** J1
Newhold *GFTH/SHER* LS25 ..... **113** J6
New Holme Rd *HWTH* BD22 ... **78** F8 🔟
Newhouse Cl *WHIT* OL12 .... **184** E8
New House La *CUL/QBY* BD13 .. **125** K5
Newhouse Pl *HUD* HD1 .... **14** D5
New House Rd *HUDN* HD2 ...... **192** E2
Newill Cl *WBOW* BD5 .... **127** H4
Newington Av *CUD/GR* S72 .... **244** D6 🔟
New Inn St *WOR/ARM* LS12 ... **108** C7
New Kirkgate *SHPY* BD18 ...... **82** D6 🔟
New Laithe Hl *HUDS* HD4 ...... **214** E4
New Laithe La *HOLM/MEL* HD7 . **254** D1
New Laithe Rd *HUDE* HD5 ...... **214** E4
HWTH BD22 .... **77** G6
WBSY BD6 .... **126** C5 🔟
Newland Av *CUD/GR* S72 .... **244** D3
CUD/GR S72 .... **262** C1
HUDN HD2 .... **14** C1
Newland La *NORM* WF6 .... **178** A5
Newland Rd *BSLYN/ROY* S71 ... **243** G7
HUDE HD5 .... **193** J7
Newlands *PDSY/CALV* LS28 .... **106** F4
Newlands Av *AWLS/ASK* DN6 .. **249** C4 🔟
BFDE BD3 .... **105** M5
HIPP HX3 .... **147** J2
KBTN HD8 .... **240** B4
RPDN/SBR HX6 .... **167** G3
WHIT OL12 .... **206** B3
YEA LS19 .... **62** C7
Newlands Cl *BRIG* HD6 ...... **170** D5 🔟
WHIT OL12 .... **206** B3
Newlands Dr *AIRE* BD20 .... **34** F7 🔟

BGLY BD16 .... **81** G1
EARD/LOFT WF3 .... **177** G1
HIPP HX3 .... **147** J3
MOR LS27 .... **152** F2
Newlands Pl *BFDE* BD3 .... **5** K3
Newlands Ri *YEA* LS19 .... **62** C7
Newlands Rd *LUD/ILL* HX2 ..... **145** H3
The Newlands *MSTN/BAR* LS15 . **167** G4
Newland St *KNOT* WF11 .... **181** K2 🔟
WKFDE WF1 .... **199** G4
Newlands Wk *EARD/LOFT* WF3 . **177** G1
Newland Vw *NORM* WF6 .... **178** B4
New La *AIRE* BD20 .... **35** H4
BEE/HOL LS11 .... **8** B8
BOW BD4 .... **105** M8
BOW BD4 .... **128** D4
CLECK BD19 .... **149** J8
COP/BISH YO23 .... **51** M1
EARD/LOFT WF3 .... **153** L6
GFTH/SHER LS25 .... **115** M8
GLE DN14 .... **161** K8
HBR HX7 .... **142** F3
HBR HX7 .... **165** M2
HEM/SK/SE WF9 .... **225** J8
HIPP HX3 .... **168** D4
HOLM/MEL HD7 .... **212** C5
HOR/CROF WF4 .... **198** A6
HUDW HD3 .... **210** F2
KBTN HD8 .... **239** K5
KNOT WF11 .... **159** M3
LUD/ILL HX2 .... **166** D1
MID LS10 .... **153** K1
MOR LS27 .... **24** F6
New Lane Crs *HEM/SK/SE* WF9 . **225** J7
Newlay Cl *IDLE* BD10 .... **84** A7 🔟
Newlay Gv *HORS* LS18 .... **85** K8
Newlay La *BRAM* LS13 .... **107** K2
HORS LS18 .... **85** K7
Newlay Lane Pl *BRAM* LS13 ... **107** K2
Newlay Wood Av *HORS* LS18 .. **85** L7
Newlay Wood Cl *HORS* LS18 .. **85** L7
Newlay Wood Dr *HORS* LS18 .. **85** L7
Newlay Wood Gdns *HORS* LS18 . **85** L7 🔟
Newlay Wood Ri *HORS* LS18 .. **85** K7
Newlay Wood Rd *HORS* LS18 .. **85** K7
New Lennerton La
  GFTH/SHER LS25 .... **117** M7
Newley Av *BTLY* WF17 .... **151** H6
Newley Mt *HORS* LS18 .... **85** K8
New Line *IDLE* BD10 .... **84** A7
New Lodge Crs *BSLYN/ROY* S71 . **243** G7
New Longley La *RPDN/SBR* HX6 . **167** J5
Newlyn Dr *BSLYN/ROY* S71 .... **261** K3
WKFDW/WTN WF2 .... **198** F4
Newlyn Rd *AIRE* BD20 .... **58** C5
Newman Av *BSLYN/ROY* S71 ... **243** G5
Newman St *BOW* BD4 ...... **127** K4 🔟
MILN OL16 .... **206** E8
New Market *OT* LS21 .... **41** J7 🔟
Newmarket Ap *OSM* LS9 .... **132** D1
Newmarket Gn *OSM* LS9 .... **110** C8
Newmarket La *EARD/LOFT* WF3 . **155** L6
OSM LS9 .... **132** D1
New Market St *LDS* LS1 .... **9** H1
Newmarket St *SKP/WHF* BD23 . **16** C2
New Mill La *BSPA/BRAM* LS23 .. **70** A1
New Mill Rd *HOLM/MEL* HD7 ... **236** D8
New Mill St *LIT* OL15 .... **207** J1
New North Pde *HUD* HD1 .... **14** E6
New North Rd *HECK* WF16 ..... **172** E1
HOLM/MEL HD7 .... **212** C4
HUD HD1 .... **14** C4
New Occupation La
  PDSY/CALV LS28 .... **106** E8
New Otley Rd *BFDE* BD3 .... **5** J4
New Oxford St *COL* BB8 .... **52** A8 🔟
New Park Av *PDSY/CALV* LS28 . **107** G3
New Park Cl *PDSY/CALV* LS28 . **107** G3 🔟
New Park Cft *PDSY/CALV* LS28 . **107** G3
New Park Ga *OSS* WF5 .... **175** K6
New Park Pl *PDSY/CALV* LS28 . **107** G3
New Park Rd *CUL/QBY* BD13 ... **124** F5
New Park Rd *MOR* LS27 .... **152** B3
New Park V *PDSY/CALV* LS28 .. **107** G3
New Park Vw *PDSY/CALV* LS28 . **106** F4
New Park Wk *PDSY/CALV* LS28 . **106** F4 🔟
New Park Wy *PDSY/CALV* LS28 . **107** G3
New Popplewell La *CLECK* BD19 . **149** H6
Newport Av *BRAM* LS13 .... **107** J4
Newport Crs *BULY* LS4 .... **108** F5
Newport Gdns *HDGY* LS6 ... **108** F3 🔟
Newport Mt *HDGY* LS6 ..... **108** F3 🔟
Newport Pl *GIR* BD8 .... **4** A3
Newport Rd *GIR* BD8 .... **4** A2
Newport Rd *PONT* WF8 .... **180** E5
Newport Vw *HDGY* LS6 ..... **108** F2 🔟
New Princess St *BEE/HOL* LS11 . **8** E5
New Rd *AIRE* BD20 .... **36** A5
AWLS/ASK DN6 .... **227** J4
BSPA/BRAM LS23 .... **69** M3
COP/BISH YO23 .... **73** L4
CUL/QBY BD13 .... **101** M6
DOD/DAR S75 .... **240** D8
DOD/DAR S75 .... **242** C4
EARD/LOFT WF3 .... **154** F3
FEA/AMT WF7 .... **178** E8
GFTH/SHER LS25 .... **136** F6
GTL/HWG HX4 .... **168** C7
GTL/HWG HX4 .... **190** C6
HBR HX7 .... **120** A8
HBR HX7 .... **143** H3
HBR HX7 .... **144** A6
HBR HX7 .... **165** M5
HEM/SK/SE WF9 .... **224** A7
HFAX HX1 .... **11** H7
HOLM/MEL HD7 .... **236** D2
HOR/CROF WF4 .... **196** B8
HOR/CROF WF4 .... **197** K5
HOR/CROF WF4 .... **201** K5
HOR/CROF WF4 .... **220** D8
HUDE HD5 .... **193** K4
HUDW HD3 .... **190** E4
KNOT WF11 .... **181** J1
LIT OL15 .... **207** G2
LUD/ILL HX2 .... **144** F5

PONT WF8 .... **204** E4
STKB/PEN S36 .... **258** A5
TAD LS24 .... **94** D1
TOD OL14 .... **140** E1
TOD OL14 .... **142** B6
TOD OL14 .... **164** C2
YEA LS19 .... **62** B7
New Road Side *HORS* LS18 .... **85** J7
YEA LS19 .... **84** D1
New Road Sq *BRIG* HD6 ... **170** A8 🔟
New Row *COL* BB8 .... **74** A1
New Row La *STKB/PEN* S36 .... **257** G6
New Royd *STKB/PEN* S36 .... **269** M3
Newroyd Rd *WBOW* BD5 .... **127** G4
Newsam Ct *MSTN/BAR* LS15 .. **111** J7 🔟
Newsam Green Rd
  MSTN/BAR LS15 .... **133** M4
RTHW LS26 .... **134** A6
New Shaw La *HBR* HX7 .... **142** B1
Newsholme La *HOR/CROF* WF4 . **198** B7
Newsholme New Rd
  HWTH BD22 .... **78** C2
New Smithy Av *STKB/PEN* S36 . **270** C2 🔟
New Smithy Dr *STKB/PEN* S36 . **270** C2 🔟
Newsome Av *HUDS* HD4 .... **214** C5
Newsome Rd *HUDS* HD4 .... **214** D2
Newsome Rd South *HUDS* HD4 . **214** D4
Newsome St *DEWS* WF13 ...... **173** K5
New Station St *LDS* LS1 .... **8** F7
Newstead Av *HEM/SK/SE* WF9 . **223** J3
HFAX HX1 .... **146** A7
WKFDE WF1 .... **176** C3
Newstead Crs *HEM/SK/SE* WF9 . **223** J2
Newstead Dr *HEM/SK/SE* WF9 . **223** J2
Newstead Gdns *HFAX* HX1 ..... **146** A7
Newstead Gv *HEM/SK/SE* WF9 . **223** J2
HFAX HX1 .... **146** A7
Newstead Heath *HFAX* HX1 .. **146** A7 🔟
Newstead La *HOR/CROF* WF4 .. **223** C6
Newstead Pl *HFAX* HX1 .... **146** A7
Newstead Rd *BSLYN/ROY* S71 . **243** G6
WKFDE WF1 .... **12** D1
Newstead Ter *HEM/SK/SE* WF9 . **223** J3
HFAX HX1 .... **146** A7
Newstead Vw *HEM/SK/SE* WF9 . **223** H3
New Temple Ga
  MSTN/BAR LS15 .... **111** J8
Newthorpe Rd *AWLS/ASK* DN6 . **227** L2
Newton Av *WKFDE* WF1 .... **176** D4
Newton Cl *AIRE* BD20 .... **35** M4 🔟
RTHW LS26 .... **154** D2
WKFDE WF1 .... **176** D5
Newton Ct *RHAY* LS8 .... **88** E8
WKFDE WF1 .... **176** D3
Newton Dr *CAS* WF10 ...... **158** D7 🔟
WKFDE WF1 .... **176** D3
Newton Garth *WKFDE* WF1 .... **110** A1
Newton Gdns *WKFDE* WF1 ..... **176** D5
Newton Gv *CHAL* LS7 .... **109** M2
TOD OL14 .... **141** M7 🔟
Newton Hill Rd *CHAL* LS7 ...... **109** M1
Newton La *CAS* WF10 .... **157** M2
WKFDE WF1 .... **176** D2
Newton Lodge Cl *CHAL* LS7 ... **109** L1 🔟
Newton Lodge Dr *CHAL* LS7 .. **109** L1 🔟
Newton Pk *BRIG* HD6 .... **148** B8
Newton Park Dr *CHAL* LS7 .... **110** A1
Newton Park Vw *CHAL* LS7 .... **110** A3
Newton Pl *WBOW* BD5 .... **127** G2 🔟
Newton Rd *CHAL* LS7 .... **110** A2
Newton St *BSLY* S70 .... **260** F4 🔟

MILN OL16 .... **228** D1
RPDN/SBR HX6 .... **167** K2 🔟
WBOW BD5 .... **127** G3
Newton Vw *CHAL* LS7 .... **109** M1
Newton Wk *CHAL* LS7 .... **110** A2
Newton Wy *BAIL* BD17 ...... **82** E2 🔟
Newtown Av *BSLYN/ROY* S71 .. **243** K2
CUD/GR S72 .... **262** D1
Newtown Gn *CUD/GR* S72 ...... **262** D1 🔟
Newtown St *COL* BB8 .... **74** A1 🔟
ROY/SHW OL2 .... **229** K8 🔟
New Wk *RHAY* LS8 .... **88** D5
New Wy *BTLY* WF17 .... **173** L1 🔟
GSLY LS20 .... **61** L3
New Wellgate *CAS* WF10 ...... **158** B8 🔟
New Windsor Dr *RTHW* LS26 .. **133** H8
New Works Rd *LM/WK* BD12 ... **148** E1
New York La *YEA* LS19 .... **84** F4
New York Rd *LDSU* LS2 .... **7** J8
New York St *LDSU* LS2 .... **9** H1
Nibshaw La *CLECK* BD19 .... **150** C6
Nibshaw Rd *CLECK* BD19 ...... **150** C6
Nice Av *RHAY* LS8 .... **110** B2
Nice St *RHAY* LS8 .... **110** C2
Nice Vw *RHAY* LS8 .... **110** B2
Nicholas Cl *GTHN* BD7 ..... **104** B7 🔟
Nicholas St *BSLY* S70 .... **260** F5 🔟
Nichols Cl *WBY* LS22 .... **47** L1
Nicholson Av *DOD/DAR* S75 ... **260** A2
Nicholson St *CAS* WF10 .... **157** L7
ROCH OL11 .... **228** D1 🔟
Nichols Wy *WBY* LS22 .... **47** K1
Nickleby Rd *OSM* LS9 ..... **110** C6 🔟
Nicolsons Pl *AIRE* BD20 .... **36** A5 🔟
Nidd Ap *WBY* LS22 .... **29** M6
Nidd Ct *AIRE* BD20 .... **36** A6
Nidderdale Cl *GFTH/SHER* LS25 . **135** K1
Nidderdale Wk *BAIL* BD17 ... **83** C2 🔟
Nields Rd *HOLM/MEL* HD7 ..... **212** B6
Nigher Moss Av *MILN* OL16 ... **206** E8 🔟
Nighthorne Av *BFDE* BD3 ...... **105** L5 🔟
Nightingale Crest
  WKFDW/WTN WF2 .... **197** L2 🔟
Nile Crs *HWTH* BD22 .... **2** A7
Nile St *HUD* HD1 .... **14** D9
HWTH BD22 .... **79** G6 🔟
HWTH BD22 .... **79** G6 🔟
LDSU LS2 .... **7** J8
MILN OL16 .... **206** C4
Nina Rd *GTHN* BD7 .... **126** B3 🔟
Ninelands La *GFTH/SHER* LS25 . **135** J1
Ninelands Sp *GFTH/SHER* LS25 . **113** H8
Ninelands Vw *GFTH/SHER* LS25 . **113** J7 🔟
Ninevah La *CAS* WF10 .... **157** H1
HEM/SK/SE WF9 .... **224** F3
Nineveh Gdns *MSTN/BAR* LS15 . **8** D5
Nineveh Pde *BEE/HOL* LS11 .... **8** D6
Nineveh Rd *BEE/HOL* LS11 ..... **8** C5
Ninth Av *LVSG* WF15 .... **171** K1
Nippet La *OSM* LS9 .... **7** M8
Nixon Av *OSM* LS9 .... **110** D7
Nixon Cl *EARL* WF12 .... **186** B5
Noble Ct *HUDS* HD4 .... **213** M8 🔟
Noble Meadow *WHIT* OL12 ... **206** F2 🔟
Noble St *GTHN* BD7 .... **126** D1 🔟
Nog La *HTON* BD9 .... **104** C2
Nook Farm Av *WHIT* OL12 .. **206** B3 🔟
Nook Gdns *MSTN/BAR* LS15 ... **90** B6
Nook Gn *EARD/LOFT* WF3 ...... **153** H7
EARL WF12 .... **195** M4
The Nooking *WKFDW/WTN* WF2 . **175** K3
Nook La *HBR* HX7 .... **143** M2
RPDN/SBR HX6 .... **166** B3
STKB/PEN S36 .... **271** G5
Nook Rd *MSTN/BAR* LS15 ...... **90** B6
The Nooks *MOR* LS27 .... **129** M7
The Nook *AL/HA/HU* LS17 ...... **87** M1
CLECK BD19 .... **150** A6
EARD/LOFT WF3 .... **153** C8
GFTH/SHER LS25 .... **138** A2
RPDN/SBR HX6 .... **167** K3
STKB/PEN S36 .... **258** C5
Nook Wk *DEWS* WF13 .... **173** H6
Noon Cl *EARD/LOFT* WF3 ...... **177** G1
Noon Sun St *WHIT* OL12 .. **206** B5 🔟
Nopper Rd *HUDS* HD4 .... **213** H7
Nora Pl *BRAM* LS13 .... **107** J3
Nora Rd *BRAM* LS13 .... **107** J3
Nora Ter *BRAM* LS13 .... **107** J3
Norbeck Dr *HWTH* BD22 ... **79** G6 🔟
Norbury Rd *IDLE* BD10 .... **106** A1
Norbury St *MILN* OL16 .... **228** D2 🔟
Norcliffe La *HIPP* HX3 .... **147** J8
Norcroft Brow *GTHN* BD7 ...... **4** C7
Norcroft La *DOD/DAR* S75 ..... **259** C3
Norcroft St *BFD* BD1 .... **4** B6
Norcross Av *HUDW* HD3 .... **191** J7
Norfield *HUDN* HD2 .... **192** C2
Norfolk Av *BTLY* WF17 ..... **173** K3 🔟
Norfolk Cl *BSLYN/ROY* S71 .... **261** K2
CHAL LS7 .... **87** M7
KNOT WF11 .... **159** K6
LIT OL15 .... **185** L6
ROY/SHW OL2 .... **229** K7 🔟
RTHW LS26 .... **155** M1
Norfolk Dr *RTHW* LS26 .... **155** M1
Norfolk Gdns *BFD* BD1 .... **4** F7
CHAL LS7 .... **87** M7
RYKW YO26 .... **32** B1 🔟
Norfolk Gn *CHAL* LS7 .... **87** M7
Norfolk Mt *CHAL* LS7 .... **87** M7
Norfolk Pl *CHAL* LS7 .... **87** M7
HFAX HX1 .... **10** D8
Norfolk St *BGLY* BD16 .... **81** D3 🔟
BTLY WF17 .... **173** K2
COL BB8 .... **74** A1
HBR HX7 .... **143** J4 🔟
ROCH OL11 .... **206** A4
Norfolk Vw *CHAL* LS7 ...... **87** M7 🔟
Norfolk Wk *CHAL* LS7 .... **87** M7 🔟
Norgarth Cl *BTLY* WF17 ... **174** B1 🔟
Norham Gv *LM/WK* BD12 ...... **148** F4
Norland Rd *RPDN/SBR* HX6 .... **167** K3
RPDN/SBR HX6 .... **167** M5
Norland St *GTHN* BD7 .... **126** B3
Norland Town Rd
  RPDN/SBR HX6 .... **167** M4

314 Nor - Oak

Norland Vw RPDN/SBR HX6 167 M2
Norman Av ECHL BD2 105 K1
ELL HX5 169 J8 2
Norman Cl BSLYN/ROY S71 261 L2 3
Norman Crs ECHL BD2 105 K1
Norman Dr MIRF WF14 172 B8
Norman Gv ECHL BD2 105 K1
ELL HX5 169 J8 3
KSTL LS5 108 C2
Norman La ECHL BD2 105 K1
Norman Mt ECHL BD2 105 K1 2
KSTL LS5 108 C2
Normanon Pl BEE/HOL LS11 8 D7
Norman Pl RHAY LS8 88 C4 6
Norman Rd KBTN HD8 257 H1
MIRF WF14 172 B8
Norman Rw KSTL LS5 108 C2
Norman St BGLY BD16 81 J3 15
ELL HX5 169 J8 2
HFAX HX1 10 A9
KSTL LS5 108 C2
SHPY BD18 82 F7
Normans Wy
WKFDW/WTN WF2 199 H5
Norman Ter ECHL BD2 105 K1 3
ELL HX5 169 J8
RHAY LS8 88 C4 7
Normanton Gv BEE/HOL LS11 8 C7
Normanton St HOR/CROF WF4 197 L6
Normanton Vw NORM WF6 178 D6
Norman Vw KSTL LS5 108 C2
Norreys St MILN OL16 206 C6 10
Norridge Bottom
HOLM/MEL HD7 254 C1 4
Norris Cl HUDE HD5 215 J2
Norristhorpe La LVSG WF15 172 C4
Nortech Cl CHAL LS7 7 K5
Northallerton Rd BFDE BD3 5 H2
North Ap TAD LS24 92 C2
North Av AIRE BD20 55 L2
CAS WF10 157 H7
HEM/SK/SE WF9 247 H4
HOR/CROF WF4 197 L5
HTON BD9 104 F3
OT LS21 41 J6
PONT WF8 180 C6
WKFDE WF1 176 E6
North Baileygate PONT WF8 180 F5
North Bank Rd BGLY BD16 103 J1
BTLY WF17 173 J1
HUDN HD2 14 C1
North Bolton LUD/ILL HX2 123 M7
North Br HFAX HX1 11 H4
North Bridge St HFAX HX1 11 H4
North Broadgate La HORS LS18 85 L7 8
Northbrook Pl CHAL LS7 87 M7
North Brook St BFD BD1 5 G4
Northbrook St CHAL LS7 87 M7
North Byland LUD/ILL HX2 124 A7 8
North Carr HUDE HD5 193 G7
North Cliffe Av CUL/QBY BD13 103 H8
North Cliffe Cl CUL/QBY BD13 103 G8 2
North Cliffe Dr CUL/QBY BD13 103 G8
North Cliffe Gv CUL/QBY BD13 103 G7
North Cliffe La CUL/QBY BD13 103 H7
Northcliffe Rd SHPY BD18 82 C8 1
North Cl BSLYN/ROY S71 243 L3
FEA/AMT WF7 179 L5
RHAY LS8 88 F8
Northcote OSS WF5 174 E5
Northcote Crs BEE/HOL LS11 8 F7
Northcote Dr BEE/HOL LS11 8 E7
Northcote Fold WBY LS22 47 K4
Northcote Gn BEE/HOL LS11 8 F7
Northcote Rd ECHL BD2 105 K4
North Ct LDSU LS2 7 H8
North Court Gv WBY LS22 30 A8 3
North Crs GFTH/SHER LS25 116 A5
HEM/SK/SE WF9 247 K2
Northcroft HEM/SK/SE WF9 247 J3
Northcroft Av HEM/SK/SE WF9 247 J2
North Croft Grove Rd ILK LS29 38 C2
Northcroft Ri HTON BD9 104 A5
North Cross Rd HUDN HD2 192 B4
North Cut BRIG HD6 170 A4
Northdale Av WBOW BD5 126 E4 6
Northdale Crs WBOW BD5 126 E4
Northdale Mt WBOW BD5 126 E4
Northdale Rd HTON BD9 104 E1 1
North Dean Av HWTH BD22 57 G7
North Dean Rd GTL/HWG HX4 168 B5
North Dene Rd AIRE BD20 36 A4
Northdowns Rd ROY/SHW OL2 229 H6
North Dr BHP/TINH LS16 64 B4
GFTH/SHER LS25 116 A5
GFTH/SHER LS25 135 K2
HOLM/MEL HD7 213 G1
Northedge La HIPP HX3 147 M5
Northedge Meadow IDLE BD10 83 K8
Northedge Pk HIPP HX3 147 M6
Northern Cl GTHN BD7 126 B4 6
Northern St LDS LS1 8 D1
North Farm Rd RHAY LS8 110 D3
North Fld DOD/DAR S75 259 H6
Northfield Av HEM/SK/SE WF9 246 D2
KNOT WF11 182 B2
OSS WF5 174 F7 2
RTHW LS26 154 E2
Northfield Cl AWLS/ASK DN6 205 H3
Northfield Ct TAD LS24 94 F7
Northfield Crs BGLY BD16 81 J7
Northfield Dr PONT WF8 181 H5
Northfield Gdns WBSY BD6 126 E5
Northfield Gv HEM/SK/SE WF9 246 D3
HUD HD1 214 A2
WBSY BD6 126 E5
North Field La KBTN HD8 239 J4 3
Northfield La AWLS/ASK DN6 205 G2
GFTH/SHER LS25 137 M1
HEM/SK/SE WF9 246 D3
HOR/CROF WF4 197 L5
KBTN HD8 216 A6
KNOT WF11 182 F8
TAD LS24 94 F6
Northfield Pl DEWS WF13 173 L5 3
GIR BD8 4 B1
RTHW LS26 154 D2
WBY LS22 30 A8
North Field Rd AWLS/ASK DN6 248 A6
Northfield Rd DEWS WF13 173 K5
HOR/CROF WF4 200 D3
KNOT WF11 182 B2
OSS WF5 174 F8
WBSY BD6 126 D5
Northfields BSPA/BRAM LS23 49 J3
Northfields St DEWS WF13 173 L5
HEM/SK/SE WF9 246 D3
Northfield Ter CUL/QBY BD13 125 J5 1
North Fold IDLE BD10 83 K6 3
North Ga MIRF WF14 193 M4
Northgate BAIL BD17 82 E2
BFD BD1 4 E5
CLECK BD19 150 A7
CUD/GR S72 223 G8
DEWS WF13 173 M6
DOD/DAR S75 260 E3
ELL HX5 169 H7
GTL/HWG HX4 190 D2
HBR HX7 143 H1
HECK WF16 172 E2
HFAX HX1 11 H4
HOLM/MEL HD7 214 D8
HOLM/MEL HD7 236 C1 1
HOR/CROF WF4 197 J4
HUD HD1 15 G4
HUDE HD5 215 H3
PONT WF8 180 F5
RTHW LS26 133 L8 3
WKFDE WF1 12 E2 3
Northgate Cl PONT WF8 180 F5 3
Northgate La WBY LS22 47 K4
Northgate Ldg PONT WF8 180 F5
Northgate Ri WBY LS22 47 K4
Northgates WBY LS22 48 A1
North Grange Ms HDGY LS6 6 A1
North Grange Mt HDGY LS6 109 G1
North Grange Rd HDGY LS6 109 G2
North Gv WBY LS22 30 A8
North Grove Av WBY LS22 30 A7
North Grove Cl RHAY LS8 88 F8 2
North Grove Crs WBY LS22 30 A7
North Grove Dr RHAY LS8 88 F8
WBY LS22 30 A7
North Grove Mt WBY LS22 30 A8
North Grove Ri RHAY LS8 88 F8
North Grove Rd WBY LS22 30 A7
North Grove Wy WBY LS22 30 A7
North Hall Av IDLE BD10 83 J4
North Hl SCFT LS14 67 M5
North Hill Dr HUDE HD5 193 L6
North Hill Rd HDGY LS6 6 A1
North Holme St BFD BD1 4 F4
North King St BTLY WF17 173 M2 3
Northlands BSLYN/ROY S71 243 L2
North La HOLM/MEL HD7 211 M5
RHAY LS8 88 E8
RTHW LS26 133 L8
STKB/PEN S36 258 B4
WHIT OL12 206 B6
Northlea Av IDLE BD10 83 J5
North Lingwell Rd MID LS10 153 L1
North Lodge Fold DEWS WF13 173 H5 3
North Lodge La PONT WF8 204 B2
North Md BHP/TINH LS16 64 B4
North Moor La HUDE HD5 193 L4
MIRF WF14 193 M3
Northolme Av BHP/TINH LS16 86 D7 1
Northolme Crs BHP/TINH LS16 86 D7
Northorpe Ct MIRF WF14 172 E7
Northorpe La MIRF WF14 172 E7
Northowram Gn HIPP HX3 147 J2
North Pde BFD BD1 4 E5
BHP/TINH LS16 86 C6
HFAX HX1 11 G5
ILK LS29 38 E2
ILK LS29 40 A4
MILN OL16 229 L2
OT LS21 41 J6
SKP/WHF BD23 16 C4
WIL/AL BD15 103 J4
North Park Av RHAY LS8 88 B6
North Park Gv RHAY LS8 88 C6
North Park La AWLS/ASK DN6 249 M3
North Park Rd HTON BD9 104 D3
RHAY LS8 88 C6
North Park St DEWS WF13 173 J5
North Park Ter HTON BD9 104 E4 2
North Pkwy SCFT LS14 111 G1
North Pl DOD/DAR S75 260 D3
North Pollard St HFAX HX1 11 H4
North Queen St KGHY BD21 3 G4
North Ri HUDN HD2 192 E4
North Rd AIRE BD20 55 L1
BSLYN/ROY S71 243 M2
DEWS WF13 172 F8
HORS LS18 85 K3
KBTN HD8 216 A7
KNOT WF11 159 J2 3
MSTN/BAR LS15 111 L4 2
OSM LS9 132 E3
WBSY BD6 126 D5 6
North Road Ter WKFDE WF1 176 D7
Northrop Cl GIR BD8 104 C5 3
North Rw KBTN HD8 237 M6
North Royds Wd
BSLYN/ROY S71 243 H5
Northside Av GTHN BD7 104 C8
Northside Rd GTHN BD7 104 C8
Northside Ter GTHN BD7 104 B8
North's Pl MIRF WF14 172 C7 3
Northstead DEWS WF13 172 F8
North St AIRE BD20 34 F7 10
AIRE BD20 36 A4
AIRE BD20 55 M1
BFD BD1 5 H5
CAS WF10 157 L6 6
CAS WF10 158 E4
CHAL LS7 7 J5
DEWS WF13 173 L5 6
GTL/HWG HX4 168 F7
GTL/HWG HX4 190 D2
HECK WF16 172 F3
HEM/SK/SE WF9 246 D3
HUD HD1 214 A2
HWTH BD22 78 D7
IDLE BD10 83 K4
ILK LS29 19 J6
KGHY BD21 3 G5
LDSU LS2 7 J7
LM/WK BD12 149 J2 3
MILN OL16 206 C6
MIRF WF14 194 B3
NORM WF6 178 C6
OT LS21 41 J6
PDSY/CALV LS28 107 G6
WBY LS22 48 A1
WMB/DAR S73 263 J8
YEA LS19 84 D2
North Ter BTLY WF17 151 H5
MSTN/BAR LS15 111 L4 5
YEA LS19 62 D7
Northumberland St HUD HD1 14 F6
Northumberland Wy
BSLYN/ROY S71 262 B6
North Vw AIRE BD20 35 H8 2
EARL WF12 173 M8 2
ILK LS29 61 J2
KNOT WF11 182 A1
WIL/AL BD15 102 E1
WIL/AL BD15 103 J5
North View Rd BFDE BD3 105 H4
BOW BD4 128 C7
North View St KGHY BD21 57 L5 6
PDSY/CALV LS28 107 G4
North View Ter HWTH BD22 78 E6
PDSY/CALV LS28 107 G4
North Wk BGLY BD16 80 C5
HEM/SK/SE WF9 223 M6
North Wy HUDN HD2 193 G2
RHAY LS8 88 F8 3
Northway MIRF WF14 172 B7
Northway Crs MIRF WF14 172 B7
Northway Gdns MIRF WF14 172 B6
Northwell Ga OT LS21 41 G5
North West Rd HDGY LS6 6 F3
North Wing BFDE BD3 5 H4
Northwood Cl PDSY/CALV LS28 129 H1
RTHW LS26 133 L7 5
Northwood Crs IDLE BD10 83 L7
Northwood Falls RTHW LS26 133 L7
Northwood Gdns
MSTN/BAR LS15 112 A7
Northwood Mt
PDSY/CALV LS28 129 H1 1
Northwood Pk KBTN HD8 216 A7
RTHW LS26 133 L7
Northwood Vw
PDSY/CALV LS28 129 H1
Norton & Kirk Smeaton Rd
PONT WF8 226 F1
PONT WF8 227 H3
Norton Cl ELL HX5 191 H1
LUD/ILL HX2 145 K7
Norton Dr LUD/ILL HX2 145 K7
Norton Mill La AWLS/ASK DN6 227 L2
Norton Rd RHAY LS8 88 C3
WHIT OL12 206 B3
WKFDE WF1 176 F7 4
Norton St AIRE BD20 35 M5
ELL HX5 191 H1
WKFDE WF1 13 K7
Norton Wy MOR LS27 130 C8 6
Norville Crs WMB/DAR S73 263 K8
Norwich Av MID LS10 131 M4
Norwich St ROCH OL11 228 C1
Norwood PONT WF8 203 J1
Norwood Av BIRK/DRI BD11 150 D2
ILK LS29 40 B5
SHPY BD18 82 D8
Norwood Bottom Rd OT LS21 23 H3
Norwood Cl ILK LS29 40 B5 1
ROY/SHW OL2 229 J6 6
Norwood Crs CLECK BD19 150 D2
PDSY/CALV LS28 107 H4
Norwood Dr BIRK/DRI BD11 150 D2
BTLY WF17 151 H6
DOD/DAR S75 260 A1
Norwood Green Hl HIPP HX3 148 B4
Norwood Gv BIRK/DRI BD11 150 D2
HDGY LS6 109 G3
Norwood La PBR HG3 24 D1
STKB/PEN S36 270 B1
Norwood Mt HDGY LS6 109 G3 24
Norwood Pk HUDW HD3 191 M5
Norwood Pl HDGY LS6 109 G3
SHPY BD18 82 D8
Nor Wood Rd HEM/SK/SE WF9 245 M1
Norwood Rd HDGY LS6 109 G3
HUDN HD2 192 A4
SHPY BD18 82 D8 4
Norwood St NORM WF6 178 F3
SHPY BD18 82 D8 5
WBOW BD5 126 F4 7
Norwood Ter HDGY LS6 109 G3
ILK LS29 40 B5
SHPY BD18 82 D8
Norwood Vw HDGY LS6 109 G3 25
Nostell Cl GIR BD8 4 C3
Nostell Fold DOD/DAR S75 260 B8 4
Nostell La HOR/CROF WF4 222 D4
Noster Gv BEE/HOL LS11 8 B9
Noster Hl BEE/HOL LS11 131 H3
Noster Pl BEE/HOL LS11 8 B9
Noster Rd BEE/HOL LS11 131 H3
Noster St BEE/HOL LS11 8 B9
Noster Ter BEE/HOL LS11 8 B9
Noster Vw BEE/HOL LS11 8 B9
Nottingham Cl BSLYN/ROY S71 262 C7
EARD/LOFT WF3 154 C3 2
Nottingham St BFDE BD3 106 A7 2
Notton La HOR/CROF WF4 221 L7
Nova La BTLY WF17 150 F4
Nowell Ap OSM LS9 110 D5 8
Nowell Av OSM LS9 110 D5
Nowell Ct OSM LS9 110 D5 9
Nowell Crs OSM LS9 110 D5 10
Nowell End Rw OSM LS9 110 D5 11
Nowell Gdns OSM LS9 110 D5 12
Nowell Gv OSM LS9 110 D5
Nowell La OSM LS9 110 D5
Nowell Mt OSM LS9 110 D5
Nowell Pde OSM LS9 110 D5
Nowell Pl HUDE HD5 215 H2
OSM LS9 110 D5
Nowell St DEWS WF13 173 K5
OSM LS9 110 D5
Nowell's Yd DEWS WF13 173 K6 4
Nowell Ter OSM LS9 110 D5
Nowell Vw OSM LS9 110 D5 13
Nowell Wk OSM LS9 110 D5
Noyna Av COL BB8 52 A5
Noyna Vw COL BB8 52 A7
Nunburnholme Wk IDLE BD10 83 L8 3
Nunington Av WOR/ARM LS12 108 E6
Nunington St WOR/ARM LS12 108 E6
Nunington Ter WOR/ARM LS12 108 E6
Nunington Vw
WOR/ARM LS12 108 E5 2
Nunlea Royd BRIG HD6 148 C8
Nunnery La BRIG HD6 169 M7
Nunns Av FEA/AMT WF7 201 L3
Nunn's Cl FEA/AMT WF7 201 L2
Nunns Ct FEA/AMT WF7 201 L3
Nunn's Cft FEA/AMT WF7 201 M2
Nunn's Gn FEA/AMT WF7 201 M2
Nunn's La FEA/AMT WF7 201 L2
Nunroyd HECK WF16 172 F1
Nunroyd Av GSLY LS20 62 B6
Nunroyd Gv AL/HA/HU LS17 87 M5 3
Nunroyd Lawn AL/HA/HU LS17 87 M5 4
Nunroyd Rd AL/HA/HU LS17 87 M5
Nunroyd St AL/HA/HU LS17 87 M5 5
Nunroyd Ter AL/HA/HU LS17 87 M5 6
Nunthorpe Rd BRAM LS13 107 H1
Nurser La WBOW BD5 126 E2
Nurser Pl WBOW BD5 126 E2 1
Nursery Av LUD/ILL HX2 146 B3
Nursery Cl AIRE BD20 57 J3 2
AL/HA/HU LS17 87 L2
BAIL BD17 82 A4 2
Nursery Gdns BSLY S70 262 A7 1
MILN OL16 206 E6 2
Nursery Garth WBY LS22 30 B8
Nursery Gv AL/HA/HU LS17 87 J2
LUD/ILL HX2 146 B3
Nursery La AL/HA/HU LS17 87 K2
HIPP HX3 146 B3
ILK LS29 19 J6
RPDN/SBR HX6 188 D3
Nursery Mt MID LS10 132 A5
Nursery Mount Rd MID LS10 132 A5
Nursery Rd GSLY LS20 61 M3
GTHN BD7 126 B4
Nursery St BSLY S70 261 G6
EARL WF12 195 L2
Nursery Wy BSPA/BRAM LS23 48 D6 1
BSPA/BRAM LS23 69 M1
Nursery Wood Rd BTLY WF17 173 M4
Nussey Av BTLY WF17 151 G4
Nutclough Rd HBR HX7 143 K2
Nutfield St TOD OL14 141 K8
Nuttall Rd BFDE BD3 5 J5
Nutter La CLECK BD19 150 E4
Nutter St CLECK BD19 149 L7 2
Nutting Grove Ter
WOR/ARM LS12 130 A1
Nutwood Wk WBSY BD6 126 B8 5

O

Oak Av BGLY BD16 81 H5
COP/BISH YO23 73 L8
EARD/LOFT WF3 177 H2
GFTH/SHER LS25 113 H7
GIR BD8 104 E4
HOLM/MEL HD7 234 E3
HUDE HD5 215 G1
HUDW HD3 213 G1
ILK LS29 40 B6
MOR LS27 152 D3
NORM WF6 178 C6 3
ROY/SHW OL2 228 F8
RPDN/SBR HX6 167 K1
TOD OL14 141 J7
Oak Bank BGLY BD16 81 H5
SHPY BD18 104 F1
Oakbank Av HWTH BD22 2 A9
Oakbank Broadway HWTH BD22 79 H2
Oakbank Ct HWTH BD22 79 H2 1
Oakbank Crs HWTH BD22 79 H2
Oakbank Dr HWTH BD22 2 A9
Oakbank Gv HWTH BD22 2 B9
Oakbank La HWTH BD22 79 H2 2
Oakbank Mt HWTH BD22 79 H2
Oakburn Rd ILK LS29 38 C3
Oakcliffe Rd WHIT OL12 206 E2
Oak Crs GFTH/SHER LS25 113 H7
MSTN/BAR LS15 111 H7 3
Oakdale BGLY BD16 81 J1
Oakdale Av SHPY BD18 82 F8
WBSY BD6 126 D5
Oakdale Cl EARD/LOFT WF3 154 D8
HIPP HX3 146 C4
IDLE BD10 106 A3 1
Oakdale Crs HUDW HD3 191 J6
WBSY BD6 126 D5
Oakdale Dr IDLE BD10 106 A3
SHPY BD18 83 G8
Oakdale Garth SCFT LS14 89 K5 3
Oakdale Gv SHPY BD18 83 G8
Oakdale Meadow SCFT LS14 89 K5 6
Oakdale Pk OT LS21 42 F8
Oakdale Rd SHPY BD18 83 G8
Oakdale Ter WBSY BD6 126 D5 7
Oakdean HUDN HD2 192 C2
Oakdene Cl PDSY/CALV LS28 129 H1
Oakdene Ct AL/HA/HU LS17 88 C2 2
Oakdene Dr AL/HA/HU LS17 88 C2
Oakdene Gdns AL/HA/HU LS17 88 C2 3
Oakdene V AL/HA/HU LS17 88 C2
Oakdene Wy AL/HA/HU LS17 88 C2
Oak Dr GFTH/SHER LS25 113 H7
HOLM/MEL HD7 212 F3
Oakenshaw Ct LM/WK BD12 148 E4
Oakenshaw La CLECK BD19 149 J3
WKFDW/WTN WF2 199 J6
Oakenshaw St WKFDE WF1 13 L9
Oakes Av HOLM/MEL HD7 236 E5
Oakes Fold KBTN HD8 216 C3
Oakes La HOLM/MEL HD7 236 E4
Oakes Rd South HUDW HD3 191 K7
Oakes St WKFDW/WTN WF2 175 M8
Oakfield HDGY LS6 109 G1
Oakfield Av BGLY BD16 81 L4
RTHW LS26 133 G8 3
Oakfield Cl ELL HX5 169 G8
GFTH/SHER LS25 113 H8
ILK LS29 40 C8
Oakfield Crs KNOT WF11 182 B3
Oakfield Dr BAIL BD17 82 F4
MIRF WF14 194 B3
Oakfield Gv HTON BD9 104 E4
KBTN HD8 239 J5
Oakfield Pk PONT WF8 225 K2
Oakfield Rd HUDN HD2 192 A5
HWTH BD22 79 J2
Oakfield Ter SHPY BD18 82 F7 2
Oakfield Wk DOD/DAR S75 260 D4
Oak Gv GFTH/SHER LS25 113 J7
HWTH BD22 79 J3
MOR LS27 152 D3
Oakhall Pk CUL/QBY BD13 102 F7 2
Oak Hall Pk HOR/CROF WF4 219 L2
Oakham Pl DOD/DAR S75 260 E3
Oakhampton Ct RHAY LS8 88 E6 1
Oak Hl LIT OL15 207 H1
RPDN/SBR HX6 167 G6
Oak Hill Rd BRIG HD6 170 D3
Oakhill Rd BTLY WF17 151 J7
Oakhurst Av BEE/HOL LS11 131 H5
Oakhurst Gv BEE/HOL LS11 131 H5
Oakhurst Mt BEE/HOL LS11 131 H5
Oakhurst Rd BEE/HOL LS11 131 J5
Oakhurst St BEE/HOL LS11 131 H5
Oakland Ct KBTN HD8 216 B7
Oakland Dr HOR/CROF WF4 218 E1
Oakland Rd HOR/CROF WF4 218 F1
WKFDE WF1 13 J9
Oaklands BRIG HD6 170 B5
EARD/LOFT WF3 154 C3
IDLE BD10 83 J6
ILK LS29 38 B4
SHPY BD18 81 M7
Oaklands Av BHP/TINH LS16 86 F3
BRAM LS13 107 G1
BSLYN/ROY S71 261 M2
HIPP HX3 147 J3
Oaklands Cl BHP/TINH LS16 86 F3
HOLM/MEL HD7 236 C7
Oaklands Cft WKFDW/WTN WF2 199 K8
Oaklands Dr BHP/TINH LS16 86 F3
BTLY WF17 174 B1
HUDE HD5 215 H1
Oaklands Fold BHP/TINH LS16 86 F3 2
Oaklands Gv BHP/TINH LS16 86 F3 3
Oaklands Rd BRAM LS13 107 G1
Oakland St AIRE BD20 35 M5 8
Oak La GIR BD8 104 E4 3
HFAX HX1 10 C5 3
RPDN/SBR HX6 167 G6
Oaklea Cl DOD/DAR S75 242 D4
Oaklea Gdns BHP/TINH LS16 86 F4
Oaklea Hall Cl BHP/TINH LS16 86 F4
Oaklea Rd MSTN/BAR LS15 90 B8
Oak Leigh DOD/DAR S75 259 G2
Oakleigh Av CLAY BD14 125 K3
HIPP HX3 168 E3
WKFDW/WTN WF2 198 A1
Oakleigh Cl CLAY BD14 125 K2 12
HOR/CROF WF4 200 E2
Oakleigh Gdns CLAY BD14 125 K3 1
Oakleigh Gv CLAY BD14 125 K3 2
Oakleigh Rd CLAY BD14 125 K3
Oakleigh Ter CLAY BD14 125 K2 13
Oakleigh Vw BAIL BD17 82 D3
Oakley St EARD/LOFT WF3 154 A5
Oakley Ter BEE/HOL LS11 131 L4
Oakley Vw BEE/HOL LS11 131 L4
Oak Mt GIR BD8 104 F4
TOD OL14 141 K8
Oak Pl GFTH/SHER LS25 113 G7
HFAX HX1 10 C6 1
RPDN/SBR HX6 167 K1 9
Oak Rdg WBY LS22 47 L1
Oakridge Av ILK LS29 61 K2
Oakridge Ct BGLY BD16 81 J2
Oak Ri CLECK BD19 149 M4
Oak Rd CHAL LS7 109 M1
CUD/GR S72 244 F4
GFTH/SHER LS25 113 G7
HUDN HD2 193 J1
MOR LS27 152 B4
MSTN/BAR LS15 111 H7
WBY LS22 30 F1
WOR/ARM LS12 109 G7
Oak Royd GFTH/SHER LS25 113 H7
Oakroyd RTHW LS26 155 H2
Oakroyd Av WBSY BD6 126 E5 14
Oakroyd Cl BIRK/DRI BD11 150 C1
BRIG HD6 170 D1 1
Oakroyd Dr BIRK/DRI BD11 150 C2
BRIG HD6 170 D1
Oakroyd Fold MOR LS27 130 E6 5
Oakroyd Mt PDSY/CALV LS28 107 G6
Oakroyd Rd WBSY BD6 126 E6
Oakroyd Ter BAIL BD17 82 F4 3
MOR LS27 130 E6 6
PDSY/CALV LS28 107 G6
Oak Scar La HOLM/MEL HD7 254 F4
Oaks Crs BSLY S70 261 L6
Oaks Dr GIR BD8 103 L6
Oaks Farm Dr DOD/DAR S75 242 B6 2
Oaksfield RTHW LS26 156 F4
Oaks Fold WBOW BD5 127 G3 15
Oaks Green Mt BRIG HD6 170 B7
Oaks La BSLY S70 261 L6
BSLYN/ROY S71 261 L5
BSPA/BRAM LS23 48 F6
GIR BD8 103 L6
Oaks Rd BTLY WF17 174 A2
The Oaks HOR/CROF WF4 200 D2
MOR LS27 130 D7
Oak St BSLY S70 260 F5
CLAY BD14 125 K2
COL BB8 52 B8
CUD/GR S72 263 K1
ELL HX5 169 H8
HBR HX7 143 J3

HECK WF16 172 E2 5
HEM/SK/SE WF9 247 G5
HOR/CROF WF4 200 C7
HWTH BD22 78 F7 9
HWTH BD22 100 E3
LIT OL15 207 L1
MILN OL16 206 B7 17
MILN OL16 229 J3 1
MOR LS27 130 D7
PDSY/CALV LS28 106 E6
ROY/SHW OL2 229 L8
RPDN/SBR HX6 167 K1
TOD OL14 163 J2
WKFDE WF1 176 E2
Oaks Wood Dr DOD/DAR S75 242 B6 5
Oak Ter LIT OL15 185 M4
Oak Tree Av CUD/GR S72 244 D7
KBTN HD8 215 M3
Oak Tree Cl DOD/DAR S75 241 M6 4
OSM LS9 110 E3
Oak Tree Ct AIRE BD20 35 M4
Oak Tree Crs OSM LS9 110 E3
Oak Tree Dr RHAY LS8 110 E3
Oak Tree Gv HEM/SK/SE WF9 224 B8
OSM LS9 110 E3
Oaktree La HEM/SK/SE WF9 224 E1
Oak Tree Meadow
WKFDW/WTN WF2 199 J8
Oak Tree Mt OSM LS9 110 E3
Oak Tree Pl OSM LS9 110 E3
Oak Tree Rd KBTN HD8 215 M3
Oak Tree Ter KBTN HD8 215 M3
Oak Tree Wk OSM LS9 110 E3
Oak Vw AIRE BD20 36 A4
Oak Vls GIR BD8 104 F4
Oakville Rd HBR HX7 142 F4
Oakway BIRK/DRI BD11 150 D2
Oakwell Av BTLY WF17 151 H8
PONT WF8 180 E8
RHAY LS8 88 C8
WOR/ARM LS12 108 F7
Oakwell Cl BIRK/DRI BD11 151 J1
GTHN BD7 126 D3 5
HEM/SK/SE WF9 223 J4
Oakwell Crs RHAY LS8 88 C8
Oakwell Dr RHAY LS8 88 C8 2
Oakwell Gdns RHAY LS8 88 C8
Oakwell Gv BRAM LS13 107 K3
Oak Well La BSLY S70 261 J6
Oakwell Mt RHAY LS8 88 C8
Oakwell Ov RHAY LS8 88 C8
Oakwell Rd BIRK/DRI BD11 151 J1
Oakwell Ter BSLYN/ROY S71 261 J6 5
PDSY/CALV LS28 106 F3 5
Oakwell Vw BSLYN/ROY S71 261 J5
Oakwell Wy BTLY WF17 151 J3
Oakwood WKFDW/WTN WF2 197 M3 1
Oakwood Av BIRK/DRI BD11 150 C1
BSLYN/ROY S71 243 K2
ECHL BD2 104 F2
RHAY LS8 88 D8
WKFDW/WTN WF2 197 M1
Oakwood Boundary Rd
RHAY LS8 88 D8
Oakwood Cl NORM WF6 178 B2 2
TAD LS24 94 E8
Oakwood Ct GIR BD8 4 A4
Oakwood Crs BSLYN/ROY S71 243 K3
Oakwood Dr BGLY BD16 81 H1
HEM/SK/SE WF9 246 B1
NORM WF6 178 B2
RHAY LS8 88 D8
RTHW LS26 132 F7
Oakwood Garth RHAY LS8 88 E8
Oakwood Gra RHAY LS8 88 E8
Oakwood Grange La RHAY LS8 88 E8
Oakwood Gn RHAY LS8 88 E8
Oakwood Gv GIR BD8 104 C5
HOR/CROF WF4 197 L5
RHAY LS8 88 D8
Oakwood La OSM LS9 110 F3
RHAY LS8 88 D8
Oakwood Mt RHAY LS8 88 D8
Oakwood Nook RHAY LS8 88 D8 3
Oakwood Pk RHAY LS8 110 E1
Oakwood Pl RHAY LS8 88 D8
Oakwood Ri RHAY LS8 88 E8
Oakwood Rd BSLYN/ROY S71 243 K2
BTLY WF17 174 A1
Oak Wood Rd WBY LS22 29 M7
Oakwood Sq DOD/DAR S75 241 K6 1
Oakwood Ter PDSY/CALV LS28 106 E8
Oakwood Vw RHAY LS8 88 E8 1
Oakwood Wk RHAY LS8 88 D8
Oakworth Cl DOD/DAR S75 260 D3 2
Oakworth Hall HWTH BD22 78 E4
Oakworth Rd HWTH BD22 79 H2 5
KGHY BD21 2 B9
Oasby Cft BOW BD4 128 A5
Oast House Cft EARD/LOFT WF3 154 D3
Oastler Av HUD HD1 14 C7
Oastler Pl LM/WK BD12 126 F8 5
Oastler Rd PDSY/CALV LS28 84 D8
SHPY BD18 82 B6
Oastler St DEWS WF13 173 K6 5
Oates St DEWS WF13 173 L6 5
Oatland Cl CHAL LS7 7 H4
Oatland Ct CHAL LS7 7 H5
Oatland Dr CHAL LS7 7 H5
Oatland Gdns CHAL LS7 7 H4
Oatland Gn CHAL LS7 7 H4
Oatland La CHAL LS7 7 G4
Oatland Pl CHAL LS7 7 G3
Oatland Rd CHAL LS7 7 G4
Oatlands Dr OT LS21 41 H5
Oban Cl EARD/LOFT WF3 152 F5
Oban Pl WOR/ARM LS12 108 D6
Oban St WOR/ARM LS12 108 D6
Oban Ter WOR/ARM LS12 108 D6
Oberon Crs WMB/DAR S73 263 H8
Occupation La BHP/TINH LS16 63 K3
DEWS WF13 173 H3
HOLM/MEL HD7 236 F5
HWTH BD22 78 F2
LUD/ILL HX2 124 A8
PDSY/CALV LS28 106 E8
TAD LS24 91 M2
Occupation Rd HUDN HD2 192 E3 1
HUDW HD3 191 K6
Ochrewell Av HUDN HD2 193 G2 5
Octagon Ter LUD/ILL HX2 168 A2
Odda La GSLY LS20 61 G5
Oddfellows' Ct BFD BD1 4 E6
Oddfellows St BRIG HD6 170 D2 4
CLECK BD19 149 H6
MIRF WF14 194 C1
Oddfellow St MOR LS27 152 C2 10
Oddy Pl WBSY BD6 126 D5 5
Oddy's Fold HDGY LS6 87 G6
Oddy St BOW BD4 128 A5
Odsal Pl WBSY BD6 126 F6 5
Odsal Rd WBSY BD6 126 F6
Offley La HEM/SK/SE WF9 201 K8
Ogden Crs CUL/QBY BD13 101 M4
Ogden La BRIG HD6 170 B6
CUL/QBY BD13 101 M4
LUD/ILL HX2 123 M4
MILN OL16 229 M1
Ogden St RPDN/SBR HX6 167 J3
Ogden View Cl LUD/ILL HX2 123 M7
Ogilby Ms RTHW LS26 133 K7 2
Old Allen Rd CUL/QBY BD13 102 C3
Old Anna Lane Or Long La
STKB/PEN S36 270 C2
Old Bank HIPP HX3 11 K5
HOLM/MEL HD7 212 B6
Old Bank Rd EARL WF12 174 A6
MIRF WF14 172 C7
Old Bar La HOLM/MEL HD7 255 K6
Old Barn Cl AL/HA/HU LS17 87 J1
Old Bent La WHIT OL12 184 C7
Old Brewery Gdns TAD LS24 72 A2
Old Bridge Ri ILK LS29 38 C2
Old Brook Cl ROY/SHW OL2 229 M6 4
Old Brow La MILN OL16 206 E3 7
Old Canal Rd BFD BD1 4 F2
Old Cawsey RPDN/SBR HX6 167 L2
Old Church St OSS WF5 196 F1 5
Old Clay Dr WHIT OL12 206 F2 5
Old Cl BEE/HOL LS11 130 F6
Old Cock Yd HFAX HX1 11 H6 2
Old Corn Mill La GTHN BD7 126 C2 14
Old Crown Rd
WKFDW/WTN WF2 197 M3
Old Dalton La KGHY BD21 3 J4
Old Earth ELL HX5 169 K7
Oldfarm Ap BHP/TINH LS16 86 B6
Oldfarm Cl BHP/TINH LS16 86 C6
Oldfarm Cross BHP/TINH LS16 86 C6
Oldfarm Dr BHP/TINH LS16 86 C6
Oldfarm Garth BHP/TINH LS16 86 C6
Oldfarm Pde BHP/TINH LS16 86 C6
Oldfarm Wk BHP/TINH LS16 86 B6
Oldfield Av WOR/ARM LS12 108 E8
Old Fieldhouse La HUDN HD2 192 F4
Oldfield La HECK WF16 172 F3
HWTH BD22 77 M6
KBTN HD8 240 B4
WBY LS22 47 M5
WOR/ARM LS12 108 F8
Oldfield Rd HOLM/MEL HD7 236 A5
Oldfield St HIPP HX3 146 C2 4
HUDS HD4 214 A2 4
WOR/ARM LS12 108 E8
Old Forge Ms BHP/TINH LS16 63 M3
Old Garth Cft KNOT WF11 159 J2
Old Ga HBR HX7 143 J3
HOLM/MEL HD7 253 G7
Oldgate La GFTH/SHER LS25 115 L2
Old Great North Rd KNOT WF11 159 M6
KNOT WF11 181 L1 4
Old Gnd HOLM/MEL HD7 211 J6
Old Guy Rd CUL/QBY BD13 124 D4
Old Hall Cl AIRE BD20 34 D8
HWTH BD22 78 E8 14
Old Hall La KBTN HD8 240 A1
Old Hall Ms BTLY WF17 151 L7 1
Old Hall Rd AIRE BD20 34 D8
AWLS/ASK DN6 249 J5 3
BTLY WF17 151 L7
EARD/LOFT WF3 153 H6
Old Hall Wy AIRE BD20 34 C8
Oldham Rd MILN OL16 206 B7
ROCH OL11 228 D6
RPDN/SBR HX6 210 C1
UPML OL3 230 C8
Oldham Wy MILN OL16 229 H5
ROY/SHW OL2 230 C4
UPML OL3 231 L3
Old Haworth La YEA LS19 62 D7 5
Old Hollings Hl BAIL BD17 61 L8
Old Laithe La HBR HX7 143 L1
Old La BEE/HOL LS11 131 H4
BHP/TINH LS16 63 J3
BIRK/DRI BD11 129 J7
BIRK/DRI BD11 150 C1
BRIG HD6 170 D3
BWCK/EAR BB18 52 B2
GSLY LS20 61 G6
HBR HX7 121 K6
HIPP HX3 10 E1
HIPP HX3 146 C4
HOLM/MEL HD7 211 M7
HOLM/MEL HD7 212 D1
HOLM/MEL HD7 252 E2
HUDN HD2 192 F2
HWTH BD22 54 E4
HWTH BD22 77 H7
ILK LS29 19 L8
ILK LS29 38 F3
LUD/ILL HX2 144 F5
RYKW YO26 33 J3
SEL YO8 139 L5
WHIT OL12 162 A8
Old Langley La BAIL BD17 82 F2
Old Lee Bank HIPP HX3 10 E2
Old Leeds Rd HUD HD1 15 H6
Old Lees Rd HBR HX7 143 J2
Old Lindley Rd HUDW HD3 190 E4
Old London Rd TAD LS24 93 K2
Old Main St BGLY BD16 81 H3 11
Old Manchester Rd
STKB/PEN S36 269 G6
Old Manor Dr STKB/PEN S36 271 K5
Old Manse Cft HWTH BD22 100 E3 5
Old Market HFAX HX1 11 H6
Old Marsh PDSY/CALV LS28 106 E7
Old Mill Cl HEM/SK/SE WF9 223 L7 5
ILK LS29 40 B4
Old Mill Dr COL BB8 74 B2
Old Mill La BSLY S70 261 G4
BSLYN/ROY S71 261 J3
CHPT/GREN S35 271 M8
MID LS10 9 M8
Old Mill Rd BAIL BD17 82 C6 7
Oldmill St WHIT OL12 206 B6 10
Old Mill Vw EARL WF12 195 K1
Old Mill Yd OSS WF5 196 E3 1
Old Moll Rd HOLM/MEL HD7 235 M1
Old Mount Farm
HOR/CROF WF4 220 C7
Old Mount Rd HOLM/MEL HD7 233 G3
Old Oak Cl BHP/TINH LS16 86 C7
Old Oak Garth BHP/TINH LS16 86 B7
The Old Orch OT LS21 42 E7
Old Oxenhope La HWTH BD22 100 D1
Old Park Horse Rd UPML OL3 231 K8
Old Park Rd IDLE BD10 83 L7
RHAY LS8 88 C7
Old Pool Bank BHP/TINH LS16 63 K2
OT LS21 63 K1
Old Popplewell La CLECK BD19 149 G6
Old Power Wy ELL HX5 169 J6
Old Quarry La GFTH/SHER LS25 137 M5
Old Riding La LUD/ILL HX2 145 H3
Old Rd AL/HA/HU LS17 44 F4
BSLYN/ROY S71 261 J1
COP/BISH YO23 73 K5
CUL/QBY BD13 101 M6
CUL/QBY BD13 103 H8
GTHN BD7 126 A4
HBR HX7 121 J4
HOLM/MEL HD7 253 L4
HOR/CROF WF4 196 B8
MILN OL16 207 G2
MOR LS27 130 E6
Oldroyd Av CUD/GR S72 245 J8
Oldroyd Crs BEE/HOL LS11 131 G4
Oldroyd Rd TOD OL14 163 M1
Oldroyd Wy DEWS WF13 173 K6
Old Run Rd MID LS10 131 M4
Old Run Vw MID LS10 131 M6 5
The Old Sawmills
RPDN/SBR HX6 188 E4 1
Old School Ct CAS WF10 179 L1
Old School La HUDE HD5 215 H3
Old School Ms MOR LS27 130 E6 7
Old Schools Gdns HIPP HX3 11 H2
Old Shaw La HBR HX7 142 B2
Old Side Ct AIRE BD20 59 G5
Old Souls Wy BGLY BD16 59 G8
Old South St HUD HD1 14 E7
Old Station Rd LUD/ILL HX2 144 F7
Old Station Wy ILK LS29 19 H6
Old Stone Brow
BWCK/EAR BB18 52 C2
Old Stone Trough La
BWCK/EAR BB18 52 C1
Old St AWLS/ASK DN6 248 B7
Old Town Mill La HBR HX7 143 K1
Old Vicarage La
GFTH/SHER LS25 138 C7
Old Village St AWLS/ASK DN6 249 J2
Old Wakefield Rd HUDE HD5 15 L8
Old Westgate EARL WF12 173 L6
Old Whack House La YEA LS19 62 B8 2
Old Wood La BGLY BD16 60 C4
The Old Woodyard
HOR/CROF WF4 218 E4
Old Yew La HOLM/MEL HD7 254 A4
Olicana Pk ILK LS29 38 C1 1
Olive Gv GIR BD8 104 A6
Oliver Cl LIT OL15 207 H1
Oliver Gdns MIRF WF14 172 B7
Oliver Hl HORS LS18 85 L7
Oliver Mdw ELL HX5 169 J6
Oliver Rd HECK WF16 173 G1
Olivers Mt PONT WF8 181 G6
Oliver St BOW BD4 5 J9
BOW BD4 127 J1 5
Olive St HUD HD1 15 G1
Ollerdale Av WIL/AL BD15 103 J3
Ollerdale Cl WIL/AL BD15 103 J4 2
Ollerton Rd BSLYN/ROY S71 243 H6
Olney St HOLM/MEL HD7 212 B5
Olympic Pk LM/WK BD12 149 G1
Omar St HECK WF16 172 E2
One Acre Garth SEL YO8 139 M4
One Ash Cl WHIT OL12 206 B4
Onslow Crs BOW BD4 127 K4
Ontario Pl CHAL LS7 87 M8
Opal St HWTH BD22 79 J2 13
Orange St BFDE BD3 105 L8 4
HFAX HX1 11 G5
Orange Tree Gv
EARD/LOFT WF3 153 L7 7
Orchan Rd TOD OL14 141 H7
Orchard Av EARD/LOFT WF3 177 H1
Orchard Cl AWLS/ASK DN6 227 M3 2
BSLYN/ROY S71 261 L1
DOD/DAR S75 242 D5
EARD/LOFT WF3 153 M8
GFTH/SHER LS25 138 A3
GFTH/SHER LS25 138 D6
HOLM/MEL HD7 235 H5
HOR/CROF WF4 197 J4 5
LUD/ILL HX2 145 M8
TAD LS24 115 M1
WKFDW/WTN WF2 176 A3
Orchard Ct BSPA/BRAM LS23 69 M4
HUDW HD3 191 H8 2
Orchard Cft DOD/DAR S75 260 C8
WKFDW/WTN WF2 176 A4 5
WKFDW/WTN WF2 199 J7
Orchard Dr AWLS/ASK DN6 227 M3
CUD/GR S72 222 F8
FEA/AMT WF7 224 C1
HOR/CROF WF4 198 B7
KNOT WF11 159 K1
SEL YO8 139 M4
WBY LS22 47 K3
Orchard Gdns HOR/CROF WF4 198 B7
Orchard Gv IDLE BD10 83 M7
ILK LS29 61 J2
ROY/SHW OL2 229 J7
Orchard Head Crs PONT WF8 181 H2 1
Orchard Head Dr PONT WF8 181 G3
Orchard Head La PONT WF8 181 G2
Orchard La ILK LS29 19 J6
PONT WF8 203 L2
TAD LS24 116 A2
Orchard Lees HUDE HD5 193 L6
Orchard Mt MSTN/BAR LS15 111 L4 5
Orchard Pl CUD/GR S72 262 E1
Orchard Ri RPDN/SBR HX6 167 H4
Orchard Rd HUDE HD5 193 L6
MSTN/BAR LS15 111 K4
WKFDW/WTN WF2 199 G5
Orchard Sq MSTN/BAR LS15 111 K4
The Orchards BGLY BD16 81 J1
CLECK BD19 150 E6 2
MSTN/BAR LS15 111 K4
RTHW LS26 156 E4 2
Orchard St EARL WF12 173 L8
HUDS HD4 214 C2
OT LS21 41 K7
Orchard St West HUDW HD3 213 J1 2
Orchard Ter DOD/DAR S75 259 H2
HUDS HD4 214 D2
The Orchard AWLS/ASK DN6 227 L6
FEA/AMT WF7 179 M5 5
HOR/CROF WF4 200 B5
KGHY BD21 58 B7 1
MIRF WF14 172 D7 2
NORM WF6 178 C6
OSS WF5 196 F1 4
PONT WF8 203 H1
WKFDW/WTN WF2 176 B3
Orchard Wk HBR HX7 144 B5
Orchard Wy BRIG HD6 170 C2
RTHW LS26 133 G8
Orchid Ct EARD/LOFT WF3 154 D4
Oriel St ROCH OL11 228 B1
Oriel Wy BSLYN/ROY S71 261 M3
Oriental St WOR/ARM LS12 108 E7
Orion Crs MID LS10 132 A7
Orion Dr MID LS10 132 A7 5
Orion Gdns MID LS10 132 B7
Orion Vw MID LS10 132 B7
Orion Wk MID LS10 132 B6
Orlando Cl MIRF WF14 172 B7
Orleans St WBSY BD6 126 B7
Ormonde Dr WIL/AL BD15 103 J6
Ormond Rd WBSY BD6 126 D6 7
Ormondroyd Av WBSY BD6 126 E6 2
Ormond St GTHN BD7 126 C2 15
Orron St LIT OL15 207 J1 5
Orville Gdns HDGY LS6 109 G2
Orwell Cl CAS WF10 180 E1
Osborne Av HOR/CROF WF4 197 L3
Osborne Ms BSLY S70 261 J6 5
Osborne Pl TOD OL14 163 L1 10
Osborne Rd HUD HD1 14 D3
Osborne St BSLY S70 261 J6
HBR HX7 143 J3 17
HFAX HX1 10 B4
HUDE HD5 15 M8
ROCH OL11 228 A1
ROY/SHW OL2 229 K8 13
WBOW BD5 126 F1 5
Osbourne Ct BRAM LS13 107 M5
Osbourne Dr CUL/QBY BD13 125 G5 12
Osmondthorpe La OSM LS9 110 E7
Osprey Cl AL/HA/HU LS17 88 B2 5
AWLS/ASK DN6 249 K8
WBY LS22 47 K5
Osprey Ct GIR BD8 103 L7 5
Osprey Dr HUDS HD4 214 A7
Osprey Gv AL/HA/HU LS17 88 B2
Osprey Meadow MOR LS27 152 F2 4
Ossett La EARL WF12 174 B7
Osterley Gv IDLE BD10 106 A1
Oswald St MILN OL16 206 C6
ROY/SHW OL2 229 L6
SHPY BD18 82 F7
Oswaldthorpe Av BFDE BD3 105 M5
Otley La YEA LS19 62 D7
Otley Mt AIRE BD20 58 F5 4
Otley Old Rd BHP/TINH LS16 86 B2
HORS LS18 63 J5
Otley Rd AL/HA/HU LS17 44 E7
BAIL BD17 82 E6
BFDE BD3 5 J1
BGLY BD16 59 J5
BHP/TINH LS16 86 D6
GSLY LS20 61 L5
HDGY LS6 108 F1
ILK LS29 40 C6
ILK LS29 61 K1
OT LS21 44 C7
PBR HC3 25 H3
SHPY BD18 82 D8
SKP/WHF BD23 16 D2
Otley St HFAX HX1 10 A5
KGHY BD21 2 F7
SKP/WHF BD23 16 C2
Ottawa Pl CHAL LS7 87 M8 12
Otterburn Cl WBOW BD5 126 F1
Otterburn Gdns BHP/TINH LS16 86 D3
Otterburn St KGHY BD21 3 G1 2
Otter Lee La RPDN/SBR HX6 166 E6
Otters Holt HOR/CROF WF4 198 B7
Otterwood Bank WBY LS22 30 B7
Ouchthorpe La WKFDE WF1 176 E3
Ouldfield Cl MILN OL16 206 D8 6
Oulton Dr CUD/GR S72 244 E7
RTHW LS26 155 L3
Oulton La RTHW LS26 155 J1
Oulton Ter GTHN BD7 4 A9
Ouse Dr WBY LS22 29 M6
Ouslethwaite Ct BSLY S70 261 G8
Ouston Cl TAD LS24 72 A3 1
Ouston La TAD LS24 72 A3
Outcote Bank HUD HD1 14 E9
Out Gang BRAM LS13 107 M3
Outgang La BRAM LS13 108 A3
Outlands Ri IDLE BD10 83 M6
Out La HOLM/MEL HD7 236 B6
KBTN HD8 217 L7
Outside La HWTH BD22 100 B4
Outwood Av HORS LS18 85 M7
Outwood Cha HORS LS18 85 M6
Outwood La HORS LS18 85 L7
TAD LS24 95 G3
Outwood Park Ct WKFDE WF1 176 D2 1
Outwood Wk HORS LS18 85 L7
Ouzelwell Crs EARL WF12 195 J3
Ouzelwell La EARL WF12 195 J3
Ouzelwell Rd EARL WF12 195 K2 1
Ouzlewell Gn EARD/LOFT WF3 154 F4
The Oval AWLS/ASK DN6 249 H8 1
BGLY BD16 81 K4
GIR BD8 104 A6
GLE DN14 183 H1
GSLY LS20 61 L6
HOLM/MEL HD7 236 B7
HOR/CROF WF4 221 K8
LVSG WF15 171 L1
MID LS10 9 K8
OT LS21 41 H5
RTHW LS26 155 H2
SCFT LS14 111 H4
SKP/WHF BD23 16 D3
Ovenden Av HIPP HX3 10 C1
Ovenden Cl HIPP HX3 10 D1 5
Ovenden Crs HIPP HX3 146 C4
Ovenden Gn HIPP HX3 146 C4
Ovenden Rd HIPP HX3 146 C3
Ovenden Ter HIPP HX3 146 C4 11
Ovenden Wy HIPP HX3 146 B4
Ovenden Wood Rd LUD/ILL HX2 145 L4
Overburn Rd AIRE BD20 55 M2 4
Overdale RPDN/SBR HX6 167 G7 1
Overdale Av AL/HA/HU LS17 88 C1
BSLY S70 261 K8
Overdale Cl WBY LS22 29 M8
Overdale Ct SKP/WHF BD23 16 C1
Overdale Dr SHPY BD18 83 H5
Overdale Mt LUD/ILL HX2 167 M1
Overdale Ter HWTH BD22 78 E7 5
MSTN/BAR LS15 111 J6 10
Overfield Wy WHIT OL12 206 B4 5
Over Hall Cl MIRF WF14 172 D8 1
Over Hall Pk MIRF WF14 172 D8
Over Hall Rd MIRF WF14 172 D8
Overland Crs IDLE BD10 83 M6
Over La YEA LS19 84 E3
Overthorpe Av EARL WF12 195 M5
Overthorpe Rd EARL WF12 195 M4
Overton Dr WBSY BD6 125 M4
Overt St ROCH OL11 228 B1 13
Ovington Dr BOW BD4 128 A4
Owen Ct BGLY BD16 59 J8
Owlcotes Dr PDSY/CALV LS28 106 E6
Owlcotes Gdns PDSY/CALV LS28 106 E6
Owlcotes Garth
PDSY/CALV LS28 106 D6
Owlcotes La PDSY/CALV LS28 106 D5
Owlcotes Rd PDSY/CALV LS28 106 D6
Owlcotes Ter PDSY/CALV LS28 106 E6
Owler Bars Rd HOLM/MEL HD7 234 E4
Owler Ings Rd BRIG HD6 170 C4
Owler La BTLY WF17 151 G3
Owler Mdw HECK WF16 172 E1
Owler Park Rd ILK LS29 20 B8
Owlers Cl HUDN HD2 193 H1
Owler's La HEM/SK/SE WF9 225 H2
Owlet Hurst La LVSG WF15 172 D4
Owlet Rd SHPY BD18 82 E7
Owlett Md EARD/LOFT WF3 154 A5
Owlett Mead Cl
EARD/LOFT WF3 154 A5
Owl La EARL WF12 174 C4
Owl Ms HUDE HD5 193 L8
Owl Rdg MOR LS27 152 E3
Owston La AWLS/ASK DN6 249 M4
Owston Rd AWLS/ASK DN6 249 L6
Ox Close La WBY LS22 29 L1
Oxfield Ct HUDE HD5 193 J8
Oxford Av GSLY LS20 61 M5
Oxford Cl CLECK BD19 150 D6
CUL/QBY BD13 124 E7
Oxford Court Gdns CAS WF10 157 L7 4
Oxford Crs CLAY BD14 125 K2
HIPP HX3 168 F2
Oxford Dr CLECK BD19 150 D6
GFTH/SHER LS25 135 J5
Oxford La HIPP HX3 168 F2
Oxford Pl BAIL BD17 83 G4 5
BFDE BD3 5 H3
BSLYN/ROY S71 262 A6 5
HUD HD1 214 A3
LDS LS1 6 E8
MILN OL16 228 C1
PDSY/CALV LS28 107 G5
Oxford Rd BTLY WF17 151 G5
CHAL LS7 7 G3
CLECK BD19 150 D3
CLECK BD19 150 E6 5
CUL/QBY BD13 124 E6 5
DEWS WF13 173 J5
ECHL BD2 105 J4
GSLY LS20 61 M5
HFAX HX1 11 G8
WKFDE WF1 176 D6
Oxford Rw LDS LS1 6 E8
Oxford St BSLY S70 261 J7
BSLYN/ROY S71 262 A6
BTLY WF17 173 K2
CLAY BD14 125 K2
COL BB8 74 A1
EARD/LOFT WF3 154 A6 5
FEA/AMT WF7 201 M1
GSLY LS20 62 A5
HBR HX7 143 H3
HEM/SK/SE WF9 247 H4
HUD HD1 14 F4
HWTH BD22 2 D6
NORM WF6 178 E3
ROY/SHW OL2 229 K7
RPDN/SBR HX6 167 M1
TOD OL14 163 K1
WKFDE WF1 13 J8
Oxford Ter BTLY WF17 173 M2 5
Oxford Wk CLECK BD19 150 D6
Oxford Wy WHIT OL12 206 A4
Ox Hey La UPML OL3 231 C5
Ox Heys Mdw CUL/QBY BD13 103 J8 1
Ox Lee La HOLM/MEL HD7 255 G6
Oxley Gdns WBSY BD6 126 E7

Oxley Rd HUDN HD2 .... 192 E2
Oxley St GIR BD8 .... 4 B4
  OSM LS9 .... 110 B7
Oxmoor La GFTH/SHER LS25 .... 117 L3
  TAD LS24 .... 95 J8
Oxspring La STKB/PEN S36 .... 271 K3
Oxspring Rd STKB/PEN S36 .... 270 F6
Oxton Dr TAD LS24 .... 72 A3
Oxton La TAD LS24 .... 72 A3
Oxton Mt OSM LS9 .... 110 B6 11
Oxton Rd BSLYN/ROY S71 .... 243 M2
Oxton Wy OSM LS9 .... 110 B6 12
Oyster Cl MOR LS27 .... 152 C3
Ozar St BEE/HOL LS11 .... 8 C5

P

Pacaholme Rd
  WKFDW/WTN WF2 .... 175 M6 4
Packer St MILN OL16 .... 206 B7 18
Pack Horse Cl KBTN HD8 .... 240 C2
Pack Horse Gn DOD/DAR S75 .... 259 H6
Padan St HIPP HX3 .... 168 F2
Pad Cote La HWTH BD22 .... 54 C6
Paddock HTON BD9 .... 104 E2 8
Paddock Br WBY LS22 .... 47 K5
Paddock Cl DOD/DAR S75 .... 242 E5
  GFTH/SHER LS25 .... 113 J8
  LM/WK BD12 .... 148 E5
Paddock Dr BIRK/DRI BD11 .... 151 C1
Paddock Foot HUD HD1 .... 14 B9
Paddock Gn AL/HA/HU LS17 .... 67 L1
Paddock Gv CUD/GR S72 .... 244 E7
Paddock House La WBY LS22 .... 46 C2
Paddock La BGLY BD16 .... 59 M8
  LUD/ILL HX2 .... 145 L6
Paddock Rd DOD/DAR S75 .... 242 E5
  HIPP HX3 .... 147 C1
  KBTN HD8 .... 216 C1
Paddocks Church BRIG HD6 .... 171 G4
The Paddocks PBR HG3 .... 28 A1
The Paddock AIRE BD20 .... 36 A5
  AL/HA/HU LS17 .... 46 E8
  AWLS/ASK DN6 .... 249 L8 6
  BAIL BD17 .... 83 H2
  CAS WF10 .... 158 E8 9
  CLECK BD19 .... 149 H6 9
  CUL/QBY BD13 .... 79 M8 7
  EARL WF12 .... 174 A4
  GFTH/SHER LS25 .... 115 M7
  HDGY LS6 .... 87 H7 5
  HOR/CROF WF4 .... 220 C7
  HUDE HD5 .... 193 L6
  KNOT WF11 .... 182 B3
  NORM WF6 .... 178 D5
  RTHW LS26 .... 155 C1
  SCFT LS14 .... 90 B1
  WMB/DAR S73 .... 263 J8
Paddock Vw CAS WF10 .... 158 E8
Paddy Bridge Rd HBR HX7 .... 143 M5 5
Padgum BAIL BD17 .... 82 E2 3
Padley Cl DOD/DAR S75 .... 260 A7 8
Padma Cl GTHN BD7 .... 104 D7
Padstow Gdns MID LS10 .... 153 J1
Pagan St MILN OL16 .... 206 B6
Page Hl LUD/ILL HX2 .... 146 A4
Page St HUD HD1 .... 15 C8
Paget Crs HUDN HD2 .... 191 M5
Paget St KGHY BD21 .... 2 D5
Pagewood Ct IDLE BD10 .... 83 J5
Painter La SEL Y08 .... 139 M3
Painthorpe La HOR/CROF WF4 .... 220 B3
Paisley Gv WOR/ARM LS12 .... 108 D6 4
Paisley Pl WOR/ARM LS12 .... 108 D6 3
Paisley Rd WOR/ARM LS12 .... 108 D6 8
Paisley St WOR/ARM LS12 .... 108 D6
Paisley Ter WOR/ARM LS12 .... 108 D6 9
Pakington St WBOW BD5 .... 126 F2 18
Palace House Rd HBR HX7 .... 143 J4
Palatine St MILN OL16 .... 206 B7
Pale La SKP/WHF BD23 .... 16 A6
Paleside La OSS WF5 .... 174 F7
Palesides Av OSS WF5 .... 174 F6
Palestine Rd HBR HX7 .... 143 J2 8
Paley Rd BOW BD4 .... 127 L2
Paley Ter BOW BD4 .... 127 L2
Palin Av BFDE BD3 .... 105 M5
Pall Ml BSLY S70 .... 261 H5 0
Palma St TOD OL14 .... 140 D5
Palm Cl WBSY BD6 .... 126 D6
Palmer Cl STKB/PEN S36 .... 270 E5 0
Palmer Rd BFDE BD3 .... 5 M4
Palmer's Av HEM/SK/SE WF9 .... 247 J4
Palmerston St ECHL BD2 .... 105 K4 0
Palm St DOD/DAR S75 .... 260 E3
  HIPP HX3 .... 146 D4
  HUDS HD4 .... 214 D2
Panelagh Br IDLE BD10 .... 106 A1
Pannal Av PBR HG3 .... 26 F3
  WKFDE WF1 .... 177 C6 0
Pannal Bank PBR HG3 .... 26 F3
Pannal Cl PBR HG3 .... 26 F2
Pannal Rd PBR HG3 .... 27 J2
Pannal St GTHN BD7 .... 126 C3
Panorama Dr ILK LS29 .... 38 A4
The Parade BGLY BD16 .... 81 J7 4
  OSM LS9 .... 11 G6
Paradise La LUD/ILL HX2 .... 145 K8
  TAD LS24 .... 92 D1
Paradise Rd HTON BD9 .... 104 B2 0
Paradise St BFD BD1 .... 4 C5
  HFAX HX1 .... 10 F7
  PDSY/CALV LS28 .... 106 F3
Parish Ghyll Dr ILK LS29 .... 38 B3
Parish Ghyll La ILK LS29 .... 38 C3
Parish Ghyll Rd ILK LS29 .... 38 C3
Parish Ghyll Wk ILK LS29 .... 38 C3 0
Parish Wy BSLYN/ROY S71 .... 261 M3
Park Av AIRE BD20 .... 55 M1
  AWLS/ASK DN6 .... 249 L6 0
  BGLY BD16 .... 81 H4
  BIRK/DRI BD11 .... 129 C8
  BSLY S70 .... 261 G5
  BSLYN/ROY S71 .... 243 H7

BSLYN/ROY S71 .... 243 M3
CAS WF10 .... 157 L2
CUD/GR S72 .... 244 D7
CUD/GR S72 .... 245 J3
CUD/GR S72 .... 245 K3
DEWS WF13 .... 173 K6
EARD/LOFT WF3 .... 154 E7
ELL HX5 .... 169 G8
GFTH/SHER LS25 .... 115 M7
GFTH/SHER LS25 .... 135 L5
HEM/SK/SE WF9 .... 246 D8
HUD HD1 .... 14 D6
IDLE BD10 .... 83 K4
KBTN HD8 .... 238 B3
KBTN HD8 .... 240 B3
KGHY BD21 .... 2 E7
LVSG WF15 .... 172 C4
MIRF WF14 .... 194 D2
MOR LS27 .... 152 B3
MSTN/BAR LS15 .... 111 M4
NORM WF6 .... 178 D4
PONT WF8 .... 180 D6
PONT WF8 .... 203 L1
RHAY LS8 .... 88 D7
RTHW LS26 .... 134 C5
SHPY BD18 .... 82 C6 0
STKB/PEN S36 .... 270 E3
WKFDE WF1 .... 176 C2
WKFDE WF1 .... 177 M7
WKFDW/WTN WF2 .... 12 D6
WOR/ARM LS12 .... 108 D6
YEA LS19 .... 62 C7
Park Copse HORS LS18 .... 85 J5
Park Ct OSS WF5 .... 197 H2
  OT LS21 .... 42 F8
Park Crs BFDE BD3 .... 105 J4
  BSLYN/ROY S71 .... 243 M3
  CAS WF10 .... 158 E7
  GSLY LS20 .... 59 J5
  HIPP HX3 .... 10 C1
  ILK LS29 .... 19 J6
  MOR LS27 .... 129 M8 3
  RHAY LS8 .... 88 D5
  RTHW LS26 .... 133 J8 2
  WOR/ARM LS12 .... 108 D6
Park Crest HEM/SK/SE WF9 .... 223 M8
Park Cft BTLY WF17 .... 173 J2
  DEWS WF13 .... 173 J6
Parkcroft PDSY/CALV LS28 .... 106 F4
Park Cross St LDS LS1 .... 6 E9
Park Dl CAS WF10 .... 158 E4
  ILK LS29 .... 61 J2
Parkdale Dr RPDN/SBR HX6 .... 167 C2
Park Dr AIRE BD20 .... 55 M1
  AWLS/ASK DN6 .... 227 M5
  BGLY BD16 .... 81 K1
  BTLY WF17 .... 151 J7 8
  EARD/LOFT WF3 .... 154 E7
  HORS LS18 .... 85 H6
  HTON BD9 .... 104 D2
  HUD HD1 .... 14 B5
  KBTN HD8 .... 238 B3
  MIRF WF14 .... 194 D2 0
Park Drive Rd KGHY BD21 .... 3 G8
Park Dr South HUD HD1 .... 14 B6
Park Edge Cl RHAY LS8 .... 88 E7
Parker Av NORM WF6 .... 178 A2
Parker La MIRF WF14 .... 194 D1
Parker Rd EARL WF12 .... 195 L3
  HOR/CROF WF4 .... 197 L5
Parker's La AIRE BD20 .... 57 K3 2
Parker St AIRE BD20 .... 34 F7 11
  BSLY S70 .... 260 F5
  EARD/LOFT WF3 .... 153 L7
  HECK WF16 .... 172 F2
  LVSG WF15 .... 172 E3
Park Fld ILK LS29 .... 61 J2
Parkfield Av BEE/HOL LS11 .... 131 J3
  ELL HX5 .... 169 H8 8
  MIRF WF14 .... 194 E2
Parkfield Cl GFTH/SHER LS25 .... 135 K4
  PDSY/CALV LS28 .... 106 F7
Parkfield Crs MIRF WF14 .... 194 D2
Parkfield Cft MIRF WF14 .... 194 E2
Parkfield Dr BSPA/BRAM LS23 .... 48 E6
  CUL/QBY BD13 .... 124 F5 0
  RPDN/SBR HX6 .... 167 M3
Parkfield Gv BEE/HOL LS11 .... 131 J3
Parkfield La FEA/AMT WF7 .... 179 L4
  RPDN/SBR HX6 .... 167 M3
Parkfield Mt BEE/HOL LS11 .... 131 H3
  PDSY/CALV LS28 .... 107 G7
Parkfield Pl BEE/HOL LS11 .... 131 H3 0
  GIR BD8 .... 104 F4
  SHPY BD18 .... 82 A6 0
Parkfield Rw BEE/HOL LS11 .... 131 J3
Park Flds LUD/ILL HX2 .... 145 K4
Parkfield St BEE/HOL LS11 .... 9 C6
  MID LS10 .... 9 H6
  ROCH OL11 .... 228 D4 0
Parkfield Ter PDSY/CALV LS28 .... 107 G5
Parkfield Vw BEE/HOL LS11 .... 131 J3
  OSS WF5 .... 197 J1
Parkfield Wy MIRF WF14 .... 194 D2
  SCFT LS14 .... 111 C3
Park Gdns LUD/ILL HX2 .... 167 M1
  OSS WF5 .... 197 H2
Park Ga BSLY S70 .... 5 H5
Parkgate HEM/SK/SE WF9 .... 246 B5
  HUDS HD4 .... 214 B6
Parkgate Av WKFDE WF1 .... 13 K2
Park Gate Cl HORS LS18 .... 85 K6

Park Gate Rd HOLM/MEL HD7 .... 211 K8
Park Gn AIRE BD20 .... 35 L4
  NORM WF6 .... 178 B5
Park Gv BSLY S70 .... 261 G6
  CUL/QBY BD13 .... 124 F5
  HOR/CROF WF4 .... 197 H4
  HORS LS18 .... 85 H6
  HTON BD9 .... 104 D2
  HUD HD1 .... 14 D7
  MIRF WF14 .... 194 D2
  MOR LS27 .... 129 M8 1
  RTHW LS26 .... 134 D6
  SHPY BD18 .... 82 B6 10
  YEA LS19 .... 62 C7
Park Grove Rd
  WKFDW/WTN WF2 .... 12 A5
Parkhead Cl BSLYN/ROY S71 .... 243 J2
Park Head La HOLM/MEL HD7 .... 254 A2
  KBTN HD8 .... 256 A1
Park Hl DOD/DAR S75 .... 241 K4
  HUDN HD2 .... 171 H8
Parkhill Crs WKFDE WF1 .... 13 K2
Park Hill Dr GIR BD8 .... 103 M5
Park Hill Gv WKFDE WF1 .... 13 J3
Park Hill La WKFDW/WTN WF2 .... 13 J3
Park House Cl LM/WK BD12 .... 127 G7
Park House Crs LM/WK BD12 .... 127 G7
Park House Dr EARL WF12 .... 195 M2
Park House Gn PBR HG3 .... 28 F4
Park House Gv LM/WK BD12 .... 127 G7 2
Park House Rd LM/WK BD12 .... 126 F8
Park House Wk LM/WK BD12 .... 127 G7
Parkin Hall La RPDN/SBR HX6 .... 166 D4
Parkin La IDLE BD10 .... 84 B6
  TOD OL14 .... 140 F8
Parkinson Ap GFTH/SHER LS25 .... 113 H6
Parkinson Cl WKFDE WF1 .... 13 K1
Parkinson Rd CUL/QBY BD13 .... 102 A5
Parkin St LVSG WF15 .... 171 L1
Parkland Av MOR LS27 .... 152 A3
Parkland Dr IDLE BD10 .... 83 L7
  TAD LS24 .... 72 A2
Parkland Gdns HDGY LS6 .... 87 J6
Parklands BHP/TINH LS16 .... 63 M3
  CAS WF10 .... 158 A7
  ILK LS29 .... 38 F2
  OSS WF5 .... 197 H2 3
Park Lands PBR HG3 .... 28 A1
Parklands ROY/SHW OL2 .... 228 E8
Parklands Av HOR/CROF WF4 .... 197 G5 3
Parklands Ct HOR/CROF WF4 .... 197 G5 4
Parklands Crs BHP/TINH LS16 .... 64 A3
  HOR/CROF WF4 .... 197 G5 3
Parklands Dr HOR/CROF WF4 .... 197 G5
  RPDN/SBR HX6 .... 167 G5
Parklands Ga BHP/TINH LS16 .... 64 A3
Parklands Wk KBTN HD8 .... 238 B3
Parkland Ter HDGY LS6 .... 87 H6
Parkland Vw YEA LS19 .... 62 D8
Park La AIRE BD20 .... 55 M1 3
  AWLS/ASK DN6 .... 205 J3
  BAIL BD17 .... 83 H2
  BVRD LS3 .... 6 B8
  CAS WF10 .... 125 K2
  CLAY BD14 .... 125 K2
  CUD/GR S72 .... 263 K3
  CUL/QBY BD13 .... 125 H5
  GFTH/SHER LS25 .... 135 L6
  GFTH/SHER LS25 .... 136 E6
  GSLY LS20 .... 61 L7
  GTL/HWG HX4 .... 190 B5
  HBR HX7 .... 143 L6
  HIPP HX3 .... 169 G4
  HOLM/MEL HD7 .... 212 F2
  HOLM/MEL HD7 .... 235 G4 2
  HOR/CROF WF4 .... 219 G7
  HUDS HD4 .... 214 C7
  HWTH BD22 .... 54 B4
  KBTN HD8 .... 239 J1
  KBTN HD8 .... 256 C1
  KGHY BD21 .... 3 H8
  LDS LS1 .... 6 E8
  MILN OL16 .... 206 B8 13
  MOR LS27 .... 130 E6
  MSTN/BAR LS15 .... 111 K6
  OSS WF5 .... 197 H2 2
  ROY/SHW OL2 .... 229 K8
  RPDN/SBR HX6 .... 167 L2
  SHPY BD18 .... 82 C6
  SKP/WHF BD23 .... 16 B7 2
  WKFDE WF1 .... 13 G4
  WOR/ARM LS12 .... 108 C6
  YEA LS19 .... 62 C7
Park Lane Ms AL/HA/HU LS17 .... 88 D1 0
Park Lea HUDN HD2 .... 171 H8
Park Lodge Crs WKFDE WF1 .... 13 J2
Park Lodge La WKFDE WF1 .... 13 J2
Park Lodge Vw KBTN HD8 .... 239 J5
Parkmere Cl BOW BD4 .... 127 K7 0
Park Ms OT LS21 .... 42 F8
Park Mill La WKFDW/WTN WF5 .... 175 J7
  WKFDW/WTN WF2 .... 175 L8
Park Mill Wy KBTN HD8 .... 240 B3
Park Mt KSTL LS5 .... 108 D2
  OT LS21 .... 63 K1
  PBR HG3 .... 28 E4
  WOR/ARM LS12 .... 108 C6
Park Mount Av BAIL BD17 .... 83 G3
Park Pde DEWS WF13 .... 173 K5
  MOR LS27 .... 152 B3 0
  ROY/SHW OL2 .... 229 L5
Park Pl IDLE BD10 .... 83 K4
  LDS LS1 .... 6 D9
  PONT WF8 .... 180 D6
Park Pl East HIPP HX3 .... 148 A7
Park Pl West HIPP HX3 .... 148 A7
Park Ri BRAM LS13 .... 107 L2
  CAS WF10 .... 158 B7
Park Rd AIRE BD20 .... 34 C7
  BGLY BD16 .... 81 H3
  BRAM LS13 .... 107 L3
  BSLY S70 .... 261 G7
  BSPA/BRAM LS23 .... 48 E6
  BTLY WF17 .... 173 M1
  CAS WF10 .... 180 C1

CUD/GR S72 .... 245 J7
CUD/GR S72 .... 245 K3
DEWS WF13 .... 173 H8
EARL WF12 .... 173 L8
EARL WF12 .... 174 A7
GSLY LS20 .... 61 L7
HECK WF16 .... 172 F2 0
HFAX HX1 .... 10 E7
HUDS HD4 .... 214 A2
HWTH BD22 .... 54 E3
IDLE BD10 .... 83 K4
IDLE BD10 .... 105 M1
ILK LS29 .... 61 J2
KBTN HD8 .... 240 B3
MSTN/BAR LS15 .... 133 M1
PONT WF8 .... 180 C3
RPDN/SBR HX6 .... 167 L2
SHPY BD18 .... 82 B7
TOD OL14 .... 141 K8
WBOW BD5 .... 126 F1
WBSY BD6 .... 126 F7
WHIT OL12 .... 206 D5
WOR/ARM LS12 .... 108 C6
YEA LS19 .... 62 C7
YEA LS19 .... 84 D2
Park Rd West HUDS HD4 .... 213 L2
Park Rw BRIG HD6 .... 170 D4 2
  LDS LS1 .... 6 F9
  PDSY/CALV LS28 .... 107 C5
Parkside BGLY BD16 .... 81 J2
  CLECK BD19 .... 149 M7
Park Side CLECK BD19 .... 150 C7 3
  HOLM/MEL HD7 .... 255 C6
  HOR/CROF WF4 .... 217 L3
  HORS LS18 .... 85 J6
  HUDE HD5 .... 193 L5
Parkside Av CUL/QBY BD13 .... 124 F5
  HDGY LS6 .... 87 H7
Park Side Av ROY/SHW OL2 .... 229 L6 4
Parkside Ct HWTH BD22 .... 79 C6
Parkside Crs HDGY LS6 .... 87 H6
Parkside Gdns HDGY LS6 .... 87 H6
  EARD/LOFT WF3 .... 177 G4
Parkside Gv HDGY LS6 .... 87 H7
  HTON BD9 .... 104 D4
Parkside Lawns HDGY LS6 .... 87 H7 4
Parkside Mt BEE/HOL LS11 .... 131 H5
Parkside Pde HDGY LS6 .... 131 J5
Parkside Pl HDGY LS6 .... 87 H6
Parkside Rd HDGY LS6 .... 87 G5
  PDSY/CALV LS28 .... 106 F4
  TOD OL14 .... 140 D5
  WBOW BD5 .... 126 F3 11
Parkside Rw BEE/HOL LS11 .... 131 J5
Parkside Ter CUL/QBY BD13 .... 79 M8
Parkside Vw HDGY LS6 .... 87 H6
Parkside Wk PDSY/CALV LS28 .... 107 G4
Park Spring Gdns BRAM LS13 .... 107 K5
Park Spring Ri BRAM LS13 .... 107 K6
Park Spring Rd CUD/GR S72 .... 263 L6
Park Sq EARD/LOFT WF3 .... 154 E8
  OSS WF5 .... 197 H2
  WBSY BD6 .... 126 B6
Park Sq East LDS LS1 .... 6 E9
Park Sq North LDS LS1 .... 6 E9
Park Sq South LDS LS1 .... 6 E9
Park Sq West LDS LS1 .... 6 E9
Parkstone HUDN HD2 .... 171 H8
Parkstone Av BHP/TINH LS16 .... 86 C5
Parkstone Dr IDLE BD10 .... 105 L1
Parkstone Gn BHP/TINH LS16 .... 86 C5
Parkstone Gv BHP/TINH LS16 .... 86 C5
Parkstone Mt BHP/TINH LS16 .... 86 C5
Parkstone Pl BHP/TINH LS16 .... 86 C5 1
Park Stone Ri HIPP HX3 .... 125 K8
Park St AIRE BD20 .... 34 F7
  BRIG HD6 .... 170 D4
  BSLY S70 .... 261 G6
  BTLY WF17 .... 151 G6
  CLECK BD19 .... 149 K8
  CLECK BD19 .... 150 C8
  DEWS WF13 .... 173 M5
  HECK WF16 .... 172 F2 7
  HOLM/MEL HD7 .... 190 E8
  HOR/CROF WF4 .... 197 J5
  HWTH BD22 .... 78 F7 0
  LDS LS1 .... 6 E8
  MILN OL16 .... 206 B8 13
  MOR LS27 .... 130 E6
  MSTN/BAR LS15 .... 111 K6
  OSS WF5 .... 197 H2 2
  ROY/SHW OL2 .... 229 K8
  RPDN/SBR HX6 .... 167 L2
  SHPY BD18 .... 82 C6
  SKP/WHF BD23 .... 16 B7 2
  WKFDE WF1 .... 13 G4
  WOR/ARM LS12 .... 108 C6
  YEA LS19 .... 62 C7
Park Ter HDGY LS6 .... 86 F8
  KGHY BD21 .... 3 K4
  OT LS21 .... 63 J1
  SHPY BD18 .... 82 C6 0
The Park DOD/DAR S75 .... 259 G2
Park Top PDSY/CALV LS28 .... 107 G5
The Park Towngate HIPP HX3 .... 169 J3
Park Vw BEE/HOL LS11 .... 131 J3
  BRAM LS13 .... 107 L3
  BSLYN/ROY S71 .... 243 M2
  CAS WF10 .... 158 E8
  CLECK BD19 .... 149 L6
  CUD/GR S72 .... 244 F3
  CUD/GR S72 .... 245 K3
  DOD/DAR S75 .... 260 B7
  EARD/LOFT WF3 .... 154 E8
  HEM/SK/SE WF9 .... 223 K5
  HIPP HX3 .... 148 A7 8
  HOLM/MEL HD7 .... 254 B1
  LIT OL15 .... 185 K8
  RTHW LS26 .... 134 C5
  WKFDW/WTN WF2 .... 176 B3 2
Park View Av HDGY LS6 .... 108 F3

HIPP HX3 .... 147 J5
HWTH BD22 .... 79 G6
Parkview Ct RHAY LS8 .... 88 D4 0
Park View Crs RHAY LS8 .... 88 D5
Park View Gv BULY LS4 .... 108 F3
Park View Rd BULY LS4 .... 108 F4
  DOD/DAR S75 .... 242 E5
  HTON BD9 .... 104 D4
Park View Ter HTON BD9 .... 104 D3
  YEA LS19 .... 84 D2
Park Vls RHAY LS8 .... 88 D3
Park Villas Dr PONT WF8 .... 180 D5
Parkville Pl BRAM LS13 .... 107 L3
Park Wy AWLS/ASK DN6 .... 249 K8
  BAIL BD17 .... 82 B5
  ILK LS29 .... 61 J2
  OT LS21 .... 42 F8
Parkway AIRE BD20 .... 35 L8
  CUL/QBY BD13 .... 124 F5
  HOR/CROF WF4 .... 200 B4
  KGHY BD21 .... 3 G9
  MOR LS27 .... 129 L8
  WBOW BD5 .... 126 F5
Parkway Cl SCFT LS14 .... 111 G2
Parkway Ms SCFT LS14 .... 111 K1 3
Parkways RTHW LS26 .... 133 K8
Parkways Av RTHW LS26 .... 155 K1
Parkways Cl RTHW LS26 .... 133 K8
Parkways Ct RTHW LS26 .... 133 K8 8
Parkways Dr RTHW LS26 .... 133 K8
Parkways Garth RTHW LS26 .... 155 K1 0
Parkways Gv RTHW LS26 .... 133 K8
Park West RTHW LS26 .... 155 H1
Park Willow HIPP HX3 .... 125 M8
Parkwood Av BEE/HOL LS11 .... 131 H7
Parkwood Av RHAY LS8 .... 88 C7
Parkwood Cl KBTN HD8 .... 238 B3
Park Wood Crs BEE/HOL LS11 .... 131 H7
Park Wood Dr BEE/HOL LS11 .... 131 H6
Parkwood Gdns
  PDSY/CALV LS28 .... 84 D8
Parkwood Ri KGHY BD21 .... 3 H7
Park Wood Rd BEE/HOL LS11 .... 131 H7
Parkwood Rd HOLM/MEL HD7 .... 191 C8
  PDSY/CALV LS28 .... 84 C8
  SHPY BD18 .... 82 B7
Parkwood Vw RHAY LS8 .... 88 C6 0
Parkwood Wy RHAY LS8 .... 88 C7
Parliament Pl WOR/ARM LS12 .... 108 F6
Parliament Rd WOR/ARM LS12 .... 108 F7
Parliament St
  WKFDW/WTN WF2 .... 12 C3
Parlington Ct MSTN/BAR LS15 .... 91 G7
Parlington Dr GFTH/SHER LS25 .... 92 A7
Parlington La GFTH/SHER LS25 .... 92 A8
Parlington Meadow
  MSTN/BAR LS15 .... 91 G8
Parlington Vls GFTH/SHER LS25 .... 92 A7
Parma St WBOW BD5 .... 127 G1
Parnaby Av MID LS10 .... 132 B5
Parnaby Rd MID LS10 .... 132 B5
Parnaby St MID LS10 .... 132 B5
Parnaby Ter MID LS10 .... 132 B5
Parratt Rw BFDE BD3 .... 105 M7
Parrock La HWTH BD22 .... 121 K8
Parrott St BOW BD4 .... 127 M5
Parry Cl BGLY BD16 .... 80 C5 3
Parry La BOW BD4 .... 127 L1
Parsonage La BFDE BD3 .... 170 C4 3
Parsonage Rd BOW BD4 .... 127 M1
  RTHW LS26 .... 156 F3
  WBOW BD5 .... 127 G3 10
Parsonage St HIPP HX3 .... 11 J7
Parsonage Wk MILN OL16 .... 207 H7 0
Parson La HOR/CROF WF4 .... 220 C7
Parsons Gn WBY LS22 .... 48 B1
Parson's La ILK LS29 .... 18 E6 0
Parsons Rd HTON BD9 .... 104 C2
Parson St KGHY BD21 .... 3 H8
Partons Pl EARD/LOFT WF3 .... 154 E8 3
Partridge Cl MOR LS27 .... 152 F2
Partridge Crs EARL WF12 .... 196 B5
The Pass MILN OL16 .... 206 C6 0
Pasture Av CHAL LS7 .... 87 M7
  GFTH/SHER LS25 .... 116 C6
  HWTH BD22 .... 78 E5
Pasture Cl CLAY BD14 .... 125 M2
  SKP/WHF BD23 .... 16 D1
Pasture Ct GFTH/SHER LS25 .... 116 B7
Pasture Crs CHAL LS7 .... 87 M7 13
Pasture Dr CAS WF10 .... 157 J8
Pasture Fold ILK LS29 .... 40 A4 2
Pasture Gv CHAL LS7 .... 87 M7 14
Pasture La CHAL LS7 .... 87 M7
  CLAY BD14 .... 125 M2
  WBY LS22 .... 46 A5
Pasture Mt WOR/ARM LS12 .... 108 D6
Pasture Pde CHAL LS7 .... 87 M7 15
Pasture Pl CHAL LS7 .... 87 M7 16
Pasture Ri CLAY BD14 .... 125 M2
Pasture Rd BAIL BD17 .... 82 F4
  RHAY LS8 .... 110 A2
Pasture Side Terrace (East)
  CLAY BD14 .... 125 M2 4
Pasture Side Terrace (West)
  CLAY BD14 .... 125 L2 8
Pasture St CHAL LS7 .... 87 M7 17
Pastures Vw HOLM/MEL HD7 .... 212 F1
Pasture Ter CHAL LS7 .... 87 M7 18
Pasture Vw GFTH/SHER LS25 .... 116 B6
  WOR/ARM LS12 .... 108 D6
Pasture View Rd RTHW LS26 .... 154 F1
Pasture Wk CLAY BD14 .... 125 L2
Pasture Wy CAS WF10 .... 157 J8
  GFTH/SHER LS25 .... 116 B6
Pateley Crs HUDN HD2 .... 192 B4
Patent St HTON BD9 .... 104 D4
Paternoster La GTHN BD7 .... 126 C2 16
Paterson Av WKFDW/WTN WF2 .... 12 B3
Patience La NORM WF6 .... 178 A3
Patterdale Ap WBY LS22 .... 47 K1
Patterdale Dr HUDE HD5 .... 15 L6
Patterdale Rd EARL WF12 .... 174 A4 4
Patte Roale Cl AWLS/ASK DN6 .... 249 L5
Patterson Ct
  WKFDW/WTN WF2 .... 176 B3

Pattie St KGHY BD21 57 K5 2
Pauline Ter CAS WF10 157 L7
Paul La HOR/CROF WF4 216 E3
HUDE HD5 193 L1
Pavement La LUD/ILL HX2 124 A7
Pavilion Cl CUD/GR S72 245 J3 2
WHIT OL12 206 B4 7
Paw Hill La STKB/PEN S36 269 L6
Paw La CUL/QBY BD13 125 H7
Pawson St BOW BD4 105 M8
EARD/LOFT WF3 154 A6 6
EARD/LOFT WF3 154 D4
MOR LS27 152 A3
Paxton Av AWLS/ASK DN6 249 M5
Peabody St HIPP HX3 10 C1 2
Peace Hall Dr HUDE HD5 215 L1 1
Peace St BOW BD4 127 L1
Peach Tree Cl PONT WF8 180 D8 1
Peacock Av WKFDW/WTN WF2 176 B7
Peacock Ct YEA LS19 62 F8 4
Peacock Gn MOR LS27 152 E3
Peacock Gv WKFDW/WTN WF2 176 B7
Peak Rd BSLYN/ROY S71 243 J7 2
Peak Vw DEWS WF13 173 H4
Pearl St BTLY WF17 151 J8
HWTH BD22 79 J2 14
Pear Pl TOD OL14 140 C5
Pearson Av HDGY LS6 109 G3
Pearson Cl MILN OL16 207 H7
Pearson Gv HDGY LS6 109 G3
Pearson La GIR BD8 103 M5 1
HTON BD9 103 M5
Pearson Rd WBSY BD6 126 F6
Pearson Rw LM/WK BD12 148 F3 3
Pearson's La EARL WF12 195 H7
Pearson St BFDE BD3 105 L8 5
CLECK BD19 149 K8
MID LS10 9 J6
MILN OL16 206 E6 3
NORM WF6 178 C1
PDSY/CALV LS28 84 D7
Pearson Ter HDGY LS6 109 G3 26
Pear St HFAX HX1 10 A7
HUDS HD4 214 A2 5
HWTH BD22 79 J3 2
HWTH BD22 100 E4 7
Pear Tree Acre
BSPA/BRAM LS23 49 G5
Pear Tree Cl CUD/GR S72 263 M4
PONT WF8 180 D8
Pear Tree Ct AIRE BD20 36 A4 13
Peartree Field La PONT WF8 225 L2
Pear Tree La
HEM/SK/SE WF9 223 M7 1
Peasborough Vw ILK LS29 40 B6 1
Pease Cl PONT WF8 180 F8
Peasefold GFTH/SHER LS25 135 K5 6
Peasehill Cl BSLY S70 261 G6
YEA LS19 84 E2
Peasehill Pk YEA LS19 84 E2 4
Peaseland Av CLECK BD19 149 L7 3
Peaseland Cl CLECK BD19 149 M7 2
Peaseland Rd CLECK BD19 149 M7
Peat Ponds HUDW HD3 191 G5
Peckett Cl HUDW HD3 191 L7
Peckover Dr PDSY/CALV LS28 106 B5
Peckover St BFD BD1 5 H6
Pedler Brow La WHIT OL12 185 G8
Peebles Cl HUDW HD3 191 J5
Peel Av BTLY WF17 173 L1 15
Peel Cl BOW BD4 128 A1
HOR/CROF WF4 197 K5
Peel Cottage Rd TOD OL14 163 J5
Peel Cott St TOD OL14 163 J6
Peel Pde BSLY S70 261 G5
Peel Park Dr ECHL BD2 105 K4
Peel Park Ter ECHL BD2 105 J4
Peel Park Vw BFDE BD3 5 J1
Peel Pl BSLYN/ROY S71 261 J3
ILK LS29 40 A5
Peel Rw GTHN BD7 126 C2 17
Peel Sq BSLY S70 261 G5 9
Peel St BGLY BD16 81 K3
BSLY S70 261 G4
CUL/QBY BD13 102 F8 19
CUL/QBY BD13 125 H5
HECK WF16 172 E2 7
HOLM/MEL HD7 233 J3
HOR/CROF WF4 197 K5
HUD HD1 14 F8
LIT OL15 207 K1
MOR LS27 152 D2
RPDN/SBR HX6 167 K2 11
WHIT OL12 206 A6
WIL/AL BD15 102 E2
Peep Green Rd LVSG WF15 171 L3
Pegholme Dr OT LS21 40 F8 1
Pelham Ct EARD/LOFT WF3 153 M3 2
ECHL BD2 105 K3 4
Pelham Rd ECHL BD2 105 K3 5
Pell Ct HOLM/MEL HD7 236 E7
Pellentine Rd PBR HG3 28 A1
Pell La HOLM/MEL HD7 236 E8
Pellon La HFAX HX1 10 A3
Pellon New Rd LUD/ILL HX2 146 A6
Pellon St TOD OL14 163 J4 3
Pellon Ter IDLE BD10 83 K5
Pellon Wk IDLE BD10 83 K5
Pemberton Dr GTHN BD7 4 C8
Pemberton Rd CAS WF10 158 D6
Pemberton Wy ROY/SHW OL2 229 K6 3
Pembroke Cl MOR LS27 152 B1 4
Pembroke Ct HUDS HD4 213 K4 2
Pembroke Ri GFTH/SHER LS25 135 L4
Pembroke Rd PDSY/CALV LS28 107 G6
Pembroke St LIT OL15 185 K8 3
SKP/WHF BD23 16 B3 4
WBOW BD5 127 G2
Pembury Mt MSTN/BAR LS15 112 B3 3
Penarth Av HEM/SK/SE WF9 225 J7
Penarth Rd MSTN/BAR LS15 111 K4 2
Penarth Ter HEM/SK/SE WF9 225 H7
Penda's Dr MSTN/BAR LS15 111 M4
Penda's Gv MSTN/BAR LS15 111 M3
Penda's Wk MSTN/BAR LS15 111 M4
Penda's Wy MSTN/BAR LS15 112 A4
Pendennis Av HEM/SK/SE WF9 247 G2
Pendil Cl MSTN/BAR LS15 111 L6
Pendle Rd BGLY BD16 81 K3
Pendle Wy COL BB8 75 G1
COL BB8 75 L5
Pendragon ECHL BD2 105 J3 3
Pendragon La ECHL BD2 105 K3 6
Penfield Gv CLAY BD14 125 L2
Penfield Rd BIRK/DRI BD11 129 H8
Pengarth BGLY BD16 81 K1
Pengeston Rd STKB/PEN S36 270 D4
Penistone Av MILN OL16 206 E8
Penistone Boundary Wk
STKB/PEN S36 257 H8
STKB/PEN S36 258 E6
STKB/PEN S36 269 K1
STKB/PEN S36 269 M1
STKB/PEN S36 271 J1
Penistone Ms HWTH BD22 78 E7 4
Penistone Rd HOLM/MEL HD7 237 H8
HOLM/MEL HD7 255 G7
HUDE HD5 215 K1
KBTN HD8 215 M7
KBTN HD8 238 A8
KBTN HD8 238 B4
KBTN HD8 256 E4
Penlands Crs MSTN/BAR LS15 111 M7
Penlands Lawn
MSTN/BAR LS15 111 M7 20
Penlands Wk MSTN/BAR LS15 111 M7
Penlington Cl
HEM/SK/SE WF9 245 M1 1
Penmore Cl ROY/SHW OL2 229 L7
Penn Cl ECHL BD2 105 K2 4
Penn Dr CLECK BD19 149 M8
Penn Gv CLECK BD19 149 M8
Pennine Cl CUL/QBY BD13 124 F7
HOLM/MEL HD7 253 M1
WKFDW/WTN WF2 198 A4
Pennine Crs HUDW HD3 191 G6
Pennine Dr KBTN HD8 239 M4
MILN OL16 207 J8
WHIT OL12 184 E8
Pennine Gdns HOLM/MEL HD7 212 F5
Pennine Gv TOD OL14 141 L8
Pennine Ri KBTN HD8 239 M4
Pennine Rd EARL WF12 174 A6
Pennine V ROY/SHW OL2 229 L6
Pennine Vw BTLY WF17 151 J3
DOD/DAR S75 242 C4
HBR HX7 142 B2
HEM/SK/SE WF9 225 J6
HOLM/MEL HD7 212 F5
HUDE HD5 193 L4
LIT OL15 185 M4
Pennine Wy DOD/DAR S75 260 D4
GLSP SK13 264 D6
HBR HX7 119 M3
HBR HX7 142 F5
HEM/SK/SE WF9 224 B7
HUDW HD3 209 L8
HWTH BD22 76 E3
KBTN HD8 239 M4
LIT OL15 186 D7
UPML OL3 231 M3
Pennington Gv HDGY LS6 6 D1 3
Pennington La RTHW LS26 155 K4
Pennington Pl HDGY LS6 6 D2
Pennington St HDGY LS6 6 D1
Pennington Ter HDGY LS6 6 D1 4
WBOW BD5 126 E2 2
Pennithorne Av BAIL BD17 82 E2
Penn St HFAX HX1 10 C4
MILN OL16 206 B6
Pennwell Fold SCFT LS14 112 A1 1
Pennwell Garth SCFT LS14 111 M1
Pennwell Gn SCFT LS14 111 M1
Pennwell Lawn SCFT LS14 111 M1
Pennygate BGLY BD16 59 M8
Penny Hill Dr CLAY BD14 125 M2
Penny La HUDE HD5 215 K1
Penny Lane Wy MID LS10 9 J8
Penny Spring HUDE HD5 215 G3
Penraevon Av CHAL LS7 7 G2
Penrhyn Wk BSLYN/ROY S71 262 C6
Penrith Crs CAS WF10 159 G4
Penrith Gv BSLYN/ROY S71 262 B6
WOR/ARM LS12 108 A4
Penrith St ROCH OL11 228 B1 14
Penrose Beck Dr
FEA/AMT WF7 224 A1 2
Penrose Dr GTHN BD7 126 B3 9
Penrose Pl WKFDW/WTN WF2 220 B1
Penryn Av HUDE HD5 193 L6
Pentland Av CLAY BD14 125 M2
KNOT WF11 182 A2
Pentland Cl HWTH BD22 2 D6 1
Pentland Dr GFTH/SHER LS25 135 H1 3
Pentland Gv WKFDW/WTN WF2 198 A3
Pentland Rd EARL WF12 173 M8
Pentland Wy MOR LS27 152 C3 2
Pepper Gdns BRAM LS13 108 A2
Pepper La BRAM LS13 107 M2
MID LS10 132 B3
Peppermint Cl MILN OL16 229 L2
Pepper Rd MID LS10 132 B4
Pepper Royd St DEWS WF13 173 M5 5
Percival St BFDE BD3 5 K6
HUDW HD3 191 H8
LDSU LS2 6 F7
Percy St BGLY BD16 81 J3
COL BB8 52 A8 3
HEM/SK/SE WF9 246 D4
HUDN HD2 192 C5
KGHY BD21 79 K2
MILN OL16 228 D1
WHIT OL12 162 A8
WOR/ARM LS12 108 F8
Peregrine Av MOR LS27 152 F2
Peregrine Ct HUDS HD4 214 A7
Peridot Fold HUDN HD2 192 E4 2
Per La LUD/ILL HX2 123 M7
Permain Ct HUDS HD4 214 D2 3
Perry Cl HWTH BD22 79 J3
Perseverance La GTHN BD7 126 C3 7
Perseverance Rd
CUL/QBY BD13 124 C3
Perseverance St BAIL BD17 82 F2 7
BSLY S70 260 F5 6
CAS WF10 157 M6 10
HUDS HD4 214 C3
LM/WK BD12 148 E2 14
PDSY/CALV LS28 106 E7
RPDN/SBR HX6 167 K2
Perseverance Ter HFAX HX1 168 C1 11
RTHW LS26 155 G2
Perseverence St HUDS HD4 213 H3 1
Perth Av ECHL BD2 105 G3
Perth Dr EARD/LOFT WF3 153 H6
Perth Mt HORS LS18 85 K2
Perth Rd ROCH OL11 228 D4
Peterborough Pl ECHL BD2 105 K3 7
Peterborough Rd ECHL BD2 105 K4 7
Peterborough Ter ECHL BD2 105 K3 8
Petergate BFD BD1 5 G6
Peter Hl BTLY WF17 173 M4 1
Peterhouse Dr OT LS21 41 L7
Peter La LUD/ILL HX2 145 K7
MOR LS27 152 F1
Petersfield Av MID LS10 132 A7
Peterson Rd WKFDE WF1 13 G3
Peter St COL BB8 74 A2 5
Pether Hl GTL/HWG HX4 190 B3
Petrel Wy MOR LS27 152 E3 4
Petrie Crs BRAM LS13 106 F1 1
Petrie Gv BFDE BD3 106 A7
Petrie Rd BFDE BD3 106 A7
Petrie St BRAM LS13 106 F1
WHIT OL12 206 B6 12
Petts Crs LIT OL15 185 J8
Petworth Cft BSLYN/ROY S71 243 K2 3
Petyt Gv SKP/WHF BD23 16 C2
Peverell Cl BOW BD4 128 A3 12
Peveril Crs BSLYN/ROY S71 243 J7 3
Peveril Mt ECHL BD2 105 L4
Pexwood Rd TOD OL14 163 H3
Pheasant Dr BTLY WF17 151 J3
Pheasant St KGHY BD21 3 J3
Philip Garth WKFDE WF1 176 D1
Philip La SEL YO8 139 L2
Philippa Wy WOR/ARM LS12 130 E3
Philip Rd BSLY S70 261 M7
Philip's Gv EARD/LOFT WF3 154 E8
Philip's La PONT WF8 203 L1
Philip St ROCH OL11 228 B1
Phillips St CAS WF10 157 K6
Phoebe La HIPP HX3 168 F2
Phoenix Av KBTN HD8 217 M8
Phoenix Ct BTLY WF17 174 B1
TOD OL14 141 M8 4
WKFDW/WTN WF2 12 A3
Phoenix St BRIG HD6 170 D4
LIT OL15 185 K8
TOD OL14 141 M8
Phoenix Wy BOW BD4 106 A8
Piccadilly BFD BD1 4 E5
WKFDW/WTN WF2 12 D3
Pickard Ct MSTN/BAR LS15 111 L6
Pickard La AIRE BD20 36 A4 14
Pickard Wy DEWS WF13 173 K5
Pickering Av GFTH/SHER LS25 113 K6
Pickering Dr OSS WF5 174 E5
Pickering La OSS WF5 174 D5
Pickering Mt WOR/ARM LS12 108 F6
The Pickerings CUL/QBY BD13 125 G6
Pickering St WOR/ARM LS12 108 F6
Pickersgill St OSS WF5 174 E6
Pickford St HUDS HD4 213 J2 6
Pick Haven Garth GLE DN14 161 M8
Pick Hill Rd HOLM/MEL HD7 234 F3
Picklesfield DEWS WF13 173 K4 2
Pickles La GTHN BD7 126 B3
KBTN HD8 239 K5
Pickles St DEWS WF13 173 K4 3
KGHY BD21 2 F8 2
Pickrowfield La
GFTH/SHER LS25 117 G3
Pickthall Ter TOD OL14 163 M1
Pickup St MILN OL16 206 C7 3
Pickwood La RPDN/SBR HX6 168 A4
Picton St GIR BD8 4 C2
Picton Wy HUDE HD5 193 J7 4
Piece Wood Rd BHP/TINH LS16 85 M3
Piethorne Cl MILN OL16 229 L2
Pigeon Cote Cl SCFT LS14 89 J8 1
Pigeon Cote Rd SCFT LS14 89 H8
Piggott St BRIG HD6 170 C3
Pighill Nook Rd
GFTH/SHER LS25 139 H7
Pighill Top La HOLM/MEL HD7 212 A4
Pike End Rd RPDN/SBR HX6 188 D6
Pike Law La HOLM/MEL HD7 212 D1
Pike Law Rd HOLM/MEL HD7 212 D1
Pike Lowe Gv DOD/DAR S75 242 F6
Pike St ROCH OL11 228 B1 15
Pildacre Brow OSS WF5 174 E8
Pildacre Cft OSS WF5 174 E8
Pildacre La EARL WF12 174 D8
Pilden La EARD/LOFT WF3 153 L7 3
Pilgrim Av DEWS WF13 173 H7
Pilgrim Crs DEWS WF13 173 H7
Pilgrim Dr DEWS WF13 173 J7 1
Pilkington St
WKFDW/WTN WF2 12 E7 2
Pilley Hl DOD/DAR S75 260 B8 5
Pilling La KBTN HD8 239 K4
Pilling Top La KBTN HD8 238 D2
Pill White La OT LS21 24 B8
Pilmer Ct WKFDW/WTN WF2 197 M2
Pilot St OSM LS9 7 L6
Pincheon St WKFDE WF1 13 G2
Pindar Oaks Cottages
BSLY S70 261 K6 4
Pindar Oaks St BSLY S70 261 J6
Pindar St BSLY S70 261 K6 3
Pinder Av WOR/ARM LS12 130 B2
Pinderfields Rd WKFDE WF1 176 E7
Pinder Gv WOR/ARM LS12 130 B1
Pinders Crs KNOT WF11 181 L1
Pinders Garth KNOT WF11 181 L1
Pinders Gn RTHW LS26 156 E5
Pinders Green Ct RTHW LS26 156 E5 1
Pinders Green Dr RTHW LS26 156 E5
Pinders Green Fold
RTHW LS26 156 E5 2
Pinder's Gv WKFDE WF1 177 G6
Pinder St WOR/ARM LS12 130 B2
Pine Cl BSLY S70 261 L8
CAS WF10 158 A8
SKP/WHF BD23 16 A2
WBY LS22 30 A7
Pine Ct HUDS HD4 213 M8
LDSU LS2 9 J1
Pine Cft KGHY BD21 2 C1
Pinedale BGLY BD16 81 H1
Pine Gv BTLY WF17 173 K2
ROY/SHW OL2 228 F8
Pinehall Dr BSLYN/ROY S71 261 M2
Pine Rd TOD OL14 141 H7
Pines Gdns ILK LS29 38 B3
The Pines AL/HA/HU LS17 43 L3
Pine St BFD BD1 5 H5
HEM/SK/SE WF9 247 G5
HFAX HX1 11 G7
HUD HD1 15 H6
HWTH BD22 78 E8 15
LIT OL15 185 K8
MILN OL16 206 D7 2
MILN OL16 229 K3 3
Pine Tree Av BSPA/BRAM LS23 49 G6
PONT WF8 180 D8
Pine Tree La GFTH/SHER LS25 138 D8
Pinewood Av
WKFDW/WTN WF2 175 M8 2
Pinewood Cl CUD/GR S72 263 M3
ILK LS29 38 C3 2
Pinewood Gdns GTL/HWG HX4 190 D2
Pinewood Pl KNOT WF11 182 A3 1
Pinfold Av GFTH/SHER LS25 116 B6
Pinfold Cl BSLYN/ROY S71 262 A6 4
EARL WF12 196 A4 2
GFTH/SHER LS25 116 B6 2
GTL/HWG HX4 189 J1
HOR/CROF WF4 217 L4
KNOT WF11 181 L1
MIRF WF14 194 D1
WBY LS22 31 L5
Pinfold Ct GFTH/SHER LS25 116 B6
MSTN/BAR LS15 111 K6 4
Pinfold Garth GFTH/SHER LS25 116 B6
Pinfold Gv MSTN/BAR LS15 111 J6 11
WKFDW/WTN WF2 198 F5
Pinfold Hl BSLY S70 261 J8
DEWS WF13 173 K7
MSTN/BAR LS15 111 K7
Pinfold La AWLS/ASK DN6 227 M3
BHP/TINH LS16 64 A8
BSLYN/ROY S71 243 L4
ELL HX5 169 M8
GFTH/SHER LS25 113 H7
HOLM/MEL HD7 212 C2
HOR/CROF WF4 217 L4
HUDW HD3 211 L1
KBTN HD8 216 C3
MIRF WF14 194 D1
MSTN/BAR LS15 111 J6
PONT WF8 226 F1
RPDN/SBR HX6 166 F2
RTHW LS26 157 G4
WKFDW/WTN WF2 199 G5
WOR/ARM LS12 108 D6
Pinfold Mt MSTN/BAR LS15 111 K7
Pinfold Ri GFTH/SHER LS25 92 B6
Pinfold Rd MSTN/BAR LS15 111 K7
Pinfold Sq MSTN/BAR LS15 111 J6 12
The Pinfold SKP/WHF BD23 16 B1
Pinfold Wy GFTH/SHER LS25 116 B6
Pingle Ri KBTN HD8 239 J7
Pinhaw Rd SKP/WHF BD23 16 C4
Pin Hill La LUD/ILL HX2 144 F5
Pink St HWTH BD22 78 E8
Pinnacle La HBR HX7 143 G5
Pinnacle Vw HWTH BD22 54 E3
Pinnar La HIPP HX3 169 H1
Pioneer St EARL WF12 195 L3
LIT OL15 207 K1 13
TOD OL14 163 J7 3
Pioneer Wy CAS WF10 179 G1
Pipe And Nook La
WOR/ARM LS12 108 B7
Pipercroft WBSY BD6 126 A8 4
Piper Hl KNOT WF11 159 J1
Piper La HWTH BD22 54 F5
OT LS21 41 H7
Piper Well La KBTN HD8 238 A8
Pipit Meadow MOR LS27 152 E3
Pippin's Ap NORM WF6 178 D3
Pippins Green Av
WKFDW/WTN WF2 175 K4
Pirie Cl ECHL BD2 105 H3
Pitchstone Ct WOR/ARM LS12 107 M7
Pitcliffe Wy BOW BD4 127 H1
WBOW BD5 127 G2
Pitfall St LDS LS1 9 H2
Pit Field Rd EARD/LOFT WF3 154 F4
Pit La CLECK BD19 150 D4
CUL/QBY BD13 101 L5
CUL/QBY BD13 124 E2
DEWS WF13 173 H4
GFTH/SHER LS25 114 C8
GFTH/SHER LS25 136 A2
ROY/SHW OL2 228 F6
RTHW LS26 156 F3
Pits La CLECK BD19 149 G8
Pitt Hill La GTL/HWG HX4 189 L4
Pitt Rw LDS LS1 9 G2
Pitts St BOW BD4 127 M2
Pitt St BSLY S70 261 G5
KGHY BD21 3 J5
LVSG WF15 172 D4 1
TOD OL14 163 M1
WHIT OL12 206 B6
Pitt St West BSLY S70 260 F5 7
Place's Rd OSM LS9 9 M2
Plaid Rw OSM LS9 7 M9
Plain La RPDN/SBR HX6 166 E4
Plains La ELL HX5 169 H5
HOLM/MEL HD7 233 J1
Plane St HUDS HD4 214 D3
TOD OL14 141 G7
Plane Tree Av AL/HA/HU LS17 88 B2
Plane Tree Cl AL/HA/HU LS17 88 B2
Plane Tree Cft AL/HA/HU LS17 88 B2
Plane Tree Gdns
AL/HA/HU LS17 88 B2 6
Plane Tree Gv YEA LS19 62 F8
Plane Tree Nest La LUD/ILL HX2 146 A8
Plane Tree Ri AL/HA/HU LS17 88 B2 7
Plane Tree Rd
RPDN/SBR HX6 167 K1 10
Plane Trees Cl CLECK BD19 149 M3
Planetrees Rd BFDE BD3 105 L8
Planetrees St WIL/AL BD15 103 J4 3
Plane Tree Vw AL/HA/HU LS17 88 B2
Planet Rd AWLS/ASK DN6 249 L7
Plantation Av AL/HA/HU LS17 88 C1
BSLYN/ROY S71 243 M3
MSTN/BAR LS15 111 H7
Plantation Dr HUDS HD4 214 C5
Plantation Gdns AL/HA/HU LS17 88 D1
Plantation Pl BOW BD4 127 L2
Plantation Wy BAIL BD17 82 F3
Platt Cl MILN OL16 229 J1
Platting La ROCH OL11 228 C2
Platt La HOLM/MEL HD7 212 C5
Playfair Rd MID LS10 131 M4
Playground WOR/ARM LS12 129 M3 3
Playhouse Sq OSM LS9 7 K9
The Pleasance RTHW LS26 134 C5
Pleasant Ct HDGY LS6 6 C2
Pleasant Mt BEE/HOL LS11 8 C5
Pleasant Pl BEE/HOL LS11 8 C5
Pleasant St BEE/HOL LS11 8 B5
GTHN BD7 126 C2
Pleasant Ter BEE/HOL LS11 8 C5
Pleasant Vw CUD/GR S72 262 E2
Pledwick Crs WKFDW/WTN WF2 198 F8
Pledwick Dr WKFDW/WTN WF2 220 F1
Pledwick Gv
WKFDW/WTN WF2 220 E1 1
Pledwick La WKFDW/WTN WF2 220 F1
Pledwick Ri WKFDW/WTN WF2 198 F8
Plevna St MID LS10 132 C4 3
Plevna Ter BGLY BD16 81 H2
Plimsoll St BOW BD4 127 J2 11
HEM/SK/SE WF9 223 M7
Ploughcroft La HIPP HX3 146 D4
Ploughmans Cft ECHL BD2 105 G2 2
Plover Dr BTLY WF17 173 H1
Plover Rd HUDW HD3 191 K6
Plover St KGHY BD21 3 H2
WBOW BD5 126 E3
Plover Wy MOR LS27 152 F3 3
Plumber St BSLY S70 261 G5 10
Plumpton Av ECHL BD2 83 H8
Plumpton Cl ECHL BD2 105 J1
Plumpton Dr ECHL BD2 83 H8
Plumpton End ECHL BD2 83 J8
Plumpton Gdns ECHL BD2 83 H8
Plumpton Lea ECHL BD2 83 H8
Plumpton Md ECHL BD2 83 H8
Plumpton Pl WKFDW/WTN WF2 12 B3
Plumpton Rd ROCH OL11 228 D6
WKFDW/WTN WF2 12 B3
Plumpton St GIR BD8 104 C6
WKFDW/WTN WF2 12 B4
Plumpton Ter WKFDW/WTN WF2 12 B4
Plumpton Wk ECHL BD2 83 H8
Plum St HFAX HX1 10 B8
HWTH BD22 79 J3 1
Plum Tree Cl PONT WF8 180 D8
Poet's Pl HORS LS18 85 L4
Pogmoor La DOD/DAR S75 260 C4
Pogmoor Rd DOD/DAR S75 260 D5
Pog Well La DOD/DAR S75 259 M4
Pohlman St HFAX HX1 10 B9 8
Pole Ga HUDW HD3 211 M3
Pole Gate Branch HUDW HD3 211 M2
Pole Rd HWTH BD22 56 B6
Pollard Av BGLY BD16 81 K1
CLECK BD19 150 D5
Pollard Cl CLECK BD19 150 D5 3
Pollard La BFDE BD3 5 M1
BRAM LS13 85 L8
Pollard's Flds KNOT WF11 181 K1
Pollard St BOW BD4 5 G9
EARD/LOFT WF3 176 E1
HUDN HD2 192 D4 2
TOD OL14 141 G7
Pollard St South HUDW HD3 213 K1
Pollard Wy CLECK BD19 150 D5
Pollit Av RPDN/SBR HX6 167 H3
Pollitt St DOD/DAR S75 260 F3
Pollyfox Wy DOD/DAR S75 260 A7
Polperro Cl NORM WF6 178 D3 5
Pomfret Pl GFTH/SHER LS25 113 K6
Pomona St ROCH OL11 228 B1 16
Pond Cl HUDS HD4 214 B4 2
Pond Common La
STKB/PEN S36 271 K8
Ponden La HWTH BD22 77 J8
Ponderosa Cl RHAY LS8 110 B3 20
Pondfields Cl GFTH/SHER LS25 135 K5
Pondfields Crest
GFTH/SHER LS25 135 K5
Pondfields Dr GFTH/SHER LS25 135 K4
Pondfields Ri GFTH/SHER LS25 135 K5
Pond La KBTN HD8 216 C4
Pond St BSLY S70 261 G6
KGHY BD21 3 H4
Ponker La KBTN HD8 239 G6
Ponker Nook La KBTN HD8 239 H5
Pontefract Av OSM LS9 110 B7
Pontefract La MSTN/BAR LS15 133 L4
OSM LS9 110 B7
Pontefract Lane Cl OSM LS9 110 B7 14
Pontefract Rd CAS WF10 158 A7
CUD/GR S72 244 E5 1
FEA/AMT WF7 201 L2
FEA/AMT WF7 202 C6
HEM/SK/SE WF9 224 B5
HOR/CROF WF4 200 B4
KNOT WF11 181 M2
MID LS10 132 C4
NORM WF6 178 F2
PONT WF8 181 J2
Pontefract St OSM LS9 110 B7
Pontefract Ter
HEM/SK/SE WF9 224 A8 7
Pontey Dr HUDE HD5 215 K1
Pontey Mt HUDE HD5 215 K1
Ponyfield Cl HUDN HD2 14 B1
Pool Bank Cl OT LS21 42 F7
Pool Bank Ct OT LS21 42 F8

Pool Bank New Rd
BHP/TINH LS16 .... 63 K2
Pool Br OT LS21 .... 42 E6
Pool Ct BFDE BD3 .... 5 K4
Poole Crs MSTN/BAR LS15 .... 111 K4
Poole La GFTH/SHER LS25 .... 160 A3
Poole Mt MSTN/BAR LS15 ..... 111 K5
Poole Rd MSTN/BAR LS15 ..... 111 K5
Poole Sq MSTN/BAR LS15 ..... 111 L5
Pool Hill La HUDN HD8 ...... 257 L1
Pool Rd OT LS21 .... 41 L6
OT LS21 .... 42 B6
Pools La BSLYN/ROY S71 ..... 244 A3
Pool St KGHY BD21 .... 3 L1 [2]
Popeley Rd HECK WF16 .... 150 E8
NORM WF6 .... 178 D1
Pope St KGHY BD21 .... 3 K3
NORM WF6 .... 178 D1
Poplar Av CAS WF10 .... 158 E7
CUD/GR S72 .... 244 E4
GFTH/SHER LS25 .... 113 G7
GTHN BD7 .... 126 B4
HOLM/MEL HD7 .... 236 E5 [1]
MSTN/BAR LS15 .... 111 M4
RPDN/SBR HX6 .... 167 K1
SHPY BD18 .... 104 E1 [3]
TOD OL14 .... 141 J7
WBY LS22 .... 30 A7
WKFDW/WTN WF2 .... 197 M1
Poplar Cl BRAM LS13 .... 108 B6
ILK LS29 .... 40 B6
Poplar Crs EARD/LOFT WF3 ... 152 E5
LUD/ILL HX2 .... 124 B7 [2]
SHPY BD18 .... 104 E1
Poplar Cft BRAM LS13 .... 108 A6
Poplar Dr AIRE BD20 .... 58 E7
HORS LS18 .... 85 H5
NORM WF6 .... 178 C1
SHPY BD18 .... 104 E1 [3]
Poplar Gdns BRAM LS13 ...... 108 A6
Poplar Garth BRAM LS13 ..... 108 A6
Poplar Ga WOR/ARM LS12 ..... 108 A6
Poplar Gv BGLY BD16 .... 80 C5
BSLYN/ROY S71 .... 262 A2
CLECK BD19 .... 149 L8
GTHN BD7 .... 126 B4
KNOT WF11 .... 182 A4
PONT WF8 .... 180 D6
SHPY BD18 .... 104 E1 [3]
Poplar Ri BRAM LS13 .... 108 A5
KBTN HD8 .... 239 K5 [1]
Poplar Rd AWLS/ASK DN6 ..... 249 K5
GTHN BD7 .... 126 C4
SHPY BD18 .... 104 E1
Poplars Park Rd ECHL BD2 ... 104 F2
Poplars Sq PDSY/CALV LS28 .. 106 F4 [7]
Poplars Rd BSLY S70 .... 261 K7
The Poplars AIRE BD20 ...... 55 L2
BHP/TINH LS16 .... 64 B4
GSLY LS20 .... 62 A4
HDGY LS6 .... 109 G2
KNOT WF11 .... 182 D4
Poplar St CUD/GR S72 .... 263 K1
HIPP HX3 .... 11 L3
HUDE HD5 .... 15 K9
HUDN HD2 .... 192 C5
Poplar Ter AIRE BD20 .... 58 F7
BSLYN/ROY S71 .... 243 M2
HEM/SK/SE WF9 .... 247 J4
HUDE HD5 .... 15 M8 [1]
Poplar Vw BRAM LS13 .... 108 A6
BRIG HD6 .... 148 C8
GTHN BD7 .... 126 A4
Poplar Wy BRAM LS13 .... 108 A6
WOR/ARM LS12 .... 108 A6
Poplarwood Gdns IDLE BD10 .. 106 A1 [3]
Popley Dr HOLM/MEL HD7 ..... 234 F5
Popples Dr LUD/ILL HX2 ..... 124 B7
Poppleton Av EARD/LOFT WF3 . 153 G5 [1]
Poppleton Dr EARD/LOFT WF3 . 153 G5
Poppleton Ri EARD/LOFT WF3 . 153 G5 [3]
Poppleton Rd EARD/LOFT WF3 . 153 G5
Poppleton Wy
EARD/LOFT WF3 .... 153 G6 [2]
Popple Wells La LUD/ILL HX2 145 H7
Poppy Ct WBSY BD6 .... 126 B8 [8]
Porritt St CLECK BD19 ...... 149 M5 [1]
Portage Av MSTN/BAR LS15 ... 111 H7
Portage Crs MSTN/BAR LS15 .. 111 H7
Portal Dr MIRF WF14 .... 172 C6
Porter Ter DOD/DAR S75 ..... 260 D4 [2]
Portland Av PONT WF8 .... 180 D5
Portland Cl HUDW HD3 .... 191 L7 [2]
Portland Crs LDS LS1 .... 6 E5
Portland Ga LDSU LS2 .... 6 E7
Portland Pl BGLY BD16 ...... 81 J4 [2]
HEM/SK/SE WF9 .... 225 J7 [1]
HFAX HX1 .... 11 M8
Portland Rd HIPP HX3 .... 11 H3
WOR/ARM LS12 .... 108 E8
Portland St BSLY S70 .... 261 K6
COL BB8 .... 74 B1
HFAX HX1 .... 11 M5
HUD HD1 .... 14 D6
HWTH BD22 .... 78 F7 [1]
LDS LS1 .... 6 E5
PDSY/CALV LS28 .... 107 J7 [3]
WBOW BD5 .... 4 F8
WKFDE WF1 .... 13 M8
Portland Wy LDSU LS2 .... 6 E7
Portman St PDSY/CALV LS28 .. 84 D8
Portobello Gv WKFDW/WTN WF2 13 G9
Portobello Rd WKFDE WF1 .... 13 G9
Portsmouth Av BFDE BD3 ..... 5 H2
Portwood St HTON BD9 .... 103 H4 [1]
Post Hill Ct WOR/ARM LS12 .. 107 M7
Post Office Rd FEA/AMT WF7 . 201 M1
IDLE BD10 .... 105 L1
Post Office St CLECK BD19 .. 150 B8 [3]
Pothouse Rd WBSY BD6 .... 126 D6
Pot La AIRE BD20 .... 35 K8
Potovens La WKFDE WF1 ...... 176 D1
WKFDW/WTN WF2 .... 176 A1
Potter Av WKFDW/WTN WF2 .... 198 A2
Potter Brow Rd BAIL BD17 ... 60 E7
Potternewton Av CHAL LS7 ... 87 K8
Potternewton Ct CHAL LS7 ... 87 L8 [3]

Potternewton Crs CHAL LS7 .. 109 K1
Potternewton La CHAL LS7 ... 109 L1 [3]
Potternewton Mt CHAL LS7 ... 87 K8
Potternewton Vw CHAL LS7 ... 87 K8 [3]
Potters Cft EARD/LOFT WF3 .. 154 E8 [3]
Potters Ga HOLM/MEL HD7 .... 255 M6
Potters Wk HOLM/MEL HD7 .... 213 G2 [3]
Potterton Av MSTN/BAR LS15 . 91 G5
Potterton Cl MSTN/BAR LS15 . 91 G6
Potterton La MSTN/BAR LS15 . 91 G7
Pottery La KNOT WF11 .... 181 M1
RTHW LS26 .... 133 M7
Pottery Rd MID LS10 .... 9 J7
Pottery St CAS WF10 .... 157 K6
Potts' Ter NORM WF6 .... 178 C6
Poulton Pl BEE/HOL LS11 .... 9 H1
Poulton St BSLYN/ROY S71 ... 243 M8
Poverty La RPDN/SBR HX6 .... 166 C5
Powell Av WBOW BD5 .... 126 C2
Powell Rd BGLY BD16 .... 81 J3
SHPY BD18 .... 104 F1
Powell St CAS WF10 .... 157 M6 [11]
HECK WF16 .... 173 G3 [3]
HEM/SK/SE WF9 .... 246 F3
HFAX HX1 .... 11 G6
Poxton Gv HEM/SK/SE WF9 .... 247 G5
Prail Cl PONT WF8 .... 181 H5
Pratt La MIRF WF14 .... 172 B4
SHPY BD18 .... 82 E8
Premiere Pk ILK LS29 .... 38 A3
Prescott St HFAX HX1 .... 11 C8
MILN OL16 .... 206 E4 [2]
Prescott Ter WIL/AL BD15 .. 103 K5 [3]
Preston La LUD/ILL HX2 ..... 145 L4
RTHW LS26 .... 135 G7
Preston Pde BEE/HOL LS11 ... 131 J4
Preston Pl HFAX HX1 .... 10 D6
Preston St BTLY WF17 .... 173 L2
EARL WF12 .... 174 A7
GTHN BD7 .... 4 A5
Preston Vw RTHW LS26 .... 134 D5
Preston Wy BSLYN/ROY S71 ... 243 M8
Prestwich Dr HUDN HD2 ...... 192 B4
Prestwick Cl OT LS21 .... 40 F8 [2]
Prestwick Fold OSS WF5 ..... 174 F7 [3]
Pretoria St CAS WF10 .... 158 A7
FEA/AMT WF7 .... 179 L8
HOLM/MEL HD7 .... 212 B5
WKFDE WF1 .... 13 H9
Priest Bank Rd AIRE BD20 ... 35 G6
Priest Croft La BSLYN/ROY S71 263 C4
Priest Hill Gdns WBY LS22 .. 29 M7
Priesthorpe Av PDSY/CALV LS28 106 D4
Priesthorpe Ct PDSY/CALV LS28 106 D2
Priesthorpe La PDSY/CALV LS28 106 D2
Priesthorpe Rd PDSY/CALV LS28 106 D2
Priest La RPDN/SBR HX6 ..... 189 G2
Priestley Av DOD/DAR S75 ... 241 L6
HECK WF16 .... 150 F8
WBSY BD6 .... 126 D6
Priestley Cl PDSY/CALV LS28 107 H6
Priestley Ct PDSY/CALV LS28 107 H6
PDSY/CALV LS28 .... 107 H6
Priestley Gdns HECK WF16 ... 172 E1
PDSY/CALV LS28 .... 107 H6 [1]
Priestley Gv HUDS HD4 ...... 214 B5
Priestley Pl RPDN/SBR HX6 .. 167 J3 [6]
Priestley Sq BTLY WF17 ..... 151 G4
Priestley St CUL/QBY BD13 .. 102 F8 [2]
Priestley Ter WBSY BD6 ..... 126 E5 [15]
Priestley Vw PDSY/CALV LS28 107 H6
Priestley Wk PDSY/CALV LS28 107 H6
Priestley Wy ROY/SHW OL2 ... 229 M7
Priestman Cl GIR BD8 .... 4 A1
Priestman St GIR BD8 .... 4 B3
Priest Royd DOD/DAR S75 .... 242 C5
Priestthorpe Cl BGLY BD16 .. 81 J2
Priestthorpe La BGLY BD16 .. 81 J2
Priestthorpe Rd BGLY BD16 .. 81 J3
Primitive St EARD/LOFT WF3 . 154 F3 [5]
HUD HD1 .... 15 G6
Primley Gdns AL/HA/HU LS17 . 87 L2
Primley Park Av AL/HA/HU LS17 87 L2
Primley Park Cl AL/HA/HU LS17 87 M1
Primley Park Ct AL/HA/HU LS17 87 L1
Primley Park Crs
AL/HA/HU LS17 .... 87 M2 [3]
Primley Park Dr AL/HA/HU LS17 87 L2
Primley Park Garth
AL/HA/HU LS17 .... 87 M1
Primley Park Gn AL/HA/HU LS17 87 M1
Primley Park La AL/HA/HU LS17 87 M2
Primley Park Mt
AL/HA/HU LS17 .... 87 M1 [1]
AL/HA/HU LS17 .... 87 M2 [6]
Primley Park Ri
AL/HA/HU LS17 .... 87 M2 [7]
Primley Park Rd AL/HA/HU LS17 87 L2
Primley Park Vw AL/HA/HU LS17 87 L1
Primley Park Wk AL/HA/HU LS17 87 L1
Primley Park Wy AL/HA/HU LS17 87 L1
Primrose Av MSTN/BAR LS15 .. 111 J6 [13]
RTHW LS26 .... 134 D5
Primrose Bank BGLY BD16 .... 81 K4
Primrose Cl MSTN/BAR LS15 .. 111 J6 [14]
PONT WF8 .... 180 F7
Primrose Crs MSTN/BAR LS15 . 111 J5 [1]
Primrose Dene KNOT WF11 .... 159 M7
Primrose Dr BGLY BD16 ...... 81 L4
CAS WF10 .... 158 D8
MSTN/BAR LS15 .... 111 J6
Primrose Gdns BTLY WF17 .... 152 A8 [1]
MSTN/BAR LS15 .... 111 J5
Primrose Garth
MSTN/BAR LS15 .... 111 H6 [2]
Primrose Gv HUDS HD4 .... 214 C3
KGHY BD21 .... 3 M4
Primrose Hl BTLY WF17 ...... 151 M8
KNOT WF11 .... 182 C1 [3]
PDSY/CALV LS28 .... 106 F6
SKP/WHF BD23 .... 16 B2 [3]
Primrose Hill Cl RTHW LS26 . 134 D5 [1]
Primrose Hill Dr RTHW LS26 . 134 D5
Primrose Hill Gn RTHW LS26 . 134 D5 [2]
Primrose Hill Rd HUDS HD4 .. 214 C2
Primrose La BEE/HOL LS11 ... 9 H9

BGLY BD16 .... 81 K5
BSPA/BRAM LS23 .... 48 C7
ECHL BD2 .... 104 F2
HOR/CROF WF4 .... 197 M6
KBTN HD8 .... 215 M6
LVSG WF15 .... 172 B2
MIRF WF14 .... 172 E7
MSTN/BAR LS15 .... 111 H7
Primrose Rd MSTN/BAR LS15 .. 111 J6
Primrose St GIR BD8 .... 4 B3
HUDS HD4 .... 214 C2 [3]
KGHY BD21 .... 3 M4
Primrose V KNOT WF11 .... 182 C2 [3]
Primrose Wk MOR LS27 .... 130 E6 [3]
Primrose Wy HIPP HX3 .... 125 M7 [1]
Prince Arthur St DOD/DAR S75 260 F4
Prince Edward Gv
WOR/ARM LS12 .... 130 C2
Prince Edward Rd
WOR/ARM LS12 .... 130 C2
Prince Henry Rd OT LS21 .... 41 J5
Princeroyd Wy GTHN BD7 ..... 104 C7
Prince's Av RHAY LS8 .... 88 D7
Prince's Crs ECHL BD2 ...... 105 G3
SKP/WHF BD23 .... 16 D2
Princes Dr SKP/WHF BD23 .... 16 C3
Prince's Ga HIPP HX3 .... 168 D2
Princess Av EARL WF12 ...... 174 C6
HEM/SK/SE WF9 .... 247 H4
WHIT OL12 .... 206 E2 [3]
Princess Cl EARL WF12 ...... 174 C6
Princess Ct AL/HA/HU LS17 .. 87 M3
NORM WF6 .... 178 E5 [3]
Princess Crs EARL WF12 ..... 174 C6
Princess La EARL WF12 ...... 174 C6
ILK LS29 .... 38 C3
MILN OL16 .... 206 F7
ROY/SHW OL2 .... 229 J8
Princess Rd EARL WF12 ...... 174 C6
Princess Royal Wy PBR HG3 .. 26 F4
Princess St BRIG HD6 .... 170 D4
BSLY S70 .... 261 G5
BTLY WF17 .... 151 L8
CAS WF10 .... 158 A5
CUD/GR S72 .... 245 J8 [2]
DOD/DAR S75 .... 242 C5
EARL WF12 .... 174 C6
GTL/HWCG HX4 .... 168 F7 [7]
HFAX HX1 .... 11 H5
HUD HD1 .... 14 D6
NORM WF6 .... 178 D4 [7]
RPDN/SBR HX6 .... 167 J2
WHIT OL12 .... 206 B5
WKFDE WF1 .... 176 D2
WKFDE WF1 .... 199 G4 [1]
YEA LS19 .... 84 C2 [3]
Princes St HECK WF16 .... 173 G2
WBSY BD6 .... 126 A7 [3]
WBSY BD6 .... 126 E6 [8]
Prince St AIRE BD20 .... 35 M5
BOW BD4 .... 127 L5
BTLY WF17 .... 151 L8 [2]
CAS WF10 .... 135 G7
DEWS WF13 .... 173 M6 [11]
HUDS HD4 .... 214 D2
HWTH BD22 .... 78 F7
MILN OL16 .... 228 C1
Prince's Wy WBOW BD5 .... 4 E7
Princeville Rd GTHN BD7 .... 104 C7
Princeville St GTHN BD7 .... 104 D7
Prince Wood La HUDN HD2 .... 191 L4
Priordale Rd ROY/SHW OL2 ... 229 K7 [12]
Prior St KGHY BD21 .... 3 K2
Priory Cl BGLY BD16 .... 81 J2 [7]
MIRF WF14 .... 172 A8
NORM WF6 .... 178 B2
OSS WF5 .... 196 F2 [3]
WBY LS22 .... 30 D8 [2]
Priory Ct GIR BD8 .... 4 C3 [1]
BSLYN/ROY S71 .... 262 A3
Priory Gv BGLY BD16 .... 81 J2
Priory Ms EARD/LOFT WF3 .... 155 H8 [2]
HUDN HD2 .... 193 H1
Priory Park Gv GFTH/SHER LS25 138 D6
Priory Pl BSLYN/ROY S71 .... 262 A2
FEA/AMT WF7 .... 201 L2
Priory Road Or Hall La
AWLS/ASK DN6 .... 227 L2
Priory Sq WKFDW/WTN WF2 .... 199 J7 [1]
Priory Wk MIRF WF14 .... 172 A8
Priory Wy MIRF WF14 .... 172 A8
Privilege St WOR/ARM LS12 .. 108 D8
Proctor St BOW BD4 .... 127 M5
Prod La BAIL BD17 .... 82 F4
Progress Av BGLY BD16 ...... 80 C5 [3]
Prospect Av BRAM LS13 ...... 107 L3
GFTH/SHER LS25 .... 116 B7
LUD/ILL HX2 .... 168 A2
NORM WF6 .... 178 D3
PDSY/CALV LS28 .... 106 F6
SHPY BD18 .... 82 E7
Prospect Bank
BSPA/BRAM LS23 .... 69 M3
Prospect Cl LUD/ILL HX2 .... 168 A2
SHPY BD18 .... 82 E7 [3]
Prospect Ct LUD/ILL HX2 .... 145 K6
TAD LS24 .... 71 M2
Prospect Crs HWTH BD22 ..... 79 G1
MID LS10 .... 131 M4
Prospect Dr HWTH BD22 ...... 79 G1 [3]
TAD LS24 .... 71 M2
Prospect Gdns
MSTN/BAR LS15 .... 111 K5
Prospect Gv PDSY/CALV LS28 . 106 F6 [3]
SHPY BD18 .... 82 E7
Prospect La BIRK/DRI BD11 .. 150 D1
Prospect Mt HWTH BD22 ...... 79 G1
SHPY BD18 .... 82 E7
Prospect Pl BRIG HD6 .... 170 C4
EARD/LOFT WF3 .... 154 D4
ECHL BD2 .... 105 L4
HORS LS18 .... 85 K6 [3]
HTON BD9 .... 104 B5
LUD/ILL HX2 .... 146 B3
RTHW LS26 .... 155 H2 [3]

SKP/WHF BD23 .... 16 B2 [14]
Prospect Rd BFDE BD3 .... 5 H3
BGLY BD16 .... 81 L1
CLECK BD19 .... 149 M6
HECK WF16 .... 150 E8
HUDW HD3 .... 191 H8
ILK LS29 .... 40 B6
LVSG WF15 .... 171 M4
OSS WF5 .... 196 F1
OSS WF5 .... 197 G1 [3]
Prospect Sq PDSY/CALV LS28 . 106 F4
Prospect St AIRE BD20 ...... 34 F7 [12]
BOW BD4 .... 5 H9
BSLY S70 .... 260 F5
BTLY WF17 .... 151 L8 [3]
CLECK BD19 .... 149 M7
CUD/GR S72 .... 244 D7
HIPP HX3 .... 11 J3
HOR/CROF WF4 .... 197 L6
HUD HD1 .... 14 D8
HWTH BD22 .... 2 A7
HWTH BD22 .... 78 E8
IDLE BD10 .... 105 L1
LIT OL15 .... 185 K8 [3]
PDSY/CALV LS28 .... 106 E6 [3]
PDSY/CALV LS28 .... 106 F5
ROCH OL11 .... 228 A2 [3]
SHPY BD18 .... 82 E7
WBSY BD6 .... 126 B7 [8]
YEA LS19 .... 84 E3 [3]
Prospect Ter BRAM LS13 ..... 107 L3
CLECK BD19 .... 149 H6 [3]
GFTH/SHER LS25 .... 114 C8
LVSG WF15 .... 172 C2
RTHW LS26 .... 155 H2 [3]
WIL/AL BD15 .... 103 L5 [3]
Prospect Vw BRAM LS13 ...... 107 L3
LVSG WF15 .... 171 M4
Prospect Wk SHPY BD18 ...... 82 E7 [3]
Prosper St MID LS10 .... 9 J7
Providence Av BAIL BD17 .... 82 E2 [3]
HDGY LS6 .... 6 D1
Providence Crs HWTH BD22 ... 78 E4
MOR LS27 .... 152 C1 [3]
Providence Gn PONT WF8 ..... 181 G3
Providence La HWTH BD22 .... 78 E4
Providence Pl BRIG HD6 ..... 170 E5
GFTH/SHER LS25 .... 113 G7
LDSU LS2 .... 7 G1
PDSY/CALV LS28 .... 107 G5 [3]
RTHW LS26 .... 157 K3
Providence Rd HDGY LS6 ..... 6 D1
Providence Rw BAIL BD17 .... 82 E2
LUD/ILL HX2 .... 146 B3
Providence St BFD BD1 ...... 4 D3
BTLY WF17 .... 173 L1 [3]
CLECK BD19 .... 149 G5 [1]
CLECK BD19 .... 150 A6 [3]
EARL WF12 .... 174 B7
ELL HX5 .... 169 J7 [2]
OSM LS9 .... 9 L1
PDSY/CALV LS28 .... 106 F4
TOD OL14 .... 163 J7 [4]
WKFDE WF1 .... 12 E2
Providence Ter
CUL/QBY BD13 .... 102 F8 [3]
LDSU LS2 .... 6 D3
Providential St
HOR/CROF WF4 .... 217 K1
Provident Rw ROY/SHW OL2 ... 229 K7 [12]
Prune Park La WIL/AL BD15 .. 103 G3
Psalters Dr STKB/PEN S36 ... 271 J5
Pudding La TOD OL14 .... 140 C4
Pudsey Rd BRAM LS13 .... 107 K7
TOD OL14 .... 140 D5
WOR/ARM LS12 .... 107 M7
Pule Green La HIPP HX3 ..... 146 D3
Pulan Av ECHL BD2 .... 105 L2
Pullan Dr ECHL BD2 .... 105 L2 [3]
Pullan Gv ECHL BD2 .... 105 L2
Pullan La BAIL BD17 .... 83 L1
Pullan St WBOW BD5 .... 126 F1
Pullman St ROCH OL11 .... 228 B1
Pumphouse La MIRF WF14 ..... 172 D8 [3]
Pump La DEWS WF13 .... 173 H6 [3]
EARD/LOFT WF3 .... 175 G1
KBTN HD8 .... 216 F7
Purbeck Ct BOW BD4 .... 128 A4 [3]
Purbeck Gv GFTH/SHER LS25 .. 113 H8
Purcell Dr AIRE BD20 .... 35 M4
Purley Wk WBSY BD6 .... 126 D6 [3]
Purlwell Av BTLY WF17 ...... 173 K3
Purlwell Crs BTLY WF17 ..... 173 K3
Purlwell Hall Rd BTLY WF17 . 173 L3
Purlwell La BTLY WF17 ...... 173 K3
Purprise La HBR HX7 .... 121 J5
Purston La FEA/AMT WF7 ..... 202 B5
Purston Park Ct FEA/AMT WF7 201 M2
Pye Av DOD/DAR S75 .... 242 C6
Pye Nest Av LUD/ILL HX2 .... 167 M1
Pye Nest Ct LVSG WF15 ...... 171 M2
Pye Nest Dr LUD/ILL HX2 .... 168 A2
Pye Nest Gdns LUD/ILL HX2 .. 168 A1
Pye Nest Gv LUD/ILL HX2 .... 167 M1
Pye Nest Ri LUD/ILL HX2 .... 168 A2
Pye Nest Rd RPDN/SBR HX6 ... 167 M2
Pyenot Av CLECK BD19 .... 150 A8
Pyenot Dr CLECK BD19 .... 150 A8
Pyenot Gdns CLECK BD19 ..... 150 A8
Pyenot Hall La CLECK BD19 .. 150 A7
Pymont Ct EARD/LOFT WF3 .... 133 K7
Pymont Gv RTHW LS26 .... 133 K7 [3]
Pymroyd La HUDS HD4 .... 213 J2 [3]
Pym St MID LS10 .... 9 L6
Pyrah Av CLECK BD19 .... 150 A8
Pyrah Rd DEWS WF13 .... 173 L5
LM/WK BD12 .... 148 F2
Pyrah St DEWS WF13 .... 173 L5

Q

Quail St KGHY BD21 .... 3 J3 [3]

Quaker La BSLYN/ROY S71 .... 262 B6
CLECK BD19 .... 149 M8
HUD HD1 .... 14 A9
LVSG WF15 .... 171 M1
WBOW BD5 .... 126 D3
Quakers La RPDN/SBR HX6 .... 188 C4
YEA LS19 .... 84 D1
Quarmby Cft HUDW HD3 .... 191 J7 [3]
Quarmby Rd HUDW HD3 .... 213 L1 [1]
Quarrie Dene Ct CHAL LS7 ... 87 L8 [3]
Quarry Av KNOT WF11 .... 182 C3
Quarry Bank Ct KSTL LS5 .... 86 B8
Quarry Bank Rd CUD/GR S72 .. 244 D8 [3]
Quarry Cl DOD/DAR S75 ...... 241 M6 [3]
Quarry Ct CAS WF10 .... 157 M8
HOLM/MEL HD7 .... 191 H7
Quarry Dene BHP/TINH LS16 .. 86 E6 [3]
Quarrydene Dr CAS WF10 ..... 158 D8 [3]
Quarry Dr HUDE HD5 .... 193 K8
Quarry Farm Rd OT LS21 ..... 63 J3
Quarryfields MIRF WF14 ..... 172 D7
Quarry Hl HOR/CROF WF4 ..... 197 H5
HUDE HD5 .... 215 K2
RPDN/SBR HX6 .... 167 K3
RTHW LS26 .... 133 L3
Quarry Hill La WBY LS22 .... 29 M8
HEM/SK/SE WF9 .... 225 J6
HUDS HD4 .... 193 K8
HUDS HD4 .... 213 L7 [3]
MOR LS27 .... 152 C7
Quarry La BTLY WF17 .... 151 H6
HEM/SK/SE WF9 .... 225 J6
HUDS HD4 .... 193 K8
HUDS HD4 .... 213 L7 [3]
MOR LS27 .... 152 C7
Quarry Mt HOR/CROF WF4 ..... 222 D5
Quarry Mount St HDGY LS6 ... 6 D1
Quarry Mount Ter HDGY LS6 .. 6 D1
Quarry Pl ECHL BD2 .... 105 K4
MIRF WF14 .... 171 M8
Quarry Rd CLECK BD19 .... 149 L7
CLECK BD19 .... 150 D7
DEWS WF13 .... 173 K7
HIPP HX3 .... 146 A4
HUD HD1 .... 14 A6
HUDS HD4 .... 213 K3
LVSG WF15 .... 172 C2
OT LS21 .... 63 J1
RTHW LS26 .... 133 M8
Quarryside Rd MIRF WF14 .... 172 A8
Quarry St BSLY S70 .... 261 H6 [3]
BSLYN/ROY S71 .... 261 J1 [3]
CUD/GR S72 .... 244 D7
FEA/AMT WF7 .... 224 B1
HDGY LS6 .... 6 D1
HTON BD9 .... 104 C2
KGHY BD21 .... 3 K5
WHIT OL12 .... 184 A1
WHIT OL12 .... 206 A5
The Quarry AL/HA/HU LS17 ... 65 J8
Quarry Vw DEWS WF13 .... 173 H5
Quayside BAIL BD17 .... 82 D6 [3]
Quay St HUD HD1 .... 15 H6
Quebec St ELL HX5 .... 169 J7 [2]
KGHY BD21 .... 2 F5
LDS LS1 .... 6 D3
TOD OL14 .... 163 J5 [11]
WKFDW/WTN WF2 .... 12 C3
Queen Elizabeth Dr
NORM WF6 .... 178 C6
Queen Elizabeth Gdns
HUD HD1 .... 14 D6
Queen Elizabeth Gv
WKFDE WF1 .... 177 G7
Queen Elizabeth Rd
WKFDE WF1 .... 177 G7
Queen Elizabeth St
WKFDE WF1 .... 176 C2
Queen Margarets Av
KNOT WF11 .... 159 M6 [2]
Queen Margarets Cl
KNOT WF11 .... 159 M6 [3]
Queen Margaret's Dr
KNOT WF11 .... 159 M6
Queen's Av CUD/GR S72 ...... 263 M7
DOD/DAR S75 .... 260 F4
ECHL BD2 .... 105 H3
PONT WF8 .... 180 C7
WHIT OL12 .... 206 E2
Queensbury Av WKFDE WF1 .... 176 E1
Queensbury Rd HIPP HX3 ..... 146 D1
Queensbury Sq
CUL/QBY BD13 .... 125 G5 [13]
Queens Cl BGLY BD16 .... 81 K4 [3]
CHAL LS7 .... 87 L6
Queen's Crs HOR/CROF WF4 ... 200 F2
OSS WF5 .... 196 F1
Queen's Dr CUD/GR S72 ...... 244 E5
CUD/GR S72 .... 244 E5
DOD/DAR S75 .... 260 F3
DOD/DAR S75 .... 260 E3
EARD/LOFT WF3 .... 175 G1
HIPP HX3 .... 169 J2 [4]
ILK LS29 .... 38 B3
OSS WF5 .... 197 G3
PDSY/CALV LS28 .... 106 F6
ROCH OL11 .... 228 A3
WKFDW/WTN WF2 .... 176 A5
Queens Drive Cl OSS WF5 .... 197 H2 [10]
Queen's Drive La ILK LS29 .. 38 B3
Queens Gdns DOD/DAR S75 .... 260 E3
ILK LS29 .... 38 C3 [3]
OSS WF5 .... 196 F1 [3]
TAD LS24 .... 71 L4
Queen's Ga HIPP HX3 .... 168 D2
Queensgate HUD HD1 .... 15 G9
Queensgate Dr ROY/SHW OL2 .. 228 E8
Queens Gv KGHY BD21 .... 2 B9
MOR LS27 .... 152 B3 [3]
Queenshill Av AL/HA/HU LS17 87 L3
Queenshill Cl AL/HA/HU LS17 87 L4 [3]
Queenshill Ct AL/HA/HU LS17 87 L4 [3]
Queenshill Crs AL/HA/HU LS17 87 L3
Queenshill Dr AL/HA/HU LS17 87 L4
Queenshill Gdns AL/HA/HU LS17 87 K4
Queenshill Garth
AL/HA/HU LS17 .... 87 L4 [7]
Queenshill Rd AL/HA/HU LS17 87 L4

Queenshill Vw AL/HA/HU LS17 ..... 87 L4 8
Queenshill Wk AL/HA/HU LS17 ..... 87 L4 9
Queenshill Wy AL/HA/HU LS17 ... 87 L4 10
Queens Md HIPP HX3 ..... 147 J3 1
Queens Mill Rd HUD HD1 ..... 214 C2
Queens Park Cl CAS WF10 ..... 158 D6
Queen's Park Dr CAS WF10 ..... 158 C7
Queen's Pl MOR LS27 ..... 152 D2 11
OT LS21 ..... 41 J7
SHPY BD18 ..... 82 B6 20
Queen's Prom MOR LS27 ..... 152 C2 11
Queen Sq LDSU LS2 ..... 7 G7
Queen's Ri ECHL BD2 ..... 105 H3
Queen's Rd AWLS/ASK DN6 ..... 249 L6
BGLY BD16 ..... 59 G8
BSLYN/ROY S71 ..... 261 H5
BSPA/BRAM LS23 ..... 48 E6
CAS WF10 ..... 158 C7
CUD/GR S72 ..... 244 E5
CUD/GR S72 ..... 245 K8
ECHL BD2 ..... 105 H4 1
HDGY LS6 ..... 109 G4
HFAX HX1 ..... 10 B4
HIPP HX3 ..... 148 B4
HUDW HD3 ..... 14 B3
ILK LS29 ..... 38 C3
KGHY BD21 ..... 2 E9
LIT OL15 ..... 207 K1
MOR LS27 ..... 152 B3
PONT WF8 ..... 180 C7 1
SHPY BD18 ..... 82 B6
Queens's Ct LDS LS1 ..... 9 H1
Queens Sq HUD HD1 ..... 15 M1
PONT WF8 ..... 180 C7
Queen's St SKP/WHF BD23 ..... 16 D2 2
Queen's Ter OSS WF5 ..... 196 F1 6
Queensthorpe Av BRAM LS13 ..... 107 M6
Queensthorpe Cl BRAM LS13 ..... 108 A6 1
Queensthorpe Ri BRAM LS13 ..... 107 M6 1
Queen St AIRE BD20 ..... 36 A5 11
AIRE BD20 ..... 56 E1
BAIL BD17 ..... 82 E5 3
BGLY BD16 ..... 81 H3 12
BSLY S70 ..... 261 H5
CAS WF10 ..... 158 A5
CLECK BD19 ..... 150 A8
CLECK BD19 ..... 150 D4
DEWS WF13 ..... 173 G8
EARD/LOFT WF3 ..... 153 M6
EARD/LOFT WF3 ..... 154 F3
EARL WF12 ..... 174 C6
GTL/HWG HX4 ..... 168 E8
HBR HX7 ..... 144 A6 2
HECK WF16 ..... 172 E3 2
HEM/SK/SE WF9 ..... 247 H4
HOR/CROF WF4 ..... 197 J5
HUD HD1 ..... 15 G7
HWTH BD22 ..... 54 E3
IDLE BD10 ..... 83 M7
KBTN HD8 ..... 239 J4
LDS LS1 ..... 8 D1
LIT OL15 ..... 207 K1
MID LS10 ..... 132 C4
MIRF WF14 ..... 194 C2
MOR LS27 ..... 152 C1
NORM WF6 ..... 178 C4
OSS WF5 ..... 196 F1
PONT WF8 ..... 180 D6
ROY/SHW OL2 ..... 229 K8
RPDN/SBR HX6 ..... 167 G3
RTHW LS26 ..... 135 G8
STKB/PEN S36 ..... 271 G3
TOD OL14 ..... 163 K1 10
WBSY BD6 ..... 126 A7 4
WHIT OL12 ..... 206 B6 13
WIL/AL BD15 ..... 102 E2
WKFDE WF1 ..... 12 E3
WKFDE WF1 ..... 176 D2
WMB/DAR S73 ..... 263 K8
YEA LS19 ..... 84 D2
Queen St South HUD HD1 ..... 15 G9
HUD HD1 ..... 214 D2 4
Queens Vw LIT OL15 ..... 207 J3 2
Queen's Wk OSS WF5 ..... 197 H1
Queens Wy KBTN HD8 ..... 238 C1
Queensway BGLY BD16 ..... 81 K4
BSLYN/ROY S71 ..... 243 L2 2
DOD/DAR S75 ..... 260 E3 4
GFTH/SHER LS25 ..... 112 F7
GSLY LS20 ..... 62 B5
HFAX HX1 ..... 10 A4
MOR LS27 ..... 152 C2
MSTN/BAR LS15 ..... 111 L6
PONT WF8 ..... 181 H3
ROCH OL11 ..... 228 C2
RTHW LS26 ..... 133 G8
YEA LS19 ..... 62 C6
Queenswood Cl HDGY LS6 ..... 86 C7
Queenswood Dr HDGY LS6 ..... 86 C8
Queenswood Gdns HDGY LS6 ..... 108 E2
Queenswood Gn HDGY LS6 ..... 86 C7
Queenswood Mt HDGY LS6 ..... 108 D1 2
Queenswood Ri HDGY LS6 ..... 108 D2 1
Queenswood Rd HDGY LS6 ..... 108 D1
Queen Victoria Crs HIPP HX3 ..... 147 K3
Queen Victoria St LDS LS1 ..... 7 H9
ROCH OL11 ..... 228 C3
Quernmore Dr BWCK/EAR BB18 ..... 52 C1
Quern Wy WMB/DAR S73 ..... 263 J8
Quincy Cl ECHL BD2 ..... 105 L2 2
Qunsworth St BOW BD4 ..... 127 K2

R

Raby Av CHAL LS7 ..... 7 J2
Raby Pk WBY LS22 ..... 47 M1
Raby St CHAL LS7 ..... 7 J2
Raby Ter CHAL LS7 ..... 7 J2
Racca Av KNOT WF11 ..... 182 D2
Racca Gn KNOT WF11 ..... 182 C2
Race Common Av
STKB/PEN S36 ..... 270 E6
Racecommon La BSLY S70 ..... 260 F7
Racecommon Rd BSLY S70 ..... 260 F6
Race Moor La HWTH BD22 ..... 78 D3
Race St BSLY S70 ..... 261 G5
Rachael St HOR/CROF WF4 ..... 197 H5
Racton St HOLM/MEL HD7 ..... 212 B5
Radcliffe Av ECHL BD2 ..... 105 J1
Radcliffe Gdns PDSY/CALV LS28 ..... 107 G7
Radcliffe La LUD/ILL HX2 ..... 144 E4
PDSY/CALV LS28 ..... 107 G7
Radcliffe Pl WKFDE WF1 ..... 12 E2
Radcliffe Rd BSLYN/ROY S71 ..... 243 H6
HOLM/MEL HD7 ..... 212 C5
HUDS HD4 ..... 213 K2
WKFDW/WTN WF2 ..... 197 M2
Radcliffe St KBTN HD8 ..... 239 H4
Radfield Dr WBSY BD6 ..... 127 G5
Radford Park Av
HEM/SK/SE WF9 ..... 246 D5
Radnor St BFDE BD3 ..... 105 L7
WOR/ARM LS12 ..... 109 G8
Radwell Dr WBOW BD5 ..... 4 E9
Raeburn Dr WBSY BD6 ..... 126 C7
Rae Ct EARD/LOFT WF3 ..... 177 G1
Rae Rd SHPY BD18 ..... 82 C8
Rafborn Av HUDW HD3 ..... 191 G5
Raglan Av HWTH BD22 ..... 2 B6
Raglan Cl CAS WF10 ..... 157 J6
Raglan Rd HDGY LS6 ..... 6 D2
LDSU LS2 ..... 6 D3
Raglan St BFDE BD3 ..... 105 M7 11
CUL/QBY BD13 ..... 125 G5 14
HFAX HX1 ..... 10 D5
HWTH BD22 ..... 2 B6
TOD OL14 ..... 163 K1
Raikes Av SKP/WHF BD23 ..... 16 B1
Raikes La BOW BD4 ..... 128 A7
BTLY WF17 ..... 151 G4
Raikes Rd SKP/WHF BD23 ..... 16 A1
Raikeswood Crs SKP/WHF BD23 ..... 16 A1
Raikes Wood Dr BOW BD4 ..... 128 A7
Raikeswood Dr SKP/WHF BD23 ..... 16 A1
Raikeswood Rd SKP/WHF BD23 ..... 16 A1
Railes Cl LUD/ILL HX2 ..... 144 F5
Railsfield Mt BRAM LS13 ..... 107 L4
Railsfield Ri BRAM LS13 ..... 107 L5
Railsfield Wy BRAM LS13 ..... 107 L4
Railway Av PONT WF8 ..... 180 E5
Railway Rd IDLE BD10 ..... 83 K6
MSTN/BAR LS15 ..... 111 M4
Railway St BOW BD4 ..... 127 L4 3
BRIG HD6 ..... 170 D5 3
CLECK BD19 ..... 149 M7 8
DEWS WF13 ..... 173 H8
EARL WF12 ..... 173 M6
HECK WF16 ..... 172 F3
HUD HD1 ..... 14 F6
KGHY BD21 ..... 57 L5 3
LIT OL15 ..... 207 K1
MILN OL16 ..... 206 C8
MILN OL16 ..... 229 L2 1
OSM LS9 ..... 9 L1
TOD OL14 ..... 141 K8
Railway Ter EARD/LOFT WF3 ..... 153 L5
HEM/SK/SE WF9 ..... 223 J3
HIPP HX3 ..... 168 C4
NORM WF6 ..... 178 C4
Railway Vw CAS WF10 ..... 157 K7
ROY/SHW OL2 ..... 229 L5 3
Rainbow Ms WBSY BD6 ..... 126 B8 7
Raincliffe Gv OSM LS9 ..... 110 C6
Raincliffe Mt OSM LS9 ..... 110 C7 12
Raincliffe Rd OSM LS9 ..... 110 C6
Raincliffe St OSM LS9 ..... 110 C6
Raincliffe Ter OSM LS9 ..... 110 C7 13
Raines Crest MILN OL16 ..... 207 J8
Raines Dr AIRE BD20 ..... 34 E1 4
Rainford Dr BSLYN/ROY S71 ..... 243 M8
Rainsborough Av KNOT WF11 ..... 181 L3
Rainton Gv DOD/DAR S75 ..... 260 D3
Raistrick Wy SHPY BD18 ..... 82 F6
Rake HBR HX7 ..... 143 H6
Rake Head Barn La TOD OL14 ..... 163 J6
Rake Head Rd HOLM/MEL HD7 ..... 253 G7
Rakehill Rd MSTN/BAR LS15 ..... 90 B7
Rake Ter LIT OL15 ..... 185 L8
Rakewood Rd LIT OL15 ..... 207 K3
Raleigh Gdns LIT OL15 ..... 185 L5 4
Raleigh St HFAX HX1 ..... 10 B9 9
Raley St BSLY S70 ..... 260 F6
Ralph Garth RYKW YO26 ..... 32 C1
Ralph St WHIT OL12 ..... 206 C5
Rampart Rd HDGY LS6 ..... 6 C2
The Rampart COP/BISH YO23 ..... 73 J8
Ramsay Pl MILN OL16 ..... 206 C6 12
Ramsay St MILN OL16 ..... 206 C6
Ramsay Ter MILN OL16 ..... 206 C6 13
Ramsden Av GTHN BD7 ..... 126 A1 1
Ramsden Cl KNOT WF11 ..... 159 L6 1
Ramsden Ct GTHN BD7 ..... 126 C2 18
Ramsden La TOD OL14 ..... 163 G7
Ramsden Mill La
HOLM/MEL HD7 ..... 213 G3
Ramsden Pl CLAY BD14 ..... 125 K1
Ramsden Rd HOLM/MEL HD7 ..... 253 L6
WHIT OL12 ..... 184 E7
Ramsden St CAS WF10 ..... 179 L1
GFTH/SHER LS25 ..... 135 H6
HIPP HX3 ..... 146 A4
HOLM/MEL HD7 ..... 213 G2
HUD HD1 ..... 14 F8
TOD OL14 ..... 163 J7
Ramsden Wood Rd TOD OL14 ..... 163 H7
Ramsey Crs HOR/CROF WF4 ..... 196 D7
Ramsey Rd HOR/CROF WF4 ..... 196 C7
Ramsey St WBOW BD5 ..... 126 F3 12
Ramsey Vw HOR/CROF WF4 ..... 196 C7
Ramsgate EARD/LOFT WF3 ..... 154 D5
Ramsgate Crs EARD/LOFT WF3 ..... 154 D5
Ramsgate St HFAX HX1 ..... 10 A5
Ramshaw Dr SKP/WHF BD23 ..... 16 C5
Ramshead Ap SCFT LS14 ..... 89 J8
Ramshead Cl SCFT LS14 ..... 89 J7
Ramshead Crs SCFT LS14 ..... 89 H6 3
Ramshead Dr SCFT LS14 ..... 89 H7
Ramshead Gdns SCFT LS14 ..... 89 H7
Ramshead Gv SCFT LS14 ..... 89 J8 2
Ramshead Hl SCFT LS14 ..... 89 J8
Ramshead Pl SCFT LS14 ..... 89 J8 3
Ramshead Vw SCFT LS14 ..... 89 J8 4
Randall Pl HTON BD9 ..... 104 C3
Randall Well St BFD BD1 ..... 4 D7
Randolph St BFDE BD3 ..... 106 A6 6
BRAM LS13 ..... 107 J4
HIPP HX3 ..... 11 G3
Random Cl HWTH BD22 ..... 2 A9
Rand Pl GTHN BD7 ..... 4 A9
Rand St GTHN BD7 ..... 4 A9
Ranelagh Av IDLE BD10 ..... 106 A1 3
Raneley Gv ROCH OL11 ..... 228 C4
Range Bank HIPP HX3 ..... 11 H2
Range Gdns HIPP HX3 ..... 11 H2
Range La HIPP HX3 ..... 11 H3
UPML OL3 ..... 230 F5
Range St HIPP HX3 ..... 11 G2
Rankin's Well Rd SKP/WHF BD23 ..... 16 D2
Ransdale Dr WBOW BD5 ..... 126 F3
Ransdale Gv WBOW BD5 ..... 126 F3 13
Ransdale Rd WBOW BD5 ..... 126 F3
Ranter's Fold HOR/CROF WF4 ..... 197 J5 5
Raper Vw GFTH/SHER LS25 ..... 92 A6
Rapes Hwy UPML OL3 ..... 231 J1
Rashcliffe Hill Rd HUD HD1 ..... 214 B2
Rastrick Common BRIG HD6 ..... 170 C6
Rathbone St MILN OL16 ..... 206 E7
Rathlin Rd EARL WF12 ..... 174 B4
Rathmell Rd MSTN/BAR LS15 ..... 111 H7 4
Rathmell St WBOW BD5 ..... 126 F5
Ratten Rw DOD/DAR S75 ..... 260 A8
Ratten Row Rd RPDN/SBR HX6 ..... 166 E5
Raven Cl FEA/AMT WF7 ..... 179 K5
Ravenfield Dr BSLYN/ROY S71 ..... 243 J8
Raven La CUD/GR S72 ..... 222 C8
Raven Rd HDGY LS6 ..... 109 G2 3
Raven Royd BSLYN/ROY S71 ..... 243 H5
Ravens Av DEWS WF13 ..... 173 J8
HUDE HD5 ..... 215 G1
Ravenscar Av RHAY LS8 ..... 88 C8 3
Ravenscar Mt RHAY LS8 ..... 88 C8 4
Ravenscar Ter RHAY LS8 ..... 88 C8 5
Ravenscar Vw RHAY LS8 ..... 88 C8 6
Ravenscar Wk RHAY LS8 ..... 88 C8 7
Ravenscliffe Av IDLE BD10 ..... 106 A1
Ravenscliffe Rd PDSY/CALV LS28 ..... 84 A8
Ravens Cl DOD/DAR S75 ..... 242 D6 3
Ravens Crs DEWS WF13 ..... 173 J8 3
Ravensdeane HUDW HD3 ..... 191 M6 1
Ravensfield Rd DEWS WF13 ..... 173 J8 4
Ravens Gv DEWS WF13 ..... 173 J8
Ravenshaw Cl DOD/DAR S75 ..... 260 D3 3
Ravenshouse Rd DEWS WF13 ..... 173 H7
Ravensknowle Rd HUDE HD5 ..... 215 G1
Ravens Lodge Ter DEWS WF13 ..... 173 J8 5
Ravensmead FEA/AMT WF7 ..... 202 B1
Ravens Mt PDSY/CALV LS28 ..... 107 H7
Ravens St DEWS WF13 ..... 173 H8 2
Ravensthorpe Rd EARL WF12 ..... 195 H2
Ravenstone Dr GTL/HWG HX4 ..... 168 E8
Raven St BGLY BD16 ..... 81 J3 3
HFAX HX1 ..... 10 B5
HUD HD1 ..... 213 M1
KGHY BD21 ..... 2 F4
Ravensville AIRE BD20 ..... 35 G8 2
Ravens Wk DEWS WF13 ..... 173 J8
Ravens Wy HOLM/MEL HD7 ..... 255 G2
Ravenswharf Rd DEWS WF13 ..... 173 J8 6
Ravensworth Cl
MSTN/BAR LS15 ..... 112 B3 4
Ravensworth Wy
MSTN/BAR LS15 ..... 112 B3 5
Raven Ter GIR BD8 ..... 103 L7
Rawden Hl OT LS21 ..... 44 A8
Rawdon Dr YEA LS19 ..... 84 D3
Rawdon Hall Dr YEA LS19 ..... 84 D3
Rawdon Rd HORS LS18 ..... 85 G5
HWTH BD22 ..... 78 E7
Rawdon St HWTH BD22 ..... 2 C7
Raw End Rd LUD/ILL HX2 ..... 145 J6
Rawfield La GFTH/SHER LS25 ..... 137 L8
Rawfolds Av BTLY WF17 ..... 151 H4
Rawfolds Wy CLECK BD19 ..... 150 A8
Rawgate Av CAS WF10 ..... 157 H6
Raw Hl BRIG HD6 ..... 170 B6 4
Raw La HBR HX7 ..... 143 M3
LUD/ILL HX2 ..... 145 M1
TAD LS24 ..... 94 A1
Rawling St KGHY BD21 ..... 2 E9
Raw Nook LM/WK BD12 ..... 149 H1 4
Raw Nook Rd HUDW HD3 ..... 191 G6
Rawroyds GTL/HWG HX4 ..... 190 E1
Rawson Av BFDE BD3 ..... 105 M6
HIPP HX3 ..... 168 D3
Rawson Pl BFD BD1 ..... 4 E5
RPDN/SBR HX6 ..... 167 J3 5
Rawson Rd BFD BD1 ..... 4 D5
Rawson Sq BFD BD1 ..... 4 E5
IDLE BD10 ..... 83 K6 10
Rawson St HFAX HX1 ..... 11 G6
LM/WK BD12 ..... 148 F2
Rawson St North HIPP HX3 ..... 10 E1
Rawson Ter BEE/HOL LS11 ..... 131 L3 26
Rawtenstall Bank HBR HX7 ..... 143 G5
Rawthorpe Crs HUDE HD5 ..... 193 G6
Rawthorpe La HUDE HD5 ..... 15 M5
HUDE HD5 ..... 193 G6 2
Rawthorpe Ter HUDE HD5 ..... 193 G6
Rayfield WKFDW/WTN WF2 ..... 198 B1 2
Ray Ga HBR HX7 ..... 122 B7
HOLM/MEL HD7 ..... 236 F6
HUDW HD3 ..... 190 F6
Raygill Cl AL/HA/HU LS17 ..... 88 D1
Raylands Cl MID LS10 ..... 132 B8
Raylands Ct MID LS10 ..... 132 B8 2
Raylands Fold MID LS10 ..... 132 B8 3
Raylands Garth MID LS10 ..... 132 B8 4
Raylands La MID LS10 ..... 132 B8
Raylands Pl MID LS10 ..... 132 B8
Raylands Rd MID LS10 ..... 132 B8
Raylands Wy MID LS10 ..... 154 B1
Rayleigh St BOW BD4 ..... 127 J2
Raymond Av CUD/GR S72 ..... 245 J8
Raymond Dr WBOW BD5 ..... 127 G4
Raymond Rd BSLY S70 ..... 261 M7
Raymond St WBOW BD5 ..... 127 G4
Raynbron Cresent
WBOW BD5 ..... 127 H4 6
Raynel Ap BHP/TINH LS16 ..... 86 B3
Raynel Cl BHP/TINH LS16 ..... 86 B2
Raynel Dr BHP/TINH LS16 ..... 86 C3
Raynel Gdns BHP/TINH LS16 ..... 86 C2
Raynel Garth BHP/TINH LS16 ..... 86 C3 1
Raynel Gn BHP/TINH LS16 ..... 86 C3
Raynel Mt BHP/TINH LS16 ..... 86 B2
Raynel Wy BHP/TINH LS16 ..... 86 B2
Rayner Av GIR BD8 ..... 104 B5
HECK WF16 ..... 150 F8
Rayner Dr BRIG HD6 ..... 170 C2
Rayner Mt WIL/AL BD15 ..... 103 K6
Rayner Rd BRIG HD6 ..... 170 C2
Rayners Av LVSG WF15 ..... 171 L2
Rayner St HOR/CROF WF4 ..... 197 J5
Raynham Crs HWTH BD22 ..... 57 G6
Raynor Cl HUDW HD3 ..... 191 L7
Raynville Ap BRAM LS13 ..... 108 A4
Raynville Av BRAM LS13 ..... 108 B3
Raynville Crs WOR/ARM LS12 ..... 108 B4
Raynville Dr BRAM LS13 ..... 108 A3
Raynville Gv BRAM LS13 ..... 108 A3
Raynville Mt BRAM LS13 ..... 108 A3
Raynville Pl WOR/ARM LS12 ..... 108 A4 2
Raynville Ri BRAM LS13 ..... 108 A4
Raynville Rd WOR/ARM LS12 ..... 108 B3
Raynville St BRAM LS13 ..... 108 A3 6
Raynville Ter BRAM LS13 ..... 108 A3
Raynville Wk BRAM LS13 ..... 108 A4
Ray St HUD HD1 ..... 15 G4
Raywood Cl YEA LS19 ..... 62 C6
Reap Hirst Rd HUDN HD2 ..... 191 M4
Reasbeck Ter BSLYN/ROY S71 ..... 261 H1 1
Rebecca Ms BSLY S70 ..... 261 H6 10
Rebecca Rw BSLY S70 ..... 261 H6
Rebecca St GIR BD8 ..... 4 C4
Recreation Av BEE/HOL LS11 ..... 8 C7 1
Recreation Crs BEE/HOL LS11 ..... 8 B7
Recreation Gv BEE/HOL LS11 ..... 8 B7
Recreation La ELL HX5 ..... 169 G8
Recreation Mt BEE/HOL LS11 ..... 8 B7
Recreation Pl BEE/HOL LS11 ..... 8 B7
Recreation Rd RPDN/SBR HX6 ..... 167 K2
Recreation Rw BEE/HOL LS11 ..... 8 B7
Recreation St BEE/HOL LS11 ..... 8 B7
Recreation Ter BEE/HOL LS11 ..... 8 B7
Recreation Vw BEE/HOL LS11 ..... 8 B7
Rectory Cl BSLYN/ROY S71 ..... 243 M5
COP/BISH YO23 ..... 73 J7
GFTH/SHER LS25 ..... 113 H7
HOLM/MEL HD7 ..... 233 H2
Rectory Dr BTLY WF17 ..... 151 J5
HUDE HD5 ..... 193 K7
Rectory Gdn KBTN HD8 ..... 217 M7
Rectory La KBTN HD8 ..... 217 M7
SKP/WHF BD23 ..... 16 C2
Rectory Rw KGHY BD21 ..... 2 F5
Rectory St CAS WF10 ..... 157 M6 12
OSM LS9 ..... 7 M6
Rectory Vw EARL WF12 ..... 196 A3
Rectory Wy BSLYN/ROY S71 ..... 261 M3 2
Red Beck Rd HIPP HX3 ..... 147 H5
Red Beck V SHPY BD18 ..... 104 C1
Red Brink La RPDN/SBR HX6 ..... 166 D4
Redbrook Ct DOD/DAR S75 ..... 260 E2 2
Redbrook Rd DOD/DAR S75 ..... 260 C2
Redbrook Vw DOD/DAR S75 ..... 260 E2
Redbrook Wk DOD/DAR S75 ..... 260 E2
Redburn Av SHPY BD18 ..... 104 C1
Redburn Dr SHPY BD18 ..... 104 C1
Redburn Rd SHPY BD18 ..... 104 C1
Redcar La AIRE BD20 ..... 56 D4
Redcar Rd IDLE BD10 ..... 84 A8
Redcar St HFAX HX1 ..... 10 A5
WHIT OL12 ..... 206 A6 16
Redcliffe Av KGHY BD21 ..... 2 D4
Redcliffe Cl DOD/DAR S75 ..... 260 D2
Redcliffe Gv KGHY BD21 ..... 2 C4
Redcliffe St KGHY BD21 ..... 2 E4
Redcote La WOR/ARM LS12 ..... 108 D5
Redcross St WHIT OL12 ..... 206 B6
Redcross St North
WHIT OL12 ..... 206 B5 19
Red Deer Park La
HOR/CROF WF4 ..... 217 G1
Reddisher Rd HOLM/MEL HD7 ..... 233 G2
Red Doles La HUD HD1 ..... 192 E5
Red Doles Rd HUDN HD2 ..... 192 E4
Reddyshore Scout Ga
TOD OL14 ..... 185 K1
Redesdale Gdns BHP/TINH LS16 ..... 86 D3
Redfearn Av HECK WF16 ..... 172 F1
Redfearn St BSLYN/ROY S71 ..... 261 H4 5
Red Hall Ap SCFT LS14 ..... 89 J5
Red Hall Av AL/HA/HU LS17 ..... 89 H5
Redhall Cl BEE/HOL LS11 ..... 131 G5
Red Hall Ct SCFT LS14 ..... 89 J5 1
Redhall Crs BEE/HOL LS11 ..... 131 G5
Red Hall Cft SCFT LS14 ..... 89 J6
Red Hall Dr SCFT LS14 ..... 89 H5
Red Hall Gdns AL/HA/HU LS17 ..... 89 H5
Red Hall Garth SCFT LS14 ..... 89 J5
Redhall Ga BEE/HOL LS11 ..... 131 G5
Red Hall Gn SCFT LS14 ..... 89 J5 2
Red Hall La AL/HA/HU LS17 ..... 89 H5
WKFDE WF1 ..... 176 D4
Red Hall Vw SCFT LS14 ..... 89 J5 3
Red Hall Wk SCFT LS14 ..... 89 J5
Red Hall Wy SCFT LS14 ..... 89 J5
Redhill Av BSLY S70 ..... 261 L7
CAS WF10 ..... 158 B8
EARD/LOFT WF3 ..... 175 G1
Redhill Cl EARD/LOFT WF3 ..... 175 G1
Redhill Crs EARD/LOFT WF3 ..... 175 G1
Redhill Dr CAS WF10 ..... 158 C7
EARD/LOFT WF3 ..... 175 G1
Redhill Gdns CAS WF10 ..... 158 C8 3
Red Hill La GFTH/SHER LS25 ..... 137 L5
Redhill Mt CAS WF10 ..... 158 C7
Redhill Rd CAS WF10 ..... 158 C7
Redhill Vw CAS WF10 ..... 158 C8
Red House La AWLS/ASK DN6 ..... 248 F8
AWLS/ASK DN6 ..... 249 J7
Redhouse La CHAL LS7 ..... 88 A7 2
Red Laithes La DEWS WF13 ..... 173 G8 5
Redland Cl LIT OL15 ..... 185 K8
Redland Crs HEM/SK/SE WF9 ..... 223 K4
Redland Dr KBTN HD8 ..... 216 A7 1
Redland Gv DOD/DAR S75 ..... 242 D4
Red La FEA/AMT WF7 ..... 201 G1
HOLM/MEL HD7 ..... 234 D4
PDSY/CALV LS28 ..... 106 E3
WHIT OL12 ..... 206 D4
WKFDE WF1 ..... 200 A1
Red Lodge Cl RHAY LS8 ..... 110 F2
Redman Garth HWTH BD22 ..... 78 D7 4
Redmayne Gv KNOT WF11 ..... 181 M2
Redmire Ct SCFT LS14 ..... 111 J2
Redmire Dr SCFT LS14 ..... 111 J2
Redmire St BFDE BD3 ..... 106 A7 5
Redmire Vw SCFT LS14 ..... 111 J2
Redruth Dr NORM WF6 ..... 178 D3
Redshaw Rd WOR/ARM LS12 ..... 108 F8
Redthorne Wy CUD/GR S72 ..... 244 D3
Redthorpe Crest DOD/DAR S75 ..... 260 C2 2
Red V CLECK BD19 ..... 150 D4 3
Redvers Cl BHP/TINH LS16 ..... 86 C5
Redwood Av BSLYN/ROY S71 ..... 243 L3
EARD/LOFT WF3 ..... 153 J6
Redwood Cl KGHY BD21 ..... 3 L8
Redwood Dr HUDN HD2 ..... 192 F1
Redwood Gv HOR/CROF WF4 ..... 200 E2 2
Redwood Park Gv MILN OL16 ..... 206 F7 9
Redwood Wy YEA LS19 ..... 62 B7
Reed Hl MILN OL16 ..... 206 B6 14
Reedling Dr MOR LS27 ..... 152 E3 5
Reed Rd WOR/ARM LS12 ..... 108 E8
Reedsdale Av MOR LS27 ..... 129 L7 4
Reedsdale Dr MOR LS27 ..... 129 L7 5
Reedsdale Gdns MOR LS27 ..... 129 L7
Reedshaw La HWTH BD22 ..... 54 B5
Reed St HUD HD1 ..... 191 M7
Rees Wy BFDE BD3 ..... 5 H3
Reeth Rd BRIG HD6 ..... 170 A6 1
Reevy Av WBSY BD6 ..... 126 B5
Reevy Crs WBSY BD6 ..... 126 A7
Reevy Dr WBSY BD6 ..... 126 C6
Reevylands Dr WBSY BD6 ..... 126 C6
Reevy Rd WBSY BD6 ..... 126 B6
Reevy Rd West WBSY BD6 ..... 126 A6
Reevy St WBSY BD6 ..... 126 C5
Reform St CLECK BD19 ..... 150 D5
WHIT OL12 ..... 206 B5
Refuge St ROY/SHW OL2 ..... 229 K8
Regal Cl RPDN/SBR HX6 ..... 188 E5
Regal Dr RPDN/SBR HX6 ..... 188 E5
Regency Ct GIR BD8 ..... 104 C6
HDGY LS6 ..... 109 G2
Regency Gdns
EARD/LOFT WF3 ..... 153 J6 2
Regency Park Gv
PDSY/CALV LS28 ..... 129 G1 3
Regency Park Rd
PDSY/CALV LS28 ..... 129 G1
Regency Rd MIRF WF14 ..... 194 C2 1
Regency Vw ECHL BD2 ..... 105 J4 4
Regent Av COL BB8 ..... 52 A8 3
HORS LS18 ..... 85 L7
SKP/WHF BD23 ..... 16 D1
Regent Cl BRIG HD6 ..... 170 A8 4
Regent Crs BSLYN/ROY S71 ..... 243 H7
HORS LS18 ..... 85 K7
SKP/WHF BD23 ..... 16 D1
Regent Cresent CUD/GR S72 ..... 245 G1
Regent Dr SKP/WHF BD23 ..... 16 D2
Regent Gdns BSLY S70 ..... 261 G4
Regent Ms BTLY WF17 ..... 174 B2 1
Regent Park Av HDGY LS6 ..... 6 B1
Regent Park Cross Av HDGY LS6 ..... 6 B1
Regent Park Ter HDGY LS6 ..... 6 B1
Regent Pl HBR HX7 ..... 143 J2 10
IDLE BD10 ..... 83 J5 4
RPDN/SBR HX6 ..... 167 K1
Regent Rd HORS LS18 ..... 85 K7
HUDE HD5 ..... 193 L4
HUDW HD3 ..... 14 A4
ILK LS29 ..... 38 C2
SKP/WHF BD23 ..... 16 D1
Regents Pk WKFDE WF1 ..... 13 J3
Regent St BSLY S70 ..... 261 G4
CAS WF10 ..... 157 L7
CHAL LS7 ..... 87 L7
CUD/GR S72 ..... 245 G1
CUL/QBY BD13 ..... 125 H5 11
FEA/AMT WF7 ..... 201 M1 3
HBR HX7 ..... 143 J3
HECK WF16 ..... 172 E3
HEM/SK/SE WF9 ..... 223 L7
HEM/SK/SE WF9 ..... 247 G3
HFAX HX1 ..... 10 F7
HOR/CROF WF4 ..... 197 H5
IDLE BD10 ..... 83 J5 3
IDLE BD10 ..... 83 M7 7
LIT OL15 ..... 207 K1
MIRF WF14 ..... 194 C3 3
NORM WF6 ..... 178 E3
OSM LS9 ..... 7 K8
TOD OL14 ..... 163 J5 12
WHIT OL12 ..... 206 B5
WKFDE WF1 ..... 13 K7
Regent Ter HDGY LS6 ..... 6 A5
Regina Crs CUD/GR S72 ..... 245 G3
HOR/CROF WF4 ..... 222 E5
Regina Dr CHAL LS7 ..... 87 M8
Reginald Mt CHAL LS7 ..... 109 M2
Reginald Pl CHAL LS7 ..... 109 M2 9
Reginald Rd BSLY S70 ..... 261 M7
Reginald Rw CHAL LS7 ..... 109 M2
Reginald St CHAL LS7 ..... 109 M2
WBOW BD5 ..... 126 F3
Reginald Ter CHAL LS7 ..... 109 M2 10
Reginald Vw CHAL LS7 ..... 109 M2 11
Reid Park Av HOR/CROF WF4 ..... 197 G5 6
Reighton Cft IDLE BD10 ..... 84 A8
Rein Gdns EARD/LOFT WF3 ..... 152 E6
Rein Ms EARD/LOFT WF3 ..... 152 E6
Rein Rd BRAM LS13 ..... 85 L8
EARD/LOFT WF3 ..... 152 E5
Reins Av BAIL BD17 ..... 82 D5
Reins Rd BRIG HD6 ..... 170 A6
Rein St MOR LS27 ..... 152 E5
The Rein SCFT LS14 ..... 89 H8
Reinwood Av HUDW HD3 ..... 191 K8
RHAY LS8 ..... 110 F1
Reinwood Rd HUDW HD3 ..... 191 K8
Rembrandt Av EARD/LOFT WF3 ..... 153 H6
Renald La STKB/PEN S36 ..... 258 A7
Renee Cl BOW BD4 ..... 127 L6
Renfield Gv NORM WF6 ..... 178 F3
Renshaw St IDLE BD10 ..... 83 K5 13

Renton Av GSLY LS20 61 M5
Renton Dr GSLY LS20 61 M6
Repton Rd AWLS/ASK DN6 249 K6
Reservoir Pl CUL/QBY BD13 124 E4
Reservoir Rd HWTH BD22 78 A7
LUD/ILL HX2 146 A6
Reservoir Side Rd
HOLM/MEL HD7 213 G7
Reservoir St DEWS WF13 173 J5
MILN OL16 206 E6
Reservoir Vw CUL/QBY BD13 102 E7 3
KBTN HD8 239 G4
Restmore Av GSLY LS20 61 M3
Retford Av MILN OL16 228 D2 3
Retford Pl GTHN BD7 4 B9
Reuben St LVSG WF15 172 C1
Reva Cl BGLY BD16 81 K2 2
Reva Syke Rd CLAY BD14 125 K3
Revel Garth KBTN HD8 257 J1
Revie Rd BEE/HOL LS11 8 A9
Reydon Wk WBSY BD6 126 B5 4
Reyhill Gv WBOW BD5 4 E9
Reyner House Ms WBOW BD5 4 F9
Reynolds Av GTHN BD7 126 A1 2
Rhine St BOW BD4 127 J2 12
Rhodes Av HECK WF16 150 F8 2
Rhodes Crs PONT WF8 180 F8
ROCH OL11 228 B3
Rhodes Gdns EARD/LOFT WF3 154 E8
Rhode's Hill La
BSPA/BRAM LS23 70 A3
Rhodesia Av HIPP HX3 168 E3
WIL/AL BD15 103 L6
Rhodesia St AIRE BD20 34 F8 4
Rhodes La BSPA/BRAM LS23 48 D8
Rhodes Pl BAIL BD17 82 D6 8
Rhodes St CAS WF10 157 K7
HFAX HX1 10 E6
LVSG WF15 172 E2
SHPY BD18 82 C6
WHIT OL12 206 D3
Rhodes Ter WOR/ARM LS12 109 G8
Rhodes Wy GIR BD8 103 M5
Rhodesway GIR BD8 103 M7
Rhondda Pl HFAX HX1 146 A7
Rhum Cl WBSY BD6 126 B8
Rhyddings Av FEA/AMT WF7 224 B1
Rhyddings Dr FEA/AMT WF7 224 B2
Rhylstone Mt GTHN BD7 104 B8 5
Rhyl St FEA/AMT WF7 179 M8
Ribble Av LIT OL15 185 H8
Ribblesdale Av
GFTH/SHER LS25 113 K8
Ribble St KGHY BD21 3 M3
Ribbleton Gv BFDE BD3 5 J4
Riber Av BSLYN/ROY S71 243 J7
Ribstone St HBR HX7 144 A5
Ribston Rd PBR HG3 29 G1
Riccall Nook IDLE BD10 83 M8 4
Rice St HUD HD1 15 G7
Richard Av BSLYN/ROY S71 243 J8
Richard Rd BSLYN/ROY S71 243 J8
DOD/DAR S75 241 M6
Richardshaw La
PDSY/CALV LS28 107 G5
Richardshaw Rd
PDSY/CALV LS28 107 H5
Richardson Av WBSY BD6 126 E6 3
Richardson Crs OSM LS9 110 D7
Richardson Rd OSM LS9 110 D7
Richardson St LM/WK BD12 149 J2 4
Richard St BRIG HD6 170 C2
BSLY S70 260 F5 8
ROCH OL11 206 B8
Richard Thorpe Av MIRF WF14 194 D1
Rich Ga HOLM/MEL HD7 254 D4
Richmond Av DOD/DAR S75 241 M7 1
HDGY LS6 109 G3
HUDN HD2 192 C4
KNOT WF11 181 K1
RPDN/SBR HX6 167 H3
Richmond Cl BRAM LS13 107 J4
HFAX HX1 10 F4
MILN OL16 228 E3
MOR LS27 152 C3 3
ROY/SHW OL2 229 K8 14
RTHW LS26 133 H7
Richmond Ct HOR/CROF WF4 200 C6
HUDS HD4 213 H3
PONT WF8 180 F5 6
RTHW LS26 133 H8 2
Richmond Cft OSM LS9 110 B7 15
Richmondfield Av
MSTN/BAR LS15 91 G8
Richmondfield Cl
MSTN/BAR LS15 91 G8 1
Richmondfield Crs
MSTN/BAR LS15 91 G8 2
Richmondfield Cross
MSTN/BAR LS15 91 G8 3
Richmondfield Dr
MSTN/BAR LS15 91 G8 4
Richmondfield Garth
MSTN/BAR LS15 91 G7
Richmondfield Gv
MSTN/BAR LS15 91 G8 5
Richmondfield La
MSTN/BAR LS15 91 G8
Richmondfield Mt
MSTN/BAR LS15 91 G8
Richmondfield Wy
MSTN/BAR LS15 91 G8
Richmond Gdns
PDSY/CALV LS28 107 J7 3
RPDN/SBR HX6 167 H3 5
Richmond Garth OSS WF5 197 H2 11
Richmond Green St OSM LS9 9 M2
Richmond Gv CLECK BD19 150 D4
Richmond Hill Ap OSM LS9 9 M2
Richmond Hill Cl OSM LS9 9 M2
Richmond Lea MIRF WF14 172 C8 3
Richmond Ms SHPY BD18 82 B6 21
Richmond Mt HDGY LS6 109 G3
Richmond Park Av LVSG WF15 172 C3
Richmond Pl SHPY BD18 82 B6 22
Richmond Rd GTHN BD7 4 B6
HDGY LS6 109 G2
HECK WF16 151 G8
HEM/SK/SE WF9 225 K7
HFAX HX1 10 F4
PDSY/CALV LS28 106 E4
SHPY BD18 82 B6 23
WKFDE WF1 176 D6
Richmond St BSLY S70 260 F5 9
CLECK BD19 149 M7
HFAX HX1 10 F4
KGHY BD21 2 E3
OSM LS9 9 L2
TOD OL14 163 L1 11
Richmond Ter OT LS21 41 H7 1
PDSY/CALV LS28 107 J7
Richmond Wy GFTH/SHER LS25 135 H1
Rickard St WOR/ARM LS12 8 A3
Ridding Ga OT LS21 41 G5
Riddings Cl HEM/SK/SE WF9 245 M1
HUDN HD2 192 F3
Riddings Ri HUDN HD2 192 F3
Riddings Rd HUDN HD2 193 G3
Riddlesden St AIRE BD20 58 B5 4
Ridehalgh La BRFD/BLYE BB10 96 B3
Rider Rd HDGY LS6 6 E1
Rider St OSM LS9 7 L8
Ridge Av HOR/CROF WF4 196 C7
Ridge Bank TOD OL14 163 K1 11
Ridge Cl GSLY LS20 61 L6
HUDS HD4 214 C3
KBTN HD8 239 J5
Ridge Crs HOR/CROF WF4 196 C8
Ridgedale Mt PONT WF8 180 E2
Ridgefield St CAS WF10 157 M7 2
Ridge Gv CHAL LS7 109 J2
Ridge Hl BRIG HD6 170 A5
Ridge La AIRE BD20 17 L7
Ridge Lea BRIG HD6 170 B5
Ridge Mt HDGY LS6 6 C1
Ridgemount Rd AIRE BD20 58 A4
Ridge Rd GFTH/SHER LS25 135 M6
HDGY LS6 6 F1
HOR/CROF WF4 196 C7
TOD OL14 163 K1
Ridgestone Av
HEM/SK/SE WF9 224 A7
Ridge St HUDS HD4 214 C3
Ridge Ter HDGY LS6 109 G1
The Ridge WBY LS22 47 K3
Ridge Vw BRAM LS13 107 L6
Ridge View Dr HUDN HD2 191 M4
Ridge View Gdns IDLE BD10 83 L7
Ridge View Rd BRIG HD6 170 C5 11
Ridgewalk Wy BSLY S70 261 H8
Ridgeway CUL/QBY BD13 125 H6
GSLY LS20 61 K6
HUDE HD5 193 G7
RHAY LS8 88 B8
Ridgeway SHPY BD18 83 C8
SKP/WHF BD23 16 A1
Ridgeway Cl HUDE HD5 193 G7
RHAY LS8 88 B8 1
Ridgeway Crs BSLYN/ROY S71 243 L5
Ridgeway Dr BTLY WF17 151 J5
Ridgeway Gdns BRIG HD6 170 A1
Ridgeway Mt HWTH BD22 2 A9
Ridgeway Sq KNOT WF11 182 B3 2
The Ridgeways
HOLM/MEL HD7 212 F6
The Ridgeway KNOT WF11 182 B3
Ridgewood Cl BAIL BD17 83 G3
Ridgill Av AWLS/ASK DN6 249 J5
Ridgway Av WMB/DAR S73 263 J8
Riding Head La LUD/ILL HX2 145 G5
Riding Hl HIPP HX3 126 A8
Riding La LUD/ILL HX2 145 L3
Ridings Av BSLYN/ROY S71 261 K1
Ridings Cl EARD/LOFT WF3 154 D8
Ridings Ct EARD/LOFT WF3 154 D8 2
Ridings Flds HOLM/MEL HD7 236 E3
Ridings Gdns EARD/LOFT WF3 154 D8 3
Ridings La EARD/LOFT WF3 154 D8
HOLM/MEL HD7 212 E2
HOLM/MEL HD7 236 E7 2
Ridings Ms EARD/LOFT WF3 154 D8
Ridings Rd EARL WF12 173 M6 12
The Ridings AIRE BD20 57 K3 3
BSLYN/ROY S71 261 L1 1
Riding St BTLY WF17 151 G8
Ridings Wy EARD/LOFT WF3 154 D8
WBSY BD6 126 A5
Ridingwood Ri KBTN HD8 240 A4 5
Ridleys Fold ILK LS29 19 H6 5
Rievaulx Av GIR BD8 4 B3
Rievaulx Cl BSPA/BRAM LS23 48 E7 2
Riffa La OT LS21 42 E3
Rifle Flds HUD HD1 14 D7
Rigg La FEA/AMT WF7 202 E6
PONT WF8 202 E7
Rightox Rd HOLM/MEL HD7 236 E3 1
Rigton Ap OSM LS9 7 M8
Rigton Bank AL/HA/HU LS17 67 M2
Rigton Cl OSM LS9 110 B6 13
Rigton Gn AL/HA/HU LS17 68 A2
OSM LS9 7 M8
Rigton Hl AL/HA/HU LS17 25 M7
Rigton Lawn OSM LS9 7 M8
Rigton Ms OSM LS9 7 M8
Rigton St WBOW BD5 126 F3 14
Riley La KBTN HD8 238 A1
LUD/ILL HX2 124 B6
Riley Pk KBTN HD8 216 B8
Riley St HUDS HD4 214 D2
Rillbank La BVRD LS3 109 G5
Rillbank St BVRD LS3 6 A6
Rillington Md IDLE BD10 83 M8
Rillside KBTN HD8 238 B5
Rills Md OT LS21 41 J7
Rilston St GTHN BD7 104 D8 6
Rimswell Holt IDLE BD10 84 A8
Ringby La HIPP HX3 146 D2
Ring Lows La WHIT OL12 206 B2
Ring Road Adel BHP/TINH LS16 86 F4
Ring Road Beeston
BEE/HOL LS11 131 G6
WOR/ARM LS12 130 E3
Ring Road Beeston Pk
BEE/HOL LS11 131 H8
Ring Road Bramley BRAM LS13 107 M6
Ring Road Cross Gates
MSTN/BAR LS15 111 L3
Ring Road Farnley
WOR/ARM LS12 107 M7
Ring Road Farsley
PDSY/CALV LS28 106 E3
Ring Road Halton
MSTN/BAR LS15 111 L5
Ring Road (Horsforth)
HORS LS18 86 A6
Ring Road Meanwood
BHP/TINH LS16 87 G4
Ring Road Middleton MID LS10 153 M1
Ring Road (Moortown)
AL/HA/HU LS17 87 J4
RHAY LS8 88 B3
Ring Road (Seacroft)
SCFT LS14 89 J6
Ring Road (Shadwell)
AL/HA/HU LS17 88 E4
Ring Road Weetwood
BHP/TINH LS16 86 E5
Ring Road West Pk
BHP/TINH LS16 86 C5
Ringstone Gv CUD/GR S72 245 J3
Ringway GFTH/SHER LS25 112 E8
Ringwood Av SCFT LS14 89 H6
Ringwood Ct WKFDE WF1 176 F1 9
Ringwood Crs SCFT LS14 89 J5
Ringwood Dr SCFT LS14 89 J6
Ringwood Edge GTL/HWG HX4 168 E8
Ringwood Gdns SCFT LS14 89 J6
Ringwood Mt SCFT LS14 89 J6 4
Ringwood Rd WBOW BD5 126 D3
Ringwood Wy HEM/SK/SE WF9 224 B7
Rink St BTLY WF17 173 M3
Ripley Cl NORM WF6 178 F4
Ripley Ct NORM WF6 178 D6
Ripley Dr NORM WF6 178 F3
Ripley Gv DOD/DAR S75 260 D2
Ripley La GSLY LS20 62 A4
Ripley Rd BOW BD4 127 H2
LVSG WF15 172 B2
Ripley St AIRE BD20 58 B5 5
BOW BD4 127 H2
HIPP HX3 148 C7
WBOW BD5 127 G2
WIL/AL BD15 103 J4 3
Ripon Av HUDN HD2 192 C4
Ripon Rd EARL WF12 174 B6
Ripon St HFAX HX1 146 A8
Ripon Ter HIPP HX3 10 F1
Ripponden New Bank
RPDN/SBR HX6 189 G2
Ripponden Old Bank
RPDN/SBR HX6 189 G2
Ripponden Old La
RPDN/SBR HX6 188 C3
Ripponden Rd UPML OL3 230 F4
Risedale Av BTLY WF17 151 K4
Risedale Cl BTLY WF17 151 K4 5
Rise La TOD OL14 163 K1
The Rise HIPP HX3 147 J4
KNOT WF11 159 L6 2
KSTL LS5 108 C1
PONT WF8 181 G7
Rishworth Av KBTN HD8 217 M8
Rishworth Cl
WKFDW/WTN WF2 176 A4 4
Rishworth Hall Cl
RPDN/SBR HX6 188 D5
Rishworthian Ct HIPP HX3 168 C5 1
Rishworth Mill La
RPDN/SBR HX6 188 F6
Rishworth New Rd
RPDN/SBR HX6 188 D5
Rishworth Ri ROY/SHW OL2 229 H5
Rishworth Rd EARL WF12 173 M6
GTL/HWG HX4 189 J3
Rishworth St EARL WF12 173 M6 13
HWTH BD22 2 B7
WKFDE WF1 12 E1
Rivadale Vw ILK LS29 38 D2
Rivelin Rd CAS WF10 157 L8
Riverdale GLE DN14 161 J7
WBY LS22 48 B2
Riverdale Av EARD/LOFT WF3 177 H4
Riverdale Cl EARD/LOFT WF3 177 H4 1
Riverdale Crs EARD/LOFT WF3 177 H4 2
Riverdale Dr EARD/LOFT WF3 177 H4 3
Riverdale Gdns OT LS21 41 J6
Riverdale Rd EARD/LOFT WF3 177 H4
OT LS21 41 J6
River Holme Vw
HOLM/MEL HD7 236 E4
Rivermead MILN OL16 229 K3
WKFDW/WTN WF2 13 G9
River Pk HOLM/MEL HD7 236 B1
River Pl MILN OL16 207 H8 2
Riverside KBTN HD8 240 A4
KGHY BD21 3 L4
Riverside Av OT LS21 41 K4
Riverside Cl OT LS21 41 K5
WMB/DAR S73 263 L8 1
Riverside Crs OT LS21 41 K5
Riverside Dr CLECK BD19 149 M5
MILN OL16 206 D4
OT LS21 41 K4
Riverside Est BAIL BD17 82 C6
Riverside Pk OT LS21 41 K5
Riverside Vls WKFDW/WTN WF2 12 F9
WKFDW/WTN WF2 198 F4 1
Riverside Wk ILK LS29 38 B1
River St BRIG HD6 170 E5
COL BB8 74 E3
HWTH BD22 78 F7 12
KGHY BD21 3 L1
MILN OL16 206 B7 19
TOD OL14 163 L1
River Vw BSPA/BRAM LS23 49 H7
MIRF WF14 171 M8
River Wk BGLY BD16 81 H3
Riverwood Dr HIPP HX3 168 D4
Riviera Gdns CHAL LS7 87 L8
Rivington Dr ROY/SHW OL2 229 M7
Rivington St WHIT OL12 206 B5 20
Rivock Av AIRE BD20 35 M8
AIRE BD20 57 H3
Rivock Gv AIRE BD20 57 H3 1
Riverside Dr MILN OL16 206 E4
Roach Grange Av
GFTH/SHER LS25 135 J3
Roach Pl MILN OL16 206 C6
Roach V MILN OL16 206 E4 3
Roads Ford Av MILN OL16 207 H7
Roaine Dr HOLM/MEL HD7 254 D3
Roans Brae IDLE BD10 84 A8
Robb Av BEE/HOL LS11 131 J5
Robbins Ter FEA/AMT WF7 179 M8
Robb St BEE/HOL LS11 131 J5
Roberson Ter CLECK BD19 150 C6
Robert Av BSLYN/ROY S71 261 M4
Robert La HOLM/MEL HD7 236 E7
Roberts Av OSM LS9 110 D4
Roberts Ct OSM LS9 110 D4
Robertsgate EARD/LOFT WF3 154 D5
Robertshaw Rd HBR HX7 143 H3 5
Robertson Av BRIG HD6 170 C6 2
Roberts Pl BFD BD1 4 D5
OSM LS9 110 D5
Robert's St CLECK BD19 149 L7
CUD/GR S72 244 D7 2
HWTH BD22 56 E8
PDSY/CALV LS28 106 F5 4
RTHW LS26 133 L8 10
Robert St BFDE BD3 5 J7
COL BB8 74 A1 3
HIPP HX3 146 C4 12
HWTH BD22 79 H6 5
MILN OL16 206 C6
Robert St North HIPP HX3 146 E4 4
Roberts Wy WKFDW/WTN WF2 199 H5
Roberttown La LVSG WF15 172 B4
Robin Cha PDSY/CALV LS28 107 H7
Robin Cl ECHL BD2 105 L2
PONT WF8 180 F3
Robin Dr AIRE BD20 35 K8
ECHL BD2 105 L2
Robin Hl BTLY WF17 151 J5
Robin Hood Av
BSLYN/ROY S71 243 M2 1
Robin Hood Crs
WKFDW/WTN WF2 197 M2
Robin Hood Gv HUDN HD2 192 E2
Robin Hood Hl HUDS HD4 214 B7
Robin Hood Rd HUDN HD2 192 E2
Robin Hood St CAS WF10 158 A7 2
Robin Hood Wy BRIG HD6 171 G4
Robin La BSLYN/ROY S71 243 M2
DEWS WF13 173 H3
DEWS WF13 173 K4 4
HEM/SK/SE WF9 245 J1
PDSY/CALV LS28 107 G7
Robin Rocks HOLM/MEL HD7 236 E4 2
Robin Royd Av MIRF WF14 172 C6
Robin Royd Cft MIRF WF14 172 C6 4
Robin Royd Dr MIRF WF14 172 C6
Robin Royd Garth MIRF WF14 172 C6 5
Robin Royd Gv MIRF WF14 172 C6 6
Robin Royd La MIRF WF14 172 C7
Robin's Gv RTHW LS26 155 H1
Robinson Ct GTHN BD7 104 B8 6
Robinson La GFTH/SHER LS25 135 K4
Robinson St CAS WF10 157 K3
HUD HD1 15 H9
MILN OL16 206 C7
PONT WF8 181 G5 2
The Robins ILK LS29 40 A6
Robin St HUD HD1 213 M1
WBOW BD5 126 E2 1
Robin Wk SHPY BD18 82 F8
Rob Royd DOD/DAR S75 260 B8 6
Rob Royd La BSLY S70 260 F8
Robson Cl PONT WF8 180 F8
Robsons Dr HUDE HD5 15 M6
Robsons Rd WKFDE WF1 12 D3 1
Rochdale Rd GTL/HWG HX4 168 A7
HUDW HD3 212 A1
LUD/ILL HX2 167 M1
MILN OL16 206 F7
MILN OL16 229 G5
ROY/SHW OL2 228 E8
ROY/SHW OL2 229 H6
RPDN/SBR HX6 167 H4
RPDN/SBR HX6 187 H5
TOD OL14 163 J3
TOD OL14 185 L2
UPML OL3 230 D3
Roche Cl BSLYN/ROY S71 261 K3 3
Rocheford Cl MID LS10 132 B3
Rocheford Gdns MID LS10 132 B3
Rocheford Gv MID LS10 132 B3
Rochester Ct HOR/CROF WF4 197 L3 1
Rochester Dr HOR/CROF WF4 197 L3
Rochester Gdns BRAM LS13 107 H2 3
Rochester Rd BSLYN/ROY S71 261 K2
BTLY WF17 151 G3
Rochester St BFDE BD3 105 L7
SHPY BD18 82 E8
Rochester Ter HDGY LS6 108 F2
Rochester Wynd
AL/HA/HU LS17 88 C2 4
Roch St MILN OL16 206 D5
Rockcliffe Av BAIL BD17 82 E5
Rock Edge LVSG WF15 172 C1
Rockery Cft HORS LS18 85 L6 6
Rockery Rd HORS LS18 85 L4
Rockfield Ter YEA LS19 62 E7
Rock Fold HOLM/MEL HD7 212 F2
Rock Hl CAS WF10 158 C8
Rockhill Cl BTLY WF17 151 H5
Rockhill La BOW BD4 127 J7
Rock House Dr DEWS WF13 173 L4
Rockingham Cl
MSTN/BAR LS15 112 B3 6
ROY/SHW OL2 229 G6 3
Rockingham Ct TAD LS24 93 M2
Rockingham La
HEM/SK/SE WF9 225 G1
Rockingham Rd
MSTN/BAR LS15 112 B3
Rockingham St BSLYN/ROY S71 261 G2
CUD/GR S72 245 J7 2
HEM/SK/SE WF9 223 K3 2
Rockingham Wy
MSTN/BAR LS15 112 B3 7
Rockland Crs GTHN BD7 126 A1
Rocklands Av BAIL BD17 82 E2 8
Rocklands Pl BAIL BD17 82 E2 9
Rock La BRAM LS13 107 K2
CUL/QBY BD13 102 E6
HOLM/MEL HD7 212 C4
Rockley Cl HUDE HD5 215 G2
Rockley Dr WKFDW/WTN WF2 198 D8
Rockley Grange Gdns
GFTH/SHER LS25 134 F1 1
Rockley Mdw BSLY S70 260 E7
Rockley St EARL WF12 173 M6 14
Rockmill Rd HOLM/MEL HD7 236 E4
Rock Side Rd STKB/PEN S36 270 C3
Rocks La LUD/ILL HX2 123 M6
Rocks Rd HIPP HX3 168 C3
Rock St BRIG HD6 170 C3 4
BSLY S70 260 F4 8
HUDW HD3 191 G7 2
Rock Ter CUL/QBY BD13 102 F8 22
HUDW HD3 191 J4
MOR LS27 152 D1
MSTN/BAR LS15 111 H6 3
Rock Vw GTL/HWG HX4 190 E2
HOLM/MEL HD7 233 H3
Rockville Ter HFAX HX1 168 C1 12
Rockwell La IDLE BD10 83 L8
Rockwood Cl DOD/DAR S75 242 B6 4
HUDN HD2 171 G8
SKP/WHF BD23 16 A2 1
Rockwood Crs HOR/CROF WF4 197 M8
PDSY/CALV LS28 106 C3
Rockwood Dr SKP/WHF BD23 16 A1
Rockwood Gv PDSY/CALV LS28 106 D3
Rockwood Ri KBTN HD8 239 J7
Rockwood Rd PDSY/CALV LS28 106 C4
Roderick St WOR/ARM LS12 108 D7
Rodger La WKFDW/WTN WF2 176 B4
Rodin Av GIR BD8 103 M7 8
Rodley La BRAM LS13 107 G1
KBTN HD8 217 M7
PDSY/CALV LS28 84 E8
Rodney Yd WKFDE WF1 12 F3
Rods Mills La MOR LS27 152 D3
Roebuck La OT LS21 41 H2
Roebuck St BTLY WF17 151 H5
Roeburn Cl DOD/DAR S75 242 C4 2
Roehampton Ri
BSLYN/ROY S71 262 B6
Roe La KNOT WF11 161 H2
Roger Ct ECHL BD2 5 M1
Roger Dr WKFDW/WTN WF2 198 F5
Roger Fold GFTH/SHER LS25 135 K5 7
Roger Ga HBR HX7 143 L5
Roger La HUDS HD4 214 D3
Roger Rd BSLYN/ROY S71 262 A4
Rogers Ct EARD/LOFT WF3 155 H8
Rogerson Sq BRIG HD6 170 C3 5
Rogers Pl PDSY/CALV LS28 107 H6
Roils Head Rd LUD/ILL HX2 145 K7
Rokeby Gdns HDGY LS6 108 E1
IDLE BD10 84 A8
Roker La PDSY/CALV LS28 129 H1
Rolleston Rd AWLS/ASK DN6 249 K6
Rolling Br TAD LS24 72 D1
Roman Av HUDW HD3 190 F5
RHAY LS8 88 C3
Romanby Shaw IDLE BD10 83 M8
Roman Cl HUDW HD3 190 F5
TAD LS24 71 M2 3
Roman Crs RHAY LS8 88 D4 7
Roman Dr HUDW HD3 190 F5
RHAY LS8 88 D4 8
Roman Gdns RHAY LS8 88 C4
Roman Gv RHAY LS8 88 D4 9
Roman Mt RHAY LS8 88 D4 10
Roman Pl RHAY LS8 88 D4 11
Roman Rdg AWLS/ASK DN6 249 G7
Roman Ri PONT WF8 202 E1 1
Roman Rd BTLY WF17 151 H6
DOD/DAR S75 241 M7
Roman Ter RHAY LS8 88 C4
Roman Vw RHAY LS8 88 D4
Rombalds Av WOR/ARM LS12 108 E6
Rombalds Crs AIRE BD20 36 B6
WOR/ARM LS12 108 E5
Rombalds Dr BGLY BD16 81 K3
SKP/WHF BD23 16 C4
Rombalds Gv WOR/ARM LS12 108 E6
Rombalds La ILK LS29 39 G3
Rombalds Pl WOR/ARM LS12 108 E6
Rombalds St WOR/ARM LS12 108 E5
Rombalds Ter WOR/ARM LS12 108 E6
Rombald's Vw ILK LS29 38 F1
OT LS21 40 F4
WOR/ARM LS12 108 E5
Romford Av MOR LS27 152 C3
Romille St SKP/WHF BD23 16 B3
Romney Av ROCH OL11 228 A4
Romney Mt PDSY/CALV LS28 129 J1
Romsey Cl HUDW HD3 191 H5
Romsey Gdns BOW BD4 127 M3 11
Romsey Ms BOW BD4 127 M3 12
Ronald Dr GTHN BD7 104 C7
Roods La HOLM/MEL HD7 253 J3
Rookdale Cl DOD/DAR S75 260 D2
Rookery La HIPP HX3 168 F3
Rookes Av WBSY BD6 126 E6
Rookes La HIPP HX3 148 C5
Rookhill Dr PONT WF8 181 G7
Rookhill Mt PONT WF8 181 H7
Rookhill Rd PONT WF8 181 H8
Rook La BOW BD4 127 K4
Rooks Av CLECK BD19 149 L6
Rooks Cl LM/WK BD12 148 F5
Rook's Nest Rd WKFDE WF1 176 E2
Rook St BGLY BD16 81 H3 13
HUD HD1 14 E5
Rookwith Pde IDLE BD10 83 M8
Rookwood Av GFTH/SHER LS25 135 J6
OSM LS9 110 E6
Rookwood Crs OSM LS9 110 E6
Rookwood Gdns OSM LS9 110 E7
Rookwood Hl OSM LS9 110 E6
Rookwood Mt OSM LS9 110 E6
Rookwood Pde OSM LS9 110 F6 1
Rookwood Pl OSM LS9 110 E6 4
Rookwood Rd OSM LS9 110 E7

Rookwood Sq *OSM* LS9 .... 110 F6
Rookwood St *OSM* LS9 .... 110 E7
Rookwood Ter *OSM* LS9 .... 110 E6
Rookwood V *OSM* LS9 .... 110 E6
Rookwood Vw *OSM* LS9 .... 110 E6
Rooley Av *WBSY* BD6 .... 126 F6
Rooley Banks *RPDN/SBR* HX6 .. 167 G3
Rooley Cl *WBOW* BD5 .... 127 G5
Rooley Crs *WBSY* BD6 .... 127 G5
Rooley Hts *RPDN/SBR* HX6 .. 166 F3
Rooley La *BOW* BD4 .... 127 K4
  RPDN/SBR HX6 .... 166 F4
  WBOW BD5 .... 126 F5
  WBOW BD5 .... 127 J5
Roomfield St *TOD* OL14 .... 163 K1
Rooms Fold *MOR* LS27 .... 130 C8
Rooms La *MOR* LS27 .... 130 B6
Ropefield Wy *WHIT* OL12 .... 206 A3
Roper Av *RHAY* LS8 .... 88 B6
Ropergate *PONT* WF8 .... 180 E6
Ropergate Service Rd
  PONT WF8 .... 180 E6
Roper Gn *LUD/ILL* HX2 .... 145 M2
Roper Gv *RHAY* LS8 .... 88 B6
Roper La *CUL/QBY* BD13 .... 124 D4
  LUD/ILL HX2 .... 124 B6
Rope St *WHIT* OL12 .... 206 C2
Rope Wk *KNOT* WF11 .... 182 C2
  LUD/ILL HX2 .... 123 H7
  SKP/WHF BD23 .... 16 C2
Roscoe St *CHAL* LS7 .... 7 J4
Roseate Gn *MOR* LS27 .... 152 E3
Rose Av *GFTH/SHER* LS25 .... 116 A8
  HEM/SK/SE WF9 .... 225 H7
  HORS LS18 .... 85 J6
  HUDS HD4 .... 213 H3
  HUDW HD3 .... 191 L8
  LIT OL15 .... 207 H3
  WMB/DAR S73 .... 263 H7
Rose Bank *ILK* LS29 .... 40 A6
Rosebank Crs *HDGY* LS6 .... 6 A5
Rosebank Gdns *BVRD* LS3 .... 6 A6
Rose Bank Pl *GIR* BD8 .... 104 A7
Rosebank Rd *BVRD* LS3 .... 6 A6
Rosebank Rw *BVRD* LS3 .... 6 A6
Rose Bank St *BTLY* WF17 .... 151 K8
Roseberry St *HWTH* BD22 .... 78 F4
  TOD OL14 .... 140 F5
Rosebery Av *HIPP* HX3 .... 168 F2
  SHPY BD18 .... 82 E3
Rosebery Mt *SHPY* BD18 .... 82 E3
Rosebery Rd *GIR* BD8 .... 104 E4
Rosebery St *ELL* HX5 .... 169 H8
  HUDN HD2 .... 14 D1
  PDSY/CALV LS28 .... 106 E6
Rosebery Ter *BSLY* S70 .... 261 H6
  HFAX HX1 .... 10 C3
  PDSY/CALV LS28 .... 107 H4
Rosebud Wk *RHAY* LS8 .... 7 L4
Rosechapel Cl *WBSY* BD6 .... 126 B8
Rosecliffe Mt *BRAM* LS13 .... 107 K5
Rosecliffe Ter *BRAM* LS13 .... 107 K4
Rose Cl *HEM/SK/SE* WF9 .... 225 J7
Rose Ct *GFTH/SHER* LS25 .... 113 J7
Rose Crs *GFTH/SHER* LS25 .... 116 A8
Rose Cft *AL/HA/HU* LS17 .... 46 E8
Rosedale *PBR* HG3 .... 26 E2
  RTHW LS26 .... 133 H8
Rosedale Av *HUDE* HD5 .... 15 M8
  LVSG WF15 .... 171 M4
  WIL/AL BD15 .... 103 H4
  WKFDW/WTN WF2 .... 199 C6
Rosedale Bank *MID* LS10 .... 131 M5
Rosedale Cl *BAIL* BD17 .... 82 C4
  HEM/SK/SE WF9 .... 225 K7
  NORM WF6 .... 178 F5
  PBR HG3 .... 26 E2
Rosedale Gdns *BSLY* S70 .... 260 E5
  MID LS10 .... 131 M5
Rosedale Gn *MID* LS10 .... 131 M5
Rosedale Ri *BSPA/BRAM* LS23 .... 48 E3
Rosedale Wk *MID* LS10 .... 131 M5
Rose Farm Ap *NORM* WF6 .... 178 B2
Rose Farm Cl *NORM* WF6 .... 178 B1
Rose Farm Fold *NORM* WF6 .... 178 B1
Rose Farm Ri *NORM* WF6 .... 178 B2
Rosefield Crs *MILN* OL16 .... 206 F2
Rose Garth *HOR/CROF* WF4 .... 200 B5
  ILK LS29 .... 39 L7
Rosegarth Av *HOLM/MEL* HD7 .... 236 E7
Rose Gv *HBR* HX7 .... 144 A6
  HEM/SK/SE WF9 .... 225 J7
  RTHW LS26 .... 132 F5
Rose Grove La *RPDN/SBR* HX6 .... 167 H1
Rose Heath *LUD/ILL* HX2 .... 123 M7
Rose Hill Cl *STKB/PEN* S36 .... 270 F4
Rosehill Ct *BSLY* S70 .... 261 C4
Rosehill Crs *LM/WK* BD12 .... 148 E2
Rose Hill Dr *DOD/DAR* S75 .... 260 B7
Rose La *FEA/AMT* WF7 .... 223 M2
  TAD LS24 .... 94 D8
Rose Lea Cl *GFTH/SHER* LS25 .... 138 D8
Roselee Cl *HIPP* HX3 .... 169 G3
Rosemary Av *WOR/ARM* LS12 .... 108 F7
Rosemary Ct *TAD* LS24 .... 71 M2
Rosemary Dr *LIT* OL15 .... 185 H8
Rosemary La *BRIG* HD6 .... 170 C6
  HIPP HX3 .... 169 G3
Rosemary Rw *TAD* LS24 .... 71 M2
Rose Mdw *HWTH* BD22 .... 79 G1
Rosemont Av *BRAM* LS13 .... 107 L4
  PDSY/CALV LS28 .... 107 H6
Rosemont Dr *PDSY/CALV* LS28 .... 107 H6
Rosemont Gv *BRAM* LS13 .... 107 L4
Rosemont La *BAIL* BD17 .... 82 F4
Rosemont Pl *BRAM* LS13 .... 107 L4
Rosemont St *BRAM* LS13 .... 107 L4
  PDSY/CALV LS28 .... 107 H6
Rosemont Ter *BRAM* LS13 .... 107 L4
  PDSY/CALV LS28 .... 107 H6
Rosemont Vw *BRAM* LS13 .... 107 L4
Rosemont Wk *BRAM* LS13 .... 107 L4
Rose Mt *ECHL* BD2 .... 105 J5
  HUDN HD2 .... 191 M5
Rosemount Av *ELL* HX5 .... 169 J8

Rose Mount Pl *WOR/ARM* LS12 .... 108 F8
Roseneath Pl *WOR/ARM* LS12 .... 108 F8
Roseneath St *WOR/ARM* LS12 .... 108 F8
Roseneath Ter *WOR/ARM* LS12 .... 108 F8
Rose Pl *LUD/ILL* HX2 .... 167 G1
Rose St *GIR* BD8 .... 104 D5
  HFAX HX1 .... 10 B6
  HORS LS18 .... 85 J6
  KGHY BD21 .... 58 B7
  TOD OL14 .... 163 K1
Rose Tree Av *CUD/GR* S72 .... 244 D7
Rose Tree Ct *CUD/GR* S72 .... 244 D7
Roseville Rd *RHAY* LS8 .... 7 L5
Roseville St *COL* BB8 .... 7 M4
Roseville Wy *RHAY* LS8 .... 7 L5
Rosewood Av *GFTH/SHER* LS25 .... 135 H3
  KGHY BD21 .... 58 B5
Rosewood Ct *RTHW* LS26 .... 133 H7
Rosewood Gv *BOW* BD4 .... 127 M1
Rosgill Dr *SCFT* LS14 .... 111 H1
Rosgill Wk *SCFT* LS14 .... 111 H1
Rosley Mt *WBSY* BD6 .... 126 B8
Rosley St *COL* BB8 .... 74 D1
Roslyn Av *HUDS* HD4 .... 213 L7
Roslyn Pl *GTHN* BD7 .... 104 D9
Rossall Gv *RHAY* LS8 .... 110 B2
Rossall Rd *RHAY* LS8 .... 110 B2
  WHIT OL12 .... 206 C4
Rossefield Ap *BRAM* LS13 .... 107 M5
Rossefield Av *BRAM* LS13 .... 107 M4
  HUDN HD2 .... 14 A1
Rossefield Cha *BRAM* LS13 .... 107 M4
Rossefield Cl *BRAM* LS13 .... 107 M4
Rossefield Dr *BRAM* LS13 .... 107 M4
Rossefield Gdns *BRAM* LS13 .... 107 M4
Rossefield Gn *BRAM* LS13 .... 107 M4
Rossefield Lawn *BRAM* LS13 .... 107 M4
Rossefield Pk *HTON* BD9 .... 104 D2
Rossefield Pl *BRAM* LS13 .... 107 M4
Rossefield Rd *HTON* BD9 .... 104 C2
Rossefield Ter *BRAM* LS13 .... 107 M4
Rossendale Cl *ROY/SHW* OL2 .... 229 M7
Rossendale La *SHPY* BD18 .... 82 C7
Rossendale Wy *BCUP* OL13 .... 162 C7
  WHIT OL12 .... 184 C3
Rosse St *GIR* BD8 .... 104 C7
  SHPY BD18 .... 82 D6
Rosett Green La *HARS* HG2 .... 26 D1
Ross Gv *BRAM* LS13 .... 107 K2
Rossington Gv *RHAY* LS8 .... 7 M1
Rossington Pl *RHAY* LS8 .... 7 M1
Rossington Rd *RHAY* LS8 .... 110 C1
Rossington St *LDSU* LS2 .... 6 F8
Rossiter Dr *KNOT* WF11 .... 181 M3
Rosslyn Av *FEA/AMT* WF7 .... 224 B1
Rosslyn Cl *FEA/AMT* WF7 .... 224 B1
Rosslyn Ct *EARL* WF12 .... 174 B7
  FEA/AMT WF7 .... 224 B1
Rosslyn Gv *FEA/AMT* WF7 .... 224 B1
  HWTH BD22 .... 78 E3
Rossmore Dr *WIL/AL* BD15 .... 103 L5
Rosy St *HWTH* BD22 .... 79 H6
Rotcher La *HOLM/MEL* HD7 .... 212 A6
Rotcher Rd *HOLM/MEL* HD7 .... 254 C2
Rothbury Gdns *BHP/TINH* LS16 .... 86 D3
Rotherham Rd *BSLYN/ROY* S71 .... 243 J8
Rothesay Ter *GTHN* BD7 .... 4 A9
  MILN OL16 .... 228 E2
Roth St *HWTH* BD22 .... 79 G6
Rothwell La *RTHW* LS26 .... 155 J1
Rothwell Mt *HFAX* HX1 .... 10 E9
Rothwell Rd *HFAX* HX1 .... 10 E9
  HFAX HX1 .... 10 E9
Rothwell St *HUDE* HD5 .... 193 G8
  WHIT OL12 .... 206 C5
Roughaw Cl *SKP/WHF* BD23 .... 16 B4
Roughaw Rd *SKP/WHF* BD23 .... 16 C4
Roughbirchworth La
  STKB/PEN S36 .... 271 J6
Rough Hall La *LUD/ILL* HX2 .... 145 C1
Rough Side La *TOD* OL14 .... 163 L2
Round Close Rd
  HOLM/MEL HD7 .... 254 D8
Roundell Av *BOW* BD4 .... 127 K6
Roundhay Crs *RHAY* LS8 .... 110 B1
Roundhay Gdns *RHAY* LS8 .... 110 B1
Roundhay Gv *RHAY* LS8 .... 110 B1
Roundhay Mt *RHAY* LS8 .... 110 B1
Roundhay Park La
  AL/HA/HU LS17 .... 88 D3
Roundhay Pl *RHAY* LS8 .... 110 B1
Roundhay Rd *CHAL* LS7 .... 7 K4
  RHAY LS8 .... 110 B3
Roundhay Vw *RHAY* LS8 .... 110 B1
Roundhead Fold *IDLE* BD10 .... 84 A6
Round Hl *DOD/DAR* S75 .... 242 C6
  LUD/ILL HX2 .... 124 B8
Roundhill Av *BGLY* BD16 .... 81 K7
Round Hill Cl *CUL/QBY* BD13 .... 125 K4
Roundhill Mt *BGLY* BD16 .... 81 K7
Roundhill Pl *BFD* BD1 .... 4 D5
Roundhill Rd *CAS* WF10 .... 157 M7
Roundhill St *WBOW* BD5 .... 126 F5
Round Ings Rd *HUDW* HD3 .... 190 B7
Round St *WBOW* BD5 .... 127 G3
  WKFDE WF1 .... 13 K7
Round Thorn Pl *GIR* BD8 .... 104 C6
Roundway *HOLM/MEL* HD7 .... 236 B2
The Roundway *MOR* LS27 .... 152 A2
Roundwell Rd *LVSG* WF15 .... 171 L1
Roundwood *SHPY* BD18 .... 82 A7
Roundwood Av *BAIL* BD17 .... 83 G1
Round Wood Av *HUDE* HD5 .... 193 H8
Roundwood Av *IDLE* BD10 .... 106 A1
Roundwood Crs
  WKFDW/WTN WF2 .... 197 L1
Roundwood Gln *IDLE* BD10 .... 84 A8
Roundwood Ri
  WKFDW/WTN WF2 .... 197 M2
Roundwood Rd *BAIL* BD17 .... 83 G2
  OSS WF5 .... 197 J2
Roundwood Vw *IDLE* BD10 .... 84 A8
Rouse Fold *BOW* BD4 .... 5 H9
Rouse Mill La *BTLY* WF17 .... 173 M2
Rouse St *LVSG* WF15 .... 172 C2
Rowan Av *BFDE* BD3 .... 106 A7
  HUDS HD4 .... 213 M8
  NORM WF6 .... 178 C7
Rowan Avenue Ms *HUDS* HD4 .. 213 M8

Rowanberry Cl *ECHL* BD2 .... 105 K2
Rowan Cl *BSLY* S70 .... 261 H7
  BTLY WF17 .... 151 J4
Rowan Ct *ECHL* BD2 .... 105 L5
  WKFDW/WTN WF2 .... 176 B6
  YEA LS19 .... 84 D1
Rowan Dr *BRIG* HD6 .... 170 E3
  DOD/DAR S75 .... 260 D3
Rowan Garth *AIRE* BD20 .... 34 F8
Rowan Pl *GFTH/SHER* LS25 .... 113 K8
The Rowans *BAIL* BD17 .... 82 B3
  BHP/TINH LS16 .... 64 D4
  BRAM LS13 .... 107 H3
Rowan St *AIRE* BD20 .... 57 J4
Rowantree Av *BAIL* BD17 .... 82 D2
Rowantree Dr *IDLE* BD10 .... 83 J3
Rowanwood Gdns *IDLE* BD10 .... 106 A1
Row Ga *KBTN* HD8 .... 237 M7
Rowgate *KBTN* HD8 .... 238 C8
Rowland Av *HEM/SK/SE* WF9 .... 225 J7
  HUDE HD5 .... 193 J3
Rowland La *HBR* HX7 .... 143 L3
Rowland Rd *BEE/HOL* LS11 .... 131 K3
  DOD/DAR S75 .... 260 E3
Rowlands Av *HEM/SK/SE* WF9 .... 225 J7
  HUDE HD5 .... 193 J3
Rowland St *BSLYN/ROY* S71 .... 243 M2
  MILN OL16 .... 206 D8
  SKP/WHF BD23 .... 16 C3
Rowland Ter *BEE/HOL* LS11 .... 131 L3
Row La *HOLM/MEL* HD7 .... 211 L6
  RPDN/SBR HX6 .... 166 F3
Rowlestone Ri *IDLE* BD10 .... 84 A8
Rowley Dr *ILK* LS29 .... 39 H5
  KBTN HD8 .... 215 M3
Rowley La *HEM/SK/SE* WF9 .... 247 J5
  KBTN HD8 .... 215 M4
Rowsley St *KGHY* BD21 .... 3 J4
Row St *HUDS* HD4 .... 214 A2
Rowton Thorpe *IDLE* BD10 .... 84 A8
Roxburgh Gv *WIL/AL* BD15 .... 103 K6
Roxby Cl *OSM* LS9 .... 7 M7
Roxby St *WBOW* BD5 .... 126 F3
Roxholme Gv *CHAL* LS7 .... 110 A1
Roxholme Pl *CHAL* LS7 .... 110 A1
Roxholme Rd *CHAL* LS7 .... 110 A1
Roxholme Ter *CHAL* LS7 .... 110 A1
Royal Cl *MID* LS10 .... 131 M4
Royal Ct *DOD/DAR* S75 .... 242 A8
  MID LS10 .... 131 M4
  PONT WF8 .... 202 D1
Royal Dr *MID* LS10 .... 131 M4
Royal Gdns *MID* LS10 .... 131 M4
Royal Park Av *HDGY* LS6 .... 6 A3
Royal Park Gv *HDGY* LS6 .... 6 A3
Royal Park Mt *HDGY* LS6 .... 6 A3
Royal Park Rd *HDGY* LS6 .... 6 A3
Royal Park Ter *HDGY* LS6 .... 109 G3
Royal Park Vw *HDGY* LS6 .... 6 A3
Royal Pl *MID* LS10 .... 131 M4
Royal St *BSLY* S70 .... 261 G5
  MILN OL16 .... 206 E4
Royal Ter *BSPA/BRAM* LS23 .... 49 G3
  HUDW HD3 .... 213 J1
Royd Av *BGLY* BD16 .... 81 K3
  CUD/GR S72 .... 244 D8
  DOD/DAR S75 .... 242 D5
  HECK WF16 .... 150 F8
  HUDW HD3 .... 191 J5
  HUDW HD3 .... 213 J1
  STKB/PEN S36 .... 269 M5
Royd Cl *AIRE* BD20 .... 34 F8
Royd Crs *HBR* HX7 .... 144 B5
  HFAX HX1 .... 10 A4
Royd Cft *HUDW* HD3 .... 191 K8
Royd Field La *STKB/PEN* S36 .... 270 F2
Roydfield St *HUDN* HD2 .... 192 D4
Royd Head Farm *OSS* WF5 .... 196 E1
Royd House Gv *KGHY* BD21 .... 3 J1
Royd House La *HOLM/MEL* HD7 .... 212 F5
Royd House Rd *KGHY* BD21 .... 3 M8
Royd House Wy *KGHY* BD21 .... 3 L8
Royd Ings Av *KGHY* BD21 .... 3 J1
Roydlands St *SHPY* HX3 .... 147 M7
Royd La *DOD/DAR* S75 .... 259 L3
  HIPP HX3 .... 146 C3
  HOLM/MEL HD7 .... 254 A1
  KGHY BD21 .... 57 K5
  LUD/ILL HX2 .... 124 A7
  RPDN/SBR HX6 .... 188 E1
  STKB/PEN S36 .... 269 M2
  TOD OL14 .... 141 K7
Royd Moor La *HEM/SK/SE* WF9 .... 224 B5
Royd Moor Rd *STKB/PEN* S36 .... 269 M1
Royd Mt *HIPP* HX3 .... 146 E4
  HOLM/MEL HD7 .... 254 C2
Roydon Gv *HTON* BD9 .... 104 C4
Royd Pl *HIPP* HX3 .... 146 E4
Royd Rd *HOLM/MEL* HD7 .... 235 G6
  TOD OL14 .... 141 J8
Royds Av *BIRK/DRI* BD11 .... 150 D1
  BRIG HD6 .... 148 D6
  CAS WF10 .... 158 E6
  HOLM/MEL HD7 .... 212 F4
  HOLM/MEL HD7 .... 236 C1
  HUDW HD3 .... 191 K8
  OSS WF5 .... 174 C6
Roydscliffe Dr *HTON* BD9 .... 104 B2
Roydscliffe Rd *HTON* BD9 .... 104 A3
Royds Cl *HOLM/MEL* HD7 .... 236 F8
Royds Crs *BRIG* HD6 .... 148 D7
Roydsdale Wy *BOW* BD4 .... 127 J8
Royds Dr *HOLM/MEL* HD7 .... 236 F8
Royds Farm Rd *BEE/HOL* LS11 .... 130 E4
Royds Gv *WKFDE* WF1 .... 176 E1
Royds Hall Av *WBSY* BD6 .... 126 E6
Royds Hall La *LM/WK* BD12 .... 148 C3
  WBSY BD6 .... 126 C8
Royds Hall Rd *WOR/ARM* LS12 .... 130 C2
Royds La *RTHW* LS26 .... 155 J2
  WOR/ARM LS12 .... 130 E2
Royds Pk *BKTN* HD8 .... 239 J8
Royds Park Crs *LM/WK* BD12 .... 148 F2
Royds Pl *MILN* OL16 .... 228 C1
Royds St *HOLM/MEL* HD7 .... 233 H5
  LIT OL15 .... 207 L1
  MILN OL16 .... 228 D1
  MILN OL16 .... 229 L1

  SKP/WHF BD23 .... 16 C3
  TOD OL14 .... 163 L1
  WBOW BD5 .... 4 D9
  WKFDE WF1 .... 12 F6
The Russets *WKFDW/WTN* WF2 .. 199 G8
Russett Gv *HUDS* HD4 .... 214 D3
Rustic Av *HIPP* HX3 .... 169 J2
Ruswarp Crs *IDLE* BD10 .... 83 M8
Ruth St *HUDS* HD4 .... 214 C4
Ruthven Vw *RHAY* LS8 .... 110 C3
Rutland Av *PONT* WF8 .... 202 F1
  WKFDW/WTN WF2 .... 198 C4
Rutland Cl *GFTH/SHER* LS25 .... 135 K4
  RTHW LS26 .... 133 M8
Rutland Dr *GFTH/SHER* LS25 .... 135 K4
  HOR/CROF WF4 .... 199 L3
Rutland Mt *BVRD* LS3 .... 6 B8
Rutland Rd *BTLY* WF17 .... 151 M8
  HOR/CROF WF4 .... 217 L3
  HUDW HD3 .... 213 H1
Rutland St *BOW* BD4 .... 127 J2
  COL BB8 .... 74 B1
  KGHY BD21 .... 2 F8
  LDS LS1 .... 6 C8
Rutland Ter *BVRD* LS3 .... 6 B8
Rutland Wy *DOD/DAR* S75 .... 260 E3
  ROY/SHW OL2 .... 229 L6
Ryan Gv *HWTH* BD22 .... 56 F6
Ryan Pl *RHAY* LS8 .... 110 C2
Ryan St *WBOW* BD5 .... 126 F3
Ryburn La *RPDN/SBR* HX6 .... 189 G1
Ryburn Pl *WKFDW/WTN* WF2 .... 12 D6
Ryburn Rd *HUDW* HD3 .... 191 K7
Ryburn St *RPDN/SBR* HX6 .... 167 K3
Ryburn Ter *HFAX* HX1 .... 10 B5
Ryburn Vw *RPDN/SBR* HX6 .... 188 E3
Rycroft Av *BGLY* BD16 .... 81 J8
  BRAM LS13 .... 107 J5
Rycroft Cl *BRAM* LS13 .... 107 K5
Rycroft Dr *BRAM* LS13 .... 107 K5
Rycroft Gdns *BRAM* LS13 .... 107 J5
Rycroft St *SHPY* BD18 .... 82 F3
Rycroft Towers *BRAM* LS13 .... 107 J5
Rydal Av *GFTH/SHER* LS25 .... 113 G8
  HTON BD9 .... 104 E2
  ROY/SHW OL2 .... 228 E6
Rydal Cl *STKB/PEN* S36 .... 270 F2
Rydal Crs *MOR* LS27 .... 152 F1
  WKFDW/WTN WF2 .... 176 A7
Rydal Dr *HUDE* HD5 .... 15 L6
  MOR LS27 .... 152 F1
  WKFDW/WTN WF2 .... 176 A7
Rydale Ct *OSS* WF5 .... 196 F2
Rydale Ms *OSS* WF5 .... 196 F2
Rydal Gv *LVSG* WF15 .... 172 C5
Rydall Pl *BEE/HOL* LS11 .... 8 B6
Rydall St *BEE/HOL* LS11 .... 8 B6
Rydall Ter *BEE/HOL* LS11 .... 8 B6
Rydal Pl *COL* BB8 .... 74 C1
Rydal Rd *AWLS/ASK* DN6 .... 249 L3
Rydal St *CAS* WF10 .... 158 F6
  HWTH BD22 .... 2 D6
Ryder Cl *PONT* WF8 .... 180 D6
Ryder Gdns *RHAY* LS8 .... 88 C7
Rydings Av *BRIG* HD6 .... 170 C3
Rydings Dr *BRIG* HD6 .... 170 B3
Rydings La *WHIT* OL12 .... 184 C8
Rydings Rd *WHIT* OL12 .... 206 D2
Ryebank *HOLM/MEL* HD7 .... 254 D6
Ryebread *CAS* WF10 .... 158 A5
Rye Close La *HOLM/MEL* HD7 .... 252 F2
Ryecroft *BSLYN/ROY* S71 .... 243 J8
Rye Cft *BSLYN/ROY* S71 .... 243 J8
  LUD/ILL HX2 .... 124 B8
Ryecroft Av *AWLS/ASK* DN6 .... 227 L1
  HOR/CROF WF4 .... 222 E4
Ryecroft Cl *WKFDE* WF1 .... 176 D1
Ryecroft Crs *LUD/ILL* HX2 .... 145 K5
Ryecroft Dr *HUDW* HD3 .... 191 K5
Ryecroft La *BRIG* HD6 .... 170 C6
  HOLM/MEL HD7 .... 254 D6
  LUD/ILL HX2 .... 145 M6
Ryecroft Rd *AIRE* BD20 .... 34 E8
  AWLS/ASK DN6 .... 227 L3
  BGLY BD16 .... 79 M4
Ryecroft St *OSS* WF5 .... 174 E8
Ryecroft Ter *LUD/ILL* HX2 .... 145 M5
Ryecroft Wy *AIRE* BD20 .... 34 E8
Ryedale *HUDE* HD5 .... 193 K4
Ryedale Av *KNOT* WF11 .... 182 A4
  WOR/ARM LS12 .... 130 D2
Ryedale Cl *NORM* WF6 .... 178 C1
  TAD LS24 .... 94 F2
Ryedale Ct *SCFT* LS14 .... 111 H1
Ryedale Holt *WOR/ARM* LS12 .... 130 D1
Ryedale Pk *ILK* LS29 .... 38 F2
Ryedale Pl *NORM* WF6 .... 178 C1
Ryedale Wy *EARD/LOFT* WF3 .... 153 C7
  WIL/AL BD15 .... 103 J4
Ryefield Av *CLAY* BD14 .... 125 K1
Rye Field La *HUDW* HD3 .... 189 H8
Rye Field La West *HUDW* HD3 .... 189 H8
Ryefields *HOLM/MEL* HD7 .... 254 F2
Ryefields Av *HUDW* HD3 .... 191 J7
Ryefields Rd *HOLM/MEL* HD7 .... 213 G2
Rye Garth *WBY* LS22 .... 29 H4
Ryeland St *MILN* OL16 .... 228 D2
Ryelands Gv *HTON* BD9 .... 103 M2
Ryeland St *AIRE* BD20 .... 34 F8
Rye La *LUD/ILL* HX2 .... 145 L5
Rye Pl *SCFT* LS14 .... 111 H5
Rye St *HWTH* BD22 .... 79 G2
Ryhill Pits La *HOR/CROF* WF4 .... 221 M5
Rylands Av *BGLY* BD16 .... 81 K3
Rylands Meadow *HWTH* BD22 .. 79 G1
Rylstone Gdns *BFDE* BD3 .... 5 K1
Rylstone Gv *WKFDE* WF1 .... 177 G6
Rylstone Rd *BAIL* BD17 .... 82 B4
Rylstone St *KGHY* BD21 .... 3 K2
Ryndieside *HUDW* HD5 .... 191 J6
Ryshworth Av *AIRE* BD20 .... 58 F7
Ryton Dl *IDLE* BD10 .... 84 A8

S

Sable Crest ECHL BD2 105 H2 5
Sackup La DOD/DAR S75 242 B5
Sackville Ap CHAL LS7 7 H3
Sackville Cl ROY/SHW OL2 229 J5
Sackville Rd AIRE BD20 36 A4
Sackville St BFD BD1 4 E6
BSLY S70 260 F4
CHAL LS7 7 H3
DEWS WF13 173 G8
DEWS WF13 195 G1
HBR HX7 143 J3 18
SKP/WHF BD23 16 C3
TOD OL14 163 L1
Saddlers Cft CAS WF10 158 D8 5
Saddlers La KNOT WF11 159 L5
Saddler St LM/WK BD12 148 E2
Saddlers Wy RYKW YO26 33 J3
Saddleworth Rd GTL/HWG HX4 169 G7
GTL/HWG HX4 189 K1
HUDW HD3 210 E3
Sadler Cl BHP/TINH LS16 86 E2
Sadler Copse BHP/TINH LS16 86 E2
Sadler Ga BSLY S70 261 G4 8
Sadler Wy BHP/TINH LS16 86 E2
Saffron Dr WIL/AL BD15 103 J5
Sagar La TOD OL14 140 F4
Sagar Pl HDGY LS6 108 F2
Sagar St CAS WF10 157 M6
Sage St WBOW BD5 126 E2
Sahara Ct GIR BD8 104 F4
St Abbs Cl WBSY BD6 126 E7
St Abbs Dr WBSY BD6 126 E7
St Abbs Fold WBSY BD6 126 E7
St Abbs Ga WBSY BD6 126 E7 1
St Abbs Wk WBSY BD6 126 E7
St Abbs Wy WBSY BD6 126 E7
St Aidan's Rd BAIL BD17 82 F4
RTHW LS26 135 G6
St Aiden's Wk OSS WF5 197 J2 3
St Alban Ap OSM LS9 110 E5 2
St Alban Cl OSM LS9 110 E5 3
St Alban Crs OSM LS9 110 E5
St Alban Gv OSM LS9 110 E5 4
St Alban Mt OSM LS9 110 E5
St Alban Rd OSM LS9 110 E5
St Alban's Av HIPP HX3 168 E3 1
HUDW HD3 191 J3 2
St Albans Cft HIPP HX3 168 F2 5
St Albans Pl LDSU LS2 7 H7
St Alban's Rd HIPP HX3 168 E3
St Alban's St MILN OL16 206 A8
St Alban Vw OSM LS9 110 E5
St Andrew's Av MOR LS27 152 A3
St Andrew's Cl BRAM LS13 107 G1
MOR LS27 152 A3 1
YEA LS19 62 E6 1
St Andrew's Crs LM/WK BD12 149 J2 5
St Andrews Cft AL/HA/HU LS17 87 K1
St Andrews Dr AL/HA/HU LS17 87 L2
BRIG HD6 170 C2
DOD/DAR S75 242 C5
FEA/AMT WF7 179 L5
HUDE HD5 193 L6 2
KNOT WF11 181 L1 5
St Andrew's Gv MOR LS27 152 B3 6
St Andrew's Pl BVRD LS3 6 B8
St Andrew's Rd CAS WF10 158 E5
HUD HD1 15 J7
YEA LS19 62 F7
St Andrew's St BVRD LS3 6 B8
St Andrew's Vls GTHN BD7 4 A6
St Andrews Wk AL/HA/HU LS17 87 L2
St Andrews Wy BSLYN/ROY S71 262 C7
St Anne's Cl EARL WF12 195 M2
St Anne's Dr BSLYN/ROY S71 243 M7
BULY LS4 108 E2
St Anne's Gn BULY LS4 108 E2
St Anne's Rd HDGY LS6 108 E1
HIPP HX3 168 E4
St Anne's St HOR/CROF WF4 222 D5
LDS LS1 6 F8
St Ann's Av BULY LS4 108 F4
St Ann's Cl BULY LS4 108 E2
St Ann's Gdns BULY LS4 108 E3
St Ann's La KSTL LS5 108 E2
St Ann's Mt BULY LS4 108 F3
St Ann's Ri BULY LS4 108 D3
St Ann's Rd MILN OL16 206 E3
St Ann's Sq BULY LS4 108 E3
OSM LS9 7 L9 1
RPDN/SBR HX6 167 L2
St Ann's Wy BULY LS4 108 E3
St Anthony's Dr BEE/HOL LS11 131 H4 1
St Anthony's Rd BEE/HOL LS11 131 G4
St Anuil GIR BD8 104 D5 12
St Augustine's Ter BFDE BD3 5 J2
St Austell Dr DOD/DAR S75 260 A2
St Barnabas Rd BEE/HOL LS11 8 F4
LVSG WF15 171 L1
St Barnabas's Dr LIT OL15 185 J8
St Bartholomew's Cl
WOR/ARM LS12 108 E7
St Bartholomews Ct
WKFDW/WTN WF2 197 L2
St Bernard's Av PONT WF8 180 D6 5
St Bevan's Rd HIPP HX3 168 E3
St Blaise Wy BFD BD1 4 F5
St Boltophs Cl KNOT WF11 182 C2 9
St Catherine's Crs BRAM LS13 107 M2
St Catherine's Dr BRAM LS13 107 M2
St Catherine's Gn BRAM LS13 107 M2
St Catherine's Hl BRAM LS13 107 M2
St Catherine St WKFDE WF1 13 K8
St Catherine's Wk RHAY LS8 88 C8 5
St Catherines Wy
DOD/DAR S75 260 D5 2
St Chad's Av BRIG HD6 170 A1 5
HDGY LS6 86 E8
St Chad's Cl MILN OL16 206 B7 20
St Chad's Dr HDGY LS6 86 E8
St Chad's Ri HDGY LS6 86 E8
St Chad's Rd GIR BD8 104 D5 13
HDGY LS6 86 F8
St Chad's Vw HDGY LS6 108 E1
St Christopher's Av
RTHW LS26 155 H1 5
St Christophers Cl
BSLYN/ROY S71 262 C7 1
St Christophers Dr ILK LS29 19 H6 5
St Clair Gn WKFDW/WTN WF2 175 M6
St Clair Rd OT LS21 41 K7
St Clair St OT LS21 41 K6
WKFDE WF1 13 G3
St Clare's Av ECHL BD2 105 M4
St Clements Av RTHW LS26 155 G1 3
St Clements Cl BSLYN/ROY S71 262 C7 2
RTHW LS26 154 F2 1
St Clements Ri RTHW LS26 154 F1
St Cuthbert's Ct FEA/AMT WF7 202 C5 1
St Cyprians Gdns OSM LS9 110 D4 15
St David's Dr BSLYN/ROY S71 262 B6
St Davids Rd OT LS21 41 G4
St Edmunds Cl CAS WF10 158 E6 1
St Edwards Av BSLY S70 260 F6
St Edwards Cl KNOT WF11 160 A7
St Elmo Gv OSM LS9 110 C6 16
St Eloi Av BAIL BD17 82 E2
St Enoch's Rd WBSY BD6 126 D5
St Francis Bvd
BSLYN/ROY S71 243 M7 4
Saint Francis Gdns HUDN HD2 192 C1
St Francis Pl BEE/HOL LS11 8 E3
St George's Av HUDW HD3 191 J3
RTHW LS26 132 E7
St Georges Ct HOR/CROF WF4 222 F4
St George's Crs HFAX HX1 10 D3
RTHW LS26 132 E7
St Georges Ms
WKFDW/WTN WF2 220 C1
St George's Rd BSLY S70 261 G5
HIPP HX3 10 D2
HOLM/MEL HD7 254 F2
LDS LS1 6 E7 1
WKFDW/WTN WF2 197 M3
St George's Sq HBR HX7 143 J3 19
HUD HD1 14 F6
St George's St HBR HX7 143 J3 20
HUD HD1 14 F7
St Georges Wk
WKFDW/WTN WF2 198 D8
St Giles Av PONT WF8 180 D6
St Giles Cl BRIG HD6 170 A1
St Giles Garth BHP/TINH LS16 63 M3
St Giles Rd HIPP HX3 148 A8
St Helena Rd WBSY BD6 126 D5
St Helens Av BHP/TINH LS16 86 F3
BSLYN/ROY S71 261 K1
HEM/SK/SE WF9 223 L7
St Helens Cl BHP/TINH LS16 86 F3
St Helens Cft BHP/TINH LS16 86 E3
St Helen's Dr GFTH/SHER LS25 114 B6
St Helen's Fld HUDS HD4 215 J4 1
St Helens Gdns BHP/TINH LS16 86 E3
St Helen's Ga HUDE HD5 215 J4
St Helen's Gv BHP/TINH LS16 86 E3
WKFDW/WTN WF2 199 H6
St Helen's La BHP/TINH LS16 86 D3
St Helen's Pl CAS WF10 158 A7 3
St Helens St MID LS10 9 K6
St Helens Wy BHP/TINH LS16 86 E3
BSLYN/ROY S71 261 M1
ILK LS29 38 F2
St Helier Dr DOD/DAR S75 260 D4
St Helier Gv BAIL BD17 82 F2
St Hilda Av BSLY S70 260 E5
St Hilda's Av OSM LS9 110 B8 22
St Hilda's Crs OSM LS9 110 B8 23
St Hilda's Gv OSM LS9 110 B8 24
St Hilda's Mt OSM LS9 110 B8 25
St Hilda's Pl OSM LS9 110 B8 26
St Hilda's Rd OSM LS9 110 B8 27
St Hilda's Ter BFDE BD3 106 A6
St Ians Cft ILK LS29 19 H7
St Ives Cl PONT WF8 180 F3
St Ives Crs CAS WF10 180 E1
St Ive's Gdns HIPP HX3 168 E3 2
St Ives Gv BGLY BD16 80 E4
Saint Ives Gv WOR/ARM LS12 108 C6 11
Saint Ives Mt WOR/ARM LS12 108 C6
St Ives Pl BGLY BD16 80 E4
St Ives Rd BGLY BD16 80 E4
HIPP HX3 168 D3
St James Ap SCFT LS14 111 J2
St James Av HORS LS18 85 L5
St Jame's Cl MILN OL16 228 E6
WOR/ARM LS12 108 A6
St James Ct HOR/CROF WF4 222 E5
St James Crs PDSY/CALV LS28 106 D7
St James Dr HORS LS18 85 M5
St James Ri WKFDW/WTN WF2 197 L2
St James Rd HFAX HX1 11 G5
ILK LS29 38 C3
St James's Ct WKFDW/WTN WF2 12 D6
St James's Ms WOR/ARM LS12 108 B6
St James's Pk WKFDE WF1 13 J3
St James's Rd HUD HD1 191 M7
St James's Sq WBOW BD5 127 G1 20
St James's St WBY LS22 48 A1
St James St BTLY WF17 173 L1 18
HECK WF16 172 F3 9
HFAX HX1 10 F5
MILN OL16 207 H8
ROY/SHW OL2 229 K7 13
St James Ter HORS LS18 85 M5
St James Wk HORS LS18 85 M5
St James Wy HOR/CROF WF4 220 A1
St John Pde DEWS WF13 173 K7 4
St Johns STKB/PEN S36 258 B8
St John's Av DOD/DAR S75 260 A2
HDGY LS6 6 B5
HUDE HD5 193 K5
HUDS HD4 214 C4
ILK LS29 19 H6
OSS WF5 197 J1
PDSY/CALV LS28 106 E4
SCFT LS14 90 B1
WKFDE WF1 176 D6
St John's Cha WKFDE WF1 176 D7 3
St Johns Cl CLECK BD19 150 A7 8
DEWS WF13 173 K6 8
DOD/DAR S75 260 A8 1
GFTH/SHER LS25 113 H8
HBR HX7 143 J3 21
HDGY LS6 6 A5
OSS WF5 197 J1 1
RPDN/SBR HX6 188 E5
STKB/PEN S36 270 E4
St John's Ct BAIL BD17 83 G4 4
KBTN HD8 216 B3 3
SCFT LS14 90 B1 1
TAD LS24 94 F1 2
YEA LS19 62 C8
St John's Crs GIR BD8 104 A6
HUD HD1 14 E3
NORM WF6 178 C7 2
OSS WF5 197 J1
St John's Cft WKFDE WF1 176 D6 5
St John's Dr AL/HA/HU LS17 25 M7
HUD HD1 14 E3
MILN OL16 206 D8
YEA LS19 62 C8
St John's Garth
GFTH/SHER LS25 92 A6
St John's Gv HDGY LS6 6 A4
WKFDE WF1 176 E6
St John's La HFAX HX1 11 G8
St Johns Ms WKFDE WF1 176 D7 4
St John's Mt WKFDE WF1 176 C6
St John's North WKFDE WF1 176 D7
St John's Pk ILK LS29 61 H1
St John's Pl BIRK/DRI BD11 128 C8 5
HFAX HX1 11 G8 1
St John's Rd AIRE BD20 57 J4
BSLY S70 261 G6
BSPA/BRAM LS23 48 F8
BVRD LS3 6 B6
CUD/GR S72 244 D8
HUD HD1 14 E2
HUDE HD5 193 L5
ILK LS29 39 G2
YEA LS19 62 C8
St John's Sq WKFDE WF1 176 D7
St John's St AIRE BD20 34 C4
AIRE BD20 36 A5
HOR/CROF WF4 197 G5
RTHW LS26 155 L1 1
St John St BRIG HD6 170 C5
DEWS WF13 173 K6 7
St John's Vw BSPA/BRAM LS23 48 E7
St John's Wk BSLYN/ROY S71 243 M3
St Johns Wy HWTH BD22 2 B7
YEA LS19 62 C8
St John Wk DEWS WF13 173 K6
St Joseph's Dr MILN OL16 228 D2 4
St Joseph's Mt PONT WF8 180 D7
St Joseph's St TAD LS24 71 L3
St Jude's St BFD BD1 4 C3
HFAX HX1 168 D1 5
St Julien's Mt DOD/DAR S75 259 G2
St Julien's Wy DOD/DAR S75 259 G2
St Laurence's Cl SHPY BD18 105 G1 1
St Lawrence Cl
PDSY/CALV LS28 106 F7 2
St Lawrence Md
PDSY/CALV LS28 106 F8
St Lawrence St CHAL LS7 87 M8 13
St Lawrence Ter
PDSY/CALV LS28 107 G8
St Leonards Cl ILK LS29 19 H7
St Leonard's Gv GIR BD8 104 B5
St Leonard's Rd GIR BD8 104 B5
St Leonards Wy
BSLYN/ROY S71 262 C7 3
St Lucius's Cl HUDS HD4 215 G8 1
St Luke's Cl BSPA/BRAM LS23 69 M1 4
BTLY WF17 174 A2 1
CLECK BD19 149 K7
St Luke's Crs BEE/HOL LS11 8 D7
St Luke's Gn BEE/HOL LS11 8 D8
St Luke's Rd BEE/HOL LS11 8 D8
St Luke's St BEE/HOL LS11 8 D8
St Luke St ROCH OL11 228 B1 17
St Luke's Vw BEE/HOL LS11 8 D8
St Lukes Wy BSLYN/ROY S71 261 L3 5
St Margaret's Av BOW BD4 127 M4
HORS LS18 85 K5
RHAY LS8 88 C8 9
RTHW LS26 156 F3 2
St Margaret's Cl HORS LS18 85 K4
St Margaret's Dr HORS LS18 85 K4
RHAY LS8 88 C8
St Margaret's Gv RHAY LS8 88 C8
St Margaret's Pl GTHN BD7 126 D1 5
St Margaret's Rd GTHN BD7 104 D8
GTHN BD7 126 D1 6
HORS LS18 85 K4
RTHW LS26 156 F3 3
St Margaret's Ter GTHN BD7 126 D1 7
ILK LS29 38 D3 3
St Margaret's Vw RHAY LS8 88 C8
St Mark's Av LDSU LS2 6 D4
LM/WK BD12 148 E1
St Mark's Rd HUDW HD3 191 J8 1
LDSU LS2 6 D3
St Mark's St LDSU LS2 6 D4
WKFDE WF1 176 E6
St Mark's Ter LM/WK BD12 148 E1
St Marks Vw HUDW HD3 191 J8 2
St Martin's Av CHAL LS7 109 L1
GTHN BD7 4 A6
OT LS21 41 H4
St Martins Cl DOD/DAR S75 260 D4
FEA/AMT WF7 201 L2
St Martin's Crs CHAL LS7 109 M1
St Martin's Dr CHAL LS7 87 M8 14
St Martin's Gdns CHAL LS7 109 L1 6
St Martin's Gv CAS WF10 157 K8
CHAL LS7 109 M1 5
St Martin's Rd CHAL LS7 109 M1
St Martin's Vw BRIG HD6 170 C3
CHAL LS7 109 M1
St Mary's Av BTLY WF17 173 J3
HOLM/MEL HD7 236 B6
LM/WK BD12 148 E4
MIRF WF14 172 E8
NORM WF6 178 B2
RTHW LS26 134 C5
St Mary's Cl CHAL LS7 109 M1 7
EARD/LOFT WF3 152 E7
GFTH/SHER LS25 113 H8
HEM/SK/SE WF9 247 J4
ILK LS29 38 E2
LM/WK BD12 148 D4
MILN OL16 228 D1
WOR/ARM LS12 108 F8
St Mary's Ct CAS WF10 157 K2
CHAL LS7 109 M1 8
St Mary's Crs HOLM/MEL HD7 236 B6
LM/WK BD12 148 D5
St Mary's Dr LM/WK BD12 148 E4
St Mary's Gdns LM/WK BD12 148 E4
St Mary's Garth AL/HA/HU LS17 67 K1
St Mary's Ga BSLY S70 261 G4 9
ELL HX5 169 H7 3
ROY/SHW OL2 229 K7 14
WHIT OL12 206 A7
St Mary's La HUDE HD5 193 L7
OSM LS9 7 L8
St Mary's Mt LM/WK BD12 148 D4 1
St Mary's Park Ap
WOR/ARM LS12 108 B6
St Mary's Park Ct
WOR/ARM LS12 108 B6 1
St Mary's Park Crs
WOR/ARM LS12 108 B6
St Mary's Park Gn
WOR/ARM LS12 108 B6 2
St Mary's Pl BSLY S70 261 G4 10
EARL WF12 173 L8 2
St Mary's Ri HOLM/MEL HD7 236 B6
St Mary's Rd AIRE BD20 58 B4
BOW BD4 127 M1 3
CHAL LS7 109 M1
GIR BD8 104 E4 9
HOLM/MEL HD7 236 B1
HOLM/MEL HD7 236 B6
HTON BD9 104 E4
NORM WF6 178 B3
St Mary's Sq HOLM/MEL HD7 236 B1 7
LM/WK BD12 148 D4
MOR LS27 152 C2 12
St Mary's St BSPA/BRAM LS23 48 F6
OSM LS9 7 K8
STKB/PEN S36 270 F3
St Mary St HFAX HX1 10 E7
St Mary's Wk GFTH/SHER LS25 114 B7
MIRF WF14 172 E8
St Mary's Wy HOLM/MEL HD7 236 B6 2
St Matthew Rd DEWS WF13 173 K6 8
St Matthews Cl WIL/AL BD15 102 D2
St Matthew's Dr HIPP HX3 147 J3 2
St Matthews Gv WIL/AL BD15 102 E2 5
St Matthew's Rd WBSY BD6 126 F5 8
St Matthew's St BEE/HOL LS11 8 C5
St Matthew's Wk CHAL LS7 87 L6
St Matthews Wy
BSLYN/ROY S71 261 L3
St Matthias' St BULY LS4 108 F4
St Merrion Crs HIPP HX3 11 M9
St Michael's Av BSLYN/ROY S71 243 M8
PONT WF8 180 D6
St Michael's Cl CAS WF10 157 M7 2
EARL WF12 196 A4
KBTN HD8 217 M7 1
WKFDW/WTN WF2 12 A4
St Michael's Crs HDGY LS6 108 F2 8
St Michael's Gdns KBTN HD8 217 L7
St Michaels Gn NORM WF6 178 C5 4
St Michael's Gv HDGY LS6 108 F2
St Michael's La HDGY LS6 108 F3
St Michael's Mt EARL WF12 196 A4
St Michael's Rd GIR BD8 4 B4
HDGY LS6 108 F2
St Michael's Ter HDGY LS6 108 F2
St Michaels Wy ILK LS29 19 H6
ILK LS29 40 B6
St Nicholas Rd ILK LS29 38 C1
St Nicholas St CAS WF10 157 M7 3
St Oswald Av PONT WF8 180 D6
St Oswald Rd
WKFDW/WTN WF2 197 L1
St Oswalds Garth GSLY LS20 62 A5
St Oswalds Pl OSS WF5 175 G7 2
St Oswald St CAS WF10 157 M6 13
St Owens Dr DOD/DAR S75 260 D4 10
St Paulinus Cl DEWS WF13 173 K6 9
St Paul's Av BIRK/DRI BD11 150 D1 1
WBSY BD6 126 D6
St Paul's Cl HEM/SK/SE WF9 225 M6 1
St Paul's Dr WKFDW/WTN WF2 175 M6
St Paul's Gv ILK LS29 38 F2
WBSY BD6 126 D6
St Paul's Pde BSLYN/ROY S71 262 B6
St Paul's Pl LDS LS1 6 E9 1
St Pauls Ri ILK LS29 19 H7
St Paul's Rd BIRK/DRI BD11 150 C1
GIR BD8 104 E4
HFAX HX1 10 A9
HUDE HD5 193 K6
KGHY BD21 3 J6
MIRF WF14 194 C2
SHPY BD18 82 C7 5
WBSY BD6 126 D6
St Paul's St HUD HD1 15 G9
LDS LS1 6 D9
MOR LS27 152 D3 5
St Paul's Ter MIRF WF14 194 C2 2
St Paul's Wk
WKFDW/WTN WF2 175 M6 5
St Peg Cl CLECK BD19 150 A7
St Peg La CLECK BD19 150 A7
St Peter's Av RPDN/SBR HX6 167 H3
RTHW LS26 155 H1 10
St Peter's Cl BTLY WF17 150 F5 2
MIRF WF14 194 B1 4
St Peters Ct BEE/HOL LS11 9 G8
BRAM LS13 107 M3
HOR/CROF WF4 197 J4 6
ILK LS29 19 H7
St Peter's Crs EARD/LOFT WF3 155 K8
HUDE HD5 193 K6
MOR LS27 130 C8 6
St Peter's Gdns BRAM LS13 107 L3
St Peter's Garth SCFT LS14 68 C8
St Peters Ga OSS WF5 174 F7 4
St Peter's Gv HOR/CROF WF4 197 K5 3
St Peter's Mt BRAM LS13 107 L4
St Peter's Sq OSM LS9 7 K9
St Peter's St HUD HD1 15 G6
LDSU LS2 7 J9
MILN OL16 206 D8
St Peter's Ter BSLY S70 261 J6 7
St Peter's Wy ILK LS29 61 H2
St Philip's Av MID LS10 153 K1
St Philip's Cl DEWS WF13 173 M5 6
ILK LS29 40 B6
MID LS10 153 L1
St Philips Ct HUDW HD3 191 K4 2
St Philip's Dr ILK LS29 40 B6
St Philip's Wy ILK LS29 40 B5
St Richards Rd OT LS21 41 H4
St Stephen's Cl SKP/WHF BD23 16 B2
St Stephen's Ct AIRE BD20 35 L8
HIPP HX3 168 C4 1
OSM LS9 110 B6 14
St Stephen's Rd AIRE BD20 56 E1
HUD HD1 214 B2 3
OSM LS9 110 B6 15
PDSY/CALV LS28 84 C7
WBOW BD5 126 F3
St Stephen's St HIPP HX3 168 C4
St Stephen's Ter WBOW BD5 127 G3 17
St Stephen's Wy COL BB8 74 B1
Saint St GTHN BD7 126 C2
St Swithins Dr EARD/LOFT WF3 177 H4
St Swithins Gv
EARD/LOFT WF3 177 H4 4
St Thomas Gdns HUDN HD2 171 H8
St Thomas Rd FEA/AMT WF7 201 M1 4
St Thomas Rw LDSU LS2 7 J7
St Thomas's Rd DOD/DAR S75 260 C2
St Vincent Av AWLS/ASK DN6 249 H8
St Vincent Rd PDSY/CALV LS28 107 G8
St Wilfred's St PDSY/CALV LS28 84 D7
St Wilfrid's Av RHAY LS8 110 C2
St Wilfrid's Circ RHAY LS8 110 D3
St Wilfrid's Cl GTHN BD7 126 B1 8
St Wilfrid's Crs GTHN BD7 126 B1
RHAY LS8 110 D2
St Wilfrid's Dr RHAY LS8 110 C2
St Wilfrid's Garth RHAY LS8 110 D3
St Wilfrid's Gv RHAY LS8 110 D2
St Wilfrid's Rd GTHN BD7 126 B1 9
St Winifred's Cl LUD/ILL HX2 145 M1 1
Salcombe Cl DOD/DAR S75 242 E6
Salcombe Pl BOW BD4 128 A4 13
Salem Pl GFTH/SHER LS25 113 G7 3
MID LS10 9 H3
Salem St BFD BD1 4 E5
CUL/QBY BD13 124 F5 7
HBR HX7 143 H3 6
Salerno Wy WMB/DAR S73 263 G8
Sale St LIT OL15 185 K8
Salford Wy TOD OL14 163 J2 1
Salik Gdns ROCH OL11 228 B1 18
Salisbury Av BAIL BD17 82 E3
WOR/ARM LS12 108 E6
Salisbury Cl EARL WF12 174 B6 5
NORM WF6 178 D3
Salisbury Gv WOR/ARM LS12 108 E6
Salisbury Ms HORS LS18 85 M4
Salisbury Pl HIPP HX3 10 F1
PDSY/CALV LS28 84 C8
Salisbury Rd CLECK BD19 149 H6
HTON BD9 104 E1
HWTH BD22 2 D7
LM/WK BD12 126 E8 5
WOR/ARM LS12 108 E6
Salisbury St DOD/DAR S75 260 F3
PDSY/CALV LS28 84 C8
ROY/SHW OL2 229 H6
RPDN/SBR HX6 167 J3
SKP/WHF BD23 16 A2
YEA LS19 84 D2
Salisbury Ter WOR/ARM LS12 108 E6
Salisbury Vw WOR/ARM LS12 108 E6 7
Salkeld St ROCH OL11 228 B1
Salmon Crs HORS LS18 85 L5
Sal Nook Cl LM/WK BD12 126 F7
Sal Royd Rd LM/WK BD12 149 G1
Saltaire Rd BGLY BD16 59 M8
BGLY BD16 81 M1
SHPY BD18 82 C6
Saltburn Pl HTON BD9 104 B4 5
Saltburn St HFAX HX1 10 A5
Salt Drake RPDN/SBR HX6 166 D6
Salterhebble Hl HIPP HX3 168 F4
Salter Hill La STKB/PEN S36 271 G8
Salter Rake Ga TOD OL14 163 K6
Salter Rw PONT WF8 180 F6
Saltersbrook Rd WMB/DAR S73 263 H7
Saltersgate Av KNOT WF11 182 A1
Salter St DEWS WF13 173 K4 5
Salter's Wy STKB/PEN S36 270 F4
Salt Horn Cl LM/WK BD12 149 H1
Saltonstall La LUD/ILL HX2 144 F1
Salt Pie Aly WKFDW/WTN WF2 12 C4
Salts Dr LIT OL15 185 J8
Salts Mill Rd BAIL BD17 82 D6 9
Salts St ROY/SHW OL2 229 K7
Salt St GIR BD8 4 A2
HFAX HX1 10 C4
Samlesbury Cl ROY/SHW OL2 229 H7 7
Sampson St LVSG WF15 172 D2 6
Samson St MILN OL16 206 E6
Samuel Dr EARD/LOFT WF3 177 G1
Samuel La ROY/SHW OL2 229 G6
Samuel Rd DOD/DAR S75 260 D3
Samuel Sq DOD/DAR S75 260 D3 4
Samuel St KGHY BD21 3 G4 2
Sandal Av WKFDW/WTN WF2 199 G5
Sandal Cliff WKFDW/WTN WF2 199 G6
Sandale Wk WBSY BD6 126 B7 9
Sandal Hall Cl
WKFDW/WTN WF2 199 H6
Sandal Hall Ms
WKFDW/WTN WF2 199 G5 2
Sandall Cl GFTH/SHER LS25 135 K4
Sandall Magna WBSY BD6 126 A7
Sandal Ri PONT WF8 225 J1 3
Sandals Rd BAIL BD17 82 E4
Sandal Wy BTLY WF17 151 H5
Sandbeck Cl BSLYN/ROY S71 261 H3 3
Sandbeck La WBY LS22 30 B7

Sandbeck Pk WBY LS22 .... 30 B7
Sandbeck Wy WBY LS22 .... 30 B7
Sandbed Ct MSTN/BAR LS15 .... 111 M3
Sandbed La MSTN/BAR LS15 .... 111 M3
Sand Beds HOLM/MEL HD7 .... 214 B8
Sandbeds CUL/QBY BD13 .... 125 C5
Sandbeds La LUD/ILL HX2 .... 146 A5
Sandbeds Rd LUD/ILL HX2 .... 146 A6
Sandbeds Ter LUD/ILL HX2 .... 146 A5
Sandene Av HUDS HD4 .... 213 L4
Sandene Dr HUDS HD4 .... 213 L4
Sanderling Ct GIR BD8 .... 103 L7
Sanderling Garth MID LS10 .... 153 M1
Sanderling Wy MID LS10 .... 153 M1
Sanderson Av NORM WF6 .... 178 C5
  WBSY BD6 .... 126 E5
Sanderson La RTHW LS26 .... 155 J6
Sanderson St WKFDE WF1 .... 13 H1
Sandfield Av HDGY LS6 .... 87 C8
Sandfield Garth HDGY LS6 .... 87 C8
Sandfield Rd BFDE BD3 .... 105 L7
  HEM/SK/SE WF9 .... 247 J1
  KSTL LS5 .... 108 D3
Sandfield Ter TAD LS24 .... 72 A2
Sandford Ct BSLY S70 .... 260 F6
Sandford Pl KSTL LS5 .... 108 C2
Sandford Rd BFDE BD3 .... 105 L7
  HEM/SK/SE WF9 .... 247 J1
  KSTL LS5 .... 108 D3
Sandforth Av HIPP HX3 .... 146 K4
Sandgate Dr GFTH/SHER LS25 .... 135 K4
Sandgate La GFTH/SHER LS25 .... 135 L5
Sandgate Ri GFTH/SHER LS25 .... 135 L4
Sandgate Ter GFTH/SHER LS25 .... 135 L5
Sandhall Av LUD/ILL HX2 .... 145 M7
Sandhall Dr LUD/ILL HX2 .... 145 M7
Sandhall Gn LUD/ILL HX2 .... 145 M6
Sandhall La LUD/ILL HX2 .... 145 M7
Sandhill Cl PONT WF8 .... 180 F2
Sandhill Crs AL/HA/HU LS17 .... 88 A2
Sandhill Dr AL/HA/HU LS17 .... 88 A2
Sandhill Gv AL/HA/HU LS17 .... 88 A1
  CUD/GR S72 .... 245 H5
Sand Hill La AL/HA/HU LS17 .... 87 M3
Sandhill Lawn PONT WF8 .... 180 E7
Sand Hill Lawns
  AL/HA/HU LS17 .... 87 M3
Sandhill Mt AL/HA/HU LS17 .... 87 M1
  IDLE BD10 .... 83 K8
Sandhill Ov AL/HA/HU LS17 .... 88 A1
Sandhill Ri PONT WF8 .... 180 F3
Sand Hole La ROCH OL11 .... 228 B5
Sandholme Crs HIPP HX3 .... 147 M7
Sandholme Dr IDLE BD10 .... 83 L8
  ILK LS29 .... 40 B7
  OSS WF5 .... 196 F4
Sandhurst Av RHAY LS8 .... 110 C3
Sandhurst Gv RHAY LS8 .... 110 C3
Sandhurst Pl RHAY LS8 .... 110 C3
Sandhurst Rd RHAY LS8 .... 110 C3
Sandhurst Ter RHAY LS8 .... 110 C2
Sandiford Cl MSTN/BAR LS15 .... 111 M3
Sandiford Ter MSTN/BAR LS15 .... 111 M3
Sandiway Bank EARL WF12 .... 195 M3
Sand La GFTH/SHER LS25 .... 138 K3
Sandleas Wy MSTN/BAR LS15 .... 112 B4
Sandlewood Cl BEE/HOL LS11 .... 8 D6
Sandlewood Gn BEE/HOL LS11 .... 8 D6
Sandmead Cl BOW BD4 .... 128 A3
  MOR LS27 .... 130 C8
Sandmead Cft MOR LS27 .... 130 C8
Sandmead Wy MOR LS27 .... 130 C8
Sandmoor Av AL/HA/HU LS17 .... 65 M8
Sandmoor Cha AL/HA/HU LS17 .... 87 M1
Sandmoor Cl AL/HA/HU LS17 .... 87 M1
  CUL/QBY BD13 .... 103 G8
Sandmoor Dr AL/HA/HU LS17 .... 65 M8
  HUDW HD3 .... 191 J5
Sandmoor Gdns HIPP HX3 .... 147 M3
Sandmoor Garth IDLE BD10 .... 83 K5
Sandmoor Gn AL/HA/HU LS17 .... 65 L8
Sandmoor La AL/HA/HU LS17 .... 65 M8
Sandmoor Ms AL/HA/HU LS17 .... 87 M1
Sandon Gv MID LS10 .... 132 A4
Sandon Mt MID LS10 .... 132 K4
Sandown Av HOR/CROF WF4 .... 200 B5
  LUD/ILL HX2 .... 146 A2
Sandown Rd LUD/ILL HX2 .... 146 A2
Sandpiper Ap MOR LS27 .... 152 E3
Sandpiper Ms GIR BD8 .... 103 L7
Sandringham HUDN HD2 .... 193 C1
Sandringham Ap
  AL/HA/HU LS17 .... 88 A3
Sandringham Av KNOT WF11 .... 181 L2
Sandringham Cl CLAY BD14 .... 125 M1
  MOR LS27 .... 152 E1
  PONT WF8 .... 202 E1
  STKB/PEN S36 .... 270 C2
Sandringham Ct CLAY BD14 .... 125 M1
Sandringham Crs
  AL/HA/HU LS17 .... 87 M3
  PDSY/CALV LS28 .... 107 G8
Sandringham Dr
  AL/HA/HU LS17 .... 88 A2
  MILN OL16 .... 207 J8
Sandringham Gdns
  AL/HA/HU LS17 .... 87 M3
Sandringham Gn
  AL/HA/HU LS17 .... 88 A3
Sandringham Mt
  AL/HA/HU LS17 .... 88 A2
Sandringham Rd CLAY BD14 .... 125 M1
  KNOT WF11 .... 159 M7
  WBY LS22 .... 30 A8
Sandringham Wy
  AL/HA/HU LS17 .... 87 M3
  ROY/SHW OL2 .... 228 E8
Sandrock Rd PONT WF8 .... 181 C4
Sandsend Cl HTON BD9 .... 103 M3
Sands House La HUDS HD4 .... 213 K5
Sandside Cl WBOW BD5 .... 127 H4
Sands La EARL WF12 .... 173 M7
  HUDE HD5 .... 194 B8
  MIRF WF14 .... 194 F3
Sands Rd EARL WF12 .... 174 A8
Sandstone Cl HOLM/MEL HD7 .... 236 B3
Sandstone Rd MILN OL16 .... 207 H2
Sand St HUD HD1 .... 15 H8
  HWTH BD22 .... 78 E8

KGHY BD21 .... 3 G3
Sandwath La TAD LS24 .... 94 D7
Sandway MSTN/BAR LS15 .... 111 K4
Sandway Gdns MSTN/BAR LS15 .... 111 K4
Sandway Gv MSTN/BAR LS15 .... 111 K4
Sandwell St HOLM/MEL HD7 .... 212 B5
Sandwich Crs HUDN HD2 .... 192 B3
Sandyacres RTHW LS26 .... 133 H8
Sandyacres Crs RTHW LS26 .... 133 H8
Sandyacres Dr RTHW LS26 .... 133 H8
Sandy Bank ROY/SHW OL2 .... 229 H6
Sandy Bank Av RTHW LS26 .... 133 H8
Sandy Banks BGLY BD16 .... 80 D6
Sandybridge La CUD/GR S72 .... 244 D2
Sandy Dyke La RPDN/SBR HX6 .... 167 G6
Sandyfields Vw AWLS/ASK DN6 .... 249 K5
Sandyfoot GTL/HWG HX4 .... 189 K7
Sandyforth La HWTH BD22 .... 53 M4
Sandy Ga AL/HA/HU LS17 .... 44 F7
  HOLM/MEL HD7 .... 254 E1
  KGHY BD21 .... 2 C2
Sandy Gate La FEA/AMT WF7 .... 202 E3
Sandygate Ter BOW BD4 .... 127 M1
Sandy Gv RTHW LS26 .... 133 H8
Sandylands HUDS HD4 .... 213 M8
Sandy La HOR/CROF WF4 .... 196 D7
  HUDS HD4 .... 213 J7
Sandy Lobby OT LS21 .... 42 E8
Sandymoor WIL/AL BD15 .... 103 J2
Sandy Wk BHP/TINH LS16 .... 64 B4
  WKFDE WF1 .... 12 C1
Sandy Wy YEA LS19 .... 62 D7
Sandywood St KGHY BD21 .... 3 G3
Sangster Wy WBOW BD5 .... 127 J5
Santa Monica Cl IDLE BD10 .... 83 J7
Santa Monica Gv IDLE BD10 .... 83 J7
Santa Monica Rd IDLE BD10 .... 83 J7
Santingley La HOR/CROF WF4 .... 200 C8
Sanworth St TOD OL14 .... 163 L1
Sapgate La CUL/QBY BD13 .... 103 G8
Saplin St GIR BD8 .... 104 D5
Sapphire Ct BTLY WF17 .... 151 J8
Sarah Butterworth St
  MILN OL16 .... 206 D8
Sarah St EARD/LOFT WF3 .... 153 M6
  ROCH OL11 .... 206 C8
Sardinia St MID LS10 .... 9 J6
Saunders Cl HUDW HD3 .... 191 L7
Saunderson Rd STKB/PEN S36 .... 270 D2
Saunters Wy NORM WF6 .... 178 C2
Savile Av CHAL LS7 .... 7 J2
  IDLE BD10 .... 83 L8
  KBTN HD8 .... 217 M7
Savile Cl BRIG HD6 .... 170 F3
Savile Ct MIRF WF14 .... 172 C8
Savile Crs HFAX HX1 .... 10 F8
Savile Dr CHAL LS7 .... 7 J2
  HOR/CROF WF4 .... 197 J4
Savile Gln HFAX HX1 .... 10 F8
Savile Gn HFAX HX1 .... 11 G8
Savile Gv EARL WF12 .... 173 L7
Savile La BRIG HD6 .... 170 F3
Savile Lea HFAX HX1 .... 10 F8
Savile Ms EARL WF12 .... 195 L1
Savile Mt CHAL LS7 .... 7 J2
Savile Pde HFAX HX1 .... 168 D1
Savile Pk HFAX HX1 .... 168 C1
  HIPP HX3 .... 168 D2
Savile Park Gdns HFAX HX1 .... 168 D7
Savile Park Rd CLECK BD19 .... 149 M3
  HFAX HX1 .... 10 F8
Savile Park St HFAX HX1 .... 168 C1
Savile Pit La EARL WF12 .... 174 C5
Savile Pl CHAL LS7 .... 7 J2
  MIRF WF14 .... 172 C8
Savile Rd CAS WF10 .... 157 L6
  CHAL LS7 .... 7 J2
  EARL WF12 .... 195 L1
  ELL HX5 .... 169 L6
  HBR HX7 .... 143 G3
  HFAX HX1 .... 10 F8
  HUDW HD3 .... 191 L6
  RTHW LS26 .... 156 F3
Savile Royd HFAX HX1 .... 10 E9
Savile St BTLY WF17 .... 173 M5
  CLECK BD19 .... 149 M5
  DEWS WF13 .... 173 L4
  HUDW HD3 .... 213 J1
  KBTN HD8 .... 217 M7
Savile Wk CUD/GR S72 .... 245 K3
Savile Wy ELL HX5 .... 169 J6
Saville Cl EARD/LOFT WF3 .... 154 E5
Saville Ct OT LS21 .... 41 H7
Saville Hall La DOD/DAR S75 .... 260 B8
Saville La STKB/PEN S36 .... 270 B3
Saville Pk OSS WF5 .... 197 H2
Saville Park Rd HFAX HX1 .... 10 E9
Saville Rd DOD/DAR S75 .... 260 C8
  KBTN HD8 .... 239 J4
Saville St CUD/GR S72 .... 244 D8
  KBTN HD8 .... 239 M5
  OSS WF5 .... 197 H2
  WKFDE WF1 .... 176 E7
Sawley Av LIT OL15 .... 185 J7
Sawley St KGHY BD21 .... 2 E3
Saw Mill St BEE/HOL LS11 .... 8 E3
Sawood La HWTH BD22 .... 101 H5
Sawrey Pl WBOW BD5 .... 4 D8
Saw Wells La TAD LS24 .... 116 A2
Sawyers Garth ILK LS29 .... 19 J6
Sawyer St WHIT OL12 .... 206 B5
Saxon Cl HEM/SK/SE WF9 .... 246 B4
Saxon Ct GFTH/SHER LS25 .... 113 H6
  KBTN HD8 .... 217 L3
Saxon Ga AL/HA/HU LS17 .... 87 K4
  HEM/SK/SE WF9 .... 246 C5
Saxon Gn AL/HA/HU LS17 .... 87 J4
Saxon Gv AL/HA/HU LS17 .... 87 J4
  HEM/SK/SE WF9 .... 246 B4
Saxon Mt AL/HA/HU LS17 .... 87 K3
  HEM/SK/SE WF9 .... 246 B4
Saxon Rd AL/HA/HU LS17 .... 87 J4
Saxon St CUD/GR S72 .... 244 D8
  GIR BD8 .... 4 A4
  HFAX HX1 .... 10 A5

TOD OL14 .... 163 J5
Saxon Wy CAS WF10 .... 158 C6
Saxton Av WBSY BD6 .... 126 B5
Saxton Ct GFTH/SHER LS25 .... 113 H6
  TAD LS24 .... 93 K7
Saxton La OSM LS9 .... 9 K1
Saxton Pl HUDE HD5 .... 215 J2
Saxton St LVSG WF15 .... 172 E1
Sayers Cl KSTL LS5 .... 108 D2
Sayle Av BOW BD4 .... 127 K6
Sayner La MID LS10 .... 9 K4
Sayner Rd MID LS10 .... 9 J4
Scalebor Park La ILK LS29 .... 40 A6
Scale HI HUDN HD2 .... 192 C4
Scaley St BFDE BD3 .... 105 M7
  OT LS21 .... 42 D3
Scaly Ga HOLM/MEL HD7 .... 255 J1
  HOLM/MEL HD7 .... 255 J4
Scammonden Rd
  GTL/HWG HX4 .... 189 H7
  RPDN/SBR HX6 .... 167 J8
Scape Vw HOLM/MEL HD7 .... 213 G2
Scarboro Mdw MIRF WF14 .... 194 C1
Scarborough Gv SHPY BD18 .... 82 C7
Scarborough La
  EARD/LOFT WF3 .... 152 F5
Scarborough Rd SHPY BD18 .... 82 C7
Scarborough St
  EARD/LOFT WF3 .... 152 F5
  EARL WF12 .... 173 M8
Scarborough Ter EARL WF12 .... 173 M8
Scar Bottom La GTL/HWG HX4 .... 168 B7
Scarbro' Jct BRAM LS13 .... 107 M5
Scarcroft Ct SCFT LS14 .... 67 M6
Scarfield Cl BSLYN/ROY S71 .... 262 B6
Scarfold HOLM/MEL HD7 .... 254 C1
Scargill Cl OSM LS9 .... 110 B5
Scar Gv HUDS HD4 .... 214 B4
Scar Head Rd RPDN/SBR HX6 .... 167 K4
Scar Hole La HOLM/MEL HD7 .... 255 J2
Scarhouse La HOLM/MEL HD7 .... 213 G2
Scar La BSLYN/ROY S71 .... 262 B6
  HOLM/MEL HD7 .... 213 H2
Scarlet Hts CUL/QBY BD13 .... 125 H5
Scarr Bottom Rd LUD/ILL HX2 .... 168 B2
Scarr Dr WHIT OL12 .... 206 B4
Scarr End La DEWS WF13 .... 173 H4
  EARL WF12 .... 196 B1
Scarr End Vw DEWS WF13 .... 173 H4
Scarr La ROY/SHW OL2 .... 229 L7
Scarsdale La AL/HA/HU LS17 .... 47 G8
Scarsdale Rdg AL/HA/HU LS17 .... 47 G8
Scarth Av OSM LS9 .... 110 C4
Scarthingwell Crs TAD LS24 .... 93 K7
Scarthingwell La TAD LS24 .... 93 K7
Scarth Ter EARD/LOFT WF3 .... 155 K8
Scar Top La HUDS HD4 .... 213 M8
Scar Top Rd HWTH BD22 .... 77 H7
Scarwood Cl BGLY BD16 .... 81 J2
Scatcherd Gv MOR LS27 .... 152 B2
Scatcherd La MOR LS27 .... 152 B3
Scatcherd Park Av MOR LS27 .... 152 C1
Scawthorpe Cl PONT WF8 .... 181 H5
Sceptone Gv CUD/GR S72 .... 244 E3
Schofield Dr WMB/DAR S73 .... 263 J8
Schofield Hall Rd LIT OL15 .... 207 M5
Schofield La HUDE HD5 .... 15 J7
Schofield Pl WMB/DAR S73 .... 263 J8
Schofield Rd WMB/DAR S73 .... 263 H8
Schofield St LIT OL15 .... 185 L8
  LIT OL15 .... 185 M4
  MILN OL16 .... 229 J1
  ROCH OL11 .... 228 C2
Scholars St WBOW BD5 .... 126 F4
Schole Av STKB/PEN S36 .... 270 D4
Scholebrook La BOW BD4 .... 128 E3
  PDSY/CALV LS28 .... 128 F2
Schole Hill La STKB/PEN S36 .... 270 D4
Scholemoor Av GTHN BD7 .... 126 A1
Scholemoor La GTHN BD7 .... 126 A1
Scholemoor Rd GTHN BD7 .... 126 B1
Scholes La CLECK BD19 .... 149 H7
  GTL/HWG HX4 .... 168 C5
  HWTH BD22 .... 78 B5
  MSTN/BAR LS15 .... 90 A6
Scholes Moor Rd
  HOLM/MEL HD7 .... 254 E5
Scholes Rd CAS WF10 .... 158 F5
  HOLM/MEL HD7 .... 255 C2
  HUDN HD2 .... 192 C4
Scholes St WBOW BD5 .... 126 F4
Scholey Av BRIG HD6 .... 170 C6
Scholey Rd BRIG HD6 .... 170 C6
Scholfield St TOD OL14 .... 141 K8
School Av DEWS WF13 .... 173 H5
School Cl HOR/CROF WF4 .... 200 C6
  LUD/ILL HX2 .... 124 B7
  RPDN/SBR HX6 .... 189 C2
  WOR/ARM LS12 .... 129 M3
School Cote Brow LUD/ILL HX2 .... 124 D8
School Crs DEWS WF13 .... 173 H5
  LUD/ILL HX2 .... 124 B7
  WKFDW/WTN WF2 .... 197 M2
School Dr KNOT WF11 .... 181 L1
Schoolgate MSTN/BAR LS15 .... 91 G7
School Gn BHP/TINH LS16 .... 64 A4
  BRIG HD6 .... 170 C6
  CUL/QBY BD13 .... 103 J8
School Green Av
  CUL/QBY BD13 .... 103 H8
School Gv DEWS WF13 .... 173 H5
School HI CUD/GR S72 .... 244 D7
  HUDS HD4 .... 213 J7
  KBTN HD8 .... 216 B8
  WKFDW/WTN WF2 .... 220 D2
School Land La HBR HX7 .... 120 B8
School La AL/HA/HU LS17 .... 66 D6
  AL/HA/HU LS17 .... 67 L1
  BSPA/BRAM LS23 .... 49 H2
  CAS WF10 .... 158 B8
  CHAL LS7 .... 87 J7
  COL BB8 .... 53 G8
  DEWS WF13 .... 173 H5
  GFTH/SHER LS25 .... 92 A7
  GFTH/SHER LS25 .... 138 A3

HDGY LS6 .... 87 G8
HIPP HX3 .... 169 J3
HOLM/MEL HD7 .... 190 D8
HOLM/MEL HD7 .... 211 L8
HOR/CROF WF4 .... 197 J5
HUD HD1 .... 14 A9
HUDE HD5 .... 193 K7
HUDS HD4 .... 214 B6
ILK LS29 .... 19 G6
KBTN HD8 .... 217 M7
KBTN HD8 .... 239 J8
LUD/ILL HX2 .... 124 B6
LVSG WF15 .... 171 M4
MILN OL16 .... 206 B7
MSTN/BAR LS15 .... 111 J6
MSTN/BAR LS15 .... 112 A7
PBR HG3 .... 28 E3
TOD OL14 .... 163 K1
WBY LS22 .... 47 K6
WKFDW/WTN WF2 .... 176 A4
WKFDW/WTN WF2 .... 197 M5
School Pl LM/WK BD12 .... 148 E2
School Rd HOLM/MEL HD7 .... 190 D8
  HWTH BD22 .... 2 A5
  PONT WF8 .... 181 G7
  WBY LS22 .... 30 B8
  WKFDW/WTN WF2 .... 197 M2
School Sq BFDE BD3 .... 105 M7
School St AIRE BD20 .... 56 E1
  AIRE BD20 .... 57 J4
  BGLY BD16 .... 81 K7
  BOW BD4 .... 127 K6
  BOW BD4 .... 127 L3
  BSLY S70 .... 261 M6
  CAS WF10 .... 157 L6
  CLAY BD14 .... 125 K2
  CLECK BD19 .... 149 L8
  CUD/GR S72 .... 244 D6
  CUL/QBY BD13 .... 79 M8
  CUL/QBY BD13 .... 102 A6
  DEWS WF13 .... 194 F1
  DOD/DAR S75 .... 242 A5
  DOD/DAR S75 .... 242 E5
  DOD/DAR S75 .... 260 F3
  EARD/LOFT WF3 .... 174 F1
  EARL WF12 .... 173 M6
  EARL WF12 .... 174 D6
  GTL/HWG HX4 .... 168 D6
  HBR HX7 .... 143 J3
  HEM/SK/SE WF9 .... 225 M6
  HFAX HX1 .... 11 J7
  HOLM/MEL HD7 .... 236 B2
  HOLM/MEL HD7 .... 236 B6
  HOLM/MEL HD7 .... 254 C1
  HUDE HD5 .... 15 M8
  LIT OL15 .... 207 G2
  LM/WK BD12 .... 126 E8
  LM/WK BD12 .... 149 J2
  LVSG WF15 .... 172 A4
  LVSG WF15 .... 172 D4
  MOR LS27 .... 130 E6
  MOR LS27 .... 152 D2
  OSS WF5 .... 174 E5
  PDSY/CALV LS28 .... 106 F3
  PDSY/CALV LS28 .... 106 F3
  WHIT OL12 .... 206 B6
  WIL/AL BD15 .... 102 E1
  WMB/DAR S73 .... 263 K8
School St West HUDW HD3 .... 191 K6
School Vw HDGY LS6 .... 109 G3
School Wk HWTH BD22 .... 2 B5
School Yard Vw HIPP HX3 .... 11 H2
Sconce La BAIL BD17 .... 60 C6
Scopsley Gn EARL WF12 .... 195 G6
Scopsley La EARL WF12 .... 194 F5
Scorcher Hills La
  AWLS/ASK DN6 .... 249 H2
Score Cft KBTN HD8 .... 239 J2
Score HI HIPP HX3 .... 147 J2
Scoresby Dr BFD BD1 .... 5 H6
Scotchman Cl MOR LS27 .... 152 B4
Scotchman La MOR LS27 .... 152 A6
Scotchman Rd HTON BD9 .... 104 B4
Scotgate Rd HOLM/MEL HD7 .... 235 M2
Scotland Cl HORS LS18 .... 85 K3
Scotland La HORS LS18 .... 85 J2
Scotland Mill La BHP/TINH LS16 .... 87 H4
  HDGY LS6 .... 87 H5
Scotland St CLECK BD19 .... 150 E5
Scotland Wy HORS LS18 .... 85 J2
Scotland Wood Rd
  AL/HA/HU LS17 .... 87 H4
Scott Av HECK WF16 .... 150 F8
Scott Cl AIRE BD20 .... 55 M1
  RTHW LS26 .... 134 C5
Scott Dr HOR/CROF WF4 .... 200 C6
Scott Gn MOR LS27 .... 129 K6
Scott Green Crs MOR LS27 .... 129 K6
Scott Green Dr MOR LS27 .... 129 K6
Scott Green Gv MOR LS27 .... 129 K6
Scott Green Mt MOR LS27 .... 129 K6
Scott Green Vw MOR LS27 .... 129 L6
Scott Hall Av CHAL LS7 .... 109 L2
Scott Hall Dr CHAL LS7 .... 7 J1
Scott Hall Gn CHAL LS7 .... 109 L1
Scott Hall Pl CHAL LS7 .... 109 L1
Scott Hall Rd AL/HA/HU LS17 .... 87 K8
  CHAL LS7 .... 87 K8
Scott Hall Rw CHAL LS7 .... 7 J1
Scott Hall Sq CHAL LS7 .... 109 L1
Scott Hall Ter CHAL LS7 .... 7 G1
Scott Hall Wk CHAL LS7 .... 109 L2
Scott HI KBTN HD8 .... 240 B3
Scott La AIRE BD20 .... 58 A4
  CLECK BD19 .... 149 M6
  CLECK BD19 .... 150 D5
  MOR LS27 .... 152 A3
  WBY LS22 .... 48 A1
Scott La West AIRE BD20 .... 57 M4
Scott Ms WBY LS22 .... 48 A1
Scotts Hill Cl SCFT LS14 .... 90 B1

Scott St KGHY BD21 .... 2 F4
  PDSY/CALV LS28 .... 107 H8
  TOD OL14 .... 163 J6
Scott V HUDN HD2 .... 192 F3
Scott Wood La CHAL LS7 .... 109 L2
Scotty Bank BRIG HD6 .... 170 C4
Scotty Croft La BRIG HD6 .... 170 C5
Scout La HBR HX7 .... 144 B6
Scout Hill Rd DEWS WF13 .... 173 J4
Scout La HOLM/MEL HD7 .... 211 K5
Scout Rd HBR HX7 .... 144 A6
Scowcroft La ROY/SHW OL2 .... 229 J8
Scrapers La TOD OL14 .... 141 K6
Scriftain La WBY LS22 .... 30 A5
Seacroft Av SCFT LS14 .... 111 K1
Seacroft Cl SCFT LS14 .... 111 K1
Seacroft Crs SCFT LS14 .... 111 K1
Seaforth Av OSM LS9 .... 110 C3
Seaforth Gv OSM LS9 .... 110 C3
Seaforth Mt OSM LS9 .... 110 C3
Seaforth Pl OSM LS9 .... 110 C3
Seaforth Rd OSM LS9 .... 110 C3
Seaforth Ter OSM LS9 .... 110 C3
Seagrave Rd HUDS HD4 .... 213 L3
Seaton St BFDE BD3 .... 5 L5
Seckar La HOR/CROF WF4 .... 220 C6
Secker St WKFDW/WTN WF2 .... 12 D8
Second Av AL/HA/HU LS17 .... 68 A1
  BFDE BD3 .... 105 L5
  HEM/SK/SE WF9 .... 223 J2
  HEM/SK/SE WF9 .... 225 J6
  HEM/SK/SE WF9 .... 246 B5
  HIPP HX3 .... 168 D2
  HOR/CROF WF4 .... 197 H5
  HUDE HD5 .... 193 H7
  KGHY BD21 .... 2 E7
  LVSG WF15 .... 171 K2
  RTHW LS26 .... 133 H7
  WBY LS22 .... 48 B1
  WKFDE WF1 .... 176 D4
  WOR/ARM LS12 .... 109 G7
  YEA LS19 .... 84 E1
Second St LM/WK BD12 .... 127 G8
Sedan St HFAX HX1 .... 11 G7
Sedbergh Cl MSTN/BAR LS15 .... 110 F7
Sedbergh Dr ILK LS29 .... 38 E3
Sedbergh Pk ILK LS29 .... 38 E3
Sedburgh Rd HIPP HX3 .... 11 J9
Sedge Gv HWTH BD22 .... 78 E6
Sedge Ri TAD LS24 .... 71 J4
Sedgewick Cl BTLY WF17 .... 151 G5
Sedgley Av MILN OL16 .... 228 D2
Sedgwick Cl GIR BD8 .... 4 C4
Seed Hill Ter LUD/ILL HX2 .... 123 L8
Seed St LM/WK BD12 .... 126 F8
Sefton Av BEE/HOL LS11 .... 131 J5
  BRIG HD6 .... 170 B1
Sefton Crs BRIG HD6 .... 170 B1
Sefton Dr BRIG HD6 .... 170 B1
  ILK LS29 .... 38 D3
Sefton Gv ECHL BD2 .... 105 K3
Sefton La HOLM/MEL HD7 .... 234 F4
Sefton Pl KGHY BD21 .... 3 G3
Sefton Ri EARL WF12 .... 195 M2
Sefton St BEE/HOL LS11 .... 131 K3
  COL BB8 .... 74 B1
  HFAX HX1 .... 10 D4
  KGHY BD21 .... 3 G2
  ROCH OL11 .... 228 A1
Sefton Ter BEE/HOL LS11 .... 131 J3
  HFAX HX1 .... 10 D4
Selborne Gv HTON BD9 .... 104 D3
  KGHY BD21 .... 2 D1
Selborne Mt HTON BD9 .... 104 E4
Selborne Ter HTON BD9 .... 104 D4
  SHPY BD18 .... 82 D8
Selborne Vis CLAY BD14 .... 125 L3
Selbourne Av EARL WF12 .... 173 L6
Selbourne Cl DOD/DAR S75 .... 260 A3
Selbourne Dr EARL WF12 .... 195 L1
Selbourne Rd EARL WF12 .... 195 L1
Selby LUD/ILL HX2 .... 123 M7
Selby Av OSM LS9 .... 111 G6
Selby Cl MILN OL16 .... 207 G8
Selby Rd BSLYN/ROY S71 .... 243 H7
  GFTH/SHER LS25 .... 134 F1
  MSTN/BAR LS15 .... 111 G6
  SCFT LS14 .... 110 F5
Selby St MILN OL16 .... 206 D6
  WKFDE WF1 .... 176 E7
Seldon St WBOW BD5 .... 126 D3
Selene Cl CLECK BD19 .... 150 E4
Sellars Fold GTHN BD7 .... 126 C2
Sellerdale Av LM/WK BD12 .... 148 F5
Sellerdale Dr LM/WK BD12 .... 148 F4
Sellerdale Ri LM/WK BD12 .... 148 F4
Sellerdale Wy LM/WK BD12 .... 148 F5
Selso Rd EARL WF12 .... 174 B5
Seminary St LDSU 6 D1
Semon Av ECHL BD2 .... 105 H1
Senior St DEWS WF13 .... 173 K7
  HUDE HD5 .... 15 M8
Senior Wy WBOW BD5 .... 4 D8
Sennen Cft BSLYN/ROY S71 .... 261 K3
Sentry HOLM/MEL HD7 .... 236 B1
Sergeantson St HUD HD1 .... 14 F7
Serpentine Rd CLECK BD19 .... 149 M6
Servia Dr CHAL LS7 .... 6 F3
Servia Gdns CHAL LS7 .... 7 G3
Servia HI CHAL LS7 .... 6 F3
Servia Rd HDGY LS6 .... 6 F3
Service Rd OSM LS9 .... 132 C5
Sessions House Yd PONT WF8 .... 180 E5
Seth Ter BSLY S70 .... 261 J6
Sevenoaks Md WIL/AL BD15 .... 103 K5
Seventh Av LVSG WF15 .... 171 K1
  RTHW LS26 .... 133 J8
Severn Dr GFTH/SHER LS25 .... 135 K1
  MILN OL16 .... 207 J8
Severn Rd ECHL BD2 .... 105 J5
  MID LS10 .... 132 B3
Sewage Works Rd OSM LS9 .... 132 C3
Sewell Rd BFDE BD3 .... 5 M7
Sewerbridge La FEA/AMT WF7 .... 179 M1
Seymour Gv MILN OL16 .... 228 D3
Seymour St BFDE BD3 .... 5 J7
  WKFDW/WTN WF2 .... 12 E7
Seymour Wk HOLM/MEL HD7 .... 235 G4

Shackleton St *TOD* OL14 .... 140 E5
Shackleton Vw *STKB/PEN* S36 ... 270 F4
Shade St *TOD* OL14 .... 163 J3
Shadwell La *AL/HA/HU* LS17 ...... 87 M4
Shadwell Park Av
AL/HA/HU LS17 .... 88 E1
Shadwell Park Cl
AL/HA/HU LS17 .... 88 E1 🔟
Shadwell Park Ct
AL/HA/HU LS17 .... 88 E2
Shadwell Park Dr
AL/HA/HU LS17 .... 88 E2
Shadwell Park Gdns
AL/HA/HU LS17 .... 88 E1
Shadwell Park Gv
AL/HA/HU LS17 .... 88 E2
Shadwell Wk *AL/HA/HU* LS17 ...... 88 A3
Shady La *AIRE* BD20 .... 34 B3
Shaftesbury Av *BRIG* HD6 .... 170 D7
  GLE DN14 .... 183 H1
  HTON BD9 .... 103 M4
  LIT OL15 .... 207 J4
  RHAY LS8 .... 88 C5
  SHPY BD18 .... 82 E7
Shaftesbury Dr *WHIT* OL12 ...... 184 F8
Shaftesbury Rd *RHAY* LS8 .... 88 C4
Shaftesbury St *BSLY* S70 .... 261 M6
Shafton Hall Dr *CUD/GR* S72 ... 244 D3
Shafton La *BEE/HOL* LS11 .... 8 A7
Shafton Pl *BEE/HOL* LS11 .... 8 A7
Shafton St *BEE/HOL* LS11 .... 8 A7
Shafton Vw *BEE/HOL* LS11 .... 8 B6
Shakespeare Ap *OSM* LS9 .... 110 B5
Shakespeare Av
  AWLS/ASK DN6 .... 227 L4
  NORM WF6 .... 178 C7 🔟
  OSM LS9 .... 110 B5
  TOD OL14 .... 141 M8
Shakespeare Cl *LIT* OL15 .... 185 L5 🔟
  OSM LS9 .... 110 B5 🔟
Shakespeare Crs *CAS* WF10 ...... 180 F1
Shakespeare Gdns *OSM* LS9 ..... 110 B5 🔟
Shakespeare Lawn *OSM* LS9 .... 110 B5
Shakespeare Rd *GSLY* LS20 .... 62 A6
Shakespeare St *HFAX* HX1 .... 11 H7 🔟
  OSM LS9 .... 110 B4
Shalimar St *HFAX* HX1 .... 10 A5
Shambles *BSLY* S70 .... 261 C5
The Shambles *WBY* LS22 .... 48 A1 🔟
Shann Av *KGHY* BD21 .... 2 B3
Shann Crs *KGHY* BD21 .... 2 B3
Shann La *KGHY* BD21 .... 2 B3
Shannon Cl *BRIG* HD6 .... 170 A7
  ILK LS29 .... 38 B3
Shannon Dr *HUDW* HD3 .... 190 F5
Shannon Rd *BRIG* HD6 .... 170 A7
  OSM LS9 .... 7 M9
Shannon St *OSM* LS9 .... 7 L9
Shann St *SHPY* BD18 .... 104 F2
Shapla Cl *HWTH* BD22 .... 2 C6
Share Hl *HOLM/MEL* HD7 .... 212 E2
Sharp Av *WBSY* BD6 .... 126 E6
Sharpe St *HECK* WF16 .... 172 F3
  WBOW BD5 .... 4 E7
Sharphaw Av *SKP/WHF* BD23 ..... 16 C4
Sharp House Rd *MID* LS10 .... 154 A2
Sharp La *EARD/LOFT* WF3 .... 154 B2
  HUDS HD4 .... 215 H5
Sharp Rw *PDSY/CALV* LS28 .... 107 H8
Sharp Royd *HUDE* HD5 .... 215 J2
Sharp St *DEWS* WF13 .... 173 M5 🔟
  WBSY BD6 .... 126 E5 🔟
Shaw Av *NORM* WF6 .... 178 E4
Shaw Barn Cft *WBY* LS22 .... 47 L1
Shaw Barn La *WBY* LS22 .... 47 L1
Shaw Booth La *LUD/ILL* HX2 ..... 145 J1
Shaw Cl *GFTH/SHER* LS25 .... 135 J1
  GTL/HWG HX4 .... 190 E6
  NORM WF6 .... 178 E4
Shawfield Av *HOLM/MEL* HD7 ... 253 M2
Shawfield Rd *BSLYN/ROY* S71 ... 243 C8
Shaw Fields La *HOLM/MEL* HD7 . 211 L6
Shaw Fold *WKFDW/WTN* WF2 .... 199 C5
Shaw Ga *HOLM/MEL* HD7 .... 212 A8
Shaw Hl *HFAX* HX1 .... 168 E1 🔟
Shaw Hill La *HIPP* HX3 .... 11 J9
Shaw La *BSLY* S70 .... 260 E5
  BSLYN/ROY S71 .... 244 A5
  DOD/DAR S75 .... 242 E5
  ELL HX5 .... 169 L7
  GSLY LS20 .... 62 B5
  GTL/HWG HX4 .... 190 D2
  HDGY LS6 .... 86 F8
  HIPP HX3 .... 125 H8
  HIPP HX3 .... 168 F2
  HOLM/MEL HD7 .... 190 D7
  HOLM/MEL HD7 .... 211 J6
  HOLM/MEL HD7 .... 253 M2
  HUDS HD4 .... 213 K2
  HUDW HD3 .... 190 E6
  KGHY BD21 .... 79 M3
  MILN OL16 .... 207 H5
  PBR HG3 .... 25 K3
  PBR HG3 .... 28 D2
  RPDN/SBR HX6 .... 167 L5
  RPDN/SBR HX6 .... 188 E4
  TOD OL14 .... 140 D3
Shaw Lane Gdns *GSLY* LS20 .... 62 B5
Shaw Leys *YEA* LS19 .... 62 C6
Shaw Rd *NORM* WF6 .... 178 E4 🔟
  MILN OL16 .... 228 D5
  MILN OL16 .... 229 K3
Shaw Royd *YEA* LS19 .... 62 C6
Shaws La *MSTN/BAR* LS15 .... 90 B8
  RPDN/SBR HX6 .... 166 C5
Shaw St *BSLY* S70 .... 149 K7 🔟
  CLECK BD19 .... 150 D6
  GTL/HWG HX4 .... 190 E2
  LM/WK BD12 .... 126 D8 🔟
  MIRF WF14 .... 194 C1 🔟
  WHIT OL12 .... 206 D4 🔟
Shaw Wood Rd *TOD* OL14 .... 142 B8
Shay Cl *HTON* BD9 .... 104 B2
Shay Ct *HOR/CROF* WF4 .... 200 B5 🔟
Shay Crs *HTON* BD9 .... 104 A2
Shay Dr *HTON* BD9 .... 104 A2
Shayfield La *EARD/LOFT* WF3 ... 154 F3 🔟
Shay Fold *HTON* BD9 .... 104 A2

Shay Gap Rd *HWTH* BD22 .... 56 E7 🔟
Shay Gra *HTON* BD9 .... 104 A1
Shay Gv *HTON* BD9 .... 104 B2
Shay La *HIPP* HX3 .... 146 C2
  HOLM/MEL HD7 .... 253 C3
  HOR/CROF WF4 .... 200 B5 🔟
  HTON BD9 .... 104 A1
  LUD/ILL HX2 .... 146 C2
  WIL/AL BD15 .... 103 G2
Shay St *HDGY* LS6 .... 6 E1
  LDSU LS2 .... 6 E1
Shay Syke *HFAX* HX1 .... 11 J8
Sheaf Ct *BSLY* S70 .... 261 M7
Sheaf St *MID* LS10 .... 9 J3
Shearbridge Rd *GTHN* BD7 .... 4 A7
Shearbridge Ter *GTHN* BD7 .... 4 B9
Sheardale *HOLM/MEL* HD7 .... 236 A2
Shearing Cross Gdns *HUD* HD1 ... 15 G3
Shed St *KGHY* BD21 .... 3 G4
Sheep Hill La *CUL/QBY* BD13 ... 125 K4
Sheepridge Gv *HUDN* HD2 .... 192 E5
Sheepridge Rd *HUDN* HD2 .... 192 E5
Sheepscar Gv *CHAL* LS7 .... 7 J1
Sheepscar St North *CHAL* LS7 .... 7 J2
Sheepscar St South *CHAL* LS7 .... 7 K5
Sheepscar Wy *CHAL* LS7 .... 7 J2
Sheep St *SKP/WHF* BD23 .... 16 B3
Sheepwalk La *SKP/WHF* WF10 .. 158 F8
  HEM/SK/SE WF9 .... 226 A6
  PONT WF8 .... 226 A6
Sheerien Cl *BSLYN/ROY* S71 ..... 243 G6
Sheffield Rd *BSLY* S70 .... 261 H6
  HOLM/MEL HD7 .... 255 H1
  STKB/PEN S36 .... 271 H4
Sheldon Rdg *BOW* BD4 .... 127 K7
Sheldrake Av *GIR* BD8 .... 103 L7
Sheldrake Rd *CAS* WF10 .... 157 M8
Shelf Hall La *HIPP* HX3 .... 147 K1
Shelfield La *BRFD/BLYE* BD10 .... 74 A7
Shelf Moor *HIPP* HX3 .... 125 L7
Shelf Moor Rd *HIPP* HX3 .... 125 L7
Shelf Rd *HBR* HX7 .... 143 H3
Shelldrake Dr *MID* LS10 .... 153 M1
Shelley Av *HECK* WF16 .... 173 G4 🔟
  STKB/PEN S36 .... 270 F2
Shelley Cl *RTHW* LS26 .... 155 L3
  STKB/PEN S36 .... 270 F2
Shelley Crs *RTHW* LS26 .... 155 L3
Shelley Dr *BSLYN/ROY* S71 .... 261 K3
  KNOT WF11 .... 181 K2
Shelley Gv *GIR* BD8 .... 104 A6 🔟
Shelley La *KBTN* HD8 .... 238 C1
Shelley Woodhouse La
  KBTN HD8 .... 239 C6
Shell La *PDSY/CALV* LS28 .... 106 C2
Shepcote Cl *BHP/TINH* LS16 ...... 86 B3
Shepcote Crs *BHP/TINH* LS16 .... 86 B3
Shepherds Gv *HUDN* HD2 .... 193 G3 🔟
  RHAY LS8 .... 7 M1
Shepherd's La *CHAL* LS7 .... 110 A2
  RHAY LS8 .... 7 M1
Shepherd's Pl *RHAY* LS8 .... 110 B2 🔟
Shepherds Thorn La
  HUDN HD2 .... 170 E8
Shepley Mt *MIRF* WF14 .... 172 D7 🔟
Shepley Rd *HUDS* HD4 .... 237 L4
Shepley St *WKFDE* WF1 .... 13 J1
Shepstye Rd *HOR/CROF* WF4 .... 197 J6
Sherborne Dr *HWTH* BD22 .... 79 C1
Sherborne Rd *GTHN* BD7 .... 4 B8
  IDLE BD10 .... 83 K5 🔟
Sherbrooke Av
  MSTN/BAR LS15 .... 111 H7
Sherburn Ap *SCFT* LS14 .... 89 L8
Sherburn Av *AWLS/ASK* DN6 ... 249 L4
  BIRK/DRI BD11 .... 128 D8
Sherburn Gv *BIRK/DRI* BD11 .... 128 D8
Sherburn Pl *SCFT* LS14 .... 89 L8
Sherburn Rd *BRIG* HD6 .... 169 M6
  BSLYN/ROY S71 .... 243 G7
  SCFT LS14 .... 89 L8
Sherburn Rd North *SCFT* LS14 ... 89 K6
Sheridan Cl *PDSY/CALV* LS28 ... 107 H8
Sheridan Ct *BSLYN/ROY* S71 .... 261 K3 🔟
  PDSY/CALV LS28 .... 107 H8 🔟
Sheridan Rd *COL* BB8 .... 52 F8
Sheridan St *BOW* BD4 .... 127 J2
  WKFDE WF1 .... 176 F1
Sheridan Wy *PDSY/CALV* LS28 . 107 G8
Sheriff La *BGLY* BD16 .... 81 L2
Sheriff St *MILN* OL16 .... 229 J1
  WHIT OL12 .... 206 A5
Sherwell Gv *WIL/AL* BD15 .... 103 L5 🔟
Sherwell Ri *WIL/AL* BD15 .... 103 L5
Sherwood Av *CLECK* BD19 .... 150 D6
  HUDN HD2 .... 193 H1
Sherwood Cl *AWLS/ASK* DN6 ... 227 L5 🔟
  BGLY BD16 .... 81 L1
  CLECK BD19 .... 150 D6 🔟
  DEWS WF13 .... 173 H3 🔟
Sherwood Gn *EARD/LOFT* WF3 . 154 D2
  HUDS HD4 .... 213 L8
  WKFDW/WTN WF2 .... 220 B1
Sherwood Gv *SHPY* BD18 .... 82 A6 🔟
  WKFDW/WTN WF2 .... 197 M2
Sherwood Pl *ECHL* BD2 .... 105 K4 🔟
Sherwood Rd *BRIG* HD6 .... 170 E4
Sherwood St *BSLYN/ROY* S71 ... 261 H5 🔟
Sherwood Wy *CUD/GR* S72 ...... 244 D5
  ROY/SHW OL2 .... 229 C6
Shetcliffe La *BOW* BD4 .... 127 M5
Shetcliffe Rd *BOW* BD4 .... 127 M5
Shetland Cl *ECHL* BD2 .... 105 H2 🔟
Shibden Dr *BTLY* WF17 .... 151 L8
Shibden Garth *HIPP* HX3 .... 147 J6
Shibden Grange Dr *HIPP* HX3 ... 147 H5
Shibden Hall Cft *HIPP* HX3 .... 147 H6
Shibden Hall Rd *HIPP* HX3 .... 147 H6
Shibden Head La
  CUL/QBY BD13 .... 124 E7
Shibden Vw *CUL/QBY* BD13 ... 124 F7 🔟
Shield Cl *MSTN/BAR* LS15 .... 112 A3
Shill Bank Av *MIRF* WF14 .... 172 E8
Shill Bank La *MIRF* WF14 .... 172 E8
Shillbank Vw *MIRF* WF14 .... 172 E8

Shilling St *WKFDE* WF1 .... 176 F7
Shipley Airedale Rd *BFDE* BD3 ..... 5 G3
Shipley Fields Rd *SHPY* BD18 .... 104 D1
Ship St *BRIG* HD6 .... 170 D4 🔟
Shipton Ms *MOR* LS27 .... 152 D3 🔟
Shire Cl *WBSY* BD6 .... 126 B7
Shire Oak Rd *HDGY* LS6 .... 109 G1
Shire Oak St *HDGY* LS6 .... 108 F1
Shires Gv *EARD/LOFT* WF3 .... 177 H1
Shires Hl *HUD* HD1 .... 14 B9
Shirland Av *BSLYN/ROY* S71 ..... 243 J8
Shirley Av *BTLY* WF17 .... 150 F4
  CLECK BD19 .... 150 D6
  LM/WK BD12 .... 148 D5
Shirley Crs *LM/WK* BD12 .... 148 D5
Shirley Dr *BRAM* LS13 .... 107 L2 🔟
Shirley Gv *CLECK* BD19 .... 150 D6
  HIPP HX3 .... 148 C7
Shirley Mt *CLECK* BD19 .... 150 D6
Shirley Pde *CLECK* BD19 .... 150 D6
Shirley Pl *CLECK* BD19 .... 150 C6
  LM/WK BD12 .... 148 D5
Shirley Rd *BOW* BD4 .... 127 M5
  CLECK BD19 .... 150 D6
  GTHN BD7 .... 104 D8 🔟
Shirley St *HWTH* BD22 .... 78 D7
  SHPY BD18 .... 82 B6 🔟
Shirley Ter *CLECK* BD19 .... 150 D6 🔟
Shirley Wk *CLECK* BD19 .... 150 D6
Shoebridge Av *AIRE* BD20 .... 35 H8 🔟
Shoebroad La *TOD* OL14 .... 163 K2
Shoe Market *PONT* WF8 .... 180 F6 🔟
Sholebroke Av *CHAL* LS7 .... 109 M2
Sholebroke Mt *CHAL* LS7 .... 109 M2 🔟
Sholebroke Pl *CHAL* LS7 .... 109 M2 🔟
Sholebroke Ter *CHAL* LS7 .... 109 M1 🔟
Sholebroke Vw *CHAL* LS7 .... 109 M2 🔟
Shoolaboards La *PONT* WF8 ..... 181 H6 🔟
Shop La *EARD/LOFT* WF3 .... 154 D6
  HUDE HD5 .... 193 L5
  HWTH BD22 .... 54 D1
Shore Av *ROY/SHW* OL2 .... 229 J4
Shore End La *HBR* HX7 .... 122 C7
Shorefield Cl *MILN* OL16 .... 207 H7 🔟
Shore Fold *LIT* OL15 .... 185 H8
Shore Gn *TOD* OL14 .... 140 E4
Shore Hall La *HBR* HX7 .... 120 A6
Shoreham Rd *WOR/ARM* LS12 . 108 E8 🔟
Shore Hl *LIT* OL15 .... 185 L8 🔟
Shore Lea *LIT* OL15 .... 185 H8
Shore Mt *LIT* OL15 .... 185 H8
Shore New Rd *TOD* OL14 .... 140 D4
Shore Rd *LIT* OL15 .... 185 H7
Shore St *MILN* OL16 .... 207 H8
Shortbank Cl *SKP/WHF* BD23 .... 16 C2
Shortbank Rd *SKP/WHF* BD23 ... 16 C2
Short Cl *LM/WK* BD12 .... 148 D1
Shortfield Ct *BSLYN/ROY* S71 ... 243 G6
Short La *CHAL* LS7 .... 87 L7 🔟
Short St *EARL* WF12 .... 174 C7
  FEA/AMT WF7 .... 201 L1 🔟
Shortway *CUL/QBY* BD13 .... 103 J8 🔟
  PDSY/CALV LS28 .... 106 C5 🔟
Showfield Cl *GFTH/SHER* LS25 . 116 A7
Shrewsbury Cl *STKB/PEN* S36 .. 270 F3
Shrewsbury Rd
  STKB/PEN S36 .... 270 F3
Shroggs Head Cl
  WMB/DAR S73 .... 263 K8 🔟
Shroggs Rd *HFAX* HX1 .... 10 D3
Shroggs St *HFAX* HX1 .... 10 D4
Shroggs Vue Ter *HFAX* HX1 .... 10 D4
Shuttleworth La *GIR* BD8 .... 103 M6
  GIR BD8 .... 104 A6 🔟
Shuttocks Cl *GFTH/SHER* LS25 . 135 J3
Shuttocks Fold
  GFTH/SHER LS25 .... 135 K3
Shutts La *HIPP* HX3 .... 148 A4
The Shutt *HOR/CROF* WF4 .... 197 K6
Sicklehome Ct *HUDN* HD2 .... 193 G1 🔟
Sickle St *CLECK* BD19 .... 150 A6
Sicklinghall Rd *WBY* LS22 .... 47 H1
Sidcop Rd *CUD/GR* S72 .... 244 D6
Siddal Gv *HIPP* HX3 .... 168 F2
Siddal La *HIPP* HX3 .... 169 G2
Siddall St *BEE/HOL* LS11 .... 8 B9
  ROY/SHW OL2 .... 229 K7 🔟
Siddal New Rd *HIPP* HX3 .... 168 F1
Siddal St *HIPP* HX3 .... 169 G3 🔟
Siddal Top La *HIPP* HX3 .... 169 G2
Siddon Dr *HUDE* HD5 .... 215 J3
Side Copse *OT* LS21 .... 41 K6
Side La *HUDW* HD3 .... 191 H8
Sides Rd *PONT* WF8 .... 180 F8
Sidgwick Ct *SKP/WHF* BD23 ...... 16 C5 🔟
The Sidings *GSLY* LS20 .... 61 M5
  SHPY BD18 .... 82 E6 🔟
Sidney St *LDS* LS1 .... 7 H9
Siegen Cl *MOR* LS27 .... 152 C2 🔟
Siena Cl *WMB/DAR* S73 .... 263 G8
Siggett La *TOD* OL14 .... 141 H8
Sigott St *HUDW* HD3 .... 191 H8
Sike Cl *DOD/DAR* S75 .... 241 M5 🔟
Sike La *HOLM/MEL* HD7 .... 254 F1 🔟
  STKB/PEN S36 .... 270 C5
  WKFDW/WTN WF2 .... 221 K1
Sikes Cl *HUDE* HD5 .... 215 H2 🔟
Silcoates Av
  WKFDW/WTN WF2 .... 176 A5 🔟
Silcoates Ct *WKFDW/WTN* WF2 . 176 A6
Silcoates Dr
  WKFDW/WTN WF2 .... 176 A5 🔟
Silcoates La *WKFDW/WTN* WF2 . 175 M5
Silcoates St *WKFDW/WTN* WF2 . 176 B6
Silk Mill Ap *BHP/TINH* LS16 ...... 86 A4
Silk Mill Av *BHP/TINH* LS16 ...... 85 M3
Silk Mill Bank *BHP/TINH* LS16 .. 85 M3
Silk Mill Cl *BHP/TINH* LS16 .... 85 M3
Silk Mill Dr *BHP/TINH* LS16 ...... 85 M4
Silk Mill Gdns *BHP/TINH* LS16 .. 85 M4
Silk Mill Gn *BHP/TINH* LS16 ...... 85 M4
Silk Mill Ms *BHP/TINH* LS16 ..... 86 A4
Silk Mill Rd *BHP/TINH* LS16 ...... 85 M4
Silk Mill Wy *BHP/TINH* LS16 ..... 86 A4
Silkstone Cl *GFTH/SHER* LS25 .. 113 K5

Silkstone Ct *MSTN/BAR* LS15 ... 111 L5
Silkstone Crs *NORM* WF6 .... 178 B2 🔟
  WKFDW/WTN WF2 .... 198 B8
Silkstone La *DOD/DAR* S75 ...... 259 H4
Silkstone Wy *MSTN/BAR* LS15 . 111 L5
Silk St *HTON* BD9 .... 104 C4
Silsden Br *AIRE* BD20 .... 35 M7
Silsden Rd *AIRE* BD20 .... 34 F1
  AIRE BD20 .... 58 B2
  ILK LS29 .... 18 D7
Silson La *BAIL* BD17 .... 83 G2
Silver Birch Av *LM/WK* BD12 .... 148 E5
Silver Birch Cl *LM/WK* BD12 ..... 148 E4
Silver Birch Dr *LM/WK* BD12 .... 148 E4
Silver Birch Gv *LM/WK* BD12 ... 148 F4 🔟
  CLECK BD19 .... 150 D6
  LM/WK BD12 .... 148 D5
Silverdale Av *AIRE* BD20 .... 58 A5
  AL/HA/HU LS17 .... 88 C1
  GSLY LS20 .... 62 A6
Silverdale Dr *BSLYN/ROY* S71 .. 261 M1
  GSLY LS20 .... 62 A7
Silverdale Gra *GSLY* LS20 .... 62 A6
Silverdale Gv *GSLY* LS20 .... 61 M6
Silverdale Mt *GSLY* LS20 .... 62 A7
Silverdale Rd *GSLY* LS20 .... 61 M7
  WBOW BD5 .... 127 G4
Silver Hl *MILN* OL16 .... 207 H8 🔟
Silverhill Dr *BFDE* BD3 .... 105 M6
Silverhill Rd *BFDE* BD3 .... 105 L5
Silver La *YEA* LS19 .... 62 D7
Silver Mill Hl *OT* LS21 .... 41 K8
Silver Royd Av *WOR/ARM* LS12 108 B8
Silver Royd Cl *WOR/ARM* LS12 . 108 B8
Silver Royd Garth
  WOR/ARM LS12 .... 108 B8
Silver Royd Gv *WOR/ARM* LS12 108 B8
Silver Royd Hl *WOR/ARM* LS12 . 108 B8
Silver Royd Pl *WOR/ARM* LS12 . 108 B8
Silver Royd Rd *WOR/ARM* LS12 108 B8
Silver Royd St *WOR/ARM* LS12 . 108 B8
Silver Royd Ter *WOR/ARM* LS12 108 B8
Silver St *BEE/HOL* LS11 .... 8 D5
  BSLY S70 .... 261 G6
  DOD/DAR S75 .... 260 B8
  GIR BD8 .... 104 C5 🔟
  HFAX HX1 .... 11 G6
  HUD HD1 .... 15 K8
  KNOT WF11 .... 159 J3
  TOD OL14 .... 163 J7
  WKFDE WF1 .... 12 E2
  WHIT OL12 .... 176 D3
Silver St East *HUD* HD1 .... 15 J8
Silver St West *HUD* HD1 .... 15 J8
Silverwood Av *LUD/ILL* HX2 ..... 145 L3
Silwood Dr *ECHL* BD2 .... 105 L3
Simbach Cl *SKP/WHF* BD23 .... 16 D3
Simeon St *TOD* OL14 .... 163 J6 🔟
Simes St *BFD* BD1 .... 4 E5
Simm Carr La *HIPP* HX3 .... 146 F2
Simmonds La *HFAX* HX1 .... 11 J8
Simmons Wy *RHAY* LS8 .... 110 D2
Simms Dene *WIL/AL* BD15 .... 103 J2
Simon Cl *BOW* BD4 .... 128 B4 🔟
Simon Green Rd
  HOLM/MEL HD7 .... 212 D3
Simon St *MILN* OL16 .... 207 H8
  WOR/ARM LS12 .... 108 F7
Simpson Gv *IDLE* BD10 .... 83 L5 🔟
  WOR/ARM LS12 .... 108 F7
Simpson Rd *HBR* HX7 .... 143 M5
  HEM/SK/SE WF9 .... 247 K2 🔟
Simpsons La *KNOT* WF11 .... 181 M3
Simpson St *EARD/LOFT* WF3 .... 154 D6
  HIPP HX3 .... 146 D4 🔟
Sim Royd La *STKB/PEN* S36 ...... 257 M7
Sinclair Garth
  WKFDW/WTN WF2 .... 199 C6
Sinclair Rd *ECHL* BD2 .... 105 H1 🔟
Sinden Ms *IDLE* BD10 .... 83 K4 🔟
Singleton St *BFD* BD1 .... 4 F3
Sion Hl *HIPP* HX3 .... 169 G3 🔟
Sir George Martin Dr
  BHP/TINH LS16 .... 86 F1
Sir Isaac Holden Pl
  GTHN BD7 .... 104 D7 🔟
Sir John's La *GFTH/SHER* LS25 . 115 M6
Sir Karl Cohen Sq
  WOR/ARM LS12 .... 108 D7
Sir Wilfred Pl *IDLE* BD10 .... 83 K6 🔟
Siskin Ct *MOR* LS27 .... 152 D3 🔟
Sisley La *TOD* OL14 .... 164 C2
Sissons Av *MID* LS10 .... 153 K2
Sissons Crs *MID* LS10 .... 153 K3
Sissons Dr *MID* LS10 .... 153 K3
Sissons Gn *MID* LS10 .... 153 K2 🔟
Sissons Gv *MID* LS10 .... 153 K2
Sissons La *MID* LS10 .... 153 J3
Sissons Mt *MID* LS10 .... 153 J3
Sissons Pl *MID* LS10 .... 153 K2
Sissons Rd *MID* LS10 .... 153 K2 🔟
Sissons Rw *MID* LS10 .... 153 K2 🔟
Sissons St *MID* LS10 .... 153 K2
Sissons Ter *MID* LS10 .... 153 J3
Sissons Vw *MID* LS10 .... 153 J3
Sitka Cl *BSLYN/ROY* S71 .... 243 K4
Siward St *HEM/SK/SE* WF9 .... 223 J4
Sixroad La *AWLS/ASK* DN6 ...... 249 J1
Sixth Av *BFDE* BD3 .... 105 L5
  LVSG WF15 .... 171 K1
  RTHW LS26 .... 133 J7
Sizers Ct *YEA* LS19 .... 84 C1
Skelbrooke Dr *PONT* WF8 .... 202 F7 🔟
Skelda Ri *ILK* LS29 .... 38 D3
Skelf St *TAD* LS24 .... 95 C5
Skellow Hall Gdns
  AWLS/ASK DN6 .... 249 H5
Skellow Rd *AWLS/ASK* DN6 ..... 249 L6
Skelton Av *DOD/DAR* S75 .... 242 D5
  OSM LS9 .... 110 D6
Skelton Crs *HUDS* HD4 .... 213 K3
  OSM LS9 .... 110 D6 🔟
Skelton Grange Rd *MID* LS10 ... 132 D4
Skelton Mt *OSM* LS9 .... 110 D6
Skelton Pl *OSM* LS9 .... 110 D6
Skelton Rd *OSM* LS9 .... 110 D6
Skeltons La *SCFT* LS14 .... 89 K5
Skelton St *COL* BB8 .... 74 A1

  OSM LS9 .... 110 D6 🔟
Skelton Ter *OSM* LS9 .... 110 D6
Skelton Wk *IDLE* BD10 .... 83 M7 🔟
Skelwith Ap *SCFT* LS14 .... 111 J4
Skibeden Ct *SKP/WHF* BD23 ..... 16 D1
Skinner La *GIR* BD8 .... 104 E4
  LDSU LS2 .... 7 K6
  PONT WF8 .... 180 F5 🔟
Skinner St *LDS* LS1 .... 6 C9
Skinpit La *STKB/PEN* S36 .... 258 C9
Skipton Av *HUDN* HD2 .... 192 D4
Skipton New Rd *COL* BB8 .... 52 A5
Skipton Old Rd *COL* BB8 .... 52 F6
  COL BB8 .... 52 F6
Skipton Ri *GFTH/SHER* LS25 .... 113 K7
Skipton Rd *AIRE* BD20 .... 16 C7
  AIRE BD20 .... 34 B3
  AIRE BD20 .... 34 E4
  AIRE BD20 .... 80 B6
  AIRE BD20 .... 57 H3
  COL BB8 .... 52 A8
  COL BB8 .... 74 D2
  ILK LS29 .... 18 F5
  ILK LS29 .... 19 G6 🔟
  ILK LS29 .... 38 A2
  KGHY BD21 .... 3 G1
  SKP/WHF BD23 .... 16 C7
Skipton St *BTLY* WF17 .... 173 L4
Skircoat Gn *HIPP* HX3 .... 168 E4
Skircoat Green Rd *HIPP* HX3 ... 168 E3 🔟
Skircoat Moor Cl *LUD/ILL* HX2 . 168 C2 🔟
Skircoat Moor Rd *LUD/ILL* HX2 . 168 C2
Skircoat Rd *HFAX* HX1 .... 11 H9
Skirrow St *BGLY* BD16 .... 81 K8 🔟
Skye Rd *HTON* BD9 .... 104 C3 🔟
Skye Vw *RTHW* LS26 .... 155 H1
Slack Bottom Rd *WBSY* BD6 .... 126 C6
Slackcote La *UPML* OL3 .... 230 E7
Slack Ga *WHIT* OL12 .... 184 A6
Slack Gate La *UPML* OL3 .... 230 F6
Slack House La *HBR* HX7 .... 121 K8
Slack La *CUD/GR* S72 .... 244 D1
  GTL/HWG HX4 .... 189 J3
  HBR HX7 .... 144 D2
  HOLM/MEL HD7 .... 254 D2
  HOR/CROF WF4 .... 200 B6
  HUDW HD3 .... 190 C6
  HWTH BD22 .... 77 J7
  RPDN/SBR HX6 .... 166 B5
  RPDN/SBR HX6 .... 188 B1
  UPML OL3 .... 230 F8
  WKFDW/WTN WF2 .... 220 D2
Slacks La *HOLM/MEL* HD7 .... 211 J6
  HOLM/MEL HD7 .... 212 C5
Slack St *MILN* OL16 .... 206 B7 🔟
Slack Top La *HOLM/MEL* HD7 .. 255 L8
Sladdin Rw *CUL/QBY* BD13 .... 124 E6 🔟
Slade Cl *BSPA/BRAM* LS23 .... 48 F7
Slade La *AIRE* BD20 .... 58 A4
  BRIG HD6 .... 170 B8
Sladen St *KGHY* BD21 .... 2 D5
  WHIT OL12 .... 206 B5
Slades La *HOLM/MEL* HD7 .... 235 G2
Slades Rd *HOLM/MEL* HD7 .... 212 D2
Slade Wk *BTLY* WF17 .... 151 H5
Slaidburn Cl *MILN* OL16 .... 229 H1 🔟
Slaithwaite Av *EARL* WF12 .... 195 L2
Slaithwaite Cl *EARL* WF12 .... 195 L2
Slaithwaite Ga *HOLM/MEL* HD7 168 C2
Slaithwaite Rd *EARL* WF12 .... 195 M2
  HEM/SK/SE WF9 .... 247 K2
Slant Ga *HOLM/MEL* HD7 .... 213 G4
  KBTN HD8 .... 216 A7
  STKB/PEN S36 .... 269 J2
Slant La *TOD* OL14 .... 141 M8
Slater Av *HBR* HX7 .... 143 J2
Slater Ing La *HBR* HX7 .... 142 E1
Slaters Rd *PDSY/CALV* LS28 .... 107 G5
Slates La *ILK* LS29 .... 20 C7
Slaymaker La *HWTH* BD22 .... 78 E3
Slead Av *BRIG* HD6 .... 170 B2
Slead Ct *BRIG* HD6 .... 170 B2
Slead Crs *BRIG* HD6 .... 170 B2
Slead Gv *BRIG* HD6 .... 170 B2
Slead Royd *BRIG* HD6 .... 170 B2
Sledbrook Crs *STKB/PEN* S36 .. 255 L8
Sledgate La *HOLM/MEL* HD7 ... 234 A1
Sledge Ga *HUDW* HD3 .... 211 H3
Sledmere Cft *SCFT* LS14 .... 89 L8
Sledmere Garth *SCFT* LS14 .... 89 L8 🔟
Sledmere La *SCFT* LS14 .... 89 L8
Sledmere Pl *SCFT* LS14 .... 89 L8
Sleep Hill La *AWLS/ASK* DN6 .. 226 D8
  HEM/SK/SE WF9 .... 226 A7
Sleights La *AL/HA/HU* LS17 .... 45 K3
The Sleights *AL/HA/HU* LS17 .... 43 K2
Sleningford Gv *SHPY* BD18 .... 82 A6
Sleningford Ri *BGLY* BD16 .... 81 H1 🔟
Sleningford Rd *BGLY* BD16 .... 81 H1
  SHPY BD18 .... 82 A6 🔟
Slice La *TAD* LS24 .... 72 D3
Slingsby Cl *IDLE* BD10 .... 83 M6 🔟
Slipper La *MIRF* WF14 .... 172 A6
Slippery Ford La *HWTH* BD22 .... 55 L7
Slippy La *LUD/ILL* HX2 .... 145 L1
Sloan Sq *GIR* BD8 .... 104 D6 🔟
Slutwell La *PONT* WF8 .... 180 F6
Smalewell Cl *PDSY/CALV* LS28 . 106 E8
Smalewell Dr *PDSY/CALV* LS28 . 106 E8 🔟
Smalewell Gdns
  PDSY/CALV LS28 .... 106 E8
Smalewell Gn *PDSY/CALV* LS28 106 D8
Smalewell Rd *PDSY/CALV* LS28 106 D8
Smallbrook Rd *ROY/SHW* OL2 . 229 L6
Small La *HOLM/MEL* HD7 .... 212 D2
  STKB/PEN S36 .... 258 D6
Small Lees Rd *RPDN/SBR* HX6 . 188 F3
Small Page Fold
  CUL/QBY BD13 .... 125 C5 🔟
Smallpage Yd *WKFDE* WF1 .... 12 F2 🔟
Small Shaw La *HBR* HX7 .... 121 H5
Smallwood Gdns *EARL* WF12 ... 174 D3 🔟
Smallwood Rd *EARL* WF12 ... 174 C4 🔟
Smawell La *HOR/CROF* WF4 ..... 221 K7
Smawthorne Av *CAS* WF10 .... 157 M7
Smawthorne Gv *CAS* WF10 ...... 157 M7
Smawthorne La *CAS* WF10 .... 157 M7
Smeatley's La *PONT* WF8 .... 205 G7

Smeaton Ap *MSTN/BAR* LS15 ..... **112** A3
Smeaton Gv *RTHW* LS26 ..... **134** C4
Smeaton Rd *HEM/SK/SE* WF9 ..... **225** M6
Smiddles La *WBOW* BD5 ..... **126** E4 ⑦
Smiddy Hl *BSPA/BRAM* LS23 ..... **49** J2
Smirthwaite St *WKFDE* WF1 ..... **176** E6 ⑧
Smirthwaite Vw *NORM* WF6 ..... **178** C5
Smith Av *WBSY* BD6 ..... **126** C5
Smith Crs *BRIG* HD6 ..... **170** A6
Smitherds St *KGHY* BD21 ..... **2** F7
Smithfield Av *HIPP* HX3 ..... **147** M6 ③
Smith Hl *MILN* OL16 ..... **207** H8
Smith House Av *BRIG* HD6 ..... **148** C8
Smith House Crs *BRIG* HD6 ..... **170** B1
Smith House Dr *BRIG* HD6 ..... **148** C8
Smith House Gv *BRIG* HD6 ..... **170** C1
Smith House La *BRIG* HD6 ..... **170** C1
Smithies La *BSLYN/ROY* S71 ..... **261** G2
BTLY WF17 ..... **151** G6
LVSG WF15 ..... **172** A4
Smithies Moor Crs *BTLY* WF17 ..... **151** H6 ⑥
Smithies Moor La *BTLY* WF17 ..... **151** H6
Smithies Moor Ri *BTLY* WF17 ..... **151** H6
Smithies St *BSLYN/ROY* S71 ..... **261** G2
Smith La *HTON* BD9 ..... **104** A4
Smith Mills La *BHP/TINH* LS16 ..... **86** F7
Smith Rd *DEWS* WF13 ..... **173** H5
GTHN BD7 ..... **126** D3 ⑩
Smiths Av *HUDW* HD3 ..... **191** M7
Smithson Av *CAS* WF10 ..... **158** D8
Smithson St *RTHW* LS26 ..... **155** H2 ②
Smith's Ter *HIPP* HX3 ..... **146** C3
Smith St *BGLY* BD16 ..... **81** K8 ②
BOW BD4 ..... **127** K6
CAS WF10 ..... **158** B5
CAS WF10 ..... **158** E3
GTHN BD7 ..... **4** C6
KGHY BD21 ..... **2** D3
LIT OL15 ..... **207** K1 ⑭
LVSG WF15 ..... **172** D3 ⑩
MILN OL16 ..... **206** B7
Smithville *AIRE* BD20 ..... **58** B5
Smithwell La *HBR* HX7 ..... **143** G1
Smithy Bridge Rd *LIT* OL15 ..... **207** G2
LIT OL15 ..... **207** J4 ⑧
Smithy Brook La *EARL* WF12 ..... **196** F5
Smithy Carr La *BRIG* HD6 ..... **170** C2
Smithy Cl *HOR/CROF* WF4 ..... **200** B6
KBTN HD8 ..... **239** J5
Smithy Clough La
RPDN/SBR HX6 ..... **188** C3
Smithy Hl *CUL/QBY* BD13 ..... **102** A8
KBTN HD8 ..... **257** H3
WBSY BD6 ..... **126** E5 ⑰
Smithy La *AL/HA/HU* LS17 ..... **67** L4
BHP/TINH LS16 ..... **64** A8
EARD/LOFT WF3 ..... **153** H6
GTL/HWG HX4 ..... **188** F7
HBR HX7 ..... **142** C1
HOLM/MEL HD7 ..... **253** L4
HOR/CROF WF4 ..... **218** B2
HUDE HD5 ..... **15** K9
ILK LS29 ..... **21** K7
ILK LS29 ..... **40** A6
KBTN HD8 ..... **239** J5
TAD LS24 ..... **95** C1 ②
WIL/AL BD15 ..... **80** E8
Smithy Mills La *BHP/TINH* LS16 ..... **86** F4
Smithy Pde *EARL* WF12 ..... **196** B5
Smithy Place La
HOLM/MEL HD7 ..... **236** D4
Smithy St *HFAX* HX1 ..... **11** J5
Smithy Wk *EARL* WF12 ..... **196** B5
Smithy Wood La *DOD/DAR* S75 ..... **260** B8
Smyth St *WKFDE* WF1 ..... **12** D3
Snail La *HBR* HX7 ..... **143** K6
Snailsden Wy *DOD/DAR* S75 ..... **242** F6
Snaith Wood Dr *YEA* LS19 ..... **84** E5
Snaith Wood Ms *YEA* LS19 ..... **84** E5
Snape Dr *GTHN* BD7 ..... **125** M4
Snapes Fold *HUDE* HD5 ..... **215** H2
Snapethorpe Crs
WKFDW/WTN WF2 ..... **197** M2 ⑤
Snapethorpe Ga
WKFDW/WTN WF2 ..... **197** L2
Snapethorpe Rd
WKFDW/WTN WF2 ..... **197** M2
Snell Gv *COL* BB8 ..... **52** B8
Snelsins La *CLECK* BD19 ..... **149** L5
Snelsins Rd *CLECK* BD19 ..... **149** L5
Snetterton Cl *CUD/GR* S72 ..... **244** E7 ⑧
Snittle Rd *HOLM/MEL* HD7 ..... **254** D7
Snowden Ap *BRAM* LS13 ..... **108** A3 ⑦
Snowden Carr Rd *OT* LS21 ..... **22** E5
Snowden Cl *BRAM* LS13 ..... **107** M4
Snowden Crs *BRAM* LS13 ..... **107** M4
Snowden Fold *BRAM* LS13 ..... **107** M4
Snowden Gv *BRAM* LS13 ..... **107** M4
Snowden Lawn *BRAM* LS13 ..... **107** M4
Snowden Royd *BRAM* LS13 ..... **107** M4
Snowden Rd *SHPY* BD18 ..... **82** F7 ③
Snowdens Wk *CLAY* BD14 ..... **125** M2 ④
Snowden V *BRAM* LS13 ..... **107** M4
Snowdon Av *KNOT* WF11 ..... **181** L2
Snowdon St *BTLY* WF17 ..... **173** K2
ROCH OL11 ..... **228** C4
Snowdrop Ms *WIL/AL* BD15 ..... **103** K6 ⑧
Snow Hill Cl *WKFDE* WF1 ..... **176** C5 ⑩
Snow Hill Ri *WKFDE* WF1 ..... **176** C5
Snow Hill Vw *WKFDE* WF1 ..... **176** D6
Snug La *HOLM/MEL* HD7 ..... **255** J5
Snydale Av *NORM* WF6 ..... **178** E5
Snydale Cl *NORM* WF6 ..... **178** E5
Snydale Ct *NORM* WF6 ..... **178** E5
Snydale Gv *NORM* WF6 ..... **178** E5
Snydale Rd *CUD/GR* S72 ..... **244** D7
NORM WF6 ..... **178** D5
Soaper House La *HIPP* HX3 ..... **147** L4
Soaper La *HIPP* HX3 ..... **125** M7
Sod House Gn *HIPP* HX3 ..... **146** C3
Soho La *WKFDW/WTN* WF2 ..... **12** A3
Soho St *HFAX* HX1 ..... **10** B6
Solid *HUDS* HD4 ..... **214** B4
Solomon Hl *LUD/ILL* HX2 ..... **144** F5
Solway Rd *BTLY* WF17 ..... **174** B1
Somerdale Cl *BRAM* LS13 ..... **107** M5 ③

Somerdale Gdns *BRAM* LS13 ..... **107** M5 ⑤
Somerdale Gv *BRAM* LS13 ..... **107** M5
Somerdale Wk *BRAM* LS13 ..... **107** M5 ⑧
Somerset Av *BAIL* BD17 ..... **82** D2
BRIG HD6 ..... **170** D7
ROY/SHW OL2 ..... **229** H7 ⑪
Somerset Rd *HUDE* HD5 ..... **15** K9
PDSY/CALV LS28 ..... **107** G6
Somerset St *BSLY* S70 ..... **260** F4 ⑧
CUD/GR S72 ..... **244** D8 ②
Somers Pl *LDS* LS1 ..... **6** D9 ②
Somers St *LDS* LS1 ..... **6** D9
Somerton Dr *BOW* BD4 ..... **127** M4
Somerville Av *SCFT* LS14 ..... **111** H4
WBSY BD6 ..... **126** D7 ③
Somerville Dr *SCFT* LS14 ..... **111** H4
Somerville Gn *SCFT* LS14 ..... **111** H4
Somerville Mt *SCFT* LS14 ..... **111** H4
Somerville Pk *WBSY* BD6 ..... **126** D7
Somerville Vw *SCFT* LS14 ..... **111** H4 ①
Sonning Rd *WIL/AL* BD15 ..... **103** K6 ②
Soothill La *BTLY* WF17 ..... **174** B1
Sorbus Wy *KBTN* HD8 ..... **216** A3
Sorrel Cl *PONT* WF8 ..... **180** F7
Sorrel Dr *LIT* OL15 ..... **185** H8
Sorrento Wy *WMB/DAR* S73 ..... **263** H8
Sorrin Cl *IDLE* BD10 ..... **83** J7
Sotheron Cft *PONT* WF8 ..... **203** L1
Soureby Cross Wy *BOW* BD4 ..... **128** B7
Sourhall Ct *TOD* OL14 ..... **140** F8
Sourhall Rd *TOD* OL14 ..... **162** F1
South Accommodation Rd
MID LS10 ..... **9** K5
Southampton St *BFDE* BD3 ..... **5** M1
South Ap *BSPA/BRAM* LS23 ..... **69** H6
GFTH/SHER LS25 ..... **92** H4
TAD LS24 ..... **92** C3
South Av *CAS* WF10 ..... **157** H7
HEM/SK/SE WF9 ..... **247** G4
HOR/CROF WF4 ..... **197** C5
HUDS HD4 ..... **213** H3
PONT WF8 ..... **180** C7
South Baileygate *PONT* WF8 ..... **181** G5
South Bank *AL/HA/HU* LS17 ..... **46** E8
CUL/QBY BD13 ..... **125** H5 ③
South Bank Rd *BTLY* WF17 ..... **151** J8
South Bolton *LUD/ILL* HX2 ..... **123** M7
South Cliffe *CUL/QBY* BD13 ..... **102** F8
Southcliffe Dr *BAIL* BD17 ..... **82** D5
Southcliffe Wy *BAIL* BD17 ..... **82** E5
South Cl *BSLYN/ROY* S71 ..... **243** L4
GSLY LS20 ..... **61** K6
South Clough Head
LUD/ILL HX2 ..... **145** J6 ⑨
Southcote Pl *IDLE* BD10 ..... **83** K6 ⑫
South Crs *DOD/DAR* S75 ..... **260** B3
South Cft *CUD/GR* S72 ..... **244** E3
KBTN HD8 ..... **257** H3
South Croft Av *BIRK/DRI* BD11 ..... **128** C8
South Croft Dr *BIRK/DRI* BD11 ..... **128** C8 ④
South Croft Ga *BIRK/DRI* BD11 ..... **128** C8
South Cross Rd *HUDN* HD2 ..... **192** B4
Southdale Rd *OSS* WF5 ..... **196** F1
Southdale Gdns *OSS* WF5 ..... **196** F2 ③
Southdown Cl *HTON* BD9 ..... **104** A4
Southdown Rd *BAIL* BD17 ..... **82** D5
Southdowns Cl
ROY/SHW OL2 ..... **229** H6 ③
South Dr *BSLYN/ROY* S71 ..... **243** L4
GSLY LS20 ..... **61** K6
PDSY/CALV LS28 ..... **106** F3
WKFDW/WTN WF2 ..... **198** F5 ②
South Drive Farm
AWLS/ASK DN6 ..... **249** J3
South Edge *KGHY* BD21 ..... **2** C3
SHPY BD18 ..... **82** A7
Southedge Cl *HIPP* HX3 ..... **147** M8
South End Av *BRAM* LS13 ..... **107** M5
AL/HA/HU LS17 ..... **88** A4
FEA/AMT WF7 ..... **201** K2
WBSY BD6 ..... **126** E6
South End Gv *BRAM* LS13 ..... **107** M5
South End Mt *BRAM* LS13 ..... **107** M5
South End Ter *BRAM* LS13 ..... **107** M5
Southern Rd *HUDS* HD4 ..... **213** J3
Southey Cl *LIT* OL15 ..... **207** H4 ②
Southey St *SKP/WHF* BD23 ..... **16** C3
South Farm Crs *OSM* LS9 ..... **110** E4
South Farm Rd *OSM* LS9 ..... **110** E4
Southfield *BHP/TINH* LS16 ..... **64** B4
HBR HX7 ..... **143** H2
Southfield Av *AIRE* BD20 ..... **58** B4
AL/HA/HU LS17 ..... **88** A4
FEA/AMT WF7 ..... **201** K2
WBSY BD6 ..... **126** E6
Southfield Cl *KBTN* HD8 ..... **216** B7
Southfield Dr *AIRE* BD20 ..... **58** C4
AL/HA/HU LS17 ..... **88** A4 ③
Southfield Fold
HOR/CROF WF4 ..... **197** K6 ⑤
Southfield La *GLE* DN14 ..... **183** M3
GTHN BD7 ..... **126** C3
HOR/CROF WF4 ..... **197** K6
ILK LS29 ..... **19** H6
South Field La *RYKW* YO26 ..... **32** A3
Southfield La *WBOW* BD5 ..... **126** C3
Southfield Mt *AIRE* BD20 ..... **58** C4 ⑦
WOR/ARM LS12 ..... **108** C7
Southfield Rd *BGLY* BD16 ..... **81** J5
CUD/GR S72 ..... **262** G2
HOR/CROF WF4 ..... **200** D2
HUDE HD5 ..... **215** H3
ILK LS29 ..... **19** H6
ILK LS29 ..... **40** A5
KNOT WF11 ..... **182** B3 ⑧
WBOW BD5 ..... **126** E3
Southfield Sq *GIR* BD8 ..... **4** B2
Southfield St *WOR/ARM* LS12 ..... **108** E7
Southfields Vw
HOR/CROF WF4 ..... **218** F1 ②
Southfield Ter *BIRK/DRI* BD11 ..... **128** C8
HIPP HX3 ..... **147** L5
ILK LS29 ..... **19** H6 ⑦
SKP/WHF BD23 ..... **16** B3
Southfield Wy *AIRE* BD20 ..... **58** C4 ③
Southgate *BFD* BD1 ..... **4** E7
CUD/GR S72 ..... **223** G8
DOD/DAR S75 ..... **260** E3

EARL WF12 ..... **173** L6 ②
ELL HX5 ..... **169** H7
GSLY LS20 ..... **61** K7
HFAX HX1 ..... **11** H6
HOLM/MEL HD7 ..... **236** D2
HUD HD1 ..... **15** C6
PONT WF8 ..... **180** F6
RTHW LS26 ..... **133** L8 ⑪
STKB/PEN S36 ..... **271** C4
WKFDE WF1 ..... **12** F1
South Gv *BRIG* HD6 ..... **169** M1
SHPY BD18 ..... **81** M7 ②
South Hill Cl *MID* LS10 ..... **132** B7
South Hill Cft *MID* LS10 ..... **132** B7 ⑩
South Hill Dr *BGLY* BD16 ..... **81** K3
South Hill Gdns *RTHW* LS26 ..... **132** B7 ⑫
South Hill Ri *MID* LS10 ..... **132** B7 ⑫
South Hill Wy *MID* LS10 ..... **132** B7
Southlands *BAIL* BD17 ..... **82** D5
HUDE HD5 ..... **193** K5
LUD/ILL HX2 ..... **124** B5
Southlands Av *AIRE* BD20 ..... **58** C5 ①
AL/HA/HU LS17 ..... **87** L6
BGLY BD16 ..... **81** J5
CUL/QBY BD13 ..... **103** L5
YEA LS19 ..... **84** F4
Southlands Cl *GFTH/SHER* LS25 ..... **138** B3
HEM/SK/SE WF9 ..... **225** C4
Southlands Crs *AL/HA/HU* LS17 ..... **87** L6
Southlands Dr *AIRE* BD20 ..... **58** C5 ③
AL/HA/HU LS17 ..... **87** L6 ③
HUDN HD2 ..... **192** C3
Southlands Gv *AIRE* BD20 ..... **58** C5
BGLY BD16 ..... **81** H5
CUL/QBY BD13 ..... **103** K5
Southlands Gv West *AIRE* BD20... **58** C4 ③
Southlands Mt *AIRE* BD20 ..... **58** C5
Southlands Rd *AIRE* BD20 ..... **58** C4
South La *DOD/DAR* S75 ..... **258** D5
ELL HX5 ..... **191** H2
HIPP HX3 ..... **125** K7
HOR/CROF WF4 ..... **218** F2
South Lane Gdns *ELL* HX5 ..... **191** H1
Southlea *AL/HA/HU* LS17 ..... **79** G4
Southlea Cl *LM/WK* BD12 ..... **149** H1
South Lee *HORS* LS18 ..... **85** K5
Southleigh Av *BEE/HOL* LS11 ..... **131** J6
Southleigh Crs *BEE/HOL* LS11 ..... **131** J6
Southleigh Cft *BEE/HOL* LS11 ..... **131** K6 ①
Southleigh Dr *BEE/HOL* LS11 ..... **131** J6
Southleigh Gdns
BEE/HOL LS11 ..... **131** J6 ②
Southleigh Gra *BEE/HOL* LS11... **131** K6
Southleigh Gv *BEE/HOL* LS11... **131** J6
Southleigh Rd *BEE/HOL* LS11 ..... **131** J6
Southleigh Vw *BEE/HOL* LS11 ..... **131** J6 ③
South Md *BHP/TINH* LS16 ..... **64** B4
Southmere Av *GTHN* BD7 ..... **126** C3
Southmere Crs *GTHN* BD7 ..... **126** C3 ⑧
Southmere Dr *GTHN* BD7 ..... **126** B3
Southmere Gv *GTHN* BD7 ..... **126** C3 ⑪
Southmere Ov *GTHN* BD7 ..... **126** B4 ⑦
Southmere Rd *GTHN* BD7 ..... **126** C3
Southmere Ter *GTHN* BD7 ..... **126** C3 ⑪
Southmoor La *KNOT* WF11 ..... **182** K4
Southmoor Rd *CUD/GR* S72 ..... **245** M4
South Mt *AL/HA/HU* LS17 ..... **46** D8
South Nelson St *MOR* LS27 ..... **152** D1
Southolme Cl *KSTL* LS5 ..... **108** B1
South Pde *CLECK* BD19 ..... **149** L6
ELL HX5 ..... **191** H1
GTL/HWG HX4 ..... **190** B3
HDGY LS6 ..... **108** F1
HFAX HX1 ..... **11** J8
ILK LS29 ..... **38** C2
LDS LS1 ..... **6** F9
MILN OL16 ..... **206** B8
MOR LS27 ..... **152** D2
OSS WF5 ..... **197** J2
PDSY/CALV LS28 ..... **107** G8
WKFDE WF1 ..... **12** E3
South Parade Cl
PDSY/CALV LS28 ..... **106** F8
South Parkway *SCFT* LS14 ..... **111** H2
South Park Wy
WKFDW/WTN WF2 ..... **176** B2
South Parkway Ap *OSM* LS9 ..... **111** G3
South Pl *DOD/DAR* S75 ..... **260** D3
South Queen St *MOR* LS27 ..... **152** D3
South Rdg *GFTH/SHER* LS25 ..... **135** J5
South Rd *CUL/QBY* BD13 ..... **101** M1
DOD/DAR S75 ..... **260** B6
HTON BD9 ..... **104** E2 ⑦
OSM LS9 ..... **132** E3
South Royde Av *HIPP* HX3 ..... **168** E3
Southroyd Ri *PDSY/CALV* LS28 ..... **129** G1
South Sq *CUL/QBY* BD13 ..... **102** F8 ⑤
South St *BRIG* HD6 ..... **170** C3
BSLY S70 ..... **260** E5 ⑤
CUL/QBY BD13 ..... **101** M6
CUL/QBY BD13 ..... **102** F7 ②
DOD/DAR S75 ..... **260** B8
EARL WF12 ..... **173** L6
HEM/SK/SE WF9 ..... **224** A5
HFAX HX1 ..... **10** F7
HOLM/MEL HD7 ..... **236** D8
HOR/CROF WF4 ..... **222** F5
HUD HD1 ..... **213** M1
HUDS HD4 ..... **213** M8
KGHY BD21 ..... **79** J2
LM/WK BD12 ..... **149** J2
LVSG WF15 ..... **172** D2 ⑦
MILN OL16 ..... **206** C6
MIRF WF14 ..... **194** B3
MOR LS27 ..... **152** D2
NORM WF6 ..... **178** C7
OSS WF5 ..... **196** F2
WBOW BD5 ..... **126** E3 ⑱
WKFDE WF1 ..... **13** H4
South Ter *OSS* WF5 ..... **197** K2
South Vw *AIRE* BD20 ..... **34** F5 ⑤
AIRE BD20 ..... **58** D5
CAS WF10 ..... **158** A4
CAS WF10 ..... **180** A1
FEA/AMT WF7 ..... **179** M8
HIPP HX3 ..... **169** J2

Spen Common La *TAD* LS24 ..... **70** G4
Spen Crs *BHP/TINH* LS16 ..... **86** B5
Spen Dr *BHP/TINH* LS16 ..... **86** C6
Spenfield Ct *LVSG* WF15 ..... **172** C4 ②
Spen Gdns *BHP/TINH* LS16 ..... **86** D6
Speng La *RYKW* YO26 ..... **33** L7
Spen Gn *BHP/TINH* LS16 ..... **86** B7
Spen La *BHP/TINH* LS16 ..... **86** B5
CLECK BD19 ..... **150** B6
HDGY LS6 ..... **86** C8
Spen Ms *BHP/TINH* LS16 ..... **86** C7
Spennithorne Av *BHP/TINH* LS16 .. **86** C5
Spennithorne Dr *BHP/TINH* LS16 .. **86** C5
Spennithorne Rd
AWLS/ASK DN6 ..... **249** G4
Spen Rd *BHP/TINH* LS16 ..... **86** D6
Spenser Ri *GSLY* LS20 ..... **62** B6
Spenser Rd *GSLY* LS20 ..... **62** B6
Spenslea Gv *MOR* LS27 ..... **152** C4
Spen Vale St *HECK* WF16 ..... **172** F3
Spen Valley Heritage Trail
BIRK/DRI BD11 ..... **128** C7
BTLY WF17 ..... **150** F5
CLECK BD19 ..... **150** A4
Spen Valley Rd *DEWS* WF13... **173** G8
Spen Vw *DEWS* WF13 ..... **173** G6
Spen View La *BOW* BD4 ..... **127** K7
Spen Wk *BHP/TINH* LS16 ..... **86** B7
Spenwood Rd *LIT* OL15 ..... **207** H8
Spey Cl *DOD/DAR* S75 ..... **242** E7
Spibey Crs *RTHW* LS26 ..... **132** F7
Spibey La *RTHW* LS26 ..... **132** F7
Spicer House La *STKB/PEN* S36... **256** D7
Spicer St *WBOW* BD5 ..... **126** E3 ⑰
Spiers Garth *WBSY* BD6 ..... **126** F5 ⑤
The Spindles *MILN* OL16 ..... **131** M6 ⑧
Spindle St *LUD/ILL* HX2 ..... **146** C1
Spinkfield Rd *HUDN* HD2 ..... **14** C3
Spink La *PONT* WF8 ..... **180** F5
Spink Pl *GIR* BD8 ..... **4** B4
Spinks Gdns *SCFT* LS14 ..... **111** K2
Spink Well La *EARD/LOFT* WF3... **153** H5
Spinkwell Rd *DEWS* WF13 ..... **173** L6 ⑩
Spinners Cha *PDSY/CALV* LS28 ... **107** G3
Spinners Wy *WHIT* OL12 ..... **206** E2
Spinners Gn *WHIT* OL12 ..... **206** B4
The Spinners *HWTH* BD22 ..... **78** E8 ⑦
Spinners Wy *CLECK* BD19 ..... **149** H6 ⑨
MIRF WF14 ..... **194** C3
Spinneyfield *HUDN* HD2 ..... **192** C3
Spinneyfield Ct *OSM* LS9 ..... **9** M2 ③
The Spinney *AIRE* BD20 ..... **58** F6
AL/HA/HU LS17 ..... **88** A4
BRIG HD6 ..... **170** C1
IDLE BD10 ..... **83** J7
OSM LS9 ..... **9** M2 ②
SKP/WHF BD23 ..... **17** M1
WBY LS22 ..... **29** M8
WKFDW/WTN WF2 ..... **197** J3
Spinning Mill Ct *SHPY* BD18 ..... **82** A6 ③
Spion Kop *SCFT* LS14 ..... **90** B1
Spire Ct *HUDW* HD3 ..... **14** A4
HUDW HD3 ..... **191** M7 ③
Spitalgap La *PONT* WF8 ..... **181** K7
Spitfire Vw *GFTH/SHER* LS25 ..... **116** D7
Spittal Hardwick La *CAS* WF10 ..... **180** K1
Spittlerush La *PONT* WF8 ..... **227** J2
Spofforth Hl *WBY* LS22 ..... **29** J2
Spofforth La *PBR* HG3 ..... **28** B1
WBY LS22 ..... **29** J2
Spofforth Wk *GFTH/SHER* LS25 ... **113** K7
Spokeshave Wy *MILN* OL16 ..... **206** E4 ④
Spout Fold *WKFDW/WTN* WF2 ..... **175** M8
Spout Hl *BRIG* HD6 ..... **170** A8
Spout House La *BRIG* HD6 ..... **148** A8
Spring Av *KGHY* BD21 ..... **3** M7
MOR LS27 ..... **129** L6
Springbank *GFTH/SHER* LS25 ..... **134** E3
Spring Bank *LUD/ILL* HX2 ..... **145** G6
Springbank Av *MOR* LS27 ..... **129** L7
PDSY/CALV LS28 ..... **107** G3
Springbank Cl *BSLYN/ROY* S71 ... **243** L6 ③
PDSY/CALV LS28 ..... **107** G3
Springbank Crs
GFTH/SHER LS25 ..... **112** E8
Spring Bank Crs *HDGY* LS6 ..... **109** G2
Springbank Crs *HUD* HD1 ..... **15** L1
MOR LS27 ..... **129** L6
Spring Bank Cft
HOLM/MEL HD7 ..... **253** M2
Springbank Dr *PDSY/CALV* LS28 .. **107** G3
Springbank Gv *PDSY/CALV* LS28... **107** G3
Springbank Ms
HOLM/MEL HD7 ..... **236** D3 ③
Spring Bank Pl *GIR* BD8 ..... **4** A2
Spring Bank Ri *KGHY* BD21 ..... **79** L2 ②
Springbank Ri *PDSY/CALV* LS28... **107** G3
Springbank Rd *HUD* HD1 ..... **15** L1
MOR LS27 ..... **129** L6
PDSY/CALV LS28 ..... **106** F3
Springcliffe *GIR* BD8 ..... **104** D5
Springcliffe St *GIR* BD8 ..... **104** D5
Spring Cl *BGLY* BD16 ..... **81** K4 ③
GFTH/SHER LS25 ..... **113** K8 ②
KGHY BD21 ..... **3** M7
MOR LS27 ..... **130** C7 ④
Spring Close Av *OSM* LS9 ..... **9** M3
Spring Close Gdns *OSM* LS9... **110** B8 ②
Spring Close St *OSM* LS9 ..... **9** M3
Spring Close Wk *OSM* LS9... **110** B8 ②
Spring Ct *WIL/AL* BD15 ..... **103** J3 ⑧
Spring Dl *HOLM/MEL* HD7 ..... **236** D3 ⑪
Springdale Crs *IDLE* BD10 ..... **83** L6
Springdale St *HUD* HD1 ..... **214** B2
Spring Dr *KGHY* BD21 ..... **3** M7
Spring Edge North *HFAX* HX1 ..... **10** C9
Spring Edge South *HFAX* HX1 ..... **168** C1
Spring Edge West *HFAX* HX1 ..... **168** B1
Spring End Rd *OSS* WF5 ..... **197** K3
Spring Farm La *BGLY* BD16 ..... **60** D7
Spring Farm Ms *WIL/AL* BD15... **102** E1 ①
Springfield *BSPA/BRAM* LS23 ..... **48** E6
HUDW HD3 ..... **190** D4
RPDN/SBR HX6 ..... **167** J3
Springfield Av *BTLY* WF17 ..... **173** K1
GTHN BD7 ..... **126** B1
HEM/SK/SE WF9 ..... **224** A8

HOLM/MEL HD7 212 A7
HOLM/MEL HD7 236 B3
ILK LS29 38 E2
KBTN HD8 240 A4
LIT OL15 185 J7
MOR LS27 130 C8
PONT WF8 181 G5
Springfield Cl HORS LS18 86 A5
KBTN HD8 240 A4
MID LS10 132 C4
Springfield Ct GFTH/SHER LS25 116 B5
KGHY BD21 2 C2
Springfield Crs MOR LS27 130 C8
PONT WF8 227 G1
Springfield Dr KBTN HD8 256 C2
LVSG WF15 171 L1
Springfield Gdns HORS LS18 85 M5
KGHY BD21 2 D2
Springfield Gra
WKFDW/WTN WF2 175 M8
Springfield Gn MID LS10 132 A4 6
Springfield Gv BGLY BD16 81 H2 8
BRIG HD6 170 C2
Springfield La BOW BD4 129 G4
KBTN HD8 216 A7 2
LVSG WF15 172 A1
MILN OL16 206 F3
MOR LS27 130 C8
ROY/SHW OL2 228 E7
Springfield Mt
HEM/SK/SE WF9 247 G5 1
HORS LS18 85 L5
ILK LS29 19 H5
LDSU LS2 6 C6
WOR/ARM LS12 108 C6 12
Springfield Pk MIRF WF14 194 D1 3
Springfield Pl BSLY S70 260 F5 10
GIR BD8 4 D3
MID LS10 132 A4
Springfield Ri HORS LS18 85 M5 2
RTHW LS26 155 H2
Springfield Rd BAIL BD17 82 D2
CUD/GR S72 245 H7
ELL HX5 169 K7
GFTH/SHER LS25 116 B5
GSLY LS20 62 A6
KGHY BD21 2 C2
MOR LS27 130 C8
Springfields KNOT WF11 182 D3
SKP/WHF BD23 16 D2 3
Springfields Av KNOT WF11 182 D2
Springfield St BSLY S70 260 E5
CUL/QBY BD13 103 G8 13
GIR BD8 4 B3
RTHW LS26 155 H2
Springfield Ter CLECK BD19 149 H5 2
DEWS WF13 173 L5
GIR BD8 4 B3 1
GSLY LS20 62 A5
PDSY/CALV LS28 106 F5 8
Spring Gdns AL/HA/HU LS17 45 J7
BFD BD1 4 D3
BIRK/DRI BD11 129 H8
BSLYN/ROY S71 261 L2 4
BTLY WF17 173 K1 3
HOLM/MEL HD7 254 A1
MOR LS27 130 E7
Spring Gardens La KGHY BD21 2 E1
Spring Gardens Mt KGHY BD21 2 E1
Spring Gardens Rd HTON BD9 104 C3 7
Spring Garden St
CUL/QBY BD13 125 G5 16
Spring Gv COL BB8 52 E8
HBR HX7 143 J2
HFAX HX1 146 A7 4
Spring Grove St HUD HD1 14 E8
Spring Grove Vw HDGY LS6 109 G4
Spring Grove Wk HDGY LS6 109 G4 20
Spring Hall Cl HIPP HX3 147 K1
Spring Hall Ct HFAX HX1 146 A6 9
Spring Hall Dr HFAX HX1 146 A8
Spring Hall Gdns HFAX HX1 146 A7
Spring Hall Gv LUD/ILL HX2 146 A7
Spring Hall La HFAX HX1 146 A7
Spring Hall Pl HFAX HX1 146 A7
Spring Head La HOLM/MEL HD7 233 H1
Spring Head Rd CUL/QBY BD13 103 G8
HWTH BD22 78 E6
Springhead Rd RTHW LS26 133 J8
Spring Hl BAIL BD17 82 B3
BHP/TINH LS16 87 G2
CHAL LS7 7 G1
SHPY BD18 83 G7
Springhill Av HOR/CROF WF4 200 C5
Springhill Cl WKFDE WF1 176 C1 2
Springhill Ct TAD LS24 71 M2 5
Springhill Dr HOR/CROF WF4 200 C5
Springhill Gv HOR/CROF WF4 200 C5 1
Springhill Mt HOR/CROF WF4 200 C6
Springhills WKFDE WF1 176 C1
Spring Holes La CUL/QBY BD13 102 E7
Springhurst Rd SHPY BD18 82 C7
Spring La BGLY BD16 59 M8
BSLYN/ROY S71 243 L6
BTLY WF17 151 K7
DOD/DAR S75 242 E2
GTL/HWG HX4 168 C7
HOLM/MEL HD7 253 M4
HOLM/MEL HD7 254 A2
HOLM/MEL HD7 255 G1
HOR/CROF WF4 200 D6
PBR HG3 26 E2
PBR HG3 45 H2
RYKW YO26 33 K4
WBY LS22 48 E1
Springlodge Pl GIR BD8 4 D2 2
Springmead Dr
GFTH/SHER LS25 113 H8
Spring Mill La OSS WF5 175 H8
Spring Mill St WBOW BD5 127 G1
Spring Mill Wk MILN OL16 206 E4
Spring Mt KGHY BD21 3 M8
Spring Park Rd WIL/AL BD15 102 E1
Spring Pl GTHN BD7 4 B9
KGHY BD21 3 M8
Spring Ri KGHY BD21 3 M7
ROY/SHW OL2 229 J5
SKP/WHF BD23 17 M1
Spring Rd HDGY LS6 108 F2
Spring Rw BGLY BD16 80 D5
KGHY BD21 2 F7
Springroyd Ter GIR BD8 104 B6
Spring Side Ri HOLM/MEL HD7 212 F1
Springs La BSPA/BRAM LS23 31 H8
ILK LS29 38 D2
Springs Rd BAIL BD17 84 A1
HOLM/MEL HD7 252 D3
The Springs WKFDE WF1 12 F2
Springstone Av
HEM/SK/SE WF9 224 A7
OSS WF5 174 F7
Spring St BRIG HD6 170 C4 7
BSLY S70 261 G6
DEWS WF13 173 L5 7
HOLM/MEL HD7 212 B6
HOLM/MEL HD7 233 H3
HUD HD1 14 D7
IDLE BD10 83 K8
KGHY BD21 3 H2
LVSG WF15 172 D2
RPDN/SBR HX6 188 F2
TOD OL14 140 E5 8
Springswood Av SHPY BD18 82 C7 9
Springswood Pl SHPY BD18 82 C7 10
Springswood Rd SHPY BD18 82 C7 11
Spring Ter HIPP HX3 11 J4
MILN OL16 229 K3 4
Springvale Ri HEM/SK/SE WF9 223 M6
Spring Vale Rd
HEM/SK/SE WF9 246 E3 1
Spring Vale Ter LIT OL15 207 K1
Spring Va PDSY/CALV LS28 107 G4
Spring Valley Av BRAM LS13 107 L5
Spring Valley Cl BRAM LS13 107 L5
Spring Valley Crs BRAM LS13 107 L5
Spring Valley Cft BRAM LS13 107 L5
Spring Valley Dr BRAM LS13 107 L5
Spring Valley St LVSG WF15 172 C1 4
Spring Valley Vw BRAM LS13 107 L5
Spring Valley Wk BRAM LS13 107 L5
Spring Vw MOR LS27 129 M6
OSS WF5 175 H8 1
Spring Vls TOD OL14 140 D5 6
Springville Gdns
HEM/SK/SE WF9 225 K7
Spring Wy KGHY BD21 3 M7
Springwell Av RTHW LS26 134 C5
Springwell Cl HWTH BD22 54 F3
YEA LS19 62 E8 4
Springwell Ct BEE/HOL LS11 8 B3
EARD/LOFT WF3 153 C5
Springwell Dr WBOW BD5 127 G2 14
Springwell Rd RTHW LS26 134 C5 1
WOR/ARM LS12 8 B3
Springwell St BEE/HOL LS11 8 B3
Springwell Vw BEE/HOL LS11 8 C4
Spring Wood Av HIPP HX3 168 D4
Springwood Av HUD HD1 14 C8
WBOW BD5 127 H3
Spring Wood Dr HIPP HX3 168 D4
Spring Wood Gdns
WBOW BD5 127 H4 8
Springwood Gv RHAY LS8 88 E8
Springwood Hall Gdns HUD HD1 14 C8
Springwood Rd
HOLM/MEL HD7 236 E6
RHAY LS8 88 D8
YEA LS19 84 C3
Springwood St HUD HD1 14 E8
Springwood Vw STKB/PEN S36 271 H4
Sprinkwell Cl BFDE BD3 5 G2
Spruce Av BSLYN/ROY S71 243 K3
Spruce Dr HUDS HD4 213 M8
Spruce Drive Ms HUDS HD4 213 M8 5
Spruce St KGHY BD21 3 J3
Sprutts La HBR HX7 121 K7
Spur Dr MSTN/BAR LS15 112 A3
Spurr Gv WKFDW/WTN WF2 199 K8
Spurrier's Av KNOT WF11 181 L3
Spurr St BTLY WF17 173 M2 7
Square Rd HFAX HX1 11 J6
TOD OL14 163 J6
Square St BOW BD4 127 J1
The Square BSLY S70 260 F6
BSPA/BRAM LS23 49 G7
CAS WF10 158 E7
CUD/GR S72 245 K8
GFTH/SHER LS25 135 J5 2
GIR BD8 103 L7 9
KNOT WF11 159 L8 1
TAD LS24 72 A2 3
Squire Gn GIR BD8 104 B5 1
Squire La HTON BD9 104 B5
Squirrel Cl DEWS WF13 173 H3
Squirrel Ct HUDN HD2 191 L4 1
Squirrel Ditch HUDS HD4 214 E3 1
Squirrel Hall Dr DEWS WF13 173 H3
Squirrel La CUL/QBY BD13 124 D1
Squirrels Drey HOR/CROF WF4 198 B7 2
Squirrel Wk DEWS WF13 173 H3 5
Stable Fold LM/WK BD12 148 F4 3
Stableford Gdns HUDN HD2 191 M4 3
Stableford Mnr
HOLM/MEL HD7 213 G1 1
Stable La HIPP HX3 10 E2
Stablers Wk NORM WF6 178 C2
Stables La BSPA/BRAM LS23 49 G7
The Stables WKFDW/WTN WF2 199 J7
Stacey Crs CUD/GR S72 245 H7
Stackgarth BRIG HD6 170 C6
Stackhills Rd TOD OL14 163 L1
Stacks La HBR HX7 166 B1
Stadium Rd WBSY BD6 126 F6
Stadium Wy BEE/HOL LS11 131 G3
HEM/SK/SE WF9 247 K1
HUDE HD5 15 J4
Stafford Av HIPP HX3 168 E2
Stafford Hill La HUDE HD5 193 L6
Stafford Pde HIPP HX3 168 E3 3
Stafford Rd HIPP HX3 168 E3
Stafford Sq HIPP HX3 168 F3
Stafford St BOW BD4 127 K2
CAS WF10 157 L5
MID LS10 9 L7
Stafford Ter WKFDW/WTN WF2 176 B8
Stainbeck Av CHAL LS7 87 H8
Stainbeck Gdns CHAL LS7 87 K8
WBSY BD6 125 M6 1
Stainbeck La CHAL LS7 87 J7
Stainbeck Rd CHAL LS7 87 J8
Stainbeck Wk CHAL LS7 87 K8
Stainborough Cl DOD/DAR S75 260 B8
Stainborough Rd DOD/DAR S75 260 B8
Stainburn Av AL/HA/HU LS17 88 A5
CAS WF10 180 C1
Stainburn Cl OT LS21 42 C4
Stainburn Crs AL/HA/HU LS17 87 M5
Stainburn Dr AL/HA/HU LS17 87 M5
Stainburn Gdns AL/HA/HU LS17 88 A5
Stainburn La OT LS21 42 C4
Stainburn Mt AL/HA/HU LS17 88 A6 5
Stainburn Rd AL/HA/HU LS17 87 M6
Stainburn Ter AL/HA/HU LS17 87 M6
Stainburn Vw AL/HA/HU LS17 88 A5
Staincliffe Cl DEWS WF13 173 J6 2
Staincliffe Crs DEWS WF13 173 H4 9
Staincliffe Hall Rd BTLY WF17 173 H3
Staincliffe Rd DEWS WF13 173 H6
Staincross Common
DOD/DAR S75 242 D4
Stainecross Av HUDS HD4 213 L4
Staines Cft HUDE HD5 193 G8
Stainland Dean GTL/HWG HX4 189 M5
Stainland Rd GTL/HWG HX4 168 E8
GTL/HWG HX4 189 J2
HUDW HD3 190 C6
Stainley Cl DOD/DAR S75 260 D2 2
Stainmore Cl DOD/DAR S75 259 H6 6
SCFT LS14 111 J3
Stainmore Pl SCFT LS14 111 J3
Stainton Cl BSLYN/ROY S71 243 G8
WBSY BD6 126 A6 3
Stainton La EARD/LOFT WF3 154 F2
Staircase La OT LS21 63 M1
Stairfoot Cl BHP/TINH LS16 86 F1
Stair Foot La BHP/TINH LS16 86 F1
Stairfoot Vw BHP/TINH LS16 86 F1
Staithe Av MID LS10 153 M1
Staithe Cl MID LS10 153 M1 9
Staithe Gdns MID LS10 153 M1 10
Staithgate La WBSY BD6 127 H5
Stake La HBR HX7 144 A7
Stake Lane Bank
HOLM/MEL HD7 254 D1
Stallabrass St GIR BD8 4 B4
Stalley Royd La
HOLM/MEL HD7 255 H3
Stamford Av CAS WF10 157 J8
Stamford St MILN OL16 206 D8
Stamford Wy DOD/DAR S75 242 D4 2
Stammergate La WBY LS22 47 K4
Stamp Hill Cl ILK LS29 18 F6 2
Stanacre Pl BFDE BD3 5 H2
Stanage La HIPP HX3 125 L7
Stanbury Cl DOD/DAR S75 260 D3
Stancliffe Wy HUDE HD5 193 K5
Standale Av PDSY/CALV LS28 106 F6
Standale Crs PDSY/CALV LS28 106 F6
Standale Ri PDSY/CALV LS28 106 F6
Standard Dr HUDS HD4 213 K4
Standbridge Cl
WKFDW/WTN WF2 220 C1
Stand Bridge Garth
HOR/CROF WF4 198 B8
Standbridge La
WKFDW/WTN WF2 198 E7
Standedge Trail
HOLM/MEL HD7 232 C5
UPML OL3 231 M7
Standhill Crs BSLYN/ROY S71 243 G7
Standiforth La HUDE HD5 193 G7
Standiforth Rd HUDE HD5 15 M7
Standish Crs HEM/SK/SE WF9 246 E2
Standroyd Dr COL BB8 74 C1
Standroyd Rd COL BB8 74 C1
Stanhall Av PDSY/CALV LS28 106 F5
Stanhope Av DOD/DAR S75 259 H1
HORS LS18 85 L4
Stanhope Cl HORS LS18 85 L4
Stanhope Dr HORS LS18 85 K6
Stanhope Gdns DOD/DAR S75 260 E3
EARD/LOFT WF3 154 A5
Stanhope Gv EARD/LOFT WF3 154 A5
Stanhope St BSLY S70 260 F5 11
KBTN HD8 239 M5 2
ROCH OL11 228 B1 19
Stanks Ap SCFT LS14 111 M2
Stanks Av SCFT LS14 111 M2
Stanks Cl SCFT LS14 112 A2
Stanks Cross SCFT LS14 111 M2
Stanks Dr SCFT LS14 89 L8
Stanks Gdns SCFT LS14 111 M1
Stanks Garth MSTN/BAR LS15 112 A2 1
Stanks Gn SCFT LS14 112 A2 2
Stanks Gv SCFT LS14 111 M2
Stanks La North SCFT LS14 89 L8
Stanks La South SCFT LS14 111 M2
Stanks Pde SCFT LS14 111 M2
Stanks Ri SCFT LS14 112 A2
Stanks Rd SCFT LS14 111 M2
Stanks Wy SCFT LS14 111 M2
Stanleigh Cft HBR HX7 143 J4 4
Stanley Av OSM LS9 110 B4 12
Stanley Cottages NORM WF6 178 C4 5
Stanley Dr RHAY LS8 88 D4
Stanley La GTL/HWG HX4 190 B3
LVSG WF15 172 C1
WKFDE WF1 176 F2
Stanley Pl BTLY WF17 173 M1
OSM LS9 110 C4 20
WHIT OL12 206 A6 17
Stanley Rd BSLY S70 262 A6
CHAL LS7 7 H2
ECHL BD2 104 F2
HFAX HX1 10 A8
HUDW HD3 191 L5
HWTH BD22 79 J2
LVSG WF15 172 C4 3
OSM LS9 110 B4
WKFDE WF1 13 H2
Stanley St BGLY BD16 81 J3
BRIG HD6 170 D3 6
BSLY S70 260 F5 12
CAS WF10 158 A6
CLECK BD19 149 M6
CUD/GR S72 262 E1
FEA/AMT WF7 179 M7
HTON BD9 104 E1 6
HUDS HD4 214 A3
HWTH BD22 79 H6 8
IDLE BD10 83 K6 13
KGHY BD21 2 F3 1
RPDN/SBR HX6 167 L2 6
WHIT OL12 206 A5
WKFDE WF1 13 H2
Stanley Ter OSM LS9 110 C4 21
Stanley Vw WOR/ARM LS12 108 E7
Stanmoor Dr EARD/LOFT WF3 155 G8
Stanmore Av BULY LS4 108 E3
Stanmore Crs BULY LS4 108 E3
Stanmore Gv BULY LS4 108 E3
Stanmore Hl BULY LS4 108 F3
Stanmore Mt BULY LS4 108 E3
Stanmore Pl BULY LS4 108 E3
GTHN BD7 126 C1 3
Stanmore Rd BULY LS4 108 E3
Stanmore St BULY LS4 108 E3
Stanmore Ter BULY LS4 108 E3
Stanmore Vw BULY LS4 108 E3
Stannard Well Dr
HOR/CROF WF4 197 K4
Stannard Well La
HOR/CROF WF4 197 K4
Stannary Pl HFAX HX1 10 F4
Stannery End La HBR HX7 144 B7
Stanneybrook Cl MILN OL16 206 D6
Stanney Cl MILN OL16 229 G1
Stanney Rd MILN OL16 206 D6
Stanningley Av LUD/ILL HX2 145 K1
Stanningley By-pass
BRAM LS13 107 M6
PDSY/CALV LS28 106 E5
Stanningley Dr LUD/ILL HX2 145 K1
Stanningley Gv HECK WF16 172 F3
Stanningley Rd BRAM LS13 107 J4
LUD/ILL HX2 145 K1
PDSY/CALV LS28 107 H4
WOR/ARM LS12 108 D6
Stansfield Cl CAS WF10 158 D5
HFAX HX1 10 D5
Stansfield Ct RPDN/SBR HX6 167 K3 3
Stansfield Dr CAS WF10 158 E6
Stansfield Hall LIT OL15 185 L5
Stansfield Hall Rd TOD OL14 141 K8
Stansfield Mill La
RPDN/SBR HX6 167 H5
Stansfield Rd CAS WF10 158 D6
TOD OL14 163 K1
Stansfield St TOD OL14 141 K8
Stan Va PONT WF8 205 G8
Stanwell Av HUDW HD3 191 M5
Stapper Gn WIL/AL BD15 80 D8
Starbeck Rd WKFDE WF1 177 G6
Starfield Av LIT OL15 207 H4
Starkey La AIRE BD20 35 G5
Starkie St KGHY BD21 2 F6
Star La BSLY S70 261 G5
Starmire HWTH BD22 54 D2
Starring La LIT OL15 207 G1
Starring Rd WHIT OL12 207 G1
Starring Wy LIT OL15 207 H1
Star St WBOW BD5 126 E3
Starwort Cl PONT WF8 180 F7
Station Ap HOLM/MEL HD7 236 D1
ILK LS29 40 A6
TOD OL14 163 K1
Station Av BRAM LS13 107 K4
Station Crs WOR/ARM LS12 108 D7
Stationers Entry MILN OL16 206 B7 22
Station Flds GFTH/SHER LS25 113 H7
Station La BIRK/DRI BD11 128 D8
EARD/LOFT WF3 153 G5 3
EARD/LOFT WF3 153 M5
FEA/AMT WF7 201 L1
HOLM/MEL HD7 212 F3
HUDS HD4 214 B6
KBTN HD8 238 B5
LVSG WF15 172 E4
PONT WF8 180 F6
RTHW LS26 133 M7
SCFT LS14 68 B8
WBY LS22 47 K5 1
Station Mt BRAM LS13 107 L4
Station Pde KSTL LS5 108 C2
TOD OL14 140 B5
Station Pl BRAM LS13 107 L4
Station Rd AIRE BD20 34 F7
AIRE BD20 35 M8
AWLS/ASK DN6 205 J4
AWLS/ASK DN6 249 M6
BAIL BD17 61 K8
BAIL BD17 82 F3
BIRK/DRI BD11 129 G8
BRIG HD6 170 E4
BSLY S70 260 F4
BSLYN/ROY S71 243 K2
BSLYN/ROY S71 262 B1
BTLY WF17 173 M2
CAS WF10 157 L2
CLAY BD14 125 L2
CUL/QBY BD13 79 L8
CUL/QBY BD13 102 A6
CUL/QBY BD13 125 G5
DOD/DAR S75 242 A5
DOD/DAR S75 260 A7
EARL WF12 174 B8
EARL WF12 195 L1
FEA/AMT WF7 202 C7
GFTH/SHER LS25 135 H6
GSLY LS20 61 M5
GTL/HWG HX4 190 D2
HBR HX7 143 J4
HECK WF16 172 F3
HEM/SK/SE WF9 224 A7
HEM/SK/SE WF9 247 J3
HIPP HX3 147 L7
HIPP HX3 148 C4
HOLM/MEL HD7 212 B5
HOLM/MEL HD7 212 F2
HOLM/MEL HD7 233 H2
HOLM/MEL HD7 236 C1
HOLM/MEL HD7 254 C1
HOR/CROF WF4 222 C5
HORS LS18 85 L4
HUDN HD2 193 J1
HUDS HD4 237 L4
HWTH BD22 78 E7
HWTH BD22 78 F4
HWTH BD22 100 E3
ILK LS29 38 D2
ILK LS29 40 A6
ILK LS29 61 J2
KBTN HD8 215 L3
KBTN HD8 238 A6
KBTN HD8 239 J2
KNOT WF11 181 L1 7
LIT OL15 207 K1 15
LM/WK BD12 149 G1
LUD/ILL HX2 144 F7
MILN OL16 229 H1
MIRF WF14 194 C2
MOR LS27 152 C1
MSTN/BAR LS15 90 B7
MSTN/BAR LS15 111 L4 7
NORM WF6 178 B3
OSS WF5 196 F1
OT LS21 41 J7
OT LS21 64 B1
PBR HG3 26 F2
ROCH OL11 206 B8
RPDN/SBR HX6 167 L3
RTHW LS26 156 D3
SHPY BD18 82 D6
TAD LS24 71 K3
TAD LS24 94 E8
TOD OL14 140 E5 9
WIL/AL BD15 102 B3
WOR/ARM LS12 108 D7
Station St HOLM/MEL HD7 234 F4
HUD HD1 14 F6
PDSY/CALV LS28 106 F8
WKFDE WF1 199 G4
Station Ter BRAM LS13 107 L4
CAS WF10 157 L2
Station to Station Wk
HOLM/MEL HD7 231 L1
LIT OL15 207 M6
Station Vw AIRE BD20 56 F1 2
HWTH BD22 100 E3 4
MSTN/BAR LS15 111 L5
Station Wy WOR/ARM LS12 108 D7
Staups La HBR HX7 142 B4
HIPP HX3 147 H5
Staveley Cl ROY/SHW OL2 229 M8
Staveley Dr SHPY BD18 81 M7 11
Staveley Gv HWTH BD22 79 J3
Staveley Rd BGLY BD16 81 H2
GTHN BD7 104 D8 9
HWTH BD22 79 J3
SHPY BD18 81 M6
Staveley Wy HWTH BD22 79 J2
Stavely Ms BGLY BD16 81 J2 9
Staverton St LUD/ILL HX2 146 A7 5
Staybrite Av BGLY BD16 81 J7
Staygate Gn WBSY BD6 127 G5 1
Staynton Crs HUDN HD2 193 H1
Stead Ga KBTN HD8 238 F4
Stead Hill Wy IDLE BD10 83 H5
Stead La HUDE HD5 193 K6
ILK LS29 39 K6
RPDN/SBR HX6 188 E4
SCFT LS14 90 C1
Steadman St BFDE BD3 5 M7
Steadman Ter BFDE BD3 5 M7
Stead Rd BOW BD4 128 A6
Stead St BAIL BD17 82 D6
HFAX HX1 10 F6 4
Stead's Yd HORS LS18 85 L4
Steanard La MIRF WF14 194 E3
Steander OSM LS9 9 K2
Steele La GTL/HWG HX4 189 L5
Steeplands HUDN HD2 171 H8
Steep La HBR HX7 166 C2
STKB/PEN S36 271 H2
Steeple Av HOR/CROF WF4 217 G2
Steep Riding HOLM/MEL HD7 236 E3
Steeton Gv AIRE BD20 35 L8
Steeton Hall Gdns AIRE BD20 35 L8 2
Steeton Wy GFTH/SHER LS25 137 L3
Steincroft Rd GFTH/SHER LS25 138 B3
Stella Gdns PONT WF8 181 H4
Stell Hl HWTH BD22 78 F1
Stephen Cl HIPP HX3 147 J5
Stephen Crs ECHL BD2 105 G3
Stephen Rd WBSY BD6 126 B4
Stephenson Cl EARL WF12 174 A5 5
Stephenson Dr
WOR/ARM LS12 130 A3 2
Stephenson Rd WIL/AL BD15 102 F4
Stephenson St GTHN BD7 126 D3 12
Stephenson Wy
WKFDW/WTN WF2 176 B1
WOR/ARM LS12 129 M3
Stepping Stones AIRE BD20 59 G5
Steps La RPDN/SBR HX6 167 L1
Steps Meadow WHIT OL12 206 E2
Sterne Hl LUD/ILL HX2 168 B2
Stevenson Av CAS WF10 180 E1 3
Stevenson Dr DOD/DAR S75 260 A2
Stewart Cl ECHL BD2 105 L1
Stewart Pl BEE/HOL LS11 8 D9 2
Stewart St HWTH BD22 79 G6 20
MILN OL16 229 K3
Sticker La BOW BD4 127 L2
Stile Common Rd HUDS HD4 214 D3
Stile Hill Wy MSTN/BAR LS15 112 A7
Stilemoor Ri TOD OL14 141 J7 2
Stile Rd TOD OL14 141 J7
Stillwell Dr WKFDW/WTN WF2 199 G6
Stillwell Garth
WKFDW/WTN WF2 199 G6
Stillwell Gv WKFDW/WTN WF2 199 G6
Stirling Crs BOW BD4 128 A3
HORS LS18 85 J2
Stirling Rd ILK LS29 39 M5
Stirling St AIRE BD20 36 A4 15
HFAX HX1 10 E7
Stirling Wy GFTH/SHER LS25 113 K7 5
Stirrup Gv ECHL BD2 105 H2 2
Stirton St WBOW BD5 126 F3 15

Stithy St OSS WF5 .... 174 E6 10
Stiups La MILN OL16 .... 228 D2
Stockeld La WBY LS22 .... 28 F8
Stockeld Rd ILK LS29 .... 38 C2
Stockeld Wy ILK LS29 .... 38 C1
Stockerhead La
    HOLM/MEL HD7 .... 212 C6
Stock Gv MILN OL16 .... 207 H7
Stockheld La MSTN/BAR LS15 ... 90 B5
Stock Hey La TOD OL14 .... 142 D8
Stockhill Fold IDLE BD10 .... 83 M6
Stockhill La IDLE BD10 .... 83 M7
Stockhill St DEWS WF13 .... 173 J6
Stockingate HEM/SK/SE WF9 ...... 246 D5
Stockinger La ILK LS29 .... 19 H7
Stocking La GFTH/SHER LS25 ...... 92 B8
    GFTH/SHER LS25 .... 138 E8
    KNOT WF11 .... 182 E2
    SEL YO8 .... 139 L5
Stock La LUD/ILL HX2 .... 145 K8
Stocks Ap SCFT LS14 .... 111 K2
Stocks Av HBR HX7 .... 143 M6
Stocksbank Dr MIRF WF14 .... 171 M8 2
Stocks Crs HBR HX7 .... 143 M6 2
Stocks Dr KBTN HD8 .... 237 L6
Stocks Gdns HBR HX7 .... 143 M6
Stocks Hl BEE/HOL LS11 .... 8 C5
    ILK LS29 .... 61 H2
    WOR/ARM LS12 .... 108 E6
Stocks Hill La AIRE BD20 .... 58 F5 5
Stocks La BTLY WF17 .... 173 L1
    CUL/QBY BD13 .... 125 K5
    DOD/DAR S75 .... 260 D1
    HBR HX7 .... 143 M6 3
    HUDS HD4 .... 237 L5
    LUD/ILL HX2 .... 145 G5
    RPDN/SBR HX6 .... 167 G3
Stocksmoor Rd
    HOR/CROF WF4 .... 218 E4
Stocks Moor Rd HUDS HD4 .... 237 K4
Stocks Ri SCFT LS14 .... 111 K2
Stocks Rd SCFT LS14 .... 111 K2
Stocks St CHAL LS7 .... 7 G2
Stockwell Dr BTLY WF17 .... 151 M8
Stocks Wy KBTN HD8 .... 237 M6
Stockton St LIT OL15 .... 207 J1
Stockwell St WF17 .... 151 M8
Stod Fold LUD/ILL HX2 .... 123 L6
Stoke St MILN OL16 .... 206 D8
Stone Acre Hts
    HOLM/MEL HD7 .... 235 H5 5
Stonebridge Ap
    WOR/ARM LS12 .... 108 A8 1
Stonebridge Av
    WOR/ARM LS12 .... 108 B8 1
Stonebridge Gv
    WOR/ARM LS12 .... 108 A8
Stonebridge La
    WOR/ARM LS12 .... 108 A8
Stonebridge Wk KBTN HD8 .... 238 B5 1
Stone Brig Gn RTHW LS26 .... 154 F2
Stone Brig La RTHW LS26 .... 155 G1
Stonechat Ri MOR LS27 .... 152 E2 5
Stonecliffe Crs WOR/ARM LS12 ... 108 A8
Stonecliffe Dr HOR/CROF WF4 .... 196 D7
    WOR/ARM LS12 .... 108 A8
Stonecliffe Garth
    WOR/ARM LS12 .... 108 A8
Stonecliffe Gv WOR/ARM LS12 ... 108 A8
Stonecliffe Mt WOR/ARM LS12 ... 108 A8
Stonecliffe Ter WOR/ARM LS12 .. 107 M8
Stonecliffe Wy WOR/ARM LS12 .. 129 M1
Stone Ct AIRE BD20 .... 58 F6
    CUD/GR S72 .... 245 G1
Stonecroft EARD/LOFT WF3 ...... 177 C1
    ECHL BD2 .... 105 L1 8
Stonecroft Gdns KBTN HD8 .... 238 A6
Stonedale Cl OT LS21 .... 43 G8
Stonedene Pk WBY LS22 .... 30 B8 8
Stonefield SCFT LS14 .... 67 M6
Stonefield Av HUDS HD4 .... 213 K3 2
Stonefield Cl IDLE BD10 .... 105 K1 6
Stonefield Pl BTLY WF17 .... 151 H5 6
Stonefield Rd HUDS HD4 .... 213 K3
Stonefield St CLECK BD19 .... 149 J8
    DEWS WF13 .... 173 L5
    MILN OL16 .... 229 H1
Stonefleece Ct
    HOLM/MEL HD7 .... 236 B5 3
Stonegarth Cl CUD/GR S72 .... 244 D8 3
Stonegate BGLY BD16 .... 81 J1
    CHAL LS7 .... 7 H2
    OSS WF5 .... 197 G3
Stonegate Ap CHAL LS7 .... 87 H8
Stonegate Cha CHAL LS7 .... 87 H7 6
Stonegate Cl AL/HA/HU LS17 ...... 87 M3
Stonegate Crs CHAL LS7 .... 87 J7
Stonegate Dr PONT WF8 .... 180 E5
Stonegate Farm Cl CHAL LS7 ...... 87 H7 6
Stonegate Gdns CHAL LS7 .... 87 H7
Stonegate Gn CHAL LS7 .... 87 H8 12
Stonegate La CHAL LS7 .... 87 H7
    FEA/AMT WF7 .... 224 A1 8
Stonegate Ms CHAL LS7 .... 87 H8 13
Stonegate Pl CHAL LS7 .... 87 H8 14
Stonegate Rd AL/HA/HU LS17 ..... 87 M4 8
    AL/HA/HU LS17 .... 87 M4 8
    IDLE BD10 .... 83 L8
Stonegate Wk CHAL LS7 .... 87 J8 4
Stone Gv AIRE BD20 .... 56 E1 8
Stone Hall Rd ECHL BD2 .... 105 C2
Stone Head La HWTH BD22 .... 53 M2
Stone Hl BGLY BD16 .... 81 K2
Stonehill Ri CUD/GR S72 .... 244 D8
    STKB/PEN S36 .... 270 E5
Stonehouse Dr CUL/QBY BD13 .. 124 E6
Stonehurst MSTN/BAR LS15 ...... 111 M2 2
Stonehurst Rd MIRF WF14 .... 172 C8 3
Stonehyrst Av DEWS WF13 .... 173 M5
Stone La HWTH BD22 .... 100 D4
Stonelea GTL/HWG HX4 .... 189 J7
Stonelea Cl DOD/DAR S75 .... 259 H6 7
Stonelea Ct CHAL LS7 .... 87 J7 2
    HDGY LS6 .... 108 F1
Stone Lea Gv HEM/SK/SE WF9 ... 247 J4 4
Stoneleigh CUL/QBY BD13 .... 125 H5 13

Stoneleigh Ct KBTN HD8 .... 238 C4 1
Stoneleigh Pl BSLY S70 .... 261 H7 11
Stonely Dr TOD OL14 .... 163 J7
Stone Mill Ap HDGY LS6 .... 87 G7
Stone Pits La MOR LS27 .... 151 M1
Stones Dr RPDN/SBR HX6 .... 188 D4
Stones La HOLM/MEL HD7 .... 212 C6
    HOLM/MEL HD7 .... 212 F3
    TOD OL14 .... 163 G2
Stones Rd TOD OL14 .... 163 H2
Stones Ter TOD OL14 .... 163 J4 4
Stone St BAIL BD17 .... 83 G4
    BFD BD1 .... 4 F5
    BSLY/ROY S71 .... 261 G2
    WIL/AL BD15 .... 103 J3
Stone Wood La KBTN HD8 .... 237 L5
Stoney Back La HUDS HD4 .... 214 A4
Stoney Bank La
    HOLM/MEL HD7 .... 236 F6
Stoney Bank St DEWS WF13 ...... 173 J8 7
Stoney Battery HFAX HX1 .... 11 H3
Stoney Battery Rd HUDW HD3 ... 213 M2
Stoneybrook Cl
    HOR/CROF WF4 .... 219 H6
Stoney Cft CLECK BD19 .... 150 D7
Stoneycroft La AIRE BD20 .... 57 K4 8
Stoney Cross St HUDS HD4 .... 214 A4
Stoney Ford La HUDE HD5 .... 193 K5 2
Stoney Hl BRIG HD6 .... 170 F6
Stoneyhurst Sq BOW BD4 .... 128 A3 8
Stoney La AL/HA/HU LS17 .... 89 J1
    BTLY WF17 .... 151 M8
    COL BB8 .... 52 A5 3
    HIPP HX3 .... 146 C3
    HIPP HX3 .... 148 C7
    HOR/CROF WF4 .... 220 B3
    HORS LS18 .... 85 K6
    HUDW HD3 .... 191 H6 8
    ILK LS29 .... 39 L8
    UPML OL3 .... 230 F7
    WKFDW/WTN WF2 .... 175 M1
Stoney Ridge Av WIL/AL BD15 ... 103 K2
Stoney Ridge Rd BGLY BD16 ...... 103 L1
Stoney Ri HORS LS18 .... 85 K6
Stoney Rock Gv OSM LS9 .... 110 B5 6
Stoney Rock La OSM LS9 .... 110 B5
Stoney Royd BSLY/ROY S71 .... 243 H5
Stoney Royd La TOD OL14 .... 141 H6
Stoneys Fold WIL/AL BD15 .... 80 D7
Stoney St AIRE BD20 .... 57 K4 8
Stoneythorpe HORS LS18 .... 85 K6 3
Stonie Heyes Av WHIT OL12 ...... 206 D4
Stony Croft La AWLS/ASK DN6 .. 249 J2
    GTL/HWG HX4 .... 189 K1
Stony Ga HOLM/MEL HD7 .... 254 A4
Stony La ECHL BD2 .... 105 L1 7
    GTL/HWG HX4 .... 168 C4
    HBR HX7 .... 142 F4
    HIPP HX3 .... 169 L2
    HOLM/MEL HD7 .... 236 B2
    RPDN/SBR HX6 .... 188 F1
    TOD OL14 .... 141 C5
    WIL/AL BD15 .... 103 H4
Stony Royd PDSY/CALV LS28 ... 106 E3
Stony Royd La HBR HX7 .... 165 J2
Stoodley Cl TOD OL14 .... 164 C1
Stoodley La TOD OL14 .... 142 F7
Stoodley Ter LUD/ILL HX2 .... 146 A8
Stopford Av LIT OL15 .... 207 G2
    WKFDW/WTN WF2 .... 199 G6
Stopford Garth
    WKFDW/WTN WF2 .... 199 G6 1
Store St ROY/SHW OL2 .... 229 L6 8
Storey Pl SCFT LS14 .... 111 G5
Storie Crs WKFDW/WTN WF2 ..... 198 A2
Stormer Hill La RPDN/SBR HX6 .. 167 M4
Storr Hl LM/WK BD12 .... 148 E2
Storrs Hill Rd OSS WF5 .... 197 G4
Storrs La STKB/PEN S36 .... 271 L4
Storrs Mill La BSLY/ROY S71 ...... 263 G4
Storrs Wood Vw CUD/GR S72 .... 262 F2
Storth Av HUDS HD4 .... 213 H3
Storthes Hall La KBTN HD8 .... 215 M7 1
Storth Pl HUDN HD2 .... 14 C1
Storths Rd HUDN HD2 .... 192 B5
Stottercliffe Rd STKB/PEN S36 .. 270 D3
Stott Rd HDGY LS6 .... 109 G5 8
    MILN OL16 .... 229 H2 4
    WHIT OL12 .... 206 B5
    WOR/ARM LS12 .... 108 F7
Stott Ter ECHL BD2 .... 105 M2
Stourton Rd ILK LS29 .... 38 B1
Stowe Gv OSM LS9 .... 110 E6
Stowell Mill St WBOW BD5 .... 126 F2 7
Stradmore Rd CUL/QBY BD13 ... 102 A6
Strafford Av BSLY S70 .... 261 H6
Strafford Rd DOD/DAR S75 .... 241 L6
Strafford Wk DOD/DAR S75 ...... 260 B8
Strafford Wy IDLE BD10 .... 84 A6
Straightacres La IDLE BD10 .... 105 M1 7
Straight La AWLS/ASK DN6 .... 248 D2
    ILK LS29 .... 36 F1
    LUD/ILL HX2 .... 145 M1
Strait La AL/HA/HU LS17 .... 43 L2
Straits BAIL BD17 .... 82 B2
Stralau St BTLY WF17 .... 151 L8 4
Strands Ct HOR/CROF WF4 .... 197 G8
The Strand ROCH OL11 .... 228 B4
Strangford Ct IDLE BD10 .... 83 M6 8
Stranglands La KNOT WF11 .... 159 J4
Stratford Av BEE/HOL LS11 .... 131 J2
    ROCH OL11 .... 228 A1
Stratford Cl HOLM/MEL HD7 ...... 213 G1
Stratford Dr GTHN BD7 .... 126 D1
Stratford St BEE/HOL LS11 .... 131 L3 6

Stratton Pk BRIG HD6 .... 170 D5
Stratton Rd BRIG HD6 .... 170 D5
Stratton Vw BOW BD4 .... 128 A2 7
Strawberry Av GFTH/SHER LS25.. 113 G8
    LVSG WF15 .... 172 C2
Strawberry Bank LVSG WF15 ...... 172 C2 8
Strawberry Flds KGHY BD21 .... 3 G3
Strawberry Gdns
    BSLY/ROY S71 .... 243 L2
Strawberry La WOR/ARM LS12 ... 108 A7
Strawberry Rd WOR/ARM LS12 .. 108 A7
Strawberry St AIRE BD20 .... 35 M5 8
    KGHY BD21 .... 3 G3
Stream Head Rd CUL/QBY BD13.. 102 D4
Streamside HDGY LS6 .... 87 G8
Streamside Fold HBR HX7 .... 144 A6 8
Street 1 BSPA/BRAM LS23 .... 49 J5
Street 2 BSPA/BRAM LS23 .... 49 K6
Street 3 BSPA/BRAM LS23 .... 49 K5
Street 5 BSPA/BRAM LS23 .... 49 K3
Street 7 BSPA/BRAM LS23 .... 49 K3
Street 8 BSPA/BRAM LS23 .... 49 L4
Street Furlong La PONT WF8 ..... 181 K2
Street Head La HWTH BD22 .... 78 A3
Street La AIRE BD20 .... 58 D3
    AL/HA/HU LS17 .... 87 M4
    MOR LS27 .... 129 L7 8
The Street ILK LS29 .... 18 F6
Strelley Rd BSLY/ROY S71 .... 243 G6 8
Strensall Gn WBSY BD6 .... 126 A6 8
Stretchgate La LUD/ILL HX2 .... 146 A6
Stretton Cl FEA/AMT WF7 .... 179 J5
Stretton Rd BSLY/ROY S71 .... 261 J1
Strickland Cl AL/HA/HU LS17 .... 89 J1
Strickland Crs AL/HA/HU LS17 .... 89 J2
Strickland Rd HEM/SK/SE WF9 .. 225 M6
Strikes La AIRE BD20 .... 56 A3
Strines Moor Rd
    HOLM/MEL HD7 .... 254 E7
Strines St TOD OL14 .... 163 J7
Stringer House La KBTN HD8 ...... 217 J7
Strong Close Gv KGHY BD21 .... 3 L4
Strong Close Rd KGHY BD21 .... 3 L4
Stuart Gv HOLM/MEL HD7 .... 212 C6
    NORM WF6 .... 178 C2
Stuart Pl HOLM/MEL HD7 .... 212 B2
Stuart Rd PONT WF8 .... 180 E5
Stuart St CAS WF10 .... 158 A4
    MILN OL16 .... 206 D8
    PONT WF8 .... 180 E5
Stubbin Fold HOLM/MEL HD7 .... 253 L3
Stubbing Brink HBR HX7 .... 143 H3
Stubbing Dr HBR HX7 .... 143 H3
Stubbing Holme Rd HBR HX7 .... 143 H3
Stubbing La GTL/HWG HX4 .... 190 A1
    RPDN/SBR HX6 .... 167 G3
Stubbings Cl HOLM/MEL HD7 .... 253 L3
Stubbings Rd BAIL BD17 .... 82 B4
Stubbing Wy SHPY BD18 .... 82 E8 4
Stubbin La HOLM/MEL HD7 .... 253 L3
    KBTN HD8 .... 239 K8
Stubbin Rd HOLM/MEL HD7 ...... 233 K2
Stubbs Br AWLS/ASK DN6 .... 248 C4
    KNOT WF11 .... 183 J3
Stubbs La AWLS/ASK DN6 .... 227 M1
    EARD/LOFT WF3 .... 154 A7
    KNOT WF11 .... 182 C7
Stubbs Rd HFAX HX1 .... 227 J1
Stubham Ri ILK LS29 .... 38 C1
Stubley Farm Rd HECK WF16 ..... 150 E8
Stubley Holme TOD OL14 .... 140 C5 8
Stubley La LIT OL15 .... 207 H2
    TOD OL14 .... 140 C5
Stubley Mill Rd LIT OL15 .... 207 H2
Stubley Rd HECK WF16 .... 150 E8
Stubley St WKFDE WF1 .... 12 D3 8
Stubs Beck La CLECK BD19 .... 149 L4
Studfold Vw SCFT LS14 .... 111 J3
Studio Rd BVRD LS3 .... 109 G5
Studley Av WBSY BD6 .... 126 D7
Studley Cl AIRE BD20 .... 58 F5
Studley Crs BGLY BD16 .... 81 K3
Studley Rd BOW BD4 .... 105 H4
Stumpcross Ct PONT WF8 .... 181 H3 1
Stumpcross La PONT WF8 .... 181 J3
Stumpcross Wy PONT WF8 .... 181 H3
Stunstead Rd CLECK BD19 .... 149 M6
Stunsteds Rd CLECK BD19 .... 149 M6
Sturges Gv HUDN HD2 .... 14 D4
Sturton Av GFTH/SHER LS25 ...... 113 J6
Sturton Grange La
    GFTH/SHER LS25 .... 113 K7
Sturton Gv LUD/ILL HX2 .... 124 A7
Sturton La GFTH/SHER LS25 ...... 113 J6
    LUD/ILL HX2 .... 124 A8
Stutely Gv HUDN HD2 .... 193 G1
Stutton Rd TAD LS24 .... 71 K6
Styebank La RTHW LS26 .... 133 H4
Stygate La AWLS/ASK DN6 .... 227 L4
Sty La BGLY BD16 .... 59 H4
Styveton Wy AIRE BD20 .... 35 K8
Sude Hl HOLM/MEL HD7 .... 237 G8
Sude Hill Ter HOLM/MEL HD7 .... 237 H8 2
Sudforth La GLE DN14 .... 183 J1
Sudlow St MILN OL16 .... 206 D4
Suffolk Av BTLY WF17 .... 173 J4
Suffolk Ct YEA LS19 .... 62 F7
Suffolk Pl ECHL BD2 .... 105 H2
Suffolk St BTLY WF17 .... 173 K4 8 1
    ROCH OL11 .... 206 B8
Sufton St HUDN HD2 .... 14 D1
Sugar Hl ILK LS29 .... 19 H6
Sugar Hill Cl RTHW LS26 .... 155 L3
Sugar La EARL WF12 .... 174 A6
    WKFDE WF1 .... 13 J7
Sugar Well Ap CHAL LS7 .... 109 J1 8
Sugar Well Mt CHAL LS7 .... 109 J1
Sugar Well Rd CHAL LS7 .... 109 J1
Sugden Cl BRIG HD6 .... 170 C6
Sugden St BFD BD1 .... 4 B5
    LM/WK BD12 .... 149 H2
Sulby Gv BSLY S70 .... 261 M8
    IDLE BD10 .... 84 A8

Sullivan Cl HUDS HD4 .... 213 M3
Sullivan Gv HEM/SK/SE WF9 ..... 246 D5
Summerbridge Cl BTLY WF17 ..... 151 M8 5
Summerbridge Crs CLECK BD19.. 150 D4
Summerbridge Dr IDLE BD10 ..... 105 M1 5
Summer Castle MILN OL16 .... 206 B7 7
Summerdale CLECK BD19 .... 150 D4 8
Summerdale Rd CUD/GR S72 ..... 262 C1
    BRIG HD6 .... 148 D8
Summerfield Av BRAM LS13 ...... 107 J3 6
    KNOT WF11 .... 160 A6 8
Summerfield Dr BAIL BD17 .... 82 D3
    BRAM LS13 .... 107 J3
    KNOT WF11 .... 159 M6
Summerfield Gdns BRAM LS13 .. 107 J3
Summerfield Gn BAIL BD17 .... 82 D3
    BRAM LS13 .... 107 J3
Summerfield Gv BAIL BD17 .... 82 C3
    KBTN HD8 .... 215 M4 8
Summerfield Pk BAIL BD17 .... 82 D3
Summerfield Pl BRAM LS13 .... 107 J3
Summerfield Rd BRAM LS13 ...... 107 H3
    IDLE BD10 .... 83 L8
    TOD OL14 .... 163 L1
Summergate Pl HFAX HX1 .... 10 A8
Summer Hall Ing LM/WK BD12 .. 148 D2
Summerhill Av AIRE BD20 .... 35 M8 8
Summerhill Dr AIRE BD20 .... 35 M8 8
Summerhill Gdns RHAY LS8 .... 88 D3 12
Summerhill Gv AIRE BD20 .... 35 M8
Summerhill La AIRE BD20 .... 35 M8
Summerhill Pl RHAY LS8 .... 88 D3 1
Summerhill Rd
    GFTH/SHER LS25 .... 112 F7
Summer Hill Rd RTHW LS26 ...... 156 F3
Summer Hill St GTHN BD7 .... 126 C1 8
Summerlands Gv WBOW BD5 .... 127 J4
Summer La BSLY S70 .... 260 E6 8
    BSLY/ROY S71 .... 243 K2
    KBTN HD8 .... 217 M8
Summer Lea IDLE BD10 .... 83 J6
Summer Meadow PONT WF8 ..... 180 E2 8
Summer Rd BSLY/ROY S71 .... 243 K2 8
Summerscale St HFAX HX1 .... 10 C4 1
Summer St BSLY S70 .... 260 F4 11
    HFAX HX1 .... 10 B9
    HUD HD1 .... 214 B2 8
    HUDS HD4 .... 213 M8
    MILN OL16 .... 206 C7 2
Summervale HOLM/MEL HD7 .... 236 C8 8
Summerville Rd GTHN BD7 .... 4 A7
    PDSY/CALV LS28 .... 106 D7
Summit St KGHY BD21 .... 2 F5 3
Sunbeam Av BEE/HOL LS11 ...... 131 K3
Sunbeam Gv BEE/HOL LS11 ...... 131 K3 13
Sunbeam Pl BEE/HOL LS11 .... 131 K3
Sunbeam Ter BEE/HOL LS11 ..... 131 K3
Sunbridge Rd BFD BD1 .... 4 B4
Sunbury Gv HUDE HD5 .... 193 G8
Sun Ct FEA/AMT WF7 .... 179 L5
Sunderland Ct BRIG HD6 .... 170 C3 7
Sunderland Rd AIRE BD20 .... 34 F1
    HTON BD9 .... 104 D4
Sunderland St HFAX HX1 .... 10 F6 8
    HWTH BD22 .... 79 H6 8
    KGHY BD21 .... 2 F7
Sunderland Ter BSLY S70 .... 261 J6 8
Sundown Av GTHN BD7 .... 126 A3
Sun Fld PDSY/CALV LS28 .... 106 F5
Sunfield Cl PDSY/CALV LS28 ..... 106 F4
Sunfield Dr PDSY/CALV LS28 ..... 106 F4 8
Sunfield Gdns PDSY/CALV LS28. 106 F4 8
Sunfield Pl PDSY/CALV LS28 ..... 106 F4
Sun Fold HFAX HX1 .... 11 J8
Sunhill Cl MILN OL16 .... 228 D3
Sun Hill Dr BAIL BD17 .... 82 A3
Sunhurst Cl HWTH BD22 .... 78 E4 8
Sunhurst Dr HWTH BD22 .... 78 E4
Sun La HWTH BD22 .... 78 A7
    ILK LS29 .... 39 M4
    WKFDE WF1 .... 13 G3
Sunmoor Dr SKP/WHF BD23 .... 16 D2
Sunningdale GFTH/SHER LS25 ... 114 B7
    GIR BD8 .... 104 F4 8
Sunningdale Av AL/HA/HU LS17 .. 87 J2
    DOD/DAR S75 .... 242 C5 8
Sunningdale Crs
    CUL/QBY BD13 .... 102 A1
Sunningdale Cft HUDN HD2 .... 192 B3 8
Sunningdale Dr AL/HA/HU LS17 .. 87 J2
    CUD/GR S72 .... 244 E5
Sunningdale Gn AL/HA/HU LS17 . 87 J2
Sunningdale Rd HUDS HD4 .... 213 M3
Sunny Av HEM/SK/SE WF9 .... 225 J7
    HEM/SK/SE WF9 .... 247 K4
Sunny Bank CHAL LS7 .... 110 B1
    HEM/SK/SE WF9 .... 223 J2
    HOR/CROF WF4 .... 222 C5
    NORM WF6 .... 178 C6
    SHPY BD18 .... 82 D7 7
Sunnybank Av BFDE BD3 .... 106 B5
    HORS LS18 .... 85 K7
Sunny Bank Av MIRF WF14 .... 172 C6 8
    WBOW BD5 .... 126 F5 10
Sunnybank Cl CLECK BD19 .... 149 M8
Sunnybank Crs GTL/HWG HX4 .. 168 D7 5
    YEA LS19 .... 62 F7
Sunny Bank Dr CUD/GR S72 ...... 262 D2
    GTL/HWG HX4 .... 168 D7
Sunny Bank Dr MIRF WF14 .... 172 B6
    RPDN/SBR HX6 .... 167 L2
Sunnybank Gv BFDE BD3 .... 106 B5
Sunny Bank Gv CHAL LS7 .... 110 A1
    MIRF WF14 .... 172 C7 8
Sunny Bank La BTLY WF17 .... 151 M7 8
Sunny Bank La GTL/HWG HX4 .... 168 D7 8
Sunny Bank La HBR HX7 .... 165 J2
    HIPP HX3 .... 147 K8
Sunny Bank Pde MIRF WF14 ...... 172 B6
Sunny Bank Rd AIRE BD20 .... 34 E8 8

BRIG HD6 .... 170 B3
    BTLY WF17 .... 151 M8
    DOD/DAR S75 .... 260 D3
Sunnybank Rd GFTH/SHER LS25.. 114 D8
    GTL/HWG HX4 .... 168 C7
Sunny Bank Rd
    HOLM/MEL HD7 .... 212 D3
    HOLM/MEL HD7 .... 234 E4
Sunnybank Rd HORS LS18 .... 85 K7 5
    HUDW HD3 .... 191 M6
Sunny Bank Rd LUD/ILL HX2 ...... 145 K1
    MIRF WF14 .... 172 C6
    WBOW BD5 .... 126 F5
Sunny Bank St OSS WF5 .... 196 E1
Sunny Bank St RPDN/SBR HX6 .. 167 L2
Sunny Bank Ter HIPP HX3 .... 11 G2 8
    TOD OL14 .... 140 D5 8
Sunny Bank Vw RHAY LS8 .... 110 B1 8
Sunny Bank Wk MIRF WF14 .... 172 C6
Sunnybrae Crs BGLY BD16 .... 81 K4 8
Sunny Brow HUDS HD4 .... 214 B6 8
Sunny Brow La HTON BD9 .... 103 M4
Sunnycliffe AIRE BD20 .... 58 F6
Sunnydale Av BRIG HD6 .... 170 C6 8
Sunnydale Crs OT LS21 .... 40 F8
Sunnydale Cft OSS WF5 .... 197 G2 8
Sunnydale Gv KGHY BD21 .... 58 B8
Sunnydale Pk AIRE BD20 .... 59 G5
    OSS WF5 .... 197 G1 8
Sunnydale Rdg OT LS21 .... 40 F8
Sunnydale Rd OSS WF5 .... 197 G1
Sunnydale Ter OSS WF5 .... 197 G1 8
Sunnydene SCFT LS14 .... 111 H5
Sunnyfield EARD/LOFT WF3 ...... 153 L7 8
Sunnyfield Dr HEM/SK/SE WF9 .. 223 J5
Sunny Gv MOR LS27 .... 130 E6 8
Sunny Heys Rd HOLM/MEL HD7.. 234 F3
Sunny Heys West
    HOLM/MEL HD7 .... 234 F3
Sunny Hl WKFDW/WTN WF2 ..... 175 M5
Sunnyhill Av HUDE HD5 .... 193 K4
Sunny Hill Av HWTH BD22 .... 2 B8
Sunny Hill Cl
    WKFDW/WTN WF2 .... 176 A4 8
Sunnyhill Crs
    WKFDW/WTN WF2 .... 175 M5
Sunnyhill Cft WKFDW/WTN WF2.. 175 M4
Sunny Hill Gv HWTH BD22 .... 2 B8
Sunny Md HUDE HD5 .... 193 J8
Sunnymead KBTN HD8 .... 239 M4
Sunny Mt AIRE BD20 .... 58 E7
    BGLY BD16 .... 80 D5 2
    KGHY BD21 .... 2 E5
Sunnyridge Av PDSY/CALV LS28.. 106 D7
Sunnyside BRIG HD6 .... 170 F6
    GTL/HWG HX4 .... 190 B5
    HECK WF16 .... 172 F3
    HUDW HD3 .... 14 A3
    TOD OL14 .... 163 J1
Sunnyside Av EARD/LOFT WF3 .. 152 F2
    LVSG WF15 .... 172 B4
Sunnyside La BFDE BD3 .... 5 H1
Sunnyside Rd BRAM LS13 .... 107 K5
Sunny Side St HIPP HX3 .... 11 H2 8
Sunnyvale Mt HEM/SK/SE WF9 . 247 G3
Sunnyview EARD/LOFT WF3 ...... 153 L7 10
Sunnyview Av BEE/HOL LS11 ..... 131 H3
Sunny View Crs HUDN HD2 .... 192 F3 8
Sunnyview Gdns BEE/HOL LS11.. 131 H3
Sunnyview Ter BEE/HOL LS11 .... 131 H3
Sunny View Ter CUL/QBY BD13 .. 124 F6 2
Sunroyd Av HOR/CROF WF4 ...... 197 K4
Sunroyd Hl HOR/CROF WF4 ...... 197 K4
Sunset Av HDGY LS6 .... 87 G6
Sunset Dr HDGY LS6 .... 87 G7 8
    ILK LS29 .... 38 F1
Sunset Hilltop HDGY LS6 .... 87 G6
Sunset Mt HDGY LS6 .... 87 G7 8
Sunset Ri HDGY LS6 .... 87 G6 7
Sunset Rd HDGY LS6 .... 87 G6
Sunset Vw HDGY LS6 .... 87 G6
Sunshine Ct WBSY BD6 .... 126 B8 8
Sun St AIRE BD20 .... 34 B4
    AIRE BD20 .... 56 B1
    BFDE BD3 .... 5 H4
    COL BB8 .... 74 A1 8
    HWTH BD22 .... 54 E3 2
    KGHY BD21 .... 3 G6
    PDSY/CALV LS28 .... 106 F5
    YEA LS19 .... 62 E7
Sun Ter TOD OL14 .... 140 D5 8
Sun Vale Av TOD OL14 .... 163 K7
Sun Wy HIPP HX3 .... 169 K1
Sun Wood Av HIPP HX3 .... 147 K2
Surat Rd HOLM/MEL HD7 .... 212 D4
Suresnes Rd KGHY BD21 .... 2 F5
Surgery St HWTH BD22 .... 78 E1 8
Surma Cl MILN OL16 .... 228 D1
Surrey Gv ROY/SHW OL2 .... 229 H7
Surrey Cl BSLY S70 .... 261 H7
Surrey Gv PDSY/CALV LS28 .... 107 G6
    WBOW BD5 .... 127 G2 15
Surrey Park Cl ROY/SHW OL2 .... 229 K6 10
Surrey Rd PDSY/CALV LS28 .... 107 G6
Surrey St BTLY WF17 .... 173 M1 8
    HFAX HX1 .... 146 A8
    KGHY BD21 .... 3 L2
    TOD OL14 .... 141 K8 8
Sussex Av HORS LS18 .... 85 L3
    MID LS10 .... 132 B3
Sussex Cl HEM/SK/SE WF9 .... 223 M6
Sussex Crs CAS WF10 .... 159 G7
Sussex Gdns MID LS10 .... 132 B3 8
Sussex Pl MID LS10 .... 132 B3
Sussex St BTLY WF17 .... 173 M1 8
    KGHY BD21 .... 3 L2
    OSM LS9 .... 9 M1
    OSM LS9 .... 110 B7 13
    ROCH OL11 .... 206 B8 14
Sutcliffe St LIT OL15 .... 185 K8
    LUD/ILL HX2 .... 146 A6
Sutcliffe Wood La HIPP HX3 .... 147 L8
Sutherland Av RHAY LS8 .... 88 C5
Sutherland Crs RHAY LS8 .... 88 C4
Sutherland Dr HUDS HD4 .... 213 L5
Sutherland Mt OSM LS9 .... 110 C4

Sutherland Rd *HIPP* HX3 .... 148 A6
   OSM LS9 .... 110 C4
Sutherland St *WOR/ARM* LS12 .. 109 G8 🔟
Sutton Ap *SCFT* LS14 .... 111 C5
Sutton Av *BSLYN/ROY* S71 .... 243 H6
   ECHL BD2 .... 105 H1
   HUDE HD5 .... 193 J6
Sutton Crs *BOW* BD4 .... 128 A2
   SCFT LS14 .... 111 G5 🟦
Sutton Dr *CUL/QBY* BD13 .... 101 M1
   HUDE HD5 .... 193 J6
Sutton Gv *BOW* BD4 .... 128 A1 🟦
   MOR LS27 .... 152 C3 🔟
Sutton La *AIRE* BD20 .... 56 A1
   KNOT WF11 .... 159 M7
Sutton Rd *AWLS/ASK* DN6 .... 227 L6
   BOW BD4 .... 128 A1
Sutton St *WOR/ARM* LS12 .... 8 B3
Suzanne Crs *HEM/SK/SE* WF9 .. 247 G3
Swadford St *SKP/WHF* BD23 .... 16 B2
Swaindrod La *LIT* OL15 .... 186 A1
Swaine Hill Crs *YEA* LS19 .... 62 C7
Swaine Hill St *YEA* LS19 .... 62 C7
Swaine Hill Ter *YEA* LS19 .... 62 C7
Swain House Crs *ECHL* BD2 .... 105 J1
Swain House Rd *ECHL* BD2 .... 105 J1
Swain Mt *ECHL* BD2 .... 105 J1
Swain St *WHIT* OL12 .... 206 A5 🟦
Swale Crs *GFTH/SHER* LS25 .... 113 K8
Swales Moor Rd *HIPP* HX3 .... 146 L1
Swales' Yd *PONT* WF8 .... 180 E6 🟦
Swallow Av *WOR/ARM* LS12 .... 108 C8
Swallow Cl *AL/HA/HU* LS17 .... 88 B2 🟦
   DOD/DAR S75 .... 241 M6
   OT LS21 .... 42 F8
Swallow Dr *AL/HA/HU* LS17 .... 88 B2
   OT LS21 .... 42 F8
Swallow Fold *GIR* BD8 .... 103 L7 🔟
Swallow Garth
   WKFDW/WTN WF2 .... 220 F1
Swallow Gv *HUDS* HD4 .... 214 A4
Swallow Hl *BTLY* WF17 .... 151 J5
Swallow Hill Rd *DOD/DAR* S75 .. 242 C7
Swallow Mt *HOLM/MEL* HD7 .... 212 C1
Swallow St *WOR/ARM* LS12 .... 108 C7
Swallow St *HECK* WF16 .... 172 F6 🔟
   KGHY BD21 .... 2 E7
Swallow V *MOR* LS27 .... 152 F2 🟦
Swan Bank Ct *HOLM/MEL* HD7 .. 254 C2
Swan Bank La *HIPP* HX3 .... 11 K9
   HOLM/MEL HD7 .... 254 C2
Swan Ct *ROY/SHW* OL2 .... 229 K8 🔟
Swanee Rd *BSLY* S70 .... 261 K8
Swanhill La *PONT* WF8 .... 180 F7
Swan La *HUDS* HD4 .... 13 K8
   HUDW HD3 .... 190 D5 🟦
Swan St *LDS* LS1 .... 7 G9
   WBOW BD5 .... 4 E9
Swarcliffe Ap *SCFT* LS14 .... 111 L2
Swarcliffe Av *SCFT* LS14 .... 111 L2
Swarcliffe Bank *SCFT* LS14 .... 111 L1
Swarcliffe Dr *SCFT* LS14 .... 111 L2
Swarcliffe Dr (East)
   MSTN/BAR LS15 .... 111 M1
Swarcliffe Gn *SCFT* LS14 .... 111 M2
Swarcliffe Gn *SCFT* LS14 .... 111 L1
Swardale Gn *SCFT* LS14 .... 111 L2 🟦
Swardale Rd *SCFT* LS14 .... 111 L2
Swarland Gv *WBOW* BD5 .... 127 G2
Swartha La *AIRE* BD20 .... 36 C3
Sweeming La *GFTH/SHER* LS25 .. 117 C3
Sweep La *HOLM/MEL* HD7 .... 254 D3
Sweetbriar Cl *ROY/SHW* OL2 ... 229 K8 🔟
Sweet Briar Cl *WHIT* OL12 .... 206 A4 🟦
Sweet Briar La *WHIT* OL12 .... 206 A4 🟦
Sweet St *BEE/HOL* LS11 .... 8 E4
Sweet St West *BEE/HOL* LS11 .... 8 E4
Swift's Fold *HOLM/MEL* HD7 .... 236 B1 🟦
Swift St *DOD/DAR* S75 .... 260 F4
Swift Wy *WKFDW/WTN* WF2 .... 220 E1
Swillington La *RTHW* LS26 .... 134 B5
Swincar Av *YEA* LS19 .... 62 D7
Swincliffe Cl *CLECK* BD19 .... 150 C2
Swincliffe Crs *CLECK* BD19 .... 150 C3
Swincroft *OSS* WF5 .... 197 L5
Swindon La *PBR* HG3 .... 26 E6
   PBR HG3 .... 45 H1
Swindon Rd *DEWS* WF13 .... 173 L6
Swinegate *LDS* LS1 .... 9 G2
Swine La *AIRE* BD20 .... 58 D6
   HOR/CROF WF4 .... 222 C3
Swine Lane Br *AIRE* BD20 .... 58 E6
Swineshead La *TOD* OL14 .... 163 K3
Swineshead Rd *TOD* OL14 .... 163 J3
Swinnow Av *BRAM* LS13 .... 107 J5
Swinnow Cl *BRAM* LS13 .... 107 J5
Swinnow Crs *PDSY/CALV* LS28 ... 107 J4
Swinnow Dr *BRAM* LS13 .... 107 J5
Swinnow Gdns *BRAM* LS13 .... 107 J5
Swinnow Garth
   PDSY/CALV LS28 .... 107 J4
Swinnow Gn *PDSY/CALV* LS28 .. 107 H5
Swinnow Gv *BRAM* LS13 .... 107 J5
Swinnow La *BRAM* LS13 .... 107 J4
   PDSY/CALV LS28 .... 107 J4
Swinnow Pl *PDSY/CALV* LS28 .... 107 J4
Swinnow Rd *PDSY/CALV* LS28 ... 107 J5
Swinnow Vw *BRAM* LS13 .... 107 J5
Swinnow Wk *BRAM* LS13 .... 107 J5
Swinton Ter *HFAX* HX1 .... 126 D1 🟦
Swinton Ter *HFAX* HX1 .... 10 A7
Swires La *AIRE* BD20 .... 34 B1
Swires Rd *ECHL* BD2 .... 5 M1
   HFAX HX1 .... 10 E8 🟦
Swires Ter *HFAX* HX1 .... 10 F7
Swiss St *CAS* WF10 .... 158 A5
Swithenbank Av *OSS* WF5 .... 174 E5
Swithenbank St *OSS* WF5 .... 174 E5
Swithen Hl *DOD/DAR* S75 .... 241 M4
Swithens Ct *RTHW* LS26 .... 155 H2
Swithens Dr *RTHW* LS26 .... 155 H2
Swithens Gv *RTHW* LS26 .... 155 H2
Swithens' La *RTHW* LS26 .... 155 H1
Swithen's St *RTHW* LS26 .... 155 H2
Swordfish Wy *GFTH/SHER* LS25 .. 116 D7
Sybil St *LIT* OL15 .... 185 J8

Sycamore Av *BGLY* BD16 .... 81 H4
   CUD/GR S72 .... 244 D7 🟦
   CUD/GR S72 .... 263 K1 🟦
   GFTH/SHER LS25 .... 135 H4
   HDGY LS6 .... 104 B7
   HOLM/MEL HD7 .... 234 F5
   HUDW HD3 .... 213 H1
   MILN OL16 .... 229 J3
   MSTN/BAR LS15 .... 111 J6
   RHAY LS8 .... 110 B1
   TOD OL14 .... 141 J2
   WKFDW/WTN WF2 .... 176 B4 🟦
   WKFDW/WTN WF2 .... 176 B7
Sycamore Cha *PDSY/CALV* LS28 .. 107 H7
Sycamore Cl *BFDE* BD3 .... 5 J3
   BHP/TINH LS16 .... 64 B5
   CHAL LS7 .... 87 H7
   HDGY LS6 .... 6 C1
   KBTN HD8 .... 216 B3 🟦
   KNOT WF11 .... 181 M4
   LIT OL15 .... 207 H1
Sycamore Copse
   WKFDW/WTN WF2 .... 198 B1
Sycamore Ct *KBTN* HD8 .... 216 B7
   RHAY LS8 .... 88 E8 🟦
Sycamore Cft *BEE/HOL* LS11 .... 8 E9
Sycamore Dr *BRIG* HD6 .... 148 C8
   BSLYN/ROY S71 .... 243 J3
   CLECK BD19 .... 149 K7
   ELL HX5 .... 168 F8
   ILK LS29 .... 19 J6 🟦
Sycamore Fold *BEE/HOL* LS11 .... 8 E9
Sycamore Gn *KBTN* HD8 .... 239 C7
Sycamore Gv *AIRE* BD20 .... 56 B1
   NORM WF6 .... 178 C6 🟦
   WKFDW/WTN WF2 .... 176 B7
Sycamore La *HOR/CROF* WF4 .... 219 H6
Sycamore Ri *HOLM/MEL* HD7 .... 236 F7 🟦
Sycamore Rd *HEM/SK/SE* WF9 ... 223 L8
Sycamore Rw *BRAM* LS13 .... 107 J2 🟦
The Sycamores *BHP/TINH* LS16 ... 64 B5
   DEWS WF13 .... 173 K4 🟦
   GSLY LS20 .... 62 A4
   HOR/CROF WF4 .... 197 L5
Sycamore St *DOD/DAR* S75 .... 260 E4 🟦
   WKFDE WF1 .... 13 K7
Sycamore Vw *HWTH* BD22 .... 2 B7
Sycamore Wk *PDSY/CALV* LS28... 106 F4
   STKB/PEN S36 .... 270 F3 🟦
Sycamore Wy *BTLY* WF17 .... 151 H5
   FEA/AMT WF7 .... 179 M8
Sydenham Pl *BFDE* BD3 .... 105 J4
Sydenham Rd *BEE/HOL* LS11 .... 8 A4
Sydenham St *BEE/HOL* LS11 .... 8 A4
Sydney Gdns *LIT* OL15 .... 185 L5
Sydney St *BGLY* BD16 .... 81 J3 🔟
   LVSG WF15 .... 172 D3
   PDSY/CALV LS28 .... 106 F4
   RTHW LS26 .... 133 M8
Syke Av *EARD/LOFT* WF3 .... 152 F7
Syke Cl *EARD/LOFT* WF3 .... 152 E7
Syke Cft *BSLYN/ROY* S71 .... 243 L1
Syke Gdns *EARD/LOFT* WF3 ..... 152 F7 🟦
Syke Gn *SCFT* LS14 .... 67 L6
Syke Gv *EARL* WF12 .... 174 B6
Syke House La *GTL/HWG* HX4 ... 168 B3 🟦
Syke Ing Cl *EARL* WF12 .... 174 C7
Syke La *CUL/QBY* BD13 .... 125 C7
   EARL WF12 .... 174 B7
   HIPP HX3 .... 148 A5
   LUD/ILL HX2 .... 123 M4
   RPDN/SBR HX6 .... 167 J3
   SCFT LS14 .... 67 L7
   WHIT OL12 .... 206 B2
Syke Rd *EARD/LOFT* WF3 .... 152 F7
   EARL WF12 .... 174 B6
   LIT OL15 .... 207 L4
   WBY LS22 .... 48 C1
   WHIT OL12 .... 206 B2
Sykes Av *DOD/DAR* S75 .... 260 F4
   MIRF WF14 .... 172 A8
Sykes Cl *BTLY* WF17 .... 152 A8
Sykes Ga *RHAY* LS8 .... 165 K7
Syke Side *AIRE* BD20 .... 57 K4 🟦
Sykes La *AIRE* BD20 .... 36 A5 🔟
   EARL WF12 .... 174 C2
   HWTH BD22 .... 78 F3
   LM/WK BD12 .... 149 J2
Sykes Rd *BTLY* WF17 .... 152 A8
Sykes St *BSLY* S70 .... 260 F7
   CAS WF10 .... 157 M6 🔟
   CLECK BD19 .... 149 M7
   MILN OL16 .... 206 D8 🟦
   MILN OL16 .... 229 J2
Syke St *EARL* WF12 .... 174 B6
Syke Vw *EARL* WF12 .... 174 B6
Sylhet Cl *BFD* BD1 .... 4 D4
Sylvan Av *CUL/QBY* BD13 .... 124 F6
Sylvester Av *NORM* WF6 .... 178 B7
Symons St *WKFDW/WTN* WF2 ... 12 D6
Syringa Av *WIL/AL* BD15 .... 103 J2
Syringa St *HUDW* HD3 .... 191 M7

T

Tabbs Ct *CLECK* BD19 .... 149 H5
Tabbs La *CLECK* BD19 .... 149 H5
Tadman St *WKFDE* WF1 .... 12 F6
Tagore Ct *BOW* BD4 .... 105 M8 🔟
Talbot & Falcon Yd
   WKFDE WF1 .... 12 E2 🟦
Talbot Av *AL/HA/HU* LS17 .... 88 A4
   BULY LS4 .... 108 E3
   HUDW HD3 .... 191 L6
Talbot Ct *RHAY* LS8 .... 88 B5
Talbot Crs *RHAY* LS8 .... 88 B4
Talbot Fold *RHAY* LS8 .... 88 B5 🟦
Talbot Gdns *RHAY* LS8 .... 88 B4
Talbot Gv *RHAY* LS8 .... 88 B4
Talbot Mt *BULY* LS4 .... 108 E3
Talbot Ri *RHAY* LS8 .... 88 B4
Talbot Rd *RHAY* LS8 .... 88 B4
Talbot Rw *BTLY* WF17 .... 173 M1 🟦

Talbot St *BTLY* WF17 .... 173 L2
   GTHN BD7 .... 104 D7
   KGHY BD21 .... 2 C5
   NORM WF6 .... 178 C4
   ROCH OL11 .... 206 B8 🟦
Talbot Ter *BULY* LS4 .... 108 E3
   RTHW LS26 .... 155 G2 🟦
Talbot Vw *BULY* LS4 .... 108 E3
Tallow Ms *KBTN* HD8 .... 239 J5
Tall Trees Dr *FEA/AMT* WF7 .... 179 M6
Tamar Cl *DOD/DAR* S75 .... 260 A3
Tamar St *WBOW* BD5 .... 126 E2
Tame Barn Cl *MILN* OL16 .... 207 J8 🟦
Tame La *UPML* OL3 .... 230 E7
Tammy Hall St *WKFDE* WF1 .... 12 E2 🟦
Tamworth St *BOW* BD4 .... 106 A8 🟦
Tandem Wy *HUD* HD5 .... 193 K8
Tandle Hill Rd *ROY/SHW* OL2 .... 228 D8
Tandlewood Pk *ROY/SHW* OL2 .. 228 D8
Tanfield Cl *BSLYN/ROY* S71 .... 243 J2
Tanfield Dr *ILK* LS29 .... 40 A4
Tanfield Rd *HUD* HD1 .... 14 D7
Tanglewood Ct *WBSY* BD6 .... 126 C5 🟦
Tanhouse Hl *HIPP* HX3 .... 147 L7
   HORS LS18 .... 86 A6 🟦
Tanhouse La *MIRF* WF14 .... 194 D7
Tan House La *WIL/AL* BD15 .... 80 D8
Tanhouse Pk *HIPP* HX3 .... 147 L7
Tanhouse St *DEWS* WF13 .... 173 H8
Tank Rw *BSLY* S70 .... 261 M5
Tan La *BOW* BD4 .... 127 K8
Tannerbrook Cl *CLAY* BD14 .... 125 M2 🟦
Tanner Hill Rd *GTHN* BD7 .... 126 A3
Tanners *HOLM/MEL* HD7 .... 212 B7
Tannery Ct *IDLE* BD10 .... 83 M6 🟦
Tanpit La *BSLYN/ROY* S71 .... 243 H3
Tanpits *HBR* HX7 .... 143 J3 🟦🟦
Tanshelf Dr *PONT* WF8 .... 180 E6
Tanton Crs *CLAY* BD14 .... 125 M2
Tanton Wk *CLAY* BD14 .... 125 M2
Tanyard Av *HUDW* HD3 .... 191 J7 🟦
Tanyard Cft *CUD/GR* S72 .... 245 J3 🟦
Tanyard Fold *HOR/CROF* WF4 .... 220 C2
Tanyard Rd *HUDS* HD4 .... 213 K2
Tarn Cl *CAS* WF10 .... 159 G5
Tarn Ct *HWTH* BD22 .... 2 A2
   WKFDE WF1 .... 176 D3
Tarnhill Ms *WBOW* BD5 .... 127 G2 🟦
Tarn Hows Wk *FEA/AMT* WF7 ... 224 A1 🟦
Tarn La *AL/HA/HU* LS17 .... 66 F7
   HWTH BD22 .... 56 E6
Tarn Rd *FEA/AMT* WF7 .... 202 A2
Tarnside Cl *MILN* OL16 .... 206 E3
Tarnside Dr *SCFT* LS14 .... 111 H5
Tarn View Rd *YEA* LS19 .... 62 E7
Tatefield Cl *GFTH/SHER* LS25 .... 135 J6
Tatefield Pl *GFTH/SHER* LS25 .... 135 J6
Tateley Cl *OSS* WF5 .... 174 F5 🟦
Tateley La *OSS* WF5 .... 174 E5
Tate Naylor St *DEWS* WF13 .... 173 K4 🟦
Tatham St *MILN* OL16 .... 206 D8
Tatham Wy *RHAY* LS8 .... 88 E8
Tatton St *SHPY* BD18 .... 82 C6
Taunton St *WBOW* BD5 .... 117 G6
Tavern St *WKFDE* WF1 .... 13 H4
Tavistock Rd *ROCH* OL11 .... 228 B3
Tavistock Wy
   WKFDW/WTN WF2 .... 220 B1
Tavora St *WKFDE* WF1 .... 176 E7 🟦
Tavy Cl *DOD/DAR* S75 .... 260 A3
Tawny Cl *BOW* BD4 .... 128 A5 🔟
Taylor Av *AIRE* BD20 .... 35 M5
Taylor Cl *OSS* WF5 .... 197 H2
Taylor Crs *CUD/GR* S72 .... 263 J2
   OSS WF5 .... 197 H2
Taylor Dr *OSS* WF5 .... 197 H2 🟦
Taylor Gv *RTHW* LS26 .... 157 G3
Taylor Hall La *MIRF* WF14 .... 172 A5
Taylor Hill Rd *HUDS* HD4 .... 214 A5
Taylor La *HOLM/MEL* HD7 .... 212 D1
   LUD/ILL HX2 .... 124 C4
   MSTN/BAR LS15 .... 90 D8
Taylor Rd *WBSY* BD6 .... 126 F6 🟦
Taylor Rw *BSLY* S70 .... 261 H6 🟦
Taylors Cl *SCFT* LS14 .... 111 K2
Taylors Pl *WHIT* OL12 .... 206 B5 🟦
Taylor St *BTLY* WF17 .... 173 L2
   CLECK BD19 .... 149 L7
   HOLM/MEL HD7 .... 213 G1
   WHIT OL12 .... 206 B5
Tealbeck Ap *OT* LS21 .... 41 K7
Tealby Cl *BHP/TINH* LS16 .... 86 A4
Teal Cl *CAS* WF10 .... 157 M8
Teal Ct *AIRE* BD20 .... 35 K8
Teal Dr *MOR* LS27 .... 152 F2
Teall Ct *OSS* WF5 .... 197 J1
Teall St *OSS* WF5 .... 197 J1
   WKFDE WF1 .... 12 F1
Teal Ms *MID* LS10 .... 153 M1
Teal St *WKFDE* WF1 .... 12 F2
Teasdale St *BOW* BD4 .... 127 K3
Teasel Cl *LM/WK* BD12 .... 149 J2
Technology Dr *BTLY* WF17 .... 174 A2
Tees St *MILN* OL16 .... 206 D8 🟦
   WBOW BD5 .... 126 E3 🟦
Telephone Pl *CHAL* LS7 .... 7 K6
Telford Cl *AIRE* BD20 .... 36 B6
   CAS WF10 .... 157 K7
   MID LS10 .... 132 A4
Telford Pl *MID* LS10 .... 132 A4 🟦
Telford Ter *MID* LS10 .... 132 A3
Telford Wy *ROCH* OL11 .... 228 C4
   WKFDW/WTN WF2 .... 176 A1
Telscombe Dr *BOW* BD4 .... 127 M4
Temperance Flds *CLECK* BD19 ... 149 H6
Tempest Av *WMB/DAR* S73 .... 263 J7
Tempest Pl *BEE/HOL* LS11 .... 8 D9
Tempest Rd *HEM/SK/SE* WF9 ... 246 E2
Templar Gdns *WBY* LS22 .... 30 B7
Templar La *LDSU* LS2 .... 7 J9
   MSTN/BAR LS15 .... 111 M2
Templar Pl *LDSU* LS2 .... 7 J9

Templars Cl *GTL/HWG* HX4 .... 168 C7
Templar St *LDSU* LS2 .... 7 J9
   WKFDE WF1 .... 13 M8 🟦
Templars Wy *GFTH/SHER* LS25 .. 113 H8
   GIR BD8 .... 104 A6
Temple Av *MSTN/BAR* LS15 .... 111 J8
   RTHW LS26 .... 133 H7
Temple Cl *HUD* HD1 .... 14 F6
   MSTN/BAR LS15 .... 111 J8
Temple Ct *MSTN/BAR* LS15 .... 111 H7
   RTHW LS26 .... 133 H7
Temple Crs *BEE/HOL* LS11 .... 8 C9
Temple Gdns *NORM* WF6 .... 178 B2
Temple Gn *MSTN/BAR* LS15 .... 111 J8
Templegate Av *MSTN/BAR* LS15 .. 111 J8
Templegate Cl *MSTN/BAR* LS15 .. 111 K8
Templegate Crs
   MSTN/BAR LS15 .... 111 K8
Temple Gate Dr
   MSTN/BAR LS15 .... 111 J7
Templegate Gn *MSTN/BAR* LS15 .. 111 J8
Templegate Ri *MSTN/BAR* LS15 .. 111 J8
Templegate Rd *MSTN/BAR* LS15 . 111 J8
Templegate Vw
   MSTN/BAR LS15 .... 111 J8
Templegate Wk
   MSTN/BAR LS15 .... 111 J8
Templegate Wy
   MSTN/BAR LS15 .... 111 K8 🟦
Temple Gn *RTHW* LS26 .... 133 J7
Temple Gv *MSTN/BAR* LS15 .... 111 J8
Temple La *LIT* OL15 .... 185 L5
   MSTN/BAR LS15 .... 111 K7
Temple Lea *MSTN/BAR* LS15 .... 111 J7
Templenewsam Rd
   MSTN/BAR LS15 .... 111 H7
Templenewsam Vw
   MSTN/BAR LS15 .... 111 H8
Temple Park Cl
   MSTN/BAR LS15 .... 111 J7 🟦
Temple Park Gdns
   MSTN/BAR LS15 .... 111 J7
Temple Park Gn
   MSTN/BAR LS15 .... 111 J7
Temple Rhydding Dr *BAIL* BD17 .. 82 E4
Temple Ri *MSTN/BAR* LS15 .... 111 J8
Temple Rd *DEWS* WF13 .... 173 J7
Temple Row Cl
   MSTN/BAR LS15 .... 112 A8 🟦
Templestowe Crs
   MSTN/BAR LS15 .... 111 L5 🟦
Templestowe Dr
   MSTN/BAR LS15 .... 111 L6 🟦
Templestowe Gdns
   MSTN/BAR LS15 .... 111 K6 🟦
Templestowe Hl
   MSTN/BAR LS15 .... 111 K5 🟦
Temple St *CAS* WF10 .... 157 L7
   COL BB8 .... 52 A8
   HTON BD9 .... 104 D4
   HUDW HD3 .... 191 K5
Temple Vw *EARD/LOFT* WF3 ..... 154 E5 🟦
Temple View Gv *OSM* LS9 .... 110 C7 🟦
Temple View Pl *OSM* LS9 .... 110 B7
Temple View Rd *OSM* LS9 .... 110 B7
Temple View Ter *OSM* LS9 .... 110 B7
Temple Wk *MSTN/BAR* LS15 .... 111 K6
Temple Wy *BSLYN/ROY* S71 ..... 261 M3 🟦
Tenbury Fold *BOW* BD4 .... 128 A3
Ten Lands La *HOR/CROF* WF4 .. 222 B7
Tennis Av *BOW* BD4 .... 128 A5
Tennis Wy *BAIL* BD17 .... 82 C5
Tennyson Av *AWLS/ASK* DN6 ... 227 L5
   EARD/LOFT WF3 .... 155 G8 🟦
   RPDN/SBR HX6 .... 167 H3
   TOD OL14 .... 141 M8
Tennyson Cl *PDSY/CALV* LS28 ... 107 J3
   STKB/PEN S36 .... 270 F2
Tennyson Pl *BFDE* BD3 .... 5 L3
   CLECK BD19 .... 149 M6 🟦
Tennyson Rd *WBSY* BD6 .... 126 D6
Tennyson St *GSLY* LS20 .... 62 B6
   HIPP HX3 .... 10 D1
   KGHY BD21 .... 2 F8 🟦
   MOR LS27 .... 152 D2 🟦
   PDSY/CALV LS28 .... 106 F3
   ROCH OL11 .... 228 C1 🟦
Tennyson Ter *MOR* LS27 .... 152 D2 🟦
Tennyson Wy *PONT* WF8 .... 180 F3
Tenter Cl *BTLY* WF17 .... 151 L8 🟦
   KBTN HD8 .... 239 J4
Tentercroft Ct *DEWS* WF13 ..... 173 M5 🟦
Tenterden Wy *MSTN/BAR* LS15 .. 112 B3
Tenterfield Ri *HIPP* HX3 .... 147 J5
Tenterfield Rd *OSS* WF5 .... 197 G1
Tenterfields *IDLE* BD10 .... 84 A6
   LUD/ILL HX2 .... 167 G1
Tenter Hl *BSPA/BRAM* LS23 ..... 69 K4
   CLAY BD14 .... 125 K2 🟦
   HOLM/MEL HD7 .... 255 H2
Tenter Hill La *HUDW* HD2 .... 192 F2
Tenter La *STKB/PEN* S36 .... 271 J8
Tenters Cl *KNOT* WF11 .... 181 L1
Tenters Gv *HUDN* HD2 .... 192 E3
Tenth Av *LVSG* WF15 .... 171 K1
Ten Yards La *CUL/QBY* BD13 .... 102 D3
Ternhill Gv *WBOW* BD5 .... 4 E9
Tern Pk *WBY* LS22 .... 47 J5
Tern St *WBOW* BD5 .... 126 E3
Terrace Gdns *HIPP* HX3 .... 10 E2
The Terrace *PDSY/CALV* LS28 .... 129 G2
Terrington Crest *CLAY* BD14 ..... 125 M2
Terry Rd *LM/WK* BD12 .... 149 G1
Tetley Dr *BIRK/DRI* BD11 .... 150 D2
Tetley La *HIPP* HX3 .... 147 L5
Tetley Pl *ECHL* BD2 .... 105 H3 🟦
Tetley St *BFD* BD1 .... 4 D6
Teville Ct *BOW* BD4 .... 127 J2 🟦
Tewit Cl *LUD/ILL* HX2 .... 124 B7
Tewit Gn *LUD/ILL* HX2 .... 124 B7
Tewit Hall Gdns *LUD/ILL* HX2 .. 124 B8 🟦
Tewit Hall Rd *BFDE* BD3 .... 105 L6
Tewit La *LUD/ILL* HX2 .... 124 B7
Tewitt Cl *AIRE* BD20 .... 35 K8 🟦
Tewitt La *BGLY* BD16 .... 59 K8
   CUL/QBY BD13 .... 102 C4
Tew St *WKFDW/WTN* WF2 .... 12 C6
Texas St *MOR* LS27 .... 152 D4

Thackeray Gv *HUDS* HD4 .... 213 M3
Thackeray Rd *IDLE* BD10 .... 105 M2
Thacker Gate Rd *HBR* HX7 .... 166 D2
Thackley Av *IDLE* BD10 .... 83 J4 🟦
Thackley Ct *SHPY* BD18 .... 82 E6 🟦
Thackley Old Rd *SHPY* BD18 ..... 82 F6
Thackley Rd *IDLE* BD10 .... 83 J4
Thackray Av *HECK* WF16 .... 173 G1
Thackray La *PONT* WF8 .... 181 G5 🟦
Thackray St *LUD/ILL* HX2 .... 145 M7
   MOR LS27 .... 152 C3
Thames Dr *GFTH/SHER* LS25 ..... 113 J8
Thames St *MILN* OL16 .... 207 J8
Thames Steet *MILN* OL16 .... 206 D8
Thanes Cl *HUDN* HD2 .... 192 A4
Thanet Garth *AIRE* BD20 .... 36 B6
Thane Wy *MSTN/BAR* LS15 .... 112 A3
Thatchers Wy *CLECK* BD19 .... 150 C5
Theaker La *WOR/ARM* LS12 ..... 108 D6
Theakston Md *CLAY* BD14 .... 125 L1
Thealby Cl *OSM* LS9 .... 7 L7
Thealby Lawn *OSM* LS9 .... 7 L7
Thealby Pl *OSM* LS9 .... 7 L7
Thearne Gn *CLAY* BD14 .... 125 M2
Theodore St *BEE/HOL* LS11 ..... 131 J5
Thewlis La *HUDS* HD4 .... 213 K4
Thickett La *STKB/PEN* S36 .... 271 G6
Thick Hollins Dr
   HOLM/MEL HD7 .... 235 H5
Thick Hollins Rd
   HOLM/MEL HD7 .... 235 H6
Thimble Cl *WHIT* OL12 .... 206 F2
The Thimbles *WHIT* OL12 .... 206 F2
Third Av *BFDE* BD3 .... 105 L5
   HEM/SK/SE WF9 .... 225 A6
   HIPP HX3 .... 168 D2
   KGHY BD21 .... 2 E7
   LVSG WF15 .... 171 K1
   RTHW LS26 .... 133 H7
   WBY LS22 .... 48 B1
   WKFDE WF1 .... 176 D4
   WOR/ARM LS12 .... 108 F8
Third St *LM/WK* BD12 .... 127 G8
Thirkleby Royd *CLAY* BD14 .... 125 L2
Thirlmere Av *COL* BB8 .... 52 B8 🟦
   ELL HX5 .... 169 K7
   LM/WK BD12 .... 149 G5
Thirlmere Cl *BEE/HOL* LS11 ..... 131 G6
Thirlmere Dr *CAS* WF10 .... 158 F7
   EARD/LOFT WF3 .... 153 J4
   WBY LS22 .... 47 K1
Thirlmere Gdns *BEE/HOL* LS11... 131 G6 🟦
   ECHL BD2 .... 105 K4 🟦
Thirlmere Gv *ROY/SHW* OL2 .... 228 F5
Thirlmere Rd *BSLYN/ROY* S71 .. 261 J8 🟦
   EARL WF12 .... 174 B4
   WKFDW/WTN WF2 .... 176 A8
Thirsk Dr *GFTH/SHER* LS25 ..... 135 J4
Thirsk Gra *CLAY* BD14 .... 125 L2
Thirsk Rw *LDS* LS1 .... 8 E1
Thirstin Rd *HOLM/MEL* HD7 ..... 236 A1
Thirteenth Av *LVSG* WF15 .... 171 K1 🟦
Thistle Cl *HUDN* HD2 .... 192 A4
Thistle Dr *HEM/SK/SE* WF9 ..... 225 H7
Thistle Hill Av *HUDE* HD5 .... 215 L1
Thistle St *HUD* HD1 .... 15 H3
Thistle Wy *MOR* LS27 .... 151 M1
Thistlewood Rd
   EARD/LOFT WF3 .... 176 F1
Thomas Ct *WBSY* BD6 .... 126 E5 🟦
Thomas St *BRIG* HD6 .... 170 C5
   BSLY S70 .... 261 G6
   BTLY WF17 .... 151 K8
   CAS WF10 .... 158 A5
   ELL HX5 .... 169 J8
   HDGY LS6 .... 6 D2
   HECK WF16 .... 172 F3
   HEM/SK/SE WF9 .... 224 A8
   HFAX HX1 .... 11 H6
   HUD HD1 .... 214 A2
   HUDW HD3 .... 191 J5
   HWTH BD22 .... 78 F8 🟦
   LVSG WF15 .... 172 C2 🟦🟦
   MILN OL16 .... 206 C6 🟦
   ROY/SHW OL2 .... 229 L8
   TOD OL14 .... 140 E5 🟦
Thomas St South *HFAX* HX1 .... 10 B7
Thomas St West *HFAX* HX1 ..... 168 C1 🟦
Thompson Av *CAS* WF10 .... 159 G8
   ECHL BD2 .... 105 H1
Thompson Dr
   WKFDW/WTN WF2 .... 176 B3
Thompson Gn *BAIL* BD17 .... 82 C4
Thompson La *BAIL* BD17 .... 82 C5 🟦
Thompson St *HFAX* HX1 .... 10 F5
   SHPY BD18 .... 82 C6 🟦
Thompson's Yd *WKFDE* WF1 .... 12 D2
Thong La *HOLM/MEL* HD7 .... 236 C6
Thoresby Av *BSLYN/ROY* S71 ... 261 M2
Thoresby Dr *CLECK* BD19 .... 150 D6
Thoresby Gv *GTHN* BD7 .... 126 A3 🟦
Thoresby Pl *LDS* LS1 .... 6 E8
Thornaby Dr *CLAY* BD14 .... 125 M1 🟦
Thornacre Crs *SHPY* BD18 .... 83 G8
Thornacre Rd *SHPY* BD18 .... 83 G7 🟦
Thorncliffe Av *ROY/SHW* OL2 ... 228 C4
Thorncliffe Est *BTLY* WF17 .... 173 J3
Thorncliffe La *KBTN* HD8 .... 217 M7
Thorncliffe Rd *BTLY* WF17 .... 173 J3
   GIR BD8 .... 4 C1
   HWTH BD22 .... 2 A6
Thorncliffe St *HUDW* HD3 .... 191 K5

Thorncliff Green Rd KBTN HD8 .... 216 D7
Thorncliff La KBTN HD8 .... 216 E7
Thorn Cl RHAY LS8 .... 110 D3
  SHPY BD18 .... 83 G8
Thorn Crs RHAY LS8 .... 110 D3
Thorncroft Rd WBSY BD6 .... 126 C5
Thorndale Ri ECHL BD2 .... 105 G2
Thorndene Wy BOW BD4 .... 128 C7
Thorn Dr CUL/QBY BD13 .... 124 E7
  HTON BD9 .... 103 M2
  RHAY LS8 .... 110 D3
Thorne Cl BSLYN/ROY S71 .... 243 G7
  NORM WF6 .... 178 E5
  PDSY/CALV LS28 .... 106 D6
Thorne End Rd DOD/DAR S75 ... 242 D4
Thornefield Crs
  EARD/LOFT WF3 .... 152 F6
Thorne Gv RTHW LS26 .... 133 H8
Thornely Av DOD/DAR S75 .... 260 B6
Thorner Gv AIRE BD20 .... 36 A4
Thorner La BSPA/BRAM LS23 .... 69 G5
  SCFT LS14 .... 67 M6
  SCFT LS14 .... 90 A4
Thorne Rd HUD HD1 .... 214 A2
Thorner Rd BSPA/BRAM LS23 .... 69 G5
Thornes Farm Ap OSM LS9 .... 132 F1
Thornes Farm Wy OSM LS9 .... 132 F1
Thornes La WKFDW/WTN WF2 .... 12 E1
Thornes Lane Whf WKFDE WF1 ...... 13 G8
Thornes Moor Av
  WKFDW/WTN WF2 .... 12 A9
Thornes Moor Cl
  WKFDW/WTN WF2 .... 12 A8
Thornes Moor Dr
  WKFDW/WTN WF2 .... 12 A9
Thornes Moor Rd
  WKFDW/WTN WF2 .... 12 A9
  WKFDW/WTN WF2 .... 198 C4
Thornes Pk BRIG HD6 .... 170 C5
  SHPY BD18 .... 104 F1
Thornes Park Ct
  WKFDW/WTN WF2 .... 12 C8
Thorne St GTL/HWG HX4 .... 190 C2
Thorney La LUD/ILL HX2 .... 144 F4
Thornfield BGLY BD16 .... 81 G2
Thornfield Av HUDS HD4 .... 214 A3
  PDSY/CALV LS28 .... 106 E3
  WBSY BD6 .... 126 F6
Thornfield Ct MSTN/BAR LS15... 111 K4
Thornfield Drive Dr
  MSTN/BAR LS15 .... 111 K4
  MSTN/BAR LS15 .... 111 K4
Thornfield Ms BGLY BD16 .... 59 G7
Thornfield Mt BTLY WF17 .... 151 J5
Thornfield Pl ECHL BD2 .... 105 L3
Thornfield Ri GTL/HWG HX4 .... 168 D7
Thornfield Rd BHP/TINH LS16 ..... 86 D6
  KGHY BD21 .... 57 J5
Thorn Gv COL BB8 .... 52 B8
  HTON BD9 .... 103 M2
  RHAY LS8 .... 110 D3
Thornham Ct MILN OL16 .... 228 E6
Thornham La ROY/SHW OL2 .... 228 C6
Thornham New Rd ROCH OL11 .... 228 B5
Thornham Old Rd MDTN M24 ... 228 B7
  ROY/SHW OL2 .... 228 C7
Thornham Rd ROY/SHW OL2 .... 228 C7
Thorn HI GTL/HWG HX4 .... 190 B4
Thornhill Av HUDW HD3 .... 191 L7
  HWTH BD22 .... 79 J3
  SHPY BD18 .... 104 F1
Thornhill Back Rd HUDW HD3.. 191 L7
Thornhill Bridge La BRIG HD6 .. 170 C3
Thornhill Cft HOR/CROF WF4...... 196 D7
  PDSY/CALV LS28 .... 84 D7
  WKFDW/WTN WF2 .... 199 J7
Thornhill Cft WKFDW/WTN WF2.. 199 J7
  WOR/ARM LS12 .... 108 D8
Thornhill Dr PDSY/CALV LS28... 84 B8
  SHPY BD18 .... 104 F1
  WKFDW/WTN WF2 .... 199 J7
Thornhill Gv AIRE BD20 .... 35 K8
  PDSY/CALV LS28 .... 84 D7
  SHPY BD18 .... 104 F1
Thornhill Hey GTL/HWG HX4 ... 190 B4
Thornhill Park Av EARL WF12 ... 195 M4
Thornhill Pl BFDE BD3 .... 106 A6
  WOR/ARM LS12 .... 108 D8
Thornhill Rd AIRE BD20 .... 35 K8
  BRIG HD6 .... 170 B6
  CAS WF10 .... 158 A8
  DEWS WF13 .... 173 K7
  EARL WF12 .... 196 C5
  HUDW HD3 .... 191 M6
  WOR/ARM LS12 .... 108 D8
Thornhills Beck La BRIG HD6 .. 170 D2
Thornhills La BRIG HD6 .... 170 C2
Thornhill St EARL WF12 .... 173 M8
  PDSY/CALV LS28 .... 84 D7
  WKFDE WF1 .... 12 F3
  WOR/ARM LS12 .... 108 D7
Thornhill Ter BFDE BD3 .... 105 M6
Thorn La HTON BD9 .... 103 L2
  RHAY LS8 .... 88 B8
Thornlea Cl YEA LS19 .... 84 B1
Thornleigh EARL WF12 .... 173 M8
Thornleigh Av
  WKFDW/WTN WF2 .... 12 E8
Thornleigh Crs
  WKFDW/WTN WF2 .... 12 E7
Thornleigh Cft
  WKFDW/WTN WF2 .... 12 E7
Thornleigh Dr LVSG WF15......... 172 D1
  WKFDW/WTN WF2 .... 12 E8
Thornleigh Gdns OSM LS9 ... 110 B8
Thornleigh Garth
  WKFDW/WTN WF2 .... 12 E8
Thornleigh Gv OSM LS9 ... 110 B8
Thornleigh Mt OSM LS9 ... 110 B8
Thornleigh Rd HUDS HD4......... 213 K3
  WKFDW/WTN WF2 .... 12 E7
Thornleigh St OSM LS9 ... 110 B8
Thornleigh Vw OSM LS9 ... 110 B8
Thornmead Rd BAIL BD17 .... 82 F4

Thorn Mt RHAY LS8 .... 110 E2
Thorn Rd EARL WF12 .... 195 L5
Thorn Royd Dr BOW BD4 .... 128 B4
Thornsgill Av BOW BD4 .... 127 L3
Thorn St BTLY WF17 .... 151 G5
  GIR BD8 .... 104 B5
  HWTH BD22 .... 79 G6
Thorn Ter RHAY LS8 .... 110 E2
Thornton Av WOR/ARM LS12 ...... 108 C7
Thornton Cl BTLY WF17 .... 151 K5
  HEM/SK/SE WF9 .... 245 M1
Thornton Gdns
  WOR/ARM LS12 .... 108 C7
Thornton Gv WOR/ARM LS12 ...... 108 C7
Thornton La WBOW BD5 .... 126 E3
Thornton Lodge Rd HUD HD1 .... 214 A2
Thornton Moor Rd HWTH BD22 ... 101 J7
Thornton Old Rd GIR BD8 .... 103 M7
Thornton Rd BRIG HD6 .... 170 A6
  BSLY S70 .... 261 K7
  CUL/QBY BD13 .... 103 H8
  CUL/QBY BD13 .... 124 B1
  EARL WF12 .... 195 K2
  GIR BD8 .... 103 M7
  GIR BD8 .... 104 C6
Thornton Ter BSLY S70 .... 261 L7
  HFAX HX1 .... 10 B9
Thornton View Rd CLAY BD14.... 125 L2
Thorntonville CLECK BD19 .... 150 B8
Thorntree Av HOR/CROF WF4 ...... 200 A5
Thorntree Cl PONT WF8 .... 203 M2
Thorntree Ct HOR/CROF WF4 ...... 200 A5
Thorntree La DOD/DAR S75....... 260 F3
Thorn Tree St HFAX HX1 .... 10 B9
  RHAY LS8 .... 144 A6
Thornville MOR LS27 .... 130 D7
Thornville Av HDGY LS6 .... 109 G4
Thornville Ct HDGY LS6 .... 109 G4
Thornville Crs HDGY LS6.......... 109 G3
Thornville Gv HDGY LS6 .... 109 G3
Thornville Mt DEWS WF13 .... 173 J8
  HDGY LS6 .... 109 G3
Thornville Pl DEWS WF13 .... 173 J8
  HDGY LS6 .... 109 G3
Thornville Rd DEWS WF13 .... 173 J8
  HDGY LS6 .... 109 G4
Thornville St DEWS WF13 .... 173 J8
  HDGY LS6 .... 109 G4
Thornville Ter DEWS WF13 .... 173 K8
  HDGY LS6 .... 109 G3
Thornville Vw HDGY LS6 .... 109 G4
Thornville Wk DEWS WF13 .... 173 J8
Thorn Wk RHAY LS8 .... 110 E3
Thornwell Gv CUD/GR S72 ...... 244 C8
Thorp Arch Pk BSPA/BRAM LS23... 49 C5
Thorp Av HOLM/MEL HD7 .... 254 D2
Thorpe Av CUL/QBY BD13 .... 103 J8
Thorpe Cl GSLY LS20 .... 61 K6
Thorpe Ct MID LS10 .... 153 L3
Thorpe Crs MID LS10 .... 153 L3
Thorpe Dr GSLY LS20 .... 61 K5
Thorpe Gdns MID LS10 .... 153 L2
Thorpe Garth MID LS10 .... 153 K3
Thorpe Green Dr
  HOLM/MEL HD7 .... 191 G8
  HUDW HD3 .... 191 G8
Thorpe Gv CUL/QBY BD13 .... 103 K8
  MID LS10 .... 153 L2
Thorpe La EARD/LOFT WF3 .... 153 G5
  GSLY LS20 .... 61 J6
  HEM/SK/SE WF9 .... 225 H3
  HUDE HD5 .... 215 J2
Thorpe Lower La
  EARD/LOFT WF3 .... 154 B4
Thorpe Mt MID LS10 .... 153 L3
Thorpe Pl MID LS10 .... 153 L2
Thorpe Rd CUL/QBY BD13 .... 103 K8
  EARD/LOFT WF3 .... 153 L7
  MID LS10 .... 153 L2
  PDSY/CALV LS28 .... 106 F6
Thorpes Av WBSY BD6 .... 239 J7
Thorpes Crs KBTN HD8 .... 239 J5
Thorpe Sq MID LS10 .... 153 M3
Thorpe St HIPP HX3 .... 146 D4
  KGHY BD21 .... 3 G2
  MID LS10 .... 153 L2
  MSTN/BAR LS15 .... 111 J6
Thorpe Ter MID LS10 .... 153 L2
Thorpe Vw EARD/LOFT WF3 .... 154 A4
  MID LS10 .... 153 L3
  OSS WF5 .... 153 L3
  WKFDW/WTN WF2 .... 176 B8
Thorp Garth IDLE BD10........... 83 K6
Thorp Vw ROY/SHW OL2 .... 229 K7
Thorverton Dr BOW BD4 .... 128 A6
Thorverton Gv BOW BD4 .... 128 A6
Threadneedle St HUD HD1 .... 14 E7
Three Nooks La CUD/GR S72 .... 244 D5
Three Sisters Sq HUD HD1 .... 14 F2
Threshfield Crs BIRK/DRI BD11... 128 C8
Thrift Wy BGLY BD16 .... 81 H4
Throstle Av MID LS10 .... 153 K3
Throstle Crest FEA/AMT WF7 .... 179 K1
Throstle Dr MID LS10 .... 153 J3
Throstle HI MID LS10 .... 153 K3
Throstle La LUD/ILL HX2 .... 167 H1
  MID LS10 .... 153 K3
Throstle Mt LUD/ILL HX2 .... 167 H1
Throstle Nest BTLY WF17 .... 173 J2
Throstle Nest Cl OT LS21 .... 40 F4
Throstle Nest Rd AIRE BD20 .... 35 M4
Throstle Nest Vw HORS LS18..... 85 L7
Throstle Pde MID LS10 .... 153 J4
Throstle Pl MID LS10 .... 153 K3
Throstle Rd MID LS10 .... 153 K3
Throstle Rw MID LS10 .... 153 K3
Throstle Sq MID LS10 .... 153 K3
Throstle St MID LS10 .... 153 K3
Throstle Ter MID LS10 .... 153 M3
Throstle Vw MID LS10 .... 153 M3

Throstle Wk MID LS10 .... 153 K3
Throxenby Wy CLAY BD14 .... 125 L2
Thrum Hall Dr HFAX HX1 .... 10 A5
Thrum Hall La HFAX HX1 .... 10 A5
  WHIT OL12 .... 206 A3
Thrumpton Rd
  BSLYN/ROY S71 .... 243 H5
Thrush Hill Rd HBR HX7 .... 143 M6
Thrush St KGHY BD21 .... 3 J2
Thruxton Cl CUD/GR S72 .... 244 E6
Thryberg St BFDE BD3 .... 5 K7
Thunder Bridge La KBTN HD8 .... 237 M3
Thunderton La RPDN/SBR HX6.... 166 D4
Thurgoland Bank
  STKB/PEN S36 .... 271 M6
Thurgory Ga KBTN HD8 .... 215 M3
Thurgory La KBTN HD8 .... 216 B2
Thurley Dr BOW BD4 .... 127 K4
Thurley Rd BOW BD4 .... 127 K4
Thurlstone Rd STKB/PEN S36 .... 270 D2
Thurnscoe Bd BFD1 .... 4 D3
Thurrish La HBR HX7 .... 121 K1
Thursby St BFDE BD3 .... 5 L6
Thurston Gdns WIL/AL BD15 ..... 103 K6
Thurstonland Bank Rd
  HOLM/MEL HD7 .... 236 F5
Thurstonland Rd HUDS HD4 ...... 237 G1
Thwaite Ga MID LS10 .... 132 B3
Thwaite La MID LS10 .... 132 C3
Thwaites Av ILK LS29 .... 38 C2
Thwaites Br KGHY BD21 .... 3 M4
Thwaites Brow Rd KGHY BD21 .. 58 B7
Thwaites La KGHY BD21 .... 3 M4
Tichborne Rd WBOW BD5....... 127 G3
Tichborne Rd West
  WBOW BD5 .... 127 G3
Tichborne St WF15 .... 172 A2
Tichbourne St BTLY WF17 .... 173 H2
Tickhill St BFDE BD3 .... 5 L7
Tickling Field La HOLM/MEL HD7 . 211 M4
Tidswell St HECK WF16 .... 173 G2
Tiflis St WHIT OL12 .... 206 A3
Tilbury Av BEE/HOL LS11 .... 8 B8
Tilbury Gv BEE/HOL LS11 .... 8 B8
Tilbury Mt BEE/HOL LS11 .... 8 B8
Tilbury Pde BEE/HOL LS11 .... 8 B8
Tilbury Rw BEE/HOL LS11 .... 8 A8
Tilbury Ter BEE/HOL LS11 .... 8 B8
Tilbury Vw BEE/HOL LS11 .... 8 B8
Tile Cl SKP/WHF BD23 .... 16 D3
Tile La BHP/TINH LS16 .... 86 F3
Tile St GIR BD8 .... 104 D5
Tiley Sq WBOW BD5 .... 127 G2
Till Carr La HIPP HX3 .... 148 C3
Tillotson Av RPDN/SBR HX6...... 166 C5
Tillotson St AIRE BD20 .... 35 M4
Timber St ELL HX5 .... 169 H8
  KGHY BD21 .... 3 L3
Timberwood KBTN HD8 .... 237 M2
Timble Dr BGLY BD16 .... 81 K2
Tim La HWTH BD22 .... 78 D5
Timmey La RPDN/SBR HX6 .... 167 J1
Timothy La BTLY WF17 .... 151 M7
Tinderley Gv HUDE HD5 .... 215 G2
Tingley Av EARD/LOFT WF3 ...... 153 G5
Tingley Common
  EARD/LOFT WF3 .... 152 F5
  MOR LS27 .... 152 D4
Tingley Crs EARD/LOFT WF3 ..... 152 E5
Tinker La HOLM/MEL HD7 .... 234 F5
Tinker's La KNOT WF11 .... 161 J3
Tinkler Stile SHPY BD18 .... 83 H6
Tinsel Rd EARL WF12 .... 174 B5
Tinshill Av BHP/TINH LS16 ...... 86 A3
Tinshill Cl BHP/TINH LS16 ...... 86 A3
Tinshill Crs BHP/TINH LS16 ..... 86 A2
Tinshill Dr BHP/TINH LS16....... 86 A1
Tinshill Garth BHP/TINH LS16 .. 86 A2
Tinshill Gv BHP/TINH LS16 ...... 86 A2
Tinshill La BHP/TINH LS16 ...... 85 M3
Tinshill Mt BHP/TINH LS16 ...... 86 A2
Tinshill Rd BHP/TINH LS16 ...... 85 M3
Tinshill Vw BHP/TINH LS16 ...... 86 A2
Tinsworth Rd
  WKFDW/WTN WF2 .... 220 C2
Tintagel Dr NORM WF6 .... 178 D3
Tintern Av GIR BD8 .... 103 M7
  HUDW HD3 .... 185 J1
  LIT OL15 .... 185 J7
  WHIT OL12 .... 206 A4
Tippaty La KNOT WF11 .... 160 C7
Tipping La KBTN HD8 .... 217 M7
Tippit La CUD/GR S72 .... 262 E1
Tisma Dr BOW BD4 .... 127 L6
Tithe Barn Cl WHIT OL12........ 206 F2
Tithe Barn La AL/HA/HU LS17 .... 67 K4
Tithe Barn Rd KNOT WF11 .... 182 C2
Tithe Barn St EARL WF12 .... 173 M6
  HOR/CROF WF4 .... 197 J5
Tithe House Wy HUDN HD2 .... 171 G8
Titus La KBTN HD8 .... 216 F8
Titus St SHPY BD18 .... 82 B6
Tivoli Pl ILK LS29 .... 38 C3
  WBOW BD5 .... 126 E3
Tivy Dl DOD/DAR S75 .... 259 G2
Tivy Dale Cl DOD/DAR S75 .... 259 G2
Tivydale Dr DOD/DAR S75 .... 242 A7
Tivy Dale Dr DOD/DAR S75....... 259 G2
Toad La MILN OL16 .... 206 B6
  WHIT OL12 .... 206 A6
Toby La GTHN BD7 .... 126 C1
Toby Wood La KBTN HD8 .... 256 F1
Tockwith La AL/HA/HU YO26 ...... 32 C2
Tockwith Rd RYKW YO26 .... 32 E1
Todd St MILN OL16 .... 206 A6
Todd Ter GTHN BD7 .... 126 D2
Todley Hall Rd HWTH BD22 ...... 56 B8
Todmorden Rd LIT OL15.......... 185 L8
  TOD OL14 .... 162 B2
Todwell La WBOW BD5 .... 126 E3
Toft La HUDS HD4 .... 215 H8
Tofts Av LM/WK BD12 .... 148 E4
Tofts Gv BRIG HD6 .... 170 B7
Tofts Grove Gdns BRIG HD6 ..... 170 B7
Toftshaw Fold BOW BD4 .... 127 M6

Toftshaw La BOW BD4 .... 128 A6
Toftshaw New Rd BOW BD4 .... 127 M6
Tofts House Cl
  PDSY/CALV LS28 .... 107 G7
Tofts La PBR HG3 .... 28 A1
Tofts Rd CLECK BD19 .... 149 M7
Toft St WOR/ARM LS12 .... 108 F8
Toll Bar Cl SEL YO8 .... 139 M4
Toll Bar La WKFDW/WTN WF2 .. 175 M5
Tollbar Cl STKB/PEN S36 .... 271 K6
Toll Bar Rd CAS WF10 .... 157 H7
Toll Bar Wy TAD LS24 .... 72 B1
Toller Dr HTON BD9 .... 104 A3
Toller Gv HTON BD9 .... 104 A3
Toller La GIR BD8 .... 104 C5
  HTON BD9 .... 104 B3
Toller Pk HTON BD9 .... 104 B3
Tollgate Wy HOL16 .... 206 E6
Tolson Crs HUDE HD5 .... 193 H7
Tolson St DEWS WF13 .... 173 L5
  OSS WF5 .... 174 D6
Tolworth Fold WIL/AL BD15...... 103 K6
Tombridge Crs
  HEM/SK/SE WF9 .... 223 K5
Tom Cat La WBY LS22 .... 31 L5
Tom Dando Cl NORM WF6 .... 179 G4
Tom La HUDS HD4 .... 213 K3
  HWTH BD22 .... 53 L1
Tomling Cote La AIRE BD20 ...... 36 C6
Tomlinson Wy GFTH/SHER LS25 .. 115 M7
Tommy La HOLM/MEL HD7 .... 213 G5
Tom Wood Ash La
  HEM/SK/SE WF9 .... 225 M7
Tonbridge Cl WBSY BD6.......... 126 B6
Tonbridge St LDS LS1 .... 6 D1
Tong Ap WOR/ARM LS12 .... 107 M8
Tong Av WOR/ARM LS12 .... 107 M7
Tonge St ROCH OL11 .... 206 C8
Tong Ga WOR/ARM LS12 .... 107 M7
Tong Gn WOR/ARM LS12 .... 107 M8
Tong La BOW BD4 .... 128 C6
Tong Rd WOR/ARM LS12 .... 129 K2
Tong St BOW BD4 .... 127 M5
Tongue La HDGY LS6 .... 87 H6
Tong Wy WOR/ARM LS12 .... 107 M7
Tootal St WKFDE WF1 .... 13 G6
Toothill Av BRIG HD6 .... 170 C7
Toothill Bank BRIG HD6 .... 170 C7
Toothill La BRIG HD6 .... 170 C8
Toot Hill La RPDN/SBR HX6...... 166 D4
Toothill La South HUDN HD2 ... 192 E1
Topaz Cl HUDN HD2 .... 192 E4
Topcliffe Av MOR LS27 .... 152 F2
Topcliffe Gv MOR LS27 .... 152 F2
Topcliffe La EARD/LOFT WF3 .... 152 E5
  MOR LS27 .... 152 E4
Topcliffe Md MOR LS27 .... 152 F2
Topfield Fold MOR LS27 .... 152 E4
Top Fold KNOT WF11 .... 159 J2
Top House Farm Ms
  KNOT WF11 .... 159 J2
Top La COL BB8 .... 74 E2
  HOR/CROF WF4 .... 218 F5
  OT LS21 .... 23 J2
Top Meadow MIRF WF14 .... 194 B4
Top Moor Side BEE/HOL LS11 .... 8 C6
Top Orch MOR LS27 .... 152 F2
Top of the HI HUDS HD4 .... 237 H5
Top O' Th' Bank HUDS HD4 ...... 237 G5
Top O'th' Close Rd TOD OL14 ... 163 K8
Top Rd KBTN HD8 .... 239 G7
Top Stone Cl GFTH/SHER LS25 .. 160 A3
Top St HEM/SK/SE WF9 .... 223 L7
Tor Av LM/WK BD12 .... 148 C5
Tor Cl BSLYN/ROY S71 .... 261 J1
Torcote Crs HUDN HD2 .... 192 E1
Tordoff Av GTHN BD7 .... 126 A1
Tordoff Gn WBSY BD6 .... 126 D6
Tordoff Rd LM/WK BD12 .... 127 G8
Tordoff Ter KSTL LS5 .... 108 C2
Toronto Pl CHAL LS7 .... 87 M8
Torre Cl OSM LS9 .... 110 D5
Torre Crs OSM LS9 .... 110 D5
  WBSY BD6 .... 125 M5
Torre Dr OSM LS9 .... 110 C5
Torre Gv OSM LS9 .... 110 C5
  WBSY BD6 .... 125 M5
Torre HI OSM LS9 .... 110 D6
Torre La OSM LS9 .... 110 D6
Torre Mt OSM LS9 .... 110 C5
Torre Pl OSM LS9 .... 110 D6
Torre Rd OSM LS9 .... 110 C5
  WBSY BD6 .... 125 M5
Torre Sq OSM LS9 .... 110 D5
Torre Vw OSM LS9 .... 110 D5
Torre Wk OSM LS9 .... 110 D5
Torridon Crs WBSY BD6 .... 126 A8
Torridon Rd EARL WF12 .... 174 A4
Torver Av LM/WK BD12 .... 148 C5
Tor Vw HOLM/MEL HD7 .... 236 E4
Totley Cl BSLYN/ROY S71 .... 243 K7
Totties La HOLM/MEL HD7 ...... 254 F1
Toulston La TAD LS24 .... 70 B4
Tower Av HEM/SK/SE WF9 .... 225 J6
Tower Cswy TOD OL14 .... 140 D6
Tower Crs TAD LS24 .... 71 K2
The Tower Dr OT LS21 .... 43 G7
Tower Gdns LUD/ILL HX2 .... 168 B2
Tower Gv WOR/ARM LS12 .... 108 B6
Tower HI RPDN/SBR HX6 .... 167 K2
Tower House St LDSU LS2 .... 7 G7
Tower La WOR/ARM LS12 .... 108 B6
Tower Pl WOR/ARM LS12 .... 108 B6
Tower Rd SHPY BD18 .... 82 A6
Towers Cl HOR/CROF WF4 .... 200 B6
Towers La HOR/CROF WF4 .... 200 D5
Towers Paddock CAS WF10 ...... 158 C7
Towers Sq HDGY LS6 .... 87 J6
Towers Wy HDGY LS6 .... 87 J6
Towlerton La
  WKFDW/WTN WF2 .... 176 A4
Town Av HUD HD1 .... 15 J3

Town Cl HORS LS18 .... 85 K5
Town Crs HUD HD1 .... 15 J3
Town End GFTH/SHER LS25 ...... 113 G6
  GTHN BD7 .... 126 C2
  HOLM/MEL HD7 .... 212 F2
  HUDE HD5 .... 215 G2
  MOR LS27 .... 129 M7
  OSS WF5 .... 196 F1
Town End Av FEA/AMT WF7 ...... 202 F7
  HOLM/MEL HD7 .... 236 E8
Town End Cl AIRE BD20 .... 34 E8
Town End Crs HOLM/MEL HD7 .. 236 F7
Town End La KBTN HD8 .... 216 C2
Townend Pl AIRE BD20 .... 34 E8
  PDSY/CALV LS28 .... 107 H6
Town End Rd CLAY BD14 .... 125 K1
  HOLM/MEL HD7 .... 236 D8
Townend Rd WOR/ARM LS12..... 130 D1
Town End Vw HOLM/MEL HD7 .. 236 D8
Townfield WIL/AL BD15 .... 102 E1
Townfield La HBR HX7 .... 143 H1
Town Fields Rd ELL HX5 .... 169 G8
Townfold OSS WF5 .... 175 G8
Town Ga CLECK BD19 .... 149 H6
  GSLY LS20 .... 62 A5
  HBR HX7 .... 143 H1
  HIPP HX3 .... 147 J3
  HOLM/MEL HD7 .... 233 H2
  HOLM/MEL HD7 .... 236 B6
  HOLM/MEL HD7 .... 253 M1
  KBTN HD8 .... 216 A6
  LUD/ILL HX2 .... 144 D5
  PDSY/CALV LS28 .... 84 D7
  RPDN/SBR HX6 .... 166 C5
Towngate BRIG HD6 .... 171 G4
  DOD/DAR S75 .... 242 D5
  DOD/DAR S75 .... 259 H6
  HIPP HX3 .... 147 L6
  HIPP HX3 .... 169 J2
  HUDS HD4 .... 214 C4
  LM/WK BD12 .... 148 E4
  MIRF WF14 .... 172 D8
  OSS WF5 .... 197 G1
  SHPY BD18 .... 82 F7
  STKB/PEN S36 .... 270 C2
Towngate Av BRIG HD6 .... 170 F3
Towngate Gv MIRF WF14 .... 194 B7
Towngate Rd BTLY WF17 .... 173 J8
Town Hall Sq YEA LS19 .... 62 D7
Town Hall St ELL HX5 .... 169 H8
  HOLM/MEL HD7 .... 254 C1
  KGHY BD21 .... 3 G5
  MIRF WF14 .... 194 C3
  RPDN/SBR HX6 .... 167 K3
Town Hall St East HFAX HX1.... 11 H5
Town Hall Yd EARL WF12 .... 173 M6
Townhead Fold ILK LS29 .... 19 G6
Town HI BSPA/BRAM LS23 .... 69 M4
Town Hill St BGLY BD16 .... 81 K8
Town House Rd LIT OL15........ 185 K8
Town La IDLE BD10 .... 83 K5
Townley Av HIPP HX3 .... 169 J2
Townley Rd MILN OL16 .... 207 H8
  WKFDW/WTN WF2 .... 197 M1
Townley St COL BB8 .... 74 A1
Town Moor HUDS HD4 .... 237 H4
Town Pl HUD HD1 .... 15 J3
Town Rd HUDE HD5 .... 193 L5
Town St BEE/HOL LS11 .... 131 G4
  BIRK/DRI BD11 .... 128 C8
  BRAM LS13 .... 107 H1
  CHAL LS7 .... 87 M7
  DEWS WF13 .... 173 L4
  EARD/LOFT WF3 .... 153 F4
  EARL WF12 .... 174 B7
  GSLY LS20 .... 62 A5
  HEM/SK/SE WF9 .... 223 L7
  HORS LS18 .... 85 K6
  MID LS10 .... 153 L1
  MOR LS27 .... 129 M7
  PDSY/CALV LS28 .... 106 F4
  WOR/ARM LS12 .... 108 C6
  YEA LS19 .... 62 D7
  YEA LS19 .... 84 F7
Town Street Ms CHAL LS7 ...... 87 M7
Town Ter HUD HD1 .... 15 J3
The Town EARL WF12 .... 195 M4
Town Wells Dr PDSY/CALV LS28 . 84 D7
Towton Dr CAS WF10 .... 157 J8
Track Mt BTLY WF17 .... 173 K4
Track Rd BTLY WF17 .... 173 K4
Trafalgar Cl HUDN HD2 .... 192 D2
Trafalgar Rd DEWS WF13 .... 173 K5
  ILK LS29 .... 38 D3
Trafalgar Sq AWLS/ASK DN6 .... 249 J1
  BFD BD1 .... 4 E4
  BTLY WF17 .... 173 J1
  HFAX HX1 .... 10 C9
  LDSU LS2 .... 7 J2
  MILN OL16 .... 206 C6
Trafford Av OSM LS9 .... 110 D4
Trafford Gv OSM LS9 .... 110 C3
Trafford Rd AWLS/ASK DN6 ..... 249 H1
Trafford St ROCH OL11 .... 228 A1
Trafford Ter OSM LS9 .... 110 D4
Tramways LM/WK BD12 .... 149 H6
Tranbeck Rd GSLY LS20 .... 61 L5
Tranfield Av GSLY LS20 .... 61 L5
Tranfield Cl GSLY LS20 .... 61 L5
Tranfield Gdns GSLY LS20 ...... 61 L5
Tranmere Ct GSLY LS20 .... 61 L5
Tranmere Dr GSLY LS20 .... 61 K5
Tranquility MSTN/BAR LS15 ..... 111 J4
Tranquillity Ct MSTN/BAR LS15.. 111 J4
Trans Pennine Trail
  BSLYN/ROY S71 .... 244 A7
  EARD/LOFT WF3 .... 177 J3
  MID LS10 .... 9 G2
  RTHW LS26 .... 156 B7
  WKFDE WF1 .... 199 J2
Transperience Wy LM/WK BD12 .. 127 H8
Transvaal Ter BTLY WF17 .... 151 K7
Trans Wk TAD LS24 .... 95 G5
Tranter Gv BOW BD4 .... 128 A3
Tranter Pl MSTN/BAR LS15 ..... 111 G6
Travis St MILN OL16 .... 229 K2
  ROY/SHW OL2 .... 229 K7

Trawden Rd COL BB8 74 D1
Tredgold Av BHP/TINH LS16 64 A4
Tredgold Cl BHP/TINH LS16 64 A4
Tredgold Crs BHP/TINH LS16 64 A4
Tredgold Garth BHP/TINH LS16 64 A4
Tredis Cl BSLYN/ROY S71 261 K3
Treecrest Ri DOD/DAR S75 261 G2
Treelands DOD/DAR S75 260 D3
Tree La LUD/ILL HX2 145 H1
Tree Top Vw CUL/QBY BD13 124 E4 5
Trefoil Wy LIT OL15 185 H8
Trelawn Av HDGY LS6 108 F1
Trelawn Pl HDGY LS6 108 F1
Trelawn St HDGY LS6 108 F1
Trelawn Ter HDGY LS6 108 F1
Tremont Gdns MID LS10 132 A4 8
Trenam Park Dr IDLE BD10 83 J4
Trenance Dr SHPY BD18 82 B7
Trenance Gdns GTL/HWG HX4 168 C8
Trenholme Av LM/WK BD12 126 D8
Trenic Crs HDGY LS6 108 F3 22
Trenic Dr HDGY LS6 108 F3
Trent Av GFTH/SHER LS25 135 J1
MILN OL16 207 J8
NORM WF6 178 C2
Trentham Av BEE/HOL LS11 131 K4
Trentham Gv BEE/HOL LS11 131 K4
Trentham Pl BEE/HOL LS11 131 K4
Trentham Rw BEE/HOL LS11 131 K4
Trentham St BEE/HOL LS11 131 K4
Trenton Dr GIR BD8 4 B2
Trenton Rd EARL WF12 174 B4
Trent Rd OSM LS9 110 B6
ROY/SHW OL2 229 J6
Trent St BEE/HOL LS11 8 E5
MILN OL16 206 D8 11
Trescoe Av WOR/ARM LS12 108 A5
Tresham Ct EARL WF12 174 B4 1
Trevelyan St BRIG HD6 170 C1 1
HUDE HD5 15 M8
Trewan Ct BSLYN/ROY S71 261 K3 6
Triath Ct BTLY WF17 151 G8
Trilby St WKFDE WF1 13 G1
Trimmingham La LUD/ILL HX2 145 M8
Trimmingham Rd LUD/ILL HX2 145 M8
Trinity Church Ga WKFDE WF1 12 F3
Trinity Cl LUD/ILL HX2 124 C8
Trinity Ct HOLM/MEL HD7 236 B2
Trinity Dr KBTN HD8 257 H1
Trinity Pl BGLY BD16 81 J4
HFAX HX1 11 G7
Trinity Ri OT LS21 41 K7
Trinity Rd HFAX HX1 11 G7
WBOW BD5 4 C9
Trinity St BTLY WF17 173 L4
HBR HX7 143 H3 7
HFAX HX1 11 G7
HUD HD1 14 E7
MIRF WF14 194 C2
PONT WF8 180 F5
WKFDE WF1 13 L8
Trinity Ter BTLY WF17 150 F5
Trinity Vw HIPP HX3 11 K8
LM/WK BD12 127 G7
OSS WF5 174 F7
Trinity Wk LM/WK BD12 127 G7
Trip Garth WBY LS22 47 K4
Trip La WBY LS22 47 H4
Tristram Av WBOW BD5 127 J4
Triumph Cl BEE/HOL LS11 8 C4
Troon Dr HUDN HD2 192 B3
Troon Wy WKFDW/WTN WF2 198 C4 2
Trooper La HIPP HX3 11 K8
Trooper Ter HIPP HX3 11 K8
Trough La HEM/SK/SE WF9 247 L3
HWTH BD22 101 J5
Trough Well La
WKFDW/WTN WF2 176 A3
Trowell Wy BSLYN/ROY S71 243 H6
Troydale Gdns PDSY/CALV LS28 129 K1
Troydale Gv PDSY/CALV LS28 129 K1
Troydale La PDSY/CALV LS28 107 J8
Troy Hl MOR LS27 152 C1 1
Troy Ri MOR LS27 152 D1
Troy Rd HORS LS18 85 L4
MOR LS27 152 C1
Trueman Av HECK WF16 173 G2
Trueman Ct LM/WK BD12 127 G8 5
Trueman Ter BSLYN/ROY S71 262 A4 2
Truncliffe WBSY BD6 126 F5
Trundles La KNOT WF11 182 D2
Truro Ct BSLYN/ROY S71 261 K3
Truro Dr NORM WF6 178 D3
Truro St WOR/ARM LS12 108 E6
Truro Wk NORM WF6 178 D3
Tubby La HUDN HD2 192 D5 3
Tudor Barn Ct SHPY BD18 82 F7 5
Tudor Cl PDSY/CALV LS28 106 E4
PONT WF8 202 E1
Tudor Ct HEM/SK/SE WF9 247 H3
Tudor Cft HUDN HD2 193 H1
Tudor Gdns BEE/HOL LS11 131 G4
Tudor Lawns RHAY LS8 88 D7 1
WKFDW/WTN WF2 176 A1 2
Tudor St HOLM/MEL HD7 212 C6
ROY/SHW OL2 229 K7
WBOW BD5 126 F2 18
Tudor Wy EARL WF12 195 K3
Tuel La RPDN/SBR HX6 167 K2
Tufton St AIRE BD20 35 M4
Tulip Gv WHIT OL12 206 A3
Tulip St HWTH BD22 100 E1
MID LS10 131 M3
Tumbling Cl OSS WF5 175 G8
Tumbling Hl PONT WF8 203 J1
Tumbling Hill St GTHN BD7 4 C7
Tumbling La BSLYN/ROY S71 244 B8
Tune St BSLY S70 261 J6
Tun La CUD/GR S72 222 F7
Tunnacliffe Rd HUDS HD4 214 D3
Tunnel St CUL/QBY BD13 101 M6
HUDS HD4 213 L7
Tunnicliffe Pl AIRE BD20 35 M5 10
Tunshill La LIT OL15 208 A7
MILN OL16 207 L7
Tunstall Gn BOW BD4 128 A3 15
Tunstall Rd BEE/HOL LS11 131 L3
Tunwell La ECHL BD2 105 L2
Tunwell St ECHL BD2 105 L2
Tup La HOR/CROF WF4 222 E6
Turbary Av PDSY/CALV LS28 107 G4
Turbid La HUDS HD4 213 J8
Turbury La GTL/HWG HX4 168 A6
Turf Ct CUL/QBY BD13 101 L1
Turf Hill Rd MILN OL16 228 D2
Turf House Cl LIT OL15 185 H7 1
Turf La CUL/QBY BD13 79 L8
Turf Ter LIT OL15 185 J8
Turgate La RPDN/SBR HX6 166 B5
Turley Cote La HUDW HD3 190 E5
Turnberry Av AL/HA/HU LS17 87 K2
Turnberry Cl AL/HA/HU LS17 87 K2
Turnberry Ct AIRE BD20 57 J3 3
NORM WF6 178 F5 3
Turnberry Dr AL/HA/HU LS17 87 K2
EARD/LOFT WF3 152 F6 3
Turnberry Gdns
EARD/LOFT WF3 152 F6
Turnberry Gv AL/HA/HU LS17 87 K2
CUD/GR S72 244 E5 2
Turnberry Pl AL/HA/HU LS17 87 K2 1
Turnberry Ri AL/HA/HU LS17 87 K2
Turnberry Vw AL/HA/HU LS17 87 K2 2
Turnbridge Rd HUDE HD5 15 J6
Turner Av BTLY WF17 173 L1 19
GTHN BD7 126 B1 10
Turner Av North LUD/ILL HX2 145 M1
Turner Av (South) LUD/ILL HX2 146 A2
Turner Cl EARD/LOFT WF3 153 G6 8
Turner Crs OT LS21 41 J5
Turner Dr EARD/LOFT WF3 153 G6
Turner La HIPP HX3 11 K2
ILK LS29 18 E8
Turner Pl GTHN BD7 126 D1 9
LUD/ILL HX2 146 A2
Turner's Ct HIPP HX3 146 D4 7
Turner's Pl WHIT OL12 206 A3
Turner St PDSY/CALV LS28 106 F3 4
WHIT OL12 206 A5 6
Turners Yd PDSY/CALV LS28 106 F3
Turney St HIPP HX3 146 C4
Turnfield Cl MILN OL16 206 F3 6
Turnhill Rd MILN OL16 228 D3 5
Turnip La EARL WF12 195 M5
Turn O'the Nook OSS WF5 174 E8 4
Turnough Rd MILN OL16 207 H7 4
Turnpike La WBY LS22 31 L5
Turnpike Rd TAD LS24 72 B1
Turnpike St ELL HX5 169 J7
Turnshaw Rd HWTH BD22 78 B4
KBTN HD8 216 C8
Turnshaws Av KBTN HD8 216 C7
Turnshaws Cl KBTN HD8 216 C7
Turnsteads Av CLECK BD19 149 K6
Turnsteads Cl CLECK BD19 149 L6 3
Turnsteads Crs CLECK BD19 149 L6
Turnsteads Dr CLECK BD19 149 L6
Turnsteads Mt CLECK BD19 149 L6
Turnstone Ct MID LS10 153 M1 11
The Turnways HDGY LS6 108 E2
Turpin La GFTH/SHER LS25 138 D3
Turret Hall Rd HBR HX7 142 E4
Turret Royd Rd HBR HX7 142 E4
Turton Gn MOR LS27 129 M7 9
Turton St WKFDE WF1 13 G3
Turton V MOR LS27 129 M8 2
Turver's La KNOT WF11 183 G2
Turvin Rd RPDN/SBR HX6 186 F4
Tuxford Crs BSLYN/ROY S71 261 M4
Twain Crs CAS WF10 180 E1 4
Tweedale Gdns DEWS WF13 173 K6 11
Tweedale St DEWS WF13 173 K6 12
ROCH OL11 228 A1
Tweed Cl BTLY WF17 151 J5
Tweedy St WIL/AL BD15 102 E1
Twelfth Av LVSG WF15 171 K1
Twibell St BSLYN/ROY S71 261 J3
Twickenham Ct GIR BD8 104 F4 1
Twinegate WHIT OL12 206 A3
Twitch Hl HOR/CROF WF4 197 K5
Twivey St CAS WF10 157 L7 5
Two Acre Dr ROY/SHW OL2 229 H6
Two Bridges Rd MILN OL16 229 K3
Two Laws Rd HWTH BD22 76 E5
Tyas Gv OSM LS9 110 D7
Tyas La HOLM/MEL HD7 211 K4
Tyburn La KBTN HD8 217 K8
Tydeman Wk MILN OL16 229 J1 6
Tyersal Av BOW BD4 106 B7
Tyersal Cl BOW BD4 106 B7
Tyersal Ct BOW BD4 106 B8
Tyersal Crs BOW BD4 106 B8
Tyersal Dr BOW BD4 106 B8
Tyersal Garth BOW BD4 106 B8 1
Tyersal Gn BOW BD4 106 B8
Tyersal Gv BOW BD4 106 B8
Tyersal La BOW BD4 128 A2
PDSY/CALV LS28 106 E8
Tyersal Pk BOW BD4 106 B8
Tyersal Rd BOW BD4 106 B8
Tyersal Ter BOW BD4 106 A8
Tyersal Vw BOW BD4 106 A8
Tyersal Wk BOW BD4 106 B8
Tyler Cl NORM WF6 179 G4
Tyndale Av HOR/CROF WF4 197 L4
Tyndale Wk BTLY WF17 173 G1
Tynedale Ct CHAL LS7 87 J8 5
Tyne St BFDE BD3 5 H4
KGHY BD21 3 K5
Tynwald Cl AL/HA/HU LS17 87 J4 1
Tynwald Dr AL/HA/HU LS17 87 J3
Tynwald Gn AL/HA/HU LS17 87 J3
Tynwald Hl AL/HA/HU LS17 87 J4
Tynwald Mt AL/HA/HU LS17 87 J3
Tynwald Rd AL/HA/HU LS17 87 J3
Tynwald Wk AL/HA/HU LS17 87 J4
Tyrrell Ct WKFDW/WTN WF2 175 M7
Tyrrel St BFD BD1 4 F6
Tyson St HFAX HX1 146 A8

U

Ulla Gn TAD LS24 95 G5
Ullswater Av EARL WF12 174 A3
ROY/SHW OL2 228 F8
Ullswater Cl EARL WF12 174 A3
Ullswater Crs MSTN/BAR LS15 111 G8
RTHW LS26 133 L8
Ullswater Dr WBSY BD6 126 B8
WBY LS22 29 L8
Ullswater Ri WBY LS22 29 L8
Ullswater Rd BSLYN/ROY S71 262 D6 8
EARL WF12 174 A4
Ulster Av ROCH OL11 228 A1 15
Una Pl HUDN HD2 14 B2
Uncouth Rd MILN OL16 207 G7
Underbank Av TOD OL14 142 D5
Underbank Old Rd
HOLM/MEL HD7 254 D2
Undercliffe La BFDE BD3 5 J2
Undercliffe Old Rd ECHL BD2 5 L1
Undercliffe Ri ILK LS29 39 G4
Undercliffe Rd ECHL BD2 105 K3
Undercliffe St BFDE BD3 5 L2
Underwood Av BSLY S70 261 K8
Underwood Dr YEA LS19 84 D5
Underwood Wy ROY/SHW OL2 229 M6
Union Ct BSLY S70 261 H6
Union Gv LVSG WF15 172 D3
Union House La CLAY BD14 125 L4
Union La LUD/ILL HX2 123 M6
Union Pl BEE/HOL LS11 8 E4
Union Rd GTHN BD7 126 D1
LVSG WF15 172 D3
WBSY BD6 126 E7
WHIT OL12 207 G2
Union Sq WKFDE WF1 12 F3
Union St BAIL BD17 83 G4 5
BGLY BD16 59 G7
BSLY S70 261 H6
BTLY WF17 151 H5 6
COL BB8 74 A1
CUL/QBY BD13 125 G5 17
DEWS WF13 173 M6 18
GTL/HWG HX4 168 F7 8
HEM/SK/SE WF9 224 A8 8
HFAX HX1 11 H7
HOLM/MEL HD7 212 B5
HUD HD1 15 G5
HUDW HD3 191 K6 5
LDSU LS2 7 H9
LVSG WF15 172 E3
MOR LS27 130 E6 10
OSS WF5 174 F8 3
OT LS21 41 H7
RPDN/SBR HX6 167 G5
WHIT OL12 206 B6
WKFDE WF1 12 F2
Union St South TOD OL14 163 K1 13
Union Ter CHAL LS7 87 L8 8
SKP/WHF BD23 16 B3 5
Union Yd IDLE BD10 83 L6 7
Unity Cl HDGY LS6 6 E1
Unity Ct DEWS WF13 173 K6
Unity St AIRE BD20 58 B4
EARD/LOFT WF3 154 F3
HBR HX7 143 J2
TOD OL14 163 J6 5
Unity St North BGLY BD16 81 H4
Unity St South BGLY BD16 81 H4
Unity Ter HFAX HX1 146 A8 4
University Rd LDSU LS2 6 C5
University St CAS WF10 157 M7 5
Unwin Crs STKB/PEN S36 270 F4
Unwin Pl HTON BD9 104 A4
Unwin St STKB/PEN S36 270 F4
Upland Crs RHAY LS8 110 C1
Upland Gdns RHAY LS8 110 C2 13
Upland Gv RHAY LS8 110 C1
Upland Rd RHAY LS8 110 C2
Uplands HUDN HD2 192 A5
KGHY BD21 57 J5
SKP/WHF BD23 16 D1
Uplands Av CUL/QBY BD13 125 K4
DOD/DAR S75 241 L6
Uplands Cl CUL/QBY BD13 125 K4
Uplands Crs CUL/QBY BD13 125 K4
Uplands Dr MIRF WF14 172 C8
Uplands Gv CUL/QBY BD13 125 K4
The Uplands PONT WF8 180 E7
Upper Accommodation Rd
OSM LS9 9 M1
Upper Ada St SHPY BD18 82 B6 25
Upper Addison St BOW BD4 5 H9
Upper Allerton La WIL/AL BD15 103 G6
Upper Ash Gv HEM/SK/SE WF9 247 J3
Upper Ashley La SHPY BD18 82 D6 10
Upper Bank End Rd
HOLM/MEL HD7 254 D3
Upper Barker St LVSG WF15 172 C2 11
Upper Basinghall St LDS LS1 6 F9
Upper Batley La BTLY WF17 151 K6
Upper Batley Low La
BTLY WF17 151 K4
Upper Battye St HECK WF16 172 F1
Upper Bell Hall HFAX HX1 168 C1
Upper Bolton Brow
RPDN/SBR HX6 167 M1
Upper Bonegate BRIG HD6 170 D3
Upper Brig Royd
RPDN/SBR HX6 188 F2
Upper Brow Rd HUDW HD3 213 M1
Upper Butts CLECK BD19 149 M7 9
Upper Calton St KGHY BD21 2 E8
Upper Camroyd St
DEWS WF13 173 M5 9
Upper Carr La PDSY/CALV LS28 84 C8
Upper Carr St LVSG WF15 172 C1
Upper Castle St WBOW BD5 127 G1
Upper Chelsea St KGHY BD21 2 E8
Upper Cliffe Rd DOD/DAR S75 260 A6
Upper Clough Rd
HOLM/MEL HD7 212 E6
Upper Commercial St
BTLY WF17 173 L1
Upper Common La KBTN HD8 240 B6
Upper Croft Rd BTLY WF17 173 K2 13
Upper Cross St DEWS WF13 173 L5 9
Upper Ellistones Ct
GTL/HWG HX4 168 C7 2
Upper Ferndown Gn
WIL/AL BD15 103 J5 3
Upperfield Dr HOLM/MEL HD7 212 E2
Upper Field House La
RPDN/SBR HX6 166 F4
Upper Field La DOD/DAR S75 240 F5
Upper Folderings
DOD/DAR S75 260 B7 3
Upper Forest Rd
BSLYN/ROY S71 243 H6
Upper Forge HFAX HX1 11 H6 3
Upper Fountaine St LDS LS1 6 F8
Upper Fountain St
RPDN/SBR HX6 167 K2
Upper Fyfe La BAIL BD17 83 G3
Upper Ga HOLM/MEL HD7 255 G4
Upper George St HECK WF16 172 F2
HUD HD1 14 D7
WBSY BD6 126 D5 9
WHIT OL12 206 B5 23
Upper Grange Av
WIL/AL BD15 103 K6 8
Upper Green Av CLECK BD19 149 H6 10
EARD/LOFT WF3 152 F7
Upper Green La BRIG HD6 170 A1
Upper Green Wy
EARD/LOFT WF3 152 F7
Upper Hagg Rd HOLM/MEL HD7 236 D5
Upper Hall Vw HIPP HX3 147 J3
Upper Hatfield Pl HOR/CROF WF4 222 F4
Upper Haugh Shaw HFAX HX1 10 D9 3
Upper Hayes Cl MILN OL16 206 E6 8
Upperhead Rw HUD HD1 14 E7
Upper Heaton La HUDE HD5 193 K3
Upper Heights Rd CUL/QBY BD13 102 E6
Upper High Royds DOD/DAR S75 242 C6
Upper House La LVSG WF15 171 L2
Upper House Rd
HOLM/MEL HD7 254 E6
Upper House St BOW BD4 127 K1 5
Upper Kirkgate HFAX HX1 11 J6 2
Upper La CLECK BD19 150 D7
HIPP HX3 147 H2
HOR/CROF WF4 218 E2
KBTN HD8 217 M8
TOD OL14 141 M5
Upper Langwith WBY LS22 47 G6
Upper Lombard St YEA LS19 84 C2 5
Upper Marsh La HWTH BD22 100 B1
Upper Martin Gn
GTL/HWG HX4 168 C7 5
Upper Mary St SHPY BD18 82 B6 26
Upper Maythorn La
HOLM/MEL HD7 255 M6
Upper Mdw CUL/QBY BD13 125 G6 3
HOLM/MEL HD7 253 M1
Uppermoor PDSY/CALV LS28 106 E7
Uppermoor Cl PDSY/CALV LS28 106 F8
Upper Mosscar St BFDE BD3 5 K6
Upper Mount St BTLY WF17 173 L3
HUD HD1 214 B2
Upper New St BSLY S70 261 H6 13
Upper Nidd St BFDE BD3 5 M7
Upper North St BTLY WF17 173 K2 14
LDSU LS2 6 F7
Upper Parish Ghyll La ILK LS29 38 B3 2
Upper Peel St DEWS WF13 173 M5 10
Upper Quarry Rd HUDN HD2 171 J8
Upper Raglan St TOD OL14 141 K8 10
Upper Rd DEWS WF13 173 K4
Upper Rushton Rd BFDE BD3 105 M5
Upper Sackville St
SKP/WHF BD23 16 C3
Upper School St AIRE BD20 56 E1 9
Upper Seymour St BFDE BD3 5 L7
Upper Sheffield Rd BSLY S70 261 J8
Upper South St DEWS WF13 173 L5 10
Upper Station Rd BTLY WF17 173 M2
Upper Stone Dr MILN OL16 206 F8 2
Upper Sutherland Rd HIPP HX3 148 A6
Upperthong La HOLM/MEL HD7 254 A1
Upper Town St BRAM LS13 107 L3
Upper Union St SKP/WHF BD23 16 B3
Upper Warrengate WKFDE WF1 13 G2
Upper Washer La LUD/ILL HX2 168 B1
Upper Wellhouse Rd
HOLM/MEL HD7 212 E3
Upper Westlock Av OSM LS9 110 C5
Upper West St BTLY WF17 174 A1 4
Upper Willow Hall LUD/ILL HX2 145 M8
Upper Woodlands Rd GIR BD8 104 C5
Upperwood Rd WMB/DAR S73 263 G8
Upper Woodview Pl
BEE/HOL LS11 131 K4 10
Upper Wortley Dr
WOR/ARM LS12 108 D7 3
Upper Wortley Rd
WOR/ARM LS12 108 D7
Upper York St WKFDE WF1 12 E1
Upton St BTLY WF17 151 K8
Upwood La AIRE BD20 58 F4
Ure Crs GIR BD8 4 B3
Ure Gv WBY LS22 29 M6
Usher St BOW BD4 127 J1
Uttley St HIPP HX3 146 D4 8

V

Vaal St BSLY S70 261 K6
Vale Av KNOT WF11 181 M2
RHAY LS8 88 C3
Vale Cl HUDE HD5 215 H3
Vale Cottages LIT OL15 207 J1 5
Vale Crs KNOT WF11 181 M2
Vale Crest KNOT WF11 181 M2
Vale Gv AIRE BD20 35 M5
CUL/QBY BD13 125 H5 14
Vale Head Gv KNOT WF11 181 M2
Vale Head Mt KNOT WF11 181 M2
Vale Mill La HWTH BD22 78 F5
Valentine Ct CUL/QBY BD13 103 G7
Vale Rd HEM/SK/SE WF9 223 K5
ROY/SHW OL2 229 M8
Valestone Av HEM/SK/SE WF9 224 A7
Vale St BRIG HD6 170 C3
KGHY BD21 3 L1
The Vale HDGY LS6 109 H1
WBY LS22 47 J6
Vale Vw FEA/AMT WF7 202 D7
Valley Av HEM/SK/SE WF9 247 K3
HIPP HX3 148 B6
Valley Cl AL/HA/HU LS17 87 J1
Valley Ct BFDE BD3 4 F1
Valley Crs WKFDW/WTN WF2 176 B4
Valley Dr EARL WF12 196 A5
ILK LS29 38 F2
MSTN/BAR LS15 111 K5
RTHW LS26 135 G6
WKFDW/WTN WF2 176 B5
Valley Farm Rd RTHW LS26 132 C5
Valley Farm Wy RTHW LS26 132 C5
Valley Fold CUL/QBY BD13 125 G6
Valley Gdns CHAL LS7 87 L6
Valley Gn PDSY/CALV LS28 107 H8
Valley Gv LUD/ILL HX2 124 B7
PDSY/CALV LS28 107 H8
Valley Head HUDW HD3 191 L4
Valley Mt BRAM LS13 107 J6
GFTH/SHER LS25 135 J4
Valley Pde GIR BD8 4 D2
Valley Pl BFD BD1 4 E1
Valley Rdg GFTH/SHER LS25 135 H3
Valley Ri BRAM LS13 107 L1
ROY/SHW OL2 229 J5
Valley Rd BFD BD1 4 F2
BRAM LS13 107 L1
CLECK BD19 150 A6
DOD/DAR S75 242 C5
EARL WF12 196 B5
GFTH/SHER LS25 135 H3
HBR HX7 143 J3
ILK LS29 38 F1
LVSG WF15 172 C1
MOR LS27 152 D1
OSS WF5 196 F2
PDSY/CALV LS28 107 H8
PONT WF8 204 A2
ROCH OL11 228 A2
SHPY BD18 82 D8
Valley Sq PDSY/CALV LS28 107 H8
Valley St HEM/SK/SE WF9 247 H4
Valley Ter AL/HA/HU LS17 88 B3
The Valley AL/HA/HU LS17 65 J8
Valley Vw AIRE BD20 34 E7
BAIL BD17 82 D5
BGLY BD16 80 C5
HEM/SK/SE WF9 247 K3
LUD/ILL HX2 124 B7
Valley View Cl HWTH BD22 79 G3
Valley View Gdns HWTH BD22 79 G6 22
Valley View Gv ECHL BD2 105 J4
Valley View Rd HBR HX7 143 H2
OSS WF5 196 F2
Valley Wy LUD/ILL HX2 124 B7
Vancouver Pl CHAL LS7 88 A8 4
Varley Rd HOLM/MEL HD7 212 B8
Varley St COL BB8 52 A8
PDSY/CALV LS28 106 F5
Vaughan Rd AWLS/ASK DN6 227 M5
DOD/DAR S75 260 D3 5
Vaughan St BFD BD1 4 C5
HFAX HX1 10 A9 4
Vavasour St MILN OL16 206 D8
Velvet Wood Cl DOD/DAR S75 260 C3
Venables Av COL BB8 52 B8
Ventnor Cl CLECK BD19 150 D4
OSS WF5 196 F1
Ventnor Dr OSS WF5 196 F1 7
Ventnor St BFDE BD3 5 K6
ROCH OL11 228 B1
Ventnor Ter HIPP HX3 168 D2
Ventnor Wy OSS WF5 196 F1
Vento Cl WBSY BD6 126 D6
Verdant Wy MILN OL16 228 E3
Verdun Rd WBSY BD6 126 C6
Vere Sq WBOW BD5 127 G2 18
Verity Sp SCFT LS14 111 G6
Verity St BOW BD4 128 B7
Verity Vw SCFT LS14 111 G5
Vermont St BRAM LS13 107 J4
Verner St FEA/AMT WF7 201 L2
Vernon Av HUD HD1 14 C5
Vernon Cl BSLY S70 261 H7
HUD HD1 14 C5
Vernon Ct KGHY BD21 2 F3
Vernon Pl ECHL BD2 105 K4 12
PDSY/CALV LS28 107 G4
WKFDW/WTN WF2 12 D8 5
Vernon Rd COL BB8 52 F8
LDS LS1 6 E6
LVSG WF15 172 E2
Vernon St BSLYN/ROY S71 261 H4
HWTH BD22 79 H6 10
LDSU LS2 7 G7 1
TOD OL14 163 J3
Vernon St North
BSLYN/ROY S71 261 H4 5
Vernon Wy DOD/DAR S75 260 D3
Vesper Cl KSTL LS5 86 B8
Vesper Ct KSTL LS5 86 A8
Vesper Gdns KSTL LS5 108 B1
Vesper Gate Crs KSTL LS5 108 B1
Vesper Gate Dr KSTL LS5 86 A8
Vesper Gate Mt KSTL LS5 86 B8
Vesper Gv KSTL LS5 108 C2
Vesper La KSTL LS5 108 B1
Vesper Mt KSTL LS5 108 C2
Vesper Pl KSTL LS5 108 C2
Vesper Ri KSTL LS5 86 A8
Vesper Rd KSTL LS5 86 A8
Vesper Ter KSTL LS5 108 C2
Vesper Wk KSTL LS5 86 A8
Vesper Wy KSTL LS5 85 M8
Vestry St BOW BD4 127 K3 4
Viaduct Rd WOR/ARM LS12 108 F5
Viaduct St HOLM/MEL HD7 212 C5
HUD HD1 14 F5
Vicarage Av KSTL LS5 108 D2
MOR LS27 129 L8
Vicarage Cl HEM/SK/SE WF9 246 E3
LM/WK BD12 148 E4
WKFDE WF1 176 D1
Vicarage Ct CLECK BD19 149 M6
Vicarage Dr MILN OL16 206 E3 8
PDSY/CALV LS28 106 F7 5
Vicarage Gdns BIRK/DRI BD11 150 C1

BRIG HD6 ... 170 B6
FEA/AMT WF7 ... 179 M6
OT LS21 ... 41 J7
Vicarage La BSLYN/ROY S71 ... 243 L3
BSPA/BRAM LS23 ... 69 M4
FEA/AMT WF7 ... 201 M1
Vicarage Meadow MIRF WF14 ... 194 E1
Vicarage Rd EARL WF12 ... 173 M6
EARL WF12 ... 195 L1
HDGY LS6 ... 6 A4
HDGY LS6 ... 109 G4
HUDW HD3 ... 191 J8
SHPY BD18 ... 83 G6
Vicarage St KSTL LS5 ... 108 D2
ROY/SHW OL2 ... 229 K7
Vicarage St North WKFDE WF1 ... 13 G1
Vicarage St South WKFDE WF1 ... 13 G1
Vicarage Ter KSTL LS5 ... 108 D2
Vicarage Vw KSTL LS5 ... 108 D2
Vicarage Wk STBK/PEN S36 ... 270 F3
Vicarage Wy ROY/SHW OL2 ... 229 J8
Vicar La BFD BD1 ... 5 G7
LDS LS1 ... 7 H9
LDSU LS2 ... 7 H8
OSS WF5 ... 197 G2
Vicar Park Dr LUD/ILL HX2 ... 145 K6
Vicar's Dr MILN OL16 ... 206 B7
Vicar's Ga MILN OL16 ... 206 B7
Vicars Rd RHAY LS8 ... 110 B2
RHAY LS8 ... 110 B2
Vicars Ter CAS WF10 ... 157 K6
Vickerman Crs HUDS HD4 ... 214 B5
Vickerman St HFAX HX1 ... 10 B7
Vickers Av HEM/SK/SE WF9 ... 247 G5
KSTL LS5 ... 108 B3
Vickersdale PDSY/CALV LS28 ... 107
Vickers St WF10 ... 157 M7
MOR LS27 ... 152 B3
Victor Dr GSLY LS20 ... 62 A6
Victoria Av BRIG HD6 ... 170 B5
BTLY WF17 ... 173 L2
CLECK BD19 ... 149 M7
ECHL BD2 ... 105 M4
ELL HX5 ... 169 G8
HFAX HX1 ... 10 A8
HORS LS18 ... 85 J7
HWTH BD22 ... 78 E6
ILK LS29 ... 38 G2
ILK LS29 ... 61 H1
KGHY BD21 ... 3 G2
MOR LS27 ... 152 C1
OSM LS9 ... 110 C7
RPDN/SBR HX6 ... 167 L1
RTHW LS26 ... 155 G2
SHPY BD18 ... 82 B6
WKFDW/WTN WF2 ... 12 A2
YEA LS19 ... 62 F7
Victoria Cl CAS WF10 ... 157 K2
HORS LS18 ... 85 J7
ILK LS29 ... 38 G2
YEA LS19 ... 62 F7
Victoria Ct HEM/SK/SE WF9 ... 225 J2
KGHY BD21 ... 2 E4
Victoria Crs BSLY S70 ... 260 F4
DEWS WF13 ... 173 J4
ELL HX5 ... 169 H8
HORS LS18 ... 85 J7
PDSY/CALV LS28 ... 106 E7
Victoria Crs West DOD/DAR S75 ... 260 F4
Victoria Dr EARL WF12 ... 195 L2
ECHL BD2 ... 105 M2
HIPP HX3 ... 147 K3
HORS LS18 ... 85 J7
ILK LS29 ... 38 B2
MOR LS27 ... 130 D8
Victoria Gdns HORS LS18 ... 85 J7
ILK LS29 ... 38 B2
PDSY/CALV LS28 ... 106 E7
ROY/SHW OL2 ... 229 K7
Victoria Grange Dr MOR LS27 ... 152 C1
Victoria Gv HORS LS18 ... 85 J8
ILK LS29 ... 38 B2
OSM LS9 ... 110 C6
WKFDW/WTN WF2 ... 197 M3
Victoria La HOLM/MEL HD7 ... 212 C2
HUD HD1 ... 15 G7
Victoria Ms HORS LS18 ... 85 J7
MOR LS27 ... 152 C1
Victoria Mt HORS LS18 ... 85 J7
Victoria Pk SHPY BD18 ... 82 B7
Victoria Park Av BRAM LS13 ... 108 A3
Victoria Park Gv BRAM LS13 ... 108 A3
Victoria Park St KGHY BD21 ... 3 J3
Victoria Park Vw KGHY BD21 ... 3 J2
Victoria Pl BRIG HD6 ... 170 D5
CAS WF10 ... 157 M6
HUDE HD5 ... 15 M8
HUDS HD4 ... 213 J5
MIRF WF14 ... 194 B1
YEA LS19 ... 62 C7
Victoria Ri PDSY/CALV LS28 ... 106 C7
Victoria Rd AIRE BD20 ... 34 E2
AWLS/ASK DN6 ... 249 M8
BEE/HOL LS11 ... 8 F3
BRIG HD6 ... 148 D7
BSLY S70 ... 260 F4
BSLYN/ROY S71 ... 243 M2
CLECK BD19 ... 150 E6
DEWS WF13 ... 173 L6
EARL WF12 ... 195 L2
ECHL BD2 ... 105 L2
ELL HX5 ... 169 G8
GSLY LS20 ... 61 M6
HBR HX7 ... 143 G2
HDGY LS6 ... 109 G3
HFAX HX1 ... 10 C5
HIPP HX3 ... 147 M7
HOLM/MEL HD7 ... 234 F4
HUD HD1 ... 214 B2
HWTH BD22 ... 54 F7
HWTH BD22 ... 78 F4
ILK LS29 ... 38 B2
KGHY BD21 ... 2 E7
KSTL LS5 ... 108 C2
LVSG WF15 ... 172 C3
MOR LS27 ... 152 C1
PDSY/CALV LS28 ... 106 E7
PDSY/CALV LS28 ... 106 F4

RPDN/SBR HX6 ... 167 K3
RTHW LS26 ... 132 F8
SHPY BD18 ... 82 B6
TOD OL14 ... 141 K8
WBSY BD6 ... 126 C6
Victoria Springs HOLM/MEL HD7 ... 254 A2
Victoria St AIRE BD20 ... 55 M1
BAIL BD17 ... 82 E5
BFD BD1 ... 4 D3
BRIG HD6 ... 170 E3
BSLY S70 ... 261 G4
BSLY S70 ... 261 M6
BTLY WF17 ... 151 H5
BTLY WF17 ... 151 K8
BVRD LS3 ... 6 B7
CAS WF10 ... 157 K2
CAS WF10 ... 157 K6
CHAL LS7 ... 87 M7
CLAY BD14 ... 125 K2
CLECK BD19 ... 149 M6
CUD/GR S72 ... 244 D7
CUL/QBY BD13 ... 80 A3
CUL/QBY BD13 ... 125 H5
DEWS WF13 ... 173 G8
ECHL BD2 ... 105 L4
FEA/AMT WF7 ... 201 M1
FEA/AMT WF7 ... 223 M1
GTL/HWG HX4 ... 168 F7
HECK WF16 ... 172 F2
HEM/SK/SE WF9 ... 224 A8
HFAX HX1 ... 11 G5
HOLM/MEL HD7 ... 233 H2
HOLM/MEL HD7 ... 254 C1
HOR/CROF WF4 ... 197 H5
HUD HD1 ... 214 C2
HUDE HD5 ... 15 M8
HUDN HD2 ... 193 G3
HUDW HD3 ... 191 J6
IDLE BD10 ... 83 K5
KBTN HD8 ... 240 A4
LIT OL15 ... 207 K1
MID LS10 ... 9 K4
MOR LS27 ... 130 E7
PDSY/CALV LS28 ... 84 C8
PONT WF8 ... 180 B5
ROY/SHW OL2 ... 229 K7
RPDN/SBR HX6 ... 167 K3
SKP/WHF BD23 ... 16 E3
STBK/PEN S36 ... 270 F3
TOD OL14 ... 140 E5
WBY LS22 ... 48 A1
WHIT OL12 ... 206 B5
WIL/AL BD15 ... 102 E2
WIL/AL BD15 ... 103 J3
WKFDE WF1 ... 176 D2
WKFDW/WTN WF2 ... 12 A1
WMB/DAR S73 ... 263 K8
Victoria Ter BSLY S70 ... 261 J6
BVRD LS3 ... 6 B7
KBTN HD8 ... 240 B4
LUD/ILL HX2 ... 167 G2
PDSY/CALV LS28 ... 107 H4
SKP/WHF BD23 ... 16 E2
Victoria Wk HORS LS18 ... 85 J7
Victoria Wy WKFDE WF1 ... 176 D3
Victor Rd HEM/SK/SE WF9 ... 246 K4
BFDE BD3 ... 106 A7
BTLY WF17 ... 173 M1
CAS WF10 ... 179 L1
HEM/SK/SE WF9 ... 247 H4
HTON BD9 ... 104 D4
Victor Ter HFAX HX1 ... 10 C3
HTON BD9 ... 104 D4
Victory Av HUDW HD3 ... 213 K1
Victory La EARD/LOFT WF3 ... 177 M4
View Croft Rd BAIL BD17 ... 82 D6
Viewland Cl CUD/GR S72 ... 262 E1
Viewlands HUDN HD2 ... 192 C2
Viewlands Cl STBK/PEN S36 ... 270 F4
Viewlands Mt ILK LS29 ... 61 M1
View Rd KGHY BD21 ... 2 D2
STBK/PEN S36 ... 270 C2
The View AL/HA/HU LS17 ... 65 K8
RHAY LS8 ... 88 B6
Vignola Ter CLAY BD14 ... 125 L3
Viking Av KBTN HD8 ... 217 M8
Viking Rd PONT WF8 ... 181 G6
Villa Cl EARL/AMT WF7 ... 202 D6
Village Av BULY LS4 ... 108 F4
Village Farm Ct GLE DN14 ... 161 K7
Village Ms WIL/AL BD15 ... 102 E1
Village Pl BULY LS4 ... 108 F4
Village Rd BHP/TINH LS16 ... 65 H4
Village St AWLS/ASK DN6 ... 249 K6
HIPP HX3 ... 148 B4
The Village St BULY LS4 ... 108 F4
Village Ter BULY LS4 ... 108 F3
The Village BSPA/BRAM LS23 ... 49 C5
HUDS HD4 ... 215 H8
HUDS HD4 ... 237 G5
Villa Gv BGLY BD16 ... 81 J2
Villa Mt LM/WK BD12 ... 148 E5
Villa Rd BGLY BD16 ... 81 J2
Villa St RPDN/SBR HX6 ... 167 L2
Villier Ct WIL/AL BD15 ... 103 K5
Vincent Av AIRE BD20 ... 56 C1
Vincent Rd BSLYN/ROY S71 ... 262 B3
Vincent St COL BB8 ... 74 B1
HFAX HX1 ... 10 B1
MILN OL16 ... 228 C1
Vine Av CLECK BD19 ... 149 L6
Vine Cl BRIG HD6 ... 170 F5
BSLYN/ROY S71 ... 261 J2
ROY/SHW OL2 ... 229 K7
Vine Ct BRIG HD6 ... 170 F4
Vine Crs CLECK BD19 ... 149 L6
Vine Garth BRIG HD6 ... 170 F4
Vine Gv BRIG HD6 ... 170 F4
Vine Pl ROCH OL11 ... 228 B1
Vinery Av OSM LS9 ... 110 C6
Vinery Cl KBTN HD8 ... 240 B4
Vinery Gv OSM LS9 ... 110 C6
Vinery Mt OSM LS9 ... 110 C7
Vinery Rd BULY LS4 ... 108 F4

Vinery St OSM LS9 ... 110 C6
Vinery Ter OSM LS9 ... 110 C7
Vine St CLECK BD19 ... 149 M6
GTHN BD7 ... 126 D1
HUD HD1 ... 15 H1
Vine Ter CUL/QBY BD13 ... 102 F8
HFAX HX1 ... 10 B7
Vine Ter (East) GIR BD8 ... 104 A6
Vine Ter (West) GIR BD8 ... 104 A6
Vineyard Cl WHIT OL12 ... 184 E7
Violet St HFAX HX1 ... 10 C5
HWTH BD22 ... 100 E1
Violet St North HFAX HX1 ... 10 C4
Virginia Cl EARD/LOFT WF3 ... 154 C8
Virginia Ct EARD/LOFT WF3 ... 154 C8
Virginia Dr EARD/LOFT WF3 ... 154 C8
Virginia Gdns EARD/LOFT WF3 ... 154 C8
Virginia Rd HUDW HD3 ... 191 L7
Virginia St CLAY BD14 ... 125 L3
ROCH OL11 ... 228 A2
Vissett Cl HEM/SK/SE WF9 ... 223 J8
Vissitt La HEM/SK/SE WF9 ... 223 J8
Vivian Pl GTHN BD7 ... 126 C3
Vivian Rd GIR BD8 ... 103 L6
Vivien Rd GIR BD8 ... 103 L6
Vulcan Cl DEWS WF13 ... 173 L6
Vulcan Gdns DEWS WF13 ... 173 L6
Vulcan Rd DEWS WF13 ... 173 K6
Vulcan St BOW BD4 ... 127 K5
BRIG HD6 ... 170 E5
TOD OL14 ... 163 J5

W

Waarburton KBTN HD8 ... 217 L8
Waddington Fold MILN OL16 ... 228 E4
Waddington Rd DOD/DAR S75 ... 260 D4
Waddington St KGHY BD21 ... 3 G7
Wade House Av HIPP HX3 ... 125 L8
Wade House La HIPP HX3 ... 147 L8
Wade St LDSU LS2 ... 7 G7
Wade St DOD/DAR S75 ... 260 D4
HFAX HX1 ... 11 H5
PDSY/CALV LS28 ... 106 F5
Wadhouse La HOR/CROF WF4 ... 198 B6
Wadlands Cl PDSY/CALV LS28 ... 106 C2
Wadlands Dr PDSY/CALV LS28 ... 106 C2
Wadlands Gv PDSY/CALV LS28 ... 106 C2
Wadlands Ri PDSY/CALV LS28 ... 106 C3
Wadman Rd HOLM/MEL HD7 ... 254 C2
Wadsworth La HBR HX7 ... 143 K3
Wadsworth St HFAX HX1 ... 10 B4
Waggon La HEM/SK/SE WF9 ... 225 K7
Wagon La BGLY BD16 ... 81 J5
Wain Brow HUDS HD4 ... 214 B6
Waincliffe Crs BEE/HOL LS11 ... 131 H5
Waincliffe Dr BEE/HOL LS11 ... 131 H6
Waincliffe Garth BEE/HOL LS11 ... 131 H6
Waincliffe Mt BEE/HOL LS11 ... 131 H6
Waincliffe Pl BEE/HOL LS11 ... 131 H6
Waincliffe Sq BEE/HOL LS11 ... 131 H6
Waincliffe Ter BEE/HOL LS11 ... 131 H6
Wain Cl GFTH/SHER LS25 ... 137 M3
Waindale Cl LUD/ILL HX2 ... 145 J3
Waindale Crs LUD/ILL HX2 ... 145 J3
Waindyke Wy NORM WF6 ... 178 F4
Waingap Ri WHIT OL12 ... 206 B2
Waingate HOLM/MEL HD7 ... 212 F6
Waingate Pk HOLM/MEL HD7 ... 212 F5
Wainhouse Rd HFAX HX1 ... 10 A9
Wainman's Cl HWTH BD22 ... 54 F2
Wainman St BAIL BD17 ... 82 D6
BAIL BD17 ... 82 F2
HFAX HX1 ... 10 B5
Wain Pk HUDS HD4 ... 214 B6
Wainscott Cl HBR HX7 ... 121 K8
Wainsgate HBR HX7 ... 121 K8
Wainsgate La HBR HX7 ... 121 K8
Wainstalls La LUD/ILL HX2 ... 145 G1
Wainstalls Lodge La LUD/ILL HX2 ... 145 G1
Wainstalls Rd LUD/ILL HX2 ... 123 H8
Waite St WKFDW/WTN WF2 ... 176 A8
Waithlands Rd MILN OL16 ... 206 D8
Wakefield Av SCFT LS14 ... 111 H5
Wakefield Crs EARL WF12 ... 174 B6
Wakefield Ga LUD/ILL HX2 ... 168 B2
Wakefield Old Rd EARL WF12 ... 173 M6
Wakefield Rd BFD BD1 ... 5 G8
BIRK/DRI BD11 ... 151 J1
BOW BD4 ... 5 K9
BRIG HD6 ... 170 F5
BSLYN/ROY S71 ... 243 H7
DOD/DAR S75 ... 242 F5
EARL WF12 ... 173 M6
FEA/AMT WF7 ... 201 H1
FEA/AMT WF7 ... 223 M1
GFTH/SHER LS25 ... 112 E8
HEM/SK/SE WF9 ... 223 J3
HIPP HX3 ... 148 B3
HIPP HX3 ... 168 C4
HIPP HX3 ... 148 B4
HOR/CROF WF4 ... 197 L4
HUDE HD5 ... 15 K8
HUDE HD5 ... 193 G8
KBTN HD8 ... 216 D3
KBTN HD8 ... 240 B3
KBTN HD8 ... 257 G1
LVSG WF15 ... 172 D2
MID LS10 ... 132 B4
NORM WF6 ... 151 L1
OSS WF5 ... 175 L7
PONT WF8 ... 180 D7
RPDN/SBR HX6 ... 168 A2
RTHW LS26 ... 134 C5
RTHW LS26 ... 154 D1
Walden Dr HTON BD9 ... 103 L3
Walden St CAS WF10 ... 157 K2
Walden Stubbs Rd AWLS/ASK DN6 ... 227 M2
Waldorf Wy WKFDW/WTN WF2 ... 12 E5
Walesby Ct BHP/TINH LS16 ... 86 A4
Walford Av OSM LS9 ... 110 C6
Walford Gv OSM LS9 ... 110 C6
Walford Mt OSM LS9 ... 110 C6

Walford Rd OSM LS9 ... 110 C6
Walford Ter OSM LS9 ... 110 C6
Walker Av GTHN BD7 ... 126 A1
WKFDW/WTN WF2 ... 176 B3
Walker Cl AIRE BD20 ... 34 D8
Walker Dr GIR BD8 ... 104 C6
Walkergate OT LS21 ... 41 J6
PONT WF8 ... 181 G5
Walker Gn EARL WF12 ... 196 A5
Walker La HBR HX7 ... 143 L1
HOR/CROF WF4 ... 197 K5
RPDN/SBR HX6 ... 167 M2
Walker Pl MOR LS27 ... 130 D7
SHPY BD18 ... 82 F6
Walker Rd HORS LS18 ... 85 K5
LM/WK BD12 ... 149 H6
Walkers Gn WOR/ARM LS12 ... 130 C2
WOR/ARM LS12 ... 130 C2
Walkers Mt BTLY WF17 ... 173 L3
HDGY LS6 ... 109 H1
Walker's Pl AIRE BD20 ... 36 A6
Walkers Rw YEA LS19 ... 62 C8
Walker's Ter WKFDE WF1 ... 12 D2
Walker St BOW BD4 ... 127 K2
CLECK BD19 ... 149 H6
CLECK BD19 ... 149 M6
DEWS WF13 ... 194 F2
EARL WF12 ... 195 M2
MILN OL16 ... 206 C7
Walker Ter BOW BD4 ... 127 K2
CUL/QBY BD13 ... 101 M1
Walkley Av HECK WF16 ... 172 F4
Walkley Gv HECK WF16 ... 172 F5
Walkley La HECK WF16 ... 173 G4
Walkley Ter HECK WF16 ... 173 G4
Walk Mill Cl WHIT OL12 ... 206 F2
Walk Royd Hl DOD/DAR S75 ... 241 K4
The Walk KGHY BD21 ... 3 H6
MILN OL16 ... 206 D8
PDSY/CALV LS28 ... 106 C7
Wallace Gdns EARD/LOFT WF3 ... 154 D8
Wallace St HFAX HX1 ... 10 A7
Wallbank Dr SHPY BD18 ... 82 E8
Waller Clough Rd HOLM/MEL HD7 ... 212 B2
Wallingford Mt WIL/AL BD15 ... 103 K7
Wallis St GIR BD8 ... 104 D7
RPDN/SBR HX6 ... 167 K2
Wall Nook La KBTN HD8 ... 237 M8
Wallroyds KBTN HD8 ... 257 G1
Wall St BSLY S70 ... 261 G6
HWTH BD22 ... 2 B7
Walmer Gv PDSY/CALV LS28 ... 129 H1
Walmer Vis GIR BD8 ... 4 C1
Walmsley Av HEM/SK/SE WF9 ... 225 K7
Walmsley Rd HDGY LS6 ... 109 H4
Walney Fold BSLYN/ROY S71 ... 243 M8
Walnut Av EARL WF12 ... 174 C7
WKFDW/WTN WF2 ... 176 B7
Walnut Cl EARL WF12 ... 174 C8
SCFT LS14 ... 89 L6
TAD LS24 ... 93 K7
Walnut Crs EARL WF12 ... 174 C7
Walnut Dr EARL WF12 ... 174 C8
NORM WF6 ... 178 C7
PONT WF8 ... 202 D1
Walnut Gv EARL WF12 ... 174 D7
Walnut La EARL WF12 ... 174 C8
Walnut Pl EARL WF12 ... 174 C7
Walnut Rd EARL WF12 ... 174 C7
Walnut St BFDE BD3 ... 105 L8
HEM/SK/SE WF9 ... 247 H5
HFAX HX1 ... 10 C6
KGHY BD21 ... 79 K2
Walpole Rd HUDS HD4 ... 213 M3
Walpole St MILN OL16 ... 206 C7
Walsham Dr HUDW HD3 ... 191 G5
Walshaw La HBR HX7 ... 120 E3
Walshaw St GTHN BD7 ... 126 C2
Walsh La BGLY BD16 ... 59 L8
HIPP HX3 ... 10 L2
WOR/ARM LS12 ... 129 L4
Walsh St HFAX HX1 ... 10 B5
Walter Clough La HIPP HX3 ... 169 K1
Walter Crs OSM LS9 ... 110 B7
Walter St BULY LS4 ... 108 F5
ECHL BD2 ... 104 F2
IDLE BD10 ... 83 K6
Waltham Dr AWLS/ASK DN6 ... 249 G4
Waltham St BSLY S70 ... 261 H6
Waltin Rd HOLM/MEL HD7 ... 254 B5
Walton Av PBR HG3 ... 27 G3
Walton Cha BSPA/BRAM LS23 ... 49 H3
Walton Cft HUDE HD5 ... 193 G8
Walton Dr BIRK/DRI BD11 ... 129 H8
Walton Garth BIRK/DRI BD11 ... 129 H1
Walton Head La PBR HG3 ... 26 F6
Walton La BRIG HD6 ... 171 G1
WKFDW/WTN WF2 ... 199 H6
Walton Pk PBR HG3 ... 26 F3
Walton Rd BSPA/BRAM LS23 ... 48 F2
HEM/SK/SE WF9 ... 225 M6
WBY LS22 ... 48 B1
Walton Station La WKFDW/WTN WF2 ... 199 G7
Walton St BEE/HOL LS11 ... 8 E4
BOW BD4 ... 5 H9
BOW BD4 ... 127 H1
DOD/DAR S75 ... 260 E3
HWTH BD22 ... 54 E3
MID LS10 ... 9 L8
RPDN/SBR HX6 ... 167 K2
SKP/WHF BD23 ... 16 E3
Walton St North DOD/DAR S75 ... 260 D3
Walton Vw HOR/CROF WF4 ... 200 B6
Waltroyd Rd CLECK BD19 ... 149 L7
Wansford Cl BOW BD4 ... 128 A4
Wanstead Crs WIL/AL BD15 ... 103 K6
Wapping Nick La HUDW HD3 ... 191 G3
Wapping Rd BFDE BD3 ... 5 G3
Ward Bank Rd HOLM/MEL HD7 ... 254 C2
Ward La EARD/LOFT WF3 ... 177 J4
MID LS10 ... 131 M5

Wardle Crs HWTH BD22 ... 2 B3
KGHY BD21 ... 2 B3
Wardle Edge WHIT OL12 ... 206 D3
Wardle Fold WHIT OL12 ... 184 E7
Wardle Gdns WHIT OL12 ... 206 E3
Wardle Rd WHIT OL12 ... 206 E1
Wardle St LIT OL15 ... 185 J8
Wardman St KGHY BD21 ... 3 L1
Ward Place La HOLM/MEL HD7 ... 254 B3
Ward's End HFAX HX1 ... 11 H7
Wards Hl BTLY WF17 ... 173 L2
Wards Hill Ct BTLY WF17 ... 173 L2
Ward St DEWS WF13 ... 173 L5
GTHN BD7 ... 126 C3
KGHY BD21 ... 2 E7
MID LS10 ... 9 J5
SKP/WHF BD23 ... 16 C2
STBK/PEN S36 ... 270 F4
Wareham Cnr BOW BD4 ... 128 A4
Wareham Gv DOD/DAR S75 ... 260 C6
Warehouse Hill Rd HOLM/MEL HD7 ... 233 H2
Warehouse St BTLY WF17 ... 173 M3
Wareings Yd ROCH OL11 ... 228 C2
War Field La WBY LS22 ... 31 G2
Warhurst Rd ELL HX5 ... 169 J6
Waring Wy EARL WF12 ... 174 A5
Warlbeck ILK LS29 ... 38 B2
Warley Av BFDE BD3 ... 105 M6
Warley Dene LUD/ILL HX2 ... 145 K8
Warley Dr BFDE BD3 ... 105 M7
Warley Edge La LUD/ILL HX2 ... 145 K7
Warley Gv BFDE BD3 ... 105 M6
LUD/ILL HX2 ... 145 M7
Warley Rd LUD/ILL HX2 ... 145 M8
Warley St HFAX HX1 ... 145 M7
LIT OL15 ... 207 K1
Warley Town La LUD/ILL HX2 ... 145 J7
Warley Vw LUD/ILL HX2 ... 145 K8
Warley Wise La COL BB8 ... 53 J3
Warley Wood Av LUD/ILL HX2 ... 167 G1
Warley Wood La LUD/ILL HX2 ... 167 G1
Warmfield La WKFDE WF1 ... 178 A7
Warmfield Vw WKFDE WF1 ... 177 H7
Warm La YEA LS19 ... 84 C1
Warmliegh Pk CUL/QBY BD13 ... 124 D5
Warneford Av OSS WF5 ... 174 C7
Warneford Mt WIL/AL BD15 ... 213 J2
Warneford Rd HUDS HD4 ... 213 J2
Warner Av DOD/DAR S75 ... 260 D4
Warner Pl DOD/DAR S75 ... 260 D4
Warner Rd DOD/DAR S75 ... 260 D4
Warrel's Av BRAM LS13 ... 107 L4
Warrel's Ct BRAM LS13 ... 107 L4
Warrel's Gv BRAM LS13 ... 107 L4
Warrel's Mt BRAM LS13 ... 107 L4
Warrel's Pl BRAM LS13 ... 107 L4
Warrel's Rd BRAM LS13 ... 107 L4
Warrel's Rw BRAM LS13 ... 107 L4
Warrel's St BRAM LS13 ... 107 L4
Warrel's Ter BRAM LS13 ... 107 L4
Warren Av BSLY S70 ... 81 K1
KNOT WF11 ... 181 M3
WKFDW/WTN WF2 ... 198 F4
Warren Cl BSLYN/ROY S71 ... 243 M1
LVSG WF15 ... 172 D4
Warren Ct WKFDE WF1 ... 13 H2
Warren Crs BSLY S70 ... 261 H7
Warren Dr BSLY S70 ... 81 K2
FEA/AMT WF7 ... 179 J6
Warrenfield Ct HUDN HD2 ... 192 F3
Warren House La HUDW HD3 ... 191 J3
YEA LS19 ... 62 F5
Warren La BGLY BD16 ... 81 K2
DOD/DAR S75 ... 242 E2
OT LS21 ... 43 J7
TAD LS24 ... 70 D5
Warren Pk BRIG HD6 ... 148 B3
Warren Park Cl BRIG HD6 ... 148 A8
Warren Pl FEA/AMT WF7 ... 201 H1
Warren Quarry La BSLY S70 ... 261 H6
Warren Rd FEA/AMT WF7 ... 201 H1
Warrenside HUDN HD2 ... 192 C3
Warrens La BIRK/DRI BD11 ... 151 G1
BTLY WF17 ... 150 F3
Warren St EARL WF12 ... 173 M8
Warrenton Pl GTHN BD7 ... 126 C1
Warsop Rd BSLYN/ROY S71 ... 243 G5
Warton Av BOW BD4 ... 127 K5
Warwick Av HOLM/MEL HD7 ... 213 G7
Warwick Cl BOW BD4 ... 127 K2
ROY/SHW OL2 ... 229 H7
Warwick Dr BOW BD4 ... 127 K2
Warwick Rd BOW BD4 ... 127 K2
BSLYN/ROY S71 ... 261 K3
BTLY WF17 ... 173 L3
Warwick St WHIT OL12 ... 206 D4
WKFDE WF1 ... 13 L9
Wasdale Crs WKFDW/WTN WF2 ... 176 A7
Wasdale Rd WKFDW/WTN WF2 ... 176 A7
Washburn Ct WBY LS22 ... 29 M1
Washburn Dr AIRE BD20 ... 34 E8
Washer La LUD/ILL HX2 ... 168 B2
Washfold Rd HBR HX7 ... 165 J7
Washington Pl BRAM LS13 ... 107 J6
Washington St BRAM LS13 ... 107 J6
BVRD LS3 ... 109 G6
GIR BD8 ... 104 D5
HIPP HX3 ... 10 D1
Washington Ter BRAM LS13 ... 107 J6
Washpit New Rd HOLM/MEL HD7 ... 254 C4
Wasp Av ROCH OL11 ... 228 C3
Wasp Nest Rd HUDN HD2 ... 14 F1
Waste La HBR HX7 ... 121 J1
HUDE HD5 ... 215 G3
MIRF WF14 ... 194 B3
Wastwater Dr WBSY BD6 ... 126 B8
Watchit Hole La PONT WF8 ... 225 L2
Watercock St BOW BD4 ... 127 J1
Watercroft HUDE HD5 ... 215 H3
Waterfield Pl BSLYN/ROY S71 ... 262 A6
Waterfront Ms IDLE BD10 ... 84 A3
Watergate HIPP HX3 ... 147 L2
HUD HD1 ... 15 H6
PONT WF8 ... 180 E6
RTHW LS26 ... 135 D5

Watergate Rd *EARL* WF12........ 173 K7 **7**
Water Green La *RPDN/SBR* HX6.. 166 C8
Water Hall La *STKB/PEN* S36.... 270 F2
Waterhall Vw *STKB/PEN* S36.... 270 F2 **1**
Waterhouse Cl *WHIT* OL12...... 206 E1
Waterhouse Gv
   WKFDW/WTN WF2.............. 12 B3
Waterhouse St *HFAX* HX1........ 11 C6
   KGHY BD21..................... 2 E4
   WHIT OL12.................. 206 B6 **18**
Watering Place Rd
   STKB/PEN S36............... 270 C3 **2**
Water La *BEE/HOL* LS11.......... 8 D3
   EARD/LOFT WF3............. 177 H2
   EARL WF12.................. 173 K8
   EARL WF12.................. 174 C7
   GFTH/SHER LS25............ 138 D6
   HEM/SK/SE WF9.............. 246 B2
   HFAX HX1..................... 11 J8
   HOR/CROF WF4.............. 196 F6
   HOR/CROF WF4.............. 220 C6
   HORS LS18.................... 85 C5
   KGHY BD21..................... 2 F6
   MILN OL16.................. 229 J1
   PDSY/CALV LS28............ 106 F3
   PONT WF8.................. 181 H3
   PONT WF8.................. 202 F4
   PONT WF8.................. 205 G8
   WOR/ARM LS12............. 107 M7
Water Lane Cl *HOR/CROF* WF4.. 196 F6
Waterloo Cl *CAS* WF10......... 179 H1
Waterloo Crs *BRAM* LS13....... 107 M3
   IDLE BD10................... 84 B6 **2**
Waterloo Fold *LM/WK* BD12.... 148 F4 **2**
Waterloo Gv *PDSY/CALV* LS28.. 106 D7
Waterloo La *BRAM* LS13........ 107 M3
Waterloo Mt *PDSY/CALV* LS28.. 106 D6
Waterloo Ri *HUDE* HD5......... 193 L7
Waterloo Rd *BGLY* BD16........ 81 H3 **14**
   BRIG HD6.................. 170 C3
   BSLY S70.................. 260 F5 **13**
   HUDE HD5.................. 193 K8
   PDSY/CALV LS28............ 106 D6
Waterloo St *MID* LS10.......... 9 H2
   WKFDE WF1.................. 13 C6
Waterloo Ter *LUD/ILL* HX2..... 145 L8
Waterloo Wy *BRAM* LS13....... 107 M3
Waterman Vw *MILN* OL16...... 206 E6 **7**
Watermill Cl *MILN* OL16....... 206 F8 **3**
Water Rw *HOLM/MEL* HD7...... 237 C8 **2**
Water Royd Av *MIRF* WF14..... 172 C8
Water Royd Crs *MIRF* WF14.... 172 C8 **6**
Water Royd Dr *DOD/DAR* S75.. 260 B7
   MIRF WF14................. 172 C8 **7**
Water Royd La *MIRF* WF14..... 172 C8
Waterside *AIRE* BD20........... 36 B6 **3**
   BGLY BD16................... 80 F1
   HIPP HX3.................... 11 J8
   HUD HD1.................... 14 B9
   HUDS HD4................. 214 B4
   HWTH BD22................ 100 E4
Waterside Fold *HBR* HX7...... 143 J2 **11**
Waterside La *MILN* OL16...... 206 D6 **8**
Waterside Rd *MID* LS10........ 132 D4
Waterside Wk *HUDE* HD5....... 193 M1
Watersole La *WBY* LS22......... 48 D2
Waters Rd *HOLM/MEL* HD7..... 232 C1
Water Stalls Rd *RPDN/SBR* HX6.. 166 A6
Water St *BRIG* HD6............ 170 D3 **7**
   HOLM/MEL HD7............. 253 M3
   HUD HD1..................... 14 D8
   HUD HD1................... 214 B3 **5**
   KBTN HD8.................. 239 M5 **3**
   MILN OL16................. 206 B7 **24**
   RPDN/SBR HX6.............. 167 K3
   SKP/WHF BD23................ 16 B2
Waterton Cl *HEM/SK/SE* WF9.. 246 F3 **1**
   WKFDW/WTN WF2............ 199 H7
Waterton Gv *WKFDW/WTN* WF2.. 198 B1 **1**
Waterton Rd
   WKFDW/WTN WF2............ 197 M2
Waterview Cl *MILN* OL16....... 229 K3 **3**
Waterwheel Ri *HUDS* HD4...... 213 M4
Waterwood Rd *BTLY* WF17..... 173 H2
Waterworks Rd *BTLY* WF17.... 173 H2 **6**
Watery La *HOLM/MEL* HD7..... 253 H6
Watford Av *HIPP* HX3.......... 148 B3
Wath La *TAD* LS24.............. 94 F2
Watkin Av *CUL/QBY* BD13...... 103 H8
Watkinson Av *LUD/ILL* HX2.... 146 B2
Watkinson Dr *LUD/ILL* HX2.... 146 B2 **9**
Watkinson Rd *LUD/ILL* HX2.... 146 B2 **2**
Watkin St *MILN* OL16......... 228 D2
Watling Rd *CAS* WF10.......... 158 C8
Watmough St *GTHN* BD7........ 126 C3 **13**
Watnall Rd *BSLYN/ROY* S71.... 243 H6 **2**
Watroyd La *HOLM/MEL* HD7.... 212 D3
Watson Av *EARL* WF12.......... 174 D6
Watson Crs *WKFDE* WF1........ 177 G7
Watson Mill La *RPDN/SBR* HX6.. 167 K3
Watson Rd *SCFT* LS14.......... 111 H5
Watson's Houses
   SKP/WHF BD23.............. 16 B2 **17**
Watson's La *TAD* LS24.......... 70 F1
Watson St *MOR* LS27.......... 152 B3
   NORM WF6.................. 178 C4 **3**
Wattle Syke *WBY* LS22.......... 47 M5
Wattlesyke *WBY* LS22........... 48 A6
Watts St *CLAY* BD14.......... 125 K2
   WHIT OL12................. 206 C6 **6**
Watt St *BOW* BD4............ 127 M1 **6**
Watty Hall Av *WBSY* BD6....... 126 C4
Watty Hall La *WBSY* BD6....... 126 C4
Watty Hall Rd *WBSY* BD6...... 126 C4
Watty La *TOD* OL14........... 163 H3
Wauchope St *WKFDW/WTN* WF2.. 12 D6 **1**
Wauds Gates *BAIL* BD17........ 82 E5 **5**
Waulkmill Cl *HEM/SK/SE* WF9.. 225 J7
Wavell Av *WKFDW/WTN* WF2.... 199 H7
Wavell Gv *WKFDW/WTN* WF2... 199 G7
Waveney Dr *DOD/DAR* S75..... 260 A3 **1**
   ROY/SHW OL2.............. 229 J8
   WOR/ARM LS12............. 108 C8
Waverley Av *AIRE* BD20........ 58 C5 **3**
   GTHN BD7................. 126 D1
Waverley Crs *HIPP* HX3....... 147 L7 **3**
Waverley Garth *BEE/HOL* LS11.. 8 E8

Waverley Pl *GTHN* BD7........ 126 D1 **10**
Waverley Rd *ELL* HX5......... 191 H1
   GTHN BD7................. 126 D1
   HUD HD2.................... 14 D5
Waverley St *EARL* WF12........ 173 L7 **3**
   HOLM/MEL HD7............. 212 B5
Waverley Ter *GTHN* BD7....... 126 D1 **11**
   HUD HD2................... 191 M7
Waverton Gn *WBSY* BD6....... 126 A7 **8**
Wavertree Park Gdns
   LM/WK BD12............... 148 E2 **15**
Waycliffe *BSLYN/ROY* S71..... 261 L3
Wayland Ap *BHP/TINH* LS16.... 86 F2
Wayland Dr *BHP/TINH* LS16.... 86 F2
Wayne Cl *BTLY* WF17.......... 151 L8
Wayside Av *SCFT* LS14........ 67 M5
Wayside Crs *IDLE* BD10....... 105 K1 **5**
   SCFT LS14.................. 67 M4
Wayside Mt *SCFT* LS14........ 67 M5
Weardale Cl *BOW* BD4........ 127 L5
Weardley La *AL/HA/HU* LS17.... 44 D8
Weatherall Pl *AWLS/ASK* DN6.. 249 H4
Weatherhead Pl *AIRE* BD20.... 36 B5 **6**
Weatherhill Crs *HUDW* HD3... 191 J4
Weather Hill La *HBR* HX7..... 166 A1
   HOLM/MEL HD7............. 254 A6
Weather Hill Rd *HUDW* HD3... 191 J3
Weatherhouse Ter *LUD/ILL* HX2.. 145 M5
Weaver Cl *DOD/DAR* S75...... 260 A3
Weaver Gdns *MOR* LS27....... 152 F3 **5**
Weavers Cft *HOLM/MEL* HD7... 235 H4 **9**
   WOR/ARM LS12............. 108 D7 **2**
Weavers Cft *IDLE* BD10........ 83 K4 **8**
   PDSY/CALV LS28............ 107 H8
Weavers Gra *GSLY* LS20........ 62 A5
Weavers Hl *HWTH* BD22........ 78 E8
Weavers Rd *PONT* WF8........ 181 G5 **4**
Weavers Rw *PDSY/CALV* LS28.. 107 H8
Weaver St *BULY* LS4........... 108 C5
Weavers Wk *AIRE* BD20........ 36 A4 **15**
   KBTN HD8.................. 239 K7
Weaverthorpe Rd *BOW* BD4.... 128 A6
Webb Dr *ECHL* BD2........... 105 J4 **3**
Webb's Ter *HIPP* HX3.......... 11 K3
Webster Hl *EARL* WF12........ 173 L6
Webster Pl *NORM* WF6........ 178 C4 **7**
Webster Rw *WOR/ARM* LS12.. 108 D8
Webster St *BFDE* BD3.......... 5 L4
   DEWS WF13................. 173 H6
Wedgemoor Cl *LM/WK* BD12... 148 E2 **10**
Wedgewood Dr *RHAY* LS8...... 88 C6
Wedgewood Gv *RHAY* LS8..... 88 C6
Weedling Ga *TAD* LS24......... 71 K6
Weedon St *MILN* OL16........ 206 D6 **8**
Weeland Av *HOR/CROF* WF4... 200 D3
Weeland Crs *HOR/CROF* WF4.. 200 C4
Weeland Dr *HOR/CROF* WF4.. 200 C4
Weeland Rd *GLE* DN14........ 183 H1
   HOR/CROF WF4............ 200 C4
   KNOT WF11................ 183 G2
Weetlands Cl *GFTH/SHER* LS25.. 135 K4 **3**
Weeton La *AL/HA/HU* LS17..... 43 M3
Weet Shaw La *CUD/GR* S72.... 244 C5
Weetwood Av *BHP/TINH* LS16.. 86 F5
Weetwood Cl *BHP/TINH* LS16.. 86 E6
Weetwood Ct *BHP/TINH* LS16.. 86 E6
Weetwood Crs *BHP/TINH* LS16.. 86 E5
Weetwood Grange Gv
   BHP/TINH LS16............. 86 D6 **2**
Weetwood La *BHP/TINH* LS16.. 86 E5
Weetwood Mill La
   BHP/TINH LS16............. 86 F6
Weetwood Park Dr
   BHP/TINH LS16............. 86 D6
Weetwood Rd *BHP/TINH* LS16.. 86 D6
   GIR BD8................... 104 C6
Weetwood Wk *BHP/TINH* LS16.. 86 E7
Weetworth Av *CAS* WF10...... 158 A8
Weetworth Pk *CAS* WF10...... 158 A8
Weir Rd *MILN* OL16.......... 207 G7
Weir Side *HOLM/MEL* HD7..... 233 H2 **2**
Weir St *TOD* OL14........... 163 J3
Welbeck Av *LIT* OL15......... 185 J8
Welbeck Dr *GTHN* BD7........ 126 C2
Welbeck Ri *GTHN* BD7........ 125 M2
Welbeck Rd *BTLY* WF17........ 151 H4
   MILN OL16................. 228 D2
   OSM LS9.................. 110 C7
Welbeck St *CAS* WF10......... 157 M6 **16**
   DOD/DAR S75.............. 260 F4
   WKFDE WF1................. 13 K8 **5**
   WKFDE WF1.................. 13 L7
Welburn Av *BHP/TINH* LS16.... 86 B7
   HIPP HX3.................. 147 M7
Welburn Cl *WKFDW/WTN* WF2.. 199 H5 **3**
Welburn Dr *BHP/TINH* LS16.... 86 B7
Welburn Gv *BHP/TINH* LS16.... 86 D7 **2**
Welburn Mt *WBSY* BD6........ 126 A6
Welbury Dr *GIR* BD8.......... 104 E4
Weldon Ct *BOW* BD4......... 128 A2 **3**
Weldon Dr *HUDW* HD3........ 190 C6 **3**
Welfare Av *MSTN/BAR* LS15.... 91 G7
Welham Wk *BFDE* BD3.......... 5 J3
Welland Ct *DOD/DAR* S75..... 260 A3
Welland Dr *GFTH/SHER* LS25.. 113 J8
Welland Rd *ROY/SHW* OL2.... 229 J6
Wellands Gn *CLECK* BD19..... 149 K7
Wellands La *CLECK* BD19..... 149 H6
Wellands Ter *BFDE* BD3...... 105 L7 **8**
Well Cl *RTHW* LS26.......... 135 G6
   YEA LS19.................... 84 E3
Well Close Ri *LDSU* LS2......... 7 G5
Well Close St *BRIG* HD6...... 170 D3 **8**
Wellcroft *OT* LS21............ 41 J7
Well Cft *SHPY* BD18.......... 82 D7
Wellcroft Gv *EARD/LOFT* WF3.. 153 H7
Wellesley La *WKFDW/WTN* WF2.. 176 A7
Wellfield Cl *HOLM/MEL* HD7.. 213 G4
   HOR/CROF WF4............ 217 G1 **1**
Wellfield Gdns *STKB/PEN* S36.. 270 F1
Wellfield Pl *ROCH* OL11...... 228 C1 **3**
Wellfield Rd *DOD/DAR* S75.... 260 F3
   HUDW HD3................. 191 L8
Wellfield Ter *TOD* OL14...... 163 K2
Wellfield Bank *HUDS* HD4.... 213 L4

Wellgarth *HFAX* HX1........... 10 F9
Well Garth *MSTN/BAR* LS15.... 111 L4
Well Garth Bank *BRAM* LS13.. 107 K2
Well Garth Mt *MSTN/BAR* LS15.. 111 L4
Well Garth Vw *BRAM* LS13.... 107 L2
Wellgate *CAS* WF10.......... 158 B8
   DOD/DAR S75.............. 242 B5
   GTL/HWG HX4.............. 168 E6
   HOLM/MEL HD7............. 212 D3
Well Green Gdns
   HOLM/MEL HD7............. 236 B7 **1**
Well Green La *BRIG* HD6...... 170 B1
Well Gv *BRIG* HD6............ 170 B1
   HUDN HD2................. 192 E3
Wellhead Cl *BHP/TINH* LS16... 64 A2
Well Head Dr *HFAX* HX1....... 11 G8
Well Head La *HFAX* HX1....... 11 G8
   RPDN/SBR HX6.............. 166 E4
Well Heads *CUL/QBY* BD13.... 102 C8
Well Hl *HOLM/MEL* HD7...... 236 B2
   OT LS21.................... 41 H7
   YEA LS19................... 62 D7
Well Hill Gv *BSLYN/ROY* S71.. 243 L2 **8**
Well Hill Rd *HOLM/MEL* HD7.. 254 D3
Wellholme *BRIG* HD6.......... 170 D3
Well Holme Md *WOR/ARM* LS12.. 130 A3
Wellhouse Av *MIRF* WF14..... 172 C7
Well House Av *RHAY* LS8..... 110 C1
Wellhouse Cl *MIRF* WF14..... 172 C7
Well House Dr *RHAY* LS8..... 110 C1 **8**
Well House Gdns *RHAY* LS8.. 110 C1 **3**
Well House La *HUDE* HD5..... 193 J5
   MIRF WF14................. 172 C7
Well House La *STKB/PEN* S36.. 257 K8
   STKB/PEN S36.............. 270 F2
Well House Rd *RHAY* LS8..... 110 C1 **1**
Wellhouse Wy *STKB/PEN* S36.. 270 F1
   WOR/ARM LS12.............. 8 B1
Wellington Bridge St *BVRD* LS3.. 6 B9
Wellington Cl *BSLYN/ROY* S71.. 261 L8
Wellington Ct *BIRK/DRI* BD11.. 128 C8
Wellington Crs *SHPY* BD18.... 82 C7 **12**
Wellington Gdns *BRAM* LS13.. 107 M3
Wellington Garth *BRAM* LS13.. 107 M2 **8**
Wellington Gv *BRAM* LS13.... 107 M2 **1**
   ECHL BD2................. 105 K4 **13**
   PDSY/CALV LS28............ 106 E7
Wellington Hl *SCFT* LS14...... 88 F5
Wellington Mt *BRAM* LS13.... 107 M2 **3**
Wellington Pl *KNOT* WF11.... 181 M2 **1**
   MILN OL16................. 206 C6 **19**
Wellington Rd *EARL* WF12.... 173 L6 **4**
   ECHL BD2................. 105 K4
   KGHY BD21.................. 3 H6
   TOD OL14................. 163 K1
   WIL/AL BD15............... 102 C2
   WOR/ARM LS12............. 109 G8
Wellington Rd East
   DEWS WF13................ 173 L6 **15**
   BFD BD1..................... 5 G5
   BGLY BD16.................. 81 H3
   BOW BD4.................. 105 M8
   BSLY S70................. 261 G5
   BTLY WF17................. 173 L2 **8**
   BVRD LS3................... 6 B9
   CAS WF10................. 157 K6 **2**
   CUL/QBY BD13............. 125 H5 **15**
   DEWS WF13................ 173 L6 **16**
   ECHL BD2................. 105 K3 **3**
   HUDW HD3................. 191 K6
   IDLE BD10.................. 83 K7 **10**
   LDS LS1.................... 8 D1
   LIT OL15.................. 207 K1
   LVSG WF15................. 172 D5 **3**
   MILN OL16................. 207 J8
   MOR LS27................. 152 C2 **14**
   SKP/WHF BD23............... 16 C5 **7**
   WHIT OL12................ 206 B5 **23**
   WIL/AL BD15............... 103 L5
   WKFDW/WTN WF2........... 176 A7
Wellington St South *HFAX* HX1.. 11 J7
Wellington St West *HFAX* HX1.. 10 F8
Wellington Ter *BRAM* LS13.... 107 M2 **7**
Well I' Th' La *ROCH* OL11.... 228 C1
Well La *BRIG* HD6............ 171 G4
   BSLYN/ROY S71............. 261 L1
   BTLY WF17................. 173 M1
   CHAL LS7................... 87 M7
   DEWS WF13................. 173 H6
   GFTH/SHER LS25............ 135 J5
   GFTH/SHER LS25............ 138 A2
   GSLY LS20.................. 62 A5
   HFAX HX1................... 11 J5
   YEA LS19................... 62 D8
Well Road Cl *LUD/ILL* HX2.... 145 L7
Well Royd Av *LUD/ILL* HX2.... 145 L7
Wells Ct *OSS* WF5........... 196 E1 **6**
Wells Cft *HDGY* LS6.......... 87 G7
Wells Mt *KBTN* HD8.......... 238 C7
Wells Prom *ILK* LS29.......... 38 D3
Wells Rd *EARL* WF12......... 195 M4
   GSLY LS20.................. 62 A5
   ILK LS29.................... 38 C4
Wells St *CUD/GR* S72........ 244 D8
   DOD/DAR S75.............. 242 A6 **8**
The Wells *LUD/ILL* HX2....... 145 L7
Wellstone Av *BRAM* LS13..... 107 K5
Wellstone Dr *BRAM* LS13..... 107 K6
Wellstone Gdns *BRAM* LS13.. 107 K6
Wellstone Garth *BRAM* LS13.. 107 K5
Wellstone Gn *BRAM* LS13.... 107 K6
Wellstone Ri *BRAM* LS13..... 107 K5
Wellstone Wy *BRAM* LS13.... 107 K6
Well St *BFD* BD1.............. 5 G6
   BSLY S70.................. 260 F5 **14**
   CUL/QBY BD13............. 104 M6
   EARL WF12................ 174 A5 **8**
   EARL WF12................ 174 A6 **8**
   GTL/HWG HX4.............. 190 D2
   HUD HD1.................... 14 C9
   KGHY BD21................... 2 F4
   LVSG WF15................. 172 C1
   ROCH OL11................ 228 C1
   TOD OL14................. 163 K2

Wells Rw *PDSY/CALV* LS28.... 107 G6 **3**
Wells Wk *OSS* WF5.......... 196 D1
Welsyke Rd *AWLS/ASK* DN6... 249 M7
Welthorne Av *MSTN/BAR* LS15.. 91 J1
Wellthorne La *STKB/PEN* S36.. 257 G5
Well Vw *SHPY* BD18........... 82 C5 **3**
Welton Gv *HDGY* LS6......... 109 G3 **10**
Welton Mt *HDGY* LS6......... 109 G3
Welton Pl *HDGY* LS6......... 109 G3
Welton Rd *HDGY* LS6......... 109 G3 **31**
Welwyn Av *BTLY* WF17........ 151 H8
   SHPY BD18................. 83 H7
Welwyn Dr *BAIL* BD17......... 82 E4
   SHPY BD18.................. 83 H7 **3**
Welwyn Rd *EARL* WF12....... 174 B3
Wembly Av *CUL/QBY* BD13.... 103 H8
Wenborough La *BOW* BD4..... 128 B3 **8**
   BOW BD4................. 128 B4 **13**
Wendel Av *MSTN/BAR* LS15.... 90 F7
Wendron Cl *LVSG* WF15....... 172 B5
Wendron Wy *IDLE* BD10....... 83 K7
Wenlock St *BFDE* BD3........... 5 J7
Wenning St *KGHY* BD21......... 3 H1
Wensley Av *CHAL* LS7......... 87 L7 **8**
   SHPY BD18................. 82 C7 **13**
Wensley Bank *CUL/QBY* BD13.. 102 E8
Wensley Bank Ter
   CUL/QBY BD13............. 102 E8
Wensley Bank (West)
   CUL/QBY BD13............. 102 E8
Wensley Crs *CHAL* LS7........ 87 L7 **5**
   WOR/ARM LS12............. 108 B4 **2**
Wensleydale Av *SKP/WHF* BD23.. 16 D2
   WOR/ARM LS12............. 108 B4
Wensleydale Crs
   WOR/ARM LS12............. 108 B4
Wensleydale Dr
   WOR/ARM LS12............. 108 B4
Wensleydale Ms
   WOR/ARM LS12............. 108 B4 **3**
Wensleydale Ri *BAIL* BD17.... 83 G2
   WOR/ARM LS12............. 108 B4
Wensleydale Rd *BFDE* BD3.... 106 A7
Wensley Dr *CHAL* LS7......... 87 K6
   PONT WF8................. 181 G8
Wensley Gn *CHAL* LS7........ 87 K7
Wensley Gv *BRIC* HD6........ 170 A6 **2**
Wensley Rd *BSLYN/ROY* S71.. 243 G7
   CHAL LS7................... 87 K6
Wensley St East
   HOR/CROF WF4............ 197 J5 **3**
Wensley Vw *CHAL* LS7........ 87 L7
Wensley Wy *MILN* OL16...... 206 D8
Went Av *AL/HA/HU* LS17...... 201 L3
Wentbridge La *PONT* WF8..... 203 L8
Wentbridge Rd *FEA/AMT* WF7.. 202 A2
Wentcliffe Rd *KNOT* WF11.... 181 K2
Went Cft *PONT* WF8......... 202 F1
Wentdale *PONT* WF8......... 205 G8
Went-dale Rd *PONT* WF8..... 202 F1
Went Fold *PONT* WF8........ 202 F1
Went Garth *PONT* WF8....... 202 F1
Went Gv *FEA/AMT* WF7....... 201 L2
Went Hill Cl *FEA/AMT* WF7... 202 C6
Went La *HOR/CROF* WF4...... 201 J8
Went Vw *PONT* WF8.......... 225 J1
Wentwell Rd *FEA/AMT* WF7... 200 E1
Wentworth Av *AL/HA/HU* LS17.. 87 K2
   ILK LS29................... 61 J2
Wentworth Cl *HOR/CROF* WF4.. 220 B7
   DOD/DAR S75.............. 242 E6 **3**
   STKB/PEN S36.............. 270 F3
Wentworth Dr *DOD/DAR* S75.. 242 E6 **10**
   HEM/SK/SE WF9............ 246 E3
   HOR/CROF WF4............ 200 C6
   KBTN HD8.................. 217 L8
   LUD/ILL HX2............... 124 B7
Wentworth Ga *WBY* LS22...... 29 K8
Wentworth Gv *LUD/ILL* HX2.. 124 B7
Wentworth Mdw
   STKB/PEN S36............. 270 E2
Wentworth Ms *STKB/PEN* S36.. 270 F3 **3**
Wentworth Park Ri
   PONT WF8................. 203 M1 **1**
Wentworth Rd *DOD/DAR* S75.. 241 L6
   DOD/DAR S75.............. 242 E6
   FEA/AMT WF7.............. 201 K2
   STKB/PEN S36.............. 270 F2
Wentworth St *BSLYN/ROY* S71.. 261 G3 **3**
   HUD HD1.................... 14 D5
   WKFDE WF1................. 176 D7
Wentworth Ter
   HEM/SK/SE WF9............ 223 K3
   WKFDE WF1................. 176 D7 **6**
Wentworth Wy *AL/HA/HU* LS17.. 87 L2 **1**
   DOD/DAR S75.............. 260 B5
   WKFDW/WTN WF2........... 199 G5
Wepener Mt *OSM* LS9........ 110 D5
Wepener Pl *OSM* LS9......... 110 D5
Wescoe Hill La *AL/HA/HU* LS17.. 43 M4
Wesleyan Ter *BOW* BD4....... 127 L3 **10**
Wesley Av *LM/WK* BD12....... 126 F7
   WOR/ARM LS12............. 108 C7
Wesley Av South *LM/WK* BD12.. 127 G8
Wesley Cl *BTLY* WF17......... 151 G5
   WHIT OL12................. 206 D4
Wesley Ct *BEE/HOL* LS11..... 131 H4 **2**
   HDGY LS6.................... 6 D2
   HFAX HX1................... 11 H5 **8**
   OSS WF5................... 174 E8
Wesley Cft *BEE/HOL* LS11...... 8 A9
Wesley Dr *LM/WK* BD12....... 127 G7
Wesley Garth *BEE/HOL* LS11.. 131 H4 **9**
Wesley Gn *BEE/HOL* LS11..... 131 H4 **8**
Wesley Gv *IDLE* BD10.......... 83 H8
Wesley Hall Ct
   EARD/LOFT WF3............ 177 H4 **8**
Wesley Pl *AIRE* BD20......... 36 A5 **13**
   DEWS WF13................ 173 L6 **17**
   FEA/AMT WF7.............. 201 M2 **1**
   KGHY BD21.................. 79 K3
   OSM LS9..................... 9 M1
   WOR/ARM LS12............. 108 C7
Wesley Rd *PDSY/CALV* LS28.. 106 C5 **3**
   WOR/ARM LS12............. 108 C7

Wesley Rw *PDSY/CALV* LS28.. 107 G6 **3**
Wesley Sq *PDSY/CALV* LS28.. 107 G6
Wesley St *BEE/HOL* LS11...... 131 G3
   BRAM LS13................. 107 H1
   BSLY S70.................. 261 H5 **11**
   CAS WF10................. 157 M6
   CAS WF10................. 179 L1 **9**
   CLECK BD19............... 149 M6
   HEM/SK/SE WF9............ 247 G4
   MILN OL16................ 207 G8 **8**
   MOR LS27.................. 152 C2
   OSS WF5................... 174 E8
   OT LS21.................... 41 J6 **7**
   PDSY/CALV LS28............ 106 F3
   WHIT OL12................ 206 D3 **6**
   WKFDE WF1.................. 13 K8
Wesley Ter *BRAM* LS13........ 107 H1
   BRAM LS13................. 107 M3
   KBTN HD8................. 239 M8
   PDSY/CALV LS28............ 107 G6 **8**
Wesley Vw *BRAM* LS13........ 107 H1 **3**
   PDSY/CALV LS28............ 107 G7 **8**
Wessenden Cl *DOD/DAR* S75.. 260 C5 **3**
Wessenden Head Rd
   HOLM/MEL HD7............. 234 D6
Wessenden Rd *HOLM/MEL* HD7.. 233 J6
Wessex Park Cl
   ROY/SHW OL2.............. 229 K6 **11**
West Acres *KNOT* WF11....... 159 M6
West Av *BAIL* BD17........... 82 E2
   BSPA/BRAM LS23............ 48 D7
   HEM/SK/SE WF9............ 225 J7
   HEM/SK/SE WF9............ 247 K2
   HIPP HX3.................. 148 C7
   HIPP HX3.................. 168 C2
   HOLM/MEL HD7............. 236 A2
   HOR/CROF WF4............ 197 L5
   HUDW HD3................. 191 L5
   RHAY LS8................... 88 E6
West Bank *LUD/ILL* HX2...... 145 M2
West Bank Cl *HWTH* BD22...... 2 A3
West Bank Gv *AIRE* BD20...... 58 A4 **2**
West Bank Ri *HWTH* BD22..... 2 A3
West Bank Rd *AIRE* BD20..... 57 M4
   SKP/WHF BD23.............. 16 C3
West Bolton *LUD/ILL* HX2.... 123 M7
Westborough Dr *LUD/ILL* HX2.. 145 M7
Westbourne Av *BEE/HOL* LS11.. 131 K3
   GFTH/SHER LS25............ 112 F8
   PONT WF8................. 180 D7 **2**
Westbourne Cl *OT* LS21....... 41 G7 **1**
   WKFDW/WTN WF2........... 198 E8 **1**
Westbourne Crs
   GFTH/SHER LS25............ 112 F8
   PONT WF8................. 180 D7
Westbourne Dr
   GFTH/SHER LS25............ 112 F8
   GSLY LS20.................. 61 L5
   ILK LS29................... 61 J1
Westbourne Gdns
   GFTH/SHER LS25............ 112 F8 **8**
Westbourne Gv
   DOD/DAR S75.............. 260 F3 **4**
   GFTH/SHER LS25............ 112 F8
   HIPP HX3.................. 168 F3 **3**
   OT LS21.................... 41 G8 **1**
Westbourne Mt
   BEE/HOL LS11............. 131 K3 **19**
   PONT WF8................. 180 E7 **5**
Westbourne Pl
   BEE/HOL LS11............. 131 K3 **20**
   PDSY/CALV LS28............ 106 F5
Westbourne Rd *GIR* BD8...... 104 D2 **2**
   HUDW HD3................. 191 M7
   PONT WF8................. 180 D7
Westbourne St *BEE/HOL* LS11.. 131 K3
Westbourne Ter *DOD/DAR* S75.. 260 E5
   GFTH/SHER LS25............ 112 F8
   HIPP HX3.................. 168 F3 **3**
Westbrook Cl *HORS* LS18...... 85 K4
Westbrook Dr *HUDE* HD5...... 193 K8
Westbrook La *HORS* LS18..... 85 K4
Westburn Av *HWTH* BD22....... 2 A8
Westburn Crs *HWTH* BD22...... 2 A8
Westburn Gv *HWTH* BD22....... 2 A8
Westburn Wy *HWTH* BD22...... 2 A8
Westbury Cl *BOW* BD4........ 127 M1
   DOD/DAR S75.............. 260 D2
Westbury Gv *MID* LS10....... 132 B4 **3**
Westbury Mt *RTHW* LS26...... 132 B5
Westbury Pl *HFAX* HX1....... 146 A8
Westbury Pl North *MID* LS10.. 132 B4
Westbury Pl South *RTHW* LS26.. 132 B5
Westbury Rd *WBSY* BD6....... 127 M1
   ELL HX5................... 169 J7
   MID LS10.................. 132 B5
Westbury Ter *HFAX* HX1...... 146 A8
   MID LS10.................. 132 B5
West Busk La *OT* LS21......... 40 F8
West Byland *LUD/ILL* HX2.... 123 M7
West Carr La *HUDW* HD3...... 211 G4
West Chevin Rd *OT* LS21...... 61 M1
Westcliffe Av *BAIL* BD17..... 82 B3
Westcliffe Dr *LUD/ILL* HX2.. 145 M7
Westcliffe Ri *CLECK* BD19.... 149 L7
Westcliffe Rd *CLECK* BD19.... 149 L6
   SHPY BD18.................. 82 C7 **14**
West Cl *HUDN* HD2.......... 192 D4
   NORM WF6................. 178 C4
   PONT WF8................. 203 G2
Westcombe Av *RHAY* LS8...... 88 C4
Westcombe Cl *LM/WK* BD12.. 148 E2 **18**
West Ct *RHAY* LS8............ 88 E7
West Crs *STKB/PEN* S36...... 271 J4
West Cft *AIRE* BD20.......... 55 L2
Westcroft *HOLM/MEL* HD7.... 236 A2
West Cft *ILK* LS29........... 19 H6 **8**
   LM/WK BD12............... 148 C3
Westcroft Av *HIPP* HX3...... 147 K2
Westcroft Dr *OSS* WF5........ 174 C5 **1**
Westcroft La *SEL* YO8........ 139 M5
Westcroft Rd *GTHN* BD7...... 126 C2
   HEM/SK/SE WF9............ 223 M7
West Di *BSPA/BRAM* LS23..... 48 C5
Westdale Dr *PDSY/CALV* LS28.. 106 F6
Westdale Gdns *PDSY/CALV* LS28.. 106 F6

Westdale Gv PDSY/CALV LS28 ...... 106 F6
Westdale Ri PDSY/CALV LS28 ...... 106 F6
Westdale Rd PDSY/CALV LS28 ...... 106 F6
West Dene AIRE BD20 ...... 36 A4
AL/HA/HU LS17 ...... 88 B1
West Dr HWTH BD22 ...... 100 E3
PONT WF8 ...... 181 G7
West Edge Rd PONT WF8 ...... 204 B8
West End BSPA/BRAM LS23 ...... 48 E6
CUL/QBY BD13 ...... 124 F6
HOLM/MEL HD7 ...... 236 B6
MOR LS27 ...... 129 F7
WOR/ARM LS12 ...... 129 M3
West End Ap MOR LS27 ...... 151 M3
TAD LS24 ...... 94 F1
West End Av BSLYN/ROY S71 ...... 243 J3
FEA/AMT WF7 ...... 179 J6
HOLM/MEL HD7 ...... 236 E8
STKB/PEN S36 ...... 269 M3
West End Cl HORS LS18 ...... 85 H5
West End Crs BSLYN/ROY S71 ...... 243 J3
HORS LS18 ...... 85 J5
West End Dr CLECK BD19 ...... 149 K8
HORS LS18 ...... 85 J5
West End Gv HORS LS18 ...... 85 H5
West End La HORS LS18 ...... 85 H4
West End Pl BEE/HOL LS11 ...... 8 C4
West End Ri HORS LS18 ...... 85 J5
West End Rd AWLS/ASK DN6 ...... 227 L3
HFAX HX1 ...... 146 A8
HOLM/MEL HD7 ...... 212 E2
PDSY/CALV LS28 ...... 84 D8
Westend St BFD BD1 ...... 4 D5
West End Ter ECHL BD2 ...... 105 K1
GSLY LS20 ...... 61 J5
HBR HX7 ...... 144 A5
SHPY BD18 ...... 82 C6 11
Westercroft La HIPP HX3 ...... 147 K3
Westercroft Vw HIPP HX3 ...... 147 K3
Westerley Cl KBTN HD8 ...... 238 C3
Westerley Crs AIRE BD20 ...... 35 L5
Westerley La KBTN HD8 ...... 238 B3
Westerly Wy KBTN HD8 ...... 238 C3
Westerman Cft FEA/AMT WF7 ...... 179 M8
WKFDE WF1 ...... 199 H4
Westerman St WKFDE WF1 ...... 13 K9
WKFDE WF1 ...... 199 H4
Western Av AIRE BD20 ...... 57 M3
BTLY WF17 ...... 151 J3
PONT WF8 ...... 181 H5
Western Ct PONT WF8 ...... 181 H5 2
Western Gales Wy NORM WF6 ...... 178 F5
Western Gv WOR/ARM LS12 ...... 130 D1
Western Mt WOR/ARM LS12 ...... 130 D1
Western Pl CUL/QBY BD13 ...... 125 K5
Western Rd HUDS HD4 ...... 213 J2
SKP/WHF BD23 ...... 16 D3
WOR/ARM LS12 ...... 130 D1
Western St BSLY S70 ...... 261 G4
WOR/ARM LS12 ...... 130 D1
Western Wy WBSY BD6 ...... 126 C7
Westerton Cl EARD/LOFT WF3 ...... 153 K7
Westerton Ct LM/WK BD12 ...... 149 K1
Westerton Rd
EARD/LOFT WF3 ...... 152 F7 3
Westerton Wk
EARD/LOFT WF3 ...... 153 K6
West Farm Av MID LS10 ...... 153 K1
Westfell Cl HWTH BD22 ...... 2 B7
Westfell Rd HWTH BD22 ...... 2 B7
Westfell Wy HWTH BD22 ...... 2 B7
Westfield CUL/QBY BD13 ...... 103 J8
HBR HX7 ...... 143 L1
PDSY/CALV LS28 ...... 106 F5
Westfield Av CAS WF10 ...... 179 L2
EARL WF12 ...... 174 C6
GFTH/SHER LS25 ...... 135 J4
HIPP HX3 ...... 147 M7
HOLM/MEL HD7 ...... 234 E3
HUDW HD3 ...... 191 K7
KBTN HD8 ...... 239 H5
KNOT WF11 ...... 182 B3
PONT WF8 ...... 180 E8
STKB/PEN S36 ...... 270 C2
WOR/ARM LS12 ...... 108 B6
YEA LS19 ...... 62 B8
Westfield Cl GFTH/SHER LS25 ... 137 M3
HECK WF16 ...... 172 F1 2
RTHW LS26 ...... 154 E2 2
YEA LS19 ...... 62 B8
Westfield Crs GFTH/SHER LS25 ... 138 B2 2
HOR/CROF WF4 ...... 197 H4
MIRF WF14 ...... 194 C1
RTHW LS26 ...... 154 E2
Westfield Crs AIRE BD20 ...... 58 B4 2
BVRD LS3 ...... 6 A6
HDGY LS6 ...... 6 A5
HOR/CROF WF4 ...... 222 C5
OSS WF5 ...... 196 E1
SHPY BD18 ...... 83 C8 2
TAD LS24 ...... 71 L3
WKFDW/WTN WF2 ...... 175 K4 2
Westfield Dr AIRE BD20 ...... 58 B5 2
HIPP HX3 ...... 147 M7
KBTN HD8 ...... 239 H5
OSS WF5 ...... 196 E1
YEA LS19 ...... 62 A8
Westfield Farm OSS WF5 ...... 174 E8 2
Westfield Gdns
GFTH/SHER LS25 ...... 135 H4
HIPP HX3 ...... 147 M7 2
Westfield Gn RYKW YO26 ...... 32 A1
Westfield Gv CAS WF10 ...... 135 J8
DEWS WF13 ...... 173 H6
FEA/AMT WF7 ...... 202 D6
IDLE BD10 ...... 83 J6
SHPY BD18 ...... 83 C8 2
WKFDE WF1 ...... 176 E6
Westfield La ECHL BD2 ...... 83 H7
GFTH/SHER LS25 ...... 135 H4
GFTH/SHER LS25 ...... 137 J4
HEM/SK/SE WF9 ...... 247 H5
West Field La IDLE BD10 ...... 83 H7 2
KBTN HD8 ...... 217 G6
LM/WK BD12 ...... 148 F5
PONT WF8 ...... 203 L3
PONT WF8 ...... 227 G3
STKB/PEN S36 ...... 270 C2

Westfield Mt YEA LS19 ...... 62 A8
Westfield Ov YEA LS19 ...... 62 A8
Westfield Pk WKFDE WF1 ...... 176 E6
Westfield Pl CLECK BD19 ...... 149 G5
HFAX HX1 ...... 10 C1
WKFDW/WTN WF2 ...... 175 K4
Westfield Rd AIRE BD20 ...... 58 B5 3
BVRD LS3 ...... 6 A6
CLAY BD14 ...... 125 K2
HECK WF16 ...... 172 E1
HEM/SK/SE WF9 ...... 223 M7
HOR/CROF WF4 ...... 197 H4
HTON BD9 ...... 104 C4
KNOT WF11 ...... 182 B3
MOR LS27 ...... 152 C2 15
RTHW LS26 ...... 154 E2
RYKW YO26 ...... 32 A1
WKFDE WF1 ...... 176 D6
Westfields BSLYN/ROY S71 ...... 243 J2
CAS WF10 ...... 179 L1
Westfields Av MIRF WF14 ...... 194 C1
Westfield Sq TAD LS24 ...... 71 L2
Westfields Rd MIRF WF14 ...... 194 C1
Westfield St BSLY S70 ...... 260 F5 15
HECK WF16 ...... 172 E1
HFAX HX1 ...... 10 E7
OSS WF5 ...... 196 E1
Westfield Ter BAIL BD17 ...... 82 E2
CAS WF10 ...... 87 L7
CHAL LS7 ...... 87 L7 7
CLAY BD14 ...... 125 K2 15
ECHL BD2 ...... 5 L1
HFAX HX1 ...... 10 C3
TAD LS24 ...... 71 L2
WKFDE WF1 ...... 176 E6 6
Westfield Vw WKFDE WF1 ...... 176 E5
West Garth TAD LS24 ...... 94 F1 3
Westgarth WBY LS22 ...... 47 K3
West Ga HOLM/MEL HD7 ...... 254 D6
WBY LS22 ...... 48 A1
Westgate BAIL BD17 ...... 82 E2
BFD BD1 ...... 4 D5
BRIG HD6 ...... 171 G4
BSLY S70 ...... 261 G2
BSLYN/ROY S71 ...... 261 K2
CLECK BD19 ...... 149 L7
EARL WF12 ...... 173 M6 20
ECHL BD2 ...... 105 L2
ELL HX5 ...... 169 H7
GIR BD8 ...... 4 C1
GSLY LS20 ...... 61 K6
HEM/SK/SE WF9 ...... 223 L8
HFAX HX1 ...... 11 H6
HOLM/MEL HD7 ...... 234 F4
HOLM/MEL HD7 ...... 236 B2
HUD HD1 ...... 14 F7
HUDE HD5 ...... 215 H4
LDS LS1 ...... 6 C9 1
LVSG WF15 ...... 172 E4
OT LS21 ...... 41 H7
SHPY BD18 ...... 82 D6
STKB/PEN S36 ...... 270 F4
TAD LS24 ...... 71 L3
WKFDE WF1 ...... 12 E2
WKFDW/WTN WF2 ...... 12 D3
Westgate Cl EARD/LOFT WF3 ...... 154 D6
Westgate End
WKFDW/WTN WF2 ...... 12 B4
Westgate Gv EARD/LOFT WF3 ...... 154 E6 2
Westgate Hill St BOW BD4 ...... 128 B6
Westgate La EARD/LOFT WF3 ...... 154 D6
Westgate Ter BOW BD4 ...... 128 C6
West Grange Av MID LS10 ...... 131 M5
West Grange Dr MID LS10 ...... 131 M5
West Grange Fold MID LS10 ...... 131 M5
West Grange Gdns MID LS10 ...... 131 M5
West Grange Garth MID LS10 ...... 131 M5
West Grange Rd MID LS10 ...... 131 M5
West Grange Wk MID LS10 ...... 131 M5
BSLYN/ROY S71 ...... 243 J2
West Grove Av HUDE HD5 ...... 15 M6
West Grove St
PDSY/CALV LS28 ...... 106 F5
West Grove Ter HFAX HX1 ...... 10 C1
West Hall Av ILK LS29 ...... 19 J4
West Hill Av CHAL LS7 ...... 87 L7
Westhill Av CUL/QBY BD13 ...... 102 A1
West Hill St HFAX HX1 ...... 10 D6
Westholme Rd HFAX HX1 ...... 10 A6
Westholme St BFD BD1 ...... 4 D7
West Ings Ct KNOT WF11 ...... 182 D1
West Ings Crs KNOT WF11 ...... 182 D1
West Ings La KNOT WF11 ...... 182 D1
West Ings Ms KNOT WF11 ...... 182 D1
West Ings Wy KNOT WF11 ...... 182 D1
Westland Cl AIRE BD20 ...... 35 G8 3
Westland Rd BEE/HOL LS11 ...... 131 J5
Westlands RYKW YO26 ...... 32 D5
Westlands Dr WIL/AL BD15 ...... 103 K5
Westlands Gv WIL/AL BD15 ...... 103 L5 7
Westland Sq BEE/HOL LS11 ...... 131 K6
West La AIRE BD20 ...... 34 B3
AIRE BD20 ...... 34 E1
AIRE BD20 ...... 55 L3
BAIL BD17 ...... 82 C4
BSPA/BRAM LS23 ...... 48 E5
CLECK BD19 ...... 150 D5
CUL/QBY BD13 ...... 102 F3
HIPP HX3 ...... 169 H3
HOR/CROF WF4 ...... 200 D5
HWTH BD22 ...... 2 A3
OT LS21 ...... 40 D1
Westlea Av KGHY BD21 ...... 58 B5
West Lea Cl AL/HA/HU LS17 ...... 87 K5
West Lea Crs EARD/LOFT WF3 ... 152 F7
YEA LS19 ...... 62 B8
West Lea Dr AL/HA/HU LS17 ...... 87 K5
EARD/LOFT WF3 ...... 152 F7
West Lea Gdns AL/HA/HU LS17 ... 87 K5
West Lea Garth AL/HA/HU LS17 ... 87 K5
West Lea Gv YEA LS19 ...... 62 B8
West Leeds St HWTH BD22 ...... 2 D1
Westleigh BGLY BD16 ...... 81 J2
Westleigh Cl BAIL BD17 ...... 82 C4
Westleigh Dr BAIL BD17 ...... 82 C4

Westleigh Rd BAIL BD17 ...... 82 C3
Westleigh Wy BAIL BD17 ...... 82 B4
Westley Av HOLM/MEL HD7 ...... 236 B6
Westlock Av OSM LS9 ...... 110 C5 3
West Lodge Crs HUDW HD3 ...... 191 K7
West Lodge Gdns CHAL LS7 ...... 87 L8
West Md CAS WF10 ...... 158 C7
Westminister Cl
ROY/SHW OL2 ...... 229 K6 2
Westminster Av CLAY BD14 ...... 125 J1
ROY/SHW OL2 ...... 228 E8
Westminster Cl BRAM LS13 ...... 107 H2
Westminster Dr BRAM LS13 ...... 107 H2 2
CLAY BD14 ...... 125 J1
PBR HG3 ...... 26 E3
Westminster Cft BRAM LS13 ...... 107 H2 2
Westminster Dr BRAM LS13 ...... 107 H2 2
CLAY BD14 ...... 125 J2
PBR HG3 ...... 26 E3
Westminster Gdns CLAY BD14 ... 125 J2 1
Westminster Ga PBR HG3 ...... 26 E2
Westminster Gv PBR HG3 ...... 26 E2 2
Westminster Pl BFDE BD3 ...... 5 H2
PBR HG3 ...... 26 E2
Westminster Ri PBR HG3 ...... 26 E2
Westminster Ter BFDE BD3 ...... 5 H2
PBR HG3 ...... 26 D2
Westmoor Av BAIL BD17 ...... 82 D2
Westmoor Cl BAIL BD17 ...... 82 D2 1
West Moor Crs DOD/DAR S75 ...... 260 C5
West Moorlands Av
DEWS WF13 ...... 173 K5
Westmoor Pl BRAM LS13 ...... 107 K3
Westmoor Ri BRAM LS13 ...... 107 K3
West Moor Rd
HEM/SK/SE WF9 ...... 223 J4
Westmoor St BRAM LS13 ...... 107 K3
Westmoreland Mt
BRAM LS13 ...... 107 M2 2
Westmoreland St
SKP/WHF BD23 ...... 16 C3
Westmorland Dr WHIT OL12 ...... 184 F3
Westmorland St WKFDE WF1 ...... 12 F7
West Mt TAD LS24 ...... 71 K4
West Mount St BEE/HOL LS11 ... 8 D9 3
Westmount St PONT WF8 ...... 180 E6
Westoff La CUL/QBY S72 ...... 222 E7
Weston Av CUL/QBY BD13 ...... 124 F6
MILN OL16 ...... 228 D2
Weston Crs OT LS21 ...... 41 G5
Weston Dr OT LS21 ...... 40 F4
Weston La OT LS21 ...... 41 G5
Weston Moor Rd OT LS21 ...... 22 E6
Weston Park Vw OT LS21 ...... 40 F4
Weston Rdg OT LS21 ...... 41 G4
Weston St HWTH BD22 ...... 2 A1
MILN OL16 ...... 207 C8 1
MILN OL16 ...... 207 H8 3
Weston Vale Rd
CUL/QBY BD13 ...... 124 E6
Westover Gdns
PDSY/CALV LS28 ...... 106 E7
Westover Gn BRAM LS13 ...... 107 L3 2
Westover Gv BRAM LS13 ...... 107 L3 3
Westover Mt BRAM LS13 ...... 107 L3 2
Westover Rd BRAM LS13 ...... 107 L3
Westover St BRAM LS13 ...... 107 L3
Westover Ter BRAM LS13 ...... 107 L3 3
Westover Vw BRAM LS13 ...... 107 L3 3
West Pde BHP/TINH LS16 ...... 86 C7
HFAX HX1 ...... 10 E7
ILK LS29 ...... 38 E2
RPDN/SBR HX6 ...... 167 M2
RTHW LS26 ...... 155 H1 11
WKFDE WF1 ...... 12 F5
West Parade St WKFDE WF1 ...... 12 F4
West Pk GSLY LS20 ...... 61 L4
West Park Av RHAY LS8 ...... 88 D3
West Park Cl RHAY LS8 ...... 88 D3
West Park Crs RHAY LS8 ...... 88 D3
West Park Dr BHP/TINH LS16 ...... 86 C6
PONT WF8 ...... 203 M4
West Park Dr (East) RHAY LS8 ... 88 C3
West Park Dr (West) RHAY LS8 ... 88 D3
RHAY LS8 ...... 88 C3
West Park Gv BTLY WF17 ...... 173 J1
RHAY LS8 ...... 88 C3
West Park Pl RHAY LS8 ...... 88 D4
West Park Rd BTLY WF17 ...... 173 J1
GIR BD8 ...... 104 B6
West Parks PDSY/CALV LS28 ... 106 F7
West Park St BRIG HD6 ...... 170 D4 2
DEWS WF13 ...... 173 K5
West Park Ter BTLY WF17 ...... 173 J1
GIR BD8 ...... 104 B6 7
West Pasture Ct HORS LS18 ...... 85 H5
West Pinfold BSLYN/ROY S71 ... 243 J3
West Pl HUDE HD5 ...... 15 M6
Westridge Dr HUDS HD4 ...... 213 H4
West Rd DOD/DAR S75 ...... 260 D4
OSM LS9 ...... 132 C3
Westroyd PDSY/CALV LS28 ...... 106 E8
West Royd WIL/AL BD15 ...... 102 K1
Westroyd Av CLECK BD19 ...... 149 M3
West Royd Av ECHL BD2 ...... 105 K2 7
HFAX HX1 ...... 10 E7
MIRF WF14 ...... 194 C1
Westroyd Av PDSY/CALV LS28 ... 106 E8
West Royd Cl SHPY BD18 ...... 82 F6
West Royd Cl HFAX HX1 ...... 10 C9
SHPY BD18 ...... 82 F6
Westroyd Crs PDSY/CALV LS28 ... 106 E8
West Royd Crs SHPY BD18 ...... 83 C6
West Royd Dr MIRF WF14 ...... 172 C6
SHPY BD18 ...... 83 C6
Westroyd Gdns
PDSY/CALV LS28 ...... 106 E8
West Royd Gv MIRF WF14 ...... 172 C8
SHPY BD18 ...... 83 G6 3
West Royd Mt SHPY BD18 ...... 83 C6 3
West Royd Pk MIRF WF14 ...... 172 C8
West Royd Rd SHPY BD18 ...... 83 C6
West Royd Ter SHPY BD18 ...... 83 C6
West Scausby Pk
LUD/ILL HX2 ...... 124 A7 10
West Shaw La HWTH BD22 ...... 100 C3

West Slaithwaite Rd
HOLM/MEL HD7 ...... 211 L7
West St BAIL BD17 ...... 82 E2 11
BFD BD1 ...... 5 G7
BIRK/DRI BD11 ...... 151 G7
BRIG HD6 ...... 148 D7
BRIG HD6 ...... 170 C3
BSLYN/ROY S71 ...... 243 M2
BTLY WF17 ...... 173 M1 1
BTLY WF17 ...... 174 A1
BVRD LS3 ...... 6 A8
CAS WF10 ...... 157 L6
CLECK BD19 ...... 149 M7 1
CLECK BD19 ...... 150 A7
COL BB8 ...... 74 A2
CUD/GR S72 ...... 245 G1
EARL WF12 ...... 173 L7
ECHL BD2 ...... 105 K3 10
GTL/HWC HX4 ...... 190 D2
HECK WF16 ...... 172 E2 7
HEM/SK/SE WF9 ...... 223 L1
HEM/SK/SE WF9 ...... 246 B4
HEM/SK/SE WF9 ...... 247 K2
HFAX HX1 ...... 10 C5
HIPP HX3 ...... 147 K2
HOR/CROF WF4 ...... 222 K5
HUDW HD3 ...... 191 J5
LIT OL15 ...... 207 K1 17
MILN OL16 ...... 206 F7 10
MOR LS27 ...... 152 D3
NORM WF6 ...... 178 C4 8
PDSY/CALV LS28 ...... 107 G6
RPDN/SBR HX6 ...... 167 K3
WKFDW/WTN WF2 ...... 198 D1
Westvale Ms BRAM LS13 ...... 108 A5
West Vw AIRE BD20 ...... 36 A4
BEE/HOL LS11 ...... 8 D9
BOW BD4 ...... 127 J2 14
CUD/GR S72 ...... 262 C6
DEWS WF13 ...... 173 K4
FEA/AMT WF7 ...... 223 M4
GFTH/SHER LS25 ...... 114 D8
GFTH/SHER LS25 ...... 116 A8
GFTH/SHER LS25 ...... 135 K4
GTL/HWC HX4 ...... 190 C2
HIPP HX3 ...... 146 D4
HUD HD1 ...... 213 M1
LIT OL15 ...... 207 L1
NORM WF6 ...... 178 B1 8
OT LS21 ...... 41 K6
OT LS21 ...... 43 H8
RTHW LS26 ...... 155 L1
SKP/WHF BD23 ...... 17 M1
WBY LS22 ...... 29 K2
WKFDW/WTN WF2 ...... 175 K4
YEA LS19 ...... 62 B7
West View Av CAS WF10 ...... 158 C7
HFAX HX1 ...... 146 A7
ILK LS29 ...... 40 A5
West View Av SHPY BD18 ...... 83 G7
West View Cl SHPY BD18 ...... 83 G7 3
Westview Cl AIRE BD20 ...... 34 C7
Westview Cl KGHY BD21 ...... 2 B5
West View Cl YEA LS19 ...... 62 B7 1
West View Crs HFAX HX1 ...... 146 A8
West View Dr LUD/ILL HX2 ...... 145 M7
Westview Gv KGHY BD21 ...... 2 B5
West View Ri HUD HD1 ...... 213 M1
ILK LS29 ...... 40 A5
West View Rd HIPP HX3 ...... 146 D4
ILK LS29 ...... 40 A5
West View Ter LUD/ILL HX2 ... 146 A6 10
West Villa Rd GSLY LS20 ...... 62 A5
Westville Av ILK LS29 ...... 38 C2
Westville Cl ILK LS29 ...... 38 C2
Westville Rd DOD/DAR S75 ...... 260 F3
ILK LS29 ...... 38 C2
Westville Wy CUL/QBY BD13 ...... 102 F8
Westward Cft HUDW HD3 ...... 191 L4
Westward Ho HIPP HX3 ...... 146 C2
MILN OL16 ...... 207 H8
West Wy BSLY S70 ...... 261 G5
SHPY BD18 ...... 81 M7
Westway BTLY WF17 ...... 174 B3
GFTH/SHER LS25 ...... 112 F8
GSLY LS20 ...... 61 K6
HTON BD9 ...... 103 L4
KGHY BD21 ...... 2 B1
MIRF WF14 ...... 172 B7
PDSY/CALV LS28 ...... 106 E3
ROY/SHW OL2 ...... 229 K8 18
Westways WKFDW/WTN WF2 ... 176 B3
Westways Cl RHAY LS8 ...... 88 C7
Westways Ri
WKFDW/WTN WF2 ...... 176 B4
West Wells Crs OSS WF5 ...... 196 E1
West Wells Rd OSS WF5 ...... 196 E1
West Winds ILK LS29 ...... 61 G1
Westwinn Garth SCFT LS14 ...... 89 L6
Westwinn Vw SCFT LS14 ...... 89 L5
Westwood Av ECHL BD2 ...... 105 K1
HOLM/MEL HD7 ...... 236 D8
Westwood Cl FEA/AMT WF7 ...... 179 M7 1
MOR LS27 ...... 130 D8
Westwood Ct BSLY S70 ...... 261 G4 13
West Wood Ct MID LS10 ...... 153 J1
Westwood Crs BGLY BD16 ...... 81 J6
Westwood Dr ILK LS29 ...... 38 B4
Westwood Edge Rd
HOLM/MEL HD7 ...... 212 C3
Westwood Fold
HOLM/MEL HD7 ...... 212 D4
Westwood Gv ECHL BD2 ...... 105 K1 2
Westwood Ri ILK LS29 ...... 38 B4
MOR LS27 ...... 130 C8
West Wood Rd CAS WF10 ...... 179 K1
OSS WF5 ...... 197 H1
Westwood Side MOR LS27 ...... 130 C7
Westwoodside MOR LS27 ...... 130 D7
Westwood St HUDN HD2 ...... 171 J8 5
Wetherby Gv BULY LS4 ...... 108 E4
Wetherby La WBY LS22 ...... 30 E1

Wetherby Pl BULY LS4 ...... 108 F4
Wetherby Rd AL/HA/HU LS17 ...... 67 M2
BSPA/BRAM LS23 ...... 49 G2
BSPA/BRAM LS23 ...... 69 L3
RHAY LS8 ...... 88 D7
RYKW YO26 ...... 32 B5
RYKW YO26 ...... 33 J3
SCFT LS14 ...... 89 H5
TAD LS24 ...... 71 L3
WBY LS22 ...... 46 F1
WBY LS22 ...... 47 M5
Wetherby Ter BULY LS4 ...... 108 E4
Wetherhill St BTLY WF17 ...... 173 K1
Wetlands Rd HOLM/MEL HD7 ... 235 G5
Wetton Ct BFDE BD3 ...... 105 M7 14
Weydale Av HUDW HD3 ...... 191 J6 3
Weyhill Dr WIL/AL BD15 ...... 103 K6
Weymouth Av HUDW HD3 ...... 191 K7
WIL/AL BD15 ...... 103 J6
Whack House Cl YEA LS19 ...... 62 C8 3
Whack House La YEA LS19 ...... 62 C8
Whales La GLE DN14 ...... 183 M1
Whaley Rd DOD/DAR S75 ...... 260 B3
Whalley Av LIT OL15 ...... 185 J8
Whalley La CUL/QBY BD13 ...... 101 M4
Wham La UPML OL3 ...... 230 F5
Whams Rd STKB/PEN S36 ...... 269 G4
Wharfe Bank WBY LS22 ...... 47 G6
Wharfe Cl BHP/TINH LS16 ...... 86 F2 1
Wharfe Ct AIRE BD20 ...... 36 A5 14
Wharfe Crs OT LS21 ...... 42 F7
Wharfedale Av CHAL LS7 ...... 109 K2
Wharfedale Cl SKP/WHF BD23 ... 16 D2 2
Wharfedale Ct OT LS21 ...... 41 K6
SCFT LS14 ...... 111 H1 3
Wharfedale Crs
GFTH/SHER LS25 ...... 135 H1 3
KBTN HD8 ...... 239 K5
Wharfedale Dr ILK LS29 ...... 38 E3
NORM WF6 ...... 178 C2
Wharfedale Gdns BAIL BD17 ... 83 G2 7
Wharfedale Gv HDGY LS6 ...... 6 E1
Wharfedale Ms OT LS21 ...... 41 K6
Wharfedale Mt HIPP HX3 ...... 125 K8
Wharfedale Ri EARD/LOFT WF3 ... 152 F7 7
HTON BD9 ...... 103 L4
Wharfedale Rd BOW BD4 ...... 127 J7
DOD/DAR S75 ...... 260 C3
Wharfedale Vw ILK LS29 ...... 19 G6 7
ILK LS29 ...... 61 J2
Wharfe Gra WBY LS22 ...... 47 M1
Wharfe Gv WBY LS22 ...... 47 M1
Wharfe La WBY LS22 ...... 45 L4
Wharfe Pk ILK LS29 ...... 19 J6
Wharfe Rein WBY LS22 ...... 47 G6
Wharfeside La ILK LS29 ...... 38 E1 1
Wharfe St OT LS21 ...... 41 K6
Wharfe Vw PBR HG3 ...... 27 K7
WBY LS22 ...... 47 M1
Wharfe View Rd ILK LS29 ...... 38 D2
Wharf St BAIL BD17 ...... 82 D6
BFDE BD3 ...... 5 G4
BRIG HD6 ...... 170 D4
BSLYN/ROY S71 ...... 261 J3 1
EARL WF12 ...... 173 M1
LDSU LS2 ...... 9 J1
RPDN/SBR HX6 ...... 167 L2
TOD OL14 ...... 165 J3
Wharncliffe DOD/DAR S75 ...... 260 C8 3
Wharncliffe Crs ECHL BD2 ...... 105 M2
Wharncliffe Dr ECHL BD2 ...... 105 M2
Wharncliffe Gv ECHL BD2 ...... 105 M2
SHPY BD18 ...... 82 D8 7
Wharncliffe Rd HOR/CROF WF4 ... 220 C2
SHPY BD18 ...... 104 D1
Wharncliffe St BSLY S70 ...... 260 F5
BSLYN/ROY S71 ...... 243 M6 3
The Whartons OT LS21 ...... 41 J4
Wharton St LVSG WF15 ...... 172 D2 3
Wheat Cl DEWS WF13 ...... 173 H6
Wheatcroft CAS WF10 ...... 158 D8 3
Wheatcroft Av BTLY WF17 ...... 173 L2
Wheater Rd GTHN BD7 ...... 126 C1 8
Wheat Field Av HUDW HD3 ...... 191 J7
Wheatfield Ct PDSY/CALV LS28 ... 106 F8
Wheat Head Crs HWTH BD22 ...... 79 G1
Wheat Head Dr HWTH BD22 ...... 2 A8
Wheat Head La HWTH BD22 ...... 79 G1
Wheathill St ROCH OL11 ...... 228 C2 12
Wheathouse Rd HUDN HD2 ...... 14 D1
Wheathouse Ter HUDN HD2 ...... 14 D1
The Wheatings OSS WF5 ...... 197 H1
Wheatlands ILK LS29 ...... 38 E1
PDSY/CALV LS28 ...... 106 E3
Wheatlands Av AIRE BD20 ...... 34 E7 2
HTON BD9 ...... 104 A4 3
Wheatlands Crs HTON BD9 ...... 104 A4 3
Wheatlands Dr HTON BD9 ...... 104 A4 3
LVSG WF15 ...... 172 B4 2
Wheatlands Gv HTON BD9 ...... 104 A4
Wheatlands La AIRE BD20 ...... 34 E7
Wheatlands Sq HTON BD9 ...... 104 A4
Wheatley Av ILK LS29 ...... 39 G3
NORM WF6 ...... 178 D5
Wheatley Cl BSLYN/ROY S71 ... 261 H2 1
Wheatley Dr MIRF WF14 ...... 194 C3
Wheatley Gdns ILK LS29 ...... 39 G3
Wheatley Gv ILK LS29 ...... 39 G3
Wheatley Hill La KBTN HD8 ...... 240 A6
Wheatley La HIPP HX3 ...... 10 C1
ILK LS29 ...... 39 G3
Wheatley Ri DOD/DAR S75 ...... 242 D4 3
ILK LS29 ...... 39 G3
Wheatley Rd BSLY S70 ...... 262 A7 2
HIPP HX3 ...... 146 B4
ILK LS29 ...... 38 E3
Wheaton Av MSTN/BAR LS15 ...... 111 J3
Wheatroyd Crs HUDW HD5 ...... 196 F3
Wheatroyd La HUDE HD5 ...... 215 C4
Wheat St HWTH BD22 ...... 79 J2 16
Wheelwright Av
WOR/ARM LS12 ...... 130 C1
Wheelwright Cl WOR/ARM LS12 ... 130 C1
Wheelwright Dr DEWS WF13 ...... 173 K4
MILN OL16 ...... 206 D3
Wheelwright St EARL WF12 ... 173 L6 3
Wheldale La CAS WF10 ...... 159 G4
Wheldon Rd CAS WF10 ...... 158 A6

CAS WF10 .... 158 F3
Whernside Mt GTHN BD7 .... 126 A4
Whernside Wy LUD/ILL HX2 .... 145 J3
Wherwell Rd BRIG HD6 .... 170 D5
Whetley Cl GIR BD8 .... 4 A3
Whetley Gv GIR BD8 .... 104 C5
Whetley Hl GIR BD8 .... 104 C5
Whetley La GIR BD8 .... 104 C5
Whetley Ter GIR BD8 .... 4 B3
Whewell St BTLY WF17 .... 151 G5
Whimbrel Cl GIR BD8 .... 103 L1
Whimbrel Ms MOR LS27 .... 152 E3
Whinbeck Av NORM WF6 .... 178 F5
Whinberry Pl BTLY WF17 .... 151 H3
Whinbrook Crs AL/HA/HU LS17 .... 87 L5
Whinbrook Gdns AL/HA/HU LS17 .... 87 L5
Whinbrook Gv AL/HA/HU LS17 .... 87 L5
Whinby Cft DOD/DAR S75 .... 260 B7
Whinby Rd DOD/DAR S75 .... 259 M6
Whin Cl HEM/SK/SE WF9 .... 245 M1
Whincop Av CAS WF10 .... 157 H7
Whincover Cl WOR/ARM LS12 .... 130 A1
Whincover Cross WOR/ARM LS12 .... 130 B1
Whincover Dr WOR/ARM LS12 .... 130 A1
Whincover Gdns WOR/ARM LS12 .... 130 B1
Whincover Gv WOR/ARM LS12 .... 130 B1
Whincover Mt WOR/ARM LS12 .... 130 B1
Whincover Rd WOR/ARM LS12 .... 130 A1
Whincover Vw WOR/ARM LS12 .... 130 B1
Whinfield Cl AWLS/ASK DN6 .... 249 K4
Whinfield BHP/TINH LS16 .... 86 D2
Whinfield Av HWTH BD22 .... 57 G6
Whinfield Cl HWTH BD22 .... 2 A3
Whinfield Dr HWTH BD22 .... 57 G6
Whingate WOR/ARM LS12 .... 108 C6
Whingate Av WOR/ARM LS12 .... 108 C7
Whingate Cl WOR/ARM LS12 .... 108 C7
Whingate Gn WOR/ARM LS12 .... 108 C7
Whingate Gv WOR/ARM LS12 .... 108 C7
Whingate Rd WOR/ARM LS12 .... 108 C7
Whingrove Av HOLM/MEL HD7 .... 234 E5
Whin Knoll Av KGHY BD21 .... 2 B7
Whin La GFTH/SHER LS25 .... 137 J3
Whinmoor Crs SCFT LS14 .... 89 H5
Whinmoor Ct SCFT LS14 .... 89 H5
Whinmoor Crs SCFT LS14 .... 89 H5
Whinmoor Dr DOD/DAR S75 .... 259 H5
Whinmoor Gdns SCFT LS14 .... 89 H5
Whin Moor La AL/HA/HU LS17 .... 258 G6
Whinmoor La AL/HA/HU LS17 .... 89 G3
Whinmoor Vw DOD/DAR S75 .... 259 H5
Whinmoor Wy DOD/DAR S75 .... 259 H6
Whinmore Gdns CLECK BD19 .... 150 E7
Whin Mt NORM WF6 .... 178 E6
Whinney Cl FEA/AMT WF7 .... 200 F1
Whinney Hill Pk BRIG HD6 .... 170 C1
Whinney La FEA/AMT WF7 .... 200 E1
Whinney Moor Av WKFDW/WTN WF2 .... 197 M3
Whinney Royd La HIPP HX3 .... 147 J1
Whinny Gill Rd SKP/WHF BD23 .... 16 D3
Whins La BSPA/BRAM LS23 .... 49 H5
PBR HG3 .... 28 E6
Whin St HWTH BD22 .... 2 C4
Whirlaw Av TOD OL14 .... 141 J7
Whirlaw La TOD OL14 .... 141 K6
Whiskers La HIPP HX3 .... 147 G3
Whisperwood Cl WKFDE WF1 .... 176 F1
Whisperwood Rd WKFDE WF1 .... 176 F1
Whitacre Cl HUDN HD2 .... 193 G3
Whitacre Rd HUDN HD2 .... 193 G3
Whitaker Av ECHL BD2 .... 105 L3
Whitaker Cl ECHL BD2 .... 105 L3
Whitaker St BTLY WF17 .... 173 M2
PDSY/CALV LS28 .... 106 F4
Whitaker Wk HWTH BD22 .... 100 E4
Whitbourne Cl BSLYN/ROY S71 .... 261 H1
Whitby Av HUDN HD2 .... 192 C4
Whitby Crs EARL WF12 .... 174 B6
Whitby Rd GIR BD8 .... 104 C5
Whitby St ROCH OL11 .... 228 C1
Whitby Ter GIR BD8 .... 104 C5
Whitcliffe Rd CLECK BD19 .... 149 L6
Whitcliffe Sq CLECK BD19 .... 149 M6
White Abbey Rd GIR BD8 .... 4 B3
White Apron St HEM/SK/SE WF9 .... 246 D4
Whitebeam Cl MILN OL16 .... 229 J3
Whitebeam La MID LS10 .... 131 M6
Whitebeam Pk MID LS10 .... 191 M4
Whitebridge Crs OSM LS9 .... 111 C5
Whitebridge Sp SCFT LS14 .... 111 C5
Whitebridge Vw OSM LS9 .... 111 C5
White Castle Ct CUL/QBY BD13 .... 124 D4
Whitechapel Cl RHAY LS8 .... 88 D4
Whitechapel Gv CLECK BD19 .... 149 J5
Whitechapel Rd CLECK BD19 .... 149 J6
Whitechapel Wy RHAY LS8 .... 88 C4
Whitecliffe Crs RTHW LS26 .... 134 C4
Whitecliffe Dr RTHW LS26 .... 134 C4
Whitecliffe Ri RTHW LS26 .... 134 C4
Whitecote Gdns BRAM LS13 .... 107 K2
Whitecote Hl BRAM LS13 .... 107 K2
Whitecote La BRAM LS13 .... 107 K1
GFTH/SHER LS25 .... 137 K2
Whitecote Ri BRAM LS13 .... 107 K2
Whitecroft Av ROY/SHW OL2 .... 229 M7
White Cross HUDN HD2 .... 193 G1
White Cross Av CUD/GR S72 .... 262 D1
White Cross Ct CUD/GR S72 .... 262 E1
White Cross Gdns CUD/GR S72 .... 222 F8
White Cross Mt CUD/GR S72 .... 262 E1
White Cross Rd CUD/GR S72 .... 262 D1
EARL WF12 .... 174 A5
Whitefield La GLE DN14 .... 183 M5
White Field La HBR HX7 .... 143 L6
Whitefield Pl GIR BD8 .... 104 C6
Whitegate AL/HA/HU LS17 .... 46 L8
HIPP HX3 .... 168 F2
White Ga HOLM/MEL HD7 .... 236 B1
Whitegate LIT OL15 .... 207 G2
White Ga LUD/ILL HX2 .... 123 M7

Whitegate Dr HIPP HX3 .... 168 F2
Whitegate Hl PONT WF8 .... 203 G6
Whitegate Rd PONT WF8 .... 203 G7
Whitegate Rd HIPP HX3 .... 168 F1
White Gate Rd HOLM/MEL HD7 .... 253 M5
Whitegate Rd HUDS HD4 .... 214 D2
Whitegates Cl WKFDW/WTN WF2 .... 176 B5
Whitegates Gv KBTN HD8 .... 215 M4
Whitegate Ter HIPP HX3 .... 168 F2
Whitegate Top HIPP HX3 .... 169 G2
White Gv RHAY LS8 .... 88 C6
Whitehall Av LM/WK BD12 .... 148 E5
MIRF WF14 .... 172 C7
WKFDE WF1 .... 176 C5
Whitehall Crs WKFDE WF1 .... 176 C5
Whitehall Cft RTHW LS26 .... 155 H1
Whitehall Gv BIRK/DRI BD11 .... 128 F8
BIRK/DRI BD11 .... 150 D1
Whitehall Quay LDS LS1 .... 8 C1
Whitehall Ri WKFDE WF1 .... 176 C6
Whitehall Rd BIRK/DRI BD11 .... 129 H7
CLECK BD19 .... 149 H5
HOLM/MEL HD7 .... 212 E6
LM/WK BD12 .... 149 M1
WOR/ARM LS12 .... 8 A3
WOR/ARM LS12 .... 130 C2
Whitehall Rd East BIRK/DRI BD11 .... 150 D1
Whitehall Rd West BIRK/DRI BD11 .... 150 C2
CLECK BD19 .... 149 M4
Whitehall St HIPP HX3 .... 147 M6
WHIT OL12 .... 206 B6
WKFDW/WTN WF2 .... 176 B8
Whitehall Wy DEWS WF13 .... 173 M6
White Hart Dr HUDS HD4 .... 214 C3
White Hart Fold HEM/SK/SE WF9 .... 225 K8
RPDN/SBR HX6 .... 188 E3
Whitehaven Cl WBSY BD6 .... 126 B7
Whitehead Gv ECHL BD2 .... 105 L5
Whitehead La HOLM/MEL HD7 .... 213 H8
HUDS HD4 .... 214 B3
Whitehead Pl ECHL BD2 .... 105 L5
Whitehead's Ter HFAX HX1 .... 10 B5
Whitehead St BFDE BD3 .... 5 M1
MILN OL16 .... 207 G7
MILN OL16 .... 229 M2
ROY/SHW OL2 .... 229 H6
White Hl HOLM/MEL HD7 .... 211 L7
White Hill Av BSLY S70 .... 260 C5
Whitehill Crs LUD/ILL HX2 .... 146 A1
Whitehill Dr LUD/ILL HX2 .... 124 A8
Whitehill Gn LUD/ILL HX2 .... 124 B8
White Hill Gv BSLY S70 .... 260 D5
Whitehill Rd HWTH BD22 .... 77 L1
LUD/ILL HX2 .... 146 A1
White Hill Ter BSLY S70 .... 260 C5
White Horse Cl BTLY WF17 .... 151 K4
White Horse Fold CAS WF10 .... 158 A1
White Horse Ms PBR HG3 .... 28 E4
White Horse Mdw MILN OL16 .... 228 E4
White Horse Yd WKFDE WF1 .... 12 E3
Whitehouse Av RTHW LS26 .... 134 E6
Whitehouse Crs RTHW LS26 .... 135 G6
Whitehouse Dr RTHW LS26 .... 134 F6
Whitehouse La RTHW LS26 .... 134 E3
YEA LS19 .... 63 H6
Whitehouse St MID LS10 .... 9 K6
White Laith Av SCFT LS14 .... 89 K6
White Laithe Cl SCFT LS14 .... 89 K6
White Laithe Cft SCFT LS14 .... 89 K6
White Laithe Gdns SCFT LS14 .... 89 L6
White Laithe Garth SCFT LS14 .... 89 K5
White Laithe Gn SCFT LS14 .... 89 L6
White Laithe Rd SCFT LS14 .... 89 K5
White Laithe Wk SCFT LS14 .... 89 L6
White Lands YEA LS19 .... 84 C2
Whitelands Crs BAIL BD17 .... 82 F3
Whitelands Rd BAIL BD17 .... 82 F3
White La HWTH BD22 .... 78 B4
WBSY BD6 .... 126 F5
White Lee Av COL BB8 .... 74 E4
White Lee Cl BTLY WF17 .... 151 G8
White Lee Gdns HBR HX7 .... 144 B5
White Lee Rd BTLY WF17 .... 151 G8
White Lee Side HECK WF16 .... 151 G8
Whitelees Rd LIT OL15 .... 207 J1
Whiteley Av RPDN/SBR HX6 .... 167 H3
White Ley Bank HOLM/MEL HD7 .... 237 J7
Whiteley Cft OT LS21 .... 41 J7
Whiteley Croft Ri OT LS21 .... 41 J7
Whiteley Croft Rd OT LS21 .... 41 J7
White Ley Rd AWLS/ASK DN6 .... 227 J5
Whiteley St FEA/AMT WF7 .... 201 L1
HFAX HX1 .... 10 F7
HUDS HD4 .... 213 K2
Whitelock St CHAL LS7 .... 7 H6
White Moss Cl FEA/AMT WF7 .... 202 B8
Whiteplatts St TOD OL14 .... 163 K1
White Rose Av GFTH/SHER LS25 .... 113 H7
HUDE HD5 .... 193 H7
Whiterose Md GFTH/SHER LS25 .... 113 J7
White Rose Wy GFTH/SHER LS25 .... 113 J7
White Slack Ga TOD OL14 .... 163 H8
White's Rd WKFDE WF1 .... 13 G2
White's Ter GIR BD8 .... 104 D5
White Walls La HOLM/MEL HD7 .... 253 H3
Whiteways HECK BD2 .... 105 G3
Whitewell Green La ELL HX5 .... 169 K7
White Wells Gdns HOLM/MEL HD7 .... 254 F3
White Wells Rd HOLM/MEL HD7 .... 254 F3
Whitewood Cl BSLYN/ROY S71 .... 243 K3
Whitfield Av MID LS10 .... 9 L8
Whitfield Crs MILN OL16 .... 229 K3
Whitfield Dr MILN OL16 .... 229 K3
Whitfield Gdns MID LS10 .... 9 L8
Whitfield Pl MID LS10 .... 9 L8

Whitfield Ri ROY/SHW OL2 .... 229 J5
Whitfield Sq CLECK BD19 .... 149 M6
RHAY LS8 .... 110 B3
Whitfield Wy MID LS10 .... 9 L7
Whitham Cl BSPA/BRAM LS23 .... 48 F6
Whitkirk Cl MSTN/BAR LS15 .... 112 A6
Whitkirk La MSTN/BAR LS15 .... 111 M6
Whitlam St SHPY BD18 .... 82 B6
Whitley Dr LUD/ILL HX2 .... 124 C8
Whitley La HIPP HX3 .... 169 J1
Whitley Pl CAS WF10 .... 157 K2
Whitley Rd EARL WF12 .... 195 G6
KGHY BD21 .... 2 C1
STKB/PEN S36 .... 256 B8
Whitley Spring Crs OSS WF5 .... 175 H8
Whitley Spring Rd OSS WF5 .... 175 H8
Whitley St BFDE BD3 .... 5 J6
BGLY BD16 .... 81 H3
Whitley Wy HOR/CROF WF4 .... 217 G1
Whittaker Dr LIT OL15 .... 207 H4
Whittaker La LIT OL15 .... 207 M2
Whitteron Cl HUDW HD3 .... 191 K5
Whittle Crs CLAY BD14 .... 125 K1
Whittle Dr ROY/SHW OL2 .... 229 M6
Whittle St LIT OL15 .... 207 H1
Whitty La LUD/ILL HX2 .... 145 K8
Whitwell Av ELL HX5 .... 169 K7
Whitwell Dr ELL HX5 .... 169 K7
Whitwell Gv ELL HX5 .... 169 K7
Whitwell St BOW BD4 .... 127 J1
Whitwood Common La CAS WF10 .... 179 H1
Whitwood La CAS WF10 .... 157 G8
CLECK BD19 .... 148 E7
Whitworth Rd DEWS WF13 .... 173 K7
WHIT OL12 .... 206 B4
Whitworth St MILN OL16 .... 206 E4
MILN OL16 .... 207 H8
Wholestone Ga HOLM/MEL HD7 .... 212 D1
Whytecote End LM/WK BD12 .... 148 E2
Wibsey Bank WBSY BD6 .... 126 F5
Wibsey Park Av WBSY BD6 .... 126 B6
Wicken Cl IDLE BD10 .... 83 L8
Wicken La CUL/QBY BD13 .... 102 E7
Wickets Cl WBSY BD6 .... 126 F6
The Wickets BTLY WF17 .... 173 K4
HDGY LS6 .... 87 H7
MSTN/BAR LS15 .... 112 A7
WKFDW/WTN WF2 .... 199 G6
Wickham Av BSPA/BRAM LS23 .... 48 E6
WBSY BD6 .... 126 E6
Wickham Cl BSPA/BRAM LS23 .... 48 F6
Wickham La BEE/HOL LS11 .... 8 D9
CLECK BD19 .... 149 H5
Wicking La RPDN/SBR HX6 .... 166 C6
Wickins La HOLM/MEL HD7 .... 235 M8
Wickleden Ga HOLM/MEL HD7 .... 254 F3
Widdop Rd HBR HX7 .... 120 E7
Wide La HWTH BD22 .... 78 C3
MOR LS27 .... 152 F2
Wigan St BFD BD1 .... 4 D5
Wigeon Ap MOR LS27 .... 152 E2
Wiggan La HUDN HD2 .... 192 F3
Wighill Garth TAD LS24 .... 71 M2
Wighill La BSPA/BRAM LS23 .... 49 L4
TAD LS24 .... 50 D7
TAD LS24 .... 51 G3
Wighill St AIRE BD20 .... 55 M1
Wightman St BFDE BD3 .... 105 J4
Wignall St KGHY BD21 .... 57 K5
Wigton Cha AL/HA/HU LS17 .... 88 C1
Wigton Ga AL/HA/HU LS17 .... 66 B8
Wigton Gn AL/HA/HU LS17 .... 66 B8
Wigton Gv AL/HA/HU LS17 .... 66 B8
Wigton La AL/HA/HU LS17 .... 88 B1
Wigton Park Cl AL/HA/HU LS17 .... 66 C8
Wike La AL/HA/HU LS17 .... 66 D3
Wike Ridge Av AL/HA/HU LS17 .... 66 C8
Wike Ridge Cl AL/HA/HU LS17 .... 66 C8
Wike Ridge Ct AL/HA/HU LS17 .... 66 C8
Wike Ridge Fold AL/HA/HU LS17 .... 66 C8
Wike Ridge Gv AL/HA/HU LS17 .... 88 D1
Wike Ridge La AL/HA/HU LS17 .... 88 D1
Wike Ridge Ms AL/HA/HU LS17 .... 88 D1
Wike Ridge Mt AL/HA/HU LS17 .... 88 D1
Wike Ridge Vw AL/HA/HU LS17 .... 88 C1
Wike Rd BSLYN/ROY S71 .... 262 A4
Wilbrook Ri DOD/DAR S75 .... 260 C2
Wilby St CLECK BD19 .... 261 J6
Wilcock La AIRE BD20 .... 35 H4
Wild Gv PDSY/CALV LS28 .... 106 C7
Wildhouse La LIT OL15 .... 207 H5
Wildspur Gv HOLM/MEL HD7 .... 255 G2
Wild St ROY/SHW OL2 .... 229 L8
Wild's Yd WKFDE WF1 .... 12 F4
Wilford Rd BSLYN/ROY S71 .... 243 G5
Wilfred Av MSTN/BAR LS15 .... 111 K6
Wilfred St CLAY BD14 .... 125 M2
MSTN/BAR LS15 .... 111 K6
Wilfrid Ter WOR/ARM LS12 .... 130 C2
Wilkinson Fold LM/WK BD12 .... 148 E2
Wilkinson St BSLY S70 .... 261 H6
Wilkinson Ter GTHN BD7 .... 104 B8
Wilkinson Wy OT LS21 .... 41 G5
Wilkin St KGHY BD21 .... 2 F4
Willans Av RTHW LS26 .... 133 G2
Willan's Rd DEWS WF13 .... 173 L6
Willerton Cl EARL WF12 .... 174 D3
Willgutter La HWTH BD22 .... 78 B5
William Av MSTN/BAR LS15 .... 111 G6
William Henry St BRIG HD6 .... 170 C3
ROCH OL11 .... 228 C2
SHPY BD18 .... 82 B6
William Hey St OSM LS9 .... 110 D4
William Horsfall St HUDS HD4 .... 213 L3
William Prince Gv WKFDE WF1 .... 13 K7
William Ri MSTN/BAR LS15 .... 111 G6
Williams Dr AIRE BD20 .... 56 D1
Williamson St HFAX HX1 .... 10 C4
Williams Rd AIRE BD20 .... 56 D1
William St BOW BD4 .... 127 M1
BOW BD4 .... 127 M5
BRIG HD6 .... 170 C1
CAS WF10 .... 157 M5
COL BB8 .... 74 A2
CUL/QBY BD13 .... 101 M5

DEWS WF13 .... 173 H3
DEWS WF13 .... 195 G1
EARL WF12 .... 174 A6
HDGY LS6 .... 109 G3
HUD HD1 .... 15 G4
HUDS HD4 .... 213 L2
LIT OL15 .... 207 J1
LVSG WF15 .... 172 C2
MILN OL16 .... 206 F2
MOR LS27 .... 130 E6
PDSY/CALV LS28 .... 106 F5
PDSY/CALV LS28 .... 107 H4
ROCH OL11 .... 206 B8
WBSY BD6 .... 126 B7
William Vw MSTN/BAR LS15 .... 111 G6
Willington Rd AWLS/ASK DN6 .... 249 J5
Willis St OSM LS9 .... 9 M2
Willman Rd BSLYN/ROY S71 .... 262 B3
Willoughby Ter BEE/HOL LS11 .... 8 B6
Willow Ap BULY LS4 .... 109 G5
Willow Av BSPA/BRAM LS23 .... 48 F8
BULY LS4 .... 109 G5
ECHL BD2 .... 83 J8
Willow Bank BSLYN/ROY S71 .... 260 F2
HFAX HX1 .... 10 C9
TOD OL14 .... 141 K8
Willow Bank Dr PONT WF8 .... 141 K8
Willowbank Gv HUDE HD5 .... 193 K5
Willow Beck HOR/CROF WF4 .... 221 J7
Willowbridge La CAS WF10 .... 157 H8
Willowbridge Rd AWLS/ASK DN6 .... 205 J7
Willowbridge Wy CAS WF10 .... 157 H8
Willowbrook AWLS/ASK DN6 .... 249 H4
Willow Brook Rd DOD/DAR S75 .... 242 C6
Willow Cl BULY LS4 .... 109 G5
CLECK BD19 .... 150 D7
CUD/GR S72 .... 244 D7
ILK LS29 .... 40 A5
LUD/ILL HX2 .... 145 M8
WBSY BD6 .... 126 E7
Willow Clough RPDN/SBR HX6 .... 188 F4
Willow Ct BTLY WF17 .... 151 L8
FEA/AMT WF7 .... 179 L5
OT LS21 .... 42 F8
WKFDW/WTN WF2 .... 175 M7
Willow Crs BSPA/BRAM LS23 .... 48 F8
ECHL BD2 .... 83 J8
MSTN/BAR LS15 .... 111 H7
NORM WF6 .... 178 C6
RPDN/SBR HX6 .... 167 L1
Willow Cft CLECK BD19 .... 149 L7
Willow Dene Av LUD/ILL HX2 .... 167 M1
Willowdene La PONT WF8 .... 180 F3
Willow Dene Rd CUD/GR S72 .... 245 J7
Willow Dr HEM/SK/SE WF9 .... 245 L1
LUD/ILL HX2 .... 145 M8
WBSY BD6 .... 126 E7
WKFDE WF1 .... 13 J9
Willow Field Av LUD/ILL HX2 .... 167 M1
Willowfield Cl LUD/ILL HX2 .... 145 M8
Willowfield Crs IDLE BD10 .... 83 J8
LUD/ILL HX2 .... 145 M8
Willowfield Dr LUD/ILL HX2 .... 167 M1
Willowfield St LUD/ILL HX2 .... 167 M1
Willowfield Ter LUD/ILL HX2 .... 168 A1
Willowfield Vw LUD/ILL HX2 .... 145 M8
Willow Gdns CAS WF10 .... 158 F8
ECHL BD2 .... 83 J8
GSLY LS20 .... 62 A5
WKFDW/WTN WF2 .... 175 M7
Willow Garth HEM/SK/SE WF9 .... 247 K4
Willow Garth Av AIRE BD20 .... 34 F6
Willowgarth Cl HOR/CROF WF4 .... 222 C6
Willow Gld BSPA/BRAM LS23 .... 69 M1
Willow Gn WKFDE WF1 .... 176 D3
Willow Gv BSPA/BRAM LS23 .... 48 F8
ECHL BD2 .... 83 J8
GFTH/SHER LS25 .... 135 H3
HOLM/MEL HD7 .... 213 G1
OSS WF5 .... 197 G2
WKFDE WF1 .... 13 J9
Willow Hall Dr RPDN/SBR HX6 .... 167 L1
Willow Hall La RPDN/SBR HX6 .... 167 L1
Willow La BSPA/BRAM LS23 .... 48 F8
FEA/AMT WF7 .... 179 L5
HUD HD1 .... 14 E2
NORM WF6 .... 177 M4
WKFDW/WTN WF2 .... 175 M7
Willow La East FEA/AMT WF7 .... 179 L5
HUD HD1 .... 15 G2
Willow Ms WKFDW/WTN WF2 .... 175 M7
Willow Mt WKFDW/WTN WF2 .... 175 M7
Willow Pk PONT WF8 .... 181 H6
WKFDE WF1 .... 176 D4
Willow Ri KBTN HD8 .... 239 H5
LIT OL15 .... 207 H3
LUD/ILL HX2 .... 145 M8
TAD LS24 .... 71 K4
Willow Rd AWLS/ASK DN6 .... 227 M5
BTLY WF17 .... 174 A2
BULY LS4 .... 109 G5
CAS WF10 .... 157 M8
KNOT WF11 .... 182 C1
PDSY/CALV LS28 .... 106 E4
WKFDW/WTN WF2 .... 175 M7
Willows La MILN OL16 .... 207 G7
The Willows AL/HA/HU LS17 .... 87 L4
BGLY BD16 .... 80 D5
HOR/CROF WF4 .... 197 J5
KBTN HD8 .... 216 C3
LUD/ILL HX2 .... 124 A7
SEL YO8 .... 139 M4
Willow St CLECK BD19 .... 149 M5
GIR BD8 .... 104 C6
HFAX HX1 .... 10 C5
RPDN/SBR HX6 .... 167 L2
Willow Terrace Rd LDSU LS2 .... 6 D1
Willow Tree Cl KGHY BD21 .... 3 K8
Willow Tree Gdns BGLY BD16 .... 81 L1
ILK LS29 .... 62 G2
Willow V WBY LS22 .... 30 A7
Willow Vls IDLE BD10 .... 83 H4
Willow Wk LVSG WF15 .... 172 C3
Willow Well Rd MSTN/BAR LS15 .... 111 H6
Wills Gill GSLY LS20 .... 62 B5
Willwood Av HUDW HD3 .... 191 K7

Wilman Dr OSS WF5 .... 174 E8
Wilman Post OSS WF5 .... 174 E8
SHPY BD18 .... 104 C1
Wilmington Gv CHAL LS7 .... 7 H1
Wilmington St CHAL LS7 .... 7 J4
Wilmington Ter CHAL LS7 .... 7 H4
Wilmot Rd ILK LS29 .... 38 E2
Wilsden Gv DOD/DAR S75 .... 260 D2
Wilsden Hill Rd WIL/AL BD15 .... 102 D1
Wilsden Old Rd BGLY BD16 .... 80 D5
Wilsden Rd BGLY BD16 .... 80 D5
WIL/AL BD15 .... 103 G3
Wilshaw Mill Rd HOLM/MEL HD7 .... 235 J6
Wilshaw Rd HOLM/MEL HD7 .... 235 J6
Wilson Av AIRE BD20 .... 35 K8
MIRF WF14 .... 194 B3
OSS WF5 .... 197 J2
STKB/PEN S36 .... 270 F4
Wilson Cl TOD OL14 .... 141 J7
Wilson Ct WKFDE WF1 .... 176 E2
Wilson Dr WKFDE WF1 .... 176 E2
Wilson Gv BSLYN/ROY S71 .... 262 A1
Wilson Rd BGLY BD16 .... 81 H2
HFAX HX1 .... 10 A9
LM/WK BD12 .... 148 F2
MIRF WF14 .... 194 B3
Wilson St AIRE BD20 .... 56 A1
CAS WF10 .... 157 L5
FEA/AMT WF7 .... 201 L1
GIR BD8 .... 4 B1
PONT WF8 .... 180 F5
WHIT OL12 .... 206 B6
Wilsons Yd PDSY/CALV LS28 .... 106 F5
Wilson Ter MIRF WF14 .... 194 B1
Wilson Wood St BTLY WF17 .... 173 K3
Wilsthorpe Av DOD/DAR S75 .... 260 E2
Wilthorpe Crs DOD/DAR S75 .... 260 E2
Wilthorpe Farm Rd DOD/DAR S75 .... 260 E2
Wilthorpe Gn DOD/DAR S75 .... 260 E2
Wilthorpe La DOD/DAR S75 .... 260 D2
Wilthorpe Rd DOD/DAR S75 .... 260 D2
Wilton Av HUDN HD2 .... 171 G8
Wilton Gv HDGY LS6 .... 87 G8
Wilton Rd ILK LS29 .... 38 C3
Wilton St BRIG HD6 .... 170 B5
EARL WF12 .... 173 M7
Wilton Ter CLECK BD19 .... 149 M7
WHIT OL12 .... 206 A6
Wimborne Dr HWTH BD22 .... 57 G6
WIL/AL BD15 .... 103 G5
Winbrooke Ter WBSY BD6 .... 126 C5
Winburg Rd GTHN BD7 .... 126 C1
Winby St ROCH OL11 .... 228 C1
Winchester Cl WKFDW/WTN WF2 .... 175 M5
Winchester St WOR/ARM LS12 .... 108 F7
Winchester Wy BSLYN/ROY S71 .... 262 C7
Winden Cl HOR/CROF WF4 .... 197 M8
WKFDE WF1 .... 176 L1
Winden Gv WKFDE WF1 .... 176 D1
ILK LS29 .... 40 C8
Windermere Av COL BB8 .... 52 B5
Windermere Cl AWLS/ASK DN6 .... 249 J5
Windermere Dr AL/HA/HU LS17 .... 65 H8
GFTH/SHER LS25 .... 113 H8
KNOT WF11 .... 182 A4
Windermere Rd BSLYN/ROY S71 .... 261 J5
CAS WF10 .... 158 F7
EARL WF12 .... 174 A3
GTHN BD7 .... 126 A3
ROY/SHW OL2 .... 228 F7
STKB/PEN S36 .... 270 F2
WKFDW/WTN WF2 .... 176 A7
Windermere Ter GTHN BD7 .... 126 A3
Winders Dl MOR LS27 .... 130 B8
Windgate AIRE BD20 .... 36 B6
Windham Cl BSLYN/ROY S71 .... 261 H3
Windham St MILN OL16 .... 206 D8
WKFDE WF1 .... 177 G6
Windhill Av DOD/DAR S75 .... 242 C3
Windhill Crs DOD/DAR S75 .... 242 C3
WKFDE WF1 .... 177 G6
Windhill Dr DOD/DAR S75 .... 242 C3
Windhill La DOD/DAR S75 .... 242 C3
Windhill Mt DOD/DAR S75 .... 242 B3
Windhill Old Rd IDLE BD10 .... 83 H4
SHPY BD18 .... 83 H5
Windhill Rd WKFDE WF1 .... 177 G6
Windhill Vw WKFDE WF1 .... 177 G6
Winding Rd HFAX HX1 .... 11 H5
Winding Wy AL/HA/HU LS17 .... 87 K1
Windle Edge STKB/PEN S36 .... 267 J8
Windle La AIRE BD20 .... 34 C5
Windle Royd La LUD/ILL HX2 .... 145 L2
Windmill Ap MID LS10 .... 132 A6
Windmill Av CUD/GR S72 .... 245 H6
Windmill Cha RTHW LS26 .... 155 G2
Windmill Cl MID LS10 .... 132 A7
Windmill Crs SCFT LS14 .... 89 K8
Windmill Crs HIPP HX3 .... 147 J2
KBTN HD8 .... 239 K5
Windmill Dr HIPP HX3 .... 147 H2
Windmill Fld Rd RTHW LS26 .... 155 G2
Windmill Gdns MSTN/BAR LS15 .... 111 M7
Windmill Gn RTHW LS26 .... 155 G2
Windmill Gv CLECK BD19 .... 150 D8
TAD LS24 .... 71 K4
Windmill Hl PDSY/CALV LS28 .... 106 E8
WBSY BD6 .... 126 C5
Windmill Hill La KBTN HD8 .... 217 H6
Windmill La AWLS/ASK DN6 .... 227 K4
BTLY WF17 .... 151 L3
ILK LS29 .... 61 M2
KBTN HD8 .... 255 M3
RTHW LS26 .... 155 G2
WBSY BD6 .... 126 E5
YEA LS19 .... 62 G2
Windmill Ri GFTH/SHER LS25 .... 92 A8
TAD LS24 .... 71 K5
Windmill Rd BSPA/BRAM LS23 .... 70 A3
MID LS10 .... 132 A6
Windmill St MILN OL16 .... 206 D8
Windmill Vw HOLM/MEL HD7 .... 254 E3

Windrose CI NORM WF6 .... 178 C2
Windsor Av AIRE BD20 .... 35 M5
  DOD/DAR S75 .... 241 J8
  FEA/AMT WF7 .... 202 E7
  MSTN/BAR LS15 .... 111 K6
  SKP/WHF BD23 .... 16 C2
  STKB/PEN S36 .... 270 C2
Windsor CI EARL WF12 .... 174 D3
  GFTH/SHER LS25 .... 135 J4
Windsor Ct AL/HA/HU LS17 .... 88 A4
Windsor Crs BSLYN/ROY S71 ... 261 K3
  CUD/GR S72 .... 263 M7
  HWTH BD22 .... 78 D4
  LUD/ILL HX2 .... 146 A5
  RTHW LS26 .... 133 G8
  WKFDE WF1 .... 176 B5
Windsor Dr DOD/DAR S75 ...... 260 B7
  HUDE HD5 .... 193 J8
  KBTN HD8 .... 239 K5
  KNOT WF11 .... 181 K1
  LVSG WF15 .... 172 D4
Windsor Gdns EARL WF12 ...... 174 D3
Windsor Gn GFTH/SHER LS25 ... 113 K7
Windsor Gv CUL/QBY BD13 ..... 102 F8
  HWTH BD22 .... 78 D4
Windsor Mt MSTN/BAR LS15 .... 111 K6
Windsor PI HUDN HD2 .... 193 D1
Windsor Ri PONT WF8 .... 202 D1
Windsor Rd BTLY WF17 .... 151 J5
  EARL WF12 .... 174 D3
  HBR HX7 .... 143 J2
  HEM/SK/SE WF9 .... 224 B8
  HUDS HD4 .... 213 H3
  HWTH BD22 .... 78 D4
  SHPY BD18 .... 82 D7
  TOD OL14 .... 141 J8
  WKFDE WF1 .... 176 A4
Windsor St BOW BD4 .... 5 J9
  COL BB8 .... 74 A1
  HEM/SK/SE WF9 .... 247 J4
  HFAX HX1 .... 11 G8
  ROCH OL11 .... 228 C1
Windsor Vw EARL WF12 .... 174 C4
  HBR HX7 .... 143 J2
Windsor Wk BRIG HD6 .... 148 C8
Windy Bank COL BB8 .... 74 A1
Windy Bank La HIPP HX3 ...... 124 D8
  LVSG WF15 .... 171 K2
Windy Gv WIL/AL BD15 .... 102 F3
Windy Harbour La TOD OL14 ... 141 K4
Windy Rdg CUL/QBY BD13 ...... 102 E7
Windyridge St HOR/CROF WF4 .. 197 H6
Wine St LDS LS1 .... 6 F9
Wine Tavern La RPDN/SBR HX6 . 166 D3
Wine Tavern Rd RPDN/SBR HX6 . 166 D3
Winewall La COL BB8 .... 74 D1
Winfield Dr HUDW HD3 .... 191 H6
Winfield Gv LDSU LS2 .... 6 F4
Winfield PI LDSU LS2 .... 6 F4
Winfield Rd BIRK/DRI BD11 ... 128 A4
Winfield Ter LDSU LS2 .... 6 F4
Wingate Av HWTH BD22 .... 2 B7
Wingate Cft WKFDW/WTN WF2 ... 199 H4
Wingate Gv WKFDW/WTN WF2 .... 199 G6
Wingate Wy HWTH BD22 .... 2 B7
Winget Av HUDS HD4 .... 213 H3
Wingfield Ct BGLY BD16 ...... 81 J2
Wingfield Mt BFDE BD3 .... 5 L3
Wingfield Rd BSLYN/ROY S71 .. 243 J8
Wingfield St BFDE BD3 .... 5 L4
Winney Bank La
  HOLM/MEL HD7 .... 254 D1
Winnipeg PI CHAL LS7 .... 87 M8
Winnow La BSPA/BRAM LS23 .... 48 D7
Winrose Ap MID LS10 .... 132 A7
Winrose Av MID LS10 .... 131 M5
Winrose CI LM/WK BD12 .... 148 E2
Winrose Crs MID LS10 .... 131 M6
Winrose Dr MID LS10 .... 131 M6
Winrose Garth MID LS10 ...... 131 M6
Winrose Gv MID LS10 .... 132 A6
Winrose HI MID LS10 .... 132 A5
Winsford Dr HUDE HD5 .... 193 K7
Winslow Rd IDLE BD10 .... 106 A2
Winston Av AIRE BD20 .... 35 G4
Winston Gdns HDGY LS6 .... 108 E1
Winston Mt HDGY LS6 .... 108 E1
Winston Ter GTHN BD7 .... 126 C1
Winter Av BSLYN/ROY S71 ..... 243 L1
  DOD/DAR S75 .... 260 E4
Winterbourne Av MOR LS27 .... 130 D8
Winterburn La LUD/ILL HX2 ... 145 J8
Winterburn St KGHY BD21 ..... 3 G2
Winterbutlee Gv TOD OL14 .... 163 J5
Winterbutlee Rd TOD OL14 .... 163 J5
Winter Ct WIL/AL BD15 .... 103 J3
Winter Rd DOD/DAR S75 .... 260 E4
Wintersett La HOR/CROF WF4 .. 222 C2
Winter's La HFAX HX1 .... 10 B9
Winter Ter DOD/DAR S75 ...... 260 E4
Winterton Dr LM/WK BD12 ..... 148 E1
Winthorpe Av EARD/LOFT WF3 .. 153 M3
Winthorpe Crs EARD/LOFT WF3 . 153 M4
Winton CI BSLY S70 .... 261 J7
Winton St HUD HD1 .... 214 A3
  LIT 207 K1
Wintoun St CHAL LS7 .... 7 J6
Wistons La ELL HX5 .... 169 J7
Witchfield HI HIPP HX3 ...... 125 M8
Witham CI SKP/WHF BD23 ...... 16 D2
Witham Rd SHPY BD18 .... 82 A6
Witham Wy GFTH/SHER LS25 .... 113 J8
Withens Ct DOD/DAR S75 ...... 242 C5
Withens End La GTL/HWG HX4 .. 189 H7
Withens Hill Cft LUD/ILL HX2 123 M7
Withens La GTL/HWG HX4 ...... 189 H6
  HBR HX7 .... 143 H5
Withens New Rd HBR HX7 ...... 164 D1
  LUD/ILL HX2 .... 123 H4
Withens Rd BTLY WF17 .... 151 G4
  LUD/ILL HX2 .... 123 H6
Within Flds HIPP HX3 .... 169 J3
Withins CI GTHN BD7 .... 126 D3
Withyside KBTN HD8 .... 239 J8
Witley Rd MILN OL16 .... 206 D7
Witmore St HEM/SK/SE WF9 .... 247 J3
Witton St WKFDE WF1 .... 12 F1

Woburn CI MILN OL16 .... 207 G8
Woburn Dr HUDE HD5 .... 193 K8
Woburn PI DOD/DAR S75 .... 260 B8
Woburn Ter BD14 .... 125 K2
Wold CI CUL/QBY BD13 .... 102 F8
Wolfstones Rd HOLM/MEL HD7 .. 235 L8
Wollaton CI BSLYN/ROY S71 ... 243 G6
Wolley Av WOR/ARM LS12 ...... 129 M3
Wolley Ct WOR/ARM LS12 ...... 129 M3
Wolley Dr WOR/ARM LS12 ...... 129 M3
Wolley Gdns WOR/ARM LS12 .... 129 M3
Wolseley Rd BULY LS4 .... 108 F4
Wolseley St CLAY BD14 .... 125 L1
  MILN OL16 .... 229 K2
Wolsey Av GFTH/SHER LS25 .... 116 B6
Wolsey CI GFTH/SHER LS25 .... 116 B6
Wolsey Cft GFTH/SHER LS25 ... 116 B6
Wolsey Gdns GFTH/SHER LS25 .. 116 B6
Wolston CI BOW BD4 .... 128 A4
Wombwell La BSLY S70 .... 262 B7
Womersley PI PDSY/CALV LS28 . 106 F8
Womersley Rd KNOT WF11 ...... 182 C3
Womersley St HFAX HX1 .... 10 B5
Wonder St WKFDE WF1 .... 13 G4
Woodacre Crs AL/HA/HU LS17 .. 67 L3
Woodacre Gn AL/HA/HU LS17 ... 67 L2
Woodacre La AL/HA/HU LS17 ... 67 L2
Wood Acres DOD/DAR S75 ...... 260 C2
Woodale Av HTON BD9 .... 103 M3
Wood Av HECK WF16 .... 172 F1
Wood Bank Rd LIT OL15 .... 207 J3
Woodbine Av PONT WF8 .... 180 E6
Woodbine Rd HUDN HD2 .... 15 G1
Woodbine St BFDE BD3 .... 5 J5
  HFAX HX1 .... 10 C9
  MILN OL16 .... 228 C1
  OSS WF5 .... 174 F7
Woodbine St East MILN OL16 .. 228 D1
Woodbine Ter BRAM LS13 ...... 107 L3
  IDLE BD10 .... 83 K7
  TOD OL14 .... 140 D5
Wood Bottom La BRIG HD6 ..... 170 A1
Wood Bottom Rd HUDS HD4 ..... 235 K1
Woodbourne Av AL/HA/HU LS17 . 87 L5
Woodbridge CI HDGY LS6 ...... 108 C1
  WKFDE WF1 .... 13 K3
Woodbridge Crs HDGY LS6 ..... 86 C8
Woodbridge Gdns HDGY LS6 .... 86 C8
Woodbridge Garth HDGY LS6 ... 108 C1
Woodbridge PI HDGY LS6 ...... 86 C8
Woodbridge Rd HDGY LS6 ...... 108 C1
Woodbrook Av LUD/ILL HX2 .... 145 L1
Woodbrook CI LUD/ILL HX2 .... 145 L1
Woodbrook PI LUD/ILL HX2 .... 145 L1
Woodbrook Rd LUD/ILL HX2 .... 145 L1
Woodburn Av EARL WF12 .... 196 B1
Woodbury Rd GIR BD8 .... 104 D4
Woodchurch Vw
  HOLM/MEL HD7 .... 236 D6
Wood CI AIRE BD20 .... 34 E1
  BAIL BD17 .... 82 D4
  BHP/TINH LS16 .... 86 F3
  CHAL LS7 .... 87 L7
  HEM/SK/SE WF9 .... 223 J4
  NORM WF6 .... 178 A3
  RTHW LS26 .... 132 F8
  SKP/WHF BD23 .... 16 A1
Woodcock CI PBR HG3 .... 26 E2
Woodcock St WKFDE WF1 .... 13 H8
Woodcock Wy AWLS/ASK DN6 .... 249 K7
Woodcot Av BAIL BD17 .... 82 F4
Wood Crs RTHW LS26 .... 132 F8
Wood Cft HDGY LS6 .... 170 B5
  RPDN/SBR HX6 .... 167 G3
Woodcroft WKFDW/WTN WF2 ..... 199 G5
Woodcross MOR LS27 .... 130 C7
Woodcross End MOR LS27 ...... 130 C7
Woodcross Fold MOR LS27 ..... 130 C8
Woodcross Gdns MOR LS27 ..... 130 C8
Woodcross Garth MOR LS27 .... 130 C7
Wood Dr RTHW LS26 .... 132 E8
Woodedge Av HUDE HD5 .... 193 J8
Woodend CAS WF10 .... 135 H8
Wood End HUDS HD4 .... 214 B3
Wood End Av STKB/PEN S36 .... 270 E5
Wood End CI HIPP HX3 .... 168 D3
Woodend Crs CAS WF10 .... 157 H1
Wood End Crs SHPY BD18 ...... 82 F6
Wood End La KBTN HD8 .... 237 L7
Woodend La WHIT OL12 .... 184 F8
Wood End Rd HUDS HD4 .... 214 A6
Wood Farm La HOLM/MEL HD7 ... 236 E4
Woodfield Av BTLY WF17 ...... 173 J2
  GTL/HWG HX4 .... 168 D7
  WHIT OL12 .... 206 A4
Woodfield CI WMB/DAR S73 .... 263 J8
Woodfield Ct HUDN HD2 .... 14 C3
Woodfield Dr AIRE BD20 ...... 34 E1
  GTL/HWG HX4 .... 168 D8
Woodfield Pk
  WKFDW/WTN WF2 .... 199 J8
Woodfield Rd AWLS/ASK DN6 ... 227 L6
  CUL/QBY BD13 .... 80 A7
  PONT WF8 .... 226 D6
Woodford Av HIPP HX3 .... 168 F2
  ROY/SHW OL2 .... 229 M7
Woodford Ct WIL/AL BD15 ..... 103 J6
Woodford Dr HUDE HD5 .... 193 J7
Woodgarth Ct AWLS/ASK DN6 ... 227 L6
Woodgarth Gdns BOW BD4 ...... 128 B3
Wood Gn AL/HA/HU LS17 .... 43 M2
Wood Gv OSS WF5 .... 174 F6
  WOR/ARM LS12 .... 107 M7
Woodhall Av BFDE BD3 .... 106 A6
Woodhall CI HOR/CROF WF4 .... 196 C8
  PDSY/CALV LS28 .... 106 C4
  WMB/DAR S73 .... 263 J8
Woodhall Ct MSTN/BAR LS15 ... 111 M8
Woodhall Cft PDSY/CALV LS28 . 106 C4
  PDSY/CALV LS28 .... 106 C1
Woodhall Dr BTLY WF17 .... 173 J2
  FEA/AMT WF7 .... 202 B8
  KSTL LS5 .... 86 A8

Woodhall Gv RTHW LS26 .... 156 F3
Woodhall La AWLS/ASK DN6 .... 205 J2
  PDSY/CALV LS28 .... 106 C2
Woodhall Park Av
  PDSY/CALV LS28 .... 106 C4
Woodhall Park Crs West
  PDSY/CALV LS28 .... 106 C5
Woodhall Park Cft
  PDSY/CALV LS28 .... 106 D5
Woodhall Park Dr
  PDSY/CALV LS28 .... 106 C5
Woodhall Park Gv
  PDSY/CALV LS28 .... 106 C5
Woodhall Park Mt
  PDSY/CALV LS28 .... 106 C4
Woodhall PI BFDE BD3 .... 106 A5
Woodhall Rd BFDE BD3 .... 106 A6
  PDSY/CALV LS28 .... 106 A3
Woodhall Ter BFDE BD3 .... 106 A6
Woodhall Vw BFDE BD3 .... 106 B5
Woodhead CI HOLM/MEL HD7 .... 192 E3
Woodhead La BRIG HD6 .... 171 G4
  MOR LS27 .... 130 C4
Woodhead Rd BTLY WF17 .... 151 K3
  GTHN BD7 .... 104 D8
  HOLM/MEL HD7 .... 236 D6
  HOLM/MEL HD7 .... 253 G8
  HOLM/MEL HD7 .... 265 M1
Woodhead St CLECK BD19 ...... 150 A8
  LUD/ILL HX2 .... 146 A6
Wood Hey Gv WOR/ARM LS12 .... 206 B2
Wood Hey La HBR HX7 .... 143 K5
Woodheys Rd LIT OL15 .... 207 J4
Wood HI RTHW LS26 .... 132 F8
Wood Hill CI BHP/TINH LS16 .. 85 M2
Wood Hill Crs BHP/TINH LS16 . 85 L3
Wood Hill Gdns BHP/TINH LS16 85 M2
Wood Hill Ri BHP/TINH LS16 .. 85 M2
Woodhill Ri IDLE BD10 .... 84 A6
Wood Hill Rd BHP/TINH LS16 .. 85 M2
Woodhill Vw WBY LS22 .... 30 A8
Woodhouse Av HUDN HD2 .... 192 E4
  KGHY BD21 .... 3 H9
Woodhouse Cliff HDGY LS6 .... 6 D1
Woodhouse CI EARD/LOFT WF3 .. 153 K8
  KGHY BD21 .... 3 H9
Woodhouse Crs NORM WF6 ...... 178 D6
Woodhouse Dr KGHY BD21 ...... 79 L2
Woodhouse Gdns BRIG HD6 ..... 170 E6
Woodhouse Gv HUDN HD2 .... 192 D4
  KGHY BD21 .... 3 G9
  TOD OL14 .... 163 M1
Woodhouse Hall Rd
  HUDN HD2 .... 192 E4
Woodhouse HI HUDN HD2 .... 192 E4
Woodhouse Hill Av HUDN HD2 .. 192 E4
Woodhouse Hill Gv MID LS10 .. 132 A4
Woodhouse Hill PI MID LS10 .. 132 A4
Woodhouse Hill Rd MID LS10 .. 132 A4
Woodhouse Hill Ter MID LS10 . 132 A4
Woodhouse La BRIG HD6 .... 170 A6
  DOD/DAR S75 .... 242 D1
  HDGY LS6 .... 6 C2
  HIPP HX3 .... 168 C3
  HOLM/MEL HD7 .... 253 M5
  LDSU LS2 .... 6 D4
  WKFDW/WTN WF2 .... 175 J3
Woodhouse Mt NORM WF6 .... 178 C6
Woodhouse Rd ROY/SHW OL2 .... 229 L5
  TOD OL14 .... 164 A1
  WKFDE WF1 .... 13 J2
Woodhouse Sq BVRD LS3 .... 6 D8
Woodhouse St HDGY LS6 .... 6 E2
Woodhouse Ter WBSY BD6 ...... 126 F6
Woodhouse Wk KGHY BD21 ...... 3 H9
Woodhouse Wy KGHY BD21 ...... 3 H9
Woodkirk Gdns EARL WF12 ..... 174 D1
Woodkirk Gv EARD/LOFT WF3 ... 152 E6
  LM/WK BD12 .... 148 E6
Woodland Av RTHW LS26 .... 134 B5
  WKFDE WF1 .... 177 L7
Woodland CI HOR/CROF WF4 .... 220 B4
  HTON BD9 .... 103 L2
  MSTN/BAR LS15 .... 111 L6
Woodland Crs BGLY BD16 ...... 80 F1
  RTHW LS26 .... 103 K2
  RTHW LS26 .... 134 C5
Woodland Cft HORS LS18 ...... 85 L4
Woodland Dr BGLY BD16 .... 80 F1
  BSLY S70 .... 260 D6
  CHAL LS7 .... 87 M7
  KBTN HD8 .... 239 K5
  LUD/ILL HX2 .... 167 M1
  RTHW LS26 .... 134 B5
  WKFDW/WTN WF2 .... 198 F8
Woodland Gv CHAL LS7 .... 110 A2
  DEWS WF13 .... 173 H6
  FEA/AMT WF7 .... 202 C5
  HTON BD9 .... 103 L1
  RTHW LS26 .... 134 B5
Woodland HI MSTN/BAR LS15 ... 111 K6
Woodland La CHAL LS7 .... 87 M7
Woodland Meadow KBTN HD8 .... 216 B7
Woodland Mt CHAL LS7 .... 110 A2
Woodland Pk ROY/SHW OL2 ..... 228 D3
  RTHW LS26 .... 155 L1
Woodland Park Rd HDGY LS6 ... 109 G3
Woodland Ri MSTN/BAR LS15 ... 111 L6
  WKFDW/WTN WF2 .... 197 M1
Woodland Rd HUDN HD2 .... 193 H4
  MSTN/BAR LS15 .... 111 K6
  WKFDW/WTN WF2 .... 175 M8
Woodlands EARD/LOFT WF3 ..... 153 L7
  HOR/CROF WF4 .... 197 L4
  ILK LS29 .... 38 F2
  OSS WF5 .... 174 F7
  RPDN/SBR HX6 .... 167 H4
Woodlands CAS WF10 .... 158 E6
  CLECK BD19 .... 150 C5
  HIPP HX3 .... 11 G1
  HOLM/MEL HD7 .... 236 E6
  PDSY/CALV LS28 .... 106 E5
  TAD LS24 .... 71 J4
  TOD OL14 .... 141 K8

Woodlands CI EARD/LOFT WF3 .. 153 L7
  GFTH/SHER LS25 .... 138 A2
  HUDN HD2 .... 171 J8
  IDLE BD10 .... 84 B5
  ILK LS29 .... 38 B2
  KBTN HD8 .... 239 J8
  SCFT LS14 .... 67 L6
Woodlands Ct BHP/TINH LS16 .. 86 D5
  HEM/SK/SE WF9 .... 224 A6
Woodlands Cft GFTH/SHER LS25 135 K6
Woodlands Dr CLECK BD19 ..... 150 C5
  EARD/LOFT WF3 .... 153 K7
  GFTH/SHER LS25 .... 113 K8
  IDLE BD10 .... 84 B5
  MOR LS27 .... 130 B8
  SKP/WHF BD23 .... 16 A1
  YEA LS19 .... 84 D4
Woodlands Fold
  BIRK/DRI BD11 .... 150 D1
Woodlands Gv BAIL BD17 ...... 82 B4
  BGLY BD16 .... 81 K7
  CUL/QBY BD13 .... 125 J5
  GFTH/SHER LS25 .... 135 L6
  HIPP HX3 .... 11 G1
  ILK LS29 .... 38 B2
  PDSY/CALV LS28 .... 106 E5
Woodlands La DEWS WF13 ...... 173 H6
Woodlands Mt HIPP HX3 .... 146 E4
Woodlands Park Rd
  PDSY/CALV LS28 .... 128 F1
Woodland Sq BRIG HD6 .... 170 E5
  WOR/ARM LS12 .... 108 B6
Woodlands Ri AWLS/ASK DN6 ... 227 L5
  HWTH BD22 .... 78 E8
  ILK LS29 .... 38 A2
Woodlands Rd BGLY BD16 ...... 81 L2
  BTLY WF17 .... 151 J6
  CLECK BD19 .... 150 C5
  CUL/QBY BD13 .... 125 J5
  ELL HX5 .... 169 H6
  GIR BD8 .... 104 C5
  KBTN HD8 .... 216 A3
  KGHY BD21 .... 3 G9
Woodlands Rd East KBTN HD8 .. 215 M3
Woodlands St GIR BD8 .... 4 B4
Woodlands Ter
  PDSY/CALV LS28 .... 106 E5
Woodlands Vw
  GFTH/SHER LS25 .... 135 L6
  MILN OL16 .... 206 E6
  TAD LS24 .... 71 K4
Woodland Ter CHAL LS7 .... 87 J7
Woodland Vw CUD/GR S72 ...... 262 D1
  PDSY/CALV LS28 .... 84 C8
  PONT WF8 .... 181 G8
Wood La AL/HA/HU LS17 .... 67 M3
  BRAM LS13 .... 107 L2
  BSLYN/ROY S71 .... 243 L5
  BSPA/BRAM LS23 .... 49 G3
  BTLY WF17 .... 173 K3
  CAS WF10 .... 179 H2
  CHAL LS7 .... 87 L7
  CUD/GR S72 .... 245 J3
  DEWS WF13 .... 173 L4
  DOD/DAR S75 .... 243 G4
  EARL WF12 .... 195 L6
  ECHL BD2 .... 105 H1
  HBR HX7 .... 122 D8
  HDGY LS6 .... 109 G1
  HIPP HX3 .... 147 K5
  HIPP HX3 .... 169 M4
  HOLM/MEL HD7 .... 234 B1
  HOLM/MEL HD7 .... 236 C8
  HOR/CROF WF4 .... 220 C3
  HORS LS18 .... 85 L6
  HUDE HD5 .... 193 M2
  HUDS HD4 .... 214 E5
  HUDS HD4 .... 237 K2
  KNOT WF11 .... 161 K3
  LUD/ILL HX2 .... 145 M5
  MSTN/BAR LS15 .... 90 A8
  PDSY/CALV LS28 .... 84 D7
  RPDN/SBR HX6 .... 167 C2
  RTHW LS26 .... 135 C8
  RTHW LS26 .... 132 B4
  WKFDW/WTN WF2 .... 198 F8

Woodliffe Dr CHAL LS7 .... 87 L7
Woodman Av ELL HX5 .... 191 H1
  HUDN HD2 .... 193 H4
Woodman Ct WBSY BD6 .... 126 A8
Woodman St MSTN/BAR LS15 .... 111 J6
Woodmoor CI HOR/CROF WF4 .... 220 A2
Woodmoor Dr HOR/CROF WF4 .... 219 M2
Woodmoor Ri HOR/CROF WF4 .... 219 M1
Wood Moor Rd
  HEM/SK/SE WF9 .... 224 B7
Woodmoor Rd
  WKFDW/WTN WF2 .... 220 C1
Woodmoor St BSLYN/ROY S71 ... 243 M6
Wood Mt HOR/CROF WF4 .... 196 B8
  RTHW LS26 .... 132 E8
Woodnook CI BHP/TINH LS16 ... 85 M4
Woodnook Dr BHP/TINH LS16 ... 85 M4
Woodnook Garth
  BHP/TINH LS16 .... 85 M4
Wood Nook La HOLM/MEL HD7 ... 235 K4
  RPDN/SBR HX6 .... 167 L1
Woodnook Rd BHP/TINH LS16 ... 85 M3
Wood Nook Ter
  PDSY/CALV LS28 .... 106 E5
Wood PI BEE/HOL LS11 .... 8 D9
  GIR BD8 .... 4 B3
Wood Rd HTON BD9 .... 104 E2
  WBOW BD5 .... 127 G2
Wood Rw RTHW LS26 .... 156 D3
Woodrow Crs RTHW LS26 .... 156 C3
Woodrow Dr LM/WK BD12 .... 149 G1
Woodroyd HOLM/MEL HD7 .... 212 E1
Woodroyd Av BSLYN/ROY S71 ... 243 L5
  HOLM/MEL HD7 .... 236 D1
  WBOW BD5 .... 127 H4
Woodroyd CI BSLYN/ROY S71 ... 243 L5
Woodroyd Dr HIPP HX3 .... 146 A4
Woodroyd Gdns ILK LS29 ...... 39 H3
  RPDN/SBR HX6 .... 167 H1
Wood Royd Hill La
  HOLM/MEL HD7 .... 255 K7
Woodroyd Rd WBOW BD5 .... 127 G3
Woodroyd Ter WBOW BD5 .... 127 H3
Woodside CAS WF10 .... 158 E6
  KBTN HD8 .... 239 J8
  KGHY BD21 .... 57 J5
  MILN OL16 .... 229 L1
  ROY/SHW OL2 .... 229 M6
  SHPY BD18 .... 82 F6
  WKFDW/WTN WF2 .... 176 A4
Woodside Av BGLY BD16 .... 81 H7
  BULY LS4 .... 108 E4
  CHAL LS7 .... 87 H7
  HOR/CROF WF4 .... 200 E3
  SHPY BD18 .... 82 A6
  WKFDW/WTN WF2 .... 176 A4
Woodside CI MOR LS27 .... 130 C8
Woodside Ct CUL/QBY BD13 .... 101 M1
  HORS LS18 .... 86 A6
Woodside Crs BGLY BD16 ...... 81 H7
  BTLY WF17 .... 173 J2
  HIPP HX3 .... 10 F2
  HOR/CROF WF4 .... 200 D2
Woodside Dr BGLY BD16 .... 81 H7
  MOR LS27 .... 130 C7
  WKFDW/WTN WF2 .... 176 A4
Woodside Gdns MOR LS27 ...... 130 C7
Woodside Gv CAS WF10 .... 135 H8
  GTL/HWG HX4 .... 168 F3
  HIPP HX3 .... 11 G3
Woodside Hill CI HORS LS18 .. 86 A6
Woodside La AIRE BD20 .... 34 B2
  HUDN HD2 .... 192 D2
  MOR LS27 .... 130 C7
Woodside Ldg HUDS HD4 .... 215 K8
Woodside Ms HUDS HD4 .... 87 H7
Woodside Mt HFAX HX1 .... 10 F3
Woodside Park Av HORS LS18 .. 85 M6
Woodside Park Dr HORS LS18 .. 85 M6
Woodside PI BULY LS4 .... 108 E4
  HIPP HX3 .... 10 F2
Woodside Rd AIRE BD20 .... 35 L5
  BSPA/BRAM LS23 .... 48 D7
  HFAX HX1 .... 10 F2
  HUDS HD4 .... 213 M5
  LM/WK BD12 .... 148 E2
Woodside St CAS WF10 .... 135 H8
Woodside Ter BULY LS4 .... 108 E4
  HIPP HX3 .... 10 F2
Woodside Veiw HUDS HD4 ...... 213 H3
Woodside Vw BGLY BD16 .... 81 H7
  BULY LS4 .... 108 E4
  HIPP HX3 .... 10 F2
  HOLM/MEL HD7 .... 253 M2
Woodsley Gn HDGY LS6 .... 6 A5
Woodsley Rd BVRD LS3 .... 109 G5
  HDGY LS6 .... 6 A5
  IDLE BD10 .... 83 J8
  LDSU LS2 .... 6 C5
Woodsome Av MIRF WF14 .... 172 A6
Woodsome Dr KBTN HD8 .... 215 M4
  MIRF WF14 .... 172 B8
Woodsome Hall La KBTN HD8 ... 215 L5
Woodsome Lees La KBTN HD8 ... 215 M7
Woodsome Pk KBTN HD8 .... 215 M4
Woodsome Rd HUDS HD4 .... 215 H7
Wood Sq HIPP HX3 .... 146 D4
Woodstock Crs HUDW HD3 ...... 191 K6
Woodstock Rd DOD/DAR S75 .... 260 F2
Wood St AIRE BD20 .... 56 E1
  BAIL BD17 .... 82 E5
  BGLY BD16 .... 59 G8
  BRIG HD6 .... 170 D4
  BSLY S70 .... 261 H6
  BTLY WF17 .... 173 L1
  CAS WF10 .... 157 L6
  CLECK BD19 .... 149 L7
  COL BB8 .... 74 A2
  CUD/GR S72 .... 223 G8
  DEWS WF13 .... 173 M5
  EARD/LOFT WF3 .... 153 M6
  ELL HX5 .... 169 J4
  HOLM/MEL HD7 .... 212 B5
  HOR/CROF WF4 .... 200 D2
  HUD HD1 .... 14 F6
  HUDE HD5 .... 15 L7
  HUDW HD3 .... 191 H8

KBTN HD8 .... 239 H4
KBTN HD8 .... 239 M5
KGHY BD21 .... 3 H7
LIT OL15 .... 207 J1
MILN OL16 .... 229 L1
MOR LS27 .... 152 B1
OSS WF5 .... 174 F7
ROCH OL11 .... 206 C8
ROY/SHW OL2 .... 229 G7
WIL/AL BD15 .... 103 L5
WKFDE WF1 .... 12 E2
Wood St North HX3 .... 146 D4
Wood Syke DOD/DAR S75 ...... 260 C7
Wood Ter HUDS HD4 .... 214 C3
Woodthorne Cft
  AL/HA/HU LS17 .... 88 C2
Woodthorpe Cl
  WKFDW/WTN WF2 .... 199 G7
Woodthorpe Dr
  WKFDW/WTN WF2 .... 199 G7
Woodthorpe Glades
  WKFDW/WTN WF2 .... 198 F7
Woodthorpe La
  WKFDW/WTN WF2 .... 198 F7
Woodthorpe Park Dr
  WKFDW/WTN WF2 .... 198 F7
Woodthorpe Ter HUD HD1 ...... 14 C8
Wood Top BRIG HD6 .... 170 A1
Wood Top Rd HBR HX7 .... 143 K4
Woodvale Cl BOW BD4 .... 128 A1
Woodvale Crs BGLY BD16 .... 81 J1
Woodvale Gv GTHN BD7 .... 126 A1
Woodvale Rd BRIG HD6 .... 170 D2
Woodview BIRK/DRI BD11 ...... 128 F7
Wood Vw HUDN HD2 .... 191 M4
  MOR LS27 .... 130 E6
Woodview Av BAIL BD17 .... 83 H2
Wood View Av CAS WF10 ...... 157 J7
Wood View Cl CAS WF10 .... 157 J7
Woodview Cl HORS LS18 .... 85 L4
Wood View Crs CAS WF10 ...... 157 J6
Wood View Dr ECHL BD2 .... 105 M4
Woodview Gv BEE/HOL LS11 .. 131 K4
Wood View Gv BRIG HD6 .... 170 B2
Woodview La DOD/DAR S75 .. 260 D3
Woodview Mt BEE/HOL LS11 .. 131 K4
Woodview Rd BEE/HOL LS11 .. 131 K4
  HWTH BD22 .... 79 H2
Woodview St BEE/HOL LS11 .. 131 K4
Woodview Ter BEE/HOL LS11 .. 131 K4
Woodville Av HOLM/MEL HD7 .. 213 G2
  HORS LS18 .... 85 M6
Woodville Ct RHAY LS8 .... 88 C5
  WKFDW/WTN LS22 .... 198 E4
Woodville Crs HORS LS18 .... 86 A6
Woodville Gv HORS LS18 .... 85 M6
  HWTH BD22 .... 79 H6
  MID LS10 .... 132 A5
Woodville Pl HORS LS18 .... 86 A6
  HTON BD9 .... 104 B2
  HUDN HD2 .... 171 G8
Woodville Rd EARL WF12 ...... 173 M6
  KGHY BD21 .... 2 E3
Woodville Sq MID LS10 .... 132 A5
Woodville St HIPP HX3 .... 10 D1
  HORS LS18 .... 86 A6
  SHPY BD18 .... 82 F6
Woodville Ter HORS LS18 ...... 85 M6
  WBOW BD5 .... 4 D9
Wood Vine Rd
  PDSY/CALV LS28 .... 106 E5
Wood Wk BSLYN/ROY S71 .... 243 H1
Woodward Ct MIRF WF14 ...... 172 D7
Woodway BGLY BD16 .... 81 H7
  HORS LS18 .... 85 L7
Woodway Dr HORS LS18 .... 85 L7
Woodworth Gv KGHY BD21 .... 79 K3
Woolcroft Dr HOLM/MEL HD7 .. 236 E8
Wooldale Cliff Rd
  HOLM/MEL HD7 .... 236 D8
Wooldale Rd HOLM/MEL HD7 .. 236 E7
Wooler Av BEE/HOL LS11 ...... 131 J4
Wooler Dr BEE/HOL LS11 ...... 131 J4
Wooler Gv BEE/HOL LS11 ...... 131 J4

Wooler Pl BEE/HOL LS11 ...... 131 H4
Wooler Rd BEE/HOL LS11 ...... 131 H4
Wooler St BEE/HOL LS11 ...... 131 H4
Woolford Wy EARD/LOFT WF3 .. 154 F8
Woolgreaves Av
  WKFDW/WTN WF2 .... 198 F8
Woolgreaves Cl
  WKFDW/WTN WF2 .... 198 F7
Woolgreaves Cft
  WKFDW/WTN WF2 .... 198 F8
Woolgreaves Dr
  WKFDW/WTN WF2 .... 198 F8
Woolgreaves Garth
  WKFDW/WTN WF2 .... 198 F8
Woolley Colliery Rd
  DOD/DAR S75 .... 242 A3
Woolley Edge La
  DOD/DAR S75 .... 242 A1
Woolley Low Moor La
  HOR/CROF WF4 .... 219 M4
Woolley Park Gdns
  HOR/CROF WF4 .... 220 C2
Woollin Av EARD/LOFT WF3 .. 175 G1
Woollin Crs EARD/LOFT WF3 .. 153 G8
Woolmarket PONT WF8 .... 180 F6
Woolpack's Yd WKFDE WF1 .... 12 D2
Woolrow La BRIG HD6 .... 148 E8
Wool Row La KBTN HD8 .... 238 E1
Woolshops Sq HFAX HX1 .... 11 H6
Woolstocks La DOD/DAR S75 .. 259 G3
Wool St HECK WF16 .... 172 F3
Wootton St WBOW BD5 .... 127 G2
Worcester Av AL/HA/HU LS17 .. 88 C2
Worcester Cl EARD/LOFT WF3 .. 153 L5
Worcester Dr
  EARD/LOFT WF3 .... 154 B2
Worcester Pl BOW BD4 .... 127 J2
Worcester St ROCH OL11 ...... 228 A2
Wordsworth Av
  AWLS/ASK DN6 .... 227 L5
  STKB/PEN S36 .... 270 E4
Wordsworth Ct RTHW LS26 .. 155 L3
Wordsworth Crs LIT OL15 ...... 207 H4
Wordsworth Dr KNOT WF11 .. 181 K1
  RTHW LS26 .... 155 L3
Wordsworth Gv
  EARD/LOFT WF3 .... 177 G1
Wordsworth Rd
  BSLYN/ROY S71 .... 261 K2
Work Bank La STKB/PEN S36 .. 270 D2
Workhouse La GTL/HWG HX4 .. 168 F8
  LUD/ILL HX2 .... 145 J7
Wormald Rw LDS LS1 .... 7 G8
Wormald St DEWS WF13 ...... 173 L6
  HUDE HD5 .... 215 H3
  LVSG WF15 .... 172 E3
Worral Cl BSLY S70 .... 261 H8
Worrall Rd WKFDW/WTN WF2 .. 220 C2
Worrall St MOR LS27 .... 152 B3
Worsley Cl BSLY S70 .... 261 K8
Worsley Pl AWLS/ASK DN6 .. 249 H4
  MILN OL16 .... 206 D7
  ROY/SHW OL2 .... 229 J8
Worsley St MILN OL16 .... 206 D7
Worsnop Buildings
  LM/WK BD12 .... 148 E2
Worsnop St LM/WK BD12 ...... 126 F8
Worstead Rd HWTH BD22 ...... 79 H6
Worth Av KGHY BD21 .... 3 M1
Worth Bridge Rd KGHY BD21 .. 3 L3
Worthing Head Cl
  LM/WK BD12 .... 148 F3
Worthing Head Rd
  LM/WK BD12 .... 148 F3
Worthing St LM/WK BD12 ...... 148 F3
Worthington St GIR BD8 .... 4 B4
Worthville Cl KGHY BD21 .... 3 H9
Worth Wy HWTH BD22 .... 79 J6
  HWTH BD22 .... 100 F2
  KGHY BD21 .... 3 G7
Wortley La WOR/ARM LS12 .... 8 A4

Wortley Moor La
  WOR/ARM LS12 .... 108 D8
Wortley Moor Rd
  WOR/ARM LS12 .... 108 D7
Wortley Pk HEM/SK/SE WF9 .. 223 C7
Wortley Rd HEM/SK/SE WF9 .. 223 L2
Wortley Rd WOR/ARM LS12 .. 108 D7
Wortley St BGLY BD16 .... 81 K3
  BSLY S70 .... 261 G5
Worts Hill La HUDW HD3 ...... 211 K2
Worts Hill Side HUDW HD3 .. 211 L2
Wrangbrook La
  HEM/SK/SE WF9 .... 225 L8
Wrangbrook Rd
  HEM/SK/SE WF9 .... 225 M6
Wrangthorn Av HDGY LS6 .... 6 A3
Wrangthorn Pl HDGY LS6 .... 6 A3
Wrangthorn Ter HDGY LS6 ...... 6 A3
Wray Pl OL16 .... 206 E8
Wrelton Cl BSLYN/ROY S71 .. 243 K5
Wren Av GTHN BD7 .... 126 A1
Wrenbeck Av OT LS21 .... 41 J4
Wrenbeck Cl OT LS21 .... 41 J4
Wrenbeck Dr OT LS21 .... 41 J4
Wrenbury Av BHP/TINH LS16 .. 85 M1
Wrenbury Crs BHP/TINH LS16 .. 85 M1
Wrenbury Dr MILN OL16 ...... 228 E2
Wrenbury Gv BHP/TINH LS16 .. 86 A1
Wren Cft PONT WF8 .... 180 F3
Wren Dr MOR LS27 .... 152 F3
Wren Garth WKFDW/WTN WF2 .. 220 E1
Wren Gn MILN OL16 .... 206 D8
Wren Hl BTLY WF17 .... 151 J6
Wren Nest Rd RPDN/SBR HX6 .. 188 C2
Wren's Nest Av ROY/SHW OL2 .. 229 L6
Wren St HUD HD1 .... 213 M1
  KGHY BD21 .... 3 H3
Wrenthorpe La
  WKFDW/WTN WF2 .... 175 L5
Wrenthorpe Rd
  WKFDW/WTN WF2 .... 176 B5
Wrexhall Rd EARL WF12 .... 174 A4
Wrexham Rd ILK LS29 .... 39 M5
Wright Av HWTH BD22 .... 78 F3
Wrights La KNOT WF11 .... 182 F7
Wright St AIRE BD20 .... 55 M1
  HWTH BD22 .... 78 F4
Wrigley Av BOW BD4 .... 127 K5
Wrigley Hl LUD/ILL HX2 .... 124 A4
Wrigley Pl LIT OL15 .... 207 H3
Wroe Crs LM/WK BD12 .... 148 E3
Wroe Pl LM/WK BD12 .... 148 E3
Wroe St DEWS WF13 .... 173 H5
Wroe Ter LM/WK BD12 .... 148 E3
Wrose Av ECHL BD2 .... 105 J1
  SHPY BD18 .... 82 F8
Wrose Brow Rd SHPY BD18 .... 82 F6
Wrosecliffe Gv SHPY BD18 .... 83 H6
Wrose Dr SHPY BD18 .... 82 F8
Wrose Gv ECHL BD2 .... 83 H8
  SHPY BD18 .... 82 F8
Wrose Hill Pl SHPY BD18 ...... 104 F1
Wrose Mt SHPY BD18 .... 83 G8
Wrose Rd SHPY BD18 .... 82 F8
Wrose Vw SHPY BD18 .... 82 F8
Wuerdle Cl MILN OL16 .... 207 G2
Wuerdle Farm Wy
  MILN OL16 .... 207 G2
Wuerdle Pl MILN OL16 .... 207 G2
Wuerdle St MILN OL16 .... 207 G2
Wycliffe Cl BRAM LS13 .... 106 F1
Wycliffe Dr AL/HA/HU LS17 .. 87 M4
Wycliffe Gdns SHPY BD18 ...... 82 C6
Wycliffe Rd SHPY BD18 .... 82 C6
Wycliffe St OSS WF5 .... 174 E7
Wycoller Rd LM/WK BD12 ...... 148 E2
Wycombe Gn BOW BD4 .... 128 A3
Wycombe St
  BSLYN/ROY S71 .... 262 A4
Wykebeck Av OSM LS9 .... 110 E7
Wykebeck Crs OSM LS9 .... 110 F6
Wykebeck Gdns OSM LS9 ...... 110 F6
Wykebeck Gv OSM LS9 .... 110 F6
Wykebeck Mt OSM LS9 .... 110 F6
Wykebeck Pl OSM LS9 .... 111 G6

Wykebeck Rd OSM LS9 .... 110 F6
Wykebeck Sq OSM LS9 .... 110 F6
Wykebeck St OSM LS9 .... 110 F6
Wykebeck Ter OSM LS9 .... 110 F6
Wykebeck Valley Rd OSM LS9 .. 110 F4
Wykebeck Vw OSM LS9 .... 110 F6
Wyke Crs LM/WK BD12 .... 148 E4
Wyke La LM/WK BD12 .... 148 E4
Wykelea Cl LM/WK BD12 ...... 148 E4
Wyke Old La BRIG HD6 .... 148 D7
Wyncliffe Gdns AL/HA/HU LS17 .. 87 M4
Wyncroft Gv BHP/TINH LS16 .. 64 B4
Wyncroft Ri SHPY BD18 .... 104 F1
Wyndham Av ECHL BD2 .... 105 H3
Wynford Av BHP/TINH LS16 .. 86 D5
Wynford Dr HEM/SK/SE WF9 .. 247 J3
Wynford Gv BHP/TINH LS16 .. 86 D5
Wynford Mt BHP/TINH LS16 .. 86 C5
Wynford Ri BHP/TINH LS16 .. 86 D5
Wynford Ter BHP/TINH LS16 .. 86 D5
Wynford Wy WBSY BD6 .... 127 G6
Wynmore Av BHP/TINH LS16 .. 64 C4
Wynmore Crs BHP/TINH LS16 .. 64 B4
Wynmore Dr BHP/TINH LS16 .. 64 B4
  HUDW HD3 .... 191 H5
Wynthorpe Rd
  HOR/CROF WF4 .... 197 K5
Wynyard Dr MOR LS27 .... 152 B2
Wyther Av
  WOR/ARM LS12 .... 108 B5
Wyther Park Av
  WOR/ARM LS12 .... 108 B5
Wyther Park Cl
  WOR/ARM LS12 .... 108 B5
Wyther Park Crs
  WOR/ARM LS12 .... 108 B5
Wyther Park Gv
  WOR/ARM LS12 .... 108 B5
Wyther Park Hl
  WOR/ARM LS12 .... 108 B4
Wyther Park Pl
  WOR/ARM LS12 .... 108 A5
Wyther Park Rd BRAM LS13 .. 108 A5
Wyther Park Sq
  WOR/ARM LS12 .... 108 A4
Wyther Park St
  WOR/ARM LS12 .... 108 B5
Wyther Park Ter
  WOR/ARM LS12 .... 108 A5
Wyther Park Vw
  WOR/ARM LS12 .... 108 B4
Wyvern Av HUDW HD3 .... 191 L8
Wyvern Cl BTLY WF17 .... 151 L8
  GTHN BD7 .... 104 B8
Wyverne Rd HOLM/MEL HD7 .. 213 G2
Wyvern Pl LUD/ILL HX2 .... 146 A6
Wyvern Ter LUD/ILL HX2 ...... 146 A6
Wyvil Crs ILK LS29 .... 39 G2
Wyvil Rd ILK LS29 .... 39 G1

Y

Yarborough Cft HIPP HX3 ...... 147 J2
Yardley Wy LM/WK BD12 ...... 127 G8
Yard No4 BTLY WF17 .... 151 H5
Yarn St MID LS10 .... 9 M6
Yarrow Cl ROCH OL11 .... 228 B1
Yarwood Gv GTHN BD7 .... 126 A3
Yate La HWTH BD22 .... 99 L1
Yates Flat SHPY BD18 .... 82 F8
Yates La HUDS HD4 .... 213 J2
Yeadon Dr HIPP HX3 .... 169 J2
Yeadon Moor Rd HORS LS18 .. 63 J7
  YEA LS19 .... 63 C8
Yealand Cl AWLS/ASK DN6 .. 249 K8
Ye Farre Cl BRIG HD6 .... 170 B2
Yeoman's Cl MILN OL16 .... 207 H7
Yewbank Cl ILK LS29 .... 38 C2
Yewbank Ter ILK LS29 .... 38 C2
Yewdall Rd BRAM LS13 .... 106 F1
Yewdall Wy IDLE BD10 .... 83 L8
Yew Green Av HUDS HD4 ...... 214 A3

Yew Green Rd HUDS HD4 ...... 214 A3
Yew Gv HUDS HD4 .... 213 H4
Yew La GFTH/SHER LS25 ...... 113 K8
Yews Hill Rd HUDS HD4 ...... 214 A2
Yews La HUDS HD4 .... 214 A2
Yews Mt HUD HD1 .... 214 B2
Yews Pl BSLY S70 .... 261 K8
Yew St HUDN HD2 .... 14 E1
Yew Tree Av GIR BD8 .... 103 M5
Yew Tree Cl AIRE BD20 .... 16 D8
  HARS HG2 .... 26 C1
  SHPY BD18 .... 82 F8
Yew Tree Crs GIR BD8 .... 104 A5
Yew Tree La HOLM/MEL HD7 .. 212 B6
  HOLM/MEL HD7 .... 213 H3
  HOLM/MEL HD7 .... 253 L3
  MSTN/BAR LS15 .... 112 A7
  WIL/AL BD15 .... 103 G6
Yew Tree Rd HUDW HD3 ...... 191 J4
Yew Trees Av HIPP HX3 .... 147 J3
Yew Trees Cft LUD/ILL HX2 .. 144 D5
Yew Tree St WKFDE WF1 .... 13 K7
York Av HUDN HD2 .... 192 C4
York Crs BGLY BD16 .... 81 J4
York Dr BTLY WF17 .... 151 M8
  HECK WF16 .... 150 F8
York Ga OT LS21 .... 62 C2
York Gv BTLY WF17 .... 151 L8
York Pl CLECK BD19 .... 149 M6
  FEA/AMT WF7 .... 202 D7
  LDS LS1 .... 6 E9
  TOD OL14 .... 163 K1
  WBY LS22 .... 30 A8
York Rd BTLY WF17 .... 151 L8
  EARL WF12 .... 174 B5
  ILK LS29 .... 40 B5
  MSTN/BAR LS15 .... 111 K3
  OSM LS9 .... 7 M9
  RYKW YO26 .... 33 K2
  SCFT LS14 .... 111 K3
  TAD LS24 .... 51 K2
  TAD LS24 .... 72 A2
  WBY LS22 .... 30 E7
  WBY LS22 .... 31 K5
Yorkshire St MILN OL16 ...... 206 B6
Yorkshire Wy GTHN BD7 ...... 126 D3
York St AIRE BD20 .... 34 F7
  BGLY BD16 .... 81 J4
  BRIG HD6 .... 170 C5
  BSLY S70 .... 261 G5
  CAS WF10 .... 157 M6
  COL BB8 .... 74 A1
  CUD/GR S72 .... 244 C8
  CUL/QBY BD13 .... 125 G5
  GIR BD8 .... 104 A7
  HBR HX7 .... 143 J4
  HEM/SK/SE WF9 .... 246 A1
  HFAX HX1 .... 10 F7
  LDSU LS2 .... 9 J1
  MILN OL16 .... 206 D8
  NORM WF6 .... 178 B3
  OSM LS9 .... 9 K1
  TOD OL14 .... 141 K8
York Ter HIPP HX3 .... 10 F1
York Vls NORM WF6 .... 178 D4
Young's Ct GFTH/SHER LS25 .. 92 A8
Young St GIR BD8 .... 104 B7

Z

Zealand St BOW BD4 .... 127 M2
Zermatt Gv CHAL LS7 .... 87 L8
Zermatt Mt CHAL LS7 .... 87 L8
Zermatt St CHAL LS7 .... 87 M8
Zermatt Ter CHAL LS7 .... 87 M8
Zetland Pl RHAY LS8 .... 110 B3
Zetland St HUD HD1 .... 15 G8
  WKFDE WF1 .... 12 F2
Zion Cl HUDW HD3 .... 191 K5
Zion Dr DOD/DAR S75 .... 242 D5
Zion St HBR HX7 .... 144 A5
Zoar St MOR LS27 .... 152 C2

Index - featured places

Abbey Grange School
  BHP/TINH LS16 .... 86 B6
Abbey Park School
  LUD/ILL HX2 .... 123 M8
A B C Cinema
  ROCH OL11 .... 228 A2
Aberford C of E
  Primary School
  GFTH/SHER LS25 .... 92 A7
Abraham Ormerod
  Day Hospital
  TOD OL14 .... 163 K1
A1 Business Park
  KNOT WF11 .... 181 L3
Ackton Pastures
  Junior & Infant School
  CAS WF10 .... 157 K8
Ackworth Business Park
  FEA/AMT WF7 .... 202 A5
Ackworth Howards
  C of E J & I (VC) School
  FEA/AMT WF7 .... 202 D7
Ackworth Mill Dam School
  FEA/AMT WF7 .... 224 C1
Ackworth School
  FEA/AMT WF7 .... 202 C7
Acorn Business Park
  AIRE BD20 .... 16 C7
Acorn Business Park
  SCFT LS14 .... 111 G5
Addingham Cricket Club
  ILK LS29 .... 19 G6
Addingham Middle School
  ILK LS29 .... 19 H5
Addingham Primary School
  ILK LS29 .... 19 G5
Adel Primary School
  BHP/TINH LS16 .... 87 G3

Adwalton Cricket Club
  BIRK/DRI BD11 .... 151 H1
Agbrigg Surgery
  WKFDE WF1 .... 13 L9
Agnes Stewart C of E
  High School
  OSM LS9 .... 7 L8
Aireborough Leisure Centre
  GSLY LS20 .... 62 A5
Aireborough Rawdon
  C of E Primary School
  YEA LS19 .... 84 F3
Airedale Business Centre
  AIRE BD20 .... 16 C6
Airedale Clinic
  CAS WF10 .... 158 E7
Airedale First & Middle School
  CAS WF10 .... 158 E7
Airedale High School
  CAS WF10 .... 158 F7
Aireside Business Centre
  LDS LS1 .... 8 E1
Aireside Retail Park
  LDS LS1 .... 8 D1
Aire Valley Business Centre
  KGHY BD21 .... 3 G3
Aire Valley Clinic
  AIRE BD20 .... 56 E1
Aireview Business Centre
  BAIL BD17 .... 82 C6
Aire View Infant School
  AIRE BD20 .... 35 M5
Aireview Primary School
  BRAM LS13 .... 107 H2
Alexander Doctors Clinic
  KSTL LS5 .... 86 B8
The Alhambra Shopping Centre
  BSLY S70 .... 261 H5

Alhambra Theatre
  BFD BD1 .... 4 D7
Alice Ingham Primary School
  MILN OL16 .... 206 M4
Allerton Bywater Business Park
  CAS WF10 .... 157 M2
Allerton Bywater Infant School
  CAS WF10 .... 157 K2
Allerton Bywater
  Primary School
  CAS WF10 .... 157 K1
Allerton Clinic
  WIL/AL BD15 .... 103 K6
Allerton First & Middle School
  WIL/AL BD15 .... 103 K6
Allerton Grange High School
  AL/HA/HU LS17 .... 88 A5
Allerton High School
  AL/HA/HU LS17 .... 87 K3
All Saints C of E First School
  WBOW BD5 .... 126 E2
All Saints C of E Junior &
  Infant School
  HIPP HX3 .... 168 A4
All Saints C of E Primary School
  WHIT OL12 .... 206 C5
All Saints First School
  ILK LS29 .... 38 D2
All Saints High School
  HUDN HD2 .... 192 E1
All Saints Industrial Estate
  PONT WF8 .... 181 G5
All Saints Infant School
  PONT WF8 .... 181 G5
All Saints Junior & Infant School
  FEA/AMT WF7 .... 179 L5

All Saints Junior &
  Middle School
  OT LS21 .... 41 J6
Allwoodley County
  Primary School
  AL/HA/HU LS17 .... 87 J3
Alma Industrial Estate
  WHIT OL12 .... 206 C5
Almondbury C of E
  Infant School
  HUDE HD5 .... 215 G4
Almondbury County
  Junior School
  HUDE HD5 .... 215 J2
Almondbury High School
  HUDE HD5 .... 215 J2
Alston Retail Park
  KGHY BD21 .... 3 K1
Altofts Middle School
  NORM WF6 .... 178 B3
Altofts Sports Club
  NORM WF6 .... 178 C1
Alverthorpe St Pauls
  C of E Aided Junior &
  Infant School
  WKFDW/WTN WF2 .... 175 M6
Alwoodley Golf Club
  AL/HA/HU LS17 .... 66 A8
Amateurs Football Club
  ELL HX5 .... 169 K6
A M F Bowling
  LDSU LS2 .... 7 G7
Apex Business Park
  BEE/HOL LS11 .... 9 G5
Ardsley Oaks Junior &
  Infant School
  BSLY S70 .... 262 B6

Area Office Town Hall
  CLECK BD19 .... 150 A7
Arlington Business Centre
  MOR LS27 .... 130 F6
Armley Clinic
  WOR/ARM LS12 .... 108 E6
Armley Link Trading Estate
  WOR/ARM LS12 .... 108 F6
Armley Primary School
  WOR/ARM LS12 .... 108 E6
Armley Sports & Leisure Centre
  WOR/ARM LS12 .... 108 D7
Armytage Road
  Industrial Estate
  BRIG HD6 .... 170 E4
Art Gallery
  ILK LS29 .... 38 D2
Art & Poetry Gallery
  SKP/WHF BD23 .... 16 B2
A S B & S Sports Club
  FEA/AMT WF7 .... 201 L1
Ashcroft Surgery
  ECHL BD2 .... 105 K4
Ashfield Medical Centre
  MSTN/BAR LS15 .... 111 L4
Ashfield School
  IDLE BD10 .... 83 L5
Ashfield Valley Primary School
  ROCH OL11 .... 228 A2
Ash Grove Surgery
  KNOT WF11 .... 182 C2
Ashlands First School
  ILK LS29 .... 38 C2
Ashley Business Centre
  LDSU LS2 .... 7 J8
Ashley Industrial Estate
  HUDN HD2 .... 193 L2

Ashley Industrial Estate
OSS WF5 .... 175 G7

Ashmount Industrial Park
HEM/SK/SE WF9 .... 223 L4

Ashton View Medical Centre
RHAY LS8 .... 110 B4

Ash Tree County Infant School
LUD/ILL HX2 .... 145 L1

Ashville Medical Centre
BSLY S70 .... 261 M6

Askwith CP School
OT LS21 .... 40 B1

Astley Surgery
RTHW LS26 .... 134 C5

Athelstan CP School
GFTH/SHER LS25 .... 116 A8

Athersley North
Primary School
BSLYN/ROY S71 .... 243 G6

Athersley South Junior School
BSLYN/ROY S71 .... 243 H7

Athletic Club
HEM/SK/SE WF9 .... 223 K3

Atlas First School
GIR BD8 .... 4 A2

Austhorpe County
Primary School
MSTN/BAR LS15 .... 112 A6

Austhorpe View Surgery
MSTN/BAR LS15 .... 111 M6

Automobilia Transport Museum
HBR HX7 .... 143 L1

Aylesham Industrial Estate
LM/WK BD12 .... 126 F8

Azam & Sender Dentist Surgery
HIPP HX3 .... 125 M7

Badsworth C of E
Junior & Infant School
HEM/SK/SE WF9 .... 225 G4

Bagshaw Museum
BTLY WF17 .... 151 K6

Baildon C of E First School
BAIL BD17 .... 82 F2

Baildon Recreation Centre
BAIL BD17 .... 82 D5

Baileygate Industrial Estate
PONT WF8 .... 181 G5

Bailiff Bridge Primary School
BRIG HD6 .... 148 D7

Baillie Street Health Centre
MILN OL16 .... 206 B6

Balderstone Community
School
ROCH OL11 .... 228 C3

Balm Road Industrial Estate
MID LS10 .... 9 K9

Bank End Junior &
Infant School
BSLY S70 .... 261 L8

Bankfield Museum
HIPP HX3 .... 11 G2

Bankfield Surgery
ELL HX5 .... 169 H7

Bankfoot First School
WBOW BD5 .... 126 F4

Bardsey County Primary School
AL/HA/HU LS17 .... 67 L2

Barkerend First School
BFDE BD3 .... 5 K4

Barkisland C of E
Junior & Infant School
GTL/HWG HX4 .... 189 J1

Barkisland Cricket Club
GTL/HWG HX4 .... 189 J2

Barnsley Borough Council
BSLY S70 .... 261 H5

Barnsley Christian School
BSLY S70 .... 261 G5

Barnsley College
BSLY S70 .... 261 G4

Barnsley College
DOD/DAR S75 .... 260 F2

Barnsley County Court
BSLY S70 .... 261 G4

Barnsley District
General Hospital
DOD/DAR S75 .... 260 E3

Barnsley Football Club
BSLYN/ROY S71 .... 261 J5

Barnsley Magistrates Court
BSLY S70 .... 261 G4

Barnsley Metropolitan Borough
Council
BSLY S70 .... 260 F7

Barnsley Metropolitan Borough
Council
BSLY S70 .... 261 H4

Barnsley Metropolitan Borough
Council
BSLYN/ROY S71 .... 243 L2

Barnsley Metropolitan Borough
Council
BSLYN/ROY S71 .... 243 H7

Barnsley Metropolitan Borough
Council
DOD/DAR S75 .... 241 M6

Barnsley Municipal Golf Club
DOD/DAR S75 .... 242 E4

Barnsley Private Clinic
DOD/DAR S75 .... 260 F3

Barras Garth Industrial Estate
WOR/ARM LS12 .... 108 D8

Barwick Infant School
MSTN/BAR LS15 .... 91 G7

Batley Art Gallery
BTLY WF17 .... 173 L1

Batley High School for Boys
BTLY WF17 .... 151 L8

Batley Manorfields
County Infant School
BTLY WF17 .... 173 J2

Batley Rugby League
Football Club Ltd
BTLY WF17 .... 173 L2

Batley Sports Centre
BTLY WF17 .... 151 K5

Battyeford C of E (C)
Junior & Infant School
MIRF WF14 .... 172 A8

kBatty Street School
HECK WF16 .... 172 F2

Bbc North Studio
BFD BD1 .... 4 F7

Bbc Studios
LDSU LS2 .... 6 F6

Beacon Business Centre
HIPP HX3 .... 11 L8

Beauty Gallery
KGHY BD21 .... 3 H4

Becca House Surgery
HEM/SK/SE WF9 .... 223 M7

Beckfoot Upper School
BGLY BD16 .... 81 J5

Beech County Junior &
Infant School
HOLM/MEL HD7 .... 213 G1

Beech Hill County Primary
School
HFAX HX1 .... 10 E4

Beech House School
ROCH OL11 .... 206 A8

Beechwood County
Primary School
SCFT LS14 .... 111 J1

Beeston Hill St Lukes School
BEE/HOL LS11 .... 8 E7

Beeston Primary School
BEE/HOL LS11 .... 131 G4

Beeston Village Surgery
BEE/HOL LS11 .... 131 H4

Beevor Industrial Estate
BSLYN/ROY S71 .... 261 K4

Belal Mosque
HUDS HD4 .... 213 M3

Belfield Community School
MILN OL16 .... 206 E6

Belle Isle Medical Centre
RTHW LS26 .... 132 B6

Belle Vue Boys School
HTON BD9 .... 103 M2

Belle Vue Girls Upper School
HTON BD9 .... 103 L1

Bell Lane Junior &
Infant School
FEA/AMT WF7 .... 224 B1

Belmont Business Centre
BFD BD1 .... 5 H5

Belmont Middle School
BAIL BD17 .... 82 D3

Ben Rhydding Sports Club
ILK LS29 .... 39 J1

Bentley Lane School
HDGY LS6 .... 87 H8

Benton Park School
YEA LS19 .... 84 D1

Bero Bu School
LDSU LS2 .... 6 F6

Beth Hamedrash
Hagadol Synagogue
AL/HA/HU LS17 .... 87 M2

The Beth Hamedrash Hagadol
Synagogue
AL/HA/HU LS17 .... 88 A4

Bierley C of E First School
BOW BD4 .... 127 K5

Bilton Medical Centre
GIR BD8 .... 4 A4

Bingley Grammar School
BGLY BD16 .... 81 G2

Bingley Health Centre
BGLY BD16 .... 81 G3

Bingley Hospital
BGLY BD16 .... 81 J3

Bingley Little Theatre
BGLY BD16 .... 81 H3

Birch Lane Medical Centre
WBOW BD5 .... 127 G3

Birdsedge First School
KBTN HD8 .... 256 C2

Birkby Junior
School/community Centre
HUD HD1 .... 14 F1

Birkenshaw
C of E (C) First School
BIRK/DRI BD11 .... 128 C8

Birkenshaw Health Centre
BIRK/DRI BD11 .... 128 C8

Birkenshaw Middle School
BIRK/DRI BD11 .... 150 D2

Birkwood First School
CUD/GR S72 .... 262 E1

Birstall Cricket Club
BTLY WF17 .... 151 J3

Birstall Junior & Infant School
BTLY WF17 .... 151 H1

Blackburn Industrial Estate
GFTH/SHER LS25 .... 116 D6

Blackgates Infant School
EARD/LOFT WF3 .... 153 C5

Blackgates Junior School
EARD/LOFT WF3 .... 153 H6

Blakehill First School
IDLE BD10 .... 83 J8

Blenheim Primary School
LDSU LS2 .... 6 F5

The Bloomfield Practice
AL/HA/HU LS17 .... 87 J2

The Bloomfield Practice
BHP/TINH LS16 .... 86 F7

B M K Industrial Estate
LVSG WF15 .... 172 D2

Bolling Road First School
ILK LS29 .... 38 F2

The Bolton Brow Gallery
RPDN/SBR HX6 .... 167 L2

Bolton Brow Primary School
RPDN/SBR HX6 .... 167 M2

Bolton Lane First School
ECHL BD2 .... 105 J3

Bolton Royd College of
Further Education
GIR BD8 .... 104 F1

Bolton Villas Cricket Club
IDLE BD10 .... 83 J8

Bolton Woods First School
SHPY BD18 .... 104 F1

Bondgate Industrial Estate
PONT WF8 .... 181 G5

Bond Street Surgery
BTLY WF17 .... 151 H5

Boothroyd Junior &
Infant School
DEWS WF13 .... 173 J7

Borough Market
HFAX HX1 .... 11 H6

Boston Spa C of E School
BSPA/BRAM LS23 .... 48 F7

Boston Spa Comprehensive
School
BSPA/BRAM LS23 .... 48 D7

Bowling Community College
BOW BD4 .... 127 K3

Bowling Green Junior &
Infant School
GTL/HWG HX4 .... 190 B3

Bowling Park First School
WBOW BD5 .... 127 H3

Bowling Pool
BOW BD4 .... 127 J3

Bowling Special School
BOW BD4 .... 127 K3

Bracken Edge Primary School
CHAL LS7 .... 110 A1

Brackenhill First School
GTHN BD7 .... 126 B2

Bradford Area Health Authority
GTHN BD7 .... 4 D7

Bradford Area Health Authority
GTHN BD7 .... 126 C2

Bradford & Bingley Rugby Club
BGLY BD16 .... 81 K5

Bradford Business Park
BFD BD1 .... 4 F3

Bradford Business Park
BFDE BD3 .... 4 F2

Bradford City A F C
GIR BD8 .... 4 D2

Bradford Community
Health N H S Trust
BFDE BD3 .... 105 L6

Bradford Community Health
N H S Trust
GIR BD8 .... 104 B6

Bradford Girls Grammar School
GIR BD8 .... 104 A5

Bradford Grammar School
HTON BD9 .... 104 E3

Bradford & Ilkley College
BFD BD1 .... 4 D7

Bradford & Ilkley College
WBOW BD5 .... 4 C9

Bradford & Ilkley
Community College
BFD BD1 .... 4 D6

Bradford & Ilkley
Community College
GTHN BD7 .... 4 B8

Bradford & Ilkley
Community College
GTHN BD7 .... 126 D2

Bradford & Ilkley
Community College
ILK LS29 .... 38 D3

Bradford Industrial &
Horses at Work Museum
ECHL BD2 .... 105 L3

Bradford Metropolitan
Borough Council
ILK LS29 .... 38 D2

Bradford Moor First School
BFDE BD3 .... 105 L6

Bradford Royal Infirmary
HTON BD9 .... 104 B4

Bradford Royal Infirmary
Remedial Unit
HTON BD9 .... 104 A4

Bradford Salem Rugby
Football Club
HTON BD9 .... 104 A2

The Bradford Synagogue
GIR BD8 .... 4 D3

Bradford University
PDSY/CALV LS28 .... 106 C5

Bradley Junction
Industrial Estate
HUDN HD2 .... 193 H2

Bradley Mills Cricket &
Bowling Club
HUD HD1 .... 15 J1

Bradleys Both CP School
AIRE BD20 .... 16 E8

Bradshaw School
LUD/ILL HX2 .... 124 A6

Braithwaite Special School
HWTH BD22 .... 57 G6

Bramham CP School
BSPA/BRAM LS23 .... 69 M2

Bramhope Junior &
Infant School
BHP/TINH LS16 .... 64 A4

Bramhope Primary School
BHP/TINH LS16 .... 64 A4

Bramley Business Centre
BRAM LS13 .... 107 K5

Bramley Grange College
SCFT LS14 .... 89 L5

Bramley Health Centre
BRAM LS13 .... 107 L3

Bramley R U F C
BRAM LS13 .... 107 L3

Bramley St Peters C of E
°Primary School
BRAM LS13 .... 107 L4

Branshaw School
HWTH BD22 .... 2 D6

Branxholme Industrial Estate
BRIG HD6 .... 148 E7

Brent Gallery
HWTH BD22 .... 54 E3

Bretton Hall College
WKFDE WF1 .... 13 H9

Brewery
MID LS10 .... 9 H3

Bridge Court Business Park
BEE/HOL LS11 .... 8 C5

Bridge Theatre
HBR HX7 .... 121 H7

Brierley C of E Junior &
Infant School
CUD/GR S72 .... 245 J3

Brighouse High School
BRIG HD6 .... 170 C3

Brighouse Sports Centre
BRIG HD6 .... 170 B1

Brighouse Sports Club
BRIG HD6 .... 170 D3

Broadgate Infant School
HORS LS18 .... 85 L5

Broad Oak Cricket & Athletic
Club
HOLM/MEL HD7 .... 213 G4

Broadway School
BSLY S70 .... 260 D6

Brockholes C of E School
HOLM/MEL HD7 .... 236 E4

Brockholes Industrial Park
HOLM/MEL HD7 .... 236 D4

Brodetsky Jewish Primary
School
AL/HA/HU LS17 .... 87 L2

Bromham Park
BSPA/BRAM LS23 .... 69 H6

Bronte House School
IDLE BD10 .... 84 B4

Bronte Parsonage Museum
HWTH BD22 .... 78 D7

Bronte School
HWTH BD22 .... 79 G3

Brookfield Infant School
IDLE BD10 .... 84 A8

Brooklands School
SKP/WHF BD23 .... 16 B4

The Brooksbank School
ELL HX5 .... 191 G1

Broomwood Middle School
BOW BD4 .... 127 L5

Brotherton County Primary
School
KNOT WF11 .... 159 L6

Broughton House Surgery
BTLY WF17 .... 173 K1

Brownhill Infant School
BTLY WF17 .... 151 J5

Brownhill Primary School
OSM LS9 .... 110 C5

Brownhill School
WHIT OL12 .... 206 A5

Brudenell Primary School
HDGY LS6 .... 109 G3

Bruntcliffe High School
MOR LS27 .... 152 A2

Bruton Gallery
LDS LS1 .... 6 E9

Buckley Road Industrial Estate
WHIT OL12 .... 206 D4

Burley Football Club
KSTL LS5 .... 86 B8

Burley In Wharfedale School
ILK LS29 .... 40 A5

Burley Middle School
ILK LS29 .... 40 B6

Burley Park Medical Centre
BULY LS4 .... 108 F4

Burley Woodhead C of E School
ILK LS29 .... 40 B6

Burmantofts Health Centre
OSM LS9 .... 7 M7

Burnley Road Primary School
HBR HX7 .... 143 M5

Burntwood School
HEM/SK/SE WF9 .... 246 E4

Burntwood Sports &
Leisure Centre
CUD/GR S72 .... 245 L4

Burton Road Junior &
Infant School
BSLYN/ROY S71 .... 261 J3

Burton Salmon CP School
GFTH/SHER LS25 .... 160 A2

Bury & Rochdale Health
Authority
MILN OL16 .... 206 B7

Bus Station (Interchange)
BFD BD1 .... 4 F7

Butterfield Industrial Estate
BAIL BD17 .... 82 F5

Buttershaw Middle School
WBSY BD6 .... 126 B7

Buttershaw Upper School
WBSY BD6 .... 126 B6

Byron Primary School
BFDE BD3 .... 5 M4

Bywell C of E Junior School
EARL WF12 .... 174 B4

Calderdale Business Centre
HFAX HX1 .... 10 B6

Calderdale Business Park
LUD/ILL HX2 .... 146 B3

Calderdale College
HFAX HX1 .... 10 C7

Calderdale Health Authority
HFAX HX1 .... 146 A8

Calderdale Metropolitan
Borough Council
HFAX HX1 .... 11 G6

Calderdale Metropolitan
Borough Council
HIPP HX3 .... 125 L8

Calderdale Metropolitan
Borough Council
LUD/ILL HX2 .... 146 A7

Calderdale Metropolitan
Borough Council
LUD/ILL HX2 .... 146 A2

Calder High School
HBR HX7 .... 144 B5

Calder Industrial Estate
BRIG HD6 .... 148 D8

Calder Trading Estate
HUDN HD2 .... 171 J8

Calder Trading Estate
RPDN/SBR HX6 .... 167 L3

Calverley C of E Primary School
PDSY/CALV LS28 .... 84 D7

Calverley Medical Centre
PDSY/CALV LS28 .... 84 C8

Calverley Parkside
Junior & Infant School
PDSY/CALV LS28 .... 84 C8

Calversyke Middle School
HWTH BD22 .... 2 A5

Campsmount School
AWLS/ASK DN6 .... 227 K4

Canalside Industrial Estate
MILN OL16 .... 228 D1

Cannon Hall Museum &
Country Park
DOD/DAR S75 .... 258 E1

Cape Industrial Estate
PDSY/CALV LS28 .... 107 G3

Carcroft Health Centre
AWLS/ASK DN6 .... 249 L6

Carcroft Industrial Estate
AWLS/ASK DN6 .... 249 M7

Cardigan Trading Estate
BULY LS4 .... 108 F5

Cardinal Heenan School
HDGY LS6 .... 87 J5

Carleton Business Park
SKP/WHF BD23 .... 16 A3

Carleton Park Junior &
Infants School
PONT WF8 .... 180 F8

Carlinghow Princess Royal
Primary School
BTLY WF17 .... 151 J7

Carlisle Business Centre
GIR BD8 .... 4 A1

Cariton Bolling College and
Sports Centre
BFDE BD3 .... 5 K3

Carlton Cricket Club
EARD/LOFT WF3 .... 154 F4

Carlton High School
PONT WF8 .... 203 G1

Carlton Industrial Estate
BSLYN/ROY S71 .... 243 L6

Carlton Junior & Infant School
BSLYN/ROY S71 .... 243 M6

Carlton Junior & Infant School
DEWS WF13 .... 173 L4

Carlton Mills Trading Estate
WOR/ARM LS12 .... 108 F6

Carlton Northfield A F C
EARD/LOFT WF3 .... 154 F4

Carlton Surgery
CHAL LS7 .... 7 H5

Carr Gate Hospital
WKFDW/WTN WF2 .... 176 A1

Carr Green County
Primary School
BRIG HD6 .... 170 B7

Carr Green Surgery
HUDE HD5 .... 15 M5

Carr Manor County
Primary School
AL/HA/HU LS17 .... 87 J6

Carr Manor High School
AL/HA/HU LS17 .... 87 J6

Carr Wood Industrial Estate
CAS WF10 .... 180 B1

Cartwright Hall Art Gallery
HTON BD9 .... 104 E3

Castleford Health Centre
CAS WF10 .... 157 M6

Castleford High School
CAS WF10 .... 158 A6

Castleford Park School
CAS WF10 .... 158 A7

Castleford Rugby Union
Football Club
CAS WF10 .... 179 H1

Castle Grove Infant School
WKFDW/WTN WF2 .... 199 G8

Castle Hall School
MIRF WF14 .... 194 D1

Castle Hill Junior & Infant
School
TOD OL14 .... 141 M8

Castle School
CAS WF10 .... 158 E7

Castleton Primary School
WOR/ARM LS12 .... 109 G7

Cas Whitwood Mere
Middle School
CAS WF10 .... 157 J4

Cathedral Retail Park
WKFDW/WTN WF2 .... 12 D5

The Cathedral School
WKFDW/WTN WF2 .... 12 A8

Cawthorne C of E Junior &
Infant School
DOD/DAR S75 .... 259 G2

Cawthorne Victoria Jubilee
Museum
DOD/DAR S75 .... 259 H2

Central Leisure Centre
MILN OL16 .... 206 C4

Central Mosque
HFAX HX1 .... 10 D6

Central Street Infant School
HBR HX7 .... 143 H3

Centre 27 Business Park
BTLY WF17 .... 151 K3

The Chandos Medical Centre
RHAY LS8 .... 88 B8

Chapel Allerton Hospital
CHAL LS7 .... 110 A1

Chapel Allerton Medical Centre
CHAL LS7 .... 87 M8

Chapel Allerton Primary School
CHAL LS7 .... 87 L8

Chapel Grange Special School
GIR BD8 .... 103 L6

Chapelthorpe Surgery
HOR/CROF WF4 .... 220 D2

Chapeltown Business Centre
CHAL LS7 .... 7 K1

Chapeltown Health Centre
CHAL LS7 .... 7 L3

Charles Street Surgery
OT LS21 .... 41 J7

Chel House Business Centre
CHAL LS7 .... 7 K4

Chellow Dene Middle School
GIR BD8 .... 103 M6

Chequerfield Infant School
PONT WF8 .... 181 H7
Chesham Building
GTHN BD7 .... 4 B8
Chevet Business Centre
KNOT WF11 .... 181 L3
Chichester Business Centre
MILN OL16 .... 206 C2
Chickenley County Junior &
Infant School
EARL WF12 .... 174 C7
Chippendale Junior School
OT LS21 .... 41 H4
Chohan Medical Centre
WBOW BD5 .... 126 F2
Christchurch C of E
Primary School
SKP/WHF BD23 .... 16 B3
Christchurch C of E
Primary School
UPML OL3 .... 230 F4
Christ Church C of E
COL BB8 .... 74 D1
Christ Church Junior &
Infant School
LUD/ILL HX2 .... 145 M6
Christ Church Junior School
RPDN/SBR HX6 .... 167 M1
Christ Church Primary School
WOR/ARM LS12 .... 108 D6
Christ Church Woodhouse
Junior & Infant School
HUDN HD2 .... 192 F3
Christ the King RC
Primary School
BRAM LS13 .... 108 A5
Church Drive Surgery
CUD/GR S72 .... 245 H3
Church Lane Surgery
BRIG HD6 .... 170 C3
Church School
CUL/QBY BD13 .... 103 G8
Church View Surgery
MSTN/BAR LS15 .... 111 L4
Churwell Junior & Infant School
MOR LS27 .... 130 D7
City Hall
BFD BD1 .... 4 F7
City Link Industrial Park
BOW BD4 .... 106 A7
City of Bradford Metropolitan
Council
ILK LS29 .... 61 J2
City of Bradford Metropolitan
District Council
AIRE BD20 .... 57 K4
City of Bradford Metropolitan
District Council
BFD BD1 .... 4 F6
City of Bradford Metropolitan
District Council
BFD BD1 .... 4 F7
City of Bradford Metropolitan
District Council
BFD BD1 .... 5 H6
City of Bradford Metropolitan
District Council
BGLY BD16 .... 81 G4
City of Bradford Metropolitan
District Council
BOW BD4 .... 128 A3
City of Bradford Metropolitan
District Council
HTON BD9 .... 104 D5
City of Bradford Metropolitan
District Council
KGHY BD21 .... 2 F5
City of Bradford Metropolitan
District Council
SHPY BD18 .... 82 D7
City of Bradford Metropolitan
District Council
WBOW BD5 .... 126 E2
City of Bradford Metropolitan
District Council
WBOW BD5 .... 126 F1
City of Bradford Metropolitan
District Council
WBOW BD5 .... 127 J5
City of Leeds School
HDGY LS6 .... 109 J2
City of Wakefield Golf Club
WKFDW/WTN WF2 .... 198 A4
City Park Industrial Estate
WOR/ARM LS12 .... 130 E3
Civic Centre
OT LS21 .... 41 J6
Civic Hall
LDSU LS2 .... 6 F7
Civic Theatre
BSLY S70 .... 261 H5
Civic Theatre
DEWS WF13 .... 173 L4
Civic Theatre
HFAX HX1 .... 11 H7
Clapgate Primary School
MID LS10 .... 154 B1
Claycliffe Business Park
DOD/DAR S75 .... 260 A1
kClayton C of E First School
CLAY BD14 .... 125 K2
Clayton Middle School
CLAY BD14 .... 125 L2
Cleckheaton Golf Course
CLECK BD19 .... 149 K4
Cleckheaton Sports Club
CLECK BD19 .... 149 L4
Clevedon House School
ILK LS29 .... 39 J4
Cliffe Avenue Surgery
BAIL BD17 .... 82 E4
Cliffe Castle Museum
KGHY BD21 .... 2 F1
Cliffe Hill School
HIPP HX3 .... 148 C8
Cliffe Middle School
BFDE BD3 .... 5 H1
Clifford Medical Centre
BSPA/BRAM LS23 .... 48 F8

Cliff School
WKFDE WF1 .... 176 D6
Clifton Forge Business Park
KNOT WF11 .... 182 A2
Clifton Infant School
HOR/CROF WF4 .... 197 H3
The Clinic
GFTH/SHER LS25 .... 116 A6
The Clinic
KBTN HD8 .... 217 L7
Clough Head Junior &
Infant School
HOLM/MEL HD7 .... 212 C2
Club House
AWLS/ASK DN6 .... 249 J2
Club House
BOW BD4 .... 128 A7
Cobblers Lane Junior &
Infant School
PONT WF8 .... 181 J6
Cobden Cp School
WOR/ARM LS12 .... 130 B2
Cocksford Golf Club
TAD LS24 .... 93 J2
Colden Primary School
HBR HX7 .... 142 C1
College Lane Surgery
FEA/AMT WF7 .... 202 B8
The College
WKFDE WF1 .... 176 E7
Collingham Parish Council
AL/HA/HU LS17 .... 67 M3
Colne Cricket Club
COL BB8 .... 74 C1
kColne Golf Club
COL BB8 .... 52 D7
Colne Side Business Park
HUDW HD3 .... 213 K1
Colne Valley High School
HOLM/MEL HD7 .... 213 G5
Colne Valley Leisure Centre
HOLM/MEL HD7 .... 212 C5
Colne Valley Museum
HOLM/MEL HD7 .... 212 E2
Colour Museum
BFD BD1 .... 4 D6
Colton County Primary School
MSTN/BAR LS15 .... 112 A8
Community Clinic
HORS LS18 .... 85 K5
Concert Hall
HUD HD1 .... 15 G8
Cononley Business Park
AIRE BD20 .... 34 D4
Cononley Primary School
AIRE BD20 .... 34 C3
Conway Medical Centre
RHAY LS8 .... 110 C3
Cookridge County Primary
School
BHP/TINH LS16 .... 86 A2
Cookridge Hospital
BHP/TINH LS16 .... 86 A4
Co-operative Museum
WHIT OL12 .... 206 A6
Cooper Gallery
BSLY S70 .... 261 G4
Cooper Lane First School
WBSY BD6 .... 125 L5
Cope Street Surgery
BSLY S70 .... 261 J7
Copley Hill Trading Estate
WOR/ARM LS12 .... 131 G1
Copley Primary School
HIPP HX3 .... 168 D5
Copperfields College
OSM LS9 .... 110 C8
Copthorne First School
GTHN BD7 .... 126 E1
Copwood Mental Health Clinic
BOW BD4 .... 128 A2
Corn Exchange
LDS LS1 .... 9 H1
Cornholme Junior & Infant School
TOD OL14 .... 140 C5
Coronation Business Centre
KGHY BD21 .... 3 J1
Corpus Christi High School
OSM LS9 .... 111 G6
The Cottage Gallery
SKP/WHF BD23 .... 16 B2
The Cottage Road Picture House
HDGY LS6 .... 86 F8
Cottingley Clinic
BGLY BD16 .... 81 J7
Cottingley Community
Health Centre
BEE/HOL LS11 .... 130 F5
Cottingley First School
BGLY BD16 .... 81 K7
Cottingley Primary School
BEE/HOL LS11 .... 130 C5
The Coulthurst Craven
Sports Centre
SKP/WHF BD23 .... 16 A3
Council for Mosques
GTHN BD7 .... 126 D1
County Borough of Halifax
HFAX HX1 .... 11 G6
County Council Hall
WKFDE WF1 .... 12 D1
County Infant School
HOLM/MEL HD7 .... 212 E5
County Police Office
MOR LS27 .... 152 B2
County Police Office
WBY LS22 .... 48 A2
County Police Station
WKFDE WF1 .... 12 D1
Cowgill House Surgery
CLAY BD14 .... 125 L2
Cowling Primary School
HWTH BD22 .... 54 D3
Craven Art Gallery
KGHY BD21 .... 2 F4
Craven Clinic
SKP/WHF BD23 .... 16 C2
Craven Road Medical Centre
HDGY LS6 .... 6 F2

Crawshaw High School
PDSY/CALV LS28 .... 107 H7
Cricket Club
MIRF WF14 .... 194 E5
Crigglestone Sports Club
HOR/CROF WF4 .... 220 B2
Croft Junior School
HOR/CROF WF4 .... 200 C6
Crofton Health Centre
HOR/CROF WF4 .... 200 B5
Crofton High School
HOR/CROF WF4 .... 200 B6
Crofton Infant School
HOR/CROF WF4 .... 200 B6
The Croft Surgery
HORS LS18 .... 85 L5
Croft & Tinshall Medical Practice
BHP/TINH LS16 .... 86 A2
Crompton Buckstones
Primary School
ROY/SHW OL2 .... 229 M6
Crompton Cricket Club
ROY/SHW OL2 .... 229 K6
Crompton Health Centre
ROY/SHW OL2 .... 229 K8
Crompton House C of E
High School
ROY/SHW OL2 .... 229 J6
Crompton Swimming Pool
ROY/SHW OL2 .... 229 K8
Crosland Heath Golf Club
HUDS HD4 .... 213 H5
Crosland Moor County Junior School
HUDS HD4 .... 213 L3
Crosland Moor Surgery
HUDS HD4 .... 213 M2
Crossflatts Cricket Club
BGLY BD16 .... 58 F8
Crossflatts First School
BGLY BD16 .... 59 G8
Cross Flatts Park Primary School
BEE/HOL LS11 .... 131 J4
Cross Gates Primary School
MSTN/BAR LS15 .... 111 J4
Cross Green Industrial Estate
OSM LS9 .... 132 C1
Cross Hall Junior & Infant School
MOR LS27 .... 152 B3
Cross Hills Group Practice
AIRE BD20 .... 34 F8
Cross Lane Business Park
LVSG WF15 .... 172 C2
Cross Lane Primary School
ELL HX5 .... 191 G1
Crossley Hall First and Middle
School
GIR BD8 .... 104 A7
Crossley Heath School
HFAX HX1 .... 168 C2
Crossley Retail Park
HFAX HX1 .... 10 E4
Crowlees C of E School
MIRF WF14 .... 194 C1
Crown Court
LDS LS1 .... 6 E8
Crown Point Retail Park
MID LS10 .... 9 H4
Cuckoo Nest Industrial Estate
GTHN BD7 .... 4 A6
Cudworth Churchfield School
CUD/GR S72 .... 244 D7
Cullingworth First School
CUL/QBY BD13 .... 79 M8
Cullingworth Medical Centre
CUL/QBY BD13 .... 79 M8
Cumberworth C of E
First School
KBTN HD8 .... 238 D8
Dalesway Gallery
ILK LS29 .... 38 D2
Dalton Surgery
HUDE HD5 .... 193 G8
Dane Royd Junior &
Infant School
HOR/CROF WF4 .... 220 A4
Dansk Way
ILK LS29 .... 38 E1
Darfield C of E Junior School
WMB/DAR S73 .... 263 K8
Darrington School
PONT WF8 .... 203 M1
Darton High School
DOD/DAR S75 .... 241 K6
Darton Junior & Infant School
DOD/DAR S75 .... 242 B6
Darton Kexborough
Infant School
DOD/DAR S75 .... 241 K6
The Dawes Family Practice
WHIT OL12 .... 206 A6
Deanfield County
Primary School
LUD/ILL HX2 .... 146 A3
Dearne Valley Health Centre
KBTN HD8 .... 239 M5
Deighton Gate Junior &
Infant School
WBY LS22 .... 30 A6
Delf Hill Middle School
LM/WK BD12 .... 126 E8
Delph End Gallery
PDSY/CALV LS28 .... 106 D7
Denby C of E First School
KBTN HD8 .... 257 G3
Denby Dale Industrial Park
KBTN HD8 .... 239 H8
Denholme Clinic
CUL/QBY BD13 .... 101 M5
Denholme First School
CUL/QBY BD13 .... 101 M5
Dental Health Centre
BSLY S70 .... 261 G5
Derby Street Junior &
Infant School
ROCH OL11 .... 228 C1
Dewsbury College
DEWS WF13 .... 173 K5
Dewsbury & District Hospital
DEWS WF13 .... 173 J4

Dewsbury Health Authority
DEWS WF13 .... 173 K6
Dewsbury Moor Infants School
DEWS WF13 .... 173 H4
Dewsbury Sports Centre
EARL WF12 .... 173 M7
Dixon Lane Medical Centre
WOR/ARM LS12 .... 130 E2
Dixons City Technology College
WBOW BD5 .... 127 G2
Dockfield Industrial Estate
BAIL BD17 .... 82 E6
Dodworth C of E School
DOD/DAR S75 .... 260 A8
Dodworth Health Centre
DOD/DAR S75 .... 260 B7
Dodworth Junior School
DOD/DAR S75 .... 260 B7
Doncaster Road Primary School
BSLY S70 .... 261 J6
Drakes Industrial Estate
LUD/ILL HX2 .... 146 C2
Dr Alim Surgery
KGHY BD21 .... 2 F2
Dr Ankers Danks Smith
Sykes & Farrell
BEE/HOL LS11 .... 8 D9
Dr Hindell Surgery
HOLM/MEL HD7 .... 212 B6
Drighlington Junior School
BIRK/DRI BD11 .... 129 H7
Dr K Coley
BFDE BD3 .... 5 J3
Dr Singhs Surgery
HIPP HX3 .... 11 G1
Dr S M Handa Surgery
HUDN HD2 .... 192 D5
Drug Addiction Clinic
LDSU LS2 .... 6 C6
Drummond Middle School
GIR BD8 .... 4 A2
Drummond Trading Estate
GIR BD8 .... 4 C3
Dr Wybrews Surgery
HUD HD1 .... 14 D5
Dudley Hill First School
BOW BD4 .... 127 L3
Durn Street Industrial Estate
LIT OL15 .... 185 L8
Dyneley House Surgery
SKP/WHF BD23 .... 16 C2
Earlsheaton County Infant
School
EARL WF12 .... 174 B7
Earlsheaton High School
EARL WF12 .... 174 A6
East Ardsley Health Centre
EARD/LOFT WF3 .... 153 K7
East Ardsley Infant School
EARD/LOFT WF3 .... 153 M6
East Ardsley Primary School
EARD/LOFT WF3 .... 153 M6
East Ardsley United Cricket &
Athletic Club
EARD/LOFT WF3 .... 153 L4
East Bierley C of E First School
BOW BD4 .... 128 B7
East Bierley Cricket Club
BIRK/DRI BD11 .... 128 A8
Eastborough School
EARL WF12 .... 173 M6
Eastburn Junior & Infant School
AIRE BD20 .... 35 H8
East Crompton St Georges C of E
Primary School
ROY/SHW OL2 .... 229 L7
East Crompton St James
C of E Junior School
ROY/SHW OL2 .... 229 K7
East Garforth County
Primary School
GFTH/SHER LS25 .... 113 K6
East Leeds Clinic
OSM LS9 .... 110 D5
East Leeds Leisure Centre
MSTN/BAR LS15 .... 111 G2
Eastmoor Health Centre
WKFDE WF1 .... 177 M6
East Morton First School
AIRE BD20 .... 58 E6
Eastwood First School
KGHY BD21 .... 3 J2
Eccleshill Clinic & Health Centre
IDLE BD10 .... 83 M8
Eccleshill Cricket Club
IDLE BD10 .... 105 M1
Eccleshill North Middle School
IDLE BD10 .... 84 A8
Eccleshill School
IDLE BD10 .... 106 A1
Eccleshill United Sports Club
ECHL BD2 .... 83 H8
Edward Sheerien School
BSLYN/ROY S71 .... 243 K8
Eldwick First School
BGLY BD16 .... 81 L1
Electronic Theatre
HUD HD1 .... 14 F5
Elizabethan Gallery
WKFDE WF1 .... 12 F2
Elland C of E School
ELL HX5 .... 169 H7
Elland Old Earth School
ELL HX5 .... 169 L7
Elland Road Industrial Park
BEE/HOL LS11 .... 130 F3
Ellen Royde Health Centre
ELL HX5 .... 169 G7
Elmfield Business Park
GFTH/SHER LS25 .... 113 J6
Elmwood Health Centre
HOLM/MEL HD7 .... 236 C7
Elmwood Surgery
MSTN/BAR LS15 .... 90 F7
Emley First School
KBTN HD8 .... 217 M7
Emley Moor Business Park
KBTN HD8 .... 217 K8
Emmanuel Trading Estate
WOR/ARM LS12 .... 8 B3

Empire Business Centre
LUD/ILL HX2 .... 146 C2
English Martyrs School
WKFDW/WTN WF2 .... 197 M1
Environmental Business Centre
MOR LS27 .... 152 C2
Ermysteds Grammar School
SKP/WHF BD23 .... 16 B2
Esholt & Aire Bronians
Sports Club
BAIL BD17 .... 83 K1
Essex Park Industrial Estate
BFDE BD3 .... 5 J8
E T Z Chaim Synagogue
AL/HA/HU LS17 .... 87 M3
Eureka the Museum for Children
HIPP HX3 .... 11 J7
The Eye Clinic
GTHN BD7 .... 4 B7
Fagley First School
ECHL BD2 .... 105 M4
Fairburn County Primary School
KNOT WF11 .... 159 J2
Fairburn Sports &
Recreation Centre
KNOT WF11 .... 159 J2
Fairfield Special School
HECK WF16 .... 173 G1
Fairway Industrial Estate
BTLY WF17 .... 151 H4
Farfield Group Practice
KGHY BD21 .... 2 F1
Farnham First School
GTHN BD7 .... 126 D1
Farnley C of E Primary School
OT LS21 .... 41 L1
Farnley Park High School
WOR/ARM LS12 .... 130 A2
Farrowdale House Preparatory
School
ROY/SHW OL2 .... 229 J8
Farrow Medical Centre
BFDE BD3 .... 5 H3
Farsley Celtic A F C
PDSY/CALV LS28 .... 107 G4
Farsley Community Clinic
PDSY/CALV LS28 .... 106 E3
Farsley Fairfield Primary School
PDSY/CALV LS28 .... 106 D4
Farsley Springbank Junior
School
PDSY/CALV LS28 .... 106 F3
Fartown Health Centre
HUDN HD2 .... 192 C5
Fartown High School
HUDN HD2 .... 192 E4
Fearnville Sports Centre
RHAY LS8 .... 110 F2
Featherbank Infant School
HORS LS18 .... 85 K6
Featherstone High School
FEA/AMT WF7 .... 202 B1
Featherstone Sports Centre
FEA/AMT WF7 .... 202 B2
Felnex Trading Estate
OSM LS9 .... 132 E1
Fernbank Special School
AWLS/ASK DN6 .... 249 L8
Ferniehurst First School
BAIL BD17 .... 82 E4
Ferrybridge Infant School
KNOT WF11 .... 181 L1
Feversham College
BFDE BD3 .... 5 J7
Feversham Street First School
BFDE BD3 .... 5 M6
Fieldhead Carr Primary School
SCFT LS14 .... 89 K5
Fieldhead Doctors
Surgery Clinic
KBTN HD8 .... 238 A6
Field Head Hospital
WKFDE WF1 .... 176 F4
Fieldhead Surgery
HOLM/MEL HD7 .... 212 F1
Fieldhouse Industrial Estate
WHIT OL12 .... 206 B4
Field Lane Infant School
BTLY WF17 .... 173 M2
Firbank County School
ROY/SHW OL2 .... 228 F7
Firgrove Business Park
MILN OL16 .... 206 F6
Fisher Medical Centre
SKP/WHF BD23 .... 16 B2
Fixby Golf Club
HUDN HD2 .... 192 A3
Fixby Junior & Infant School
HUDN HD2 .... 192 C2
Flanshaw Junior &
Infant School
WKFDW/WTN WF2 .... 176 B7
Flockton C of E School
HOR/CROF WF4 .... 217 L3
The Flockton Surgery
HOR/CROF WF4 .... 217 K4
Flower Gallery
BFD BD1 .... 4 F6
Flushdyke Primary School
OSS WF5 .... 175 H7
Follifoot C of E Primary School
PBR HG3 .... 27 M1
Forster Square Retail Park
BFD BD1 .... 4 F4
The Foulstone School
WMB/DAR S73 .... 263 K8
The Fountain Medical Centre
MOR LS27 .... 152 C3
Four Lanes Business Park
GIR BD8 .... 104 B6
Fowler Street Industrial Estate
BOW BD4 .... 127 K1
Foxhill First School
CUL/QBY BD13 .... 124 F4
Friars Industrial Estate
IDLE BD10 .... 83 K7
Friarwood Surgery
PONT WF8 .... 180 F6
Frizinghall First & Middle School
HTON BD9 .... 104 E1

Frizinghall Medical Centre
HTON BD9 .... 104 D2
The Froebelian School
HORS LS18 .... 85 K7
Fulford Grange Hospital
YEA LS19 .... 84 C3
Fulneck School
PDSY/CALV LS28 .... 129 G1
The Gables Surgery
PDSY/CALV LS28 .... 107 J6
The Galleries
EARL WF12 .... 173 L7
The Gallery
KSTL LS5 .... 108 C3
Garforth Clinic
GFTH/SHER LS25 .... 113 G8
Garforth Community College
GFTH/SHER LS25 .... 113 G8
Garforth Green Lane
Primary School
GFTH/SHER LS25 .... 113 K8
Garforth Leisure Centre
GFTH/SHER LS25 .... 113 J7
Garforth Medical Centre
GFTH/SHER LS25 .... 113 G7
Garforth St Benedicts RC
Primary School
GFTH/SHER LS25 .... 113 H6
Garforth Surgery
GFTH/SHER LS25 .... 113 G7
Gateways School
AL/HA/HU LS17 .... 45 J8
Gawber Junior & Infant School
DOD/DAR S75 .... 260 C3
Gawthorpe Primary School
OSS WF5 .... 174 E5
Gawthorpe Surgery
OSS WF5 .... 174 E5
Gelderd Trading Estate
WOR/ARM LS12 .... 131 G1
Gemini Business Park
CHAL LS7 .... 7 J3
General Practice
LDSU LS2 .... 6 C6
Ghyll Royd School
ILK LS29 .... 38 B3
Gibson Lane Junior School
GFTH/SHER LS25 .... 135 K5
Gildersome Birchfield
Primary School
MOR LS27 .... 129 K8
Gildersome Junior School
MOR LS27 .... 129 L7
Gilstead Middle School
BGLY BD16 .... 81 L2
Gilthwaites First School
KBTN HD8 .... 239 J7
Girlington First School
GIR BD8 .... 104 C5
Girlington Industrial Centre
GIR BD8 .... 104 B6
Girls High School
SKP/WHF BD23 .... 16 A2
Girnhill Infant School
FEA/AMT WF7 .... 201 L2
Glasshoughton First School
CAS WF10 .... 158 A7
The Gleddings School
HIPP HX3 .... 168 C3
Gledholt Business Park
HUD HD1 .... 14 A8
Gledhow County Primary School
RHAY LS8 .... 88 A6
Glenaire First School
BAIL BD17 .... 82 C4
Gleniea Surgery
PDSY/CALV LS28 .... 107 H4
Glenrhydding Gallery
OT LS21 .... 41 J7
Glusburn Cp School
AIRE BD20 .... 34 E8
Goddard Wybor Practice
RHAY LS8 .... 88 A7
Golden Mosque
WHIT OL12 .... 206 A6
Golf Club Bungalow
CLAY BD14 .... 125 M3
Gomersal C of E Middle School
CLECK BD19 .... 150 E5
The Good Health Centre
RHAY LS8 .... 88 C4
Gordon Street Junior &
Infant School
FEA/AMT WF7 .... 179 M7
Gorrells Industrial Estate
ROCH OL11 .... 228 A3
Grafton Special School
HDGY LS6 .... 6 F2
Grand Theatre & Opera House
LDSU LS2 .... 7 G8
Grangefield Industrial Estate
PDSY/CALV LS28 .... 107 H5
Grange Gate Junior School
BSLYN/ROY S71 .... 262 A4
Grange Lane Industrial Estate
BSLYN/ROY S71 .... 262 A6
The Grange Medical Centre
SCFT LS14 .... 111 K1
Grange Middle School
AIRE BD20 .... 58 A5
Grange Park Surgery
ILK LS29 .... 40 B5
Grange Road Business Park
BTLY WF17 .... 174 A2
Grange Road Industrial Estate
BTLY WF17 .... 174 A2
Grange Surgery
EARL WF12 .... 174 C7
Grange Upper School
WBOW BD5 .... 126 D4
Great Horton Cricket Club
GTHN BD7 .... 126 C3
Great Horton Industrial Estate
WBSY BD6 .... 125 M4
Great Horton Middle School
GTHN BD7 .... 126 C2
Great & Little Preston C of E
Infant School
RTHW LS26 .... 135 G7

Great & Little Preston
Primary School
CAS WF10 .... 135 H7
Great & Little Preston
Primary School
RTHW LS26 .... 135 G7
Great Northern Retail Park
HUD HD1 .... 15 H4
Greatwood Primary School
SKP/WHF BD23 .... 16 C3
Greenbank Cp School
WHIT OL12 .... 206 B5
Greenfield School
IDLE BD10 .... 83 K5
Greengates First School
IDLE BD10 .... 84 A7
Greenhead College
HUD HD1 .... 14 C7
Greenhead Grammar School
AIRE BD20 .... 57 J4
Greenhill Cp School
BRAM LS13 .... 107 M6
Green Leas School
PONT WF8 .... 203 G1
Green Meadows School
GSLY LS20 .... 61 L5
Greenmount School
BEE/HOL LS11 .... 8 E9
Greetland Cricket &
Bowling Club
GTL/HWG HX4 .... 168 C2
Greetland Junior & Infant School
GTL/HWG HX4 .... 168 C7
Greetland Mixed School
GTL/HWG HX4 .... 168 C7
Gregory Middle School
WBOW BD5 .... 127 J3
Grimethorpe Hall
CUD/GR S72 .... 245 H6
Grimethorpe Ladywood First
School
CUD/GR S72 .... 245 K8
Group Surgery
OSS WF5 .... 174 F8
Grove House First School
ECHL BD2 .... 105 J2
Grove House Surgery
BTLY WF17 .... 173 M1
Grove Mills Industrial Estate
ELL HX5 .... 169 J7
Grove Street Junior & Infant
School
BSLYN/ROY S71 .... 261 J5
Guiseley A F C
GSLY LS20 .... 61 L5
Guiseley County Infant School
GSLY LS20 .... 62 A5
Guiseley School
GSLY LS20 .... 61 M6
Gulsyke Medical Centre
MSTN/BAR LS15 .... 111 J7
Gunthwaite Hall
STKB/PEN S36 .... 257 K4
Hade Edge Primary School
HOLM/MEL HD7 .... 254 D6
Haggs Business Park
PBR HG3 .... 27 M3
Haigh Hall Medical Centre
IDLE BD10 .... 83 M7
Haigh Hospital Lodge
RTHW LS26 .... 133 G8
Hainsworth Moor Junior &
Infant School
CUL/OBY BD13 .... 124 F6
Halal Mosque
HUD HD1 .... 214 B2
Half Acres J & I School
CAS WF10 .... 157 L7
Halfpenny Lane Junior &
Infant School
PONT WF8 .... 180 C6
Halifax Catholic High School
LUD/ILL HX2 .... 124 C8
Halifax General Hospital
HIPP HX3 .... 168 E3
Halifax High School
HFAX HX1 .... 11 G8
Halifax Industrial Centre
HFAX HX1 .... 10 D4
Halifax Leisure Centre
HFAX HX1 .... 11 H7
Halifax Rugby Union Football
Club
LUD/ILL HX2 .... 146 B2
Halifax Swimming Pool
HFAX HX1 .... 11 H8
Halifax Town FC
HFAX HX1 .... 11 H9
Hall Bower Athletic Club
HUDS HD4 .... 214 D5
Hall Bower Cricket Club
HUDS HD4 .... 214 D5
Halton Building
GTHN BD7 .... 4 B7
Hambledon First School
BOW BD4 .... 127 K6
Hanging Heaton C of E School
BTLY WF17 .... 174 B3
Hanson Upper School
ECHL BD2 .... 105 H2
Harambee Surgery
COL BB8 .... 74 D3
Harden First School
BGLY BD16 .... 80 C5
Harehills Middle School
RHAY LS8 .... 110 B3
Harehills Primary School
RHAY LS8 .... 110 C3
Harewood C of E Primary School
AL/HA/HU LS17 .... 45 J7
Harewood House
AL/HA/HU LS17 .... 45 G8
Hartington Middle School
HWTH BD22 .... 78 E7
Hartshead Junior & Infant School
LVSG WF15 .... 171 L4
Hatfield Hall Golf Club
EARD/LOFT WF3 .... 177 G3
Havercroft Health Centre
HOR/CROF WF4 .... 222 D6

Havercroft Junior &
Infant School
HOR/CROF WF4 .... 222 D6
Hawkins Clinic
MILN OL16 .... 206 B7
Hawksworth C of E School
GSLY LS20 .... 61 G6
Hawksworth Cp School
KSTL LS5 .... 86 A7
Haworth Junior & Infant School
HWTH BD22 .... 78 E7
Haycliffe Special School
WBSY BD6 .... 126 D4
Headfield Junior & Infant School
EARL WF12 .... 195 L1
Headingley Primary School
HDGY LS6 .... 108 F1
Headlands C of E (C) J I & N
School
WKFDE WF15 .... 172 C2
Headway Business Park
WKFDW/WTN WF2 .... 12 D9
Healey Junior School
BTLY WF17 .... 173 H1
Healey Primary School
WHIT OL12 .... 206 A3
Healey Surgery
WHIT OL12 .... 206 A3
Heather Grove First School
HTON BD9 .... 103 M3
Heathfield Industrial Estate
ELL HX5 .... 169 J8
Heath House Surgery
HFAX HX1 .... 168 E2
Heath View Middle School
WKFDE WF1 .... 13 K1
Heaton Middle School
HTON BD9 .... 103 M2
Heaton Royds Hospital
HTON BD9 .... 103 M1
Heaton Royds Special School
SHPY BD18 .... 104 C1
Hebble Brook Business Park
LUD/ILL HX2 .... 123 L7
Hebden Bridge Health Centre
HBR HX7 .... 143 J3
Hebden Royd Cragg Vale
County Primary School
HBR HX7 .... 165 L3
Hebden Royd Primary School
HBR HX7 .... 143 G2
Heckmondike Mosque
HECK WF16 .... 172 G2
Heckmondwike Grammar
School
HECK WF16 .... 172 F2
Heckmondwike Sports Club
HECK WF16 .... 172 F2
Helme C of E Junior &
Infant School
HOLM/MEL HD7 .... 234 F2
Hemsworth Fitzwilliam School
HEM/SK/SE WF9 .... 223 K2
Hemsworth Grove Lea
Junior & Infant School
HEM/SK/SE WF9 .... 223 M7
Hemsworth R U F C
HEM/SK/SE WF9 .... 224 B7
Hemsworth Town Council
HEM/SK/SE WF9 .... 223 M7
Henry Moore Clinic
CAS WF10 .... 157 M7
Henry Moore Junior School
CAS WF10 .... 157 M8
Heponstall County
Primary School
HBR HX7 .... 143 H1
Hepworth Junior & Infant
School
HOLM/MEL HD7 .... 255 G5
Hewiston Surgery
HUDW HD3 .... 191 M7
Heybrook CP School
WHIT OL12 .... 206 C5
Highbank First School
LVSG WF15 .... 171 K1
High Burton Junior & Infant
School
KBTN HD8 .... 216 A6
Highcliffe Industrial Estate
MOR LS27 .... 152 B1
High Crags First School
SHPY BD18 .... 82 E8
High Crompton St Marys C of E
School
ROY/SHW OL2 .... 229 H6
High Fernley First School
LM/WK BD12 .... 148 E3
Highfield County Primary School
AL/HA/HU LS17 .... 88 A2
Highfield Middle School
KGHY BD21 .... 2 D1
Highfield School
OSS WF5 .... 174 F5
The Highfields Medical Centre
BRAM LS13 .... 107 M2
Highfields School
HUD HD1 .... 14 D4
Highfields Special School
HUD HD1 .... 14 D4
Highfield Surgery
BHP/TINH LS16 .... 86 A1
Highlander Sports Centre
KBTN HD8 .... 216 D3
High Royds Hospital
ILK LS29 .... 61 J3
High Street Surgery
NORM WF6 .... 178 D4
High Trees School
BSPA/BRAM LS23 .... 49 G8
Hill Brow Surgery
DOD/DAR S75 .... 242 C5
Hillcrest Primary School
CHAL LS7 .... 7 M1
Hillfoot Surgery
PDSY/CALV LS28 .... 106 D1
Hill Top C of E First School
LM/WK BD12 .... 126 E8

Hill Top Infant School
EARD/LOFT WF3 .... 174 F1
Hinchliffe Mill County School
HOLM/MEL HD7 .... 253 L4
Hindu Temple
HUD HD1 .... 15 G8
Hipperholme Clinic
HIPP HX3 .... 147 M6
Hipperholme Grammar School
HIPP HX3 .... 147 L6
Hipperholme & Lightcliffe
High School
HIPP HX3 .... 148 B7
Hm Young Offender Institution
WBY LS22 .... 30 D7
Holgate School
BSLY S70 .... 260 E5
Hollies Surgery
HECK WF16 .... 172 F2
Hollingwood First School
GTHN BD7 .... 126 A3
Hollybank Natural Health Centre
HUDW HD3 .... 191 K5
Holly Bank Surgery
HDGY LS6 .... 86 F8
Hollywood Bowl
BULY LS4 .... 108 F5
Holmefield First School
BOW BD4 .... 128 B2
Holme Middle School
BOW BD4 .... 127 M3
Holme School
HOLM/MEL HD7 .... 253 G5
Holme Valley Clinic
HOLM/MEL HD7 .... 236 B1
Holme Wood Health Centre
BOW BD4 .... 128 A3
Holmfirth Craft Market
HOLM/MEL HD7 .... 254 B1
Holmfirth Secondary School
HOLM/MEL HD7 .... 236 E6
Holmfirth Swimming Pool
HOLM/MEL HD7 .... 236 D7
Holycroft First School
KGHY BD21 .... 2 E7
Holy Cross Deanery C of E
Junior & Infant School
BSLYN/ROY S71 .... 243 K8
Holy Family Primary School
ROCH OL11 .... 228 C3
Holy Family RC School
PONT WF8 .... 181 J5
Holy Family RC School
WOR/ARM LS12 .... 108 F7
Holy Family School
KGHY BD21 .... 2 D1
Holy Name RC School
BHP/TINH LS16 .... 86 B3
Holyrood RC Junior &
Infant School
BSLY S70 .... 260 F6
Holy Rosary & St Annes RC
Primary School
CHAL LS7 .... 7 K3
Holy Trinity C of E First School
BGLY BD16 .... 81 J4
Holy Trinity C of E Primary
School
BHP/TINH LS16 .... 85 M1
Holy Trinity C of E School
OSS WF5 .... 174 F8
Holy Trinity C of E Senior School
LUD/ILL HX2 .... 124 B8
Holy Trinity Infant School
HFAX HX1 .... 10 E8
Holy Trinity Junior School
HFAX HX1 .... 10 E8
Holywell Green School
GTL/HWG HX4 .... 190 D2
Homestead Clinic
WKFDW/WTN WF2 .... 176 B8
Honley Business Centre
HOLM/MEL HD7 .... 236 C2
Honley C of E Infant School
HOLM/MEL HD7 .... 236 D2
Honley C of E Junior School
HOLM/MEL HD7 .... 236 D2
Honley High School & Sixth
Form School
HOLM/MEL HD7 .... 236 C1
Hopton County Primary School
MIRF WF14 .... 194 B2
Hopwood Hall College
WHIT OL12 .... 206 A7
Horbury Junction Industrial
Estate
HOR/CROF WF4 .... 197 L6
Horbury Junior School
HOR/CROF WF4 .... 197 L5
Horbury School
HOR/CROF WF4 .... 197 L5
Horsforth Hall Park Cricket Club
HORS LS18 .... 86 A6
Horsforth Newlaithes Junior
School
HORS LS18 .... 85 J8
Horsforth St Margarets C of E
Primary School
HORS LS18 .... 85 K5
Horsforth School & Further
Education Centre
HORS LS18 .... 85 K4
Horsforth Village Museum
HORS LS18 .... 85 J6
Horsforth Woodside C of E
Primary School
HORS LS18 .... 85 M5
Horton Bank Top First School
GTHN BD7 .... 126 A4
Horton Bank Top Surgery
GTHN BD7 .... 125 M4
Horton Park First School
WBOW BD5 .... 126 D2
Hothfield Street Junior School
AIRE BD20 .... 35 M5
Hot Shots Ten Pin Bowl & Bar
HUD HD1 .... 14 E9
Hovingham Primary School
RHAY LS8 .... 110 C2

Howden Clough
Industrial Estate
BTLY WF17 .... 151 K3
Howley Hall Golf Club
MOR LS27 .... 152 A7
Hoyers Industrial Estate
HUD HD1 .... 192 F5
Hoyle Court First School
BAIL BD17 .... 83 G3
Huddersfield Golf Club
HUDN HD2 .... 192 A3
Huddersfield Lawn Tennis &
Squash Club
HUD HD1 .... 14 C4
Huddersfield New College
HUDW HD3 .... 191 G7
Huddersfield Rugby Union
Football Club
HUDS HD4 .... 214 A4
Huddersfield Sports Centre
HUD HD1 .... 15 G6
Huddersfield Technical College
HOLM/MEL HD7 .... 236 C8
Huddersfield Technical College
HUD HD1 .... 14 E6
Huddersfield Technical College
HUDN HD2 .... 192 F4
Huddersfield Technical College
HUDS HD4 .... 214 B4
Huddersfield Town A F C Ltd
HUDE HD5 .... 15 K3
Huddersfield University
HUD HD1 .... 15 G6
Huddersfield University Annexe
HUD HD1 .... 14 D4
Hudds School of Theatre
HUDS HD4 .... 214 A6
Hugh Gaitskell Middle School
BEE/HOL LS11 .... 131 G4
Hugh Gaitskell Primary School
BEE/HOL LS11 .... 131 G4
Hungate County Primary
School
GFTH/SHER LS25 .... 116 A6
Hunningley Junior &
Infant School
BSLY S70 .... 262 A7
Hunslet Carr CP School
MID LS10 .... 132 A4
Hunslet C of E Primary School
MID LS10 .... 9 L9
Hunslet Health Centre
MID LS10 .... 9 M8
Hunslet Moor Primary School
BEE/HOL LS11 .... 9 G9
Hunslet St Josephs Primary
School
MID LS10 .... 9 L7
Hunslet Trading Estate
MID LS10 .... 132 B2
Hutton Junior & Infant School
IDLE BD10 .... 105 L1
Hutton Middle School
ECHL BD2 .... 105 L1
Hyde Park Picture House
HDGY LS6 .... 109 G3
Hyrstmount Junior School
BTLY WF17 .... 173 L3
Ida & Robert Arthington
Hospital
BHP/TINH LS16 .... 86 A4
Idle C of E School
IDLE BD10 .... 83 K5
Idle Cricket Club
IDLE BD10 .... 83 K7
Idle Medical Centre
IDLE BD10 .... 83 K6
Ilkley Grammar School
ILK LS29 .... 38 E3
Ilkley Health Centre
ILK LS29 .... 38 E3
Ilkley Middle School
ILK LS29 .... 39 G2
Ilkley Swimming Baths
ILK LS29 .... 38 D1
Immaculate Heart of Mary RC
Primary School
AL/HA/HU LS17 .... 87 L5
Industrial Estate
HEM/SK/SE WF9 .... 246 F4
Ingfield Business Centre
HUDN HD2 .... 193 G3
Inglebrook School
PONT WF8 .... 180 F5
Ingram Road Primary School
BEE/HOL LS11 .... 8 A6
Ingrow First & Infant School
HWTH BD22 .... 79 J2
Inland Revenue Office
BFD BD1 .... 4 F5
Intake High School
BRAM LS13 .... 107 J2
Ireland Wood County Primary
School
BHP/TINH LS16 .... 86 C2
Islamia Girls High School
HUD HD1 .... 214 A2
Iveson Primary School
BHP/TINH LS16 .... 86 C2
Jacksons Estate
OSS WF5 .... 175 G2
Jalalia Mosque
MILN OL16 .... 206 C4
Jamia Islamia Mosque
GTHN BD7 .... 126 D2
Jawbone Industrial Estate
RTHW LS26 .... 132 D7
Jerry Clay Lane Junior & Infant
School
WKFDW/WTN WF2 .... 175 M4
Joe Dean Recreation Centre
WOR/ARM LS12 .... 108 F2
John Jamieson Special School
RHAY LS8 .... 110 E1
John O Gaunts Trading Estate
RTHW LS26 .... 133 G2
John Smeaton School
MSTN/BAR LS15 .... 112 A3
John Smeaton Sports Centre
MSTN/BAR LS15 .... 112 A2

John Street Market
 BFD BD1 .... 4 E5
Joseph Priestley College
 MOR LS27 .... 152 D2
Kayes First School
 KBTN HD8 .... 240 B4
Keelham First School
 CUL/QBY BD13 .... 124 B1
Keighley Business Centre
 KGHY BD21 .... 2 F8
Keighley College
 KGHY BD21 .... 3 K3
Keighley College
 KGHY BD21 .... 3 G4
Keighley Cricket Club
 KGHY BD21 .... 3 H1
Keighley Industrial Park
 KGHY BD21 .... 57 L5
Keighley Leisure Centre
 KGHY BD21 .... 3 J2
Keighley Rugby Union
 Football Club
 AIRE BD20 .... 57 H3
Kelbrook Primary School
 BWCK/EAR BB18 .... 52 C1
Kendray Hospital
 BSLY S70 .... 261 L6
Kendray Infant School
 BSLY S70 .... 261 L7
Kendray Primary School
 BSLY S70 .... 261 K7
Kensington Street
 Health Centre
 GIR BD8 .... 104 C6
Kents Sports Club
 ECHL BD2 .... 105 K2
Keresforth Primary School
 DOD/DAR S75 .... 260 C8
Kermackie Primary School
 RHAY LS8 .... 88 C7
Kershaw Drive Health Centre
 LUD/ILL HX2 .... 144 F6
Kettlethorpe High School
 WKFDW/WTN WF2 ...... 198 E8
Kexborough Junior School
 DOD/DAR S75 .... 241 K6
Kildwick C of E Primary School
 AIRE BD20 .... 35 G6
Killinghall First School
 BFDE BD3 .... 105 L5
Kilmeny Surgery
 HWTH BD22 .... 79 J2
Kiln Hill Industrial Estate
 HOLM/MEL HD7 .... 212 C6
King James's School
 HUDS HD4 .... 215 J4
Kings Cross Surgery
 HFAX HX1 .... 10 C9
Kingsdale Shopping Centre
 HUD HD1 .... 15 H7
Kings High School
 PONT WF8 .... 180 E7
Kingsway West Business Park
 MILN OL16 .... 228 E1
Kingsway West Business Park
 ROCH OL11 .... 228 C1
Kingswear Galleries
 MSTN/BAR LS15 .... 111 M5
Kinsley Industrial Estate
 HEM/SK/SE WF9 .... 223 L5
Kippax Greenfield Primary
 School
 GFTH/SHER LS25 .... 135 J4
Kippax Hall Surgery
 GFTH/SHER LS25 .... 135 K5
Kippax Health Centre
 GFTH/SHER LS25 .... 135 K4
Kippax Infant School
 GFTH/SHER LS25 .... 135 J5
Kippax Leisure Centre
 GFTH/SHER LS25 .... 135 H6
Kippax North Junior & Infant
 School
 GFTH/SHER LS25 .... 135 H2
Kirkburton C of E (A) School
 KBTN HD8 .... 216 B1
Kirkburton Cricket Club
 KBTN HD8 .... 216 B8
Kirkburton Middle School
 KBTN HD8 .... 216 C2
Kirkby Overblow C of E Primary
 School
 PBR HG3 .... 27 J7
Kirk Fenton C of E Primary
 School
 TAD LS24 .... 94 E7
Kirkfields Business Centre
 YEA LS19 .... 62 C7
Kirkgate Business Centre
 WKFDE WF1 .... 13 H5
Kirkgate Market
 LDS LS1 .... 7 H9
Kirkgate Shopping
 Centre & Market
 BFD BD1 .... 4 E6
Kirkgate Surgery
 BTLY WF17 .... 150 F5
Kirkhamgate Junior &
 Infant School
 WKFDW/WTN WF2 ...... 175 K4
Kirkheaton County Junior &
 Infant School
 HUDE HD5 .... 193 K5
Kirkheaton Cricket &
 Bowling Club
 HUDE HD5 .... 193 K5
Kirkheaton Surgery
 HUDE HD5 .... 193 M4
Kirklees Metropolitan Council
 BTLY WF17 .... 173 K1
Kirklees Metropolitan Council
 DEWS WF13 .... 173 G8
Kirklees Metropolitan Council
 DEWS WF13 .... 173 L6
Kirklees Metropolitan Council
 HECK WF16 .... 172 E3
Kirklees Metropolitan Council
 MIRF WF14 .... 194 C1
Kirklees Open Market
 HUD HD1 .... 14 F5

Kirkroyd Infant School
 HOLM/MEL HD7 .... 236 F7
Kirk Smeaton C of E
 Primary School
 PONT WF8 .... 204 F8
Kirkstall Health Clinic
 KSTL LS5 .... 108 C2
Kirkstall Industrial Park
 BULY LS4 .... 108 F5
Kirkstall Leisure Centre
 KSTL LS5 .... 108 C2
Kirkstall St Stephens C of E
 School
 KSTL LS5 .... 108 C2
Kirkstall Valley Primary School
 BULY LS4 .... 108 E4
Kitchen Surgery
 KNOT WF11 .... 182 D2
Knottingley C of E (C)
 Junior & Infant School
 KNOT WF11 .... 182 C2
Knowle Spring Industrial Estate
 KGHY BD21 .... 2 F8
La Bowl
 BEE/HOL LS11 .... 8 E4
Ladderbank Middle School
 BAIL BD17 .... 83 C2
Lady Elizabeth Hastings
 C of E School
 BSPA/BRAM LS23 .... 49 G5
Lady Elizabeth Hastings C of E School
 WBY LS22 .... 47 J5
Lady Lane Park School
 BGLY BD16 .... 81 J1
Laisterdyke Clinic
 BFDE BD3 .... 105 M7
Laisterdyke Middle School
 BFDE BD3 .... 105 M7
Lakeside Industrial Estate
 WOR/ARM LS12 .... 108 A7
Laneshawbridge CP School
 COL BB8 .... 52 F8
Langdale Primary School
 RTHW LS26 .... 133 K7
Lapage Middle School
 BFDE BD3 .... 105 L6
Lascelles Hall Cricket Club
 HUDE HD5 .... 215 L1
Latchmore Industrial Park
 WOR/ARM LS12 .... 130 E3
Latchmore Industrial Park
 WOR/ARM LS12 .... 131 G2
Laura Mitchell Health Centre
 HFAX HX1 .... 11 G5
Laurel Bank Surgery
 HDGY LS6 .... 108 E2
Law Courts
 BFD BD1 .... 5 G7
Lawefield First School
 WKFDW/WTN WF2 .... 12 B4
Lawns Park Primary School
 WOR/ARM LS12 .... 130 A1
Lawnswood Business Park
 BHP/TINH LS16 .... 86 B5
Lawnswood School
 BHP/TINH LS16 .... 86 D6
Lawrence Batley Theatre
 HUD HD1 .... 15 G7
Laycock First School
 HWTH BD22 .... 56 E7
L C Museum
 LDS LS1 .... 9 G2
Leaventhorpe Middle School
 WIL/AL BD15 .... 103 K7
Leeds Area Health Authority
 HDGY LS6 .... 6 C2
Leeds Area Health Authority
 LDSU LS2 .... 7 H8
Leeds Area Health Authority
 MID LS10 .... 9 M8
Leeds Area Health Authority
 MOR LS27 .... 129 L7
Leeds Bradford International
 Airport
 YEA LS19 .... 63 H7
The Leeds Business Centre
 MOR LS27 .... 152 A2
Leeds City Art Gallery
 LDS LS1 .... 6 F8
Leeds City Council
 AL/HA/HU LS17 .... 88 B3
Leeds City Council
 BEE/HOL LS11 .... 8 C2
Leeds City Council
 BEE/HOL LS11 .... 8 D7
Leeds City Council
 BEE/HOL LS11 .... 131 K6
Leeds City Council
 BRAM LS13 .... 107 M3
Leeds City Council
 CHAL LS7 .... 109 L2
Leeds City Council
 GFTH/SHER LS25 .... 113 G7
Leeds City Council
 HDGY LS6 .... 6 F2
Leeds City Council
 KSTL LS5 .... 108 C2
Leeds City Council
 LDS LS1 .... 6 F8
Leeds City Council
 LDS LS1 .... 8 E1
Leeds City Council
 LDSU LS2 .... 7 G8
Leeds City Council
 MID LS10 .... 9 K4
Leeds City Council
 MID LS10 .... 9 L8
Leeds City Council
 MID LS10 .... 9 L5
Leeds City Council
 OSM LS9 .... 110 B6
Leeds City Council
 OSM LS9 .... 110 C6
Leeds City Council
 OSM LS9 .... 132 D1
Leeds City Council
 OT LS21 .... 41 J6
Leeds City Council
 PDSY/CALV LS28 .... 107 H4

Leeds City Council
 PDSY/CALV LS28 .... 107 G7
Leeds City Council
 PDSY/CALV LS28 .... 107 G6
Leeds City Council
 RHAY LS8 .... 7 L4
Leeds City Council
 RTHW LS26 .... 155 G1
Leeds City Council
 SCFT LS14 .... 89 J8
Leeds City Council
 SCFT LS14 .... 89 K8
Leeds City Council
 SCFT LS14 .... 111 J2
Leeds City Council
 SCFT LS14 .... 111 G5
Leeds City Council
 WBY LS22 .... 48 A1
Leeds City Council
 WOR/ARM LS12 .... 129 M1
Leeds City Council
 YEA LS19 .... 84 D2
Leeds City Council
 YEA LS19 .... 84 D1
Leeds City Museum
 LDS LS1 .... 6 F8
Leeds Civic Theatre
 LDSU LS2 .... 6 F7
Leeds College of Art & Design
 LDSU LS2 .... 6 F7
Leeds College of Art & Design
 LDSU LS2 .... 6 E4
Leeds College of Building
 LDSU LS2 .... 7 J7
Leeds College of Technology
 BEE/HOL LS11 .... 131 J6
Leeds College of Technology
 OSM LS9 .... 9 L2
Leeds Community &
 Mental Health Services
 PDSY/CALV LS28 .... 107 G7
Leeds Community &
 Mental Health Services
 Teaching NHS Trust
 HDGY LS6 .... 6 A5
Leeds Community &
 Mental Health Services
 Teaching NHS Trust
 OSS WF5 .... 175 G8
Leeds County Council
 WOR/ARM LS12 .... 109 G8
Leeds County Council
 WOR/ARM LS12 .... 108 E7
Leeds & District Workpeoples
 Hospital Fund
 LDS LS1 .... 6 E9
Leeds General Infirmary
 LDSU LS2 .... 6 D7
Leeds Girls High School
 HDGY LS6 .... 6 A1
Leeds Grammar School
 AL/HA/HU LS17 .... 66 B7
Leeds Grammar School
 HDGY LS6 .... 6 B5
Leeds Health Authority
 LDS LS1 .... 6 C9
Leeds Health Authority
 MOR LS27 .... 152 D2
Leeds Hospital Fund
 LDS LS1 .... 6 E9
Leeds & Hull Business Centre
 LDSU LS2 .... 6 E5
Leeds Industrial Museum
 WOR/ARM LS12 .... 108 E6
Leeds International Swimming
 Pool
 LDS LS1 .... 6 D9
Leeds Metropolitan University
 HDGY LS6 .... 86 D8
Leeds Metropolitan University
 KSTL LS5 .... 108 B2
Leeds Metropolitan University
 LDSU LS2 .... 6 E6
Leeds Metropolitan University
 LDSU LS2 .... 7 G7
Leeds Mosque
 HDGY LS6 .... 6 A5
Leeds Road Hospital
 BFDE BD3 .... 5 L6
Leeds Road Retail Park
 HUD HD1 .... 15 L2
Leeds Rugby Union
 Football Club
 RHAY LS8 .... 88 A6
Leeds Shopping Plaza
 LDS LS1 .... 9 G4
The Leeds Teaching
 Hospitals N H S Trust
 BVRD LS3 .... 6 D8
Leeds Twenty-Seven
 Industrial Estate
 MOR LS27 .... 152 A4
Leeds United A F C
 BEE/HOL LS11 .... 131 G3
Leeds University
 BHP/TINH LS16 .... 86 E5
Leeds University
 LDSU LS2 .... 6 E6
Lee Mount County Primary
 School
 HIPP HX3 .... 10 C2
Lees First School
 HWTH BD22 .... 79 G6
Leopold Primary
 CHAL LS7 .... 7 L3
Lepton Surgery
 KBTN HD8 .... 216 A3
Lidget Green First School
 GTHN BD7 .... 104 B8
Lidget Green Middle School
 GTHN BD7 .... 104 B8
Lightcliffe C of E Primary School
 HIPP HX3 .... 148 A7
Lightcliffe Preparatory School
 HIPP HX3 .... 147 M6
Light Waves Sports Centre
 WKFDE WF1 .... 12 F1
Lilycroft First School
 HTON BD9 .... 104 D4
Lindley C of E Infant School
 HUDN HD3 .... 191 K5

The Lindley Group Practice
 HUDW HD3 .... 191 K6
Lindley Junior School
 HUDN HD3 .... 191 K5
The Lindley Village Surgery
 HUDN HD3 .... 191 K5
Linguard Business Park
 ROCH OL11 .... 206 D2
Lingwell Croft Surgery
 MID LS10 .... 153 M1
Linthwaite Business Centre
 HOLM/MEL HD7 .... 212 F5
Linthwaite C of E Junior & Infant
 School
 HOLM/MEL HD7 .... 213 G1
Littleborough CP School
 LIT OL15 .... 185 K7
Littleborough Cricket Club
 LIT OL15 .... 185 K8
Little London CP School
 CHAL LS7 .... 7 H4
Littlemoor County Primary School
 YEA LS19 .... 84 E2
Littlemoor Mills Business Park
 HUD HD1 .... 214 C2
Little Theatre
 HBR HX7 .... 143 J3
Little Theatre
 SKP/WHF BD23 .... 16 B3
Little Town Junior & Infant
 School
 CLECK BD19 .... 172 C1
Littleworth Lane Infant School
 BSLYN/ROY S71 .... 261 M3
Liversedge Cricket Club
 LVSG WF15 .... 172 B4
Lockwood Surgery
 HUDS HD4 .... 214 B3
Lofthouse Gate Junior &
 Infant School
 EARD/LOFT WF3 .... 154 E7
Lofthouse Surgery
 EARD/LOFT WF3 .... 154 E6
Longcar Junior & Infant School
 BSLY S70 .... 260 F6
Longlands Trading Estate
 OSS WF5 .... 175 G8
Long Lee Junior & Infant School
 KGHY BD21 .... 3 M8
Long Lee Surgery
 KGHY BD21 .... 3 M8
Longley Park Golf Club
 HUD HD1 .... 15 J9
Longley School
 HUDE HD5 .... 214 E2
Longley Tennis Club
 HUDE HD5 .... 214 F2
Long Marston C of E
 Primary School
 RYKW YO26 .... 33 J3
Longroyde Junior School
 BRIG HD6 .... 170 B5
Longroyde Surgery
 BRIG HD6 .... 170 B5
Lord Chancellors Department
 LDS LS1 .... 6 D9
Lorne First School
 BOW BD4 .... 127 K2
Lotherton Hall
 GFTH/SHER LS25 .... 114 D1
Low Ash First School
 SHPY BD18 .... 82 F8
Lowerfields Middle School
 BOW BD4 .... 127 L2
Lower Grange Medical Centre
 GIR BD8 .... 103 L7
Lowerhouses C of E School
 HUDE HD5 .... 214 F2
Lower Place School
 MILN OL16 .... 228 D2
Lower Wortley CP School
 WOR/ARM LS12 .... 130 D1
Low Moor C of E First School
 LM/WK BD12 .... 126 F8
Low Road Primary School
 MID LS10 .... 9 M8
Lowtown Primary School
 PDSY/CALV LS28 .... 107 H7
Luddendenfoot Junior &
 Infant School
 LUD/ILL HX2 .... 167 G1
Luddenden Primary School
 LUD/ILL HX2 .... 144 F6
Lundwood Medical Centre
 BSLYN/ROY S71 .... 261 M4
Lupset Group Medical Centre
 WKFDW/WTN WF2 ...... 197 M3
Lydgate Junior & Infant School
 BTLY WF17 .... 174 B1
Lynfield Mount Hospital
 HTON BD9 .... 103 M4
Mackie Hill Junior & Infant
 School
 HOR/CROF WF4 .... 219 M2
Madni Muslim Girls School
 EARL WF12 .... 173 M8
Magnet Sports Club
 TAD LS24 .... 71 L4
Malsis School
 AIRE BD20 .... 34 B8
Mandale Middle School
 WBSY BD6 .... 125 M6
Manningham Baths &
 Sports Centre
 GIR BD8 .... 104 D5
Manningham Clinic
 GIR BD8 .... 4 C1
Manningham Middle School
 GIR BD8 .... 4 C2
Manor Leisure Centre
 YEA LS19 .... 62 C7
Manor Park Industrial Estate
 BIRK/DRI BD11 .... 129 G7
Manor Park Surgery
 BRAM LS13 .... 107 L3
Manston C of E School
 MSTN/BAR LS15 .... 111 M3
Manston Primary School
 MSTN/BAR LS15 .... 111 L3

Maple Industrial Estate
 DOD/DAR S75 .... 242 F6
Mapplewell Health Centre
 DOD/DAR S75 .... 242 D6
Margaret Mcmillan First School
 HTON BD9 .... 104 C4
Margram Business Centre
 HFAX HX1 .... 10 E4
Markazi Mosque
 EARL WF12 .... 173 M8
Market Cross Surgery
 RTHW LS26 .... 155 G1
Market Hall
 COL BB8 .... 74 A1
Mark Street Surgery
 WHIT OL12 .... 206 D5
Marsden County Junior School
 HOLM/MEL HD7 .... 233 J2
Marsden Health Centre
 HOLM/MEL HD7 .... 233 H2
Marsden Infant School
 HOLM/MEL HD7 .... 233 J2
Marshfield First School
 WBOW BD5 .... 126 E3
Masjidomar Mosque
 HUDN HD2 .... 14 D2
Masonic Temple
 DEWS WF13 .... 173 L5
Masonic Temple
 MOR LS27 .... 152 A4
Matthew Murray High School
 BEE/HOL LS11 .... 8 A7
Maybrook Industrial Park
 WOR/ARM LS12 .... 8 A1
Maybush Surgery
 WKFDE WF1 .... 13 G8
Mayfield Surgery
 HDGY LS6 .... 108 F4
Meanwood C of E School
 HDGY LS6 .... 87 G7
Meanwood Health Centre
 HDGY LS6 .... 87 H8
Meanwood Park Hospital
 HDGY LS6 .... 87 G5
The Medical Centre
 BIRK/DRI BD11 .... 129 G8
The Medical Centre
 BTLY WF17 .... 151 G5
The Medical Centre
 GFTH/SHER LS25 .... 116 A6
The Medical Centre
 KNOT WF11 .... 181 L1
The Medical Centre
 MSTN/BAR LS15 .... 111 K3
Meltham C of E School
 HOLM/MEL HD7 .... 235 G5
Meltham County Primary
 School
 HOLM/MEL HD7 .... 234 E3
Meltham Cricket & Athletic Club
 HOLM/MEL HD7 .... 235 G3
Meltham Golf Club
 HOLM/MEL HD7 .... 235 H5
Meltham Mills Industrial Estate
 HOLM/MEL HD7 .... 235 H4
Meltham Road Surgery
 HUDS HD4 .... 214 A3
Menston Cricket Club
 ILK LS29 .... 61 K1
The Menston & Guiseley Practice
 ILK LS29 .... 61 J2
Menston Primary School
 ILK LS29 .... 61 J2
Mental Health Service & Child
 Guidance Clinic
 WBOW BD5 .... 4 D8
Merrion Shopping Centre
 LDSU LS2 .... 7 G8
Methley C of E Infant School
 RTHW LS26 .... 156 E4
Methley County Junior School
 RTHW LS26 .... 157 G3
Methley Park Hospital
 RTHW LS26 .... 156 C3
Metronomesports &
 leisurecomplex
 BSLYN/ROY S71 .... 261 J4
Middlestown Health Centre
 HOR/CROF WF4 .... 196 D7
Middlestown Surgery
 HOR/CROF WF4 .... 196 C7
Middleton C of E School
 MID LS10 .... 153 L1
Middleton County Primary
 School
 MID LS10 .... 153 K3
Middleton Junior & Infant
 School
 HOR/CROF WF4 .... 196 D7
Middleton Park High School
 MID LS10 .... 153 M2
Middleton Park Leisure Centre
 MID LS10 .... 153 M1
Mid York Golf Club
 PONT WF8 .... 204 A1
Mid Yorkshire Nuffield Hospital
 HORS LS18 .... 85 M6
Miles Hill County Primary
 School
 CHAL LS7 .... 87 J7
Milestone School
 PDSY/CALV LS28 .... 107 G4
Milford R U F C
 KSTL LS5 .... 108 C2
Millbridge School
 LVSG WF15 .... 172 D2
Mill Hill Community
 Health Centre
 HUDE HD5 .... 193 J7
Mill Lane Junior & Infant School
 BTLY WF17 .... 173 M3
Mill Trading Estate
 BSLYN/ROY S71 .... 261 K5
Milnrow Cricket Club
 MILN OL16 .... 229 H1
Milnrow Crossgates School
 MILN OL16 .... 207 J7
Milnrow Health Centre
 MILN OL16 .... 229 H1

Minerva Industrial Estate
RTHW LS26 .... **134** A7
Minsthorpe Community College
HEM/SK/SE WF9 .... **247** H2
Minsthorpe Swimming Pool
HEM/SK/SE WF9 .... **247** J2
Minstral Gallery
AL/HA/HU LS17 .... **26** C6
Mirfield Parish Cricket Club
MIRF WF14 .... **172** D8
Mixenden Clinic
LUD/ILL HX2 .... **145** M2
Mixenden County Primary School
LUD/ILL HX2 .... **123** K8
Moderna Business Park
HBR HX7 .... **144** B6
Monk Bretton Health Centre
BSLYN/ROY S71 .... **261** L2
Monk Fryston C of E Primary School
GFTH/SHER LS25 .... **138** D6
Moor Allerton Hall Primary School
AL/HA/HU LS17 .... **88** A5
Moorcroft Surgery
AL/HA/HU LS17 .... **87** J2
Moorfield Business Park
YEA LS19 .... **62** F8
Moorfield First School
BFDE BD3 .... **105** L7
Moorfield School
ILK LS29 .... **38** E3
Moorhouse CP School
MILN OL16 .... **207** L6
Moorlands School
BHP/TINH LS16 .... **86** F5
Moorlands Small Business Centre
CLECK BD19 .... **149** M5
Moor Park Business Centre
WKFDW/WTN WF2 .... **12** B9
Moorside School
LUD/ILL HX2 .... **146** B2
Moorside Surgery
ECHL BD2 .... **105** K2
The Moors Shopping Centre
ILK LS29 .... **38** C2
Moortop Special School
FEA/AMT WF7 .... **224** B4
Moortown Golf Club
AL/HA/HU LS17 .... **87** M1
Moortown Primary School
AL/HA/HU LS17 .... **87** M4
Moortown R U F C
AL/HA/HU LS17 .... **87** J1
Moorview Business Park
IDLE BD10 .... **83** J5
Morgan Gallery
BULY LS4 .... **108** F5
Morley High School
MOR LS27 .... **152** B3
Morley Leisure Centre
MOR LS27 .... **152** B2
Morley Victoria Primary School
MOR LS27 .... **152** C1
Morley Western County Primary School
EARD/LOFT WF3 .... **152** F7
Moslem School
BTLY WF17 .... **173** L2
Mosque
BFD BD1 .... **4** D4
Mosque
EARL WF12 .... **173** L8
Mosque
GTHN BD7 .... **126** D1
Mosque
HDGY LS6 .... **6** A3
Mosque
HUD HD1 .... **214** B2
Mosque
KGHY BD21 .... **3** J3
Mosque
WKFDE WF1 .... **13** H3
The Mosque
MILN OL16 .... **206** C6
Moss Industrial Estate
MILN OL16 .... **228** D1
Mountjoy House School
HUD HD1 .... **14** C7
The Mount Junior & Infant School
WKFDW/WTN WF2 .... **198** B3
Mount Osborne Industrial Park
BSLYN/ROY S71 .... **261** K5
Mount Pellon Junior & Infant School
HFAX HX1 .... **10** A4
Mount St Marys High School
OSM LS9 .... **9** L2
Mount St Marys RC Primary School
OSM LS9 .... **110** C6
Mount Skip Golf Course
HBR HX7 .... **143** M3
Mount Vernon Hospital
BSLY S70 .... **261** H8
Municipal Baths
BRIG HD6 .... **170** D4
Museum of Industry & Science
WOR/ARM LS12 .... **108** E5
Museum Stores
CHAL LS7 .... **7** G2
The Museum
HIPP HX3 .... **147** H5
Muslem Mosque
WOR/ARM LS12 .... **108** E7
Muslim Girls School
WHIT OL12 .... **206** A6
Muslim Mosque
DEWS WF13 .... **173** M4
Myrtle Park Primary School
BGLY BD16 .... **81** H4
Mytholmroyd Health Centre
HBR HX7 .... **144** A5
Nab Wood Grammar School
BGLY BD16 .... **81** L7
Nab Wood Middle School
BGLY BD16 .... **81** L7

Napoleon Business Park
BOW BD4 .... **127** K1
National Coal Mining Museum for England
HOR/CROF WF4 .... **218** A1
National Film Theatre North
LDS LS1 .... **9** H2
National Museum of Photography Film & Television
GTHN BD7 .... **4** D8
National School
RPDN/SBR HX6 .... **188** E6
Neil Hunt Memorial Ground & Rugby Club
BOW BD4 .... **127** L1
Nessfield First School
HWTH BD22 .... **2** A8
Netherleigh School
HTON BD9 .... **104** B4
Netherthong County Primary School
HOLM/MEL HD7 .... **236** C6
Netherton Sitlington Junior & Infant School
HOR/CROF WF4 .... **197** G8
Newbarn Infant School
ROY/SHW OL2 .... **229** J8
New Barn Junior School
ROY/SHW OL2 .... **229** J8
Newbridge Industrial Estate
KCHY BD21 .... **3** J5
Newby First School
WBOW BD5 .... **126** F3
New College
PONT WF8 .... **180** D5
New Cross Street Health Centre
WBOW BD5 .... **126** F3
Newhaven Business Park
HUDW HD3 .... **213** J1
Newhey County School
MILN OL16 .... **229** J3
New Hey Surgery
BOW BD4 .... **127** K2
Newlands County Junior School
RPDN/SBR HX6 .... **167** G3
Newlands Industrial Estate
BAIL BD17 .... **82** E6
Newland Surgery
NORM WF6 .... **178** C5
New Line Clinic
IDLE BD10 .... **84** A7
Newsome Junior School
HUDS HD4 .... **214** C5
The Newsome Surgery
HUDS HD4 .... **214** C4
Newspaper Office
BFD BD1 .... **5** G6
New Street Health Centre
BSLY S70 .... **261** G6
The New Surgery
WOR/ARM LS12 .... **130** C2
Newton Hill Junior & Infant School
WKFDE WF1 .... **176** E4
Newton Surgery
CHAL LS7 .... **109** M1
Ninelands Lane Cp School
GFTH/SHER LS25 .... **113** J7
Norcroft Industrial Estate
BFD BD1 .... **4** B6
Norland C of E Junior & Infant School
RPDN/SBR HX6 .... **167** M4
Normanton C of E School
NORM WF6 .... **178** D4
Normanton Freeston High School
NORM WF6 .... **178** D5
Normanton Health Centre
NORM WF6 .... **178** C5
Normanton Lee Brigg First School
NORM WF6 .... **178** A3
Normanton Martin Frobisher First School
NORM WF6 .... **178** B2
Normanton Public Baths
NORM WF6 .... **178** D4
Normanton Town Middle School
NORM WF6 .... **178** C5
Normanton Woodlands Middle School
NORM WF6 .... **178** C6
Norristhorpe Junior & Infant School
LVSG WF15 .... **172** D4
North Bridge Leisure Centre
HFAX HX1 .... **11** H4
North Dean Business Park
GTL/HWG HX4 .... **168** F5
North Dean R F C
GTL/HWG HX4 .... **168** F7
Northern Ballet Theatre
BHP/TINH LS16 .... **86** C6
Northern Ballet Theatre
BRAM LS13 .... **107** M2
Northfield School
HEM/SK/SE WF9 .... **246** E3
The North Halifax Grammar School
LUD/ILL HX2 .... **124** B8
North Leeds Cricket Club
RHAY LS8 .... **88** C6
The North of England College
LDS LS1 .... **7** G9
Northowram Hall Hospital
HIPP HX3 .... **147** J2
Northowram School
HIPP HX3 .... **147** J3
Northowram Surgery
HIPP HX3 .... **147** J3
North Parade Surgery
BHP/TINH LS16 .... **86** C6
North Rigton C of E Primary School
AL/HA/HU LS17 .... **26** A7
Northside Retail Park
CHAL LS7 .... **87** H7

North View Mosque
EARL WF12 .... **173** M8
Northwest Business Park
HDGY LS6 .... **6** F3
North York Craven Institute of Further Education
SKP/WHF BD23 .... **16** B2
Norton County Junior & Infant School
AWLS/ASK DN6 .... **227** L3
Nortonthorpe Hall School
KBTN HD8 .... **239** M5
Nortonthorpe Industrial Estate
KBTN HD8 .... **239** M5
Notre Dame High School
LDSU LS2 .... **6** E3
Nova Scotia Medical Centre
CAS WF10 .... **157** J1
Oakbank School
HWTH BD22 .... **79** H2
Oakdale First School
SHPY BD18 .... **82** F8
Oakley Terrace Surgery
BEE/HOL LS11 .... **131** L4
Oaktree Business Park
SCFT LS14 .... **89** J7
Oak Tree School
FEA/AMT WF7 .... **224** B2
Oakwell Business Centre
BSLYN/ROY S71 .... **261** K5
Oakwood Primary School
RHAY LS8 .... **110** E3
Oakwood Surgery
RHAY LS8 .... **88** C8
Oakworth Health Centre
HWTH BD22 .... **78** F4
Oakworth Junior & Infant School
HWTH BD22 .... **78** E4
Odeon Cinema
BFD BD1 .... **4** D7
Odeon Cinema
BSLY S70 .... **261** H4
Odeon Cinema
LDS LS1 .... **7** G8
Old Bank School
MIRF WF14 .... **172** C7
Old College of Technology
BSLY S70 .... **261** G4
Oldfield First School
HWTH BD22 .... **77** L6
Old Rishworthians R U F C
HIPP HX3 .... **168** C4
Old Roundhegians R U F C
AL/HA/HU LS17 .... **88** A4
The Open University
LDS LS1 .... **9** G1
Optimax Eye Clinic
LDS LS1 .... **6** F8
Orchard Business Park
HBR HX7 .... **144** A6
Orchard Croft Medical Centre
HOR/CROF WF4 .... **197** K5
Orchard Head Junior & Infant School
PONT WF8 .... **181** G3
Osmondthorpe Primary School
OSM LS9 .... **110** E6
Ossett Cricket & Athletic Club
OSS WF5 .... **196** F2
Ossett Dimplewell Infant School
OSS WF5 .... **196** F2
Ossett Health Centre
OSS WF5 .... **196** F1
Ossett School
OSS WF5 .... **196** F2
Otley All Saints Infant School
OT LS21 .... **41** K7
Otley Road Medical Centre
BFDE BD3 .... **5** H2
Otley R U F C
OT LS21 .... **41** K6
Otley Town FC & Old Otlienisans RUFC
OT LS21 .... **41** L6
Oulton Health Centre
RTHW LS26 .... **133** L8
Oulton Park Golf Course
RTHW LS26 .... **155** K2
Oulton Primary School
RTHW LS26 .... **133** K8
Our Lady of Lourdes RC Primary Junior & Infant School
HUDN HD2 .... **192** E2
Our Lady of Victories RC Junior & Infant School
HWTH BD22 .... **2** B4
Outlane Junior & Infant School
HUDW HD3 .... **190** F5
Outwood Junior & Infant School
WKFDE WF1 .... **176** D2
Overthorpe C of E Junior & Infant School
EARL WF12 .... **195** L4
Owston Skellow First School
AWLS/ASK DN6 .... **249** K4
Oxenhope C of E First School
HWTH BD22 .... **100** D3
Oxspring Junior & Infant School
STKB/PEN S36 .... **271** K4
Oyster Park Infant School
CAS WF10 .... **158** F5
Oyster Park Middle School
CAS WF10 .... **158** F6
Paddock Cricket & Bowling Club
HUDW HD3 .... **213** L1
Pannal C P School
PBR HG3 .... **26** F2
Pannal Golf Club Ltd
PBR HG3 .... **27** G3
Paragon Industrial Estate
LIT OL15 .... **207** H3
The Park CP School
COL BB8 .... **74** B1
Park High School
COL BB8 .... **52** B8
Parkhouse Industrial Estate
LM/WK BD12 .... **127** C6
Parkinson Lane School
HFAX HX1 .... **10** C8

Parkland First & Middle School
IDLE BD10 .... **83** M7
Parklands County Primary School
SCFT LS14 .... **111** J2
Parklands Girls High School
SCFT LS14 .... **111** K2
Park Lane College
HORS LS18 .... **85** H7
Park Lane College
LDSU LS2 .... **7** H8
Park Lane College
MSTN/BAR LS15 .... **111** L4
Park Lane College of Further Education
BVRD LS3 .... **6** C8
Park Lane College of Further Education
CHAL LS7 .... **110** A1
Park Road County Primary School
BTLY WF17 .... **173** M1
Park Road Medical Centre
WBOW BD5 .... **127** G1
The Park School
WKFDW/WTN WF2 .... **12** C5
Parkside Middle School
CUL/QBY BD13 .... **80** A8
Park Spring CP School
BRAM LS13 .... **107** L6
Parkwood First School
KGHY BD21 .... **3** J6
Parkwood Street Industrial Estate
KGHY BD21 .... **3** M4
Parl Lane College
PDSY/CALV LS28 .... **107** G6
Pavilion Business Centre
PDSY/CALV LS28 .... **107** H4
Pavilion Business Park
WOR/ARM LS12 .... **130** E3
Pecket Well College
HBR HX7 .... **121** K7
Pecketwell College
HFAX HX1 .... **10** F5
Peel Mill Business Centre
MOR LS27 .... **152** C2
Peel Park Surgery
BFDE BD3 .... **5** H1
Pellon Industrial Estate
HFAX HX1 .... **10** B4
Penistone Grammar School
STKB/PEN S36 .... **270** E1
Penistone Group Practice
STKB/PEN S36 .... **270** F3
Penistone Sports Centre
STKB/PEN S36 .... **270** E2
Penistone Springvale Jmi School
STKB/PEN S36 .... **271** H3
Penistone Thurlstone Jmi School
STKB/PEN S36 .... **270** C2
Pennine Industrial Estate
WOR/ARM LS12 .... **108** D7
Pennyfield Special School
HDGY LS6 .... **87** H5
Penraevon Industrial Estate
CHAL LS7 .... **7** H3
Pentland County Infant School
EARL WF12 .... **195** M1
Pentland Road Clinic
EARL WF12 .... **173** M8
Peter Laycock Industrial Estate
CHAL LS7 .... **7** H2
Phoenix Works Estate
HOR/CROF WF4 .... **197** G5
Picture Drome Cinema Museum
HOLM/MEL HD7 .... **254** B1
Picture House
CHAL LS7 .... **7** K5
Picture House
HBR HX7 .... **143** J3
Picture House
NORM WF6 .... **178** C4
Picture House
WKFDE WF1 .... **176** F7
Piece Hall Art Gallery
HFAX HX1 .... **11** J6
Pilot Theatre
CAS WF10 .... **158** B8
Pinderfield Hospital
WKFDE WF1 .... **176** F5
Pinderfields & Pontefract Hospital NHS Trust
EARD/LOFT WF3 .... **177** H5
Pine Trees Gallery
LVSG WF15 .... **172** D2
Plane Trees Group Practice
LUD/ILL HX2 .... **145** M6
Playhouse & Film Theatre
BFD BD1 .... **5** H6
Playhouse Theatre
HFAX HX1 .... **10** F6
Police HQ
BFD BD1 .... **4** E7
Police Sports Ground
RHAY LS8 .... **88** B7
Pollard Park Middle School
BFDE BD3 .... **5** M4
Pomfret Gallery
PONT WF8 .... **180** E6
Pontefract C of E School
PONT WF8 .... **180** F5
Pontefract & District Golf Club
PONT WF8 .... **180** A5
Pontefract General Infirmary
PONT WF8 .... **180** F6
Pontefract Museum
PONT WF8 .... **180** E6
Pontefract Race Course
PONT WF8 .... **180** C4
Pontefract Road Junior & Infant School
CUD/GR S72 .... **244** D6
Pool C of E Primary School
OT LS21 .... **42** F7
Poplars Farm First School
ECHL BD2 .... **105** G2

P O Sorting Office
BFD BD1 .... **4** F1
Potternewton Primary School
CHAL LS7 .... **109** K1
Priestman Middle School
WBOW BD5 .... **126** E4
Priestthorpe First School
BGLY BD16 .... **81** J3
Priestthorpe Medical Centre
BGLY BD16 .... **81** J2
Primrose High School
OSM LS9 .... **7** M6
Primrose Hill Junior & Infant School
PDSY/CALV LS28 .... **106** F5
Primrose Lane Primary School
BSPA/BRAM LS23 .... **48** F7
Prince Henrys Grammar School
OT LS21 .... **41** J5
Prince of Wales Business Park
BRIG HD6 .... **170** D4
Princess Royal Health Centre
HUD HD1 .... **14** D7
The Princess Street Surgery
NORM WF6 .... **178** D4
Princeville First School
GTHN BD7 .... **104** D7
Princeville Road Industrial Estate
GIR BD8 .... **104** C7
Priory Business Park
HEM/SK/SE WF9 .... **223** M8
Proper Job Theatre Co
HUD HD1 .... **14** F6
Prospect Business Centre
HUD HD1 .... **14** E8
Prospect Road Surgery
OSS WF5 .... **196** F1
Public Baths & Recreation Centre
BTLY WF17 .... **173** L1
Public Health Laboratory Service Seacroft Hospital
SCFT LS14 .... **111** H4
Pudsey Grangefield School
PDSY/CALV LS28 .... **107** G6
Pudsey Greenside Junior & Infant School
PDSY/CALV LS28 .... **106** F8
Pudsey Leisure Centre
PDSY/CALV LS28 .... **107** G7
Pudsey St Lawrence Cricket Club
PDSY/CALV LS28 .... **106** F7
Pudsey Southroyd Primary School
PDSY/CALV LS28 .... **107** G8
Pudsey Tyersal Primary School
BOW BD4 .... **128** B1
Pudsey Waterloo Junior School
PDSY/CALV LS28 .... **106** E7
Purlwell County Primary School
BTLY WF17 .... **173** K3
Python Industrial Estate
LIT OL15 .... **185** L8
Q F Industrial Estate
BOW BD4 .... **127** K2
Quality Foods Industrial Park
BOW BD4 .... **127** M1
Quarry Hill Industrial Estate
HOR/CROF WF4 .... **197** G5
Quarry House
OSM LS9 .... **7** K9
Queen Elizabeth Grammar School
WKFDE WF1 .... **176** E7
Queen Elizabeth Junior School
WKFDE WF1 .... **176** D7
Queensbury Golf Course
CUL/QBY BD13 .... **125** H6
Queensbury Health Centre
CUL/QBY BD13 .... **124** F5
Queensbury School
CUL/QBY BD13 .... **125** G6
Queens Mill Business Centre
HUD HD1 .... **214** C2
Queens Mill Industrial Estate
HUD HD1 .... **214** C2
Queens Road Clinic
BSLYN/ROY S71 .... **261** H5
Queens Road School
HFAX HX1 .... **10** A5
Queens Sports Club
HFAX HX1 .... **10** E9
Queen Street Infant School
MOR LS27 .... **152** C2
Queen Street Junior & Infant School
NORM WF6 .... **178** C4
Queensway CP School
ROCH OL11 .... **228** D2
Queensway Primary School
GSLY LS20 .... **62** C6
Raglan Industrial Estate
CAS WF10 .... **157** K6
Railwaymens Sports Club
BSLYN/ROY S71 .... **244** A2
Ralph Thoresby High School
BHP/TINH LS16 .... **86** B2
Ralph Williams Clinic
WHIT OL12 .... **206** E8
Ramgarhia Sikh Sports Centre
CHAL LS7 .... **7** J4
Ramgarhia Sikh Temple
BFDE BD3 .... **105** H4
Rastrick High School
BRIG HD6 .... **170** B5
Ravensbridge Industrial Estate
DEWS WF13 .... **173** H8
Ravenscliffe First School
IDLE BD10 .... **106** A2
Ravenscliffe High School
HIPP HX3 .... **168** D4
Ravensthorpe C of E Junior School
DEWS WF13 .... **194** F1
Rawdon Cricket Club
YEA LS19 .... **84** E2
Rawdon Surgery
YEA LS19 .... **84** D2

Rawfolds Industrial Estate
 CLECK BD19 .... 150 B8
Rawson J & I School
 HIPP HX3 .... 146 D4
Rawson Market
 BFD BD1 .... 4 D5
Rawthorpe Junior School
 HUDE HD5 .... 15 M4
Raynville School
 BRAM LS13 .... 108 A4
Redbrook Business Park
 DOD/DAR S75 .... 260 D1
Redhill Infant School
 CAS WF10 .... 158 E6
Red Ledge Business Centre
 HOLM/MEL HD7 .... 236 D6
Reevy Hill Primary School
 WBSY BD6 .... 126 B5
Registry Office
 BFD BD1 .... 4 E5
Reinwood County Infant &
 Junior School
 HUDW HD3 .... 191 K7
Renji Chinese Medical Centre
 HUDN HD2 .... 192 D5
Revival Industrial Estate
 BOW BD4 .... 5 J9
Rhodesway School
 GIR BD8 .... 103 L6
Richard Dunn Sports Centre
 WBOW BD5 .... 126 F5
Richard Newman Infant School
 BSLYN/ROY S71 .... 243 H4
Richard Oastler School
 BULY LS4 .... 108 F4
Richmond Building
 GTHN BD7 .... 4 C7
Richmond Hill County
 Primary School
 OSM LS9 .... 110 B8
Richmond House School
 BHP/TINH LS16 .... 86 E7
Richmond Medical Centre
 OSM LS9 .... 9 M2
Riddlesden C of E School
 AIRE BD20 .... 58 B4
Riddlesden Infants School
 AIRE BD20 .... 58 B4
The Ridge Medical Practice
 GTHN BD7 .... 126 C2
Ridings Business Park
 HFAX HX1 .... 10 A7
The Ridings School
 LUD/ILL HX2 .... 146 A3
Ringway Industrial Estate
 HUD HD1 .... 14 E3
Ripponden Junior & Infant
 School
 RPDN/SBR HX6 .... 189 G1
Rishworth School
 RPDN/SBR HX6 .... 188 K1
Riverside Business Park
 BAIL BD17 .... 82 E6
Riverside Business Park
 KBTN HD8 .... 239 M4
Riverside CP School
 TAD LS24 .... 71 L2
Riverside Industrial Estate
 HOR/CROF WF4 .... 197 G6
Riverside Junior School
 HBR HX7 .... 143 J3
Riverside Medical Centre
 CAS WF10 .... 157 L6
Rochdale Curtain Theatre
 ROCH OL11 .... 206 A8
Rochdale Healthcare N H S
 Trust
 LIT OL15 .... 207 J1
Rochdale Healthcare N H S
 Trust
 WHIT OL12 .... 206 F1
Rochdale Infirmary
 WHIT OL12 .... 206 A5
Rochdale Metropolitan Borough
 Council
 MILN OL16 .... 206 C7
Rochdale Metropolitan Borough
 Council
 ROCH OL11 .... 228 B4
Rochdale Metropolitan Borough
 Council
 WHIT OL12 .... 206 B6
Rock Hill Sports Club
 CAS WF10 .... 158 C8
Rockley Mount School
 BSLY S70 .... 260 E7
Rodillian School
 EARD/LOFT WF3 .... 154 E5
Rodley Primary School
 BRAM LS13 .... 107 H1
The Rookeries Carleton Junior &
 Infant School
 PONT WF8 .... 181 H8
Rosemeade School
 HUDE HD5 .... 215 G1
Roseville Business Park
 RHAY LS8 .... 7 M4
Rossefield School
 HTON BD9 .... 104 C2
Rossett Business Park
 BRAM LS13 .... 107 K2
Rotherham Road Medical Centre
 BSLYN/ROY S71 .... 243 J8
Rothwell C of E Primary School
 RTHW LS26 .... 133 G8
Rothwell Haigh Road
 Infant School
 RTHW LS26 .... 133 G8
Rothwell Health Centre
 RTHW LS26 .... 155 G1
Rothwell Methley Cp
 Infant School
 RTHW LS26 .... 156 E4
Rothwell Primary School
 RTHW LS26 .... 155 G2
Rothwell Sports Centre
 RTHW LS26 .... 155 L2
Rothwell Victoria Primary
 School
 RTHW LS26 .... 132 F8

Rothwell West Junior School
 RTHW LS26 .... 154 F2
Royal Armouries Museum
 MID LS10 .... 9 K3
Royal Halifax Infirmary
 HFAX HX1 .... 168 E1
Royal Infirmary
 HUDW HD3 .... 191 L6
Royal Park Primary School
 HDGY LS6 .... 109 G4
Royd Business Park
 BRIG HD6 .... 170 E4
Royd Mount Middle School
 CUL/QBY BD13 .... 102 E8
Royds Hall High School
 HUDW HD3 .... 191 L8
Royds School
 RTHW LS26 .... 155 K4
Royston Clinic
 BSLYN/ROY S71 .... 243 L3
Royston Comprehensive School
 BSLYN/ROY S71 .... 243 L2
Royston Meadstead
 Junior School
 BSLYN/ROY S71 .... 243 K3
Royston Midland Junior & Infant
 School
 BSLYN/ROY S71 .... 243 L2
Royston St John Baptist C E (A)
 Primary School
 BSLYN/ROY S71 .... 243 L3
Rugby Union Club
 PONT WF8 .... 203 H2
Rushcroft CP School
 ROY/SHW OL2 .... 229 K6
Russell Hall First School
 CUL/QBY BD13 .... 125 G5
Ryan Middle School
 BOW BD4 .... 127 H3
Ryburn County Secondary
 School
 RPDN/SBR HX6 .... 167 G4
The Rydings Hall Surgery
 BRIG HD6 .... 170 D3
Rydings School
 WHIT OL12 .... 206 D2
Ryecroft First School
 BOW BD4 .... 128 B4
Ryecroft Primary School
 WOR/ARM LS12 .... 108 A8
Ryhill County Primary School
 HOR/CROF WF4 .... 222 D5
Ryshworth Middle School
 BGLY BD16 .... 59 G7
Sacred Heart Primary School
 BGLY BD16 .... 108 D3
Sacred Heart RC Primary School
 MILN OL16 .... 206 E8
Sai Medical Centre
 GIR BD8 .... 104 E4
St Agnes School
 HDGY LS6 .... 86 F8
St Aidans C of E First School
 KBTN HD8 .... 239 J5
St Andrew C of E Infant School
 BRIG HD6 .... 170 C2
St Andrews C of E Junior School
 BRIG HD6 .... 170 C3
St Andrews C of E Primary
 School
 WHIT OL12 .... 207 G2
St Annes Cathedral
 LDSU LS2 .... 6 F8
St Annes RC School
 KCHY BD21 .... 2 F3
St Anthonys RC First School
 CLAY BD14 .... 125 M1
St Anthonys RC Junior &
 Infant School
 SHPY BD18 .... 83 H6
St Augustines C of E First School
 BFDE BD3 .... 5 J2
St Augustines C of E Primary
 School
 HFAX HX1 .... 10 C4
St Augustines RC School
 RHAY LS8 .... 110 C3
St Austins RC Junior & Infant
 School
 WKFDE WF1 .... 176 F7
St Barnabas C of E School
 HTON BD9 .... 104 C2
St Bartholomews C of E Primary
 School
 WOR/ARM LS12 .... 108 E7
St Bedes Grammar School
 HTON BD9 .... 104 C3
St Chads C of E Primary School
 BHP/TINH LS16 .... 86 C7
St Chads C of E Primary School
 BRIG HD6 .... 170 A1
St Clares Roman Catholic School
 ECHL BD2 .... 105 M4
St Columbas RC Primary School
 BOW BD4 .... 127 M4
St Cuthberts RC High School
 MILN OL16 .... 228 E5
St Edwards RC School
 BSPA/BRAM LS23 .... 48 F6
St Francis RC First School
 ECHL BD2 .... 105 J2
St Francis RC School
 BEE/HOL LS11 .... 8 F7
St George's Hall
 BFD BD1 .... 5 G7
St Gregorys RC School
 SCFT LS14 .... 111 M1
St Helens Junior & Infant School
 BSLYN/ROY S71 .... 261 M1
St Hildas School
 HOR/CROF WF4 .... 197 J4
St Ignatius RC School
 OSS WF5 .... 197 G3
St James C of E Junior &
 Infant School
 HOR/CROF WF4 .... 198 A8
St James C of E Primary School
 WHIT OL12 .... 184 E8
St James C of E School
 WBY LS22 .... 30 B8

St James Market
 BFDE BD3 .... 5 J8
St James's University Hospital
 OSM LS9 .... 110 B4
St John Fisher High School
 DEWS WF13 .... 173 K5
St Johns C of E First School
 BOW BD4 .... 127 M5
St Johns C of E Infants School
 STKB/PEN S36 .... 270 E4
St Johns C of E Junior &
 Infant School
 HOLM/MEL HD7 .... 212 F1
St Johns C of E Junior &
 Infant School
 RPDN/SBR HX6 .... 188 D5
St Johns C of E Primary School
 BRIG HD6 .... 171 G4
St Johns C of E School
 DEWS WF13 .... 173 J6
St Johns Primary School
 RHAY LS8 .... 88 E8
St Johns RC Primary School
 ROCH OL11 .... 206 B8
St John the Baptist C of E
 (Aided) Junior School
 STKB/PEN S36 .... 270 E4
St John the Baptist C of E
 Primary School
 BHP/TINH LS16 .... 86 F2
St John the Baptist R C
 Aided Primary School
 NORM WF6 .... 178 D4
St John the Evangelist RC School
 WBSY BD6 .... 126 A5
St John with St. Michael School
 WHIT OL12 .... 184 A1
St Josephs College
 HTON BD9 .... 104 E3
St Josephs Primary School
 DEWS WF13 .... 173 J4
St Josephs RC First School
 WBOW BD5 .... 126 F2
St Josephs RC Infants School
 HUDE HD5 .... 193 H8
St Josephs RC Primary School
 PDSY/CALV LS28 .... 107 H6
St Josephs RC Primary School
 TAD LS24 .... 71 L2
St Josephs RC Primary School
 TOD OL14 .... 141 J8
St Josephs RC Primary School
 WBY LS22 .... 30 A8
St Josephs RC School
 BGLY BD16 .... 81 J3
St Josephs RC School
 CAS WF10 .... 158 A6
St Josephs RC School
 HIPP HX3 .... 11 J3
St Josephs RC School
 KGHY BD21 .... 2 E9
St Josephs RC School
 OT LS21 .... 41 J6
St Josephs RC Primary School
 BRIG HD6 .... 170 B1
St Lukes C of E First School
 CLECK BD19 .... 149 K7
St Lukes Eccleshill C of E
 First School
 ECHL BD2 .... 105 M2
St Lukes Hospital
 HUDS HD4 .... 213 M3
St Lukes Hospital
 WBOW BD5 .... 126 F2
St Malachys RC School
 LUD/ILL HX2 .... 146 A3
St Martins Practice
 CHAL LS7 .... 109 M1
St Marys Catholic Primary
 School
 HFAX HX1 .... 10 E8
St Marys Catholic School
 ILK LS29 .... 38 F2
St Marys C of E Junior &
 Infant School
 DOD/DAR S75 .... 260 E4
St Marys C of E Primary School
 RPDN/SBR HX6 .... 166 E7
St Marys Hospital
 WOR/ARM LS12 .... 108 B6
St Marys RC Infant School
 HFAX HX1 .... 10 E7
St Marys RC Primary School
 BFD BD1 .... 5 G5
St Marys RC Primary School
 RTHW LS26 .... 155 H2
St Marys RC School
 BTLY WF17 .... 151 K8
St Marys RC School
 HORS LS18 .... 85 L5
St Marys RC School
 ILK LS29 .... 61 L3
St Marys RC School
 LIT OL15 .... 207 J1
St Matthews C of E First
 School
 WBOW BD5 .... 127 G5
St Matthews C of E Primary
 School
 CHAL LS7 .... 87 L7
St Matthews Infant School
 DOD/DAR S75 .... 260 E4
St Matthews RC Primary School
 WIL/AL BD15 .... 103 K6
St Michael & All Angels C
 of E Primary School
 COL BB8 .... 52 A6
St Michael & All Angels C
 of E Primary School
 HIPP HX3 .... 125 M8
St Michaels C of E
 Primary School
 HDGY LS6 .... 109 G1
St Michaels College
 BVRD LS3 .... 6 B6
St Michaels RC
 Comprehensive School
 BSLYN/ROY S71 .... 243 K7
St Nicholas RC School
 OSM LS9 .... 110 F3

St Oswalds C of E Junior School
 GSLY LS20 .... 62 A6
St Patricks R C Primary School
 ELL HX5 .... 168 F8
St Patricks RC Primary School
 HUDW HD3 .... 14 A2
St Patricks RC Primary School
 WHIT OL14 .... 206 C5
St Paul Apostle RC School
 AL/HA/HU LS17 .... 87 J2
St Peter C of E Primary School
 OSM LS9 .... 7 K8
St Peters Cathedral
 BFD BD1 .... 5 G5
St Peters C of E Infant School
 RPDN/SBR HX6 .... 167 G3
St Peters C of E School
 MILN OL16 .... 228 E1
St Peters Junior & Infant School
 BTLY WF17 .... 151 G4
St Peters RC First School
 BFDE BD3 .... 5 M6
St Philips C E First School
 WIL/AL BD15 .... 103 J4
St Philips RC School
 MID LS10 .... 153 K1
St Saviours C of E Junior School
 BTLY WF17 .... 151 J5
St Stephens RC Primary School
 SKP/WHF BD23 .... 16 B2
St Stephens Special School
 WBOW BD5 .... 127 G3
St Theresas RC Primary School
 MSTN/BAR LS15 .... 111 L3
St Thomas à Becket RC City High
 School
 WKFDW/WTN WF2 .... 199 C5
St Thomas's C E Junior School
 FEA/AMT WF7 .... 201 L1
St Thomas's C of E School
 MILN OL16 .... 229 K2
St Urbans R C Primary School
 HDGY LS6 .... 87 J5
St Walburgas RC First School
 SHPY BD18 .... 82 B7
St Wilfrids Catholic High School
 FEA/AMT WF7 .... 179 L5
St Williams RC Primary School
 GIR BD8 .... 104 C7
Salendine Nook High School
 HUDW HD3 .... 191 H6
Salford Industrial Estate
 TOD OL14 .... 163 J1
Saltaire First School
 SHPY BD18 .... 82 B6
Saltaire Medical Centre
 SHPY BD18 .... 82 B6
Salterhebble School
 HIPP HX3 .... 168 F3
Salter Lee School
 HIPP HX3 .... 147 H4
Salt Grammar School
 BAIL BD17 .... 82 B4
Sandal Castle
 WKFDW/WTN WF2 .... 198 F5
Sandal Endowed C of E
 Junior School
 WKFDW/WTN WF2 .... 199 G6
Sandal First School
 BAIL BD17 .... 82 E3
Sandal Magna Junior &
 Infant School
 WKFDE WF1 .... 199 G4
Sandal Medical Centre
 WKFDW/WTN WF2 .... 198 E7
Sandal Rugby Union
 Football Club
 WKFDW/WTN WF2 .... 198 F7
Sandbeck Industrial Estate
 WBY LS22 .... 30 C7
Sandbeck Park Industrial Estate
 WBY LS22 .... 30 B7
Sandifords Gallery
 MILN OL16 .... 206 B7
Sandlands Business Centre
 SKP/WHF BD23 .... 16 A3
Sandy Lane First School
 WIL/AL BD15 .... 103 J2
Savile Business Centre
 EARL WF12 .... 173 M7
Savile Park Junior & Infant
 School
 HFAX HX1 .... 168 C1
Savile Town C of E Infant School
 EARL WF12 .... 173 L8
Savoy Squash Club
 KBTN HD8 .... 239 J4
Saxton C of E Primary School
 TAD LS24 .... 93 J8
Scalebor Park Hospital
 ILK LS29 .... 39 M6
Scammonden Sailing Club
 HUDW HD3 .... 211 H2
Scapegoat Hill Junior &
 Infant School
 HOLM/MEL HD7 .... 190 D8
Scholes Cricket Club
 HOLM/MEL HD7 .... 254 F3
Scholes Elmete Junior School
 MSTN/BAR LS15 .... 90 A8
Scholes Junior & Infant School
 HOLM/MEL HD7 .... 254 F3
School Lane Health Centre
 DEWS WF13 .... 173 H5
Schreiber Business Centre
 WKFDE WF1 .... 13 H5
Scissett Middle School
 KBTN HD8 .... 239 M4
Scissett Swimming Baths
 KBTN HD8 .... 240 A4
Scotchman Middle School
 HTON BD9 .... 104 C4
Scotch Park Trading Estate
 WOR/ARM LS12 .... 108 F6
Scout Road County
 Primary School
 HBR HX7 .... 144 B6
Seacroft Clinic
 SCFT LS14 .... 111 K1

Seacroft Industrial Estate
 SCFT LS14 .... 89 K7
Selby Gas & Leisure Centre
 KNOT WF11 .... 159 L6
Sevenhills Primary School
 MOR LS27 .... 152 D2
Shade Junior & Infant School
 TOD OL14 .... 163 J3
Shadwell County
 Primary School
 AL/HA/HU LS17 .... 89 H2
Shadwell Medical Centre
 AL/HA/HU LS17 .... 88 A3
Shafton Lane Surgery
 BEE/HOL LS11 .... 8 C6
Shafton Two Gates Junior &
 Infant School
 CUD/GR S72 .... 244 E4
Shakespeare Primary School
 OSM LS9 .... 110 B5
Shariston Junior &
 Infants School
 HOR/CROF WF4 .... 200 D2
Shariston Surgery
 HOR/CROF WF4 .... 200 D3
Sharma Park Industrial Estate
 RHAY LS8 .... 7 L5
Shawclough CP School
 WHIT OL12 .... 206 A3
Shawcross County
 Primary School
 EARL WF12 .... 174 C3
Shawcross Health Centre
 EARL WF12 .... 174 C3
Shaw House School
 HTON BD9 .... 104 C3
Shaw Lane Surgery
 HDGY LS6 .... 86 F8
Shay Lane Infant School
 HOR/CROF WF4 .... 200 A5
Sheibarg Industrial Estate
 BOW BD4 .... 127 M2
Shelf Health Centre
 HIPP HX3 .... 125 L8
Shelley High School
 KBTN HD8 .... 239 G4
Shelly First School
 KBTN HD8 .... 238 C3
Shenstone House Surgery
 MSTN/BAR LS15 .... 130 D7
Shepley First School
 KBTN HD8 .... 238 A6
Sherburn High School
 GFTH/SHER LS25 .... 116 A8
Shibden Hall
 HIPP HX3 .... 147 H6
Shibden Head First School
 CUL/QBY BD13 .... 124 E7
Shipley Baths
 SHPY BD18 .... 82 D7
Shipley C of E First School
 SHPY BD18 .... 82 D8
Shipley College
 SHPY BD18 .... 82 C6
Shipley College of Education
 SHPY BD18 .... 82 B5
Shipley Health Centre
 SHPY BD18 .... 82 C7
Shipley Hospital
 SHPY BD18 .... 82 C7
Shopping Centre
 BSLY S70 .... 261 H5
Shopping Centre
 HFAX HX1 .... 11 H6
Showcase Cinemas
 BTLY WF17 .... 151 K2
Sicklinghall Cp School
 WBY LS22 .... 46 D1
Siddal Infant School
 HIPP HX3 .... 169 G3
Siddal Junior School
 HIPP HX3 .... 169 G3
Siddal Surgery
 HIPP HX3 .... 169 G3
Sikh Leisure Centre
 HUD HD1 .... 14 E8
Sikh Temple
 BFDE BD3 .... 5 K6
Sikh Temple
 CHAL LS7 .... 110 A1
Sikh Temple
 HUD HD1 .... 14 E9
Sikh Temple
 HUD HD1 .... 15 C2
Silsden Cricket Club
 AIRE BD20 .... 35 M6
Silsden Health Centre
 AIRE BD20 .... 35 M5
Silver Blades Ice Rink
 WBOW BD5 .... 4 E8
Silver Court Industrial Estate
 HUD HD1 .... 15 K8
Silver Lane Surgery
 YEA LS19 .... 62 D7
Simpson Lane Junior &
 Infant School
 KNOT WF11 .... 181 M3
Simpson Lane Junior &
 Infant School
 KNOT WF11 .... 182 B3
Skelmanthorpe Business Park
 KBTN HD8 .... 239 J4
Skipton Castle
 SKP/WHF BD23 .... 16 C2
Skipton General Hospital
 SKP/WHF BD23 .... 16 B3
Skipton High School
 SKP/WHF BD23 .... 16 A1
Skipton Hospital
 SKP/WHF BD23 .... 16 A3
Skipton L M Sports Club
 SKP/WHF BD23 .... 16 B3
Skipton Parish Church School
 SKP/WHF BD23 .... 16 C3
Slaithwaite Health Centre
 HOLM/MEL HD7 .... 212 C5
Slaithwaite School
 HOLM/MEL HD7 .... 212 A6
Slaithwaite Swimming Baths
 HOLM/MEL HD7 .... 212 C5

Smallbridge Health Centre
  WHIT OL12 .... 206 E3
Smallbridge Industrial Park
  MILN OL16 .... 206 D4
Smallbridge St Johns C of E
  School
  WHIT OL12 .... 206 D2
Smallbridge School
  WHIT OL12 .... 206 D3
Smith Art Gallery
  BRIG HD6 .... 170 C3
Smithy Bridge Primary School
  LIT OL15 .... 207 H3
Snapethorpe Junior &
  Infant School
  WKFDW/WTN WF2 .... 197 L2
Snaygill Industrial Estate
  SKP/WHF BD23 .... 16 B5
Soothill Cricket Club
  BTLY WF17 .... 174 A1
South Bradford Golf Course
  WBSY BD6 .... 127 G6
South Craven School
  AIRE BD20 .... 34 F8
South Crosland Junior School
  HUDS HD4 .... 213 M7
South Elmsall Ash Grove Junior
  & Infant School
  HEM/SK/SE WF9 .... 247 J2
South Elmsall Health Centre
  HEM/SK/SE WF9 .... 247 H3
South Halifax High School
  HIPP HX3 .... 169 G4
South Kirkby Common
  Road School
  HEM/SK/SE WF9 .... 246 C5
South Kirkby First School
  HEM/SK/SE WF9 .... 247 C3
South Leeds Sports Centre
  BEE/HOL LS11 .... 8 F6
Southmere First School
  GTHN BD7 .... 126 C3
South Milford CP School
  GFTH/SHER LS25 .... 138 A3
South Milford Surgery
  GFTH/SHER LS25 .... 138 B2
South Ossett Infant &
  Junior School
  OSS WF5 .... 197 G2
Southowram Surgery
  HIPP HX3 .... 169 J2
South Parade Junior &
  Infant School
  OSS WF5 .... 197 H2
South View Business Centre
  GSLY LS20 .... 62 A4
Southview Business Park
  GSLY LS20 .... 62 A4
South View Infant School
  YEA LS19 .... 62 D8
South View Junior School
  YEA LS19 .... 62 D8
Sovereign Business Centre
  HUDS HD4 .... 214 B3
Sowerby Bridge Clinic
  RPDN/SBR HX6 .... 167 L3
Sowerby Bridge C of E Junior
  School
  RPDN/SBR HX6 .... 167 K2
Sowerby Bridge Cricket Club
  RPDN/SBR HX6 .... 167 J2
Sowerby Bridge High School
  RPDN/SBR HX6 .... 167 L1
Spa Baths
  BSPA/BRAM LS23 .... 49 G6
Spa Fields Industrial Estate
  HOLM/MEL HD7 .... 212 D5
Sparrow Hill Community School
  MILN OL16 .... 206 A7
Special School
  HUDS HD4 .... 214 E2
Speedwell Surgery
  HUD HD1 .... 14 A9
Spenborough Gomersal School
  CLECK BD19 .... 150 D5
Spenborough Moorend
  C of E School
  CLECK BD19 .... 149 L5
Spenborough Whitcliffe Mount
  School
  CLECK BD19 .... 149 K6
Spen Valley High School
  LVSG WF15 .... 172 C3
Spen Valley Industrial Park
  CLECK BD19 .... 150 A8
Spen Victoria Cricket Bowling &
  Athletic Club
  CLECK BD19 .... 150 B6
Spofforth Primary School
  PBR HG3 .... 28 E4
Sports Centre
  GTHN BD7 .... 4 B8
Springfield Surgery
  BGLY BD16 .... 81 H2
Springhill High School
  MILN OL16 .... 228 D1
Spring Ram Business Park
  BTLY WF17 .... 151 J2
Springwood First School
  GIR BD8 .... 4 B2
Stainbeck Surgery
  CHAL LS7 .... 87 L8
Stairfoot Health Centre
  BSLY S70 .... 261 M7
Standard Industrial Estate
  ECHL BD2 .... 105 L3
Standbridge Primary School
  WKFDW/WTN WF2 .... 220 C1
Stanley Grove Junior &
  Infant School
  EARD/LOFT WF3 .... 177 H3
Stanley Health Centre
  EARD/LOFT WF3 .... 177 G1
Stanley Mills Business Park
  HOLM/MEL HD7 .... 213 H2
Stanley Peters Junior &
  Infant School
  EARD/LOFT WF3 .... 177 H1

Stanley Rugby League
  Football Club Headquarters
  EARD/LOFT WF3 .... 155 H8
Stanningley Industrial Centre
  PDSY/CALV LS28 .... 106 F5
Stanningley Primary School
  PDSY/CALV LS28 .... 107 H4
Stanningley R L F C
  PDSY/CALV LS28 .... 107 J3
Stansfield Hall Cp School
  LIT OL15 .... 185 L6
Stansfield House Surgery
  HIPP HX3 .... 168 C3
Station Approach
  Business Estate
  ROCH OL11 .... 206 B8
Station Road Industrial Estate
  GFTH/SHER LS25 .... 135 H7
Station Road Surgery
  RPDN/SBR HX6 .... 167 K3
Steed Court Business Park
  HEM/SK/SE WF9 .... 225 L6
Steeton Hallgatehouse
  GFTH/SHER LS25 .... 137 L3
Steeton Health Centre
  AIRE BD20 .... 56 E1
Steeton Junior & Infants School
  AIRE BD20 .... 56 F1
Stephen H Smith Garden & Leisure
  Centre
  BGLY BD16 .... 80 D6
Stile Common Junior School
  HUDS HD4 .... 214 C3
Stitch Gallery
  TAD LS24 .... 71 M3
Stockingate First School
  HEM/SK/SE WF9 .... 246 C5
Stockingate Surgery
  HEM/SK/SE WF9 .... 246 D4
Stocks Lane First School
  CUL/QBY BD13 .... 125 K4
Stonefield Street Surgery
  MILN OL16 .... 229 H1
Stonegate School
  AL/HA/HU LS17 .... 87 J6
Stoney Lee Middle School
  BGLY BD16 .... 81 K8
Stoney Ridge Hospital
  BGLY BD16 .... 103 L1
The Strand Medical Centre
  ROCH OL11 .... 228 B4
Streethouse Junior &
  Infant School
  HOR/CROF WF4 .... 200 L1
Street Lane Practice
  RHAY LS8 .... 88 C4
Sues Health Centre
  BSLYN/ROY S71 .... 243 J6
Summerfield Primary School
  BRAM LS13 .... 107 H3
Summerfields Junior &
  Infants School
  BSLYN/ROY S71 .... 243 J2
Sunday School
  HBR HX7 .... 121 K6
The Sunday School
  HBR HX7 .... 120 F8
Sunfield Medical Centre
  PDSY/CALV LS28 .... 106 F1
Sunni Mosque
  WKFDE WF1 .... 176 F7
Sunny Hill House School
  WKFDW/WTN WF2 .... 176 A5
Surgery Savile Centre
  EARL WF12 .... 195 M4
Sutton County Primary School
  AIRE BD20 .... 55 L1
Sutton In Craven Cp School
  AIRE BD20 .... 55 M1
Swain House Middle School
  ECHL BD2 .... 105 J2
Swillington Primary School
  RTHW LS26 .... 134 C4
Swinnow Shopping Centre
  BRAM LS13 .... 107 J6
Swire Smith Middle School
  KGHY BD21 .... 3 K7
Sycamore Industrial Estate
  HECK WF16 .... 172 F4
Syril Academy of Theatre Arts
  YEA LS19 .... 62 C7
Tadcaster Albion F C
  TAD LS24 .... 71 M3
Tadcaster Cricket Club
  TAD LS24 .... 71 L3
Tadcaster East CP School
  TAD LS24 .... 72 A2
Tadcaster Grammar School
  TAD LS24 .... 70 F4
Tadcaster Medical Centre
  TAD LS24 .... 71 M3
Tadcaster Sports &
  Leisure Centre
  TAD LS24 .... 71 L3
Tainton Park Trading Estate
  WOR/ARM LS12 .... 109 G8
Taison Industrial Park
  GTHN BD7 .... 126 D3
Takalani Dance Theatre
  RHAY LS8 .... 110 J2
Talbot Road CP School
  RHAY LS8 .... 88 B4
Tandem Industrial Estate
  HUDE HD5 .... 193 K8
Tannery Business Park
  HIPP HX3 .... 147 J3
Tanyard Industrial Estate
  HUDW HD3 .... 213 K2
Technical College
  AIRE BD20 .... 36 A5
Temple Bank Special School
  HTON BD9 .... 104 A4
Temple Moor High School
  MSTN/BAR LS15 .... 111 K7
Temple Newsam
  MSTN/BAR LS15 .... 133 K1
Temple Newsam Golf Club
  MSTN/BAR LS15 .... 111 H8
Tenterfields Business Park
  LUD/ILL HX2 .... 167 G1

Tetley Brewery Wharf
  .... 9 J2
Thackley A F C
  IDLE BD10 .... 83 J4
Thackley Cricket Club
  IDLE BD10 .... 83 K4
Thackley First School
  IDLE BD10 .... 83 K4
Thackray Medical Museum
  OSM LS9 .... 7 M6
Thomas Danby College
  CHAL LS7 .... 7 K4
Thongsbridge Tennis Club
  HOLM/MEL HD7 .... 236 D6
Thornbury First School
  BFDE BD3 .... 105 M6
Thornbury Middle School
  BFDE BD3 .... 106 A6
Thorner C of E Primary School
  SCFT LS14 .... 68 C8
Thornham St James C of E Primary
  School
  ROY/SHW OL2 .... 228 F6
Thornhill High School
  EARL WF12 .... 196 A5
Thornhill Junior & Infant School
  EARL WF12 .... 195 M5
Thorn Park School
  HTON BD9 .... 103 M2
Thornton Baths
  CUL/QBY BD13 .... 103 C8
Thornton First School
  CUL/QBY BD13 .... 102 F8
Thornton Lodge Health Centre
  HUD HD1 .... 214 B2
Thornton Medical Centre
  CUL/QBY BD13 .... 103 C8
Thornton Upper School
  CUL/QBY BD13 .... 103 K8
Thorpe First & Middle School
  IDLE BD10 .... 83 K6
Thorpe Primary School
  EARD/LOFT WF3 .... 154 A4
Throstle Farm Junior &
  Infant School
  KNOT WF11 .... 182 B4
Thrum Hall Industrial Park
  LUD/ILL HX2 .... 146 A7
Thurstonland Endowed Primary
  School
  HUDS HD4 .... 237 H4
Thwaite Mills Museum
  OSM LS9 .... 132 D3
Tinshill Primary School
  BHP/TINH LS16 .... 86 A3
Tip Toes Complimentary Health
  Centre
  MILN OL16 .... 207 H8
Tockwith C of E Primary School
  RYKW YO26 .... 32 B1
Todmorden Community College
  TOD OL14 .... 163 K1
Todmorden Cricket Club
  TOD OL14 .... 141 J8
Todmorden Health Centre
  TOD OL14 .... 163 K1
Todmorden High School
  TOD OL14 .... 141 H8
Tolson Memorial Museum
  HUDE HD5 .... 193 G8
Tong Park First School
  BAIL BD17 .... 83 H2
Tong Sports Centre
  BOW BD4 .... 128 C6
Top Rank Theatre
  HFAX HX1 .... 11 G5
Towngate J & I School
  OSS WF5 .... 175 H8
Townville Infants School
  CAS WF10 .... 158 E7
Trading Estate
  BSPA/BRAM LS23 .... 49 K4
Tranmere Park Primary School
  GSLY LS20 .... 61 K6
Trawden Cp School
  COL BB8 .... 74 E4
Treefield Industrial Estate
  MOR LS27 .... 151 M1
Triangle Business Park
  BTLY WF17 .... 151 J3
Triangle C of E Primary School
  RPDN/SBR HX6 .... 167 G5
Trinity & All Saints College
  HORS LS18 .... 85 J3
Trinity Medical Centre
  WKFDE WF1 .... 12 F3
Tuel Lane County
  Primary School
  RPDN/SBR HX6 .... 167 K2
Tulip Street Retail Park
  MID LS10 .... 131 M3
Turnshaws Special School
  KBTN HD8 .... 216 C8
Two Ways Gallery
  ILK LS29 .... 38 D2
Tyersal Family Clinic
  BOW BD4 .... 106 B8
Tyersal First School
  BOW BD4 .... 127 M1
Undercliffe Cricket Club
  ECHL BD2 .... 105 L4
Undercliffe First School
  ECHL BD2 .... 5 L1
Union Business Centre
  ECHL BD2 .... 105 M2
University of Bradford
  GTHN BD7 .... 4 B7
University of Huddersfield
  HUD HD1 .... 15 G8
University of Huddersfield
  HUDW HD3 .... 191 L5
University of Huddersfield
  KBTN HD8 .... 215 K8
University of Leeds
  BHP/TINH LS16 .... 86 E6
University of Leeds
  HDGY LS6 .... 6 C4
University of Leeds
  HDGY LS6 .... 109 H2

University of Leeds
  LDSU LS2 .... 6 D6
University of Leeds
  LDSU LS2 .... 6 C6
University of Leeds
  MID LS10 .... 9 L4
University Sports Centre
  LDSU LS2 .... 6 D6
Upper Abrigg Special School
  HOLM/MEL HD7 .... 236 F7
Upperthong Junior &
  Infant School
  HOLM/MEL HD7 .... 254 A2
Upper Whitley Junior &
  Infant School
  HOR/CROF WF4 .... 217 G2
Upperwood Junior &
  Infant School
  WMB/DAR S73 .... 263 H8
Upper Wortley Primary School
  WOR/ARM LS12 .... 108 D8
Upton A R L F C
  HEM/SK/SE WF9 .... 225 K6
Upton Clinic
  HEM/SK/SE WF9 .... 225 M6
Upton Surgery
  HEM/SK/SE WF9 .... 225 L6
Utley Junior & Infant School
  AIRE BD20 .... 57 K4
Vale School
  KNOT WF11 .... 181 M2
Valley Medical Centre
  HBR HX7 .... 143 J2
Venlo Industrial Estate
  BOW BD4 .... 127 L4
Victoria Baths
  ELL HX5 .... 169 J8
Victoria Park School
  BRAM LS13 .... 108 A3
Victoria Primary School
  OSM LS9 .... 110 D6
The Victoria Theatre
  HFAX HX1 .... 11 G6
Victoria Walk
  LDS LS1 .... 7 G9
Victory Medical Centre
  LIT OL15 .... 207 K1
The Village Surgery
  TOD OL14 .... 163 J5
Vine Industrial Estate
  BRIG HD6 .... 170 B3
Vintage Railway
  Carriage Museum
  HWTH BD22 .... 78 E7
Wadsworth Old Town
  Primary School
  HBR HX7 .... 143 L1
Wainstalls School
  LUD/ILL HX2 .... 145 H1
Wakefield Art Gallery
  WKFDE WF1 .... 176 D7
Wakefield Cathedral
  WKFDE WF1 .... 12 F2
Wakefield City Baths
  WKFDE WF1 .... 13 G2
Wakefield City High School
  WKFDE WF1 .... 177 H7
Wakefield College
  CAS WF10 .... 157 K8
Wakefield College
  FEA/AMT WF7 .... 201 M1
Wakefield College
  HEM/SK/SE WF9 .... 224 A7
Wakefield College
  WKFDE WF1 .... 12 C1
Wakefield Girls High School
  WKFDE WF1 .... 12 D1
Wakefield Golf Club
  WKFDW/WTN WF2 .... 199 G8
Wakefield Health Authority
  WKFDE WF1 .... 176 D1
Wakefield Independent
  Junior School
  HOR/CROF WF4 .... 201 H8
Wakefield Independent School
  HOR/CROF WF4 .... 201 G6
Wakefield Methodist First
  School
  WKFDW/WTN WF2 .... 12 E8
Wakefield Metropolitan District
  Council
  HEM/SK/SE WF9 .... 223 M7
Wakefield Metropolitan District
  Council
  HEM/SK/SE WF9 .... 247 H4
Wakefield Metropolitan District
  Council
  WKFDE WF1 .... 12 D2
Wakefield Museum
  WKFDE WF1 .... 12 E2
Wakefield Road Surgery
  BOW BD4 .... 127 K3
Wakefield St Johns C of E
  (Aided) Junior & Infant
  School
  WKFDE WF1 .... 176 D6
Wakefield St Marys C of E School
  WKFDE WF1 .... 13 H3
Wakefield Sports Club
  WKFDE WF1 .... 176 E6
Wakefield Superbowl 2000
  WKFDE WF1 .... 13 L8
Wakefield Theatre Royal & Opera
  House
  WKFDE WF1 .... 12 D3
Wakefield Tutorial
  Preparatory School
  MOR LS27 .... 152 C2
Wakefield Yamaha Music School
  WKFDE WF1 .... 12 E2
Walsden C of E (E) Infant School
  TOD OL14 .... 163 K5
Walsden Cricket Club
  TOD OL14 .... 163 J6
Walsden Industrial Estate
  TOD OL14 .... 163 K7
Walsden Junior Mixed School
  TOD OL14 .... 163 J5
Walton Grove Infant School
  WKFDW/WTN WF2 .... 199 K7

Walton Primary School
  WKFDW/WTN WF2 .... 199 J7
Wapping First School
  BFDE BD3 .... 5 H3
Wardle High School
  WHIT OL12 .... 206 F1
Warley Road Junior &
  Infant School
  LUD/ILL HX2 .... 146 A8
Warley Town School
  LUD/ILL HX2 .... 145 K8
War Memorial
  HFAX HX1 .... 11 J6
Warren House Surgery
  BSLY S70 .... 261 H6
The Watergate Clinic
  MILN OL16 .... 206 B7
The Waterloo Practice
  HUDE HD5 .... 193 J8
Waterside Industrial Estate
  COL BB8 .... 74 A2
Waterside Industrial Park
  OSM LS9 .... 132 D3
Water Street CP School
  SKP/WHF BD23 .... 16 B2
Waterton Junior & Infant School
  WKFDW/WTN WF2 .... 197 M2
Waterton Park Golf Club
  WKFDW/WTN WF2 .... 199 L8
Waverley Middle School
  GTHN BD7 .... 126 D1
Wax Museum
  BFD BD1 .... 4 D5
Weetwood County Primary School
  BHP/TINH LS16 .... 86 F7
Wellfield Surgery
  ROCH OL11 .... 228 C1
Wellgate Infant School
  DOD/DAR S75 .... 242 D5
Wellhouse Junior & Infant School
  HOLM/MEL HD7 .... 212 E3
Wellhouse Middle School
  MIRF WF14 .... 172 D7
Wellington Business Centre
  ELL HX5 .... 169 J7
Wellington First School
  ECHL BD2 .... 105 K3
Wellington House Surgery
  BTLY WF17 .... 173 L1
Wellington Middle School
  ECHL BD2 .... 105 K3
Wellington Road Industrial
  Estate
  WOR/ARM LS12 .... 6 B9
Wellington Street Business Park
  CAS WF10 .... 157 L6
Well Lane Business Centre
  BTLY WF17 .... 173 L1
Wellwoman Clinic
  HFAX HX1 .... 11 G4
Westborough High School
  DEWS WF13 .... 173 J5
Westbourne Surgery
  HUDW HD3 .... 191 M7
West Bowling Golf Club Ltd
  WBOW BD5 .... 127 J5
West Bretton Junior &
  Infant School
  HOR/CROF WF4 .... 219 H6
Westbrook Lane Junior & Infant
  School
  HORS LS18 .... 85 K3
Westcliffe Medical Centre
  SHPY BD18 .... 82 C7
West End Industrial Estate
  MOR LS27 .... 151 M3
West End Junior & Infant School
  HORS LS18 .... 85 H5
West End Middle School
  CLECK BD19 .... 149 L7
Westfield Medical Centre
  CHAL LS7 .... 109 M3
Westfield Primary School
  BVRD LS3 .... 6 A7
West Garforth Junior School
  GFTH/SHER LS25 .... 113 G8
Westgate Gallery
  WBY LS22 .... 48 A1
Westgate Hill First School
  BOW BD4 .... 128 C7
Westgate Infant School
  OT LS21 .... 41 G7
Westgate Medical Centre
  OT LS21 .... 41 J6
West Hall Special School
  EARD/LOFT WF3 .... 155 K8
West Leeds High School
  WOR/ARM LS12 .... 108 B7
West Leeds Medical Practice
  WOR/ARM LS12 .... 130 C1
Westmoor County School
  DEWS WF13 .... 173 H5
West Oaks Special School
  BSPA/BRAM LS23 .... 48 E7
West Park Bramhope R U F C
  BHP/TINH LS16 .... 64 C5
West Park Surgery
  DEWS WF13 .... 173 K5
West Riding Magistrates Court
  BTLY WF17 .... 151 G5
Westroyd Infant School
  PDSY/CALV LS28 .... 106 F4
West Side Retail Park
  GSLY LS20 .... 62 B7
West Street County
  Junior & Infants School
  COL BB8 .... 74 A2
West Vale Junior &
  Infant School
  GTL/HWG HX4 .... 168 C2
Westville House
  Preparatory School
  ILK LS29 .... 20 F7
Westwood County
  Primary School
  MID LS10 .... 153 J2
West Yorkshire
  Metropolitan County Council
  GIR BD8 .... 4 C4

West Yorkshire Metropolitan
   County Council
   KGHY BD21 .... **2** E7
West Yorkshire Playhouse
   OSM LS9 .... **7** K9
Wetherby High School
   WBY LS22 .... **48** B1
Wetherby Junior School
   WBY LS22 .... **30** A8
Wetherby Race Course
   WBY LS22 .... **30** E8
Wetherby Town Council
   WBY LS22 .... **48** A1
Wharfebank Business Centre
   OT LS21 .... **41** G7
Wharfedale General Hospital
   OT LS21 .... **41** H4
The Whartons Primary School
   OT LS21 .... **41** J4
Whetley Middle School
   GIR BD8 .... **104** C6
Whinburn Residential School
   AIRE BD20 .... **57** H4
Whingate Business Centre
   WOR/ARM LS12 .... **108** C7
Whingate Business Park
   WOR/ARM LS12 .... **108** D7
Whingate Primary School
   WOR/ARM LS12 .... **108** C7
Whinmoor Surgery
   SCFT LS14 .... **89** K6
Whitebridge School
   OSM LS9 .... **110** F7
Whitechapel Middle School
   CLECK BD19 .... **149** L5
Whitecote CP School
   BRAM LS13 .... **107** M2
Whitehall Industrial Estate
   WOR/ARM LS12 .... **130** B2
Whitehill County Infant School
   LUD/ILL HX2 .... **124** A8

White Horse Leisure Centre
   WKFDE WF1 .... **12** D3
White Rose House
   WKFDE WF1 .... **12** F4
White Rose Surgery
   HEM/SK/SE WF9 .... **247** H3
Whitkirk Medical Centre
   MSTN/BAR LS15 .... **111** M6
Whitwood Business Centre
   CAS WF10 .... **157** J6
Wibsey First School
   WBSY BD6 .... **126** D5
Wibsey Middle School
   WBSY BD6 .... **126** D5
Wiggan Lane Trading Estate
   HUDN HD2 .... **192** F2
Wigton Moor School
   AL/HA/HU LS17 .... **88** B1
Wilberlee Junior & Infant School
   HOLM/MEL HD7 .... **211** M4
Wild Goose Gallery
   KNOT WF11 .... **159** J2
William Henry Smith School
   BRIG HD6 .... **170** A6
The Willows Medical Centre
   CUL/QBY BD13 .... **125** G5
Wilsden Medical Practice
   WIL/AL BD15 .... **102** D1
Wilsden Primary School
   WIL/AL BD15 .... **102** E1
Wilthorpe Junior School
   DOD/DAR S75 .... **260** E2
Windhill C of E First School
   SHPY BD18 .... **82** F6
Windhill Cricket Club
   SHPY BD18 .... **82** F5
Windhill Green Medical Centre
   SHPY BD18 .... **82** E6
Windmill Primary School
   MID LS10 .... **132** A6

Windsor House Surgery
   MOR LS27 .... **152** B2
Windsor Medical Centre
   EARL WF12 .... **174** A6
Wira Business Park
   BHP/TINH LS16 .... **86** B5
Withinfields Junior & Infants
   School
   HIPP HX3 .... **169** H1
Womersley C of E Primary
   School
   AWLS/ASK DN6 .... **205** H3
Woodbank Special School
   LUD/ILL HX2 .... **145** C6
Woodhall Hills Golf Club
   PDSY/CALV LS28 .... **106** B2
Woodhill Middle School
   SHPY BD18 .... **82** F6
Woodhouse Cricket Club
   CHAL LS7 .... **87** H8
Woodhouse Grove School
   IDLE BD10 .... **84** B5
Woodhouse Health Centre
   HDGY LS6 .... **6** F3
Woodhouse Primary School
   BRIC HD6 .... **170** D6
Woodkirk High School
   EARD/LOFT WF3 .... **152** E5
Woodland Glade Leisure Centre
   HUDN HD2 .... **192** F1
Woodlands C of E First School
   LM/WK BD12 .... **149** J1
Woodlands Cricket Club
   LM/WK BD12 .... **149** H1
Woodlands Primary School
   OSM LS9 .... **110** D3
Woodroyd Industrial Estate
   LM/WK BD12 .... **149** G1
Woodroyd Middle School
   WBOW BD5 .... **127** G3

Woodside Clinic
   WBSY BD6 .... **126** C8
Woodside First School
   WBSY BD6 .... **126** C8
Woodside Middle School
   WBSY BD6 .... **126** C8
Woodside Trading Estate
   HORS LS18 .... **86** A5
Wooldale Junior School
   HOLM/MEL HD7 .... **236** F7
Woolley Hall College
   HOR/CROF WF4 .... **220** D7
Worsbrough Common County
   Primary School
   BSLY S70 .... **261** H8
Worthinghead First School
   LM/WK BD12 .... **148** F3
Worth Valley Middle School
   HWTH BD22 .... **79** J3
W R C C Clinic
   HOLM/MEL HD7 .... **212** F5
Wrenthorpe Health Centre
   WKFDW/WTN WF2 .... **176** A4
Wrenthorpe Primary School
   WKFDW/WTN WF2 .... **176** B4
Wrenthorpe Sports Club
   WKFDW/WTN WF2 .... **176** B3
Wrose Health Centre Ltd
   ECHL BD2 .... **105** H1
Wycliffe Middle School
   SHPY BD18 .... **82** C6
Wykebeck Infant School
   OSM LS9 .... **110** A4
Wykebeck Primary School
   OSM LS9 .... **110** F4
Wyke Manor Upper School
   LM/WK BD12 .... **148** F3
Wyke Middle School
   LM/WK BD12 .... **148** E3
Wyther Lane Industrial Estate
   KSTL LS5 .... **108** C3

Wyther Park CP School
   WOR/ARM LS12 .... **108** B4
Yarnbury Rugby Union
   Football Club
   HORS LS18 .... **85** J3
Yeadon Cricket Club
   YEA LS19 .... **62** E7
Yeadon Curtain Gallery
   YEA LS19 .... **62** E7
Yeadon Health Centre
   YEA LS19 .... **62** D7
Yeadon Westfield Junior School
   YEA LS19 .... **62** B8
York Road Industrial Estate
   WBY LS22 .... **30** B8
Yorkshire Amateurs
   Football Club
   CHAL LS7 .... **88** B8
Yorkshire Bank Sports Ground
   AL/HA/HU LS17 .... **87** M4
Yorkshire Clinic
   BGLY BD16 .... **81** L7
Yorkshire County Cricket Club
   HDGY LS6 .... **108** F2
Yorkshire Martyrs Collegiate
   School
   BOW BD4 .... **128** C6
Yorkshire Post Offices
   LDS LS1 .... **8** C1
Yorkshire Post Sports Club
   BHP/TINH LS16 .... **86** E7
Yorkshire Sculpture Park
   HOR/CROF WF4 .... **219** G7
Yorkshire Television Studios
   BVRD LS3 .... **109** G5
Young Street Industrial Estate
   GIR BD8 .... **104** B6
Zakaria Muslim Girls
   High School
   BTLY WF17 .... **173** M2

Page 16

B2 1 Albert Ter 2 Back Bridge St 3 Back Of The Beck 4 Bay Horse Yd 5 Canal Yd 6 Castle View Ter 7 Coach Street Yd 8 Crossley Pl 9 Devonshire Pl 10 Elliot St 11 Hallam's Yd 12 Park St 13 Primrose St 14 Prospect Pl 15 Victoria St 16 Victoria Ter 17 Watson's Houses

Page 34

F7 1 Anderton St 2 Back Station Rd 3 Campbell St 4 Church St 5 Hall St 6 Ivy Pl 7 James St 8 Newby St 9 Newlands Dr 10 North St 11 Parker St 12 Prospect St 13 York St

Page 35

M5 1 Barrett St 2 Beech Gv 3 Fairfax St 4 Hawthorne St 5 Haythorns Av 6 Haythorns St 7 Monkmans Wharfe 8 Oakland St 9 Strawberry St 10 Tunnicliffe Pl

Page 36

A4 1 Back Briggate 2 Back La 3 Bell Sq 4 Brierdene 5 Briggate 6 Browcliff 7 Buckden Ct 8 Chapel St 9 Cragg Vw 10 Fletcher Av 11 Ghyllbank 12 Highfield La 13 Pear Tree Ct 14 Pickard La 15 Stirling St 16 Weavers Wk

A5 1 Albert Sq 2 Clog Br 3 Don Ct 4 King St 5 The Mallards 6 Mill Banks 7 Mitchell La 8 Mitchell Sq 9 New Close Av 10 Nicolsons Pl 11 Queen St 12 Sykes La 13 Wesley Pl 14 Wharfe Ct

Page 56

A1 1 Dixon St

C1 1 Bracken Rd 2 Harefield Cl 3 Vincent Av

D1 1 Williams Dr

E1 1 Game Scar La or Goose Eye Brow

E1 1 Beech St 2 Burley Ms 3 Croft St 4 Dale Vw 5 Dixon Cl 6 Falcon Cliffe 7 Forge Vw 8 Stone Gv 9 Upper School St 10 Wood St

E7 1 Shay Gap Rd

F1 1 Ash Gv 2 Station Vw

Page 57

G6 1 Bankfield Rd

G7 1 Bankfield Mt 2 Bankfield Wk

H3 1 Rivock Gv

H6 1 Coronation Wk 2 Heather Gv 3 Tarn Cf

H7 1 Braithwaite Wy 2 Guard House Gv 3 Hill Top Wy 4 School Rd

H8 1 Chestnut Ct 2 Durrance St 3 Holme Wood Rd 4 Nile St 5 Prospect St 6 Sycamore Vw 7 Wall St 8 Westfield Cl 9 Wingate Av 10 Wingate Wy

J3 1 The Fairways 2 Nursery Cl 3 Turnberry Ct

J4 1 Aireville St 2 Ashgrove St 3 Back Aireville St 4 Back Croft House La 5 Birchwood Dr 6 Croft House La 7 Howden Av 8 Lydget Ct 9 School St

J5 1 Hawkstone Dr 2 High Meadow 3 Woodside

J6 1 Albany Ct 2 Avondale 3 Cartmel Rd 4 Frances St 5 Huntsmans Cl 6 Springfield Ct 7 Westview Ct

J7 1 Back Ada St 2 Back Cartmel Rd 3 Back Edensor Rd 4 Back Grant St 5 Back Paget St 6 Back Simpson St 7 Back Sladen St 8 Cartmel Rd 9 Cashmere St 10 Grant St 11 Greenfield Ct 12 Lime St 13 Paget St 14 Redcliffe Gv 15 Simpson St 16 Sladen St 17 Spencer St 18 Talbot St 19 West Leeds St

M7 1 Alpha St 2 Ambler St 3 Back Buxton St 4 Back Rowsley St 5 Beecroft St 6 Berry St 7 Buxton St 8 Grace St 9 Rowsley St

M8 1 Brow St 2 Carlisle St 3 Delph Croft Vw 4 Dundas St 5 Elm Tree Cl 6 Haynes St 7 St Paul's Rd

Page 78

E8 1 Addison Dr 2 Alice St 3 Ashfield Ter 4 Clarendon St 5 Drill St 6 Earl St 7 Emmott Farm Fold 8 Fir St 9 Ghyll Dr 10 Hall St 11 Ivy Bank La 12 Jackly La 13 New St 14 Old Hall Cl 15 Pine St 16 Rosslyn Gv 17 The Spinners 18 Surgery St

F4 1 Clough Ga 2 East Royd 3 Green La 4 Hall St 5 Hamworth Dr 6 Larch Cl 7 Lark St 8 Meadow Vw 9 Roseberry St 10 Victoria Rd 11 Wright St

F7 1 Aire St 2 Ashlar Cl 3 Back River St 4 Chatsworth St 5 Duke St 6 Fairfax St 7 Lark St 8 Oak St 9 Park St 10 Portland St 11 River St

Page 79

G6 1 Arctic St 2 Cecil St 3 Chatsworth St 4 Collins Cl 5 Daisy St 6 Douglas St 7 East Ter 8 Fellwood Cl 9 Frith St 10 Gordon St 11 Janet St 12 Leaf St 13 Lees Bank Dr 14 Lonpacres 15 Nares St 16 Nile St 17 Nortbeck Dr 18 Roth St 19 Rylands Meadow 20 Stewart St 21 Thorn St 22 Valley View Gdns

H6 1 Albert St 2 Canberra Cl 3 Garden St 4 Cott St 5 Lorne St 6 Robert St 7 Rupert St 8 Stanley St 9 Sunderland St 10 Vernon St 11 Woodville St

J2 1 Aylesbury St 2 Back Aylesbury St 3 Back Eaton St 4 Back Malt St 5 Broomhill La 6 Broomhill St 7 Diamond St 8 Eaton St 9 Emerald St 10 Exley Wy 11 Hemsby St 12 Malt St 13 Opal St 14 Pearl St 15 Ruby St 16 Wheat St

K1 1 Arcadia St 2 Back Cromer St 3 Bransdale Cl 4 Deepdale Cl 5 Brook St 6 Broomhill Wk 7 Calton St 8 Catherine St 9 Chandos St 10 Samuel St 11 Sand St 12 Clarendon St 13 Cromer Rd 14 Cromer St 15 Grafton St 16 Hird St 17 Hope Pl 18 Knowle Spring Rd 19 Pickles St 20 Queens Gv 21 Tennyson St 22 Upper Calton St 23 Upper Chelsea St

L1 1 Alma St 2 Dawson Pl 3 Hainworth Wood Rd 4 Park Cl 5 Parkway 6 Woodhouse Av 7 Woodhouse Cl 8 Woodhouse Rd 9 Woodhouse Wk 10 Worthville Cl

M6 1 Aire St 2 Austin St 3 Back Compton St 4 Back Crouse St 5 Back Hyde St 6 Back Kirby St 7 Brown St 8 Caledonia Rd 9 Kirby St 10 Landor St 11 Linnet St 12 Marlborough St 13 Mitchell St 14 Mulberry St 15 Neville St 16 Pheasant St 17 Quail St 18 Spruce St 19 Swallow St 20 Thrush St 21 Victoria Park St 22 Victoria Park Vw

L2 1 Khus Wk 2 Spring Bank Ri

M8 1 Adam Cft 2 Blantyre Cl 3 Church St 4 Dellside Fold 5 George's Sq 6 Lodge St 7 The Paddock 8 School St

Page 81

H3 1 Airedale St 2 Arthur St 3 Bradley St 4 Burrage St 5 Dryden St 6 Foundry Hl 7 Lark St 8 Market St 9 Old Main St 10 Rook St 11 Waterloo Rd

H4 1 Back Balfour St 2 Back Gladstone St 3 Back Sycamore Av 4 Back Unity St North 5 Back Unity St South 6 Balfour St 7 Gladstone St 8 Myrtle Av

J2 1 Bramham Rd 2 Claremont Gdns 3 Foulds' Ter 4 Langley Gv 5 Leyburn Gv 6 Monk Barn Cl 7 Priory Cl 8 Scarwood Cl 9 Stavely Ms 10 Wingfield Gv

J3 1 Amy St 2 Barran St 3 Britannia St 4 Elizabeth St 5 Delgh Hl 6 Heath St 7 Jardine Rd 8 Lee St 9 Lund St 10 Lyndon Ter 11 Marion St 12 Myrtle St 13 Nether Moor Vw 14 Norfolk St 15 Norman St 16 Raven St 17 Sydney St

M7 1 Bank Crest Ri 2 Bankfield Av 3 Glenview Gv 4 Nab Wood Ms 5 Nab Wood Pl 6 Nab Wood Ri 7 South Gv 8 New Close Rd 9 South Wy 10 Staveley Dr

C7 1 Alexandra Rd 2 Avondale Gv 3 Back St Paul's Rd 4 Iver Wy 5 Marlborough Rd 6 Rossendale Pl 7 St Paul's Rd 8 Springswood Av 9 Springswood Pl 10 Springswood Rd 11 Wellington Crs 12 Wensley Av 13 Westcliffe Rd

C8 1 Northcliffe Rd

D2 1 Westmoor Cl

D3 1 Summerfield Dr 2 Summerfield Gn

D6 1 Ashley St 2 Atkinson St 3 Cross Rosse St 4 Mount Pl 5 Murgatroyd St 6 New Kirkgate 7 Quayside 8 Rhodes Pl 9 Salts Mill Rd 10 Upper Ashley La 11 Wainman St

D7 1 Bank St 2 Birklands Ter 3 Central Av 4 Dale St 5 Manor La 6 Market St 7 Sunny Bank 8 Windsor Rd

D8 1 Argyle St 2 Briggate 3 Grange Ter 4 Norwood Rd 5 Norwood St 6 Selborne Ter 7 Wharncliffe Gv

E2 1 Ashburn Gv 2 Carlton Dr 3 Delgh Hl 4 Highfield Ms 5 Newton Wy 6 Padgum 7 Providence Av 8 Rocklands Av 9 Rocklands Pl 10 West Gv 11 West St

E3 1 Hillside Ter 2 South View Ter

E5 1 Albert St 2 George St 3 Queen St 4 Victoria St 5 Wauds Gates 6 Wood St

F1 1 Hilton Crs 2 Kingsley Crs

F2 1 Wharfe Cl

F3 1 Adel Wood Pl 2 Oaklands Fold 3 Oaklands Gv

F7 1 Hollin Ct 2 Linden Ct

F8 1 Back Burton Crs 2 Sowden's Yd

Page 82

A4 1 Ellenthorpe Rd 2 Nursery Gn

A6 1 Highfield Ter 2 Parkfield St 3 Sherwood Gv 4 Sleningford Rd 5 Spinning Mill Ct 6 Woodside Av

A7 1 Beechwood Av 2 Beechwood Gv 3 Colliers Ct 4 Fairmount Pk 5 Hollin Wood Cl 6 Moorhead Cl 7 Nab Wood Cl 8 Nab Wood Gdns

B5 1 Amelia St 2 Edward St 3 Fanny St 4 Herbert St

B6 1 Ada St 2 Carlton Wk 3 Constance St 4 Dallam Wk 5 Dove St 6 Ferncliffe Rd 7 George St 8 Higher School St 9 Jane St 10 Katherine St 11 Lockwood St 12 Lower School St 13 Mary St 14 Mawson St 15 Park Gv 16 Queens Pl 17 Richmond Ms 18 Richmond Pl 19 Shelley St 20 Upper Ada St 21 Upper Mary St 22 Whitlam St 23 William Henry St

B7 1 Fern Hill Gv 2 Fern Hill Rd

B8 1 Beechtree Ct 2 Bransdale Cl 3 Deepdale Cl 4 Highmoor Wk 5 Rosedale Cl 6 Westleigh Cl

C5 1 Thompson La

C6 1 Aire View Av 2 Back Baker St 3 Belmont Crs 4 Belmont St 5 Belmont Ter 6 Maddocks St 7 Melbourne St 8 Old Mill Rd 9 Park Av 10 Park Ter 11 West End Ter

Page 83

G2 1 Acrehowe Ri 2 Bartle Gill Ri 3 Bartle Gill Vw 4 Back Kirkgate 5 Gill Beck Cl 6 Littondale Ct 7 Nidderdale Wk 8 Wharfedale Gdns

C6 1 Bescaby Gv 2 Hartlington Ct 3 Kirklands Gdns

G4 1 Ada St 2 Kirklands Cl 3 Oxford Pl 4 St John's Ct 5 Union St

G5 1 Dale Gv 2 Helen Rose Ct

G6 1 Lynfield Mt 2 Lywood Av 3 West Royd Gv 4 West Royd Mt

G7 1 Durling Dr 2 Low Ash Crs 3 Thornacre Rd 4 West View Cl

A4 1 Birchtree Wy

G8 1 Claremont Crs 2 Westfield Crs 3 Westfield Sq

H5 1 Cote Farm La 2 Frederick St 3 Glenside Rd 4 Near Crook

H6 1 Longroyd 2 Tinkler Stile

H7 1 Lyndale Dr 2 Moorview Dr 3 Welwyn Dr 4 Westfield La 5 Westcliffe Rd

H8 1 Livingstone Cl

J4 1 Brackendale 2 Brackendale Gv 3 Thackley Av 4 Thackley Rd

J5 1 Aire St 2 Baddeley Gdns 3 Brighton St 4 Regent Pl 5 Regent St

J7 1 Briarfield Cl 2 Briarfield Gv 3 Chrismoor 4 Santa Monica Crs 5 Santa Monica Gv

J8 1 Willow Gv

K4 1 Beech Cl 2 Sinden Ms 3 Weavers Cft

K5 1 Ashfield Rd 2 Blenheim Pl 3 Booth Royd 4 Booth Royd Dr 5 Bourne St 6 Charterhouse Rd 7 Dawson St 8 Gordon Ter 9 Harehill Cl 10 Harper Gv 11 Hyde St 12 Lenton Vls 13 Renshaw St 14 Sandmoor Garth 15 Sutherland St 16 Victoria St

K6 1 Calpin Cl 2 Emmeline Cl 3 Hampton Pl 4 Highdale Cft 5 Jasper St 6 Louisa St 7 Lumby St 8 Moorfield Pl 9 North Fold 10 Rawson Sq 11 Sir Wilfred Pl 12 Southcote Pl 13 Thorp Garth 14 Walter St

K7 1 Back Cavendish Rd 2 Booth St 3 Brecon Cl 4 Buckfast Ct 5 Cobden St 6 Dunkhill Cft 7 Leyton Crs 8 Leyton Gv 9 Leyton Ter 10 Wellington St

K8 1 Arthur St

L5 1 Ashfield Cl 2 Mitchell Cl 3 Simpson Gv

L6 1 Coleridge Gdns 2 Fourlands Cl 3 Fourlands Ct 4 Fourlands Dr 5 Fourlands Gdns 6 Fourlands Gv 7 Green La 8 Union Yd

L7 1 Allanbridge Cl 2 Fairhaven Gn 3 Garsdale Av 4 Hawthorn Dr

L8 1 Abbotside Cl 2 Friar Ct 3 Nunburnholme Wk 4 Wicken Cl

M6 1 The Covet 2 Slingsby Cl 3 Strangford Ct 4 Tannery Ct

M7 1 Brunswick Pl 2 Cherry Tree Av 3 Calloway Rd 4 The Grove 5 Haigh Hall 6 Haigh Hall Rd 7 Regent St 8 Skelton Wk

M8 1 Dorian Cl 2 The Drive 3 Fir Tree Gdns 4 Riccall Nook 5 Ruswarp Wk

Page 85

L7 1 Newlay Wood Gv 2 Throstle Nest Vw

M2 1 Dale Park Av

M4 1 Haigh Wood Gn

M5 1 Broadgate Av 2 Springfield Ri

M6 1 Woodville Av 2 Woodville Gv 3 Woodville Ter

M8 1 Hawksworth Gv

Page 86

A1 1 Kirkwood Ri 2 Kirkwood Wy

A2 1 Grove Farm Cft 2 Tinshill Crs

A4 1 Birchtree Wy

A6 1 Tanhouse Hl 2 Woodside 3 Woodside Hill Cl 4 Woodside Cres 5 Woodside Pl

B1 1 Holtdale Fold 2 Holtdale Gdns 3 Holtdale Lawn

B3 1 Edale Wy

B4 1 Iveson Gv

B6 1 Latchmere Crest

B8 1 Hawkswood Ter 2 Monkswood

C1 1 Holt Garth 2 Holt Park Ap 3 Holt Park Cl 4 Holt Park Ct 5 Holt Park Dr 6 Holt Park Ga 7 Holt Park La 8 Holt Park Ri 9 Holt Park Wy 10 Kenworthy Cl 11 Kenworthy Garth 12 Kenworthy Ri

C3 1 Raynel Garth

C7 1 Parkstone Pl

D1 1 Latchmere Av

D4 1 Hawthorne Gdns

D5 1 Lawnswood Gdns

D6 1 Chalfont Rd 2 Weetwood Grange Gv

D7 1 Northolme Av 2 Welburn Av

Page 87

E4 1 Adel Grange Cft 2 Adel Grange Ms

E6 1 Quarry Dene

E7 1 Hollin Gdns

E8 1 Drummond Ct

F1 1 East Causeway Crs

F2 1 Sand Hill Lawns

F3 1 Allerton Gv 2 Arncliffe Gra 3 Broomhill Crs 4 Hadleigh Ct 5 Moor Allerton Gdns 6 Stonegate Rd 7 Wycliffe Dr

F7 1 Hollin Cl 2 Linden Cl

F8 1 Back Burton Crs 2 Sowden's Yd

G6 1 Holmwood Dr 2 Sunset Ri

G7 1 Back Greenwood Mt 2 Green Cha 3 Green Vw 4 Greenwood Ct 5 Green Wood Pk 6 Sunset Dr 7 Sunset Mt

G8 1 Back Wilton Gv 2 Brookfield Rd 3 Grove Gdns 4 Mill Pond Gv 5 Sandfield Av

H1 1 The Court

H2 1 Buck Stone Gn 2 Buck Stone Vw

H3 1 Deanswood Gn

H5 1 Woodlea Fold

H6 1 Holmwood Cl 2 Holmwood Gv 3 Holmwood Mt 4 Woodlea Cha

H7 1 Elwood Cl 2 Green Cl 3 The Paddock 4 Parkside Lawns 5 Stonegate La 6 Stonegate Farm Cl 7 The Wickets 8 Woodside Ms

H8 1 Authorpe Rd 2 Back Bentley Av 3 Back Clipston Av 4 Back Gordon Ter 5 Back Monk Bridge Dr 6 Bentley Mt 7 Bentley Pde 8 Meanwood Valley Dr 9 Meanwood Valley Mt 10 Stonegate Ga 11 Stonegate Pl

Page 88

C6 1 Heron Cl 2 Highthorne Cl 3 Kestrel Cl 4 Kingfisher Cl 5 Plane Tree Cl 6 Plane Tree Gdns 7 Plane Tree Ri 8 Swallow Cl

C6 1 Parkwood Vw

C8 1 Back Ravenscar Av 2 Oakwell Dr 3 Ravenscar Av 4 Ravenscar Mt 5 Ravenscar Ter 6 Ravenscar Vw 7 Ravenscar Wk 8 St Catherine's Wk 9 St Margaret's Av

D1 1 Longwood Wy 2 Middlethorne Cl 3 Middlethorne Ms 4 Park Lane Ms 5 Wike Ridge La

A5 1 Box Tree Cl

A6 1 Shelley Gv 2 Shuttleworth La 3 Vine Ter (East) 4 Vine Ter (West)

D3 1 Summerhill Pl

K6 1 Carr Manor Gdns 2 Carr Manor Pl

K7 1 Bank View Ter

K8 1 Beckhill Gv 2 Potternewton Ln

L2 1 Wentworth Wy

L4 1 Fieldhouse Wk 2 Fieldhouse Wk 3 Highwood Gv 4 Moorland Wk 5 Queenshill Ct 6 Queenshill Ct 7 Queenshill Garth 8 Queenshill Vw 9 Queenshill Wk 10 The Willows

L5 1 Falkland Mt 2 Falkland Rd 3 Moorland Garth 4 Whinbrook Crs 5 Whinbrook Gv

L6 1 Allerton Grange Cl 2 Carr Manor Vw 3 Gledhow Vale Rd 4 North Gv Cl 5 North Wy

L7 1 Grosvenor Pk 2 Moor Farm Gdns 3 Short La 4 Wensley Av 5 Wensley Cres 6 Westfield Ter 7 Woodcliffe Dr

M1 1 Primley Park Mt

M4 1 Belvedere Gv 2 Hawk's Nest Gdns East 3 Hawk's Nest Gdns South 4 Hawk's Nest Gdns West 5 Primley Park Crs 6 Primley Park Ri

M5 1 Back Nunroyd Rd 2 Nunroyd Av 3 Nunroyd Gv 4 Nunroyd Lawn 5 Nunroyd Rd 6 Nunroyd St 7 Nunroyd Ter

M6 1 Allerton Grange Wk

M7 1 Back Pasture Gv 2 Gledmow Lane End 3 Hawthorn Cl 4 Hawthorn La 5 Hawthorn Mt 6 Hawthorn Pl 7 Hawthorn Ter 8 Hawthorn Vw 9 Hill View Pl 10 Hill View Ter 11 King George Gdns 12 Norfolk Vw 13 Pasture Gv 14 Pasture Pde 15 Pasture Pl 16 Pasture Ri 17 Pasture Ter 18 Pasture Vw 19 Town Street Ms 20 Victoria St 21 Woodland Dr

M8 1 Back Methley Dr 2 Back Potters Ct 3 Branford St 4 Edmonton Pl 5 Garmont Ms 6 Hardwick Cft 7 Harrogate Rd 8 Ivy Garth 9 Methley Mt 10 Methley Vw 11 Ottawa Pl 12 St Martin's Dr 13 Winnipeg Pl 14 Zermatt Ter

Page 89

D4 1 Back Ingleden Crs 2 Back Roman Pl 3 Cross Ingleden Crs 4 Ingleden Crs 5 Parkview Ct 6 Roman Cres 7 Roman Gv 8 Roman Mt 9 Roman Pl 10 Roman Rd 11 Summerhill Gdns

D7 1 Tudor Lawns

D8 1 Back Oakwood Dr 2 Back Oakwood Dr 3 Oakwood Nook 4 Whitechapel Wy

E1 1 Shadwell Park Ct

E6 1 Oakwood Vw 2 Sycamore Ct

E8 1 Ladywood Gra 2 North Grove Ct 3 North Wy

M8 1 Langbar Garth 2 Langbar Gv

Page 102

F8 1 Ackroyd St 2 Alderscholes Cl 3 Back Fld 4 Back Heights Rd 5 Chapel St 6 Enderley Rd 7 Fountain St 8 Friendly St 9 Henry St 10 Hugill St 11 King Edward Rd 12 Kipping La 13 Kipping Pl 14 Lane End 15 Lower Kipping La 16 Market St 17 Mary St 18 Peel St 19 Priestley St 20 Providence St 21 Rock Ter 22 South Sq 23 Sowden Gra 24 Vine Ter 25 Windsor Dr

Page 103

G8 1 Bronte St 2 Commercial St 3 Corrie St 4 Craven Av 5 Green La 6 Green Mount Rd 7 Havelock Sq 8 Market St 9 Prospect St 10 Prospect Ter 11 Sandmoor Ct 12 Sappate La 13 Springfield

C5 1 Back Girlington Rd 2 Back Kensington St 3 Firethorn Ct 4 Hoxton St 5 Round Thorn Pl 6 Thornton Rd 7 Whitefield Pl

L3 1 Dene Mt 2 Grape St 3 James St 4 Prospect Ter 5 Rossmore Dr 6 Sherwell Gv 7 Westlands Gv

L6 1 Falcon Ms 2 Grange Ter 3 Grangeway 4 Linnet St

H1 1 Brindley Gv 2 Dunlin Wy 3 Fulmar Ms 4 Kite Ms 5 Mallard Ct 6 Osprey Ct 7 Sanderling Ct 8 Sandpiper Ms 9 The Square 10 Swallow Fold 11 Whimbrel Cl

L8 1 Millbeck Cl

M2 1 Flower Hvn 2 Highfield Gdns 3 Thorn Gv

M3 1 Galsworthy Av 2 Hathaway Av 3 Woodale Av 4 Mossdale Av

M4 1 Portwood St

M5 1 Pearson La

M7 1 Arthur Av 2 Blackburn Ct 3 Crossley Hall St 4 Leaventhorpe St 5 Middlebrook Dr 6 Middlebrook Hl 7 Middlebrook Rd 8 Rodin Ct

D7 1 Sir Isaac Holden Pl

Page 104

A7 1 Bellshaw St 2 Crossley Hall Ms 3 Glynda Ct 4 Green Top St

A8 1 Abelia Mt 2 Camellia Mt

B2 1 Paradise Rd 2 Roydscliffe Dr

B4 1 Branksome Ct 2 Hartman Pl 3 Jesmond Gv 4 Masham Pl 5 Saltburn Pl

B5 1 Squire Gn

B6 1 Agar Ter 2 Clement St 3 Como Gdns 4 Iris St 5 Lingwood Ter 6 Loft St 7 West Park Ter

B7 1 Barnes Rd 2 Nicholas Cl

C3 1 Exley Mt 2 Glendare Rd 3 Glendare Ter 4 Mallory Cl 5 Rhylstone Mt 6 Robinson St 7 Wilkinson Ter

C5 1 Alum Ct 2 Firth Rd 3 Garden Ter 4 Garth Barn Cl 5 Milford Pl 6 Skye Rd 7 Spring Gardens Rd

D1 1 Brunel Ct 2 Graham St 3 Heidelberg Rd 4 Mannheim Rd 5 Mitcham Dr

C6 1 Fairbank Ter 2 Lower Westfield Rd 3 Northrop Cl 4 Whitby Rd 5 Woodlands Rd

D2 1 Heaton Gv

D4 1 Akam Rd 2 Angel Wy 3 Ashton St 4 Baptist Pl 5 Blythe St 6 Butcher St 7 Chain St 8 Fulton St 9 Grattan Rd 10 Greenaire Pl 11 Hey St 12 Holmfield St 13 Infirmary St 14 Listerhills Rd 15 Longcroft Link 16 Longcroft Pl 17 Longlands St 18 Lower Grattan Rd 19 One St 20 Providence St 21 Roundhill Pl 22 St Thomas's Rd 23 Sedgfield Ter 24 Silver St 25 Simes St 26 Soho St 27 Tetley St 28 Vincent St 29 Westend St

D5 1 Anvil St 2 Ashwell St 3 Atlas St 4 Barden St 5 Cross Rd 6 Farcliffe Pl 7 Glenholme Rd 8 Jarratt St 9 Jarratt St (East) 10 Mactuick Gv 11 Middleton St 12 St Chad's Rd 13 Silver St 14 White's Vw

D6 1 Belvedere Ter 2 Dalton Ter 3 Feamsides Ter 4 Glynn Ter 5 Grandage Ter 6 Harriet St 7 Holker St 8 Hollings Sq 9 Hollings St 10 Sloan Sq 11 White's Vw

D7 1 Carlton St 2 Edmund St 3 Grove Ter 4 Howard St 5 Lansdowne Pl 6 Longside Av 7 Manville Ter 8 Norcroft Brow 9 Sherborne Rd 10 South Brook Ter 11 Tumbling Hill St 12 Wilton St

D8 1 Burdale Pl 2 Cottam Av 3 Cottam Ter 4 Ireton St 5 Kirkburn Pl 6 Rilston St 7 Roslyn Pl 8 Shirley Rd 9 Staveley Rd 10 Willowfield St

E1 1 Northdale Mt 2 Poplar Av 3 Poplar Dr 4 Poplar Gv 5 Russell St 6 Stanley St

E2 1 Bradley St 2 Buxton St 3 Buxton La 4 Frizley Gdns 5 Paddock 6 Royal Av 7 South Rd 8 South Vw 9 Snowden St

Page 105

E4 1 Back Blenheim St 2 Back Lindum St 3 Blenheim St 4 Dartmouth Ter 5 Devonshire Ter 6 Fairmount 7 North Park Ter 8 Oak La 9 Selborne Mt

E5 1 Anderson St 2 Arnold St 3 Century Pl 4 Church St 5 Conduit St 6 Cowgill St 7 Laburnum Pl 8 Leyburne St 9 Lincoln Ct 10 Newport St 11 Newton Rd 12 Priestman Cl 13 Priestman St 14 Southfield Sq 15 Trees St 16 Wilson St

E6 1 Back Wood St 2 Denby St 3 Fraser St 4 Globe Fold 5 Hind St 6 Jasmin Ter 7 Juniper Cl 8 Lincoln Rd 9 Menstone St 10 Oxley St 11 Preston St 12 Primrose St 13 Rievaulx Av 14 Stallabrass St 15 Whetley Cl 16 Wood Pl 17 Wood St

E7 1 Back Great Russell St 2 Fieldhead St 3 Legrams Ter 4 Marion St 5 Milne St 6 Milton St 7 Monk St 8 Morpeth St 9 Musselburgh St 10 St Andrew's Vls 11 Thornton St 12 Water La

E8 1 Back Laisteridge La 2 St Andrew's Pl 3 Shearbridge Ter

F1 1 Laburnum Rd 2 Mexborough Rd 3 Wrose Hill Pl

F2 1 Bute St 2 Lang La

F4 1 Twickenham Ct

F5 1 Cornwall Pl 2 Cornwall Ter 3 Cottingley Ter 4 Drill Pl 5 Grosvenor Ter 6 Mornington Vls 7 Picton St 8 South Pde 9 Springlodge Pl 10 Valley Pde

G1 1 St Laurence's Cl

G2 1 Badgers Wy 2 Ploughmans Cft

G5 1 King's Ga 2 Lupton St

G6 1 Brearton St 2 Grammar School St 3 Hallfield Rd 4 Hallfield St 5 Hallgate 6 North Holme St 7 Salem St 8 Singleton St 9 Snowden St

G7
1 Albion St
2 Barry St
3 Broad St
4 Charles St
5 Commerce St
6 Darley St
7 Fountain St
8 Grattan Rd
9 Hustlergate
10 James Ga
11 Kirkgate
12 Mawson Ct
13 Middle St
14 Millergate
15 New John St
16 Northgate
17 North Pde
18 Oddfellows' Ct
19 Piccadilly
20 Rawson Pl
21 Rawson Rd
22 Rawson Sq
23 Sackville St
24 St Blaise Wy
25 Southgate
26 Sunbridge Rd
27 Tyrrel St
28 Upper Piccadilly
29 Wade St
G8
1 Aldermanbury
2 Channing Wy
3 Chester St
4 Glydegate
5 Market St
6 Morley St
7 Neal St
8 Norfolk Gdns
9 Pictureville
10 Portland St
11 Prince's Wy
12 Quebec St
13 Swan St
14 William St
H1
1 Finsbury Dr
2 Hirst Lodge Ct
3 Semon Av
4 Sinclair Rd
H2
1 Ashbourne Cl
2 Camargue Fold
3 Flower Bank
4 Gresham Av
5 High Poplars
6 Sable Crest
7 Shetland Cl
8 Stirrup Gv
H3
1 Armidale Wy
2 Ashbourne Bank
3 Ashbourne Gv
4 Ashbourne Mt
5 Ashbourne Ri
6 Geelong Cl
7 Kingsdale Gv
8 Luther Wy
9 Tetley Pl
H4
1 Queen's Rd
H5
1 Falmouth Av
2 Portsmouth Av
3 Southampton St
4 Westminster Pl
5 Westminster Ter
H6
1 Arnford Cl
2 Cambridge Pl
3 Craven St
4 Cross Sun St
5 Holdsworth St
6 Lawson St
7 Lingard St
8 North Brook St
9 Priestley St
10 Stanacre Pl
11 Tyne St
H7
1 Aked St
2 Anne Ga
3 Balme St
4 Captain St
5 Cater St
6 Chapel St
7 Charles St
8 East Pde
9 Field St
10 Forster Ct
11 Green St
12 Hick St
13 Jermyn St
14 Kornla Cl
15 North St
16 Park Ga
17 Petergate
18 Upper Park Ga
19 Vicar La
20 Wellesley St
21 Wellington St
H8
1 Adolphus St
2 Bedford St
3 Chandos St
4 Eastbrook La
5 Ebenezer St
6 Filey St
7 Frederick St
8 Great Cross St
9 Greenwood Ct
10 Hardy St
11 West St
J1
1 Howarth Crs
2 Milligan Av
3 Mirfield Av
4 Moser Crs
J2
1 Ashbourne Garth
2 Greenwood Dr
3 Greenwood Mt
4 Grove House Crs
J3
1 Bolton Rd
2 Grove House Dr
3 Pendragon
4 Severn Rd
J4
1 Harrogate Av
2 Harrogate Pl
3 Harrogate Ter
4 Regency Vw
5 Webb Dr
J5
1 Airedale College Ter
2 St Augustine's Ter
J6
1 Avenham Wy
2 Hill Side Ter
J7
1 Bardsey Crs
2 Bath St
3 Edderthorpe St
4 Gobind Marg
5 Heap St
6 Hill Side Rd
7 Humboldt St
8 Marley St
9 Percival St
10 Pool Ct
11 Richard St
12 Thryberg St
13 Upper Mosscar St
14 Whitley St
15 Woodbine St
J8
1 Banner St
2 Downham St
3 Robert St
4 Wenlock St
K1
1 Acre Gv
2 Norman Mt
3 Norman Ter
4 Stonefield Cl
5 Wayside Crs
6 West End Ter
7 Westwood Gv
K2
1 Back Stone Hill Rd
2 Bolton Gv
3 Bromet Pl
4 Penn Cl
5 Rowanberry Cl
6 Thornbridge Ms
7 West Royd Av
K3
1 Airedale St
2 Back Manor St
3 Manor St
4 Pelham Ct
5 Pelham Rd
6 Pendragon La
7 Peterborough Pl
8 Peterborough Ter
9 Wellington St
10 West St
K4
1 Back Dudley Hill Rd
2 Beldon Pl
3 Elbow La
4 Fletton Ter
5 Green Pl
6 Palmerston St
7 Peterborough Rd
8 Sherwood Pl
9 Sowden Buildings
10 Sturges Gv
11 Thirlmere Gdns
12 Vernon Pl
13 Wellington Gv
K5
1 Fernbank Rd
2 Heath Rd
3 Killinghall Av
4 Killinghall Gv
5 Roger Ct
6 Westfield Ter
K6
1 Alcester Garth
2 Beech Ter
3 Burnsall Rd
4 Hinchcliffe St
K7
1 Abaseen Cl
2 Barlow St
3 Downing Cl
4 Mavis St
5 Netherby St
6 Webster St
K8
1 Allan St
2 Arlington St
3 Cracoe Rd
4 Gledhill Rd
5 Kilnsey Rd
6 Nidd St
7 Whitehead St
L1
1 Caythorne Wk
2 Deanery Gdns
3 Granary Ct
4 Lands La
5 Lavender Hl
6 Stonecroft
7 Stony La
L2
1 Pullan Dr
2 Quincy Cl
L3
1 Farlea Dr
2 Gaythorne Rd
3 Moorside Cl
4 Thornfield Pl
5 Whitaker Cl
L4
1 Charnwood Cl
2 Charnwood Gv
3 Charnwood Rd
4 Fagley Crs
5 Intake Gv
6 Intake Ter
7 Museum Ct
8 Musgrave Gv
9 Musgrave Mt
L5
1 Fagley Ter
2 Glenmore Cl
3 Moorgate Av
4 Nighthorne Av
5 Rowan Ct
6 Whitehead Gv
L6
1 Chelmsford Rd
2 Dalby St
3 Moor Park Rd
L7
1 Bower Gn
2 Granton St
3 Greenhill St
4 Hazelhurst Ct
5 Manse St
6 Wellands Ter
L8
1 Almond St
2 Kimberley St
3 Lapage Ter
4 Orange St
5 Pearson St
6 Walnut St
M1
1 Bridgegate Wy
2 Straightacres La
3 Summerbridge Dr
M2
1 Elvey Cl
2 Inkerman St
3 Victoria Dr
4 Wharncliffe Crs
M3
1 Ashington Cl
2 Firbank Gn
M4
1 Moorside Av
2 Moorside Ter
3 Wood View Dr
M5
1 Addison Av
2 Moorgarth Av
3 Moorlands Av
4 Moorthorpe Av
5 Moorville Av
M6
1 Grenfell Rd
2 Roydstone Rd
3 Warley Gv
M7
1 Beswick Cl
2 Charles Av
3 Hudson St
4 Johnson St
5 Marton Ct
6 Moorside La
7 Moorside Pl
8 Moorside Rd
9 Napier St
10 Napier Ter
11 Raglan St
12 Scaley St
13 School Sq
14 Wetton Ct
M8
1 Blanche St
2 Blucher St
3 Chapman St
4 Dewhirst Pl
5 Hetton Dr
6 Iqbal Ct
7 Latimer St
8 Lilac Gv
9 Mortimer Rw
10 Tagore Ct

Page 106

A1
1 Lambourne Av
2 Poplarwood Gdns
3 Ranelagh Av
4 Rowanwood Gdns
A2
1 Larwood Av
A3
1 Oakdale Cl
A5
1 Burlington Av
2 Woodhall Pl
A6
1 Barberry Av
2 Hawthorn Av
3 Hawthorn St
4 Herbert Pl
5 Melbourne Gv
6 Randolph St
A7
1 Courtenay Cl
2 Nottingham St
3 Redmire St
4 Victor St
A8
1 Back Tamworth St
2 Tamworth St
B5
1 Daleside Cl
2 Woodhall Vw
B6
1 Grange Gv
2 Grange Vw
B8
1 Tyersal Garth
C5
1 Shortway
C6
1 Chatsworth Av
2 Chatsworth Dr
D5
1 Woodhall Park Cft
D6
1 Inghams Ter
2 Ingham's Vw
E3
1 Frederick St
E4
1 Farfield Dr
2 Fieldhouse Gv
E5
1 Beechwood St
2 Carlisle St
3 Woodlands Av
4 Woodlands Gv
5 Woodlands Ter
6 Wood Vine Rd
E6
1 Highcroft Cl
2 Highfield Ter
3 Prospect St
E7
1 Mount Tabor St
E8
1 Moorfield Gv
2 Smalewell Dr
F1
1 Petrie Crs
2 Yewdall Rd
F2
1 Kirklees Cft
2 Kirklees Ri
F3
1 Andrew St
2 Hainsworth Sq
3 Oakwell Ter
4 Turner St
F4
1 Armstrong St
2 Arncliffe Garth
3 Beckbury Cl
4 Beckbury St
5 Gilbert St
6 New Park Wk
7 Poplar Sq
8 Sunfield Gdns
9 Victoria Rd
F5
1 Dawson St
2 Hudson St
3 Laburnum St
4 Roberts St
5 Springfield Ter
6 West Grove St
7 William St
8 Wilsons Yd
F6
1 Prospect Gv
F7
1 Meadowhurst Gdns
2 St Lawrence Cl
3 Vicarage Dr
F8
1 Armitage Sq
2 Smalewell Gn

Page 107

G3
1 New Park Cl
G4
1 Bransby Ct
2 Grove St
G5
1 Ashfield Gv
2 Boocock St
3 Providence Pl
G6
1 Croft House Ct
2 Dorset Gv
3 Mount Ct
4 Wesley Rw
5 Wesley Ter
G7
1 Hutton Ter
2 Longfield Ter
3 Mulberry St
4 Mulberry Street Sq
5 Spinners Cha
6 Tofts House Cl
7 Wesley Vw
G8
1 Sandringham Crs
H1
1 Keldholme Rd
2 Longfield Garth
3 Wesley Vw
H2
1 Airedale Cft
2 Horton Garth
3 Rochester Gdns
4 Westminster Cft
5 Westminster Dr
H3
1 The Rowans
H4
1 Britannia Cl
2 Granville St
3 Half Mile Ct
4 Harrisons Av
5 Rosebery Ter
6 Victoria Ter
H6
1 Priestley Gdns
2 Rosemont Av
3 Rosemont Ter
4 Townend Pl
H7
1 Hammerton Gv
2 Longfield Av
3 Longfield Ct
4 Longfield Gv
5 Longfield Mt
H8
1 Littlemoor Ct
2 Sheridan Ct
J2
1 Calverley Gdns
2 Langley Garth
3 Langley Pl
4 Sycamore Rw
J3
1 Beecroft Mt
2 Bramstan Cl
3 Summerfield Av
J4
1 Back Atlanta St
J5
1 Rycroft Towers
J6
1 Montreal Ter
2 Washington Ter
J7
1 Cavendish Ri
2 Cavendish St
3 Hillside Gv
4 Portland St
5 Richmond Gdns
K3
1 Calverley Ct
2 Calverley Gv
3 Calverley Ter
K4
1 Nansen Ter
L1
1 Back Pollard La
L2
1 Blairsville Gv
2 Ganners Gn
3 Hillcourt Cft
4 Moorside St
5 Shirley Dr
L3
1 Back Parkville Rd
2 Westover Gn
3 Westover Gv
4 Westover Mt
5 Westover Ter
6 Westover Vw
7 Woodbine Ter
L4
1 Ashdown St
2 Back Bath Rd
3 Back Melbourne Gv
4 Back Rosemont Wk
5 Bath Gv
6 Hough Ter
7 Melbourne Gv
8 Rosemont Av
9 Rosemont Wk
10 Warrel's Rw
L5
1 Avondale St
2 Clarence St
3 Elder Mt
M2
1 Back Broad La
2 Fallswood Gv
3 Ganners Gv
4 Ivy Gdns
5 Wellington Garth
6 Wellington Mt
7 Wellington Ter
8 Westmoreland Mt
M3
1 Bellmount Gn
2 Landseer Ri
M4
1 Ashby Sq
2 Ashby Vw
3 Daisyfield Rd
4 Eightlands Av
5 Highfield St
6 Mclaren Flds
7 Rossefield Av
8 Rossefield Cl
9 Rossefield Gv
10 Rossefield Lawn
11 Rossefield Pl
M5
1 Hough End Cl
2 Hough End Ct
3 Hough End Gdns
4 Somerdale Cl
5 Somerdale Gdns
6 Somerdale Wk
M6
1 Queensthorpe Ri
M7
1 Hare Farm Cl

Page 108

A3
1 Back Landseer Av
2 Back Landseer Gv
3 Back Landseer Ter
4 Back Raynville Mt
5 Landseer Ter
6 Raynville St
7 Snowden Ap
A4
1 Aston Av
2 Raynville Pl
A5
1 Martindale Dr
A6
1 Queensthorpe Cl
A8
1 Stonebridge Ap
B4
1 Houghley Sq
2 Wensleydale Av
3 Wensleydale Ms
4 Wensleydale Ri
5 Wyther Park Hl
B5
1 Cockshott Cl
B6
1 St Mary's Park Ct
2 St Mary's Park Gn
B8
1 Stonebridge Av
C1
1 Kepstorn Ri
C2
1 Back Church La
2 Morris Mt
3 Tordoff Ter
C3
1 Gilbert Cha
2 Hutchinson's Pl
C6
1 Armley Grange Vw
2 Back Highthorne Gv
3 Back Moorfield Ter
4 Back Springfield Mt
5 Greenock Rd
6 Halliday Dr
7 Halliday Mt
8 Highthorne Gv
9 Highthorne Vw
10 Moorfield Gv
11 Saint Ives Gv
12 Springfield Mt
C7
1 Albany Ter
2 Back Barden Pl
3 Barden Cl
4 Thornton Gdns
C8
1 Cliffe Park Cha
D1
1 Foxcroft Gn
2 Queenswood Mt
D2
1 Queenswood Ri
D3
1 Gilbert Mt
D6
1 Back Christ Church Vw
2 Burnsall Gdns
3 Highthorne St
4 Paisley Gv
5 Paisley Pl
6 Paisley Rd
7 Paisley Ter
D7
1 Back Esmond Ter
2 Lawson St
3 Upper Wortley Dr
4 Weavers Ct
D8
1 Green Hill Holt
2 Thornhill Cft
E1
1 Grimthorpe Av
2 Winston Mt
E2
1 Greyshiels Cl
E3
1 Back Stanmore St
E4
1 Argie Ter
2 Back Wetherby Gv
3 Bankfield Gdns
4 Bankfield Rd
E5
1 Back Nunington Vw
2 Nunington Vw
E6
1 Arksey Pl
2 Aviary Rd
3 Back Salisbury Gv
4 Back Salisbury Vw
5 Beech Dr
6 Chichester St
7 Salisbury Vw
E7
1 Athlone Gv
2 Athlone St
3 Athlone Ter
4 Back Athlone Av
5 Back Athlone Gv
6 Back Athlone Ter
7 Back Colton Rd
8 Brentford Gv
9 Brentwood St
10 Brentwood Ter
11 Cedar Cl
12 Colton St
13 Cricketers Ter
14 Laurel Fold
15 Laurel Pl
E8
1 Lansdowne St
2 Shoreham Rd
F1
1 Chapel St
2 Cross Chapel St
3 Cross Granby Ter
4 Grunberg St
F2
1 Back Granby Gv
2 Back Rochester Ter
3 Broomfield Crs
4 Cross St Michael's La
5 Granby Rd
6 Headingley Crs
7 Headingley Vw
8 Newport Vw
9 St Michael's Crs
F3
1 Back Ashville Gv
2 Back Ashville Rd
3 Back Ashville Ter
4 Back Beechwood Rd
5 Back Newport Gdns
6 Back Newport Mt
7 Back Newport Pl
8 Back Park View Av
9 Beechwood Pl
10 Beechwood Rd
11 Beechwood Rw
12 Broomfield St
13 Cardigan La
14 Graham Mt
15 Knowle Av
16 Knowle Gv
17 Knowle Pl
18 Lumley Av
19 Lumley Vw
20 Newport Gdns
21 Newport Mt
22 Trenic Crs
F4
1 Greenhow Cl
2 Knowle Rd
F7
1 Back Masham St
2 Back Middle Cross St
3 Back Mitford Rd
4 Back Model Rd
5 Back Model Ter
6 Back Model Vw
7 Crasmere Ct
8 Rosemary Av
F8
1 Cross Albert Pl
2 Elmfield Gv

Page 109

G1
1 Back Woodland Park Rd
G2
1 Buckingham Dr
2 Buckingham Gv
3 Raven Rd
G3
1 Back Ashville Av
2 Back Brudenell Rd
3 Back Hessle Av
4 Back Hessle Mt
5 Back Hessle Ter
6 Back Hessle Vw
7 Back Mayville Pl
8 Back Mayville St
9 Back Mayville Ter
10 Back Meadow Vw
11 Back Welton Gv
12 Back Welton Pl
13 Chestnut Gv
14 Chestnut Pl
15 Chestnut St
16 Hessle Av
17 Hessle Mt
18 Hessle Pl
19 Hessle Rd
20 Hessle Ter
21 Hessle Vw
22 Hessle Wk
23 Manor Dr
24 Norwood Mt
25 Norwood Vw
26 Pearson Ter
27 Royal Park Rd
28 Stott Rd
29 Thornville Crs
30 Welton Gv
31 Welton Rd
G4
1 Alexandra Gv
2 Alexandra Rd
3 Autumn Ter
4 Back Albert Ter
5 Back Autumn Rd
6 Back Beamsley Gv
7 Back Beamsley Mt
8 Back Beamsley Ter
9 Back Chiswick Ter
10 Back Spring Grove Wk
11 Beamsley Mt
12 Beamsley Ter
13 Branksome Pl
14 Branksome St
15 Branksome Ter
16 Burley Lodge Rd
17 Cross Burley Lodge Rd
18 Hopewell Pl
19 The Maltings
20 Spring Grove Wk
21 Thornville Av
22 Thornville Ct
23 Thornville Rd
24 Thornville St
G5
1 Back Boundary Ter
2 Burley Lodge Pl
G6
1 Allinson St
2 Clyde Ap
3 Clyde Vw
4 Copley St
5 Copley Yd
6 Driver Pl
7 Hainsworth St
8 Herbalist St
9 Sutherland St
H2
1 Back Mount Vw
2 Back Regent Park Ter
3 Regent Park Cross Av
H3
1 Back Kensington Ter
2 Back Midland Rd
3 Back Welton Av
4 Brudenell St
5 Royal Park Mt
6 Wrangthorn Ter
H4
1 Back Kelso Rd
2 Back Rosebank Crs
3 Kelso Pl
4 Rosebank Crs
5 Westfield Crs
H5
1 Consort Ter
2 Consort Vw
3 Cross Westfield Rd
4 Hanover Mt
5 Westfield Crs
6 Westfield Ter
H6
1 Burley St
2 Rutland Ter
H8
1 Springwell Rd
J1
1 Back Ridge Vw
2 Farm Hill Ri
3 Sugar Well Ap
J2
1 Back Clarkson Vw
2 Back Hartley Gv
3 Back Providence Av
4 Clarkson Vw
5 Cross Quarry St
6 Providence Rd
7 Quarry Mount Pl
8 Quarry Mount St
9 Quarry Mount Ter
10 Ridge Mt
11 Sycamore Cl
12 Woodhouse Cliff
J3
1 Bussey Ct
2 Holborn Gdns
3 Holborn Gn
4 Low Close St
5 Marsh V
6 Midgley Pl
7 Moorfield St
8 Pennington Ter
9 Pleasant Ct
10 Providence Ter
11 Spenceley St
12 Thomas St
J4
1 Back Westbourne Ter
2 Clarendon Pl
J5
1 Back Claremont Av
2 Claremont Av
3 Claremont Gv
4 Claremont Vw
5 Kendal Rd
6 Woodhouse Sq
J6
1 Back Burley St
2 Cropper Ga
3 Hanover La
4 Hanover Wy
5 Inner Ring Rd
6 Leighton La
J8
1 Springwell Vw
K2
1 Back Glossop St
2 Elm St
3 Glossop Vw
4 Rider Rd
5 Wharfedale Gv
K3
1 Beulah Mt
2 Beulah Ter
3 Beulah Vw
4 Cross Speedwell St
5 Eltham Cl
6 Eltham Gdns
7 Moseley Pl
K4
1 Archery Pl
2 Archery Rd
3 Archery St
4 Archery Ter
5 Back Archery Rd
6 Back Archery St
7 Back Archery Ter
8 Back Blenheim Av
9 Back Woodstock St
10 Blenheim Ct
11 Blandford Gv
12 Blenheim Av
13 Blenheim Sq
14 Churchill Gdns
15 Constance Wy
16 Devon Cl
17 Devonshire Gdns
18 Leicester Cl
19 Marlborough Gdns
20 Marlborough Gv
21 Winfield Ter
K5
1 Back Ibbetson Pl
2 Lodge St
3 St George's Rd
K6
1 Cookridge St
2 Leighton Pl
3 Park Sq South
4 Park St
5 St Paul's Pl
6 Somers Pl
7 South Pde
8 York Pl
K7
1 Aire St
2 City Sq
3 Infirmary St
L1
1 Newton Lodge Cl
2 Newton Lodge Dr
3 Potternewton La
4 St Martin's Gdns
L2
1 Lorry Bank
2 Scott Hall Wk
L4
1 Carlton Gv
2 Grosvenor Hl
3 Wilmington Ter
L5
1 Brunswick Ter
2 Hartley Hl
3 Howarth Pl
4 Jacob St
5 Lovell Park Ga
6 Lovell Park Hl
7 Morpeth Ter
8 Queen Sq
9 St Albans Pl
10 Tower House St
L6
1 Cross Belgrave St
2 Harrison St
3 Inner Ring Rd
4 Merrion Pl
5 St Anne's St
6 Sidney St
7 Swan St
8 Wormald Rw
L7
1 Albion St
2 Assembly St
3 Bank St
4 Blayd's Ms
5 Blayd's Yd
6 Cloth Hall St
7 Crown St
8 Gascoigne St
9 Navigation Wk
10 New Market St
11 Pitfall St
12 Queens's Ct
M1
1 Back Oak Rd
2 Back Sholebroke Rw
3 Back Sholebroke Ter
4 Chapel Rd
5 Laurel Mt
6 St Martin's Gv
7 St Mary's Cl
8 St Mary's Ct
9 Sholebroke Ter
M2
1 Back Grange Vw
2 Back Reginald Mt
3 Back Reginald Pl
4 Back Reginald St
5 Back Sholebroke Mt
6 Back Sholebroke Pl
7 Back Sholebroke Vw
8 Cross Reginald Mt
9 Reginald Pl
10 Reginald Ter
11 Reginald Vw
12 Savile Av
13 Sholebroke Pl
14 Sholebroke Vw
M4
1 Cross Wingham St
2 Holroyd St
3 Wilmington St
M5
1 Barclay St
2 Brunswick Ct
3 Henbury St
4 Lovell Park Cl
5 Lower Brunswick St
6 Melbourne St
7 St Thomas Rw
8 Telephone Pl
M6
1 Bell St
2 Centenary Sq
3 Cross Bell St
4 Cross Union St
5 Harper Pl
6 Lady Beck Cl
7 Lydia St
8 Millgarth St
9 Nile St
10 Playhouse Sq
11 St Peter's Pl
12 Templar La
13 Templar Pl
M7
1 Armouries Wy
2 Back York St
3 Brick St
4 The Chandlers
5 Cross Maude St
6 Cross York St
7 Harper St
8 High Court La
9 Kirk Ings Yd
10 New York St
11 Pine Ct
12 Steander

Page 110

A2
1 Back Grange Crs
2 Back Hamilton Vw
3 Back Harehills Av
4 Back Hillcrest Vw
5 Back Rossington Gv
6 Back Rossington Pl
7 Back Shepherd's La
8 Gathorne St
9 Hamilton Vw
10 Hares Mt
11 Hillcrest Pl
12 Rossington Gv
13 Rossington Pl
14 Shepherd's Gv
15 Woodland Mt
A3
1 Back Gathorne St
2 Cross Roseville Rd
3 Frankland Pl
4 Jackie Smart Ct
5 Leopold St
A4
1 Anderson Av
2 Anderson Mt
3 Gledhow Mt
4 Gledhow Pl
5 Gledhow Ter
6 Roseville St
A5
1 Accommodation Rd
2 Alma Pl
3 Chapman St
4 Cromwell Mt
5 Lindsey Gdns
6 Naseby Garth
7 Roxby Cl
8 Ruby St
9 Thealby Lawn
A6
1 Plaid Rw
2 Rigton Gn
3 Rigton Lawn
4 Rigton Ms
5 St Ann's Sq
6 St Mary's La
7 Thealby Cl
8 Thealby Pl
A7
1 Cotton St
2 Dolphin Ct
3 Dolphin St
4 East King St
5 Foundry St
6 Greenfield Rd
7 Meadowcroft Ms
8 Morpeth Pl
9 Place's Rd
10 Providence St
11 Railway St
12 Richmond Green St
13 Richmond Hill Cl
14 The Spinney
15 Spinneyfield Ct
16 Sussex St
A8
1 Hammond St
2 Spring Close St
B1
1 Back Roundhay Av
2 Back Roundhay Crs
3 Back Roundhay Gv
4 Back Roundhay Pl
5 Back Roundhay Vw
6 Cross Hilton Gv
7 Roundhay Pl
8 Roundhay Vw
9 Sunny Bank Vw
B2
1 Alcester Pl
2 Alcester Rd
3 Alcester St
4 Alcester Ter
5 Back Airlie Av
6 Back Airlie Pl
7 Back Alcester Pl
8 Back Alcester Rd
9 Back Alcester Ter
10 Back Baldovan Ter
11 Back Ellers Gv
12 Back Ellers Rd
13 Back Hares Av
14 Back Hares Ter
15 Back Hares Vw
16 Back Hilton Gv
17 Back Hilton Pl
18 Back Hilton Rd
19 Back Lambton Gv
20 Back Lunan Pl
21 Back Lunan Ter
22 Back Markham Av
23 Back Nice Vw
24 Back Shepherd's Pl
25 Back Vicars Rd
26 Baldovan Mt
27 Baldovan Pl
28 Baldovan Ter
29 Cross Alcester Rd
30 Cross Beck Rd
31 Ekota Pl
32 Ellers Gv
33 Gathorne Ter
34 Hares Ter
35 Hares Vw
36 Hill Top Pl
37 Hilton St
38 Hilton Ter
39 Lambton Gv
40 Lambton Pl
41 Lambton St
42 Lambton Ter
43 Lambton Vw
44 Lunan Pl
45 Lunan Ter
46 Rossall Gv
47 Shepherd's Pl
48 Vicars Rd
49 Vicars Ter
B3
1 Back Banstead St
2 Back Harehills Pl
3 Back Milan Av
4 Banstead St East
5 Banstead St West
6 Banstead Ter West
7 Conway Av
8 Conway Mt
9 Conway Ter
10 Cross Banstead St
11 Cross Elford St
12 Darfield Gv
13 Elford Rd
14 Lascelles Mt
15 Lascelles Pl
16 Lascelles Rd East
17 Lascelles Rd West
18 Lascelles St
19 Lascelles Vw
20 Ponderosa Cl
B4
1 Back Stanley St
2 Bexley Mt
3 Bexley Pl
4 Bexley Vw
5 Edgware Av
6 Edgware Gv
7 Edgware Mt
8 Edgware Pl
9 Edgware Rw
10 Edgware Ter
11 Edgware Vw
12 Stanley Av
B5
1 Alma St
2 Beckett Ter
3 Cross Alma St
4 Shakespeare Cl
5 Shakespeare Gdns
6 Stoney Rock Gv
B6
1 Haslewood Ct
2 Haslewood Dene
3 Haslewood Dr
4 Haslewood Gdns
5 Haslewood Gn
6 Haslewood Ms
7 Haslewood Pl
8 Haslewood Sq
9 Haslewood Vw
10 Keeton St
11 Oxton Mt
12 Oxton Wy
13 Rigton Cl
14 St Stephen's Ct
15 St Stephen's Rd
B7
1 Aysgarth Cl
2 Aysgarth Dr
3 Aysgarth Pl
4 Aysgarth Wk
5 Back Dent St
6 Back Kitson St
7 Back Prospect Ter
8 Butterfield St
9 Danby Wk
10 East Park Dr
11 Hampton Pl
12 Hampton Ter
13 Mullins Ct
14 Pontefract Lane Cl
15 Richmond Cft
16 Sussex St
B8
1 Back Cross Green Crs
2 Back Cross Green La
3 Cavalier Cl
4 Cavalier Ct
5 Cavalier Gdns
6 Cavalier Ga
7 Cavalier Gn
8 Clark Vw
9 Copperfield Av
10 Copperfield Crs
11 Copperfield Dr
12 Copperfield Pl
13 Copperfield Rw
14 Copperfield Wk
15 Cross Easy Rd
16 Cross Green Av
17 Cross Green Crs
18 Cross Green Gv
19 Cross Green Rd
20 May Ter
21 Milner Gdns
22 St Hilda's Av
23 St Hilda's Crs
24 St Hilda's Gv
25 St Hilda's Mt
26 St Hilda's Pl
27 St Hilda's Rd
28 Spring Close Gdns
29 Spring Close Wk
30 Thornleigh Gdns
31 Thornleigh Gv
32 Thornleigh Mt
33 Thornleigh St
34 Thornleigh Vw
C1
1 Gledhow Wood Ct
2 Well House Crs
3 Well House Gdns
4 Well House Rd
C2
1 Back Dorset Mt
2 Back Dorset Rd
3 Back Hovingham Gv
4 Back Hovingham Mt
5 Back Hovingham Ter
6 Back Rossall Rd
7 Dorset Rd
8 Dorset St
9 Hovingham Av
10 Hovingham Gv
11 Hovingham Mt
12 Hovingham Ter
13 Upland Gdns
C3
1 Back Berkeley Ter
2 Back Chatsworth Rd
3 Back Cowper Gv
4 Back Dorset Ter
5 Back Milan St
6 Back Sandhurst Gv
7 Back Sandhurst Pl
8 Back Sandhurst Rd
9 Back Seaforth Ter
10 Berkeley Crs
11 Berkeley Vw
12 Chatsworth Cl
13 Cross Milan Rd
14 Seaforth Gv
15 Seaforth Mt
C4
1 Ashley Ter
2 Back Ashley Av
3 Back Ashley St
4 Back Bellbrooke Ter
5 Back Broughton Av
6 Back Broughton Ter
7 Broughton Av
8 Compton Gv
9 Compton Gv
10 Compton Mt
11 Compton Pl
12 Compton St
13 Compton Ter
14 Compton Vw
15 Cowper Av
16 Cowper Crs
17 Florence Av
18 Florence Mt
19 Florence Pl
20 Stanley Pl
21 Stanley Ter
22 Strathmore Av
C5
1 Back Westlock Av
2 Hudson Gv
3 Hudson Pl
4 Hudson St
5 Westlock Av
C6
1 Back Glenthorpe Ter
2 Back Ivy Av
3 Back Ivy Mt
4 Back St Elmo Gv
5 Cross Ivy Mt
6 Glenthorpe Av
7 Glenthorpe Ter
8 Ivy Crs
9 Ivy Vw
10 Lupton Av
11 Nickleby Rd
12 St Elmo Gv
13 Vinery Gv
14 Vinery St
15 Walford Av
16 Walford Gv
17 Walford Mt
18 Walford Ter
C7
1 Back Charlton Rd
2 Back East Park Rd
3 Back Ecclesburn St
4 Back Garton Rd
5 Back Garton Ter
6 Ecclesburn Rd
7 Ecclesburn Ter
8 Garton Rd
9 Garton Vw
10 Ivy Crs
11 Londesboro Gv
12 Raincliffe Mt
13 Raincliffe Ter
14 Temple View Gv
C8
1 Copperfield Mt
D2
1 Easterly Garth
2 Easterly Vw
3 Moynihan Cl
D3
1 Easterly Cl
D4
1 Back Bellbrooke Gv
2 Back Bellbrooke Pl
3 Back Clifton Ter
4 Back Coldcotes Av
5 Back Harehills Park Vw
6 Back Seaforth Av
7 Back Trafford Av
8 Bellbrooke Av
9 Bellbrooke Gv
10 Bellbrooke Pl
11 Cross Bellbrooke Av
12 Harehills Park Av
13 Harehills Park Vw
14 Kimberley Pl
15 St Cyprians Gdns
16 Trafford Av
17 Trafford Ter
18 William Hey Ct
D5
1 Back Nowell Crs
2 Back Nowell Mt
3 Kimberley Vw
4 Kitchener Av
5 Kitchener Mt
6 Kitchener Pl
7 Kitchener St
8 Nowell Ap
9 Nowell Ct
10 Nowell Crs
11 Nowell End Rw
12 Nowell Gdns
13 Nowell Vw
14 Torre Crs
15 Torre Sq
16 Torre Wk
D6
1 Back Victoria Av
2 Dawlish Pl
3 Dawlish Rw
4 Skelton Crs
5 Skelton Mt
6 Skelton St
D7
1 Back Ecclesburn Gv
2 Back Ivy Gv
3 Back Ivy St
4 Kirkwall Av
E1
1 Amberton Cl
2 Montagu Gv
E2
1 Amberton Crs
2 Montagu Ri
3 Thorn Ter
E5
1 Back St Alban Crs
2 St Alban Ap
3 St Alban Cl
4 St Alban Gv
E6
1 Back Osmondthorpe La
2 Green Pasture Cl
3 Greenwell Ct
4 Rookwood Pl
E8
1 Neville Rw
F1
1 Grange Park Pl
2 Grange Park Ri
3 Grange Park Wk
F5
1 Brecon Ap
2 Selby Rd
F6
1 Rookwood Pde
2 Wykebeck Gdns
3 Wykebeck Gv
4 Wykebeck Sq
5 Wykebeck Vw
F7
1 Sedbergh Cl

Page 111

G1
1 Foundry Mill Gdns
2 Fox Wood Av
3 Foxwood Farm Wy
G5
1 Chenies Cl
2 High Ways
3 Sutton Crs
4 Whitebridge Vw
G6
1 Back William Av
2 Dence Pl
3 Dunhill Crs
4 Harefield East
5 Harefield West
6 Tranter Pl
7 William Av
G7
1 Coronation Pde
2 Fremantle Pl
G8
1 Coniston Gdns
2 Esthwaite Gdns
3 Halton Moor Rd
4 Levens Garth
5 Newsam Dr
H1
1 Airedale Ct
2 Ryedale Ct
3 Wharfedale Ct
H2
1 Brooklands Vw
2 Southwaite Cl
3 Southwaite Pl
H4
1 Somerville Vw
H5
1 Back Sunnydene
H6
1 Boldmere Rd
2 Primrose Garth
3 Rock Ter
H7
1 Howard Ct
2 Irwin Ap
3 Oak Crs
4 Rathmell Rd
J1
1 Bailey's Ct
2 Baileys Lawn
3 Elizabeth Pl
J3
1 Brathay Gdns
2 Casterton Gdns
J4
1 Bridle Path Wk
2 Maryfield Gdns
3 Maryfield Ms
J5
1 Primrose Crs
J6
1 Back Graveley St
2 Back Overdale Ter
3 Barley Field Ct
4 Brooksbank Dr
5 Chapel Ct
6 Chapel Fold
7 Cross Park St
8 Cross St
9 Field Ter
10 Overdale Ter
11 Pinfold Gv
12 Pinfold Sq
13 Primrose Av
14 Primrose Cl
15 School La
16 Woodman St
J7
1 Field End Cl
2 Field End Gn
3 Newsam Ct
4 Temple Park Cl
K1
1 Eastdean Ga
2 Hansby Bank
3 Parkway Ms
K2
1 Courtenays
K3
1 Croftside Cl
2 Fairfax Cl
K4
1 Maryfield Ct
2 Penarth Rd
3 Sandway Gv
4 Thornfield Ct
5 Thornfield Drive Dr
6 Thornfield Ms
K5
1 Clapham Dene Rd
2 Cold Well Sq
3 Graveleythorpe Ri
4 Hermon St
5 Templestowe Hl
K6
1 Cricklegate
2 Field End Gv
3 Mayfield Rd
4 Pinfold Ct
5 Prospect Gdns
6 Templestowe Gdns
7 Wilfred St
K8
1 Templegate Wy
L1
1 Farndale Cl
2 Mill Green Garth
L2
1 Southwood Cl
2 Swardale Gn
L4
1 Back Austhorpe Rd
2 Back Marshall Ter
3 East Vw
4 North Rd
5 North Ter
6 Orchard Mt
7 Station Rd
8 Tranquility
9 Tranquility Ct
L5
1 Back Carter Ter
2 Back Kennerleigh Wk
3 Carter Ter
4 Greenway
5 Greenway Cl
6 Kennerleigh Gln
7 Kennerleigh Wk
8 Templestowe Crs
L6
1 Back Hollyshaw Ter
2 Hollyshaw Ter
3 Templestowe Dr
L7
1 Manor Cft
2 Manor Garth
L8
1 Cranewells Gn
2 Cranewells Ri
3 Cranewells V
4 Darnley La
5 Hertford Lawn
M1
1 Ash Tree Bank
2 Ash Tree Cl
3 Ash Tree Gv
M2
1 Ashfield Cl
2 Stonehurst
M4
1 Back Austhorpe Rd
2 Back Chestnut Av
3 Back Chestnut Av
4 Back Poplar Av
M5
1 Kennerleigh Gv
2 Kennerleigh Ri
3 Kingswear Cl
4 Kingswear Gln
5 Kingswear Ri
6 Lulworth Cl
M6
1 Bennet Ct
2 Gray Ct
3 Knightshill
4 Lulworth Garth
5 Nettleton Ct
M7
1 Burr Tree Dr
2 Burr Tree V
3 Chantry Cft
4 Colton Ct
5 Colton Cft
6 Colton Garth
7 Cranewells Dr
8 Gypsy Wood Cl
9 Gypsy Wood Crest
10 High Bank Ga
11 High Bank Pl
12 High Bank Vw
13 Kirkfield Gdns
14 Laurel Hill Cft
15 Laurel Hill Gdns
16 Laurel Hill Gv
17 Laurel Hill Vw
18 Maltby Ct
19 Meynell Ct
20 Penlands Lawn
21 Windmill Gdns
M8
1 Addison Ct
2 Chesterton Ct
3 Hertford Cl
4 Laurel Hill Wy
5 Milne Ct
6 Woodhall Ct

Page 124

A7
1 East Bolton
2 Eastwood Cl
3 Eastwood Gv
4 Illingworth Crs
5 Illingworth Gv
6 Illingworth Wy
7 Moor Top Gdns
8 Natty Fields Cl
9 North Byland
10 West Scausby Pk
E6
1 Clarendon Pl
2 High Bury Cl
3 Moor Close Av
4 Moor Close Farm Ms
5 Oxford Rd
6 Sladdin Rw
7 Sunny View Ter

Page 157

M6
1 Aire Ter
2 Back Bank St
3 Back Wesley St
4 Bradley St
5 Castlefield Ct
6 Commercial St
7 Florence St
8 Greaves St
9 Hope St East
10 Perseverance St
11 Powell St
12 Rectory St
13 St Oswald St
14 Sykes St
15 Victoria Pl
16 Welbeck St

Page 158

C6
1 Meadow Wy

D7
1 Graham Dr
2 Hastings Wk
3 Henry Moore Ct
4 Hopwood Gv
5 Newton Dr

D8
1 Farriers Pl
2 Fryston Rd
3 Holywell Mt
4 Quarrydene Dr
5 Saddlers Cft
6 Wheatcroft

Page 163

J4
1 Copperas House Ter
2 Farnboro St
3 Pellon St
4 Stones Ter

J5
1 Barnes St
2 Chapel St South
3 Clough Rd
4 Dampier St
5 Granville St
6 Hollins Pl
7 Industry St
8 Knowsley Av
9 Lacy Av
10 Montreal St
11 Quebec St
12 Regent St
13 Saxon St
14 Vulcan St
15 Winterbutlee Gv
16 Winterbutlee Rd

J7
1 Cooperative St
2 Maple St
3 Pioneer St
4 Providence St

K1
1 Back Ridge St
2 Bath St
3 Bond St
4 Bridge St
5 Buckley Wood Bottom
6 Calder St
7 Crossley St
8 George St
9 Hazelwood St
10 Queen St
11 Ridge Bank
12 Roomfield St
13 Union St South
14 Whiteplatts St

L1
1 Back Commerical St
2 Back Der St
3 Beaconsfield St
4 Cross Stone Rd
5 Der St
6 Erringden St
7 Hallroyd Pl
8 Haven St
9 Holderness St
10 Osborne Pl
11 Richmond St
12 Russell St
13 Sanworth St

Page 167

H3
1 Beechwood Crs
2 Beechwood Dr
3 Flower Bank
4 Moorland Vw
5 Richmond Gdns

J3
1 Egremont St
2 Jerry La
3 Montague St
4 Priestley Pl
5 Rawson Pl

K1
1 Beech Vw
2 Blackwall Ri
3 Byron Av
4 Byron St
5 Chatham St
6 Dalton St
7 Elm Pl
8 Fern Lea St
9 Oak Pl
10 Plane Tree Rd

K2
1 Annie St
2 Arnold St
3 Belgrave St
4 Charles St
5 Chester St
6 Clement St
7 Egerton St
8 Greenups Ter
9 Hollins Bank
10 Newton St
11 Peel St

Page 168

B1
1 Akroyd Ter
2 Autumn St
3 Burleigh St
4 Cannon St
5 Cromer St
6 Dowker St
7 Dundas St
8 Hampton St
9 Highfield Pl
10 Hornby St
11 Knight St
12 Leadenhall St
13 Lynwood Crs
14 Maple St
15 Moorgate St
16 Norman St
17 Pohlman St
18 Raleigh St
19 Summergate St
20 Thornton St
21 Thornton Ter
22 Vaughan St
23 Winter St

C1
1 Bell Hall Mt
2 Bell Hall Ter
3 Constitutional St
4 Eldroth Mt
5 Elmwood St
6 Emscote Gdns
7 Green Terrace Sq
8 Hawthorn St
9 Hyde Park St
10 Laurel Mt
11 Perseverance Ter
12 Rockville Ter
13 Savile Pk
14 Thomas St West
15 Upper Haugh Shaw
16 Willow Bank
17 Woodbine St

D1
1 Back Savile Pde
2 Clover Hill Vw
3 Industrial Ter
4 Rothwell Rd
5 St Jude's St
6 Savile Pde
7 Savile Park Gdns
8 Savile Royd

D4
1 Copley Gln
2 Copley Ter
3 Greenroyd Cl

E7
1 Lindwell Gv

F1
1 Shaw Hl
2 Shaw Hill La
3 Simmonds La
4 Trooper La

F2
1 Browning Av
2 Cheltenham Ct
3 Cleveland Av
4 Longbottom Ter
5 St Albans Cft
6 Whitegate Ter
7 Woodford Av

F3
1 Bristol St
2 Doncaster St
3 Dyson Pl
4 Falcon St
5 Westbourne Gv
6 Westbourne Ter

F4
1 Dudwell Av

F6
1 Coronation St

F7
1 Clay House La
2 Cross St
3 Elizabeth St
4 George St
5 High St
6 Hollynsmill
7 Princess St
8 Union St

F8
1 Exchange St
2 Featherbed Cl
3 Woodside Gv

Page 169

H8
1 Bedford St
2 Dean St
3 Duke St
4 Flower Acre
5 Granville St
6 Grosvenor St
7 John William St
8 Parkfield Av
9 Timber St
10 Town Hall St

Page 170

B2
1 Granny Hall Gv

B6
1 Jumble Dyke
2 Longroyde Cl
3 Longroyde Gv
4 Raw Hl

C3
1 Barton St
2 Bond St
3 Frances St
4 Rock St
5 Rogerson Sq
6 Rydings Cl
7 Sunderland Ct
8 William Henry St

C4
1 Church La
2 Croft St
3 Daisy St
4 Heaton St
5 Parsonage La
6 Scotty Bank
7 Spring St

C5
1 Back Close Lea
2 Back Close Lea Dr
3 Bryan St
4 Capel St
5 Closes Rd
6 Denham St
7 George St
8 Green End
9 Harley St
10 Laura St
11 Ridge View Rd
12 Scotty Croft La

D1
1 Oakroyd Cl

D4
1 Mellor St
2 Park Rw
3 Ship St
4 West Park St

E3
1 Ash Gv
2 Hawthorn Cl

E4
1 Alegar St

E5
1 Providence Pl
2 Vulcan St
3 Woodland Sq

F4
1 Cannon Hall Cl

Page 172

A2
1 Highfield Dr

A8
1 Lady Heton Cl
2 Monkfield
3 Moor Top

B2
1 Lower Hall Dr
2 Lower Hall Mt

B4
1 Highfield Ct
2 Wheatlands Dr

B5
1 Ashby Cl
2 Malham Dr
3 Moorfield Vw

B8
1 Fox Royd La
2 Kings Head Dr
3 Moorlands Av
4 Woodsome Dr

C1
1 Edward St
2 Garden Cl
3 Garden Wk
4 Spring Valley St

C2
1 Albion St
2 Alexandra St
3 Ashton Clough Rd
4 Churchfield Cl
5 George St
6 The Hustings
7 Lonsdale Ter
8 Rouse St
9 Strawberry Bank
10 Thomas St
11 Upper Barker St

C3
1 Dymond Gv
2 Dymond Vw
3 Headlands St
4 Willow Wk

C4
1 Lincoln Dr
2 Spenfield Ct
3 Stanley Rd

C6
1 The Coppice
2 Finching Gv
3 Portal Crs
4 Robin Royd Cft
5 Robin Royd Garth
6 Robin Royd Gv

C7
1 Eastway Pk
2 James St
3 North's Pl
4 Sunny Bank Gv
5 Whitehall Av

C8
1 Fernhurst Cl
2 Fernhurst Wy
3 Richmond Lea
4 Savile Ct
5 Stonehurst Rd
6 Water Royd Crs
7 Water Royd Dr

D1
1 Bradd Cl
2 Firthcliffe Mt
3 Firthcliffe Vw

D2
1 Alfred St
2 Barker St
3 Bennett St
4 Ings Crs
5 Keir Hardy Cl
6 Sampson St
7 South St
8 Wakefield Rd
9 Wharton St
10 William St

D3
1 Benjamin St
2 Birchwood Ct
3 Frederick St
4 John William St
5 Melbourne St
6 Wellington St

D4
1 Pitt St
2 Warren Cl
3 Windsor Dr

D7
1 Greenside Mt
2 The Orchard
3 Shepley Mt

D8
1 Fernhurst Crs
2 Fernhurst Lea
3 Over Hall Cl
4 Pumphouse La

E1
1 Almondroyd
2 Firthcliffe Pl
3 Saxton St

E2
1 Carr St
2 Centre St
3 Chapel St
4 Greenside
5 John William St
6 Oak St
7 Peel St
8 West St

E3
1 Albert St
2 Queen St

E4
1 Ings Vil

F1
1 Grosvenor St
2 Milton St
3 Westfield Cl

F2
1 Back La
2 Darley St
3 Frank Peel Cl
4 George St
5 Grosvenor Ter
6 Park Rd
7 Park St
8 Royle Fold

F3
1 Alfred St
2 Brewery St
3 Brooke St
4 Brunswick St
5 Croft St
6 Garden St
7 John St
8 Kaye St
9 St James St
10 Swallow St
11 Walkley Gv

Page 173

G1
1 Chalcroft Cl

G2
1 Cambridge St
2 The Homestead
3 Hutton Dr
4 Lavender Cft
5 Longfield Ct
6 Lyndale Crs
7 Tidswell St

G3
1 Badgers Wk
2 Capas Heights Wy
3 Forster Dr
4 Harewood Gv
5 Lascelles Rd
6 Powell St

G4
1 Shelley Av

G8
1 Beacon St
2 Clarkson St
3 Dearnley St
4 Field St
5 Garden Dr
6 Red Laithes La

H1
1 Crowther St
2 Havercroft Wy
3 Healey Cl

H2
1 Beaumont Pl
2 Easby Av
3 Kilpin Hill La
4 Tichbourne St

H3
1 Churwell Av
2 Garnett St
3 Hillary St
4 Lyndale Ms
5 Mavis Rd
6 North Lodge Fold
7 Sherwood Cl
8 Squirrel Wk

H4
1 Boundary Rd
2 Byron Gv
3 Dray Vw
4 Hollins Rd
5 Knowles Hl
6 Laburnum Rd
7 Moorside Crs
8 Scarr End Vw
9 Staincliffe Crs

H5
1 Clifton Ct

H6
1 Barley Cft
2 Charles St
3 Coney Wk
4 George St
5 Pump La
6 Woodland Gv
7 Woodlands La

H7
1 Beaver Dr
2 Beckett Gv
3 Beckett Wk

H8
1 Commercial St
2 Ravens St

J1
1 Healey La
2 Holyoake Av
3 Linton Av
4 Nelson St
5 West Park Gv

J2
1 Hazel Gv

J3
1 Ashmead

J4
1 Victoria Crs

J5
1 Anroyd St
2 Back Brunswick St
3 Back Leatham St
4 Blenheim Dr
5 Fairfield Crs
6 Moorcroft

J6
1 Mitre St
2 Staincliffe Cl

J7
1 Pilgrim Dr

J8
1 Back Ravens St
2 Mavis St
3 Ravens Crs
4 Ravensfield Rd
5 Ravens Lodge Ter
6 Ravenswharf Rd
7 Stoney Bank St
8 Thornville Mt
9 Thornville Pl
10 Thornville St
11 Thornville Wk

K1
1 Barden Cl
2 Hayburn Gdns
3 Spring Gdns

K2
1 Alfred St
2 Alpine Cl
3 Belvedere Rd
4 Brown's Pl
5 Brown's St
6 Clerk Green St
7 Hamza St
8 Kensington Cl
9 Knowles La
10 Knowles Rd
11 Lower North St
12 Suffolk St
13 Upper Croft Rd
14 Upper North St

K3
1 Grange Av
2 Norfolk Av

K4
1 Marlborough Gdns
2 Picklesfield
3 Pickles St
4 Robin La
5 Salter St
6 The Sycamores
7 Tate Naylor St

K5
1 Jesmond Gv
2 Moorlands Av
3 West Moorlands Av

K6
1 Boothroyd Gn
2 Greenwood St
3 Hanover Gdns
4 Nowell's Yd
5 Oastler St
6 St Johns Cl
7 St John St
8 St Matthew Rd
9 St Paulinus Cl
10 Speakers Ct
11 Tweedale Gdns
12 Tweedale St

K7
1 Brook Rd
2 Brooks Yd
3 Fearnley St
4 St John Pde
5 Senior St
6 Thornhill Rd
7 Watergate Rd
8 Whitworth Rd

K8
1 Thornville Ter

L1
1 Back Henrietta St
2 Back Providence St
3 Bank Field Rd
4 Bank Foot Pl
5 Bank Foot St
6 Bayldons Pl
7 Brunswick St
8 Churchfield St
9 East St
10 Fleming St
11 Henrietta St
12 Hume Crest
13 Mayman Cl
14 New Wy
15 Peel Av
16 Providence St
17 Russell Cl
18 St James St
19 Turner Av
20 Wards Hl
21 Wards Hill Ct
22 Wood St

L2
1 Back Beaumont St
2 Beaumont St
3 Charles St
4 Denison St
5 George St
6 Wellington St

L3
1 Crossmount St
2 Hartington St
3 Howard Pl

L4
1 Carlisle Cl
2 Carr St
3 Jenkinson St
4 John St
5 Lidgate Cl
6 Maxwell Av
7 Savile St
8 Wood La

L5
1 Bright St
2 Bryer St
3 Lower Peel St
4 Low St
5 Northfield Pl
6 North St
7 Spring St
8 Tolson St
9 Upper Cross St
10 Upper South St
11 Ward St

L6
1 Ashworth Cl
2 Ashworth Gdns
3 Back Webster St
4 Central St
5 Eightlands Rd
6 George St
7 Nelson St
8 Oates St
9 Southgate
10 Spinkwell Rd
11 Vulcan Cl
12 Vulcan Gdns
13 Webster St
14 Wellington Rd
15 Wellington Rd East
16 Wellington St
17 Wesley Pl
18 Wheelwright St

L7
1 Anchor Bridge Wy
2 Grosvenor St
3 Waverley St

L8
1 Chapel St
2 St Mary's Pl

M1
1 Blackburn Pl
2 Clarence St
3 Cross St
4 Surrey St
5 Sussex St
6 Talbot Rw
7 West St

M2
1 Albion St
2 Back Station Rd
3 Bar St
4 Eyre St
5 North King St
6 Oxford Ter
7 Spurr St
8 Warehouse St
9 Whitaker St

M3
1 Cross Rink St
2 Savile St

M4
1 Peter Hl

M5
1 Bradford St
2 Crackenedge Ter
3 Eastborough Crs
4 Greaves Rd
5 Pepper Royd St
6 St Philip's Cl
7 Sharp St
8 Tentercroft Ct
9 Upper Camroyd St
10 Upper Peel St
11 Wood St

M6
1 Branch Rd
2 Church St
3 Cloth Hall St
4 Corporation St
5 Ernest St
6 Foundry St
7 Highgate Rd
8 Longcauseway
9 Manor St
10 Market St
11 Prince St
12 Ridings Rd
13 Rishworth St
14 Rockley St
15 School St
16 Tithe Barn St
17 Town Hall Wy
18 Union St
19 Wakefield Old Rd
20 Westgate
21 Woodville Rd

M7
1 Cross St

M8
1 Kaye St
2 North Vw
3 Scarborough Ter
4 Thornleigh

Page 174

A2
1 St Lukes Cl

A4
1 Lowdale
2 Matterdale Cl
3 Matterdale Rd
4 Patterdale Rd

A5
1 Alfred St
2 Coates Cl
3 Ings Rd
4 Moor Park Ct
5 Stephenson Cl
6 Well St

B1
1 Norgarth Cl

B7
1 Chatsworth Ct
2 Commercial St
3 Manor Garth Rd

C4
1 John Ormsby V C Wy
2 Manor Gdns
3 Smallwood Rd

D6
1 Co-operative St
2 Earl St
3 Heath Cl
4 Heath Wk
5 Kirk Cl
6 Tolson St

D7
1 Hazel Dr
2 Lord St
3 Maple Wk

E5
1 Howroyd's Yd
2 Milner St
3 Nettleton Cha
4 Westcroft Dr

E6
1 Ashleigh Gdns
2 Bridle Av
3 Heathfield Rd
4 Hillcrest Av
5 Kings Cft
6 Kings Lea
7 Moorlands Av
8 Moorroyd St
9 Naylor St
10 Stithy St

E7
1 Hirstlands Av
2 Meadow Ct
3 Meadow Vw

E8
1 Horton St
2 Love La
3 Millfields
4 Turn O'the Nook
5 Westfield Farm
6 Wilman Dr

F1
1 School St

F5
1 High Cl
2 Neston Wy
3 Tateley Cl

F6
1 Berryfield Garth
2 Holly Dene
3 Holly Mede

F7
1 Howard St
2 Northfield Av
3 Prestwick Fold
4 St Peters Ga

F8
1 Carlton Ct
2 Gordon Av
3 Union St

Page 176

A5
1 Silcoates Av
2 Silcoates Dr
3 Southfield Cl

A8
1 Mona St
2 Park Vw
3 Waite St

B4
1 Bowling Av
2 Greenfield Cl
3 Ruskin Ct
4 Sycamore Av
5 Westways Cl
6 Westways Ri

C8
1 Anderson St
2 Moorhouse Crs
3 Plumpton Pl
4 Plumpton St
5 Plumpton Ter
6 Waterhouse Gv

D6
1 Arlington St
2 Belmont St
3 Clifton Pl
4 Lonsdale Rd
5 St John's Cft

D7
1 Cathedral Cl
2 Hodgson St
3 St John's Cha
4 St Johns Ms
5 Sandy Wk
6 Wentworth Ter

D8
1 Brooksbank
2 Cliff Pde
3 Parliament St
4 Piccadilly
5 Salt Pie Alley
6 Smyth St
7 Stubley St
8 Walker's Ter

E1
1 Belfry Ct
2 Holly Ct
3 Meadow Garth

E2
1 Binks St
2 Jubilee Av
3 Kingswell Av
4 Moxon Wy
5 Wilson Ct
6 Wilson Dr

E6
1 College Grove Cl
2 College Grove Vw
3 Dickinson Ct
4 Elizabeth Gdns
5 Smirthwaite St
6 Westfield Ter

E7
1 Arundel St
2 Back Hambleton St
3 Back Hatfeild St
4 Berne Gv
5 Cardigan Ter
6 Clarendon Ct
7 Clarendon St
8 College Gv
9 Elvey St
10 Geneva Gv
11 Gill's Yd
12 Hope St
13 Howard St
14 Industrial St
15 Marizon Gv
16 Providence St
17 Tavora St
18 Union St
19 Upper York St

E8
1 Albion Ct
2 Almshouse La
3 Barstow Sq
4 Bread St
5 Bull Ring
6 Chancery La
7 Frederick St
8 George & Crown Yd
9 Gill St
10 Kirkgate
11 Lee St
12 Radcliffe Pl
13 Saw Yd
14 Silver St
15 Smallpage Yd
16 The Springs
17 Talbot And Falcon Yd
18 Tammy Hall St
19 West Pde

F1
1 Brackenwood Ct
2 Briarwood Cl
3 Grangewood Ct
4 Hazelwood Ct
5 Hazelwood Rd
6 Heather Cl
7 Meadowcroft Cl
8 Meadowcroft Ct
9 Ringwood Ct
10 Whisperwood Cl

F2
1 Mountbatten Gv

F6
1 Belgrave Ter
2 Haigh Moor St

F7
1 Back Duke Of York St
2 Edward St
3 Governor's Yd
4 Norton Rd
5 Witton St

F8
1 Avison Yd
2 Back Mount Pleasant
3 Brunswick Gv
4 Burrell St
5 Crystal Pl
6 Dixon's Yd
7 Hardy Cft
8 Johnston St
9 John St
10 Lower Warrengate
11 Marsland Pl
12 Pincheon St
13 Sun La
14 Trinity Church Ga
15 Turton St
16 Upper Warrengate
17 Warren Ct
18 White's Rd

Page 178

B3
1 Ash Tree Gdns
2 Greenbank Gv
3 High St
4 York St

C2
1 Bransdale Cl
2 Bransdale Ms
3 Bransdale Wk
4 Broome Cl
5 Clayton Ms
6 Clayton Pl
7 Crinan Ct
8 Eskdale Cl
9 Eskdale Ct
10 Eskdale Cft
11 Langdale Dr
12 Langdale Ms

C4
1 Cross Queen St
2 Exchange St
3 Market Pl
4 Sovereign Gdns
5 Stanley Cottages
6 Watson St
7 Webster Pl
8 West St

C6
1 Beech Gv
2 Hope St
3 Oak Av
4 Sycamore Gv

D7
1 Alder Gv
2 Greenwood Cl

E5
1 Newfield Av
2 Newfield Cl
3 Princess Ct

F6
1 Augusta Dr
2 Magdalene Flds

Page 180

D7
1 Armstrong Ter
2 Beechwood Crs
3 East Av
4 Westbourne Av

E1
1 Andersen Ct
2 Eliots Cl
3 Stevenson Av
4 Twain Crs

E6
1 Banks Av
2 Cliff St
3 Crag Mt
4 Crown & Anchor Yd
5 Elm Ter
6 Granville Av
7 Ropergate Service Rd
8 Swales' Yd
9 Westmount St
10 Woodbine Av

F6
1 Bridge St
2 Church La
3 Cross St
4 Friarwood La
5 Gillygate
6 Shoe Market
7 Woolmarket

F7
1 Celandine Cl
2 Mayors Walk Cl

F8
1 Barnswick Cl
2 Moxon Cl

Page 181

G6
1 Grove Av
2 Grove Mt
3 Grove Ri
4 Harewood Vw

H3
1 Stumpcross Ct

H4
1 Dandy Mill Cft

L1
1 Argyle Rd
2 Doncaster Rd
3 High St
4 Old Great North Rd
5 St Andrews Dr
6 School Dr
7 Station Rd

Page 191

L4
1 Squirrel Ct

L7
1 Marsham Gv
2 Portland Cl
3 Saunders Cl

M4
1 Birchroyd Cl
2 Grimescar Mdw
3 Stableford Gdns

M6
1 Ravensdeane

M7
1 Broomfield Ter
2 Marsh Grove Rd
3 Spire Ct
4 Waverley Ter

M8
1 Batley Av
2 Dudley Av

Page 192

A8
1 Springwood Hall Gdns

B8
1 Back Fitzwilliam St
2 Queen Elizabeth Gdns
3 Springwood Hall Gdns

C6
1 Ash St
2 Bay Hall Common Rd
3 Common Rd
4 Eleanor St
5 Three Sisters Sq

C8
1 Back Cecil St
2 Back Greenhead Rd
3 Back Spring St
4 Brook's Yd
5 George St
6 Half Moon St
7 Little Brunswick St
8 Lockwood's Yd
9 St George's Sq
10 Sergeantson St
11 Temple Cl
12 Threadneedle St
13 Upper George St

D5
1 Back Beech Ter
2 Moorfield Rd
3 Tubby La

D6
1 Hebble St
2 Shearing Cross Gdns

D7
1 Back Union St
2 Beaumont St
3 Bradford Rd
4 Broadway
5 Knight St
6 Lower Fitzwilliam St
7 Lower Viaduct St
8 Myrtle St
9 William St

D8
1 Beast Market
2 Bradley St
3 Church St
4 Cross Church St
5 Friendly St
6 St Peter's St
7 Southgate
8 Venn St
9 Victoria La

E2
1 Bracken Sq

E3
1 Occupation Rd
2 Woodhead Cl

E4
1 Ashmere Gv
2 Peridot Fold
3 Woodhouse Hall Rd

E6
1 Bradley Mills Rd
2 Fieldhouse Rd

F3
1 Sunny View Crs
2 Warrenfield Ct

F7
1 Edge Hill Cl
2 Heathergrove Fold

F8
1 Green Mt
2 Mount Pleasant St

Page 193

G2
1 Greyfriars Av
2 Hurstwood
3 Ochrewell Av

H4
1 Woodland Rd

H7
1 Second Av

Page 194

B4
1 Brendon Ct
2 Brook Fld
3 Chiltern Dr

C1
1 The Embankment
2 Knowl Gv
3 Scarboro Mdw
4 Shaw St

Page 195

H1
1 Albion St
2 Great Pond St

Page 197

G2
1 Fairfield Ter
2 King St
3 Sunnydale Cft

G5
1 Audsley's Yd
2 Holyoake Ter
3 Parklands Av
4 Parklands Ct
5 Parklands Crs
6 Reid Park Av

G8
1 Church Crs
2 Hall Cft
3 High Rdg
4 Netherton Hall Gdns

H2
1 Bankfield Cl
2 Charlotte Gv
3 Fairfield Gdns
4 Fairfield Mt
5 Georgia Ms
6 Lee Ct
7 Lombardi Ct
8 Parklands
9 Park St
10 Queens Drive Cl
11 Richmond Garth
12 Saville Pk
13 Taylor Dr

H3
1 Brook Cl
2 Heather Cl
3 Manor Gv

H5
1 Laburnum Ct
2 Mortimer Rw

J5
1 Clubhouses Cft
2 Co-operative St
3 Cross Park St
4 Fearnside's Cl
5 Ranter's Fold
6 Wensley St East
7 The Willows

L2
1 Benjamin Sykes Wy
2 Hallamshire Ms
3 Holby Sq
4 Nightingale Crest

L4
1 Addison Ct
2 Ashwood Gv
3 Chesterton Ct
4 Shelley Ct

M1
1 Gloucester Gv
2 Gloucester Pl

M2
1 Snapethorpe Crs

M3
1 Oakwood

Page 198

C4
1 Thornes Moor Rd
2 Troon Wy

D3
1 Thornes Park Ct

F3
1 Abbott Ter
2 Acme Ter
3 Emblem Ter
4 Kimberley St
5 Manygates Crs
6 Manygates Pk

Page 199

G3
1 Anderton St
2 Ashdown Rd
3 Claremont St
4 Welbeck St

Page 206

A2
1 Calverley Wy
2 Coptrod Head Cl

A3
1 Cardigan St
2 Chatsworth St
3 Daffodil Cl
4 Earnshaw Av
5 Lytham St
6 Ropefield Wy

A4
1 Bassett Wy
2 Blackthorn Cl
3 Bradley Smithy Cl
4 Campbell St
5 Dew Meadow Cl
6 Heights Cl
7 Sweet Briar Cl
8 Sweet Briar La
9 Woodfield Av

A5
1 Augusta St
2 Headlands St
3 Henley St
4 Moorfield Pl
5 Moorland St
6 Swain St
7 Turner St

A6
1 Ashworth St
2 Beswicke St
3 Brook's Pl
4 Clement Royds St
5 Cromer St
6 Daisy St
7 Falinge Ms
8 Greenhill Av
9 Green La
10 Halliwell St
11 Jane St
12 Knowsley St
13 Leamington St
14 Littledale St
15 Mount St
16 Redcar St
17 Stanley Pl
18 Tiflis St
19 Wilton Ter

A7
1 Fenwick St

A8
1 Broadfield Stile
2 Castle Hill Crs
3 Castlemere Ter

B2
1 Dewhirst Wy
2 Highcroft Wy
3 Middle Hl

B3
1 Carlisle St
2 Nantwich Av
3 Nook Farm Av

B4
1 Barnfield St
2 Bowlers Wk
3 Isabella St
4 Leyton St
5 Mountside Cl
6 Overfield Wy
7 Pavilion Cl

B5
1 Alma St
2 Bunyan St
3 Cedar St
4 Clementina St
5 David St North
6 Denton St
7 Derwent St
8 Elm St
9 Grasmere St
10 Hendriff Pl
11 Industry Rd
12 Inkerman St
13 Jepheys Pl
14 Laurie Pl
15 Lomax St
16 Medley St
17 Milford St
18 Noon Sun St
19 Redcross St North
20 Rivington St
21 Sawyer St
22 Taylors Pl
23 Upper George St
24 Victoria St
25 Wellington St

B6
1 Bell St
2 Blossom Pl
3 Cheetham St
4 East Gate St
5 Goose La
6 Greenlees St
7 Howard Pl
8 Hunter's La
9 New Buildings Pl
10 Oldmill St
11 Park La
12 Petrie St
13 Queen St
14 Reed Hl
15 School St
16 Shepherd St
17 Toad La
18 Waterhouse St
19 Whitehall St
20 Wilson St

B7
1 Baillie St
2 The Butts Av
3 Chancel Pl
4 Church La
5 Constantine Rd
6 Faulkner St
7 Fleece St
8 Great George St
9 Greenwood St
10 Ink St
11 Junction Alley
12 Kenion St
13 Lyceum Pas
14 Mason St
15 Moore St
16 Nelson St
17 Oak St
18 Packer St
19 River St
20 St Chad's Cl
21 Slack St
22 Stationers Entry
23 Summer Castle
24 Water St

B8
1 Ann St
2 Broadfield St
3 Caton St
4 Coventry St
5 Devon St
6 Dorset St
7 Essex St
8 Kent St
9 Lower Tweedale St
10 Maclure Rd
11 Milkstone Pl
12 Monmouth St
13 Park St
14 Sussex St
15 Talbot St

C4
1 Eva St
2 Grace St
3 Holden St
4 Low's Pl
5 Maureen St

C5
1 Acton St
2 Aden St
3 Birley St

C6
1 Beverley Pl
2 Bradshaw St
3 Briton St
4 Copenhagen Sq
5 Denmark St
6 Flannel St
7 Hugh St
8 James St
9 Kitchen St
10 Norreys St
11 The Pass
12 Ramsay Pl
13 Ramsay Ter
14 Thomas St
15 Wellington Pl

C7
1 Guildford St
2 Hill St
3 Pickup St
4 Summer St

C8
1 Ainsworth St
2 Back Oldham Rd
3 Haigh St
4 Lincoln Cl
5 Sarah St
6 Tonge St

D3
1 Armstrong Hurst Cl
2 Kentmere Av
3 Kitter St
4 Wesley St

D4
1 Buckley Brook St
2 Clayton St
3 Dover St
4 Hamer Hall Crs
5 Merryman Hall
6 Shaw St

D5
1 Bath St
2 The Cloisters
3 Deacon St
4 Ernest Ter
5 Harvey St
6 John Ashworth St
7 Mark St
8 Mayfield St

D6
1 Aboukir St
2 Cooper Ter
3 Heybrook St
4 Lower Wheat End
5 Waterside La
6 Weedon St

D7
1 Cayley St
2 Pine St
3 Worsley Pl

D8
1 Bangor St
2 Channing Sq
3 Mc Naught St
4 Millfield Gv
5 Morningside Cl
6 Ouldfield Cl
7 Rowland St
8 Sarah Butterworth St
9 Sykes St
10 Tees St
11 Trent St
12 Wren Gn

E2
1 Birch Hey Cl
2 Corn Mill Cl
3 Little Howarth Wy
4 Princess Av

E3
1 Holmes St
2 Howarth Farm Wy
3 Louise Cl
4 Maitland Cl
5 Martha's Ter
6 Mitchell St
7 Old Brow La
8 Vicarage Dr

E4
1 Harold St
2 Prescott St
3 Roach V
4 Spokeshave Wy
5 Whitworth St

E6
1 Belfield Cl
2 Nursery Gdns
3 Pearson St
4 Thornbush Wy
5 Tollgate Wy
6 Upper Hayes Cl
7 Waterman Vw

E7
1 Canon Flynn Ct
2 Clover Vw
3 Hesketh Rd
4 Kenworthy St
5 Kenworthy Ter
6 Merinall Cl

E8
1 Burnside Rd
2 Cotton Fold
3 Nigher Moss Av

F1
1 Homestead Gdns

F2
1 Brook Hey Cl
2 Cooper St
3 Edward St
4 Great Bent Cl
5 Holland St
6 Hurstead Gn
7 Mill House Cl
8 Noble Meadow
9 Old Clay Dr
10 Tithe Barn Cl
11 William St

F3
1 Brownside Cl
2 Carrington Cl
3 Church St
4 Green Grove Bank
5 Laycock St
6 Turnfield Cl

F7
1 Belfield La
2 Brocklebank Rd
3 Chadwick St
4 Cross St
5 Dalton Av
6 East St
7 Hartley St
8 Leigh St
9 Redwood Park Gv
10 West St

F8
1 Knowl Rd
2 Upper Stone Dr
3 Watermill Cl

Page 207

G2
1 Belvoir Mdw
2 Crowther St
3 Mount Av
4 Wuerdle Cl
5 Wuerdle Farm Wy
6 Wuerdle St

G7
1 Whitehead St
2 Willows La

G8
1 Brakehouse Cl
2 Entwisle St
3 Hallcroft Gdns
4 Hebble Butt Cl
5 Hoyle's Ter
6 Laythe Barn Cl
7 Moorhouse Farm
8 Wesley St
9 Weston St
10 Woburn Cl

H1
1 Bamford St
2 Beaumont Cl
3 Bents Farm Cl
4 Clay St
5 Farm Wk
6 Hawthorn Wk
7 Meadow Wk

H2
1 Finance St

H3
1 Blyth Av
2 Brentwood Cl
3 Bridgenorth Dr
4 Brown Bank Rd
5 Edward Av
6 Excelsior Ter
7 Greenbank Dr
8 Johnston Av
9 Lodge Bank Rd
10 Willow Ri
11 Wrigley Pl

H4
1 Garden Cl
2 Southey Cl
3 Wordsworth Crs

H7
1 Parsonage Wk
2 Sandstone Rd
3 Shorefield Cl
4 Turnough Rd

H8
1 Kiln La
2 River Pl
3 Silver Hl
4 Weston St

J1
1 Albion St
2 Butterworth St
3 Hanover St
4 Orron St
5 Vale Cottages
6 Wood St

J3
1 Higher Bank Rd
2 Queens Vw

J4
1 Smithy Bridge Rd

J8
1 Cambrian Dr
2 Sandringham Dr
3 Tame Barn Cl

K1
1 Chapel Hl
2 Eastwood St
3 George St
4 Greenwood St
5 Heber Pl
6 Industry St
7 James Hill St
8 Jerrold St
9 Leah St
10 Maden's Sq
11 Morgan St
12 Nelson St
13 Pioneer St
14 Smith St
15 Station Rd
16 Warley St
17 West St
18 Winton St

L1
1 Beswicke St
2 Brook St
3 East St
4 Haliwell St
5 Royds St

Page 213

G2
1 Ainley Pk
2 Heathfield Ms
3 Potters Wk
4 Woodville Av

J2
1 Barlbro' Pl
2 Bowling St
3 Crown Gn
4 Francis Av
5 Mount St
6 Pickford St

K1
1 Hope St
2 Lipscomb St

K2
1 Bridge Cft
2 John St
3 Lockbridge Wy

M8
1 Elder Grove Ms
2 Noble Ct
3 Rowan Av
4 Rowan Avenue Ms
5 Spruce Drive Ms

Page 214

A2
1 Church Av
2 George St
3 Keat St
4 Oldfield St
5 Pear St

B3
1 Crowther St
2 Dockery
3 Water St
4 Wood End

C1
1 Albert Yd
2 Corporation St
3 Dale St
4 Manchester Rd
5 Outcote Bank
6 Princess St

D3
1 Ashenhurst Cl

E1
1 Carforth St
2 Dog Kennel Bank
3 Gelder Ter
4 Smithy La

E3
1 Squirrel Ditch

E4
1 New Laithe Cl

F1
1 Almondbury Bank
2 Bankfield Ct
3 Chapel St
4 Diamond St
5 Old Wakefield Rd

F2
1 Chatsworth Cl

Page 215

H3
1 Brickbank
2 Hallows Ct
3 Hudroyd
4 Stocks Wk

J4
1 St Helen's Fld

L1
1 Peace Hall La

M3
1 The Clough
2 Fields Rd
3 Greave House La
4 Greaves Cft
5 Hawthorne Cl

Page 228

A1
1 Ashton St
2 Barclyde St
3 Craven Gdns
4 Dunsterville Ter
5 Elm Gv
6 Fenton Ms
7 Gales Ter
8 Grandidge St
9 Grove St
10 Henley Ter
11 John Roberts Cl
12 Merefield Av
13 Sefton St
14 Trafford St
15 Ulster Av
16 Vivian St

A2
1 Haddon St
2 Laburnum Ter
3 Langton Ter
4 Prospect St
5 Virginia St

B1
1 Aubrey St
2 Broomfield Sq
3 Deeplish St
4 Eastbourne St
5 Ellesmere St
6 Hastings St
7 Ipswich St
8 Lincoln Leach Ct
9 Lucknow St
10 Maldon St
11 Midhurst St
12 Nicholson St
13 Overt St
14 Penrith St
15 Pike St
16 Pomona St
17 St Luke St
18 Salik Gdns
19 Stanhope St
20 Thornton St
21 Welburn St

B2
1 Green Bridge Cl

B4
1 Lilac Rd
2 Mornington Rd

C1
1 Albany St
2 Back Durham St
3 Back Royds St
4 Bright St
5 Clifton St
6 Crossfield Pl
7 Deeplish Rd
8 Falmouth St
9 Fletcher St
10 Gordon St
11 Gorrel St
12 Healing St
13 Hume St
14 Leicester St
15 Royds Pl
16 Tennyson St
17 Vincent St
18 Wellfield Pl
19 Whitby St
20 Winby St
21 Windsor St

C2
1 Argyle St
2 Brow St
3 Burlington St
4 Calf Hey North
5 Calf Hey South
6 Chapel St
7 Exmouth Sq
8 Field St
9 Harvard St
10 Marcroft Pl
11 Warings Yd
12 Wheathill St
13 William Henry St

C3
1 Exmouth Pl
2 Exmouth St

D1
1 Crown Gdns
2 Franklin St
3 Lockhart St

D2
1 Carpenters Wy
2 Norbury St
3 Retford Av
4 St Joseph's Dr

D3
1 Brookland St
2 Brook La
3 Connaught Av
4 Hughtredle St
5 Turnhill Rd

D4
1 Fairlands St
2 Harrow St
3 Holy St
4 Parkfield St

D5
1 Ashgrove

E2
1 Birkdale Rd
2 Bishopsgate Wk
3 Burnet Cl

E3
1 Brockway
2 Milingate Cl

E4
1 White Horse Mdw

E6
1 Grisedale Av
2 Lakeland Dr
3 Langdale Av
4 Rydal Av
5 Thornham Ct

E7
1 Ennerdale Av

E8
1 Castlerigg Dr
2 Kingston Dr
3 Lewisham Cl
4 Sandringham Wy

F7
1 Buttermere Gv

F8
1 Cameron Ct
2 Chapelway Gdns
3 Devine Cl
4 Highbury Wy

Page 229

G5
1 Moss Gv

G6
1 Acre Barn
2 Braemore Cl
3 Rockingham Cl

G7
1 Bowland Cl
2 Cherry Hall Dr

H1
1 Chipping Fold
2 Lambourne Gv
3 Leach St
4 Slaidburn Cl

H2
1 Bowland Gv
2 Cartmel Av
3 Grange Av
4 Stott St

H5
1 Greenway

H6
1 Glenavon Dr
2 Leonardin Cl
3 Maple Cl
4 Mendips Cl
5 Southdowns Cl
6 Whitehead St

H7
1 Astley Cl
2 The Gabriels
3 Hereford Cl
4 Markenfield Dr
5 Moorfield Hamlet
6 Norfolk Cl
7 Samlesbury Cl
8 Somerset Av

J1
1 Butterworth Hall
2 Church Ter
3 Clegg St
4 Holt St
5 Schofield St
6 Tydeman Wk

J2
1 Beech St
2 Bentfield Crs

J3
1 Oak St

J6
1 Bourne Rd
2 Clevlands Cl
3 Hawkshead Rd
4 Ingleby Cl
5 Ingleby Wy
6 Norwood Cl

J7
1 Albert St
2 Allenby St
3 Newbarn Cl

J8
1 Egerton Pl

K2
1 Beresford St
2 Broomfield Ter
3 Travis St
4 Wolseley St

K3
1 Gordon St
2 Granville Ct
3 Pine St
4 Spring Ter
5 Waterview Cl

K6
1 Bellingham Cl
2 Buckingham Park Cl
3 Chertsey Cl
4 Gilderdale Cl
5 Goldbourne St
6 Helmshore Wy
7 Hertfordshire Park Cl
8 Kingston Cl
9 Pemberton Wy
10 Surrey Park Cl
11 Wessex Park Cl
12 Westminister Cl

K7
1 Chapel St
2 Collinge St
3 Co-operative St
4 Cromer St
5 Crompton St
6 Crown St
7 Elizabeth Gv
8 Harrow Ms
9 Kershaw St East
10 King Albert St
11 Moorfield Ms
12 Provident St
13 St James St
14 St Mary's Ga
15 Siddall St
16 Sweetbriar Cl
17 Victoria Gdns

K8
1 Cedar Gv
2 Cheetham Hl
3 Dawn St
4 Diggle St
5 Durden Ms
6 Fardale
7 Hawthorn Crs
8 Henthorn St
9 High St
10 Margaret St
11 Milne St
12 Newtown St
13 Osborne St
14 Richmond Cl
15 Swan Ct
16 Westway

L3
1 Railway St

L5
1 Cross Field Cl
2 Jordan St
3 Railway Vw
4 Woodhouse Rd

L6
1 Bridge St
2 Copley St
3 Dunwood Av
4 Park Side Av
5 Store St
6 Wren's Nest Av

L7
1 Belgravia Ms
2 Buckley St
3 Chancery La
4 Cyril St
5 Edmund St
6 Gillemere Gv
7 Greaves St
8 Moorlands St

L8
1 The Knoll

M6
1 Bluefields
2 Burnside
3 Forrester Dr
4 Old Brook Cl
5 Woodside

M7
1 Betjeman Pl
2 Blueberry Dr
3 Heversham Av
4 Rossendale Cl
5 Woodford Av

Page 236

B1
1 Brooke Fold
2 Crown St
3 Doctor Fold
4 France Fold
5 Jessop Fold
6 Lower Fold
7 St Mary's Sq
8 Spring Dl
9 Swift's Fold

B2
1 Cross St
2 Exchange
3 High St
4 Marsh
5 Roundway
6 School St

B7
1 Well Green Gdns

E7
1 Co-operative Ter
2 Ridings La
3 Town End Crs

F7
1 Bromley Av
2 Sycamore Ri

Page 242

E5
1 Butterton Cl
2 Cherry Tree Cl
3 Church St
4 Greenside
5 Greenside Wk

Page 243

G7
1 Burn Pl
2 Cayton Cl
3 Hatfield Cl
4 Malton Pl
5 Murdoch Pl
6 Thorne Cl

H6
1 High Croft Dr
2 Watnall Rd

J7
1 Dale Cl
2 Peak Rd
3 Peveril Crs

J8
1 Kingsley Cl

M7
1 Baycliff Cl
2 Cartmel Cl
3 Kirkham Pl
4 St Francis Bvd

M8
1 Edenfield Cl
2 Formby Ct
3 Longridge Rd
4 Walney Fold

Page 244

D7
1 Bank St
2 Roberts St
3 School Hl
4 Sycamore Av
5 Willow Cl

Page 260

A1
1 Four Lanes Cl
2 Langdale Rd
3 Selbourne Cl
4 Tavy Cl

A2
1 Longley Cl

A3
1 Waveney Dr

A7
1 Barnsley Rd
2 Cliffe Crs
3 Edale Ri
4 Eyam Cl
5 Padley Cl

A8
1 St John's Cl

B7
1 Laithe Cft
2 Rose Hill Dr
3 Upper Folderings
4 Whinby Cft
5 Windsor Dr

B8
1 Chatsworth Ri
2 Hardwick Gv
3 Needlewood
4 Nostell Fold
5 Pilley Hl
6 Rob Royd
7 Saville Hall La
8 Woburn Pl

C2
1 Barcroft
2 Redthorpe Crest

C4
1 Bradshaw Cl
2 Britland Cl
3 Edmonton Cl

C5
1 Ancote Cl
2 Crowden Wk
3 Drury Farm Ct
4 Mickelden Wy
5 Wessenden Cl
6 White Hill Ter

C6
1 Birchfield Crs

C7
1 Cinder Hills Wy
2 Cramlands
3 Far Townend
4 Hannas Royd
5 Heather Knowle
6 Lambert Fold
7 Lingthwaite
8 Middlewoods

C8
1 Hazelshaw
2 Wharncliffe

D2
1 Belridge Cl
2 Stainley Cl
3 Wilsden Gv
4 Wilthorpe La

D3
1 Little New Cl
2 Oakworth Cl
3 Ravenshaw Cl
4 Samuel Sq
5 Vaughan Rd
6 Woodview La

D4
1 Birchfield Wk
2 Cotswold Cl
3 Grampian Cl
4 Greaves Fold
5 Hambleton Cl
6 Malvern Cl
7 Mary's Pl
8 Mendip Cl
9 Porter Ter
10 St Owens Dr

D5
1 Daleswood Av
2 St Catherines Wy
3 White Hill Gv

D6
1 Broomfield Cl
2 Glenmoor Av

E2
1 Huddersfield Rd
2 Moorbank Cl
3 Redbrook St
4 Wilthorpe Gn

E3
1 Cottesmore Cl
2 Grenville Pl
3 Ketton Wk
4 Queensway

E4
1 Helensburgh Cl
2 The Lindales
3 Myrtle St
4 Sycamore St

E5
1 South St

E7
1 Keresforth Hill Rd

F2
1 Dearnley Vw

F3
1 Carrington St
2 Lingard St
3 Thorntree La
4 Westbourne Gv

F4
1 Buckden Rd
2 Darley Ter
3 Hilton St
4 Johnson St
5 Keir Ter
6 Lingard Ct
7 Newton St
8 Rock St
9 Somerset St
10 Southwell St
11 Summer St

F5
1 Dean St
2 Hindle St
3 Knowsley St
4 Mclintock Wy
5 Nicholas St
6 Perseverance St
7 Pitt St West
8 Richard St
9 Richmond St
10 Springfield Pl
11 Stanhope St
12 Stanley St
13 Waterloo Rd
14 Well St
15 Westfield St

F6
1 Cranbrook St
2 Fife St
3 Havelock St
4 Helena St
5 Leopold St
6 Sandford St

F7
1 Dyson St
2 Ellington St
3 Kingstone Pl

Page 261

G3
1 Burton St
2 Cavendish Rd
3 Lombard Cl
4 Wentworth St

G4
1 Aireton Rd
2 Churchfield
3 Church La
4 Church St
5 Eastgate
6 Lancaster Ga
7 Rosehill St
8 Sadler Ga
9 St Mary's Ga
10 St Mary's Pl
11 Victoria St
12 Westwood Ct

G5
1 Beaconsfield St
2 Fenton St
3 George Sq
4 Graham's Orch
5 Holden Ct
6 Lower Castlereagh St
7 Mark St
8 Nelson St
9 Peel Sq
10 Plumber St
11 Royal St
12 Wortley St
13 York St

G6
1 Fleming Pl
2 Lower Thomas St

G7
1 California Ter
2 Highstone V

G8
1 Mayfield Crs

H1
1 Reasbeck Ter
2 Whitbourne Cl

H2
1 Wheatley Cl

H3
1 Aylesford Cl
2 Leighton Cl
3 Sandbeck Cl
4 Windham Cl

H4
1 Denton St
2 Hanson St
3 Harborough Hill Rd
4 Redfearn St
5 Vernon St North

H5
1 Burleigh Ct
2 Burlington Ar
3 Cheapside
4 Freemans Yd
5 Hayes Cft
6 Malthouse Rd
7 May Day Gn
8 Midland St
9 Pall Mall
10 Sherwood St
11 Wesley St

H6
1 Britannia Cl
2 Buckley Ct
3 Copper Cl
4 Denison Ct
5 Duke Crs
6 Duke St
7 Freeman St
8 Providence Ct
9 Quarry St
10 Rebecca Ms
11 Rosebery Ter
12 Taylor Rw
13 Upper New St
14 Wilkinson St

H7
1 California Crs
2 Chestnut Ct
3 Dickinson Pl
4 Dickinson Rd
5 Essex Rd
6 Frederic Pl
7 Hornby St
8 Howard St
9 Kelsey Ter
10 Kenworthy Rd
11 Stoneleigh Cft
12 Warren Pl

H8
1 Coach House La
2 Highfield Av
3 Kingwell Crs
4 Locke Av

J1
1 Dunmere Cl
2 Edgecliffe Pl
3 Quarry St

J3
1 Wharf St

J5
1 Grasmere Rd
2 Market Cl
3 Thirlmere Rd
4 Windermere Rd

J6
1 Clifton St
2 Gold Cft
3 Henshall St
4 Milnes St
5 Oakwell Ter
6 Osborne Ms
7 St Peter's Ter
8 Seth Ter
9 Sunderland Ter
10 Victoria Ter
11 Wilby La

J7
1 Crown Av
2 Crown St
3 Harriet Cl
4 Winton Cl

K1
1 Browning Cl

K2
1 Edinburgh Cl

K3
1 Carbis Cl
2 Haworth Cl
3 Roche Cl
4 Sennen Cft
5 Sheridan Ct
6 Trewan Ct

K5
1 Beevor St

K6
1 Applehurst Bank
2 Evelyn Ter
3 Lulworth Cl
4 Pindar Oaks Cottages
5 Pindar St

L1
1 The Ridings

L2
1 Farm Cl
2 Hunt Cl
3 Norman Cl
4 Spring Gdns

L3
1 Bude Ct
2 Chapter Wy
3 Cliffe La
4 Mylor Ct
5 St Lukes Wy

L6
1 Lambert Wk

L7
1 Colley Pl
2 Thornton Ter

M1
1 Blundell Cl
2 Larchfield Pl
3 Morton Cl

M3
1 Brookvale
2 Rectory Wy
3 Temple Wy

M6
1 Doncaster Rd
2 Kenwood Cl
3 Malcolm Cl

M7
1 Hunningley La
2 Neville Cl

M8
1 Brookside Dr
2 Butterley Dr
3 Foxfield Wk
4 Lepton Gdns
5 Rylstone Wk

Page 262

A6
1 Bridge St
2 New St
3 Oxford Pl
4 Pinfold Cl
5 Waterfield Pl

B6
1 Alexandra Ter
2 Chapel St
3 Crown Well Hl
4 Foxroyd Cl
5 Scarfield Cl